SEVENTH CANADIAN EDITION

UNDERSTANDING HUMAN SEXUALITY

Janet Shibley Hyde
University of Wisconsin—Madison

John D. DeLamater
University of Wisconsin—Madison

E. Sandra Byers
University of New Brunswick

Mc
Graw
Hill
Education

Understanding Human Sexuality
Seventh Canadian Edition

Statistics Canada information is used with the permission of Statistics Canada. Users are forbidden to copy this material and/or redisseminate the data, in an original or modified form, for commercial purposes, without the expressed permission of Statistics Canada. Information on the availability of the wide range of data from Statistics Canada can be obtained from Statistics Canada's Regional Offices, its Website at www.statcan.gc.ca and its toll-free access number 1-800-263-1136.

The Internet addresses listed in the text were accurate at the time of publication. The inclusion of a website does not indicate an endorsement by the authors or McGraw-Hill Ryerson, and McGraw-Hill Ryerson does not guarantee the accuracy of information presented at these sites.

ISBN-13: 978-1-25-927380-3
ISBN-10: 1-25-927380-6

1 2 3 4 5 6 7 8 9 0 WEB 22 21 20 19 18

Printed and bound in Canada

Care has been taken to trace ownership of copyright material contained in this text; however, the publisher will welcome any information that enables it to rectify any reference or credit for subsequent editions.

Portfolio Director, Humanities, Social Sciences & Languages, International: *Rhondda McNabb*
Portfolio Manager : *Scott Hardie*
Senior Marketing Manager: *Kelli Legros*
Content Development Manager: *Denise Foote*
Content Developer: *Tammy Mavroudi*
Senior Portfolio Associate: *Marina Seguin*
Supervising Editors: *Stephanie Gibson, Jeanette McCurdy, & Janie Deneau*
Photo/Permissions Researcher: *Monika Schurmann*
Copy Editor: *Michael Kelly*
Plant Production Coordinator: *Michelle Saddler*
Manufacturing Production Coordinator: *Sheryl MacAdam*
Cover and Interior Design: *Liz Harasymczuk*
Composition: *SPi Global*
Cover Photo: *"The Box" © Jessica Tanzer. All rights reserved. Used by permission of The Human Sexuality Collection, Cornell University.*
Printer: Webcom, Ltd.

Author Biographies

Janet Shibley Hyde, the Helen Thompson Woolley Professor of Psychology and Gender & Women's Studies at the University of Wisconsin–Madison, received her education at Oberlin College and the University of California, Berkeley. She has taught a course in human sexuality since 1974, first at Bowling Green State University, then at Denison University, and now at the University of Wisconsin. Her research interests are in gender differences and gender-role development in childhood and adolescence. Author of the textbook *Half the Human Experience: The Psychology of Women,* she is a past president of the Society for the Scientific Study of Sexuality and is a Fellow of the American Psychological Association and the American Association for the Advancement of Science. She has received many other honours, including an award for excellence in teaching at Bowling Green State University, the Chancellor's Award for teaching at the University of Wisconsin, and the Kinsey Award from the Society for the Scientific Study of Sexuality for her contributions to sex research. In 2000–2001 she served as one of the three scientific editors for U.S. Surgeon General David Satcher's report *Promoting Sexual Health and Responsible Sexual Behavior.* She is married to John DeLamater.

John D. DeLamater, Conway-Bascom Professor of Sociology at the University of Wisconsin–Madison, received his education at the University of California, Santa Barbara, and the University of Michigan. He created the human sexuality course at the University of Wisconsin in 1975 and has since taught it regularly. His current research and writing are focused on the biological, psychological, and social influences on sexual behaviour and satisfaction in later life. He has published papers on the influence of marital duration, attitudes about sex for elders, and illness and medications on sexual expression. He co-edited the *Handbook of the Sociology of Sexualities.* He is the co-author of the textbook *Social Psychology.* He is a Fellow of the Society for the Scientific Study of Sexuality and the 2002 recipient of the Kinsey Award from the Society for Career Contributions to Sex Research. He has received awards for excellence in teaching from the Department of Sociology and the University of Wisconsin and is a Fellow and past Chair of the Teaching Academy at the University of Wisconsin. He regularly teaches a seminar for graduate students on teaching undergraduate courses. He is married to Janet Hyde.

E. Sandra Byers is a Professor and Chair of the Department of Psychology at the University of New Brunswick (UNB). She was honoured by UNB with a University Research Scholar Award in 2008. Dr. Byers grew up in Montreal and received her university education at the University of Rochester and West Virginia University. She created the human sexuality course at the University of New Brunswick in 1979 and has taught it annually since then. She is the author or co-author of more than 160 journal articles and book chapters, and has supervised 52 honours, masters, and doctoral theses. Much (but not all) of her research has been in the areas of sexual satisfaction, sexual communication, sexual violence, and attitudes toward sexual health education. She also has a private practice in clinical psychology specializing in the treatment of sexual problems and concerns, and she regularly teaches a graduate seminar on sex therapy. She has won several awards, most recently the Kinsey Award from the Society for the Scientific Study of Sexuality in 2013, the Distinguished Scientific Contributions Award from the Society for the Scientific Study of Sexuality in 2009, and the Distinguished Contributions to Psychology as a Profession Award from the Canadian Psychological Association in 2010. She is president of the International Academy of Sex Research, a past president of the Canadian Sex Research Forum, a Fellow of the Canadian Psychological Association and the Society for the Scientific Study of Sexuality, a member of the Advisory Board of the Sex Information and Education Council of Canada, an editorial board member of four sexuality journals, and the founding director of the Muriel McQueen Fergusson Centre for Family Violence Research. Dr. Byers has given many invited addresses and workshops, and has been interviewed about sexual issues by numerous radio and television stations, magazines, and newspapers. As a sexuality educator, researcher, and therapist in Canada, Dr. Byers is uniquely placed to provide a Canadian perspective on human sexuality. She has been with her husband Dr. Larry Heinlein, also a clinical psychologist, for 44 years, has two daughters, Krista and Alyssa, and one granddaughter, Julia. To learn more about Dr. Byers and her research, you can visit her website at http://www.unb.ca/fredericton/arts/departments/psychology/people/byers.html.

Contents in Brief

Contents

Preface

Continuing a Research-Based Tradition in Sexuality

Since its conception, *Understanding Human Sexuality* has achieved distinction and success by following the science of human sexuality. The first of the modern sexuality textbooks, *Understanding Human Sexuality* introduced this topic to students through the science that has uncovered what we know about the field. Groundbreaking when it first appeared, this research-based tradition continues to result in a contemporary, balanced introduction to human sexuality in an integrated learning system that engages students to learn about the content of the course, others, and themselves.

Our goal in creating the seventh Canadian edition of *Understanding Human Sexuality* was to maintain the best features of the highly regarded American textbook while continuing to provide a truly Canadian focus. Over the past two decades, *Understanding Human Sexuality* has been widely recognized for its comprehensive and multidisciplinary coverage of a broad range of topics, its commitment to excellent scholarship, and its appeal and accessibility to students. The seventh Canadian edition retains these strengths while incorporating the latest information about a range of sexual topics, including Internet issues related to sexuality, updated statistics, adolescent sexual behaviour, transgender individuals, the causes and treatment of sexual disorders, and legal decisions related to sex work. This inclusivity makes this seventh Canadian edition a comfortable and informative resource for many audiences.

Following the Science to Understand Human Sexuality

Understanding Human Sexuality is grounded in science and the research that informs this science. This foundation, drawn from several perspectives, is reflected by us, as the authors. We bring these differing perspectives to our introduction to human sexuality. Janet's background is in psychology and biology. John's is in sociology. Sandra's is in clinical psychology. The importance we place on science comes from the desire to provide students with a holistic understanding of human sexuality based on the best available research and also on what we see and do as researchers ourselves. We each have active research careers and focus on differing aspects of human sexuality.

The quality of sex research is highly variable. One of our responsibilities as authors is to sift through available studies and present only those of the best quality and the greatest relevance and currency to this course. We are thrilled to observe that the quality of sex research improves every decade. In this edition, as much as possible, we continued to feature up-to-date studies of excellent quality in terms of their sampling, research design, and measurements.

A Book for Students

First and foremost, we have kept in mind that students want to learn about sexuality and that our job as writers is to help them do so effectively. We have covered topics completely, with as clear a presentation as possible, and have made a special effort to use language that is inclusive and will ultimately enlighten instead of intimidate. In the selection and preparation of illustrations for the book, our goal has always been to convey as much information as possible, simply and clearly, and to ensure that students with a range of gender and sexual identities can see themselves in the material they read.

This book assumes no prior university or college courses in biology, psychology, or sociology. It is designed as an introduction following the four major objectives of our own courses in human sexuality:

1. To provide students with an understanding of the methods and results of research that have contributed to our scientific knowledge about human sexuality, as well as the tools to read research reports and evaluate claims both critically and intelligently.

2. To provide practical information needed for everyday living, such as information on sexual anatomy,

contraception, sexually transmitted infections, and ways in which to deal with problems in sexual functioning.

3. To help students appreciate the fabulous diversity of human sexuality along many dimensions, including but not limited to age, gender identity, sexual orientation and identity, and ethnicity within Canada and in cultures around the world.

4. To help students feel more comfortable with thinking and talking about sex, both to broaden their knowledge base and to help them become responsible decision makers in their personal lives and in their roles as citizens and voters.

All of the above information is supported by research so that students feel confident that what they are learning is fact-based and can be easily applied to their lives or those around them.

Thinking Critically about Sexuality

Critical thinking is a well-developed area of psychological research with proven methods, and it is a new feature explored in this edition. Since we are not experts in critical thinking, we consulted with Dr. Diane Halpern, former president of the American Psychological Association and a faculty member at Claremont McKenna College in California. With Dr. Halpern's guidance, a critical thinking skill feature is included for each chapter in this seventh Canadian edition to ensure that the material continues to be accessible to all students. In Chapter 1, the first feature introduces students to the concepts and principles of critical thinking; in later chapters, specific skills are explained and applied to sexuality. Examples of these include the importance of sampling in research (Chapter 3), understanding the difference between anecdotal evidence and scientific evidence (Chapter 4), evaluating alternatives in making a health care decision (Chapter 6), understanding the concept of probability (Chapter 7), and decision making and problem solving (Chapter 10), to name a few.

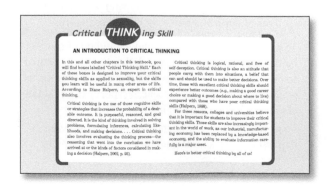

What Makes the Seventh Canadian Edition of *Understanding Human Sexuality* Unique?

A Commitment to Canadian Content

First and foremost is the Canadian content. There are many ways in which sexuality in Canada is different from sexuality in other parts of the world—whether it's rates of breast-feeding, teenage pregnancy, and STIs; attitudes toward same-sex relationships; or laws regulating sexuality. These differences are reflected throughout the text in every chapter. Students are provided with information that is relevant to their own lives, their own experiences, and the communities they live in. By featuring research conducted in Canada, this textbook sheds light on the important work Canadian researchers continue to do on our behalf. Professors who reviewed past editions of this text have been extremely positive about the inclusion of Canadian content, enthusiastically praising both the extent and the relevance of Canadian information compared with other texts available. We have maintained these features in the seventh Canadian edition.

A Focus on Diversity and an Inclusive Approach

Second, in the seventh Canadian edition we have continued to pay special attention to making the text as inclusive as possible. Canada is a diverse nation with diverse sexual identities, so it is paramount that we use language that respects this diversity and does not make normative assumptions. We use "partner" rather than "spouse," and language that applies equally to gay, lesbian, bisexual, and heterosexual students as well as to both cisgender and transgender individuals. We have also highlighted sexuality in Canadian ethnocultural communities, including the Chinese, South Asian, Caribbean, and First Nations communities, as well as highlight regional differences between Canadians living in Quebec and those living in other provinces.

Canadian Legal Information in Every Chapter

Third, students will find discussion of Canadian laws and Canadian legal issues in each chapter. This includes the current laws related to same-sex relationships, sexual assault, child sexual abuse, contraception and abortion, pornography, and prostitution, among others. We have provided a complete list of the sexually related statutes in the *Criminal Code of Canada*, as well as a history of the evolution of some of these statutes.

Relevant, Engaging Pedagogy

Fourth, to understand human sexuality fully, one must recognize one's own sexuality, as well as the diversity of others. We highlight research and issues that are of particular interest to Canadian students in each chapter and provide support for student understanding of personal sexuality in several ways:

- The frank presentation of information helps students feel more at ease with thinking and talking about sex, increasing their comfort with a tension-causing topic and helping them make responsible decisions.
- **First Person** boxes share how sexuality may be experienced on the personal level. One such box features Fran Odette, a sexual health educator, whose mission is to educate people about sexuality and disabilities and the assumptions and misconceptions that are often made about this specific group.

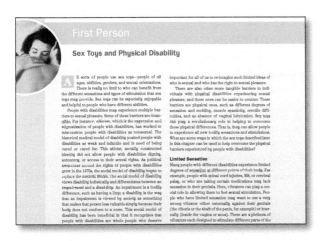

- **A Sexually Diverse World** boxes present an appreciation of the fabulous diversity of human sexuality along many dimensions, including but not limited to age, sexual orientation, gender identity, and ethnicity within Canada and around the world.

- **Milestones in Sex Research** boxes provide students with an extended look at classic and new studies that influence our understanding of human sexuality, and the people that pioneered these developments.

- **Learning Objectives** at the beginning of each chapter provide a preview of topics to help students prepare for reading and studying.

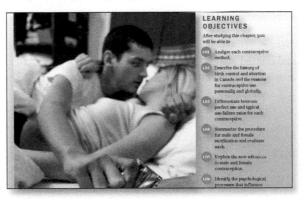

- **Key terms** are defined and placed on each page close to where the term is introduced for easy reference. In addition, all key terms are included in the Glossary.

- **End-of-chapter review tools** in each chapter include a chapter summary that reviews the main points discussed.

Our own courses are surveys, designed to provide students with a broad range of information about sexuality. Reflecting that approach, this book is intended to be complete and balanced in its coverage. For instructors who lack the time or resources to cover the entire book, or for those who prefer to rearrange the order of topics, we have written all the chapters to be fairly independent of one another.

What's New in the Seventh Canadian Edition?

Building on the first six editions, this text provides Canadian data wherever possible. It features Canadian research and researchers, describes sexuality in the major Canadian ethnocultural communities, highlights issues important to Canadian students, and ensures that inclusive language and visuals appear throughout. Some of the major content changes and additions to the seventh Canadian edition include the following:

Chapter 1 Sexuality in Perspective

- Updated statistics throughout chapter
- Updated images
- Introduced concept of *microaggressions* in the context of ethnic minorities, with extensions to sexual minorities
- Introduced concept of *intersectionality* and its impact
- Updated information on regional differences in sexuality between Quebec and the rest of Canada, as well as differing attitudes between Canada and the U.S.
- NEW Critical Thinking Skill box introduction

Chapter 2 Theoretical Perspectives on Sexuality

- Significantly reorganized and expanded chapter content
- Updated images
- Added new section on *critical theories*
- Introduced new sections on *feminist theory* and *queer theory*
- Substantially revised section on *sociological theories:* Order of presentation updated from the most specific social influences to the most general
- Added summary of *field theory*
- Updated Table 2.1: Summary of the Sexual Offences in the *Criminal Code of Canada* in 2017
- NEW Critical Thinking Skill box on the difference between truth and validity

Chapter 3 Sex Research

- Updated images
- Revised discussion on *meta-analysis*

- Updated discussion of *ethical issues* with new research on people who participate in sex research
- Added data on British (Natsal) and Australian (ASHR) surveys
- Included new section on the *validity of self-report data*
- NEW Critical Thinking Skill box on the importance of sampling

Chapter 4 Sexual Anatomy

- Revised feature on *female genital mutilation*
- Updated research on new drugs used in the prevention and treatment of breast cancer
- Updated recommendations by the Canadian Paediatric Society on male circumcision images
- NEW Critical Thinking Skill box on differences between anecdotal and scientific evidence

Chapter 5 Sex Hormones, Sexual Differentiation, and Menstruation

- Added study on epigenetic changes in the brain during prenatal sexual differentiation added
- Introduced information on recently discovered hormone *kisspeptin* and its role during puberty
- Added content from *DSM-5*
- Increased discussion on menstrual cycle fluctuations in mood
- NEW Critical Thinking Skill box on how scientific research can be applied to making policy decisions

Chapter 6 Conception, Pregnancy, and Childbirth

- Updated statistics throughout the chapter
- Updated coverage of psychological changes in fathers during pregnancy
- Revised discussion on effects of alcohol consumption during pregnancy
- Broadened discussion distinguishing *fetal alcohol spectrum disorder* and *fetal alcohol syndrome*
- Updated data on use of anesthetics during childbirth
- Added images on midwifery and home births
- Updated data on risks of HSV transmission to fetus during birth
- NEW Critical Thinking Skill box on evaluating health care alternatives

Chapter 7 Contraception and Abortion

- Introduced LARC (long-acting reversible contraceptives) category
- Introduced new methods of birth control: Ella and Skyla

- Added data on women denied abortions
- Added Ontario focus group study on female orgasm
- Updated images
- Updated material on cybersex
- NEW Critical Thinking Skill box on the concept of probability with respect to contraceptives

Chapter 8 Sexually Transmitted Infections

- Updated statistics throughout the chapter
- Complete revision of discussion on HIV/AIDS reflecting new view of HIV as manageable long-term disease
- Featured new developments in antiretroviral therapy (ART), treatment as prevention, and preexposure prophylaxis
- Updated discussion on HPV vaccine
- Added First Person feature describing cool lines about safer sex
- NEW Critical Thinking Skill box on the concept of probability with respect to sexually transmitted infections

Chapter 9 Sexual Arousal

- Updated statistics throughout chapter
- Section on brain imaging studies rewritten for greater clarity and accessibility
- NEW Critical Thinking Skill box on defending against everyday persuasive techniques

Chapter 10 Sexuality and the Life Cycle: Childhood and Adolescence

- Updated statistics throughout chapter, with special attention to frequencies of behaviours
- Improved coverage on trans individuals
- Expanded discussion of first intercourse
- Expanded coverage on casual sex in college
- Updated discussion of multi-person sex in late adolescence
- Revised First Person feature: Becoming a Teen Mother: An Indigenous Woman's Story
- Added coverage of adolescent views of ideal romantic relationships
- Updated discussion of postrelationship sex
- NEW Critical Thinking Skill box on decision making and problem solving

Chapter 11 Sexuality and the Life Cycle: Adulthood

- Added more inclusive language of cohabitating and same-sex relationships

- Expanded coverage of extra-dyadic sex
- Expanded discussion on use of electronic apps (e.g., Grindr and Tinder) to meet people, and the impact of this technology on initiating, maintaining, and terminating relationships
- Extensively revised discussion on menopause
- Added information on long-term relationships
- NEW Critical Thinking Skill box on hypothesis testing

Chapter 12 Attraction, Love, and Communication

- Updated statistics throughout the chapter
- Added research on the role of the Internet regarding where mixed-sex and same-sex individuals meet
- Increased discussion of the role of physical attractiveness and its relative importance in selecting mates
- Added new material on cross-cultural research testing hypothesis on sexual strategies theories and mating preferences
- Added new subsection on relationship education programs, their effectiveness, and their applications to military couples
- NEW Critical Thinking Skill box on the importance of clear communication

Chapter 13 Gender and Sexuality

- Introduced new term: *gender binary*
- Extensively revised transgender discussion
- Revised language to be much more inclusive to those who fall outside the gender binary
- Chapter content revised by authors in consultation with trans research expert and genderqueer individual
- Updated DSM-5 terminology and concepts
- Expanded discussion on vomeronasal organ and human pheromones
- Presented new evidence on recently identified gene coding for pheromone receptors
- NEW Critical Thinking Skill box on stereotyping

Chapter 14 Sexual Orientation and Identity: Gay, Lesbian, Bi, Straight, or Asexual?

- Updated statistics about attitudes on homosexuality around the world
- New Milestones in Sex Research feature: Does Gaydar Exist?
- Expanded discussion of the sexuality of sexual-minority women

- Added data on the resilience of LGB individuals
- Added new hypothesis on epigenetic factors in prenatal development
- Introduced new data on bisexuality
- Expanded research and discussion on "mostly heterosexuals"
- Expanded discussion on attitudes toward asexuality
- NEW Critical Thinking Skill Box on interpreting research findings

Chapter 15 Variations in Sexual Behaviour

- Updated research and statistics throughout the chapter
- Significantly revised language and discussion throughout chapter to align with DSM-5 criteria
- Added new research on *kink* communities and their varied practices
- Substantially revised Milestones in Sex Research feature on sexual addictions
- Expanded discussion on *hypersexuality* types and treatments
- Added more nuanced discussion of pornography use and types/categories of misuse
- Clarified differentiation between compulsive and addictive behaviours
- Revised section on treatments of sexual variations
- Clearly distinguished definitions of paraphilias and paraphilic disorders
- Added research on effectiveness of AA and 12-step treatment programs
- NEW Critical Thinking Skill Box on using diagnostic labels accurately

Chapter 16 Sexual Coercion

- Updated statistics throughout the chapter
- Added new section on the role of alcohol in sexual assault
- Added new material on sexual harassment and assault in the Canadian Armed Forces and the RCMP
- Added new section on consent
- Revised First Person box: What to Do after a Sexual Assault
- NEW Critical Thinking Skill box on analyzing an argument

Chapter 17 Sex for Sale

- Updated statistics throughout the chapter
- Added material on the intersection of social class and race in sex work venues

- Expanded discussion on role of technology in commercial sex work
- Added research on sex work as a career
- New First Person box: Working Their Way through University
- Expanded discussion of male sex workers and the venues in which they work
- Updated discussion on online pornography and the effects of exposure
- Added new subsection on pornographic producers
- Reorganized and updated material on consumers
- Introduced discussion of pornography addiction
- NEW Critical Thinking Skill box on identifying the differences between everyday beliefs and scientific evidence

Chapter 18 Sexual Disorders and Sex Therapy

- Updated DSM-5 terminology and concepts, while noting controversies over DSM-5 criteria
- Updated discussion of Viagra and similar drugs that are PDE5 inhibitors
- New discussion on *flibanserin*, the so-called "pink Viagra"
- Revised male hypoactive sexual desire disorder section
- Updated data on the effectiveness of various treatments
- NEW Critical Thinking Skill box on using diagnostic labels accurately

Chapter 19 Sexuality Education

- Updated statistics throughout the chapter
- Updated information on parental attitudes toward sexual health education
- NEW Critical Thinking Skill box on using science in forming public policy

Chapter 20 Ethics, Religion, and Sexuality

- Updated pro-life and pro-choice statements of religious groups
- New information on religious groups performing same-sex marriages
- NEW Critical Thinking Skill box on the difference between questions that can be decided by religious beliefs versus those that can be decided by scientific data

Superior Learning Solutions and Support

The McGraw-Hill Education team is ready to help you assess and integrate any of our products, technology, and services into your course for optimal teaching and learning performance. Whether it's helping your students improve their grades or putting your entire course online, the McGraw-Hill Education team is here to help you do it. Contact your Learning Solutions Consultant today to learn how to maximize all of McGraw-Hill Education's resources!

For more information, please visit us online at http://www.mheducation.ca/he/solutions.

Acknowledgements

I am extremely fortunate to have been able to call on a wide network of Canadian scholars in preparing the Canadian editions of *Understanding Human Sexuality*. Many of my colleagues and friends have been as generous with their time and expertise as I prepared this seventh Canadian edition as they were for the previous editions. I appreciate their contributions enormously. I am also appreciative that so many people were willing to provide me with copies of their scholarly work—their work is cited throughout this book. I have also benefited from the students in my classes. They keep me up to date on what university students are thinking and wondering about sexuality.

I am indebted to the current and former members of my sexuality research group at the University of New Brunswick who provided input for one or more of the six editions. Thank you especially to Shannon Glenn, Marvin Claybourn, Jacqueline Cohen, Lyndsay Foster, Kaitlyn Goldsmith, Miranda Fudge, Cindy Letts, Christie Little, Sheila MacNeil, Sarah McAulay, Lorna Scott, Krystelle Shaughnessy, Deanne Simms, Sara Thornton, Jennifer Thurlow, Sarah Vannier, Ashley Thompson, and Angela Weaver. I am indebted to the various people who helped me identify the individuals whose life experiences are highlighted in the First Person boxes. These individuals often wrote or edited these stories themselves. Others willingly wrote Milestones in Sex Research boxes reflecting their expertise. This includes Lori Brotto, James Cantor, Jacqueline Cohen, Lyndsay Foster, Peggy Kleinplatz, Gayle MacDonald, Dana Menard, Krystelle Shaughnessy, Cory Silverberg, Kaleigh Trace, and Kris Wells. I am particularly grateful to the people (all Canadians) who agreed to share their own experiences in these boxes, including Laurie Alpert, Josh Byers, Cheryl Dobinson, William Fisher, Trevor Jacques, Kim McKay-McNab, Fran Odette, Faizal Suhukhan, Ayesha Suhukhan, Paul Vasey, and Richard Wassersung, as well as the people who chose to remain anonymous.

I would like to thank Mary Byers (no relation) who was enormously helpful in tracking down information. I am also enormously grateful to Susan Voyer, who served as my research assistant for the previous four editions of the textbook. This book would be noticeably poorer without her contributions over the years.

The seventh Canadian edition of *Understanding Human Sexuality* has benefited from the careful reviews and valuable feedback of the following instructors:

Anne Almey, Concordia University

Cynthia Clarke, University of Guelph

Shaniff Esmail, University of Alberta

Derek Fisher, Mount Saint Vincent University

Elena Hannah, Memorial University of Newfoundland

Lisa Henry, University of Ottawa

Carla Labella, Mohawk College

Anick Legault, Dawson College

Dawn More, Algonquin College

Hiliary Rose, Concordia University

Kim Regehr, Conestoga College

Kate Salters, Simon Fraser University

Renu Sharma-Persaud, University of Windsor

Brandy Wiebe, University of British Columbia

I also owe many thanks to the editors and staff at McGraw-Hill Education: Scott Hardie, portfolio manager; Tammy Mavroudi, content developer; Stephanie Gibson, Jeanette McCurdy, and Janie Deneau, supervising editors; Michelle Saddler and Sheryl MacAdam, production coordinators; Mike Kelly, copy editor; and Monika Schurmann, photo researcher and permissions editor.

Finally, I could not have written this book without the enthusiastic support of my family. The love and gratitude I feel toward my husband, Larry, our daughters Krista and Alyssa, and now our granddaughter Julia, are immeasurable.

E. Sandra Byers

connect·2

The Complete Course Solution

We listened to educators from around the world, learned about their challenges, and created a whole new way to deliver a course.

Connect2 is a collaborative teaching and learning platform that includes an instructionally designed complete course framework of learning materials that is flexible and open for instructors to easily personalize, add their own content, or integrate with other tools and platforms

- Save time and resources building and managing a course.
- Gain confidence knowing that each course framework is pedagogically sound.
- Help students master course content.
- Make smarter decisions by using real-time data to guide course design, content changes, and remediation.

MANAGE — Dynamic Curriculum Builder

Quickly and easily launch a complete course framework developed by instructional design experts. Each Connect2 course is a flexible foundation for instructors to build upon by adding their own content or drawing upon the wide repository of additional resources.

- Easily customize Connect2 by personalizing the course scope and sequence.
- Get access to a wide range of McGraw-Hill Education content within one powerful teaching and learning platform.
- Receive expert support and guidance on how best to utilize content to achieve a variety of teaching goals.

MASTER — Student Experience

Improve student performance with instructional alignment and leverage Connect2's carefully curated learning resources. Deliver required reading through Connect2's award-winning adaptive learning system.

- Teach at a higher level in class by helping students retain core concepts.
- Tailor in-class instruction based on student progress and engagement.
- Help focus students on the content they don't know so they can prioritize their study time.

MEASURE — Advanced Analytics

Collect, analyze and act upon class and individual student performance data. Make real-time course updates and teaching decisions backed by data.

- Visually explore class and student performance data.
- Easily identify key relationships between assignments and student performance
- Maximize in-class time by using data to focus on areas where students need the most help.

Course Map

The flexible and customizable course map provides instructors full control over the pre-designed courses within Connect2. Instructors can easily add, delete, or rearrange content to adjust the course scope and sequence to their personal preferences.

Implementation Guide

Each Connect2 course includes a detailed implementation guide that provides guidance on what the course can do and how best to utilize course content based on individual teaching approaches.

Instructor Resources

A comprehensive collection of instructor resources are available within Connect2. Instructor Support and Seminar Materials provide additional exercises and activities to use for in-class discussion and teamwork.

For more information, please visit www.mheconnect2.com

CHAPTER 1

Sexuality in Perspective

©Michael DeFreitas South America / Alamy

LEARNING OBJECTIVES

After studying this chapter, you will be able to

LO1 Identify some of the issues surrounding the terms sex and gender.

LO2 Show the influences on sexuality of religion, science, the media, and the Internet.

LO3 Describe the contributions of the major sex researchers to sex research and education.

LO4 Differentiate between sexual attitudes and behaviours in Canada and other cultures.

LO5 Identify the influences of social class, gender, ethnicity, and geographic region in the sexual behaviour of Canadians.

LO6 Compare sexual behaviour in humans and other species.

LO7 Explain the principles of the sexual health and sexual rights perspectives.

Are YOU Curious?

1. Do people in other cultures have sex the same way as people do in Canada?
2. Is Quebec a distinct society sexually speaking?
3. Is same-sex sexual behaviour found in other species?

Read this chapter to find out.

"You're so beautiful," he whispered. "I want a picture of you just like this with your face flushed and your lips wet and shiny." . . . He tore open a foil packet he'd retrieved from his pocket. Mesmerized, she watched him sheath himself, amazed at how hard he was. She reached out to touch him, but he moved back, made sure she was ready, and then slid neatly inside her, so deeply she gasped. She contracted her muscles around him, and he closed his eyes and groaned, the sound so primal, it made her skin tingle.*

Human sexual behaviour is a diverse phenomenon. It occurs in different physical locations and social contexts, consists of a wide range of specific activities, and is perceived differently by different people. An individual engages in sexual activity on the basis of a complex set of motivations and organizes that activity on the basis of numerous external factors and influences. Thus, it is unlikely that the tools and concepts from any single scientific discipline will suffice to answer all or even most of the questions one might ask about sexual behaviour.†

Having children and healthy families are important goals to most Canadians, but some people cannot reach those goals without help. If there are technologies that can be used to help, a caring society should provide these. But there are misuses and harms, as well as benefits, that may come from use of the technologies—harms to both individuals and society.‡

---

* Debbi Rawlins. (2003). *Anything goes.* New York, NY: Harlequin Blaze.
† Laumann et al. (1994).
‡ Royal Commission on New Reproductive Technologies (1993).

Strikingly different though they may seem, all of the above quotations are talking about the same thing— sex. The first quotation is from a romance novel. It is intended to stimulate the reader's fantasies and arousal. The second is from a scholarly book about sex. It aims to stimulate the brain but not the genitals. The third is from a Royal Commission on the treatment of infertility. It points out the complexity of many sexual issues. From reading these brief excerpts, we can quickly see that the topic of sexuality is diverse, complex, and fascinating.

Why study sex? Most people are curious about sex, particularly because exchanging sexual information is somewhat taboo in our culture, so curiosity motivates us to study sex. Sex is an important force in many people's lives, so we have practical reasons for wanting to learn about it. Finally, most of us at various times experience concerns about our sexual functioning or wish that we could function better, and we hope that learning more about sex will help us. This book is designed to address all these needs. We'll consider several perspectives on sexuality: the effects of religion, science, the media, and culture on our understanding of sexuality, as well as a sexual health perspective. These perspectives make it clear that the study of sexuality is

not confined to one discipline but rather is multidisciplinary. However, first we must draw an important distinction between *sex* and *gender*.

 L01

Sex and Gender

Sometimes the word *sex* is used ambiguously. In some cases sex refers to being male or female, and sometimes it refers to sexual behaviour or reproduction. In most cases, of course, the meaning is clear from the context. If you are filling out a job application form and one item says "Sex," you don't write, "I like it" or "As often as possible." It is clear that your prospective employer wants to know whether you are a male or a female. In other cases, though, the meaning may be ambiguous. For example, when a book has the title *Sex and Temperament in Three Primitive Societies,* what is it about? Is it about the sexual practices of primitive people and whether having sex frequently gives them pleasant temperaments? Or is it about the kinds of personalities that males and females are expected to have in those societies? Not only does this use of the word sex create ambiguities, but it also clouds our thinking about some important issues.

To remove—or at least reduce—this ambiguity, the term *sex* will be used in this book in contexts referring to sexual anatomy and sexual behaviour, and the term **gender** will be used to refer to being male or female. Almost all of the research that we discuss in this book has been based on scientists assuming the "gender binary," the idea that there are only two genders, male and female.

This is a book about sex, not gender; it is about sexual behaviour and the biological, psychological, and social forces that influence it. Of course, although we are arguing that sex and gender are conceptually different, we would not try to argue that they are totally independent of each other. Certainly, gender roles—the ways in which males and females are expected to behave—exert a powerful influence on the way people behave sexually, and so one chapter will be devoted to gender connections to sexuality.

How should we define sex, aside from saying that it is different from gender? A biologist might define sexual behaviour as "any behavior that increases the likelihood of gametic union [union of sperm and egg]" (Bermant & Davidson, 1974). This definition emphasizes the reproductive function of sex. However, medical advances, such as the birth control pill, have allowed us to separate reproduction from sex. Most Canadians now have sex not only for procreation but also for pleasure and intimacy.[1]

Noted sex researcher Alfred Kinsey defined sex as behaviour that leads to orgasm. Although this definition has some merits (it does not imply that sex must be associated with reproduction), it also presents some problems. If one person has intercourse with another person but does not have an orgasm, was that not sexual behaviour for her or him? If an individual has an orgasm through oral–genital stimulation, is that sex? Indeed, researchers in Canada have shown that undergraduate students have a very narrow definition of the term sex. Whereas almost everybody thought that penile–vaginal and penile–anal intercourse constituted having sex, only about one-quarter of participants thought that oral sex resulting in orgasm would be defined as sex (Byers,

Henderson, & Hobson, 2009; Randall & Byers, 2003; Trotter & Alderson, 2007). Our definition in this textbook includes much more than that, though.

To try to avoid some of these problems, **sexual behaviour** will be defined in this book as *behaviour that produces arousal and increases the chance of orgasm.*[2]

Influences on Sexuality

Religion

Religion is a source of values and ethics regarding sexuality and, as such, is a powerful influence on the sexual attitudes and behaviour of many individuals. The moral code for each religion is unique—each religion has different views on what is right and what is wrong with respect to sexuality. Throughout most of recorded history, at least until about 100 years ago, religion (and rumour) provided most of the information that people had about sexuality, and in some cultures it still does. Here are a few historical examples of how different religions understood sexuality.

The ancient Greeks openly acknowledged both heterosexuality and homosexuality in their society and explained the existence of the two in a myth in which the original humans were double creatures with twice the normal number of limbs and organs; some were double males, some were double females, and some were half male and half female (LeVay, 1996). The gods, fearing the power of these creatures, split them in half, and forever after each one continued to search for its missing half. Heterosexuals were thought to have resulted from the splitting of the half male, half female; male homosexuals, from the splitting of the double male; and female homosexuals, from the splitting of the double female. It was through this mythology that the ancient Greeks understood sexual orientation and sexual desire.

Fifteenth-century Christians believed that "wet dreams" (nocturnal emissions) resulted from intercourse with tiny spiritual creatures called *incubi* and *succubi*, a notion put forth in a papal bull (an official document) of 1484 and a companion book, the *Malleus Maleficarum* ("witch's hammer"). The *Malleus* became the official manual of the Inquisition, in which people, particularly women, were tried as witches. Wet dreams, sexual dysfunction, and sexual lust were seen to be caused by witchcraft (Hergenhahn, 2001).

Over the centuries, Muslims have believed that sexual intercourse is one of the finest pleasures of life, reflecting the teachings of the great prophet Muhammad. Sexuality is regarded primarily as a source of pleasure and only secondarily

---

[1] Actually, even in former times sex was not always associated with reproduction. For example, a man in 1850 might have fathered 10 children; using a very conservative estimate that he engaged in sexual intercourse 1500 times during his adult life (once a week for the 30 years from age 20 to age 50), only 10 in 1500 of those acts, or fewer than 1 percent, resulted in reproduction.

[2] This definition, though an improvement over some, still has its problems. For example, consider a woman who feels no arousal at all during intercourse. According to the definition, intercourse would not be sexual behaviour for her. However, intercourse would generally be something we would want to classify as sexual behaviour. It should be clear that defining sexual behaviour is difficult.

---

gender: Being male, female, or some other gender such as trans.

sexual behaviour: Behaviour that produces arousal and increases the chance of orgasm.

First Person

Paul: The Story of a Gay Anglican Priest

Paul was born in 1950, the second of two children, to upper-middle-class parents in Nova Scotia. His parents stressed the importance of education, and there was no question that Paul would go to university, something his parents had not done. Paul described his parents as old-fashioned—more like parents were in the 1930s than like parents in the 1950s.

By the age of five, Paul realized two things about how he was different than other children. First, he wasn't interested in typical childhood activities, such as sports. Second, he was attracted to boys, not girls. As a result, he was a loner and turned to reading, art, music, and painting. It also became very important to Paul to receive the approval of adults. Growing up, Paul's parents attended the Anglican Church every week, but religion was not emphasized in his home. Nonetheless, Paul was drawn to religion, especially the ritual, music, and artistic forms that were part of it.

Paul's parents never talked to him about sex. Indeed, he never heard his father mention anything sexual. He did hear his mother whisper and giggle about sexual issues with her friends. This lack of communication made him realize that his parents couldn't handle sexuality issues. Sexuality also was never mentioned by anyone connected with the Anglican Church, although Paul got the impression that "it was seen as an unpleasantness." He played sex games, such as "You show me yours and I'll show you mine" with other boys, but he had no interest in playing these games with girls. He did not have bad feelings about his sexual orientation but sensed that this was something he should definitely not discuss with either his parents or his priest. The fact that he could not be open about his sexual orientation made him feel increasingly lonely as a teenager.

Paul's first sexual experimentation occurred in university with "no strings attached, conveniently available" partners. He found the opportunity to express his sexuality fulfilling. He fell in love three times but says he "got hurt every time." When he was 37, he became engaged to a woman who had been kind to him when he had been ill and wanted to marry him even though she knew that he was gay. In the end, he realized that he was confusing kindness with love and that he could never be faithful to her, so he called the engagement off.

At first Paul fought the idea of entering the ministry. However, in his 20s he realized that "he had no choice" but to study for the priesthood. According to Paul, his sexuality went underground as a result because he was aware that being gay was not something the Anglican

as a means of reproduction, although the way the laws of the Quran are carried out has varied considerably from country to country (Boonstra, 2001; Ilkkaracan, 2001).

People of different religions hold different understandings of human sexuality, and these religious views often influence behaviour profoundly. The impact of religion on Canadians is particularly apparent in the discussion of homosexuality and abortion. For example, conservative Christians often use their interpretation of the Bible, an interpretation that is not shared by other Christian denominations, to justify their opposition to same-sex sexual behaviour and same-sex marriage. Other Canadians feel that these arguments have more to do with anti-gay prejudice and homophobia than with religion. A detailed discussion of religion and sexuality is provided in Chapter 20 (also see the First Person box).

L03 Science

It was against this background of religious understandings of sexuality that the scientific study of sex began in the nineteenth century, although, of course, religious notions continue to influence our ideas about sexuality. In addition, the groundwork for an understanding of the biological aspects of sexuality had already been laid by the research of physicians and biologists. Dutch microscopist Anton van Leeuwenhoek (1632–1723) had discovered sperm swimming in human semen. In 1875 Oskar Hertwig (1849–1922) first observed the fertilization of the egg by the sperm in sea urchins, although the ovum in humans was not directly observed until the twentieth century.

Figure 1.3 presents a timeline of scientific research in sexuality since 1900. A major advance in the scientific understanding of the psychological aspects of human sexuality came with the work of Viennese physician Sigmund Freud (1856–1939; see Figure 1.1), founder of psychiatry and psychoanalysis. His ideas will be discussed in detail in Chapter 2.

It is important to recognize the cultural context in which Freud and the other early sex researchers crafted their research and writing. They began their work in the

Church would tolerate. When he was ordained as a priest at age 26, he resigned himself to never living in a loving, long-term relationship with another man. At the time, he felt that he could accept this because he had "married the church." Nonetheless, he continued to have uncommitted sex (celibacy is not required of Anglican priests).

Paul feels that because he was not married to a woman, the church hierarchy assumed he was gay. However, they were careful to "never ask the question so that they would not have to deal with the answer." Nonetheless, he feels that his career in the church was clearly impeded by his sexual orientation. For example, in contrast to married priests, he was not given the opportunity to move to other diocese to take on new challenges or to assume positions of leadership. He believes that the people in his parish also assumed he was gay. He heard reports of criticism of his sexual orientation by some of his parishioners, but these complaints did not go anywhere because there was never proof that he was gay. Nonetheless, the secrecy and lack of acceptance took their toll on Paul, and he developed an addiction to alcohol. Paul knew other gay priests, including a gay bishop who was a good friend and lover, who also were forced to hide their sexual orientation. Through it all, Paul never wavered in his commitment to his religion.

According to Paul, the official policy of the Anglican Church of Canada with respect to sexual orientation is that "heterosexual sex may be exercised within the confines of heterosexual marriage. Homosexuals must be celibate. Human rights do not enter the issue." However, Paul feels that the actual reception that homosexual church members get depends on whom they talk to. Whereas some clergy are open and welcoming to people of all sexual orientations, others appear to be "waging a vendetta against anyone who is not heterosexual."

Paul retired from the church at the age of 44 because of illness, although he remains a priest. Since that time, he has been more open about his sexuality. He has taken on the task of promoting the rights of non-heterosexuals within the church, trying to make the church more inclusive. This task was something he did not feel he could do when he was a parish priest. He would like the church to provide a safe environment in which people find spiritual sustenance and give support to one another without fear of reprisal. The Anglican Church appears to be moving in that direction; in 2016 it voted to accept same-sex marriage. However, there will need to be a second vote in 2020 before this becomes official policy.

Source: Based on an interview by Sandra Byers.

Victorian era, the late nineteenth century, both in North America and in Europe. Norms about sexuality were extraordinarily rigid and oppressive (see Figure 1.2). Historian Peter Gay characterized this repressive aspect of Victorian cultural norms as

> a devious and insincere world in which middle class husbands slaked their lust by keeping mistresses, frequenting prostitutes, or molesting children, while their wives, timid, dutiful, obedient, were sexually anesthetic and poured all their capacity for love into their housekeeping and their child-rearing. (Gay, 1984, p. 6)

Yet at the same time, the sexual behaviour of Victorians was sometimes in violation of societal norms and expectations. Dr. Clelia Mosher was a physician who spent 30 years conducting a sex survey of Victorian women in the United States. Although the sample was small (47 women) and nonrandom, her results provide an alternative description of female sexuality during this period. For example, despite the Victorian

stereotype that women felt no sexual desire, 80 percent of women who answered the question said that they felt a desire for sexual intercourse. Similarly, 72 percent of women indicated that they experienced orgasm. One woman commented that sex had been unpleasant for her for years because of her "slow reaction" but "orgasm [occurs] if time is taken." In his history of sexuality in the Victorian era, Gay (1984) documented the story of Mabel Loomis Todd, who, though married, carried on a lengthy affair with Austin Dickinson, a community leader in Amherst, Massachusetts. Many people knew about the "secret" affair, yet Mrs. Loomis Todd did not become an outcast.

An equally great—though not so well known—early contributor to the scientific study of sex was Henry Havelock Ellis (1859–1939; see Figure 1.1). A physician in Victorian England, he compiled a vast collection of information on sexuality—including medical and anthropological findings and case histories—which was published in a series of volumes entitled *Studies in the Psychology of Sex* beginning in 1896. Havelock Ellis was

Figure 1.1   Two important early sex researchers. *(a)* Sigmund Freud. *(b)* Henry Havelock Ellis.

Figure 1.2   The Victorian era, from which Freud and Ellis emerged, was characterized by extreme sexual repression. Here is an apparatus that was sold to prevent *onanism* (masturbation).

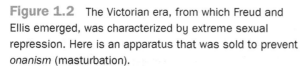

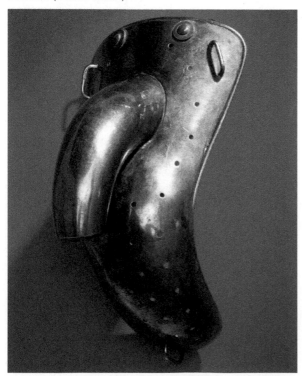

a remarkably objective and tolerant scholar, particularly for his era. He believed that women, like men, are sexual creatures. A sexual reformer, he believed that sexual variations from the norm are often harmless, and he urged society to accept them. In his desire to collect information about human sexuality rather than to make judgments about it, he can be considered the forerunner of modern sex research (for his autobiography, see Ellis, 1939; numerous biographies exist).

Another important figure in nineteenth-century sex research was German psychiatrist Richard von Krafft-Ebing (1840–1902) (Oosterhuis, 2000). His special interest was so-called pathological sexuality. He managed to collect more than 200 case histories of "pathological" individuals, which appeared in his book entitled *Psychopathia Sexualis*. His work tended to be neither objective nor tolerant. Nonetheless, it has had a lasting impact. He created the concepts of sadism, masochism, and pedophilia. The terms *heterosexuality* and *homosexuality* entered the English language in the 1892 translation of his book (Oosterhuis, 2000). One of his case histories is presented in Chapter 15.

One other early contributor to the scientific understanding of sexuality deserves mention: German physician Magnus Hirschfeld (1868–1935). He founded the first sex research institute and administered the first large-scale sex survey, obtaining data from 10 000 people on a 130-item questionnaire. Unfortunately, most of the information he amassed was destroyed by the Nazis.

Figure 1.3 The history of scientific research on sex.

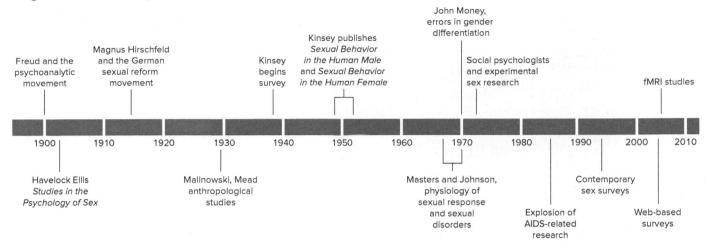

Hirschfeld also established the first journal devoted to the study of sexuality, established a marriage counselling service, worked for legal reforms, and gave advice on contraception and sex problems. His special interest, however, was homosexuality. He made important contributions as a pioneer sex researcher (Bullough, 1994).

In the twentieth century, major breakthroughs in the scientific understanding of sex came with the massive surveys of human sexual behaviour in the United States conducted by Alfred Kinsey and his colleagues in the 1940s, and with William Masters and Virginia Johnson's investigations of sexual disorders and the physiology of sexual response. These studies changed how people thought about sex and led to more open public discussion of sexuality (Connell & Hunt, 2006). At about the same time that the Kinsey research was being conducted, some anthropologists—most notably Margaret Mead and Bronislaw Malinowski—were beginning to collect data on sexual behaviour in other cultures. The 1990s saw a significant increase in research on sexuality in close relationships (Christopher & Sprecher, 2000).

A major national survey of the sexual behaviour of Canadians has never been conducted. However, Statistics Canada has included some questions about sexuality in several national surveys, such as the Canadian Community Health Survey, the National Population Health Survey, the General Social Survey, and the National Longitudinal Survey of Children and Youth. Canadian researchers have also conducted a large number of smaller investigations that have provided important information on a rich array of sexual topics (see Chapter 3 for a description of the work of some of these researchers).

The scientific study of sexuality has not emerged as a separate, unified academic discipline like biology or psychology or sociology, although some researchers do call themselves sexologists. Rather, it tends to be interdisciplinary—a joint effort by biologists, psychologists, sociologists, anthropologists, and physicians (see Figure 1.3). This approach to understanding sexuality gives us a better view of humans in all their sexual complexity.

The Media

In terms of potency of influence, the mass media in North America today may play the same role that religion did in previous centuries. Canadians are influenced both by Canadian programs and, perhaps more so, by American prime-time television. Adolescents spend 11 hours per day with some form of mass media (Rideout, Foehr, & Roberts, 2010). Television viewing occupies the most time of all leisure activities, an average of 2.8 hours per day for those aged 15 and older (Bureau of Labor Statistics, 2016). An analysis of the 25 television programs most frequently viewed by adolescents indicated that, in a typical hour of viewing, adolescents are exposed to an average of 17 instances of sexual talk or sexual behaviour (Schooler et al., 2009). References to safer sex—both for sexually transmitted infection and pregnancy prevention—are rare. Only 2 percent of sexual scenes portray any sexual precautions. Many, but not most, Canadians (47 percent) think there is too much sexually explicit programming on prime-time TV (*Maclean's/Global Poll*, 2000; see Figure 1.4).

In short, the average Canadian's views about sexuality are likely to be much more influenced by the mass media than by scientific findings. Communications theorists believe that the media can have three types of influence (Brown, 2002; Kunkel et al., 2007). The first, called **cultivation**, refers to the notion that people begin to think that what they see on television and in other media really represents the mainstream of what happens

Figure 1.4 Sexual portrayals in the media have become much more explicit, as in this scene from *Twilight.*

©AF archive / Alamy

in our culture (Gerbner, Gross, & Morgan, 2002). For example, university students who watch soap operas are more likely than non-viewing students to overestimate the incidence of divorce. The second influence is **agenda-setting**. News reporters select what to report and what to ignore and, within the stories they report, what to emphasize. For example, in 1998 the U.S. media chose to highlight the sexual dalliances of President Bill Clinton, suggesting to the public that these matters were important. In contrast, the Canadian media have rarely focused on the sexual activities of Canadian politicians. The media in many ways tell us what agenda to pay attention to. The third influence is **social learning**, a theory we will take up in detail in Chapter 2. The contention

cultivation: In communications theory, the view that exposure to the mass media makes people think that what they see there represents the mainstream of what really occurs.
agenda-setting: In communications theory, the idea that the media define what is important and what is not by which stories they cover.
social learning: In communications theory, the idea that the media provide role models whom we imitate.

here is that characters on television, in the movies, or in romance novels may serve as models whom we imitate, perhaps without even realizing it. Research has found, for example, that teens who watch more sexy television engage in first intercourse earlier than do other teens (Brown, 2002).

The Internet

The Internet is a powerful, mass media influence. Computer and Internet use is spreading more rapidly than any previous technology, and most North American homes with children have Internet access. In 2012, 83 percent of Canadian adults were online, for personal, non-business reasons (Statistics Canada, 2014); use of social networking sites, such as Facebook, and the viewing of videos on YouTube are especially common among youth. Many individuals engage in sexual activity online. For example, research in New Brunswick found that 86 percent of male students and 39 percent of female students had viewed erotic pictures or videos on the Internet; 25 percent of the men and 13 percent of the women had engaged in sexual activity with a partner online (Shaughnessy, Byers, & Walsh, 2011). Thus, people, and especially young people, not only access sexual material that is posted on the Internet by others but also share explicit information and pictures of themselves through webcams, instant messaging, and smartphones (i.e., sexting); engage in sexual activity with known and anonymous partners; and engage in sexual activity through virtual worlds, such as Second Life.

As we will discuss in later chapters, the Internet has the potential for both positive and negative effects on sexual health. A number of sites, such as that for the Society of Obstetricians and Gynaecologists of Canada (see www.sexualityandu.ca), provide excellent information about sexuality and promote sexual health. At the same time, a repeated, well-sampled study of youth between the ages of 10 and 17 indicated that, whereas in 2000, 19 percent had been sexually solicited on the Internet, by 2010 this had fallen to 9 percent (Mitchell et al., 2013). Most youth who received a solicitation responded by removing themselves from the situation (blocking the solicitor, leaving the site) or telling the solicitor to stop. Experts believe that there is greater online safety for youth today than in the past, for a number of reasons. One is that they receive more talks about online safety from teachers and police (Mitchell et al., 2013).

In the chapters that follow, we will examine the content of the media and the Internet on numerous sexual issues, and we will consider what effects exposure to this media content might have on viewers.

Let us now consider the perspectives on sexuality that are provided by scientific observations of humans in a wide variety of societies.

LO4

Cross-Cultural Perspectives on Sexuality

Humans are a cultural species (Heine & Norenzayan, 2006). Although some other species are capable of learning from others, humans are unique in the way that cultural learning accumulates over time. What do anthropologists mean by the term *culture*? Generally, **culture** refers to traditional (that is, passed down from generation to generation) ideas and values transmitted to members of the group by symbols (such as language). These ideas and values then serve as the basis for patterns of behaviour observed in the group (S. Frayser, personal communication, 2004; Kroeber & Kluckhohn, 1963).

Ethnocentrism tends to influence people's understanding of human sexual behaviour. Most of us have had experience with sexuality in only one culture—Canada, for example—and we tend to view our sexual behaviour as the only pattern in existence and certainly as the only "natural" pattern. But anthropologists have discovered wide variations in sexual behaviour and attitudes from one culture to the next. There are even significant differences between Canada and the United States. For example, Canadians tend to have more permissive attitudes toward sexuality than Americans do. Some of these differences are summarized later in the chapter in Table 1.3. Considering variations across cultures should help us to put our own sexual behaviour in perspective.

The major generalization that emerges from cross-cultural studies (see Figure 1.5) is that all societies regulate sexual behaviour in some way, though the exact regulations vary greatly from one culture to the next (DeLamater, 1987). Apparently, no society has seen fit to leave sexuality totally unregulated, perhaps fearful that social disruption would result. As an example, **incest taboos** are nearly universal: Sex is regulated in that intercourse between blood relatives is prohibited (Gregersen, 1996). Most societies also condemn forced sexual relations, such as rape. Both incest and sexual assault are illegal in Canada.

Beyond this generalization, though, regulations vary greatly from one society to the next, and sexual behaviour and attitudes vary correspondingly (see the A Sexually Diverse World box. In fact, a comparison of data from 59 countries concluded that there are currently large differences in patterns of sexual behaviour from one region of the world to another (Wellings et al., 2006). Let's look at the ways in which various societies treat some key areas of human sexual behaviour.

Figure 1.5 Margaret Mead, an anthropologist, contributed much to the early cross-cultural study of sexuality.

AP Photo

Variations in Sexual Techniques

Kissing is one of the most common sexual techniques in our culture. It is also very common in most other societies (Gregersen, 1996). In a few societies, though, kissing is unknown. For example, when the Thonga of Africa first saw Europeans kissing, they laughed and said, "Look at them; they eat each other's saliva and dirt." There is also some variation in techniques of kissing. For example, among the Kwakiutl of British Columbia and the Trobriand Islanders, kissing consisted of sucking the lips and tongue of the partner, permitting saliva to flow from one mouth to the other.

Cunnilingus (mouth stimulation of the female genitals) is fairly common in our society, and it occurs in a few other societies as well, especially in the South Pacific. A particularly interesting variation is reported on the island of Ponape: The man places a fish in the woman's vulva and then gradually licks it out prior to coitus.

> **Do people in other cultures have sex the same way as people do in Canada?**

> **culture:** Traditional ideas and values passed down from generation to generation within a group and transmitted to members of the group by symbols (such as language).
> **ethnocentrism:** The tendency to regard our own ethnic group and culture as superior to others' and to believe that its customs and way of life are the standards by which other cultures should be judged.
> **incest taboos:** Regulations prohibiting sexual interaction between close blood relatives, such as brother and sister or father and daughter.

A Sexually Diverse World

How Much Can Behaviours Vary? Sexuality in Two Societies

Inis Beag

Inis Beag is a small island off the coast of Ireland. It is probably one of the most naive and sexually repressive societies in the world.

The people of Inis Beag seem to have no knowledge of a number of sexual activities, such as French kissing, mouth stimulation of the breast, or hand stimulation of the partner's penis, much less oral sex or same-sex activity. Sex education is virtually nonexistent; parents do not seem to be able to bring themselves to discuss such embarrassing matters with their children, and they simply trust that, after marriage, nature will take its course.

Menstruation and menopause are sources of fear for the island women because they have no idea of their physiological significance. It is commonly believed that menopause can produce insanity; to ward off this condition, some women have retired from life in their mid-40s, and a few have confined themselves to bed until death years later.

The men believe that intercourse is hard on one's health. They will abstain from sex the night before they are to do a job that takes great energy. They do not approach women sexually during menstruation or for months after childbirth; a woman is considered dangerous to the male at these times.

The islanders abhor nudity. Only babies are allowed to bathe while nude. Adults wash only the parts of their bodies that extend beyond their clothing—face, neck, lower arms, hands, lower legs, and feet.

Premarital sex is essentially unknown. In marital sex, foreplay is generally limited to kissing and rough fondling of the buttocks. The husband invariably initiates the activity. The male-on-top is the only position used, and both partners keep their underwear on during the activity. The man has an orgasm quickly and falls asleep immediately. Female orgasm either is believed not to exist or is considered deviant.

Mangaia

In distinct contrast to Inis Beag is Mangaia, an island in the South Pacific. For the Mangaians, sex—for pleasure and for procreation—is a principal interest.

The Mangaian boy first hears of masturbation when he is about seven, and he may begin to masturbate at age eight or nine. At around age 13 he undergoes the superincision ritual (in which a slit is made on the top of the penis, along its entire length). This ritual initiates him into manhood; more important, however, the expert who performs the superincision gives him sexual instruction. He shows the boy how to perform oral sex, how to kiss and suck breasts, and how to bring his partner to orgasm several times before he has his own. About two weeks after the operation, the boy has intercourse with an experienced woman, which removes the scab from the superincision. She provides him with practice in various acts and positions and trains him to hold back until he can have simultaneous orgasms with his partner.

After this, the Mangaian boy actively seeks out girls, or they seek him out; soon he has coitus every night. The girl, who has received sexual instruction from an older woman, expects demonstration of the boy's virility as proof of his desire for her. What is valued is the ability of the male to continue vigorously the in-and-out action of coitus over long periods while the female moves her hips "like a washing machine." Nothing is despised more than a "dead" partner who does not move. A good man is expected to continue his actions for 15 to 30 minutes or more.

Between the ages of 13 and 20, the average girl will have three or four successive boyfriends; the average boy may have 10 or more girlfriends. Mangaian parents encourage their daughters to have sexual experiences with several men. They want them to find marriage partners who are congenial.

At around age 18, the Mangaians typically have sex most nights of the week, with about three orgasms per night. By about age 48, they have sex two or three times per week, with one orgasm each time.

All women in Mangaia apparently learn to have orgasms. Bringing his partner to orgasm is one of the man's chief sources of sexual pleasure.

Sources: Gregor, 1985; Marshall, 1971; Messenger, 1993

Inflicting pain on a partner is also a part of the sexual technique in some societies; most commonly, men and women mutually inflict pain on each other. The Apinaye woman of the Brazilian highlands may bite off bits of her partner's eyebrows, noisily spitting them aside. Ponapean men usually tug at the woman's eyebrows, occasionally yanking out tufts of hair. People of various societies bite their partners to the point of drawing blood and leaving scars (Frayser, 1985).

The frequency of intercourse for married couples varies considerably from one culture to the next. The lowest frequency seems to be among the Irish natives of Inis Beag, discussed in the A Sexually Diverse World box, who engage in intercourse perhaps only once or twice a month; however, the anthropologists who studied them were unable to determine exactly how often couples did have sex because so much secrecy surrounds the act. At the opposite extreme, the Mangaians, also described in the A Sexually Diverse World box, have intercourse several times a night, at least among the young. The Santals of southern Asia engage in sexual intercourse as often as five times per day every day early in marriage (Gregersen, 1996). Surveys of Canadian sexuality in the 1990s indicated that our frequency of intercourse was then about in the middle compared with other societies (e.g., "Doing It," 1999).

Very few societies *encourage* people to engage in sexual intercourse at particular times (Frayser, 1985). Instead, most groups have restrictions that *forbid* intercourse at certain times or in certain situations. For example, almost every society has a postpartum sex taboo—that is, a prohibition on sexual intercourse for a time after a woman has given birth, with the taboo lasting from a few days to more than a year (Gregersen, 1996).

Masturbation

Attitudes toward **masturbation**, or sexual self-stimulation of the genitals, vary widely across cultures. Some societies tolerate and some encourage masturbation during childhood and adolescence, whereas others condemn the practice at any age. Almost all human societies express some disapproval of adult masturbation, ranging from mild ridicule to severe punishment (Gregersen, 1996). Yet at least some adults in all societies appear to practise it.

Female masturbation certainly occurs in many societies. The African Azande woman uses a phallus made of a wooden root; however, if her husband catches her masturbating, he may beat her severely. The following is a description of the Lesu of the South Pacific, one of the few societies that express no disapproval of adult female masturbation:

A woman will masturbate if she is sexually excited and there is no man to satisfy her. A couple may be having intercourse in the same house, or near enough for her to see them, and she may thus become aroused. She then sits down and bends her right leg so that her heel presses against her genitalia. Even young girls of about six years may do this quite casually as they sit on the ground. The women and men talk about it freely, and there is no shame attached to it. It is a customary position for women to take, and they learn it in childhood. They never use their hands for manipulation.

(Powdermaker, 1933, pp. 276–277)

Premarital and Extramarital Sex

Societies differ considerably in their rules regarding premarital sex[3] (Frayser, 1985). At one extreme are the Marquesans of eastern Polynesia. Both boys and girls in that culture have participated in a wide range of sexual experiences before puberty. Their first experience with intercourse occurs with a partner of the other gender who is 30 to 40 years old. Mothers are proud if their daughters have many lovers. Only later does marriage occur. In contrast are the Egyptians of Siwa. In this culture a girl's clitoris is removed at age seven or eight to decrease her potential for sexual excitement and intercourse. Premarital intercourse is believed to bring shame on the family. Marriage usually occurs around the age of 12 or 13, shortening the premarital period and any temptations it might contain.

These two cultures are fairly typical of their regions. According to one study, 90 percent of Pacific Island societies permit premarital sex, as do 88 percent of African and 82 percent of Eurasian societies. In contrast, 73 percent of Mediterranean societies prohibit premarital sex (Frayser, 1985).

Extramarital sex is more complex and conflicted for most cultures. Extramarital sex ranks second only to incest as the most strictly prohibited type of sexual contact. One study found that it was forbidden for one or both partners in 74 percent of the cultures

masturbation: Self-stimulation of the genitals to produce sexual arousal.

[3] Although marriage as an institution is found in most, if not all, cultures, some people never marry or marry late in life. Some people choose not to marry; others are in same-sex relationships and cannot marry legally, as many countries do not permit same-sex marriages. For these individuals the terms *premarital sex* and *extramarital sex* do not have much meaning. For example, is a 50-year-old who has never been married engaging in premarital sex? Is a person who is having sex outside a common-law relationship engaging in extramarital sex? Nonetheless, the pervasiveness of marriage as an institution (for example, 90 to 95 percent of Canadians marry) makes it meaningful to discuss cultural rules regarding premarital and extramarital sex.

surveyed (Frayser, 1985). Even when extramarital sex is permitted, it is subjected to regulations; the most common pattern of restriction is to allow extramarital sex for husbands but not wives.

Sex with Same-Sex Partners

A wide range of attitudes toward same-sex sexual expression exists in various cultures (Murray, 2000). At one extreme are societies that strongly disapprove of same-sex sexual behaviour for people of any age. In contrast, some societies tolerate the behaviour in children but disapprove of it in adults. Still other societies actively encourage all their male members to engage in some same-sex sexual behaviour, usually in conjunction with puberty rites (Herdt, 1984). A few societies have a formalized role for the adult gay man that gives him status and dignity.

Even across European nations, attitudes about homosexuality vary considerably (Lottes & Alkula, 2011). For example, people in Denmark, the Netherlands, and Sweden have the most positive attitudes. Positive attitudes are also found in a large group of countries that includes Austria, Belgium, France, Germany, Great Britain, Greece, Italy, and Spain. Attitudes are more negative in Belarus, Bulgaria, Estonia, and Russia, and the cluster of countries with the most negative attitudes includes Croatia, Lithuania, Poland, Portugal, Romania, and Ukraine.

Although wide variation exists in attitudes toward homosexuality and in same-sex sexual activity, two general rules do seem to emerge (Ford & Beach, 1951; Murray, 2000; Whitam, 1983): (1) No matter what the society's views are, same-sex behaviour always occurs in at least some individuals—that is, same-sex sexuality is found universally; and (2) same-sex sexual activity is never the predominant form of sexual behaviour for adults in any of the societies studied.

The first point, that same-sex sexual behaviour is found universally in all cultures, is so well established that there was quite a stir in 2010 when a team of anthropologists reported that a group of people, the Aka foragers of the Central African Republic (Hewlett & Hewlett, 2010), were not aware of such practices and had no term for them. In fact, it was difficult for the anthropologists to convey what they meant. We may need to amend the earlier statement to say that same-sex sexual behaviour is nearly universal across societies.

In Canada and other Western nations, most people hold an unquestioned assumption that people have a sexual identity, whether gay, lesbian, bisexual, heterosexual, asexual, or pansexual. Yet sexual identity as an unvarying, lifelong characteristic of the self is unknown or rare in some cultures, such as Indonesia (Stevenson, 1995). In those cultures, the self and

individualism, so prominent in Canadian culture, are downplayed. Instead, a person is defined in relation to others, and behaviour is seen as much more the product of the situation than of lifelong personality traits. In such a culture, having a "gay identity" just doesn't make sense. Sexual orientation is discussed in detail in Chapter 14.

Standards of Attractiveness

In all human societies, physical characteristics are important in determining whom one chooses as a sex partner. What is considered attractive varies considerably, though (see Figure 1.6). For example, the region of the body that is judged for attractiveness varies from one culture to the next. For some peoples, the shape and colour of the eyes are especially significant. For others, the shape of the ears is most important. Some societies go directly to the heart of the matter and judge attractiveness by the appearance of the external genitals. In a few societies, elongated labia majora (the pads of fat on either side of the vaginal opening in women) are considered sexually attractive, and it is common practice for a woman to pull on hers to make them longer. Among the Nawa women of Africa, elongated labia majora are considered a mark of beauty and are quite prominent.

Our society's standards are in the minority in one way: In most cultures, a plump woman is considered more attractive than a thin one. In Canada and other Western nations today, the ideal for women, particularly as portrayed in the media, is unrealistically and unhealthily thin.

One standard does seem to be a general rule: A poor complexion is considered unattractive in the majority of human societies. Research on sexual attraction is discussed in detail in Chapter 12.

L05 Regional and Cultural Variation in Sexuality

The discussion so far may have seemed to imply that there is one uniform standard of sexual behaviour in Canada and that all Canadians behave alike sexually. But the Canadian population is composed of many cultural and ethnic groups. These groups have both differences and similarities in sexual behaviour. Some of these subcultural variations can be classified as social-class differences and some as ethnic differences. Here we discuss variations in sexual behaviour and attitudes between French-speaking and English-speaking Canadians of European descent. We also examine sexual behaviour and attitudes among Indigenous Canadians and in six of the largest ethnocultural communities in Canada.

Figure 1.6 Cross-cultural differences, cross-cultural similarities. *(a)* Woman of West Africa. *(b)* Miss Universe Canada 2013, Riza Santos. The custom of female adornment is found in most cultures, although the definition of beauty varies from culture to culture.

(a) ©Delbars/Shutterstock

(b) ©WENN Ltd / Alamy Stock Photo

Social Class and Sex

Table 1.1 shows data on some social-class variations in sexuality. There was little difference in the percentage of respondents who had engaged in sexual intercourse ever or in the past 12 months based on social class—most respondents in all social classes had done so. However, respondents from the lower social classes were more likely to have first engaged in intercourse when they were 15 years old or younger and to have had one or more sexually transmitted infections. There also are some differences in sexual behaviour across social classes. A study conducted in Montreal using a francophone sample found that manual workers engaged in both sexual intercourse and oral–genital sex more frequently than respondents with office and professional jobs (Samson et al., 1991, 1993).

Regional Differences in Sexuality

A number of surveys have examined whether regional differences in sexual behaviour and attitudes exist across provinces and territories. These results are based on self-report surveys and typically are conducted in English or French, so they may not be totally accurate.

For example, respondents may not remember their behaviour accurately or may give the answer that they think is more socially acceptable (see Chapter 3 for a discussion of possible biases in self-report data). The results of various surveys do not show consistent differences from one province to another, with one exception: francophones in Quebec often are more liberal in many of their attitudes and behaviour than Canadians in other provinces. Just how different are Quebecers from Canadians in other parts of Canada? See Figure 1.7.

Table 1.2 compares Quebecers to Canadians as a whole on a number of attitudes and behaviours related to sexuality. The data for Quebec include not only francophones but also anglophones and allophones (people whose first language is neither English nor French) living in Quebec; these groups differ in many ways from the Québécois. These data show that Quebecers are more liberal in many of their attitudes. For example, Quebec parents are more accepting of teenagers engaging in sexual activity, and more people in Quebec believe that it is morally acceptable for unmarried people to engage in sexual activity,

Is Quebec a distinct society sexually speaking?

Table 1.1   Social-Class Variations in Sexual Behaviour in Canada

	Low and Low-Middle Income	Middle Income	Upper-Middle and High Incomes
Percentage who have ever had intercourse			
Men	87%	91%	94%
Women	93%	92%	94%
Percentage who had intercourse in the last 12 months			
Men	90%	92%	94%
Women	78%	88%	92%
Percentage who had first sexual intercourse before age 16			
Men	31%	23%	19%
Women	23%	16%	12%
Percentage who had at least one sexually transmitted infection			
Men	4%	1%	1%
Women	3%	2%	2%

Source: This analysis is based on the Statistics Canada National Population Health Survey Public Use Microdata File, 1996–1997. All computations, use, and interpretation of these data are entirely that of the authors. Percentages are based only on members of the sample who responded to the question.

for married men and women to have an affair, and for people to engage in same-sex sexual activity. In addition, among students studying in the Ottawa-Gatineau area, franco-Quebec students have less sex guilt than do anglo-Canadian students, in part because they have parents who have more permissive sexual attitudes (Gravel, Young, Olavarria-Turner, & Lee, 2011).

A higher percentage of Quebecers live in common-law relationships; a smaller percentage live in marital relationships. In terms of sexual health indicators, Quebec women are equally likely to breast-feed compared with the national average; the teenage pregnancy rate in Quebec is at the national average; and Quebec has a lower rate of chlamydia, a common STI, than the national average,

Figure 1.7   Sexual attitudes in Quebec are more liberal than in the rest of Canada. This advertisement for a Montreal conference on childhood sexuality included a drawing of two children that showed their genitals. Consistent with cultural attitudes, the French-language newspaper in Montreal published the drawing at the left. The children's genitals are not shown in the advertisements run by the English-language newspaper in Toronto (right).

©Courtesy of Prof. Robert Gemme, Departement de sexologie, Université du Quebec

Table 1.2 Comparison of Sexuality in Quebec to Sexuality in Canada Overall

	Quebec	Rest of Canada
Parents who agree that teens should be allowed to spend the night together in their home with their sex partner	41%	13%
Parents who agree that it's appropriate for 16-year-olds to have sex outside of marriage	35%	6%
Believe that married men and women having an affair is morally acceptable.	62%	54%
Believe that gay or lesbian relations are morally acceptable	87%	79%
Fantasized about having sex with a person of the same sex	5%	7%
Believe that sex between an unmarried man and woman is morally acceptable	91%	84%
Couples living in common-law relationships	32%	17%

Sources: Abacusdata, 2016; Bibby et al. (2009), Driedger (2002), Ipsos (2013), Pew Research (2013), Statistics Canada (2012).

but so do Ontario and the Atlantic provinces. This result suggests that Quebecers are not distinct from the rest of Canada in their likelihood of engaging in safer sex.

Comparing Canada and the United States

The United States is our closest neighbour. Yet, when it comes to sexual attitudes and behaviour, Canada and the United States are quite different. Some of these differences are depicted in Table 1.3. In general, Canadians are more liberal than Americans are. For example, we are more accepting of birth control, pornography, sex between unmarried partners, same-sex sexual activity, and even extramarital sex. Women in Canada also have lower rates of adolescent pregnancy and STIs and higher rates of breast-feeding than do women in the United States.

Indigenous Peoples and Sexuality

Before contact with Europeans, most First Nations populations were considered egalitarian and sexually permissive by European standards (Reeves & Reading, 2013). For example, among First Nations peoples, women were encouraged to take the initiative, and premarital and extramarital sex were acceptable. In many cultures, gay men, lesbians, and Two Spirit people who assumed

Table 1.3 Percentage of People in Canada and the United States Who Find Each of the Following Morally Acceptable

	Canada	United States
Birth control	95%	89%
Pornography	49%	34%
Married men and women having an affair	16%	10%
Gay or lesbian relations	81%	60%
Sex between an unmarried man and woman	86%	67%

Source: Abacusdata (2016); Gallup (2016)

cross-gender roles were respected and admired. Sex was considered a magical spiritual gift to humans designed to bring pleasure—a gift that should be used only with respect for others and for ourselves (Newhouse, 1998).

Depictions of Canadian Indigenous peoples in the popular media over the last century have portrayed them as noble savages who are both exotic and erotic (Bird, 1999). Indigenous men have been shown nearly naked, emphasizing well-developed, masculine bodies. In romance novels of the 1990s, they became cultural icons for vanishing standards of masculinity—handsome and virile yet tender and vulnerable and magnificent lovers for white women (Van Lent, 1996).

Indigenous women have been less visible in the popular media. When present, they are stereotyped as princesses or squaws (Bird, 1999). The princess is noble, beautiful, and erotic. The Disney animated film *Pocahontas* features such a voluptuous princess. The stereotypical squaw, in contrast, is unattractive, uninteresting, and ignored.

The sexual behaviour and attitudes of most Indigenous communities have been influenced by the Judeo-Christian tradition, abusive experiences in residential schools, living on or off the reserve, and the poor economic and crowded living conditions (Reeves & Reading, 2013). For example, Indigenous women experience a disproportionally high rate of negative sexual health outcomes, including high rates of STIs, unwanted pregnancy, low-birth-weight infants, and sexual violence (Yee, Apale, & Deleary, 2011). Traditional Indigenous cultures had strict courtship rules that regulated premarital sex. Today there is great pressure in the youth culture to have sex (Hellerstedt, Peterson-Hickey, Rhodes, & Garwick, 2006). Unfortunately, there have been few studies of sexual behaviour within Indigenous communities or of the influence of Indigenous culture on sexual behaviour. Filling this gap is important because a study of First Nations people living on-reserve in Ontario found that cultural variables, such as the traditions of learning through the telling of stories by Elders, had an important influence on sexual behaviour. For example, in many communities AIDS was seen as a gay white man's disease. As a result, safer sex behaviours, such as consistent condom use, are rare (Myers et al., 1994, 1999). However, data from the Canadian Community Health Survey indicate that Indigenous youth were as likely as non-Indigenous youth to have used a condom the last time they had intercourse (Rotermann, 2005). Nonetheless, to be effective in addressing the sexual health needs of Indigenous peoples, it is important to develop culturally safe and sensitive services by using the knowledge of Elders in the community (Hampton, McKay-McNabb, Racette, & Byrd, 2007; Yee et al., 2011).

Ethnocultural Communities in Canada and Sexuality

Changing patterns of immigration to Canada in recent years have resulted in a Canadian population that is becoming more and more ethnically diverse. According to the 2011 census, 21 percent of Canadians were not born in Canada. There have been few studies of sexual behaviour in Canadian ethnocultural communities (Statistics Canada, 2013b). However, a federally funded study, Ethnocultural Communities Facing AIDS, which focused on preventing HIV and AIDS in communities with high levels of recent immigration, examined selected aspects of sexual behaviour and attitudes in six ethnic communities. Participants were from the Chinese, South Asian, Horn of Africa, English-speaking Caribbean, North African Muslim, and Latin American communities.[4] The researchers made sure that the sample was representative of the community in terms of age and how long respondents had lived in Canada. The study used both focus groups (a research procedure in which participants discuss their answers to the research questions in small groups) and questionnaires (Cappon et al., 1996; Manson Singer et al., 1996).

The sexual behaviour of individuals from ethnic minorities is influenced both by the culture of their country of origin and by the process of adapting to Canada's majority culture. The study found that, in many ways, sexual attitudes and behaviour in these Canadian

communities resemble attitudes and behaviour in the countries of origin. Generally, men and women are seen as having distinct roles, with men expected to be the head of the family and women expected to be the caregivers. Sex is not talked about in the family, even between husbands and wives. Women are expected to be passive and inexperienced, and to fulfill men's sexual needs, whereas men are expected to be sexually active and experienced. Women have little power in sexual relationships to refuse sex or to insist on condom use. In many of these communities, it is expected that men, but not women, will have extramarital affairs or use prostitutes. Homosexuality is often considered abnormal and shameful. Thus, most gay men and lesbians keep their same-sex relationships and feelings secret.

Expectations regarding adolescent dating and sexual behaviour in these ethnocultural communities are different from those in the dominant Canadian culture. In general, virginity at marriage is highly valued in women but is not expected of men. In the South Asian communities, girls may not be allowed to date. On the other hand, young people do not always conform to these expectations and adopt some aspects of the dominant culture after learning about them from friends and the media. This rebellion often creates conflict between youth and their more traditional parents. Parents may see their children's adoption of Canadian norms as threatening their values and way of life (Shirpak, Maticka-Tyndale, & Chinichian, 2007). For example, Chinese youth, including girls, are becoming increasingly likely to engage in sexual activity. However, a Vancouver study found that both male and female Asian university students are more conservative and less experienced than are non-Asians in their sexual behaviour. Notably, half as many Asian students (36 percent) as non-Asian students (66 percent) had engaged in sexual intercourse (Meston, Trapnell, & Gorzalka, 1996). However, the attitudes of Asian Canadians become more liberal as they become more acculturated (Brotto, Chik, Ryder, Gorzalka, & Seal, 2005; Brotto, Woo, & Ryder, 2007; Meston, Trapnell, & Gorzalka, 1998).

Of course, in many ways the behaviour and attitudes of members of one ethnocultural community are also different from those of other communities. For example, single South Asian men were more likely than single men from Latin America or the English-speaking Caribbean to report having had more than one sexual partner in the previous year. In contrast, married South Asian men were the least likely to report having had more than one partner in the previous year (Maticka-Tyndale et al., 1996).

Racial Microaggressions

Old-fashioned, obvious, overt racism has become rare in Canada. It has been replaced by more subtle forms of prejudiced attitudes and behaviours. **Racial microaggressions** are subtle insults directed at people

---

[4] The researchers studied communities in Vancouver (Chinese and South Asian), Toronto (English-speaking Caribbean and Horn of Africa), and Montreal (North African Muslim and Latin American). The Chinese participants came from Hong Kong, Taiwan, and the People's Republic of China. Most of the participants from the South Asian communities were from India and Pakistan. The English-speaking Caribbean participants were from all the English-speaking Caribbean islands and Guyana. Participants from the Horn of Africa came largely from Ethiopia, Eritrea, and Somalia. The North African Muslim participants came mostly from North Africa and the Middle East. The Latin American participants came primarily from Peru, Chile, Guatemala, and El Salvador.

of color, often done unconsciously (Sue et al., 2007; Sue, 2010). Members of ethnic minorities in Canada experience them frequently, and they can be a source of stress. Consider the following example:

> Neil Henning, a white professor, had just finished a lecture on Greco-Roman contributions to the history of psychology. He asked for questions. A black student raised his hand. The student seemed frustrated and said that the history of psychology was ethnocentric and Eurocentric, and that it left out contributions fro African, Asian, and Latin American cultures and psychologies.
>
> The professor responded, "Aidan, please calm down. We are studying North American psychology. We will eventually address how it has influenced and been adapted to Asian and other societies" (adapted from Sue, 2010, p. 3).

Can you spot the microaggressions? Telling a person to calm down is often an expression of dominance that invalidates the legitimacy of the person's feelings. Then, the professor implied that North American psychology was the norm and it influenced other societies, with no consideration of the possibility that other societies might have developed psychological concepts and principles on their own. All of this was very subtle, though. Aidan undoubtedly felt dissatisfied with the interaction, but it would be difficult for him to say that the professor said something overtly offensive. The subtlety and ambiguity of microaggressions makes them even more difficult to deal with.

As we will see in later chapters, the concept of microaggressions also extends to *gender microaggressions, sexual-orientation microaggressions,* and *microaggressions against trans people.*

The Significance of Cross-Cultural Studies

What relevance do cross-cultural data have to an understanding of human sexuality? They are important for two basic reasons. First, they give us a notion of the enormous variation that exists in human sexual behaviour, and they help us put our own standards and behaviour in perspective. Second, these studies provide impressive evidence concerning the importance of culture and learning in the shaping of our sexual behaviour; they show us that human sexual behaviour is not completely determined by biology or drives or instincts. For example, a woman of Inis Beag and a woman of Mangaia presumably have vaginas that are similarly constructed and clitorises that are approximately the same size and have the same nerve supply. But the woman of Inis Beag never has an orgasm, and all Mangaian women orgasm.[5] Why? Their cultures are different, and they and their partners learned different things about sex as they were growing

Figure 1.8 Sexual norms for women are restrictive in Muslim-Canadian families.

©Robert Nickelsberg/Getty Images

up. Culture is a major determinant of human sexual behaviour (see Figure 1.8).

The point of studying sexuality in different groups is to remind ourselves that each group has its own culture, and this culture has a profound influence on the sexual expression of the women and men who grow up in it. We will return with more examples in many of the chapters that follow.

LO6

Cross-Species Perspectives on Sexuality

Humans are just one of many animal species, and all of them display sexual behaviour. To put our own sexual behaviour in evolutionary perspective, it is helpful to explore the similarities and differences between our own sexuality and that of other species. (See Chapter 2 for a discussion of evolutionary perspectives.) There is one other reason for this particular discussion. Some people classify sexual behaviours as "natural" or "unnatural," depending on whether other species do or do not exhibit those behaviours. Sometimes, though, the data are twisted to suit the purposes of the person making the argument, and so there is a need for a less biased view. Let's see exactly what some other species do!

> **racial microaggressions:** Subtle insults directed at people of colour and often done unconsciously.

---

[5] We like to use the word *orgasm* not only as a noun but also as a verb. The reason is that alternative expressions, such as "to achieve orgasm" and "to reach orgasm," reflect the tendency of Canadians to make sex an achievement situation (an idea to be discussed further in Chapter 9). To avoid this, we use "to have an orgasm" or "to orgasm."

Figure 1.9   The sexual behaviour of animals. *(a)* Females have various ways of expressing choice. Here a female Barbary macaque presents her sexual swelling to a male. He seems to be interested. *(b)* Same-sex sexuality in animals: two male giraffes "necking." They rub necks and become aroused.

(a) ©Meredith F. Small

(b) ©Thomas Michael Corcoran/PhotoEdit

Masturbation

Humans are definitely not the only species that masturbates. Masturbation is found among many species of mammals, particularly among the primates (monkeys and apes). Male monkeys and apes in zoos can be observed masturbating, often to the horror of the proper folk who have come to see them. At one time it was thought that this behaviour might be the result of the unnatural living conditions of zoos. However, observations of free-living primates indicate that they, too, masturbate. Techniques include hand stimulation of the genitals or rubbing the genitals against an object. In terms of technique, monkeys and nonhuman apes have one advantage over humans: Their bodies are so flexible that they can perform mouth–genital sex on themselves.

Female masturbation is also found among many species besides our own. The prize for the most inventive technique probably should go to the female porcupine. She holds one end of a stick in her paws and walks around while straddling the stick; as the stick bumps against the ground, it vibrates against her genitals (Ford & Beach, 1951). Human females are apparently not the only ones to enjoy vibrators.

Is same-sex sexual behaviour found in other species?

Same-Sex Sexual Behaviour

Same-sex behaviour is found in many species besides our own (Bagemihl, 1999; Leca et al., 2014; MacFarlane, Blomberg, & Vasey, 2010; Wallen & Parsons, 1997; see Figure 1.9). Indeed, observations of other species indicate that our basic mammalian heritage is bisexual, composed of both heterosexual and homosexual elements (Bagemihl, 1999).

Males of many species will mount other males, and anal intercourse has been observed in some male primates (Wallen & Parsons, 1997). Among domestic sheep, 9 percent of adult males strongly prefer other males as sex partners (Ellis, 1996; Roselli, Resko, & Stormshak, 2002). In a number of primate species, including bonobos and Japanese macaques, females mount other females and derive sexual rewards from these behaviours (Vasey, Leca, Gunst, & VanderLaan, 2014; Vasey & Duckworth, 2008).

In What Ways Are Humans Unique?

Are humans in any way unique in their sexual behaviour? The general trend is for sexual behaviour to be more hormonally (instinctively) controlled among the lower species, such as fish or rodents, and to be controlled more by the brain (and therefore by learning and social content) in the higher species, like primates (Wallen, 2001). However, environmental influences are much more important in shaping primate—especially human—sexual behaviour than they are in shaping the sexual behaviour of other species.

Nonetheless, research has shown that in addition to instinctual or hard-wired preferences (such as the preference of males for sexually receptive females), learning affects the sexual preferences of a number of different species. For example, Quebec psychologist James Pfaus and his colleagues have shown in laboratory experiments that male rats can be conditioned (see Chapter 2 for an explanation of classical conditioning) to prefer female rats with a particular neutral odour, such as almond or lemon extract, to unscented females by first pairing the neutral odour with ejaculation (Pfaus, Kippin, & Coria-Avila, 2003; Pfaus et al., 2012). They have found similar results in female rats.

An illustration of this fact is provided by studies of the adult sexual behaviour of animals raised in deprived environments. If mice are reared in isolation, their adult sexual behaviour will nonetheless be normal (Scott, 1964). But if rhesus monkeys are reared in isolation, their adult sexual behaviour is severely disturbed, to the point that they may be incapable of reproducing (Harlow, Harlow, & Hause, 1963). Thus, environmental experiences are crucial in shaping the sexual behaviour of higher species, particularly humans; for us, sexual behaviour is a lot more than just "doing what comes naturally."

Female sexuality provides a particularly good illustration of the shift in hormonal control from lower to higher species. Throughout most of the animal kingdom, female sexual behaviour is strongly controlled by hormones. In virtually all mammals, females do not engage in sexual behaviour at all except when they are in *heat* (estrus), which is a particular hormonal state. In contrast, human females are capable of engaging in sexual behaviour— and actually do engage in it—during any phase of their hormonal (menstrual) cycle. Thus, the sexual behaviour of human females is not nearly as much under hormonal control as that of females of other species.

Traditionally, it was thought that female orgasm is unique to humans and does not exist in other species. Then some studies found evidence of orgasm in macaques (monkeys), as indicated by the same physiological responses indicative of orgasm in human females—specifically, increased heart rate and uterine contractions (Burton, 1970; Goldfoot, Westerberg-van Loon, Groeneveld, & Koos Slob, 1980; Zumpe & Michael, 1968). Thus, humans can no longer claim to have a corner on the female orgasm market. This fact has interesting implications for understanding the evolution of sexuality. Perhaps the higher species, in which the females are not driven to sexual activity by their hormones, have the pleasure of orgasm as an incentive.

In summary, then, little in human sexuality is completely unique to humans, except for elaborate, complex cultural influences. In other respects, we are on a continuum with other species.

The Nonsexual Uses of Sexual Behaviour

Two male baboons are locked in combat. One begins to emerge as the victor. The other *presents* (the "female" sexual posture, in which the rump is directed toward the other and is elevated somewhat).

Two male monkeys are members of the same troop. Long ago they established which one is dominant and which is subordinate. The dominant one *mounts* (the "male" sexual behaviour) the subordinate one.

These are examples of animals sometimes using sexual behaviour for nonsexual purposes (Small, 1993; Wallen & Zehr, 2004). Commonly, such behaviour signals the end of a fight, as in the first example. The loser indicates his surrender by presenting, and the winner signals victory by mounting. Sexual behaviours can also symbolize an animal's rank in a dominance hierarchy. Dominant animals mount subordinate ones. As another example, male squirrel monkeys sometimes use an exhibitionist display of their erect penis as part of an aggressive display against another male in a phenomenon called *phallic aggression* (Wickler, 1973).

The bonobo, an ape that is perhaps our closest genetic relative, is a particularly interesting example of the use of sexual behaviour for nonsexual purposes (de Waal, 1995). Bonobos live in female-centred, egalitarian groups and use sex for peacemaking in situations that might lead to aggression among other animals, such as situations involving food or jealousy. Since sex is a key part of their social life, bonobos engage in a wide range of sexual behaviours (including oral sex, massage of another's genitals, and intense tongue-kissing) with a wide range of partners, both same sex and other sex. The female is sexually attractive and sexually active during most of her cycle, rather than for just a few days around estrus.

All this is perfectly obvious when we observe it in monkeys. But do humans ever use sexual behaviour for nonsexual purposes? Consider the rapist, who uses sex as an expression of aggression against and power over a woman or a man (Zurbriggen, 2010). Another example is the exhibitionist, who uses a display of his erect penis to shock and frighten women, much as the male squirrel monkey uses such a display to shock and frighten his opponent. Humans also use sex for economic purposes; the best examples are male and female sex workers.

There are also less extreme examples. Consider the couple who have a fight and then make love to signal an end to the hostilities.[6] Or consider the person who goes to bed with an influential—though unattractive—politician because this gives him or her a vicarious sense of power.

---

[6] It has been our observation, particularly for couples in therapy, that this practice may not mean the same thing to men and women. To men it can mean that everything is fine again, but women can be left feeling dissatisfied and not at all convinced that the issues are resolved. Thus, this situation can be a source of miscommunication in mixed-sex couples.

You can probably think of other examples of the nonsexual use of sexual behaviour. Humans, just like members of other species, can use sex for a variety of nonsexual purposes. Indeed, included in the reasons men and women give for why they have sex are wanting to celebrating a special occasion, wanting to increase the emotional connection, doing a favour for someone, wanting to increase their social status, and wanting to feel loved (Armstrong & Reissing, 2015; Meston & Buss, 2007; Wood, Milhausen, & Jeffrey, 2014).

The Sexual Health Perspective

Sexual health is an important new concept and a social and political movement that is gaining momentum worldwide. Although many discussions of sexual health are actually about sexual diseases, such as HIV infection, **sexual health** is a much broader concept that involves a vision of positive sexual health (Black, Bucio, Butt, Crangle, & Lalonde, 2009; Edwards & Coleman, 2004; Parker et al., 2004; Public Health Agency of Canada [PHAC], 2008a). The World Health Organization (WHO) definition is as follows:

> Sexual health is a state of physical, emotional, mental and social well-being in relation to sexuality; it is not merely the absence of disease, dysfunction or infirmity. Sexual health requires a positive and respectful approach to sexuality and sexual relationships, as well as the possibility of having pleasurable and safe sexual experiences, free of coercion, discrimination and violence. For sexual health to be attained and maintained, the sexual rights of all persons must be respected, protected and fulfilled.

(World Health Organization (WHO, 2006), p5

Notice that this definition includes not only sexual physical health but also sexual mental health and positive sexual relationships. Therefore, public health efforts to prevent HIV or chlamydia infection, programs to promote women's reproductive rights, efforts to enhance romantic relationships, implementation of sex education curricula, and activism to end discrimination and violence against sexual and gender minorities all fall under the umbrella of sexual health.

Notice also that the definition includes both negative and positive rights. With the growth of the sexual health movement, the concept of **sexual rights** has also come to centre stage and, in fact, the term is used in the WHO definition and in the Public Health Agency of Canada guidelines. The idea here is that all human beings have certain basic, inalienable rights regarding sexuality that stem from basic human rights, such as those guaranteed in the *Canadian Charter of Rights and Freedoms*. The question, then, is, what are our basic sexual rights? The principles are new and evolving, but they generally include such elements as a right to reproductive self-determination and freedom from sexual violence, as well as the right to sexual self-expression (providing, of course, that it doesn't interfere with someone else's sexual rights) (Sandfort & Ehrhardt, 2004). According to the WHO, those rights also include the right to access reproductive health care service, receive sex education, consent or not consent to marriage, and experience a satisfying, safe, and pleasurable sex life (for a complete list of sexual rights, see Chapter 20). Negative rights are freedoms *from*—for example, freedom from sexual violence. Positive rights are freedoms *to*—for example, the freedom to experience sexual pleasure or the freedom to express sexuality with same-sex partners. The greatest sexual health benefits will be achieved by emphasizing promotion of sexual and reproductive health and prevention of problems (PHAC, 2008a).

Many, particularly Western, cultures have laws to protect individuals' sexual rights and freedoms, although many societies protect some but not all sexual rights. For example, in Canada, the *Charter of Rights and Freedoms* protects against discrimination based on sex or sexual orientation. Unfortunately, in many parts of the world people, particularly women, do not have these rights (Maticka-Tyndale & Smylie, 2008). Women may be forced to marry, have no recourse if they experience sexual assault, be expected to tolerate their husband having sex with sex workers even when it puts them at risk for disease, and receive little or no sex education. To ensure that human beings and societies develop healthy sexuality, these sexual rights must be recognized, promoted, respected, and defended by all societies through all means. Sexual health is the result of an environment that recognizes, respects, and exercises these sexual rights. In Canada, particular attention needs to be paid to protecting groups whose sexual rights are not well protected—for example, individuals with disabilities and Indigenous people (Silverberg & Odette, 2011).

The concepts of sexual health and sexual rights provide yet another broad and thought-provoking perspective on sexuality.

> **sexual health:** A state of physical, emotional, mental, and social well-being related to sexuality.
> **sexual rights:** Basic, inalienable rights regarding sexuality, both positive and negative, such as rights to reproductive self-determination and sexual self-expression, and freedom from sexual abuse and violence.

AN INTRODUCTION TO CRITICAL THINKING

In this and all other chapters in this textbook, you will find boxes labelled "Critical Thinking Skill." Each of these boxes is designed to improve your critical thinking skills as applied to sexuality, but the skills you learn will be useful in many other areas of life. According to Diane Halpern, an expert in critical thinking,

> Critical thinking is the use of those cognitive skills or strategies that increases the probability of a desirable outcome. It is purposeful, reasoned, and goal directed. It is the kind of thinking involved in solving problems, formulating inferences, calculating likelihoods, and making decisions. . . . Critical thinking also involves evaluating the thinking process—the reasoning that went into the conclusion we have arrived at or the kinds of factors considered in making a decision (Halpern, 2002, p. 93).

Critical thinking is logical, rational, and free of self-deception. Critical thinking is also an attitude that people carry with them into situations, a belief that can and should be used to make better decisions. Over time, those with excellent critical thinking skills should experience better outcomes (e.g., making a good career choice or making a good decision about where to live) compared with those who have poor critical thinking skills (Halpern, 1998).

For these reasons, colleges and universities believe that it is important for students to improve their critical thinking skills. Those skills are also increasingly important in the world of work, as our industrial, manufacturing economy has been replaced by a knowledge-based economy, and the ability to evaluate information carefully is a major asset.

Here's to better critical thinking by all of us!

UNDERSTANDING THAT OTHER CULTURES THINK DIFFERENTLY ABOUT SOME ISSUES

One way to improve critical thinking skills is to understand that some cultures have different ideas about certain issues than we have in our culture. This cross-cultural view widens our perspective and helps us to think more rationally about unspoken assumptions in our culture. For example, in Canada, if you get married in a place of worship, then, after signing some papers, you are also legally married—that is, the religious and the civil or legal parts of marriage are combined. In many European countries, however, including some Catholic countries, things are done very differently. The civil ceremonies and the religious ceremonies are separate, often

occurring on different days. For example, in France couples go to city hall for the legal ceremony and then, separately, to a church or other place of worship for the religious ceremony. Those who are religious do both, and those who are not go just to the city hall part. Either way, they have a party afterward.

How does knowing about these practices apply to how we do things in Canada? For example, some religious groups object to same-sex marriage. How would that debate change if we separated religious marriage from civil marriage?

SUMMARY

Sexual activity is activity that produces arousal and increases the chance of orgasm. *Sex* (sexual behaviour and anatomy) is distinct from *gender* (being male or female).

Historically, religion was the main source of information concerning sexuality. Important early sex researchers were Sigmund Freud, Havelock Ellis, Richard von Krafft-Ebing, and Magnus Hirschfeld, all emerging from the Victorian era. By the 1990s, major, well-conducted sex surveys were available. Today, the mass media—whether television, magazines, or the Internet—are a powerful influence on most people's understanding of sexuality. The mass media may have an influence through cultivation, agenda-setting, and social learning.

Studies of various human cultures around the world provide evidence of the enormous variations in human sexual behaviour. Frequency of intercourse may vary from once a week in some cultures to three or four times a night in others. Attitudes regarding premarital and extramarital sex, masturbation, same-sex sexual behaviour, and gender roles vary considerably across cultures. The great variations provide evidence of the importance of learning in shaping sexual behaviour. Yet all societies regulate sexual behaviour in some way.

Within Canada, sexual behaviour varies with one's social class and ethnic and linguistic group. Canada's ethnocultural communities are characterized by traditional gender roles and restrictions on female sexuality but not on male sexuality. Studies of sexual behaviour in various animal species show that masturbation, mouth–genital stimulation, and same-sex sexual behaviour are by no means limited to humans. In many species, sexual behaviour may be used for a variety of nonsexual purposes, such as expressing dominance.

A new international movement is focusing on sexual health and principles of sexual rights.

CHAPTER 2
Theoretical Perspectives on Sexuality

©Getty/Punchstock

LEARNING OBJECTIVES

After studying this chapter, you will be able to

LO1 Describe the concepts associated with the evolutionary perspective.

LO2 State the strengths and weaknesses of the various Freudian psychoanalytic concepts.

LO3 Discuss the concepts of learning theory as they relate to the learning of sexual behaviours.

LO4 Show how social exchange theory explains sexual relationships and their satisfaction, stability, and change.

LO5 Demonstrate the relationship between cognition and sexuality and gender.

LO6 Describe the critical theory perspective, including feminist theories and queer theory.

LO7 Describe symbolic interaction theory and its relationship to the concept of sexual scripts and sexual fields.

LO8 Describe the sociological perspective, including the social importance of sexuality and its relationship to the social institutions.

LO9 Show the ways in which laws in the *Criminal Code of Canada* regulate sexual conduct.

Are YOU Curious?

1. Could natural selection account for people's tendency to prefer more physically attractive partners?
2. What theory accounts for how the smell of perfume or cologne becomes sexually arousing?
3. Why do most sexual interactions in our society follow the same pattern?

Read this chapter to find out.

One of the discoveries of psychoanalysis consists of the assertion that impulses, which can only be described as sexual in both the narrower and the wider sense, play a peculiarly large part, never before sufficiently appreciated, in the causation of nervous and mental disorders. Nay, more, that these sexual impulses have contributed invaluably to the highest cultural, artistic, and social achievements of the human mind.*

From an evolutionary perspective, no single decision is more important than the choice of a mate. That single fork in the road determines one's ultimate reproductive fate.†

---

* Sigmund Freud. (1924). *A general introduction to psychoanalysis.* New York: Permabooks, 1953 (Boni & Liveright edition, 1924), pp. 26–27.
† David Buss. (2000). *The dangerous passion: Why jealousy is as necessary as love and sex.* New York: Free Press, p. 10.

Imagine, for a moment, that you are sitting in a bedroom watching two people making love. Imagine, too, that sitting with you in the room are Sigmund Freud (creator of psychoanalytic theory), E. O. Wilson (a leading sociobiologist), Albert Bandura (a prominent social learning theorist), and John Gagnon (a proponent of script theory). The scene you are imagining may evoke arousal and nothing more in you, but your imaginary companions would have a rich set of additional thoughts as they viewed the scene through the lenses of their own theoretical perspectives. Freud might be marvelling at how the biological sex drive, the *libido*, expresses itself so strongly and directly in this couple. Wilson would be thinking how mating behaviour in humans is similar to such behaviour in other species of animals, and how it is clearly the product of evolutionary selection for behaviours that lead to successful reproduction. Bandura might be thinking how sexual arousal and orgasm act as powerful positive reinforcers that will lead the couple to repeat the act frequently, and how they are imitating a technique of neck nibbling that they saw in an erotic video last week. Finally, Gagnon's thoughts might be about the social scripting of sexuality; this couple begins with kissing, moves on to stroking and fondling, and finishes up with intercourse, following a script written by society.

Some of the major theories in the social sciences have had many—and different—things to say about sexuality, and it is these theories that we consider in this chapter. Theories provide us with answers to the question of why. We often wonder why others do or do not engage in particular sexual behaviours and relationships.

> Could natural selection account for people's tendency to prefer more physically attractive partners?

sociobiology: The application of evolutionary biology to understanding the social behaviour of animals, including humans.

evolution: A theory that all living things have acquired their present forms through gradual changes in their genetic endowment over successive generations.

natural selection: A process in nature resulting in greater rates of survival of those plants and animals that are adapted to their environment.

We sometimes ask the "why" question about our own sexuality. Creative minds have developed theories to answer such questions. Given the diversity of human sexuality, we need a range of theories to understand it.

LO1

Evolutionary Perspectives

Evolutionary perspectives use principles from evolutionary biology to explain why certain patterns of social behaviour and psychological mechanisms have evolved in animals, including humans (Barash, 1982; Buss, 1991). The idea that some behaviours are a result of evolution is called **sociobiology**. Sexual behaviour, of course, is a form of social behaviour, so sociobiologists, often based on observation of other species, argue that certain sexual behaviours evolved because they gave our ancestors an evolutionary advantage. Before we proceed, we should note that in terms of **evolution**, what counts is producing lots of healthy, viable offspring who will carry on our genes. Evolution occurs via **natural selection**, the process by which the individuals who are best adapted to their environment are more likely to survive, reproduce, and pass on their genes to the next generation.

How do humans choose mates? One major criterion is the physical attractiveness of the person (see Chapter 12). The sociobiologist argues that many of the characteristics we evaluate in judging attractiveness—for example, physique and complexion—are indicative of the health and vigour of the individual. These in turn are probably related to the person's reproductive potential; people who are unhealthy are less likely to produce many vigorous offspring. Natural selection would favour individuals preferring mates who would have maximum reproductive success. Thus, perhaps our concern with physical attractiveness is a product of evolution and natural selection. (See Barash, 1982, for an extended discussion of this point and the ones that follow.) We choose an attractive, healthy mate who will help us produce many offspring. Can you guess why it is that the sociobiologist thinks most men are attracted to women with large breasts?

If attractiveness is an indicator of health, it should be more important in mate selection in societies where more people are unhealthy. An online survey obtained ratings of the attractiveness of images of male faces from 4800 women, aged 21 to 40, from 30 countries. Facial masculinity, manipulated by computer, had more impact on attractiveness ratings in countries with poorer health, as measured by mortality, life expectancy, and communicable disease (DeBruine, Jones, Crawford, Welling, & Little, 2010).

From this viewpoint, hanging out, playing sports, getting engaged, and similar customs are much like the courtship rituals of other species (see Figure 2.1). For example, many falcons and eagles have a flying courtship in which objects are exchanged between the pair in midair. The sociobiologist views this courtship as an opportunity for each member of the prospective couple to assess the other's fitness. For example, any lack of speed or coordination would be apparent during the airborne acrobatics. Perhaps that is exactly what we are doing in our human courtship rituals. The expenditure of money by men on dates indicates their ability to support a family. Dancing permits the assessment of physical prowess, and so on.

Sociobiologists can also explain why the nuclear family structure of a man, a woman, and their offspring is found in every society. Once a man and a woman mate, there are several obstacles to reproductive success, two being infant vulnerability and maternal death. Infant vulnerability is greatly reduced if the mother provides continuing physical care, including breast-feeding. It is further reduced if the father provides resources and security from attack for mother and infant. Two mechanisms that facilitate these conditions are a *pair-bond* between mother and father, and *attachment* between infant and parent (Miller & Fishkin, 1997). Thus, an offspring's chances of survival are greatly increased if the parents bond emotionally (i.e., love each other) and if the parents have a propensity for attachment. Further, an emotional bond might lead to more frequent sexual interaction; the pleasurable consequences of sex in turn will strengthen the bond. Research with small mammals, including mice and voles, demonstrates the advantages of biparental care of offspring and the critical role of bonding (Morell, 1998).

According to this theory, parents are most interested in the survival and reproductive success of their genetic offspring. *Parental investment* refers to the behaviour and resources invested in offspring to achieve this end. Because of the high rates of divorce and remarriage

(a) ©J.H. Robinson/Science Source

(b) ©Creatas Images/Picture Quest

Figure 2.1 (a) The courtship rituals of great egrets. (b) Dancing is a human dating custom. According to sociobiologists, human customs of dating and becoming engaged are biologically produced and serve the same functions as courtship rituals in other species: They allow potential mates to assess each other's fitness.

in Canada, many men have both biological children and stepchildren. This situation leads to the prediction that men will tend to invest more in their genetic children than in their stepchildren. Do research results support this prediction? Fathers have been found to invest the most money in the genetic children of their current union and the least money in stepchildren from a past relationship, as would be predicted from parental investment theory. However, they spend an equal amount on their genetic children and the stepchildren of their current relationship, perhaps to cement the pair-bond with their current partner (Anderson, Kaplan, & Lancaster, 2001).

Canadian researchers have found that, in men, physiological sexual arousal is specific to stimuli depicting their preferred sexual partner, whereas women show physiological arousal to stimuli depicting both their preferred and nonpreferred sex partners, and even to stimuli of animals (Chivers, 2005; Chivers, Rieger, Latty, & Bailey, 2004; Chivers, Seto, & Blanchard, 2007). Some Canadian researchers have argued that natural selection can account for these findings; that is, one explanation is that historically women who automatically responded physiologically with vasocongestion and vaginal lubrication were less likely to be injured during unwilling penile–vaginal intercourse or sexual activity with a chosen partner whom they did not find subjectively attractive (Chivers et al., 2007; Suschinsky, Lalumière, & Chivers, 2009). In contrast, lack of lubrication in these situations could lead to vaginal injury or infection, which, in turn, could result in sterility and even death. Thus, natural selection would have favoured women with an automatic or reflexive physiological response to a range of sexual stimuli.

In addition to natural selection, Darwin also proposed a mechanism that is less well known: **sexual selection** (Buss, 2009; Gangestad & Thornhill, 1997). Sexual selection is selection that results from differences in traits affecting access to mates. It consists of two processes: (1) competition among members of one gender (usually males) for mating access to members of the other gender, and (2) preferential choice by members of one gender (usually females) for certain members of the other gender. In other words, in many, though not all, species, males compete among themselves for the right to mate with females; females, for their part, prefer certain males and mate with them while refusing to mate with

> **sexual selection:** Selection that results from differences in traits affecting access to mates.
> **evolutionary psychology:** The study of psychological mechanisms that have been shaped by natural selection.

other males (Clutton-Brock, 2007).[1] Researchers have tested some of the predictions that come from the theory of sexual selection with humans. For example, the theory predicts that men should compete with each other in ways that involve displaying material resources that should be attractive to women, and should engage in these displays more than women do (Buss, 1988). Examples might be giving impressive gifts to potential mates, showing off possessions (e.g., cars, stereos), or displaying personality characteristics that are likely to lead to the acquisition of resources (e.g., ambition). Research shows that men engage in these behaviours significantly more than women do and that both men and women believe these tactics are effective (Buss, 1988).

Evaluation of Sociobiology

Many criticisms of sociobiology have been made. Some critics object to the biological determinism that it implies. Sociobiology also has been criticized for resting on an outmoded version of evolutionary theory that modern biologists consider naive (Gould, 1987). For example, sociobiology has focused mainly on the individual's struggle for survival and efforts to reproduce; modern biologists focus on more complex issues, such as the survival of the group and the species. Further, sociobiologists assume that the central function of sex is reproduction; this may have been true in our evolutionary past, but it probably is not true today.

Recent research does not support some of the evidence that is widely cited in support of the theory. Singh (1993) reported that the winners of the Miss America contest and *Playboy's* centrefold models have consistently had a waist-to-hip ratio of 0.7, arguing that this reflected a universal standard related to reproductive fitness. A closer look at the data showed that the average is not 0.7 but 0.66. The average for Miss America winners steadily declined from 0.78 in 1921 to 0.64 in 1986, contradicting the claim that a preference for a ratio of 0.7 was hard-wired by evolution thousands of years ago (Freese & Meland, 2002). Research analyzing waist-to-hip ratios across a large number of cultures, Western and non-Western, has found that the 0.7 ratio is most common in societies where women are economically dependent on men, not in all cultures as the theory asserts (Cashdan, 2008).

Evolutionary Psychology

A somewhat different approach is taken by **evolutionary psychology**, which focuses on how natural selection has shaped psychological mechanisms and processes (that is, the mind) rather than on how it has shaped sexual behaviour directly (Buss, 1991). If behaviours evolved in response to selection pressures, it is plausible to argue

---

[1] Sociobiologists use this mechanism to explain gender differences.

that cognitive or emotional structures evolved in the same way. Thus, a man who accurately judged whether a woman was healthy and fertile would be more successful in reproducing. If his offspring exhibited the same ability to judge accurately, they in turn would have a competitive advantage.

One line of research has concentrated on *sexual strategies* (Buss & Schmitt, 1993). According to this theory, women and men face different adaptive problems in short-term, or casual, mating and in long-term mating and reproduction. These differences lead to different strategies or behaviours designed to solve these problems. In short-term mating, a woman may choose a partner who offers her immediate resources, such as food or money. In long-term mating, a woman may choose a partner who appears able and willing to provide resources for the indefinite future. A man may choose a sexually available woman for a short-term liaison but avoid such women when looking for a long-term mate.

According to the theory, women engage in intrasexual competition for access to men. Women pursuing a long-term strategy should respond negatively to women who make sex easily available to men (a "slut"?) An experimental study found that undergraduate women reacted negatively to a female confederate dressed sexily (cleavage, very short skirt), but not to the same person engaged in the same behaviour dressed in a loose shirt and jeans (Vaillancourt & Aanchai, 2011). On the other hand, women pursuing a short-term strategy want to appear sexy. Women at ovulation choose sexier and more revealing clothing from an online catalogue than they did three or more days before or seven days after ovulation (Durante, Griskevicius, Hill, Perilloux, & Li, 2011).

Buss (1994) and others have reported data that support a number of specific predictions based on this theory. However, other research using the same measures with both men and women and, controlling for confounding effects, has found that men and women are very similar in their stated mating preferences. Both prefer long-term mating strategies and few or no short-term partners (Pedersen, Miller, Putcha-Bhagavatula, & Yang, 2002). Another criticism of evolutionary psychology is that some of the characteristics we observe that are assumed to have some adaptive significance may be simply "design flaws" or side effects of other adaptations (de Waal, 2002).

Like evolutionary psychology, sexual strategies theory is based on assumptions about what the ancestral environment was like. Although we can't study it directly, we can study very traditional societies, such as the Mayan and Asche. Research suggests that male sexual strategies are not consistent but change in response to personal characteristics and environmental contingencies (Waynforth, Hurtadoa, & Hillary, 1998).

Similarly, evidence from the U.S. suggests that the sex ratio influences female long-term mating strategies; women place more emphasis on a man's resources in selecting a husband when men are plentiful compared to women (Pollet & Nettle, 2008).

Critics also question the data used to support much of this research. Although these theories claim that the processes and behaviours are the result of human evolution, and therefore universal, most of the data testing them comes from WEIRD (Western, educated, industrialized, rich, democratic) societies (Henrich, Heine, & Norenzayan, 2010). We don't know whether these results can be applied to persons in other societies. Further, tests of sexual strategies theory rely heavily on data from undergraduate students; note that this criticism applies to research testing other theories as well.

Psychological Theories

Four of the major theories in psychology are relevant to sexuality: psychoanalytic theory, learning theory, social exchange theory, and cognitive theory.

Psychoanalytic Theory

Sigmund Freud's **psychoanalytic theory** has been one of the most influential of all psychological theories. Because Freud saw sex as one of the key forces in human life, his theory gives full treatment to human sexuality.

Freud termed the sex drive or sex energy **libido**, which he saw as one of the two major forces motivating human behaviour (the other being *thanatos*, or the death instinct).

Id, Ego, and Superego

Freud described the human personality as being divided into three major parts: the id, the ego, and the superego. The **id** is the basic part of personality and is present at birth. It is the reservoir of psychic energy (including libido). Basically it operates on the *pleasure principle*—that is, the instinct to seek pleasure and avoid pain to satisfy basic needs.

While the id operates only on the pleasure principle and can thus be pretty irrational, the **ego** operates on the *reality principle* and tries to keep the id in line. The ego functions to make the person have realistic, rational interactions with others.

> **psychoanalytic theory:** A psychological theory originated by Sigmund Freud; it contains a basic assumption that part of human personality is unconscious.
>
> **libido (lih-BEE-doh):** In psychoanalytic theory, the term for the sex energy or sex drive.
>
> **id:** According to Freud, the part of the personality containing the libido.
>
> **ego:** According to Freud, the part of the personality that helps the person have realistic, rational interactions.

Finally, the **superego** is the conscience. It contains the values and ideals of society that we learn, and it operates on *idealism*. Thus, its aim is to inhibit the impulses of the id and to persuade the ego to strive for moral goals rather than realistic ones.[2]

To illustrate the operation of these three components of the personality in a sexual situation, consider the case of the CEO of a corporation who is at a meeting of the board of directors; the meeting is also attended by her handsome, buff, hot colleague. She looks at him, and her id says, "He's a real hunk. I want to throw him on the table and make love to him immediately. Let's do it!" The ego intervenes and says, "We can't do it now because the other members of the board are also here. Let's wait until 5 p.m., when they're all gone, and then do it." The superego says, "I shouldn't make love to this hot guy at all because I'm a married woman." What actually happens? It depends on the relative strengths of this woman's id, ego, and superego.

The id, ego, and superego develop sequentially. The id contains the set of instincts present at birth. The ego develops a few years later, as the child learns how to interact realistically with his or her environment and the people in it. The superego develops last, as the child learns moral values.

Erogenous Zones

Freud saw the libido as being focused in various regions of the body known as **erogenous zones**. An erogenous zone is a part of the skin or mucous membrane that is extremely sensitive to stimulation; touching it in certain ways produces feelings of pleasure. The lips and mouth are one such erogenous zone, the genitals a second, and the rectum and anus a third.

Stages of Psychosexual Development

Freud believed that children pass through a series of stages of development. In each of these stages, a different erogenous zone is the focus of pleasure.

According to Freud, the first stage, lasting from birth to about one year of age, is the *oral stage*. The child's chief pleasure is derived from sucking and otherwise stimulating the lips and mouth. Anyone who has observed children of this age knows how they delight in putting anything they can into their

superego: According to Freud, the part of the personality containing the conscience.

erogenous (eh-RAH-jen-us) zones: Areas of the body that are particularly sensitive to sexual stimulation.

Oedipus (EH-di-pus) complex: According to Freud, the sexual attraction of a little boy for his mother.

female Oedipus complex: According to Freud, the sexual attraction of a little girl for her father; sometimes called the *Electra complex*.

mouths. The second stage, which occurs during approximately the second year of life, is the *anal stage*. During this stage, the child's interest is focused on elimination.

The third stage of development, lasting from age three to perhaps age five or six, is the *phallic stage*. Boys' and girls' interest is focused on the genital area—the boy on his phallus (penis) and the girl on her clitoris—and they derive great pleasure from masturbating.[3] Perhaps the most important occurrence in this stage according to Freud is the development of the **Oedipus complex**, which derives its name from the Greek story of Oedipus, who unknowingly killed his father and married his mother. In the male Oedipus complex, the boy loves his mother and desires her sexually. He hates his father, whom he sees as a rival for the mother's affection. The boy's hostility toward his father grows, but eventually he comes to fear that his father will retaliate by castrating him—cutting off his prized penis. Thus, the boy feels *castration anxiety*. Eventually, the castration anxiety becomes so great that he stops desiring his mother and shifts to identifying with his father, taking on the father's gender role and acquiring the characteristics expected of males by society. Freud considered the Oedipus complex and its resolution to be one of the key factors in human personality development.

The **female Oedipus complex** (sometimes called the *Electra complex*, although not by Freud) is similar to the male Oedipus complex, beginning with the girl's love for her mother and her focus on her clitoris. The little girl realizes, perhaps after observing her father or her brother, that she has no penis. She feels envious and cheated, and she suffers from *penis envy*, wishing that she too had a wonderful wand and the privileges that go along with being male. Thus, she shifts her desire for her mother onto her father, forming the female Oedipus complex. The girl resolves penis envy by identifying with her mother and switching her erogenous zone from her clitoris to her vagina in order to have a baby, a son, as a substitute for a penis. Unlike the boy, the girl is not driven by castration anxiety to resolve her Oedipus complex. Thus the girl's resolution of the Oedipus complex is not as complete as the boy's, and Freud wrote that for the rest of her life, a woman's superego is not as developed as a man's.

Freud said that following the resolution of the Oedipus complex, children pass into a prolonged stage known as *latency*, which lasts until adolescence. During this stage, the sexual impulses are repressed or are in a quiescent state, and so nothing much happens sexually. The postulation of this stage is one of the weaker parts

---

[2] Fans of the television show *The Simpsons* might have noticed that Homer seems to be ruled primarily by his id and the pleasure principle, Lisa by her superego, and Marge by her ego and the reality principle.

---

[3] Masturbation to orgasm is physiologically possible at this age, although males are not capable of ejaculation until they reach puberty (see Chapter 5).

of Freudian theory, because it is clear from the data of modern sex researchers that children do continue to engage in behaviour with sexual components during this period (see Chapter 10).

With puberty, sexual urges reawaken and the child moves into the *genital stage*. During this stage, sexual urges become more specifically genital and the oral, anal, and genital urges all fuse together to promote the biological function of reproduction.

According to Freud, people do not always mature from one stage to the next as they should. A person might remain permanently fixated, for example, at the oral stage; symptoms of such a situation would include incessant cigarette smoking or fingernail biting, which gratify oral urges. Most adults have at least traces of earlier stages remaining in their personalities.

Evaluation of Psychoanalytic Theory

From a scientific point of view, one of the major problems with psychoanalytic theory is that most of its concepts cannot be evaluated scientifically to see whether they are accurate. Freud postulated that many of the most important forces in personality are unconscious and thus cannot be studied by using the scientific techniques common to the twentieth century. Recent advances in our ability to image brain activity—for example, with high-powered magnetic resonance imagery—have opened the possibility of testing Freud's ideas (see Figure 2.2). He believed that dreams provide a window into the person's id and that during sleep the activity of the ego and superego are reduced. Research in the developing area of *neuropsychoanalysis* suggests that it is activity in the prefrontal area of the brain that

Figure 2.2 What does a magnetic resonance imaging machine have to do with psychoanalytic theory? The answer is that by studying patterns in brain waves, we can test some of Freud's ideas about the relationship between the id and the ego.

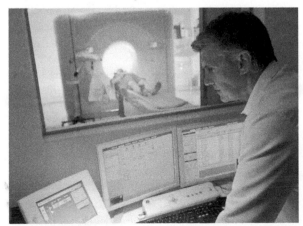

©Chris Ryan / age fotostock

constrains the sometimes bizarre imagery that is generated by the limbic and postcortical regions. During rapid eye movement (REM) sleep, there is a reduction of activity in the former (the ego?) and vivid and bizarre dreams are at times associated with activity in the latter (the id?) (Solms, 1997).

A key concept in psychoanalytic theory is *repression*, a defensive act preventing people from remaining aware of certain information, or motivated forgetting. It has been widely criticized as untestable. However, neural inhibition triggered by social factors could account for repression. Imaging evidence has identified the frontal lobes as the area that mediates the influence of social factors on impulse control, suggesting the neural basis of repression (Boag, 2007).

Another criticism is that Freud derived his data almost exclusively from his work with patients who sought therapy from him. Thus, his theory may provide a view not so much of the human personality as of *disturbances* in the human personality.

Feminists also have been critical of Freudian theory as a male-centred theory that may cause harm to women (Lerman, 1986). They object to Freud's assumption that because they do not have a penis, women are biologically inferior to men. One could just as easily argue that men have a powerful envy of women's reproductive capacity, which is just what psychoanalyst Karen Horney (1973) did when she coined the concept of *womb envy*, although this notion is equally open to criticism. They also criticize the distinction Freud made between *vaginal orgasm* (obtained through heterosexual intercourse with the penis stimulating the vagina) and clitoral orgasm (obtained through *clitoral stimulation*) in women. Research by Masters and Johnson (reviewed in Chapter 9) has shown that there is little or no physiological difference between orgasms resulting from clitoral stimulation and those resulting from heterosexual intercourse. Further, Freud's assertion that vaginal orgasm is more mature is not supported by findings that most adult women orgasm as a result of direct or indirect clitoral stimulation.

Nonetheless, Freud did make some important contributions to our understanding of human behaviour and many of his concepts have become part of everyday language. (Which ones can you think of?) He managed to rise above the sexually repressive Victorian era of which he was a member and teach that the libido is an important part of personality (although he may have overestimated its importance). His recognition that humans pass through stages in their psychological development was a great contribution. Perhaps most important from the perspective of this text, Freud took sex out of the closet, brought it to the attention of the general public, and suggested that we could talk about it and that it was an appropriate topic for scientific research.

Of course, psychoanalytic theory has evolved since Freud did his writing. Most contemporary psychoanalysts feel that Freud overemphasized the biological determinants of behaviour and instincts and that he gave insufficient recognition to the importance of environment and learning. For example, Erikson (1950), an influential theorist in developmental psychology, described how development continues throughout life rather than ending around age five. Most recent psychoanalytic theories, some of which are called object-relations theories, also describe relationships with other people, particularly the child's relationship with his or her primary caretaker (usually his or her mother or father), as crucial to development, although they have not totally abandoned Freud's view that sexuality is important to development. In particular, the type of attachment relationship children have to their mother and/or father in infancy and childhood may have a profound effect on their romantic relationships in adulthood (see Chapter 12 for more about the attachment theory of love).

L03 Learning Theory

Although psychoanalytic and sociobiological theories are based on the notion that much of human sexual behaviour is biologically controlled, it is also quite apparent that much of it is learned. Some of the best evidence for this point comes from studies of sexual behaviour across different human societies, which were considered in Chapter 1. Here the various principles of modern learning theory will be reviewed, because they can help us understand our own sexuality.

Classical Conditioning

What theory accounts for how the smell of perfume or cologne becomes sexually arousing?

Classical conditioning is a concept usually associated with the work of the Russian scientist Ivan Pavlov (1849–1936). Think of the following situations: You salivate in response to the sight or smell of food, you blink in response to someone poking a finger in your eye, or you experience sexual arousal in response to stroking the inner part of your thigh. In all these cases, an unconditioned stimulus (US; for example, appealing food) automatically, reflexively elicits an unconditioned response (UR; for example, salivation). The process of learning that occurs in classical conditioning takes place when a new stimulus, the conditioned stimulus (CS; for example, the sound of a bell) repeatedly is paired with the original unconditioned stimulus (food). After this happens many times, the conditioned stimulus (ringing bell) can eventually be presented without the unconditioned stimulus (food) and will evoke the original response, now called the conditioned response (CR; salivation).

As an example, suppose that Nadia's first serious boyfriend in high school always wears Erotik cologne when they go out. As they advance in their sexual intimacy, they have many pleasant times in the back seat of the car, where he strokes her thighs and other sexually responsive parts of her body and she feels highly aroused, always with the aroma of Erotik in her nostrils. One day she enters an elevator full of strangers in her office building, and someone is wearing Erotik. Nadia instantly feels sexually aroused, although she is not engaged in any sexual activity. From the point of view of classical conditioning, this makes perfect sense, although Nadia may wonder why she is feeling so aroused in the elevator. The thigh-stroking and sexy touching were the US. Her arousal was the UR. The aroma of the cologne, the CS, was repeatedly paired with the US. Eventually, the aroma by itself evoked arousal, the CR. See Figure 2.3.

Classical conditioning of sexual arousal has been demonstrated in an experiment using male students at Queen's University (Lalumière & Quinsey, 1998). Participants were first shown 20 slides of partially clothed women; a slide rated as 5 on a scale of sexual attractiveness ranging from 1 to 10 was selected as the target slide. Men in the control group saw only the target slide for 11 trials; men in the experimental group were shown the target slide followed by a 40-second segment of a sexually explicit videotape for 11 trials. Each man then rated the 20 original slides again. Arousal was measured by a penile strain gauge, which measures the extent of engorgement or erection of the penis (see Chapter 13). In the control group, men were less aroused by the target slide following the repeated exposure, whereas in the experimental group, the target slide was associated with an increase in arousal as measured by the strain gauge. Subsequent research has also demonstrated classical conditioning of sexual arousal in women (Hoffmann, Janssen, & Turner, 2004).

Classical conditioning is useful in explaining a number of phenomena in sexuality. One example is fetishes, discussed in Chapter 15.

Operant Conditioning

Operant conditioning, a concept that is often associated with psychologist B. F. Skinner, refers to the following process. A person performs a particular behaviour (the operant). That behaviour may be followed by either a reward (positive reinforcement) or a punishment. If a reward follows, the person will be likely to repeat the

---

classical conditioning: The learning process in which a previously neutral stimulus (conditioned stimulus) is repeatedly paired with an unconditioned stimulus that reflexively elicits an unconditioned response. Eventually, the conditioned stimulus itself will evoke the response.

operant (OP-ur-unt) conditioning: The process of changing the frequency of a behaviour (the operant) by following it with positive reinforcement (which will make the behaviour more frequent in the future) or punishment (which should make the behaviour less frequent in the future).

Figure 2.3   In this example of classical conditioning, Erotik cologne (the CS) eventually evokes sexual arousal by itself after it is repeatedly paired with kissing (the UCS).

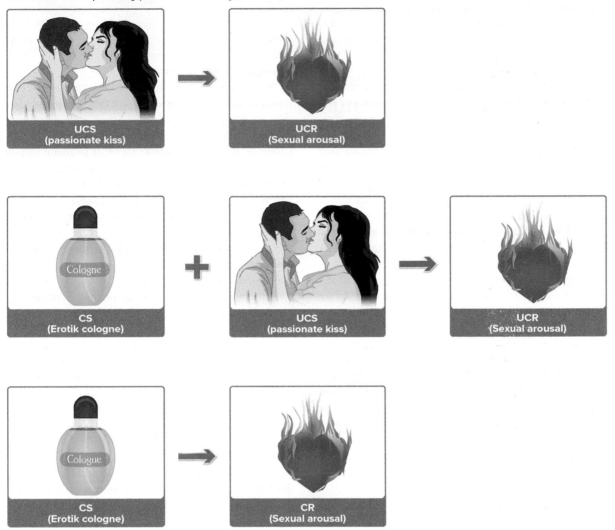

behaviour again in the future; if a punishment follows, the person will be less likely to repeat the behaviour. Thus, if a behaviour is repeatedly rewarded, it may become very frequent, and if it is repeatedly punished, it may become very infrequent or even be eliminated.

Some rewards are considered to be primary reinforcers; that is, there is something intrinsically rewarding about them. Food is one such primary reinforcer; sex is another. Male rats, for example, can be trained to learn a maze if they find a willing sex partner at the end of it. Thus, sexual behaviour plays dual roles in learning theory: it can itself be a positive reinforcer, but it can also be the behaviour that is rewarded or punished.

Simple principles of operant conditioning can help explain some aspects of sex. For example, if a woman repeatedly experiences pain when she has intercourse, she will probably want to have sex infrequently or not at all. In operant conditioning terms, sexual intercourse has repeatedly been associated with a punishment (pain), and so the behaviour becomes less frequent.

Another principle of operant conditioning that is useful in understanding sexual behaviour holds that consequences, whether reinforcement or punishment, are most effective in shaping behaviour when they occur immediately after the behaviour. The longer they are delayed after the behaviour has occurred, the less effective they become. As an example, consider a young man who has had gonorrhea three times yet continues to have unprotected sexual intercourse. The pain associated with gonorrhea is certainly punishing, so why does he persist in having sex without a condom? The delay principle suggests the following explanation. Each time he engages in unprotected intercourse, he finds it highly rewarding; this immediate reward maintains the behaviour; the punishment, gonorrhea, does not occur until several days later and so is not effective in eliminating that behaviour.

A Sexually Diverse World

Ritualized Same-Sex Sexual Activity in a Non-Western Society

Melanesia is an area of the southwest Pacific that includes the islands of New Guinea and Fiji as well as many others. Anthropologists' research on same-sex sexual behaviour in those cultures provides great insight into the ways in which sexual behaviours are the products of the scripts of a culture, as well as of social learning theory. This research is rooted in sociological and anthropological theory. As such, the analysis focuses on the norms of the society and the symbolic meaning that is attached to sexual behaviours.

Among Melanesians, same-sex sexual behaviour has a very different symbolic meaning from the one it has in Western culture. It is viewed as natural, normal, and indeed necessary. The culture actually prescribes the behaviour, in contrast to Western cultures, in which it is forbidden or proscribed. Among Melanesians, age organizes the same-sex sexual behaviour. It is not to occur between two men of the same age. Instead, it occurs between an adolescent and a preadolescent, or between an adult man and a pubertal boy. The older partner is always the inserter for the acts of anal intercourse, the younger partner is the receiver.

Ritualized same-sex sexual behaviour serves several social purposes in these cultures. It is viewed as a means by which a boy at puberty is incorporated into the adult society of men. It is also thought to "finish off" a boy's growth in puberty. In these societies, semen is viewed as a scarce and valuable commodity. Therefore, the same-sex sexual behaviours are viewed as helpful and honourable, a means of passing on strength to younger men and boys. As one anthropologist observed:

> Semen is also necessary for young boys to attain full growth to manhood. . . . They need a boost, as it were. When a boy is eleven or twelve years old, he is engaged for several months in homosexual intercourse with a healthy older man chosen by his father. (This is always an in-law or unrelated person, since the same notions of incestuous relations apply to little boys as to marriageable women.) Men point to the rapid growth of adolescent youths, the appearance of peach fuzz beards, and so on, as the favorable results of this child-rearing practice. (Schieffelin, 1976, p. 124)

In all cases, these men are expected later to marry and father children. These observations defy the commonly held, although not necessarily accurate, view in Western societies that sexual orientation is a permanent

---

A third principle that has emerged in operant conditioning studies is that, compared with rewards, punishments are not very effective in shaping behaviour. Often, as in the case of the child who is punished for taking an illicit cookie, punishments do not eliminate a behaviour but rather teach the person to be sneaky and engage in it without being caught. As an example, some parents, as many commonly did in earlier times in our culture, punish children for masturbating; yet most of those children continue to masturbate, perhaps learning instead to do it under circumstances in which they are not likely to be caught (such as in a bathroom with the door locked).

behaviour therapy: A set of techniques based on principles of classical or operant conditioning used to modify human behaviour, in which the focus is on the problem behaviour and how it can be modified or changed.

One important difference between psychoanalytic theory and learning theory should be noted. Psychoanalytic theorists believe that the determinants of human sexual behaviour occur in early childhood, particularly during the Oedipal complex period. Learning theorists, in contrast, believe that sexual behaviour can be learned and changed at any time in one's lifespan—in childhood, in adolescence, in young adulthood, or later. When we try to understand what causes certain sexual behaviours and how to treat people with sex problems, this distinction between the theories has important implications.

Behaviour Therapy

Behaviour therapy involves a set of techniques, based on principles of classical or operant conditioning, that

characteristic throughout life. This points out the contrast between sexual identity and sexual behaviour. The sexual behaviours are ones that we would surely term "homosexual," yet these cultures are so structured that the boys and men who engage in same-sex sexual behaviours do not form a homosexual identity. Indeed, the very concepts of having a "heterosexual identity" or "homosexual identity" are not present in these cultures.

Can social learning theory also explain these patterns of sexual behaviour? It can, according to the analysis of John and Janice Baldwin. First, positive conditioning in the direction of heterosexuality occurs early in life. The boy spends the first seven to ten years of his life with his family. He has a close, warm relationship with his mother. In essence, he has been conditioned to have positive feelings about women.

Second, observational learning occurs. In those same first seven to ten years, the boy observes closely the heterosexual relationship between two adults, his mother and father. This observational learning can be used a decade later when it is time for him to marry and form a heterosexual relationship.

Third, the boy is provided with much cognitive structuring, a notion present in social learning theory and in cognitive psychology. He is instructed that a boy must pass through a series of stages to become a strong, masculine man. These stages include first being the

receptive partner to fellatio, then being the inserting partner to fellatio, marrying, defending himself from his wife's first menstruation (girls are usually married before puberty and undergo no homosexual stage of development), and then fathering a child by her. Essentially, he is given all the cognitive structures necessary to convince him that it is perfectly natural, indeed desirable, to engage in sex with men for ten years and then switch to women. Finally, there is some aversive conditioning to the homosexual behaviour that leads it to be not particularly erotic. The boy performs fellatio for the first time after several days of initiation, when he is exhausted. The activities are staged so that the boy feels fearful about it. He must do it in darkness with an older boy who may be an enemy, and he is required to do it with many males in succession. In essence, unpleasantness or punishment is associated with some of the same-sex sexual behaviour.

Ritualized same-sex sexual behaviours are declining as these cultures are colonized by Westerners. It is fortunate that anthropologists were able to make their observations over the last several decades to document these interesting and meaningful practices before they disappear.

Sources: Baldwin & Baldwin, 1989; Herdt, 1982, 1984.

---

are used to change (or modify) human behaviour. In particular, these methods can be used to modify problematic sexual behaviours—that is, sexual disorders, such as orgasm problems (see Chapter 18) or compulsive sexual behaviour (see Chapter 15). Behaviour therapy methods differ from more traditional methods of psychotherapy, such as psychoanalysis, in that the behavioural therapist considers only the problem behaviour and how to modify it using learning-theory principles; the therapist does not worry about an in-depth analysis of the person's personality to see, for example, what unconscious forces might be motivating the behaviour. Most often, treatment programs combine behaviour therapy techniques with cognitive therapy approaches—called cognitive behaviour therapy.

Social Learning

Social learning theory (Bandura, 1977; Bandura & Walters, 1963) is a somewhat more complex form of learning theory. It is based on principles of operant conditioning, but it also recognizes that people learn by observing others, called *observational learning*, whether in person or in the media. This kind of social learning involves two other processes: *imitation* and *identification*. These two processes are useful in explaining the development of gender identity, or our sense of maleness or femaleness. For example, a little girl acquires many characteristics of the female role by identifying with her mother and imitating her, as when she plays at dressing up after observing her mother getting ready to go to a party. Also, various forms of sexuality may be learned through imitation (see Figure 2.4). In high school, for example, the

Figure 2.4 According to social learning theory, children learn about sex and gender in part by imitation. These children may be imitating their parents or a scene they have watched on TV.

©Girl Ray/The Image Bank/Getty Images

sexiest girl in the senior class may find that other girls are imitating her behaviours and the way she dresses. Or a boy might see a movie in which the hero's technique seems to "turn women on," and then he tries to use this technique with his own dates. The latter example points to the importance of mass media as a source of images of sexuality that young people imitate and personalities that they identify with. Unfortunately, media images are often inaccurate and unrealistic.

Once a behaviour is learned, the likelihood of its being performed depends on its consequences. The young man who imitates actor Brad Pitt's romantic technique may not succeed in arousing his companion. If the behaviour is not reinforced, he will stop performing it. If it is reinforced, he will repeat it. Successful experiences with an activity over time create a sense of competence or **self-efficacy** at performing the activity (Bandura, 1982). If a woman feels efficacious at using the female condom, she will expend more effort (going to the drugstore to buy one) and will show greater persistence in the face of difficulty (continuing to adjust it until it fits properly) than she did before. The concept of self-efficacy has been widely used in designing health intervention programs, such as those that encourage individuals to use condoms to prevent transmission of sexually transmitted infections and HIV (e.g.,

self-efficacy: A sense of competence at performing an activity.

social exchange theory: A theory that assumes people will choose actions that maximize rewards and minimize costs.

DeLamater, Wagstaff, & Havens, 2000). These programs provide opportunities for participants to practise the behaviours that are being promoted and be successful.

Social learning can also explain phenomena, such as birth rates (see also the A Sexually Diverse World box). Many adults want to have children; that is, they have *fertility intentions.* They also recognize that infant mortality may deprive them of offspring. Most adults are not aware of the infant mortality rate in their country or community. However, they are aware of the fertility outcomes of couples they know and interact with. If women are influenced by the birth and survival experiences of women around them, this would reflect the impact of social experience and learning on reproduction. Researchers identified the social networks of a group of Nepalese women and assessed the experiences of members of a woman's network on her fertility. As expected, experiences of network members were related to the timing of a woman's births, demonstrating the effects of social learning on birth rates (Sandberg, 2006).

L04 Social Exchange Theory

An important process based on the principle of reinforcement is social exchange. **Social exchange theory** (Cook & Rice, 2003) has emerged out of social learning theory and uses the concept of reinforcement to explain satisfaction, stability, and change in relationships among people. It is also useful in explaining *sexuality* in close relationships (Byers & Wang, 2004). The theory assumes that we have freedom of choice and often face choices among alternative actions. Every action provides some rewards and entails certain costs. There are many kinds of rewards (money, goods, services, sexual gratification, approval by others) and costs (time, effort, money, embarrassment, emotional distance). The theory states that we try to maximize rewards and minimize costs when we act. Thus, we choose actions that produce a favourable balance of rewards to costs or profits (profits equalling rewards minus costs), and avoid actions that produce poor profits.

As its name indicates, social exchange theory views social relationships primarily as exchanges of goods and services among persons. People participate in relationships only if they find that the relationships provide profitable outcomes. An individual judges the attractiveness of a relationship by comparing the profits it provides against both the profits he or she thinks should be received in the relationship and the profits available in alternative relationships. The level of expected outcomes is called the *comparison level;* the level of outcomes in the best alternative relationship is called the *comparison level for alternatives* (Byers & Wang, 2004). These ideas have been applied to personal relationships. Studies of heterosexual couples in long-term relationships have found that the concepts of rewards and costs can explain whether people stay in a relationship (Rusbult, 1983; Rusbult, Johnson, & Morrow, 1986). Individuals are more likely to stay in when the partner is physically and personally attractive, when the relationship does not entail undue costs (such as high monetary commitments, broken promises, or arguments), and when romantic relationships with attractive others are not available. In other words, they are more likely to stay in a relationship when its rewards are high, its costs are low, rewards and costs compare favourably to expectations, and the comparison level for alternatives is low.

Social exchange theory also predicts the conditions under which people try to change their relationships. A central concept is *equity or equality* (Walster, Walster, & Berscheid, 1978; Hatfield, Walster, & Berscheid, 1978). A state of equity exists when participants in a relationship believe that the rewards they receive from it are proportional to the costs they bear. Equality exists when both partners experience the same balance of rewards to costs (profit). If a person feels that the allocation of rewards and costs is inequitable or unequal, then the relationship is unstable. People find inequity unpleasant and may feel cheated or angry. As we will see in Chapter 11, a person experiencing inequity may engage in *extradyadic* sex (i.e., sex with someone other than their partner) as a result.

Social exchange theory has also been used to explain various other aspects of sexuality in close relationships such as partner selection, sexual frequency, and sexual satisfaction (for a review, see Byers & Wang, 2004). For example, one of this book's authors, New Brunswick psychologist Sandra Byers, and her colleagues have shown that, in both dating and long-term relationships, sexual satisfaction is higher the more sexual rewards exceed sexual costs (i.e., profit is high), sexual rewards and costs compare favourably to expectations, and sexual rewards and costs between partners are equal (Byers, Demmons, & Lawrance, 1998; Byers & MacNeil, 2006; Lawrance & Byers, 1995).

Social exchange theories have been criticized for applying the ideas of rewards and costs to romantic relationships. Some people believe that love is not and should not be about what one can get out of a relationship (i.e., its rewards). A related criticism is that social exchange theories downplay other motivations. Because of the emphasis on rewards and costs, such theories cannot explain, for example, selfless behaviours, such as altruism and martyrdom.

L05 Cognitive Theory

In the 1980s and 1990s, a "cognitive revolution" swept through psychology. In contrast to the older behaviourist tradition (which insisted that psychologists should study only behaviours that could be directly observed), cognitive psychologists believe that it is very important to study people's cognitions—that is, the way people perceive and think.

Cognition and Sexuality

Cognitive psychology can readily explain some aspects of human sexuality. A basic assumption is that what we think influences what we feel. If we think happy, positive thoughts, we will tend to feel better than if we think negative ones. Therapists using a cognitive approach believe that psychological distress is often a result of negative thoughts that do not reflect reality and include misconceptions, distortions, exaggerations of problems, and unreasonably negative evaluations of events.

To the cognitive psychologist, how we perceive and evaluate a sexual event makes all the difference in the world (Walen & Roth, 1987). For example, suppose that a man engaged in sexual activity with his partner does not get an erection. Starting from that basic event, his thoughts might take one of two directions. In the first, he thinks that it is quite common for a man in his age group (50s) not to get an erection every time he has sex; this has happened to him a few times before, once every two or three months, and it's nothing to worry about. At any rate, the oral sex was fun, and his partner had an orgasm from that, so all in all it was a nice enough encounter. In the second possibility, he began the sexual activity thinking that he had to have an erection, had to have intercourse, and had to have an orgasm. When he didn't get an erection, he mentally labelled it *impotence* and worried that he would never again have an erection. He thought of the whole episode as a frustrating disaster because he never had an orgasm. Who do you think would be more likely to experience sexual problems the next time he has sex?

As cognitive psychologists point out, our perception, labelling, and evaluation of events are crucial. In one case, the man perceived a slight problem, labelled it a temporary erection problem, and evaluated his sexual experience as pretty good. In the other case, the man perceived a serious problem, labelled it impotence, and evaluated the experience as horrible.

We will see cognitive psychology several times again in this book, as theorists use it to understand the cycle of sexual arousal (see Chapter 9); the causes of some sexual variations, such as fetishes (see Chapter 15); and the causes and treatment of sexual disorders (see Chapter 18). Before we leave cognitive psychology, however, we will look at one cognitive theory, schema theory, that has been used especially to understand issues of sex and gender.

Gender Schema Theory

Psychologist Sandra Bem (1981, 1993) proposed a schema theory to explain gender-role development and the impact of gender on people's daily lives and thinking. *Schema* is a term taken from cognitive psychology. A **schema** is a general knowledge framework that a person has about a particular topic. A schema organizes and guides perception; it helps us remember, but it sometimes also distorts our memory, especially if the information is inconsistent with our schema. Thus, for example, you might have a hockey game schema, the set of ideas you have about what elements should be present at the game (two teams, spectators, stands, etc.) and what kinds of activities should occur (opening face-off, occasional goal, penalties, power plays, etc.).

It is Bem's contention that all of us possess a *gender schema*—a cognitive structure comprising the set of attributes (behaviours, personality, appearance) that we associate with males and females. Children learn not only about appropriate roles for men and women but also that the distinctions between men and women and between masculine and feminine are extremely important ways to understand reality. Thus our gender schema, according to Bem, predisposes us to process information on the basis of gender. That is, we tend to think of things as gender-related and to want to dichotomize them on the basis of gender. A good example is the case of the infant whose gender isn't clear when we meet him or her. We eagerly seek out the information or feel awkward if we don't, because we seem to need to know the baby's gender to continue to process information about it.

schema (SKEE-muh): A general knowledge framework that a person has about a particular topic.

Bem (1981) has done a number of experiments that provide evidence for her theory, and there are confirming experiments by other researchers as well, although the evidence is not always completely consistent (Ruble & Stangor, 1986). In one of the most interesting of these experiments, five- and six-year-old children were shown pictures of males or females performing activities that were either stereotype-consistent activities (such as a girl baking cookies) or stereotype-inconsistent (such as girls boxing) at that time (Martin & Halverson, 1983; see Figure 2.5 for examples). One week later the children were tested for their recall of the pictures. The results indicated that the children distorted information by changing the gender of people in the stereotype-inconsistent pictures, while not making such changes for the stereotype-consistent pictures. That is, children tended to remember a picture of girls boxing as having been a picture of boys boxing. These results are just what would be predicted by gender schema theory. The schema helps us remember schema-consistent (stereotype-consistent) information well, but it distorts our memory of information that is inconsistent with the schema (stereotype-inconsistent).

Our gender schema influences many everyday behaviours, for example, what we look at in magazines. Male and female undergraduate students completed a measure of the masculinity-femininity of their self-concept. They were later allowed to select from three male-typed (*Men's Health, Game Informer, Sports Illustrated*), three female-typed (*Shape, Us Weekly, Glamour*), and three gender-neutral news magazines. Gender schema

Figure 2.5   Pictures like these were used in the Martin and Halverson research on gender schemas and children's memory. *(a)* A girl engaged in a stereotype-consistent activity. *(b)* Girls engaged in a stereotype-inconsistent activity. In a test of recall a week later, children tended to distort the stereotype-inconsistent pictures to make them stereotype consistent; for example, they remembered that they had seen boys boxing.

(b)

(a)

(masculinity-femininity) influenced what they read in the selected magazine(s) (Knobloch-Westerwick & Hoplamazian, 2012).

One of the interesting implications of gender schema theory is that stereotypes—whether they are about males and females, or heterosexuals and homosexuals, or other groups—may be very slow to change. The reason is that our schemas tend to filter out stereotype-inconsistent (that is, schema-inconsistent) information so that we don't even remember it.

Critical Theories

The theories we have considered so far focus on understanding the nature of various behaviours and types of persons. Since 1990, a new perspective has emerged, the *social constructionist* viewpoint. It calls our attention to the fact that these behaviours and types of people are social constructions, categories that are developed by groups and subcultures and then applied to objects in the world around them. Theories that use this perspective are more interested in understanding how these categories are created and their consequences for individuals and groups. Two theories are especially relevant to a broad understanding of sexuality: feminist theory and queer theory.

Feminist Theory

Feminist theory was not proposed by a single theorist but rather by many independent scholars (for an overview, see Enns, 2004). Here we crystallize four of the essential assertions of feminist theory.

Gender as Status and Inequality

According to the theory, gender signals status in a culture, with men having greater status and power (Ridgeway & Bourg, 2004). As such, gender is a dimension of inequality, just as race and social class are. Evidence of this inequality can be seen at many levels, from the low representation of women in Parliament to discrimination against women in promotions in the workplace. A closely related concept is the *inequality of power* between women and men, with women having less power (Pratto & Walker, 2004). Feminist analysis extends the power principle to other areas—for example, to viewing sexual assault not as a sexual act but as an expression of men's power over women.

Sexuality

Sexuality is a central issue in feminist theory (MacKinnon, 1982) and includes many specific issues including sexual assault, abortion, birth control, sexual harassment on the job, and pornography. According to feminist analysis, women's sexuality has been repressed and depressed, but rarely expressed. These problems are the result of men's control of women's sexuality; for example, men dominate the legislatures that pass laws regulating abortion. We will revisit feminist analysis of some of these issues in later chapters.

Gender Roles and Socialization

Feminist theory highlights the importance of gender roles and gender socialization. Our culture has well-defined roles for males and for females. From their earliest years, children are socialized to conform to these roles. On these points, feminist theory is in agreement with social learning theory. The problem is that gender roles tell individuals that they may not do certain things. A boy, for example, cannot grow up to be a nurse or—horrors—a ballet dancer. A girl cannot grow up to be a physicist. Because gender roles restrict people in these ways, feminist theorists argue that we would be better off without gender roles, or at least that gender roles need to be modified and made much more flexible.

Intersectionality

The experiences of women, for example, are not all the same, nor are the experiences of men all the same. They vary by the person's race/ethnicity, sexual orientation, social class, and so on. **Intersectionality** is an approach that says that we should simultaneously consider a person's multiple group memberships and identities, including gender, race, social class, and sexual orientation (Cole, 2009). For example, to understand a person's sexuality, it matters not only that the person is a woman, but also that she is Asian Canadian and a lesbian. She has multiple identities—as an Asian, as a woman, and as a lesbian. All of these identities intersect and are part of her, and in different situations, one may be more important than another.

Queer Theory

Over the years, "queer" has been used as a derogatory term referring to homosexuals. Why is it now a theory? Contemporary gays have re-appropriated the term and given it a positive meaning. A gay person may self-label as queer, and the major contemporary theorizing about sexual orientation is termed queer theory (for overviews, see Sullivan, 2003; Tolman & Diamond, 2014). Queer theory is broader than just the topic of sexual orientation, though, and includes other topics that have been considered "deviant," such as intersex and transgender.

> **intersectionality:** An approach that simultaneously considers the consequences of multiple group membership, such as the intersection of gender and ethnicity.

Queer theory questions the social categorization of sexuality and gender. It challenges binaries (the idea that people fall into one of just two categories), especially the sexual orientation binary; that is, it questions the assumption that people are either homosexual or heterosexual and there are no other possibilities or spaces in between. Similarly, it questions the *gender binary* that separates people into male and female, as if they were opposites, with no recognition of similarities or other gender possibilities. It also argues that sexual identities are not fixed for the individual; that is, sexual identities may vary depending on the situation or time in one's life. We will return to this idea in Chapters 13 and 14.

The use of "queer" in the theory has a second meaning, though. Another definition of queer is peculiar or odd–that is, different from the norm. In this sense, queer theory questions what is categorized as peculiar and what is not. It questions norms. It uses this approach to challenge **heteronormativity**, the belief that heterosexuality is the only pattern of sexuality that is normal and natural. Queer theory argues that social norms privilege heterosexuality and marginalize other sexual orientations.

Sociological Perspectives

Sociologists are most interested in the ways in which society or culture shapes human sexuality. (For a detailed articulation of the sociological perspective, see DeLamater, 1987; the arguments that follow are taken from that source.)

 Symbolic Interaction Theory

An important sociological theory is **symbolic interaction theory** (Charon, 1995; Stryker, 1987). Its premise is that human nature and the social order are products of symbolic communication among people. A person's behaviour is constructed through his or her interactions with others. People can communicate successfully with one another only to the extent that they ascribe similar meanings to objects and people. An object's meaning for a person depends not on the properties of the object but on what the person might do with it; an object takes on meaning only in relation to a person's plans. Thus, the theory views people as proactive and goal-seeking. Achieving most goals requires the cooperation of others. This is especially true of many forms of sexual expression. For example, suppose a woman invites a person she is dating to her apartment; what meaning does this invitation have? Does she want to prolong the conversation or engage

heteronormativity: The belief that heterosexuality is the only pattern that is normal and natural.

symbolic interaction theory: A theory that proposes human nature and the social order are products of communication among people.

in intimate sexual activity? The woman and her partner will have to achieve an agreement about the purpose of the visit before joint activity is possible. In terms of the theory, they have to develop a *definition of the situation.* Thus, to fit their actions together and achieve agreement, people interacting with each other must continually reaffirm old meanings or negotiate new ones.

Central to social interaction is the process of *role-taking* in which an individual imagines how he or she looks from the other person's viewpoint. By viewing the self and potential actions from the perspective of the other person, we are often able to anticipate what behaviour will enable us to achieve our goal. One consequence of role-taking is self-control; we see ourselves from the viewpoint of others and so strive to meet their standards. In the process, we exercise control over our behaviour.

Can a woman go to a strip club and get a lap dance? It depends on whether she can, in interaction with one of the dancers, create a definition of herself as a *patron.* Many strippers are oriented toward male customers and pass over women because they perceive them as unlikely to pay for a dance. A few perceive the situation as different and negotiate with women; the result may be more intimate contact than the typical male lap dance (Wosick-Correa & Joseph, 2008).

This perspective emphasizes the importance of symbolic communication (see Chapter 12). It alerts us to the mutual effort required to arrive at a definition of the situation. Criticisms of this theory include the fact that it emphasizes rational, conscious thought, whereas in the realm of sexuality, emotions are very important in many interactions. Also, this perspective portrays humans as *other-directed individuals*, concerned primarily with meeting other people's standards. A third criticism is that we don't always consciously role-take and communicate in an effort to achieve agreement. Sometimes we rely on past experience and habit. Situations such as these are the province of script theory which is discussed next.

Sexual Scripts

The outcome of these social influences, according to symbolic interaction theories, is that each of us learns the meanings of various behaviours through our interactions with others (Plummer, 1975). We also learn a set of *sexual scripts* (Gagnon, 1990; Gagnon & Simon, 1973). The idea is that sexual behaviour is a result of extensive prior learning that teaches us sexual etiquette and how to interpret specific situations. According to this concept, we have all learned an elaborate script that tells us the who, what, when, where, and why of sexual behaviour. For example, the "who" part of the dominant Canadian script tells us that sex should occur with someone of the other gender, of approximately our own age, of our own race, and so on. Even the sequence of sexual

Figure 2.6 According to some people's sexual scripts, a man taking a woman to dinner is one scene of the first act in a heterosexual sexual script that features intercourse as the finale.

©Steve Mason/Getty Images

activity is scripted. *Scripts*, then, are plans that people carry around in their heads for what they are doing and what they are going to do (see Figure 2.6); they are also devices for helping people remember what they have done in the past (Gagnon, 1977, p. 6).

How can we study these scripts? How can we find out if there are widely shared beliefs about how we should behave in a specific situation? One way is to ask people to describe what a person should do in such a situation. Researchers asked male and female college students to describe a typical "hook-up" (Holman & Sillars, 2012). The hypothetical script written by many participants included a basic sequence: attending a party, friends present, drinking alcohol, flirting, hanging out/talking, dancing, and a sexual encounter. Reflecting the ambiguity of a hook-up, the sexual encounter might include oral, anal, or vaginal intercourse; just "fooling around" (not intercourse); or "only hugging and kissing." The results also reflect contemporary gender roles; men were more likely to provide a script than were women. The widely shared nature of this script enables relative strangers to interact smoothly.

One study attempted to identify the sequence of sexual behaviours that is scripted for male–female relationships in our culture (Jemail & Geer, 1977; see also Edgar & Fitzpatrick, 1993). People were given 25 sentences, each describing an event in a heterosexual interaction. They were asked to rearrange the sentences in a sequence that was the most likely to occur. There was a high degree of agreement among the participants about what the sequence should be. There was also high agreement between men and women. The standard sequence was kissing, hand stimulation of the breasts, hand stimulation

of the genitals, mouth–genital stimulation, intercourse, and orgasm. Does this sound familiar? Interestingly, not only is this the sequence in a sexual encounter, it is also the sequence that occurs as a couple progresses in a relationship. These results suggest that there are culturally defined sequences of behaviours that we all have learned, much as the notion of a script suggests.

Researchers collected data from several hundred young adults in 2010 (Sakaluk et al., 2014). The participants endorsed most elements of the traditional heterosexual script identified by past research, suggesting little change.

Although the hook-up script provides guidelines, each couple will enact the script in a unique way. What they talk about, what they eat or drink, and whether they dance will reflect the desires and expectations of each, and the course of their interaction. Whether they kiss, fool around, or engage in intercourse will depend on each person's past experience, current desire and arousal, and how much each has had to drink.

Scripts also tell us the meaning we should attach to a particular sexual event (Gagnon, 1990). Television programs and films frequently suggest but do not show sexual activity between people. How do we make sense out of these implicit portrayals? A study of how women interpret such scenes in films found that they use scripts. If the film showed a couple engaging in two actions that are part of the accepted script for sexual intercourse (e.g., kissing and undressing each other) and then faded out, viewers inferred that intercourse had occurred (Meischke, 1995).

Why do most sexual interactions in our society follow the same pattern?

Sexual Fields

Sexual interactions are not only guided by scripts, they are influenced by the social context in which they occur. Most young couples would never take off their pants and underwear and perform oral sex on each other in a crowded bar. But the same couple in certain bars in the Gay Village in Toronto or in a swingers club might do just that. In all three cases, the couple is in a bar with many other individuals and couples engaging in various forms of symbolic or real intimacy. The difference in the degree of intimacy reflects the nature of the sexual field in each bar. A *field* is a physical site characterized by a distinct set of actors, institutionalized modes of interaction (scripts) managed by participants, and positions that confer advantage on some and disadvantage on others. A **sexual field** is a site populated with people with erotic dispositions that they project on the space and each other, creating a system of sexual stratification; the resulting interaction reflects each actor's desires, mediated by the acceptable modes of interaction and each actor's status in that field (Green, 2014).

Most interactions that lead to sexual intimacy begin or occur in a sexual field. Coffee shops; college bars; clubs; private parties; bathhouses; bars populated by gays, lesbians, leathermen, or furries; dating websites; chat rooms—all are sexual fields. People who enter a field are motivated by sexual desire and assess others who are present in terms of sexual desirability. Each field will have specific objects of evaluation—breast size, amount of skin displayed, symbolic markers like piercings or tattoos, hair style, styles of dress or undress, gait, posture, what one is drinking, or photos and text in one's profile, style, and content of messages—that are assessed by others present to create a hierarchy of desire. Actors assess their position in the hierarchy, and their opportunities for intimacy and behaviour depend on their placement in the hierarchy. In other words, fields structure the opportunities for each person to experience fulfillment of his/her sexual desire. In some sites, actors with particular attributes and desires will congregate in distinct spaces (Grazian, 2008). Groups of singles may congregate at the bar, which allows surveillance of who is coming and going and facilitates circulating around the room. The dance floor may be peopled by couples in some fields or by singles looking to hook up in others. The tables in the back may be full of undergraduates living in residence looking for an FWB among the other students in residence. There may be different dimensions of evaluation in each section. A buff male student may get more attention at the bar than he does at the tables. Some people can move seamlessly from field to field recognizing that their ranking changes as they cross invisible social boundaries. What kind(s) of sexual fields do you spend time in?

sexual field: A site populated with people with erotic dispositions that they project on the space and each other, creating a system of sexual stratification.

Social Institutions

Sociologists approach the study of sexuality with three basic assumptions:

1. Every society regulates the sexuality of its members. (For a discussion of the reasons why, see Horrocks, 1997.)
2. Basic institutions of society (such as religion, economy, the family, medicine, and law) affect the rules governing sexuality in that society.
3. The appropriateness or inappropriateness of a particular sexual behaviour depends on the institutional context in which it occurs.

Each of these institutions supports a sexual ideology, or discourse, about sexual activity. The ideology affects the beliefs and behaviours of those affiliated with the institution.

Religion

Historically, the Judeo-Christian religious tradition has been a powerful shaper of sexual norms in Western culture. A detailed discussion of that religious tradition and its teachings on sexuality is provided in Chapter 20. Suffice it to say here that the Christian religion (but not the Jewish religion) has contained within it a tradition of asceticism, in which abstinence from sexual pleasures—especially by certain persons, such as monks and priests—is seen as virtuous. The tradition, at least until recently, has also been oriented toward procreation—that is, a belief that sexuality is legitimate only within traditional heterosexual marriage and only with the goal of having children, a *procreational ideology*. This view has created within our culture a set of norms, or standards for behaviour, that say, for example, that sex before marriage, outside of marriage, and with a same-sex partner is wrong. The procreational ideology is one argument that some people use for asserting that marriage is exclusively for a man and a woman, since only a mixed-sex couple can procreate without intervention. Many of these norms are changing, so that today many Canadians do not subscribe to some of these views. Further, many Canadians come from non-Christian traditions, such as Judaism, Islam, Hinduism, Buddhism, or humanism, that have their own views about sexuality. These traditions are also described in Chapter 20.

The Economy

The nature and structure of the economy is another macro-level influence on sexuality. Before the industrial revolution, most work was done in the family unit in the home or farm. This kind of togetherness permitted rather strict surveillance of family members' sexuality, and thus strict norms could be enforced. However, with the industrial revolution, people—most frequently men—spent many hours per day at work away from the home. Thus they were under less surveillance, and scripts such as extramarital affairs and same-sex sexual activity could be acted out more often.

Today we see evidence of the extent to which economic conditions can affect sexuality. For example, the average monthly wage is very low in Russia. As a result, few people can afford to use condoms, and the rate of STIs is very high. Economic conditions have also led to a major increase in the number of prostitutes. It is difficult to support a family on the salary earned in most jobs, including professional jobs. In contrast, a Russian sex workers may earn the equivalent of the average monthly salary in just a few hours. As a result, many Russian sex workers are highly educated and choose prostitution for financial reasons. Many Russians see prostitution as a viable way of earning a living (Byers & Slattery, 1997).

In a capitalist economy, such as Canada, goods and services become commodities that can be sold for a price (an exchange). Not surprisingly, this includes sexual images and sexual gratification, giving rise to the sale of sexually explicit materials in stores and on the Internet, and to commercial sex work. The increasing globalization of the economy has led to the development of sex tourism, in which affluent men and women travel to other cultures, such as Thailand, to purchase sexual gratification from exotic (e.g., Asian) sex workers (see Chapter 17).

The Family

The family is a third institution influencing sexuality (see Figure 2.7). As we noted earlier, before the industrial revolution, the family was an important economic unit, producing the goods necessary for survival. As that function waned after the industrial revolution, there was increased emphasis on the quality of interpersonal relationships in the family. At the same time, love was increasingly seen as an important reason for marriage. Thus, a triple linkage between love, marriage, and sex was formed. Ironically, the linkage eventually became a direct one between love and sex so that, by the 1970s, some people were arguing that sex outside of marriage, if in the context of a loving relationship, was permissible, as was same-sex sexual activity, again if the relationship was a loving one. This is the *relational ideology.*

The family exerts a particularly important force on sexuality through its *socialization* of children. That is, parents socialize their children—teach them appropriate norms for behaviour—in many areas, including sexuality. Others, of course, such as the peer group, also have important socializing influences.

Medicine

The institution of medicine has become a major influence on our sexuality over the last 100 years. Physicians tell us what is healthy and what is unhealthy. In the late

Figure 2.7 Families today are no longer defined by traditional stereotypes. Here, a lesbian couple enjoy the park with their son.

2009 Jupiter Images Corporation

nineteenth century, physicians warned that masturbation could cause various pathologies. Today sex therapists tell us that sexual expression is natural and healthy and sometimes even "prescribe" masturbation as a treatment. Another example is provided by childbirth; until the end of the nineteenth century, most babies were born at home, with an experienced woman (a midwife) providing assistance to the labouring woman. Today the vast majority of births occur in hospitals and birthing facilities, with medical personnel in charge. We tend to have great confidence in medical advice, so the pronouncements of the medical establishment, based on a *therapeutic ideology*, have an enormous impact on sexuality.

The increasing influence of medicine on sexuality has not been taken lying down. The domination of contemporary theory and research by the biomedical model is referred to as the **medicalization of sexuality** (Tiefer, 2004). Medicalization has two components: Certain behaviours or conditions are defined in terms of health and illness; and these "problematic behaviours" are then given medical treatment (Polzer & Knabe, 2012). The medicalization of male sexuality is being hastened by the development of drugs to treat erectile dysfunction, and many physicians

medicalization of sexuality: The process by which certain sexual behaviours or conditions are defined in terms of health and illness, and problematic experiences or practices are given medical treatment.

and pharmaceutical companies are seeking to medicalize female sexual dysfunction by finding a pill that will "cure" them (discussed further in Chapter 18). In contrast, the sexual health perceptive described in Chapter 1 is geared toward enhancing health and preventing illness; it takes a biopsychosocial perspective, acknowledging the interaction of biological, psychological, and social factors on sexual health. There are efforts in the medical community in Canada to encourage health care providers to take a broader perspective, for example, the *Female Sexual Health Guidelines* developed by the Society of Obstetricians and Gynaecologists of Canada (Lamont et al., 2012).

LO9 The Law

The legal system is another institution influencing sexuality at the macro level. From a sociological perspective, the law influences people's sexual behaviour in a number of ways. First, laws help to determine norms. Generally, we think that what is legal is right and what is illegal is wrong. In Canada, only the federal government has the right to pass criminal laws, and all sexual offences are contained in the *Criminal Code of Canada* and apply to all Canadians regardless of the province or territory in which they live (Roach, 2000). Provincial, territorial, and municipal governments have the right to enact regulatory offences, such as zoning bylaws and licensing requirements, to help them govern matters within their jurisdiction, as long as these regulations do not stray into the criminal area. In contrast, in the United States and Australia, states have the right to enact criminal laws, resulting in significant differences in sexual offences from one state to another.

A major change to Canadian criminal law occurred in 1969 when, under Prime Minister Pierre Elliott Trudeau, the House of Commons passed an omnibus bill that introduced sweeping changes to the *Criminal Code of Canada* (see Figure 2.8). This bill removed provisions that had made consensual sexual behaviours between adults done in private illegal, such as use of contraception, oral sex, and anal sex. These changes may have reflected the fact that laws that go against prevailing social or subcultural norms are often ignored, and most Canadians agreed with Trudeau when he said, "The state has no business in the bedrooms of the nation." In contrast, although arrests for criminal sexual conduct are rare in the United States, in many states oral intercourse, anal intercourse (sodomy), sex with someone who is legally married to someone else (adultery), cohabitation, sex between two unmarried persons (fornication), and sexual contact between two persons of the same gender are crimes (Posner, 1992). Thus, every day millions of Americans engage in sexual behaviours that are illegal.

Figure 2.8 In 1969, under Prime Minister Pierre Elliott Trudeau, Parliament decriminalized consensual sexual behaviour between two adults in private, including providing birth control information and engaging in anal or oral sex.

©Chuck Mitchell/CP Images

Second, laws are the basis for the mechanisms of social control. They may specify punishments for certain acts and thus discourage people from engaging in them. It seems obvious that people ought to be free from sexual assault and coercion and that children should not be exploited, and, indeed, the *Criminal Code of Canada* has a number of laws prohibiting sexual assault of adults and children (see Table 2.1). However, sex laws also have been designed to control other behaviours that are more open to debate. For example, historically one rationale for laws against adultery or desertion of a spouse was that these laws would preserve the family as the principal unit of the social order. A current example is the law

Table 2.1 Summary of the Sexual Offences in the *Criminal Code of Canada* in 2017

Section of the Code	Offence	Description	Maximum Sentence
151	Sexual interference	Direct or indirect touching (for a sexual purpose) of a person under the age of 16 using a part of the body or an object.	10 years
152	Invitation to sexual touching	Inviting, counselling, or inciting a person under the age of 16 to touch (for a sexual purpose) the body of any person directly or indirectly with a part of the body or with an object.	10 years
153	Sexual exploitation	Sexual interference or invitation to sexual touching by a person in a position of trust or authority toward a young person age 16 to 18 with whom the young person is in a position of dependency or toward a person with a disability.	10 years
154	Incest	When an individual has sexual intercourse with a person that has a known defined blood relationship with them.	14 years
159	Anal intercourse	Anal intercourse between two people if either is under 18 or if more than two people take part or are present or if engaged in a public place.	10 years
160	Bestiality	Having sex with an animal, compelling someone to have sex with an animal, or having sex with an animal in the presence of a child.	10 years
162	Voyeurism	Surreptitiously observing or making a visual recording of a person in a private place who is nude or engaging in sexual activity. Also anyone who distributes such visual recordings or who knowingly distributes an image without consent.	5 years
162	Distributing intimate images	Publishing, distributing, transmitting, selling, making available an intimate image (visual recording) of a person knowing that the person depicted in the image did not give their consent. This includes images in which the person is nude, exposing his or her genitals or breasts, or engaging in explicit sexual activity.	5 years
163	Corrupting morals	Making, publishing, or distributing any obscene written matter, photograph, videotape, etc.	2 years
163.1	Child pornography	Possessing, making, or distributing any material that shows a person under 18 or who is depicted as being under 18 engaging in sexual activity or shows their genitals for a sexual purpose unless the material has artistic merit or an educational, scientific, or medical purpose.	10 years
167	Immoral theatrical performance	Taking part in or presenting an immoral, indecent, or obscene performance or entertainment.	2 years
168	Mailing obscene matter	Mailing anything that is obscene, indecent, immoral, or scurrilous.	2 years
170	Procuring	Procuring or enticing or forcing another person to engage in prostitution or living on the income of another person's prostitution activities. Also purchasing the sexual services of someone under 18.	16 years
171	Parent or guardian procuring, permitting sexual activity, or corrupting children	A parent or guardian or other person enticing or forcing a person under 18 to engage in an act prohibited under the Code or permitting them to engage in such an act on their premises. Also making sexual explicit material available to a child.	5 years
172	Corrupting children	A parent or guardian or other person enticing or forcing a person under 18 to engage in an act prohibited under the Code or permitting them to engage in such an act on their premises.	2 years
172.1	Luring a child	Using a computer to facilitate the commission of a sexual offence against a child under 18 years.	10 years
173	Indecent acts	Committing an indecent act in a public place or exposing genitals to a person under the age of 16.	2 years
174	Nudity	Being nude in a public place or in public view on private property.	6 months and/or $2000
210	Bawdy-house offence	Keeping, transporting a person to, or occupying a place used for the practice of acts of indecency.	2 years

(continued)

(continued)

Section of the Code	Offence	Description	Maximum Sentence
213	Offering, providing, or obtaining sexual services in a public place	Communicating with any person for the purpose of offering, providing, or obtaining sexual services in a place open to public view that is next to a school, playground, or daycare centre.	6 months and/or $5000
271	Sexual assault	Sexual assault involving minor or no physical injuries to the complainant.	10 years
272	Sexual assault with a weapon or threats	Sexual assault with a weapon, threats, or causing bodily harm, use of restricted or prohibited firearm, or use of any firearm if the offence involves a criminal organization.	14 years
273	Aggravated sexual assault	Sexual assault resulting in wounding, maiming, or disfiguring or endangering the life of the complainant, use of restricted or prohibited firearm, or use of any firearm if the offence involves a criminal organization.	Life
286.1	Obtaining sexual services	Communicating with another person in public to buy sexual services.	5 years/10 years if from a child
286.2	Material benefit from sexual services	Receiving financial or other material benefit from the purchase of sexual services. Also procuring or advertising another person to offer a service.	14 years

Based on *Criminal Code*, R.S.C., 1985, c. C-46, Department of Justice Canada

prohibiting nudity in a public place. One wonders how many people would prefer to be nude at the beach if they did not fear arrest and the possible embarrassing publicity, such as having their names in the paper as the result of an arrest.

Third, the law reflects the interests of the powerful, dominant groups within a society. In part, the law functions to confirm the superiority of the ideologies of these dominant groups although the arguments in favour of these laws often centre on the protection of society's morals. The concern for public morality results in laws against nonprocreative sex, for reasons outlined in Chapter 20. Thus, there have been laws against same-sex sexual activity, bestiality, and contraception. In fact, same-sex couples had to challenge the law that restricted marriage to the union of one man and one woman province by province to establish their legal right to marry (see Chapter 14). Consider also the Mormons in Canada and the United States. In the past, their religion approved of polygyny (a man having several wives). Mormons did not become the dominant group in North America. Rather, the Judeo-Christian tradition was the ideology of the dominant group and that tradition takes a dim view of polygyny. Accordingly, polygyny is illegal in both Canada and the United States. However, there is a breakaway sect of the Mormon Church, called the Fundamentalist Church of Jesus Christ of Latter Day Saints, located in Bountiful, British Columbia. This sect of about 1000 people practises polygyny. In 2010 the B.C. government asked the B.C. Supreme Court to rule on whether the federal law banning polygamy violates

the *Charter of Rights and Freedoms*. In 2011 the Court ruled that the ban against polygamy is constitutional. Even though the law violates freedom of religion, the harm to women and children from the practice outweighs that concern. Canadian immigrants from some African cultures that practise polygyny cannot do so in Canada because it is illegal. Nonetheless, in keeping with ethnocultural norms, many of these men have multiple relationships although they are married to only one woman, and this is accepted in their community (Maticka-Tyndale et al., 1996).

It can also be argued that another principal source of sex laws is sexism, which is deeply rooted in Western culture. Men have historically held the power and made the laws. One scholar has suggested that the history of the regulation of sexual activity could as well be called the history of the double standard (Parker, 1983). In fact, women were considered "not persons in matters of rights and privileges" under Canadian law before 1929. The Supreme Court of Canada had ruled that the word "persons" in the *British North America Act of 1867* referred only to men. On October 18, 1929, this decision was overturned by the Judicial Committee of the Privy Council of Britain, the highest court of appeal, which ruled that the word "persons" included both men and women. It is probably not coincidental that the movement for sex-law reform has gone hand in hand with the movement for the equality of women.

The *Canadian Charter of Rights and Freedoms* guarantees freedom of conscience and religion as well as equality. Therefore, criminal law cannot be based on the religious views and practices of one specific religion or be used to enforce morality per se (Roach, 2000). To the extent that today's laws are derived from the Judeo-Christian (or any other) religious tradition, they violate this principle. Increasingly, statutes in the *Criminal Code* that reflected specific moral values have been eliminated or rewritten, in part as the result of Supreme Court of Canada decisions based on *Charter* rights. For example, the Supreme Court found that statutes on abortion and those that did not extend the same benefits to same-sex couples as to mixed-sex couples violated the equality guarantees in the *Charter*. Some experts argue that other laws, such as those pertaining to prostitution and obscenity, stem from a particular moral view or ideology.

In summary, then, the sociological perspective focuses on how society or culture shapes and controls our sexual expression, from institutional levels, such as those of religion and the law, to the interpersonal level of socialization by family and peers.

Theoretical Perspectives Revisited

We started this chapter by showing how differently various theorists might view the same behaviour. Does this mean that only one of these theories is correct? No it doesn't. Rather, there is at least some truth in all of these theories. One theory might apply best in a particular situation. Another theory might play a role at a particular time in a person's life but not at another stage. Yet another theory might be best for developing treatments to help people deal with their sexual problems. Human sexual development and behaviour are complex, and there is no one theory that explains everything. As a result, we will refer to each of these theories at different places in this textbook—that is, where they provide the best explanations for people's sexual behaviour.

Critical THINKing Skill

UNDERSTANDING THE DIFFERENCE BETWEEN TRUTH AND VALIDITY

In this chapter, we presented several theories about human sexuality. A common reaction by students is to ask, "So which one is right?" That question reflects the belief that a theory is correct or incorrect, true or false. Truth can be defined as consistent with facts or reality. The belief that some things are true and others are not is one that most of us rely on as we navigate the world, so we often try to sort out truth from falsity.

However, this belief will not serve us well if we apply it to evaluating theory. A theory is an abstraction, a simplification, an intentional focus on one or a few elements of a complex situation in order to make sense of that situation. We noted at the beginning of the chapter that our four theorists, Freud, Wilson, Bandura, and Gagnon, are all watching the same couple make love, but each views that scene through the lens of his particular theory. Freud may focus on the strength of the sex drive and the vigour of the bodily movements. Wilson may be focused on the potential (or lack thereof) for reproduction inherent in their activities. Bandura is reflecting on where they learned a special technique of nibbling each other's

necks. Gagnon is marvelling at how this couple is repeating the same sequence of behaviour he has observed many times before. Each theorist's observations are consistent with some of the reality they are observing, so in this sense each theory is "true." So asking "Which one is true?" doesn't help us evaluate the different theories.

Instead, we evaluate theories in terms of their validity. We look for *evidence*. We use the theory to generate testable questions or hypotheses, collect observations (data) that are relevant to the hypotheses, and evaluate the consistency between the observations and the hypotheses. To the extent that evidence is consistent with the theory each time the theory is tested, we develop confidence that the theory is valid. Evidence that is not consistent, or evidence reported by one researcher/group that cannot be confirmed by subsequent research, gives us less confidence in the validity of the theory. We provided several examples in this chapter of claims by various theories that were not verified by evidence. So the next time you meet a new theory, what question will *you* ask?

SUMMARY

Theories provide explanations for sexual phenomena. Sociobiologists view human sexual behaviours as the product of natural selection in evolution, and thus view these behavioural patterns as being genetically controlled. Contemporary evolutionary theorists view behaviour as the result of an interaction between evolved mechanisms and environmental influence.

Among the psychological theories, Freud's psychoanalytic theory views the sex energy, or libido, as a major influence on personality and behaviour. Freud introduced the concepts of erogenous zones and psychosexual stages of development. Learning theory emphasizes how sexual behaviour is learned and modified through reinforcements and punishments according to principles of operant conditioning. Behaviour therapy techniques—therapies based on learning theory—are used in treating sexual variations and sexual disorders. Social learning theory adds the concepts of imitation, identification, and self-efficacy to learning theory. Social exchange theory highlights the role of rewards and costs in relationships. Cognitive psychologists focus on people's thoughts and perceptions—whether positive or negative—and how these influence sexuality.

Critical theory focuses our attention on the social construction of categories, the ways they are applied to people, and the consequences for individuals and society. Feminist theory systematically analyzes the meaning of gender in contemporary society. Gender is a status characteristic, and men have greater status than women. Their higher status has generally allowed men to repress women's sexual expression. Gender roles perpetuate status inequality by virtue of the restrictions they place on men's and women's behavior. Queer theory challenges the gender binary and the sexual orientation binary, arguing that gender expression and sexual orientation are both dimensions along which individuals vary.

Sociologists study the ways in which society influences our sexual expression. Symbolic interaction theory calls attention to the processes of communication and interaction which influence behaviour. Sexual scripts provide us with concrete guidelines for romantic and sexual interactions. Most sexual interactions occur in a field in which individual desires interact to create a hierarchy of sexual desire. At the macro level, sociologists investigate the ways in which institutions such as religion, the economy, the family, medicine, and the law influence sexuality.

CHAPTER 3

Sex Research

©Punchstock

LEARNING OBJECTIVES

After studying this chapter, you will be able to

LO1 Compare and evaluate the different methods that are used in sex research.

LO2 Evaluate the basic ethical principles employed by sex researchers.

LO3 Explain the basic statistical concepts necessary for understanding sex research results.

LO4 Summarize the methods and limitations of the major research projects described in this chapter.

LO5 Illustrate how media analysis is done and its importance.

LO6 Differentiate between qualitative research and quantitative research.

LO7 Compare the concepts of independent variables and dependent variables and how they relate to drawing causal inferences.

LO8 Summarize the methods used in conducting a meta-analysis.

Are *YOU* Curious?

1. How would you conduct an effective sex survey?
2. What types of sex research are taking place in Canada?
3. Is it possible to study sexuality scientifically with methods other than questionnaires?

Read this chapter to find out.

What is research, but a blind date with knowledge.

—William Henry

Over the last several decades, sex research has made great advances, and the names Kinsey and Masters and Johnson have become household words. This chapter is about sex research. You might be thinking, why do we need sex research? What are its goals? Don't we already know everything we need to know about human sexuality? Isn't common sense sufficient?

The reality is there are still many things we do not know about human sexuality. People often have opinions and views about these issues and believe that their opinions are based on fact. Yet too often they are based on misinformation and sometimes even on stereotypes or prejudice. Research is important because it creates accurate knowledge. Research puts beliefs, opinions, and theories to the systematic test.

Sex research has a number of goals. First, it can be geared toward creating basic knowledge and understanding. For example, we might want to know what percentage of 15-year-olds have engaged in sexual activity, how often long-term couples have sex, or how effective the male condom is in preventing sexually transmitted infections.

Second, research can be directed toward enhancing our understanding and can influence sexual behaviour. For example, we might want to identify risk factors for individuals who might commit a sexual offence so that we can prevent child sexual abuse; we might want to determine factors that affect sexual satisfaction in long-term relationships to help couples maintain satisfying sexual relationships; or we might want to find out whether prepared childbirth techniques are effective in reducing anxiety and discomfort during labour and delivery. How can we provide effective prevention or intervention programs without this kind of knowledge on which to base these programs?

Third, research can be geared toward public policy. For example, sexual health education is often a very controversial topic. An important question is whether individuals opposed to comprehensive sexual health education represent a majority of parents or a vocal minority of parents. Research can answer this question, thus allowing governments and school boards to take the wishes of the majority of parents into account when designing their sexual health education curriculum. Similarly, research can inform laws and regulations on a variety of issues, including access to emergency contraception, new reproductive technologies, pornography, and sex work.

How exactly do sex researchers do it? How valid are their conclusions? The answer is that sex research takes on many forms. However, basically the techniques vary in terms of the following: (1) how sex is measured, whether from people's self-reports, through observation of behaviour, or by using biological measures; (2) whether large numbers of people are studied in surveys or a smaller number of people are studied in laboratory studies and qualitative research; (3) whether the studies are conducted in the laboratory or in the field; and (4) whether sexual behaviour is studied as it occurs naturally or some attempt is made to manipulate it experimentally. Examples of studies that use all these techniques are considered and evaluated later in this chapter.

It is important to understand the techniques of sex research and their strengths and limitations. This knowledge will help you evaluate the studies that are cited as evidence for various conclusions in later chapters and will also help you decide how willing you are to accept these conclusions. Perhaps more important, this knowledge will help you evaluate future sex research. Much sex research has been conducted already, but much more will be done. The information in this chapter should help you understand and evaluate sex research that appears 10 or 20 years from now. Moreover, the media often report poor-quality research as enthusiastically as high-quality research. You should be equipped to tell the difference.

Measuring Sex

The first thing that researchers have to decide is how to measure the particular aspect of sexuality that they want to study. Multiple methods are available, including self-reports, behavioural measures, implicit measures, and biological measures, each of which is discussed in the sections that follow.

Self-Reports

The most common method for measuring sexuality is self-reports, in which the participants are asked questions about their sexual behaviour, such as the following:

- At what age did you begin masturbating?
- Did you use a condom the last time you had sex?

Self-reports are also used to measure attitudes about sexuality:

Regarding gay marriage, I (circle the number that applies)

Strongly disapprove	Moderately disapprove	Neither approve nor disapprove	Moderately approve	Strongly approve
1	2	3	4	5

Self-reports can be collected in a number of ways, including paper questionnaires, interviews, and online surveys. The strengths and weaknesses of self-reports are discussed in the section Issues in Sex Research later in the chapter.

Behavioural Measures

Several alternatives are available for behavioural measures of sexuality. One is **direct observation**, in which the scientist directly observes the behaviour and records it. As one example, sex researcher Charles Moser observed S/M (sadomasochistic) interactions in semi-public settings, attending more than 200 S/M parties (Moser, 1998). Masters and Johnson (1966), in research discussed later in this chapter, collected direct observations of sexual behaviour in laboratory studies of sexual intercourse and masturbation. As described in First Person, a number of Canadian researchers conduct similar psychophysiological research.

Psychologists have devised other clever behavioural measures. One of these is **eye-tracking**, in which participants, in the laboratory, wear an eye-tracking device that measures their point of gaze over time, as they are shown pictures on a computer. For example, in one study, researchers tracked the eye movements of adult men as they were shown photos of a front-posed naked woman, with multiple photos created through Photoshop to show different sized breasts and different waist-to-hip ratios (e.g., small waist relative to hips) (Dixson, Grimshaw, Linklater, & Dixson, 2011). With this method, the researchers could answer such questions as, Where do men look first? It turns out that the first thing men look at is the breasts or the waist, not the genitals. Relatedly, Canadian psychologists measured the amount of time individuals spent viewing pictures of naked and clothed men and women as a behavioural measure of bisexual sexual interest (Ebsworth & Lalumière, 2012). They found that bisexuals did not look longer at pictures of one sex, but heterosexual and homosexual men and women did.

For those studying illegal sexual behaviours, such as sexual assault or child pornography, one possible behavioural measure to use is police reports. The problem with this sort of measure, though, is that it detects only cases that are reported to or identified by the police. In the case of sexual assault, for example, we know that only a small proportion of cases are reported, and the great majority go unreported.

Implicit Measures

Most researchers who measure attitudes about sexuality use self-reports. However, newer measures are available. For example, a method used to measure implicit stereotypes and underlying associations between constructs is the Implicit Association Test (IAT), which measures the relative strength of association an individual makes between different pairs of concepts (Nosek, Banaji, & Greenwald, 2002). The key to measuring these associations is reaction time, measured on a computer in milliseconds. We react quickly to two concepts that we associate strongly, and we react more slowly to two concepts that we do not associate strongly. One of the great features of this measure is that people can't fake their reaction times. For example, they cannot hide their socially unacceptable stereotyped ideas.

In one New Brunswick experiment, the researchers developed an IAT to compare young adult men and women's attitudes toward sex and romance (Thompson & O'Sullivan, 2012). Their IAT comprised five phases: three practice phases and two test phases. The three practice phases were designed to introduce participants to the stimuli by having them sort the stimuli into their appropriate categories. So, for example, in one practice phase participants had to distinguish between sexual images (e.g., sexual intercourse, oral sex) and romantic images (e.g., a couple walking on a beach holding hands) by using the left key for sexual images and the right key for romantic images (or vice versa; see Figure 3.1). In another practice phase, they had to distinguish between pleasant words (e.g., good, beautiful) and unpleasant words (e.g., bad, gross). The test then had participants pair the images and attributes. For example, in the first test phase, participants were required to press the left key if they saw either a sexual image or a pleasant word and the right key if they saw either a romantic image or an unpleasant word (or vice versa). In the second test phase, the attributes (words) were reversed: Participants had to press the left key if they saw either a sexual image or an unpleasant word and the left key for either a romantic image or a pleasant word. The researchers measured how quickly and accurately these different pairings were sorted. The results allowed the researchers to determine whether men and women had a stronger association between

direct observation: A behavioural measure in which the scientist directly observes the behaviour being studied.

eye-tracking: A behavioural measure in which a device measures the participant's point of gaze over time.

Figure 3.1 The Implicit Association Test measures the relative strength of the association that an individual makes between different pairs of concepts. For example, researchers might compare the strength of the association between the concepts of pleasant and unpleasant with images depicting romance compared to images depicting sex.

Lane Oatey/Getty Images; ©krivenko/Shutterstock

sex and pleasant or between romance and pleasant. Based on gender stereotypes, the authors predicted that women would be quicker and more accurate when romantic images and pleasant words occurred together than when sexual images and pleasant words occurred together; they expected the reverse for men. However, they found that both men and women more strongly associated romantic images, not sexual images, with the pleasant category, suggesting that both implicitly preferred romance over sex.

If you want to try an IAT yourself, you can do it online at www.implicit.harvard.edu.

Biological Measures

Masters and Johnson (1966) pioneered the biological measurement of sexual response (see Milestones in Sex Research). Today, many biological measures are available.

Genital measures of sexual response assess arousal by using devices that measure erection in men and vaginal changes in women (Chivers, Seto, Lalumière, Laan, & Grimbos, 2010). In men, penile plethysmography is used, in which a flexible loop is placed around the penis that measures changes in volume. In females, a vaginal photoplethysmograph inserted into the vagina is used to optically measure blood flow to the vagina. (See Figure 13.6 to find out what these devices look like.) Ontario researchers have recently developed a clitoral photoplethysmograph that assesses changes in clitoral blood volume (Suschinsky et al., 2015). Quebec researchers have shown that *thermography*—that is, assessing temperature change—is also useful for measuring sexual arousal (Kukkonen, Binik, Amsel, & Carrier, 2007, 2010). The advantage of thermography is that it does not require any genital manipulation or contact—a camera pointed at the genitals detects changes in temperature with arousal.

MRI (magnetic resonance imaging) and fMRI (functional magnetic resonance imaging) are being used increasingly in sex research. MRI looks at *anatomy,* such as the size of shape of specific brain regions or the genitals, by using magnets to send and receive signals that give information, while participants lie in the centre of the magnet (scanner). For example, an MRI scan that shows the internal structure of the clitoris is shown in Figure 4.3. One strength of an MRI is that it provides good contrast between different soft tissues of the body. Another strength is that it is noninvasive—that is, in the old days, to get at brain structure, anatomists had to dissect the brain of a dead person. Today, researchers can look inside the brain of a living person, without disturbing it! An fMRI looks at brain *activity* by measuring relative levels of blood flow. In this way, scientists can measure the difference in activity in different regions of the brain when the person is looking at, for example, a sexual picture versus a boring picture. An example of fMRI research is given in Chapter 9 in the Milestones in Sex Research box, "What Happens in the Brain During Sex?" Some regions of the brain are very active, with large changes in blood flow, when the person looks at a sexual stimulus, and other regions have less blood flow or no change in blood flow. Because fMRI does not measure neural activity directly but rather measures blood flow, fMRI is an indirect measure of neural activity. In addition, fMRI data has a lot of "noise," and complex statistical analyses are required to get at the important patterns. Two limitations that affect fMRI use in sex research are that (1) participants must lie very still to get good images, and (2) fMRI depends on contrasting the difference between two stimuli (for example, blood flow while looking at sexual stimuli versus other stimuli). Therefore, the results depend very much on the choice of each set of stimuli.

Other biological measures include measures of pupil dilation. Devices are available that detect and record the amount of dilation. Our pupils dilate when we look at something that is especially interesting or arousing or that puts a big load on our brain. Pupil dilation is sometimes used with sex offenders, for example, to determine whether they are especially interested in children (Flak, Beech, & Fisher, 2007). If we asked a sex offender about his interest in children by using a self-report measure, he might very well lie about his illegal and taboo behaviour. Experts hope that pupil dilation measures will get around this problem, although they are not perfect.

LO2

Issues in Sex Research

Sampling

An important step in conducting sex research is identifying the appropriate **population** of people to be studied. Does the population in question consist of all adult human beings, all adults in Canada, all adolescents in Saskatchewan, all people guilty of sex crimes, or all married couples who engage in swinging? Generally, of course, the scientist is unable to get data for all the people in the population, and so a **sample** is taken.

At this point, things begin to get sticky. If the sample is a representative sample of the population in question and if it is a reasonably large sample, results obtained from it can safely be generalized to the population that was originally identified. One way of obtaining a representative sample is by using **probability sampling**. The simplest form of probability sampling is **random sampling**. That is, if a researcher has really randomly selected 1 out of every 50 adolescents in Canada, then the results obtained from that sample are probably true of all adolescents in Canada. Another technique that is sometimes used to get such a sample is **stratified random sampling**.[1] But if the sample consists only of adolescents with certain characteristics—for example, only those whose parents agree to let them participate in sex research—then the results obtained from that sample may not be true of all adolescents. Sampling has been a serious challenge in sex research.

Typically, sampling proceeds in three phases: The population is identified, a method for obtaining a sample is adopted, and the people in the sample are contacted and asked to participate. What is perhaps the thorniest problem occurs in the last phase: getting the people identified for the sample to participate. If any of the people refuse to participate, then the great probability sample is ruined. This is called the **problem of refusal or nonresponse**. As a result, the researcher is essentially studying volunteers—that is, people who agree to be in the

population: A group of people a researcher wants to study and make inferences about.

sample: A part of a population.

probability sampling: A method of sampling in research in which each member of the population has a known probability of being included in the sample.

random sampling: An excellent method of sampling in research in which each member of the population has an equal chance of being included in the sample.

stratified random sampling: A method of sampling in which the population is divided into groups and then random sampling occurs in each group.

problem of refusal or nonresponse: The problem that some people will refuse to participate in a sex survey, thus making it difficult to have a random sample.

[1] A detailed discussion of stratified random sampling is beyond the scope of this book. For a good description of this method as applied to sex research, see Cochran et al. (1953). In brief, with a random sample, each individual in the population has an equal probability of being chosen. With a stratified random sample, the researchers can set a higher probability of inclusion for certain groups, a technique called oversampling. For example, if we had funds to interview 1000 people in Canada, a random sample would yield about 30 Aboriginal individuals and 30 Chinese-Canadian individuals because each group constitutes about 3 percent of the Canadian population. We might not feel confident reaching conclusions about Aboriginal individuals or Chinese Canadians based on only 30 people, so we could decide to use stratified random sampling and give each of these groups a higher probability of inclusion compared with Whites. If we tripled the probability of including these ethnocultural minority groups, the resulting sample of 1000 would include 90 Aboriginal individuals, 90 Chinese Canadians, 82 individuals from other visible ethnocultural minority groups (e.g., South Asian, Black), and 738 Canadians from non-visible-minority groups. Although these minority samples are still small, we would feel more confident about making conclusions about each group. We could do even more oversampling of Aboriginal individuals or of other ethnocultural groups that constitute even smaller percentages of the Canadian population to increase our confidence in our conclusions.

Milestones in Sex Research

Masters and Johnson: How Did They Study Sexual Response in the Laboratory?

William Masters began his research on the physiology of sexual response in 1954. No one had ever studied human sexual behaviour in the laboratory before, so he had to develop all the necessary research techniques from scratch. He began by interviewing 188 female prostitutes, as well as 27 male prostitutes working for a gay clientele. They gave him important preliminary data in which they "described many methods for elevating and controlling sexual tensions and demonstrated innumerable variations in stimulative techniques," some of which were useful in the later program of therapy for sexual disorders.

Meanwhile, Masters began setting up his laboratory and equipping it with the necessary instruments: an electrocardiograph to measure changes in heart rate over the sexual cycle, an electromyograph to measure muscular contractions in the body during sexual response, and a pH meter to measure the acidity of the vagina during the various stages of sexual response.

Sampling

Masters made a major breakthrough when he decided that it should be possible to recruit participants from the general population and have them engage in sexual behaviour in the laboratory, where their behaviour and physiological responses could be carefully observed and measured. This approach had never been used before, as even the daring Kinsey had settled for people's verbal reports of their behaviour.

Masters let it be known in the medical school and university community that he needed volunteers for laboratory studies of human sexual response. Some people volunteered because of their belief in the importance of the research. Some, of course, came out of curiosity or because they were exhibitionists; they were weeded out in the initial interviews. Participants were paid for their

hours in the laboratory, as is typical in medical research, so many medical students and graduate students participated because it was a way to earn money.

Initially, all prospective participants were given detailed interviews by Masters and his colleague, Virginia Johnson (see Figure 3.2). People who had histories of emotional problems or who seemed uncomfortable with the topic of sex either failed to come back after this interview or were eliminated even if they were willing to proceed. Participants were also assured that the anonymity and confidentiality of their participation would be protected carefully. In all, 382 women and 312 men participated in the laboratory studies reported in *Human Sexual Response* (Masters & Johnson, 1966). The men ranged in age from 21 to 89, while the women ranged from 18 to 78.

Certainly, the group of people Masters and Johnson studied were not a random sample of the population of the United States. In fact, one might imagine that people

Figure 3.2   Masters and Johnson pioneered the biological measurement of sexual response.

©Bettmann/Getty

research. The outcomes of the research may therefore contain distortions, called **volunteer bias**. The problem of refusal in sex research is difficult, since there is no ethical way of forcing people to participate when they do not want to.

The problem of volunteer bias would not be so great if those who refused to participate were identical in their sexual behaviour to those who participated. But it is likely that those who refuse to participate differ in some ways from those who agree to, and that means the

who would agree to participate in such research would be rather unusual. The data indicate that they were more educated than the general population, and the sample was mostly white, with only a few persons from ethnic minority groups participating. Paying the participants probably helped broaden the sample since it attracted some people who simply needed the money. The sample omitted two notable types of people: those who were not sexually experienced or did not respond to sexual stimulation, and those who were unwilling to have their sexual behaviour studied in the laboratory. Therefore, the results Masters and Johnson obtained might not generalize to such people.

In defence of their sampling techniques, even if Masters and Johnson had identified an initial probability sample, they still almost surely would have had a very high refusal rate, higher than in survey research, and the probability sample would have been ruined. At present, this seems to be an unsolvable problem in this type of research.

Data Collection Techniques

After they were accepted for the project, participants proceeded to the laboratory phase of the study. First, they had a "practice session," in which they engaged in sexual activity in the laboratory in complete privacy, with no data being recorded and no researchers present. The purpose of this was to allow the participants to become comfortable with engaging in sexual behaviour in a laboratory setting.

The physical responses of the participants were then recorded during sexual intercourse, masturbation, and "artificial coition." Masters and Johnson made an important technical advance with the development of the artificial coition technique. In it, a female participant stimulates herself with an artificial penis constructed of clear plastic; it is powered by an electric motor, and the woman can adjust the depth and frequency of the thrust. There is a light and a recording apparatus inside the artificial penis, so the changes occurring inside the vagina can be photographed.

Measures such as these avoid the problems of distortion that are possible with self-reports. They also answer much different questions. That is, it would be impossible from such measures to tell whether the person had engaged in same-sex sexual activity or how frequently he or she masturbated. Instead, they ascertain how the body responds to sexual stimulation, with a kind of accuracy and detail that would be impossible to obtain through self-reports.

One final potential problem also deserves mention. It has to do with the problems of laboratory studies: Do people respond the same sexually in the laboratory as they do in the privacy of their own homes?

Ethical Considerations

Masters and Johnson were attentive to ethical principles. They were careful to use informed consent. Potential participants were given detailed explanations of the kinds of things they would be required to do in the research and were given ample opportunity at all stages to withdraw from the research if they so desired. Furthermore, Masters and Johnson eliminated people who appeared too anxious or distressed during the preliminary interviews.

It is also possible that participating in the research itself might have been harmful in some way to some people. Masters and Johnson were particularly concerned with the long-term effects of participating in the research. Accordingly, they made follow-up contacts with the participants at five-year intervals. In no case did a participant report developing a sexual disorder. In fact, many of the couples reported specific ways in which participating in the research enriched their marriages. Thus, the available data seem to indicate that such research does not harm the participants and may in some ways benefit them, not to mention the benefit to society from gaining information in such an important area.

sample is biased. Evidence suggests that volunteers who participate in sex research hold more permissive attitudes about sexuality and are more sexually experienced than those who don't; for example, they masturbate more frequently and have had more sexual partners (Bogaert, 1996; Boynton, 2003; Dunne et al., 1997). In addition, women are less likely to volunteer for some but not all types of sex research than men are (Boynton, 2003; Gaither, Sellbom, & Meier, 2003; Senn & Desmarais, 2001) so that female samples are even more highly selected

Table 3.1   The Percentage of People Reporting Having Sex at Least Once a Week: Comparing a Convenience Sample with a Probability Sample

Age	Men		Women	
	Convenience Sample (Janus Report)	**Probability Sample (General Social Survey)**	**Convenience Sample (Janus Report)**	**Probability Sample (General Social Survey)**
18–26	72%	57%	68%	58%
27–38	83	69	78	61
39–50	83	56	68	49
51–64	81	43	65	25
Over 65	69	17	74	6

Review of the Janus Report on Sexual Behavior by Samuel S. Janus & Cynthia L. Janus in *Contemporary Sociology*, Vol. 23, no. 2 (March 1994), p. 222, table 1. Reprinted by permission of the American Sociological Association and Andrew M. Greeley.

than male samples. In sum, volunteer bias is potentially a serious problem when we try to reach conclusions based on sex research.

Table 3.1 shows how different the results of sex surveys can be, depending on how carefully the sampling is done (Greeley, 1994). The table shows results from two American surveys. The Janus report (Janus & Janus, 1993) used sampling methods so haphazard that the researchers ended up with what some call a **convenience sample**. It included volunteers who came to sex therapists' offices and friends recruited by the original volunteers. In contrast, the General Social Survey conducted in 1993 by the University of Chicago obtained a probability sample. Notice that a considerably higher level of sexual activity is reported by the convenience sample in the Janus report, compared with the probability sample. This difference is especially pronounced among older adults. Convenience samples simply do not give us a very good picture of what is going on in the general population.

Accuracy of Measurement

Earlier we described various methods for measuring sexuality. How accurate are those measures? We focus mainly on self-reports because they are used so frequently in sex research.

Purposeful Distortion

If you were an interviewer in a sex research project and a 90-year-old man said that he and his wife made love twice a day, would you believe him, or would

you suspect that he might be exaggerating slightly? If a 35-year-old woman told you that she had never masturbated, would you believe her, or would you suspect that she had masturbated but was unwilling to admit it?

Respondents in sex research may, for one reason or another, engage in **purposeful distortion**, intentionally giving self-reports that are distortions of reality. These distortions may be in either of two directions. People may exaggerate their sexual activity (a tendency toward *enlargement*), or they may minimize their sexual activity or hide the fact that they have done certain things (*concealment*). Participants will often distort responses in the direction that they believe will be seen as more acceptable by the researcher, called **social desirability**. For example, an individual in a long-term relationship who believes that he or she engages in sexual activity with his or her partner much less often and masturbates much more often than other people do may exaggerate his or her sexual frequency but minimize his or her masturbation frequency. Participants are often not aware that social desirability is affecting their answers.

Distortion is a basic problem when using self-reports (McCallum & Peterson, 2012). To minimize distortion, participants must be strongly reminded of the fact that because the study will be used for scientific purposes, their reports must be as accurate as possible. They must also be assured that their responses will be completely anonymous. If they are not anonymous, people will be likely to hide behaviours that they do not want other people to know about or that embarrass them, such as an extramarital affair or a history of sex with animals. Researchers sometimes include additional scales or items that detect whether people are purposefully distorting their answers—for example, by giving only socially desirable responses. The phrasing of questions may also affect how likely people are to give honest answers (Figure 3.3). For example, people are more

volunteer bias: A bias in the results of sex surveys that arises when some people refuse to participate so that those who are in the sample are volunteers who may in some ways differ from those who refused to participate.
convenience sample: A sample chosen in a haphazard manner relative to the population of interest; not a random or probability sample.
purposeful distortion: Purposely giving false information in a survey.
social desirability: The tendency to distort answers to a survey in the direction perceived to be more acceptable.

Figure 3.3 The reliability of self-reports of sexual behaviour: If you were interviewing this man in a sex survey and he said that he had never masturbated, would you believe him, or would you think that he was concealing a taboo behaviour?

©Digital Vision

likely to honestly answer questions that first normalize the behaviour (e.g., Many people engage in oral sex. How many oral sex partners have you had?). They are also more likely to report behaviour when the question is asked in a neutral way (e.g., How often have you engaged in oral sex in the previous six months? rather than Have you engaged in oral sex in the previous six months?).

But even if all respondents were very truthful and tried to give as accurate information as possible, three factors might still cause their self-reports to be inaccurate: memory, difficulties with estimates, and interpreting the question in a different way than the researcher intended.

Memory

Some of the questions asked in sex surveys require respondents to recall what their sexual behaviour was like many years before. For example, some of the data we have on sexual behaviour in childhood come from the Kinsey study in which adults were asked about their childhood sexual behaviour. This might involve asking a 50-year-old man to remember at what age he began masturbating and how frequently he masturbated when he was 16 years old. It might be difficult to remember such facts accurately. The alternative is to

ask people about their current sexual behaviour, but getting data like these from children raises serious ethical and practical problems. However, people may also have difficulty accurately remembering recent behaviour, such as the number of times they had sex in the past month. One solution to this is the *daily diary* method in which people report their behaviour every day for the previous 24 hours and so are more likely to remember it accurately (Gilmore, Leigh, Hoppe, & Morrison, 2010; Vannier & O'Sullivan, 2008). For example, Canadian psychologists used daily diaries completed online to study changes in women's fantasies across the menstrual cycle (Dawson, Suschinsky, & Lalumière, 2012).

> **How would you conduct an effective sex survey?**

Difficulties with Estimates

One of the questions sex researchers have asked is, How long, on average, do you spend in precoital foreplay? If you were asked this question, how accurate a response do you think you could give? It is rather difficult to estimate time to begin with, and it is even more difficult to do so when engaged in an absorbing activity. For example, New Brunswick researchers found that, on average, men estimated the duration of foreplay as 13.4 minutes, which was significantly longer than the 11.3 minutes estimated by their female partners, suggesting that the men or the women or both were not accurate in the estimates of the duration of foreplay (Miller & Byers, 2004). The men and women both estimated the duration of intercourse at between seven and eight minutes, however. The point is that in some sex surveys, people are asked to give estimates of things that they probably cannot estimate very accurately. This may be another source of inaccuracy in self-report data.

Interpreting the Question

One of the questions that sex researchers often ask is, How many sexual partners have you had? This question assumes that participants all give the same meaning to the term *sexual partner* as the research intended. Yet research in New Brunswick has shown that university students do not agree in their definitions of sexual terms including the terms *having sex, sexual partner,* and *abstinence* (Byers et al., 2009; Randall & Byers, 2003). For example, about two-thirds of students would call a person they engaged in oral sex with a sexual partner, but one-third would not. Thus, estimates that participants provide about the number of sexual partners will be affected not only by the accuracy of their memory but also by how they define *sexual partner.*

Evidence on the Reliability of Self-Reports

Scientists have developed several methods for assessing how reliable or accurate people's self-reports are (Catania, Binson, Van Der Straten, & Stone, 1995). One is the method of **test–retest reliability.** The respondent is asked a series of questions and then is asked the same set of questions after some time has passed, for example, a week or a month. The correlation between answers at the two times (test and retest) measures the reliability of responses; correlations are discussed later in this chapter.

In one study, urban African-American and Latina girls between the ages of 12 and 14 were interviewed about their sexual experiences and then were interviewed again three weeks later (Hearn, O'Sullivan, & Dudley, 2003). The test–retest reliability was .84 for the age at which they had their first crush and .95 for the age at which they first touched a penis, which indicates excellent reliability (a value of 1.0 indicates

test–retest reliability: A method for testing whether self-reports are reliable or accurate; participants are interviewed (or given a questionnaire) and then interviewed a second time some time later to determine whether their answers are the same both times.
computer-assisted self-interview method (CASI): A method of data collection in which the respondent fills out questionnaires on a computer. Headphones and a soundtrack reading the questions can be added for young children or poor readers.
validity: Whether a self-report measure assesses what it is supposed to measure.

perfect reliability). Other research generally indicates that respondents give their best estimates about short, recent time intervals (Catania, Gibson, Marin, Coates, & Greenblatt, 1990).

Another method for assessing reliability involves obtaining independent reports from two different people who share sexual activity, such as both members of a couple. One study found that on a simple item, such as whether a couple had engaged in intercourse in the last month, there was 93 percent agreement. Agreement on the number of times they had had intercourse in the last month, something that requires more difficult estimation, was .80, which is lower but still good (Hyde, DeLamater, Plant, & Byrd, 1996). Similarly, researchers in Quebec asked partners to indicate the behaviours that had occurred during lovemaking. The partners agreed 87 percent of the time on average, which is a high level of agreement (Ochs & Binik, 1999).

A recent innovation is the **computer-assisted self-interview method (CASI),** which can be combined with an audio component so that the respondent not only reads but also hears the questions. This method offers the privacy of the written questionnaire while accommodating poor readers. The computer can be programmed to follow varying sequences of questions depending on respondents' answers, just as a human interviewer does. In a survey of 15-year-old boys, 16 percent reported in a personal interview that they had engaged in vaginal intercourse, but 25 percent said they had done so when CASI was used (Mosher, Chandra, & Jones, 2005). Although these findings suggest that CASI produces more honest responses, it is also possible that the some boys exaggerated their sexual history on the computer. (For similar results with adults, see Lau, Tsui, & Wang, 2003.)

Evidence for the Validity of Self-Reports

Scientists have also developed ways to determine the **validity** of self-report measures. Validity refers to whether a scale or questionnaire actually measures what it is supposed to measure. For example, if researchers developed a scale that they said measured sexual satisfaction but it only asked questions about how often individuals engaged in various sexual activities, we might suspect that they are actually measuring sexual frequency, not sexual satisfaction. There is no one way to establish the validity of a scale. Rather, researchers accumulate evidence that together demonstrates that the scale actually measures what it is supposed to measure. One way to do this is to compare groups that would be expected to differ on the measure; for example, on average, individuals with a sexual disorder would be expected to report lower sexual satisfaction than individuals without a sexual disorder. Another way is to compare the scores on the new scale to existing scales that measure the same construct. A third way is to show that the scale is correlated (but not too highly correlated) with other constructs that it should theoretically be related to (this is called *convergent validity*) and not correlated with other constructions that it should not theoretically be related to (this is called *divergent validity*). We might expect sexual satisfaction to be correlated with sexual frequency, sexual pleasure, and relationship satisfaction, for example. However, we would not expect differences in sexual satisfaction based on ethnicity or intelligence.

Canadian researchers have developed many scales assessing different aspects of sexuality and have demonstrated that these scales have good reliability and validity. There are way too many such scales to list them all here, but here are a few that were published recently (check them out if the names interest you): Motives for Feigning Orgasm Scale (Séguin, Milhausen, & Kukkonen, 2015), Sexual Contingent Self-Worth Scale (Glowacka, Rosen, Vannier, & MacLellan, 2016), Sexual Motivation Scale (Gravel, Pelletier, & Reissing, 2016), Response to Sexual Difficulties Scale (Fallis, Purdon, & Rehman, 2013).

Web-Based Surveys

The possibility of administering questionnaires over the Internet has opened a whole new era in sex research. Compared with other methods for administering surveys, web-based surveys have many advantages but also some disadvantages (Bowen, 2005; Gosling, Vazire, Srivastava, & John, 2004; Kraut et al., 2004; Ochs, Mah, & Binik, 2002).

Web-based sex surveys can recruit much larger samples than can traditional interview or questionnaire studies. For example, one web survey of men who have sex with men yielded 1052 completed surveys in less than two months (Matthews, Stephenson, & Sullivan, 2012). In addition, web surveys can potentially produce broader samples than traditional survey methods can. For example, researchers in New Brunswick conducted an online survey on the sexual well-being of individuals with autism spectrum disorders living in the community, a group that is hard to research (Byers, Nichols, & Voyer, 2013; Byers, Nichols, Voyer, & Reilly, 2012). By using a web-based survey, they were able to recruit participants from across Canada, as well as from the United States, Australia/New Zealand, the United Kingdom, and Europe. These new methods open up exciting possibilities for cross-cultural research.

Web-based surveys have particular advantages for studying special populations defined by their sexual behaviour, particularly if the behaviour is taboo. For example, traditional studies of gays and lesbians have used methods such as recruiting the sample through gay activist organizations and gay bars. These methods have been criticized because they omit from the sample individuals who are in the closet and those who do not actively participate in organizations or go to bars. Closeted gays have equal access to web-based surveys and can answer them in a highly anonymous way, respecting their own decision to remain closeted. Therefore, web methods can access this population that had previously been studied very little and can yield a much wider sample of gays and lesbians. Web methods can also locate stigmatized sexual minorities, such as those involved in sadomasochism, bondage, and discipline, by recruiting participants through virtual communities and websites specialized for that particular sexual group.

Web-based surveys have the ability to eliminate extraneous influences on responding (discussed in the next section). For example, the gender or ethnicity of the interviewer may influence an individual's responses, but these factors are eliminated in a web-administered questionnaire. In addition, web-based surveys can be used in diary studies in which participants record their behaviour at fixed intervals (for example, every day or even several times a day) to avoid problems of faulty memory. An innovative way of doing this is with tablets or cellphones (Vannier & O'Sullivan, 2008).

Web-based surveys, then, have substantial strengths on the issue of sampling. Do all these substantial advantages come with any disadvantages? They still rely on self-reports, which as we saw earlier can be inaccurate to some degree. Some bias is introduced because not everyone has Internet access. Access grows every day, but Internet users still, on average, have incomes above the national average. Internet samples are nonetheless considerably more diverse than the university-student samples used in much research. The researcher lacks control of the environment in which the respondent completes the survey—something that can be controlled in personal interviews but cannot in mailed-out questionnaires. One can imagine, for example, a group of students living in residence filling out a web sex survey together and having fun faking the answers. Individuals might complete the survey more than once or might actually try to sabotage or skew the results to show a particular outcome. Internal checks can be built into the sequence of questions that can detect faked patterns of answers, and methods have been devised to detect repeat responders and spam bots. Nonetheless, these issues continue to be a concern.

On balance, web-based surveys offer substantial advantages over traditional survey methods. Researchers will have to continue to monitor and control potential problems, such as repeat responders.

Accuracy of Behavioural Observations

As we noted earlier, one of the major ways of classifying techniques of sex research is by whether the scientist relied on people's self-reports of their behaviour or observed the sexual behaviour directly.

The problems of self-reports have just been discussed: Self-reports may be inaccurate, although the evidence indicates that they are generally accurate. Direct observations have a major advantage over self-reports in that they are accurate. No purposeful distortion or inaccurate memory can intervene. On the other hand, direct observations have their own set of problems. They are expensive and time-consuming, with the result that generally only a rather small sample is studied. Furthermore, obtaining a representative sample of the population is even more difficult than in survey research. Although some people are reticent about completing a questionnaire concerning their sexual behaviour, even more would be unwilling to come to a laboratory where their sexual behaviour would be observed by a scientist or where they would be hooked up to recording instruments while they engaged in sex. Thus, results obtained from the unusual group of volunteers who would be willing to do this might not be generalizable to the rest of the population. One study showed that volunteers for a laboratory study of sexual arousal reported lower levels of sex guilt and were more sexually experienced than non-volunteers (Plaud, Gaither, Hegstadc, Rowan, & Devitt, 1999). Moreover, only 27 percent of men and 7 percent of women volunteered, showing how selective the sample was.

Extraneous Factors

Various extraneous factors, such as the gender, race, or age of the interviewer, may influence the outcome of sex research. Questionnaires do not get around these problems, since such simple factors as the wording of a question may affect the results. In one study, respondents were given either standard or supportive wording of some items (Catania et al., 1995). For the question about extramarital sex, the standard wording was as follows:

> At any time while you were married during the past 10 years, did you have sex with someone other than your (husband/wife)?

The supportive wording was as follows:

> Many people feel that being sexually faithful to a spouse is important, and some do not. However, even those who think being faithful is important have found themselves in situations where they ended up having sex with someone other than their (husband/wife). At any time while you were married during the past 10 years, did you have sex with someone other than your (husband/wife)?

The supportive wording significantly increased reports of extramarital sex from 12 percent with the standard wording to 16 percent with the supportive wording if the interviewer was of the same gender as the respondent; the wording made no difference when the interviewer and respondent were of different genders. Sex researchers must be careful to control these extraneous factors so that they influence the results as little as possible.

L02 Ethical Issues

Ethical problems are always a possibility in doing research. Ethical problems are particularly difficult in sex research, because people are more likely to feel that their privacy has been invaded when you ask them about sex than when you ask them to name their favourite political candidate or memorize a list of words. All research conducted at Canadian universities must conform to the *Tri-Council Policy Statement: Ethical Conduct for Research Involving Humans,* developed by the three federal granting agencies, which sets standards for conducting ethical research involving human participants. The cardinal ethical principle is respect for human dignity: researchers must keep this in mind when they are establishing the goals and the procedures of their research. The principle of respect for human dignity leads to several other ethical principles, including respect for free and informed consent and protection from harm.

Free and Informed Consent

According to the principle of **free and informed consent**, participants have a right to be told, before they participate, what the purpose of the research is and what they will be asked to do. They can choose not to participate or not to continue. An investigator may not coerce people to be in a study, and it is the scientist's responsibility to see to it that all participants understand exactly what they are agreeing to do. In the case of children who may be too young to give truly informed consent, the parents usually give consent.

The principle of informed consent was adopted by scientific organizations in the 1970s. It was violated in some of the earlier sex studies, as will be discussed later in this chapter.

Protection from Harm

Investigators should minimize the amount of physical and psychological stress to people in their research. Thus, for example, if an investigator must shock participants during a study, there should be a good reason for

free and informed consent: An ethical principle in research, in which people have a right to be informed, before participating, of what they will be asked to do in the research.

doing this. Questioning people about their sexual behaviour may be psychologically stressful to them and might conceivably harm them in some way, so sex researchers must be careful to minimize the stress involved in their procedure. The principle of respect for privacy and confidentiality of response, for example, by making sure that responses are anonymous, is important to ensure that participants will not suffer afterward for their participation in research.

Another important way that researchers reduce harm is by avoiding bias. One way to avoid *heterosexist bias* is by including options that correspond to the identities of sexual and gender minorities (Blair, 2016). For example, researchers who give only male and female as options when asking about participants' sex or gender may make gender-minority individuals re-experience that marginalization and stigmatization that they experience in other aspects of their life.

Justice

The **justice principle** in research ethics holds that the risks of participating in research and the benefits of the results of the research should be distributed fairly across groups in society. For example, early testing of the birth control pill was done on poor women in Puerto Rico, not on wealthy women in Vancouver. The risks were not distributed fairly, and a particular group bore a disproportionate burden. As a second example, research on the potential benefits of taking Aspirin for preventing heart attacks was conducted with an all-male sample. Whether this effect works for women as well remains unknown. Thus, the benefits of the research did not extend fairly to everyone. Researchers have an obligation to make sure that they conduct their research in a way that benefits as wide a range of persons as possible.

Balancing Harms and Benefits

Considering the possible risks involved in sex research, is it ethical to do such research? Officials in universities and government agencies sponsoring sex research must answer this question for every proposed sex research study. In doing so, they must do a **harms–benefits analysis**; that is, the stress to research participants should be minimized as much as possible, but some stresses will remain, which are the harms. This is particularly true in sex research because most people consider sexuality very private, and they may find it embarrassing or distressing to disclose their sexual experiences, behaviour, and attitudes. The questions then become, Will the benefits that result from the research be greater than the harm? Will the participants benefit in some way from being in the study, and will science and society in general benefit from the knowledge resulting from the study? Do these benefits outweigh the potential harms? If they do, the research is justifiable; otherwise, it is not.

As an example, Masters and Johnson considered these issues carefully and concluded that their research participants benefited from being in their research; they collected data from former participants that confirm this belief. Thus, a harms–benefits analysis would suggest that their research was ethical, even though their participants might have been temporarily stressed by it. In another study, 15- to 25-year-old participants completed a questionnaire about sex; later they rated how distressing and how positive the experience had been for them (Kuyper et al., 2012). Participants reported little distress and predominantly positive feelings. Overall, 89 percent agreed that surveys like this should be carried out. The one group that reported distress was people who had experienced sexual coercion in the past.

In all research, the potential harms to the participants should be weighed against the benefits that accrue to society from being informed about this aspect of sexual behaviour. The "Tuskegee Study of Untreated Syphilis in the Negro Male" is an example of a study in which this was not done. Between 1932 and 1972, the U.S. government followed 399 poor, uneducated African-American men living in a rural area of Alabama to learn about the course of untreated syphilis. Participants did not give informed consent, did not get the treatment they were promised, and were offered incentives that would have been coercive for people who were so poor (e.g., hot meals, burial insurance, treatment for minor ailments) to continue in the experiment. When penicillin became available as an effective treatment for syphilis, participants were denied access to it and were warned not to take it (Walker, 2009). Although we learned a great deal about syphilis from the experiment, clearly the harm to participants far outweighed the benefits. In 1997, President Bill Clinton issued a formal apology for the wrongs done to these men by the American government.

Some Statistical Concepts

Before you can understand reports of sex research, you need to understand some basic statistical concepts.

Average

Suppose we get data from a sample of common-law couples on how many times per week they have sexual intercourse. How can we summarize the data? One way to do this is to compute some average value;

> **justice principle:** An ethical principle in research that holds that the risks of participation should be distributed fairly across groups in society, as should the benefits.
>
> **harms–benefits analysis:** An approach to analyzing the ethics of a research study, based on weighing the harms of the research (such as stress to subjects) against the benefits of the research (gaining knowledge about human sexuality).

Figure 3.4   Two hypothetical graphs of the frequency of intercourse for common-law couples in a sample. In both, the average frequency is about three times per week, but in *(a)* there is little variability (almost everyone has a frequency between two and four times per week), whereas in *(b)* there is great variability (the frequency ranges from 0 to 15 or more times per week). The graph for most sexual behaviour looks like *(b),* with great variability.

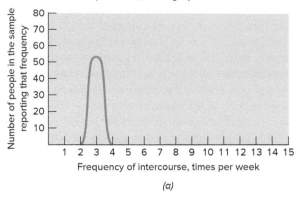

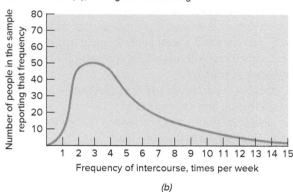

(a)   *(b)*

this will tell us how often, on average, these people have intercourse. In sex research, the number that is usually calculated is either the mean or the median, although the mode is sometimes used; all of these give us an indication of approximately where the average value for that group of people is. The **mean**, or average, is calculated by adding up all the scores and dividing by the number of people. The **median** is the score that splits the sample in half, with half the respondents scoring below that number and half scoring above it. The **mode** is the score with the greatest number of responses. People whose thoughts, feelings, and behaviour are close to the average for their group might be said to be typical of that group.

Variability

In addition to having an indication of the average for the sample of respondents, it is also important to know how much variability there is from one respondent to the next in the numbers reported. That is, it is one thing to say that the average common-law couple in a sample had intercourse three times per week, with a range in the sample from two to four times per week, and it is quite another thing to say that the average was three times per week, with a range from zero to 15 times per week. In both cases the mean is the same, but in the first there is little variability, and in the second there is a great deal of variability. These two alternatives are shown graphically in Figure 3.4. Great variability exists in virtually all sexual behaviour.

Average versus Normal

It is interesting and informative to report the average frequency of a particular sexual behaviour, but this also introduces the danger that people will confuse *average* with *normal.* That is, there is a tendency, when reading a statistic like "the average person has intercourse twice per week" to think of our own sexual behaviour, compare it with that average, and then conclude that we are abnormal if we differ much from the average. If you read that statistic and your frequency of intercourse is only once a week, you may begin to worry that you are undersexed or that you are not getting as much as you should. If you are having intercourse seven times per week, you might begin worrying that you are oversexed. Such conclusions are a mistake: First, because they can make you miserable, and second, because so much variability exists in sexual behaviour that any behaviour (or frequency or length of time) within a wide range is perfectly normal. Don't confuse average with normal.

Incidence versus Frequency

In sex statistics, the terms *prevalence* and *frequency* are often used. **Prevalence** refers to the percentage of people who have engaged in a certain behaviour. **Frequency** refers to how often people do something. Thus, we might say that the prevalence of masturbation among males is 92 percent (meaning that 92 percent of all males masturbate at least once in their lives), whereas the average frequency of masturbation among males between the ages of 16 and 20 is about once per week.

A closely related concept is that of *cumulative incidence.* If we consider a sexual behaviour according to the age at which each person in the sample first engaged in it, the cumulative incidence refers to the percentage of people who have engaged in that behaviour before a certain age. Thus, the cumulative incidence of masturbation in males might be 10 percent by age 11; 25 percent by age 12; 80 percent by age 15; and 95 percent by

mean: The average of respondents' scores calculated by adding the scores and dividing by the number of people.
median: The middle score.
mode: The most frequent score.
prevalence: The percentage of people giving a particular response.
frequency: How often a person does something.

Figure 3.5 A cumulative-incidence curve for masturbation in males. From the graph, you can read off the percentage of males who report having masturbated by a given age. For example, about 82 percent have masturbated to orgasm by age 15.

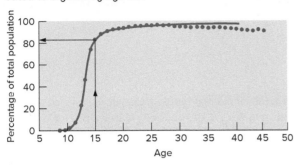

age 20. Graphs of cumulative incidence always begin in the lower left-hand corner and move toward the upper right-hand corner. An example of a cumulative-incidence curve is shown in Figure 3.5.

Correlation

The term *correlation* is used by laypeople in contexts such as the following: "There seems to be a correlation here between how warm the days are and how fast the corn is growing." But what do statisticians mean by the term *correlation*? A **correlation** is a number that measures the relationship between two variables. A correlation can be positive or negative. A positive correlation occurs when a positive relationship exists between the two variables; that is, people who have high scores on one variable tend to have high scores on the other variable, and low scores go with low scores. A negative correlation occurs when an opposite relationship exists between the two variables; that is, people with high scores on one variable tend to have low scores on the other variable. We might want to know, for example, whether there is a correlation between the number of years a couple has been together and the frequency with which they have sexual intercourse. In this case we might expect that there would be a negative correlation, and that is just what researchers have found. That is, the *greater* the number of years together, the *lower* the frequency of intercourse.

Correlations range between +1.0 and −1.0. A correlation of +1.0 indicates a perfect positive relationship between two variables, meaning that the person in the sample who scores highest on one variable also has the highest score on the other variable, the person with the second highest score on the first variable also has the second highest score on the other variable, and so on. A correlation of 0 indicates no relationship between the two variables. Knowing a person's score on one variable

tells us nothing about whether the person will have a high or a low score on the other variable. Positive correlations between 0 and +1.0—for example, +.62—say that the relationship is positive but not a perfect relationship.

As discussed earlier in this chapter, we use correlations to assess test–retest reliability. Suppose we administer a questionnaire to a sample of adults. One of the questions asks, "How many times did you masturbate to orgasm during the month of September?" We ask this question of the sample on October 1 and again on October 8. If each person in the sample gives us exactly the same answer on October 1 and on October 8, the correlation between the two variables (the number given on October 1 and the number given on October 8) would be +1.0 and the test–retest reliability would be a perfect +1.0. Test–retest reliabilities for questions about sex typically range between +.60 and +.90, indicating that people's answers on the two occasions are not identical but are very similar.

LO4

The Major Sex Surveys

In the major sex surveys, the data were collected from a large sample of people by means of questionnaires or interviews. Unfortunately, no large-scale, comprehensive sex surveys have been done in Canada with the exception of a few questions contained in the National Population Health Survey and other general surveys. However, such surveys have been conducted in a number of other countries including the United States, the United Kingdom, Australia, and France. The best known of these studies is the U.S. survey done by Alfred Kinsey, so we will consider it first. His data were collected in the late 1930s and 1940s in the United States, and thus the results are now largely of historical interest. However, Kinsey documented his methods with extraordinary care, so his research is a good example to study for both the good and the bad points of surveys.

The Kinsey Report

The Sample

Kinsey (see Milestones in Sex Research) and his colleagues interviewed 5300 men and 5940 women between 1938 and 1949 in the United States.

Initially, Kinsey was not much concerned with sampling issues. His goal was simply to collect sex histories from as wide a variety of people as possible. In the 1953 volume on women, Kinsey said that he and his colleagues had deliberately chosen not to use probability sampling methods because of

> **correlation:** A number that measures the relationship between two variables.

Milestones in Sex Research

What Is the Legacy of Alfred C. Kinsey?

A lfred C. Kinsey was born in 1894 in New Jersey, the first child of uneducated parents. In high school, he did not date, and a classmate recalled that he was "the shyest guy around girls you could think of."

His father was determined that Kinsey become a mechanical engineer. From 1912 to 1914, he tried studying mechanical engineering at Stevens Institute, but he showed little talent for it. At one point he was close to failing physics, but a compromise was reached with the professor, who agreed to pass him if he would not attempt any advanced work in the field! In 1914, Kinsey made his break and enrolled at Bowdoin College to pursue his real love: biology. Because this went against his father's wishes, Kinsey was left on his own financially.

In 1916, he began graduate work at Harvard. There he developed an interest in insects, specializing in gall wasps. While still a graduate student, he wrote a definitive book on the edible plants of eastern North America.

In 1920, he went to Bloomington, Indiana, to take a job as assistant professor of zoology at Indiana University. That fall he met Clara McMillen, whom he married six months later. They soon had four children.

With his intense curiosity and driving ambition, Kinsey quickly gained academic success. He published a high school biology text in 1926, which received enthusiastic reviews. By 1936, he had published two major books on gall wasps; they established his reputation as a leading authority in the field.

Kinsey came to the study of human sexual behaviour as a biologist. His shift to the study of sex began in 1938, when Indiana University began a "marriage" course; Kinsey chaired the faculty committee teaching it. When confronted with teaching the course, he became aware of the appalling lack of information on human sexual behaviour. Thus, his research resulted in part from his realization of the need of people, especially young people, for sex information. In 1939, he made his first field trip to collect sex histories in Chicago. His lifetime goal was to collect 100,000 sex histories.

His work culminated in the publication of the Kinsey reports in 1948 (*Sexual Behavior in the Human Male*) and 1953 (*Sexual Behavior in the Human Female*). While the scientific community generally received them as a landmark contribution, they also provoked hate mail.

In 1947, Kinsey founded the Institute for Sex Research (known popularly as the Kinsey Institute) at Indiana University. It was financed by a grant from the Rockefeller

the problems of non-response. This is a legitimate point. But as a result, we have almost no information on how adequate the sample was; the sampling was haphazard but not random. Generally, the following kinds of people were overrepresented in the sample: university students, young people, well-educated people, Protestants, people living in cities, and people living in Indiana and the northeast United States. Underrepresented groups included manual labourers, less-well-educated people, older people, Roman Catholics, Jews, members of racial minority groups, and people living in rural areas.

The Interviews

Although scientists generally regard Kinsey's sampling methods with some dismay, his face-to-face interviewing techniques are highly regarded. More than 50 percent of the interviews were done by Kinsey himself and the rest by his associates, whom he trained carefully. The interviewers made every attempt to establish rapport with the people they spoke to, and they treated all reports matter-of-factly. They were also skillful at phrasing questions in language that was easily understood. Questions were worded so as to encourage people to report anything they had done. For example, rather than asking, "Have you ever masturbated?" the interviewers asked, "At what age did you begin masturbating?" They also developed a number of methods for cross-checking a person's report so that false information would be detected. Wardell Pomeroy recounted an example:

Kinsey illustrated this point with the case of an older Negro male who at first was wary and evasive in

Foundation and, later, by book royalties. But in the 1950s, United States Senator Joseph McCarthy, the communist baiter, was in power. He made a particularly vicious attack on the institute and its research, claiming that its effect was to weaken American morality and thus make the nation more susceptible to a communist takeover. Under his pressure, the Rockefeller Foundation terminated its support.

Kinsey's health began to fail, partly as a result of the heavy workload he set for himself and partly because he saw financial support for the research collapsing. He died in 1956 at the age of 62 of heart failure while honouring a lecture engagement when his doctor had ordered him to convalesce.

By 1957, McCarthy had been discredited and the grant funds returned. The Kinsey Institute was then headed by Paul Gebhard (see Figure 3.6), an anthropologist who had been a member of the staff for many years. The Kinsey Institute continues to do research today; it also houses a large library on sex and an archival collection that includes countless works of sexual art.

In a highly publicized, tell-all biography of Kinsey, James Jones (1997) argued that, although Kinsey's public self was a heterosexual married man, he was homosexual (more accurately, bisexual) and practised masochism. According to Jones, this discredits Kinsey's research. Jones's logic is poor, though, because we can evaluate

Figure 3.6 Alfred C. Kinsey (second from right, holding the folder), with colleagues Martin, Gebhard, and Pomeroy.

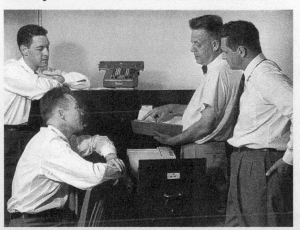

Reprinted by permission of the Kinsey Institute for Research in Sex, Gender and Reproduction, Inc., photo by Bill Dellenback.

the quality of the research methods independent of our views about Kinsey's personal sex life. Moreover, Kinsey's sexual experimenting may have contributed to the innovativeness of his research.

Sources: Bancroft, 2004; Christensen, 1971; Gathorne-Hardy, 2000; Gebhard, 1976; Jones, 1997.

his answers. From the fact that he listed a number of minor jobs when asked about his occupation and seemed reluctant to go into any of them [Kinsey] deduced that he might have been active in the underworld, so he began to follow up by asking the man whether he had ever been married. He denied it, at which Kinsey resorted to the vernacular and inquired if he had ever "lived common law." The man admitted he had, and that it had first happened when he was 14.

"How old was the woman?" [Kinsey] asked.

"Thirty-five," he admitted, smiling.

Kinsey showed no surprise. "She was a hustler, wasn't she?" he said flatly.

At this the subject's eyes opened wide. Then he smiled in a friendly way for the first time, and said, "Well,

sir, since you appear to know something about these things, I'll tell you straight."

After that, [Kinsey] got an extraordinary record of this man's history as a pimp. . . .

(Pomeroy, 1972, pp. 115–116)

Put simply, the interviewing techniques were probably very successful in minimizing purposeful distortion.

Kinsey took strict precautions to ensure that responses were anonymous and that they remained anonymous. The data were stored on IBM cards but used a code that had been memorized by only a few people directly involved in the project and was never written down. The research team had even made contingency plans for destroying the data in the event that the police tried to demand access to the records for prosecuting people.

How Accurate Were the Kinsey Statistics?

How accurate were the statistics presented by Kinsey? The American Statistical Association appointed a blue-ribbon panel to evaluate the Kinsey reports (Cochran, Mosteller, & Tukey, 1953; for other evaluations, see Terman, 1948; Wallin, 1949). While the panel members generally felt that the interview techniques had been excellent, they were dismayed by Kinsey's failure to use probability sampling and concluded, somewhat pessimistically:

> In the absence of a probability-sample benchmark, the present results must be regarded as subject to systematic errors of unknown magnitude due to selective sampling (via volunteering and the like). (Cochran et al., 1953, p. 711)

However, they also felt that this was a nearly insoluble problem for sex research; even if a probability sample were used, refusals would still create serious problems.

The statisticians who evaluated Kinsey's methods felt that one aspect of his findings might have been particularly subject to error: the generally high levels of sexual activity and particularly the high incidence of same-sex sexual activity These conclusions might, they felt, have been seriously influenced by sampling problems, particularly Kinsey's tendency to seek out persons with unusual sexual practices.

It is impossible to say how accurate the Kinsey statistics are; some may be very accurate and some may contain serious errors. Probably the single most doubtful figure is the high incidence of homosexuality.

Sexual Behaviour in the United States Today

U.S. researchers identified a need to conduct a large-scale, national survey of sexuality using probability sampling methods to determine what Americans' patterns of sexual behaviour are today. Such a study appeared in 1994. The research team was headed by Edward Laumann, a distinguished sociologist at the University of Chicago, and was conducted by the National Opinion Research Center, one of the best-respected survey organizations in the United States. The survey was called the National Health and Social Life Survey (NHSLS) (Laumann et al., 1994; Michael, Gagnon, Laumann, & Kolata, 1994).

The research method involved a probability sampling of households in the United States. This sampling excluded less than 3 percent of Americans but did exclude people living in institutions (e.g., prisons,

university dormitories) and the homeless. People were eligible if they were adults between the ages of 18 and 59.

The researchers obtained an impressive 79 percent response rate. Apparently, the great majority of people are willing to respond to a carefully conducted sex survey. The response rate is particularly impressive in view of the fact that today even surveys of more neutral topics, such as political opinions, generally have a response rate of only about 75 percent.

The data were obtained in face-to-face interviews supplemented by brief written questionnaires, which were handed to the respondents for particularly sensitive topics (such as masturbation) and sealed in a "privacy envelope" when they had been completed. The researchers chose the face-to-face interview because they felt that it would yield a higher response rate than a written questionnaire alone, and it allowed the researchers to ask more complex, detailed sequences of questions than would have been possible with just a written questionnaire or a telephone interview.

The NHSLS is one of the best sex surveys of the general population of the United States available today, and its findings will be referred to in many chapters in this book. The researchers made outstanding efforts to use the best sampling methods and interview techniques.

Nonetheless, the study has some limitations. It sampled only people between 18 and 59, giving us no information about the sexuality of older adults. The sample did not include enough people from some minority groups to compute reliable statistics for them (see Figure 3.7). No doubt some respondents engaged in concealment and perhaps also in enlargement, because self-reports were used. The skill of the interviewers and their ability to build rapport are crucial in overcoming such problems.

The most recent major national U.S. sex survey is the National Survey of Sexual Health and Behavior (NSSHB), with data collected in 2009 from people between the ages of 14 and 94 (Herbenick et al., 2010a; Reece et al., 2010a). A probability sample was identified based on a combination of random-digit dialing of telephone numbers and sampling of residential addresses from the U.S. Postal Service's list of deliverable addresses. For the adolescent part of the sample, parents were contacted first to provide consent, and 62 percent agreed, and 62 percent of the eligible adolescents participated, for a sample of 820 adolescents. In addition, 9600 potential adult participants were contacted, and just over half provided data. The overall sample size, then, combining adults and adolescents, was 5865. Participants completed the survey on the Internet, and those without computers were provided them for completing the questionnaire. Results from the survey will be presented in many chapters that follow.

Figure 3.7 Research conducted among members of racial and ethnic minority groups must be culturally sensitive. Ideally, for example, interviewers should be of the same cultural background as research participants.

How good was the NSSHB? The methods for identifying the initial probability sample—random-digit dialing of phone numbers and sampling of residential addresses—were excellent. The response rate was 50 percent, which is considerably lower than what the NHSLS obtained, but it is probably getting more difficult to recruit participants because Americans are increasingly oversaturated with solicitations from fundraising organizations, telemarketers, and so on. Statistically, with a 50 percent response rate, we cannot be sure that the results generalize to the whole population, but volunteer bias is always a problem with sex research. And, generally, administering sex questionnaires online is a good idea because respondents feel more anonymous and therefore presumably answer more truthfully.

Sexual Behaviour in Britain and Australia

Stimulated by a need for better information about sexual behaviour to improve sexual and reproductive health, Britain conducts a major sex survey once every ten years. Called the National Survey of Sexual Attitudes and Lifestyles (Natsal), the most recent one is Natsal-3, based on data collected between 2010 and 2012 (Erens et al., 2014). The survey used excellent sampling methods by conducting probability sampling of addresses within postal codes and achieved a response rate of 58 percent. Funding from the British government allowed researchers to collect a very large sample, with 15 162 completed interviews. Although the data collection method was called interviews, in fact interviewers went to homes and respondents completed the questionnaires on computers to ensure anonymity. In addition, with a

subsample of about 4000 people, researchers collected urine samples to test for sexually transmitted infections (STIs) and saliva samples to test for testosterone. Space limitations do not allow us to report all of the extensive findings here, so we will give just one example. Among participants between the ages of 16 and 44, the percentage of women who reported a sexual experience involving genital contact with another woman went from 1.8 percent in Natsal-1 (1990) to 4.9 percent in Natsal-2 (2000) to 7.9 percent in Natsal-3 (2010) (Mercer et al., 2013). Natsal-3 is one of the largest well-conducted sex surveys to date, along with the Australian survey described next.

Another team of researchers conducted a major sex survey in Australia (Rissel et al., 2003a, 2003b; Smith, Rissel, Richters, Grulich, & de Visser, 2003) called the Australian Study of Health and Relationships (ASHR). Using computer-assisted telephone interviews, the researchers recruited a sample of 19 307 men and women aged 16 to 59. The survey's response rate was 73 percent, which is comparable to the NHSLS. The findings indicate that the age of first intercourse has declined over the last several decades, consistent with trends in North America (Rissel et al., 2003b). In the youngest cohort, respondents aged 16 to 19, 27 percent of the men and 25 percent of the women reported that they had engaged in intercourse before age 16. Finally, 38 percent of the men and 27 percent of the women reported that they used no contraception the first time they had intercourse, a pattern that is also similar to North America and is of great concern.

Sexual Behaviour in Canada

Because no large-scale comprehensive Canadian sex surveys have been done, we often use the American surveys to draw conclusions about the situation in Canada. However, Canadians differ from Americans in ways that are likely to affect sexual behaviour, such as attitudes (see Chapter 1 for some examples), family patterns, laws, attitudes, and health (Barrett, King, Levy, Maticka-Tyndale, & McKay, 1997). Thus, it is impossible to be certain of the extent to which these data reflect the sexual behaviour of Canadians. This makes it difficult to develop a clear picture of the sexual behaviour of adult Canadians. In contrast, as just described, the United States, Britain, and Australia have all conducted this kind of large-scale survey in recent years. Many of the statistics in the British surveys (and some surveys done in France) match quite closely those from the United States. Thus, it is likely that a Canadian survey would also have similar, but not identical, findings.

What types of sex research are taking place in Canada?

Many sex researchers, however, are active in Canada (see First Person). These researchers have conducted surveys of selected groups, such as university students, teenagers, Indigenous peoples, sex trade workers, people living with chronic illnesses, and sexual and gender minorities, some of which are described in this chapter.

The Canada Youth, Sexual Health, and HIV/AIDS Study

Researchers from four Canadian universities—Queen's, Acadia, Laval, and the University of Alberta—conducted a study on youth sexuality and sexual health called the Canada Youth, Sexual Health, and HIV/AIDS Study, or CYSHHAS for short (Boyce, Doherty-Poirier, Fortin, & MacKinnon, 2003). It examined a number of factors thought to influence adolescent sexual knowledge, attitudes, and behaviour. Many of these questions were also used in the Canada Youth and AIDS Study conducted in 1987 by Alan King and his colleagues (King et al., 1988), allowing comparisons between the two studies. Because the CYSHHAS focused on sexual health, it is not a comprehensive survey of adolescent sexual behaviour and attitudes.

The researchers collected data in all ten provinces, as well as in Yukon and the Northwest Territories. They surveyed 11 074 youth in Grades 7, 9, and 11. However, to be acceptable to school administrations, the Grade 7 version included only one question about sexual experiences. The study was conducted in both French and English. The researchers used excellent sampling methods. They designed their sampling procedure so that the data would be representative of Canada as a whole and so they would have enough participants to present the findings separately for each province. However, some selected schools refused to participate. This resulted in a sample that was not equally representative of the whole country and was too small to analyze by province or territory. There also were some problems related to potential volunteer bias. For example, 18 percent of students either failed to return their signed permission slip or had parents who refused to give them permission to participate, and 5 percent of the students refused to participate. The students who did participate may differ in some important ways from those who did not.

The researchers found that many youth had begun engaging in sexual intercourse by age 14. For example, 23 percent of boys and 19 percent of girls in Grade 9 and 40 percent of boys and 46 percent of girls in Grade 11 reported having engaged in sexual intercourse at least once. These percentages are similar to, and if anything somewhat lower than, those obtained in the Canada Youth and AIDS Study in 1987, indicating that the percentage of students engaging in sexual intercourse does not appear to be increasing. However, the students who are engaging in sexual intercourse reported doing so more frequently than did students in 1987. Although 78 percent of the boys and 68 percent of the girls said that they had used a condom at last intercourse, between 5 and 10 percent had not used any form of birth control. Further, students who participated in 2002 were less accurate in their sexual knowledge than were the students who participated in 1987. Although this study assessed both anglophone and francophone youth, the researchers did not assess ethnicity. Thus, we do not know how cultural background affects the sexual attitudes and behaviours of Canadian youth.

Magazine Surveys

Many large-scale sex surveys have been conducted through magazines. Often the survey is printed in one issue of the magazine and readers are asked to respond. The result can be a huge sample—perhaps 20 000 people—which sounds impressive. But are these magazine surveys really all they claim to be?

Sampling is just plain out of control with magazine surveys. The survey is distributed just to readers of the magazine, and different magazines have different clienteles. No one magazine reaches a representative sample of Canadians. If the survey appeared in *Chatelaine*, it would go to certain kinds of women; if it were in *Canadian Living*, it would go to others. It would be risky to assume that women who read *Chatelaine* have the same sexual patterns as those who read *Canadian Living*. To make matters worse, the response rate is unknown. We can't know how many people saw the survey and did not fill it out compared with the number who did. We do not, therefore, even have a random sample of readers of that magazine.

As an example, let's consider a survey that was reported in the August 2009 issue of *Cosmopolitan*. The headline on the cover announces "Guys Rate 125 Sex Moves." The description of the methods in the article says that *Cosmo* "paired up with AskMen.com and got thousands of guys between the ages of 18 and 35 to confess what they want in bed." A subtitle clarifies that "thousands" actually means 6000 horny guys. That sample is twice the size of the NHSLS, but in sex surveys as in some other aspects of sexuality, bigger is not always better. What we can't tell from the article is who these 6000 horny guys are. Are they representative of all North American men between the ages of 18 and 35? That's highly unlikely, because only men who go to AskMen.com saw the survey. How can we know the response rate? Among the respondents, how many were married? Single? What about their ethnic backgrounds? Of course, these details are not the sort of thing that *Cosmo* probably thinks will entertain its readers. Nonetheless, they could have printed the information in a small box at the end of the article. More important, these details are crucial in evaluating whether one can take their claims seriously.

One question asked about the absolute sexiest sight she can treat you to. Of the men who were polled, the most frequent choice (34 percent of those polled) was "touching herself in front of me." From this, can we conclude that 34 percent of men are most turned on by the sight of their partner touching herself? That conclusion would require a leap of logic that is too big for safety. *Cosmo* wasn't even close to having a random sample in this survey.

For all these reasons, it would not be legitimate to infer that these statistics characterize North American men in general. We could continue with more examples of magazine surveys, but the general conclusion should be clear by now. Although they may appear impressive because of their large number of respondents, magazine sex surveys actually are poor in quality because the sample generally is seriously biased.

Studies of Special Populations

In addition to the large-scale surveys of Americans and of Canadian youth discussed earlier, many studies of special populations have been done. One example is the study done by Elizabeth Saewyc and her colleagues (2014) on sexual minority Indigenous youth in Canada, New Zealand, and the United States. The purpose of this study was to determine whether experiences of stigma were associated with HIV risk behaviours.

The data were collected by a team of researchers that included Indigenous and sexual minority members (both Indigenous and non-Indigenous). In order to take the unique concerns of both Indigenous and sexual minority individuals into account, the researchers also consulted with Indigenous advisory groups and community groups working on the issue of HIV and AIDS to guide study design, data analysis, interpretation of the findings, and dissemination of the results. The results also were presented to Indigenous youth as well as at Indigenous HIV/AIDS conferences for comments and feedback before the study was published.

The researchers conducted secondary analysis of well-sampled school surveys conducted in each of the three countries. The researchers found that Indigenous sexual minority youth were more likely to report having experienced stigma, such as bullying, discrimination, exclusion, harassment, and school-based violence,

compared to their heterosexual peers. They were also more likely to report engaging in behaviours that would put them at risk for contracting HIV, such as not using condoms, having multiple sexual partners, and using injection drugs.

This research demonstrates an important principle that needs to be kept in mind in doing research with different minority groups—representatives of the target communities participated in the design and management of the study. This has two advantages. First, it allows the communities to have input into the research design and methodology to ensure that the research takes the unique concerns of each community into account. Second, it makes it more likely that conclusions drawn from the research and recommendations based on the research are appropriate and relevant.

There are other important guidelines for conducting interview studies related to sexuality with different cultural groups (Ford & Norris, 1991). First, respondents should be interviewed by an interviewer of the same gender and ethnic background as they are. This practice is important for building rapport and establishing trust during the interview, both of which are critical in obtaining honest answers. Language is another important issue in constructing interviews. Many people, including those from the majority Canadian culture, do not know scientific terms for sexual concepts. Interviewers therefore have to be ready with a supply of slang terms so that they can switch to these if a respondent does not understand a question. This problem becomes more complex when interviewing people whose first language is not English.

In conclusion, doing sex research with people from diverse ethnocultural communities in Canada requires more than just administering the same old surveys to samples of people from these groups. It requires revisions to methodology that are culturally sensitive to issues such as the ethnicity of the interviewer, the language used in the interview, and the special sensitivity of some groups regarding some topics.

Media Content Analysis

So far, we have focused on methods used to analyze people's sexuality and have touched on the profound impact of the mass media on Canadians' sexuality. To be able to understand this impact, we need to be able to analyze the media. As an example, let's suppose that your friend Rachel says that it is deeply disturbing that women are shown in nothing but traditional roles on

First Person

Where Can I Go in Canada to Become a Sex Researcher?

Canada has many active sex researchers, and their numbers are growing. Most are in academic departments within specific disciplines, such as psychology, sociology, family studies, or medicine. Most supervise students. The only Department of Sexology located in Canada operates in French at l'Université du Québec à Montréal. However, York University has a program in sexuality studies. Although it is impossible to name all Canadian sex researchers, here are some of the most active researchers (from east to west)—only researchers who also supervise student research have been included.

At Acadia University in Nova Scotia, psychologist Lisa Price studies sexual coercion and risky sexual behaviour among adolescents. At Dalhousie University, psychologist Natalie Rosen studies the influence of relationship factors on sexual pain disorders. At St. Francis Xavier University, psychologist Angela Weaver studies body image, alternative sexualities, and sexuality in film; psychologist Karen Blair studies the social determinants of the health of individuals with diverse sexual and gender identities. At the University of New Brunswick, psychologist Sandra Byers is particularly well known for her research on sexual interactions in close relationships, including sexual satisfaction, sexual dysfunction, and sexual coercion; Lucia O'Sullivan is an expert in adolescent sexual health; and Scott Ronis conducts research on childhood sexual experiences. At St. Thomas University, psychologist Monika Stelzl studies sexual knowledge and women's sexual pleasure.

In Quebec, psychologist Francine Lavoie of Laval University studies high school students' sexually coercive experiences. In the Département de sexologie, l'Université du Québec à Montréal, Joseph Levy and Joanne Otis have been active in assessing the sexual behaviour of Quebecers. In the same department, Martine Hébert investigates child sexual abuse, Marie-Aude Boislard studies adolescent sexuality, and Line Chamberland studies sexual minorities. In the Département de psychologie at UQAM, Danielle Julien studies sexual and gender minorities (see www.sexologie.uqam.ca/personnel/ for a complete list of faculty at UQAM). At l'Université de Montréal, psychologist Sophie Bergeron studies women's sexual pain disorders, and psychologist Katherine Péloquin studies couples' sexual relationships. At McGill University, psychologist Yitzchak Binik studies sexual pain in women. At Concordia University, sociologist Frances Shaver is a leading researcher on sex work, and James Pfaus studies the neurochemical and molecular events underlying sexual behaviour.

A number of Ontario universities have active sex research programs. At Queen's University, psychologist Caroline Pukall does research related to sexual pain and its effects on sexual and marital functioning, and psychologist Meredith Chivers studies sexual psychophysiology. At the University of Ottawa, psychologist Elke Reissing investigates sexual pain disorders and sexual adjustment following treatment for cancer, Martin Lalumière does research on sexual aggression, Krystelle Shaughnessy studies online sexual activity, and Peggy Kleinplatz does research on optimal sexuality. At the Centre for Addiction and Mental Health, Clarke Division, in Toronto, psychologist James Cantor does his work on pedophilia. At the University of Toronto, Michael Seto studies sexual offenders, Emily Impett studies how authenticity shapes sexual well-being, and Ted Myers does research related to HIV. At York University, Nick Mulé and Maurice Kwong-Lai Poon conduct research on sexual orientation, and psychologist Amy Muise studies how couples maintain fulfilling sexual relationships over time. At Ryerson University, Maria Gurevich studies constructions of gender, sexuality, and identity, and Trevor Hart does research related to HIV and sexual-minority men.

Psychologist Anthony Bogaert at Brock University is well known for his work on the origins of sexual orientation and on asexuality. Psychologist Terry Humphreys at Trent University does research related to human sexuality and social psychology, including sexual consent. At the University of Waterloo, B.J. Rye studies HIV/AIDS and attitudes toward sexual minorities, Christine Purdon examines the role of anxiety in sexual functioning, and Uzma Rehman studies sexuality in intimate relationships. At the University of Guelph, Robin Milhausen does research related to sexual arousal and sexual health, Tuuli Kukkonen studies biological and social factors affecting sexual health, and Serge Demarais investigates sexual coercion. Psychologist William Fisher at the University of Western Ontario has an international reputation for his work on the prevention of teen pregnancy, STIs, and HIV infection (see Milestones in Sex Research to learn more about him). At the University of Windsor, sociologist Eleanor Maticka-Tyndale is well known for her qualitative and multimethod research on risk behaviour related to pregnancy and STI/HIV infection, sociologist Barry Adam does research on HIV and same-sex relationships, and psychologist Charlene Senn studies sexual violence.

At the University of Saskatchewan, psychologist Melanie Morrison studies prejudice and discrimination toward sexual minorities, and psychologist Todd Morrison studies gay and lesbian psychology. At the University of Alberta, Kris Wells conducts research on sexual and gender minority youth. Paul Vasey at the University of

Lethbridge studies sexuality and gender from a biocognitive perspective.

At the University of British Columbia, psychologist Lori Brotto studies women with sexual dysfunction and cross-cultural issues in women's sexual health, psychologist Judith Daniluk is well known for her research on infertility, psychologist Boris Gorzalka conducts psychophysiological sex research, and nursing professor Elizabeth Saewyc studies stigma and adolescent sexual health. Cari Miller, a professor of health sciences at Simon Fraser University, studies adolescent sexual and reproductive health nationally and internationally. Sociologist Aaron Devor at the University of Victoria has made important contributions with his work on conceptualization of gender dysphoria, and psychologist John Sakaluk studies health and well-being in the context of sexual relationships.

Canadian sex researchers publish their findings in both national and international journals. One Canadian journal is committed to the dissemination of sex research: the quarterly *Canadian Journal of Human Sexuality*. Many researchers belong to the Canadian Sex Research Forum, the only national association for sex researchers, as well as to international sexological organizations. The Canadian Sex Research Forum also welcomes students who are interested in sex research (for more information, visit www.canadiansexresearchforum.com). Finally, the Guelph Sexuality Conference is held each year at the University of Guelph and features Canadian and international speakers who provide research-based education and training to practitioners working in sexual health.

Milestones in Sex Research

Confessions of a Scientist: The Career of Dr. William Fisher

As listed in the First Person box, many excellent sex researchers work in Canada. Here we share the story of how one of the Canadian leaders in the field, Dr. William Fisher (see Figure 3.8), became a sex researcher. Dr. Fisher is a professor in the Department of Psychology and the Department of Obstetrics and Gynaecology at the University of Western Ontario. He received his PhD in social psychology from Purdue University in 1978. He is world-renowned for the information–motivation–behavioural skills model, his conceptualization of the factors that drive sexual and reproductive health behaviour, and his work on HIV/AIDS prevention and on the effects of pornography on men's and women's behaviour. Dr. Fisher's work is described throughout this book (see Chapters 7, 10, and 17). He has received a National Health Scientist Award from Health Canada and the Hellmuth Award for Achievement in Science from the University of Western Ontario, and he is a Fellow of the Society for the Scientific Study of Sexuality. Here he reflects, with humour, on how he came to be a sexuality researcher.

Coming out of the chaos, commitment, and politics of the Vietnam and Civil Rights era in the 1960s, I resolved, naively, to try to understand and improve the human condition, a delusional state from which I have yet to recover. Accordingly, I applied for admission to a graduate school that featured stellar researchers in the areas of human attraction and human aggression—which seemed to me at the time to be the issues we need to understand if we are to have any chance to survive as a species. Astoundingly, Donn Byrne, one of the world's premier scientists in the area of love and attraction, accepted me for graduate study. He had just shifted his research focus from interpersonal attraction to sexual behaviour—a natural progression, in retrospect—and we were off to the races.

As a graduate student I conducted research on the effects of pornography (what else?), and two things caught my eye immediately. First, I found that men and women who viewed pornography and who were most revolted by it showed large increases in their sexual activity levels in the days following exposure. (As an aside, the study was published in both the *Journal of Personality and Social Psychology* and in *Screw* magazine. Fortunately, the publication in *Screw* magazine did not turn out to be a career ender—no prospective employer ever admitted to having seen it.) Second, I found that men and women who responded to pornography with the most pronounced negative emotions also, and puzzlingly, had the most children. At first it was difficult to understand why—and indeed how—this happened. Then we realized that erotophobic persons—that is, people who are emotionally negative to sex—have a really tough time doing just about everything you need to do to not have children.

---

prime-time TV and that this situation hasn't improved a bit over the years. Your other friend Monique disagrees, saying that there may still be some traditional images of women, but there are many examples of women in nontraditional roles, such as doctors, and the media's portrayals of women have changed a lot over the years. How can you decide who is right? Arguing won't settle the debate. However, you could use a technique called **content analysis** to analyze how the media portray women today and how they have portrayed women in the past (Krippendorff, 2004).

Content analysis refers to a set of procedures used to make valid inferences about text (see Figure 3.9). The "text" might be romance novels, advice columns in *Chatelaine* magazine, lyrics from rap music, or scripts from movies or prime-time television programs. As it turns out, many of the same methodological issues discussed earlier also come into play with content analysis. Here, we have used a recently published study by Canadian researchers on descriptions in popular

content analysis: A set of procedures used to make valid inferences about text.

That is, they find it hard to learn about contraception, talk with a partner about it, acquire it from a physician or a pharmacy, and use it consistently.

That was my start, and since graduate school, building on this observation, I have worked toward development of a theory of the basic psychological factors that drive human sexual behaviour. My research has been aimed at improving people's sexual and reproductive health by applying this theory in areas as diverse as adolescent pregnancy prevention, HIV prevention, and reproductive health care seeking. I have been fortunate to do this work in settings as varied and challenging as inner-city high schools in the United States, South African AIDS treatment centres, and Israeli–Palestinian HIV containment programs. I've been at this work for years. I've published more than 150 papers in this area, and I feel like I've barely begun.

Why I Do What I Do

I do what I do because I believe that the development and application of psychological theory in the area of sexual and reproductive health is important for the human condition. I do what I do because I enjoy creating conceptual models that can, with power and precision, be used to predict and promote human sexual and reproductive health outcomes. I do what I do because my work has had the unintended but often enjoyable effect of inflaming both the political right (see my work on contraceptive behaviour and how to promote it) and the political

Figure 3.8 Dr. William Fisher is a well-known psychologist and sex researcher.

Courtesy of Dr. William Fisher

left (see my work on pornography and failure to find that it has negative effects), so I know I must be doing something right.

Proudest Achievements

Catching the occasional fish. Not really. My proudest achievements involve my resolute insistence on following my data, regardless of their political correctness or incorrectness, and insisting on maintaining fundamental human values and principles, regardless of my data.

magazines of how to achieve "great sex" (Ménard & Kleinplatz, 2008).

Sampling is one such issue. The first thing the researchers conducting this study needed to do was define the population. Were they interested in all magazines or particular types of magazines? Next, they needed to define the time period of interest: magazines published in the current year, the past five years, the past ten years, and so on. Finally, they needed to decide whether to analyze all magazines that met these criteria or a sample of these magazines, and whether to analyze the entire magazine or selected parts of the magazine. The researchers decided to include the issues from 2005 of an equal number of male and female magazines targeted at single readers between the ages of 18 and 35 and that regularly include sexual content.

The next step is to create a coding protocol. First, the researchers needed to define the recording unit—was it the magazine, the article, or specific statements? The authors chose to use explicit tips on how to have great sex within an article or blurb—that is, specific statements. Next, perhaps more importantly, they needed to define

Figure 3.9 Precise methods have been developed for analyzing the content of the media.

© Janet Hyde

Is it possible to study sexuality scientifically with methods other than questionnaires?

coding categories. Creating the coding scheme involves defining the basic content categories, the presence or absence of which will be recorded; the coding categories used depend on the research questions. In this instance, the researchers developed their coding categories by doing a qualitative analysis in which they read and reread the articles and blurbs. This resulted in five major categories: technical/mechanical/physical factors, variety, relationship factors including sexual communication and emotional connection, personal and psychological factors, and presex preparation.

Researchers doing content analysis must demonstrate that their data are reliable and objective and not biased. Usually, a measure called **intercoder or interrater reliability** is used. Two or more trained individuals independently code all or some of the text in the sample. This is done to ensure that the coding is accurate and the coder is not either overreporting (e.g., recording statements as a sexual technique when they did not actually include

intercoder or interrater reliability: In content analysis, the correlation or percentage of agreement between two coders independently rating the same texts.

a technical suggestion) or underreporting (e.g., failing to record statements that include a technique). To give a measure of the interrater reliability, the researcher computes a correlation or percentage agreement between the two coders' results. In this study, the percent agreement for assigning specific tips to one of the five categories was 73 percent. This result is sufficiently high to consider the coding to be reliable but not as high as it could be, since if the coders agreed exactly the percent agreement would be 100 percent.

Content analysis is a powerful scientific technique that allows us to know how the media portray sexuality. For example, in this study, researchers found 443 tips in the magazines. Overall, most advice was related to technical/mechanical/physical factors, such as sexual technique and duration of sex. In fact, between 25 and 40 percent of the tips in the magazines were in this category. Another strong focus was on sexual variety, including use of different props, engaging in "kinky" activities, and watching sexually explicit movies. These tips accounted for between 16 and 41 percent of the tips across the different magazines. Interestingly, what these magazines identified as great sex was quite different from the components identified by people who report having experienced "great sex" (Kleinplatz, Ménard, Paquet, et al., 2009). You can find the results of the interviews with these individuals in Chapter 11.

A related topic to content analysis is *critical discourse analysis,* which analyzes written texts for their underlying meaning. One such study examined how HIV/AIDS was portrayed in the 20 highest-circulating Canadian magazines in 1991, 1996, and 2001 (Clarke, 2006). The results showed that these stories were still characterized by heterosexism and homonegativity, although more subtly than in the past (see Chapter 14 for a discussion of heterosexism and homonegativity).

LO6
Qualitative Methods

Most of the research methods discussed so far are **quantitative methods**; that is, people's responses are quantified or given numerical values. For example, respondents rate their attitudes about gay marriage on a scale from (1) strongly disapprove to (7) strongly approve, or participants report their number of sexual partners in the past year.

An alternative to quantitative methods is **qualitative research**, in which the results are conveyed not in numbers but in words—what is sometimes called *thick description* (Berg, 2007; Denzin & Lincoln, 2005). Qualitative research actually encompasses a collection of methods that may involve the researcher's participation in a setting, direct observation, or in-depth and open-ended interviews. In qualitative research, the researchers try to make sense of experiences in terms of the meanings that people give to them (Denzin & Lincoln, 1994). It seeks to understand people in their natural environment, not in a lab or an experiment, and it seeks a complete picture of the participants and their context, not focusing just on one or two variables. Thus, qualitative researchers emphasize the participant's point of view and represent this point of view by providing quotations from participants rather than by giving statistics.

An example of qualitative research is conducted by Eleanor Maticka-Tyndale and her colleagues in a study of exotic dancers working at strip clubs in Southern Ontario (Lewis & Maticka-Tyndale, 1998; Maticka-Tyndale, Lewis, Clark, Zubick, & Young, 1999). Their goal was to determine whether the dancers' activities, both inside and outside the club, put them at risk for STIs, including HIV infection. They interviewed 30 female exotic dancers who had been dancing from 1 to 22 years.

It is difficult to recruit a representative sample of sex workers because of the stigma attached to the work and because sex workers are often distrustful of researchers (Benoit, Jannson, Millar, & Phillips, 2005). Therefore, the researchers used a procedure called *nonprobability purposive sampling* to maximize the diversity in the small sample. They wanted to make sure that the conclusions drawn from the research would reflect all the situations in which dancers find themselves. Participants were identified by key informants, by research assistants who had worked as dancers themselves, and by dancers who participated in the study, a technique called **snowball sampling** (Salganik & Heckathorn, 2004). Thus, as with all qualitative research, this was not a random or representative sample, and we cannot draw conclusions about frequencies and prevalence. Nonetheless, it provides an in-depth understanding of the world of exotic dancers. Participants responded to an informal set of open-ended questions that allowed them to freely express themselves. The interviews were analyzed to identify themes that emerged from the sex workers' responses.

The researchers found that women begin dancing primarily for the money, with the view that it will be temporary. There were two different types of dancers. Goal-oriented dancers continue to treat dancing as a temporary job and usually do not use alcohol or drugs or engage in sexual activity as part of the job. College and university students are one group of goal-oriented dancers. Dancing is attractive to them because it pays well and can fit into their class schedule. However, some women shift from viewing dancing as a temporary job to viewing it as a career. These career dancers are usually part of the strip club culture, are often heavy drinkers, and may be involved in drug use. They may have sex with customers as part of the dancing or on dates with the men they meet while dancing at the clubs.

Qualitative research generally differs from quantitative research in several ways. Qualitative researchers typically do not use random or probability samples, and they typically have small samples, perhaps only 20 people. Compared with quantitative research, qualitative research is more likely to be exploratory and to focus on generating hypotheses rather than testing hypotheses. Qualitative methods and quantitative methods can therefore be used together.

A qualitative research method used by anthropologists and sociologists

quantitative methods: Research in which people's responses are quantified or given numerical values.
qualitative research: Research, usually involving interviews, in which the researchers try to make sense of the meanings that people give to their experiences.
snowball sampling: A method for acquiring a sample of people where current participants suggest names of future participants to be recruited.

is the **participant-observer technique**. In this type of research, the scientist tries to become a part of the community to be studied, and she or he makes observations from inside the community. In the study of sexual behaviour, the researcher thus may be able to get direct observations of sexual behaviour combined with interview data.

Examples of this type of research are studies of sexual behaviour in other cultures, such as those done in Mangaia and Inis Beag, which were discussed in Chapter 1. One other example is Charles Moser's study of S/M (sadomasochistic) parties.

Sex researcher Charles Moser observed S/M interactions in semi-public settings in the United States, attending more than 200 S/M parties (Moser, 1998). Parties are typically highly scripted. The person who gives the party may advertise it widely (e.g., on the Internet) or may issue personal invitations to only a very select list. The parties may have a particular theme, such as female dominant/male submissive only or women only. The party might be held at a person's home or in a rented space.

Each party has a particular set of rules, which vary from one party to another, and guests may be required to sign a written agreement to follow the rules. Issues covered in these rules include who may talk to whom (Can a submissive be spoken to?), who may play with whom, who may have sex with whom, prohibited S/M or sexual behaviours, what constitutes safer sex, not blocking equipment by sitting on it, and so on. Drunkenness is never acceptable; some parties allow wine or beer, but others ban all alcohol.

Some individuals plan to have a first "date" at a party. Parties clearly have the function of ensuring safety for participants, since others are always present if an interaction goes too far. Potential partners negotiate what kind of interaction they desire—for example, pain versus humiliation.

Perhaps most interesting is the fact that coitus and genitally focused activity designed to produce orgasm are very rare at these parties. The participants describe the S/M experience as highly sexual, but orgasm typically is not the goal.

Moser did not report that he obtained informed consent from the people he observed. However, their behaviour was public, leading to a relaxation of human subjects regulations.

participant-observer technique: A research method in which the scientist becomes part of the community to be studied and makes observations from inside the community.
correlational studies: Studies in which the researcher does not manipulate variables but rather studies naturally occurring relationships (correlations) among variables.
experiment: A type of research study in which one variable (the independent variable) is manipulated by the experimenter while all other factors are held constant; the researcher can then study the effects of the independent variable on some measured variable (the dependent variable); the researcher is permitted to make causal inferences about the effects of the independent variable on the dependent variable.

In his report, he was careful not to divulge any identifying information about individuals.

LO7
Experiments

All the studies discussed so far have had one thing in common: They were all studies of people's sexual behaviour as it occurs naturally, conducted by means of either self-reports or direct observations. Such reports are **correlational studies**; that is, at best the data they obtain can tell us that certain factors are related. They cannot tell us, however, what causes various aspects of sexual behaviour.

For instance, suppose we conduct a survey and find that women who masturbated to orgasm before marriage are more likely to have a high consistency of orgasm in marriage than women who did not. From this it would be tempting to conclude that practice in masturbating causes women to have more orgasms in heterosexual sex. Unfortunately, this is not a legitimate conclusion to draw from the data, since many other factors might also explain the results. For example, it could be that some women have a higher sex drive than others, which causes them to masturbate and also to have orgasms with a partner. Therefore, the most we can conclude is that masturbation experience is related to (or correlated with) orgasm consistency in marital sex.

An alternative method that does allow researchers to determine the causes of various aspects of behaviour is the **experiment**. According to its technical definition, in an experiment one factor must be manipulated while all other factors are held constant. Thus, any differences among the groups of people who received different treatments on that one factor can be said to be caused by that factor. For obvious reasons, most experimental research is conducted in the laboratory.

As an example of an experiment, let us consider a study that investigated whether being interviewed face-to-face causes children to underreport their sexual experiences (Romer et al., 1997). The participants were approximately 400 low-income children between the ages of 9 and 15. Some were assigned to a face-to-face interview with an experienced adult interviewer of their own gender. Others were assigned to be interviewed by a "talking computer," which had the same questions programmed into it. The questions appeared on the screen and, simultaneously, came through headphones for those who were not good readers (Figure 3.10). Presumably in the talking computer condition, the child feels more of a sense of privacy and anonymity and therefore responds more truthfully.

Figure 3.10 An innovation in surveys of children is the use of "talking computers" to ask questions, with the child entering answers by using the mouse or the keyboard.

© JGI/Jamie Grill/Getty Images

Among 13-year-old boys interviewed by the talking computer, 76 percent said they had "had sex," compared with only 50 percent of the boys in the face-to-face interview. Forty-eight percent of 13-year-old girls interviewed by computer said they had had sex, compared with 25 percent of those interviewed by a human. The children clearly reported more sexual activity to the computer than to a human interviewer.

In the language of experimental design, the *independent variable* (manipulated variable) was the type of interview (computer or human interviewer). The *dependent variable* (the measured variable) was whether the children reported that they had had sex (there were a number of other dependent variables as well, but a discussion of them would take us too far afield).

The results indicated that children interviewed by humans reported significantly less sexual activity than those interviewed by computer. Because the research design was experimental, we can make causal inferences. We can say confidently that the type of interview had an effect on children's answers. We might also say that a face-to-face interview causes children to underreport their activity. That statement is a bit shakier than the previous one, because it assumes that the answers given to the talking computer were true. It is possible that children overreported or exaggerated in responding to the computer and that their answers to the human interviewer were accurate.

Experimental sex research permits us to make much more powerful statements about the causes of various kinds of sexual phenomena. That is, it allows us to make a **causal inference**—inferring that the independent variable actually influences the dependent variable. As for disadvantages, much of the experimental sex research, including the study described here, still relies on self-reports. Experimental sex research is time-consuming and costly, and it can generally be done only on small samples of participants. Sometimes in their efforts to control all variables except the independent variable, researchers control too much. Finally, experiments cannot address some of the most interesting, but most complex, questions in the field of sexual behaviour, such as what factors cause people to be attracted to men, women, both men and women, transgender individuals, or no one.

LO8

Meta-Analysis

At this point in the field of sex research, there can be dozens or even hundreds of studies investigating a particular question. Let's say our question is whether there are differences between males and females in attitudes about homosexuality (Petersen & Hyde, 2010). Studies can contradict each other. With this example, some might show that women are more approving of homosexuality than men are and others might show that there is no gender difference. What is a scientist or a student to conclude?

1. The researcher locates all previous studies on the question being investigated (e.g., gender differences in attitudes toward homosexuality). This step is typically done using searches of databases such as PsycINFO or Web of Science.

2. For each study, the researcher computes a statistic that measures how big the difference between males and females was, and what the direction of the difference was (males scored higher or females scored higher). This statistic is called *d*. The formula for it is:

$$d = \frac{M_M - M_F}{s}$$

where M_M is the mean or average score for males, M_F is the mean or average score for females, and *s* is the average standard deviation of the male scores and the female scores. If you've studied statistics, you know what a standard deviation is. If you haven't, the standard deviation is a measure of how much variability there is in a set of scores. For example, if the average score for students on

causal inference: Concluding that one factor actually causes or influences an outcome.

Quiz 1, is 20 and all scores fall between 19 and 21, then there is little variability and the standard deviation would be small. If, in contrast, the average score for students is 20 and scores range from 0 to 40, then there is great variability and the standard deviation will be large. The d statistic, then, tells us, for a particular study, how big the difference between the male and female means was, relative to the variability in scores. If d is a positive number, then males scored higher; if d is negative, females scored higher; and if d is zero, there was no difference.

3. The researcher averages all the values of d over all the studies that were located. This average d value tells us, when all studies are combined, what the direction of the gender difference is (whether males score higher or females score higher) and how large the difference is. Although there is some disagreement among experts, a general guide is that a d of 0.20 is a small difference, a d of 0.50 is a moderate difference, and a d of 0.80 or more is a large difference (Cohen, 1988).

Many meta-analyses of gender differences are now available. In addition, meta-analysis can be used to synthesize the results of any group of studies that all used a two-group design to investigate the same question. For example, meta-analysis could be used for all studies on the effectiveness of Viagra compared with a placebo pill. Whenever possible in the chapters that follow, we will present evidence based on meta-analyses.

UNDERSTANDING THE IMPORTANCE OF SAMPLING

As we have explained in this chapter, recruiting a random or probability sample is an important aspect of high-quality sex research. The quality of the sampling has an enormous impact on the conclusions that we can reach from a particular study. Consider the following example.

Researchers were interested in learning about the motivations for extramarital sex among individuals actively involved in extramarital relationships (Omarzu, Miller, Schultz, & Timmerman, 2012). The researchers recruited their sample by posting a message on a website aimed at adults who engage in extramarital infidelity. A sample of 22 men and 55 women agreed to participate. According to the results, for both women and men, sexual needs, emotional needs, and falling in love were the top reasons for beginning affairs.

The population of interest here is all adults who have engaged in extramarital relationships. Did the researchers recruit a random sample of that population? If not, who did they miss?

What can we conclude from this study? Given that 22 men and 55 women participated, could we conclude that women are more than twice as likely as men to engage in extramarital relationships? Could we conclude that sexual needs, emotional needs, and falling in love are the top reasons for beginning affairs among the population of people who engage in extramarital sex? After you have answered these questions for yourself, read on to the next paragraph, which provides some answers.

The researchers did not recruit a random sample of the population of those who engage in extramarital sex. Instead, they recruited a sample of people who participate on a website aimed at this topic. Therefore, we can't reach any statistical conclusions, such as that women are more than twice as likely to engage in extramarital affairs. We only know about the people who spend time on that website and were motivated to participate in the study. It is likely that certain categories of people are missing from the sample, such as the person who had an extramarital fling once while away from home and drunk at a convention, who feels terribly guilty about it, and never wants to think about it again, much less go to a website to discuss it. Therefore, the motives that the researchers found in their sample might not characterize the whole population, including all the people who were missed.

A random, or representative, or probability sample is crucial if we are to make valid conclusions from research.

Critical *THINK*ing Skill

UNDERSTANDING THE IMPORTANCE OF EXPERIMENTS

In this chapter, you learned how it is crucial to have a true experiment—with an independent variable that is manipulated, and with random assignment of participants to experimental groups—to be able to make causal inferences from a study. By causal inference we mean a conclusion that one variable causes or influences another variable. Suppose we want to determine whether substantial exposure to pornography as an adolescent leads men to commit sex crimes. Notice here that the word "leads" is a causal term. It is equivalent to saying that exposure causes or influences men to commit sex crimes.

To find an answer to the question, we recruit two samples from a prison. One is a group of sex offenders who are in prison because they committed a sex crime. The second group is composed of offenders who are in prison for some other offence (for example, murder or robbery) but have not committed a sex crime (or at least haven't been convicted of a sex crime). Both groups fill out a questionnaire that asks about their use of pornography while they were adolescents, and sure enough, the sex offenders had twice as much exposure to pornography as the other offenders. From this, can we conclude that exposure to pornography in adolescence makes men commit sex crimes? Was this a true experiment? The

answer to both questions is no. It is tempting to conclude that this was a true experiment because there were two groups, sex offenders and non–sex offenders. The problem, though, is that men were not randomly assigned to be in one group or the other. Moreover, here the hypothesized independent variable, the causal variable, is pornography exposure, not sex offending, and the men were also not randomly assigned to pornography exposure or not. Therefore, this is actually a correlational study, and all we can conclude is that there is an association between pornography exposure and sex offending, not that pornography causes sex offending.

To clarify why a causal conclusion is not warranted with a correlational study like this, it is often helpful to think of another explanation for the findings. Often this is a third-variable explanation; that is, there might be some third variable that influences both of the variables that were studied. In this case, the third variable may be genetics or experiences of child sexual abuse that influence men to commit sex offences and increase their desire to use pornography. This explanation makes it even clearer why we cannot conclude that substantial exposure to pornography makes men commit sex crimes. The effects of pornography are discussed in detail in Chapter 17.

SUMMARY

Researchers measure various aspects of human sexuality by using (1) self-reports, (2) behavioural measures (e.g., direct observation, eye-tracking), (3) implicit measures (e.g., the IAT), and (4) biological measures (e.g., plethysmography, fMRI, pupil dilation). In web-based research, sex researchers collect data online, which is especially useful in tapping hidden populations.

Three crucial methodological issues in sex research are the following:

1. *Sampling:* Random samples or probability samples are best but are difficult to obtain because some people refuse to participate.

2. *The accuracy of measurement:* Much sex research relies on people's reports of their own sexual behaviour. Research shows that these self-reports are generally accurate (i.e., reliable and valid), but they can also be distorted in several ways, such as purposeful distortion, faulty memory, and difficulty estimating.

3. *Ethical issues:* Sex researchers, like all researchers, are bound by the rules of informed consent, protection from harm, and justice.

Statistical concepts that are important for understanding reports of sex research include average, mean, median, mode, variability, incidence, frequency, and correlation.

No major national sex surveys have been conducted in Canada. However, there are three large-scale U.S. surveys of sexual behaviour: Kinsey's interview study, and the NHSLS and NSSHB, the latter two of which were based on probability sampling. Similar surveys have been conducted in the United Kingdom and Australia. The CYSHHAS assessed adolescent sexuality across Canada. Canadian studies of special populations include a survey of First Nations peoples headed by Saewyc.

Media content analysis involves a set of scientific procedures used to make valid inferences about some aspects of the media, such as sexuality in prime-time television programs or the content of advice columns.

Qualitative methods yield results that are conveyed not in numbers but in words and aim at an in-depth description of people in their natural environment from their own perspective. Participant-observer studies are one kind of qualitative method. The scientist becomes a part of the community to be studied and makes observations from inside the community.

Experiments are a type of research in which one variable (the independent variable) is manipulated so that the researcher can study the effects on the dependent variable. Experiments allow us to draw conclusions about the causes of sexual behaviour.

Meta-analysis is a statistical technique for combining all of the studies that have been done on a particular question, such as gender differences in attitudes about casual sex.

CHAPTER 4

Sexual Anatomy

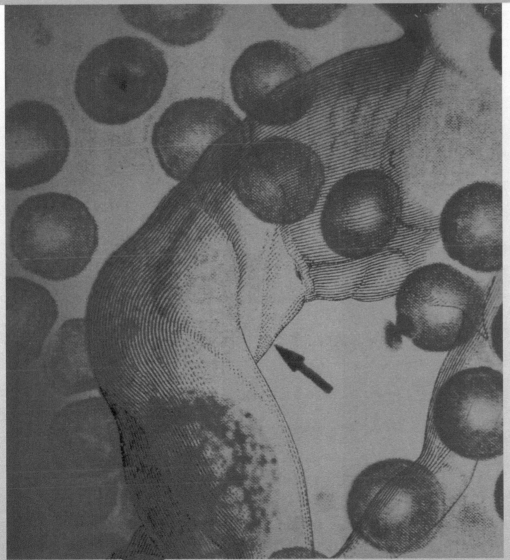

© Digital Vision/Getty Images

LEARNING OBJECTIVES

After studying this chapter, you will be able to

LO1 Describe the relationship between genital self-image and genital cosmetic surgery.

LO2 Describe the major structures of the female external and internal genitalia and their functions.

LO3 Describe the forms of female genital cutting and their health consequences.

LO4 Illustrate the structure and function of the breast.

LO5 Describe the major structures of the male external and internal genitalia and their functions.

LO6 Restate the history and evaluate the practice of male circumcision.

LO7 Differentiate between the different types of, detection of, and treatments for the reproductive cancers.

Are YOU Curious?

1. Do women ejaculate?
2. Are there any medical advantages to circumcising baby boys?
3. Do any cancers of the sex organs affect young men?

Read this chapter and find out.

Men and women, all in all, behave just like our basic sexual elements. If you watch single men on a weekend night they really act very much like sperm—all disorganized, bumping into their friends, swimming in the wrong direction.

"I was first."

"Let me through."

"You're on my tail."

"That's my spot."

We're like the three billion stooges.

But the egg is very cool: "Well, who's it going to be? I can divide. I can wait a month. I'm not swimming anywhere."[*]

---

[*]Jerry Seinfeld. (1993). *SeinLanguage.* New York: Bantam Books, p. 17.

Everyone needs more information about their own body. This is consistent with the sexual health perspective described in Chapter 1. The purpose of this chapter is to provide basic information about the structure and functions of the parts of the body that are involved in sexuality and reproduction. In this way, you will be in a better position to identify the myths and misinformation about breast and genital size and shape that are so prevalent in the media and can lead people to have a poor genital self-image. Some readers may anticipate that this will be a boring exercise. Everyone, after all, knows what a penis is and what a vagina is. But even today, we find some bright college and university students who think a woman's urine passes out through her vagina. And how many of you know what the epididymis and the seminiferous tubules are? Even if you know, keep reading. You may find out a few interesting things that you were not aware of.

LO1

Genital Self-Image

You may have heard of body image (how we feel about our bodies), but have you thought about how people feel about their genitals? Our **genital self-image** is our attitudes and feelings about our genitals. Research has shown that although on average the genital self-image of most people is positive, some people see their own genitals quite negatively, and many more have mixed feelings about their genitals (Berman et al., 2003; Fudge & Byers, 2016; Morrison et al., 2006). People's feelings about their genitals may be affected by whether they perceive that their genitals fit with general cultural norms (too big, too small), their sexual experiences (e.g., child sexual abuse), and medical conditions

genital self-image: Our attitudes and feelings toward our genitals.

(such as genital surgery). For example, an Alberta study found that men who viewed pornography on the Internet had more negative feelings about their genitals (Morrison et al., 2006). This may be because they came to see their penises as "too small" after viewing the very large penises of men on the Internet. Having a negative genital self-image may negatively affect men's and women's sexual well-being. Women with a more negative genital self-image are more self-conscious during sexual activity and report lower sexual self-esteem and sexual satisfaction, as well as more sexual problems (Herbenick & Reece, 2010; Schick et al., 2010). Similarly, men who are dissatisfied with the size of their penis are less likely to undress in front of their partner and more likely to hide their penis during sexual activity (Lever, Frederick, & Peplau, 2006).

Perhaps as a result, some people with poor genital body image are choosing to undergo genital cosmetic surgery. For example, vulval surgery is the fastest-growing trend in cosmetic surgery (Laliberté, 2006). Women choose to have this surgery because they believe that it will make their vulva more beautiful and erotic. So-called *vaginal enhancement surgery* includes vaginoplasty (tightening of the vagina), hoodectomy (removing the clitoral hood), labia minora reduction, labia majora remodelling, and pubis tuck (removing excess skin above the pubic area to elevate the pubis). Most popular among the patients of one Toronto plastic surgeon and costing thousands of dollars is the "Toronto Trim," which involves reduction of the labia and clitoral hood (Laliberté, 2006). Note that even though surgeons sometimes talk about creating "designer vaginas," this is a misnomer since the surgery is to the vulva (external genitals) not to the vagina (an internal organ). Similarly, some Canadian men are undergoing penis enlargement surgery because they believe (often incorrectly) that their partners would be more satisfied if they had a larger penis. Such surgery results in cosmetic penis enlargement, not actual penis enlargement.

Why is genital cosmetic surgery so controversial? First, men and women are opting for genital surgery because they feel that they are defective in some way. Yet there is wide variation in genital appearance. Most individuals undergoing surgery feel insecure about their genital appearance even though they have genitals that are perfectly normal. They feel that their genitals do not match the "cultural ideal" (Tiefer, 2008). Second, marketing of genital surgery (and there has been a great deal of marketing) promises better sex and fails to mention the potential risks and complications, such as infection, altered sensation, pain, adhesions, and scarring (American Congress of Obstetricians and Gynecologists [ACOG], 2007). Yet there is no evidence that this kind of surgery results in sexual enhancement or that these procedures are safe (ACOG, 2007; Tiefer, 2008).

Although not specifically related to poor genital self-image, some people seek to enhance the appearance of their genitals and sexual pleasure by getting a genital piercing. People seeking genital piercing should make themselves aware of the possible complications. If they choose to go ahead, they should ensure that the piercing is done by a trained professional under sterile conditions to avoid infections.

LO2

Female Sexual Organs

The female sexual organs can be classified into two categories: the *external organs* and the *internal organs*.

External Organs

The external genitals of the female consist of the clitoris, the mons pubis, the inner lips, the outer lips, and the vaginal opening (see Figure 4.1). Collectively, they are known as the **vulva** (*crotch;* other terms, such as *cunt* and *pussy* may refer either to the vulva or to the vagina, and some ethnic groups use *cock* for the vulva—slang, alas, is not as precise as scientific language).[1] Vulva is a wonderful term but, unfortunately, it tends to be underused—the term, that is. The appearance of the vulva varies greatly from one woman to another (see Figure 4.2).

The Clitoris

The **clitoris** is a sensitive organ that is exceptionally important in female sexual response (Figure 4.3). It consists of the *tip,* a knob of tissue situated externally in front of the vaginal opening; the *urethral opening,* a

[1] For a discussion of slang terms for female and male genitals, see Braun and Kitzinger (2001).

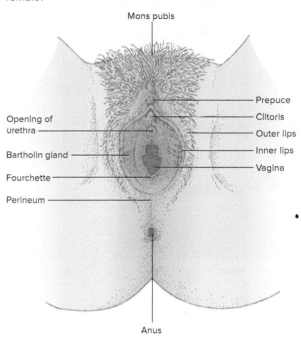

Figure 4.1   The vulva: The external genitals of the female.

Mons pubis

Opening of urethra

Bartholin gland

Fourchette

Perineum

Prepuce

Clitoris

Outer lips

Inner lips

Vagina

Anus

shaft consisting of two corpora cavernosa (spongy bodies similar to those in the male's penis) that extends perhaps 2.5 cm (1 in.) into the body; and two crura, longer spongy bodies that lie deep in the body and run from the tip of the clitoris to either side of the vagina, under the major lips (Clemente, 1987). Some refer to the entire structure as having a wishbone shape. Close to the crura are the vestibular bulbs, which will be discussed in the section on internal organs.

As discussed in Chapter 5, female sexual organs and male sexual organs develop from similar tissue before birth; thus we can speak of the organs of one gender as being homologous (in the sense of developing from the same source) to the organs of the other gender. The female's clitoris is homologous to the male's penis; that is, both develop from the same embryonic tissue. The clitoris and the penis are similar in several ways. They both have corpora cavernosa, they vary in size from one person to the next, and they are erectile because their internal structures contains corpora cavernosa that fill with blood. The corpora cavernosa and the mechanism of erection will be considered in more detail in the discussion of the male sexual organs. The clitoris has a rich supply of nerve endings, making it very sensitive to stroking. Most women find it to be more sensitive to erotic stimulation than any other part of the body.

The clitoris is unique in that it is the only part of the sexual anatomy with no known

vulva (VULL-vuh): The collective term for the external genitals of the female.

clitoris (KLIT-or-is): A highly sensitive sexual organ in the female; the glans is found in front of the vaginal entrance and the rest of the clitoris extends deeper into the body.

Figure 4.2   Genital diversity: The shape of the vulva varies widely from one woman to the next.

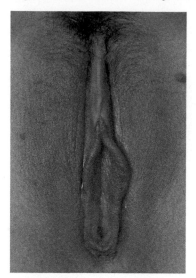 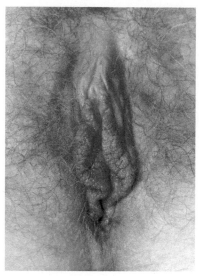 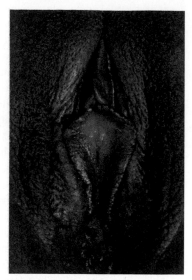

Nick Karras, www.ilovemypetals.com   © H.S. Photos/Alamy   Nick Karras, www.ilovemypetals.com

reproductive function. All the other sexual organs serve sexual and reproductive functions. For example, not only is the vagina used for sexual intercourse, but it also receives the sperm and serves as the passageway through which the baby travels during childbirth. The penis not only produces sexual arousal and pleasure but also is responsible for ejaculation and impregnation. The clitoris clearly has an important function in producing sexual arousal. Unlike the other sexual organs, however, it appears to have no direct function in reproduction. (See A Sexually Diverse World for a discussion on clitoridectomy and other ritualized genital cutting of young girls.)

The Mons

Other parts of the vulva are the mons pubis, the inner lips, and the outer lips. The **mons pubis** (also called the *mons* or the *mons veneris,* for "mountain of Venus") is the rounded, fatty pad of tissue, covered with pubic hair, at the front of the body. It lies on top of the pubic bones.

The Labia

The **outer lips** (or *labia majora,* for "major lips") are rounded pads of fatty tissue lying along both sides of the vaginal opening; they are covered with pubic hair. The **inner lips** (or *labia minora,* for "minor lips") are two hairless folds of skin lying between the outer lips and running right along the edge of the vaginal opening. Sometimes they are folded over, concealing the vaginal opening until they are spread apart. The inner lips extend forward and come together in front, forming the clitoral hood. The inner and outer lips are well supplied with nerve endings and thus are also important in sexual stimulation and arousal.

Speaking of pubic hair, people are giving it a lot of attention these days. Some women trim theirs, and others remove some or all of it, using methods ranging from shaving to waxing. In one study, 60 percent of Australian undergraduate women reported that they removed some of their pubic hair, and 48 percent said they removed most or all of it (Tiggemann & Hodgson, 2008). The women gave a number of reasons for removing pubic hair, including feeling cleaner, feeling attractive, feeling sexy, and making the sexual experience better. Some experts attribute increases in pubic hair removal to increased access to pornography on the Internet (Ramsey et al., 2009). Female porn stars invariably have some form of pubic hair removal, and they therefore show women what they should look like, in addition to teaching men what to expect from women. Many women remove their pubic hair because they believe that this is expected of them by their male partners. Men, too, both gay and straight, are increasingly likely to remove pubic hair (Martins, Tiggemann, & Churchett, 2008).

A pair of small glands, the **Bartholin glands**, lie just inside the inner lips (refer back to Figure 4.1). Their function is unknown, and they are of interest only because they sometimes become infected.[2]

mons pubis (PYOO-bis): The fatty pad of tissue under the pubic hair.
outer lips: Rounded pads of fatty tissue lying on either side of the vaginal entrance.
inner lips: Thin folds of skin lying on either side of the vaginal entrance.
Bartholin glands: Two tiny glands located on either side of the vaginal entrance.

---

[2] And there is a limerick about them: There was a young man from Calcutta / Who was heard in his beard to mutter, / "If her Bartholin glands / Don't respond to my hands, / I'm afraid I shall have to use butter." Actually, there is a biological fallacy in the limerick. Can you spot it? If not, see Chapter 9.

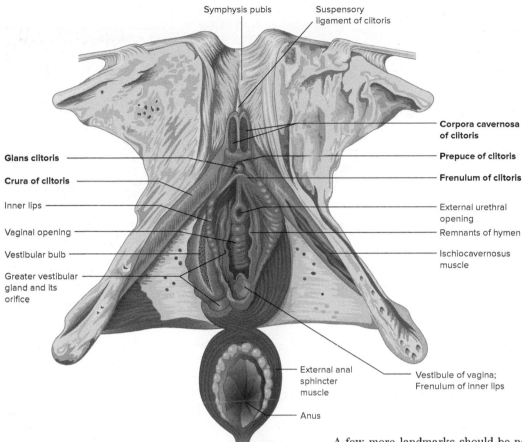

Symphysis pubis

Suspensory ligament of clitoris

Corpora cavernosa of clitoris

Glans clitoris

Prepuce of clitoris

Crura of clitoris

Frenulum of clitoris

Inner lips

External urethral opening

Vaginal opening

Remnants of hymen

Vestibular bulb

Ischiocavernosus muscle

Greater vestibular gland and its orifice

External anal sphincter muscle

Vestibule of vagina; Frenulum of inner lips

Anus

(a)

(b)

Figure 4.3 *(a)* The structure of the clitoris and *(b)* an MRI scan of the same region.

From H. O'Connell. "Clitoral Anatomy In Nulliparous, Healthy, Premenopausal Volunteers Using Unenhanced Magnetic Resonance Imaging," *Journal of Urology, 173,* 2060–2063 (June 2005).

A few more landmarks should be noted (see Figure 4.1). The place where the inner lips come together behind the vaginal opening is called the *fourchette.* The area of skin between the vaginal opening and the anus is called the **perineum**. The vaginal opening itself is sometimes called the **introitus**. Notice also that the urinary opening lies about midway between the clitoris and the vaginal opening. Thus urine does not pass out through the clitoris (as might be expected from analogy with the male) or through the vagina, but instead through a separate pathway, the *urethra,* with a separate opening.

The Vulvar Vestibule

The area enclosed by the inner lips is called the **vestibule** ("entranceway"). It contains the openings to the vagina and the urethra. This area is highly sensitive to pleasurable stimulation because it is well supplied with nerve endings. However, some women develop vulvar vestibulitis, in which the vestibule gets extremely sensitive and red such that any touch of the area around the vaginal opening elicits moderate to severe pain. For women with vulvar vestibulitis, pain can result from genital touching during sexual activity and vaginal penetration, but also from biking, exercise, tight clothing, and tampon insertion. Sexual pain disorders are discussed in Chapter 18.

> **perineum (pair-ih-NEE-um):** The skin between the vaginal entrance and the anus.
> **introitus:** The vaginal entrance.
> **vestibule:** Area of the vulva enclosed by the inner lips.

A Sexually Diverse World

What Is Female Genital Cutting? L03

A worldwide sexual health controversy rages over female genital cutting (FGC, also known as female genital mutilation, or FGM). FGC is practised in many African nations as well as in several countries in the Middle East and among Muslim populations in Indonesia and Malaysia. According to the World Health Organization (WHO), 200 million girls and women worldwide have been subjected to these procedures in 30 countries in Africa, the Middle East, and Asia (WHO, 2016). Typically, FGC is performed on girls between infancy and age 15. Often it is performed by a native woman without anaesthetic and under unsanitary conditions.

FGC is practised in several forms, depending on the customs of the particular culture. The simplest is clitoridectomy, the partial or total removal of the clitoris, and sometimes just the prepuce. The WHO classifies this as Type 1. Excision (Type 2) involves the partial or total removal of the clitoris and the inner lips. The most extreme form is infibulation (Type 3), in which the clitoris and all of the inner lips are removed, part of the outer lips are removed, and the raw edges of the outer lips are stitched together to cover the urethral opening and the vaginal entrance, with only a small opening left for the passage of urine and menstrual fluid. Type 4 refers to all other female genital procedures for nonmedical purposes, including nicking or piercing the prepuce, which is favoured by some as preserving the tradition but injuring the body the least. The term *female circumcision* is also used, although its definition is less clear; generally it means the Type 1 procedure.

All these procedures pose health risks, and infibulation creates especially severe problems. Hemorrhaging may occur, leading to shock and even to bleeding to death. Because of unsanitary conditions present during the procedure, tetanus and other infections are risks. The same instrument may be used on multiple girls, so HIV and hepatitis B can be transmitted. A common problem is that the pain of the wound is so severe and the stitching so tight that the girl avoids urinating or cannot urinate properly, leading to urinary tract infections. A tightly infibulated woman can only urinate drop by drop, and

Figure 4.6 Twenty-five African nations practise some form of ritualized genital cutting of young girls as an initiation into womanhood. Clitoridectomy is also practised in Muslim countries outside Africa and was practised in the United States during the Victorian era. Today there is a grassroots movement in Africa to end the practice. The sign says, "let's stop excision!"

© Jamie Carstairs/Alamy

her menstrual period may take ten days and be extremely painful. Women who have undergone FGC are at higher risk of infections such as herpes and bacterial vaginosis.

The sexual and reproductive health consequences are no less severe. Infibulation is an effective method for ensuring virginity until marriage, but on the wedding night the man must force an opening through stitching and scar tissue. It is painful and may take days; a midwife may be called to cut open the tissue. Orgasm would be only a remote possibility for a woman whose clitoris has been removed. Infibulated women have a substantial risk of complications during childbirth and of newborn deaths (WHO, 2016).

FGC has declined in some nations, such as Egypt, Burkino Faso, Kenya, and Liberia (UNICEF, 2016). In 2016, Nigeria banned FGC. Nonetheless, it persists in many places. If the procedures are so harmful, why do people continue them? Why do girls submit to them, and even ask for them, and why do their parents permit or even encourage it? The answer lies in the complex and powerful interplay of culture and gender. Infibulation indicates not only virginity but also a woman's loyalty to her culture and its traditions, a particularly sensitive issue for people long dominated by European colonizers. A woman who is not infibulated is not marriageable in these cultures, in which marriage is the only acceptable way of life for an adult woman. When those are the rules of the game, it is less surprising that girls submit or even want to be circumcised and that their parents require them to do it. Some communities may also hold certain beliefs that make these procedures seem necessary. Some Muslims mistakenly believe that it is required by their faith, although it is not mentioned in the Quran. Research also shows that the more empowered women are, the less they favour FGC (Afifi, 2009).

FGC raises a number of dilemmas for Canadians. As a multicultural country, we generally encourage the approach of cultural relativism, an openness to and appreciation of the customs of other cultures. If we apply standards of cultural relativism, we should say, "Great, if that's what those people want." But should cultural relativism have limits? Can one oppose certain practices that pose well-documented, serious health risks, even though they are popular in the culture? Medical personnel in Canada face difficult dilemmas. Immigrant women whose daughters are born in Canada may request that a physician perform an excision, knowing that the procedure will be far safer if done by a physician in a hospital. However, the World Health Organization and the organizations that regulate the practice of medicine in Canada have condemned the practice of FGC. Both the parents who arrange FGC and the person who performs it may be charged with sexual assault under Canadian law. Recent immigrants to Canada from countries that practise FGC may feel torn between loyalty to their native culture and the realities of Canadian law in deciding about FGC for their daughters. In addition, many immigrant women from these areas who were subjected to FGC before arriving in Canada may have physicians who are not knowledgeable about the practice. Although physicians may cut open an infibulated woman to permit childbirth, they are not allowed to reconstruct the infibulation following childbirth, regardless of the wishes of the woman.

On a more hopeful note, a grassroots movement of women that is dedicated to eliminating these practices has sprung up in a number of African nations, including Kenya, Gambia, Senegal, Sudan, and Somalia (see Figure 4.6). And some surgeons in Western nations are developing reconstructive surgeries to restore anatomy and function to women who experienced FGC; scar tissue is removed and the clitoris is uncovered. These procedures seem to be effective in reducing pain and restoring pleasure (Foldès, Cuzin, & Andro, 2012).

Several points help to put matters into perspective. First, only about 15 percent of cultures that practise FGC do the severe form, infibulation. The remaining cultures practise the milder forms ranging from a slit in the prepuce to clitoridectomy. Second, far more cultures practise male genital modifications than female genital modifications. An example is Canada where about a third of infant boys are circumcised, but FGC is extremely rare. However, there are important differences between the reasons for male circumcision and FGC.

Third, as discussed in this chapter, a growing trend in Canada advocates genital cosmetic surgeries, such as removal of the inner or outer lips, because people believe that the vulva is more beautiful and erotic that way (Miklos & Moore, 2008). More broadly, genital plastic surgery has become widely available and is raising controversies in the medical community (Liao & Creighton, 2010). Although this is not as extreme as FGC, the message about female genitals is similar: Women need to undergo a surgical procedure to make the appearance of their vulva more acceptable. How should a surgeon respond to requests for genital cosmetic surgery? Would education and psychotherapy achieve a better result? And why are these genital plastic surgeries legal in Western nations where FGC is prohibited (Johnsdotter & Essén, 2010)?

Sources: Afifi, 2009; Almroth, Almroth-Berggren, & Hassancin, 2001; Chalmers & Hashi, 2000; Gruenbaum, 2000; Laliberté, 2006; Leonard, 2000; Morrison et al., 2001; Shell-Duncan, 2008; Tag-Eldin et al., 2008; Yoder, Abderrahim, & Zhuzhuni, 2004.

Self-Knowledge

One important difference between the male sex organs and the female sex organs—and a difference that has some important psychological consequences—is that the female's external genitals are much less visible than the male's. A male can view his external genitals directly either by looking down at them or by looking into a mirror while naked. Either of these two strategies for the female, however, will result at best in a view of the mons. The clitoris, the inner and outer lips, and the vaginal opening remain hidden. Indeed, many women have never taken a direct look at their own vulva. This obstacle can be overcome by the simple method of using a mirror. The genitals can be viewed either by putting a mirror on the floor and sitting in front of it or by standing up and putting one foot on the edge of a chair, bed, or something similar and holding the mirror up near the genitals (see Figure 4.4). We recommend that all women use a mirror to identify on their own bodies all the parts shown in Figure 4.1.

The Hymen

The **hymen** (*cherry, maidenhead*) is a thin membrane, which, if present, partially covers the vaginal opening. The hymen may be one of a number of different types (see Figure 4.5), although it generally has some openings in it; otherwise the menstrual flow would not be able to pass.[3] For many women, the hymen is broken or stretched at the time of first intercourse as the penis moves into the vagina. This may cause bleeding and possibly some pain. Typically, though, it is an untraumatic occurrence and goes unnoticed in the excitement of the moment. For a woman who is very concerned about her hymen and what will happen to it at first coitus, there are two possible approaches. A physician can cut the hymen neatly

hymen (HYE-men): A thin membrane that may partially cover the vaginal entrance.

Figure 4.4   Body education: The mirror exercise lets women see their own genitals.

© Thomas Michael Corcoran/PhotoEdit

so that it will not tear at the time of first intercourse, or the woman herself can stretch it by repeatedly inserting a finger into the vagina and pressing on it.

The hymen, and its destruction at first intercourse, has captured the interest of people in many cultures. In Europe during the Middle Ages, the lord might claim the right to "deflower" a peasant bride on her wedding night before passing her on to her husband (the practice is called *droit du seigneur* in French for "right of the lord," and *jus primae noctis* in Latin for "law of the first night"). The hymen has been taken as evidence of virginity. Thus, bleeding on the wedding night was proof that the bride had been delivered intact to the groom; the parading of the bloody bed sheets on the wedding night,

---

[3] The rare condition in which the hymen is a tough tissue with no opening is called imperforate hymen and can be corrected with fairly simple surgery.

Figure 4.5   There are several types of hymens.

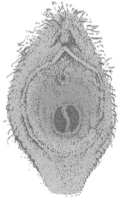

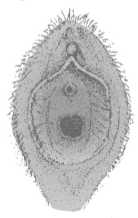

Annular hymen   Septate hymen   Cribriform hymen   Imperforate hymen

a custom of the Kurds of the Middle East, is one ritual based on this belief.

Such practices rest on the assumption that a woman without a hymen is not a virgin. However, we now know that this is not true. Some girls are simply born without a hymen, and others may tear it in active sports, such as horseback riding. Unfortunately, this means that in cultures that prize female virginity, some women have been humiliated unjustly for their lack of a hymen. Some women who do not have a hymen (because they engaged in sexual intercourse or for some other reason)

are choosing to have plastic surgery to have their hymen "restored," called *hymenoplasty*. After this procedure the woman will then have minor bleeding with her next intercourse, "proving" that she is a virgin.

Internal Organs

The internal sex organs of the female consist of the vagina, the vestibular bulbs, the Skene's glands, the uterus, a pair of ovaries, and a pair of fallopian tubes (see Figure 4.7).

Figure 4.7 Internal sexual and reproductive organs of the female from a side view (top) and a front view.

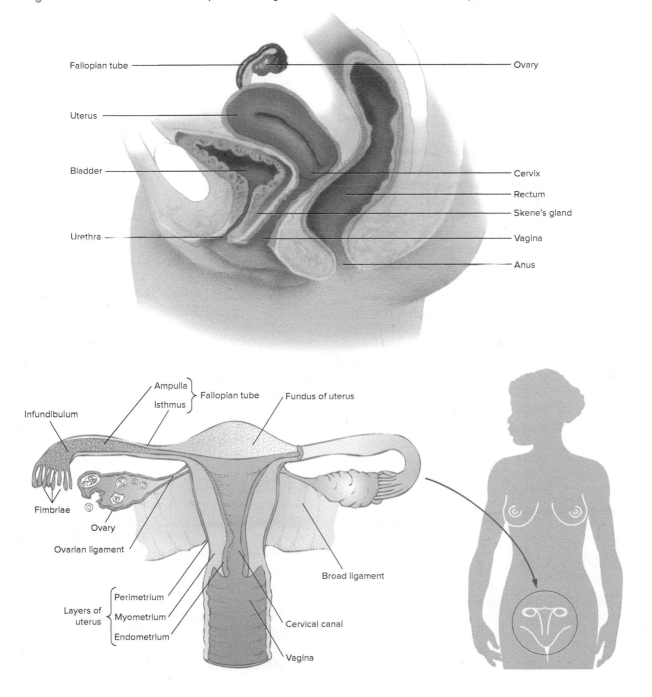

Figure 4.8   Appearance of the vulva of a woman who is a virgin (see Figure 4.5 for other appearances); a woman who has had intercourse but has not had a baby (nulliparous); and a woman who has (parous) and has delivered it vaginally.

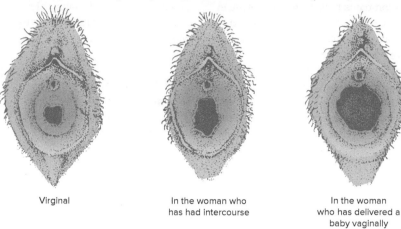

Virginal

In the woman who
has had intercourse

In the woman
who has delivered a
baby vaginally

The Vagina

The **vagina** is the tube-shaped organ into which the penis is inserted during coitus; it also receives the ejaculate. Because it is the passageway through which a baby travels during birth, it is sometimes also called the *birth canal*. In the resting or unaroused state, the vagina is about 8 to 10 cm (3 to 4 in.) long and tilts slightly backward from the bottom to the top. At the bottom it ends in the vaginal opening, or *introitus*. At the top it connects with the *cervix* (the lower part of the uterus). The vagina is a very flexible organ that works somewhat like a balloon. In the resting state, its walls lie against each other like the sides of an uninflated balloon; during arousal it expands like an inflated balloon, allowing space to accommodate the penis.

> **Do women ejaculate?**

The walls of the vagina have three layers. The inner layer, the vaginal *mucosa*, is a mucous membrane similar to the inner lining of the mouth. The middle layer is muscular, and the outer layer forms a covering. The walls of the vagina are extremely elastic and are capable of expanding to the extent necessary during intercourse and childbirth, although with age they become thinner and less flexible.

The nerve supply of the vagina is mostly in the lower one-third, near the introitus. That part is sensitive to erotic stimulation. The inner two-thirds of the vagina contains almost no nerve endings and is therefore relatively insensitive except to feelings of deep pressure. Some women have a spot on the front wall of the vagina that is more sensitive than the rest of the vagina, but even it is not nearly so sensitive as the inner lips, outer lips, or clitoris (Schultz et al., 1989). This spot is referred to by some as the G-spot (see Chapter 9).

vagina (vuh-JINE-uh): The tube-shaped organ in the female into which the penis is inserted during coitus and through which a baby passes during birth.
pubococcygeus (pyoo-bo-cox-ih-GEE-us) muscle: A muscle around the vaginal entrance.
vestibular bulbs: Erectile tissue running under the inner lips and Skene's gland.
Skene's gland: The female prostate; also called the paraurethral gland.

The number of slang terms for the vagina (e.g., *beaver, cunt*) and the frequency of their usage testify to its power of fascination across the ages. One concern has been with size: whether some vaginas are too small or too large. As noted earlier, though, the vagina is highly elastic and expandable. Thus, at least in principle, any penis can fit into any vagina. The penis is, after all, not nearly so large as a baby's head, which manages to fit through the vagina. The part of the vagina that is most responsible for a man's sensation, that is "tight," "too tight," or "too loose," is the introitus. One of the things that can stretch the introitus is childbirth; indeed, there is a considerable difference in the appearance of the vulva of a woman who has never had a baby (*nulliparous*) and the vulva of a woman who has (*parous*) (see Figure 4.8).

Surrounding the vagina, the urethra, and the anus is a set of muscles called the *pelvic floor muscles*. One of these muscles, the **pubococcygeus muscle**, is particularly important. It may be stretched during childbirth, or it may simply be weak. However, it can be strengthened through exercises in which the woman contracts the muscle ten times in a row, six times a day, and this is recommended by sex therapists as well as by many popular sex manuals. Details of how to do these exercises are provided in Chapter 18.

The Vestibular Bulbs

The **vestibular bulbs** (or bulbs of the clitoris) are two organs about the size and shape of a pea pod (refer to back Figure 4.3). They lie on either side of the vaginal wall, near the entrance, under the inner lips (O'Connell & DeLancey, 2005). They are erectile tissue and lie close to the crura of the clitoris.

The Skene's Gland, or Female Prostate

The **Skene's gland**, or *female prostate* (also called the *paraurethral gland*), lies between the wall of the urethra and the wall of the vagina (Zaviačič et al., 2000b).

Its ducts empty into the urethra, but it can be felt on the front wall of the vagina. Although controversial in the past, the evidence indicates that, in some women, it secretes fluid that is biochemically similar to male prostate fluid. Many women find it to be a region of special erotic sensitivity on the wall of the vagina. The size of the female prostate varies considerably from one woman to the next, as does the amount of its secretions. Some women experience no secretion, whereas others have an actual ejaculation when they orgasm. This is the organ dubbed the G-spot, which is responsible for female ejaculation, discussed in Chapter 9.

The Uterus

The **uterus** (womb) is about the size and shape of an upside-down pear. It is usually tilted forward and is held in place by ligaments. The narrow lower third, called the *cervix*, opens into the vagina. The top is the *fundus*, the main part the *body*. The entrance to the uterus through the cervix is very narrow, about the diameter of a drinking straw, and is called the *os* (or cervical canal). The major function of the uterus is to hold and nourish a developing fetus.

The uterus, like the vagina, consists of three layers. The inner layer, or *endometrium*, is richly supplied with glands and blood vessels. Its state varies according to the age of the woman and the phase of the menstrual cycle. It is the endometrium that is sloughed off at menstruation and creates the menstrual discharge. The middle layer, the *myometrium*, is muscular. The muscles are very strong, creating the powerful contractions of labour and orgasm, and also highly elastic, capable of stretching to accommodate a nine-month-old fetus. The outer layer—the *perimetrium*—forms the external cover of the uterus.

The Fallopian Tubes

Extending out from the sides of the upper end of the uterus are the **fallopian tubes**, also called the *oviducts* ("egg ducts") (refer back to Figure 4.7). The fallopian tubes are extremely narrow (0.2 to 0.5 mm) and are lined with hairlike projections called *cilia*. The fallopian tubes are the pathway by which the egg travels toward the uterus and the sperm reach the egg; it is the fallopian tubes that are cut when a woman has her "tubes tied" (called a *tubal ligation*) (see Chapter 7). Fertilization of the egg typically occurs in the infundibulum, the section of the tube closest to the ovary; the fertilized egg then travels the rest of the way through the tube to the uterus. The infundibulum curves around toward the ovary; at its end are numerous fingerlike projections called *fimbriae*, which extend toward the ovary.

The Ovaries

The **ovaries** are two organs about the size and shape of unshelled almonds; they lie on either side of the uterus.

The ovaries have two important functions; they produce eggs (*ova*), and they manufacture the sex hormones *estrogen* and *progesterone*.

Each ovary contains numerous follicles. A follicle is a capsule that surrounds an egg (not to be confused with hair follicles, which are quite different). A female is born with an estimated 1 million immature eggs (Federman, 2006). Beginning at puberty, one or several of the follicles mature during each menstrual cycle. When the egg has matured, the follicle bursts open and releases the egg. The ovaries do not actually connect directly to the fallopian tubes. Rather, the egg is released into the body cavity and reaches the tube by moving toward the fimbriae. If the egg does not reach the tube, it may be fertilized outside the tube, resulting in an abdominal pregnancy (see the discussion of ectopic pregnancy in Chapter 6). Cases have been recorded of women who, although they were missing one ovary and the opposite fallopian tube, nonetheless became pregnant. Apparently, in such cases the egg migrates to the tube on the opposite side.

LO4 The Breasts

Although they are secondary sex characteristics and not actually sex organs, the breasts deserve discussion here because of their erotic and reproductive significance. The breast consists of about 15 or 20 clusters of mammary glands, each with a separate opening to the nipple, and fatty and fibrous tissue that surrounds the clusters of glands (see Figure 4.9). The nipple, into which the milk

> **uterus (YOO-tur-us):** The organ in the female in which the fetus develops.
> **fallopian (fuh-LOW-pee-un) tubes:** The tubes extending from the uterus to the ovaries; also called the oviducts.
> **ovaries:** Two organs in the female that produce eggs and sex hormones.

Figure 4.9   The internal structure of the breast.

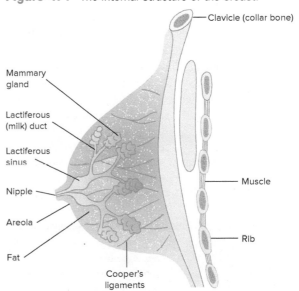

Labels: Clavicle (collar bone), Mammary gland, Lactiferous (milk) duct, Lactiferous sinus, Nipple, Areola, Fat, Cooper's ligaments, Muscle, Rib

ducts open, is at the tip of the breast. It is richly supplied with nerve endings and therefore very important in erotic stimulation for many women. The nipple consists of smooth muscle fibres; when they contract, the nipple becomes erect. The darker area surrounding the nipple is called the *areola*. There is wide variation among women in the size and shape of the breasts (see Figure 4.10). One thing is fairly consistent, though: Many women are not satisfied with the size of their breasts. Many women think they are either too small, too large, or too droopy (Frederick, Peplau, & Lever, 2008). It is good to

Figure 4.10   Breasts come in many sizes and shapes.

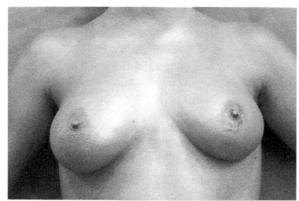

(a) © Jessica Abad de Gail/AGE Fotostock

(b) © Chris Rout/Alamy Stock Photo

(c) © Chris Rout / Alamy Stock Photo

remember that there are the same number of nerve endings in small breasts as in large breasts. It follows that small breasts are actually more erotically sensitive per square centimetre than are large ones.

Breasts may take on enormous psychological meaning; they can be a symbol of femininity or a means of attracting men. Ours is a very breast-oriented culture. Many Canadian men develop a powerful interest in, and attraction to, women's breasts. The social definition of beauty is a compelling force; many women strive to meet the ideal and a few overadapt (Sansone & Sansone, 2007). As a result, breast augmentation surgery has increased steadily, while other women undergo breast reduction surgery, in both cases to meet a socially defined standard of beauty. Breast reduction is also done for medical reasons—for example, to reduce back pain.

L05

Male Sexual Organs

Externally, the most noticeable parts of the male sexual anatomy are the penis and the scrotum, or scrotal sac, which contains the testes (see Figure 4.11).

External Organs

The Penis

The penis (*phallus, prick, cock, johnson,* and many other slang terms too numerous to list) serves important functions in sexual pleasure, reproduction, and elimination of body wastes by urination. It is a tubular organ with an end or tip called the glans. The opening at the end of the glans is the *meatus,* or *urethral opening,* through which urine and semen pass. The main part of the penis is called the *shaft.* The raised ridge at the edge of the glans is called the *corona* ("crown"), or *coronal ridge.* While the entire penis is sensitive to sexual stimulation, the corona and the rest of the glans are the most sexually excitable regions of the male anatomy.

Internally, the penis contains three long cylinders of spongy tissue running parallel to the *urethra,* which is the pathway through which semen and urine pass. The two spongy bodies lying on top are called the **corpora cavernosa**, and the single one lying on the bottom of the penis is called the **corpus spongiosum** (the urethra runs through the middle of it). During erection, the corpus spongiosum can be seen as a raised column on the lower side of the penis. As the names suggest, these bodies are tissues filled with many spaces and cavities, much like a sponge. They are richly supplied with blood vessels and nerves. In the flaccid (unaroused, not erect) state, they contain little blood. *Erection,* or *tumescence,* occurs when they become filled with blood (engorged) and expand, making the penis stiff.[4]

Figure 4.11 The male sexual and reproductive organs from a side view.

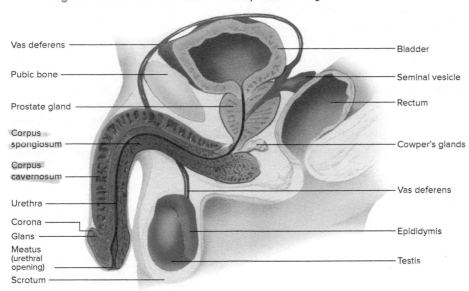

Vas deferens
Pubic bone
Prostate gland
Corpus spongiosum
Corpus cavernosum
Urethra
Corona
Glans
Meatus (urethral opening)
Scrotum

Bladder
Seminal vesicle
Rectum
Cowper's glands
Vas deferens
Epididymis
Testis

Erection is purely a vascular phenomenon; that is, it results entirely from blood flow. It is commonly believed that the penis of the human male contains a bone. This is not true, although in some other species—for example, dogs—the penis does contain a bone, which aids in intromission (insertion of the penis into the vagina). In human males, however, there is none.

The skin of the penis usually is hairless and is arranged in loose folds, permitting expansion during erection. The **foreskin**, or *prepuce*, is an additional layer of skin that forms a sheathlike covering over the glans; it may be present or absent in the adult male, depending on whether he has been circumcised (see Figure 4.12). Under the foreskin are small glands (Tyson's glands) that produce a substance called *smegma*, which is cheesy in texture. The foreskin is easily retractable,[5] and its retraction is extremely important for proper hygiene. If it is not pulled back and the glans washed thoroughly, the smegma may accumulate, producing an unpleasant smell.

The penis has been the focus of quite a lot of attention throughout history. Not surprisingly, the male genitals were often seen as symbols of fertility and thus were worshipped for their powers of procreativity. In ancient Greece, phallic worship centred on Priapus, the son of Aphrodite (the goddess of love) and Dionysus (the god of fertility and wine). Priapus is usually represented as a grinning man with a huge penis.

In contemporary Canadian society, phallic concern often focuses on the size of the penis. Internet users are bombarded with e-mail spam that promises products to increase penis size. It is commonly believed that a man with a large penis is a better lover and can satisfy a woman more than can a man with a small penis. Masters and Johnson (1966), however, found that this is not true. While the length of the penis varies considerably from one man to the next—the average penis is generally somewhere between 6 cm (2 in.) and 10 cm (4 in.) in length when flaccid (not erect) (Shamloul, 2005)—there is a tendency for the small penis to grow more in erection than one that starts out large. As a result, there is little correlation between the length of the penis when flaccid and its length when erect. As the saying has it, "Erection is the great equalizer." The average erect penis is 15 cm (6 in.) long. Further, as noted earlier, the vagina has relatively few nerve endings and is relatively insensitive. Hence, penetration to the far reaches of the vagina by a very long penis is not essential and may not even be noticeable. Many other factors are more important than penis size in giving a woman pleasure (see Chapters 9 and 18).

[4] Normally, after stopping psychological and physical stimulation or orgasms, the man loses his erection (see Chapter 9). Priapism is a painful and potentially harmful medical condition in which the erect penis does not return to its flaccid state within about four hours despite stopping stimulation.

[5] In a rare condition, the foreskin is so tight that it cannot be pulled back; this condition is called *phimosis* and requires correction by circumcision.

penis: The male external sexual organ, which functions both in sexual activity and in urination.
corpora cavernosa: Spongy bodies running the length of the top of the penis.
corpus spongiosum: A spongy body running the length of the underside of the penis.
foreskin: A layer of skin covering the glans or tip of the penis in an uncircumcised male; also called the prepuce.

Figure 4.12 *(a)* A circumcised penis and *(b)* an uncircumcised penis, showing the foreskin.

(a) © John Henderson/Alamy

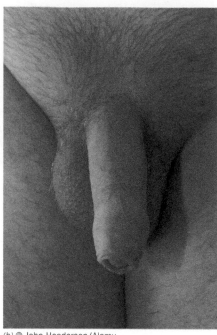

(b) © John Henderson/Alamy

Phallic concern has also included an interest in the variations in the shape of the penis when flaccid and when erect, as reflected in this limerick:

There was a young man of Kent
Whose kirp in the middle was bent.
To save himself trouble
He put it in double,
And instead of coming, he went.

L06 Circumcision

Circumcision refers to the surgical cutting away or removal of the foreskin. Circumcision is practised in many parts of the world. According to a report by the World Health Organization (2007), globally 30 percent of males over the age of 15 are circumcised. However, the rates vary considerably from country to country. For example, almost all men are circumcised in the countries in the Middle East, Central Asia, and Muslim Asian countries, as well as in some African countries. In contrast, circumcision rates are very low (less than 20 percent) in Central and South America, Europe, and many parts of Asia. In Canada, when parents choose to circumcise their sons, it is usually done within a few days after birth.

Circumcision may be done for cultural and religious reasons. Circumcision has been a part of Jewish religious practice for thousands of years. It symbolizes the covenant between God and the Jewish people and is done on the eighth day after birth,

> **Are there any medical advantages to circumcising baby boys?**

circumcision: Surgical removal of the foreskin of the penis.

according to scriptural teaching (Genesis 17:9–27). Circumcision is also common in Muslim cultures. In some cultures, circumcision is done at puberty as an initiation ritual, or *rite de passage*. The ability of the young boy to stand the pain may be seen as a proof of manhood.

In the 1980s, an anti-circumcision movement began gaining momentum in North America. Its proponents argue that circumcision does not have any health benefits and does entail some health risk and psychological trauma. According to this view, circumcision is nothing more than cruel mutilation. (For a statement of this anti-circumcision position, see Wallerstein, 1980.) In 1996, the Canadian Paediatric Society reviewed the literature and recommended against routine circumcision of newborn boys. Reflecting this advice from Canadian physicians, the controversy about circumcision, and the fact that circumcision is not usually covered by provincial health insurance plans, the rate of infant circumcision in Canada has been decreasing. Currently, 32 percent of infant boys are circumcised, although the rate varies considerably across provinces and territories (Public Health Agency of Canada [PHAC], 2009a).

In 2015, the Canadian Paediatric Society reviewed the literature on circumcision again. They concluded that the risks and benefits of routine circumcision of newborn boys were fairly equal (Sorokan, Finlay, & Jefferies, 2015). Therefore, they recommended against routine circumcision and instead suggested parents be provided with the most up-to-date, unbiased, and personalized information so they could make an informed decision for their own baby.

What are the benefits to circumcision? One is that uncircumcised male babies are ten times more likely to get urinary tract infections than are circumcised babies; however, the risk of urinary tract infections is still low. Another is that there is growing evidence that uncircumcised men have a higher risk of infection with HIV, the virus that causes AIDS, and their partners have a higher risk of cervical cancer (Sorokan et al., 2015). It is thought that the foreskin can harbour HIV and other viruses. For example, in a five-nation study including Spain, Colombia, Brazil, Thailand, and the Philippines, circumcised men showed lower rates of HPV infection (Catellsagué et al., 2002). HPV is the virus that causes genital warts and predisposes women to cervical cancer. In this same study, the monogamous female partners of the circumcised men had lower rates of cervical cancer. Circumcision also reduces the risk of prostate cancer (Wright, Lin, & Stanford, 2012). In Kenya and Uganda, adult men who wanted to be circumcised were randomly assigned to either be circumcised immediately or in two years (Bailey et al., 2007; Roehr, 2007). The circumcised men had half the rate of HIV infection compared with the men waiting to be circumcised. Therefore, the trial was halted early over ethical concerns about withholding circumcision from those who wanted it.

Other arguments have focused on whether the circumcised or the uncircumcised man receives more pleasure from sexual intercourse. Two groups of Canadian researchers have found no differences in how sensitive the penises of circumcised and uncircumcised men were to touch (Bossio, Pukall, & Steele, 2016; Payne et al., 2007).

Other forms of male genital cutting are done throughout the world. In fact, male genital cutting is done in more cultures than is female genital cutting (Gregersen, 1996). A common form across most of Polynesia is **supercision** (also known as *superincision*), which involves making a slit on the length of the foreskin on the top, with the foreskin otherwise remaining intact (Gregersen, 1996). With **subincision**, which is common in some tribes in central Australia, a slit is made on the lower side of the penis along its entire length and to the depth of the urethra. Urine is then excreted at the base rather than at the tip of the penis.

The Scrotum

The other major external genital structure in the male is the **scrotum**; this is a loose pouch of skin, lightly covered with hair, which contains the **testes** (*balls* or *nuts* in slang).[6] The testes themselves are considered part of the internal genitals.

Internal Organs

The testes are the *gonads*, or reproductive glands, of the male, which are analogous to the female's ovaries. Like the ovaries, they serve two major functions: to manufacture germ cells (*sperm*) and to manufacture sex hormones, in particular *testosterone*. Both testes are about the same size, although the left one usually hangs lower than the right one.

In the internal structure of the testes, two parts are important: the *seminiferous tubules* and the *interstitial cells* (see Figure 4.13). The **seminiferous tubules** carry out the important function of manufacturing and storing sperm, a process called *spermatogenesis*. They are a long series of threadlike tubes curled and packed densely into the testes. The testes have about 1000 of these tubules, which, if they were stretched out end to end, would be several hundred metres in length.

The **interstitial cells** carry out the second important function of the testes, the production of testosterone. These cells are found in the connective tissue lying between the seminiferous tubules. The cells lie close to the blood vessels in the testes and pour the hormones they manufacture directly into the blood vessels. Thus, the testes are endocrine (hormone-secreting) glands.

One of the clever tricks that the scrotum and testes can perform, as any male will testify, is to move up close to the body or down away from it. These changes are brought about mainly by changes in temperature (although emotional factors may also produce them). If a man plunges into a cold lake, the scrotum

supercision (superincision): A form of male genital cutting in which a slit is made the length of the foreskin on top.
subincision: A form of male genital cutting in which a slit is made on the lower side of the penis along its entire length.
scrotum (SKROH-tum): The pouch of skin that contains the testes in the male.
testes: The pair of glands in the scrotum that manufacture sperm and sex hormones.
seminiferous (sem-ih-NIFF-ur-us) tubules: Tubes in the testes that manufacture sperm.
interstitial (int-er-STIH-shul) cells: Cells in the testes that manufacture testosterone.

---

[6] This brings to mind another limerick: There once was a pirate named Gates / Who thought he could rhumba on skates. / He slipped on his cutlass / And now he is nutless / And practically useless on dates.

Figure 4.13 Schematic cross-section of the internal structure of a testis.

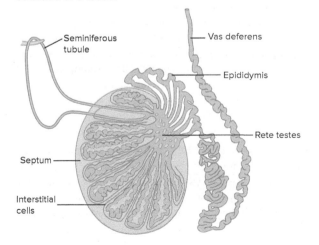

will shrivel and move close to the body.[7] If the man is working in an extremely hot place, the scrotum will hang down and away from the body. This mechanism is important because the testes should remain at a fairly constant temperature, slightly lower than normal body temperature. This constancy of temperature is necessary to protect the sperm, which may be injured by extremes of temperature. Thus, if the air is cold, the testes move closer to the body to maintain warmth, but if the air is too hot, they move away from the body to keep cool. The mechanics of this movement are made possible by the *cremasteric reflex,* named for the cremaster muscle connecting the scrotum to the body wall. Reflex contraction of this muscle pulls the testes up.

Many people believe that taking hot baths, wearing tight athletic supporters, or having a high fever can cause infertility. Indeed, in some countries, men take long, hot baths as a method of contraception. Such a practice has some basis in biological fact, because sperm can be damaged by heat (Paul, Teng, & Saunders, 2008). However, as a method of contraception, this practice has not been particularly effective. On the other hand, men with problems of infertility can sometimes increase the chance of conception by getting out of their tight jockstraps and jockey shorts.

Following initial cell division in the seminiferous tubules, the male germ cells go through several stages of maturation. At the earliest stage, the cell is called a *spermatogonium.* Then it becomes a *spermatocyte* (first primary and then secondary) and then a *spermatid.* Finally, when fully mature, it is a *spermatozoan,* or **sperm.** *Spermatogenesis,* the manufacture of sperm, occurs continuously in adult men. An average ejaculate contains about 200 million sperm (Bang et al., 2005).

A mature sperm is very tiny—about 60 micrometres, or 60/10,000 mm (0.0024 in.), long. A normal human sperm carries 23 chromosomes in the head. These 23 are half the normal number in the other cells of the human body. When the sperm unites with the egg, which also carries 23 chromosomes, the full complement of 46 for the offspring is produced. (See Chapter 6 for a discussion of the sperm's role in conception.)

After the sperm are manufactured in the seminiferous tubules, they proceed into the *rete testes,* a converging network of tubes on the surface of the testis toward the top. The sperm then pass out of the testis and into a single tube, the *epididymis.* The **epididymis** is a long tube (about 6 m, or 20 ft., in length) coiled into a small crescent-shaped region on the top and side of a testis. The sperm are stored in the epididymis, in which they mature, possibly for as long as six weeks.

On ejaculation, the sperm pass from the epididymis into the **vas deferens** (it is the vas that is cut in a vasectomy—see Chapter 7). The vas passes up and out of the scrotum and then follows a peculiar circular path as it loops over the pubic bone, crosses beside the urinary bladder, and then turns downward toward the prostate. As the tube passes through the prostate, it narrows and at this point is called the *ejaculatory duct.* The ejaculatory duct opens into the *urethra,* which has the dual function of conveying sperm and transporting urine; sperm are ejaculated out through the penis via the urethra.

Sperm have little motility of their own while in the epididymis and vas. That is, they are not capable of movement on their own until they mix with the secretions of the prostate (Breton et al., 1996). Up to this point, they are conveyed by the cilia and by contractions of the epididymis and vas.

The **seminal vesicles** are two saclike structures that lie above the prostate, behind the bladder, and in front of the rectum. They produce about 60 percent of the *seminal fluid,* or *ejaculate.* The remaining 40 percent is produced by the prostate (Ndovi et al., 2007). They empty their fluid into the ejaculatory duct to combine with the sperm.

The **prostate** lies below the bladder and is about the size and shape of a chestnut. It is composed of both muscle and glandular tissue. The prostate secretes a milky alkaline fluid that is part of the ejaculate. The alkalinity of the secretion provides a favourable environment for the sperm and helps prevent their destruction by the acidity of the vagina. The prostate is fairly small at birth, enlarges at puberty, and typically shrinks in old age. It may become enlarged enough so that it interferes with urination, in which case surgery or drug therapy is required. Its size can be determined by rectal examination.

Cowper's glands, or the *bulbourethral glands,* are located just below the prostate and empty into the urethra. During sexual arousal these glands secrete a small amount of a clear, alkaline fluid, which appears as droplets at the tip of the penis before ejaculation occurs. It is thought that the function of this secretion is to neutralize the acidic urethra, allowing safe passage of the sperm. Generally, it is not produced in sufficient quantity to serve as a lubricant in intercourse. The fluid

---

sperm: The mature male reproductive cell, capable of fertilizing an egg.

epididymis (ep-ih-DIH-dih-mus): A highly coiled tube located on the edge of a testis, where sperm mature.

vas deferens: The tube through which sperm pass on their way from the testes and epididymis, out of the scrotum, and to the urethra.

seminal vesicles: Saclike structures that lie above the prostate, which produce about 60 percent of the seminal fluid.

prostate: The gland in the male, located below the bladder, that secretes some of the fluid in semen.

Cowper's glands: Glands that secrete a clear alkaline fluid into the male's urethra.

---

[7] Fans of the television show *Seinfeld* may recall an episode depicting George's exclamation "Shrinkage" after a woman saw his penis while he was changing after a cold swim.

often contains some stray sperm. Thus, it is possible (though not likely) for a woman to become pregnant from the sperm in this fluid even though the man has not ejaculated.

L07

Cancers of the Sex Organs

Breast Cancer

Cancer of the breast is the most frequently diagnosed cancer (excluding non-melanoma skin cancer) in Canadian women. About one in nine Canadian women is expected to develop breast cancer in her lifetime (Figure 4.14). Every year, about 25 000 women are diagnosed with and 5000 women die of breast cancer in this country (Canadian Cancer Society, 2016a). The risk is higher for the woman whose mother, sister, or grandmother has had breast cancer. Although it is much more common in women, men can also develop breast cancer.

Causes

Approximately 5 to 10 percent of the cases of breast cancer in women are due to genetic factors (American Cancer Society, 2014). Other risk factors include long-term use of menopausal hormone replacement therapy (MHT) and obesity (American Cancer Society, 2014). The evidence indicates that abortion does not increase the risk.

Great breakthroughs have occurred in research into the genetics of breast cancer. First, researchers in Canada and in Britain identified ten new cancer subtypes based on their genetic characteristics. Second, scientists identified two breast cancer genes, BRCA1 (for BReast CAncer 1) on chromosome 17 and BRCA2 on chromosome 13 (Ezzell, 1994; Miki et al., 1994; Shattuck-Eidens et al., 1995). Mutations of these genes create a high risk of breast cancer. BRCA1 and BRCA2 mutations also increase susceptibility to ovarian cancer. In one study of women having a mutation in BRCA1 or BRCA2, 82 percent eventually developed breast cancer and 54 percent developed ovarian cancer (King, Marks, & Mandell, 2003). Further, among men carrying mutations of these genes, 16 percent develop prostate cancer. Genetic screening tests are available that detect BRCA mutations in women who have a family history of breast cancer. If a BRCA mutation is found, the woman can be monitored closely or choose to have preventive surgery; if it is not found, she can feel relieved (see Figure 4.15).

Diagnosis

The Canadian Cancer Society recommends that women examine their own breasts visually and physically.

Figure 4.14 Symbols used to create awareness of breast cancer and prostate cancer. The pink ribbon *(a)* is linked to breast cancer awareness while Movember *(b)* is linked to men's health issues.

(a) © Gary Woodard | Dreamstime.com

(b) © Movember

Women need to learn about how their breasts feel normally so that they can detect any changes and report them to their doctor. Although self-exams are no substitute for exams by clinicians and mammograms, many women discover their own cancer through changes in the look and feel of their breasts. There isn't a right or wrong way to check your breasts as long as you become familiar with the whole area of breast tissue.

There are three kinds of breast lumps: *cysts* (fluid-filled sacs, also called *fibrocystic* or *cystic mastitis*), *fibroadenomas*, and *malignant tumours*. About 80 percent of breast lumps are cysts or fibroadenomas and are benign—that is, not dangerous. Therefore, if a lump is found in your breast, the chances are fairly good that it is not malignant; of course, you cannot be sure of this until a doctor has performed a biopsy.

Figure 4.15 Angelina Jolie revealed that she chose to undergo a double mastectomy after tests revealed she has the two breast cancer genes.

© WENN Ltd / Alamy Stock Photo

The main technique for early detection of breast cancer is the mammography. Basically, *mammography* involves taking an X-ray of the breast. This technique is highly accurate, although some errors are still made. The major advantage, though, is that it is capable of detecting tumours that are so small that they cannot yet be felt; thus, it can detect cancer in very early stages, making recovery more likely. Nonetheless, mammography involves some exposure to radiation, which itself may increase the risk of cancer. The question is, Which is more dangerous—having mammography or not detecting breast cancer until a later stage? Experts agree that the benefits outweigh the risk for women over 50. The Canadian Cancer Society recommends that women between 50 and 69 have a screening mammogram every two years. However, scientists disagree about the effectiveness of mammography screening for women who are between 40 and 49. All women should learn how their breasts feel normally and should report any changes to their health care professional.

Recently, MRI scans have been developed to detect breast tumours. They are generally recommended only for high-risk women.

Once a lump is discovered, one of several diagnostic procedures may be carried out. One is *needle aspiration,* in which a fine needle is inserted into the breast; if the lump is a cyst, the fluid in the cyst will be drained out. If the lump disappears after this procedure, then it was a cyst; the cyst is gone, and there is no need for further concern. If the lump remains, it must be either a fibroadenoma or a malignant tumour.

Most physicians feel that the only definitive way to differentiate between a fibroadenoma and a malignant tumour is to do a *biopsy.* A small slit is made in the breast, and the lump is removed. A pathologist then examines it to determine whether it is cancerous. If it is simply a fibroadenoma, it has been removed and there is no further need for concern.

Treatment

Several forms of surgery may be performed when a breast lump is found to be malignant. If the lump is small and has not spread, the surgery may involve only a **lumpectomy**, in which the lump and a small bit of surrounding tissues are removed. The breast is thus preserved. In most cases of early breast cancer, when the cancer has not spread beyond the breast (e.g., to the lymph nodes), a lumpectomy followed by radiation therapy is highly effective (Canadian Cancer Society, 2013b). In simple mastectomy, the breast and possibly a few lymph nodes are removed. In a modified radical mastectomy, the breast and the underarm lymph nodes are removed; this procedure is used when there is evidence that the cancer has spread to the lymph nodes. If the cancer has spread more, the surgery is a **radical mastectomy**, in which the entire breast, the underlying pectoral muscle, and the underarm lymph nodes are removed.

Following surgery, radiation therapy or chemotherapy or both are used. These may be followed by drug therapy, such as tamoxifen. Researchers in New Brunswick have shown that most women who take tamoxifen experience menopausal symptoms, sometimes very severe, including sexual side effects, such as decreased sexual desire and pain during intercourse related to vaginal dryness (Archibald et al., 2006).

Treatments generally are highly effective and breast cancer deaths have been decreasing. Overall, the survival rate is more than 88 percent five years after treatment (Canadian Cancer Society, 2016a). If the cancer is localized, the survival rate is more than 98 percent five years after treatment.

lumpectomy: A surgical treatment for breast cancer in which only the lump and a small bit of surrounding tissue are removed.
radical mastectomy (mast-ECT-uh-mee): A surgical treatment for breast cancer in which the entire breast, as well as underlying muscles and lymph nodes, is removed.

Psychological Aspects

A lot more is at stake with breast cancer and mastectomy than technical details about diagnosis and surgery. The psychological impact of breast cancer and mastectomy and other treatments can be enormous. There seem to be three sources of the trauma: (1) finding out that one has cancer (of any kind), (2) having the surgery and possible amputation of the breast, and (3) experiencing severe menopausal symptoms.

The typical emotional response of breast cancer patients is depression, often associated with anxiety (Compas & Lueken, 2002; Montazeri, 2008). These responses are so common that they can be considered normal. The woman who has a mastectomy must make a number of physical and psychological adaptations, including different positions for sleeping and lovemaking, and for many women, a change to less revealing clothing. Relationship tensions and sexual problems may increase. Reconstruction surgery is available, though (see Figure 4.16), and scientists are exploring the possibility of using stem cells so that breast tissue can be regrown in the body (Findlay et al., 2011).

Long-term studies, however, indicate that most women gradually adapt to the stresses they have experienced. One study found that breast cancer survivors did not differ from controls on measures of depression (Cordova et al., 2001). Many women manage to find meaning in the cancer experience, and some show post-traumatic growth, such as finding new meaning in relationships and appreciating life more.

Educational classes providing relevant information can be very helpful. However, peer support groups, though popular, have not fared well in tests of their effectiveness in improving mental health (Helgeson, Cohen, & Schulz, 2001). For women who are more severely distressed, cognitive behavioural therapy with a trained therapist can be very effective (Antoni et al., 2001).

Cancer of the Cervix, Endometrium, and Ovaries

Cancers of the cervix, endometrium, and ovaries are also common cancers, accounting for about 12 percent of all new cancers in women. About 10 600 Canadian women were diagnosed with and 3180 died of these cancers in 2015 (Canadian Cancer Society, 2016a). Other cancers of the female sexual-reproductive organs include cancer of the vulva, vagina, and fallopian tubes; these are all relatively rare.

Approximately 95 percent of cases of cervical cancer are caused by the human papillomavirus, HPV (see Chapter 8 for a discussion of HPV and the vaccine to prevent it) (Janicek & Averette, 2001). Early initiation of penile-vaginal intercourse during the teenage years is a known risk factor for cervical cancer, as is intercourse with multiple partners. Both early intercourse and multiple partners, of course, increase the risk of HPV infection. Research shows that tumour-suppressor genes are active in normal cells, preventing them from becoming cancerous. HPV interferes with the activity of those tumour-suppressor genes (Janicek & Averette, 2001).

It is encouraging to note that the death rate from cervical cancer has decreased 78 percent since the mid-1960s, and more than 2 percent since 1994, mainly as a result of the Pap test (invented by G.N. Papanicolaou) and more regular checkups (American Cancer Society, 2009). The Pap test is performed during a pelvic examination (described in Figure 4.17). This highly accurate test can detect cancer long before the person has any symptoms. Therefore, current Canadian recommendations are that all women between ages of 21 and 70 should have routine screening every three years; women with risk factors should be screened more frequently. Unfortunately, women from ethnocultural communities in Canada, such as the Indo-Canadian community and the Chinese Canadian community, are less likely than those of European descent to have a Pap test (Brotto, Chou, et al., 2008; Chang et al., 2010; Woo, Brotto, & Gorzalka, 2009).

There is considerable variation in the incidence of cervical and endometrial cancers across Canada. For example, the incidence of cervical cancer among Indigenous groups is 1.7 to 3.5 times higher than in other groups of Canadian women, probably because historically fewer Indigenous women received regular pelvic exams (Demers et al., 2012). However, screening rates have improved significantly among Indigenous women. As with most cancers, the likelihood of a woman having

Figure 4.16 Appearance of a breast reconstructed after mastectomy.

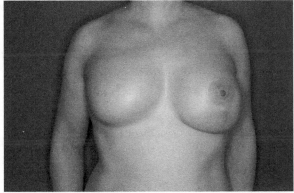

© David J. Green - lifestyle themes/Alamy

Figure 4.17 The two primary procedures used during a pelvic exam: *(a)* The speculum, a plastic or metal instrument, is inserted into the vagina to hold the vaginal walls apart to permit examination. The Ayre spatula is used to get a sample of cells from the cervix for the Pap test for cervical cancer. *(b)* The bimanual pelvic exam in which the health care provider slides the index and middle fingers of one hand into the vagina and then, with the other hand, presses down from the outside on the abdominal wall to feel the uterus, tubes, and ovaries.

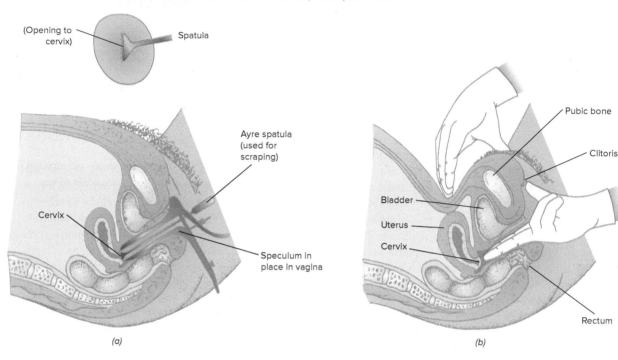

(a) (b)

a reproductive tract cancer increases with age, although cervical cancer is relatively common among women in their 20s. A vaccine is now available that prevents the most common HPV infections that cause cervical cancer (see Chapter 8). It is approved for use in Canada for females between the ages of 9 and 26, and all girls and women in this group should receive the vaccine, ideally at age 11 or 12. Because of this, it is offered free to girls in Grades 7 and 8 in all Canadian provinces and territories. Health Canada also approved the vaccine for boys between the ages of 9 and 26 in 2010, and six provinces are offering the vaccine free to boys.

Endometrial and ovarian cancers have multiple symptoms, making diagnosis difficult. Endometrial cancer may be suspected when a woman has vaginal bleeding during times in the menstrual cycle other than her period or after menopause. Ovarian cancer symptoms—abdominal bloating and cramping, vomiting, and diarrhea—can be (and usually are) indicative of less serious conditions like a stomach virus or irritable bowel syndrome. Imaging techniques, such as pelvic sonogram and MRI, and minimally invasive surgical techniques, such as hysteroscopy, can help diagnose these cancers. Recent research in Quebec had demonstrated that the deadliest subtype of ovarian cancer

hysterectomy (his-tuh-REK-tuh-mee): Surgical removal of the uterus.

originates in the fallopian tubes not in the ovaries (Gilbert et al., 2012).

Treatment for cervical cancer varies according to how advanced it is when diagnosed. If it is detected very early, it is quite curable with methods such as cryotherapy, a nonsurgical technique that uses extreme cold to destroy just the abnormal cells. Another common treatment is cone biopsy, in which a segment of the cervix is surgically removed, leaving the cervix largely intact. For women with advanced cervical cancer that has spread beyond a small, localized spot, **hysterectomy** (surgical removal of the uterus) is the usual treatment, although radiation therapy may be an alternative.

For women with endometrial cancer, hysterectomy is the standard treatment. Ovarian cancer is treated by oophorectomy (surgical removal of the ovaries), often accompanied by hysterectomy. These surgeries are typically followed by radiation treatments or chemotherapy.

It is important to note some facts about hysterectomy. Although it carries risks similar to those of any major surgery, hysterectomy does not leave a woman "masculinized," with a beard and deep voice. Beard growth is influenced by testosterone, not estrogen or progesterone. And it is the ovaries that manufacture estrogen and progesterone. They are not removed in a hysterectomy, except in rare cases when the cancer has spread to them.

First Person

Prostate Cancer, Gonadal Hormones, and My Brain

R arely do we have eureka moments in our lives that give us grand insights into how the world works. But most of us have experiences that direct or redirect our interests for years to come. In my case, being treated for prostate cancer propelled me as a scientist who had spent most of his life studying tadpoles, into studying how androgens and estrogens affect human sex drive, mood, and gender identity.

Assumptions and presumptions are rampant about how hormones affect our thoughts and feelings. Clearly, how a person responds to changes in sex hormone levels is influenced by what they believe beforehand about these compounds. Thus, for example, many male-to-female transsexuals, who desire a more feminine body form, take estrogen as part of the transitioning process. They typically become elated when they develop breasts after starting on estrogen. In addition, many prostate cancer patients take drugs to slow the growth of prostate cancer cells, some of which can have estrogenic effects. These men may become distraught, and rarely become thrilled, at any breast growth they experience. Members of both groups may credit the hormones with directly influencing their mood. But were these mood changes truly a direct effect of the hormones on emotional centres in the brain? Or were they actually a result of the individual's response to desired versus dreaded side effects?

Being diagnosed with and treated for prostate cancer gave me a chance to explore these questions first-hand. Although my sample size of one is hardly definitive science, I have strived to be as open-minded and objective as possible about how these hormones affected my mood and sex drive.

My chance to personally explore how gonadal hormones influence thought processes began when I was diagnosed with prostate cancer in my early 50s. To control my cancer, I started on androgen-deprivation therapy with drugs that drove both my testosterone (T) and estradiol (E) into the castrate range—that is, in the range of men who have no functional testicles. (Although estradiol is the main gonadal hormone for females, males have some too, derived from our testosterone.) Technically I became a *eunuch*, the correct term for a castrated individual. It is rare these days for a prostate cancer patient,

a transsexual, or for that matter anyone in the western world to self-identify as a eunuch. The label "eunuch" is now derogatory and meant to indicate an exceedingly ineffective individual.

However eunuchs, as a distinct class of citizens, have existed in various societies for thousands of years. Indeed, they have been the most recognized third gender category throughout human history (Wassersug, McKenna, & Lieberman, 2012). As part of accepting my situation, I published a personal "coming out as eunuch" essay in the *New York Times* (www.nytimes.com/2007/03/27/health/27case.html) built upon the realization that historically eunuchs were not globally impotent as presumed in contemporary society. To the contrary, for most of the last 3000 years they were diplomats, generals, and senior government officials in all major dynastic regimes of Asia (Aucoin & Wassersug, 2006). I found it therapeutic to know that my hormonal status didn't necessarily park me in the class of the totally incompetent.

As a eunuch, my mood and sex drive dropped. This was not surprising because castrating drugs, like the one I (along with about 600 000 other prostate cancer patients in North America) was taking depress men's libido. In fact, they do that so well that they are offered to individuals with extreme paraphilic disorders who want to be free of their sexual thoughts. And that is not something that patients on those drugs are particularly comfortable talking about (Wassersug, 2010).

I also quickly learned how strongly T influenced how I viewed women. Free of T (and E), I felt that I owed many of the women I had dated earlier in my life an apology for objectifying them so much. Since puberty, I had been particularly attentive to breasts and waist-to-hip ratios of women . . . and, embarrassingly I admit, not much else.

With my brain deprived of both T and E, I also felt like I was in something of a fog. Therefore, after a few years I decided to shift to taking just high-dose E as an alternative strategy for androgen deprivation. Both T and E bind to receptors in the brain, and at high concentrations, either hormone can shut down the signal from the brain to the gonads to make these hormones. To my surprise I found that on supplemental E not only did my mood improve and the mental fog lift, but some of my sex

(continued)

(continued)

drive returned. In fact, I felt so similar with high E as I did with high T that I wasn't sure the androgen-deprivation therapy with pure E was controlling my cancer. But blood tests confirmed that my T was indeed at castrate levels and that my cancer's growth was still arrested.

This was my eureka moment. I began to study estrogen's effects in castrated males. A graduate student and I experimented with giving supplemental E to castrated male rats. We were able to show that the E indeed helped to elevate the rats' sexual interest above the castrate level (and we can be confident that the rats had no expectations about how these hormones affected their behaviour). Shortly after we published our rodent results (Wibowo & Wassersug, 2013), a research team at Harvard, working with volunteers on reversible chemical castrating drugs, confirmed that not only T but also E can positively influence men's libido. I happily stayed on the supplemental E for more than a decade and along the way entertained myself with the thought that I was either a very lucky prostate cancer patient or an indifferent male-to-female transsexual, who dressed in (male) drag and declined to shave.

So what have I really learned from my own experience? Both T and E can contribute to libido. My sense is that the male brain (well, my male brain) fuelled with either T or E functions quite similarly. The odd-man out (literally and figuratively) is the neutered (i.e., the eunuchoid) brain deprived of both gonadal hormones. Although I await more experimental data with a larger sample size, as I see it, emasculation and feminization are not the same. Adding high-dose E to the male brain produces a far less drastic effect than removing both the T and E that the male brain normally experiences.

Source: Richard J. Wassersug. (2014). Prostate cancer, gonadal hormones, and my brain. *Journal of Sex & Marital Therapy, 40*(5), 355–357. doi:10.1080/0092623X.2014.921477

Women who have their ovaries removed before age 50 can take hormone replacement therapy (HRT) to avoid the effects of premature menopause but should discontinue treatment at least by the time of expected natural menopause. Another fallacy about hysterectomy is that it prevents a woman from enjoying or even having— sex. However, about half the women who undergo a hysterectomy for cervical or endometrial cancer report significant sexual problems (Brotto, Heiman et al., 2008).

Cancer of the Prostate

Cancer of the prostate is the most common form of cancer in Canadian men; one in seven men will develop prostate cancer in his lifetime. Annually, about 24 000 men are diagnosed with and 4100 die from prostate cancer in Canada (Canadian Cancer Society, 2016b). Most cases are not lethal, however, and survival rates are high because it generally affects older men (25 percent of men over 90 have prostate cancer), and because the tumours are small and spread (metastasize) very slowly. On the other hand, a percentage of prostate tumours (about 5 percent), particularly in younger men, do spread and are lethal. A prostate cancer gene (HPC1, for hereditary prostate cancer) has been discovered, but it accounts for only about 3 percent of all cases (Pennisi, 1996; Smith et al., 1996). Men of African ancestry are 60 percent more likely to develop prostate cancer than are Caucasian men. They are also likely to be diagnosed at a younger age with more advanced tumours (Canadian Cancer Society, 2013a). Men of Asian ancestry have the lowest rates.

Early symptoms of prostate cancer are frequent urination (especially at night), difficulty in urination, and difficulty emptying the bladder. These are also symptoms of benign prostate enlargement, which itself may require treatment by surgery or drugs but is not cancer. These symptoms result from the pressure of the prostate tumour on the urethra. In the early stages, there may be frequent erections and an increase in sex drive; however, as the disease progresses, there are often problems with sexual functioning.

Preliminary diagnosis of prostate cancer is by a rectal examination, which is simple and causes no more than minimal discomfort. The physician (wearing a lubricated glove) inserts one finger into the rectum and palpates (feels) the prostate. All men over 50 should have a rectal exam at least once a year; men with a family history of the disease should start having exams at 40. If the rectal exam provides evidence of a tumour, further laboratory tests can be conducted as confirmation. The rectal exam has its disadvantages, though. Some men dislike the discomfort it causes, and it is not 100 percent accurate.

Do any cancers of the sex organs affect young men?

A blood test for PSA (prostate-specific antigen) is also available and can be done as well.

Treatment often involves surgical removal of some or all of the prostate, and some type of hormone therapy, radiation therapy, or anti-cancer drugs. Because prostate cancer is often a slow-growing cancer, it may be left untreated, particularly if the man is a senior. Surgery often results in erection problems (Perez, Skinner, & Meyerowitz, 2002). Androgen-deprivation therapy is typically used for advanced prostate cancer. It results in a number of physical changes, including loss of erection, lower libido, shrinking of the penis, loss of body hair, hot flashes, and breast growth because of the loss of testosterone (Aucoin & Wassersug, 2006; Elliott et al., 2010). These changes affect both patients and their partners (Hamilton, Van Dam, & Wassersug, 2015; Lee et al., 2015). It is important that patients and their partners are provided with education that help them maintain their sexual relationship despite these changes (Walker, Wassersug, & Robinson, 2015). The First Person box in this chapter gives one man's experience with androgen-deprivation therapy. Just as research has found that a greater number of sexual partners increases women's risk of cervical cancer, new research indicates that men with a greater number of female partners have an increased risk of prostate cancer (Rosenblatt, Wicklund, & Stanford, 2001).

Cancer of the penis is another cancer of the male sexual-reproductive system, but it is rare compared with prostate cancer. It seems to be more common among uncircumcised men than among circumcised men, suggesting that the accumulation of smegma under the foreskin may be related to its cause. Treatment may consist of surgery or radiation therapy.

Cancer of the Testes

Cancer of the testes is not a particularly common form of cancer. Every year in Canada, 1050 men are diagnosed with this form of cancer, and about 40 men die from it (Canadian Cancer Society, 2016b). However, cancer of the testes tends to be a disease of cancer in young men. The mortality rate from cancer of the testes in Canada has decreased because, although there have been more cases of testicular cancer identified, treatments have improved. The survival rate is 95 percent five years after treatment.

The cause of testicular cancer is not known for certain. An undescended testis has a much greater risk of developing cancer. The first sign is usually a painless lump in the testes, or a slight enlargement or change in consistency of the testes. There may be pain in the lower abdomen or groin. Unfortunately, many men do not discover the tumour, or if they do, they do not see a physician soon after, and in most cases the cancer has spread to other organs by the time a physician is consulted. When a lump is reported to a physician early, the five-year survival rate is 96 percent (Biggs & Schwartz, 2007). Therefore, the Canadian Cancer Society recommends that men do regular testicular self-examinations every month starting at puberty (see Figure 4.18). The exam should be done during or right after a bath or shower because the scrotal skin is more relaxed and the contents can be felt more easily. However, if the lump is not discovered, or the man waits to see a physician and the cancer has progressed to Stage III, the survival rate is between 70 and 75 percent (Biggs & Schwartz, 2007). Unfortunately, men from some ethnocultural communities, such as Chinese Canadians, are less likely to do testicular self-examinations (Woo, Brotto, & Gorzalka, 2010).

Not every lump in the testes is cancerous. Some lumps are *varicoceles,* that is, varicose veins. Diagnosis is made by a physician's examination of the testes and by ultrasound. Final diagnosis involves surgical removal of the entire testis. This is also the first step in treatment. Fortunately, the other testicle remains so that hormone production and sexual functioning can continue unimpaired. An artificial, gel-filled testicle can be implanted to restore a normal appearance.

Figure 4.18 The technique used in the testicular self-exam.

© Teri L. Stratford/Science Source

UNDERSTANDING THE DIFFERENCE BETWEEN ANECDOTAL EVIDENCE AND SCIENTIFIC EVIDENCE

Maria is 50 years old. According to the Canadian Cancer Society, she should have a mammogram every two years to screen for breast cancer. Maria's doctor has told her that she needs to start having mammograms. Maria's best friend, Daphne, is 52 and had a small, cancerous lump in her breast a year ago. The lump was not detected on a mammogram, but Daphne found it herself, received prompt treatment, and is healthy. Daphne says that mammograms are worthless because they did not detect her lump, and she tells Maria not to bother with them. What should Maria do?

In this case, Daphne's experience, although real, represents a single case or an anecdote. The sample size is 1. Daphne's evidence, then, is anecdotal evidence, which stands in contrast to scientific evidence, based on carefully conducted research with large samples. Maria needs to find out what the scientific evidence is on the effectiveness of mammograms. One approach would be trust an expert, such as her doctor, or trust a well-respected organization such as the Canadian Cancer Society. She could also ask her doctor about the scientific information. How accurate are mammograms? What is their rate of false positives (saying you have a tumour when you don't)? What is their rate of false negatives (saying you have no tumour when you actually do)?

With access to the Internet, Maria could also dig out the scientific evidence herself. One strategy would be to visit the website of the Canadian Task Force on Preventive Health Care established by the Public Health Agency of Canada (canadiantaskforce.ca). We did that just now, and quickly found that the results of their systematic review of the research indicated that the false negative rate (that is, when the radiologist says there is no cancer when there is cancer) is extremely low. Cases such as Daphne's false negative do occur, but they are very, very rare, occurring less than 1 percent of the time (Paliwal et al., 2006).

If Maria goes with the anecdotal evidence from her friend, she will conclude that mammograms are inaccurate and worthless. If Maria goes with the scientific evidence, she will conclude that they are highly accurate. Good critical thinking involves going with the scientific evidence.

SUMMARY

The external sexual organs of the female are the clitoris, the mons, the inner lips, the outer lips, and the vaginal opening. Collectively these are referred to as the vulva. The clitoris is highly sensitive and is very important in female sexual response. Clitoridectomy and infibulation are rituals that involve cutting of the clitoris and inner and outer lips, and are practised widely in some African nations and elsewhere. The hymen has taken on great symbolic significance as a sign of virginity, although its absence is not a reliable indicator that a woman is not a virgin. The important internal structures are the vagina; the uterus, which houses the developing fetus; the ovaries, which produce eggs and manufacture sex hormones; and the fallopian tubes, which convey the egg to the uterus. The breasts also function in sexual arousal.

The external sexual organs of the male are the penis and the scrotum. The penis contains the corpora cavernosa and the corpus spongiosum which, when filled with blood, produce an erection. Circumcision, or surgical removal of the foreskin of the penis, is a debated practice in Canada but has some health advantages. The scrotum contains the testes, which are responsible for the manufacture of sperm (in the seminiferous tubules) and sex hormones (in the interstitial cells). Sperm pass out of the testes during ejaculation via the vas deferens, the ejaculatory duct, and the urethra. The seminal vesicles and prostate manufacture most of the fluid that mixes with the sperm to form semen.

Breast cancer is the most common form of cancer in women. Women should do a monthly self-exam, but it is no substitute for exams by a clinician and regular mammograms between ages 50 and 69. The Pap test is used to detect cervical cancer. Prostate cancer is the most common form of cancer in men, but it generally affects older men. Cancer of the testes, although rare, is the most common cancer in men between the ages of 29 and 35. Men should do a monthly testicular self-exam.

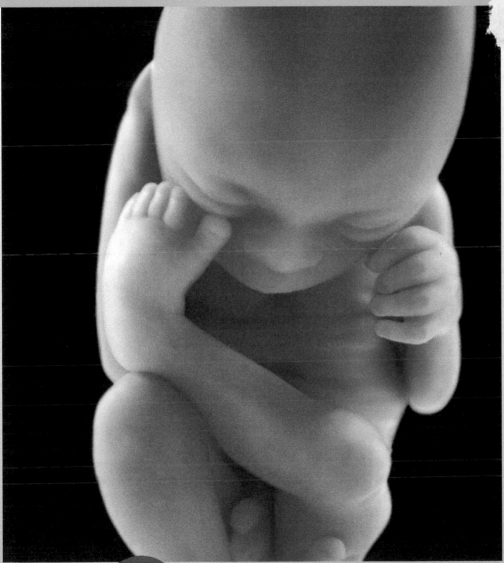

©Arno Massee/Science Source

LEARNING OBJECTIVES

After studying this chapter, you will be able to

LO1 Identify the sources and function of each of the sex hormones and how they are regulated.

LO2 Describe the changes that occur across the four phases of the menstrual cycle.

LO3 State the causes of symptoms of the most common menstrual problems.

LO4 Summarize the process of prenatal sexual differentiation.

LO5 Classify the homologous and analogous sex organs in males and females.

LO6 Distinguish the eight variables of gender and their relationship to normal and abnormal gender development.

LO7 Describe the process of puberty in boys and girls.

LO8 Summarize the research surrounding fluctuations in mood, performance, and sexuality across the menstrual cycle and their possible causes.

Are YOU Curious?

1. Can chemicals in our environment affect sexual development?
2. What is an *intersex* condition?
3. What determines the age at which a girl first menstruates?

Read this chapter to find out.

^This way

I have AIS, I guess,
Because there is a god,
And he or she or both,
Peered deep into my heart
To see
That all that I can be
Is best expressed
In female form.
The alternative for me
Would be XY, and I
Would be virilized;
So all that's soft and tender
Would instead surrender

To a strand of DNA.
In the lie of X and Y
I came to challenge the
Immutability
Of "he" and the certainty
Of "she." Blended and infused,
A ruse of gender
That upends
A different fate.
Non-functioning receptors
Have rescued me
Not a failed mess
But a smashing success of
Nature!*

Poem "This Way" by Sherri Groveman Morris in *Hermaphrodites with Attitude*, 1995, p. 2. Reprinted by permission of the author.

One of the marvels of human biology is that the complex and different male and female anatomies—males with a penis and scrotum; females with a vagina, uterus, and breasts—arise from a single cell, the fertilized egg, which varies only in whether it carries two X chromosomes (XX) or one X and one Y (XY). Many of the structural differences between males and females arise before birth, during the **prenatal period**, in a complex and delicate process called *prenatal sexual differentiation*.

Yet as the poem on this page suggests, gender is not always a simple matter. Sex and gender and their development are complex and vulnerable to disturbances. This results in further variety in the human condition.

In this chapter we examine the process of sexual differentiation both prenatally and during puberty. We also consider the biological and psychological aspects of the menstrual cycle. Let's start, however, with a basic biological system, the endocrine or hormonal system, paying particular attention to the sex

hormones. They play a major role in the differentiation process (see Milestones in Sex Research for discussion of how chemicals can disrupt the endocrine system).

LO1

Sex Hormones

Hormones are powerful chemical substances manufactured by the *endocrine glands* and secreted directly into the bloodstream. Because they go into the blood, their effects are felt fairly rapidly and at places in the body quite distant from where they were manufactured. The most important sex hormones are **testosterone** (one of a group of hormones called **androgens**) and **estrogens** and **progesterone**. The thyroid, the adrenals, and the pituitary are examples of endocrine glands. We are interested here in the gonads, or sex glands: the testes in the male and the ovaries in the female. The **pituitary gland** and a closely related region of the brain, the **hypothalamus**, are also important to our discussion because the hypothalamus regulates the pituitary, which regulates the other glands, in particular the testes and ovaries. Because of its role, the pituitary has been called the "master gland" of the endocrine system. The pituitary is a small gland, about the size of a pea, which projects down from the lower side of the brain. It is divided into three lobes: the anterior, the intermediary, and the posterior lobe. The anterior lobe is the one that interacts with the gonads. The hypothalamus is a region at the base of the brain just above the pituitary (see Figure 5.1). It plays

prenatal (pree-NAY-tul) period: The time from conception to birth.

hormones: Chemical substances secreted by the endocrine glands into the bloodstream.

testosterone: A hormone secreted by the testes in the male (and also present at lower levels in the female).

androgens: The group of "male" sex hormones, one of which is testosterone.

estrogens (ESS-troh-jens): The group of "female" sex hormones.

progesterone (pro-JES-tur-ohn): A "female" sex hormone secreted by the ovaries.

pituitary (pih-TOO-ih-tair-ee) gland: A small endocrine gland located on the lower side of the brain below the hypothalamus; the pituitary is important in regulating levels of sex hormones.

hypothalamus (hy-poh-THAL-ah-mus): A small region of the brain that is important in regulating many body functions, including the functioning of the sex hormones.

Figure 5.1 The hypothalamus–pituitary–gonad feedback loop in women, which regulates production of the sex hormones.

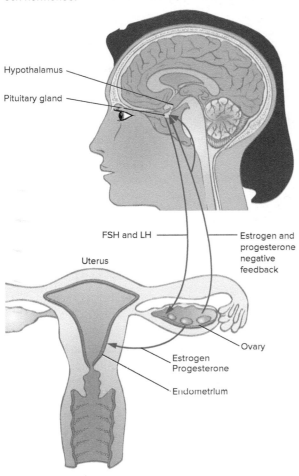

Hypothalamus

Pituitary gland

FSH and LH

Uterus

Estrogen and progesterone negative feedback

Ovary

Estrogen Progesterone

Endometrium

a part in regulating many vital behaviours, such as eating, drinking, and sexual behaviour,[1] and is important in regulating the pituitary.

These three structures, then—the hypothalamus, pituitary, and gonads (testes or ovaries)—function together. They influence such important sexual functions as the menstrual cycle, pregnancy, the changes of puberty, and sexual behaviour.

Sex Hormone Systems in Males

The pituitary and the testes both produce hormones. The important hormone produced by the testes is *testosterone*. Testosterone, a "male" or masculinizing sex hormone, has important functions in stimulating and

---

[1] One psychologist summarized the functions of the hypothalamus as being the four Fs: fighting, feeding, fleeing, and, ahem, sexual behaviour.

maintaining the secondary sex characteristics (such as beard growth), maintaining the genitals and their sperm-producing capability, and stimulating the growth of bone and muscle.

The pituitary produces several hormones, two of which are important in this discussion: **follicle-stimulating hormone (FSH)** and **luteinizing hormone (LH)**. These hormones affect the functioning of the testes. FSH controls sperm production, and LH controls testosterone production.

Testosterone levels in males are relatively constant. The hypothalamus, pituitary, and testes operate in a negative feedback loop that maintains these constant levels (see Figure 5.2a). The levels of LH are regulated by a substance called **gonadotropin-releasing hormone (GnRH)**, which is secreted by the hypothalamus (FSH levels are similarly regulated by GnRH). The system comes full circle because the hypothalamus monitors the levels of testosterone present, and in this way testosterone influences the output of GnRH. This feedback loop is sometimes called the **HPG axis**, for hypothalamus–pituitary–gonad axis.

This negative feedback loop operates much like a thermostat-furnace system. If a room is cold, certain changes occur in the thermostat, and it signals the furnace to turn on. The action of the furnace warms the air in the room. Eventually, the air becomes so warm that another change is produced in the thermostat, and it sends a signal to the furnace to turn off. The temperature in the room then gradually falls until it triggers another change in the thermostat, which then turns on the furnace, and the cycle is repeated. This cycle is a *negative* feedback loop because increases in temperature turn *off* the furnace, and *decreases* in temperature turn *on* the furnace.

The hypothalamus, pituitary, and testes work together in a similar negative feedback loop, ensuring that testosterone is maintained at a fairly constant level, just as the temperature of a room is kept fairly constant. The pituitary's production of LH stimulates the testes to produce testosterone. But when testosterone levels get high, the hypothalamus reduces its production of GnRH; the pituitary's production of LH is then reduced, and the production of testosterone by the testes consequently decreases. When testosterone levels fall, the hypothalamus again increases the production of GnRH and the process starts again.

follicle-stimulating hormone (FSH): A hormone secreted by the pituitary; it stimulates follicle development in females and sperm production in males.

luteinizing hormone (LH): A hormone secreted by the pituitary; it regulates estrogen secretion and ovum development in the female and testosterone production in the male.

gonadotropin-releasing hormone (GnRH): A hormone secreted by the hypothalamus that regulates the pituitary's secretion of gonad-stimulating hormones.

HPG axis: Hypothalamus–pituitary–gonad axis, the negative feedback loop that regulates sex hormone production.

Figure 5.2 Schematic diagram of hormonal control of sex hormones. Note how similar they are in men and women: *(a)* Testosterone secretion and sperm production by the testes. The negative signs indicate that testosterone inhibits LH production, both in the pituitary and in the hypothalamus. *(b)* Estrogen secretion and ovum production by the ovaries (during the follicular phase of the menstrual cycle).

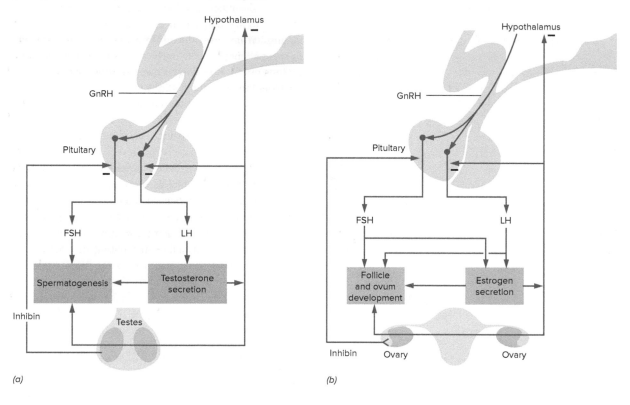

(a)

(b)

Inhibin is another hormone produced in the testes (by cells called the *Sertoli cells*). It acts to regulate FSH levels in a negative feedback loop just as testosterone does with LH (Lue et al., 2009). Interest in inhibin has been intense because it shows great promise, at least theoretically, as a male contraceptive. That is, because inhibin suppresses FSH production, sperm production in turn is inhibited.

Cycles in Men

The traditional assumption of both laypeople and scientists has been that monthly biological and psychological cycles are the exclusive property of women and that men experience no monthly cycles. These assumptions are made, at least in part, because men have no obvious signs like menstruation to call attention to the fact that some kind of periodic change is occurring. One study, in fact, found no differences between men and women in day-to-day mood changes—men were no more or less changeable than women (McFarlane, Martin, & Williams, 1988; see also

inhibin: A substance secreted by the testes and ovaries that regulates FSH levels.

McFarlane & Williams, 1994). However, one study found that men's testosterone levels displayed weekly fluctuations, peaking on weekends (Hirschenhauser et al., 2002). Men who had a female partner and wanted to have a child with her displayed a 28-day cycle of testosterone levels, leading the researchers to hypothesize that the men's hormone cycles might have synchronized with their partner's. Strikingly, men's testosterone levels also vary with sexual activity. In this same study, men who had sex with an unfamiliar partner showed a 100 percent increase in their testosterone levels the following morning!

Sex Hormone Systems in Females

The ovaries produce two important hormones: estrogen[2] and progesterone. Estrogen brings about many of the changes of puberty (stimulating the growth

---

[2] We really should say *estrogens*, because they are a group of hormones. Estradiol is one of the estrogens. To keep things simple, we will just use the term *estrogen*.

of the uterus and vagina, enlarging the pelvis, and stimulating breast growth). Estrogen is also responsible for maintaining the mucous membranes of the vagina and stopping the growth of bone and muscle, which accounts for why women generally are smaller than men.

In women the levels of estrogen and progesterone fluctuate according to the phases of the menstrual cycle and during various other stages, such as pregnancy and menopause. The two pituitary hormones, FSH and LH, regulate the levels of estrogen and progesterone. In this way, the levels of estrogen and progesterone are controlled by a negative feedback loop of the hypothalamus, pituitary, and ovaries, that is similar to the negative feedback loop in the male (look back to Figure 5.2b). For example, as shown in Figure 5.2b, increases in the level of GnRH increase the level of LH, and the increases in LH eventually produce increases in the output of estrogen. Finally, the increases in the level of estrogen inhibit (decrease) the production of GnRH and LH.

Inhibin is produced by the ovaries, just as it is by the testes. It inhibits FSH production and participates in the feedback loop that controls the menstrual cycle.

The pituitary produces two other hormones: *prolactin* and *oxytocin*. Prolactin stimulates production of milk by the mammary glands after a woman has given birth to a child. Oxytocin stimulates ejection of that milk from the nipple. Oxytocin also stimulates contractions of the uterus during childbirth. In addition, oxytocin has gained a popular reputation as the "snuggle chemical" because it seems to promote affectionate bonding, for example, with one's newborn baby (Feldman et al., 2007). Oxytocin is produced in both males and females. In fact, in cotton-top tamarins, a species of monogamous monkeys, males and females have similar oxytocin levels, and oxytocin secretion is stimulated by touching, grooming, and sex (Snowdon et al., 2010).

The female sex hormone system functions much like the male sex hormone system (and their endocrine systems can be affected in similar ways). The ovaries and testes produce many of the same hormones but in different amounts. The functioning of the female sex hormone system and the menstrual cycle will now be described in more detail.

Biology of the Menstrual Cycle

Women's sexual and reproductive lives have a rhythm of changes. One notable sign that marks the changes is menstruation. The events surrounding it are not only biological but also psychological. The biological aspects are discussed here; the psychological aspects are discussed later in this chapter.

Humans are nearly unique among species in having a menstrual cycle. Only a few other species of apes and monkeys also have menstrual cycles. All other species of mammals (e.g., horses and dogs) have *estrous* cycles. What are the differences between estrous cycles and menstrual cycles? First, in animals that have estrous cycles, there is no menstruation; there is either no bleeding or only a slight spotting of blood (as in dogs), which is not real menstruation. Second, the timing of ovulation in relation to bleeding is different in the two cycles. For estrous animals, ovulation occurs while the animal is in "heat," or *estrus*, which is also the time of slight spotting. In the menstrual cycle, however, ovulation occurs about midway between the periods of menstruation. A third difference is that female animals with estrous cycles engage in sexual behaviour only when they are in heat—that is, during the estrus phase of the cycle. Females with menstrual cycles are capable of engaging in and enjoying sexual activity throughout the cycle.

The Phases of the Menstrual Cycle

The menstrual cycle has four phases, each characterized by a set of hormonal, ovarian, and uterine changes. Because menstruation is the easiest phase to identify, it is tempting to call it the first phase, but biologically it is actually the last phase. (Note, however, that in numbering the days of the menstrual cycle, the first day of menstruation is counted as day 1 because it is the most identifiable day of the cycle.)

The first phase of the menstrual cycle is called the **follicular phase** (or sometimes the *proliferative phase*). At the beginning of this phase, the pituitary secretes relatively high levels of FSH. As the name of this hormone implies, its function is to stimulate follicles in the ovaries. At the beginning of the follicular phase, it signals one follicle (occasionally more than one) in the ovaries to bring an egg to the final stage of maturity. At the same time, the follicle secretes estrogen.

The second phase of the cycle is **ovulation**, which is the phase during which the follicle ruptures open, releasing the mature egg (see Figure 5.4). By this time, estrogen has risen to a high level, which inhibits FSH production, and so FSH has fallen back to a

> **follicular (fuh-LIK-you-lur) phase:**
> The first phase of the menstrual cycle, beginning just after menstruation, during which an egg matures in preparation for ovulation.
> **ovulation:** Release of an egg from the ovaries; the second phase of the menstrual cycle.

Is Environmental Pollution Affecting the Endocrine System?

Male Florida panthers have low sperm counts and the same levels of estradiol as females. Frogs are born hermaphroditic, with mixed male and female organs. Along the Oldman River in Alberta, 90 percent of the longnose dace (a small fish) are female. Male turtle doves display reduced courtship and nesting behaviours. A preschool girl begins growing pubic hair. These cases and dozens of others have appeared in the news in the last decade. Are they unrelated bizarre occurrences, or is there a common link?

Scientists believe that underlying all these troubling cases is the phenomenon of **endocrine disrupters**, which are chemicals found in the environment that affect the endocrine system, as well as the biological functioning and behaviour of animals, including humans. Evidence of the effects of endocrine disrupters (also called endocrine disrupting chemicals or EDCs) comes from both studies of animals in the wild and carefully controlled laboratory experiments.

> **Can chemicals in our environment affect sexual development?**

What chemicals are the culprits? Some are pesticides, such as atrazine and DDT, used by farmers and others to kill unwanted insects and weeds. Bisphenol A (BPA) is another endocrine disrupter. It is used in making plastics and can be found in some older plastic baby bottles. PCBs, which were banned from production in Canada in 1977, were used in making products such as paints, plastics, and printing ink. Some have a half-life of more than 1000 years and so they are still abundant in the environment despite being banned.

Fracking (hydraulic fracturing to extract oil from the earth) involves the use of fracking chemicals, 35 percent of which are endocrine disruptors (Alcid & Miller, 2014). These chemicals have been linked to infertility, miscarriage, birth defects, and cancer of the reproductive organs.

How do these chemicals exert their effects on sexual biology and behaviour? All of them affect the endocrine system and, specifically, the sex hormone system. Many have multiple effects. Atrazine, for example, affects both estrogen and testosterone and inhibits their binding to estrogen receptors and androgen receptors. It also depresses the LH surge that causes ovulation. The insecticide DDT affects estrogen, progesterone, and testosterone by mimicking estrogen and binding to estrogen receptors, as well as by altering the metabolism of both progesterone and testosterone. PCBs are both anti-estrogens and anti-androgens. These chemicals are in the food we eat and the water and milk that we drink.

Why should we care about a few hermaphroditic frogs or preschoolers with pubic hair? Scientists see these cases as examples of the proverbial canary in the mine shaft. In other words, they are small signs that something terribly dangerous is happening. A carefully controlled study showed that pregnant women with high exposure to phthalates (found in plastics and hairspray) are more likely to give birth to baby boys with hypospadias, a condition in which the urethral opening is not at the tip of the penis but somewhere else along it (see Figure 5.3). Studies in both the United States and Denmark show that breast development in girls is occurring one year earlier than it did a few decades ago (Aksglaede et al., 2009). The pesticide residues in fruits and vegetables have been linked to lower sperm counts in men (Chiu et al., 2015). And on a Chippewa reservation in a part of Ontario that is heavily populated with chemical manufacturing plants, only 35 percent of the babies born today are boys. According to an official statement by the Endocrine Society, "The evidence for adverse reproductive outcomes (infertility, cancers, malformations) from endocrine disrupting chemicals is strong" (Diamanti-Kandarakis & Gore, 2009).

Figure 5.3 An example of hypospadia, in which the urethral opening is not at the tip of the penis.

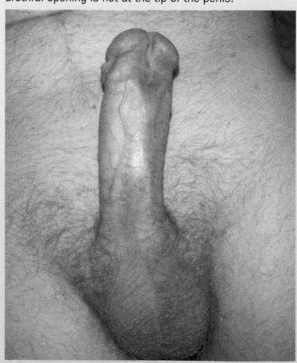

Sources: Aksglaede et al., 2009; Diamanti-Kandarakis & Gore, 2009; Hayes et al., 2002; Iwaniuk et al., 2006; Kloas et al., 2009; Ormond et al., 2008; Propper, 2005; Sanghavi, 2006; Toppari & Juul, 2010; Zala & Penn, 2004.

endocrine disrupters: Chemicals found in the environment that affect the endocrine system and the biological functioning and behaviour of animals, including humans.

Figure 5.4 Ovulation, showing the egg bursting forth from the wall of the ovary.

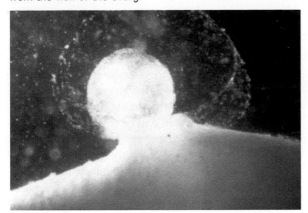

© C. Edelmann/Science Source

low level. The high levels of estrogen also stimulate the hypothalamus to produce GnRH, which causes the pituitary to begin production of LH.[3] A surge of LH triggers ovulation.

The third phase of the cycle is called the **luteal phase** (also called the *secretory phase*). After releasing an egg, the follicle, under stimulation of LH, turns into a glandular mass of cells called the **corpus luteum**[4] (hence the names *luteal phase* and *luteinizing hormone*). The corpus luteum manufactures progesterone, so progesterone levels rise during the luteal phase. But high levels of progesterone also inhibit the pituitary's secretion of LH, and as LH levels decline, the corpus luteum degenerates. With this degeneration comes a sharp decline in estrogen and progesterone levels at the end of the luteal phase. The falling levels of estrogen stimulate the pituitary to begin production of FSH, and the whole cycle begins again.

The fourth and final phase of the cycle is **menstruation**. Physiologically, menstruation is a shedding of the inner lining of the uterus (the endometrium), which then passes out through the cervix and the vagina. During this phase, estrogen and progesterone levels are low and FSH levels are rising. Menstruation is triggered by the sharp decline in estrogen and progesterone levels at the end of the luteal phase.

What has been happening in the uterus while the ovaries and endocrine system were going through the four phases that we just described? During the first, or follicular, phase, the high levels of estrogen stimulate the endometrium of the uterus to grow, thicken, and form glands that will eventually secrete substances to nourish the embryo. In other words, the endometrium proliferates (giving us the alternative name for this first phase, the *proliferative phase*). During the luteal phase, the progesterone secreted by the corpus luteum stimulates the glands of the endometrium to start secreting the nourishing substances (hence the name *secretory phase*). If the egg is fertilized and the timing goes properly, about six days after ovulation the fertilized egg arrives in a uterus that is well prepared to cradle and nourish it.

The corpus luteum continues to produce estrogen and progesterone for about 10 to 12 days. If pregnancy has not occurred, its hormone output declines sharply at the end of this period. The uterine lining thus cannot be maintained, and it is shed, resulting in menstruation. Immediately afterward, a new lining starts forming in the next proliferative phase.

The menstrual fluid itself is a combination of blood (from the endometrium), degenerated cells, and mucus from the cervix and vagina. Normally the discharge for an entire period is only about 60 mL (2 oz. or 4 Tbsp.). Common practice is to use sanitary pads, which are worn externally, or tampons, which are worn inside the vagina, to absorb the fluid. However, some women use a menstrual cup (brand names include The Keeper, The DivaCup, and Moon Cup) instead of disposable pads or tampons (see Figure 5.5). This is a small

> **luteal (LOO-tee-uhl) phase:** The third phase of the menstrual cycle, following ovulation.
> **corpus luteum:** The mass of cells of the follicle remaining after ovulation; it secretes progesterone.
> **menstruation:** The fourth phase of the menstrual cycle, during which the endometrium of the uterus is sloughed off in the menstrual discharge.

---

[3] This statement may seem to contradict the earlier statement that high estrogen levels cause a decline in LH. Both of these effects occur, but at different times in the menstrual cycle (Molitch, 1995). There are two centres in the hypothalamus: One produces a negative feedback loop between estrogen and LH, and the other produces a positive feedback loop between the two.

[4] *Corpus luteum* is Latin for "yellow body." The corpus luteum is so named because the mass of cells is yellowish in appearance.

Figure 5.5 The DivaCup is a reusable menstrual cup made of healthcare-grade silicone. It is an environmentally friendly alternative to disposable pads and tampons.

© Diva International, Inc.

Figure 5.6 The biological events of the menstrual cycle.

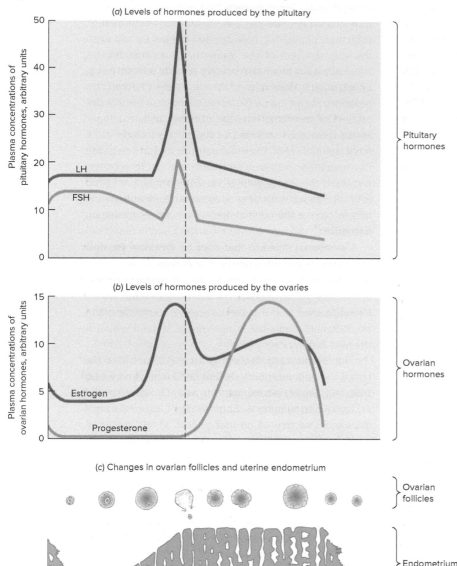

Length and Timing of the Cycle

How long is a normal menstrual cycle? Generally anywhere from 20 to 36 days is considered within the normal range (Figure 5.6). The average is about 28 days, but somehow this number has taken on more significance than it deserves. There is enormous variation from one woman to the next in the average length of the cycle, and for a given woman there can be considerable variation in length from one cycle to the next. Some recent Canadian research suggests that women with greater variability in the length of their cycle have higher levels of androgens (Van Anders & Watson, 2006).

What is the timing of the four phases of the cycle? In a perfectly regular 28-day cycle, menstruation begins on day 1 and continues until about day 4 or 5. The follicular phase extends from about day 5 to about day 13. Ovulation occurs on day 14, and the luteal phase extends from day 15 to the end of the cycle, day 28.

But what if the cycle is not a perfect 28-day one? In cycles that are shorter or longer than 28 days, the principle is that the length of the *luteal* phase is relatively constant. In other words, the time from ovulation to menstruation is always 14 days, give or take only a day or two. Thus, for example, if a woman has a 44-day cycle, she ovulates on about day 30. If she has a 22-day cycle, she ovulates on about day 8.

Some women report that they can actually feel themselves ovulate, a phenomenon called *Mittelschmerz* (*middle pain*). The sensation described is a cramping on one or both sides of the lower abdomen, lasting for about a day.

It is also true that ovulation does not occur in every menstrual cycle. That is, menstruation may take place without ovulation. When this happens the woman is said to have an *anovulatory cycle*. Such cycles occur once or twice a year in women in their 20s and 30s and are fairly common among girls during puberty and among women during menopause.

Other Cyclic Changes

Two other physiological processes that fluctuate with the menstrual cycle deserve mention: the cervical mucus cycle and the basal body temperature cycle.

The cervical mucus cycle involves glands in the cervix that secrete mucus throughout the menstrual cycle. One function of the mucus is to protect the entrance to

reusable device made of flexible rubber or soft medical-grade silicone that has been approved for sale by Health Canada. It has a stem at the bottom to facilitate removal. It should be washed in gentle, perfume and oil-free cleansers to ensure that the silicone is not compromised and to help prevent vaginal irritation. Because it is reusable, it is more economical and environmentally friendly. Other environmentally friendly options include reusable menstrual pads made of cotton and sea sponge.

the cervix, helping to keep bacteria out. These glands respond to the changing levels of estrogen during the cycle. As estrogen increases at the start of a new cycle, the mucus is alkaline, thick, and viscous. When LH production begins, just before ovulation, the cervical mucus changes markedly. It becomes even more alkaline, thin, and watery. These changes make the environment for sperm passage most hospitable just at ovulation. After ovulation, the mucus returns to its former viscous, less alkaline state. If a sample of mucus is taken just before ovulation and is allowed to dry, the dried mucus takes on a fern-shaped pattern. After ovulation, during the luteal phase, the fernlike patterning will not occur. Thus the *fern test* is one method for detecting ovulation.

A woman's *basal body temperature,* taken with a thermometer before getting up in the morning, also fluctuates with the phases of the menstrual cycle. The temperature is low during the follicular phase and takes a dip on the day of ovulation. Then, on the day after ovulation it rises noticeably, generally by 0.3°C or more, and continues at the higher level for the rest of the cycle. Progesterone raises body temperature, so the higher temperature during the luteal phase is due to the increased production of progesterone during that time (Baker et al., 2002). This change in basal body temperature is important when a couple are using the fertility awareness method of birth control (Chapter 7) and when a woman is trying to determine the time of ovulation so that she may become pregnant (Chapter 6).

LO3 Menstrual Problems

The most common menstrual problem is painful menstruation, known as **dysmenorrhea**. Almost every woman experiences at least some menstrual discomfort at various times in her life, but the frequency and severity of the discomfort vary considerably from one woman to the next. Cramping pains in the pelvic region are the most common discomfort; other symptoms may include headaches, backaches, nausea, and a feeling of pressure and bloating in the pelvis.

Dysmenorrhea is caused by **prostaglandins**, hormone-like substances produced by many tissues of the body, including the lining of the uterus (Deligeor-Oglov, 2000). Prostaglandins can cause smooth muscle to contract and can affect the size of blood vessels. Women with severe menstrual pain have unusually high levels of prostaglandins. The high levels cause intense uterine contractions, which in turn choke off some of the uterus's supply of oxygen-carrying blood. Prostaglandins may also cause greater sensitivity in nerve endings. The combination of the uterine contractions, lack of oxygen, and heightened nerve sensitivity produces menstrual cramps.

The best treatment for menstrual cramps is nonsteroidal anti-inflammatory drugs (NSAIDS), such as ibuprofen (Advil) or Naproxen (Aleve) (Hatcher et al., 2007). These drugs are anti-prostaglandins, so they interrupt the basic cause of cramps. Interestingly, Aspirin is also an anti-prostaglandin. Some women find complementary/alternative therapies, such as fish oil, herbs, or acupressure, to be useful; however, research has not yet clearly demonstrated their effectiveness (Stevinson & Ernst, 2001).

A somewhat more provocative remedy suggested by, among others, Masters and Johnson is masturbation. This makes good physiological sense because part of the discomfort of menstruation—the pressure and bloating—results from pelvic edema (a congestion of fluids in the pelvic region). During sexual arousal and orgasm, pelvic congestion increases and after orgasm, the congestion dissipates (see Chapter 9). Thus orgasm, whether produced by masturbation or some other means, should help to relieve the pelvic edema that causes menstrual discomfort. And it's a lot more fun than taking medicine!

A menstrual problem that may be mistaken for dysmenorrhea is **endometriosis**. The endometrium, or lining of the uterus, grows during each menstrual cycle and is sloughed off in menstruation. Endometriosis occurs when the endometrial tissue grows in a place other than the uterus—for example, the ovaries, fallopian tubes, rectum, bladder, vagina, vulva, cervix, or lymph glands. The symptoms vary depending on the location of the growth. Very painful periods that last an unusually long time, pain during sexual activity, and infertility are the most common symptoms. Endometriosis is fairly serious and should be treated by a physician. If left untreated it can lead to sterility. Hormones are generally used in treatment, but if the problem is severe, surgery may be required. Laser surgery is a treatment option.

Another menstrual problem is **amenorrhea**, or the absence of menstruation. It is called *primary amenorrhea* if the girl has not yet menstruated by about age 18. It is called *secondary amenorrhea* if she has had at least one period. Some of the causes of amenorrhea include pregnancy, congenital defects of the reproductive system, hormonal imbalance, cysts or tumours, disease, stress, and emotional factors related to puberty. Amenorrhea can also result from programs of strenuous exercise and from anorexia nervosa.

Prenatal Sexual Differentiation

Sex Chromosomes

At the time of conception, the future human being consists of only a single cell, the fertilized egg. What is the difference between the fertilized egg that will become a female and the

dysmenorrhea (dis-men-oh-REE-uh): Painful menstruation.

prostaglandins: Chemicals secreted by the uterus that cause the uterine muscles to contract; they are a likely cause of painful menstruation.

endometriosis: A condition in which the endometrium grows abnormally outside the uterus; the symptom is unusually painful periods with excessive bleeding.

amenorrhea: The absence of menstruation.

fertilized egg that will become a male? The only difference is the sex chromosomes carried in that fertilized egg. If there are two X chromosomes, the result will typically be a female; if there is one X and one Y, the result will typically be a male. While incredibly tiny, the sex chromosomes carry a wealth of information that they transmit to various organs throughout the body, giving them instructions on how to differentiate in the course of development. Because the Y chromosome is smaller (see Figure 5.7), it has fewer genes and carries less information than the X. The Y chromosome has about 80 genes compared with 1090 on the X (Federman, 2006).[5]

Occasionally, individuals receive at conception a sex chromosome combination other than XX or XY. Such atypical sex chromosome complements may lead to a variety of clinical syndromes, such as *Klinefelter's syndrome.* In this syndrome, a genetic male has an extra X chromosome (XXY). As a result, the testes are abnormal, no sperm are produced, and testosterone levels are low (Winter & Couch, 1995).

During development, the single cell divides repeatedly, becoming a two-celled organism, then a four-celled organism, then an eight-celled organism, and so on. By 28 days after conception, the embryo is about 1 cm (less than half an inch) long, but the male and female embryos are still identical, save for the sex chromosomes. In other words, the embryo is still in the undifferentiated state. However, by the seventh week after conception, some basic structures have been formed that will eventually become either a male or a female reproductive system. At this point, the embryo has a pair of gonads (each gonad has two parts, an outer cortex and an inner medulla), two sets of ducts (the Müllerian ducts and the Wolffian ducts), and rudimentary external genitals (the genital tubercle, the urethral folds, and the genital swelling) (see Figure 5.8, top).

Gonads

In the seventh week after conception, the sex chromosomes direct the gonads to begin differentiation. In the male, the undifferentiated gonad develops into a testis at about seven weeks. In the female, the process occurs somewhat later, with the ovaries developing at around 10 or 11 weeks.

> **sex-determining region, Y chromosome (SRY):** A gene on the Y chromosome that causes testes to differentiate prenatally.
> **Müllerian ducts:** Ducts found in both male and female fetuses; in males they degenerate and in females they develop into the fallopian tubes, the uterus, and the upper part of the vagina.

[5] Although all mammals have X and Y chromosomes as humans do, sex is determined in different exotic ways in different species. For example, in some reptiles, such as alligators and turtles, sex is determined by the temperature at a critical period in development: Cooler nests all develop into males; warmer nests hatch as females. Some snails start out male then become female. Earthworms are hermaphrodites (have both male and female sex organs).

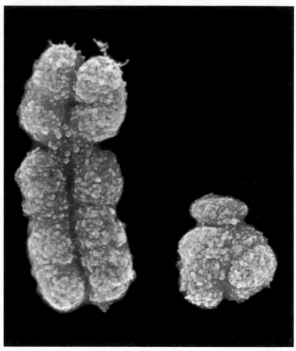

SCIENCE PHOTO LIBRARY

An important gene that directs the differentiation of the gonads, located on the Y chromosome, is called **sex-determining region, Y chromosome (SRY)** (Skaletsky et al., 2003). If SRY is present, it causes the manufacture of a substance called testis-determining factor (TDF), which makes the gonads differentiate into testes, and male development occurs. If TDF is not present, female development occurs, making female development the default option. The X chromosome carries a number of genes that control normal functioning of the ovaries (Winter & Couch, 1995). Surprisingly, a number of genes on the X chromosome affect cells in the testes that manufacture sperm (Wang et al., 2001).

Prenatal Hormones and the Genitals

Once the ovaries and testes have differentiated, they begin to produce different sex hormones, which then direct the differentiation of the rest of the internal and external genital system (see Figure 5.8).

In the female, the Wolffian ducts degenerate, and the **Müllerian ducts** turn into the fallopian tubes, the uterus, and the upper part of the vagina. The tubercle becomes the clitoris, the folds become the inner lips, and the swelling develops into the outer lips.

The testes secrete Müllerian inhibiting substance (MIS; Vilain, 2000). MIS causes the Müllerian ducts to

Figure 5.8 Development of the male and female external genitals from the undifferentiated stage. This occurs during prenatal development. Note homologous organs in the female and male.

UNDIFFERENTIATED

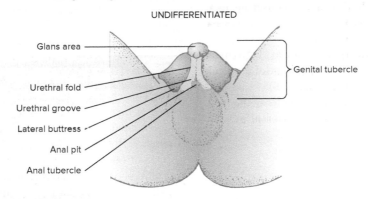

Glans area
Urethral fold
Urethral groove
Lateral buttress
Anal pit
Anal tubercle
Genital tubercle

PARTIALLY DEVELOPED

MALE   FEMALE

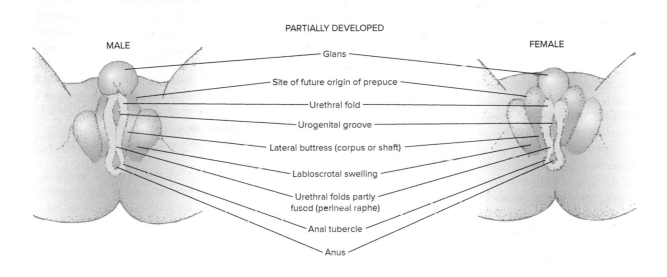

Glans
Site of future origin of prepuce
Urethral fold
Urogenital groove
Lateral buttress (corpus or shaft)
Labioscrotal swelling
Urethral folds partly fused (perineal raphe)
Anal tubercle
Anus

FULLY DEVELOPED

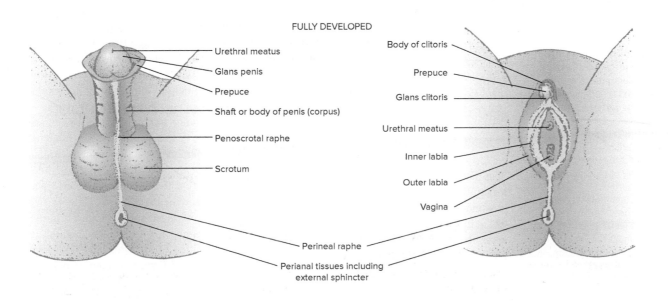

Urethral meatus
Glans penis
Prepuce
Shaft or body of penis (corpus)
Penoscrotal raphe
Scrotum

Body of clitoris
Prepuce
Glans clitoris
Urethral meatus
Inner labia
Outer labia
Vagina

Perineal raphe
Perianal tissues including external sphincter

degenerate, while the **Wolffian ducts**, supported by testosterone, turn into the epididymis, the vas deferens, and the ejaculatory duct. The tubercle becomes the glans penis, the folds form the shaft of the penis, and the swelling develops into the scrotum.

At least six different genes are involved in prenatal sexual differentiation. A mutation in any one of them can cause an error in development (Vilain, 2000).

By 12 weeks after conception, the gender of the fetus is clear from the appearance of the external genitals (refer again to Figure 5.8).

Descent of the Testes and Ovaries

As these developmental changes are taking place, the ovaries and testes are changing in shape and position. At first, the ovaries and testes lie near the top of the abdominal cavity. By the 10th week, they have grown and have moved down to the level of the upper edge of the pelvis. The ovaries remain there until after birth and later shift to their adult position in the pelvis.

The testes must make a much longer journey, down into the scrotum via a passageway called the *inguinal canal*. Normally, this movement occurs around the seventh month after conception. The inguinal canal closes off after the testes have descended.

Two problems may occur in this process. First, one or both testes may have failed to descend into the scrotum by the time of birth, a condition known as *undescended testes*, or **cryptorchidism**. This condition occurs in about 3 percent of all males. Most frequently, only one testis is undescended and the other is in the normal position. In most of these cases, the testes do descend by the first birthday. If the testes do not descend spontaneously, however, the condition is usually corrected by surgery soon after the first birthday. The optimum time for doing this is before age five. Otherwise, if both testes fail to descend, the man will be sterile because, as discussed in Chapter 4, the high temperature of the testes inside the body inhibits the production of sperm. Undescended testes are also more likely to develop cancer (Canadian Cancer Society, 2013c).

The second possible problem occurs when the inguinal canal does not close off completely. It may then reopen later in life, creating a passageway through which loops of the intestine can enter the scrotum. This condition, called *inguinal hernia*, can be remedied by simple surgery.

Wolffian ducts: Ducts found in both male and female fetuses; in females they degenerate and in males they develop into the epididymis, the vas deferens, and the ejaculatory duct.

cryptorchidism: Undescended testes; the condition in which the testes do not descend to the scrotum as they should during prenatal development.

epigenetics: A functional change to DNA that does not alter the genetic code itself, but leads to changes in gene expression. Often, an epigenetic change involves methylation; that is, a methyl group is attached to the base cytosine in the DNA.

Brain Differentiation

During the prenatal period, when sex hormones are having a big impact on genital anatomy, they are also acting on the brain (Arnold, 2003). The results of many experiments with animals indicate that, in certain regions, there are differences between male and female brains. The primary sex-differentiated structure is the hypothalamus, particularly a region of it called the *preoptic area* (Fitch & Bimonte, 2002). The hypothalamus is gender-differentiated in humans as well (Cahill, 2005; Swaab, Gooren, & Hofman, 1995).

One of the most important effects of this early sexual differentiation is determination of the estrogen sensitivity of certain cells in the hypothalamus. Estrogen passes into these cells and binds to specific molecules in the nucleus, called *estrogen receptors* (Choi et al., 2001; McEwen, 2001). If testosterone is present during fetal development, these specialized cells in the hypothalamus become insensitive to estrogen. If estrogen is present, these cells become highly sensitive to levels of estrogen in the bloodstream. This sensitivity is crucial to the hypothalamic–pituitary–gonad feedback loop discussed earlier. Male hypothalamic cells are relatively insensitive to estrogen levels, whereas female hypothalamic cells are highly sensitive to them. Male hypothalamic cells have more androgen receptors (Donahue, Stopa, & Chorsky, 2000).

A major new study in 2015 reported evidence of epigenetic changes during prenatal sexual differentiation of the brain (Spiers et al., 2015). **Epigenetics** refers to a functional change to DNA that does not alter the genetic code itself, but leads to changes in gene expression. Often an epigenetic change involves *methylation;* that is, a methyl group is attached to the base cytosine in the DNA. Differences between male and female brains in DNA methylation were found for a number of genes. These results suggest that prenatal sexual differentiation of the brain may involve more than anatomical differences in structures and androgen receptors, but may also involve epigenetic factors that can lead genes to be expressed or silenced. The researchers hope that this research will eventually help to explain why, for example, autism affects so many more males than females.

New magnetic resonance imaging (MRI) studies are giving us a view into the brains of alive, awake humans, in contrast to earlier techniques that dissected the brains of dead people and animals (see Chapter 3). The trade-off, at least for now, is that the MRI measures are relatively crude, simple assessments of the volume or size of certain regions. One of these studies found a larger volume of the hypothalamus and amygdala—both brain regions with high densities of estrogen and androgen receptors—in men compared with women (Goldstein et al., 2001). Regions of the brain that have few estrogen

Table 5.1 Homologous and Analogous Organs of the Male and Female Reproductive Systems

Embryonic Source	Homologous Organs		Analogous Organs	
	In the Adult Male	In the Adult Female	In the Adult Male	In the Adult Female
Gonad (medulla plus cortex)	Testes (from medulla)	Ovaries (from cortex)	Testes (from medulla)	Ovaries (from cortex)
Genital tubercle	Glans penis	Clitoris	Glans penis	Clitoris
Genital swelling	Scrotum			
Müllerian duct		Outer lips, fallopian tubes, uterus, part of vagina		
Wolffian duct	Epididymis, vas deferens, seminal vesicles			
Urethral primordia	Prostate, Cowper's glands	Skene's glands, Bartholin glands	Prostate, Cowper's glands	Skene's glands, Bartholin glands

and androgen receptors did not show these gender differences in size.

The brains of men and women are actually quite similar in most regions, but a few brain structures show gender differentiation (Eliot, 2009; Joel, 2011). These structures include the hypothalamus, which we have already discussed, and the amygdala, which is important in emotion (Cahill, 2005; Ngun et al., 2011). Modern neuroscientists, however, reject the notion that these represent "hard-wired" differences present from birth (Eliot, 2009). Instead, neuroscientists emphasize the *plasticity* of the brain, which is constantly changing in response to experiences that the person has. For example, an 8-year-old boy has a father who practises tossing footballs with him every day, whereas the father of the 8-year-old girl next door doesn't toss footballs with her. Within weeks, the neural circuits in the boy's brain involved in catching and throwing will have strengthened, whereas the same circuits in the girl's brain will not have. Their brains will now be different in that region, but as a result of their different experiences, not hard-wiring present from birth.

LO5 Homologous Organs

Our discussion of sexual differentiation highlights the fact that although adult men and women appear to have very different reproductive anatomies, their reproductive organs have similar origins. When an organ in the male and an organ in the female both develop from the same embryonic tissue, the organs are said to be **homologous organs**. When the two organs have similar functions, they are said to be **analogous organs**. Table 5.1 summarizes the major homologies and analogies of the male and female reproductive systems. For example, ovaries and testes are homologous (they develop from an undifferentiated gonad) and analogous (they produce gametes and sex hormones).

  ## Atypical Prenatal Gender Differentiation

Gender is not a simple matter, as you may have noted from the preceding discussion. Most people, however, assume that it is. That is, people typically assume that if a person is female, she will have feminine traits; will think of herself as a woman; will be sexually attracted to men; will have a clitoris, vagina, uterus, and ovaries; and will have sex chromosomes XX. They also assume that all males have masculine traits; think of themselves as male; are sexually attracted to women; have a penis, testes, and scrotum; and have sex chromosomes XY.

A great deal of research over the last several decades challenges these assumptions and provides much information about sexuality and gender and their development. Before we discuss the results of this research, however, some background information is helpful.

We can distinguish among the following eight variables of gender (Money, 1987):[6]

1. *Chromosomal gender:* XX in females; XY in males
2. *Gonadal gender:* Ovaries in females; testes in males
3a. *Prenatal hormonal gender:* Testosterone and MIS in males but not females before birth
3b. *Prenatal and neonatal brain differentiation:* Testosterone present for masculinization, absent for feminization
4. *Internal organs:* Fallopian tubes, uterus, and upper vagina in females; prostate, vas, and seminal vesicles in males

> **homologous (huh-MOLL-uh-gus) organs:** Organs in the male and female that develop from the same embryonic tissue.
> **analogous (an-AL-uh-gus) organs:** Organs in the male and female that have similar functions.

---

[6] The distinction between the terms *gender* and *sex*, discussed in Chapter 1, is being maintained here.

5. *External genital appearance:* Clitoris, inner and outer lips, and vaginal opening in females; penis and scrotum in males

6. *Pubertal hormonal gender:* At puberty, estrogen and progesterone in females; testosterone in males

7. *Assigned gender:* The announcement at birth, "It's a girl" or "It's a boy," based on the appearance of the external genitals; the gender the parents and the rest of society believe the child to be; the gender in which the child is reared

8. *Gender identity:* The person's private, internal sense of maleness or femaleness

These variables might be subdivided into biological variables (the first six) and psychological variables (the last two). (Gender roles, or the way people of one gender are expected to behave, are discussed in Chapter 13.)

What is an intersex condition?

In most cases, of course, all the variables are in agreement in an individual. However, there is great variability between individuals (and species, see Figure 5.9), and as a result of any one of a number of factors during the course of prenatal sexual development, the gender indicated by one or more of these variables may disagree with the gender indicated by others. When the contradictions are among several of the biological variables (1 through 6), the person is said to have an **intersex** condition, also called a **disorder of sexual development (DSD)** (Berenbaum, 2006; Hughes et al., 2006; Reis, 2007).[7] Biologically, the gender of such a person is ambiguous. The reproductive structures may be partly male and partly female, or they may be incompletely male or female. Approximately 2 percent of births have an intersex condition (Blackless et al., 2000). The controversy over whether and how to treat intersex individuals is described in A Sexually Diverse World. Individuals whose assigned gender does not match their gender identity are discussed in Chapter 13.

A number of syndromes can cause an intersex condition. Two of the most common are congenital adrenal hyperplasia and the androgen-insensitivity syndrome. In **congenital**

intersex: A condition in which an individual has a mixture of male and female reproductive structures, so that it is not clear at birth whether the individual is a male or a female; formerly called a *pseudohermaphrodite*.

disorder of sexual development (DSD): A newer term for an intersex condition.

congenital adrenal hyperplasia (CAH): A condition in which a genetic female produces abnormal levels of testosterone prenatally and therefore has male-appearing genitals at birth.

androgen-insensitivity syndrome (AIS): A genetic condition in which the body is unresponsive to androgens so that a genetic male may be born with a female-appearing body.

---

[7] The term *hermaphrodite* is taken from Hermaphroditos, the name of the mythological son of Hermes and Aphrodite. The latter was the Greek goddess of love. A true hermaphrodite has both ovarian and testicular tissues.

Figure 5.9 Diversity in prenatal sexual differentiation. The female spotted hyena has a clitoris as large as a penis and no vaginal opening because the labia fuse together like a scrotum. Urine passes out through the clitoris and she gives birth through the clitoris. Pregnant female hyenas produce high levels of an androgen (A_4), and the hyena placenta produces an enzyme that converts the A_4 to testosterone, leading to the masculinized genitals of daughters (Drea, 2009).

© Ingram Publishing

adrenal hyperplasia (CAH), a genetic female develops ovaries normally as a fetus; later in the course of prenatal development, however, the adrenal gland begins to function abnormally (as a result of a recessive genetic condition unconnected with the sex chromosomes), and produces an excess amount of androgens. Prenatal sexual differentiation then does not follow the typical female course. As a result, the external genitals are partly or completely male in appearance. The labia are partly or totally fused (so there is no vaginal opening), and the clitoris is enlarged to the size of a small penis or even a full-sized one. Hence, at birth these genetic females are sometimes identified as males. Long-term follow-ups indicate that girls with CAH have a female gender identity, tend toward male-stereotyped toy and game preference, and generally function well as girls and women (Meyer-Bahlburg et al., 2004; Meyer-Bahlburg et al., 2006).

In androgen-insensitivity syndrome (AIS) (Wisniewski et al., 2000), a genetic male fetus produces normal levels of testosterone; however, as a result of a genetic condition, the body tissues are insensitive to the testosterone, and prenatal development is feminized, although this can occur with different levels of severity. Thus, the individual is born with the external appearance of a female: a small vagina (but no internal reproductive organs) and undescended testes. The individual whose poem appears at the beginning of this chapter has AIS.

Intersex persons provide good evidence of the great complexity of sex and gender and their development. Many variables are involved in gender and sex, and there are many steps in gender differentiation, even before birth. Because the process is complex, it is vulnerable to variations, creating conditions such as intersex. Indeed, the research serves to question our basic notions of what it means to be male or female. In CAH, is the genetic female who is born with male external genitals a male or a female? What makes a person male or female? Chromosomal gender? External genital appearance? Gender identity?

A related phenomenon was first studied in a small community in the Dominican Republic (Imperato-McGinley et al., 1974). Because of a genetic-endocrine problem, a large number of genetic males were born there who, at birth, appeared to be females. The syndrome is called *5-alpha reductase deficiency syndrome*. They had a vaginal pouch instead of a scrotum and a clitoris-sized penis. The uneducated parents, according to the researchers, were unaware that there were any problems, and these genetic males were treated as typical females. At puberty, a spontaneous biological change caused a penis to develop. Significantly, the psychological identity of most of these individuals also changed. Despite their rearing as females, their gender identity switched to male, and they developed heterosexual interests. In their culture, these people are called *Guevodoces* ("penis at 12").

Anthropologist Gilbert Herdt (1990) is critical of the research and interpretations about the Guevodoces. The major criticism is that the Western researchers assumed that this culture is a two-gender society, as in Canada, and that people have to fall into one of only two categories, either male or female. Anthropologists, however, have documented the existence of three-gender societies—that is, societies in which there are three, not two, gender categories—and the society in which the Guevodoces grow up is a three-gender society. The third gender is the Guevodoces. Their gender identity is not male or female, but Guevodoce. The 5-alpha reductase deficiency syndrome has also been found among the Sambia of New Guinea, who also have a three-gender culture. Again we see the profound effect of culture on our most basic ideas about sex and gender.

LO7

Sexual Differentiation During Puberty

Puberty is not a point in time, but rather a process during which further sexual differentiation occurs. It is the stage in life during which the body changes from that of a child into that of an adult, with secondary sexual characteristics and the ability to reproduce sexually. **Puberty** can be scientifically defined as the time during which there is sudden enlargement and maturation of the gonads, other genitalia, and secondary sex characteristics (such as breasts or a beard), leading to reproductive capacity (Tanner, 1967). It is the second important period—the other being the prenatal period—during which sexual differentiation takes place. Perhaps the most memorable single event in the process is the first ejaculation for boys and the first menstruation for girls. Note that first menstruation is not necessarily a sign of reproductive capability since girls typically do not produce mature eggs until a year or two after the first menstruation.

The physiological process that underlies puberty in both genders is a marked increase in level of sex hormones. Thus the hypothalamus, pituitary, and gonads control the changes.

Adolescence is a socially defined period of development that bears some relationship to puberty. Adolescence represents a psychological transition from the behaviour and attitudes of a child to the behaviour, attitudes, and responsibilities of an adult. In Canada it corresponds roughly to the years from age 10 to age 20. Modern Canadian culture has an unusually long period of adolescence (Steinberg, 2011). A century ago, adolescence was much shorter; the lengthening of the educational process has served to prolong adolescence. In some cultures, in fact, adolescence does not exist. Instead, the child shifts to being an adult directly, with only a *rite de passage* in between.

Before describing the changes that take place during puberty, we should note two points. First, the timing of the pubertal process differs considerably for boys and girls. Girls begin the change at around 8 to 12 years of age, while boys do so about two years later. Girls reach their full height by about age 16, while boys continue growing until about age 18 or later. Second, there are large individual differences in the age at which puberty begins (Bogaert, 2005). Experiences may also affect the timing of puberty. For example, girls who have been sexually abused tend to experience earlier puberty than do girls who have not been abused (Turner, Runtz, & Galambos, 1999). There is no one normal time to begin menstruating or growing a beard. Thus, we give age ranges in describing the timing of the process.

Changes in Boys

A summary of the physical changes of puberty in boys and girls is provided in Table 5.2. The physical causes of puberty in boys parallel those in girls. They are initiated by increased production of FSH and LH by the pituitary. At the beginning of

> **puberty:** The time during which there is sudden enlargement and maturation of the gonads, other genitalia, and secondary sex characteristics, so that the individual becomes capable of reproduction.

A Sexually Diverse World

Can Gender Be Assigned? The Story of David Reimer

In Winnipeg in 1965, Janet Reimer gave birth to twin boys, Bruce and Brian. Six months later, the boys developed problems urinating, and their doctor suggested that they be circumcised. However, the doctor did not use the standard procedure for circumcision and botched the surgery, burning off Bruce's entire penis. The Reimers were told that Bruce would have to live without a penis. Some months later, Janet Reimer saw a television program describing the pioneering work of Dr. John Money of Johns Hopkins University in Baltimore, Maryland. Money believed that gender is determined by how a child is raised, not by his or her biology, providing that assignment is done in infancy and the necessary surgeries and hormone treatments occur.

The Reimers consulted with Money and made the decision to raise Bruce as female even though they had been raising him as a boy up to that time. At the age of 21 months, Bruce's testicles were removed. The Reimers renamed their son Brenda, and following the counsel of Dr. Money, resolved not to tell their child the truth. However, despite taking hormones and receiving numerous surgeries, Brenda never really fit in as a girl. She preferred stereotypically male play (e.g., climbing trees) over playing with dolls, and she was frequently made fun of by other children for her masculine mannerisms. Brenda even complained of feeling like a boy. When she reached puberty and was scheduled to have a final surgery to construct a vagina, Brenda refused, despite Money's urging, indicating she would prefer to die. A psychiatrist suggested to Mr. and Mrs. Reimer that they tell Brenda the truth, who later commented about this revelation, "Suddenly it all made sense why I felt the way I did."

Within months of learning the truth about his sex, Bruce/Brenda cut his hair, began wearing masculine clothing, and changed his name to David (see Figure 5.10). He underwent a series of surgeries to give him a more male body, including a mastectomy to remove the breasts

Figure 5.10 David Reimer underwent gender reassignment after a botched surgery when he was six months old.

© CP Picture Archive/Winnipeg Free Press

he had grown as a result of taking estrogen. Although David was much happier with his gender, he struggled with depression, in part because he thought he would not find a partner who would love him for who he was. However, as a young adult, David met and married Jane and became the father to her three children. David continued to battle depression, which worsened in his late 30s following the death of his twin brother. He also experienced marital and work-related difficulties, and failed financial investments. On May 4, 2004, at the age of 38, David committed suicide.

Babies who are born with genitals that are not clearly male or female (intersex individuals) typically are treated like David was, using a protocol that became standard in the 1960s. The treatment, which is based on Money's work, generally involves surgically altering the infant's genitals to make them clearly male or female. In Canada, such procedures are covered under Medicare. However, Accord Alliance, which promotes integrated care for those with disorders of sexual development and their families, and the Organisation Internationale des Intersexués (OII, founded in Quebec) have argued that intersexuality represents genital variability—as opposed to genital abnormality. The medical standard is that an infant's organ that is 0.9 cm or less should be considered a clitoris and 2.5 cm or more should be considered a penis, and an infant's gender is assigned accordingly. Activists argue that these cutoffs are arbitrary. What is wrong with a clitoris that is 1.7 cm long, for example? Ontario psychologist Morgan Holmes believes that the surgeries are conducted because doctors and parents are uncomfortable with the idea of a child not having genitals that fit a narrow definition of what genitals should look like. Is it ethical to conduct such surgeries and gender assignments with infants who cannot give informed consent and who may later prefer another gender than that chosen for them by their parents and doctors? Should parents be encouraged to lie to their child, as David Reimer's parents were?

Sex researcher Milton Diamond conducted long-term follow-up studies on several individuals who were treated using Money's standard protocol, including David Reimer. Diamond found that, contrary to Money's published paper describing these individuals as well adjusted, many of them had significant adjustment problems that they traced directly to the medical "management" of their condition. Diamond's research sparked a debate over proper treatment of disorders of sexual development. Diamond proposed an alternative protocol for dealing with infants with these disorders in which he urges physicians (1) to make their most informed judgment about the child's eventual gender identity and counsel the parents to rear the child in that gender; (2) not to perform surgeries that might later need to be reversed; and (3) to provide honest counselling and education to the parents and child as he

or she grows up so that the child can eventually make an informed decision regarding treatment.

More systematic follow-up studies on individuals with disorders of sexual development have followed. Many individuals who underwent surgery as infants were dissatisfied with their genitals and reported poor sexual functioning (Creighton, Minto, & Steele, 2001; Minto et al., 2003; Wisniewski et al., 2001). The results of these studies also seem to support Money's idea that gender is partly determined by environment. Recognizing these new developments, the American Academy of Pediatrics (2000; Lee et al., 2006) issued guidelines for pediatricians on how to care for newborns with genitals that are not clearly male or female. They include what tests to run to determine the cause of the ambiguous genitals, when the baby should be referred to a centre specializing in disorders of sexual development, and what factors should be used to decide the sex of rearing. These factors include fertility potential (e.g., a girl with congenital adrenal hyperplasia is potentially fertile and should be raised as a girl) and capacity for normal sexual functioning. Only with long-term studies will we learn whether these new treatments will yield better results for individuals with disorders of sexual development.

In keeping with the latest thinking about delaying surgical treatment of individual with disorders of sexual development, Germany became the first European country to legally recognize a third gender. Parents of babies with intersex conditions can choose to register their babies as having an undermined or unspecified gender on their birth certificate rather than being forced to identify them as male or female. Australia allows a passport holder to indicate X instead of F or M.

Sources: American Academy of Pediatrics, 2000; CBC News, 2004; Colapinto, 2004; Creighton & Minto, 2001; Creighton et al., 2001; Diamond, 1996, 1999; Diamond & Sigmundson, 1997; Holmes, 2002; Meyer-Bahlburg et al., 2004; Money & Ehrhardt, 1972; Wisniewski et al., 2000.

Table 5.2   Summary of the Changes of Puberty and Their Sequence

Girls			Boys		
Characteristic	**Average Age of First Appearance (Years)**	**Major Hormonal Influence**	**Characteristic**	**Average Age of First Appearance (Years)**	**Major Hormonal Influence**
Growth of breasts	9–10	Pituitary growth hormone, estrogens, progesterone, thyroxine	Growth of testes, scrotal sac	9–10	Pituitary growth hormone, testosterone
Growth of pubic hair	9–10	Adrenal androgens	Growth of pubic hair	11–12	Testosterone
Body growth	9.5–14.5	Pituitary growth hormone, adrenal androgens, estrogens	Body growth	10.5–16	Pituitary growth hormone, testosterone
Menarche	12–12.5	GnRH, FSH, LH, estrogens, progesterone	Growth of penis	11–14.5	Testosterone
			Change in voice (growth of larynx)	About the same time as penis growth	Testosterone
Underarm hair	About two years after pubic hair	Adrenal androgens	Facial and underarm hair	About two years after pubic hair	Testosterone
Oil- and sweat-producing glands (acne occurs when glands are clogged)	About the same time as underarm hair	Adrenal androgens	Oil- and sweat-producing glands, acne	About the same time as underarm hair	Testosterone

puberty, the increase in LH stimulates the testes to produce testosterone, which is responsible for most of the changes of puberty in boys.

The first noticeable pubertal change in boys is the growth of the testes and scrotal sac, which begins at an average age of 9 to 10 as a result of testosterone stimulation. The growth of pubic hair begins at about the same time. About a year later the penis begins to enlarge, first thickening and then lengthening. This change also results from testosterone stimulation. As the testes enlarge, their production of testosterone increases even more, leading to rapid growth of the penis, testes, and pubic hair at ages 13 and 14.

The growth of facial and axillary (underarm) hair begins about two years after the beginning of pubic hair growth. The growth of facial hair begins with the appearance of fuzz on the upper lip; adult beards do not appear until two or three years later. Indeed, by age 17, 50 percent of North American males have not yet shaved. These changes also result from testosterone stimulation, which continues to produce growth of facial and chest hair beyond 20 years of age.

Erections increase in frequency and sometimes occur at inopportune times. The organs that produce the fluid of semen, particularly the prostate, enlarge considerably at about the same time the other organs are growing. By age 13 or 14, the boy is capable of ejaculation.[8] By about age 15, the ejaculate contains mature sperm, and the male is now fertile. The pituitary hormone FSH is responsible for initiating and maintaining the production of mature sperm.

Beginning about a year after the first ejaculation, many boys begin having nocturnal emissions, or *wet dreams*. For the boy who has never masturbated, a wet dream may be his first ejaculation.

At about the same time that penis growth occurs, the *larynx* (voice box) also begins to grow in response to testosterone. As the larynx enlarges, the boy's voice drops, or "changes." Typically, the transition occurs at around age 13 or 14.

A great spurt of body growth begins in boys at around 11 to 16 years of age (Figure 5.11). Height increases rapidly. Body contours also change. While the changes in girls involve mainly the increase in fatty tissue in the breasts and hips, the changes in boys involve mainly an increase in muscle mass. Eventually testosterone brings the growth process to an end, although it permits the growth period to continue longer than it does in girls.

---

[8] Note that orgasm and ejaculation are two separate processes, even though they generally occur together, at least in males after puberty (see Chapter 9). But orgasm may occur without ejaculation, and ejaculation may occur without orgasm.

Figure 5.11 There is great variability in the onset of puberty and its growth spurt. Each pair of children are the same age.

(a) © PNC/Media Bakery

(b) © Skjold Photographs/The Image Works

Puberty brings changes and also problems. One problem is *acne,* a distressing skin condition that is stimulated by androgens and affects boys more frequently than girls. It is caused by a clogging of the sebaceous (oil-producing) glands, resulting in pustules, blackheads, and redness on the face and possibly the chest and back.

Gynecomastia (breast enlargement) may occur temporarily in boys, creating considerable embarrassment. About 80 percent of boys in puberty experience this growth, which is probably caused by small amounts of female sex hormones being produced by the testes. Obesity may also be a temporary problem, although it is more frequent in girls than boys.

In various cultures around the world, puberty rites are performed to signify the adolescent's passage to adulthood (see Figure 5.12). Many Indigenous cultures celebrate this life transition for boys and girls. In Canada, the other remaining vestiges of such ceremonies are the Jewish bar mitzvah for boys and bat mitzvah for girls. In a sense, it is unfortunate that we do not give more formal recognition to puberty. Puberty rites probably serve an important psychological function in that they are a formal, public announcement of the fact that the boy or girl is passing through an important period of change. In the absence of such rituals, the young person may think that his or her body is doing strange things. This may be particularly problematic for boys, who lack an obvious sign of puberty like the first menstruation (the first ejaculation is probably the closest analogy) to help them identify the stage they are in.

Changes in Girls

The first sign of puberty in girls is the beginning of breast development, on average around 9 to 10 years of age (Sun et al., 2002). The ducts in the nipple area swell, and there is growth of fatty and connective tissue, causing the small, conical buds to increase in size. These changes are produced by increases in the levels of the sex hormones. The average age at which girls start puberty—that is begin to develop breast tissue—has dropped significantly in recent years, although the average age

Figure 5.12 Most cultures celebrate puberty, but cultures vary widely in the nature of the celebration. *(a)* Canadian Jewish youth celebrate a bar mitzvah (for boys) or bat mitzvah (for girls). *(b)* Boys wear ceremonial skirts for their circumcision ceremonies in Democratic Republic of Congo. During their gruelling initiation into manhood, boys about 9 to 12 years old are circumcised and then marched into the forest, where they spend several months hunting and fishing. Each morning the boys are whipped by their elders to instill toughness.

(a) © Blair Seitz/Science Source

(b) © Randy Olson/National Geographic/Getty Images

at which girls begin to menstruate has not changed (Euling et al., 2008). Exposure to endocrine disrupting chemicals may be one cause of this decline; increased obesity may be another factor (Mouritsen et al., 2010). Girls who reach puberty significantly earlier than their peers may be at risk to experience some negative psychosocial consequences including depression, unhealthy behaviours, and school problems (Posner, 2006). On the other hand, reaching puberty significantly later than one's peers may also have negative psychosocial consequences for girls (and boys).

As the growth of fatty and supporting tissue increases in the breasts, a similar increase takes place at the hips and buttocks, leading to the rounded contours that distinguish adult female bodies from adult male bodies. Individual females have unique patterns of fat deposits, so there are also considerable individual differences in the resulting female shapes.

Another visible sign of puberty is the growth of pubic

hair, which occurs shortly after breast development begins. About two years later, axillary (underarm) hair appears.

Body growth increases sharply during puberty, during the approximate age range of 9.5 to 14.5 years. The growth spurt for girls occurs about two years before the growth spurt for boys (see Figure 5.13). This is consistent with girls' general pattern of maturing earlier than boys.

Estrogen eventually applies the brakes to the growth spurt in girls. The presence of estrogen also causes the growth period to end sooner in girls, thus accounting for the lesser average height of adult women as compared with adult men.

On average, girls in Canada experience **menarche** (first menstruation) when they are 12.7 years old (Al-Sahab, Ardern, et al., 2010). This age is somewhat higher than in the United States but somewhat lower than in other developed countries, such as Australia, Russia, and Norway. However, 15 percent of girls experience menarche when they are less than 11.5 years old; most (67 percent) when they are between 11.5 and

What determines the age at which a girl first menstruates?

menarche (MEN-ar-key): First menstruation.

Figure 5.13 The adolescent spurt of growth for boys and girls. Note that girls experience their growth spurt earlier than boys do.

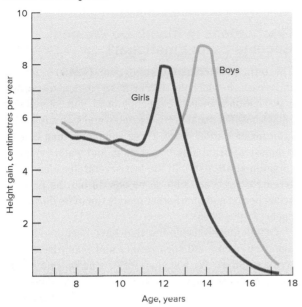

the first time and for it to be maintained. Thus, very thin adolescent girls would tend to be late in the timing of first menstruation. **Leptin**, a hormone, is related to the onset of puberty in girls and in boys (Israel et al., 2012; Terasawa et al., 2012). In pre-pubertal girls and boys, leptin levels rise as body fat increases. Leptin simulates the growth of skeletal bone and the release of LH.

The hot new hormone that has been discovered to be involved in the initiation of puberty is **kisspeptin** (Ojeda & Lomniczi, 2014). It is encoded by a gene called KISS1. Don't you just love the way these biologists name things! Other genes control when the KISS1 gene starts to be expressed so that it produces kisspeptin. Kisspeptin then stimulates the hypothalamus to produce more GnRH and to produce it in a "pulsatile" fashion—that is, in pulses. This initiates a cascade of secretion of hormones, including LH and FSH, which stimulates the ovaries to produce estrogen, and the pubertal race is on!

The percent body fat hypothesis also helps to make sense of two related phenomena: the cessation of menstruation in women with anorexia nervosa and the cessation of menstruation in female distance runners. *Anorexia nervosa* is a condition in which the person—most commonly an adolescent girl—engages in compulsive, extreme dieting and exercise, perhaps to the point of starving herself to death. As anorexia progresses, the percentage of body fat declines and menstruation ceases. It is also fairly common for women who are runners, and all women who exercise seriously to the point where their body fat is substantially reduced, to cease menstruating. It seems that when the percentage of body fat falls below a critical value, the biological mechanisms that control the menstrual cycle shut down menstruation.[9]

Before leaving the topic of running, we should note that there is some evidence that serious exercise also affects the male reproductive system. One study of male distance runners found that their testosterone levels were only about 68 percent as high, on the average, as a control group's testosterone levels, and many other studies have found similar effects (Hackney, 2008; Wheeler et al., 1984). There are some reports of male long-distance runners complaining of a loss of sex drive, but it is unclear whether this results from reduced testosterone levels or from the perpetual feelings of fatigue from their intensive training (Wheeler et al., 1984).

Other body changes in girls during puberty include a development of the blood supply to the clitoris, a thickening of the walls of the vagina, and a rapid growth of the uterus,

13.9 years old; and 17 percent when they are older than 13.9 years old. Although the average age of menarche has decreased in the past 150 years, likely because of improved nutrition, it has remained constant over the past 50 years (Posner, 2006). Girls are not capable of becoming pregnant until ovulation begins. Typically, girls do not ovulate regularly for one to two years after first ovulation (Metcalf et al., 1983). The first menstruation is not only an important biological event but also a significant psychological one. Various cultures have ceremonies recognizing its importance. In some families, it is a piece of news that spreads quickly to the relatives. Girls themselves display a wide range of reactions to the event, ranging from negative ones, such as fear, shame, or disgust, to positive ones, such as pride and a sense of maturity and womanliness.

Some of the most negative reactions occur when the girl has not been prepared for the menarche, which is still the case surprisingly often. Parents who are concerned about preparing their daughters for the first menstruation should remember that there is a wide range in the age at which it occurs. It is not unusual for a girl to start menstruating in Grade 5, and instances of menarche during Grade 4, while rare, do occur.

What determines the age at which a girl first menstruates? One explanation is the *percent body fat hypothesis* (Frisch & McArthur, 1974; Hopwood et al., 1990; Lassek & Gaulin, 2007). During puberty, deposits of body fat increase in females. According to the percent body fat hypothesis, the percentage of body weight that is fat must rise to a certain level for menstruation to occur for

leptin: A protein that is related to the onset of puberty.
kisspeptin: A hormone involved in the initiation of pubertal development.

---

[9] On the other hand, moderate exercise has been associated with reduced menstrual problems, such as cramps (Hightower, 1997).

which doubles in size between age 10 and age 18. The pelvic bone structure grows and widens, contributing to the rounded shape of the female and creating a passageway large enough for an infant to move through during birth.

The dramatic changes that occur during puberty are produced, basically, by the endocrine system and its upsurge in sex hormone production during puberty. The process begins with the hypothalamus releasing pulses of GnRH, which triggers an increase in secretion of FSH by the pituitary gland. FSH in turn stimulates the ovaries to produce estrogen. Estrogen is responsible for many of the changes that occur; it stimulates breast growth and the growth of the uterus and vagina.

Also involved in puberty are the paired **adrenal glands**, which are located just above the kidneys. In the female, the adrenal glands are the major producer of androgens, which exist at low levels in females. Adrenal androgens stimulate the growth of pubic and axillary hair and are related to the female sex drive. **Adrenarche**—the time of increasing secretion of adrenal androgens—generally begins slightly before age 8 (Grumbach & Styne, 1998).

Changes in Behaviour

Puberty brings not only changes in the body but changes in behaviour as well (Forbes & Dahl, 2010). Puberty has both organizing effects and activating effects. Pubertal development results in changes in the brain and genitals (organizing effects) and also activates certain behaviours. The research evidence indicates that puberty increases sensation-seeking behaviours—that is, wanting high-intensity, exciting experiences—and sex is one sensation that might be sought. Puberty also reorients social behaviour so that adolescents are motivated to seek social experiences with their peers and with potential romantic partners.

LO8 Psychological Aspects of the Menstrual Cycle

It is part of the folk wisdom of our culture that women experience fluctuations in mood over the phases of the menstrual cycle. In particular, women are supposed to be especially cranky and depressed just before and during their periods. In France, if a woman commits a crime during her premenstrual phase, she may use the fact in her defence, claiming "temporary impairment of sanity."

adrenal (uh-DREE-nul) glands: Endocrine glands located just above the kidneys; in the female they are the major producers of androgens.
adrenarche (AD-ren-ar-key): A time of increased secretion of adrenal androgens, usually just before age 8.

What is the scientific evidence concerning the occurrence of such fluctuations in mood, and, if they do occur, what causes them?

Fluctuations in Mood: Do Women Become Extra Emotional?

The term **premenstrual syndrome (PMS)** refers to those cases in which the woman has a particularly severe combination of physical, psychological, and behavioural symptoms that occur premenstrually and stop a few days after menstruation starts. These symptoms may include depression, irritability, breast pain, and water retention (Stanton et al., 2002). In the last several decades, much research has been done on moods during the premenstrual period and on whether moods fluctuate during the cycle (Taylor, 2006).

Of the numerous studies that have been conducted, many offer contradictory results and many have used weak methods. We will therefore focus on one recent study that used the best design of any to date. The researchers collected data from a random sample of Canadian women daily for six months (Romans et al., 2013). Notice that by collecting data every day, the researchers overcame problems of memory distortion in self-report. Each participant received a handheld Palm device loaded with mental health telemetry software. *Telemetry* refers to a method in which data are collected at remote locations and transmitted to a central computer for data storage and analysis. This method allows researchers to verify that each woman actually completed the questionnaire each day, and it allows the women to go about their usual daily routines without having to go to a lab. The questionnaire—which had to be kept short so participants would cooperate and complete it daily—included four negative mood items; four positive mood items; nine items assessing physical activity, health, social support, and stress; and one item about whether they had their menstrual period that day. The diverse items were used to disguise the fact that the study was about mood and the menstrual cycle; had participants known the point of the study, it might have activated their stereotypes about menstrual cycle fluctuations in mood, leading them to respond in a stereotyped way.

The results were surprising: No positive mood items showed cycle fluctuations. Only two negative mood items, sadness and irritability, showed significant variations across the cycle. Irritability was greater both premenstrually and during menses, compared with mid-cycle. Notice that greater irritability was not just *premenstrual*, challenging the basic concept of PMS. Sadness was greater premenstrually, but it was more strongly associated with stress, physical health, and social support than it was with cycle phase.

According to this study, there is no scientific evidence of PMS, although there are plenty of stereotypes about it. That said, it may be that a small percentage of women do experience PMS. Averaging across data from a random sample of women, there are too few with PMS to produce average mood fluctuations. The best conclusion seems to be that the great majority of women do not experience menstrual cycle fluctuations in mood, but a small percentage may.

Despite this study and other similar ones, the American Psychiatric Association has formalized severe PMS with the diagnosis **premenstrual dysphoric disorder (PMDD)** in the *Diagnostic and Statistical Manual of Mental Disorders* (5th ed.), or *DSM-5* (American Psychiatric Association, 2013a). Symptoms must occur during the week before the beginning of menstruation and must improve a few days after menstruation starts. The woman must have at least five symptoms, such as marked mood swings, sadness or hopelessness, tension or anxiety, irritability or anger, difficulty concentrating, decreased interest in usual activities, and marked changes in appetite. These symptoms have to have occurred most months for the past year, be as severe as those of other mental disorders, and result in impairment. Thus, only 3 to 5 percent of women would meet the criteria for PMDD (American Psychiatric Association, 2010). This diagnostic category is very controversial, however (Caplan, 1995). Some argue that it represents nothing but a medicalizing and pathologizing of women's experience (Offman & Kleinplatz, 2004; Poulin & Gouliquer, 2003). Others point out that there is no scientific basis for PMDD and that some studies fail to confirm it (Gallant et al., 1992). Still others argue that the PMDD diagnosis is useful for the minority of women who experience such extreme symptoms that their quality of life is affected (Di Giulio & Reissing, 2006).

Fluctuations in Performance

So far, our discussion has concentrated on fluctuations in psychological characteristics, such as depression, anxiety, and irritability. However, in some situations performance is of more practical importance than mood. For example, is a female mechanic's work less accurate premenstrually and menstrually? Is a female athlete's coordination or speed impaired during the premenstrual–menstrual period?

Research on performance—such as intellectual or athletic performance—generally shows no fluctuations over the cycle (Burrows & Bird, 2005). Research has found no fluctuations in academic performance, problem solving, memory, or creative thinking (Epting & Overman, 1988; Stanton et al., 2002).

In one study, 31 percent of female athletes said they believed that they experienced a decline in performance

during the premenstrual or menstrual phases; yet when their actual performance was measured, they showed no deficits in strength (weightlifters) or swimming speed (swimming team members) (Quadagno et al., 1991). Thus, there is no reliable evidence indicating that the kinds of performance required in a work situation or an athletic competition fluctuate over the menstrual cycle.

Fluctuations in Sex Drive

Another psychological characteristic that has been investigated for fluctuations over the cycle is women's sex drive or arousability. Studies have yielded contradictory results. Some have found a peak frequency of intercourse around ovulation, which would be biologically functional—that is, increase the chances of conception occurring. But others have found peaks just before and just after menstruation (Zillmann, Schweitzer, & Mundorf, 1994).

Of course, one should be cautious about using frequency of intercourse as a measure of a woman's sex drive. Intercourse requires some agreement between partners and thus reflects not only a woman's desires but her partner's as well. One study assessed both heterosexual women's activity with a partner and self-rated sexual desire (Bullivant, Sellergren, & Stern, 2004). The results indicated that sexual activity initiated by the woman—but not by the man—peaked during the three days before and three days after ovulation. Sexual desire showed the same pattern.

In a sophisticated study conducted by Alberta researchers, women kept daily electronic diaries on a website, reporting their sexual fantasies each day (Dawson et al., 2012). They also completed self-administered urine tests for LH to determine the day of ovulation. The fantasies were then content analyzed, using methods like those described in Chapter 3. The results indicated that both the frequency and the arousability of sexual fantasies was highest at ovulation. The number of males in the fantasies even increased at the time of ovulation. These results seem to indicate that maximum sexual arousability does occur at the time of peak fertility. Interestingly, testosterone levels also peak at ovulation (Van Goozen et al., 1997).

If there is a link between phase of the menstrual cycle and sexual interest, it most likely reflects an association between testosterone levels and sexuality with a peak in sexual interest around the time of ovulation. But with humans, psychological and

premenstrual syndrome (PMS): A combination of severe physical and psychological symptoms, such as depression and irritability, occurring just before menstruation.
premenstrual dysphoric disorder (PMDD): A diagnostic category in the *DSM-V*, characterized by symptoms such as sadness, anxiety, and irritability in the week before menstruation.

social factors—such as some couples' dislike of intercourse when the woman is menstruating—play a strong role as well (Allen & Goldberg, 2009).

What Causes the Fluctuations in Mood: Why Do Some Women Get Emotional?

For women who do experience fluctuations in mood during the menstrual cycle, the question arises about what causes these fluctuations. This raises the nature–nurture, or biology–environment, controversy. That is, some researchers argue that mood fluctuations are caused primarily by biological factors—in particular, fluctuations in levels of hormones. Others argue that environmental factors, such as menstrual taboos and cultural expectations, are the primary cause.

On the biology side, changes in mood appear to be related to changes in hormone levels during the cycle (Ross & Steiner, 2003). The fact that depression is more frequent in women premenstrually, at menopause, and postpartum (after having a baby) suggests that there is at least some relationship between sex hormones and depression. The exact hormone–mood relationship is not known, but low or declining levels of estrogen or progesterone or both are the likeliest culprits. Neither is it known exactly what the mechanism is by which hormones influence mood (Golub, 1992). Research does indicate that the estrogen–progesterone system interacts with the production of the neurotransmitters norepinephrine, serotonin, and dopamine, and neurotransmitter levels are linked to mood disorders such as depression (Halbreich & Kahn, 2001; Steiner et al., 2003).

Critics of the hormone point of view note that causality is being inferred from correlational data. In other words, the data show a correlation between cycle phase (hormonal levels) and mood, but they do not show that hormone levels cause the mood shift.

Those arguing the other side—that the fluctuations are due to cultural forces—note the widespread cultural expectations and taboos surrounding menstruation (Stanton et al., 2002; Stubbs, 2008). In some nonindustrialized cultures, women who are menstruating are isolated from the community and may have to stay in a menstrual hut at the edge of town during their period. Often the menstrual blood itself is thought to have supernatural, dangerous powers, and the woman's isolation is considered necessary for the safety of the community. Among the Lele of the Congo, for example:

> A menstruating woman was a danger to the whole community if she entered the forest. Not only was her menstruation certain to wreck any enterprise in the forest that she might undertake, but it was thought to produce unfavorable conditions for men. Hunting would be difficult for a long time after, and rituals based on forest plants would have no efficacy.

Women found these rules extremely irksome, especially as they were regularly short-handed and late in their planting, weeding, harvesting, and fishing. (Douglas, 1970, p. 179)

Such practices do not occur only among non-Western people. Note that there is a history of similar practices in our own culture as well. For example, the following passage is from the book of Leviticus in the Bible:

> When a woman has a discharge of blood which is her regular discharge from her body, she shall be in her impurity for seven days, and whoever touches her shall be unclean until the evening. . . . And whoever touches her bed shall wash his clothes, and bathe himself in water, and be unclean until the evening; whether it is the bed or anything upon which she sits, when he touches it he shall be unclean until the evening. (Leviticus 15:19–23)

Among the most common menstrual taboos are those prohibiting sexual intercourse with a menstruating woman. For example, the continuation of the passage from Leviticus just quoted is this:

> And if any man lies with her, and her impurity is on him, he shall be unclean seven days; and every bed on which he lies shall be unclean. (Leviticus 15:24)

Couples who violated the taboo could be stoned. Orthodox Jews still abstain from sex during the woman's period and for seven days afterward. At the end of this time, the woman goes to the *mikvah* (ritual bath) to be cleansed, and only after this cleansing may she resume sexual relations (Guterman, 2008).

Advocates of the cultural explanation argue, then, that women become anxious and depressed around the time of menstruation because of the many cultural forces, such as menstrual taboos, that create negative attitudes toward menstruation. For example, in an Ontario study, one-third of the university women sampled, all of whom were in a romantic relationship, had never engaged in sexual activity during menstruation (Rempel & Baumgartner, 2003).

It's important to realize that, in some cultures, separation of women during menstruation is a form of celebration. For example, in many Canadian First Nations communities, women were honoured for their role as life givers; Moon Time (menstruation; Figure 5.14) was seen as a gift from the Creator (McKenna et al., 2010) and symbolic of Grandmother Moon, which becomes full once a month just as women do. Women are seen as having powerful energy and being at their greatest strength during the Moon Time. Traditionally, they gathered in the Moon Lodge during their Moon Time. At the Moon Lodge they were taught about various aspects of women's lives, including about birth and menopause, by the Grandmothers (female elders). According to Elder Betty:

Figure 5.14 In some cultures, separation of women during menstruation is a form of celebration. For example, in many Canadian First Nations communities, women were honoured for their role as life givers and gathered in the Moon Lodge during their Moon Time. At the Moon Lodge they were taught about various aspects of women's lives, including about birth and menopause, by the Grandmothers (female Elders).

© INTERFOTO/Alamy

Figure 5.15 Does advertising for menstrual drugs contribute to negative stereotypes about women and PMS?

© Amy Etra/Photo Edit

When women are in that Moon Lodge you learn how the concept of Grandmother Moon is so vital. . . . We need Grandmother Moon just as much as we need the sun. Grandmother Moon is so powerful that the water will rise up and follow her. The women had all that knowledge and it was passed from the Grandmother to mother and to daughter to granddaughter, aunty to niece. But very rarely did it ever go out to the males because the males lead a different life. It's also important to know that your energy at the Moon Time is powerful. We think of ourselves as a connection to that Mother Earth, that we are a product of Mother Earth, we come from her, we go back to her. (McKenna et al., 2010, p. 232)

Colonialism changed this experience in many Indigenous cultures. Some Indigenous women are trying to reclaim this traditional view of Moon Time.

Women's expectations may play a role in their response to menstruation (Stanton et al., 2002). Our culture is filled with teachings that women are supposed to behave strangely just before and during their periods—for example, drug company ads that ask "Why am I so emotional?" (see Figure 5.15). According to this line of reasoning, women are taught that they should be depressed around the time of menstruation, and because they expect to become depressed, they do become depressed. Researchers in British Columbia have proposed an additional role for expectations (McFarlane et al., 1988). Women (and men) experience variability in their moods. Because of cultural stereotypes about PMS, women attribute their negative mood to hormones when they occur premenstrually. However, they attribute their negative moods at other times in their cycle to other causes (e.g., work or family).

Surely such forces do exist in our culture. But is there any evidence that they really have an effect on women's moods and behaviour? Psychologist Diane Ruble (1977; see also Klebanov & Jemmott, 1992) did a clever experiment to determine whether women's culturally induced expectations influence their reporting of premenstrual symptoms. University students were tested on the sixth or seventh day before the onset of their next menstrual period. They were told that they would participate in a study on a new technique for predicting the expected date of menstruation by using an electroencephalograph (EEG). After the EEG had been run (it actually wasn't), the woman was informed of when her next period was to occur, depending on which of three experimental groups she had randomly been assigned to: (1) she was told she was "premenstrual" and her period was due in one or two days; (2) she was told she was "intermenstrual" or "mid-cycle" and her period was not expected for at least a week to ten days; or (3) she was given no information at all about the predicted date of menstruation (control group). The women then completed a self-report menstrual distress questionnaire. The results indicated that women who had been led to believe they were in the premenstrual phase reported significantly more water retention, pain, and changes in eating habits than did women who had been led to believe they were around mid-cycle. (In fact, women in these groups did not differ significantly in when their periods actually arrived.) There were no significant differences between the groups in ratings of negative moods, however. This study indicates that, probably because of learned beliefs, women overstate the changes in body states that occur over the menstrual cycle. When they think they are in the premenstrual phase, they report more problems than when they think they are at mid-cycle.

This nature–nurture argument will not be easily resolved, particularly because there is evidence for both points of view. Perhaps the best solution is to say that both biology and culture contribute to women's mood fluctuations during the menstrual cycle. In other words, some women probably do experience mood shifts caused by hormonal and possibly other physical factors and, for many others, slight biological influences are magnified by psychological and cultural influences (Hampson & Moffat, 2004). A woman's premenstrual hormonal state may act as a sort of trigger.

Critical THINKing Skill

UNDERSTANDING HOW SCIENTIFIC RESEARCH CAN BE APPLIED TO MAKING POLICY DECISIONS

Environmental activists want to do much to clean up the environment, including banning the use of certain substances in manufacturing. Manufacturers often oppose these efforts, arguing that they are too costly, that they will handicap Canadian business, and that the risks are minimal or nonexistent anyway. How should the average person, or a government official, decide?

The best way to make a good decision is to use the best available scientific evidence and think clearly about it. The evidence might come from field studies as well as laboratory experiments. Suppose that the substance that is causing concern is the pesticide atrazine, and the worry is that it inhibits sperm production. In a field study, scientists might recruit a sample of men who live in different locations, both urban and rural. The scientists would take a sample of soil from each man's location and also get a sperm count from each one. The researchers would then see if there is a correlation between atrazine levels and sperm count. Suppose that the correlation is negative and significant—that is, the higher the atrazine level, the lower the sperm count. That result is consistent with the hypothesis, but the problem is that it is a correlational study.

Another way to get at the question would be with a laboratory experiment—in this case, for obvious ethical reasons, this research would have to be done with animals. Scientists would expose the experimental group of rats to atrazine in a concentration equivalent to what is found in the natural environment, while the control group of rats does not receive atrazine. After two months

of exposure (or not, for the control group), the sperm counts of the rats are measured. Suppose that the rats in the experimental group have significantly lower average sperm counts than those in the control group. From that result, we can make a causal inference, that atrazine decreases sperm count in rats. The problem here is that it is a laboratory experiment with rats. Perhaps it does not apply to humans in a natural environment.

We can be most confident of a conclusion if there is converging evidence from multiple studies, both field studies and laboratory experiments. Putting these two hypothetical studies together gives us more confidence in the conclusion that atrazine has real negative effects. Each study addresses some of the limitations of the other.

How can these studies inform a policy decision? The manufacturers and farmers are still saying that it would be way too expensive to eliminate atrazine. Without it, the pests will gobble up the crops. At this point, a good policy decision would involve a cost–benefit analysis. The costs of eliminating atrazine have already been calculated. We would also want to calculate the costs of the lower sperm counts. How many cases of infertility do they cause? What is the cost of the infertility treatments—both financial and psychological? We might also want to compute the benefit, over many years, of the elimination of atrazine.

In general, when making policy decisions where scientific evidence is available, we should evaluate the quality of that evidence and then weigh the costs and benefits of implementing policies based on the evidence.

SUMMARY

The major sex hormones are testosterone, which is produced in males by the testes, and estrogen and progesterone, which are produced in females by the ovaries, although both men and women have both testosterone and estrogen. Levels of the sex hormones are regulated by two hormones secreted by the pituitary: FSH (follicle-stimulating hormone) and LH (luteinizing hormone), which in turn are regulated by GnRH (gonadotropin releasing hormone) secreted by the hypothalamus. The gonads, pituitary, and hypothalamus regulate one another's output through a negative feedback loop.

Biologically, the menstrual cycle is divided into four phases: the follicular phase, ovulation, the luteal phase, and menstruation. Corresponding to these phases, there are changes in the levels of pituitary hormones (FSH and LH) and in the levels of ovarian hormones (estrogen and progesterone), as well as changes in the ovaries and the uterus. A fairly common menstrual problem is dysmenorrhea (painful menstruation).

At conception, males and females differ only in the sex chromosomes (XX in females and XY in males). As the male fetus grows, the SRY gene on the Y chromosome directs the gonads to differentiate into the testes. In the absence of the SRY gene, ovaries develop. The ovaries and testes then secrete different hormones in females and males, respectively, and these hormones stimulate further differentiation of the internal and external reproductive structures of males and females. A male organ and a female organ that derive from the same embryonic tissue are said to be homologous to each other.

Intersex conditions (disorders of sex development) are generally the result of various syndromes (such as CAH) and accidents that occur during the course of prenatal sexual differentiation. Currently, there is a debate over the best medical treatment of these individuals.

Puberty is characterized by a great increase in the production of sex hormones. Pubertal changes in both males and females include body growth, the development of pubic and axillary hair, and increased output from the oil-producing glands. Changes in the male include growth of the penis and testes, the beginning of ejaculation, and a deepening of the voice. Changes in the female include breast development and the beginning of menstruation.

Research indicates that some, although not all, women experience changes in mood over the phases of the menstrual cycle. For those who experience such changes, their mood is generally positive around the middle of the cycle (around ovulation), whereas depression and irritability are more likely just before and during menstruation. These negative moods and physical discomforts are termed premenstrual syndrome (PMS). However, research indicates that there are no fluctuations in performance over the cycle. Evidence does suggest that fluctuations in mood are related to changes in hormone levels as well as to cultural factors.

CHAPTER 6

Conception, Pregnancy, and Childbirth

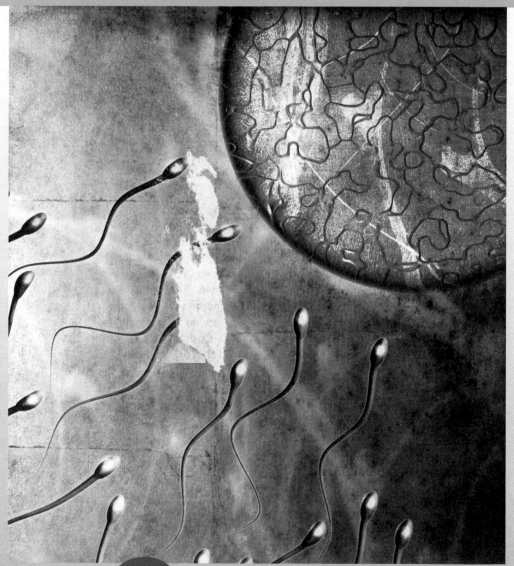

©Brand X Pictures

Are **YOU** Curious?

1. How does sexual activity change during pregnancy?
2. What substances, if taken during pregnancy, threaten the fetus?
3. What training do midwives receive?

Read this chapter to find out.

LEARNING OBJECTIVES

After studying this chapter, you will be able to

LO1 Illustrate the independent voyages of the sperm and the ovum up to and including the moment of conception.

LO2 Describe the changes that occur in the fetus, the mother, and the father during each of the three trimesters of pregnancy.

LO3 Demonstrate the importance of good nutrition and the effects of different teratogenic drugs on fetal development.

LO4 Distinguish the three stages of labour and differentiate vaginal birth procedures from Caesarean section procedures.

LO5 Compare various childbirth options.

LO6 Discuss the physical, sexual, and psychological changes that occur for the mother and father during the postpartum period, including breast-feeding.

LO7 Identify the types of problems and pathologies that can occur during conception and pregnancy.

LO8 Discuss the causes of, effects of, and treatments for infertility.

I remember feeling very sexy. We were trying all these different positions. Now that we were having a baby, I felt a lot looser. I used to feel uptight about sex for its own sake, but when I was pregnant I felt a lot freer.

I thought it would never end. I was enormous. I couldn't bend over and wash my feet. And it was incredibly hot.*

---

* Boston Women's Health Book Collective. (1998). *Our bodies, ourselves for the new century.* New York: Simon and Schuster, pp. 443, 446.

Chapter 5 described the remarkable biological process by which a single fertilized egg develops into a male or a female human being. This chapter is about some equally remarkable processes involved in creating human beings: conception, pregnancy, and childbirth.

Several things people can do to improve the odds of having a healthy mother and baby are listed in First Person.

Conception

Sperm Meets Egg: The Incredible Journey

In a 28-day menstrual cycle, the woman ovulates on about day 14 (see Chapter 5). The egg is released from the ovary into the body cavity. Typically, it is then picked up by the fimbriae (long fingerlike structures at the end of the fallopian tube—see Figure 6.1) and enters the fallopian tube. It then begins a leisurely trip down the tube toward the uterus, reaching it in about five days if it has been fertilized. Otherwise, it disintegrates in about 48 hours. The egg, unlike the sperm, has no means of moving itself and is propelled by the cilia (hairlike structures) lining the fallopian tube. The egg has begun its part of the journey toward conception.

The woman's cervix secretes mucus that flushes the passageways to prepare for the arrival of the sperm. Meanwhile, the woman has sexual intercourse, and the man has an orgasm and ejaculates inside the woman's vagina. Alternatively, the woman uses assisted insemination to place semen in the vagina.[1] Either way, the sperm are deposited in the vagina, there to begin their journey toward the egg. But they have made an incredible trip even before reaching the vagina. Initially, they were manufactured in the seminiferous tubules of the testes (see Chapter 4). They were then collected and stored in the epididymis. During ejaculation they moved up and over the top of the bladder in the vas deferens; then they travelled down through the ejaculatory duct, mixed with seminal fluid, and went out through the urethra.

The sperm is one of the tiniest cells in the human body. It is composed of a *head,* a *midpiece,* and a *tail* (see Figure 6.2). The head is about 5 micrometres long, and the total length, from the tip of the head to the tip of the tail, is about 60 micrometres (about 0.06 mm, or 2/1000 in.). The DNA, which is the sperm's most important contribution when it unites with the egg, is contained in the nucleus, which is in the head of the sperm. Sperm also contain RNA carrying the instructions for early embryonic development, as well as a large number of proteins (Ainsworth, 2005). The *acrosome,* a chemical reservoir, is also in the head of the sperm. The midpiece contains *mitochondria,* tiny structures in which chemical reactions occur that provide energy. This energy is used when the sperm lashes its tail back and forth. The lashing action (called *flagellation*) propels the sperm forward.

A typical ejaculate has a volume of about 3 mL, or about a teaspoonful, and contains about 200 million sperm. Although this might seem to be a wasteful amount of sperm if only one is needed for fertilization, the great majority of the sperm never even get close to the egg. Some of the ejaculate, including half of the sperm, will flow out of the vagina as a result of gravity. Other sperm may be killed by the acidity of the vagina, to which they are very sensitive. Others are deformed. Of those that make it safely into the uterus, half swim up the wrong fallopian tube (the one typically containing no egg).

But here we are, several hours later, with a hearty band of sperm swimming up the fallopian tube toward the egg, against the currents that are bringing the egg down. Sperm are capable of swimming 1 to 3 cm (about 1 in.) per hour, although it has been documented that sperm may arrive at the egg within an hour and a half after ejaculation, which is much sooner than would be expected, given their swimming rate. By the time a sperm reaches the egg, it has swum approximately 3000 times its own length. This feat would be comparable to a swim of more than 4 km (about 2.5 mi.) for a human being.

Contrary to the popular belief that conception occurs in the uterus, typically it occurs in the outer third (the

---

[1] Increasing numbers of Canadian women are becoming pregnant using assisted reproductive technologies. These are described later in this chapter.

Figure 6.1   Sexual intercourse in the man-on-top position, showing the pathway of sperm and egg from manufacture in the testes and ovary to conception, which typically occurs in the fallopian tube.

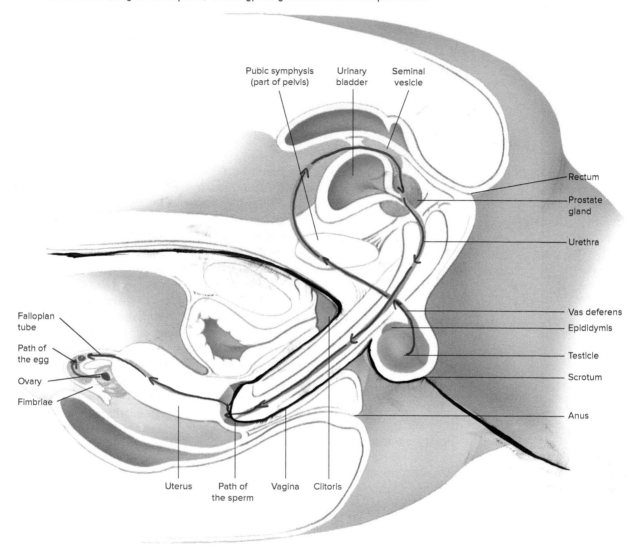

part near the ovary) of the fallopian tube. Of the original 200 million sperm, only about 2000 reach the tube containing the egg. As they approach, a chemical secreted by the egg attracts the sperm to the egg. Chemical receptors on the surface of the sperm respond to the attractant, and the sperm swim toward the egg (Spehr et al., 2003). The egg is surrounded by a thin, gelatinous layer called the *zona pellucida.* Sperm swarm around the egg and secrete an enzyme called **hyaluronidase** (produced by the acrosome located in the head of the sperm—refer to Figure 6.2); this enzyme dissolves the zona pellucida,

hyaluronidase: An enzyme secreted by the sperm that allows one sperm to penetrate the egg.
zygote: The developing organism from the time of the union of the sperm and the egg to about the second week of gestation.

permitting one sperm to penetrate the egg.[2] Conception has occurred (Figure 6.3).

The fertilized egg, called the **zygote,** continues to travel down the fallopian tube. About 36 hours after conception, it begins the process of cell division, by which the original one cell becomes a mass of two cells, then four cells, then eight cells, and so on. About five to seven days after conception, the mass of cells implants itself in the lining of the uterus, there to be nourished and grow.

[2] Thus, while only one sperm is necessary to accomplish fertilization, it appears that it is important that a lot of other sperm are present to secrete a chemical that facilitates penetration of the egg. Therefore, maintaining a high sperm count seems to be important for conception.

Figure 6.2 The structure of a mature human sperm.

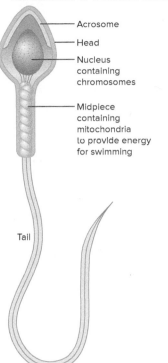

- Acrosome
- Head
- Nucleus containing chromosomes
- Midpiece containing mitochondria to provide energy for swimming

Tail

Figure 6.3 The egg is fertilized by one sperm as many sperm cluster about.

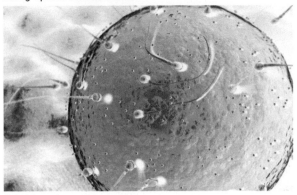

© 3D4Medical.com/Getty Images

For the first two weeks of gestation, the *conceptus* (product of conception) is called a zygote, between weeks two and eight it is called an **embryo**, and from then until birth it is called a **fetus**.

Improving the Chances of Conception: Making a Baby

Some couples choose not to have children. However, for couples wanting to conceive, the following are points to keep in mind.

The trick, of course, is to time intercourse so that it occurs around the time of ovulation. To do this, it is necessary to determine when the woman ovulates. For the vast majority of women, the time of ovulation can best be determined by keeping a *basal body temperature chart*. To do this, the woman takes her temperature every morning immediately on waking (that means before getting up and moving around or drinking a cup of coffee). She then keeps a graph of her temperature. The most reliable indicator of ovulation is the rise in temperature the day after it occurs. From this, the woman can determine the day of ovulation, and that determination should be consistent with menstruation occurring about 14 days later. Other methods for determining when a woman is ovulating are the cervical mucus and sympto-thermal methods, as well as home tests for the detection of ovulation, described in Chapter 7.

Sperm live inside the woman's body for up to five days (Wilcox, Weinberg, & Baird, 1995). The egg is capable of being fertilized for about the first 12 to 24 hours after ovulation. Allowing the sperm some swimming time, this means that intercourse should be timed right at ovulation or one or two days before.

Assuming you have some idea of the time of ovulation, how frequent should intercourse be? While more may be merrier, more is not necessarily more effective. The reason for this is that it is important for the man's sperm count to be maintained. It takes a while to manufacture 200 million sperm—at least 24 hours. And as mentioned earlier, maintaining a high sperm count appears to be important in accomplishing the task of fertilizing the egg. For purposes of conceiving, then, it is probably best to have intercourse about every 24 to 48 hours, or about two to three times during the week in which the woman is to ovulate (Mayo Clinic, 2012a).

It is also important to take some steps to ensure that once deposited in the vagina, the sperm get a decent chance to survive and to find their way into the fallopian tubes. Position during and after intercourse is important. For purposes of conceiving, the best position for intercourse is with the woman on her back (man-on-top, or *missionary*, position—see Chapter 9). If the woman is on top, much of the ejaculate may run out of the vagina because of the pull of gravity. After intercourse, she should remain on her back, possibly with her legs pulled up and a pillow under her hips, preferably for about a half hour to an hour. This allows the semen to remain in a pool in the vagina, which gives the sperm a good chance to swim up into the uterus. Because sperm are very sensitive to the pH (acidity-alkalinity) of the vagina, this factor also requires some consideration. Acidity kills sperm. Douching with commercial preparations or with acidic solutions (such as vinegar) should be avoided. Finally, lubricants and suppositories should not be used; they may kill sperm or block their entrance into the uterus (Mayo Clinic, 2012b). On the other hand, lubricants may be necessary to make sex comfortable.

embryo: The developing organism between the second and eighth weeks of gestation.
fetus: The developing organism from the eighth week of gestation through delivery.

First Person

Planning a Pregnancy?

Research has identified a number of things that can cause harm to mother or fetus during pregnancy. Some of these are preventable. Here is a preconception checklist for women.

1. Folic acid can prevent birth defects. Take a multivitamin containing 400 micrograms of folic acid every day.
2. Get your vaccinations up-to-date. Get catch-up vaccines for rubella and varicella at least one month before trying to get pregnant. Tdap, which protects infants against whooping cough, and flu vaccines can be taken in early pregnancy.
3. Women with a family history of sickle cell anemia, thalassemia, Tay-Sachs disease, and cystic fibrosis should consider genetic screening.
4. Healthy moms are more likely to have healthy babies; aim for a healthy weight before you get pregnant. Obese pregnant women are at greater risk for pre-eclampsia, stillbirth, preterm delivery, and Caesarean sections (C-sections).
5. Women with diabetes need to maintain tight control of blood sugar.
6. No drinking and no smoking; stop before you get pregnant. (Your partner should stop, too.)

Source: Fryhofer, 2012.

LO2

Development of the Conceptus

For the nine months (38 weeks, actually) of pregnancy, two organisms—the conceptus and the pregnant woman—coexist. In the past, the relationship between the two has been viewed as harmonious. In recent years, a new perspective has been gaining support—pregnancy as a silent struggle (Haig, 1996). Both fetus and mother need a variety of nutrients and may be competing for them. Nature should favour the development of characteristics of each that would give it the edge in such competitions, enabling it to win (e.g., struggles over calcium). Research with mice suggests that the placenta plays a role in regulating the flow of nutrients to protect the fetus (Broad & Keverne, 2011). Such a struggle can explain aspects of pregnancy that are inconsistent with the view of harmonious coexistence, such as gestational diabetes and pre-eclampsia. Both of these conditions carry serious risk to both the mother and the infant if not treated. Gestational diabetes is the same as other forms of diabetes in that the woman has high blood sugar because the body is not able to make and use all the insulin it needs, but it appears during pregnancy. Pre-eclampsia is a condition that occurs during the third trimester and involves a sharp rise in blood pressure, the presence of protein in the urine, and swelling of the hands, feet, and face.

During pregnancy, the two organisms undergo parallel, dramatic changes. The changes that occur in the developing conceptus will be discussed in this section; later in the chapter we will discuss the changes that take place in the pregnant woman.

Pregnancy lasts for approximately nine months (38 weeks) and is typically divided into three equal periods of three months, called *trimesters*. Thus, the first trimester is months one to three, the second trimester is months four to six, and the third (or last) trimester is months seven to nine.

The Embryo and Its Support Systems

We left the conceptus, which began as a single fertilized egg cell, dividing into many cells as it passed down the fallopian tube, finally arriving in the uterus and implanting itself in the uterine wall. Tendrils from the zygote begin to penetrate the blood vessels in the wall of the uterus.

During the embryonic period of development (the first eight weeks), most of the major organ systems are formed in processes that occur with amazing speed. The inner part of the ball of cells implanted in the uterus now differentiates into two layers, the endoderm and the ectoderm. Later, a third layer, the mesoderm, forms between them. The various organs of the body differentiate themselves out of these layers. The *ectoderm* will form the entire nervous system and the skin. The *endoderm* differentiates into the digestive system—from the pharynx, to the stomach and intestines, to the rectum—and the respiratory system. The muscles, skeleton, connective tissues, and reproductive and circulatory systems derive from the *mesoderm*, Development generally proceeds in a cephalocaudal order; that is, the head develops first, and the lower body last. For this reason, the head of an embryo is enormous compared with the rest of the body.

Meanwhile, another group of cells has differentiated into the *trophoblast*, which has important functions in maintaining the embryo and which will eventually become the placenta. The **placenta** develops out of the mass of tissues that surrounds the conceptus early in development and nurtures its growth by producing tendrils that penetrate the blood vessels in the wall of the uterus. As these tendrils become larger and more complex, they form a separate structure. The placenta has a number of important functions, perhaps the most important of which is that it serves as a site for the exchange of substances between the woman's blood and the fetus's blood. It is important to note that the woman's circulatory system and the fetus's circulatory system are completely separate; that is, with only rare exceptions, the woman's blood never circulates inside the fetus, nor does the fetus's blood circulate in the woman's blood vessels. Instead, the fetus's blood passes out of its body through the umbilical cord to the placenta (the spot where the umbilical cord attaches to the fetus becomes the navel or belly button after birth). There it circulates in the numerous *villi* (tiny fingerlike projections in the placenta). The woman's blood circulates around the outside of these villi. Thus, a membrane barrier exists between the two blood systems. Some substances are capable of passing through this barrier, whereas others are not. Oxygen and nutrients can pass through the barrier, and thus the woman's blood supplies oxygen and nutrients to the fetus, providing substitutes for breathing and eating. Carbon dioxide and waste products similarly pass back from the fetal blood to the woman's blood. Some viruses and other disease-causing organisms can pass through the barrier, including those for rubella and syphilis. But other organisms cannot pass through the barrier; thus the woman may have a terrible cold, but the fetus will remain completely healthy. Various drugs can also cross the placental barrier, and the woman should therefore be careful about drugs taken during pregnancy (we will discuss substances to avoid during pregnancy later in this chapter).

Another major function of the placenta is that it secretes hormones. The placenta produces large quantities of estrogen and progesterone. Many of the physical symptoms of pregnancy may be caused by these elevated levels of hormones. Another hormone manufactured by the placenta is **human chorionic gonadotropin (hCG)**. This is the hormone that is detected in pregnancy tests.

The **umbilical cord** is formed during the fifth week of embryonic development. The fully developed cord is about 55 cm (20 in.) long. Normally, it contains three blood vessels: two arteries and one vein. Some people believe that the fetus's umbilical cord attaches to the woman's navel; actually, the umbilical cord attaches to the placenta, thereby providing for the interchanges of substances just described.

Two membranes surround the fetus, the *chorion* and the *amnion*, the amnion being the innermost. The amnion is filled with a watery liquid called **amniotic fluid**, in which the fetus floats and can readily move. It is the amniotic fluid that is sampled when an amniocentesis (discussed shortly) is performed. The amniotic fluid maintains the fetus at a constant temperature and, most important, cushions the fetus against possible injury. Thus, even if the woman falls down, the fetus will probably remain undisturbed. Indeed, the amniotic fluid might be considered the original waterbed.

Fetal Development

Table 6.1 lists the major milestones of fetal development. It is obvious that the development of the fetus during the first trimester is more remarkable than its development during the second and third trimesters. That's because during the first trimester the small mass of cells implanted in the uterus develops into a fetus with most of the major organ systems present and with recognizable human features (see Figure 6.4).

At the end of the 12th week (end of the first trimester), the fetus is unmistakably human and looks like a small infant. It is about 10 cm (4 in.) long and weighs about 19 g (0.75 oz.). From this point on, development consists mainly of the enlargement and differentiation of structures that are already present. By the 18th week, the woman has been able to feel movement for two to four weeks.

During the seventh month, the fetus typically turns in the uterus to assume a head-down

placenta (plah-SEN-tuh): An organ formed on the wall of the uterus through which the fetus receives oxygen and nutrients and gets rid of waste products.
human chorionic gonadotropin (hCG): A hormone secreted by the placenta; it is the hormone detected in pregnancy tests.
umbilical cord: The tube that connects the fetus to the placenta.
amniotic fluid: The watery fluid surrounding a developing fetus in the uterus.

Figure 6.4   *(a)* This embryo has divided into four cells and would still be travelling down the fallopian tube. *(b)* The embryo after four weeks of development. The major organs are forming; the bright red, blood-filled heart is just below the lower jaw. *(c)* At nine weeks the human fetus is recognizable as a primate. Limbs have formed and ears are clearly visible. *(d)* By about three months the fetus is approximately 10 cm long and weighs about 19 g. Muscles have formed, which move the limbs and body.

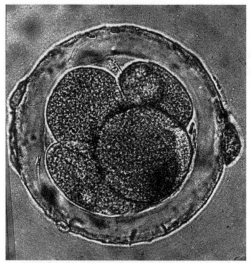

(a) © Petit Format/Nestle/Science Source

(b) © Petit Format/Nestle/Science Source

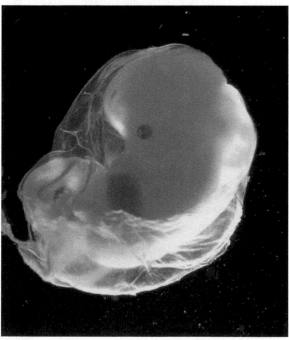

(c) © Science Pictures Ltd./Science Source

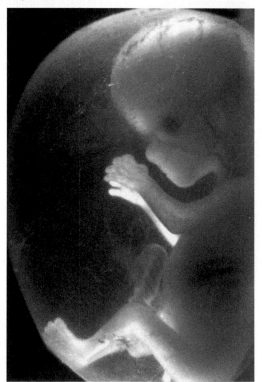

(d) © Claude Edelmann/Science Source

position. If this turning does not occur by the time of delivery, there will be a *breech presentation*, Women can try assuming various positions to aid the turning (Boston Women's Health Book Collective, 2005). Physicians and midwives can also perform certain procedures to turn the fetus.

The fetus's growth during the last two months is rapid. Canadian babies born at a gestational age of 36 weeks (about eight months) weigh an average of 2804 g (6 lbs., 3 oz.) (Kramer et al., 2001). The average full-term baby (after 38 weeks of pregnancy) weighs 3562 g (7 lb., 14 oz.) and is 50 cm (20 in.) long. Research in British Columbia found that infants of European descent weighed significantly more than infants of Chinese or South Asian descent (Janssen et al., 2007).

Table 6.1 Milestones of Fetal Development

First Trimester	
Weeks 3 and 4	Development of the head
	Nervous system begins to form
	Backbone is constructed
Week 5	Formation of the umbilical cord
Weeks 4 to 8	External body parts develop—eyes, ears, arms, hands, fingers, legs, feet, and toes
	Liver, lungs, pancreas, kidneys, and intestines form, and begin limited functioning
Second Trimester	
Week 14	Fetal movement or quickening
Week 18	Fetal heartbeat detected by examiner
Week 24	Fetus is sensitive to light and sound in utero
Third Trimester	
Week 28	Fat deposits form—gains chubby baby appearance
Weeks 29 to birth	Rapid growth

Pregnancy

The Stages of Pregnancy

The First Trimester (the First 12 Weeks)

Symptoms of pregnancy. For most women, the first symptom of pregnancy is a missed menstrual period. Of course, there may be a wide variety of reactions to this event. For the woman who has not planned the pregnancy or who feels that she already has enough children, the reaction may be depression, anger, and fear. For the woman who has been trying to conceive, the reaction may be joy and eager anticipation.

There are many other reasons besides pregnancy for a woman to have a late period or miss a period. Illness or emotional stress may delay a period, and women occasionally skip a period for no apparent reason.

It is also true that a woman may continue to experience some cyclic bleeding or spotting during pregnancy. This is not particularly a danger sign, except that in some cases it is a symptom of a miscarriage so the woman should consult her physician.

If the woman has been keeping a basal body temperature chart, it can provide a very early sign that she is pregnant. If her temperature rises abruptly at about the time ovulation would normally occur and then stays up for more than two weeks—say, about three weeks—the chances are fairly good that she is pregnant. The increased temperature results from the high level of progesterone manufactured by the corpus luteum and, later, the placenta.

Other early symptoms of pregnancy are tenderness of the breasts—a tingling sensation and special sensitivity

of the nipples—and nausea and vomiting (called *morning sickness,* although these symptoms may actually happen any time during the day). More frequent urination, feelings of fatigue, and a need for more sleep are other early signs of pregnancy. Not all pregnant women experience all of these symptoms.

Pregnancy tests. It is important that early, accurate pregnancy tests be available and that women make use of them. This is true for several reasons. A woman needs to know that she is pregnant as early as possible so that she can see a physician or midwife, begin getting good prenatal care, and get the nutrition she requires during pregnancy (see the section on nutrition later in the chapter). If she does not want to carry the baby to term, she needs to know as soon as possible, because abortions are much safer and simpler when performed in the first trimester than in the second.

A pregnancy test may be done in a physician's office, at a Planned Parenthood or sexual health centre, or at a medical laboratory. The most common pregnancy test is an immunologic test based on detecting the presence of hCG (human chorionic gonadotropin, secreted by the placenta) in the woman's urine. It can be done in a matter of minutes and is very accurate. It involves mixing a drop of urine with certain chemicals, either on a slide or in a tube.

The laboratory tests for pregnancy are 98 to 99 percent accurate. A laboratory test may produce a false negative (i.e., tell the woman she is not pregnant when she really is) if it is done too early or if errors are made in processing. Also, some women simply do not show positive signs in the tests or do not do so until the second or third test. The modern urine tests are 98 percent accurate seven days after implantation (just when a period is missed).

A different type of test, called the *beta-hCG radio-immunoassay*, assesses the presence of beta-hCG in a blood sample. It can detect hCG at very low levels, so it can reliably detect pregnancy seven days after fertilization. It is much more expensive than the urine tests and is available only in laboratories associated with hospitals or large clinics.

Home (over-the-counter) pregnancy tests are widely available in drug stores and on the Internet. They are sold under such names as Clearblue and First Response; all are urine tests designed to measure the presence of hCG. They cost from $10 to $45, depending on the number of tests in the package. There are also hCG test strips sold under a variety of names. The charm lies in their convenience and the privacy of getting the results. Manufacturers claim their tests will accurately detect a pregnancy on the first day of the missed period. Laboratory tests of 18 brands found that only 1 of the 18 detected low levels of hCG and only 8 detected high levels of hCG (Cole et al., 2004). Thus 10 of the 18 would produce a false negative result. This compares to an error rate of 1 or 2 percent for laboratory tests. A comparison of six OTC tests found that two of them were accurate at 99 percent, but the accuracy of the other four ranged from 54 to 67 percent (Cole, 2011). A high rate of false negatives is very serious because it leads a pregnant woman to think she is not pregnant; as a result she might take substances or medicines that would harm the fetus, and she would not seek prenatal care. Rare but dangerous conditions, such as an ectopic pregnancy (discussed below), could go undetected. The accuracy of a test depends on its *sensitivity*, the level of hCG in the urine required to obtain a positive result. Available tests vary from 10 mLU/mL to 100 mLU/mL; the lower the number, the higher the sensitivity (Phillips, 2012; the hCG hormone is measured in milli-international units per millilitre or mLU/mL). Complicating matters is the fact that levels of hCG in early pregnancy vary from one woman to the next. Accuracy also depends on following directions *exactly*. Overall, relying on such tests is not a good idea.

The signs of pregnancy may be classified as *presumptive signs, probable signs,* and *positive signs.* Amenorrhea, breast tenderness, nausea, and so on, are presumptive signs. The pregnancy tests discussed previously all provide probable signs. Three signs are interpreted as positive signs, that is, as definite indications of pregnancy: (1) beating of the fetal heart, (2) active fetal movement, and (3) detection of a fetal skeleton by ultrasound. These signs cannot be detected until the fourth month, with the exception of ultrasound, which can be used in the first trimester.

Once the pregnancy has been confirmed, the woman generally is very interested in determining her expected delivery date (called EDC for a rather antiquated expression, "expected date of confinement"). The EDC is calculated by using *Nägele's rule.* The rule says to take the date of the first day of the last menstrual period, subtract three months, add seven days, and finally add one year. Thus, if the first day of the last menstrual period was September 10, 2017, the expected delivery date would be June 17, 2018: subtracting three months from September 10 gives June 10, adding seven days yields June 17, and adding one year gives June 17, 2018. These days, most women have at least one ultrasound during the pregnancy. Since ultrasounds are more accurate than Nägele's rule (although they also have a margin of error), these results are often used to revise the due date. Of course, the due date is rarely the delivery date—many factors influence the date on which the baby is actually born.

Physical changes. The basic physical change that takes place in the woman's body during the first trimester is a large increase in the levels of hormones, especially estrogen and progesterone, that are produced by the placenta. Many of the other physical symptoms of the first trimester arise from these endocrine changes.

The breasts swell and tingle. This results from the development of the mammary glands, which is stimulated by hormones. The nipples and the area around them (areola) may darken and broaden.

Women often feel a need to urinate more frequently. This is related to changes in the pituitary hormones that affect the adrenals, which in turn change the water balance in the body so that more water is retained. The growing uterus also contributes by pressing against the bladder.

Some women experience morning sickness—feelings of nausea, perhaps to the point of vomiting and revulsion toward food or its odour. The nausea and vomiting may occur on waking or at other times during the day. Their exact cause is not known. One theory is that nausea and vomiting cause pregnant women to expel and subsequently avoid foods containing toxic chemicals (Flaxman & Sherman, 2000). Supporting evidence includes a lower rate of miscarriage among women who experience morning sickness. While these symptoms are quite common, about 25 percent of pregnant women experience no vomiting at all.

Vaginal discharges may also increase at this time, partly because the increased hormone levels change the pH of the vagina and partly because the vaginal secretions are changing in their chemical composition and quantity.

The feelings of fatigue and sleepiness are probably related to the high levels of progesterone, which is known to have a sedative effect.

Psychological changes. Our culture is full of stereotypes about the psychological characteristics of pregnant women. According to one view, pregnancy is supposed to be a time of happiness and calm. Radiant contentment, the "pregnant glow," is said to emanate from the woman's face, making this a good time for her to be photographed. According to another view, pregnancy is a time of emotional ups and downs. The pregnant woman swings from very happy to depressed and crying, and back again. She is irrational, sending her partner out in a blizzard for kosher dill pickles.

Research indicates that the situation is more complex than these stereotypes suggest. A woman's emotional state during pregnancy, often assessed with measures of depression, varies according to several factors. First, her attitude toward the pregnancy makes a difference; women who desire the pregnancy are less anxious than women who do not (Kalil et al., 1993). Women who want to be pregnant are more likely to get prenatal care and less likely to smoke (Cheng et al., 2009). A second factor is social class. Several studies have found that low income is associated with depression during pregnancy. For example, a study involving interviews with 192 poor, inner-city pregnant women found that they were twice as likely as their middle-income counterparts to be depressed (Hobfoll et al., 1995). The depression may be due to the economic situation these women face, or there may be more unwanted pregnancies among low-income women. A third influence is the availability of social support. Women with a supportive partner are less likely to be depressed, perhaps because the partner serves as a buffer against stressful events (Chapman, Hobfoll, & Ritter, 1997).

Research also shows that a woman's emotional state during pregnancy may have an effect on the developing fetus. In one study, women who experienced multiple stressful events during pregnancy had babies who showed small cognitive deficits at 18 months (Bergman et al., 2007). This result may occur because the stress hormone cortisol crosses the placenta (Talge et al., 2007). In a study of Danish women, high stress at 30 weeks was associated with increased risk of **stillbirth**—delivery of a dead fetus (Wisborg et al., 2008). A longitudinal study of 2900 women found that the experience of stressful events—divorce, residential move—during pregnancy was associated with ADHD behaviours in both boys and girls at age 2, and independently with autistic traits in boys at age 2 (Ronald, Pennell, & Whitehouse, 2011)

Depression is not uncommon during this time. Women who led very active lives before becoming pregnant may find fatigue and lack of energy especially distressing. Depression during the first trimester is more likely among women experiencing other stressful life events, such as moving, changes in their jobs, changes in relationships, or illnesses (Kalil et al., 1993). In this trimester, women's anxieties often centre on concerns about miscarriage.

The Second Trimester (Weeks 13 to 26)

Physical changes. During the fourth month, the woman becomes aware of the fetus's movements ("quickening"). Many women find this a very exciting experience.

The woman is made even more aware of the pregnancy by her rapidly expanding belly. There are a variety of reactions to this. Some women feel that it is a magnificent symbol of womanhood, and they rush out to buy maternity clothes and wear them before they are even necessary. Other women feel awkward and resentful of their expanding abdomen.

Most of the physical symptoms of the first trimester, such as morning sickness, disappear, and discomforts are at a minimum. Physical problems at this time include constipation and nosebleeds (caused by increased blood volume). **Edema**—water retention and swelling—may be a problem in the face, hands, wrists, ankles, and feet; it results from increased water retention throughout the body.

By about mid-pregnancy, the breasts, under hormonal stimulation, have essentially completed their development in preparation for nursing. Beginning about the 19th week, thin amber or yellow fluid called **colostrum** may come out of the nipple, although there is no milk yet.

Psychological changes. Although the first trimester can be relatively tempestuous, particularly with morning sickness, the second trimester is usually a period of relative calm and well-being. The discomforts of the first trimester are past, the tensions associated with labour and delivery not yet present. Fear of miscarriage diminishes as the woman feels fetal movement (Leifer, 1980).

Depression is less likely during the second trimester if the pregnant woman has a cohabiting partner or spouse (Hobfoll et al., 1995). Furthermore, women who report more effective partner support report less anxiety in the second trimester (Rini et al., 2006). Interestingly, women who have had a previous pregnancy are more distressed during this time than women who have not (Wilkinson, 1995). This emotion may reflect the impact of the demands associated with the care of other children when a woman is pregnant. Research also indicates that feelings of nurturance, or maternal responsiveness to the infant, increase steadily from the prepregnant to the postpartum period (Fleming et al., 1997). This increase does not appear to be related to changes in hormone levels during pregnancy.

stillbirth: Delivery of a dead fetus, especially after the 28th week of gestation.

edema (eh-DEE-muh): Excessive fluid retention and swelling.

colostrum: A watery substance that is secreted from the breasts at the end of pregnancy and during the first few days after delivery.

The Third Trimester (Weeks 27 to 38)

Physical changes. The uterus is very large and hard by the third trimester. The woman is increasingly aware of her size and of the fetus (Figure 6.5), which is becoming more and more active. In fact, some women are kept awake at night by its kicks and hiccups.

The extreme size of the uterus puts pressure on a number of other organs, causing some discomfort. There is pressure on the lungs, which may cause shortness of breath. The stomach is also being squeezed, and indigestion is common. The navel is pushed out. The heart is being strained because of the large increase in blood volume. At this stage most women feel low in energy.

Health Canada recommends a woman should gain between 6.5 and 18 kg (15 and 40 lbs.) depending on the woman's weight before the pregnancy. Women who are underweight (body mass index [BMI] of less than 18.5) should gain at the high end, 12.5 to 18 kg; women who are obese (BMI 30 or more) should gain less, 5 to 10 kg. The average Canadian full-term infant at birth weighs 3562 g (7 lbs., 14 oz.); the rest of the weight gain is accounted for by the placenta (about 450 g, or 1 lb.), the amniotic fluid (about 900 g, or 2 lbs.), enlargement of the uterus (about 900 g, or 2 lbs.), enlargement of the breasts (about 750 g, or 1.5 lbs.), and the additional fat and water retained by the woman (3.5 kg, or 8 lbs., or more). Physicians recommend limited weight gain (but not too limited) because the incidence of complications, such as high blood pressure and strain on the heart, is much higher in women who gain an excessive amount of weight. Also, excessive weight gained during pregnancy can be very hard to lose afterward.

The woman's balance is somewhat disturbed because of the large amount of weight that has been added to the front part of her body. She may compensate for this by adopting the characteristic "waddling" walk of the pregnant woman, which can result in back pain.

The uterus tightens occasionally in painless contractions called **Braxton-Hicks contractions**. These contractions are not part of labour. It is thought that they help to strengthen the uterine muscles, preparing them for labour.

In a first pregnancy, around two to four weeks before delivery, the head drops into the pelvis. This movement is called *lightening, dropping,* or *engagement.* Engagement usually occurs during labour in women who have had babies before.

Some women are concerned about the appropriate amount of activity they should engage in during pregnancy—whether some things constitute "overdoing it." Current thinking holds that for a healthy pregnant woman, moderate activity is not dangerous and is actually psychologically and physically beneficial. Modern methods of

Braxton-Hicks contractions: Contractions of the uterus during pregnancy that are not part of actual labour.

Figure 6.5 A generation ago, women tried to hide their pregnancies by wearing loose tops. Women now proudly show their pregnant bellies.

© Gareth Cattermole/Getty Images

childbirth encourage sensible exercise for the pregnant woman so that she will be in shape for labour (see the section on childbirth options later in this chapter). The matter, of course, is highly individual.

Psychological changes. The patterns noted earlier continue into the third trimester. Psychological well-being is greater among women who have social support (often from their partner), have higher incomes or are middle class, and experience fewer concurrent stressful life events. A Quebec study found that women who reported more anxiety, daily hassles, and stress during pregnancy were more likely to experience pregnancy complications (Da Costa, Brender, & Larouche, 1998).

What happens to the relationship of the pregnant woman with her partner? A comparison of women pregnant for the first time with women who had experienced previous pregnancies found that first-time mothers reported a significant increase in dissatisfaction with their husbands from the second to the third trimester (Wilkinson, 1995).

The Father's Experience in Pregnancy

To date, most research has focused on the male partner of the pregnant woman, and there is little research on the experiences of the female partner of pregnant women. One particular issue for lesbian couples is heterosexist assumptions and attitudes from health care providers (Dahl et al., 2013; Larsson & Dykes, 2009; McManus, Hunter, & Renn, 2006). Because of the lack of research on female partners, only male partners' experiences are discussed below.

Physical changes. Some men experience pregnancy symptoms, including indigestion, gastritis, nausea, change in appetite, and headaches (Kiselica & Scheckel, 1995), referred to as a *couvade syndrome.* These symptoms may be caused by hormonal changes in the male. A longitudinal study of 34 couples collected blood samples from both the men and the women before and after the birth of the infant (Storey et al., 2000). Men and women displayed stage-specific hormone differences, including high levels of prolactin prenatally and low levels of testosterone postnatally. Men with more pregnancy symptoms had higher levels of prolactin prenatally.

In some cultures, this phenomenon takes a more dramatic form, known as *couvade ritual.* In this ritual, the husband retires to bed while his wife is in labour. He suffers all the pains of delivery, moaning and groaning as she does. Couvade is still practised in parts of Asia, South America, and Oceania (Gregersen, 1996).

Psychological changes. In Canada in the twenty-first century, many men expect to be actively involved in fathering (Figure 6.6). Men report engaging in many activities in preparation for becoming fathers. A review of 25 articles about father's experiences during pregnancy identified several patterns (Poh, Koh, & He, 2014). Early in the pregnancy, fathers wanted to connect with the unborn child. Feeling fetal movements and viewing an ultrasound examination gives fathers a sense of the reality of the pregnancy. As pregnancy progresses, many fathers interact with the fetus by talking to them, and feeling and responding to their movement. Fathers may be worried about the challenges that the child will create. As the due date approaches, first-time fathers worry about how to help during delivery; experienced fathers worry about the pain their partners may experience. Fathers—especially first-time ones—wanted information about pregnancy and childbirth; many of them spent hours searching the media. Late in the pregnancy, many fathers express an increased sense of maturity as they reflect on how they met their increasing responsibilities.

Many couples take some form of classes in preparation for childbirth. The classes often specifically address the partner's role in late pregnancy and during labour and delivery. These joint activities contribute to the bond between the partners, which in turn provides a better foundation for the arrival of the new member of the family.

Figure 6.6   Dad learns to change his daughter's diaper at a course for new fathers, which helps new or prospective fathers adjust to their new role.

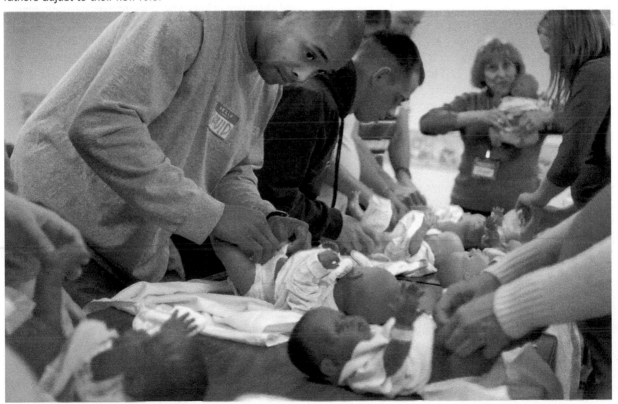

AP Photo/The Free Lance-Star, Scott Neville

Recall our discussion in Chapter 2 of the reproductive advantages of a father–infant bond. The likelihood of such a bond depends partly on the father's responsiveness to the infant. In the study of hormonal changes during pregnancy just described, men viewed videotapes with auditory and visual cues from newborns before the blood sample was drawn. Men who showed higher levels of responsiveness had higher levels of prolactin prenatally and lower levels of testosterone postnatally (Storey et al., 2000). Lower levels of testosterone may facilitate paternal behaviour.

Diversity in the Contexts of Pregnancy

Women have babies in many family contexts these days besides the traditional one of being married to the baby's father. These include living in a common-law relationship; not living with the baby's father but seeing him regularly; being a single mother-to-be who has no contact with the baby's father; being a mother-to-be who is pregnant as a result of assisted insemination or other reproductive technologies; and being a woman in a stable relationship with another woman, who is pregnant as a result of assisted insemination or other technologies. Therefore, we use the term *partner* in the following sections.

Sex during Pregnancy

Couples can and do continue to pleasure each other sexually in many ways throughout the pregnancy. However, many mixed-sex couples are concerned about whether it is safe or advisable for a pregnant woman to have sexual intercourse, particularly during the later stages of pregnancy. Medical opinion is that—given a normal, healthy pregnancy—intercourse can continue safely (Jones, Chan, & Farine, 2011). There is no evidence that intercourse or orgasm is associated with preterm labour (Sayle et al., 2001). In fact, a study involving interviews with pregnant women at 28 weeks gestation and again following delivery found that recent intercourse and orgasm was associated with reduced risk of preterm birth (Sayle et al., 2001; Schaffir, 2006). The only exception is a case where the risk of a miscarriage or preterm labour is already high. Whether and how frequently to engage in sexual activity is a matter for a couple to decide, perhaps in consultation with a physician or midwife.

> How does sexual activity change during pregnancy?

Most pregnant women with male partners continue to have intercourse throughout the pregnancy (Reamy & White, 1987). The most common pattern is a decline in the frequency of intercourse during the first trimester, variation in the second trimester, and an even greater decline in the third trimester (Fox, Gelber, & Chasen, 2008). Some women report increased arousal during the second trimester. In some cases, the decline in frequency

in the third trimester is affected by the partner's perceptions. Although some partners find the pregnant woman extremely sexy, others are not attracted to women in the later stages of pregnancy. Little is known about the sexual frequency of pregnant women with female partners.

During the later stages of pregnancy, the woman's shape makes intercourse increasingly awkward, particularly using the man-on-top position. The side-to-side position (see Chapter 9) is probably the most suitable one for intercourse during the late stages of pregnancy. Couples should also remember that they have many ways of experiencing sexual pleasure and orgasm besides having intercourse; hand–genital stimulation or oral–genital sex may be good alternatives.[3] The best guide in this matter is the woman's feelings and comfort.

Some women experience genito-pelvic pain during pregnancy (Glowacka et al., 2014).

L03 Nutrition during Pregnancy

During pregnancy, another living being is growing inside the woman, and she needs lots of energy, protein, vitamins, and minerals at this time. Therefore, diet during pregnancy is extremely important. If the woman's diet is good, she has a much better chance of remaining healthy during pregnancy and of bearing a healthy baby; if her diet is inadequate, she stands more of a chance of developing one of a number of diseases during pregnancy herself and of bearing a child whose weight is low at birth. This difference is a result of the silent struggle for nutrients between mother and fetus discussed earlier. Babies with low birth weights do not have as good a chance of survival as babies with normal birth weights.

On the other hand, overweight and obese women are at increased risk of negative outcomes for both themselves and the fetus. Risks to the mother include hypertension, gestational diabetes, and Caesarean delivery (Practice Committee of the American Society for Reproductive Medicine, 2008). Risks to the fetus include congenital abnormalities, such as spina bifida, cleft palate, and hydrocephaly (Stothard et al., 2009).

It is particularly important that a pregnant woman get enough protein, folic acid, calcium, magnesium, and vitamin A (Luke, 1994). Protein is important for building new tissues. Folic acid is important for growth; symptoms of folic acid deficiency are anemia and fatigue. A pregnant woman needs much more iron than usual because the fetus draws off iron for itself from the blood that circulates to the placenta. Muscle cramps, nerve pains, uterine ligament pains, sleeplessness, and irritability may all be symptoms of a calcium deficiency. Severe calcium deficiency during pregnancy is associated with increased

---

[3] There is, however, some risk associated with cunnilingus for the pregnant woman, as discussed in Chapter 9.

Figure 6.7 The effects of prenatal exposure to alcohol and other drugs. *(a)* A child born with fetal alcohol syndrome. *(b)* A preterm baby whose mother used crack cocaine during pregnancy.

(a) © Rick's Photography/Shutterstock

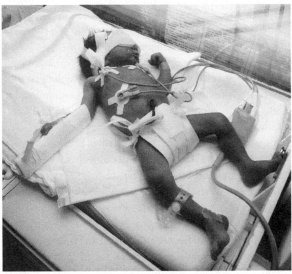

(b) © John Chiasson/Gamma Liaison/Getty Images

blood pressure, which may lead to a serious condition called eclampsia, discussed later in this chapter (Repke, 1994). Deficiencies of calcium and magnesium are associated with premature birth. Sometimes even an excellent diet does not provide enough iron, calcium, or folic acid, in which case the pregnant woman should take supplements.

Daily consumption of artificially sweetened soft drinks is linked to increased likelihood of preterm birth (Halldorsson et al., 2010). Women who drank four per day were more likely to have a preterm birth than were women who drank one per day. There was no effect of drinking sugar-sweetened soft drinks.

Substances That May Result in Birth Defects

Substances Taken during Pregnancy

We are such a pill-popping culture that we seldom stop to think about whether we should take a certain drug. The pregnant woman, however, needs to know that when she takes a drug, it not only circulates through her body, but also may circulate through the fetus. Because the fetus develops so rapidly during pregnancy, drugs may produce severe consequences, including serious malformations. Drugs that produce such defects are called **teratogens**.[4] Of course, not all drugs can cross the placental barrier, but many can. Pregnant women should be cautious in using a number of drugs and other substances.

A substantial amount of research has documented the risk to a child of maternal alcohol drinking during

[4] Teratogen is from the Greek words *teras*, meaning "monster," and *gen*, meaning "cause."

pregnancy. Alcohol consumed by the woman passes through the membrane barrier in the placenta and circulates through the fetus, so it can have pervasive effects on fetal growth and development (Jones, 2006). In turn, these can cause somatic, behavioural, and neurological impairments extending into adulthood (Dorrie et al., 2014). The Public Health Agency of Canada ([PHAC], 2012b) has identified maternal drinking as one of the leading causes of preventable birth defects and developmental delays in children; according to the National Longitudinal Survey of Children and Youth, 15 percent of pregnant Canadian women drink some alcohol.

Fetal alcohol spectrum disorder is an umbrella term covering all outcomes associated with any amount of alcohol exposure in utero (Sokol, Delaney-Black, & Nordstrom, 2007). The effects of prenatal alcohol consumption are dose-dependent; that is, the more alcohol the mother drinks, the larger the number and severity of effects (Figure 6.7). Male infants whose mothers had five or more drinks per week were more likely to be born with cryptorchidism, or undescended testes (Damgaard et al., 2006). Consuming the equivalent of one mixed drink or two glasses of wine per day was associated with slower information processing times in 6-month-old infants (Jacobson et al., 1993). The children of mothers who had taken at least one drink per day in mid-pregnancy had poorer gross and fine motor skills (e.g., catching and throwing a ball)

> **What substances, if taken during pregnancy, threaten the fetus?**

> **teratogens (ter-AH-te-jens):** Substances that produce defects in a fetus.
> **fetal alcohol spectrum disorder:** All outcomes associated with any amount of alcohol exposure during pregnancy.

at 4 years of age (Barr et al., 1990; O'Connor, Sigman, & Kasari, 1993). Data from a longitudinal study indicate that maternal drinking (an average of 3.6 drinks per occasion, 8 occasions per month) is associated with numerous academic and behaviour problems among children at age 14 (Streissguth et al., 1999).

The most serious effects are a pattern of malformations termed **fetal alcohol syndrome**, which is characterized by prenatal and postnatal growth deficiencies; a small brain; small eye openings; joint, limb, and heart malformations; and cognitive impairment. Fetal alcohol syndrome affects 1 percent of Canadians (PHAC, 2005).

"Risk drinking" (seven or more drinks per week or five or more drinks on one occasion) poses a serious health threat to the fetus. In a Danish study of 89 201 pregnant women, women who reported three or more binge drinking episodes (five or more drinks on one occasion) were more likely to experience stillbirth (Strandberg-Larsen, 2008). A study of 655 979 births in the United States found that women who drank during pregnancy were 40 percent more likely to experience a stillbirth (Aliyu et al., 2008). A meta-analysis of empirical studies found a negative relationship between binge drinking (four to five drinks per occasion) and diverse aspects of cognitive functioning in children aged 6 months to 14 years (Flak et al., 2014)

According to the Public Health Agency of Canada (2012b), there is no safe amount of alcohol during pregnancy. Perhaps understandably, well-intentioned bartenders, waitstaff, and patrons approach pregnant women consuming alcohol and ask them not to drink. Men should stop drinking before attempting to conceive. Alcohol damages sperm count, concentration and quality, and the degree of damage is dose dependent (Jensen et al., 2014).

Tobacco use during pregnancy retards fetal growth and increases the risk of infant illness, disability, and death. Maternal smoking is associated with prematurity; low birth weight; cardiovascular anomalies; conditions involving arteries, veins, or the heart; and asthma (Jaakkola & Gissler, 2004; Kai & Pourier, 2001; Woods & Raju, 2001). Results from the Maternity Experience Survey indicate that 11 percent of Canadian women smoke during pregnancy (Al-Sahab, Saqib, et al., 2010).

Other substances that may produce low birth weight, birth complications, or defects in the fetus include steroids; some antihistamines; long-term use of antibiotics; excessive amounts of vitamin A, D, B6, and K; caffeine; antidepressant medication; lithium; cocaine; and marijuana. These effects are summarized in Table 6.2.

As with alcohol, the best rule for the pregnant woman considering using a prescription or over-the-counter drug, herbal product, or other substance is to consult her physician. Up-to-date information on the effects of various legal substances is available from the Motherisk Information Line at the Hospital for Sick Children by telephone at 1-877-439-2744 or on the Internet at www.motherisk.org.

fetal alcohol syndrome: Serious growth deficiency and malformations in the child of a mother who abuses alcohol during pregnancy.

Dads and Drugs

Most research has focused on the effects of drugs taken by the pregnant woman. However, new theorizing suggests that drugs taken by men before conception may also cause birth defects, probably because the drugs damage the sperm and their genetic contents (Narod et al., 1988). For example, marijuana use has been linked to a decreased sperm count, more damaged sperm, and reduced fertility (Gorzalka & Hill, 2006). In addition, one study found that not only did a mother's smoking during the first trimester of pregnancy increase her offspring's risk of cancer in childhood, but a father's smoking during the pregnancy in the absence of the mother's smoking also increased this risk (John, Savitz, & Sandler, 1991).

Viral Illness during Pregnancy

Certain viruses may cross the placental barrier from the woman to the fetus and cause considerable harm, particularly if the illness occurs during the first trimester of pregnancy. The best known example is rubella. If a woman gets rubella during the first month of pregnancy, there is a 50 percent chance that the infant will be born deaf or have cognitive deficits, cataracts, or congenital heart defects. The risk then declines, so that by the third month of pregnancy the chance of abnormalities is only about 10 percent. Although most women have an immunity to rubella because they either had it when they were children or were immunized, a woman who suspects that she is not immune can receive a vaccination that will give her immunity; she should do this well before she becomes pregnant.

Herpes simplex is also *teratogenic*—that is, capable of producing defects in the fetus. The risk of infection to the infant is affected by the nature of the mother's infection (newly acquired or recurrent), the mode of delivery, the duration of the rupture of the membranes, and the use of forceps or vacuum-assisted delivery (Allen, Robinson, et al., 2014). Usually, the infant contracts the disease by direct contact with the sore; delivery by Caesarean section can prevent this. Women with herpes genitalis also have a high risk of spontaneously aborting.

A woman who is infected with HIV, the virus that causes AIDS, can pass the virus on to her child during pregnancy, delivery, or after birth through her breast milk. In Canada, pregnant women are given the option of being tested for HIV, but testing is not required. It is important that pregnant women know if they are HIV positive. Without treatment, 28 percent of their babies will become infected; however, if the infected mother

Table 6.2   Teratogenic Effect of Frequently Used Substances on Prenatal Development

Legal Drugs	Potential Negative Effects
Nicotine	Prematurity; low birth weight; delayed intellectual and behavioural development; risk of pneumonia, bronchitis, laryngitis, and inner ear infections; fathers' smoking may transmit risk of cancer to offspring.
Alcohol	Fetal alcohol syndrome (physical defects, short stature, mental retardation, hyperactivity, stereotypical behaviours, congenital addiction leading to withdrawal syndrome); father's abuse of alcohol may cause genetic damage that leads to birth defects. The combination of parental smoking and drinking may cause miscarriage, prematurity, low birth weight, and sudden infant death syndrome (SIDS).
Illegal Drugs	
Heroin, morphine, methadone, oxycodone	In mother, difficulty conceiving; in infant, prematurity, low birth weight, addiction, withdrawal, death.
Marijuana	In mother, difficulty conceiving; in infant, prematurity, low birth weight, high-pitched crying; no long-term effects.
Cocaine	In mother, difficulty conceiving; in infant, prematurity, low birth weight, neurological deficits, small head circumference; in father, may lead to reduced sperm count and decreased fertility.
Lysergic acid diethylamide (LSD)	Chromosomal breakage.
Medications/Treatments	
Steroids	Heart and circulatory problems; masculinization of female fetus.
Diethylstilbestrol (DES)	In mother, miscarriage; in infant, prematurity, low birth weight; female child may develop cancer of the cervix; male child may have reproductive abnormalities and increased risk of testicular cancer.
Reserpine (tranquilizer)	Respiratory problems in infant.
Antibiotics	Defective skeletal growth in infant, hearing loss, jaundice.
Aspirin	Blood disorders in infant.
Some anticonvulsant medications	Cleft lip and palate in infant; failure of blood coagulation.
Lithium	Cardiovascular abnormalities.
SSRI antidepressant medication	Feeding and breathing difficulties at birth; low birth weight.

Adapted from E. Hetherington and R. Parke, *Child Psychology*, Table 4.2. © McGraw-Hill Companies, Inc. (2003).

takes AZT, an antiretrovirus drug, the likelihood of such perinatal transmission is reduced by two-thirds to 8 percent (Canadian Paediatric Society, 2013).

Detecting Birth Defects

As has been noted, a number of factors, such as substances taken during pregnancy and illness during pregnancy, may cause defects in the fetus. Other causes include genetic defects (e.g., phenylketonuria, PKU, which causes cognitive impairment) and chromosomal defects (e.g., Down syndrome, which causes cognitive impairment as well as other problems). Genetic defects are more likely to occur as the age of the mother or the father increases (Society of Obstetricians and Gynaecologists of Canada [SOGC], 2012). As noted earlier, obesity in the mother is associated with congenital abnormalities (Stothard et al., 2009).

About 4 to 5 percent of all babies in Canada are born with a birth defect or anomaly. About one-fourth of miscarried fetuses are malformed. The cause of more than half of these defects is unknown (O'Shea, 1995).

However, amniocentesis, chorionic villus sampling, and genetic counselling are options for detecting.

Amniocentesis involves inserting a fine tube through the pregnant woman's abdomen and removing some amniotic fluid, including cells sloughed off by the fetus, for analysis. The technique is capable of providing an early diagnosis of most chromosomal abnormalities, some genetically produced biochemical disorders, and sex-linked diseases carried by females but affecting males (hemophilia and muscular dystrophy), although it cannot detect all defects. If a defect is discovered, the woman may then decide to terminate the pregnancy with an abortion.

Amniocentesis should be performed between the 13th and 16th weeks of pregnancy. If a defect is discovered and an abortion is to be performed, it should be done as early as possible (see Chapter 7). Because amniocentesis itself involves some risk, it is generally thought (although the matter is controversial) that it should be performed only on

amniocentesis (am-nee-oh-sen-TEE-sus): A test to determine whether a fetus has birth defects; done by inserting a fine tube into the woman's abdomen to obtain a sample of amniotic fluid.

women who have a high risk of bearing a child with a birth defect. A woman is in this category if (1) she has already had one child with a genetic defect; (2) she believes that she is a carrier of a genetic defect, which can usually be established through genetic counselling; and (3) she is over 35, in which case she has a greatly increased chance of bearing a child with a chromosomal abnormality.

Chorionic villus sampling (CVS) is an alternative to amniocentesis for prenatal diagnosis of genetic defects (Doran, 1990; Kolker, 1989). A major problem with amniocentesis is that it cannot be done until the second trimester of pregnancy; if genetic defects are discovered, there may have to be a late abortion. Chorionic villus sampling, in contrast, can be done in the first trimester of pregnancy, usually around 9 to 11 weeks postconception. Chorionic villus sampling can be performed in one of two ways: transcervically, in which a catheter is inserted into the uterus through the cervix, as shown in Figure 6.8; and transabdominally, in which a needle (guided by ultrasound) is inserted through the abdomen. In either case a sample of cells is taken from the chorionic villi (the chorion is the outermost membrane surrounding the fetus, the amnion, and the amniotic fluid), and these cells are analyzed for evidence of genetic defects. Studies indicate that CVS is as accurate as amniocentesis. Like amniocentesis, it carries with it a slight risk of fetal loss (caused, for example, by miscarriage). For both amniocentesis and CVS, the fetal loss rate is between 1 and 1.5 percent, but can be as low as 0.02 percent in experienced hands (SOGC, 2007a).

Serious ethical questions are raised when amniocentesis and CVS are used to determine the sex and are followed by an abortion if the fetus is not the desired sex.

Birth

The Beginning of Labour

The signs that labour is about to begin vary from one woman to the next. There may be a discharge of a small amount of bloody mucus (the "bloody show"). This is the mucus plug that was in the cervical opening during pregnancy, its purpose being to prevent germs from passing from the vagina up into the uterus. In about 10 percent of women, the membranes containing the amniotic fluid rupture (the bag of waters bursts), and there is a gush of warm fluid down the woman's legs.

Figure 6.8 Chorionic villus sampling (CVS) and amniocentesis are both available for prenatal diagnosis of genetic defects. CVS (shown here) is able to detect chromosomal abnormalities and sex-linked diseases.

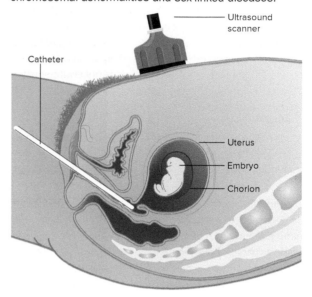

Labour usually begins within 24 hours after this occurs. More commonly, the amniotic sac does not rupture until the end of the first stage of labour. The Braxton-Hicks contractions may increase before labour and actually may be mistaken for labour. Typically, they are distinct from the contractions of labour in that they are very irregular.

The biological mechanism that initiates and maintains labour is not completely understood. The progesterone-withdrawal theory is the leading hypothesis (Schwartz, 1997). Progesterone is known to inhibit uterine contractions. It has been proposed that some mechanism, such as increased production of antiprogesterone, reduces the inhibiting effect of progesterone and labour begins.

The Stages of Labour

Labour is typically divided into three stages, although the length of the stages may vary considerably from one woman to the next. The whole process of childbirth is sometimes referred to as *parturition*.

First-Stage Labour

First-stage labour begins with the regular contractions of the muscles of the uterus. These contractions are responsible for producing two changes in the cervix, both of which must occur before the baby can be delivered. These changes are called **effacement** (thinning out) and **dilation** (opening up). The cervix must dilate until it has an opening 10 cm (4 in.) in diameter before the baby can be born.

chorionic villus sampling (CVS): A technique for prenatal diagnosis of birth defects; involves taking a sample of cells from the chorionic villus and analyzing them.
effacement: A thinning out of the cervix during labour.
dilation: An opening up of the cervix during labour; also called dilatation.

First-stage labour itself is divided into three stages: early, late, and transition. In *early first-stage labour,* contractions are spaced far apart, with perhaps 15 to 20 minutes between them. A contraction typically lasts 45 seconds to a minute. This stage of labour is fairly easy, and the woman is quite comfortable between contractions. Meanwhile, the cervix is effacing and dilating.

Late first-stage labour is marked by the dilation of the cervix from 5 to 8 cm (2 to 3 in.). It is generally shorter than the early stage, and the contractions are more frequent and more intense.

The final dilation of the cervix from 8 to 10 cm (3 to 4 in.) occurs during the **transition** phase, which is both short and difficult. The contractions are very strong, and it is during this stage that women report the most pain and exhaustion.

The first stage of labour can last anywhere from 2 to 24 hours. It averages about 12 to 15 hours for a first pregnancy and about 8 hours for later pregnancies. (In most respects, first labours are the hardest; later ones are easier.) Women having a physician-assisted birth are usually told to go to the hospital when the contractions are four to five minutes apart. Women having a hospital birth are put in the labour room or birthing room for the rest of first-stage labour. Midwives tell their clients to page them when their contractions are five minutes apart, last one minute, and have been that way for an hour. When the woman calls, the midwife does an individual assessment and makes a recommendation about assessing her at home, meeting her at the hospital, or waiting through what sounds like early labour and paging the midwife again when the contractions get stronger.

Second-Stage Labour: Delivery

Second-stage labour (see Figure 6.9) begins when the cervix is fully dilated and the baby's head (or whichever part comes first, if the baby is in some other position; see Figure 6.10) begins to move into the vagina, or birth canal. It lasts from a few minutes to a few hours and is generally much shorter than the first stage. If you have never seen a birth, a number of videos are available on the Internet showing women's birth experiences and choices (e.g., www.givingbirthnaturally .com).

> **first-stage labour:** The beginning of labour, during which there are regular contractions of the uterus; the stage lasts until the cervix is dilated 8 cm.
> **transition:** The most difficult part of labour at the end of the first stage, during which the cervix dilates from 8 to 10 cm.
> **second-stage labour:** The stage during which the baby moves out through the vagina and is delivered.

Figure 6.9 Second-stage labour. *(a)* Baby's head crowning and then *(b)* moving out.

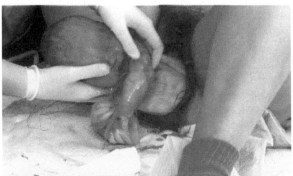

(a) © D. Van Rossum/Petit Format/Science Source

(b) © O.V.N./Petit Format/Science Source

Figure 6.10 Possible positions of the fetus during birth. *(a)* A breech presentation (4 percent of births). *(b)* A transverse presentation (fewer than 1 percent). *(c)* A normal, head-first or cephalic presentation (96 percent of births).

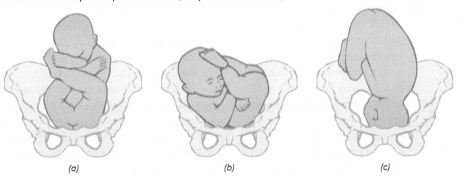

(a)   *(b)*   *(c)*

During this stage, many women feel an urge to push or bear down, and if done properly, this may be of great assistance in pushing the baby out. With each contraction the baby is pushed farther along.

When the baby's head has traversed the entire length of the vagina, the top of it becomes visible at the vaginal entrance; this is called *crowning*, It is at this point that some physicians perform an **episiotomy**, in which an incision or a slit is made in the perineum, the skin just behind the vagina; in Canada, episiotomy rates are decreasing so that currently 17 percent of vaginal deliveries involve an episiotomy (PHAC, 2012b). Most women do not feel the episiotomy being performed because the pressure of the baby against the pelvic floor provides a natural anaesthetic. The incision is stitched closed after the baby is born. The reason physicians give for performing an episiotomy are that it will prevent impaired sexual functioning in later life, reduce the severity of perineal lacerations, and reduce postdelivery pain and medication use. However, a review of relevant research conducted between 1950 and 2004 found no evidence that any of these benefits result from episiotomies (Hartmann et al., 2005). Critics claim that it is unnecessary and is done merely for the doctor's convenience, while causing the woman discomfort later as it is healing. Midwives reduce the likelihood of vaginal tears during childbirth by massaging the vaginal area and applying ointments during delivery (Maticka-Tyndale & Bicher, 1996). Perineal support, including massage or warm compresses, reduces the risk of third- and fourth-degree lacerations by half (Aasheim et al., 2011). Research in Quebec has shown that perineal massage performed by the woman or her partner during the last few weeks of pregnancy also significantly reduces the risk of tears in the perineum, but only for women who have not had a previous vaginal birth (Eason et al., 2000; Labrecque et al., 1999).

The baby is finally eased completely out of the mother's body. At this point, the baby is still connected to the mother by the umbilical cord, which runs from the baby's navel to the placenta, and the placenta is still inside the mother's uterus. As the baby takes its first breath of air, the functioning of its body changes dramatically. Blood begins to flow to the lungs, there to take on oxygen, and a flap closes between the two atria (chambers) in the heart. This process generally takes a few minutes, during which time the baby changes from a somewhat bluish colour to a healthy, pink hue. At this point, the baby no longer needs the umbilical cord, which is clamped and cut off about 7 cm (3 in.) from the body. The stub gradually dries up and falls off.

episiotomy (ih-pees-ee-ah-tuh-mee): An incision made in the skin just behind the vagina, allowing the baby to be delivered more easily.

third-stage labour: The stage during which the afterbirth is expelled.

Caesarean section (C-section): A method of delivering a baby surgically, by an incision in the abdomen.

To avoid the possibility of transmitting gonorrhea or other eye infections from the mother to the baby, drops of silver nitrate or a similar drug are placed in the baby's eyes (see Chapter 8).

Third-Stage Labour

During **third-stage labour**, the placenta detaches from the walls of the uterus, and the afterbirth (placenta and fetal membranes) is expelled. This stage may take from a few minutes to an hour. Several contractions may accompany the expulsion of the placenta. The episiotomy or any tears are sewn up.

Caesarean Section (C-section)

Caesarean section (C-section) is a surgical procedure for delivery; it is used when normal vaginal birth is impossible or undesirable. Caesarean section may be required for a number of different reasons: if the baby is too large, or if the mother's pelvis is too small to allow the baby to move into the vagina; if the labour has been very long and hard and the cervix is not dilating, or if the mother is nearing the point of total exhaustion; if the umbilical cord *prolapses* (moves into a position such that it is coming out through the cervix ahead of the baby); if there is a D (Rh) incompatibility; or if there is excessive bleeding or the mother's or the infant's condition suddenly becomes life-threatening. Another condition requiring a C-section is *placenta previa*, in which the placenta is attached to the wall of the uterus close to or covering the cervix.

In a Caesarean section, an incision is first made through the abdomen and then through the wall of the uterus. The physician lifts out the baby and then sews up the uterine wall and the abdominal wall. It is not true that once a woman has had one delivery by Caesarean she must have all subsequent deliveries by the same method. Vaginal births after Caesareans (VBAC) are possible (Miller, Nair, & Wadhera, 1996). Up to 60 percent of women with a prior Caesarean attempt a subsequent vaginal birth (Lydon-Rochelle et al., 2001). Of these, 63 percent are successful, and the success rate increases with each prior VBAC (Mercer et al., 2008). In 2014, 28 percent of Canadian births were by Caesarean section (CIHI, 2016a). The lowest rate of Caesarean delivery was in Nunavut (10 percent); the highest was in British Columbia (34 percent). The rate of Caesarean delivery in Canada is considerably higher than in most Western European countries.

There is concern about the high and increasing Canadian Caesarean rates. Reasons that have been proposed to explain the high rates include the following: (1) more older women giving birth, and they may have more difficult labours necessitating Caesareans; (2) fetal monitors are used increasingly and can give the physician early warning if the fetus is in distress, necessitating a Caesarean to save the fetus; and (3) more women are requesting (and are having) a Caesarean without clear medical reasons for it. In fact, an analysis of 540 174 primary C-sections and 371 683 repeat Caesarean births in the United States in 2001 classified 11 percent of the former and 55 percent of the latter as potentially unnecessary (Kabir et al., 2005).

There is considerable controversy about these elective C-sections—that is, Caesarean on-demand. On the one hand, some people argue that benefits of elective Caesarean delivery are that not having vaginal deliveries reduces women's risk of urinary incontinence, protects them from fear and pain, and protects the fetus from birth-related injuries (Minkoff & Chervenak, 2003). Thus, they feel that women should be given the choice of having a Caesarean if they want one. On the other hand, opponents argue that having a Caesarean increases health risks to both the mother and the fetus and should be performed only for specific problem situations (Canadian Association of Midwives, 2004). Caesarean deliveries are associated with higher rates of obstetrical trauma (Hines & Jiang, 2012) and of complications requiring hospitalization of mother or infant (Stranges, Wier, & Elixhauser, 2011) than vaginal deliveries. Thus, they argue that women should not be given the choice of a Caesarean delivery, and Caesarean surgery should only be performed when medically necessary. Education of both pregnant women and of medical staff can reduce rates of unnecessary Caesarean sections (Hollander, 1996).

L05 Childbirth Options

Pregnant women and their partners can choose from a variety of childbirth options. In some provinces they can select a midwife or a physician to provide prenatal care and catch the infant. They can take childbirth classes to prepare mentally and physically for labour and delivery. Several options are available regarding the use of anaesthesia during childbirth. Finally, depending on the province or territory, women can often choose to give birth at home, in a birthing centre, or in a hospital labour room.

Prepared Childbirth

There are several methods of prepared childbirth. Most are based on the assumption that fear causes tension and tension causes pain. Thus, programs attempt to eliminate the pain of childbirth by providing education (to eliminate the woman's fears of the unknown) and teaching relaxation techniques (to eliminate tension).

One of the most widely used methods of *prepared childbirth* was developed by French obstetrician Fernand Lamaze. Classes teaching the Lamaze method or variations of it are now offered in most areas of the world. The **Lamaze method** involves two basic techniques, *relaxation* and *controlled breathing* (see Figure 6.11). The woman learns to relax all the muscles in her body. Knowing how to do this has a number of advantages, including conservation of energy during an event that requires considerable endurance and, more important, avoidance of the tension that increases the perception of pain. The woman also learns a series of controlled breathing exercises, which she will use to help her during each contraction.

Some other techniques are taught as well. One, called *effleurage*, consists of a light, circular stroking of the abdomen with the fingertips. Exercises can strengthen specific muscles, such as the leg muscles, which undergo considerable strain during labour and delivery. Finally, because of the assumption that fear and the pain it causes are best eliminated through education, women learn a great deal about the processes involved in pregnancy and childbirth.

One other important component of several methods is the requirement that the woman be accompanied during the training and during childbirth itself by her partner or some other person, who serves as coach. The coach plays an

> **Lamaze method:** A method of "prepared" childbirth involving relaxation and controlled breathing.

Figure 6.11 Practice in relaxation and breathing techniques are important parts of prepared childbirth.

© Jiang Jin/Purestock

integral role in the woman's learning of the techniques and her use of them during labour. The coach is present during labour and delivery. The coach times contractions, checks on the mother's state of relaxation and gives her feedback, suggests breathing patterns, helps elevate her back as she pushes the baby out, and generally provides encouragement and moral support. Aside from the obvious benefits to the mother, this represents real progress in that it allows the partner to play an active role in the birth of the child and to experience more fully one of the most basic and moving of all human experiences—either as the coach or following the coach's suggestions. The presence of a companion of the woman's choice during labour and delivery has a positive influence on women's satisfaction with the birth process and does not interfere with other events (Bruggemann et al., 2007).

Some couples have a **doula** (a Greek word meaning "woman's servant") present during childbirth to provide supportive care before and during labor and delivery. A doula can provide education and emotional and physical support but does not perform clinical tasks. Six hundred women giving birth for the first time were randomly assigned to receive care from a doula of the woman's choice or standard care. Women supported during labour by a doula experienced significantly shorter labours, and their infants received higher Apgar scores (overall health rating) at one and five minutes after birth (Campbell et al., 2006).

One common misunderstanding about prepared childbirth is the belief that the use of anaesthetics is prohibited. In fact, the goal is to teach each woman the techniques she needs to control her reactions to labour so that she will not need an anaesthetic; however, it affirms her right to have an anaesthetic if she wants one. The topic of anaesthetics in childbirth, which has become quite controversial in recent years, is discussed in the next section.

A number of studies indicate that childbirth training, such as the Lamaze method, has several desirable results. These include reduction in the length of labour, decreased incidence of birth complications, decreased use of anaesthetics, a more positive attitude after birth, increased self-esteem, and a heightened sense of being in control (e.g., Felton & Segelman, 1978; Zax, Sameroff, & Farnum, 1975). Lamaze training is associated with increased tolerance for pain and reduced anxiety both before birth and four weeks after birth (Markman & Kadushin, 1986; McClure & Brewer, 1980; Worthington et al., 1983).

Prepared childbirth has undoubtedly improved the childbirth experiences of thousands of women and men. On the other hand, some advocates are so idealistic that they may create unrealistic expectations about delivery, especially for women having their first baby (**primipara**). The use of

What training do midwives receive?

prepared childbirth reduces pain in childbirth but does not eliminate it completely. Primiparas often experience a discrepancy between their positive expectations for delivery and the actual outcomes (Booth & Meltzoff, 1984). Thus, while these methods produce excellent outcomes and help women control pain, childbirth still involves some pain, as well as unexpected complications in some cases.

Midwives

Although most babies worldwide are delivered by midwives, in Canada in 2006, only 6 percent of women received prenatal care from a midwife (PHAC, 2009a). However, the status of midwives in Canada is in transition in that it is being recognized as an independent professional in more and more provinces. In 2016, midwifery was a legal and regulated profession in all Canadian provinces except Prince Edward Island (although some provinces had no or few licensed midwives). Midwives practise independently in these provinces and territories, managing the care of women with low-risk pregnancies. Further, midwives are publicly funded in all of these provinces and territories so that women can choose to be followed by a physician or by a midwife. According to the Canadian Midwifery Regulators Consortium (2007), registered midwives typically have an undergraduate degree in midwifery; some also have a nursing degree. Seven Canadian universities in five provinces offer this program. To be registered, a midwife must show that she (there is only one male midwife in Canada) is able to deliver competent care as a primary caregiver to women who are considered low risk. Many women are not familiar with midwifery. Nonetheless, more and more women are requesting to have their pregnancy and birth in the care of a midwife—so much so that the demand for midwives far exceeds the supply. (See one woman's experience with a midwife in First Person.) Research indicates that care by a midwife, compared to standard care, is safe for women and their babies (Tracy et al., 2013).

The Use of Anaesthetics in Childbirth

Throughout most of human history, childbirth has taken place without anaesthetics and in the woman's home or other familiar surroundings. The pattern in North America began to change about 250 years ago when male physicians rather than midwives began to assist during birth. A major change came around the middle of the nineteenth century, with the development of anaesthetics for use in surgery. When their use in childbirth was suggested, there was initial opposition from physicians. Opposition to the use of anaesthetics virtually ceased, however, when Queen Victoria gave birth under chloroform anaesthesia in 1853. Since then, the use of anaesthetics has become routine (too routine, according to some) and effective. Before discussing the arguments for and against the use of anaesthetics, let us briefly

doula: An individual who provides physical and emotional support during childbirth.

primipara: A woman having her first baby.

review some of the common techniques of anaesthesia used in childbirth.

The medications most commonly used during labour are regional and local anaesthetics, which numb only a specific region of the body. A *spinal* block is a regional anaesthetic used to provide pain relief late in the first stage of labour. The medication is injected in the back into a sac of fluid below the spinal cord. It provides complete pain relief for one to two hours, and is usually given only once. The *epidural* block numbs the body from the waist down. It is administered via an injection in a small area near the spinal cord (the epidural space). It may be given during labour, or before a cesarean section, or during a delivery using forceps. A *pudendal* block (named for the pudendum or vulva) involves an injection into the vaginal wall which relieves pain in the lower vagina and perineum for up to one hour. It may be given shortly before delivery. A local anaesthetic injection does not relieve labour pain but is used to numb an area if an incision or repair is necessary. Pain relief during labour may be provided by various narcotics—opioids—such as fentanyl. They may be injected into a muscle or given through an IV. If an IV is used, the woman may be able to control the dosage. Tranquilizers are rarely used during labour; they may be used if the woman is extremely anxious, or needs some rest due to the length of the labour.

In 2014–15, 59 percent of Canadian women with a vaginal delivery received an epidural. However, the rates vary considerably across jurisdictions. For example, 72 percent of vaginal births in Quebec and 65 percent of births in Ontario involved an epidural. However, only 40 percent of births in Manitoba and 36 percent in B.C. and the Yukon included one (CIHI, 2016a).

The routine use of anaesthetics has been questioned by some. Proponents of the use of anaesthetics argue that with modern technology, women no longer need to experience pain during childbirth and that they shouldn't suffer unnecessarily. Opponents argue that anaesthetics have a number of well-documented dangerous effects on both mother and infant. Anaesthetics in the mother's bloodstream pass through the placenta to the infant. Thus, while they have the desired effect of depressing the mother's central nervous system, they also depress the infant's nervous system. Anaesthetics prevent the mother from using her body as effectively as she might to help push the baby out. If administered early in labour, anaesthetics may inhibit uterine contractions, slow cervical dilation, and prolong labour. They also numb a woman to one of the most fundamental experiences of her life. However, research shows that the negative effects of epidural anaesthesia, such as the increased likelihood of the use of instruments during delivery and longer second-stage labour, can be reduced by using low dosages and techniques that allow the woman to move around (Comet, 2001).

Perhaps the best resolution of this controversy is to say that a pregnant woman should participate in prepared childbirth classes and should use those techniques during labour. If, when she is in labour, she discovers that she cannot control the pain and wants an anaesthetic, she should be able to request it and to do so without guilt; the anaesthetic should then be administered with great caution.

Home Birth versus Hospital Birth

We noted in Chapter 2 the process of *medicalization,* in which various life conditions and events are defined in medical terms, as requiring medical treatment. Childbirth is a process that was medicalized in Canada, resulting in the shift of almost all births from homes to hospitals. Further, various interventions, including induction of labour, use of anaesthesia, and C-sections, have become more common in the past 50 years (Laughon et al., 2012). Bucking this trend are advocates of home birth who argue that the atmosphere in a hospital—with its forbidding machines, regulations, and general lack of homeyness—is stressful to the woman and detracts from what should be a joyous, natural human experience (see Figure 6.12). Furthermore, hospitals are meant to deal with illness, and the delivery of a baby should not be viewed as an illness; hospital births may encourage the

Figure 6.12 A home birth.

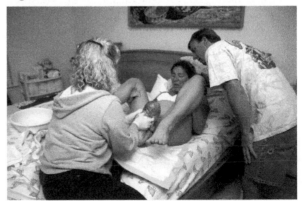

© Inga Spence/Photolibrary/Getty Images

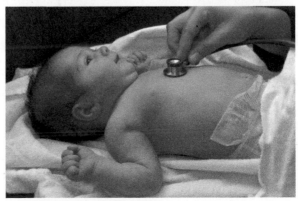

© CSP_lucidwaters/AGE Fotostock RF

First Person

Giving Birth at Home: One Couple's Experience

By the time I got pregnant with my first child (we now have two), I knew I wanted to try to have a natural birth, ideally at home. I had started to notice that pregnancy and childbirth is often talked about with the same language reserved for illness and disease as if birth cannot occur without the "help" of modern medicine. I recognized an overwhelming sensation of *fear* that dominates all talk and messages about labour and childbirth and I knew I wanted to escape that mentality or I would likely have a terrifying experience. Thank goodness I learned I actually had options when it came to childbirth! I learned over 90 percent of pregnancies and births are healthy and normal and don't require any kind of intervention at all, and that often interventions lead to more interventions, which I knew I didn't want unless I absolutely needed them. I gained confidence from reading Ina May Gaskin's books about birthing and was reminded that my body was literally *made* to do this!

I chose to have a midwife for many reasons, but one of the big drivers was to have a home birth. When I learned giving birth at home was actually a modern-day option and not just something dangerous that happens to people when they don't get to the hospital on time, I started to look into it more. In the beginning, I romanticized it after watching videos like *Orgasmic Birth,* which gives the impression that if done "right" you can actually orgasm from labour contractions. As I probed deeper into the experience of women around me and sought out birth stories from as many people as I could, from different eras, and from different parts of the world, I dropped the fantasy of having an orgasm during labour but the appeal of giving birth at home grew stronger. If I wanted a home birth, I would need a midwife.

Admittedly, I remained partly on the fence about a home birth until close to my third trimester. Before I was fully on board, I still needed to know just how safe it is, how well trained the midwives are, what would happen if things go "wrong," and if/when I could change my mind about being at home. A few things helped. First, we lived a ten-minute walk from the local hospital where I would be admitted if I needed hospital care. My midwife would still be the care provider unless a problem developed that was beyond her scope. Second, my midwife told me I could start labouring at home but ask to go to the hospital at *any* time right up until the actual birth, and that she could continue to assist the delivery with me at the hospital. Third, I learned all about how midwives are trained and educated and regulated, and how the limits of their scope is clearly outlined so they know exactly when to refer and transfer care. And finally, I learned about how they are fully integrated into the medical system in such a way that if a medical doctor is needed, the transfer of care happens safely and efficiently.

Regardless of where I ended up delivering my baby, I wanted a natural birth and I knew working with a midwife was my best bet to make that happen. I had heard my local hospital had a 98 percent rate of giving epidurals, which would make my natural approach very unusual, and I would likely face resistance. Where I live in Ontario, midwives are the only birthing professionals who deliver babies at home, where epidurals are not an option, so they typically have more experience assisting a natural birth and only suggest interventions when absolutely necessary. I knew a natural birth was more likely if I was truly comfortable to labour uninhibited and knowing and trusting my caregiver was paramount to this comfort. Throughout my prenatal appointments, I got to know all three midwives involved in my care so that at the time of birth nobody would be a stranger. Once I went into labour, my midwife was with us until the end. She didn't have to go check on other people or get called away to something more urgent; she stayed present and available with us until several hours after the baby was born. The consistency of care my midwife provided me from the time I was six weeks pregnant to having a six-week-old baby was a key ingredient to my comfort level throughout the birthing process.

I clearly wanted a midwife so I could attempt a "natural" birth, hopefully at home, but there were other reasons I wanted a midwife to support me through my pregnancy and labour. For one, the amount of time they spend with you at appointments was significantly longer than a typical experience with an MD. I met with my midwife monthly, and then bi-weekly, and then weekly as the pregnancy progressed. Each visit was 30 minutes. My midwife proposed and discussed each standard test, providing me an opportunity to ask questions, understand the rationale behind it, and consent to any benefit or risk associated with it before moving forward. I felt like an active participant in the process, with a significant amount of control and choice regarding what was happening to my baby and me. Second, as the actual time of birth approached during labour, a second midwife arrived so that there would be one midwife to fully attend to my medical needs and one to fully attend to the baby should we each require special attention simultaneously. At my second birth, there was also a fourth-year midwifery student intern, so in that case we were all *very* well cared for and attended to, with the full attention of three medical birthing specialists!

There were so many perks to giving birth at home that I could only have done with a midwife, I don't know where to start. I got to eat my own food the whole time and immediately afterwards instead of hospital food. I was able to move around freely and wear whatever I was comfortable in. I gave birth once on my own bed, and once in a birthing pool right next to my bed. I didn't have to get dressed afterwards until I wanted to. I had my own private bathroom and bedroom. I didn't have to go outside until I wanted to. I didn't have to bathe or dress my baby until we were ready. We didn't have to put him/her into a car seat within the first 48 hours. We could change the lighting as we pleased, and set up music or candles if we wanted. We could control the flow of people/visitors in and out of the room and the house. The midwives came to our home for the first two weeks after birth for follow-up appointments—again no bundling up baby or car-seat fussing in the very early days—I didn't even have to get out of bed if I didn't want to.

Both of my children were born naturally at home with midwives (and doulas). Their care was incredible: It was nurturing, supportive, professional, and proficient. My birthing experiences were wild and painful and animalistic, but they were also warm and beautiful and uninhibited, thanks to the team of caregivers surrounding me. I would do it again in a heartbeat.

His Perspective

I guess I should have expected an alternative birth experience seeing that I married a naturopathic doctor, but to be honest, at the time I didn't know that there were options when it came to childbirth. Like so many other people, I assumed that when the time came, we would go to the hospital where the baby would be delivered and then we would go back home. The idea of having the baby at home with midwives and doulas (neither of which I had heard of before) was way beyond anything I would have considered.

When Laurie and I met the midwives and they started to explain the process, it helped dispel some of my concerns (which were primarily that somehow a home birth meant that I would be responsible for delivering the baby personally). The more time I spent with our midwives, the more I understood the potential benefits of a home birth, and my comfort with not giving birth at a hospital grew. During the birth itself, the support they provided to Laurie and me was so much more than I imagined I would need or would have received had we done it in a traditional manner. The midwives' and the doulas' previous birthing experience helped reassure us and support Laurie through the most difficult parts of the birth. What was abundantly apparent was that the well-being of Laurie and the unborn baby was their primary focus. Just as important was the fact that they were with us throughout the entire process. Both of our children were born at home with midwives and doulas, and I can't imagine having done it any other way.

Source: Written by Dr. Laurie Alpert, Doctor of Naturopathic Medicine.

use of procedures, such as forceps deliveries and episiotomies, that can themselves be dangerous.

Either a physician or a midwife (in provinces and territories in which midwifery is a legal profession) may assist in a home birth. Birth at home is likely to be more relaxed and less stressful; friends and other children are often present. A study comparing the outcomes of planned home births with a licensed midwife to planned hospital births for low-risk women in Ontario (where midwives are well established and integrated into the health care system; see Figure 6.13) found that negative outcomes were low for both groups and that the two groups did not differ in maternal or fetal outcomes (Hutton, Reitsma, & Kaufman, 2009). Nonetheless, nearly all births in Canada (98 percent) occur in a hospital or clinic (PHAC, 2009a).

On the other side of the argument, hospital practices in labour and delivery have changed radically, particularly with the increased popularity of prepared childbirth; thus, hospitals are not the forbidding, alien environments they once were. Most hospitals, for example, allow partners and loved ones to be present for the entire labour and delivery, and many allow the partner to be present in the operating room during Caesarean

Figure 6.13 Alyssa Byers-Heinlein, a registered midwife working in Ontario, poses with some of the equipment she brings to all home births.

© Joshua Durbin, 2017

deliveries. Many hospitals have created birthing rooms, containing comfortable beds and armchairs, that permit labour and delivery to occur in a relaxed atmosphere and in the position the woman chooses, while being only a minute away from emergency equipment if it is required. Further, women can still have a midwife and choose to give birth in a hospital.

For any home birth, careful screening is essential. Only women with low risk pregnancies and anticipated low risk deliveries should attempt a home birth. A qualified physician or midwife must be part of the planning. Finally, there must be access to a hospital in case an emergency arises.

Why do women choose to have their baby delivered by a midwife rather than a physician? First, midwives provide care from early pregnancy to six weeks after the baby is born, therefore providing continuity of care. Thus, the midwife and the family get to know each other well. Second, prenatal visits are typically 45 minutes long (longer than the typical medical visit). As part of these visits, the midwife presents information so that the woman and her family can make informed decisions about the care they receive and their birth experience. Third, midwives offer women a choice of birth place, either a home or hospital or birthing centre birth, depending on the jurisdiction. Finally, the midwife stays with the woman throughout her labour and birth and manages all aspects of her care. Typically, two midwives are present at the birth—the primary midwife and a second midwife who takes care of the baby after it is born. Midwives are trained to know when to refer to a medical specialist when complications arise that are outside their scope of practice, although they stay involved in a supportive way even if they make a referral. Midwives support birth as a normal physiological process and are trained to manage various emergencies.

Research suggests that women who have their baby delivered by a midwife are the most satisfied with the birth experience. A survey of Canadian women giving birth during a three-month period found that 71 percent of women who had a midwife as their primary caregiver during the birth rated their experience as "very positive," while only 53 percent of women whose primary caregiver was a physician or nurse rated it as "very positive" (Statistics Canada, 2008a).

After the Baby Is Born: The Postpartum Period

Physical Changes

With the birth of the baby, the woman's body undergoes a drastic physiological change. During pregnancy the placenta produces high levels of both estrogen and progesterone. When the placenta is expelled, the levels of these hormones drop sharply, and thus the postpartum period is characterized by low levels of both estrogen and progesterone. The levels of these hormones gradually return to normal over a few weeks to a few months. Other endocrine changes include an increase in hormones associated with breast-feeding (breast-feeding is discussed later in this chapter).

In addition, the body undergoes considerable stress during labour and delivery, and the woman may feel exhausted. Discomfort from an episiotomy or laceration is common in the first postpartum weeks. Some women experience postpartum genito-pelvic pain (see Chapter 18) (Glowacka et al., 2014; Rosen & Pukall, 2016).

Psychological Changes

On average, Canadian women remain in the hospital for two or three days after parturition; the average length of stay following a Caesarean delivery is three to four days (PHAC, 2012a). For the first two days, women often feel elated; the long pregnancy is over, they have been successful competitors in a demanding athletic event and are pleased with their efforts, and the baby is finally there, to be cuddled and loved.

Following childbirth, many women experience some degree of depression. The depressed mood and other experiences range from mild to severe; the medical literature identifies three types. In the mildest, *postpartum blues* (or "baby blues"), women experience mood swings, with periods of feeling depressed, feeling irritable, and crying, alternating with positive moods. The symptoms usually begin a few days after delivery, are most intense one week postpartum, and lessen or disappear by two weeks postpartum. Between 50 and 80 percent of women experience these mild baby blues (Kennedy & Suttenfield, 2001). **Postpartum depression** is more severe, characterized by depressed mood, insomnia, tearfulness, feelings of inadequacy, and fatigue. It usually begins two to three weeks postpartum but may occur anytime after delivery. Between 8 and 15 percent of women will experience it, with symptoms lasting six to eight weeks (Morris-Rush & Bernstein, 2002; O'Hara & Swain, 1996). The most severe disturbance is *postpartum psychosis*, with early symptoms including restlessness, irritability, and sleep disturbance; later ones include disorganized behaviour, mood swings, delusions, and hallucinations. Its onset can be dramatic, within 72 hours of delivery or four to six weeks postpartum. It is very rare, affecting only 1 or 2 women out of 1000 (Kennedy & Suttenfield, 2001).

It appears that many factors contribute to postpartum depression. Being in a hospital

> **postpartum depression:** Mild to moderate depression in women following the birth of a baby.

in and of itself is stressful. Once the woman returns home, another set of stresses await her. She has probably not yet returned to her normal level of energy, yet she must perform the tiring task of caring for a newborn infant. For the first several weeks or months she may not get enough sleep, rising several times during the night to tend to a baby that is crying because it is hungry or sick, and she may become exhausted. Clearly, she needs help and support from her partner and friends at this time. Some stresses vary depending on whether this is a first child or a later child. The first child is stressful because of the woman's inexperience; while she is in the hospital she may become anxious, wondering whether she will be capable of caring for the infant when she returns home. In some cases, the mother may become depressed because she did not really want the baby. Risk factors for more severe depression include personal or family history of psychiatric disorder, unwanted pregnancy, serious complications following birth, and lack of social support (Morris-Rush & Bernstein, 2002). Women experiencing multiple births have higher depression symptoms nine months postpartum compared with mothers of singletons (Choi, Bishai, & Minkovitz, 2009).

Physical stresses are also present during the postpartum period; hormone levels have declined sharply, and the body has been under stress. Thus, it appears that postpartum depression is caused by a combination of psychological, physical, and social factors.

Postpartum depression and psychosis should be treated; for most women, depression improves in response to antidepressant drugs, individual psychotherapy, partner and peer support, and nurse home visits (Gjerdingen, 2003; Mehta & Sheth, 2006). A review of the research using randomized controlled trials to assess psychological interventions reported that the most promising is intensive professional postpartum support (Dennis, 2005).

Fathers, too, sometimes experience depression after the birth of a baby. A study in Great Britain assessed depression in both mothers and fathers eight weeks after delivery. Ten percent of the mothers and 4 percent of the fathers attained high scores. Parents with a history of depression, younger parents (ages 15 to 24), and those living in depressed neighbourhoods are at greater risk of depression (Davé et al., 2010). Paternal depression at eight weeks was associated with having a child with more adverse emotional and behavioural outcomes at 3.5 years of age, over and above the mother's level of depression (Ramchandani et al., 2005).

Attachment to the Baby

While much of the traditional psychological research has focused on the baby's developing attachment to the mother, more recent interest has been about the development of the mother's attachment (bond) to the infant (see Chapter 10). Research shows clearly that this process begins even before the baby is born. Two studies of women expecting their first child found that feelings of nurturance grew during pregnancy, and increased further at birth (Fleming et al., 1997). In this sense, pregnancy is in part a psychological preparation for motherhood.

In the 1970s, pediatricians Marshall Klaus and John Kennell (1976) popularized the idea that there is a kind of "critical period" or "sensitive period" in the minutes and hours immediately after birth, during which the mother and infant should "bond" to each other. Scientists later concluded that there is little or no evidence for the sensitive-period-for-bonding hypothesis (e.g., Goldberg, 1983; Lamb & Hwang, 1982; Myers, 1984). That outcome is fortunate. Otherwise, mothers who give birth by Caesarean section (and may therefore be asleep under a general anaesthetic for an hour or more after the birth) and adoptive parents would have inadequate bonds with their children. We know that, in both cases, strong bonds of love form between parents and children despite the lack of immediate contact following birth. Nonetheless, 73 percent of Canadian hospitals have a policy to facilitate parent–infant bonding by ensuring that the baby stays with the parents immediately after the birth, most for an unlimited amount of time (PHAC, 2012a).

Sex during Postpartum

The birth of a child has a substantial effect on a couple's sexual relationship. Following the birth, the mother is at some risk of infection or hemorrhage (Cunningham et al., 1993), so the couple should wait at least two weeks before resuming penetrative sex. Of course, there is no problem engaging in noncoital intimacy if both partners desire it. When coitus is resumed, it may be uncomfortable or even painful for the woman, and for some women, the pain may persist in the long term (Rosen & Pukall, 2016). If she had an episiotomy or lacerations, she may experience vaginal discomfort; if she had a Caesarean birth, she may experience abdominal discomfort. Fatigue of both the woman and her partner also may influence when they resume sexual activity.

A longitudinal study of the adjustment of heterosexual couples to the birth of a child collected data from 570 women (and 550 partners) four times: during the second trimester of pregnancy, and at one, four, and twelve months postpartum (Hyde et al., 1996). Data on the sexual relationship are displayed in Table 6.3. In the month following birth, only 17 percent had resumed intercourse. By the fourth month, nine out of ten couples had—the same percentage as reported intercourse during the second trimester. Reports of cunnilingus showed a similar pattern, while reports of fellatio did not indicate

Table 6.3 Sexual Behaviours within the Previous Month, Reported by Mothers during Pregnancy and the Year Postpartum

Behaviour	Pregnancy 2nd Trimester	Postpartum		
		1 Month	4 Months	12 Months
Intercourse	89%	17%	89%	92%
Mean frequency of intercourse/month	4.97	0.42	5.27	5.1
Fellatio	43%	34%	48%	47%
Cunnilingus	30%	8%	44%	49%
Satisfaction with sexual relationship*	3.76	3.31	3.36	3.53

* Satisfaction with the relationship was rated on a scale from 1 (very dissatisfied) to 5 (very satisfied).

Source: Hyde et al. (1996), pp. 143–151.

a marked decline. Note that although sexual behaviour was much less frequent in the month following birth, satisfaction with the sexual relationship remained high. A major influence on when the couple resumed intercourse was whether the mother was breast-feeding. At both one month and four months after birth, breast-feeding women reported significantly less sexual activity and lower sexual satisfaction. One reason is that lactation suppresses estrogen production, which in turn results in decreased vaginal lubrication; this can make intercourse uncomfortable. This problem can be resolved by the use of vaginal lubricants. Androgen production is also reduced, which may result in reduced sexual desire (LaMarre, Paterson, & Gorzalka, 2003).

A study of Swedish couples in the six months and four years postpartum found that, at both times, the average frequency of sex was one to two times per month, and that sexual contentment did not vary over time. Being too tired for sex was reported as a problem by 42 to 56 percent of the couples (Ahlborg et al., 2008).

A study of women's postpartum sexuality used data from an online survey completed by 310 women. The women reported on their experience in the first three months after their most recent birth. In addition to the nature of the birth experience and fatigue, results identified women's perceptions of their partner's sexual desire as an influence on resuming sexual activity (Hipp, Low, & van Anders, 2012).

L06

Breast-Feeding

Biological Mechanisms

Two hormones, both secreted by the pituitary, are involved in lactation (milk production). One, *prolactin,* stimulates the breasts to produce milk. Prolactin is produced fairly constantly for whatever length of time the woman breast-feeds. The other hormone, *oxytocin,* stimulates the breasts to eject milk. Oxytocin is produced reflexively by the pituitary in response to the infant's sucking of the breast. Thus, sucking stimulates nerve cells in the nipple; this nerve signal is transmitted to the brain, which then relays the message to the pituitary, which sends out the messenger oxytocin, which stimulates the breasts to eject milk. Interestingly, research with animals indicates that oxytocin stimulates maternal behaviour (Jenkins & Nussey, 1991).

Milk is not produced for a few days after delivery. At first, the breast secretes colostrum, discussed earlier, which is high in protein and gives the baby temporary immunity to infectious diseases. Two or three days after delivery, true lactation begins; this may be accompanied by discomfort for a day or so because the breasts are swollen and congested.

It is also important to note that, much as in pregnancy, substances ingested by the mother may be transmitted through the milk to the infant. The nursing mother thus needs to be cautious about using alcohol and other substances.

Physical and Mental Health

The Canadian Paediatric Society, Dietitians of Canada, and the Public Health Agency of Canada recommend that babies be fed breast milk exclusively for the first six months, and continue breast-feeding after introduction of solid foods up to 2 years of age and older. This is because breast milk is the ideal food for a baby (Figure 6.14). It provides the baby with the right mixture of nutrients, it contains antibodies that protect the infant from some diseases, and it may help prevent asthma and allergies. It is free from bacteria, and is always the right temperature. Breast-feeding is associated with a reduced risk of obesity at ages 5 and 6 (Von Kries et al., 1999). Researchers in Ontario showed that breast milk also helps boost the baby's own immune system

Figure 6.14 Breast-feeding.

© Digital Vision/Getty Images

(Filipp et al., 2001). Thus, there is little question that normally it is superior to cow's milk and commercial formulas. Nonetheless, the vast majority of babies who are not breastfed grow up healthy.

The percentage of Canadian infants who are breastfed, at least initially, rose from 38 percent in 1963 to 89 percent in 2011 (Statistics Canada, 2013a). However, there are large regional differences in breast-feeding rates, ranging from a low of 57 percent in Newfoundland and Labrador to a high of 96 percent or above in British Columbia and Yukon. Further, about 21 percent of mothers who initiate breast-feeding stop by one month. Only 26 percent of babies are fed only breast milk for their first six months as recommended. Mothers who do not breast-feed at all tend to be younger, have less formal education, and single than do mothers who initiate breast-feeding (Statistics Canada, 2013a). In terms of the main reasons they give for why they did not attempt to breast-feed, many women say that they did not have enough milk or had difficulty with breast-feeding techniques, which speaks to the importance of providing supports to help mothers breast-feed successfully (Statistics Canada, 2013a). Others say that breast-feeding is "unappealing" or "disgusting" or that bottle-feeding is easier (Statistics Canada, 2011a).

A systematic review of programs designed to promote breast-feeding concluded that educational sessions that review benefits, lactation, and common problems and solutions, and also provide skills training as well as in-person or telephone support programs, improve initiation rates and the maintenance of breast-feeding at six months

(Guise et al., 2003). Programs that involve only giving out materials at the time the new mother leaves the hospital may actually reduce the likelihood that she will breast-feed. Direct encouragement by a health care professional is associated with a much greater likelihood of breast-feeding. The attitudes of the partner are also important. A longitudinal study of 317 first-time mothers and their male partners in Ontario found that male partners' beliefs about breast-feeding affected the women's breast-feeding decisions (Rempel & Rempel, 2004). Women can also use a breast pump to express their milk so that the partner can give the baby a bottle. In this way, the partner can share in the experience of feeding the baby, the mother can get needed sleep if the partner takes over the night-time feeding, or the mother can go out for a few hours without fear that the baby will get hungry.

From the mother's point of view, breast-feeding has several advantages. These include a quicker shrinking of the uterus to its normal size, reduced postpartum bleeding, and more rapid loss of the weight gained during pregnancy. Breast-feeding reduces the likelihood of pregnancy by inhibiting ovulation. Full breast-feeding, short intervals between feedings, night feedings, and the absence of supplemental feedings are all associated with greater delay in ovulation (Hatcher et al., 2011). However, breast-feeding is not an effective means of birth control—it delays but does not prevent ovulation. Thus, a woman can become pregnant again before she has a period; recall from Chapter 5 that ovulation precedes menstruation. Research indicates that breast-feeding reduces negative moods and perceived stress

(Mezzacappa & Katkin, 2002). Breast-feeding is associated with reduced risk of breast cancer; the relative risk decreases by 4 percent for every 12 months of breast-feeding (Collaborative Group on Hormonal Factors in Breast Cancer, 2002).

Some women report sexual arousal during breast-feeding, and a few report having orgasms. Unfortunately, this sometimes produces anxiety in the mother, leading her to discontinue breast-feeding. However, there is nothing wrong with this arousal, which appears to stem from activation of hormonal mechanisms. Clearly, from an adaptive point of view, if breast-feeding is important to the infant's survival, it would be wise for nature to design the process so that it is rewarding to the mother.

The La Leche League is devoted to encouraging women to breast-feed their babies and has helped spread information on breast-feeding. The organization tends to be highly enthusiastic in its advocacy of breast-feeding. Some women are physically unable to breast-feed. Others may experience difficulties with breast-feeding, such as pain during breast-feeding or feeling that the baby is nursing poorly, and need support and information to be able to overcome these difficulties. Others may feel psychologically uncomfortable with the idea, perhaps because of the prevalence of negative messages in our culture about breast-feeding, particularly in public, as well as the labelling of breasts as sexual organs. Also, breast-feeding can be inconvenient for the woman who works outside the home, although working women can express their breast milk or supplement morning and evening feeding with formula while they are at work.

LO7

Pregnancy-Related Problems

Ectopic Pregnancy

An **ectopic pregnancy** (misplaced pregnancy) occurs when the fertilized egg implants somewhere other than the uterus. Most commonly, ectopic pregnancies occur when the egg implants in the fallopian tube (tubal pregnancy). In rare cases, implantation may also occur in the abdominal cavity, the ovary, or the cervix.

A tubal pregnancy may occur if, for one reason or another, the egg is prevented from moving down the tube to the uterus, as when the tubes are obstructed—for example, as a result of scarring from a chlamydia infection. Early in a tubal pregnancy, the fertilized egg implants in the tube and begins development, forming a placenta and producing the normal hormones of pregnancy. The woman may experience the early symptoms of pregnancy, such as nausea and amenorrhea, and think

she is pregnant, or she may experience some bleeding that she mistakes for a period and think that she is not pregnant. It is therefore quite difficult to diagnose a tubal pregnancy early.

A tubal pregnancy may end in one of two ways. The embryo may spontaneously abort and be released into the abdominal cavity, or the embryo and placenta may continue to expand, stretching the tube until it ruptures. Symptoms of a rupture include sharp abdominal pain or cramping, dull abdominal pain, possibly pain in the shoulder, and vaginal bleeding. Meanwhile, hemorrhaging is occurring, and the woman may go into shock and, possibly, die; thus, it is extremely important for a woman displaying these symptoms to see a doctor quickly.

The rate of ectopic pregnancy in Canada was 12 cases reported per 1000 pregnancies in 2004–05 (PHAC, 2008b). The rates vary across Canada, from a low of 6 per 1000 reported pregnancies in Prince Edward Island to 32 per 1000 pregnancies in the Northwest Territories. It is thought that high rates are due to (1) increased rates of sexually transmitted infections (STIs), particularly chlamydia, which can lead to blocking of the fallopian tubes; and (2) increased use of contraceptives, such as the IUD and progestin-only methods, that prevent implantation in the uterus but do not necessarily prevent conception. Women with a history of STIs and heavy smoking (more than 20 cigarettes per day) are more likely to have an ectopic pregnancy (Bouyer et al., 2003).

Molar Pregnancy

A *molar pregnancy* is a mass of abnormal tissue (*hydatidiform mole*) inside the uterus. It is thought to be caused either by fertilization of an ovum with no genetic information or when two sperm fertilize the same egg. The woman usually thinks she is pregnant because she experiences all the same pregnancy symptoms during the first trimester as do women with a normal pregnancy, including a missed menstrual period, breast tenderness, and nausea. She may also experience a vaginal discharge, vaginal bleeding, and other symptoms that are unique to a molar pregnancy. A molar pregnancy can be diagnosed with a blood test assessing hCG levels or with an ultrasound. Women who are over age 35, who have a history of molar pregnancy or miscarriage, and who are low in vitamin A are at increased risk for a molar pregnancy.

Pseudocyesis

In **pseudocyesis**, or *false pregnancy*, the woman believes that she is pregnant and shows the signs and symptoms of

ectopic pregnancy: A pregnancy in which the fertilized egg implants somewhere other than the uterus.
pseudocyesis: False pregnancy, in which the woman displays the signs of pregnancy but is not actually pregnant.

pregnancy without really being pregnant. She may stop menstruating and may have morning sickness. She may begin gaining weight, and her abdomen may bulge. The condition may persist for several months before it goes away, either spontaneously or as a result of psychotherapy. In rare cases it persists until the woman goes into labour and delivers nothing but air and fluid.

Pregnancy-Induced Hypertension

Pregnancy may cause a woman's blood pressure to rise to an abnormal level. *Pregnancy-induced hypertension* includes three increasingly serious conditions: (1) hypertension, (2) pre-eclampsia, and (3) eclampsia. Hypertension refers to elevated blood pressure alone. **Pre-eclampsia** refers to elevated blood pressure accompanied by generalized edema (fluid retention and swelling) and proteinuria (protein in the urine). The combination of hypertension and proteinuria is associated with an increased risk of fetal death. In severe pre-eclampsia, the earlier symptoms persist and the woman may also experience vision problems, abdominal pain, and severe headaches. In *eclampsia*, the woman has convulsions, may go into a coma, and may die (Cunningham et al., 1993).

Pre-eclampsia may reflect the silent struggle between mother and fetus for resources. It is hypothesized that the fetus, perhaps because of insufficient nutrition, releases a protein that increases the mother's blood pressure, and therefore the flow of nutrients to the placenta. Indeed, research finds elevated levels of the protein sFlt1 associated with pre-eclampsia (Widmer et al., 2007).

Pre-eclampsia usually does not appear until after the 20th week of pregnancy. It is more likely to occur in women who have not completed a pregnancy before. It is especially common among teenagers. The risk of pre-eclampsia rises steadily as pregnancy body mass index increases. For overweight women, a reduction in pre-pregnancy weight may reduce the risk (Bodner et al., 2004). The possibility of pre-eclampsia emphasizes the need for proper medical care before and during pregnancy. Hypertension and pre-eclampsia can be managed well during their early stages. Most maternal deaths occur among women who do not receive prenatal medical care.

pre-eclampsia: A serious disease of pregnancy, marked by high blood pressure, severe edema, and proteinuria.
miscarriage: The termination of a pregnancy before the fetus is viable, as a result of natural causes (not medical intervention).

D (Rh) Incompatibility

D antigen (formerly called the Rh factor) is a substance in the blood; if it is present, the person is said to be D positive (D+); if it is absent, the person is said to be D negative (D−). The D antigen is genetically transmitted, with D+ being dominant over D−.

The presence or absence of the D antigen does not constitute a health problem except when a D− person receives a blood transfusion or when a D− woman is pregnant with a D+ fetus (which can happen only if the father is D+). A blood test is done routinely early in pregnancy to determine whether a woman is D−. Fortunately, about 85 percent of whites, 93 percent of blacks, and 99 percent of Aboriginals are D+; thus, the problems associated with being D− are not very common (Beaulieu, 1994).

If some D+ blood gets into D− blood, the D− blood forms antibodies as a reaction against the D antigen in the invading blood. During parturition, considerable mixing can occur between the mother and fetus, and the blood of a D+ baby causes the formation of antibodies in a D− woman's blood. During the next pregnancy, some of the woman's blood enters the fetus and the antibodies attack the fetus's red blood cells. The baby may be stillborn, severely anemic, or developmentally delayed. Thus, there is little risk for a D− woman with the first pregnancy because antibodies have not yet formed; however, later pregnancies can be extremely dangerous.

Fortunately, techniques for dealing with this situation have been developed. An injection of a substance called *D immunoglobulin* prevents the woman's blood from producing antibodies. D− women should receive D immunoglobulin at 28 to 29 weeks gestation, within 72 hours after delivery of a D+ infant, and after induced abortion or amniocentesis (Beaulieu, 1994). If necessary, the fetus or newborn infant may get a transfusion.

Miscarriage (Spontaneous Abortion)

Miscarriage, or *spontaneous abortion*, occurs when a pregnancy terminates through natural causes, before the conceptus is viable (capable of surviving on its own). It is not to be confused with *therapeutic abortion*, in which a pregnancy is terminated by mechanical or medicinal means (what is commonly called *abortion*—see Chapter 7), or with *prematurity*, in which the pregnancy terminates early, but after the infant is viable.

Many people assume that most conceptions lead to a live birth. But, in fact, only a minority do. About 50 percent of preclinical (not medically diagnosed) pregnancies are terminated by an early miscarriage. Very early spontaneous abortions are usually not detected. The woman may not know she is pregnant, and may mistake the products of the miscarriage for a menstrual period. It is estimated that 20 to 25 percent of clinically diagnosed pregnancies are lost (Kwak-kim et al., 2013). Most spontaneous abortions (80 percent) occur during the first trimester of pregnancy. Women who experience a miscarriage in the first 24 weeks of their first pregnancy are at greater risk of obstetrical complications—pre-eclamsia, preterm birth, assisted delivery—in their next pregnancy (Bhattacharya et al., 2008).

Most spontaneous abortions occur because the conceptus is defective. Studies of spontaneously aborted fetuses indicate that 61 percent showed abnormalities that were incompatible with life; for example, many had chromosomal abnormalities (Ljunger et al., 2005). Thus, contrary to popular belief, psychological and physical traumas are not common causes of miscarriage. In fact, spontaneous abortions seem to be functional in that they naturally eliminate many defective fetuses. However, research indicates that maternal obesity, body mass index greater than 30, is associated with spontaneous abortion, and with infant death in the year following the birth (Tennant, Rankin, & Bell, 2011).

Preterm Birth

A major complication during the third trimester of pregnancy is premature labour and delivery of the fetus. When delivery occurs before 37 weeks' gestation, it is considered *preterm*, About 8 percent of the births in Canada are preterm (PHAC, 2008b).

Preterm birth is a cause for concern because the premature infant is much less likely to survive than the full-term infant. It is estimated that 60 to 80 percent of the deaths of newborn babies in Canada are due to preterm birth (PHAC, 2008b). Preterm infants are particularly susceptible to respiratory infections and must receive expert care. Advances in medical techniques have considerably improved survival rates for preterm infants. About 99 percent of infants weighing 2500 g at birth survive, as do 64 percent of those weighing 1000 g (Cunningham et al., 1993). However, prematurity may cause damage to an infant who survives. Disability occurs in 60 percent of survivors born at 26 weeks and 30 percent of those born at 31 weeks (Swamy, Ostbye, & Skjaerven, 2008). In children born at 22 to 32 weeks of gestation, cognitive and motor impairment at 5 years of age increase with younger gestational age. Many of these children require specialized care (Larroque et al., 2008).

Maternal factors such as poor health, poor nutrition, obesity, heavy smoking, cocaine use, and syphilis are associated with prematurity. Pregnancy-induced hypertension can also lead to preterm birth. Young teenage mothers, whose bodies are not yet ready to bear children, are also very susceptible to premature labour and delivery. The more risks a pregnant women is exposed to, the greater the risk of preterm birth (Ahluwalia et al., 2001).

Infertility

Infertility refers to a woman's inability to conceive and give birth to a living child, or a man's inability to impregnate a woman. About 12 percent of Canadian couples trying to get pregnant are unable to do so (Bushnik et al., 2012). When fertile couples are purposely attempting to conceive a child, about 20 percent succeed within the first menstrual cycle, and about 50 percent succeed within the first six cycles (Hatcher et al., 2007). A couple is considered infertile if they have not conceived after one year of frequent, unprotected intercourse, or after six months if the woman is over 35 (Barrett, 2006). The term *sterile* refers to an individual who has an absolute factor preventing conception. Unfortunately, most people lack knowledge about infertility (Daniluk & Koert, 2013, 2015; Daniluk, Koert, & Cheung, 2012).

Causes of Infertility

In about 40 percent of infertile couples, male factors are responsible, and female factors are responsible in an additional 40 percent. In the remaining 20 percent, either both have problems or the cause is unknown (for a detailed discussion, see Liebmann-Smith, 1987).

Causes in Women

The most common cause of infertility in women is pelvic inflammatory disease (PID) caused by a sexually transmitted infection, especially gonorrhea or chlamydia. Problems with ovulation cause 18 to 30 percent of cases. Ovulation disorders are associated with poor diet, high body mass index, and low activity levels (Chavarro et al., 2007; Practice Committee, 2008). Other causes include blockage of the fallopian tubes, and "hostile mucus," meaning cervical mucus that blocks the passage of sperm. Less common causes include poor nutrition; eating disorders; exposure to toxic chemicals, such as lead or pesticides; smoking; and use of alcohol, narcotics, or barbiturates. Age may also be a factor; fertility declines in women after 32 years of age, the decline being especially sharp after age 40 (SOGC, 2012). Women who are older than 35 also have an increased likelihood of miscarriage, spontaneous abortion, stillbirth, and pregnancy complications.

infertility: A woman's inability to conceive and give birth to a living child, or a man's inability to impregnate a woman.

Causes in Men

The most common cause of infertility in men is infections in the reproductive system caused by sexually transmitted infections. Another cause is low sperm count (often due to varicoceles—varicose veins in the testes). Couples concerned about low sperm count may decide to abstain from vaginal intercourse in the hopes of increasing the count, but research indicates that this does not work. In men with low sperm count, the sperm become less mobile and begin showing signs of become stale after only 24 hours of abstinence (Levitas et al., 2003). Another cause is sperm motility, which means that they are not good swimmers. Cigarette smoking has been linked to reduced motility, decreased sperm concentration, and mid-levels of DNA damage in sperm (Pasqualotto et al., 2008). Less common causes include exposure to toxic agents, such as lead; alcohol and marijuana use; and use of some prescription drugs (Hatcher et al., 2007). Obesity in men is associated with abnormalities in sperm (Practice Committee, 2008). Exposure to environmental estrogens causes sperm to mature too fast, reducing their fertilizing capacity (Adoya-Osiguwa et al., 2003). Exposure to environmental estrogens comes through contact with substances such as beer and pesticides. Exposure to bisphenol A (BPA) and phthalates, chemicals found in most everyday products containing plastics, is associated with a 20 percent decline in male fecundity (Buck et al., 2014).

Research also reports that the quality of semen declines with age. As men age, the volume of the semen as well as the number and motility of the sperm decline (SOGC, 2012). Also, the rate of sperm with various genomic abnormalities increases with age. Finally, women whose partners are over 40 are more likely to experience a spontaneous abortion (Kleinhaus et al., 2006).

Combined Factors

In some situations, a combination of factors in both the man and the woman causes the infertility. One such factor is an immunologic response. The woman may have an allergic reaction to the man's sperm, causing her to produce antibodies that destroy or damage the sperm. Or her immune system may react to the fetus or placenta. According to one controversial theory, an immune reaction may create the high blood pressure that is associated with pre-eclampsia (Fox, 2002). Immune reactions occur in response to novel cells entering the body; if the body has been exposed to the cells frequently in the past, the reaction is less likely. Frequent prior exposure of a woman to a specific man's semen would reduce the likelihood of rejecting his sperm. So frequent vaginal intercourse without a condom (Robertson & Sharkey, 2001) or oral sex in which the woman swallows the ejaculate (Koelman et al., 2000) before the attempt to get pregnant may increase the chances of a successful pregnancy.

Sperm have a chemical sensor that causes them to swim toward the egg, attracted by a chemical on the surface of the egg (Spehr et al., 2003). Researchers have already identified one chemical that disrupts this process by shutting down the receptor. This chemical, or chemicals, that influence the surface of the egg can cause infertility. Finally, a couple may also simply lack knowledge; for instance, they may not know how to time intercourse correctly so that conception may take place.

Psychological Aspects of Infertility

At some point, most adults in Canadian society attempt to have a child, and infertility may put significant stresses on a couple (Daniluk, 2001a). Because in our society the male role is defined partly by the ability to father children, the man may feel that his masculinity or virility is in question. Similarly, the female role is defined largely by the ability to bear children and be a mother, so infertility may affect a woman's sense of self-worth, adequacy, and femininity (Daniluk, 1999). Historically, in most cultures fertility has been encouraged—and, indeed, demanded; hence, pressures on infertile couples may be high, particularly in traditional cultures, leading to more psychological stress. The psychological stress is greatest for the partner identified as the source of the infertility and for couples whose infertility remains unexplained (Daniluk, 2001a). Research indicates that, among couples entering fertility treatment programs, women perceive themselves as experiencing greater emotional and social stress than do men (Stanton et al., 2002). A study of 545 couples undergoing assisted reproduction found that 31 percent of the women and 10 percent of the men had a psychiatric disorder. Depression was found in 11 percent of the women and 5 percent of the men. Couples whose first attempt at treatment is unsuccessful show elevated levels of anxiety and depression (Schmidt, 2006). Couples whose first attempt is successful report improved emotional well-being (Holter et al., 2006). Only 20 percent of those with a diagnosis had received treatment for it (Volgsten et al., 2008).

Infertility does not significantly reduce relationship satisfaction, but it can lower sexual satisfaction, pleasure, and spontaneity as couples shift from "making love" to "making babies" (Daniluk, 1999, 2001a). As emphasis on population control increases in our society, and being childfree[5] becomes an acceptable and more recognized option, the stress on infertile couples may lessen.

Treatment for infertility also can be long and stressful. British Columbia psychologist Judith Daniluk (2001a)

---

[5] Semantics can make a big difference here. Many couples who choose not to have children prefer to call themselves *childfree* rather than *childless*.

interviewed 65 infertile couples who had received medical intervention for infertility for an average of five years. Couples described their experience with fertility treatments as an emotional rollercoaster. At first they were optimistic that the medical profession, time, and effort could fix the problem. As the process continued, they (particularly the women) experienced a sense of failure every time menstruation occurred and they had to accept that the treatment had, once again, not worked. Couples whose attempts to conceive were unsuccessful after years of medical intervention described being faced with the difficulty of deciding when "enough is enough"—that is, to stop medical interventions and accept their infertility. They also described the stress in deciding whether to pursue other options to parenthood, a decision that caused conflict between some partners. However, they also described gains that had resulted from treatment, including strengthening their relationship and personal growth. Further, when asked whether they would make the decision to undergo fertility treatments if they had to do it again, all but one couple said yes.

Treatment of Infertility

Some physicians and clinics specialize in the evaluation and treatment of infertility. An infertility evaluation should include an assessment of the couple's knowledge of sexual behaviour and conception, and lifestyle factors such as regular drug use. Infertility caused by such factors can be easily treated.

If the infertility problem stems from the woman's failure to ovulate, the treatment may involve the so-called fertility drugs. The drug of first choice is clomiphene (Clomid). It stimulates the pituitary to produce LH and FSH, thus inducing ovulation. The treatment produces a pregnancy in about half the women who are given it. Multiple births occur about 8 percent of the time with Clomid, compared with 1.2 percent with natural pregnancies. If treatment with Clomid is not successful, a second possibility is injections with *human menopausal gonadotropin* (HMG, a combination of LH and FSH), which may help trigger ovulation.

If the infertility is caused by blocked fallopian tubes, delicate microsurgery can sometimes be effective in removing the blockage. Laparoscopy procedures are less invasive and less likely to cause side effects than abdominal entry (Coughlan, 2008). Endometriosis and endometrial adhesions can also be successfully treated surgically.

If the infertility is caused by varicoceles in the testes, the condition can usually be treated successfully by a surgical procedure known as varicocelectomy.

Finally, a number of new reproductive technologies, such as in vitro fertilization, are now available for those with fertility problems, as discussed in the next section.

A Canadian study is helpful in putting issues of the treatment of infertility into perspective. Among infertile couples seeking treatment, 65 percent subsequently achieved a pregnancy with *no treatment* (Rousseau et al., 1983). For some couples conception just takes a bit longer. However, for those who meet the medical definition of infertility (unable to conceive after 12 months of unprotected intercourse), only about half will conceive a child with treatment (Daniluk, 2001b). Thus, the risks associated with treatments need to be weighed against the possibility that a pregnancy can be achieved without treatment.

Assisted Reproductive Technologies

Reproductive technologies developed in the last four decades mean that there are many ways to conceive and birth babies besides sexual intercourse and pregnancy (see Figure 6.15). These are collectively referred to as assisted reproductive technologies (ART). These options can be used by infertile couples, single individuals, and same-sex couples. The equality provisions in the

Figure 6.15 Explaining reproduction to children was a lot easier in 1977 when "Where Did I Come From?" was first published. With the development of assisted reproductive technologies, it has made this discussion much more complex.

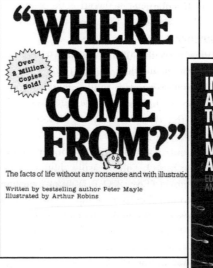

Left: © Kensington Publishing Corp, Right: © Jessica Kingsley Publishers

Canadian Charter of Rights and Freedoms guarantee that access to new reproductive technologies cannot discriminate on the basis of family status, marital status, sexual orientation, and so on (Law Reform Commission of Canada, 1992). Canada has more than 30 fertility clinics that provide assistance with reproduction by using a range of technologies (Gunby et al., 2011).

Assisted Insemination

Assisted insemination (also called *artificial insemination*) involves artificially placing semen in the vagina, uterus, or fallopian tubes to produce a pregnancy; thus, it is a means of accomplishing reproduction without having sexual intercourse. Assisted insemination in animals was first done in 1776. In 1949, when British scientists successfully froze sperm without any apparent damage to them, a new era of reproductive technology began.

There are two kinds of assisted insemination: assisted insemination by the male partner or husband (AIH) and donor insemination (AID). AIH can be used when the man has a low sperm count. Several samples of his semen are collected and pooled to make one sample with a higher count. This sample is then usually placed in the woman's vagina at the time of ovulation. To increase the number of sperm that reach the fallopian tubes, the sperm can also be washed, concentrated, and injected into the woman's uterus. This is called **intrauterine insemination**, or IUI.[6] AID is used when the male partner is sterile or when the woman does not have a male partner. A donor provides semen to impregnate the woman. The success rate is about 60 percent after six months for women under the age of 35; it decreases for women who are older. The cost of each donor semen specimen sample is between $400 and $800; there are also other expenses associated with AID that can raise the cost substantially.

Of course, it is not always necessary to do AID in a fertility centre or medical facility; some people choose home insemination. The donor ejaculates into a clean glass jar and keeps the sperm at body temperature. Within one to two hours, the woman injects the sperm into her vagina while lying on her back using a nonlatex syringe without a needle. Women who attempt home insemination with fresh sperm run the risk of contracting an STI just as they would if they had unprotected sex, so they should make sure that the donor has not had unprotected sex since being tested. A study of lesbians in Victoria planning to become parents found that 44 percent were planning to use self-insemination at home (McNair et al., 2002).

Surrogacy is also called preconception arrangement or contract motherhood, and occurs when a woman agrees to conceive and carry a baby for someone else (Norris, 2006). Traditionally, surrogate mothers have been used by heterosexual couples in which the woman has a problem with fertility. In this case, the male partner provides the sperm and the surrogate mother becomes pregnant through assisted insemination. However, increasing numbers of gay male couples are using surrogate mothers to become parents through assisted insemination using the sperm of one of the fathers.

Sperm Banks

Because it is possible to freeze sperm, it is also possible to store it, which is just what some people are doing: using frozen human *sperm banks*. The sperm banks open up many reproductive choices. For example, suppose that a couple decide, after having had two children, that they want a permanent method of contraception. The husband then has a vasectomy. A few years later the couple decides that they very much want to have another baby, or the couple has divorced and the man wants to have a baby with a new partner. If the man has stored semen in a sperm bank, they can.

Young men can use sperm banks to store sperm before they undergo radiation therapy for cancer. They can later father children without fearing that they will transmit damaged chromosomes (as a result of the radiation) to their offspring.

Since the mid-1990s, sperm banks have gone online, making their services available to millions of people around the world (Springen & Noonan, 2003). Canada has three sperm banks that are compliant with Health Canada's screening requirements; they all import sperm from other countries. However, there are many more sperm banks in the United States. Many of these sperm banks have websites that allow prospective parents to browse through a good deal of information about each potential donor, enabling them to select on the basis of not only height, weight, and eye and hair colour but also education and family medical history. As recipients demand more information about prospective donors, it has become harder to maintain the donor's anonymity. Some donors of eggs or sperm advertise directly on the Internet; although the costs may be lower than the costs associated with clinic services, as is often true on the

assisted insemination: A procedure in which sperm are placed into the vagina by means other than sexual intercourse.
intrauterine insemination: A procedure in which sperm are washed, concentrated, and injected into a women's uterus.

---

[6] After taking a human sexuality course in which this textbook was used, a student contacted one of the authors to say that her mother had taken part in a pilot study involving IUI. She was born in 1981 and was one of the first babies, if not the first, born in Canada through IUI.

Internet, there is no guarantee that the donor has given accurate information. It is estimated that some 70 percent of the money spent on sperm-bank services in the United States in 2002 (US$65 million) was for purchases via the Internet.

Embryo Transfer

With **embryo transfer**, a fertilized, developing egg (embryo) is transferred from the uterus of one woman to the uterus of another woman. Dr. John Buster of UCLA perfected the technique for use with humans, and the first two births resulting from the procedure were announced in 1984 (Brotman, 1984).

This technique may enable a woman who can conceive but who always miscarries early in the pregnancy to transfer her embryo to another woman who serves as the *surrogate mother;* that is, the person who provides the uterus in which the fetus grows (and whom the media, somewhat callously, have called a "rent-a-womb"). The embryo transfer procedure also essentially can serve as the opposite of assisted insemination. That is, if a woman produces no viable eggs, her male partner's sperm can be used to artificially inseminate another woman (who donates her egg), and the fertilized egg is then transferred from the donor to the mother.

In Vitro Fertilization

It is possible for scientists to make sperm and egg unite in a dish outside the human body. The scientific term for this procedure is **in vitro fertilization (IVF)** (*in vitro* is Latin for "in glass"). The fertilized egg or embryo can then be implanted in the uterus of a woman and carried to term. This technique can be of great benefit to couples who are infertile because the woman's fallopian tubes are blocked. It can also be used for cases of unexplained infertility, ovulation disorders, endometriosis, or severe male infertility. A process called *intracytoplasmic sperm injection* (ICSI) can be used if the man has no sperm or no healthy sperm in his ejaculate. This involves collecting sperm from the epididymis or testes, injecting a single healthy sperm into the ovum, and then using the fertilized egg for IVF (Pinheiro et al., 1999).

A milestone was reached with the birth of Louise Brown, the first test-tube (IVF) baby, in England on July 25, 1978. Obstetrician Patrick Steptoe and physiologist Robert Edwards had fertilized the mother's egg with her husband's sperm in a laboratory dish and implanted the embryo in the mother's uterus. The pregnancy went smoothly, and Louise was born healthy and normal. The first IVF children conceived in Canada were born

in Vancouver in 1983. IVF is now performed in a number of countries, with 26 clinics in Canada (Figure 6.16). Edwards was awarded the 2010 Nobel Prize in Physiology and Medicine for developing the technique (Abbott, 2010).

embryo transfer: Procedure in which an embryo is transferred from the uterus of one woman into the uterus of another.

in vitro fertilization (IVF): A procedure in which an egg is fertilized by sperm in a laboratory dish.

Figure 6.16 New reproductive technologies. *(a)* With in vitro fertilization, conception is more likely if the egg is scratched, allowing the sperm to enter more easily. *(b)* Vicken Sahakian, MD, medical director of a fertility centre, collects eggs from Deborah, 38. She and her husband, Eric, came in for in vitro fertilization. Out of 13 eggs produced by her, five became fertilized and were reintroduced into Deborah.

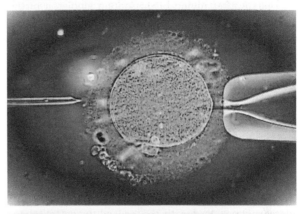

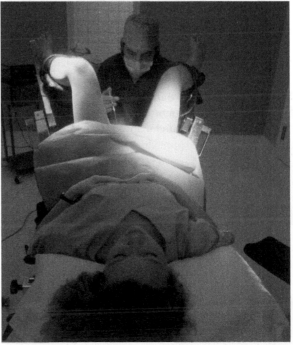

© ISM/Phototake; © Eric Preau/Getty Images

On average across Canadian clinics, 29 percent of all procedures are successful—that is, they resulted in a live birth—and 30 percent of these were multiple births, mostly twins (Gunby et al., 2011). The success rate is higher when the woman is under 40 years old. It is also higher when two embryos are transferred than only one embryo is transferred. The procedure is expensive, about $10 000 per attempt, not including the cost of medication, which can run from $2000 to $8000. The cost is even higher for ICSI. Quebec, Manitoba, and Ontario are the only provinces that cover some or all of the cost of IVF.

There is also evidence that babies born as a result of IVF are more likely to be low birth weight and have congenital abnormalities (Cohen et al., 2009). A study in Finland found a 30 percent greater risk of abnormalities with IVF babies (Klemetti et al., 2006). In another study, mothers were interviewed by telephone six weeks to two years after giving birth. Among singleton births, babies conceived by ART were two to four times as likely to have heart defects, cleft lip, and esophageal and anorectal defects (Reefhuis et al., 2009). Using Australian data, researchers assessed the occurrence of nine specific birth defects for five years following 308 974 births. The rate of defects was 8.3 for babies conceived via ART versus 5.8 for unassisted conceptions (Davies et al., 2012). However, analyses suggested that defects in children conceived via IVF were due to parental factors rather than the procedure. The risk of defects for babies conceived via ICSI remained after controls for parental characteristics. It is not clear whether the increased risk is due to the procedure or to related factors—for example, mothers are typically older (Kovacs, 2002a). These adverse outcomes are more common in babies born after procedures using donor eggs (Wright et al., 2005).

It is also possible to freeze eggs that have been fertilized in vitro (unfertilized eggs do not freeze well), resulting in frozen embryos. This procedure creates the possibility of donated embryos; the birth of a baby resulting from this procedure was first announced in 1984 in Australia. Research finds that babies born after procedures using thawed embryos were less likely to be low birth weight but more likely to be preterm (Wright et al., 2005). The legal and moral status of the frozen embryo is a difficult question, and some worry about "embryo wastage."

Several Canadian reproductive groups have reviewed the literature and made recommendations regarding the number of embryos to be transferred in IVF (Canadian Fertility & Andrology Society Guidelines, 2013). This is because

GIFT: Gamete intrafallopian transfer, a procedure in which sperm and eggs are collected and then inserted together into the fallopian tube.

multiple births, especially triplets or more, are associated with adverse outcomes. In general, the number depends on the age of the mother, varying from one embryo in women under 35 and in excellent health to no more than three embryos in women over 40 with a poor prognosis (Joint SOGC-CFAS Guidelines, 2008).

GIFT and ZIFT

GIFT (for gamete intra-fallopian transfer) is an improvement, in some cases, over IVF. Sperm and eggs (gametes) are collected and then inserted together into the fallopian tube, where natural fertilization can take place, followed by natural implantation. Less than 1 percent of the procedures performed in 2002 were of this type (Wright et al., 2005). Because the number is so small, success rates are not reported.

Yet another improvement is ZIFT (zygote intra-fallopian transfer) in which an egg is fertilized with sperm in a laboratory dish, and the developing fertilized egg (zygote) is placed into the fallopian tube, again allowing natural implantation. Again, less than 1 percent of the procedures performed in 2002 involved this technique (Wright et al., 2005).

Assisted reproduction is more likely to be successful if the woman is younger (under 34) and if fresh embryos rather than frozen ones are used. Success rates do not vary by the cause of the infertility. However, success rates vary across racial and ethnic groups (Fujimoto et al., 2008).

Assisted reproduction is likely to result in multiple births—up to 50 percent of infants born through assisted reproduction technology (Wright et al., 2005). These deliveries are associated with greater health risks for mother and infants. The multiple births result from the common practice of transferring several embryos at one time. Medical and public health authorities are increasingly concerned about the problem (see Figure 6.17).

Reproductive Cloning

Cloning is the reproduction of an individual from a single cell taken from a "donor" or "parent." The technique, called intracellular nuclear transfer, involves replacing the nucleus of an ovum with the nucleus from a donor, thus producing an embryo that is genetically identical to the donor. Normally, of course, a child has only half of its genes in common with the mother; the other half come from the father. Therefore, children are never genetically identical to either parent. But in cloning, no sperm is necessary and the result is an individual who is genetically identical to the donor.

Figure 6.17 Multiple births, such as these triplets, are a common consequence of ART, resulting from implanting multiple fertilized eggs. Many specialists now agree that no more than two embryos should be implanted.

© Ocean/Corbis

In 1997, researchers announced the birth of Dolly, a sheep cloned from a single cell of an adult ewe. In 2000, six cloned piglets were born, significant because pigs are physiologically close to humans (Prather, 2000). Cloning has great potential—for example, as a source of organs that could be transplanted to replace failing ones, stem cells, or as an alternative in cases of infertility. But it has great risks as well; fewer than 3 percent of cloning efforts succeed, and those that do sometimes suffer from grave, unpredictable genetic defects (Kolata, 2001). In 2004, the federal government passed legislation, the *Assisted Human Reproduction Act,* prohibiting human cloning.

Gender Selection

There is much interest in techniques that will allow couples to choose whether to have a boy or a girl. Such a technology would be useful to parents who have six girls and really want a boy, or for people who would like to have two children, one of each sex. Problems might arise, though. Some scientists fear that the result of being able to choose gender would be a great imbalance in our population, with many more males than females, because many couples prefer their first child to be a boy. This is already happening in some Asian countries, such as China and India, in which there is a particularly strong preference for sons. For example, a Canadian-led study in India examined the ratio of male to female births for women who already have a

daughter compared with women who already have a son. They concluded that, even though gender selection is illegal in India, about half a million female fetuses are aborted each year in India by couples trying for a boy (Jha et al., 2006). An Ontario study demonstrated that gender selection may be happening in Canada as well—women born in India who already had one or more children were significantly more likely than were women born in Canada to have a boy (Ray, Henry, & Urquia, 2012).

There is a good deal of conventional wisdom about various home methods of increasing the likelihood that a fetus will be male or female. One technique is timing intercourse in relation to ovulation, based on the belief that sperm carrying a Y chromosome swim faster; thus, intercourse at the time of ovulation should increase the chances of a male, whereas intercourse at a time before and remote from ovulation should favour the slow but hardy sperm carrying an X chromosome, resulting in a female. Several studies have tried to test these ideas, relying on indirect measures of time of ovulation (cervical mucus changes, basal body temperature). They suggest that a female is more likely when intercourse coincides with ovulation. Thus, conventional wisdom is wrong. Studies have also investigated the effect of douching; conventional wisdom has it that douching with vinegar will change the vaginal pH, increasing the chances of a boy. Neither of these (or other) "natural" methods will reliably affect the offspring's gender (Kovacs, 2002b).

As usual, entrepreneurs are taking advantage of people's desire to pick the baby's sex and selling kits that promise results. Some of these kits capitalize on the natural methods, providing the purchaser with thermometers, douching solutions, and other paraphernalia. At least one company is selling kits via the Internet. Again, there is no evidence that these kits will produce the expected results. *Caveat emptor* (buyer beware)!

Several scientific laboratory procedures can be used to separate sperm containing male and female chromosomes. Older techniques involved separation based on swimming speed or immunologic characteristics; these work with 70 to 80 percent accuracy. The latest sorting technique, the Micro-Sort method, uses the fluorescence-activated sorter, which can select sperm with an X chromosome with 90 percent accuracy; this technique greatly reduces sperm count and requires ART. Little data exists on the long-term outcomes of using this procedure (Kovacs, 2002b).

The most reliable method of gender selection is *pre-implantation genetic diagnosis* (PGD). This technique involves removing eggs from the woman and fertilizing them via IVF. After three days, a cell is taken from each embryo and its chromosomal makeup is determined. An embryo of the preferred type would then be implanted via ART. This method is very invasive to the woman's body and very expensive. The likelihood that the implanted egg would result in the live birth of a healthy infant is the same as for other ART pregnancies. PGD is banned in Canada and in the United Kingdom.

Prenatal Genetic Diagnosis

Prenatal genetic diagnosis, determining a fetus's genotype at a specific locus, has been done on a small scale for decades. In the past, amniocentesis and CVS, discussed earlier, have been the primary procedures. Both are invasive, carry a slight risk of harm, and allow only limited analysis of the cells retrieved. As a result, less than 2 percent of pregnant women undergo these tests, primarily to detect a marker for Down syndrome. In the near future, NIPD—non-invasive, prenatal diagnosis—may become a reality, allowing a sample of maternal blood to be tested for hundreds of fetal traits.

During pregnancy, some fetal cells pass through the placenta into the mother's blood stream (Greely, 2011), including cells containing fetal DNA. If samples of fetal DNA can be isolated in the mother's blood, cheap and sensitive genetic sequencing techniques can be used to analyze the fetal genome. This type of analysis is currently used to determine the D (Rh) type of the fetus (see earlier discussion). Two scientists have developed techniques to analyze fetal cell–free DNA and have published proof that fetal genotype can be identified for thousands of sites. Thus, tests are now feasible for many single cell diseases, such as cystic fibrosis, sickle cell anemia, and Tay-Sachs disease. Theoretically, the same techniques could be used to identify fetal sex and sexual orientation, not to mention hair and eye colour and IQ.

Two factors will determine how quickly NIPD becomes readily available—its accuracy as an indicator of the specific disease or trait, and its cost. When and if it becomes available, it will be very controversial, raising serious religious, social, and political issues. One fundamental issue will be whether it should be used to determine which fetuses should be aborted.

The Legal and Ethical Challenges of New Reproductive Technologies

The technologies discussed here require expert practitioners and appropriate facilities. Further, these and other procedures raise complex legal and ethical questions (discussed in Chapter 20). The federal government passed legislation in 2004 to regulate the new reproductive technologies and to deal with some of these issues. The *Assisted Human Reproduction Act* prohibits identifying the sex of an embryo created for reproductive purposes except for medical reasons, paying a woman to be a surrogate mother, paying a donor for sperm or eggs, and buying or selling human embryos. Health Canada announced in 2016 that it plans to strengthen the Act by updating several of its regulations.

However, a number of other legal questions remain. One set of questions is to be found in the matter of kinship and parental rights and responsibilities. When a child is born as a result of these techniques, who exactly are the parents? What legal claim do donors and surrogates have to contact with "their" children after birth?

There are also a host of procedural and ethical issues (O'Neill & Blackmer, 2015). What will the standards of confidentiality be, especially about the identity of non-parent donors? If something goes wrong during one of these procedures—and they are risky—who is liable? Who will take responsibility for a child with a serious disability born through one of these techniques? What should happen to frozen embryos that are not needed and have been abandoned by clinic patients? Should they be made available to infertile couples or destroyed? Finally, there is the question of who should pay for treatment of infertility. Investigations of the causes of infertility are covered by medicare. In addition, the provinces fund some costly treatments for infertility such as tubal surgery in women and repair of varicocele in men (Leader, 1999). However, DI, IVF, and drugs used to treat infertility are not covered by Medicare for most Canadians, which makes most infertility treatments unavailable to the majority of Canadians, who cannot afford them. In 2010, the Supreme Court ruled that many of these regulatory issues fall under provincial rather than federal jurisdiction; however, there is a need for national standards (O'Neill & Blackmer, 2015).

Critical *THINK*ing Skill

EVALUATING ALTERNATIVES IN MAKING A HEALTH CARE DECISION

One of our goals in writing this book is to enable you to make the best decisions about your health care. To do that, you need to (1) know the alternatives, (2) collect valid information about the pros and cons of each alternative, and (3) weigh the alternatives with respect to your circumstances.

Midwives provide care to clients during labour and birth in the client's home, a birth centre, or a hospital. A very important decision facing a pregnant woman is where to have her baby. In this chapter we discussed two alternatives: hospital birth and home birth. Let's collect information about them. The major benefit of choosing a hospital birth is proximity to sophisticated instruments and medical treatment. This may make clients feel safer and more relaxed. What are the cons? One is that various obstetric interventions are more common in hospital deliveries—interventions that sometimes are themselves dangerous. The pros of home birth include the comfort, intimacy, and reduced stress of giving birth at home, and proximity to friends and family. Another pro is the lowest likelihood of receiving medical interventions such as C-section, epidural, or episiotomy. The major con is

distance from sophisticated instruments (although midwives do bring equipment similar to that available in a hospital with them) and medical treatment, if needed. We cited the research conclusion that home birth is not more risky than hospital birth for women who are "low risk, have qualified birth attendants, and have timely access to specialized care." In provinces that licence midwives, both options are covered by Medicare, so cost is not a factor.

Now it is up to you to evaluate these alternatives. Are you a worrier? Are you at some risk for difficulty during birth? Do you live 20 miles or more from a labour and delivery facility? All of these support a hospital-birth decision.

On the other hand, does the peace and quiet of home appeal to you as a birth setting? Has a medical professional determined that you are at "low risk"? Do you live fairly close to a hospital where you can be taken if complications arise? All of these support a home-birth decision with a qualified home-birth provider. If you or your partner were pregnant, what decision seems the best for you?

SUMMARY

Sperm are manufactured in the testes and ejaculated out through the vas deferens and urethra into the vagina. Then they begin their swim through the cervix and uterus and up a fallopian tube to meet the egg, which has already been released from the ovary. When the sperm and egg unite in the fallopian tube, conception occurs. The single fertilized egg cell then begins dividing as it travels down the tube, and finally it implants in the uterus. Various techniques for improving the chances of conception are available.

The placenta, which is important in transmitting substances between the woman and the fetus, develops

early in pregnancy. The most remarkable development of the fetus occurs during the first trimester (first three months), when most of the major organ systems are formed and human features develop.

For the woman, early signs of pregnancy include amenorrhea, tenderness of the breasts, and nausea. The most common pregnancy tests are designed to detect hCG in the urine or blood. Physical changes during the first trimester are mainly the result of the increasing levels of estrogen and progesterone produced by the placenta. Despite cultural myths about the radiant contentment of the pregnant woman, some women do have negative feelings during the first trimester. During the second trimester, the woman generally feels better, both physically and psychologically.

Despite many people's concerns, sexual intercourse is generally quite safe during pregnancy. Nutrition is exceptionally important during pregnancy because the woman's body has to supply the materials to create another human being. Pregnant women also must be very careful about ingesting substances because some can penetrate the placental barrier and enter the fetus, possibly causing damage.

Labour is typically divided into three stages. During the first stage, the cervix undergoes effacement (thinning) and dilation. During the second stage, the baby moves out through the vagina. The placenta is delivered during the third stage. Caesarean section is a surgical method of delivering a baby.

Prepared childbirth has become very popular; it emphasizes the use of relaxation and controlled breathing to control contractions and minimize the woman's discomfort. Anaesthetics may not be necessary, which seems desirable, since they are potentially dangerous.

During the postpartum period, hormone levels are very low. Postpartum depression may arise from a combination of this hormonal state and the many environmental stresses on the woman at this time.

Two hormones are involved in lactation: prolactin and oxytocin. Breast-feeding has a number of psychological as well as health advantages.

Problems of pregnancy include ectopic (misplaced) pregnancy, pseudocyesis (false pregnancy), pre-eclampsia and eclampsia, illness (such as rubella), a defective conceptus, D (Rh) incompatibility, spontaneous abortion, and preterm birth.

The most common cause of infertility in men and women is infection related to sexually transmitted infections (STIs).

Assisted reproductive technologies include assisted insemination, frozen sperm banks, embryo transfer, in vitro fertilization, and GIFT (gamete intrafallopian transfer), all of which are now a reality. These procedures are expensive and have low success rates. In addition, the practice of transferring multiple embryos often results in multiple births, which are riskier for both mother and infants.

On the horizon is widespread use of NIPD to determine fetal genotype. If the technique is used to determine whether a fetus should be aborted, it will create a host of social and ethical debates.

CHAPTER 7

Contraception and Abortion

© BananaStock/Punchstock

Are YOU Curious?

1. I'd like to use the birth control pill, but I worry about remembering to take a pill every day. What are my other options?
2. Can a man still ejaculate after a vasectomy?
3. Are there any hormonal contraceptive methods for men?
4. What is the difference between a surgical abortion and a medical abortion?

Read this chapter to find out.

LEARNING OBJECTIVES

After studying this chapter, you will be able to

LO1 Analyze each contraceptive method.

LO2 Describe the history of birth control and abortion in Canada and the reasons for contraceptive use personally and globally.

LO3 Differentiate between perfect use and typical use failure rates for each contraceptive.

LO4 Summarize the procedure for male and female sterilization and evaluate each.

Explain the new advances in male and female contraception.

LO6 Identify the psychological processes that influence contraception use.

LO7 Describe the abortion procedures currently available in Canada, and illustrate the unequal accessibility for women across the country.

LO8 Describe the typical psychological outcomes of abortion and compare abortion views from a cross-cultural perspective.

For a short time I worked in an abortion clinic. One day I was counseling a woman who had come in for an abortion. I began to discuss the possible methods of contraception she could use in the future (she had been using rhythm), and I asked her what method she planned to use after the abortion. "Rhythm," she answered. "I used it for eleven months and it worked!"[*]

Source: Paula Weideger. (1976). *Menstruation and menopause.* New York: Knopf, p. 42.

The average student of today grew up in the pill era and simply assumes that highly effective methods of contraception are available. It is sometimes difficult to remember that this has not always been true and that previously contraception was a hit-or-miss affair at best. Contraception is less controversial now than it once was: The use of contraceptives was illegal until 1969 when, under Prime Minister Pierre Trudeau, Parliament amended many of the laws pertaining to sexual behaviour (see First Person for a brief history of birth control in Canada).

Before 1969, a person who sold, advertised, or published an advertisement about any "means, instructions, medicine, drug or article intended or represented as a method of preventing conception or causing abortion" could be jailed for up to two years. This statute came under the subheading "Offences Tending to Corrupt Morals" and as such was intended to protect the public and preserve social values (Appleby, 1999). The 1969 amendments to the *Criminal Code of Canada* also allowed abortion under certain restrictive circumstances. The process by which the abortion law was declared unconstitutional by the Supreme Court of Canada in 1988 (abortion is now legal in Canada) is discussed later in this chapter in the section on abortion. These contraception and abortion laws are clear examples of yesterday's values being enshrined in the statute books. They arise from an understanding of reproduction as the only legitimate purpose of sex and the belief in the necessity of vigorous propagation of the species.

Today, people use contraceptives for a variety of reasons. Both babies and mothers are healthier if pregnancies are spaced three to five years apart (Setty-Venugopal & Upadhyay, 2002). Most couples want to limit the size of their family—usually to one or two children. People who are not in a relationship typically want to avoid pregnancy. In some cases, a couple knows, through genetic counselling, that they have a high risk of bearing a child with a birth defect, and they want to prevent pregnancy. And in this era of successful career women, many women feel that it is essential to be able to control when and whether to have children. Of course, a woman's age and relationship status affect her contraceptive use. For example, Canadian women under 30 who are single are more likely than older women and women who are married or cohabiting to use oral contraceptives or condoms or both (Black, Bucio, et al., 2009).

There are other important reasons for encouraging the use of contraceptives at the level of society as a whole. In 2010, 2.8 percent of adolescent girls in Canada got pregnant, and some of these were girls under 15 years old (McKay, 2012); adolescent pregnancy is a major social problem. Physicians do not need a parent's or guardian's permission to prescribe contraceptives, providing the teenager is able to understand the risks and benefits of the decision and thus to provide informed consent.

On the global level, overpopulation is a serious problem. In 1900, the world's population was 1.6 billion—and it had taken millions of years to reach that level (Townsend, 2003). By 1950, it had increased to 2.5 billion. In 2016, the world population hit 7.4 billion, an alarming increase, and experts estimate that it will reach 9.9 billion by 2050. With the resulting destruction of the environment and increased consumption of natural resources, grave concerns arise about the ability of the planet to sustain such a large population, even in the near future. Most experts believe that it is important to limit the size of the world population. Although contraceptives are used by most married or in-union women around the world, the rates are lowest in developing countries, particularly in Africa (U.N., 2015). This is, in part, due to a lack of access to modern contraceptive methods. For a summary of contraceptive practices among married women around the world, see Table 7.1.

In this chapter we discuss various methods of birth control, how each works, how effective they are, what side effects they have, and their relative advantages and disadvantages. We also discuss abortion and advances in contraceptive technology.

Table 7.1 Contraception around the World, Reported by Married and In-Union Women Ages 15–49
The great variations reflect differences among cultures in such factors as availability of medical service, people's education about contraception, and gender roles.

Region, Country	Voluntary Sterilization		Pill	IUD	Male Condom	Injectables[*]	Vaginal Barrier Methods[**]	Fertility Awareness Methods	All Methods
	Male	Women							
North America									
Canada	22	11	21	1	15	1	1	<1	73
United States	11	22	16	5	12	0	<1	1	75
Europe									
France	1	4	40	18	8	1	<1	2	74
Netherlands	7	3	39	8	9	0	2		68
Africa (Sub-Saharan)									
Kenya	0	3	9	4	2	28	0	1	57
Somalia	0	0	4	1	0	1	0	1	24
Asia									
China	4	28	1	40	8	0	<1	1	83
Bangladesh	1	4	33	1	4	14	0	5	64
India	1	39	4	2	6	<1	0	5	60
Latin America									
Colombia	3	34	8	7	7	9	<1	2	78
Middle East and North Africa									
Egypt	0	1	16	31	1	9	<1	<1	60
Morocco	0	3	38	5	1	<1	3		58

[*]Includes injections, such as Depo-Provera.

[**]Includes ring, diaphragm, cervical cap, sponges, and spermicides

Based on data from United Nations (2015). Trends in Contraceptive Use World Wide 2015.

Hormonal Methods

Hormonal methods of contraception are highly effective and come in a number of forms: the pill, the patch, the vaginal ring, implants, and injections.

The Combination Pill

With **combination birth control pills** (sometimes called *oral contraceptives*), such as Alesse and Yasmin, the woman takes a pill that contains estrogen and progestin (a synthetic progesterone), both at doses higher than natural levels, for 21 days. Then she takes no pill or a placebo for seven days, after which she repeats the cycle.

The traditional 21-on, 7-off pattern is still very common, but variations have been introduced. One is Seasonale, which provides 84 days of combined hormones and 7 days of placebo; this means that the woman has a period only once in three months. Seasonale was approved by Health Canada in 2007. Some women take two packets of pills back-to-back—that is, they start the second packet without taking the seven placebo pills to delay getting their period. Continuous or extended pill use is as effective as the traditional pill and results in fewer menstrual days (Society of Obstetricians and Gynaecologists of Canada [SOGC], 2007b).

The preferred method for a woman starting the pill is quick start; that is, she starts taking the pill the first day she gets the prescription, regardless of the day of the menstrual cycle.

How It Works

The pill works mainly by preventing ovulation. Recall from Chapter 5 that in a natural menstrual cycle, the low levels of estrogen during and just after the menstrual period trigger the pituitary to produce FSH, which stimulates the process of ovulation. When a woman starts taking the birth control pills, estrogen levels are pushed high. This high level of estrogen inhibits FSH production, and the message to ovulate is never sent out. The high level of progesterone inhibits LH production, further preventing ovulation.

combination birth control pills: Birth control pills that contain a combination of estrogen and progestin (progesterone).

A Brief History of Birth Control in Canada

I n the early nineteenth century in Canada and in other Western countries, birth control and abortion early in pregnancy were not illegal. Laws were then passed to prohibit the use of birth control and the spread of contraceptive information. In the 1892 Canadian *Criminal Code*, a person who sold, advertised, or published an advertisement about any "medicine, drug, or article" intended to prevent conception could be jailed for up to two years. Abortion was also made illegal.

The movement toward legalizing birth control in Canada was started by women's groups in British Columbia that recognized the toll that unwanted pregnancies were having on women's health and well-being. They joined together to form the Canadian Birth Control League. This group was influenced by Margaret Sanger, who had founded the American Birth Control League in 1914, thereby launching the birth control movement in the United States.

A number of other organizations began calling for the legalization of birth control during the 1920s and 1930s, including the Saskatchewan section of the United Farmers of Canada, the Seventh Labour Women's Society and Economic Conference, and the National Council of Jewish Women. A. H. Tyler, a Protestant minister who wrote sex education and birth control publications in the 1930s and 1940s, was responsible for starting the birth control movement in Toronto and founded the Canadian Voluntary Parenthood League in 1931.

The first birth control clinic in Canada was established in Hamilton, Ontario, in 1932 by Mary Hawkins. This clinic, called the Birth Control Society of Hamilton, served hundreds of patients. To allay criticisms by members of the medical profession, a physician was always in attendance. Dr. Elizabeth Bagshaw (see Figure 7.1), one of Hamilton's few female physicians at the time, served the clinic for more than 30 years. The clinic was so successful that the hospital in Hamilton began cooperating with the clinic in 1935. By 1937 there were also birth control clinics in Windsor and Kitchener.

In 1936, Dorothea Palmer, an Ottawa social worker, was charged with distributing birth control information in poor neighbourhoods. She was acquitted in 1937, partly through the efforts of the birth control lobby. The court recognized that the provision of birth control

Figure 7.1 Dr. Elizabeth Bagshaw served as a physician for more than 30 years with the clinic run by the Birth Control Society of Hamilton, the first birth control clinic in Canada.

Special Collections Department, Hamilton Public Library

information was permissible if it were done in the interest of the "public good." However, the sale and distribution of contraceptives was still technically illegal until 1969. In fact, as recently as 1960, a Toronto pharmacist was jailed for selling condoms.

In 1967, Pierre Elliott Trudeau, then the justice minister, introduced the *Omnibus Bill,* making large-scale changes to the Canadian *Criminal Code,* including in the sections relating to contraception and abortion. In defending the bill, Trudeau made his now-famous statement: "The state has no business in the bedrooms of the nation." The *Omnibus Bill* was passed in 1969 when Trudeau was prime minister. Among other changes, it made the use of contraceptives legal and allowed abortion under certain restrictive circumstances.

Sources: CARAL, n.d.; Chesler, 1992; Planned Parenthood Federation of Canada, n.d.

The progestin provides additional backup effects. It keeps the cervical mucus very thick, making it difficult for sperm to get through, and it changes the lining of the uterus in such a way that even if a fertilized egg were to arrive, implantation would be unlikely.

When the estrogen and progestin are withdrawn (after day 21 in the traditional pill), the lining of the uterus disintegrates, and withdrawal bleeding or menstruation occurs. The flow is typically reduced because the progestin has inhibited development of the endometrium.

Effectiveness

To understand the effectiveness of the pill, you'll need to understand several technical terms that are used in communicating data on contraceptive effectiveness. If 100 women use a contraceptive method for one year, the number of them who become pregnant during that first year of use is called the **failure rate** or *pregnancy rate.* That is, if 5 women out of 100 become pregnant during a year of using contraceptive A, then A's failure rate is 5 percent. *Effectiveness* is 100 minus the failure rate; thus contraceptive A would be said to be 95 percent effective. We can also talk about two kinds of failure rate: the *failure rate for perfect users* and the *failure rate for typical users.* The perfect-user failure rate refers to studies of the best possible use of the method—for example, when the user has been well-taught about the method, uses it with perfect consistency, and so on. The failure rate for typical users is just that—the failure rate when people actually use the method, perhaps imperfectly when they forget to take a pill or do not use a condom every time. The good news is that if you are very responsible about contraception, you can anticipate close to the perfect-user failure rate for yourself.

Combination pills are one of the most effective methods of birth control (see Figure 7.2). The perfect-user failure rate is 0.3 percent (that is, the method is essentially 100 percent effective), and the typical-user failure rate is

Figure 7.2 Birth control pills.

The McGraw-Hill Companies, Inc./Christopher Kerrigan, photographer

3 percent (Hatcher et al., 2011). Failures occur primarily as a result of forgetting to take a pill for two or more days or not taking it at the same time every day. If a woman forgets to take a pill, she should take it as soon as she remembers and take the next one at the regular time; this does not appear to increase the pregnancy risk appreciably. If she forgets for two days, she should do the same thing—take one as soon as possible and then continue taking one a day. If she forgets for three or more days, she should follow the same instructions, taking one pill as soon as possible and then one pill a day, but in addition she should use condoms or abstain from sex until she has taken hormonal pills for seven days in a row, at which point she will again be well protected (Salem, 2005).

Side Effects

You may have seen reports in the media on the dangerous side effects of birth control pills. Many of these reports are no more than scare stories with little or no evidence behind them. However, the use of the pill does have some well-documented side effects, and women who are using it or who are contemplating using it should be aware of them.

Among the serious side effects associated with use of the pill are slight but significant increases in certain diseases of the circulatory system. One of these is problems of blood clotting (thromboembolic disorders or venous thromboembolism). Women who use the pill have a higher chance than nonusers of developing blood clots (thrombi), particularly women over 35 who smoke. Symptoms of blood clots are severe headaches, severe leg or chest pains, and shortness of breath. For some women, the pill can cause high blood pressure. There is no evidence that the pill is associated with infertility or difficulty conceiving after the woman goes off the pill.

Although the pill actually protects women from endometrial cancer and ovarian cancer (Hatcher et al., 2011), it may aggravate some already existing cancers, such as breast cancer. While these problems are relatively rare, for women who have taken the pill for more than five years, the risk of benign liver tumours increases (Hatcher et al., 2011).

The pill increases the amount of vaginal discharge and the susceptibility to vaginitis (vaginal inflammations, such as *monilia*—see Chapter 8) because it alters the chemical balance of the lining of the vagina. Women on the pill have an increased susceptibility to chlamydia and gonorrhea. Although the matter is controversial, some good evidence indicates that use of the pill—or any hormonal contraceptive— increases the risk of HIV infection (Heffron et al., 2012).

The pill may cause some nausea, although this almost always goes away after the first

failure rate: The pregnancy rate occurring when using a particular contraceptive method; the percentage of women who will be pregnant after a year of use of the method.

month or two of use. Some brands of pills can also cause weight gain, by increasing appetite or water retention, but this side effect can often be reversed by switching to another brand.

Finally, there may be some psychological effects. About 20 percent of women on the pill report increased irritability and depression, which become worse with the length of time it is used. These side effects are probably related to the progesterone in the pill. Women may also experience changes in sexual desire. Some women report an increase in sexual interest. But others report a decrease in sexual desire, vaginal lubrication, and arousal. Switching brands may be helpful for these effects.

In short, the pill does have some serious potential side effects. However, so do pregnancy and many other medications we take regularly. For example, the risk of blood clots is higher during pregnancy than from the pill (SOGC, 2013a). Thus, it may not be a good choice for high-risk individuals, but for many others it is an extremely effective means of contraception that poses little or no danger.

Advantages and Disadvantages

The pill has a number of advantages. It is close to 100 percent effective if used properly. It does not interfere with intercourse, as do some other methods, such as the cervical cap, the condom, and foam. It is not messy. Some of its side effects are also advantages; it reduces the amount of menstrual flow and thus reduces cramps. Indeed, it is sometimes prescribed for the noncontraceptive purpose of regulating menstruation and eliminating cramps. Iron deficiency anemia is less likely to occur among pill users. The pill can clear up acne and has a protective effect against some rather serious things, including endometriosis and ovarian and endometrial cancer (Hatcher et al., 2011).

The side effects of birth control pills, discussed earlier, are, of course, major disadvantages. Another disadvantage is the cost, which is about $30 a month for as long as they are used, although many women (41 percent) do not pay the full cost (Boroditsky et al., 1996). They also place the entire burden of contraception on the woman. In addition, taking the pill correctly is a little complicated; the woman must understand that it is to be taken at the same time every day, and she must remember when to take it and when not to take it. This effort is not too taxing for a well-educated woman from a culture that is familiar with various contraceptives. However, currently available information on the use of birth control pills might be inadequate to meet the needs of a woman from a developing country. Appropriate information and direction on how to use the pill is also important for women with intellectual disabilities.

One other criticism of the pill is that for a woman who has intercourse only infrequently (say, once or twice a month or less), it represents contraceptive overkill; that is, the pill makes her infertile every day of the month, and yet she needs it only a few days each month. Women in this situation might consider a method that is used only when needed, such as the cervical cap or condom.

Finally, it is important to recognize that, although it is an excellent contraceptive, the pill provides absolutely no protection against sexually transmitted infections (STIs).

Reversibility

When a woman wants to become pregnant, she simply stops taking pills after the end of one cycle. Some women experience a brief delay (two or three months) in becoming pregnant, but pregnancy rates are about the same as for women who never took the pill.

Drug Interactions

If you are taking birth control pills, you are taking a prescription drug, and it can have interactions with other prescription drugs you take (Hatcher et al., 2011). Some of the interactions are mentioned here, but women on the pill should always consult a pharmacist before taking any new medication, including over-the-counter medication. Some anticonvulsant drugs, for example, decrease the effectiveness of the pill, as do some antiretroviral drugs used to treat HIV infection.

The pill may also increase the metabolism of some drugs, making them more potent (Hatcher et al., 2007). Examples include some anti-anxiety drugs, corticosteroids used for inflammation, and theophylline (a drug used for asthma). Therefore, women using the pill may require lower doses of these drugs.

Some over-the-counter drugs may also interact with the pill. St. John's wort, for example, can decrease the effectiveness of the pill substantially.

Other Kinds of Pills

To this point, the discussion has centred chiefly on the *combination pill,* so named because it contains both estrogen and progestin. This variety of pill is the most widely used, but many kinds of combination pills and several kinds of pills other than combination ones are available.

Combination pills vary from one brand to the next in the dosages of estrogen and progestin. The dose of estrogen is important because higher doses are more likely to induce blood-clotting problems. Most women do well on pills containing no more than 30 to 35 micrograms of estrogen, such as Alesse, Demulen 30, Min-Ovral, and Minestrin (Dickey, 2000). Because of concerns about side effects due to the estrogen in the pill, current pills have considerably lower levels of estrogen than early pills; for example, Ortho 1/35 has one-third the amount of estrogen of the early pill Enovid 10. In January 2005, Yasmin, a type of contraceptive pill that combines a low dose of estrogen with a synthetic form of progestin (drospirenone), was approved for sale by Health Canada, although in 2011, Health Canada also issued a warning that some women taking Yaz or Yasmin have an increased risk of blood clots. High-progestin brands are related to such symptoms as vaginitis and depression. Thus, depending on what side effects the woman wants to avoid, she can choose a brand for its high or low estrogen or progesterone level. (See Hatcher et al., 2011, p. 312, for a list of symptoms related to dosages of estrogen and progestin.)

The **triphasic pill** (e.g., Ortho 7/7/7) contains a steady level of estrogen like the combination pill does, but the levels of progesterone have three phases. The idea is to reduce total hormone exposure, although they do not appear to have an advantage over monophasic pills (Grimes et al., 2006).

Progestin-only pills (Micronor is the only one available in Canada) have also been developed. They are sometimes called *mini-pills*. The pills contain only a low dose of progestin and no estrogen, and were designed to avoid the estrogen-related side effects of the combination pill. The woman takes one beginning on the first day of her period and one every day thereafter; it is important that she takes it at the same time each day. Progestin-only pills work by changing the cervical mucus so that sperm cannot get through, inhibiting implantation, and inhibiting ovulation (although while taking mini-pills about 40 percent of women ovulate consistently).

Progestin-only pills have a typical-user failure rate of 5 percent, which is higher than that of combination pills. Their major side effect is that they produce very irregular menstrual cycles. The mini-pill is probably most useful for women who cannot take combination pills—for example, women over 35 who smoke, or women with a history of high blood pressure or blood-clotting problems.

Progestin-only pills are also useful for women who are breast-feeding and cannot use combination pills because they reduce milk production. Neither kind of pill should be used in the first six weeks after birth when breast-feeding, because trace amounts of the hormones can reach the infant through the breast milk. After that time, though, progestin-only pills are a good choice.

The Patch

The patch (Evra) contains the same hormones as combination birth control pills but is administered transdermally—that is, through the skin. The patch itself is thin, beige, and about the size of a double Band-aid. It consists of an outer protective layer of polyester, an adhesive layer that contains the hormones, and a polyester liner that is removed before applying.

The patch lasts for seven days, so the woman places a new one on once a week for three weeks, and then has

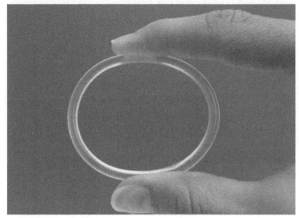

Figure 7.3 NuvaRing, the vaginal contraceptive ring.

© vario images GmbH & Co.KG/Alamy Stock Photo

a patch-free week. The first time it is used, it takes a couple of days for the hormones to reach effective levels, so a backup method, such as a condom, should be used. One advantage of the patch is that women using it do not have to remember to take a pill every day, only to replace the patch every week. In addition, with the patch, the hormones enter the body through the skin, rather than going to the stomach and needing to be digested.

The patch is relatively new (it became available in Canada in 2004), so we do not have extensive data on it yet. Because the hormones are the same as in the pill, the expectation is that the benefits and side effects will be quite similar to those of the pill (Hatcher et al., 2011). It is somewhat less effective in women weighing more than 90 kg (198 lbs.). There is also concern that a woman gets more estrogen from the patch than she would from the combination pill.

> I'd like to use the birth control pill, but I worry about remembering to take a pill every day. What are my other options?

The Vaginal Ring

It's not the latest in body piercing. Rather, the vaginal ring (NuvaRing; Figure 7.3) is a flexible, transparent ring made of plastic and filled with the same hormones as those in the combination pill, at slightly lower doses. The woman squeezes the two sides of the ring together, and then gently pushes the folded ring into her vagina so that it comes to rest high up in her the vagina. It remains in place for 21 days after which she removes it and goes ring-free for—you guessed it—7 days. She then inserts a new ring. This method requires even less remembering than the patch does.

The ring, too, was only recently introduced, so the scientific data on it are limited. Because the hormones in it are the same as those in the

triphasic pill: A birth control pill containing a steady level of estrogen and three phases of progesterone, intended to mimic more closely women's natural hormonal cycles.

combination pill, the side effects should be the same. It acts mainly by stopping ovulation. Although it was hoped that its typical-user failure rate would be lower than the pill (because of less need to remember to use it), in fact it is about the same as the pill (Hatcher et al., 2011). In 2014, Health Canada put out safety information about NuvaRing including that it should not be used by women who are over 35 and smoke, experience migraines, and have a number of other medical conditions.

Emergency Contraception

Emergency contraception (EC) is available in pill form for emergencies involving unprotected intercourse that might result in an unwanted pregnancy, such as from forced intercourse or a condom breaking (Public Health Agency of Canada [PHAC], 2007a). In Canada, its brand name is Plan B. Plan B contains levonorgestrel (a progestin), which is also found in some regular birth control pills, although the dose is higher in Plan B (Dunn & Guilbert, 2003). The treatment is most effective if begun within 12 to 24 hours and cannot be delayed longer than 120 hours (five days) after unprotected intercourse. Nausea is a common side effect, but Gravol can be taken to prevent it. EC may also result in irregular vaginal bleeding, fatigue, headache, dizziness, and breast tenderness (PHAC, 2007a).

Ella, which contains a different drug, ulipristal acetate, is another type of pill for emergency contraception. Yet another alternative is to take multiple combination birth control pills. The exact number depends on the brand of pill; for a listing, see http://ec.princeton.edu.

Emergency contraception may work in any of several ways, depending on when in the cycle it is taken. It may stop ovulation, inhibit the functioning of sperm, prevent fertilization, or inhibit the development of a nourishing endometrium. Its action is to prevent pregnancy, and it will not cause an abortion if the woman is already pregnant (PHAC, 2007a).

Emergency contraception is between 75 and 89 percent effective (Hatcher et al., 2007). Those statistics underestimate the actual effectiveness, though, because they refer to effectiveness during the most fertile part of the cycle. Actual pregnancy rates are between 0.5 and 2 percent (von Hertzen et al., 2002). Emergency contraception is highly effective.

As of May 2008, the emergency contraceptive pill became available over the counter without a written prescription from a physician, with the option, but not a requirement, of speaking with a pharmacist. Opponents of Plan B had argued that making EC widely available in this way would lead women, and especially teenagers, to become irresponsible about contraception. Research in British Columbia, where EC has been available from pharmacists without a prescription since December 2000, found that making it available without a prescription

more than doubled its use (Soon et al., 2005). However, this increase was not because women were being irresponsible. The vast majority of these women used EC only once during the period of the study, most often because of birth control failure. Further, research indicates that making Plan B available to teenagers has no effect on whether they have unprotected intercourse or on their number of sexual partners (Harper et al., 2005).

The Canadian Paediatric Society is solidly behind making emergency contraception available to adolescents, including providing information during routine visits such as that it is available from pharmacists without a prescription (Katzman & Taddeo, 2010).

An IUD can also be used for emergency contraception for a woman who wants continuing protection (Cleland et al., 2012). The failure rate is less than 1 percent if inserted within five days of unprotected intercourse.

LARC

LARC stands for long-acting, reversible contraceptives; that is, the methods last for more than a year, and they can also be reversed, unlike sterilization. The LARC methods include implants and IUDs. LARC is rapidly growing in popularity and is recommended by family planning experts because these methods are even more effective than the pill. The LARC methods are safe for adolescents and are used by 7 percent of teenagers seeking contraception (Romero et al., 2015).

Implants

Implants are thin rods or tubes containing progestin. They are inserted under the skin in a woman's arm and are effective for three years. Norplant was the first implant available but was removed from the market because of health concerns. One implant is currently available in the United States, Implanon, which uses just a single rod that is four centimetres long and two millimetres wide (Hatcher et al., 2011). It is not approved for use in Canada.

Depo-Provera Injections

Depo-Provera (DMPA) is a progestin administered by injection by any health care provider licensed to provide injections. The injections must be repeated every three months for maximum effectiveness. Depo-Provera was approved for use as a contraceptive in Canada in 1997. A study of women in Saskatchewan using Depo-Provera found that most did so because of its convenience; for example, they did not have to worry about forgetting to take the birth control pill (Hampton et al., 2000).

How It Works

Depo-Provera works like the other progestin-only methods, by inhibiting ovulation, thickening the cervical mucus, and inhibiting the growth of the endometrium.

Depo-Provera is highly effective, with a typical-user failure rate of 6 percent, making it a little less effective than the pill.

Advantages and Disadvantages

Depo-Provera has many advantages. It does not interfere with lovemaking. It requires far less reliance on memory than birth control pills do, although the woman must remember to have a new injection every three months. It is available for women who cannot use the combination pill, such as those over 35 who smoke and those with blood pressure problems.

A disadvantage of Depo-Provera is that most users experience amenorrhea (no menstrual periods). Sometimes they have just some spotting. However, this may be an advantage. It can relieve anemia caused by heavy menstrual periods, and Depo-Provera can be used in the treatment of endometriosis.

Side Effects

No lethal side effects of Depo-Provera have been found, although long-term studies have not yet been done. However, in 2005 Health Canada put out a warning that Depo-Provera can result in irreversible bone loss after only two years on the drug and that it should only be used by women who are unable to use other contraceptive methods. To protect against bone loss, women on Depo-Provera should make sure they get enough calcium and vitamin D in their diet or through vitamin supplements.

Reversibility

The method is reversible simply by not getting another injection. Many women are infertile for 6 to 12 months after stopping its use but then are able to become pregnant at normal rates (Hatcher et al., 2007).

The IUD and IUS

The **intrauterine device (IUD)** is a small piece of plastic; it comes in various shapes. Metal or a hormone may also be part of the device. An IUD is inserted into the uterus by a doctor or nurse practitioner, and it then remains in place until the woman wants to have it removed. One or two plastic strings hang down from the IUD through the cervix, enabling the woman to check to see whether it is in place.

The basic idea for the IUD has been around for some time. In 1909, Burton Richter reported on the use of an IUD made of silkworm gut. In the 1920s, German physician Ernst Gräfenberg reported data on 2000 insertions of silk or silver wire rings. In spite of its high effectiveness (98.4 percent), his work was poorly received. Not until the 1950s, with the development of plastic and stainless-steel devices, did the method gain much popularity. In the 1970s and 1980s, the use of the IUD in North America was sharply reduced by numerous lawsuits against manufacturers by women claiming to have been

Figure 7.4 Copper T IUD.

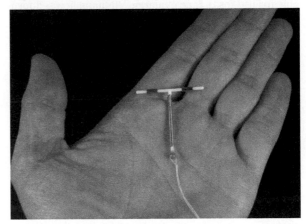

The McGraw-Hill Companies, Inc./Jill Braaten, photographer

damaged by the device, specifically by the IUD known as the Dalkon Shield, which was taken off the market (Hubacher, 2002). Some companies stopped producing IUDs, and others declared bankruptcy. Only three IUDs are available in Canada today (Nova-T, Flexi-T, and Liberté). All contain copper (Figure 7.4).

The intrauterine system (IUS) is also available in Canada (Mirena). It also contains progesterone. Thus, it is inserted like an IUD, but it is actually a hormonal method of contraception. Currently, 106 million women worldwide are using an IUD or IUS, 40 million of them in the People's Republic of China, and experts predict a resurgence of enthusiasm for them (Hubacher, 2002).

How It Works

The foreign body in the uterus creates an environment that is toxic to both sperm and eggs (Hatcher et al., 2011). In the rare event of fertilization, the IUD prevents implantation. The small amount of copper that is added to the copper T is thought to have an additional contraceptive effect. It seems to alter the functioning of the enzymes involved in implantation. It is also used as an emergency contraceptive within seven days of unprotected intercourse.

The IUS (Mirena) releases progesterone directly into the uterus. One effect is to reduce the endometrium. This results in reduced menstrual flow and reduced risk of anemia, thus overcoming two undesirable side effects of other IUDs. The progestin thickens cervical mucus, disrupts ovulation, and changes the endometrium.

Effectiveness

The IUD is extremely effective; it is in the same category as the pill (and sterilization) in effectiveness. The pregnancy rate for the copper IUD is 0.7 percent for the first year of use; after that, the

> **intrauterine device (IUD):** A plastic device sometimes containing metal or a hormone that is inserted into the uterus for contraceptive purposes.

failure rate is even lower (Hatcher et al., 2011). It is available for use for 3, 5, or 12 years. Mirena is licensed for 5 years. Most failures occur during the first three months of use, either because the IUD/IUS is expelled or for other, unknown reasons. Expulsion is most likely in women who have never been pregnant, in younger women, and in women during menstruation. The expulsion rate is about 2 to 10 percent during the first year (Hatcher et al., 2011).

Side Effects

The most common side effects of the copper T are increased menstrual cramps, irregular bleeding, and increased menstrual flow. These symptoms occur in 10 to 20 percent of women using it and are most likely immediately after insertion. Mirena, in contrast, reduces menstruation flow, and about 20 percent of users stop bleeding altogether. Women who are sensitive to progesterone may experience weight gain, depression, or decreased sexual interest. There is no evidence that the IUD or IUS causes cancer.

Advantages and Disadvantages

Because insertion of the IUD/IUS by a physician is covered by Medicare, the initial cost is about $60 for an IUD and $350 for an IUS—the cost of purchasing the device. Thus, the IUD/IUS is a fairly cheap means of contraception over a long time of use, since the cost is incurred only once and the IUD/IUS lasts 5 to 12 years.

The effectiveness of the IUD/IUS is a major advantage. The typical-user failure rate is only 0.8 percent, making it more effective than combination birth control pills and Depo-Provera.

Once inserted, the IUD/IUS is perfectly simple to use. The woman has only to check periodically to see that the strings are in place. Thus it has an advantage over methods like the diaphragm or condom in that it does not interrupt intercourse in any way. It has an advantage over the pill in that the woman does not have to remember to use it. The IUD is a method that can be used safely by women after giving birth and while breast-feeding. Contrary to what some people think, the IUD/IUS does not interfere with the use of a tampon during menstruation; nor does it have any effect on intercourse.

Reversibility

When a woman who is using an IUD/IUS wants to become pregnant, she simply has a physician remove the device. She can become pregnant immediately.

Cervical Caps and the Sponge

FemCap: A method of birth control involving a rubber cap that fits snugly over the cervix.

The diaphragm was the mainstay of contraception until about 1960. Although diaphragms are still being manufactured, they hard to find in Canada because most women prefer using a cervical cap or the sponge. However, a single-size SILCS contoured diaphragm was approved by Health Canada in 2014 and is now available.

Cervical Caps

FemCap is a vaginal barrier device. It is shaped like a sailor's cap (see Figure 7.5), is made of silicone, and has a brim, a dome, a groove between the dome and the brim, and a removal strap. It comes in three sizes. A woman needs a prescription from a health care provider, who will recommend the correct size based on the woman's obstetric history: the smallest size for women who have never been pregnant, the medium size for women who have been pregnant but have not had a vaginal delivery, and the largest size for women who have had a vaginal delivery. It can be inserted several hours before sexual activity and left in place for up to 48 hours. It costs about $90 and can be used for about two years. It should be used with a spermicide or one of the new microbicides.

How It Works

The primary action of FemCap is mechanical; it blocks the entrance to the uterus so that sperm cannot swim up into it. The cream kills any sperm that manage to get past the barrier. Any sperm remaining in the vagina die after about eight hours (this is why it should not be removed until at least six hours after intercourse).

Effectiveness

The typical-user failure rate of the FemCap for women who have never given birth has been estimated to be about 20 percent. Most failures are due to improper use:

Figure 7.5 FemCap is a silicone rubber barrier contraceptive shaped like a sailor's hat, with a dome that covers the cervix and a brim that conforms to the vaginal walls.

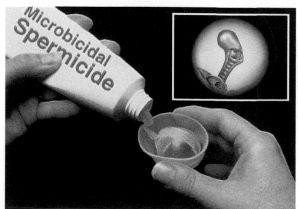

The McGraw-Hill Companies, Inc./Bob Coyle, photographer

A woman may not use it every time; it may not fit well; she may not leave it in long enough; or she may not use contraceptive cream or jelly. Even with perfectly proper use, there is still a 9 percent failure rate. To get closer to 100 percent effectiveness, FemCap can be combined with a condom around the time of ovulation or throughout the cycle. For women who have had children, the failure rates can be higher.

Side Effects

FemCap has few side effects. One is the possible irritation of the vagina or the penis; this is caused by the cream or jelly and can be relieved by switching to another brand.

Advantages and Disadvantages

Some women dislike touching their genitals and inserting their fingers into their vagina. Use of the cervical cap is not a good method for them. Cervical caps require some thought and presence of mind on the woman's part. She must remember to put it in ahead of time or have it and a supply of cream or jelly with her when she needs it. She also needs to avoid becoming so carried away with passion that she forgets about it or decides not to use it.

The cost of FemCap is about $90 plus the cost of the contraceptive cream; the office visit is covered by Medicare. With proper care, FemCap should last about two years and thus itself is not expensive.

The major advantages of cervical caps are that they have few side effects and, when used properly, are very effective. For this reason, women who are worried about the side effects of the pill or the IUD/IUS should seriously consider a cervical cap as an alternative. They also do not interfere with sensations or sensitivity of either partner, so some people may prefer using a cervical cap to using a condom. There is also evidence of a reduction in the rate of cervical cancer among long-time users of the diaphragm, which may also apply to users of cervical caps. And the cervical cap provides some protection against STIs such as chlamydia because it covers and protects the cervix; it does not protect against most other STIs, however.

Reversibility

If a woman wants to become pregnant, she simply stops using the cervical cap. Its use has no effect on her later chances of conceiving.

The Sponge

The **contraceptive sponge** (see Figure 7.6) is another vaginal barrier method like the FemCap. Made of polyurethane, the sponge is small and shaped like a pillow with a concave dimple on one side. The other side has a woven loop to aid in removal. The sponge contains a spermicide and is inserted much like a cervical cap, with

Figure 7.6 The contraceptive sponge.

© McGraw-Hill Education/Christopher Kerrigan

the concave side over the cervix. The sponge is effective for 24 hours, even with multiple acts of intercourse. It should not be left in place for more than 24 hours, though, because of a risk of toxic shock syndrome. It comes in one size and is available over the counter without prescription. The cost is about $15 for four.

Condoms

The Male Condom

The **male condom** (*rubber, prophylactic, jimmy hat, safe*) is a thin sheath that fits over the penis (see Figure 7.7). It comes rolled up in a little packet and must be unrolled onto the penis before use. It may be made of latex (*rubber*), polyurethane, or the intestinal tissue of lambs (*skin*). The polyurethane condom (Avanti, Trojan Supra) is a recent innovation that is helpful to people who are allergic to latex.

> **contraceptive sponge:** A contraceptive method made of polyurethane that contains a spermicide and is placed over the cervix.
> **male condom:** A contraceptive sheath that is placed over the penis.

Figure 7.7   A variety of male condoms.

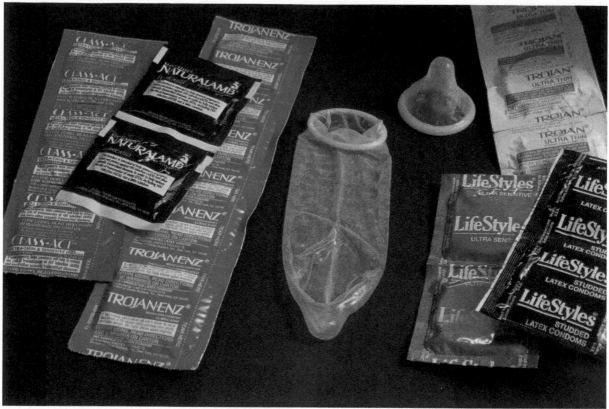

© Stock Connection Distribution/Alamy

The widespread use of the modern condom, both for contraception and for protection against diseases, dates from about 1843, when vulcanized rubber was developed; however, the use of a sheath to cover the penis has been known throughout most of recorded history.[1] Casanova (1725–1798) was one of the first to popularize the condom for its contraceptive ability, as well as its protective value. Condoms have become increasingly popular because they help protect against STIs, including HIV.

To be effective, the condom must be used properly (see Figure 7.8). It must be unrolled onto the erect penis before the penis ever enters the vagina—*not* just before ejaculation, since long before then some drops containing a few thousand sperm may have been produced. To be effective in preventing STIs, too, it must be put on before genital-to-genital contact. Condoms come in two shapes: those with plain ends and those with a protruding tip that catches the semen. If a plain-ended one is used, about a centimetre or (half-inch) of air-free space should

be left at the tip to catch the ejaculate. Care should be taken that the condom does not slip during intercourse. After the man has ejaculated, he must hold the rim of the condom against the base of the penis as he withdraws. It is best to withdraw soon after ejaculation, while the man still has an erection, to minimize the chances of leakage. A new condom must be used with each act of intercourse.

Condoms may be either lubricated or unlubricated. Some further lubrication for intercourse may be necessary. A sterile, water-based lubricant such as K-Y Jelly or Sensilube may also be used.

How It Works

The condom catches the semen and thus prevents it from entering the vagina. Spermicide-coated condoms are no longer recommended. They may create allergies to the spermicide for the man or his partner, and the amount of spermicide is probably not sufficient to be very effective. For couples who want to improve on the effectiveness of the condom, it is probably wiser for the woman to use a contraceptive foam or, better yet, a cervical cap.

Effectiveness

Condoms are actually much more effective as a contraceptive than most people think. The perfect-user failure rate is about 2 percent. The typical-user failure rate is

---

[1] Condoms have also been the stimulus for humour throughout history, an example being this limerick: There was a young man of Cape Horn / Who wished he had never been born / And he wouldn't have been / If his father had seen / That the end of the rubber was torn.

Figure 7.8 Putting on a condom correctly. *(a)* The tip is pinched to keep air out. *(b)* The condom is then rolled down over the erect penis.

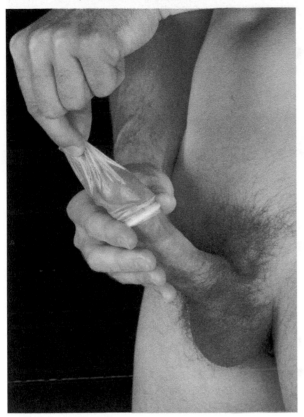

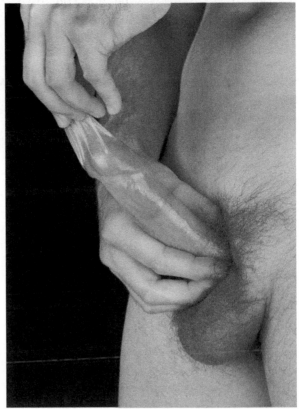

(a) © H.S. Photos/Alamy

(b) © H.S. Photos/Alamy

about 18 percent, but many failures result from improper or inconsistent use. Health Canada controls the quality of condoms carefully, and thus the chances of a failure caused by a defect in the condom itself are small. Combined with a contraceptive foam or cream or a cervical cap, the condom is close to 100 percent effective.

Side Effects

The condom has no side effects, except that some users are allergic to latex. For them, non-latex condoms made of polyurethane or other plastics are available.

Advantages and Disadvantages

One disadvantage of the condom is that it must be put on just before intercourse, raising the spontaneity problem again. If the couple can make an enjoyable, erotic ritual of putting it on together, this problem can be minimized.

Some men complain that the condom reduces their sensation and thus lessens their pleasure in intercourse ("It's like taking a shower with a raincoat on"). However, adding a drop or two of lubricant inside the condom will increase the man's sensations. Further, the reduction in sensation may be an advantage for some; for example, it may help the man who ejaculates more quickly than

he or his partner wants. Polyurethane condoms are thinner and should provide more sensation. However, today, condoms come in all shapes, sizes, and thinnesses, so if one brand doesn't work well for you, try another.

There are several advantages to condoms. They are the only contraceptive currently available for men except sterilization. They are cheap (around $1.50 to $2.50 for three), they are readily available without a prescription at any drugstore and some convenience stores, and they are fairly easy to use, although the man (or woman) must plan ahead so that one will be available when it is needed.

Finally, a major advantage of condoms is that they provide protection against many STIs (Hatcher et al., 2011). Unlubricated condoms can also easily be made into a *dental dam* to provide protection against STIs during oral–genital activity (see Chapter 8). Over the past several years, some far-right political groups, particularly in the United States, have mounted a campaign to convince the public that condoms are completely ineffective at STI prevention. However, the scientific data say otherwise. Condoms are highly effective protection against STIs that are transmitted mainly through genital secretions (cervical and vaginal secretions as well as semen) because they keep the secretions away from the other person. STIs in this category include chlamydia, gonorrhea, trichomoniasis, hepatitis B, and HIV (Hatcher et al., 2011; McKay, 2007). Condoms can and should be used during anal intercourse for protection against STIs.

Condoms also provide substantial, although not perfect, protection against STIs that are transmitted mainly by skin-to-skin contact, such as herpes, syphilis, and human papillomavirus (McKay, 2007). They won't protect against these diseases, of course, if the area producing the microbe is not covered by the condom—for example, if herpes blisters are on the scrotum. Latex and polyurethane condoms are the effective ones; animal-skin condoms are much less effective because they have larger pores that allow some viruses, such as HIV, to pass through them. For a more complete discussion of the effectiveness of condoms in STI prevention, see Chapter 8.

Reversibility

The method is easily and completely reversible. The man simply stops using condoms if conception is desired.

The Female Condom

The female condom (Reality or FC) became available in 1996. It is made of polyurethane and resembles a clear balloon (see Figure 7.9). There are two rings in it, one at either end. One ring is inserted into the vagina; the other is spread over the vaginal entrance. The inside is prelubricated, but additional lubrication may be applied. The penis must be guided into the female condom so that the penis does not slip in between the condom and the vaginal wall. The condom is removed after intercourse, before the woman stands up. The outer ring is squeezed together and twisted to keep the semen inside. A new female condom must be used with each act of intercourse. A new version, FC2, was approved for use in Canada in 2009. It makes less noise during intercourse and costs less than Reality.

How It Works

The female condom works by preventing sperm from entering the vagina and by blocking the entrance to the uterus.

Effectiveness

The typical-user failure rate is 21 percent (Hatcher et al., 2011), which is unacceptably high for many women. The perfect-user failure rate is 5 percent.

Side Effects

There are few if any side effects with the female condom. A few women experience vaginal irritation, and a few men experience irritation of the penis as a result of using it.

Figure 7.9 The female condom. One ring fits over the cervix, and the other goes outside the body, over the vulva, so that the condom lines the vagina and partly covers the vulva.

© Keith Brofsky/Getty Images RF

Advantages and Disadvantages

The female condom is made of polyurethane, not the latex used in most male condoms. Polyurethane is less susceptible to tearing and does not deteriorate with exposure to oil-based substances in the way that latex does. It does not create the allergic reactions that some people have to latex.

One major advantage is that the female condom is a method that a woman can use herself to reduce her risk of contracting an STI. The polyurethane is impermeable to HIV and to the viruses and bacteria that cause other STIs. Another advantage is that it can be inserted up to eight hours before sexual intercourse.

For disadvantages, the spontaneity problem presents itself again. The female condom, at least the original, is awkward to insert and makes rustling noises while in use, although additional lubricant reduces this problem. It makes the male condom seem sophisticated and unobtrusive by comparison. Also, it is the least effective of the methods discussed so far in this chapter. Another disadvantage is the cost, about $15 for three condoms, which is considerably higher than the cost for male condoms.

Reversibility

The method is easily and completely reversible. The woman simply stops using the condom.

Spermicides

Contraceptive foams, creams, and jellies (e.g., VCF Foam, Contragel Green Gel) are all classified as **spermicides**—that is, sperm killers (Figure 7.10). Most contain nonoxynol-9 (N-9). They come in a tube or a can, along with a plastic applicator. The applicator is filled and inserted into the vagina. The applicator's plunger is then used to push the spermicide out into the vagina near the cervix, so the spermicide is inserted much as a tampon is. It must be left in for six to eight hours after intercourse. One application provides protection for only one act of intercourse.

Figure 7.10   Contraceptive foams, creams, and jellies are all spermicides.

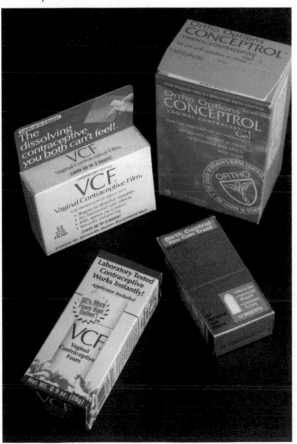

The McGraw-Hill Companies, Inc./Christopher Kerrigan, photographer

Spermicides are not to be confused with the various feminine hygiene products (vaginal deodorants) on the market. The latter are not effective as contraceptives.

How They Work

Spermicides consist of a spermicidal chemical in an inert base, and they work in two ways: chemical and mechanical. The chemicals in them kill sperm, while the inert base itself mechanically blocks the entrance to the cervix so that sperm cannot swim into it.

Effectiveness

Failure rates for spermicides can be as high as 28 percent. Put simply, they are not very effective. Foams tend to be more effective, and creams and jellies less so. Spermicidal tablets and suppositories are also available, but they are the least effective. Spermicides are highly effective only when used with a cervical cap or condom.

Side Effects

Some people experience an allergic reaction—irritation of the vagina or penis—to spermicides. Because we couldn't find any scientific studies on the incidence of these allergies, we surveyed our sexuality classes. We found that, of the students who had used spermicides, about 2 percent of the men reported an allergic reaction, as did 26 percent of the women.

Advantages and Disadvantages

The major advantage of spermicides is that they are readily available, without a prescription, in any drugstore. Thus, they can be used as a stop-gap method until the woman can see a health care provider and get a more effective contraceptive. Their failure rate is so high, though, that we cannot recommend using them by themselves; always combine them with a second method, such as a condom.

Spermicides provide no protection against bacterial STIs, such as chlamydia and gonorrhea. Neither do they protect against HIV, and there is some evidence that their frequent use increases susceptibility to HIV (Hatcher et al., 2011).

Their major disadvantage is that by themselves, they are not very effective. They also interrupt the spontaneity of sex, although only briefly. Some women dislike the sensation of the spermicide leaking out after intercourse, and some are irritated by the chemicals. Finally, some people find that they taste terrible, so their use interferes with oral sex.

Douching

Some people mistakenly believe that **douching** (flushing the vagina with a liquid) with any

spermicides (SPERM-ih-sides): Substances that kill sperm.
douching (DOOSH-ing): Flushing out the inside of the vagina with a liquid.

one of a variety of solutions is an effective contraceptive technique. A popular rumour among teenagers is that douching with Coca-Cola after intercourse will prevent pregnancy. Unfortunately, although it is true that acidic solutions will kill sperm, it takes only seconds for some of the sperm to reach the cervical mucus; once there, they are free to continue moving up into the uterus, and no douching solution will reach them. The woman would have to be a champion sprinter to get herself up and douched soon enough. And the douche itself may even push some sperm up into the uterus. Douching, therefore, is just not effective as a contraceptive method.

Withdrawal

Withdrawal (*coitus interruptus, pulling out*) is probably the most ancient form of birth control. (A reference to it is even found in the Bible in Genesis 38:8–9.) Withdrawal is still widely used throughout the world. The man withdraws his penis from his partner's vagina before he has an orgasm and thus ejaculates outside the vagina. To be effective as contraception, the ejaculation must occur completely away from the woman's vulva.

Effectiveness
Withdrawal is not very effective as a method of birth control. The failure rate is around 22 percent. Failures occur for several reasons: The few drops of fluid that come out of the penis during arousal may carry enough sperm for conception to occur; if ejaculation occurs outside the vagina but near or on the vulva, sperm may still get into the vagina and continue up into the uterus; and sometimes the man simply does not withdraw in time.

Side Effects
Withdrawal produces no direct physical side effects. However, over long periods of time, worry about ejaculating before withdrawal may contribute to sexual dysfunctions in the man, such as premature ejaculation, and also sexual dysfunction in the woman (e.g., low arousal) because of anxiety about pregnancy.

Advantages and Disadvantages
The major advantage of withdrawal is that it is the only last-minute method; it can be used when nothing else is available, although if the situation is that desperate, one might consider abstinence or some other form of sexual expression, such as oral–genital sex as alternatives. Obviously, withdrawal requires no prescription and is completely free.

One major disadvantage is that withdrawal is not very effective. In addition, it requires exceptional motivation on the part of the man, and it may be psychologically stressful to him. He must constantly maintain a kind of self-conscious control (Figure 7.11). The woman may worry about whether he really will withdraw in time, and the situation is certainly less than ideal for her to become aroused and orgasm.

Fertility Awareness (Rhythm) Methods

Fertility awareness (rhythm) methods, although they are not very effective, are the only form of "natural" birth control. They require abstaining from intercourse during the woman's fertile period (around ovulation). There are several fertility awareness methods, and in each the woman's fertile period is determined in a different way: the calendar method, the basal body temperature method, and the cervical mucus method (Hatcher et al., 2011).

The **calendar method** is based on the assumption that ovulation occurs about 14 days before the onset of menstruation (see Chapter 5). It works best for the woman with the perfectly regular 28-day cycle. She should ovulate on day 14 and almost surely on one of days 13 to 15. Three days are added in front of that period (previously deposited sperm may result in conception), and two days are added after it (to allow for long-lasting eggs); thus, the couple must abstain from sexual intercourse from day 10 to day 17. Therefore, even for the woman with perfectly regular cycles, eight days of abstinence are required in the middle of each cycle. Research shows that sperm can live up to five days inside the female reproductive tract, and eggs live less than a day (Hatcher et al., 2011).

Figure 7.11 Male responsibility is a key issue in birth control.

Stockbrokerxtra/Dreamstime.com

---

withdrawal: A method of birth control in which the man withdraws his penis from his partner's vagina before he orgasms.

fertility awareness (rhythm) methods: Methods of birth control that involve abstaining from intercourse around the time the woman ovulates.

calendar method: A type of fertility awareness method of birth control in which the woman determines when she ovulates by keeping a calendar record of the length of her menstrual cycles.

The woman who is not perfectly regular must keep a record of her cycles for at least six months and preferably a year. From this she determines the length of her shortest cycle and longest cycle. The preovulatory safe period is then calculated by subtracting 18 from the number of days in the shortest cycle, and the postovulatory safe period is calculated by subtracting 11 from the number of days in the longest cycle. Thus for a woman who is somewhat irregular—say, with cycles varying from 26 to 33 days in length—a period of abstinence from day 8 to day 22 (a total of 15 days) would be required.

A somewhat more accurate method for determining ovulation is the **basal body temperature (BBT) method**. The principle behind this was discussed in Chapters 5 and 6. The woman takes her temperature every day immediately on waking. During the preovulatory phase, her temperature will be at a fairly constant low level. On the day of ovulation, it drops (although this does not always occur), and on the day after ovulation, it rises sharply, staying at that high level for the rest of the cycle. Intercourse would be safe beginning about three days after ovulation. Some of the psychological stresses involved in using this method have been noted previously. As a form of contraception, the BBT method has a major disadvantage in that it determines safe days only *after* ovulation; theoretically, according to the method, there are no safe days before ovulation. Thus, the BBT method is best used in combination with the calendar method or the cervical mucus method, which determine the preovulatory safe period; the BBT method determines the postovulatory safe period.

Another fertility awareness method, the **cervical mucus method**, is based on variations over the cycle in the mucus produced by the cervix. There are generally a few days just after menstruation during which no mucus is produced, and there is a general sensation of vaginal dryness. This is a relatively safe time. Then there are a number of days of mucus discharge around the middle of the cycle. On the first days, the mucus is white or cloudy and tacky. The amount increases, and the mucus becomes clearer, until there are one or two *peak days*, when the mucus is like raw egg white—clear, slippery, and stringy. There is also a sensation of vaginal lubrication. Ovulation occurs within 24 hours after the last peak day. Abstinence is required from the first day of mucus discharge until four days after the peak days. After that, the mucus, if present, is cloudy or white, and intercourse is safe. Combination of the cervical mucus method with BBT is called the **sympto-thermal method**.

Home Ovulation Tests

Recently, home tests for the detection of ovulation have been developed (e.g., Clear Blue). Most such tests have been designed for use by couples wanting to conceive; however, a few are now available for contraception

(Hatcher et al., 2011). One kind (PG53, PC 2000, and Maybe Baby) involves mini-microscopes to examine saliva or cervical mucus. Others involve temperature computers that work on the BBT method. Hormone computers (e.g., Persona) assess hormone levels in urine. Costs range between $13 and $169. The effectiveness of these tests is not yet well enough researched for us to recommend them as reliable.

Effectiveness

The effectiveness of the fertility awareness method varies considerably, depending on a number of factors, but basically it is not very effective with typical users (giving rise to its nickname, *Vatican roulette*, and a number of old jokes like, "What do they call people who use the rhythm method?" Answer: "Parents"). Although the typical-user failure rate is around 25 percent for all methods, ideal-user failure rates vary considerably. They are 5 percent for the calendar method, 2 percent for BBT, 2 percent for the sympto-thermal method, and 3 percent for the cervical mucus method (Hatcher et al., 2011). Failure rates are lower when the woman's cycle is very regular and when the couple are highly motivated and have been well instructed in the methods.

Advantages and Disadvantages

The method has no side effects except possible psychological stress, and it is inexpensive. It is easily reversible. It also helps the woman become more aware of her body's functioning. The method requires cooperation from both partners, which may be considered either an advantage or a disadvantage.

Its main disadvantages are its high failure rate and the psychological stress it may cause. Periods of abstinence of at least eight days, and possibly as long as two or three weeks, are necessary, which is an unacceptable requirement for many couples. A certain amount of time, usually several months, is required to collect the data needed to make the method work. Thus, one cannot simply begin using it on the spur of the moment.

 LO4

Sterilization

Sterilization, or voluntary surgical contraception, is a surgical procedure whereby an individual is made permanently sterile, that is, unable to reproduce. Some people confuse sterilization with castration, though the two are quite different. Sterilization is an emotion-laden

basal body temperature (BBT) method: A type of fertility awareness method of birth control in which the woman determines when she ovulates by keeping track of her temperature.
cervical mucus method: A type of fertility awareness method of birth control in which the woman determines when she ovulates by checking her cervical mucus.
sympto-thermal method: A type of fertility awareness method of birth control combining the basal body temperature method and the cervical mucus method.
sterilization: A surgical procedure by which an individual is made sterile, that is, incapable of reproducing.

topic for a number of reasons. Sterilization means the end of a person's capacity to reproduce, and the ability to impregnate and the ability to bear a child are very important in cultural definitions of manhood and womanhood. We hope that as gender roles become more flexible in our society and as concern about reproduction is replaced by a concern for limiting population size, the word *sterilization* will no longer carry such emotional overtones.

> **Can a man still ejaculate after a vasectomy?**

Most physicians are conservative about performing sterilizations; they want to make sure that the patient has made a firm decision on his or her own and will not be back a few months later wanting to have the procedure reversed. The physician has an obligation to follow the principle of "informed consent." This means explaining the procedures involved, telling the patient about the possible risks and advantages, discussing alternative methods, and answering any questions the patient has.

Despite this conservatism, both male sterilization and female sterilization have become increasingly popular as methods of birth control. Sterilization is the most common method of birth control for long-term couples in their fertile years in Canada: as shown in Table 7.1, 22 percent of men and 11 percent of women. As you would expect, sterilization is more common among couples who are older (Boroditsky et al., 1996).

Male Sterilization

vasectomy (vas-EK-tuh-mee): A surgical procedure for male sterilization involving severing of the vas deferens.

The male sterilization operation is called a **vasectomy**, so named for the vas deferens, which is tied or cut. It can be done in a physician's office under local anaesthesia and requires only about 20 minutes to perform. In the traditional procedure, the physician makes a small incision on one side of the upper part of the scrotum. The vas is then separated from the surrounding tissues, tied off, and cut. The procedure is then repeated on the other side, and the incisions are sewn up. For a day or two, the man may have to refrain from strenuous activity and be careful not to pull the incision apart.

A newer *no-scalpel vasectomy* procedure has been developed (Hatcher et al., 2011). It involves making just a tiny pierce in the scrotum and has an even lower rate of complications than a standard vasectomy (see Figure 7.12).

Typically, the man can return to having intercourse within a few days. It should not be assumed that he is sterile yet, however. Some stray sperm may still be lurking in his ducts beyond the point of the incision. Men should not rely completely on the vasectomy until three months after it was performed (Hatcher et al., 2011). Until then, an additional method of birth control should be used. Ideally, the man should have a semen analysis after three months to confirm that his ejaculate is sperm-free.

Misunderstandings about the vasectomy abound. A vasectomy creates no physical changes that interfere with erection. Neither does it interfere in any way with sex hormone production; the testes continue to manufacture testosterone and secrete it into the bloodstream. Nor does a vasectomy interfere with the process or sensation of ejaculation. As we noted in Chapter 4, virtually all the fluid of the ejaculate is produced by the seminal vesicles and prostate, and the incision is made long before that point in the duct system. Thus the ejaculate is completely normal, except that it does not contain any sperm.

Figure 7.12   The no-scalpel vasectomy. (a) The vas (dotted line) is grasped by special ring forceps and the scrotum is pierced by sharp-tipped forceps. (b) The forceps stretch the opening slightly. (c) The vas is lifted out and then tied off. The other vas is then lifted out through the same small hole and the procedure is repeated.

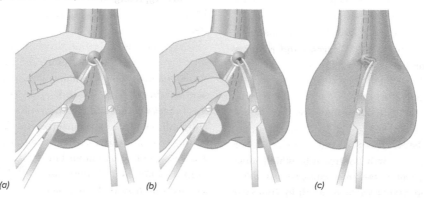

(a)   *(b)*   *(c)*

How It Works

The vasectomy makes it impossible for sperm to move beyond the cut in the vas. Thus the vasectomy prevents sperm from being in the ejaculate.

Effectiveness

The vasectomy is essentially 100 percent effective; it has a failure rate of 0.1 percent. Failures occur because stray sperm are still present during the first months after surgery, because the physician did not completely sever the vas, or because the ends of the vas have grown back together.

Side Effects

The physical side effects of the vasectomy typically are minimal. In rare cases there is a minor complication from the surgery, such as infection of the vas (Hatcher et al., 2011). Some psychologically based problems may arise. Thus, the man's attitude toward having a vasectomy is extremely important. Only about 5 percent of men regret having had a vasectomy (Hatcher et al., 2011).

Reversibility

Quite a bit of effort has been devoted to developing techniques for reversing vasectomies (the surgical procedure for reversal is termed *vasovasostomy*) and to developing vasectomy techniques that are more reversible. At present, with sophisticated microsurgery techniques, pregnancy rates following reversal are between 38 and 89 percent in various studies (Hatcher et al., 2011). In making a decision about whether to have a vasectomy, though, a man should assume that it is irreversible. After a vasectomy some men begin forming antibodies to their own sperm. Because these antibodies destroy sperm, they might contribute further to the irreversibility of the vasectomy.

Advantages and Disadvantages

The major advantages of the vasectomy are its effectiveness and its minimal health risks. Once performed, it requires no further thought or planning on the man's part. It is a permanent, long-term method of contraception and is free. The operation itself is simple—simpler than the female sterilization procedures—and requires no hospitalization or absence from work. Finally, it is one of the few methods that allow the man to assume contraceptive responsibility.

The permanency of the vasectomy may be either an advantage or a disadvantage. If permanent contraception is desired, the method is certainly much better than something like the birth control pill, which must be used repeatedly. But if the man changes his mind and decides that he wants to have a child (perhaps with a new partner), the permanence is a distinct disadvantage. Some men freeze several samples of their sperm in a sperm bank so that assisted insemination can be performed if they do decide to have a child after a vasectomy.

Another disadvantage of the vasectomy is the various psychological problems that might result if the man sees sterilization as a threat to his masculinity or virility. However, studies done around the world show that the majority of vasectomized men say that they have no regrets about having had the sterilization performed, they would recommend it to others, and there has been no change or else an improvement in their happiness and sexual satisfaction in their relationship.

Finally, if a couple use the vasectomy as a permanent method of birth control, the woman is not protected if she has intercourse with someone other than her partner. Similarly, the man is not protected from STIs.

Female Sterilization

Several surgical techniques (sometimes called tubal ligation or "having the tubes tied") are used to sterilize a woman, including minilaparotomy, laparoscopy, and the transcervical approach. These techniques differ in terms of the type of procedure used (see Figure 7.13). They are performed under local or general anaesthesia, and involve blocking the fallopian tubes in some way so that sperm and egg cannot meet.

With **laparoscopy**, a magnifying instrument is inserted in the abdomen. The doctor uses it to identify the fallopian tubes and then blocks them with clips. A variation on this procedure is the *minilaparotomy*, which is used immediately after a woman has given birth. Either procedure takes only about 10 to 20 minutes and does not require that the woman spend the night in the hospital.

Another procedure is the *transcervical approach*, which does not require an incision. Instead, the instruments enter through the cervix and uterus, and a blockage device is placed in each fallopian tube. The devices that are typically used today are called Essure and Adiana. Scar tissue forms around it, blocking the fallopian tube.

The female sterilization procedures do not interfere with the ovaries, and therefore the production of sex hormones continues normally; thus, female sterilization does not bring on premature menopause. Some of the misunderstandings arise from confusion of female sterilization procedures with hysterectomy (surgical removal of the uterus) or oophorectomy (surgical removal of the ovaries, which does impair hormonal functioning). These latter two operations do produce

laparoscopy: A method of female sterilization.

Figure 7.13 Tubal ligation using the laparoscopic method.

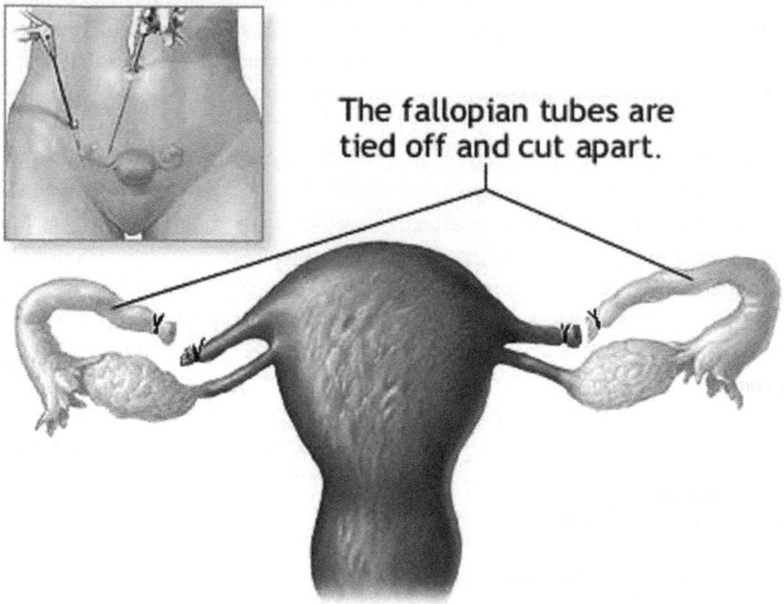

The fallopian tubes are tied off and cut apart.

sterility, but they are generally performed for purposes other than sterilization, such as treatment of cancer.

How It Works

Female sterilization procedures make it impossible for the egg to move down the fallopian tube toward the uterus. They also prevent sperm from reaching the egg.

Effectiveness

These procedures are essentially 100 percent effective. The failure rate of 0.5 percent is due to an occasional rejoining of the ends of the fallopian tubes, and rare cases in which the woman was pregnant before the sterilization procedure was performed.

Side Effects

Occasionally, there are side effects arising from the surgery, such as infections, hemorrhaging, and problems related to the anaesthetic. Generally, only 1 percent of women undergoing the surgery experience complications.

Reversibility

Highly refined microsurgery techniques make it possible to reverse female sterilization in some cases. The success rate varies considerably, depending on the method that was used to perform the sterilization. Pregnancy rates range between 50 and 75 percent, depending on the woman's age and other factors (Gordts et al., 2009). However, in deciding whether to have sterilization surgery, a woman should assume that it is irreversible. Five years

after sterilization, only 7 percent of women regret having had the procedure (Jamieson et al., 2002).

Advantages and Disadvantages

Female sterilization has some of the same advantages as male sterilization in terms of effectiveness, permanence, and cost (it's free) when used for long-term contraception. One disadvantage is that it offers no protection from STIs.

LO5

New Advances in Contraception

According to some, a really good method of contraception is not yet available (see Milestones in Sex Research). The highly effective methods either are permanent (sterilization) or have associated health risks (the pill). Other, safer methods (such as the condom and the cervical cap) have failure rates that cannot be ignored. Most of the methods are for women, not men. With the exception of the condom, none of the methods provide protection from STIs. Because of the limitations of the currently available methods, contraception research continues. Next, we discuss some of the more promising possibilities for the future.

Male Methods

Several possibilities for new or improved male contraception are being explored (Hatcher et al., 2011; Institute of Medicine, 2004; Wenk & Nieschlag, 2006).

Milestones in Sex Research

History of the Development of Sophisticated Methods of Contraception

Late 1700s	Casanova (1725–1798) popularizes and publicizes use of the sheath, or *English riding coat*.
1798	Malthus urges "moral restraint" orabstinence.
1840s	Goodyear vulcanizes rubber. Production of rubber condoms soon follows.
1883	Mensinga invents the diaphragm.
1893	Harrison performs the first vasectomy.
1909	Richter uses the intrauterine silkworm gut.
1910–1920	Sanger pioneers in New York City; the term *birth control* is coined.
1930	Gräfenberg publishes information documenting his 21 years of experience with the ring (silver and copper) and catgut as IUDs.
1930–1931	Knaus and Ogino elucidate "safe and unsafe" periods of the woman's menstrual cycle: the rhythm method.
1932	First birth control clinic in Canada opens in Hamilton, Ontario.
1934	Corner and Beard isolate progesterone.
1937	Makepeace demonstrates that progesterone inhibits ovulation.
1950s	Abortions are used extensively in Japan.
1960s	Many Western nations liberalize abortion laws. Modern IUDs become available. Contraceptive sterilization becomes more acceptable. The laparoscopic tubal ligation technique is developed.
1969	Changes to the *Criminal Code of Canada* legalize contraceptive use and allow abortions under some circumstances.
1970s	Depo-Provera contraceptive injections become available in more than 50 nations (though not in Canada until 1997).
1988	The Supreme Court of Canada rules on abortion.
1996	The female condom becomes available over the counter.
2004	NuvaRing and Ortho Evra patch are approved by Health Canada.
2007	Seasonale is approved by Health Canada.
2008	Plan B emergency contraception is approved for sale over the counter by Health Canada.

Sources: Hatcher et al. (1976); Institute of Medicine (2004).

New Condoms

Several new models of condoms are being tested. To deal with the problem of allergies to latex, polyurethane condoms have been developed, as noted earlier. They are thinner than latex, so they should provide more sensation. Another model is one that could be put on before erection.

Male Hormonal Methods

The basic idea underlying the development of male hormonal methods is to suppress the production of LH and FSH by the pituitary so that sperm would not be produced or would not develop properly (Wenk & Nieschlag, 2006). Unfortunately, many of the hormone preparations that have been tried shut down sperm production but also shut down the user's sex drive, making them unacceptable to most men. Current drugs being tested involve a combination of a testosterone and a progestin (such as DMPA, used in the Depo-Provera shot for women); the latter would suppress FSH and LH production, leading to the suppression of spermatogenesis (Page et al., 2006). Another group of drugs is the GnRH antagonists. By reducing GnRH activity, they would reduce the production of FSH and LH, which would stop spermatogenesis.

Are there any hormonal contraceptive methods for men?

RISUG

RISUG is the name for *reversible inhibition of sperm under guidance,* a method that has been developed mainly in India (Kogan & Wald, 2014; Lohiya et al., 2014). It involves injection of a porous polymer into the vas through a small incision. Sperm can pass through the polymer, but the polymer disrupts the membranes of the sperm cells as they pass through, so that they are not viable. RISUG, then, is somewhat like a vasectomy except that it is easily reversible. Test results with monkeys look promising. RISUG is being evaluated in preclinical trials in the U.S. under the trade name Vasalgel. It has been shown to be effective in preventing conception in adult male rhesus monkeys, with few side effects (Colagross-Schouten et al., 2017).

Immunocontraceptives

Scientists have been working on a contraceptive vaccine that would induce the individual's immune system to react in a way that would interrupt one of the steps in the fertility system, for example, one of the stages in the production or maturation of sperm. One option is a vaccine targeting sperm antigens (Naz, 2011). Another is a vaccine for men that would target pituitary FSH, which would block sperm production without stopping the manufacture of testosterone. None of these are in trials yet.

Male Contraceptive Implant

Health Canada has approved a clinical trial for an intra-vas device (IVD) in which two tiny plugs that block sperm are inserted into the vas deferens. Unlike a vasectomy, for which reversal is often not successful, these devices could be removed if the man later decided he wanted to father a child.

Female Methods

Microbicides

Microbicides are substances that kill microbes (bacteria and viruses) and, preferably, sperm. Experts had hoped that current contraceptive foams and gels that contain nonoxynol-9 (N-9) would be effective microbicides, but it turns out that N-9 is ineffective and may actually make women more vulnerable to infection by irritating the vagina. What we need is a microbicide that is highly effective at killing the viruses and bacteria that cause STIs *and* is effective at killing sperm *and* does not irritate the vagina. Several promising microbicides are in clinical trials (Hatcher et al., 2011). One example is BufferGel. These microbicides could be used by themselves or with a cervical cap or condom.

Several microbicides, with trade names such as BufferGel and PRO 2000, are in clinical trials now. To this point, though, they have proven ineffective against HIV, chlamydia, and gonorrhea (Guffey et al., 2014; Obiero et al., 2012).

A Better Pill

The combination birth control pill tends to lower women's testosterone levels, which may explain why some women experience a loss of sexual desire while they are on it. A new pill is being developed that adds an androgen to the combination pill (Zimmerman et al., 2015).

Vaginal Rings

The NuvaRing, discussed earlier, is already available in Canada and contains a combination of estrogen and progestin. A new ring, NES-EE, is being developed and would last 12 months (Ringheim & Gribble, 2009). The NES stands for Nestorone, a progestin.

One company is developing a ring that contains both contraceptive hormones and tenofovir, an antiretroviral that protects against HIV (Hatcher et al., 2011). The idea is to produce multipurpose technologies that work as contraceptives and protect from STIs.

Reversible, Nonsurgical Sterilization

This method involves injecting liquid silicone into the fallopian tubes. The silicone hardens and forms a plug. The plugs could later be removed if the woman wanted to become pregnant. It might also be used to plug the vas in men. It is being studied in the Netherlands.

LO6

Psychological Aspects: Attitudes toward Contraception

It is a favourite old saying that contraceptives are only as effective as the people who use them. That is, no contraceptive method is effective if it is not used or if it is used improperly. Thus, the user is at least as important as all the technology of contraception.

About 2.8 percent of teenage girls in Canada or about 31 000 girls (most of them single) became pregnant each year (McKay, 2012). The rate of teenage pregnancy in Canada has been decreasing in most provinces and territories. However, it increased between 2001 and 2010 in Newfoundland and Labrador, Nova Scotia, New Brunswick, and Yukon. The rate (28.2 per 1000) is considerably higher than in many European countries (e.g., German, Finland, Switzerland) and much lower than in England and the United States (McKay, 2012). Approximately 53 percent of teenage pregnancies are terminated by abortion, 45 percent result in live births (often to single teenagers), and 2 percent end in miscarriage. Of the teenagers who give birth, most choose to keep the baby.

Most unwanted pregnancies are the result of failure to use contraceptives responsibly. The Canada Youth Sexual Health and HIV/AIDS Study (CYSHHAS) found that between 5 and 10 percent of high school students in

Figure 7.14 Reasons given by Canadian Grade 11 students for not using condoms the last time they had intercourse.

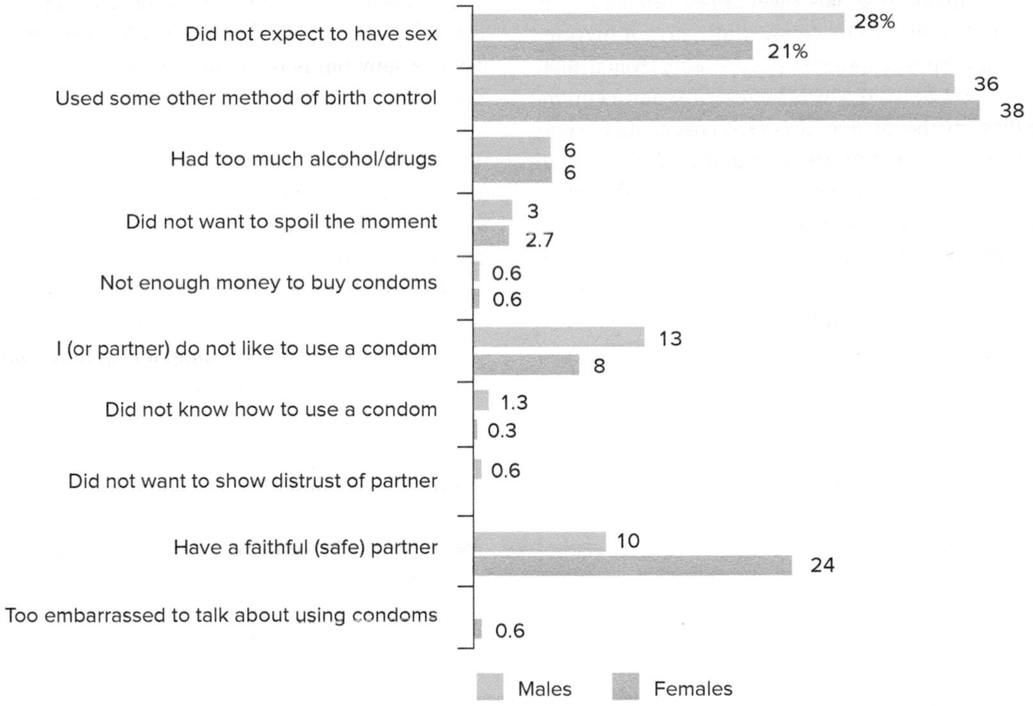

Did not expect to have sex — 28% / 21%
Used some other method of birth control — 36 / 38
Had too much alcohol/drugs — 6 / 6
Did not want to spoil the moment — 3 / 2.7
Not enough money to buy condoms — 0.6 / 0.6
I (or partner) do not like to use a condom — 13 / 8
Did not know how to use a condom — 1.3 / 0.3
Did not want to show distrust of partner — 0.6
Have a faithful (safe) partner — 10 / 24
Too embarrassed to talk about using condoms — 0.6

Males   Females

Councils of Ministers of Education, (2003). Canadian Youth, Sexual Health and HIV/AIDS Study: Factors influencing knowledge, attitude, and behaviours.

Grades 9 and 11 had used no contraceptive method the last time they engaged in sexual intercourse (Boyce et al., 2006). Further, only about three-quarters of Canadian adolescents who engaged in sexual intercourse report always using contraception (Black, Yang, et al., 2009; Fisher et al., 2004). Others do not use contraceptives consistently.[2] Research in five Western countries, including Canada, indicates that in all five countries, adolescents from low-income families are more likely to become pregnant (Darroch et al., 2001).

If we are to understand this issue and take effective steps to address it, we must understand the psychology of contraceptive use and nonuse. Many researchers have been investigating this issue. Why don't adolescents use contraceptives? The CYSHHAS asked Canadian high school students why they did not used condoms the last time they had sexual intercourse (Boyce et al., 2006). As shown in Figure 7.14, one important reason for both Grade 9 and Grade 11 students was that they did not

expect to have sex. Another important reason was that they used another method of birth control. Other common reasons were having had too much alcohol or drugs, not wanting to spoil the moment, not having enough money to buy condoms, their or their partner not wanting to use condoms, and feeling that they had a faithful partner. Few students said that they did not know how to use a condom or that they were too embarrassed to talk about condom use. The study did not ask students about some other reasons that adolescents sometimes give for not using contraceptives, such as believing that they could not get pregnant. And some think that pregnancy would not be such a bad thing and might even be a good thing.

What factors affect whether teens are consistent users of contraception? William Fisher, a psychologist at the University of Western Ontario, has developed the information–motivation–behavioural skills (IMB) model to explain such sexual health behaviour as contraceptive use (Camilleri et al., 2015; Fisher & Fisher, 1992, 1998). The first component of this model is *information* that is relevant to using condoms effectively. People who lack information about contraceptives and their correct use can scarcely use them effectively. People need the information to be presented in a way that makes it easy for them to put it into practice. That is, people need basic and understandable information about fertility and

---

[2] Myths teenagers hold about when a woman can and cannot get pregnant may contribute to their inconsistent use of contraception. For example, when she was in high school, the daughter of one of this text's authors (ESB) regularly heard other kids state with certainty that a female cannot get pregnant the first time she has intercourse or if she has intercourse standing up or in water. What have you heard?

contraceptives, but they also need specific, practical information about where to acquire contraceptives and how to use them correctly to prevent pregnancy.

The second component of the IMB is *motivation*. People are more motivated to use contraceptives if they have positive attitudes toward the use of contraception, perceive that the use of contraception is socially acceptable, and have the expectation that intercourse could result in pregnancy. Individuals who believe that contraception interferes with lovemaking, think that their friends disapprove of sex or of the use of contraceptives, or believe that there is little chance of pregnancy will be less likely to practise effective contraception. A person's motivation to engage in contraceptive behaviour is also influenced by his or her emotional responses to sexual cues, called *erotophobia-erotophilia* (Byrne, 1983; Fisher et al., 1983). **Erotophobes** tend to have negative emotions related to sex, such as guilt and fear of social disapproval. **Erotophiles** are just the opposite—they feel comfortable with and positive toward sex and sexual stimuli. Most people are somewhere in between.

The third component of the IMB is having the *behavioural skills* to engage in the actions needed to use contraceptives effectively. This includes the skills to acquire contraceptives, discuss contraceptive use with a partner, and refuse to engage in sexual intercourse if contraception is not available. Before individuals will engage in these behaviours, they must accept the fact that they are sexually active and that pregnancy (or STIs) can result from intercourse. They also need to set preventing pregnancy as a personal goal and have confidence that they can enact their skills (Camilleri et al., 2015; Fisher & Fisher, 1998).

As shown in Figure 7.14, having information is a necessary but not sufficient condition to ensure that people will use condoms consistently. According to this model, people with more information and motivation are more likely to acquire the needed skills that, in turn, result in more consistent condom sue. Research has shown that, compared to people who are erotophilic, people who are erotophobic are less likely to engage in a number of the steps essential for effective contraception (Byrne, 1983; Fisher et al., 1988), including obtaining information, acknowledging that sex might occur, obtaining contraceptives, communicating with their partner, and using condoms consistently.

Although it is generally recognized that fantasy is an important part of sexual expression, fantasy may also play an important role in contraceptive behaviour. Most of us have fantasies about sexual encounters, and we often try to make our real-life sexual encounters turn out like the *scripts* of our fantasies. An important shaper of our fantasies is the

erotophobes: People with a negative orientation toward sexuality, who feel guilty and fearful about sex.
erotophiles: People with a positive orientation toward sexuality, who feel comfortable with and positive toward sex.

mass media. Through movies, television, the Internet, and romance novels, we learn idealized techniques for kissing, holding, and lovemaking. But the media's idealized versions of sex almost never include a portrayal of the use of contraceptives (American Academy of Pediatrics, 2010). In the popular TV show *Grey's Anatomy*, Cristina has sex for the first time with a new partner with no contraception in sight, and she's a doctor! One content analysis of media (television, magazines, music, and movies) that are popular with adolescents found that on the rare occasion when contraception was presented, it was portrayed as embarrassing or humiliating (Hust et al., 2008).

There were a number of positive examples of discussion of condoms in the original *Degrassi* series (M. Byers, 2005). For example, Caitlin tells Joey that she's ready to have sex with him by slipping a condom into his hand while they are having a romantic dinner in a nice restaurant. More recently, positive examples have come from the television series *Sex and the City*. In one sequence, Miranda has "mercy sex" with her ex-boyfriend Steve, who had just undergone treatment for testicular cancer. They don't use a condom, and Miranda gets pregnant. After that, she frequently reminds her friends to use a condom, using herself as an example of the consequences of not using one. These episodes were excellent in showing that negative consequences do occur when contraception is not used, and they provide examples of honest discussions of contraception. If teenagers saw lots of instances of their heroes and heroines behaving responsibly about contraception, it would probably influence their behaviour. But right now that is not what the media usually give them. However, things may be slowly moving in the right direction: 25 percent of television programs that show or strongly imply sexual intercourse also include a reference to safer sex (Kaiser Family Foundation, 2001). For example, in an episode of *Friends*, Monica and Rachel fought over the last condom when both of their boyfriends were staying over.

What are the solutions? Can this research and theorizing on the psychology of contraceptive use be applied to reducing unwanted teenage pregnancy? The most direct solution would be to have better programs of sex education in the schools. In Canada, the nature and extensiveness of school-based sexual health education varies considerably among and within provinces and territories (Barrett et al., 1997). Sex education programs should include a number of components that are typically missing, including legitimizing presex communication about sex and contraception (Milan & Kilmann, 1987); legitimizing the purchase and carrying of contraceptives; discussing how to weigh the costs and benefits of pregnancy, contraception, and abortion; legitimizing noncoital kinds of sexual pleasure, such as masturbation and oral–genital sex; encouraging men to accept equal responsibility for contraception; and enhancing skills through role-playing and other skill-building activities. Some suggestions on how to negotiate safer sex are presented in the Chapter 8, and sexuality education is discussed in more depth in Chapter 19.

So far we have focused only on why many adolescents do not use contraceptives consistently. Before leaving this discussion, it is important to note that it is not just single teenagers who have unwanted pregnancies, and many of the same factors just discussed also apply to older individuals. Further, some single teenage mothers make good parents, whereas some single women in their 20s and 30s do not. For example, a Nova Scotia study found no differences between the children of single teenage mothers and those of older single mothers in either parenting skills or the children's educational achievements (Bissell, 2000; Nova Scotia Department of Community Services, 1991). Research has shown that it is poverty and lack of education, rather than age per se, that create difficulties for single mothers (Luong, 2008; Maticka-Tyndale, 2001; Singh et al., 2001).

Abortion

In the past several decades, **abortion** (the termination of a pregnancy) has been a topic of considerable controversy in North America. Canada currently has no laws related to abortion and so, legally, abortion is treated like any other medical procedure (see First Person for a short history of abortion in Canada). However, some groups would like to see abortion recriminalized. Opposition to abortion comes from a coalition of anti-abortion groups that prefer to call themselves *pro-life* groups. Those seeking to preserve the right of women to legal abortions, who call themselves *pro-choice*, have also organized. Action Canada for Sexual Health and Rights, for example, has been active in trying to ensure reproductive freedom for women in Canada and around the world.

What do most Canadians think about abortion? An Angus Reid poll in 2014 found that the vast majority of Canadians are in favour. Specifically, 59 percent believe abortion should be legal in all circumstances—that is, to any woman who wants one—and 23 percent believe that abortion should be permitted but should be subject to greater restrictions that it currently is. Some Canadians are opposed to abortion: 10 percent would like abortion to be available only in special circumstances, and 6 percent would like to see abortion outlawed except when the life of the mother is in danger.

In 2014, 81 897 Canadian women obtained a legal abortion in one of the 94 abortion facilities (hospitals or clinics) across Canada (Canadian Institute for Health Information [CIHI], 2015). Nonetheless, all Canadian women do not have equal access to abortion services.

Several factors limit Canadian women's access to abortion. One factor is a lack of abortion services in many areas. In particular, with the exception of B.C. and Quebec, abortions are more available in urban than in rural areas (Norman et al., 2016). Women in the Atlantic provinces as well as women in Canada's rural, Northern, and coastal communities have the least access (Sethna & Doull, 2013). Further, most hospitals do not perform abortions. Women may prefer to have an abortion in a free-standing clinic due to confidentiality issues, but many women do not have easy access to a clinic. As a result, many women have to travel long distances at considerable cost to access an abortion (Sethna & Doull, 2013). The process for obtaining an abortion varies across jurisdictions and may make it difficult for some women to receive abortions in a timely fashion. In some provinces, abortions are fully funded by Medicare; however, in other provinces, only hospital abortions are covered, and women have to pay between $500 and $800 for a clinic abortion. Finally, the activities of anti-abortion groups, such as picketing outside abortion clinics or the homes of physicians who provide abortions, have discouraged some physicians from providing abortion services. They have some reason to be fearful. In the past, at least three Canadian physicians have been wounded in their homes by snipers, and the Toronto Morgentaler clinic was destroyed by a firebomb in 1992. There are still protests outside clinics by anti-abortion groups, but there has been little harassment of or violence against providers recently (Norman et al., 2016).

In other countries, policies on abortion vary widely. Abortion is legal and widely practised in Russia and Japan, parts of eastern and central Europe, and South America. The use of abortion in Africa and Asia is limited because of the scarcity of medical facilities, and many women in these countries undergo unsafe abortions. The World Health Organization estimates that there are 19 million unsafe abortions each year and that 68 000 women die as a result (WHO, 2004). Table 7.2 gives rates of abortion in various countries, including Canada. The Canadian abortion rate has remained fairly stable over the past decade (PHAC, 2008b). We discuss methods of abortion and the psychological aspects of abortion here; the ethical aspects will be discussed in Chapter 20.

Abortion Procedures

Several methods of abortion are available; which one is used depends on how far the pregnancy has progressed.

Vacuum Aspiration

The **vacuum aspiration** method (also called *vacuum suction* or *vacuum curettage*)

> **abortion:** The termination of a pregnancy.
> **vacuum aspiration:** A method of abortion that is performed during the first trimester and involves suctioning out the contents of the uterus.

A History of Abortion in Canada: Focus on Dr. Henry Morgentaler

anada currently has no abortion legislation, and abortion is legal in Canada. However, this has not always been the case. For example, from 1969 to 1988, women could obtain a legal abortion only under certain restricted circumstances. Under this law, many women were not able to get legal abortions. Dr. Henry Morgentaler was instrumental in bringing changes to Canada's abortion laws through a campaign of civil disobedience (Figure 7.15).

Henry Morgentaler was born in Poland in 1923. Both of his parents were killed by the Nazis, and he himself was interned in two concentration camps before being liberated by U.S. forces. He immigrated to Canada and graduated with a degree in medicine from l'Université de Montréal in 1953. In 1955 he opened a general medical practice. At first, Dr. Morgentaler refused to perform abortions. However, in 1968, moved by the desperation of some of his poor female patients with unwanted pregnancies, he opened his first abortion clinic in Montreal in violation of Canadian law. He believed that the abortion law was unjust and harmed women. At the time, physicians convicted of performing an abortion could receive a life sentence.

In 1973, Dr. Morgentaler started a campaign of civil disobedience to challenge Canada's abortion laws and provide Canadian women with access to safe legal abortions. At the same time, in his clinics, he developed the vacuum-suction method for performing abortions; this is the procedure that is used for 97 percent of abortions in Canada today. Dr. Morgentaler was charged several times between 1973 and 1986, and was acquitted by juries in Quebec, Ontario, and Manitoba. However, he did spend ten months in Quebec prisons in 1975–1976, after the Quebec Court of Appeal overturned his jury acquittal and substituted a guilty verdict. (It is no longer legal for an appeal court to substitute a guilty verdict for a jury acquittal, because of this case.)

In 1988, after this series of court cases, the Supreme Court of Canada struck down Canada's abortion law as unconstitutional, calling it the "Morgentaler Decision." This decision effectively decriminalized abortion in Canada and provided most women with easier access to a legal abortion should they want one. In June 2005, Dr. Morgentaler was awarded his first honorary degree by the University of Western Ontario, and he was awarded the Order of Canada in 2008. It's because of the actions of Dr. Morgentaler that abortion is legal in Canada. He continued to fight to increase woman's access to abortion through legal action against provincial governments who refuse to fund abortions performed in clinics until his death in 2013.

Figure 7.15 Dr. Henry Morgentaler was instrumental in decriminalizing abortion in Canada. Legal challenges against Morgentaler began in 1970 and ended in 1988 when the Supreme Court of Canada found that the section of the *Criminal Code* dealing with abortion was unconstitutional.

© CP Picture Archive/Paul Chiasson

Table 7.2   Abortion Rates around the World

Country	Number of Abortions per Year	Abortion Rate*	% of Pregnancies Ending in Abortion
Bulgaria	24 900	16	21
Canada	94 000	14	14
China	9 173 000	29	N/A
Denmark	16 200	15	18
Israel	19 600	13	10
New Zealand	17 900	20	20
Russian Federation	1 208 700	38	N/A
Spain	115 800	12	16
United States	1 210 000	20	19

*The abortion rate is the number of abortions per 1000 women aged 15 to 44. Statistics are for legal abortions

Sources: Jones & Kooistra, 2011; Sedgh et al., 2011

can be performed during the first trimester of pregnancy and up to 14 weeks' gestation. It is done on an outpatient basis with a local anaesthetic. The procedure itself takes only about ten minutes, and the woman stays in the doctor's office, clinic, or hospital for a few hours. It is the most widely used abortion procedure in Canada today, accounting for 97 percent of abortions (Baird & Flinn, 2001).

The woman is prepared as she would be for a pelvic exam, and an instrument is inserted into the vagina; the instrument dilates (stretches open) the opening of the cervix. A tube is then inserted into this opening until one end is in the uterus (see Figure 7.16). The other end is attached to a suction-producing apparatus, and the contents of the uterus, including the fetal tissue, are sucked out.

Vacuum aspiration is a simple procedure and entails little risk. There are rare risks of uterine perforation, infection, hemorrhaging, and failure to remove all the fetal material.

Dilation and Evacuation

Dilation and evacuation (D&E) is used mostly for later second-trimester abortions (Hatcher et al., 2011). It is somewhat similar to vacuum aspiration, but it is more complicated because the fetus is relatively large by the second trimester.

Induced Labour

During the late part of the second trimester, abortion is usually performed by inducing labour and a miscarriage. The most commonly used version of this method is the saline-induced abortion. A fine tube is inserted through the abdomen into the amniotic sac and saline solution is injected. Within several hours, the solution causes labour to begin. A variation on this technique is

Figure 7.16   A vacuum aspiration abortion.

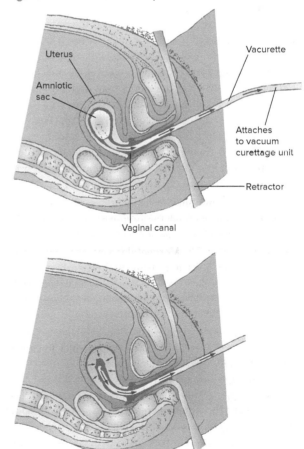

the prostaglandin abortion. Prostaglandins (hormone-like substances that cause contractions) are injected and cause labour. Misoprostol can also be used to induce labour for second-trimester abortions (Autry et al., 2002).

Induced labour is used for abortion only if pregnancy has progressed late into the second trimester, and it accounts for only 1 percent of abortions in Canada (Statistics Canada, 1995). This method is both more hazardous and more costly than the previous methods.

Medical Abortion

Medical abortion involves only the administration of a drug. The two drugs commonly used are mifepristone and methotrexate. Medical abortions account for 3 percent of the abortions in Canada (CIHI, 2010). This compares with 17 percent in the United States, 47 percent in the United Kingdom, and 86 percent in Finland (Heino & Gissler, 2013; Jones & Kooistra, 2011; London Department of Health, 2013). This may be in part because mifepristone has only recently become available in Canada.

> **What is the difference between a surgical abortion and a medical abortion?**

Mifepristone

In 1986, French researchers announced the development of a new drug called **RU-486**, or mifepristone (Couzinet et al., 1986; Ulmann et al., 1990). It can induce a very early abortion. It has a powerful anti-progesterone effect, causing the endometrium of the uterus to be sloughed off and thus bringing about an abortion (see Figure 7.17). It is administered as a tablet and followed two days later by a small dose of prostaglandin (misoprostol), which increases contractions of the uterus, helping to expel the embryo. It can be used during the first seven to nine weeks of pregnancy. Research shows that it is effective in 92 to 96 percent of cases when combined with prostaglandin (Hatcher et al., 2007). It is most effective when the woman has been pregnant less than 49 days. Early research has found little evidence of side effects, although the woman experiences some cramping as the uterine contents are expelled.

In France today, more than half of women who decide to terminate an early pregnancy choose mifepristone rather than conventional abortion methods (Jones & Henshaw, 2002). Mifepristone is also widely used in Britain, Sweden, China, and the United States. Mifegymiso was approved for use in Canada in 2015. Mifegymiso is a combination of two medications sold together: mifepristone and misoprostol. Misoprostol is taken taken 24 to 48 hours after the woman takes mifepristone and induces contractions similar to a natural miscarriage.

Mifegymiso was approved by Health Canada in 2015, but it only became available in 2017, a year and a half later. To prescribe it, physicians have to complete a six-hour online course. This required level of training is very unusual for medications, and only about 300 physicians have completed the course so far, so it is not readily available to women who need it. The drug

> **RU-486 (mifepristone):** The "abortion pill."

Figure 7.17   How RU-486, or mifepristone, works.

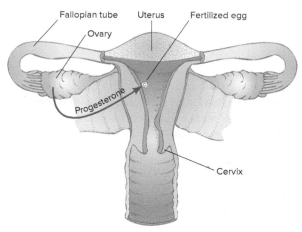

Progesterone, a hormone produced by the ovaries, is necessary for the implantation and development of a fertilized egg.

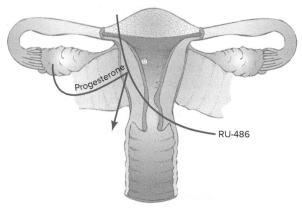

Taken early in pregnancy, RU-486 blocks the action of progesterone and makes the body react as if it isn't pregnant.

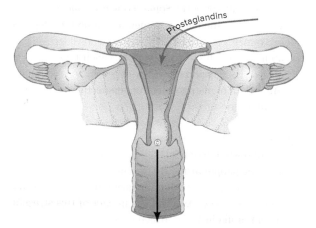

Prostaglandins, taken two days later, cause the uterus to contract and the cervix to soften and dilate. As a result, the embryo is expelled in 97 percent of the cases.

is expensive (about $300), but several provinces have committed to covering the cost, including Alberta, Ontario, and New Brunswick. The abortion rate is not expected to increase but it is expected that many women will choose a medical abortion over a surgical one. A study of Canadian women who had received an abortion before mifepristone was available indicated that many would have chosen mifepristone if it had been available (Vogel et al., 2016).

Methotrexate

Another alternative in drug-induced early abortion involves the use of a combination of the drug methotrexate, which is toxic to the embryo, with misoprostol, which causes uterine contractions that expel the dead embryo (Hatcher et al., 2007). Both of these drugs are already widely used for treatment of other diseases and so are available to be used for medical abortions. Like mifepristone, they permit the early induction of abortion in a physician's office rather than an abortion clinic or a hospital. Methotrexate is also used to treat ectopic pregnancy, which is a life-threatening condition.

LO8 Psychological Aspects

The discovery of an unwanted pregnancy triggers a complicated set of emotions, as well as a complex decision-making process. Initially, women tend to feel anger and some anxiety. They then embark on the decision-making process studied by psychologist Carol Gilligan (1982). In this process, women essentially weigh the need to think of themselves and protect their own welfare against the need to think of the welfare of the fetus. Even focusing only on the welfare of the fetus can lead to conflicting conclusions: Should I complete the pregnancy because the fetus has a right to life, or should I have an abortion because the fetus has a right to be born into a stable family with two parents who have completed their education and can provide good financial support? Some women consider whether to give birth to the baby and then give it up for adoption. Many women in Gilligan's study showed considerable psychological growth over the time in which they wrestled with these issues and made their decision. See A Sexually Diverse World for a cross-cultural perspective on abortion.

What is the impact of abortion on women's mental health? Anti-abortion activists claim that women are psychologically traumatized by having an abortion, which they call post-abortion syndrome (Bazelon, 2007). However, other people argue that abortion is a stressful life event that is similar to other types of stressful events that women experience. As such, the impact of this stressful life event is likely to be affected by the woman's social and cultural context (e.g., what others around her think of abortion), as well as by other factors in the woman's life (e.g., whether she has a history of emotional problems) (Major et al., 2009; Munk-Olsen et al., 2011). From this perspective, only some women would experience negative psychological consequences from abortion, and those that do would be ones who have poor coping skills or emotional difficulties, or live in a society that stigmatizes abortion (Major et al., 2009).

What do the scientific data say? The best scientific evidence indicates that most women do not experience severe negative psychological responses to abortion (Major et al., 2009; Schmiege & Russo, 2005). Most women show good adjustment. Typically, they do not feel guilt or sorrow over the decision. Instead, they report feeling relieved, satisfied, and relatively happy, and say that if they had the decision to make over again, they would do the same thing. Nonetheless, some women benefit from talking about their experience, and it is important that post-abortion support groups be available (Lewis, 1997). This may be particularly true of women who have had one or more abortions in the past. An Ontario study found that women who were undergoing repeat abortions were significantly more likely to have experienced physical and sexual violence from a male partner and to have a history of child sexual abuse (Fisher et al., 2005).

Research in this area raises many interesting questions. Women generally show good adjustment after having an abortion, but good adjustment compared with what? It is important to compare the psychological responses of women who undergo abortion to women facing an unwanted pregnancy who choose other alternatives. The American Psychological Association reviewed all the research on the relationship between abortion and women's mental health and concluded that women who have a single, legal, first-trimester abortion are not at greater risk for mental health problems than women who deliver an unwanted pregnancy. However, the minority of women who experience significant distress about their decision to have an abortion may experience mental health problems following the abortion (Fergusson et al., 2009).

What is the consequence of being denied an abortion on the children born to these women? It is impossible to do this research in Canada now because abortion has been legal since 1988. However, in some other countries, access to abortion depends on obtaining official approval. One such country was the former Czechoslovakia. Researchers followed up 220 children born to women denied abortion (the study group) and 220 children born to women who had not requested abortion; the children were studied when they were 9 years old and again when they were 14 to 16 years old, 21 to 23, 30, and 35 (David et al., 2003). By age 14, 43 children from the study group, but only 30 of the controls, had been referred for counselling. Although there were no differences between the groups in tested intelligence, children in the study group did less well in school and were more likely to drop out. Teachers described them as less sociable and more hyperactive compared with the control group. At age 16, the boys (but not the girls) in the study group more frequently rated themselves as feeling neglected or rejected by their mothers and felt that their

A Sexually Diverse World

Abortion in Cross-Cultural Perspective

Beliefs about abortion show dramatic variation in different cultures around the world. The following is a sampling from two very different cultures.

Ekiti Yoruba

The Ekiti Yoruba, many of whom have a high school or post-secondary education, live in southwest Nigeria. For them, abortion is not a distinct category from contraception but rather is on a continuum with it (Renne, 1996).

Traditionally in the Ekiti Yoruba culture, the ideal was for a woman to have as many children as possible, spaced at two- to three-year intervals. The spacing of children is made possible by a period of sexual abstinence for two years postpartum. The Ekiti Yoruba believe that sexual intercourse while a woman is still breast-feeding a baby causes illness or death to the child; men whose children have died in infancy have been blamed for breaking the postpartum sex taboo and causing the death. Because of the high value placed on fertility, use of contraceptives and abortion must be kept secret. Even though condoms, foam, and birth control pills are available at a local clinic, few people take advantage of the service because they would not want others to know that they engaged in such practices. Abortion then becomes the chief method of birth control. Estimates are that between 200 000 and 500 000 pregnancies are aborted each year in Nigeria and that about 10 000 women die each year from botched abortions.

If a woman has an unwanted pregnancy, she generally will consult a local divine healer or herbalist first, to "keep the pregnancy from staying." They generally provide pills or substances to insert in the vagina. If the treatment does not work, the woman then goes to a clinic and has a dilation and curettage (D&C; a procedure that is similar to D&E) abortion.

Women who abort generally fall into two categories: single high school or post-secondary students who want to finish their education, and married women who are pregnant because of an affair. Here is one woman's story:

> In 1991, when awaiting entrance into university, I became pregnant by one boyfriend whom I later decided not to marry in favor of another. Since I did not want my chosen fiancé to know of the pregnancy, I decided to abort it. I first used 3 Bee-codeine tablets, Andrew's Liver Salt, and Sprite, mixing them together and then drinking them. When this did not work, I went to a clinic in a neighboring town for D&C. The abortion cost N80 and was paid for by my boyfriend. There were no after effects. (Renne, 1996, p. 487)

The ease with which Ekiti Yoruba people rely on abortion is related in part to their understanding of prenatal development. Many believe that the "real child" is not formed until after the fourth month of pregnancy and before that the fetus is lizard-like.

Greece

Birth control for women was legalized in Greece only in 1980, and abortion was legalized in 1986. Yet Greece has had a sharply declining birth rate since World War II, accounted for, in large part, by abortion (Georges, 1996). Among European nations, Greece is unique in its combination of very little use of medical contraception, a low fertility rate, and the highest abortion rate in Europe.

Three powerful institutions—the government, the Greek Orthodox Church, and the medical profession—have exerted a strong pronatalist (in favour of having babies) influence. The Greek Orthodox Church equates abortion with murder and prohibits all methods of birth control except fertility awareness methods and abstinence. The government, for its part, encourages large

mothers were less satisfied with them. By their early 20s, the study group reported less job satisfaction, more conflicts with co-workers and supervisors, and fewer and less satisfying friendships. Several other studies have found results similar to the Czech one (David et al., 2003). These results point to the serious long-term consequences for some children whose mothers would have preferred to have an abortion.

Men and Abortion

Only women become pregnant, and only women have abortions, but where do men enter the picture? Do they have a right to contribute to the decision to have an abortion? What are their feelings about abortion?

A large survey of women who had abortions indicated that 82 percent of the male partners knew that they

families by a variety of measures, including paying a monthly subsidy to families with more than three children, making daycare centres widely available, and keeping female methods of contraception illegal (until 1980). Despite all this, Greek women achieved a low fertility rate, which is regarded by the government as a threat to the Greek "race," Greek Orthodoxy, and the military strength of Greece in relation to hostile neighbours, such as the extremely fertile Turks.

Despite the illegality of abortion in Greece until 1986, abortion was widespread and a very open secret. Abortions were not back-alley affairs but rather were performed by gynecologists in private offices. Physicians, as members of a powerful and prestigious profession, were successful at legal evasion. As a result, Greek women did not have to face the life-threatening risks that occur with illegal abortion in other countries. They had access to safe illegal abortion.

Why is there so much reliance on abortion and so little access to contraception in this modern European nation? As noted earlier, the Greek Orthodox Church opposes all medical contraception, and the Greek government kept contraception illegal until 1980. But even then, contraception did not become widespread. In 1990, only 2 percent of women of reproductive age were using the pill. Some blame this on the medical profession, which is thought to block access to contraception to continue a thriving, more lucrative abortion practice. Greek women, too, resist contraception. They distinguish between *contraception* (such as birth control pills) and *being careful* (withdrawal and condoms). They reject contraception, but being careful—especially the use of withdrawal—is widespread. Fertility awareness methods are not widely used and would not be very successful if they were, since Greek women commonly believe that they are most fertile for the four to seven days just before and after the menstrual period. The mass media have spread scare messages about the pill, and many women believe that it causes cancer.

How do Greek women, the great majority of whom are Orthodox, deal with the contradiction between their church's teaching—that abortion is murder and that a woman who has had an abortion may not receive communion—and their actual practice of having abortions? First, the Greek Orthodox Church is not as absolutist in its application of doctrines regarding abortion as the Roman Catholic Church is. Some attribute this to the fact that Orthodox priests can be married and are therefore more in touch with the realities of family life. In some cases, women do abstain from receiving communion following an abortion but then later make a confession to the priest. Priests typically are forgiving.

In Greece, motherhood is highly esteemed and idealized, yet abortion is not considered contradictory to the high value placed on motherhood. Good motherhood today is thought to require an intense investment of time and energy in the children; by definition, then, the good mother limits family size, and abortion is a means to achieve that goal.

Cross-Cultural Patterns

Several patterns emerge from the study of abortion in these quite distinct cultures and other cultures (e.g., Gursoy, 1996; Johnson et al., 1996; Rigdon, 1996; Rylko-Bauer, 1996). First, no matter how strict the prohibitions against abortion, some women in all cultures choose and manage to obtain abortions. Second, the meaning of abortion is constructed in any particular culture based on factors such as beliefs about prenatal development, when life starts, and how much large families are valued. Third, the legality and morality of abortion in any culture is determined in part by political forces, such as the Greek government's desire to expand the size of the Greek population.

Sources: Georges, 1996; Gursoy, 1996; Johnson et al., 1996; Renne, 1996; Rigdon, 1996; Rylko-Bauer, 1996.

---

were having an abortion, although the percentage was lower for women in an abusive relationship (Jones et al., 2011). Among the men who knew, 80 percent were supportive of the decision.

A recent Swedish study surveyed 75 men ranging in age from 18 to 50 who were involved in legal abortion (Kero et al., 1999). The majority were in a long-term relationship with the pregnant woman. Among the men, 64

percent indicated that they wanted the woman to have an abortion; 27 percent felt that it was the woman's decision. The main reasons why these men wanted an abortion were related to family planning, such as conflict with life plans (e.g., schooling), feeling unable to offer a child a caring environment, or socio-economic reasons. The second most common reason was feeling that their relationship with the woman was not stable. What were these men's reactions to the abortion? The most common words the men used to describe their feelings were *anxiety, responsibility, guilt, relief,* and *grief.* That is, more than half the men expressed both positive and negative emotions about the abortion.

Although counselling for women undergoing abortion is a standard procedure, counselling is rarely available for the men who are involved. These findings suggest that some men also need such counselling (see, for example, Coyle & Enright, 1997).

Critical THINK*ing Skill*

UNDERSTANDING THE CONCEPT OF PROBABILITY LO3

Concepts of probability are often misunderstood and misused, yet they are crucial for good decision-making. For example, we are grateful to Environment Canada and the forecasts it provides, especially if a storm bringing a major snowfall is approaching. However, a pet peeve is a weather forecast of a 70 percent chance of rain today when it is currently raining outside. If it is currently raining, then the probability of rain today is 100 percent! It is definitely going to rain and, in fact, it already is.

Understanding concepts of probability is crucial in understanding the effectiveness of contraceptives and in deciding which one you should use. Probability refers to the chance that an event will occur. Probabilities can range between 0 (no chance) and 1.0 (definitely will occur). Often probabilities are stated as percentages ranging between 0 percent and 100 percent. For example, if we toss a fair coin, the probability that it will come up heads is 0.5, or 50 percent. Statisticians tend to talk a lot about tossing coins and rolling dice. Here we will think about rolling the pregnancy dice.

As explained earlier in the chapter, contraception experts define the failure rate of a contraceptive method as follows: If 100 people use the method for one year, the number of them who become pregnant is the failure rate. If 100 women use the vaginal ring for a year and 8 of them become pregnant during that time, then the ring has a failure rate of 8, or 8 percent. That 8 percent is really a probability. It means that if Samantha uses that method for a year (and is of reproductive age and engages in sexual intercourse regularly), her probability of pregnancy at some time during that year is 8 percent. The effectiveness of a method is 100 minus the failure rate. If the ring has an 8 percent failure rate, then it is 92 percent effective, which means that Samantha has a 92 percent probability of not getting pregnant during that year.

Suppose that your friend Eunjung comes to you wanting advice, knowing that you are taking a human sexuality course. She is considering using the vaginal ring. She is an unmarried undergraduate student, and her parents would be furious if she got pregnant. Her boyfriend attends a college 500 kilometres away, so they get together only once a month. So far, they have abstained from sex, but both of them really want to do it next month. Eunjung, who has a good understanding of probability and statistics but not contraception, asks you the probability that she will get pregnant this one time she has sex if she is using the vaginal ring. What would you tell her?

It is tempting to say that the answer would be 8 percent, but the 8 percent probability of pregnancy while using the ring is over a whole year, assuming intercourse two to three times per week, or perhaps 100 to 150 times over the year. The probability of pregnancy from a single act of intercourse is therefore much less than 8 percent, but we can't know exactly what it is from the information we have. You could explain all of that to Eunjung. She could then weigh the likelihood of pregnancy (which might be 1 percent or less) against the seriousness of the costs of pregnancy.

The other complication in thinking about the probability of pregnancy is that it depends not only on the contraceptive method but also on some other factors. Mathematicians call this *conditional probability,* which is the probability of an event occurring given some other event. If Eunjung has one act of intercourse while using the ring and the act of intercourse occurs one day before she ovulates, that carries a higher probability of pregnancy than if the intercourse occurred the day before her period, long after she ovulated.

People engage in the best decision-making if they understand and use concepts of probability.

SUMMARY

Table 7.3 provides a comparative summary of the various methods of birth control discussed in this chapter.

Table 7.3 Summary of Information on Methods of Contraception and Abortion

Method	Failure Rate, Perfect Use, %	Failure Rate, Typical Use, %	Death Rate (per 100,000 women)	Yearly Costs, $[*]	Advantages	Disadvantages
Implant	0.05	0.05		NA	Requires less remembering	Not available in Canada
Depo-Provera	0.3	6		140–180	Requires less remembering	
Combination birth control pills	0.3	3	1.6	0–360	Highly effective; not used at time of coitus; improved menstrual cycles	Cost; possible side effects; must take daily; no STI protection
Patch	0.3	8		0–430	Requires less remembering than the pill	
Vaginal ring	0.3	9	—	200–480		
IUD, copper T	0.6	0.8	1.0	30–175[‡]	Requires no remembering or motivation	May be expelled
Progesterone T	0.1	0.1				
Condom, male	2	18	1.7	75[*]	Easy to use; protection from STIs	Used at time of coitus; continual expense
Condom, female	5	21	2.0	0–750[*]	Protection from STIs	Awkward
Diaphragm with spermicide	6	16	2.0[§]	250[*]	No side effects; Inexpensive	Aesthetic objections
FemCap with spermicide						
Parous women	26	32	2.0[§]	250	No side effects; inexpensive	—
Nulliparous women	9	20	2.0[§]			
Vaginal foam, cream	18	28	2.0[§]	40[*]	Easy to use; availability	Messy; continual expense
Sponge	9–20	16–32		750[*]		
Withdrawal	4	22	2.0	None	No cost	Requires high motivation
Fertility awareness	3–5	25	2.0	None	No cost	Requires high motivation, prolonged - abstinence; not all women can use
Unprotected intercourse	85	85	9	None[¶]		
Legal abortion, first trimester	0	0	0.5	0–800[**]	Available when other methods fail	Expense
Sterilization, male	0.1	0.1	0.3	0–100[***]	Permanent; highly effective	Permanence
Sterilization, female	0.5	0.5	1.5	None	Permanent; highly effective	Permanence

[*]Based on 150 acts of intercourse.

[‡]Based on a cost of $60–$400 for the IUD/IUS and the assumption that the IUD/IUS will be used for two years.

[§]Based on the death rate for pregnancies resulting from the method. Of every 100,000 live births, 12 women die (Cheng et al., 2003).

[¶]But having a baby is expensive.

[**]All hospital abortions are covered by medicare. Only Newfoundland and Labrador, Quebec, Ontario, Manitoba, Alberta, and British Columbia cover abortions done in free-standing clinics.

[***]Although vasectomy is covered by medicare, in some provinces there is an additional fee for those done in doctors' offices.

CHAPTER 8

Sexually Transmitted Infections

Can you tell someone has HIV just by looking at them?

Protect yourself. Six in ten Canadians with multiple partners did not use a condom the last time they had sex.

Learn More at **Kisses4CANFAR.com**

Kisses 4 CANFAR campaign 2013. Image created by Three Chairs.

Are **YOU** Curious?

1. How can I know whether I have chlamydia?
2. Is there a cure for herpes?
3. Why isn't there a vaccine against HIV?
4. My partner has no symptoms of any STI. Should we still practise safer sex?

Read this chapter to find out.

Maria and Louis get home after an evening on the town and enter the house hungry for passion. The two embrace, clinging to each other, longing for each other. Louis slowly undresses Maria, hungry for the silky flesh he feels beneath him. As their passion grows, she begins reaching for him, ripping his clothes off as she explores his body with her tongue. As Louis gets more and more excited, Maria rips a condom package open with her teeth and slowly slides the condom over Louis's erect penis. After an hour of incredible lovemaking, Louis, exhausted with pleasure, turns to Maria and says, "You were right, the BEST sex is SAFER sex with LATEX!"*

* From a student essay.

As noted in Chapter 1, according to the World Health Organization, sexual health is a state of physical, emotional, mental, and social well-being related to sexuality. One aspect of this is the absence of disease, of which sexually transmitted infections (STIs) are an example. Not only do STIs affect an individual's physical sexual health, but the psychological aspects of dealing with an STI also may challenge the emotional, mental, and social aspects of a person's sexual health and well-being. In keeping with the Public Health Agency of Canada, we use the term STI rather than STD (sexually transmitted disease). STD refers only to infections that cause symptoms. STI is more encompassing because it includes infections for which people have symptoms and those for which they have no symptoms—that is, are asymptomatic.

The sexual scene is not the same as it was 30 or 40 years ago. The human papillomavirus (HPV) and HIV/AIDS pose real threats. We need to do many things to combat these dangers. One is that we must rewrite our sexual scripts, as the opening box illustrates. We also need to inform ourselves, and the goal of this chapter is to provide you with the important information you need to make decisions about your sexual activity.[1]

Your health is very important, and a good way to harm it or cause yourself suffering is to have an STI. Although in 1997 it appeared that there would be a continuing gradual decline in the rates of many STIs, that trend ended and instead there has been an increase in the incidence of newly acquired STIs in Canada (MacDonald & Wong, 2007). Consequently, it is very important to know the symptoms of the various kinds of STIs so that you can seek treatment if you develop one. Also, there are some ways to prevent STIs or at least reduce your chances of getting them, and these are certainly worth knowing about. Finally, after you have read

some of the statistics on how many people contract STIs every year and on your chances of getting one, you may want to modify your sexual behaviour somewhat. For example, according to the 2013–2014 Canadian Community Health Survey, 19 percent of women and 12 percent of men who had multiple partners in the previous year reported that they had been diagnosed with an STI (Statistics Canada, 2015). If you love, love wisely.

One of the most disturbing things about the STI epidemic in Canada is that it disproportionately affects teens and young adults. For example, in 2010 the rate of chlamydia for women between 20 and 24 years old was more than five times the rate for women overall. For people in this age group, three infections—human papillomavirus, trichomoniasis, and chlamydia—account for the majority of cases, although of these only chlamydia is a reportable infection. Canadian youth with low incomes and from ethnocultural minority groups are at a greater risk of contracting STIs (Wong et al., 2012). Worldwide, of the 37 million people living with HIV, about half became infected between the ages of 15 and 24; 34 percent of new infections (excluding neonatal transmission) occurred in this age group despite accounting for just 11 percent of the adult population (UNAIDS, 2016). Clearly, prevention efforts, including sexuality education for youth, must be accorded a higher priority than they have been given in the past.

The STIs are presented in this chapter in the following order. First we look at three—chlamydia, HPV, and herpes—that are frequent among university students. Following that is a discussion of HIV infection and AIDS, which is less common among university students but is one of the world's major public health problems and is generating an enormous amount of research. Next we discuss gonorrhea, syphilis, viral hepatitis, and trichomoniasis. Then comes not an infection but a bug: the pubic louse. After a practical section on preventing STIs, the chapter ends with a section about various other genital infections that, for the most part, are not sexually transmitted.

Some STIs are caused by *bacteria*, some are caused by *viruses*, and a few are caused by other organisms. The distinction between bacterial infections and viral infections

[1] The diagnosis and treatment of sexually transmitted infections is an area of furiously active research. New discoveries are announced almost monthly. Therefore, by the time you read this book, some of the statements in this chapter may have been superseded by newer research.

is important because bacterial infections can be cured by using antibiotics. Viral infections cannot be cured but they can be treated to reduce symptoms. Chlamydia, gonorrhea, and syphilis are caused by bacteria. Herpes, HIV/AIDS, HPV, and hepatitis B are caused by viruses.

Many statistics throughout this chapter come from the Public Health Agency of Canada (PHAC) website at www.phac-aspc.gc.ca. Data from the PHAC are used so frequently throughout the chapter that we do not provide a citation every time. Information on STIs changes quickly, so to get the most up-to-date information, check the website. Only some STIs, not all, must be reported. Therefore, there are no national data on some of the most common STIs, such as genital herpes and HPV. STI rates vary considerably across provinces and territories. You can look up the rates for the province or territory you live in on the PHAC website.

One final note before we proceed: Many photos in this chapter show the symptoms of various STIs, and some students find them distressing. The photos are not meant to scare you but to help you recognize the symptoms of STIs so that you can spot them on a prospective sexual partner and on you. You should consult your physician if you see any change in your genitals, even if it does not look like any of the pictures in this book—most of these photos are of severe cases.

L01

Chlamydia

Chlamydia trachomatis is a bacterium that is spread by sexual contact and infects the genital organs of both males and females (Figure 8.1). **Chlamydia** has become the most prevalent bacterial STI in Canada. According to the PHAC, there were 95 690 reported cases of chlamydia, a rate of 278 cases per 100 000 people in the population, the most common reported STI in Canada. However, a study that examined the rate of chlamydia in a nationally representative Canadian sample found a much higher rate: 700 cases per 100 000 people (Rotermann et al., 2013). None of these individuals had ever been diagnosed with chlamydia. This is because many young people who are at risk for chlamydia are not screened for it (Mitchell et al., 2015). The rate of chlamydia has been rising steadily since 1997. Adolescent girls have a particularly high rate of infection, more than seven times the national rate.

> **How can I know whether I have chlamydia?**

chlamydia (klah-MIH-dee-uh): An organism causing a sexually transmitted infection; the symptoms in men are a thin, clear discharge and mild pain on urination; women are frequently asymptomatic.
asymptomatic (ay-simp-toh-MAT-ik): Having no symptoms.

Symptoms

The main symptoms in men are a thin, usually clear discharge

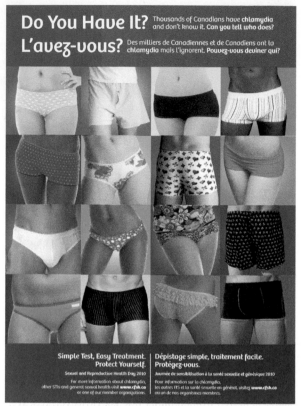

Figure 8.1   Poster developed by the Canadian Federation of Sexual Health for Sexual and Reproductive Health Day.

and mild discomfort on urination appearing 7 to 21 days after infection (Stamm, 2008). The symptoms are somewhat similar to the symptoms of gonorrhea in men. When a man consults a physician because of a urethral discharge, his chances of having chlamydia are greater than his chances of having gonorrhea. It is important that the correct diagnosis be made because chlamydia does not respond to the drugs used to cure gonorrhea. Gonorrhea tends to produce more painful urination and a more profuse, puslike discharge. Diagnosis is made from a urine sample in men and from a sample of cells from the vagina (or urine sample) in women. Tests are then used to detect the bacterium. Unfortunately, 75 percent of the cases of chlamydia infection are **asymptomatic** in women. This means that the woman never goes to a clinic for treatment, and she goes undiagnosed and untreated. The consequences of untreated chlamydia in women are discussed in the next section. Even among men, 50 percent of the cases are asymptomatic.

Treatment

Chlamydia is quite curable. It is treated with azithromycin or doxycycline (Workowski & Berman, 2010); it does not respond to penicillin. Poorly treated or undiagnosed cases may lead to a number of complications: urethral damage, epididymitis (infection of the epididymis), Reiter's syndrome,[2] and proctitis in men who have had anal intercourse. Women with untreated or undiagnosed chlamydia may experience serious complications if not treated: **pelvic inflammatory disease (PID)** and possibly infertility caused by scarring of the fallopian tubes. A baby born to an infected mother may develop pneumonia or an eye infection.

Prevention

Scientists doing research on chlamydia have a major goal of developing a vaccine that would prevent infection (Berry et al., 2004). Vaccines have been developed that are effective in mice, but certain technical obstacles prevent their use with humans. An effective vaccine for humans should be available in the next decade.

Until a vaccine is available, one of the most effective tools for prevention (in addition to safer sex) is screening. The problem with chlamydia is that so many infected people are asymptomatic and spread the disease unknowingly. In screening programs, asymptomatic carriers are identified, treated, and cured so that they do not continue to spread the disease. More asymptomatic women are being tested routinely. In fact, the PHAC recommends routine testing by the family doctor of all sexually active women under age 25. However, research in Ontario indicates that only a minority of physicians do any sexual health assessment and that physicians infrequently suggest chlamydia testing (Hardwick et al., 2007). Further, far fewer men than women are screened, even though it is important to screen both men and women if screening is to be effective at reducing the prevalence of chlamydia (McKay, 2006a).

In an innovative program in rural Nova Scotia, self-test screen kits were made available in a private setting to all high-school girls. Girls did not have to first see a nurse for counselling to get a kit (Langille et al., 2008). The girls collected vaginal swabs themselves, and the swabs were subjected to laboratory tests with no names attached. Of the 163 girls who had vaginal intercourse at least once during the study period, only 27 used the self-help kit. Two of the tests were positive, which would have gone undetected if the girls had not been screened. Of the girls who did use the kit, the most common reason for screening was wanting the reassurance of a negative test; few girls said that they were concerned about infection. Even though most students knew that chlamydia is often asymptomatic, the most common reasons for not getting screened was not having any symptoms. Similarly, researchers in Ontario piloted a urine drop-off

testing kit for gonorrhea and chlamydia at two bath-houses, studying men who have sex with men (O'Byrne & Dias, 2008). Anonymous self-testing is a promising method for screening individuals who would not see a medical professional for testing, perhaps because of perceived STI-related stigma. On an individual level, the best method of prevention is the consistent use of a condom.

HPV

HPV stands for *human papillomavirus*. There are more than 40 different types of HPV that are sexually transmitted (Winer & Koutskley, 2008). Some types (6 and 11) cause genital warts and are called low risk because they do not cause cancer; other types cause cervical cancer and are called high risk. Some types have no symptoms at all. In fact, the majority of people infected with HPV are asymptomatic. But a person without symptoms can still transmit the virus.

Infection with HPV is widespread. HPV is not a reportable disease and thus there are no national Canadian data. However, Health Canada estimates that in the pre-vaccine era between 20 and 33 percent of women had HPV. Not all of these, though, were the cancer-causing types. Again, in the pre-vaccine era, between 11 and 25 percent of women had the cancer-causing types of HPV. Two studies tested women having routine Pap tests in Newfoundland and Labrador and Ontario (Ratnam et al., 2000; Sellors et al., 2000). They found that the highest rate of HPV was among women under 25: 16 percent of the young Newfoundland and Labrador women and 24 percent of the young Ontario women had HPV infections. There are no good estimates of the prevalence of HPV in men, although it is likely lower than in women (PHAC, 2012c). The disease is highly infectious, and although condoms reduce the risk of infection, they do not eliminate it. HPV is transmitted through skin-to-skin contact, most often from contact with the penis, scrotum, vagina, vulva, or anus of the infected person. Research suggests that the rate has gone down significantly in the vaccine era, despite the fact that many people are not getting vaccinated. Just think what we could do if everyone was vaccinated!

Genital warts are cauliflower-like warts appearing on the genitals (Figure 8.2), usually around the urethral opening of the penis, the shaft of the penis, or the scrotum in the male, and on the vulva, the walls of the vagina, or the cervix in the female; warts may also occur on the anus. Typically they appear three to eight months after intercourse with an infected person. A Canadian

> **pelvic inflammatory disease (PID):** An infection and inflammation of the pelvic organs, such as the fallopian tubes and the uterus, in women.
> **HPV:** Human papillomavirus, the organism that causes genital warts.
> **genital warts:** A sexually transmitted infection causing warts on the genitals and cervical cancer.

---

[2] Reiter's syndrome involves the following symptoms: urethritis, eye inflammations, and arthritis.

Figure 8.2 Genital warts *(a)* on the penis and *(b)* on the vulva.

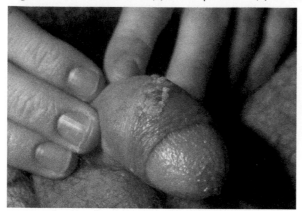

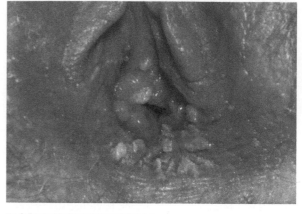

(a) © Dr. P. Marazzi/Science Source

(b) © Bart's Medical Libarary/Phototake

study showed that experiencing genital warts had a negative impact on quality of life, including completing usual activities, experiencing pain and discomfort, experiencing anxiety and depression, creating a poor self-image, and reducing sexual activity (Drolet et al., 2011).

Research shows that oral sex can transmit HPV. Individuals infected this way have an increased rate of oral cancers—that is, cancer of the mouth or throat (D'Souza et al., 2007). HPV causes almost all cases of cervical cancer. HPV 16 and 18 account for 70 percent of the cases of cervical cancer (Dailard, 2006). HPV infection is also associated with cancer of the penis and anus, although many Canadian men who have sex with men are not aware of this (Moores et al., 2015).

It is also true that about 90 percent of HPV infections are asymptomatic and go away by themselves within two years (CDC, 2014a). Does this mean there's no need for vaccination of safer sex practices? Of course not, because you don't want to be in the 10 percent who continue to harbour the virus, transmit it to others, or get warts or cervical or other cancers.

Diagnosis

Diagnosis can sometimes be made simply by inspecting the warts, because their appearance is distinctive. However, some strains of warts are flat and less obvious. Also, the warts may grow inside the vagina and may not be detected there. However, HPV is a silent infection because many individuals with HPV show no obvious signs of infection. Thus, for many women the first indication of HPV is abnormal cells on a Pap test. Men are not routinely tested for HPV.

Treatment

Several treatments for genital warts are available. Chemicals such as podophyllin (Podofilm) or bichloroacetic acid (BCA) can be applied directly to the warts.

Typically, these treatments have to be repeated several times, and the warts then fall off. With cryotherapy (often using liquid nitrogen), the warts are frozen off; again, it is typically necessary to apply more than one treatment. Drugs such as Podofilox cream can be applied by the patient. In many cases, HPV symptoms go away on their own, but others persist for long periods.

Vaccine

As noted, almost all cases of cervical cancer are linked to HPV infection. Anal cancer, although relatively rare, is also linked to HPV infection (Moores et al., 2015). Therefore, a vaccine against HPV would prevent most cases of cervical cancer. Two such vaccines are now available in Canada, Gardasil and Cervarix, and must be administered in three shots over six months. The goal is to administer it to youth around ages 11 to 12 (or as early as 9 years old), before they have engaged in sexual activity, as well as to women up to the age of 25 who have not had an HPV infection or abnormalities on their Pap tests. The vaccine is also approved for boys and young men for whom it prevents penile and anal cancers. Gardasil protects against HPV types 16 and 18 that between them cause 70 percent of cervical cancers, and against two other HPV types that cause most cases of genital warts. Cervarix also protects against types 16 and 18. Randomized controlled trials show the vaccine to be highly (95 percent) effective in stopping infection with these strains of HPV (Winer & Koutsky, 2008). A newer Gardasil vaccine protects against four cancer-causing types of HPV.

The federal government has provided funding to the provinces and territories to establish HPV immunization programs. All Canadian provinces and Yukon now have publicly funded school-based programs in place to administer the vaccine to girls in Grades 6, 7, or 8 with parental consent. The vaccine is free. However, it is not without controversy. Some parents argue that it will encourage young people to engage in sexual activity or that it has not been tested sufficiently to use on youth. Advocates for administering the vaccine point out the potential health benefits and that vaccines have been around for a long time and have been shown to be safe. They argue that the decision to make Gardasil available is no different from the decision to introduce other new vaccines (e.g., a vaccine for chicken pox was recently made available), yet there has been no controversy about those vaccines. An Ontario study demonstrated that parents who were less knowledgeable about the vaccine were less likely to consent to their daughter receiving it (Okoronkwo et al., 2012). In keeping with the National Advisory Committee on Immunization, we recommend that all youth be given the HPV vaccine in order to protect them against cancer.

Genital Herpes

Genital herpes is a disease of the genital organs caused by the herpes simplex virus, **HSV**. Genital herpes is transmitted by sexual intercourse and by oral–genital sex. Two strains of HSV are circulating: HSV-1 and HSV-2. In simpler times, HSV-2 caused genital herpes and HSV-1 caused cold sores around the mouth. Today, however, there is more crossing over. Genital herpes, then, can be caused by either HSV-1 or HSV-2.

The Canadian Health Measures Survey tested a representative Canadian sample between the ages of 14 and 59 for HSV-2 antibodies between 2009 and 2011. They found that 13.6 percent of the sample were infected (Rotermann et al., 2013), about 2.9 million Canadians. The rate was higher in women (16 percent) than in men (11 percent). The rate increased with age. Only 6 percent of individuals who tested positive for HSV-2 were aware that they had the infection. That is, the great majority of people with HSV are asymptomatic and are not aware that they are infected. These persons transmit the disease to others unknowingly.

Symptoms

The symptoms of genital herpes caused by HSV-2 are small, painful bumps or blisters on the genitals. Typically they appear within two to three weeks of infection. In women, they are usually found on the vaginal lips; in men, they usually occur on the penis (Figure 8.3). They may be found around the anus if the person has had anal intercourse. The blisters burst and can be quite painful. Fever, painful urination, and headaches may occur. The blisters heal on their own in about three weeks in the first episode of infection. The virus continues to live in the body, however. It may remain dormant for the rest of the person's life. But the symptoms may recur unpredictably, so that the person repeatedly undergoes 7- to 14-day periods of sores. HSV-1 infection tends to be less severe.

People with herpes are most infectious when they are having an active outbreak. However, people are infectious even when there is no outbreak or if they have never been symptomatic. Therefore, there is no completely safe period.

> **Is there a cure for herpes?**

Treatment

Unfortunately, no known drug kills the virus; that is, there is no cure. Researchers are pursuing two solutions: drugs that would treat symptoms in someone who is already infected, and vaccinations that would prevent herpes. The drug acyclovir (Zovirax) prevents or reduces the recurring symptoms, although it does not actually cure the disease.

Valacyclovir (Valtrex) and famciclovir (Famvir) are newer drugs that are even more effective at shortening outbreaks and suppressing recurrences (Corey & Wald, 2008). They, as well as acyclovir, also reduce rates of transmission from an infected partner to an uninfected one. Scientists are actively working to create a method for immunization against herpes (Corey & Wald, 2008).

> **genital herpes (HER-pees):** A sexually transmitted infection, the symptoms of which are small, painful bumps or blisters on the genitals. **HSV:** The herpes simplex virus.

Figure 8.3 *(a)* Herpes blisters on the penis. *(b)* Herpes infection of the vulva.

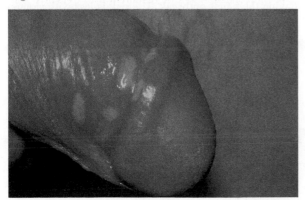

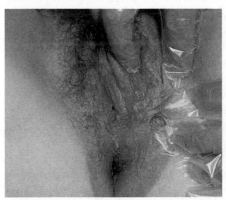

(a) © Biophoto Associates/Science Source

(b) © Biophoto Associates/Science Source

First Person

Coping with Herpes

It's cliché to say, but I think at some point we all think it: "I just didn't think it could happen to me." I am an intelligent, responsible young adult living in Atlantic Canada while I complete my undergraduate degree. And I have herpes.

I had been seeing my partner exclusively for some time. We were honest and open with each other and cared very much for one another. So after some discussion, we decided to stop using condoms during sex. We both had had a number of previous partners and had both engaged in unprotected sex before. However, we also had both been tested, neither of us had symptoms, and we trusted each other.

One morning, after a particularly wonderful night together, I woke up with a small sore on my genitals. I looked at it carefully. It looked somewhat like an ingrown hair, which I had had before, but it was also somehow different. I was worried because I instantly realized it could be something sexually transmitted. I found myself thinking of my partner. I needed to tell her. I also found my thoughts drifting to her sexual history. Did I get this from her or had I given this to her? What was I going to say? How would she react? I was more scared than I thought possible about the situation.

I waited until we were alone. There wasn't really an easy way to say what I had to say. So I turned to her and just spit it out: "I have a sore." She looked a little shocked. She turned and said to me that she had one too. She had also been waiting to say something in private. We spent the next hour talking about it; what it looked like, what we knew about herpes and HPV, and what we were going to do. It seemed odd that both of us had one sore, and had gotten it at the same time. But the coincidence both relieved and worried us. We took turns that day calming each other down. I was worried but more than that, I was annoyed and I knew she was too. How could two careful people let this happen to them? We knew that if it was going to be an STI there was nothing we could do to change it. We also knew that we wouldn't know anything for sure until we saw a doctor. I called and made an appointment with my doctor right away.

As time went by, I started to get more signs that something was wrong. I had a burning sensation when I urinated which seemed to subside if I drank a lot of water. My urethral opening sometimes burned, and I felt sore in my groin area. The doctor sent me for all kinds of tests; urine tests, blood tests, and swabbed the sore. She told me that if the tests came back negative, I'd be sent to a different clinic for more tests.

The first round of tests came back negative. By the time my partner got in for tests, her sore had healed, and all her

Long-Term Consequences

Either men or women with recurrent herpes may develop complications, such as meningitis or narrowing of the urethra caused by scarring, leading to difficulties with urination. However, such complications do not affect the majority of those with herpes. There are two more serious long-term consequences. One is that having a herpes infection increases the risk of becoming infected with HIV, probably because the open blisters during an outbreak make it easy for HIV to enter the body. Therefore, people who have herpes should be especially careful to use safer sex practices.

The other serious risk involves the transfer of the virus from mother to infant in childbirth, which in some cases leads to serious illness or death in the baby (Brown et al., 2005). The risk of transmission to the infant is highest in women who have recently been infected and are having their first outbreak. The risk is less with women who have had the disease longer and is low if the woman is not having an outbreak. C-sections are therefore usually performed on women with an outbreak, but vaginal delivery is possible if there is not an outbreak.

Psychological Aspects: Coping with Herpes

The psychological consequences of herpes need to be taken as seriously as the medical consequences (see First Person). The range of psychological responses is enormous. At one end of the spectrum are persons with

other tests came back negative. For over a month, we didn't know what had happened and assumed that the sores were ingrown hairs. The anxiety I felt at the onset slowly subsided. Then one day my doctor called. The swab tests had finally come back and I needed to go in for an appointment. The swab had come back positive for herpes. I couldn't believe it. Yet, I could. How did I get this? I had read a lot online, trying to sort out my symptoms and realized there was a chance I had herpes. Still, how did I get this? Again, I wondered whether I got it from my partner. If not, did I give it to her? And if not, where did I get it? I was angry; angry that the tests had taken so long, angry that they had come back positive, angry that my partner didn't have the same news, but most of all angry at myself for thinking I was okay to not use condoms in the first place. I called my partner as soon as I left the doctor's office and told her what I found out. I told her she needed to get tested. But she didn't have any sores. There was nothing she could do.

A short time later I had another outbreak. It was just like the first one, so I knew what it was. I was frustrated and upset. How could I let this happen to me? I had been cautious in so many ways. I found myself thinking of all kind of things, my future sex life, having these sores pop up whenever they wanted, knowing that I would always have to be extra careful. I was sad and worried about future partners; when and how would I let them know, how will they react, would I even be able to tell them. I spent a lot of time reading information on herpes. I

thought that if I knew more I might feel better. My partner and I talked about it a lot. She was sympathetic and supportive, letting me know I had every right to be frustrated. And she apologized for the fact that we were dealing with this.

As I read about herpes, I learned that I could re-infect myself in other areas, and I could infect or re-infect my sexual partner. I had to be very careful when I had an outbreak. But I also had to be careful at other times. I read about learning to feel changes in my body, and how keeping my stress level down and living a healthy, active life could help prevent breakouts. I also read about medications that could treat symptoms, help prevent outbreaks, and help sores heal faster. After some consideration, I decided the cost of the medication was worth getting rid of my current sore and controlling future outbreaks.

For now, I've come to terms with having herpes. I still get frustrated with myself sometimes but I'm not devastated by it. The reality is that almost one in four people in Canada have it. I am cautious when I have signs of sores, making sure to use barriers for any sexual activity, and washing my hands well if they come in contact with the sore. Now, I use medications to help the sore heal and prevent future outbreaks.

Source: As told to Krystelle Shaughnessy.

asymptomatic herpes, who are not aware that they have the disease and are happily sexually active—and at the same time possibly unknowingly spreading the disease to others. At the other end of the spectrum are persons who experience frequent, severe, painful recurrences. These difficulties are aggravated by the fact that outbreaks are often unpredictable, and current scientific evidence indicates that people are at least somewhat infectious even when they are not having an active outbreak. The impact of having herpes is also exacerbated by the fact that many people with herpes feel stigmatized because of their disease and believe that they should abstain from sex to avoid infecting others (Nack, 2008; Ross, 2008). Infections on the genitals are more likely to be stigmatized than a similar infection elsewhere on the body, such

as a cold sore (which is also caused by the herpes virus) precisely because they are sexually transmitted. New Brunswick researchers found that individuals who experienced more self-stigma and public stigma experienced poorer sexual well-being (Foster & Byers, 2016). On the other hand, the researchers found that most people with herpes and other STIs are able to cope, and most experience good sexual well-being.

Psychologists are exploring therapies for herpes patients. One highly effective treatment program consists of a combination of information on herpes, relaxation training, instruction in stress management, and instruction in an imagery technique in which the patient imagines that the genitals are free of lesions and that he or she is highly resistant to the virus (Longo et al., 1988).

HIV Infection and AIDS

In 1981 a physician in Los Angeles reported a mysterious and frightening new disease identified in several gay men. The first AIDS case in Canada was reported in February 1982. Within two years, the number of cases had escalated sharply. The disease was named **AIDS**, an acronym for acquired immune deficiency syndrome.

A major breakthrough came in 1984 with the identification of the virus causing AIDS. The virus is called **HIV**, for human immunodeficiency virus. Another strain of the virus, HIV-2, has been identified; it is found almost exclusively in Africa. HIV-1 accounts for almost all infections in North America.

As the name implies, HIV destroys the body's natural system of immunity to diseases. Once HIV has damaged an individual's immune system, opportunistic diseases may take over. They can kill.

An Epidemic?

In 2015, approximately 59 600 Canadians had received a positive test result and were living with HIV. This included about 2500 people newly diagnosed in 2014. However, these statistics represent only the tip of the iceberg, for they do not count persons who are infected with HIV but have never been tested for it or people who had died of AIDS. The PHAC estimates that almost 15 800 people are infected with HIV and don't know it. Experts estimate that 33 million persons worldwide are infected with HIV, although the majority of them show no symptoms yet and are unaware that they are infected (Duerr et al., 2008).

Worldwide about 2.1 million people became newly infected with HIV in 2015, and 36.7 million people were living with HIV (UNAIDS, 2016). The hardest-hit part of the world is sub-Saharan Africa, accounting for 72 percent of all new HIV infections. According to UNAIDS, an agency of the United Nations, 1.4 million people in sub-Saharan Africa became newly infected with HIV in 2015 alone. This brought the total number of adults and children living with HIV/AIDS in this region to 25.5 million. In contrast, approximately 1.5 million people in Eastern Europe and Central Asia, 230 000 people in the Middle East and North Africa, 2.0 million people in Latin America and the Caribbean, 5.1 million people in Asia and the Pacific, and 2.4 million people in Europe and North America were living with HIV/AIDS in 2015. Thus, the terms *global epidemic* and *pandemic* (a widespread epidemic) have been used, with reason. The somewhat encouraging news is that although the number of people with HIV worldwide continues to grow, the number of new infections each year has been decreasing. This suggests that HIV prevention efforts are working in at least some countries. Also, more people have access to antiretroviral therapy, although still only 46 percent of people with HIV had access to treatment. As a result, AIDS-related deaths have fallen dramatically.

Transmission

When people speak of HIV being transmitted by an exchange of body fluids, the body fluids they are referring to are semen and blood and possibly secretions of the cervix and vagina. HIV is spread in four ways: (1) by sexual intercourse (either penis-in-vagina intercourse or anal intercourse);[3] (2) by contaminated blood (a risk for people who receive a blood transfusion if the blood has not been screened); (3) by contaminated hypodermic needles (a risk for those who inject drugs, or health care workers who receive accidental sticks); and (4) from an infected woman to her baby during pregnancy or childbirth or through her breast milk.

Supporting these assertions, statistics indicate that Canadians who were diagnosed with HIV/AIDS in 2014 are primarily from the following exposure categories: (1) men who have sex with men (54 percent); (2) people who inject drugs (13 percent); (3) heterosexuals who have had sexual contact with an infected person (19 percent); and (4) heterosexuals that come from an HIV-endemic country (14 percent). About 21 percent were under the age of 30, and 32 percent were between 30 and 40, indicating that they were likely exposed to HIV in their early 20s. Worldwide, 70 percent of the cases result from heterosexual transmission.

How great is your risk of becoming infected with HIV? In essence, it depends on what your sexual practices are (leaving aside the issues of injection drug use, which are beyond the scope of this book) (Varghese et al., 2002). *The sexual behaviour most likely to spread HIV is anal intercourse, and the receiving partner is most at risk.* This is true for both men and women, regardless of sexual orientation. Penile–vaginal intercourse without a condom is a high-risk activity for contracting HIV as well. Whether you are gay or straight, statistically *the greater your number of sexual partners, the greater your risk of getting infected with HIV.* You may have heard the saying "six degrees of separation." It turns out that it is true for HIV as well. One study found that most people are just a few degrees of sexual separation from someone who is HIV-infected

AIDS (acquired immune deficiency syndrome): A sexually transmitted disease that destroys the body's natural immunity to infection so that the person is susceptible to and may die from another disease, such as pneumonia or cancer.
HIV: Human immunodeficiency virus, the virus that causes AIDS.

---

[3] There is also a chance that oral–genital sex can spread AIDS, particularly if there is ejaculation by an infected person into the mouth.

(Liljeros et al., 2001). The greater your number of partners, the greater your chances of connecting with that HIV-positive person. However, some people have contracted HIV from their first sexual partner. The risk varies considerably depending on whom you have sex with and whether you use a condom or a dental dam. Penile–vaginal or anal intercourse is riskier if it is with a person who is infected with HIV (seropositive), who has engaged in high-risk behaviours (unprotected anal or vaginal sex, injection drug use), who is hemophiliac, or who is from a country where there is a high rate of HIV infection, or if condoms are not used.

Table 8.1 summarizes the STI infection risk when condoms are not used, broken down by type of activity. Perhaps the risk is lower than you thought for some of these STIs—researchers in Quebec have shown that a large majority of university students and health care providers are not aware of the transmissibility of HIV and chlamydia (Knäuper & Kornik, 2004; Rosen et al., 2005). However, even if the chance of contracting an STI from one unprotected sexual encounter is low, the chances add up with each additional unprotected sexual encounter. This is called the **cumulative risk**. Unfortunately, people tend to underestimate their cumulative risk of contracting an STI, particularly if the partner is appealing to them (Knäuper et al., 2005).

A study of heterosexual transmission of HIV among 415 Ugandan couples in which one partner was infected at the beginning and one was not indicated that 22 percent of the uninfected became infected over a two-year period (Quinn et al., 2000). The male-to-female transmission rates and female-to-male rates were about equal. The higher the viral count in the infected person, the greater the rate of transmission. Interestingly, none of the circumcised men became infected. In fact, based on the results of three studies, the World Health Organization concluded that male circumcision reduces the risk of HIV transmission by as much as 60 percent. Importantly, condoms are 80 to 95 percent effective in protecting against HIV transmission during heterosexual intercourse if used consistently (Steiner et al., 2008). This isn't perfect protection, but it's darned good, and far better than no protection.

The Virus

HIV is one of a group of retroviruses. Retroviruses reproduce only in living cells of the host species, in this case humans. They invade a host cell, and each time the host cell divides, copies of the virus are produced along with more host

cumulative risk: The likelihood of contracting an STI after repeated unprotected exposure.

| **Table 8.1** | Sexually Transmitted Infection Risk Chart When Condoms Are Not Used |

STI	Anal Sex	Vaginal Sex	Giving Oral Sex	Getting Oral Sex	Deep (French) Kissing	Mutual Masturbation (without exchanging body fluids)	Hugging, Dry Kissing, Massage, Self-Masturbation
Chlamydia	SR	HR	SR	NR	NR	NR	NR
Genital warts/ HPV	HR	HR	SR (but low)	SR (but low)		SR	NR
Gonorrhea	HR	HR	HR	SR	SR	NR	NR
Hepatitis B	HR	HR	HR	HR	SR	NR	NR
Herpes	HR	HR	HR	HR	SR	SR	NR (except for kissing if you come into contact with infected area)
HIV/AIDS	HR	HR	SR (but low)	TR	TR	NR	NR
Pubic lice	HR	HR	SR	SR	NR	SR	NR (Except for massage)
Syphilis	HR	HR	HR	SR	SR	NR	NR
Vaginitis (yeast infection, bacterial vaginosis, trichomoniasis	NA	HR	NA	NR	NA	NR	NR

HR = high risk; NR = no risk; SR = some risk; TR = theoretical risk.

Note: Using condoms for anal and vaginal sex and condoms and dental dams for oral sex reduce but do not completely eliminate the risk of contracting an STI. Theoretical risk means that in theory a person could contract a given STI through a particular activity but no one has been reported as contracting the STI through that activity. Theoretical risk activities are considered low risk.

Source: PHAC (Public Health Agency of Canada). (2007). Sexually transmitted infections. Retrieved from www.publichealth.gc.ca/sti.

cells, each containing the genetic code of the virus (see Figure 8.4 for more detail on the biology of HIV). Current research is aimed at finding drugs that will prevent the virus from infecting new cells. At least two strains of HIV are found in North America, HIV-1 and HIV-2, and there are several subgroups of HIV-1 that differ genetically (Harrington & Swanstrom, 2008).

HIV specifically invades a group of white blood cells (lymphocytes) called CD4+ T-lymphocytes. We'll just call them T cells. These cells are critical to the body's immune response in fighting off infections. When HIV reproduces, it destroys the infected T cell. Eventually the HIV-positive person's number of T cells is so reduced that infections cannot be fought off.

Scientists have pressed hard to understand the functioning of HIV. They have identified two *coreceptors* for HIV, CCR5 and CXCR4, which allow HIV to enter T cells (Harrington & Swanstrom, 2008). CCR5 seems to be the important coreceptor in the early stages of the disease and CXCR4 in the later stages. This discovery may lead to advances in treatment if drugs can be used that block these coreceptors.

The Disease

The *Canadian Guidelines on Sexually Transmitted Infections* define four stages of HIV infection (PHAC, 2013):

1. *Primary/acute infection.* This stage is from the initial infection to development of antibodies to it over the next two to four weeks. Most (90 percent) people have some symptoms that are often mild and not specific to HIV, such as a fever, headache, or sore throat. These people may be highly infectious.

2. *Chronic asymptomatic infection.* During this stage, the person is infected with the virus and the virus

Figure 8.4   During infection, the AIDS virus binds to and injects its cone-shaped core into cells of the human immune system. It next uses reverse transcriptase to copy its RNA genome into double-stranded DNA molecules in the cytoplasm of the host cell. The double helixes then travel to the nucleus where another enzyme inserts them into a host chromosome. Once integrated into a host-cell chromosome, the viral genome can do one of two things. It can commandeer the host cell's protein synthesis machinery to make hundreds of new viral particles that bud off from the parent cell, taking with them part of the cell membrane and sometimes resulting in the cell host's death. Alternately, it can lie latent inside the host chromosome, which then copies and transmits the viral genome to two new cells with each cell division.

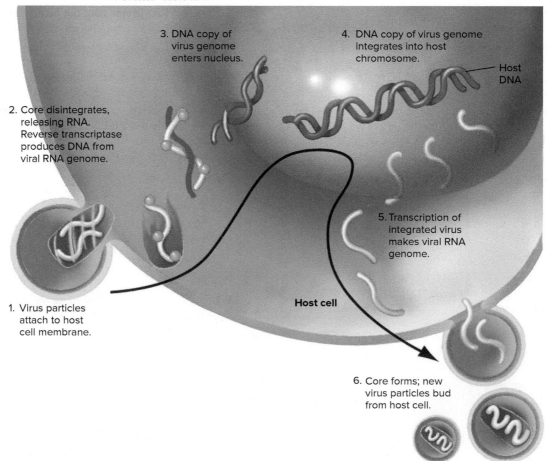

is replicating, but the person shows no symptoms. However, the T4 cell count is dropping. People may develop symptoms that are not immediately life-threatening, such as swollen lymph glands, fever, diarrhea, persistent yeast infections in the throat or vagina, shingles, fatigue, abnormal cells in the cervix, and night sweats. These asymptomatic carriers can infect other persons.

3. *Chronic symptomatic HIV infection.* During this stage, the virus has greatly reduced the T4 cell count so that the person's immune system is not able to fight off infections. Many infected persons go on to develop symptoms that are not immediately life-threatening: fever, chronic diarrhea, unexplained weight loss, fatigue, chronic yeast infections in the throat or vagina, shingles, or abnormal or cancerous cells in the cervix.

4. *AIDS-defining conditions.* The diagnosis of AIDS is applied when the person is affected by life-threatening opportunistic infections (infections that occur only with severely reduced immunity). Examples are *Pneumocystis carinii* pneumonia (a rare form of pneumonia) and Kaposi's sarcoma (a rare form of skin cancer).

Diagnosis

The blood test that detects the presence of antibodies to HIV uses the ELISA (for enzyme-linked immunosorbent assay) technique. It is easy and cheap to perform. It can be used in two important ways:

1. To screen donated blood. All donated blood in Canada is now screened with ELISA, so infections because of transfusions should rarely occur. However, 1200 Canadians were infected with HIV from infected blood between 1978 and 1985, and a tiny risk remains even with ELISA.[4]

2. To help people determine whether they are infected (HIV positive) but are asymptomatic carriers.

The latter use is important because if people suspect that they are infected and find through the blood test that they are, they should either abstain from sexual activity or, at the very least, use a condom consistently, so they do not spread the disease to others. Only by responsible behaviour of this kind can the epidemic be brought under control.

ELISA is a very sensitive test; that is, it is highly accurate in detecting HIV antibodies (it has a very low rate of false negatives, in statistical language). However, it does produce a substantial number of false positives—the test saying HIV antibodies are present when they really are not. Thus, positive results on ELISA should always be confirmed by a second, more specific test.

The other major test, using the Western blot or immunoblot method, provides such confirmation. It is more expensive and difficult to perform, so it is not practical for mass screening of blood, as ELISA is. However, it is highly accurate (false positives are rare), and thus it is very useful in confirming or disconfirming a positive test from ELISA.

It should be emphasized that both tests detect only the presence of HIV antibodies. They do not predict whether the person will develop symptoms or will progress to the AIDS classification.

One of the drawbacks to the ELISA test is that it involves a long waiting period—more than a week—before test results are known. A rapid test has been approved for use in Canada. The test takes 60 seconds and only detects antibodies to HIV-1. This test is intended as a screening test and, as with the ELISA test, must be confirmed by a more accurate test. The Canadian AIDS Society (2011) has raised concerns that if these tests are done in doctors' offices rather than in sexual health centres, they fear that people may not be given enough pretest counselling to give true informed consent or be given sufficient posttest counselling should they receive a positive test result.

There is now a home test kit for HIV available in the United States, but it is not authorized for use in Canada (although they are available on the Internet). It involves a finger prick and then dried blood spots are mailed to a laboratory for anonymous testing. Introduced in 2012, Ora Quick uses a swab from the mouth and gives results in 20 minutes. The Canadian AIDS Society opposes the use of home test kits because some of them are unreliable, individuals using a home test kit would not have access to counselling and support, and individuals should not have to pay for HIV testing.

Treatment

There is not yet any cure for AIDS. However, treatments are available to control the disease. One antiviral drug, **AZT** (azidothymidine, also called zidovudine or ZDV), has been used widely. It has the effect of stopping the virus from multiplying. However, even when it stops replication of the virus, it cannot repair the person's damaged immune system. Unfortunately, AZT has many side effects and cannot be used by some people or can be used only for limited periods. Therefore, there has been a concerted

> **AZT:** A drug used to treat HIV-infected persons; also called ZDV.

---

[4] The risk that ELISA will miss occasional cases of infected blood results from the fact that it detects antibodies to HIV, not HIV itself. It takes six to eight weeks for antibodies to form. Thus, if a person donates blood within a few weeks of becoming infected and before antibodies form, ELISA will not detect the infection. Usually ELISA is positive within three months of infection.

effort to find new drugs that will slow or stop the progression of the disease.

DDI (dideoxyinosine or didanosine) and DDC (dideoxycytidine) are two examples. Like AZT, they slow the progression of the disease by preventing replication of the virus. D4T is yet another, similar drug. Collectively, these drugs are called ART, for antiretroviral therapy.

A major breakthrough came in 1996 with the availability of a new category of drugs, *protease inhibitors* (Kempf et al., 1995). Protease inhibitors attack the viral enzyme protease, which is necessary for HIV to make copies of itself and multiply. Another breakthrough came in 2006 with the introduction of darunavir, a drug that acts on viruses that are resistant to the protease inhibitors (Simon et al., 2006).

Today, patients take a "drug cocktail" of one of the protease inhibitors combined with AZT and one other anti-HIV drug. This combination is called HAART, for highly active antiretroviral therapy. Within a year of the introduction of HAART, thrilling reports emerged that the HIV count had become undetectable in the blood of persons taking the drug cocktail (Cohen, 1997). Some believed that the cure had been found. The number of deaths from AIDS declined in 1996 for the first year since the disease had been identified. Because in Canada most people with HIV/AIDS are now taking the drug cocktail, in 2011 there were only 303 deaths from AIDS, compared with 1764 deaths in 1995 (the year with the highest number of deaths) when the cocktail was not available.

HIV research, unfortunately, is much like a roller-coaster ride, with elated highs followed by plunges to the depths. HIV mutated to drug-resistant forms. And although HIV had become undetectable in the blood of persons treated with the drug cocktail, it was hiding out in T cells and the lymph nodes and in organs, such as the brain, eyes, and testes (Cohen, 1998; Wong et al., 1997). In short, it is not eradicated by the drug cocktail treatment.

Today, HAART is making HIV infection a manageable disease for many persons who are surviving much longer than they would have without this treatment. A person diagnosed with HIV who receives treatment can now expect to live 20 to 30 years. For others, long-term HAART treatment causes serious side effects, such as diabetes-like problems, brittle bones, and heart disease, which means that they have to stop the treatment or switch to another one (Cohen, 2002). Others simply stop responding to the HAART regimen, and there is concern about the emergence of further resistant strains.

On another front, progress is also being made with drugs that prevent the opportunistic infections that strike people living with AIDS. The drug pentamidine, for example, in aerosol form, is a standard treatment to prevent *Pneumocystis carinii* pneumonia.

 ## Women, Children, Ethnic Minorities, and AIDS

In the early days of the HIV/AIDS epidemic, men accounted for most cases in Canada, but the picture has changed considerably and the number of infected women is rapidly rising (Figure 8.5). Whereas between 1985 and 1995 women accounted for only 11 percent of positive HIV tests, in 2014, 23 percent of individuals who tested positive for HIV were women. Most contracted HIV through heterosexual contact. About a third of women

Figure 8.5 AIDS is a multicultural disease. *(a)* A North American man with AIDS. *(b)* An African woman with AIDS.

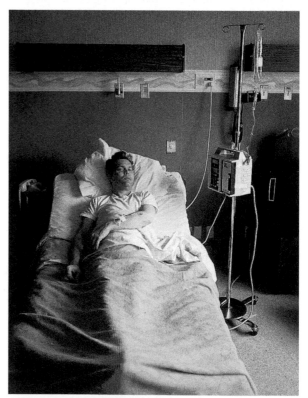

(a) Thomas Bowman/PhotoEdit

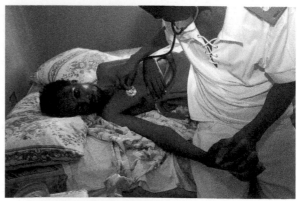

(b) © Alexander Joe/AFP/Getty Images

diagnosed with HIV are under 30 years old. The urgency of addressing the needs of women with HIV infection is thus increasing.

New cases of women with AIDS and HIV infection are most likely to be the result of heterosexual contact (64 percent); injection drug use is the second-largest cause at 25 percent (PHAC, 2009b). Women need far more recognition in AIDS research, and intervention programs tailored to their needs should be developed. Such programs should include sexual assertiveness training, in which women are empowered to insist that their sex partners use condoms. Women also need to be included in clinical trials of drug treatments.

Some of the saddest cases are children with AIDS, known as pediatric AIDS. Babies born to infected mothers are often, but not always, infected. Although since 1984, 607 babies have been infected with HIV from their mothers, the number is dropping dramatically: Only six HIV-infected babies were born in Canada in 2014. One bright spot is the finding that if a woman uses antiretroviral therapy during pregnancy, it can substantially reduce the rate of infection in their babies to less than 2 percent (PHAC, 2010a). AIDS in infants has nearly been eliminated through helping pregnant women know their HIV status and, for those who test positive, the use of antiretroviral therapy, reduction of HIV exposure during delivery, and avoidance of breast-feeding. Therefore, the Canadian Paediatric Society (2013) recommends that all pregnant women be offered confidential HIV testing.

Worldwide, people of colour have borne a disproportionate burden of the cases of AIDS. In Canada in 2014, of reported HIV/AIDS cases for which ethnic identity was recorded, 45 percent identified their ethnic background as white, 20 percent as black, 16 percent as Aboriginal, and 6 percent as Latin American. Although the annual number of reported AIDS cases has declined among all ethnic groups since 1993, the decline has been lowest among minority groups, resulting in an increase in the proportion of people with HIV who are black and Aboriginal. For example, the percentage of newly diagnosed cases of HIV infection among blacks went from 5 percent in 1989 to 16 percent in 2014.

The problem is particularly severe among Indigenous Canadians. In 1989, Indigenous people constituted only 1 percent of reported HIV/AIDS cases, compared with 22 percent in 2014. However, in 2014, 16 percent of new HIV infections in Canada were in Indigenous people, even though Indigenous peoples make up less than 3.8 percent of the population. This means that in 2014 the overall infection rate among Indigenous people was more than 3.5 times the rate in non-Indigenous people. Indigenous people also tend to be infected at an earlier age than non-Indigenous. The percentage of Indigenous women diagnosed with HIV is more than twice as high as in the non-Indigenous population.

A lack of prevention programs and poor access to testing are two factors that contribute to the increasing rate of HIV in the Indigenous population. Some Indigenous people, particularly in remote communities, also lack basic AIDS information. Mobility between inner cities and rural or reserve communities is an important factor in the introduction and spread of HIV to unexposed populations (Health Canada, 2001).

There is an urgent need to develop education and prevention programs for Aboriginal and other culturally distinct Canadian communities (Poon et al., 2011). These programs must be culturally sensitive, with substantial community involvement in program development and implementation to ensure that the programs are culturally appropriate (Health Canada, 1996b, 1996c; Myers et al., 1999). Researchers in Ontario developed and tested one such program. It was designed for Spanish-speaking gay and bisexual newcomers to Canada because of the steep rise in HIV diagnoses among Latino men who have sex with men (Adam et al., 2011). It addressed both HIV prevention and life skills. The results of the initial evaluation demonstrate that the program has the potential to be effective.

L03 Psychological Considerations in HIV/AIDS

Psychological issues for those infected with HIV and for people with AIDS are profound. There are some analogies to people who receive a diagnosis of an incurable cancer, for AIDS is—at least at present—incurable. Many patients experience the typical reactions for such situations, including a denial of the reality, followed by anger, depression, or both. However, the analogy to cancer patients is not perfect, for AIDS is a socially stigmatized disease in a way that cancer is not. Thus, the revelation that one has AIDS must often be accompanied by the announcement that one is gay or drug-addicted or engaged in extra-dyadic sex (that is, sex outside the relationship). It may make it more difficult for the person to fill the human need for emotional and physical intimacy. Also, as the person becomes sicker, he or she is unlikely to be able to hold a job, and financial worries become an additional strain.

Research in Ontario has shown that individuals living with HIV also experience stigmatization from the health care system (Wagner et al., 2016). Overt acts of discrimination were less common than were the less overt stigmatization. Such experiences increase the probability that people living with HIV will receive sub-optimal care and/or be less likely to seek care.

There is a great need to be sensitive to the psychological needs of people living with HIV/AIDS. Most cities have support groups for people living with HIV/AIDS patients and their families. Social and psychological support from others is essential as people weather this crisis (Pakenham et al., 1994). Research with gay men in Alberta has shown that after sometimes years of struggle with their diagnosis, most come to view their lives more positively (Harris & Alderson, 2006).

Research in Ontario sheds light on the experiences with sexual intimacy of people living with HIV or AIDS (Maticka-Tyndale et al., 2002). The researchers conducted in-depth interviews with 31 men and 4 women who were taking combination antiviral therapies. (See Gurevich et al., 2007, for the impact of an HIV diagnosis on the sexual well-being of Canadian women.) Individuals who were living with a partner described a drop in sexual interest soon after diagnosis. For some participants sexual desire returned over time; for others it did not. According to one woman:

> Toward the very beginning, it [sex] was almost nonexistent. We were afraid to. Now we're getting back to our regular sexual relationship—protected sex and it's much better than in the beginning. (Maticka-Tyndale et al., 2002, p. 35)

Some single individuals worried about finding an accepting partner. Others preferred to remain single, often because of concerns about disclosing their HIV-positive status. As one man said:

> I just don't want to bother. . . . You don't realize what it's like to meet someone and find them attractive physically and all and then have to one day look at them and say, "By the way, I'm HIV-positive." (Maticka-Tyndale et al., 2002, p. 37)

Finally, participants discussed the negative impact of both the symptoms of HIV and the side effects of therapies on sexual intimacy. Nonetheless, sexuality continues to be an important part of the lives of many individuals living with HIV. Thus, it is important that HIV-prevention efforts and research are directed at ensuring that HIV-positive individuals do not infect their partners (Fisher et al., 2009).

Psychological treatments can be helpful for people living with HIV in several ways (Heckman et al., 2011; Lovejoy & Heckman, 2014). Interventions such as motivational interviewing can improve people's adherence to the drug treatment regimen that is necessary to keep AIDS at bay. Even with ART, HIV-infected people who are depressed have worse medical outcomes than do those are infected but are not depressed (Hartzell et al., 2008). Psychotherapy can reduced depression in infected persons, improving their quality of life and their medical outcomes, as well as increasing their adherence to ART (Sin & DiMatteo, 2014). Therapy also needs to focus on improving sexual satisfaction among persons living with HIV without increasing risk of transmission, as this is an important aspect of quality of life (Maticka-Tyndale et al., 2002).

Why isn't there a vaccine against HIV?

In Chapter 16 we discuss the phenomenon of *posttraumatic growth* following sexual assault. Between 60 and 80 percent of people living with HIV infection report positive psychological growth following diagnosis; people who experience posttraumatic growth and are optimistic tend to have higher T-cell counts, helping them to fight disease progression (Milam, 2006).

Recent Progress in HIV/AIDS Research

As this discussion makes clear, much more research on HIV/AIDS is needed. We need better treatments to control this disease, we need a cure for it, and we need a vaccine against it. Those are pretty tall orders, and it is unlikely that any of them will appear in the next few years.

Vaccine

Researchers have been working hard to develop a vaccine against HIV, but the job has turned out to be much more difficult than expected (Duerr et al., 2008; Shattock et al., 2011). Researchers in Ontario have developed one vaccine based on genetically modified dead whole virus, and it has been approved for clinical trials. The problem is that HIV has many forms, and to make matters worse, it mutates rapidly and recombines, creating even more forms. In effect, the virus doesn't hold still long enough for a vaccine to take effective aim at it.

One strategy in developing a vaccine is to first develop a vaccine that works with monkeys, which can be infected by an analogue to HIV called SIV (simian immunodeficiency virus). Progress toward developing vaccines that protect monkeys from infection with SIV has been slow but steady (Hessell & Haigwood, 2015).

Two other strategies involve developing a vaccine that stimulates the body to form resistance (i.e., antibodies) to HIV, or a vaccine that acts at the cellular level by stimulating the production of specialized T cells that are toxic to HIV (Korber & Gnanakaram, 2011; Luzuriaga et al., 2006). Another possibility is a vaccine that combines both. Yet another possibility is to develop a vaccine to be administered to infants that would prevent transmission through breast milk, as well as later infection when they become sexually active. Several of these vaccines have moved into clinical trials with humans and one partially effective vaccine has been identified (Cohen, 2009; Graham, 2009; Haynes et al., 2012).

Treatment as Prevention

Science magazine called it the scientific breakthrough of the year for 2011. Cohen and his colleagues (2011) conducted a large-scale clinical trial in several African nations, Brazil, India, Thailand, and the United States. They studied discordant heterosexual couples—that is, one member of the couple was infected with HIV and the other one wasn't. Those in the treatment group started

ART (antiretroviral treatment) immediately (even though their T-cell count had fallen only to between 350 and 550), whereas those in the control group did not (their treatment was delayed). Of those partners who became infected during the study period, only one was in the treatment group and all others were in the control group. That is, the ART treatment for the infected person prevented transmission to the sexual partner, with only one exception. Biologically, the result makes sense, because ART reduces the amount of HIV in the infected person's body, but until this trial, no one had an idea that it could be so effective in preventing transmission.

Preexposure Prophylaxis

Preexposure prophylaxis (prophylaxis means prevention) refers to giving an uninfected person antiretrovirals so that they *don't* become infected. This has been a major new prevention strategy for people who are in high-risk situations, such as an HIV-negative person whose partner is HIV-positive. In a clinical trial, preexposure prophylaxis was effective as long as the person took a pill every day or at least four times per week (Grant et al., 2014).

Research on Nonprogressors

Some specific groups of people are being studied for clues to breakthroughs in the war against AIDS. One such group is *nonprogressors* (Duerr et al., 2008). Approximately 5 percent of HIV-infected people go for ten years or more without symptoms and with no deterioration of their immune system. Their T-cell count remains higher than 500. Nonprogressors turn out to have less HIV in their bodies, even though they have been infected for over a decade. Why? One possibility is that these people have unusually strong immune systems that have essentially managed to contain the virus. Scientists are investigating the mechanism that might account for the strong immune reaction.

Killer T Cells and Chemokines

Certain lymphocytes (CD8+ T cells) battle HIV in the body. They do so by secreting chemokines (which are molecules) (Chaterjee et al., 2012). The chemokines can bind to the coreceptor CCR5, blocking HIV from entering cells. Scientists hope that this discovery may lead to improved treatments for HIV-infected persons and possibly to vaccines that boost the level of chemokines and therefore boost the body's resistance to HIV infection.

Genetic Resistance

Scientists have discovered a mutation of a gene, and the mutation creates strong resistance to HIV infection (Cohen, 2011a; Novembre et al., 2005). The gene is called CCR5 because it is the gene for the CCR5 receptor that, as discussed earlier, allows HIV to enter cells. The mutation occurred some time in history as humans spread out of Africa. The evidence indicates that the mutation was strongly selected for during the bubonic plague or smallpox plagues that occurred in Europe, and the mutation is much more common there than in other parts of the world. People with two copies of the mutation (homozygotes) are resistant to infection, whereas people with one copy (heterozygotes) may become infected but show much slower disease progression.

Microbicides

Microbicides are substances, usually in ointment form, that kill microbes such as HIV. These ointments could be put into the vagina or anus or spread on the penis to battle HIV transmission. The old standby nonoxynol-9 was thought to be effective in killing HIV some years ago, but today we know that it is not only ineffective but actually makes women more vulnerable to infection by irritating the lining of the vagina. Much effort is now going into developing effective microbicides that will attack HIV as well as other sexually transmitted viruses. Tenofovir gel (tenofovir is an antiretroviral drug) used vaginally by women reduced infection rates by 39 percent (Abdool Karim et al., 2010; Nicol, 2015). That isn't perfect, but it's progress.

Behavioural Prevention

In the last analysis, prevention is better than cure. Until we have a highly effective vaccine, our best hope is interventions that aim to change people's behaviour, because it is behaviour (sexual activity, injection drug use) that spreads HIV. Many successful interventions have been designed that increase condom use, communication with the partner, and other behaviours that help to prevent infection (e.g., Hidalgo et al., 2015).

Gonorrhea

Historical records indicate that **gonorrhea** (*the clap, the drip*) is the oldest of the sexual diseases. Its symptoms are described in the Old Testament, in Leviticus 15 (about 3500 years ago). The Greek physician Hippocrates, some 2400 years ago, believed that gonorrhea resulted from "excessive indulgence in the pleasures of Venus," the goddess of love (hence the term "venereal" disease). Albert Neisser identified the bacterium that causes it, the gonococcus *Neisseria gonorrhoeae*, in 1879.

Gonorrhea has always been a particular problem in wartime, when it spreads rapidly among the soldiers and the prostitutes they patronize. In the twentieth

preexposure prophylaxis: The use of antiretroviral drugs to prevent infection in people who are HIV negative and are in a high-risk category.

gonorrhea (gon-uh-REE-uh): A sexually transmitted infection that usually causes symptoms of a puslike discharge and painful, burning urination in the male but is frequently asymptomatic in the female.

century, a gonorrhea epidemic occurred during World War I, and gonorrhea was also a serious problem during World War II. Then, with the discovery of penicillin and its use in curing gonorrhea, the disease became much less prevalent in the 1950s.

There was a resurgence in the incidence of gonorrhea in the 1970s. It is clear that one of the reasons for the resurgence was the shift in contraceptive practices to use of the pill, which (unlike the condom) provides no protection from gonorrhea and actually increases a woman's susceptibility. However, in Canada the reported rate of gonorrhea has declined 93 percent since 1980 through the use of condoms, improved diagnostic services, partner notification, and treatment. In 2009, there were 11 178 reported cases, more than half of which were among 15- to 24-year-olds. The highest rates are among young women between 15 and 19 years old. This is a rate of 33 per 100 000 people in the population—the rate of chlamydia is almost eight times the rate for gonorrhea.

Symptoms

Most cases of gonorrhea result from penis-in-vagina intercourse. In the male, the gonococcus invades the urethra, producing *urethritis* (inflammation of the urethra). White blood cells rush to the area and attempt to destroy the bacteria, but the bacteria soon win the battle. In most cases, symptoms appear two to five days after infection, although they may appear as early as the first day or as late as two weeks after infection (Hook & Handsfield, 2008). Initially a thin, clear mucous discharge seeps out of the meatus (the opening at the tip of the penis). Within a day or so it becomes thick and creamy and may be white, yellowish, or yellow-green (see Figure 8.6). This

Figure 8.6 Symptoms of gonorrhea in men include a puslike discharge. About 80 percent of women, however, are asymptomatic.

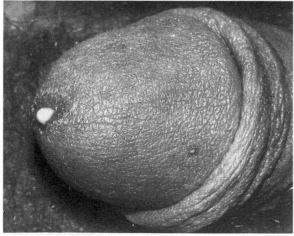

Centers for Disease Control

is often referred to as a purulent (puslike) discharge. The area around the meatus may become swollen. About half of infected men experience a painful burning sensation when urinating.

Because the early symptoms of gonorrhea in men are obvious and often painful, most men seek treatment immediately and are cured. If the disease is not treated, however, the urethritis spreads up the urethra, causing inflammations in the prostate (prostatitis), seminal vesicles (seminal vesiculitis), urinary bladder (cystitis), and epididymis (epididymitis). Pain on urination becomes worse and is felt in the whole penis. Then these early symptoms may disappear as the disease spreads to the other organs. If the epididymitis is left untreated, it may spread to the testicles and the resulting scar tissue may cause sterility.

Asymptomatic gonorrhea (gonorrhea with no symptoms) does occur in men, but its incidence is low. In contrast, about 50 to 80 percent of women infected with gonorrhea are asymptomatic during the early stages of the disease. Many women are unaware of their infection unless they are told by a male partner. Therefore, it is extremely important for any man who is infected to inform all his contacts.

The gonorrheal infection in the woman invades the cervix. Pus is discharged, but the amount may be so slight that it is not noticed. When present, it is yellow-green and irritating to the vulva, but it is generally not heavy (it is not to be confused with normal cervical mucus, which is clear or white and nonirritating, or with discharges resulting from the various kinds of vaginitis—discussed later in this chapter—which are irritating but white). Although the cervix is the primary site of infection, the inflammation may also spread to the urethra, causing burning pain on urination (not to be confused with cystitis). If the infection is not treated, the Bartholin glands may become infected. The infection may also be spread to the anus and rectum.

Because so many women are asymptomatic in the early stages of gonorrhea, many receive no treatment, and thus there is a high risk of serious complications. In about 20 percent of women who go untreated, the gonococcus moves up into the uterus. From there it infects the fallopian tubes (Hook & Handsfield, 2008). The tissues become swollen and inflamed, and thus the condition is also called pelvic inflammatory disease (PID)—although PID can be caused by diseases other than gonorrhea. The major symptom is pelvic pain and, in some cases, irregular or painful menstruation. If PID is not treated, scar tissue may form, blocking the tubes and leaving the woman sterile. Indeed, untreated gonorrhea is one of the most common causes of infertility in women. If the tubes are partially blocked, so that sperm can get up them but eggs cannot move down, ectopic pregnancy can result, because the fertilized egg is trapped in the tube.

There are three other major sites for non-genital gonorrhea infection: the mouth and throat, the anus and rectum, and the eyes. If fellatio is performed on an infected man, the gonococcus may invade the throat. (Cunnilingus is less likely to spread gonorrhea, and mouth-to-mouth kissing rarely does.) Such an infection is often asymptomatic; the typical symptom, if there is one, is a sore throat. Rectal gonorrhea is contracted through anal intercourse and thus affects both women in heterosexual relations and, more commonly, men who have sex with men. Symptoms include some discharge from the rectum and itching, but many cases are asymptomatic. Gonorrhea may also invade the eyes. This occurs only rarely in adults, when they touch the genitals and then transfer the bacteria-containing pus to their eyes by touching them. This eye infection is much more common in newborn infants. The infection is transferred from the mother's cervix to the infant's eyes during birth. For this reason, most provinces require that silver nitrate, or erythromycin or some other antibiotic, be put in every newborn's eyes to prevent any such infection. If left untreated, the eyes become swollen and painful within a few days, and there is a discharge of pus. Blindness was a common result in the pre-antibiotic era.

Diagnosis

A urine test is available for men. If gonorrhea in the throat is suspected, a swab should be taken and tested. People who suspect that they may have rectal gonorrhea should request that a swab be taken from the rectum, since many physicians will not automatically think to do this.

A urine test is also available for women. However, a pelvic examination should also be performed because pain during this exam may indicate PID. Women who suspect throat or rectal infection should request that samples be taken from those sites as well.

Treatment

The traditional treatment for gonorrhea was a large dose of penicillin, or tetracycline for those who were allergic to penicillin. However, strains of the gonococcus that are resistant to penicillin and tetracycline have become so common that newer antibiotics, such as ceftriaxone or ciprofloxacin (Cipro), must now be used. They are highly effective, even against resistant strains.

Syphilis

There has been considerable debate over the exact origins of **syphilis**. The disease, called the Great Pox, was present in Europe during the fifteenth century and became a pandemic by 1500. The bacterium that causes syphilis is called *Treponema pallidum*. It is spiral-shaped and is thus often called a *spirochete*.

In 2012 there were 2003 cases of syphilis reported in Canada. Although the rate of syphilis remains low, there has been an increase in cases in the last few years; for example, there were only 174 reported cases in 2000. The increase is largely due to outbreaks in Vancouver involving sex trade workers, in Yukon and northern Alberta among heterosexuals, and in Calgary, Ottawa, and Montreal among men who have sex with men.

Although syphilis is not nearly as common as chlamydia or gonorrhea, its effects are much more serious if left untreated. In most cases, chlamydia or gonorrhea cause only discomfort and, sometimes, sterility; syphilis, if left untreated, can damage the nervous system and even cause death. There are many cases today of co-infection, in which the person is infected with both syphilis and HIV. Syphilis infection makes a person more vulnerable to HIV and vice versa.

Symptoms

The major early symptom of syphilis is the **chancre**. It is a round, ulcerlike lesion with a hard, raised edge, resembling a crater. One of the distinctive things about the chancre is that although it looks terrible, it is painless. It appears about three weeks (as early as ten days or as late as three months) after intercourse with an infected person. The chancre appears at the point where the bacteria entered the body. Typically, the bacteria enter through the mucous membranes of the genitals. Thus, in men the chancre often appears on the penis or scrotum. In women, the chancre often appears on the cervix, and thus the woman does not notice it and is unaware that she is infected (nature's sexism again). The chancre may also appear on the vaginal walls or, externally, on the vulva (see Figure 8.7).

If oral sex or anal intercourse with an infected person occurs, the bacteria can also invade the mucous membranes of the mouth or rectum. Thus, the chancre may appear on the lips, tongue, or tonsils or around the anus. Finally, the bacteria may enter through a cut in the skin anywhere on the body. Thus, it is possible (though rare) to get syphilis by touching the chancre of an infected person. The chancre would then appear on the hand at the point where the bacteria entered through the break in the skin.

The progress of the disease once the person has been infected is generally divided into four stages: primary-stage syphilis, secondary-stage syphilis, latent syphilis, and late syphilis. The phase just described, in which the chancre forms, is *primary-stage syphilis*. If left

> **syphilis (SIFF-ih-lis):** A sexually transmitted infection that causes a chancre to appear in the primary stage.
> **chancre (SHANK-er):** A painless, ulcerlike lesion with a hard, raised edge that is a symptom of syphilis.

Figure 8.7 The chancre characteristic of primary-stage syphilis *(a)* on the labia majora and *(b)* on the penis.

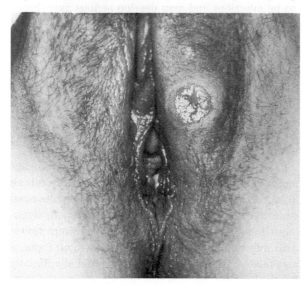

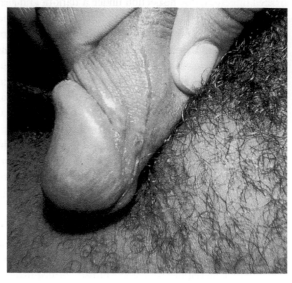

(a)

(b)

Centers for Disease Control

untreated, the chancre goes away by itself within one to five weeks after it appears. This marks the end of the primary stage. However, the disease has not gone away just because the chancre has healed; it has only gone underground.

Beginning a few months after the original appearance of the chancre, a generalized body rash develops, marking the beginning of *secondary-stage syphilis*. The rash is variable in its appearance, the most distinctive feature being that it does not itch or hurt. Hair loss may also occur during the secondary stage. Usually, the symptoms are troublesome enough to cause the person to seek medical help. With appropriate treatment at this stage, the disease can still be cured, and there will be no permanent effects. Even without treatment, the secondary-stage symptoms go away in a few weeks, leading people to believe mistakenly that the disease has gone away. Instead, it has entered a more dangerous stage.

After the symptoms of the secondary stage have disappeared, the disease is in the latent stage; *latent syphilis* may last for years. Although there are no symptoms in this stage, *T. pallidum* is busily burrowing into the tissues of the body, especially the blood vessels, central nervous system (brain and spinal cord), and bones. After the first year or so of the latent stage, the disease is no longer infectious, except that a pregnant woman can still pass it on to the fetus.

About half of the people who enter the latent stage remain in it permanently, living out the rest of their lives without further complications. The other half, however, move into the dangerous *late syphilis*. In

congenital (kun-JEN-ih-tul) syphilis: A syphilis infection in a newborn baby resulting from transmission from an infected mother.

cardiovascular late syphilis the heart and major blood vessels are attacked; this occurs 10 to 40 years after the initial infection. Cardiovascular syphilis can lead to death. In *neurosyphilis* the brain and spinal cord are attacked, leading to insanity and paralysis, which appear 10 to 20 years after infection. Neurosyphilis may be fatal.

If a pregnant woman has syphilis, the fetus may be infected when the bacteria cross the placental barrier, and the child gets **congenital syphilis** (meaning present from birth). The infection may cause early death of the fetus (spontaneous abortion) or severe illness at or shortly after birth. It may also lead to late complications that show up only at 10 or 20 years of age. Women are most infectious to their baby when they have primary- or secondary-stage syphilis, but they may transmit the infection to the fetus in utero as long as eight years after the mother's initial infection. If the disease is diagnosed and treated before the fourth month of pregnancy, the fetus will not develop the disease. For this reason, a syphilis test is done as a routine part of the blood analysis in a pregnancy test. In 2012 there were only three cases of congenital syphilis in all of Canada (PHAC, 2016).

Diagnosis

Syphilis is somewhat difficult to diagnose from symptoms because, as noted earlier, its symptoms are like those of many other diseases. The physical exam should include inspection not only of the genitals but also of the entire body surface. Women should have a pelvic exam so that the vagina and the cervix can be checked for chancres. If the patient has had anal intercourse, a rectal exam should also be performed.

If a chancre is present, some of its fluid is taken and placed on a slide for inspection under a dark-field microscope. If the person has syphilis, *T. pallidum* should be present. The most common tests for syphilis are blood tests, all of which are based on antibody reactions. The VDRL (venereal disease research laboratory test) is one of these blood tests. It is fairly accurate, cheap, and easy to perform.

Treatment

The treatment of choice for syphilis is penicillin (Workowski & Berman, 2010). *T. pallidum* is actually rather fragile, so large doses are not necessary in treatment. The recommended dose is two shots of penicillin G, one in each of the buttocks. Latent, later, and congenital syphilis require larger doses. For those allergic to penicillin, the recommended treatment is tetracycline or doxycycline, but these should not be given to pregnant women.

Viral Hepatitis

Viral hepatitis is a disease of the liver. One symptom is an enlarged liver that is somewhat tender. The disease can vary greatly in severity from asymptomatic cases to ones in which there is a fever, fatigue, jaundice (yellowish skin), and vomiting, much as one might experience with a serious case of the flu. There are five types of viral hepatitis: hepatitis A, B, C, D, and E. The one that is of most interest in a discussion of STIs is hepatitis B. Hepatitis C and D (or delta) can also be transmitted sexually, but they are rare compared with B.

The virus for **hepatitis B (HBV)** can be transmitted through blood, saliva, semen, vaginal secretions, and other body fluids. The behaviours that spread it include sharing needles by people who inject drugs, sharing toothbrushes and razors, getting tattoos and body piercings, having acupuncture, having vaginal and anal intercourse, and having oral–anal sex. It has many similarities to AIDS, although hepatitis B is about 100 times as contagious.

Hepatitis B is more common than most people think because it receives relatively little publicity compared with AIDS and herpes. In 2013 there were 178 new cases of hepatitis B in Canada. The good news is that the rates of HBV are decreasing in Canada (PHAC, 2013). This may be because increasing numbers of people have received the HBV vaccine. People who have had the disease continue to have a positive blood test for it for the rest of their lives.

Many adults infected with HBV are asymptomatic; their bodies fight off the virus and they are left uninfected, with permanent immunity. Others develop an early, acute (short-term) illness and display a variety of symptoms but recover from the illness. A third group develops chronic (long-term) hepatitis B. They continue to be infectious and may develop serious liver disease involving cirrhosis or cancer. Fortunately, antiviral treatments are now available for those with chronic hepatitis B (PHAC, 2010b). Symptoms of hepatitis B can include jaundice (yellowing of the skin and eyes), fatigue, loss of appetite, nausea, dark urine, pale stools, joint pain, and pain in the stomach area. Symptoms typically appear between two and six months after infection. However, about half of people infected with Hepatitis B do not have any symptoms.

The good news is that there is a vaccine against hepatitis B. The current recommendation is that all children be vaccinated and all provinces have school-based immunization programs. The vaccine is also recommended for individuals who are at risk of contracting an HBV infection. As a result of these vaccination programs, the rate of HBV infection has decreased significantly, particularly among children and youth (PHAC, 2011). We urge you to be vaccinated if you are a person who has had a number of partners. You should be tested if there is even a hint that you have been exposed.

Trichomoniasis

Trichomoniasis (*trich*) is caused by a protozoan, *Trichomonas vaginalis* (Hobbs et al., 2008). The organism can survive for a time on toilet seats and other objects, so it is occasionally transmitted nonsexually, but it is transmitted mainly through sexual intercourse.

For women, the symptom is vaginal discharge that irritates the vulva and has an unpleasant smell. In men, there may be irritation of the urethra and a discharge from the penis, but some men are asymptomatic. It is important that accurate diagnosis be made, because the drugs used to cure trichomoniasis are different from those used to treat other STIs that have similar symptoms, and the long-term effects of untreated trichomoniasis can be serious, with untreated trich possibly leading to PID and problems with birth (Swygard et al., 2004). It also increases susceptibility to HIV infection. The treatment of choice is metronidazole (Flagyl) taken orally.

Pubic Lice

Pubic lice (*crabs* or *pediculosis pubis*) are tiny lice that attach themselves to the base of pubic hairs and there feed on blood from their human host. They

hepatitis B (HPV): A liver disease that can be transmitted sexually or by needle sharing.

trichomoniasis (trick-oh-moh-NYus-is): A form of vaginitis causing a frothy white or yellow discharge with an unpleasant odour.

pubic lice: Tiny lice that attach themselves to the base of pubic hairs and cause itching; also called crabs.

Figure 8.8 A pubic louse, enlarged. The actual size is about the same as the head of a pin.

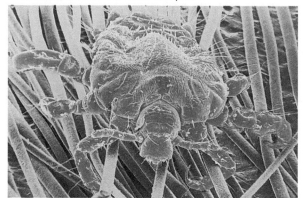

© E. Gray/Science Photo Library/Science Source

are about the size of a pinhead and, under magnification, resemble a crab (see Figure 8.8). They lay their eggs frequently and live for about 30 days, but they die within 24 hours if they are taken off a human host. Lice are transmitted by sexual contact, but they may also be picked up from sheets, towels, sleeping bags, or toilet seats. (Yes, there *are* some things you can catch from toilet seats.)

The major symptom of pubic lice is fierce itching in the region of the pubic hair. Diagnosis is made by finding the lice or the eggs attached to the hairs. Pubic lice are treated with the drugs Nix and Rid, which are available without prescription. Both kill the lice. After treatment, the person should put on clean clothing. Since the lice die within 24 hours, it is not necessary to disinfect clothing that has not been used for longer than 24 hours. However, the eggs can live up to six days, and in difficult cases it may be necessary to boil or dry clean one's clothing or use a spray, such as R and C.

LO4

Preventing STIs

While most of the literature on STIs concentrates on their rapid diagnosis and treatment, prevention would be much better than cure, and there are some ways in which we can avoid getting STIs or at least reduce the chances of doing so. The most obvious, of course, is limiting yourself to a monogamous relationship with an uninfected person or abstaining from sexual activity. However, many people in committed monogamous relationships have engaged in behaviours that put them at risk for STIs in the past. They may not be aware that they are infected and thus can pass on the STI to their partner if they engage in unprotected sex even if both partners are monogamous (Misovich et al., 1997). As described in the First Person

> **My partner has no symptoms of any STI. Should we still practise safer sex?**

earlier in this chapter, just because a partner has no obvious symptoms like herpes blisters or warts, don't assume that the person is uninfected. We have seen in this chapter how many of these infections—for example, chlamydia, herpes, and warts—can be asymptomatic. The only way to really know is for both you and your partner to have a complete battery of tests for STIs when you enter a new relationship, a choice people are increasingly making. Not every STI is tested in the standard battery—for example, herpes and HPV usually are not—but still testing will catch most infections.

However, if you are not *sure* that your partner is uninfected, there are other techniques available. People tend to perceive less risk of acquiring an STI when they are more familiar with their partner, even if the person is a new partner (Sparling & Cramer, 2015). Because it is sometimes difficult to negotiate with a partner, particularly a partner you know well, who is not committed to engaging in safer sex if both of you have not been tested, the First Person below provides responses to some objections that your partner may have.

The latex condom, in addition to being a decent contraceptive, gives good (although not perfect) protection against HIV, HPV, chlamydia, gonorrhea, herpes, syphilis, and other STIs (Baldwin et al., 2004; Steiner & Cates, 2006; Wald et al., 2005; Winer et al., 2006). With the rise of the STI epidemic, the condom is again becoming popular. The key is to eroticize condom use (Ploem & Byers, 1997). The diaphragm (although it isn't available in Canada) also provides some protection for women, as does the female condom.

A dental dam gives protection from the spread of STIs during cunnilingus (oral stimulation of the vulva) or anilingus (oral stimulation of the anus). Some stores sell them or you can make them yourself from an unlubricated condom: First, carefully unroll the condom. Then cut off the tip and the rim. Finally, cut down the length of the tube and open the condom. Voila, you have a rectangular piece of latex that can be used during oral sex.

Some simple health precautions are also helpful. Successful prostitutes, who need to be careful about STIs, take such precautions. Washing the genitals before intercourse helps remove bacteria. This may not sound like a romantic prelude to lovemaking, but you can make a sensuous game out of soaping the man's genitals, possibly as part of taking a shower or bath with your partner. Urinating both before and after intercourse also helps to keep bacteria out of the urethra.

Another important technique is inspecting your partner's genitals. If you see a chancre, a wart, a herpes blister, or a discharge, put on your clothes and leave or, at the very least, immediately start a conversation about STI status (do not fall for the "it's only a pimple" routine). This technique may sound a little crude or embarrassing, but if you are intimate enough with someone to have sex with that person, you ought to be intimate enough to look

First Person

Cool Lines about Safer Sex

Partner	*You*
What's that?	A condom, baby.
What for?	To use when we're making love.
I don't like using them.	Why not?
Rubbers are gross.	Being pregnant when I don't want to be is worse. So is getting AIDS.
Don't you trust me?	Trust isn't the point. People carry sexually transmitted infections without knowing it.
I'll pull out in time.	Women can get pregnant from precum. It can also carry sexually transmitted infections.
I thought you said using condoms made you feel cheap.	I decided to face facts. I like having sex, and I want to stay healthy and happy.
Rubbers aren't romantic.	Making love and protecting each other's health sounds romantic enough to me.
Making love with a rubber on is like taking a shower with a raincoat on.	Doing it without a rubber is playing Russian roulette.
It just isn't as sensitive.	With a condom you might last even longer, and that'll make up for it.
I don't stay hard when I put on a condom.	I can do something about that.
Putting it on interrupts everything.	Not if I help put it on.
I'll try, but it might not work.	Then you'll help me protect myself.
I guess you don't really love me.	I'm not going to prove my love by risking my life.
I'm not using a rubber, no matter what.	Well, then I guess we're not having sex.
Just this once without it.	It only takes once to get pregnant. It only takes once to get AIDS.
It won't fit.	Condoms come in all different sizes.

Source: www.teenwire.com, June 22, 2004.

at her or his genitals. Once again, if you are cool about it, you can make this an erotic part of foreplay. Of course, you should also inspect your own genitals on a regular basis to make sure you're not inadvertently passing on an STI to a partner. Women will need to use a hand-held mirror to do so.

One factor that has interfered with efforts to prevent STIs is the stigma and shame associated with being diagnosed with one of these infections (Wong et al., 2012), something we must combat. **STI-related stigma** refers to people's awareness that others will judge them negatively for having an STI. **STI-related shame** refers to the negative feelings people have about themselves when they receive an STI diagnosis (Fortenberry et al., 2002). For example, a young woman in a Toronto study was clearly aware of the stigma associated with an STI diagnosis:

It's gross. It's scornful. Once you're in that room and the doctor says, "You have chlamydia," you're not going to sit there, you're going to want to go home and bathe your skin and sit in a pot of

> **STI-related stigma:** Awareness that people are judged negatively for contracting an STI.
>
> **STI-related shame:** The negative feelings people have about themselves as a result of receiving an STI diagnosis.

hot boiling water. You're going to think about it. It's always there. You don't talk about it but you'll always remember it. (Wong et al., 2012, p. 82)

People with higher STI-related stigma and shame are less likely to be tested or screened for STIs (Mihan et al., 2016). They are also less likely to have an open discussion of sexual histories with their sexual partners. Research in New Brunswick has shown that people who are more socially and sexually conservative experience greater STI-related stigma and shame (Foster & Byers, 2008). This research also identifies a means to reduce stigma and shame—individuals who had received better sexual health education in school reported less STI-related stigma and shame.

Finally, each person needs to recognize that it is his or her ethical responsibility to seek out early diagnosis and treatment. Table 8.2 provides information about STI testing, including what the test involves, how soon after infection the test becomes accurate, and who should get tested. Probably the most important responsibility is that of informing prospective partners if you have an STI and of informing past partners as soon as you discover that you have one. For example, because so many women are asymptomatic for chlamydia, it is particularly important for men to take the responsibility of informing their female partners if they find that they have the infection. It is important to take care of your own health, but it is equally important to take care of your partner's health.

> **vaginitis (vaj-in-ITE-is):** An irritation or inflammation of the vagina, usually causing a discharge.
> **candida:** A form of vaginitis causing a thick, white discharge; also called monilia or yeast infection.

 L05

Other Genital Infections

Vaginitis (vaginal inflammation or irritation) is very common among women and is endemic in university populations. Two kinds of vaginitis, as well as prostatitis, will be considered here. None of these infections are STIs, because they are not transmitted by sexual contact; they are, however, common infections of the sex organs.

A few simple steps can help prevent vaginitis. Every time you shower or take a bath, wash the vulva carefully and dry it thoroughly. Do not use feminine hygiene deodorant sprays; they are unnecessary and can irritate the vagina. Wear cotton underpants; nylon and other synthetics retain moisture, and vaginitis-producing organisms thrive on moisture. Avoid wearing pants that are too tight in the crotch; they increase moisture and may irritate the vulva. Wipe the anus from front to back so that bacteria from the anus do not get into the vagina. For the same reason, never go immediately from anal intercourse to vaginal intercourse. Finally, if an attack of vaginitis seems to be coming on, placing some plain yogurt with active cultures into the vagina can help restore the good bacteria.

Candida

Candida (also called *yeast infection* and *moniliasis*) is a form of vaginitis caused by the yeast fungus *Candida. Candida* is normally present in the vagina, but if the

Table 8.2	Getting Tested: Handy Information about STI Testing		
STI	**What does the test involve?**	**How soon is the test accurate?**	**Who should get tested?**
Chlamydia	Men: urine sample or urethral swab Women: urine sample, vaginal swab, or cervical swab	1–2 weeks after infection	Sexually active women under 25 Men who have sex with men People with symptoms, at high risk, or recently exposed
Genital herpes	Blood test or swab of herpes sore	2–6 weeks after infection	People with symptoms
Gonorrhea	Men: urine sample or urethral swab Women: urine sample, vaginal swab, or cervical swab Other sites: swab of throat or rectum	1–2 weeks after infection	Sexually active women under 25 Men who have sex with men People with symptoms, at high risk, or recently exposed
Hepatitis B	Blood test	6–12 weeks	Certain high-risk individuals Pregnant women Persons with symptoms or exposed
HIV	Blood test or saliva swab	2–12 weeks from infection	Everyone
HPV	Cervical swab	varies	Women over age 30 as part of a routine Pap smear
Syphilis	Blood test	1–6 weeks after infection	Pregnant women Men who have sex with men Persons who are exposed
Trichomoniasis	Vaginal swab	1–4 weeks after infection	Persons with symptoms

delicate environmental balance there is disturbed (e.g., if the pH is changed), the growth of Candida can get out of hand. Conditions that encourage the growth of Candida include long-term use of birth control pills, menstruation, diabetes or a prediabetic condition, pregnancy, and long-term use of antibiotics, such as tetracycline. It is not a sexually transmitted infection, although intercourse may aggravate it.

The major symptom is a thick, white, curdlike vaginal discharge found on the vaginal lips and the walls of the vagina. The discharge can cause extreme itching, to the point where the woman is not interested in having intercourse.

Treatment is by the drugs miconzole or elotrimazole, both available over the counter. Flucomazole, a single-dose treatment, is available by prescription. If a woman has Candida while she is pregnant, she can transmit it to her baby during birth. The baby gets the yeast in its digestive system, a condition known as *thrush*. Thrush can also result from oral–genital sex.

Bacterial vaginosis is another vaginal infection that produces a similar discharge. The distinctive feature is that the discharge has a foul odour.

Prostatitis

Prostatitis is an inflammation or swelling of the prostate gland. It used to be thought that it was almost always caused by an infection by the bacterium *E. coli*, but it is now known that it can be caused by several different conditions. It can also be caused by gonorrhea or chlamydia. The typical symptoms are fever; chills; pain above the penis or around the scrotum, anus, or rectum; difficulty starting urination; and a need for frequent urination. Research in Ontario has shown that prostatitis may produce sexual dysfunction (Smith et al., 2007). In some cases, prostatitis may be chronic (long-lasting) and may have no symptoms, or only lower-back pain. Antibiotics are used in treatment.

> **prostatitis (pros-tuh-TY-tis):** An infection, inflammation, or swelling of the prostate gland.

Critical **THINK** *ing Skill*

UNDERSTANDING THE CONCEPT OF PROBABILITY

In this chapter, we revisit a critical thinking skill introduced in Chapter 7. As we saw in that chapter, probability refers to the chance that an event will occur. Probabilities can range between 0 (no chance) and 1.0 (definitely will occur). Often probabilities are stated as percentages ranging between 0 and 100 percent. For example, if we toss a fair coin, the probability that it will come up heads is 0.5, or 50 percent. Consider the following case:

> Ryan is planning to go to a party at a fourth-year student's house close to campus. He thinks that Molly, an attractive woman whom he has noticed in one of his classes, will be there, and he hopes for a hookup with her, including intercourse. Then he starts thinking about how he has heard that chlamydia is widespread on university campuses. Will it be safe to have sex with Molly? Should he use a condom?

Ryan needs to assess some probabilities. The first is the probability that Molly has chlamydia. He doesn't really know that probability. How could he find out? He could ask Molly if she has any of the symptoms, but Molly might not be happy with that line of conversation. Then Ryan remembers that a high percentage of women with chlamydia are asymptomatic and don't even know that they have it. He could ask her if she has been tested for STIs recently. That might not sound romantic, but he needs to protect his health, and he could frame it in terms of his commitment to both her health and his health. He could volunteer that he was tested just a month ago and had nothing. In the end, though, he may not be able to know precisely the probability that she is infected. He could go with a statistic from this chapter, that the rate of reported cases of chlamydia among adolescent girls is about 5 percent.

Some people make a mistake at this stage and assume that if Molly looks healthy and attractive, the probability that she is infected is 0. That is a bad assumption. Why?

Another probability that Ryan needs to know, especially if he can't know precisely whether she is infected, is the probability of infection from a single act of intercourse. Even scientists cannot give very precise estimates of these probabilities, and the probabilities depend greatly on factors such as whether the man uses a condom (Garnett, 2008). Gonorrhea, for example, is highly infectious, with a probability of transmission from an infected woman to an uninfected man of 25 percent from one act of unprotected intercourse (but a 50 percent risk of transmission in the reverse direction, from an infected man to an uninfected woman). Ryan probably can't know the exact probability of transmission if Molly is infected.

Overall, then, Ryan faces a great deal of uncertainty. He does know, though, that condoms are highly effective in preventing transmission of STIs like chlamydia. After assessing all of these factors, if Ryan is applying good critical thinking skills, he will use a condom.

SUMMARY

Table 8.3 provides a summary of the information about the STIs discussed in this chapter.

Table 8.3 Summary of Information about STIs

STI Description & Cause	Primary Symptoms	Primary Complications	Treatment
Chlamydia Caused by the bacterium *Chlamydia trachomatis*	*In men* A thin clear discharge from the penis and mild pain on urination *In women* Most have no symptoms	If untreated: *In men* Urethral damage, epididymitis, Reiter's syndrome, proctitis *In women* Pelvic inflammatory disease and infertility	Cured with antibiotics (azithromycin or doxycycline)
HPV Caused by the *human papillomavirus*	Cauliflower-like warts on the genitals Many people have no symptoms	*In men* Cancer of the penis and anus *In women* Cervical cancer	Podofilox or bichloroacetic acid, cryotherapy, laser therapy for warts Vaccine available No cure available
Genital herpes (HSV) Caused by the virus *herpes simplex*	Small painful bumps or blisters on the genitals Fever, painful urination, headaches	Reoccurrences Increased risk of HIV infection Transmission during childbirth	Acyclovir, valacyclovir, and famciclovir to minimize symptoms No cure available
HIV/AIDS Caused by the *human immunodeficiency virus*	Flu-like symptoms (e.g., fever or sore throat) may occur at the initial infection Most people have no symptoms for years	Destroys the immune system, resulting in vulnerability to opportunistic infections	Combination of drugs (protease inhibitor, azidothymidine, and one other drug) called HAART to slow progression No cure
Gonorrhea Caused by the bacterium *Neisseria gonorrhoeae*	*In men* Inflammation of the urethra, thin clear white or yellow discharge from the penis, burning pain on urination *In women* Most (and some men) have no symptoms Vaginal discharge, pain on urination in some	Infertility if left untreated	Cured with antibiotics (penicillin or tetracycline)
Syphilis Caused by the bacterium *Treponema pallidum*	Painless sore with hard, raised edge (chancre) in primary stage A generalized body rash in secondary stage	If left untreated, progresses through several stages that may lead to brain infection and death Infection of the fetus	Cured with antibiotics (penicillin)
Hepatitis B Caused by the virus *hepatitis B*	Jaundice, fatigue, loss of appetite, nausea Many people are asymptomatic	Liver disease involving cirrhosis or cancer	Antiviral drugs to treat chronic cases; vaccine available No cure
Trichomoniasis Caused by protozoan *Trichomonas vaginalis*	*In men* Irritation of the urethra, discharge from the penis *In women* Abundant white or yellowish vaginal discharge with unpleasant smell	*In men* Increased risk of HIV infection *In women* Pelvic inflammatory disease Problems with birth Increased risk of HIV infection	Cured with antibiotics (Flagyl)
Pubic lice Caused by the genital crab louse, *pediculosis pubis*	Intense itching in region of the pubic hair	None	Special soap (Nix, Rid)

CHAPTER 9

Sexual Arousal

© Rawpixel.com/Shutterstock

LEARNING OBJECTIVES

After studying this chapter, you will be able to

LO1 Explain the two basic physiological processes and physiological changes that occur during each of the three stages of the sexual response cycle for men and for women.

LO2 Compare the similarities and differences between the various models of sexual response.

LO3 Illustrate how the brain and spinal cord reflexes affect sexual response in men and women.

LO4 Identify how hormones and pheromones influence sexual response in men and women.

LO5 Give examples of the techniques that men and women use during one-person sex.

LO6 Describe the techniques that men and women use during two-person sex with same-sex and other-sex partners.

LO7 Differentiate between aphrodisiacs and anaphrodiasics.

LO8 Explain the difference between *sex as work* and *exceptional sex*.

Are YOU Curious?

1. What happens, biologically, when a man has an erection? When a woman's vagina lubricates?
2. What hormone is most important to sexual desire in men? In women?
3. What is tantric sex?

Read the chapter to find out.

Here are some colors of different people's orgasms: champagne, all colors and white and gray afterward, red and blue, green, beige and blue, red, blue and gold. Some people never make it because they are trying for plaid.[*]

[*] Eric Berne. (1970). *Sex in human loving*. New York: Simon & Schuster, p. 238.

In this chapter, we focus on the ways the body becomes sexually aroused, how it responds during arousal and orgasm, and the physiological, hormonal, neurological, and social processes involved in these responses. Satisfying sexual expression is essential to good physical and mental health (WHO, 2006). Understanding the processes involved is essential on the social level to providing quality reproductive and sexual health care, and on a personal level to developing mutually pleasurable lovemaking techniques. This information is also important in understanding sexual variations (Chapter 15) and treating sexual dysfunctions (Chapter 18).

First, we examine how the body responds physiologically during arousal and orgasm. Our basic knowledge of these processes comes from the classic research of Masters and Johnson. One of the virtues of science is that it advances because of its public and cumulative character. In this case, criticisms of Masters and Johnson's work led to the development of alternative, expanded models. More recently, research has identified the hormonal and neuroanatomical aspects of the processes Masters and Johnson described. We also consider research on pheromones and their influence on sexual behaviour in animals and humans. Finally, we discuss sexual techniques.

> **What happens biologically when a man has an erection and when a women's vagina lubricates?**

The Sexual Response Cycle

Sex researchers William Masters and Virginia Johnson provided one of the first models of the physiology of human sexual response. Their research culminated in 1966 with the publication of *Human Sexual Response*, which reported data on 382 women and 312 men observed in more than 10 000 sexual cycles of arousal and orgasm. Recent biological research has confirmed many of their findings while questioning a few and augmenting many. All this research is the basis for the sections that follow.

vasocongestion (vay-so-con-JES-tyun): An accumulation of blood in the blood vessels of a region of the body, especially the genitals; a swelling or erection results.

myotonia (my-oh-TONE-ee-ah): Muscle contraction.

excitement: The first stage of sexual response, during which erection in the male and vaginal lubrication in the female occur.

Sexual response typically progresses in three stages: *excitement*, *orgasm*, and *resolution*. (Masters and Johnson originally proposed that there are four phases: excitement, plateau, orgasm, and resolution. Most researchers now consider the plateau phase to be the late part of the excitement phase.) The two basic physiological processes that occur during these stages are vasocongestion and myotonia. **Vasocongestion** occurs when a great deal of blood flows into the blood vessels in a region, in this case the genitals, as a result of dilation of those blood vessels. **Myotonia** occurs when muscles contract, not only in the genitals but also throughout the body. Let's now consider in detail what occurs in each of the stages.

Excitement

The **excitement** phase is the beginning of erotic arousal. The basic physiological process that occurs during excitement is vasocongestion, which produces the obvious arousal response in men—erection. Erection results when the corpora cavernosa and the corpus spongiosum fill (becoming engorged) with blood (see Figure 9.1). Erection may be produced by direct physical stimulation of the genitals, by stimulation of other parts of the body, or by erotic thoughts. Vasocongestion occurs rapidly, and in young men erection may occur within a few seconds of stimulation, although it may take place more slowly as a result of a number of factors, including age, intake of alcohol, and fatigue. As the man gets closer to orgasm, a few drops of fluid (for some men quite a few) secreted by the Cowper's gland appear at the tip of the penis. Although they are not ejaculate, they may contain active sperm.

Research in the last decade—stimulated, in part, by the search for Viagra—has given us much more detailed information about the physiological processes involved in erection (Adams et al., 1997; Heaton, 2000). Several arteries supply the corpora cavernosa and spongiosum (look back at Figure 4.11). For an erection to occur, these arteries must dilate (vasodilation), allowing a strong flow of blood into the corpora. At the same time, the veins carrying blood away from the penis are compressed, restricting outgoing blood flow. The arteries dilate because the smooth muscle surrounding the arteries relaxes. Multiple neurotransmitters are involved in this process including, especially, nitric oxide (NO). Viagra acts on the NO system.

Figure 9.1 Changes during the sexual response cycle in the male.

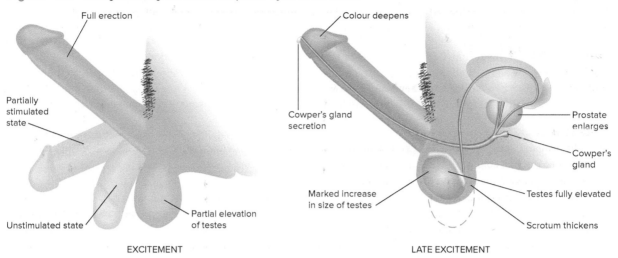

EXCITEMENT

- Full erection
- Partially stimulated state
- Unstimulated state
- Partial elevation of testes

LATE EXCITEMENT

- Colour deepens
- Cowper's gland secretion
- Marked increase in size of testes
- Prostate enlarges
- Cowper's gland
- Testes fully elevated
- Scrotum thickens

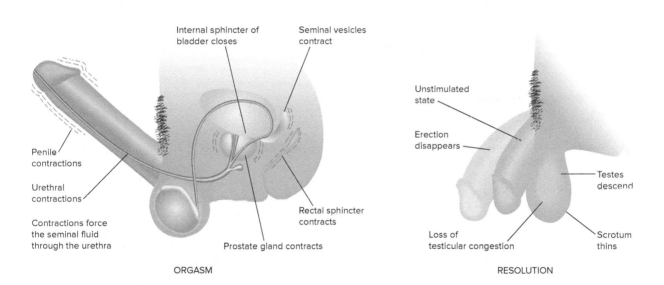

ORGASM

- Internal sphincter of bladder closes
- Seminal vesicles contract
- Penile contractions
- Urethral contractions
- Contractions force the seminal fluid through the urethra
- Prostate gland contracts
- Rectal sphincter contracts

RESOLUTION

- Unstimulated state
- Erection disappears
- Loss of testicular congestion
- Testes descend
- Scrotum thins

Of course, erections, nice though they are, would become a pain if they lasted forever, so there is a reverse process—vasoconstriction—that makes an erection go away—for example, following orgasm. The neurotransmitters epinephrine and norepinephrine are involved. These processes occur in the resolution phase, discussed shortly.

An important response to sexual stimulation of women in the excitement phase is lubrication of the vagina. Laboratory studies in Ontario show that women who are more sexually aroused produce more lubrication (Dawson et al., 2015). Although this response might seem much different from the man's, actually they both result from the same physiological process: vasocongestion. During excitement, the capillaries in the walls of the vagina dilate and blood flow through them increases

(Levin, 2005). Vaginal lubrication results when fluids seep through the semipermeable membranes of the vaginal walls, producing lubrication as a result of vasocongestion in the tissues surrounding the vagina. This response to arousal is also rapid, though not quite so fast as the man's; lubrication usually begins 10 to 30 seconds after the onset of arousing stimuli. Like the male sexual response, female responding can be affected by factors, such as age, intake of alcohol, and fatigue.

As the woman becomes more aroused and gets closer to orgasm, the **orgasmic platform** forms. This is a tightening of the **bulbospongiosus muscle** around the entrance to the

orgasmic platform: A tightening of the entrance to the vagina caused by contractions of the bulbospongiosus muscle (which covers the vestibular bulbs) that occur late in the arousal stage of sexual response.

vagina (Figure 9.2). Thus, the size of the vaginal entrance actually becomes smaller, and there may be a noticeable increase in gripping of the penis.

During the excitement phase, the glans of the clitoris (the tip) swells. This results from engorgement of its corpora cavernosa and is similar to erection in men. The clitoris feels larger and harder than usual under excitement. The crura of the clitoris, lying deeper in the body (refer back to Figure 4.3), also swell as a result of vasocongestion. The vestibular bulbs, which lie along the wall of the vagina, are also erectile and swell during the excitement phase. Late in the excitement phase, elevation of the clitoris may occur. The clitoris essentially retracts or draws up into the body.

Vasocongestion in women results from the same underlying physiological processes as in men. That is, relaxation of the smooth muscles surrounding the arteries supplying the glans and crura of the clitoris and the vestibular bulbs occurs, allowing a great deal of blood flow to the region (Berman et al., 2000). As in the male, nitric oxide is a key neurotransmitter involved in the process (Traish et al., 2002). Estrogen helps the vasodilation. In the unaroused state, the inner lips are generally folded over, covering the entrance to the vagina, and the outer lips lie close to each other. During excitement, the inner lips swell and open up (a vasocongestion response).

Under excitement, the nipples become erect; this results from contractions of the muscle fibres (myotonia) surrounding the nipple. The breasts themselves swell and enlarge somewhat in the late part of the excitement phase (a vasocongestion response). Thus, the nipples may not actually look erect but may appear somewhat flatter against the breast because the breast has swollen. Many men also have nipple erection during the excitement phase.

Figure 9.2 Changes during the sexual response cycle in the female.

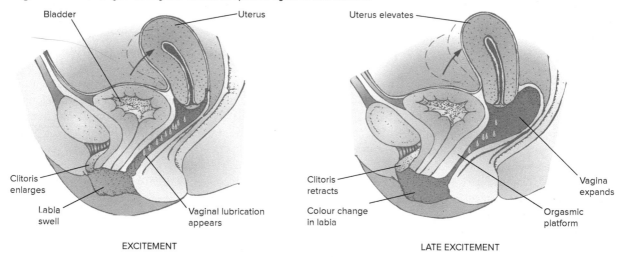

EXCITEMENT

LATE EXCITEMENT

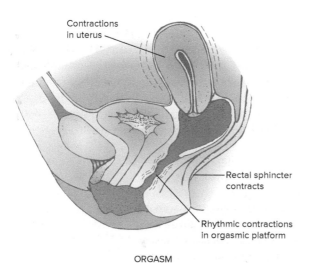

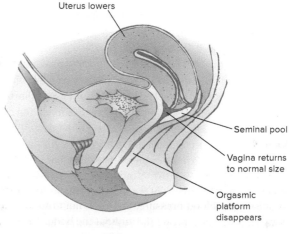

ORGASM

RESOLUTION

The vagina shows an important change during excitement. Think of the vagina as being divided into two parts, an upper (or inner) two-thirds and a lower (or outer) one-third. In the unaroused state, the walls of the vagina lie against each other, much like the sides of an uninflated balloon. During the excitement phase, the upper two-thirds of the vagina expands dramatically in what is often called a *ballooning response;* that is, it becomes more like an inflated balloon (see Figure 9.2). This helps accommodate penetration. As part of the ballooning, the cervix and uterus also pull up.

During excitement, a *sex flush* may appear on the skin of both men and women, though more commonly of women. The sex flush resembles a measles rash; it often begins on the upper abdomen and spreads over the chest. It may also appear later in the sexual response cycle. Other changes that occur in both men and women include increases in pulse rate and in blood pressure.

In men, the skin of the scrotum thickens. The scrotal sac tenses, and the scrotum is pulled up and closer to the body (Figure 9.1). The spermatic cords shorten, pulling the testes closer to the body. Late in the excitement phase, the process of vasocongestion and myotonia continue to build until there is sufficient tension for orgasm.

Orgasm

In men, **orgasm** consists of a series of rhythmic contractions of the pelvic organs at 0.8-second intervals. Actually, male orgasm occurs in two stages. In the preliminary stage, the vas, seminal vesicles, and prostate contract, forcing the ejaculate into a bulb at the base of the urethra (Figure 9.1). Masters and Johnson call the sensation in this stage one of *ejaculatory inevitability* ("cumming"); that is, there is a sensation that ejaculation is just about to happen and cannot be stopped. And, indeed, although men can learn to delay reaching the emission stage of ejaculation, ejaculation cannot be stopped once the man has reached this point. In the second stage, the urethral bulb, muscles at the base of the penis, and the urethra contract rhythmically, forcing the semen through the urethra and out the opening at the tip of the penis. There may also be a difference between ejaculation and the sensation of orgasm (Mah & Binik, 2001). For example, researchers in Quebec have shown that feelings of pleasure and satisfaction from orgasm were more strongly related to psychological and social factors than to physical factors (Mah & Binik, 2005).

In both men and women, the greater the build-up of sexual arousal and desire, the more pleasurable the orgasm (Paterson et al., 2014). There are sharp increases in pulse rate, blood pressure, and breathing rate during orgasm. Muscles contract throughout the body. The face may be contorted in a grimace; the muscles of the arms, legs, thighs, back, and buttocks may contract; and the muscles of the feet and hands may contract in *carpopedal spasms*. Generally, in the passion of the moment, one is not really aware of these occurrences.

The process of orgasm in women is basically similar to that in men. It is a series of rhythmic muscular contractions of the orgasmic platform. The contractions generally occur at about 0.8-second intervals; there may be three or four in a mild orgasm or as many as a dozen in a very intense, prolonged orgasm. The uterus also contracts rhythmically. Other muscles, such as those around the anus, may also contract.

Female orgasm typically leaves no tangible evidence (except for those women who experience emission of fluid), and women often do not reach orgasm as quickly as men do, a point to be discussed in more detail in Chapter 13. As a result, some women, particularly young women, may think they are having an orgasm when they are not; they have never had an orgasm, and they mistake intense arousal for orgasm.

Just what does orgasm in the female feel like? The main feeling is a spreading sensation that begins around the clitoris and then spreads outward through the whole pelvis. There may also be sensations of falling or opening up. The woman may be able to feel the contraction of the muscles around the vaginal entrance. The sensation is more intense than just a warm glow or a pleasant tingling. In one study, university men and women gave written descriptions of what an orgasm felt like to them (Vance & Wagner, 1976). Interestingly, a panel of experts (medical students, obstetrician-gynecologists, and clinical psychologists) could not reliably figure out which of the descriptions were written by women and which by men. This suggests that the sensations are quite similar for men and women.

Some of the men in our classes have asked how they can tell whether a woman has really had an orgasm. Their question in itself is interesting. It reflects, in part, a cultural skepticism about female orgasm. There is usually obvious proof of male orgasm: ejaculation. But there is no consistent proof of female orgasm except that some women do ejaculate. The question also reflects the fact that men know that women sometimes fake orgasm. So do men. A survey of 281 university students reported that 25 percent of the men and 51 percent of the women had faked an orgasm during heterosexual activity (Muehlenhard & Skippee, 2010). Most had pretended during penile–vaginal intercourse. People vary in their reasons for feigning orgasm including being intoxicated, concerns about their partner's self-esteem, poor partner technique, and having sex without desire (Séguin et al., 2015). Faking also reflects a shared sexual script (see Chapter 2) in which

orgasm: The second stage of sexual response; an intense sensation that occurs at the peak of sexual arousal and is followed by release of sexual tensions.

women should orgasm first, and men are responsible for the orgasms.

A focus group study in Ontario sheds further light on beliefs and concerns about female orgasm (Salisbury & Fisher, 2014). The results showed that both women and men believe that men are responsible for stimulating their partner to orgasm. Men confirm that it is important to them that their female partner have an orgasm and that they are distressed if she doesn't have one. Women are concerned that if they don't have an orgasm, their male partner will feel bad about himself or inadequate. New Brunswick researchers have shown that women sometimes fake orgasm to end unwanted or unpleasurable sexual encounters (Thomas et al., 2016). In short, faking is a complex issue. It is not a good practice because it prevents the partner from getting valid feedback about sexual technique. On the other hand, we can appreciate that people do it because of the pressures created by the script.

But back to the question: How can a person tell? There really is not any very good way. From a scientific point of view, a good method would be to have the woman hooked up to an instrument that registers pulse rate; there is a sudden sharp increase in the pulse rate at orgasm, and that would be a good indicator. That doesn't seem like a very practical or desirable approach. Probably rather than trying to check up on each other, it would be better for partners to establish good, honest communication and avoid setting up performance goals in sex, points that will be discussed further in later chapters. Unfortunately, direct communication about women's lack of orgasms is the exception not the rule (Salisbury & Fisher, 2014)

Resolution

Following orgasm is the **resolution** phase, during which the body returns physiologically to the unaroused state. Orgasm triggers a massive release of muscular tension and of blood from the engorged blood vessels. Resolution, then, represents a reversal of the processes that build up during the excitement stage.

The first change in women is a reduction in the swelling of the breasts. In the five to ten seconds after the end of the orgasm, the clitoris returns to its normal position, although it takes longer for it to shrink to its normal size. The orgasmic platform relaxes and begins to shrink. The resolution phase generally takes 15 to 30 minutes, but it may take much longer—as much as an hour—in women who have not had an orgasm.

resolution: The third stage of sexual response, in which the body returns to the unaroused state.

refractory (ree-FRAK-toh-ree) period: The period following orgasm during which the man cannot be sexually aroused.

clitoral orgasm: Freud's term for orgasm in the female resulting from stimulation of the clitoris.

vaginal orgasm: Freud's term for orgasm in the female resulting from stimulation of the vagina in heterosexual intercourse; Freud considered vaginal orgasm to be more mature than clitoral orgasm.

In both males and females, resolution brings a gradual return of pulse rate, blood pressure, and breathing rate to the unaroused levels.

In men, the most obvious occurrence in the resolution phase is *detumescence,* the loss of erection in the penis. This happens in two stages, the first occurring rapidly but leaving the penis still enlarged (this first loss of erection results from an emptying of the corpora cavernosa) and the second occurring more slowly, as a result of the slower emptying of the corpus spongiosum and the glans.

During the resolution phase, men enter a **refractory period**, during which they are refractory to further arousal; that is, they are incapable of being aroused again, having an erection, or having an orgasm. The length of this refractory period varies considerably from one man to the next; in some it may last only a few minutes, and in others it may go on for 24 hours. The refractory period tends to become longer as men grow older. Women usually do not have a refractory period, making it possible for them to experience multiple orgasm, which is discussed in the next section.

Oxytocin is secreted during sexual arousal, and a surge of prolactin occurs at orgasm in both women and men (Exton et al., 1999; Krüger et al., 2002; Levin, 2003). Some researchers think that prolactin is the off switch to sexual arousal and that it creates the refractory period in males, although that does not explain why females do not have a refractory period. Interestingly, in both women and men, much more prolactin is secreted following orgasm from intercourse than orgasm from masturbation (Kruger, 2006).

An important component of the resolution phase for most couples is engaging in affectionate behaviour such as cuddling, caressing, and shared intimacy after sex. Researchers in Ontario showed that couples who spend longer engaging in *post sex affection* report higher sexual and relationship satisfaction (Muise et al., 2014). The bottom line is that orgasm is not the end of *satisfying* sex, and couples should not just roll over and go to sleep after one or both have reached orgasm.

More on Women's Orgasms

Some people believe that women can have two kinds of orgasm: **clitoral orgasm** and **vaginal orgasm**. The words *clitoral* and *vaginal* refer to the locus of stimulation: an orgasm resulting from clitoral stimulation versus an orgasm resulting from vaginal stimulation. The distinction was originated by Sigmund Freud. Freud believed that in childhood little girls masturbate and thus have orgasms by means of clitoral stimulation, or clitoral orgasms. He thought that as women grow older and mature, that is, after the Oedipal stage, they shift their erogenous zone from their clitoris to their vagina. Consequently, they shift from having orgasms as a result of clitoral stimulation to having them as a result of heterosexual intercourse, that is, by means of vaginal stimulation. Thus he considered vaginal orgasms "mature" and clitoral orgasms "immature" in a developmental sense. Not only were there two types of orgasms, but "mature" has been taken to mean "better," such that many people view one kind of orgasm (orgasms through intercourse alone) as better than the other.

According to the results of Masters and Johnson's research, there is no difference between clitoral and vaginal orgasms. This conclusion is based on two findings. First, their results indicate that all female orgasms are physiologically the same, regardless of the site of stimulation. That is, an orgasm always consists of contractions of the orgasmic platform and the muscles around the vagina whether the stimulation is clitoral or vaginal. Indeed, they found a few women who could orgasm purely through breast stimulation, and that orgasm was the same as the other two. Thus, physiologically there is only one kind of orgasm. (Of course, this does not mean that psychologically there are not different kinds; the experience of orgasm with a partner may be quite different from the experience of orgasm during masturbation.)

Second, clitoral stimulation is almost always involved in producing orgasm, even during vaginal intercourse. The deep structure of the clitoris (refer again to Figure 4.3) ensures that the crura of the clitoris are stimulated as the penis moves through the vaginal entrance. Thus, even the purely vaginal orgasm results from quite a bit of clitoral stimulation. Clitoral stimulation is usually the trigger to orgasm; the orgasm itself occurs in the vagina and surrounding tissues.

Stimulation of the glans of the clitoris by a thrusting penis in the vagina could contribute to an orgasm. Look again at Figure 4.1. The glans and the vaginal opening are some distance apart, and this distance varies from woman to woman. In 1924 psychoanalyst Marie Bonaparte proposed that a shorter distance would be associated with greater likelihood of experiencing an orgasm during penile–vaginal intercourse. In the interest of standardizing measurement by using two fixed points (instead of the variable "top" of the vaginal opening), she measured the clitoral–urethral meatus distance (CUMD). Wallen and Lloyd (2011) obtained two data sets containing measures of CUMD and measures of orgasm for 78 adult women. Shorter distances were associated with increased likelihood of orgasm. Genital anatomy can make a difference!

Masters and Johnson also discovered that women do not enter into a refractory period, and with continued stimulation they can have **multiple orgasms** within a short time. Actually, women's capacity for multiple orgasms was originally discovered by Kinsey in his interviews with women (Kinsey et al., 1953; see also Terman et al., 1938). The scientific establishment, however, dismissed these reports as another instance of Kinsey's supposed unreliability.

The term *multiple orgasm*, then, refers to a series of orgasms occurring within a short time. They do not differ physiologically from single orgasms. Each is a real orgasm, and they are not minor experiences.

How does multiple orgasm work physiologically? Immediately following an orgasm, both males and females move into the resolution phase. In this phase, males typically enter into a refractory period, during which they cannot be aroused again. But women usually do not enter a refractory period, perhaps because after orgasm it takes longer for vasocongestion to return to baseline in women than in men (Mah & Binik, 2001). That is, if stimulation continues, most women can immediately be aroused and have another orgasm if they choose to.

Multiple orgasm with a partner is more likely to result from hand–genital or mouth–genital stimulation than from intercourse. Regarding capacity, Masters and Johnson found that through masturbation, women might have 5 to 20 orgasms. In some cases, they quit only when physically exhausted. When a vibrator is used, less effort is required, and some women were capable of having 50 orgasms in a row.

It should be noted that some women who are capable of multiple orgasms are satisfied with one, particularly in intercourse, and do not want to continue. We should be careful not to set multiple orgasm as another of the many goals in sexual performance.

Some men are capable of having multiple orgasms (e.g., Hartman & Fithian, 1984; Zilbergeld, 1992). In one study, 21 men were interviewed, all of whom had volunteered for research on multiply orgasmic men (Dunn & Trost, 1989). Some of the men reported having been multiply orgasmic since they began having sex, whereas others had developed the pattern later in life, and still others had worked actively to develop the capacity after reading about the possibility. The respondents reported that multiple orgasm did not occur every time they engaged in sexual activity. For these men, detumescence did not always follow an orgasm, allowing for continued stimulation and an additional orgasm. Some reported that some of the orgasms included ejaculation and others in the sequence did not. This study cannot tell us the incidence of multiply orgasmic men in the general population, but it does provide evidence that multiply orgasmic men exist.

Other Models of Sexual Response

Some experts on human sexuality are critical of Masters and Johnson's model. One important criticism is that the Masters

multiple orgasms: A series of orgasms occurring within a short period of time.

and Johnson model ignores the cognitive and subjective aspects of sexual response (Zilbergeld & Evans, 1980). That is, Masters and Johnson focused almost entirely on the physiological aspects of sexual response, ignoring what the person is thinking and feeling emotionally. Desire and passion are not part of the model, and it omits the subjective qualities of arousal and orgasm. An individual's subjective experience may be influenced by the context and the quality of the relationship in which sexual activity occurs as well as by a variety of psychological factors (Mah & Binik, 2001). The omission of the subjective element may be particularly problematic in understanding women's sexual response because women tend to emphasize subjective arousal rather than physical arousal (Working Group for a New View of Women's Sexual Problems, 2001). Women's sense of being aroused is often unrelated to awareness of genital changes (Laan et al., 1994). Research in Quebec has shown that there are two components to orgasm for both men and women: a sensory dimension, made up of the physical sensations, and a cognitive-affective dimension, consisting of pleasure, satisfaction, emotional intimacy, and feelings of ecstasy (Mah & Binik, 2002).

A second important criticism concerns how research participants were selected and how this process may have created a self-fulfilling prophecy for the outcome (Tiefer, 1991). To participate in the research, participants were required to have a history of orgasm both through masturbation and through coitus. Essentially, anyone whose pattern of sexual response did not include orgasm—and therefore did not fit Masters and Johnson's model—was excluded from the research. As such, the model cannot be generalized to the entire population. Masters and Johnson themselves commented that every one of their participants was characterized by high and consistent levels of sexual desire. Yet sexual desire is certainly missing among some members of the general population, or it is present at some times and absent at others. The research, in short, claims to be objective and universal when it is neither (Tiefer, 1991).

Once these difficulties with the Masters and Johnson research and model of sexual response were recognized, alternative models were proposed. We will examine three of them in the following sections.

Kaplan's Triphasic Model

On the basis of her work on sex therapy (discussed in Chapter 18), Helen Singer Kaplan (1974, 1979) proposed a **triphasic model** of sexual response. Rather than thinking of the sexual response as having successive stages, she conceptualized it as having three relatively independent phases or

triphasic model: Kaplan's model of sexual response, in which there are three components: sexual desire, vasocongestion, and muscular contractions.

components: *sexual desire, vasocongestion* of the genitals, and the reflex *muscular contractions* of the orgasm phase. Notice that two of the components (vasocongestion and muscular contractions) are physiological, whereas the other (sexual desire) is psychological. Therefore, Kaplan's model adds the cognitive component, desire, that was missing in Masters and Johnson's model.

Kaplan's approach has a number of justifications. First, the two physiological components are controlled by different parts of the nervous system. Vasocongestion—producing erection in the male and lubrication in the female—is controlled by the parasympathetic division of the autonomic nervous system. In contrast, ejaculation and orgasm are controlled by the sympathetic division.

Second, the two components involve different anatomical structures: blood vessels for vasocongestion and muscles for the contractions of orgasm.

Third, vasocongestion and orgasm differ in their susceptibility to being disturbed by injury, drugs, or age. For example, the refractory period following orgasm in the male lengthens with age. Accordingly, there is a decrease in the frequency of orgasm with age. In contrast, for many men, the capacity for erection is relatively unimpaired with age, although the erection may be slower to make its appearance. A much-older man may have nonorgasmic sex several times a week, with a firm erection, although he may have an orgasm only once a week.

Fourth, the reflex of ejaculation in the male can be brought under voluntary control by most men, but the erection reflex generally cannot.

Finally, the impairment of the vasocongestion response or the orgasm response produce different disturbances (sexual disorders). Erection problems in men are caused by an impairment of the vasocongestion response, whereas rapid ejaculation and delayed ejaculation are disturbances of the orgasm response. Similarly, many women show a strong arousal and vasocongestion response, yet have trouble with the orgasm component of their sexual response.

Kaplan's triphasic model is useful both for understanding the nature of sexual response and for understanding and treating disturbances in it. Her writing on the desire phase is particularly useful in understanding problems of low sexual desire, discussed in Chapter 18.

The Intimacy Model

Kaplan's model assumes that desire comes before arousal, motivating the person toward sexual activity and excitement. Vancouver therapist physician Rosemary Basson (2001a) has developed an intimacy-based model of sexual response that does not make this assumption (see Figure 9.3). She argues that some people in long-term relationships, particularly women, may not be motivated to engage in sexual activity by their experience

Figure 9.3 Basson's intimacy model of sexual response showing that desire sometimes comes after arousal or excitement.

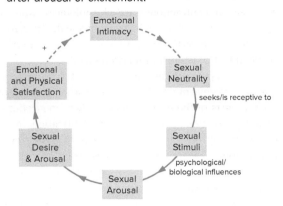

of spontaneous sexual desire. Rather they are motivated to engage in sexual activity to enhance intimacy, closeness, and commitment with their partner; to enhance their sense of attractiveness; or to share physical sexual pleasure. That is, they begin sexual activity in a sexually neutral state, but are receptive to sexual stimuli that will arouse them. Once sexual activity has begun, the person becomes aroused. This leads them to experience sexual desire and enhanced sexual arousal. Thus, according to Basson, some people may begin sexual activity for intimacy reasons but then continue for sexual as well as intimacy reasons. Basson also acknowledges that even in long-term relationships, both men and women can and do experience spontaneous sexual desire outside of this intimacy model that may lead to sexual activity with their partner, casual sex, or self-stimulation.

A recent study by Canadian researchers described the Masters and Johnson, Kaplan, and Basson models to women and asked them which fit their experience best (Sand & Fisher, 2007). About equal numbers of women chose each of the three models.

The Dual Control Model

John Bancroft and his colleagues introduced the **dual control model** of sexual response (Bancroft et al., 2009). The model proposes that two basic processes underlie human sexual response: excitation (responding with arousal to sexual stimuli) and inhibition (inhibiting sexual arousal). The Bancroft team argues that almost all sex research has focused on the excitation component, and certainly the Masters and Johnson research falls in that category. They believe that it is equally important to understand the inhibition component. They observe that inhibition of sexual response is adaptive across species; sexual arousal can be a powerful distraction that could become disadvantageous or even dangerous in certain situations.

According to the dual control model, propensities toward sexual excitation and sexual inhibition vary widely from one person to the next. Most people fall in the moderate range on both and function well. At the extremes, however, problems can occur. People who are very high on the excitation component and low on the inhibition component may engage in high-risk sexual behaviours. People who are very high on inhibition and low on excitation may be more likely to develop sexual disorders, such as erectile dysfunction or low sexual desire.

Bancroft and his colleagues have developed scales to measure individuals' tendencies toward sexual excitation and sexual inhibition (Janssen et al., 2002a, 2002b). These are some examples of *excitation* items:

- When I think of a very attractive person, I easily become sexually aroused.
- When I am taking a shower or a bath, I easily become sexually aroused.
- When a sexually attractive stranger accidentally touches me, I easily become aroused.

These are examples of *inhibition* items (male version/female version):

- I need my penis to be touched to maintain an erection/I need my clitoris to be stimulated to continue feeling aroused.
- Putting on a condom can cause me to lose my erection/Using condoms or other safe-sex products can cause me to lose my arousal.
- If I am masturbating on my own and I realize that someone is likely to come into the room at any moment, I will lose my erection/my sexual arousal.

Data collected with large samples by using these scales support the model's assumption that individuals do vary widely in their tendencies toward excitation and inhibition.

The dual control model also recognizes that, although both excitation and inhibition have biological bases, early learning and culture are critical factors for both men and women because they determine which stimuli the individual will find to be sexually exciting or will set off sexual inhibition (Figure 9.4). For example, media images communicate standards of what women are *supposed* to look like to be considered sexually attractive and desirable, which likely affects what body types men find most attractive. In Canada these models are typically overly thin women with large breasts. Conversely, most men in our culture have learned that children are not appropriate sexual stimuli, so any sexual response to them is inhibited.

dual control model: A model that holds that sexual response is controlled both by sexual excitation and by sexual inhibition.

Figure 9.4   Can the dual control model of sexual arousal explain our response to this? Here a man touches a woman's breast, but it is not sexual. Why not? The context, a medical office, leads us not to perceive the woman's breast as a sexual stimulus nor the man's touch as sexual.

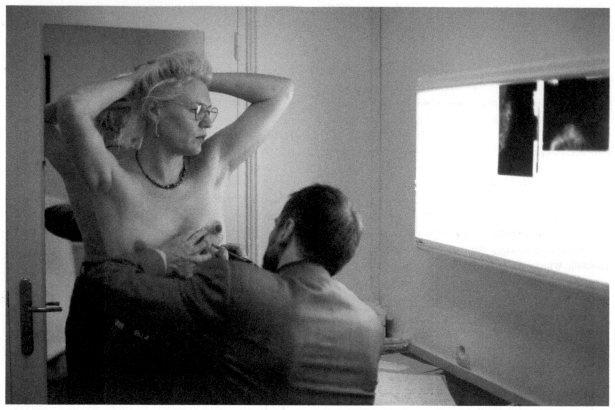

© Owen Franken/Getty Images

Wouldn't evolution have selected purely for sexual excitation? It is the engine that drives reproduction and passing our genes to the next generation. Would inhibition therefore be dysfunctional in an evolutionary sense? Not according to the dual control model. First, sexual activity in some situations could be downright dangerous. Imagine, for example, that the King and Queen are locked in a lusty embrace while the castle is being stormed by enemies, who are eager to kill them both. Sexual inhibition would be very adaptive at that point, so that the King and Queen could engage in non-sexual behaviours that would save their lives. Second, sometimes the environment is not conducive to repro-duction and it is better to wait for a better day or a better season. An example is conditions of drought and famine in which women's fertility is usually sharply reduced because any baby that was born would likely die, and the mother might die as well in the attempt to provide food. Inhibiting sexual response and waiting until condi-tions improve would be the best strategy. Third, exces-sive sexual behaviour in men, perhaps with ejaculations several times a day, reduces fertility. The body cannot produce sperm quickly enough to have a high sperm count in each of those ejaculations, so the high rate of

sexual behaviour would not be adaptive in an evolution-ary sense.

Data support many aspects of this model. We will review some of these data in the later section and then return to it in the chapter on sexual disorders, because it is helpful in understanding them.

Emotion and Arousal

A major criticism of Masters and Johnson's model of sexual response was that it was all physiological, ignor-ing the psychological aspects of sexual responding. The three alternative models that we have reviewed so far—Kaplan's three-component model, the intimacy model, and the excitation–inhibition model—make major strides in filling in some of the psychological missing pieces. Cognitive processes are added with Kaplan's component of sexual desire; motivation and relationship factors are added with the intimacy model; and the excitation–inhibition model emphasizes the importance of culture and early learning in shaping the way the individual pro-cesses and evaluates sexual stimuli.

What is still missing, though, is a recognition of the importance of emotion in sexual arousal. No one has proposed a formal model of emotion and arousal, so here we will review one study that provides a preview of what these effects might look like. Researchers recruited 81 mixed-sex and 106 same-sex couples (Ridley et al., 2008). A daily diary method was used in which each participant logged onto a website at the same time each day for 14 days. The daily questionnaire contained questions about emotions and sexual behaviours. Members of the couple were asked to fill it out separately and independently. The results indicated that, over time, positive emotions (e.g., happiness) showed a strong positive association with reports of sexual arousal. That is, when people were happier, they also had more thoughts of sexual arousal. The surprising result was that negative emotions (e.g., anger, anxiety, sadness) were also positively correlated with reports of sexual arousal. When people experienced stronger negative emotions, they also had more thoughts of arousal. The researchers believe that this is because emotions like anxiety and anger involve generalized arousal, which intensifies arousal responses to sexual stimuli. (For other studies investigating the relationship between emotion and sexual expression, see Burleson et al., 2007, and Fortenberry et al., 2005.)

Research in British Columbia suggests that the propensity toward excitement or inhibition as proposed in the dual control model may play a role in the impact of emotion on the sexual response (Winters et al., 2009). However, so far this research has only been done with men. Clearly there is much intriguing research to be done about the role of emotions in sexual responding.

LO3 Hormonal and Neural Bases of Sexual Behaviour

Up to this point we have focused on the psychological and genital responses that occur during sexual activity. We have not yet considered the underlying neural and hormonal mechanisms that make this possible; they are the topic of this section.

The Brain, the Spinal Cord, and Sex

The brain and the spinal cord both have important interacting functions in sexual response. First, the relatively simple spinal reflexes involved in sexual response will be discussed, and then the more complex brain mechanisms will be considered.

Spinal Reflexes

Several important components of sexual behaviour, including erection and ejaculation, are controlled by fairly simple spinal cord reflexes (see the lower part of Figure 9.5). A reflex has three basic components: the *receptors*, which are sensory neurons that detect stimuli and transmit the message to the spinal cord (or brain); the *transmitters*, which are centres in the spinal cord (or brain) that receive the message, interpret it, and send out a message to produce the appropriate response; and the *effectors*, neurons or muscles that respond to the stimulation. The jerking away of the hand when it touches a hot object is a good example of a spinal reflex.

Mechanism of Erection

Erection can be produced by a spinal reflex with a similar mechanism, although it can also be produced by cognitive factors (McKenna, 2000). Tactile stimulation (stroking or rubbing) of the penis (which has lots of receptor neurons) or nearby regions, such as the scrotum or thighs, produces a neural signal that is transmitted to an *erection centre* in the sacral, or lowest, part of the spinal cord (there may also be another erection centre higher in the cord). This centre then sends out a message via the parasympathetic division of the autonomic nervous system to the muscles (the effectors) around the walls of the arteries in the penis. In response to the message, the muscles relax; the arteries then expand, permitting a large volume of blood to flow into them, and erection results. Furthermore, the valves in the veins and the compression of the veins caused by the swelling in

Figure 9.5 Nervous system control of erection. Note both the reflex centre in the spinal cord and brain control.

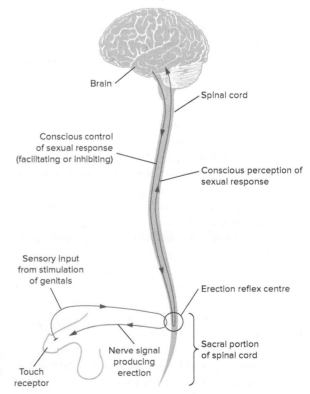

Brain

Spinal cord

Conscious control of sexual response (facilitating or inhibiting)

Conscious perception of sexual response

Sensory input from stimulation of genitals

Erection reflex centre

Touch receptor

Nerve signal producing erection

Sacral portion of spinal cord

the tissue around them reduce the blood flow out of the penis (Adams et al., 1997).

The existence of this reflex is confirmed by the responses of men who have had their spinal cords completely severed, as a result of accidents, at a level above that of the reflex centre. They are capable of having erections and ejaculations produced by rubbing their genitals, although it is clear that no brain effects can be operating, since signals from the brain cannot move past the point at which the spinal cord was severed. (In fact, these men cannot feel anything because neural signals cannot be transmitted up the spinal cord either.) Thus, erection can be produced simply by tactile stimulation of the genitals, which triggers the spinal reflex.

Erection may also be produced by conditions other than tactile stimulation of the genitals; for example, fantasy or other purely psychological factors may produce erection. This points to the importance of the brain in producing erection, a topic that will be discussed in a later section.

Mechanism of Ejaculation

The ejaculation reflex is similar, except that there are two ejaculation centres and they are located higher in the spinal cord, the sympathetic and parasympathetic divisions of the nervous system are involved, and the response is muscular not vasocongestion (Giuliano & Clement, 2005; Rowland & Slob, 1997). In the ejaculation reflex, the penis responds to stimulation by sending a message to the *ejaculation centre,* which is located in the lumbar portion of the spinal cord. A message is then sent out via the nerves in the sympathetic nervous system, and this message

retrograde ejaculation: A condition in which orgasm in the male is not accompanied by an external ejaculation; instead, the ejaculate goes into the urinary bladder.

triggers muscle contractions in the internal organs that are involved in ejaculation.

Ejaculation can often be controlled voluntarily by controlling the approach to ejaculation (see Chapter 18 for more information). This fact highlights the importance of brain influences on the ejaculation reflex (Truitt & Coolen, 2002).

The three main problems of ejaculation are rapid ejaculation, male orgasmic disorder (delayed ejaculation), and retrograde ejaculation. Rapid ejaculation, which is by far the most common problem, and male orgasmic disorder will be discussed in Chapter 18. **Retrograde ejaculation** occurs when the ejaculate, rather than going out through the tip of the penis, empties into the bladder (Kothari, 1984). A "dry orgasm" results, since no ejaculate is emitted. This problem can be caused by some illnesses, by tranquilizers and drugs used in the treatment of psychoses, and by prostate surgery. The mechanism that causes it is fairly simple (see Figure 9.6). Two sphincters are involved in ejaculation: an internal one, which closes off the entrance to the bladder during a normal ejaculation, and an external one, which opens during a normal ejaculation, allowing the semen to flow out through the penis. In retrograde ejaculation, the actions of these two sphincters are desynchronized; the external one closes, and thus the ejaculate cannot flow out through the penis, and the internal one opens, permitting the ejaculate to go into the bladder. The condition itself is quite harmless, although some men are disturbed by the lack of sensation of emitting semen.

Mechanisms in Women

Unfortunately, there is far less research on similar reflex mechanisms in women. We know that sensory input—such as touch—travels along the dorsal nerve of the clitoris

Figure 9.6 How a retrograde ejaculation occurs.

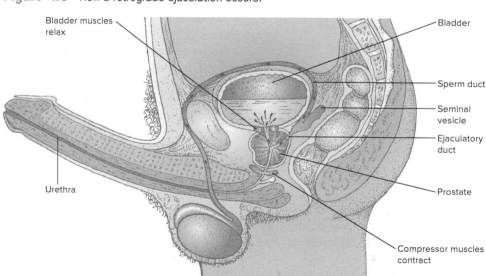

and continues within the pudendal nerve to a reflex centre in the sacral portion of the spinal cord (Berman et al., 2000). Research with nonhumans—mainly male and female rats—has investigated the urethrogenital reflex, which results in muscle contractions similar to orgasm in humans (Meston et al., 2004). This research suggests that the neural circuits for orgasm in women are very similar to those for orgasm and ejaculation in men. The clitoris has both sympathetic and parasympathetic nerve fibres. The vagina, too, is supplied by both sympathetic and parasympathetic nerves. The limbic system of the brain is crucial to both female and male sexual arousal.

Research indicates that some women emit fluid during orgasm, often referred to as *female ejaculation* (Addiego et al., 1981; Belzer, 1981; Perry & Whipple, 1981). The region responsible is the **Gräfenberg spot or G-spot**, also called the *female prostate* or the *Skene's glands* (Schubach, 2002). It is located on the top side of the vagina (with the woman lying on her back, which is the best position for finding it), about halfway between the pubic bone and the cervix (see Figure 9.7). Its ducts open into the urethra. Stroking it produces an urge to urinate, but if the stroking continues for a few seconds more, it begins to produce sexual pleasure. The original researchers, Perry and Whipple, argued that continued stimulation of it produces a uterine orgasm, characterized by deeper sensations of uterine contractions than the clitorally induced vulvar orgasm investigated in the Masters and Johnson research.

In one survey of women, 40 percent reported having experienced ejaculation at the time of orgasm at least once, and 66 percent reported having an especially sensitive area on the front wall of the vagina (Darling et al., 1990). Biochemical analyses indicate that the female prostate produces *prostate-specific antigen* (PSA), just as the male prostate does (Zaviačič, Zajíčkovà, et al., 2000). In the most recent study, MRI scans identified a female prostate in six of seven women studied (Wimpissinger et al., 2009).

Figure 9.7 The Gräfenberg spot, or G-spot: hypothesized to produce ejaculation in some women.

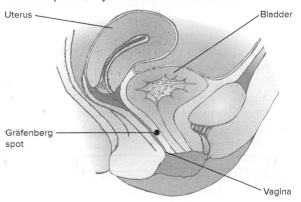

Uterus
Bladder
Gräfenberg spot
Vagina

Brain Control of Sexual Response

Sexual responses are controlled by more than simple spinal reflexes. They may be brought under voluntary control, and they may be initiated by purely psychological forces, such as fantasy. Environmental factors, such as having been taught as a child that sex is dirty and sinful, may also affect one's sexual response. All these phenomena point to the critical influence of the brain and its interaction with the spinal reflexes in producing sexual response (see Figure 9.5). As once scientist commented, the most important sex organ is the brain.

Research using sophisticated imaging techniques is revealing a great deal about brain control of sexual response (see Milestones in Sex Research). The results indicate that distinct brain regions and networks are associated with desire/interest, arousal, orgasm, and the refractory period (Georgiadis & Kringelbach, 2012; Pfaus, 2014; Poeppl et al., 2014). Interestingly, these neural networks are quite similar to other pleasure networks in the brain such as those involved in the pleasure of eating food. The researchers in this field organize the phases of sexual response differently from the Masters and Johnson model of excitement, orgasm, and resolution. The brain-imaging researchers instead think about (1) an *anticipatory phase* that includes sexual interest, desire, and the beginnings of arousal; (2) a *consummatory phase* that involves sexual activity (whether with a partner or solo) and orgasm; and (3) a *post-orgasmic period* that corresponds to Masters and Johnson's resolution phase and includes a refractory period in males.

Anticipatory Phase

Brain imaging research frequently uses visual sexual stimuli to produce arousal, either still photos or video clips of sexual activity.

Still photos presented to heterosexual men create neural activity in the *sexual interest network*, which includes the nucleas accumbens (NAcc, which is the centre of the brain very close to the hypothalamus), amygdala, anterior cingulate cortex (pACC), and hypothalamus (see Figure 9.8). These are all part of the **limbic system**. Interestingly, erection is not associated with activity in these regions, suggesting that the role of the interest network is to recognize sexual opportunities in the environment.

In contrast to still photos, videos depicting sexual activity produce stronger arousal and erection. The *sexual arousal network* involves activity in different regions of the brain, as described in Milestones in Sex Research.

Gräfenberg spot (GRAY-fen-berg) or G-spot: A small region on the front wall of the vagina, emptying into the urethra and responsible for female ejaculation. Also called the female prostate or the Skene's glands.
limbic system: A set of structures in the interior of the brain, including the amygdala, hippocampus, and fornix; believed to be important for sexual behaviour in both animals and humans.

Figure 9.8 The limbic system of the brain, which is important in sexuality.

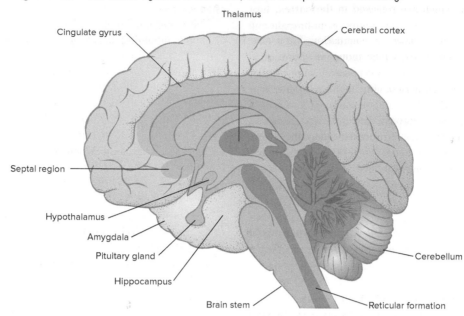

Most of this research has involved men. The few studies of heterosexual women suggest that their brain activity is similar to men's, expecially in response to photos (the sexual interest network) (Stoleru et al., 2012). When women look specifically at men's faces, activity occurs in the medial orbitofrontal cortex (mOFC). One study demonstrated that subliminal presentation of visual sexual stimuli to women created the same vaginal responses as viewing a photo (Ponseti & Bosinski, 2010), suggesting that activation of the sexual interest network is automatic (nonconscious).

Consummatory Phase: Brain Activity during Sexual Activity

When the clitoris or penis is stimulated, yet another pattern of brain electrical activity is detected (Georgiadis & Kringelbach, 2012). In relation to Masters and Johnson's stages, this would correspond roughly to excitement and late excitement. Genital stimulation creates activity in the motor cortex, not surprisingly, given that pelvic muscles are so involved in sexual activity. There is also activity in the somatosensory cortex as we respond to the feel of the stimulation. Patterns of brain activation during sexual activity are correlated with both objective measures of arousal (using a plethysmograph) and subjective measures of arousal based on self-report. Interestingly, there is reduced activity in the amygdala, indicating a different brain response during sexual activity than in the desire/interest phase.

During excitement and late excitement, of course, there can be small waves of decreased excitement or de-arousal. When a wave of decreased arousal occurs and the penis becomes less erect, there is activity in the

ventromedial prefrontal cortex (vmPFC), amygdala, and parahippocampal gyrus (which surrounds the hippocampus and lies next to the amygdala), as well as one region of the hypothalamus.

Orgasm

The most prominent brain response related to orgasm is decreased activity in the prefontal cortex, which is associated with subjective ratings of pleasure.

Resolution and Post-Orgasmic Period

This period is more easily studied in men because they almost always have an orgasm in response to sexual activity. Using fMRI to scan men's brains 3 to 30 minutes post-orgasm, activity was observed in the septal area, temporal lobe, and amygdala. The results suggest a *de-arousal neural network* including these areas and others as well.

Neurochemical Influences on Sexual Response

We just described activity in various regions of the brain that are associated with sexual response. This neural activity is closely related to neurochemical processes. Distinctive neurochemicals are involved in sexual excitation and sexual inhibition.

During excitation, or the anticipatory and consummatory phases of sexual response, dopamines, melanocortins, oxytocin, and norepinephrine are involved (Pfaus, 2009). Dopamine and melanocortin stimulate attention to sexual stimuli and sexual desire within the limbic system. Noradrenalin and oxytocin stimulate sexual arousal and erection. In part, the activation of these neurochemicals also block the action of inhibitory processes.

Neurochemicals involved in inhibitory processes include opioids, which are released in the cortex, limbic system, hypothalamus, and midbrain in response to sexual pleasure and orgasm or ejaculation. They also include endocannabinoids, which induce sedation (and counteract stress!), and serotonin, which induces satiety and the refractory period. (For more detail and diagrams, see Pfaus, 2009.)

The sex hormones androgen, estrogen, and progestin facilitate or prime the brain to respond to sexual incentives by binding to specific hormone receptor complexes, which in turn leads to the synthesis of these neurochemicals.

L04 Hormones and Sex

The sex hormones are another important physiological force that interacts with the nervous system to influence sexual response.

Organizing versus Activating Effects

Endocrinologists generally make a distinction between the organizing effects of hormones and their activating effects. As discussed in Chapter 5, hormones present during prenatal development have important influences on genital anatomy, creating male or female genitals. Effects such as these are called the **organizing effects of hormones** because they cause a relatively permanent change in the organization of some structure, whether in the nervous system or in the reproductive system. Typically there are critical periods during which these hormone effects may occur.

It has also been known for some time that if an adult male mouse or rat is castrated (has the testes removed, which removes the source of testosterone), it will cease engaging in sexual behaviour (and will be less aggressive). If that animal is then given injections of testosterone, it will start engaging in sex again. Effects such as these are called the **activating effects of hormones** because they activate (or deactivate) certain behaviours.

The organizing effects of sex hormones on sexual behaviour have been well documented (Keefe, 2002). In a classic experiment, testosterone was administered to pregnant female guinea pigs. The female offspring that had been exposed to testosterone prenatally[1] were, in adulthood, incapable of displaying "female" sexual behaviour (in particular, lordosis, which is a sexual posturing involving arching of the back and raising of the hindquarters so that intromission of the male's penis is possible) (Phoenix et al., 1959). It is thought that this result occurred because the testosterone "organized" the brain tissue (particularly the hypothalamus) in a male fashion. These female offspring were also born with masculinized genitals, and thus their reproductive systems had also been organized in the male direction. But the important point here is that the prenatal doses of testosterone had masculinized their sexual behaviour. Similar results have been obtained in experiments with many other species.

These hormonally masculinized females in adulthood displayed mounting behaviour, a male sexual behaviour.[2] When they were given testosterone in adulthood, they showed about as much mounting behaviour as males did. Thus, the testosterone administered in adulthood *activated* male patterns of sexual behaviour.

The analogous experiment on males would be castration at birth, followed by administration of ovarian hormones in adulthood. When this was done with rats, female sexual behaviour resulted; these males responded to mating attempts by other males essentially in the same way females do (Harris & Levine, 1965). Their brain tissue had been organized in a "female" direction during an early critical period when testosterone was absent, and the female behaviour patterns were activated in adulthood by administration of ovarian hormones.

It thus seems that males and females initially have capacities for both male and female sexual behaviours; if testosterone is present early in development, the capacity for exhibiting female behaviours is suppressed. Sex hormones in adulthood then activate the behaviour patterns that were differentiated early in development.

How relevant is this research to humans? Generally, the trend is for the behaviour of lower species to be more under hormonal control and for the behaviour of higher species to be more under brain (neural) control. Thus, human sexual behaviour is less under hormonal control than rat sexual behaviour; human sexual behaviour is more controlled by the brain, and thus learning from past experiences and cultural conventions, which are stored in the brain, are more likely to have a profound effect (Wallen, 2001).

Let us now consider in more detail the known activating effects of sex hormones on the sexual behaviour of adult humans.

Testosterone and Sexual Desire

Testosterone has well-documented effects on libido, or sexual desire, in humans (Carani et al., 1990; Carter, 1992; Everitt & Bancroft, 1991). In men deprived of their main source of testosterone by

> **What hormone is most important to sexual desire in men? In women?**

> **organizing effects of hormones:** Effects of sex hormones early in development, resulting in a permanent change in the brain or reproductive system.
> **activating effects of hormones:** Effects of sex hormones in adulthood, resulting in the activation of behaviours, especially sexual behaviours and aggressive behaviours.

---

[1] Note the similarity of these experiments to John Money's observations of human intersex individuals (Chapter 5).

[2] The term *male sexual behaviour* is being used here to refer to a sexual behaviour that is displayed by normal males of the species and either is absent in females of that species or is present at a much lower frequency. Normal females do mount, but they do so less frequently than males do. *Female sexual behaviour* is defined similarly.

Milestones in Sex Research

What Happens in the Brain during Sex?

Exciting advances in the technology of neuroimaging are giving us inside views of the human brain during various phases of sexual response. Methods such as PET (positron emission tomography) and fMRI (functional magnetic resonance imaging) show which regions of the brain "light up" (have neurons most actively firing) while the individual is solving a math problem or thinking about something sad.

Sex researchers have adopted these techniques, with the goal of learning which regions of the brain are most involved in various aspects of sexuality. One of the challenges they have faced is that the participant cannot move while in an MRI scanner. Researchers have dealt with the problem by showing erotic videos to the person inside the scanner.

In one experiment, heterosexual men viewed erotic video clips, relaxing clips, and sports clips in random order (Arnow et al., 2002). Meanwhile, their brains were being scanned in an MRI machine and the erection of the penis was measured. One has to admire these men for being able to become aroused while in an MRI scanner! Pictures from the brain scans are shown in Figure 9.9. When the men were exposed to erotic clips and were sexually aroused, as indicated by erection, intense brain activity was found in the right insula and claustrum, striatum (left caudate nucleus and putamen), cingulate gyrus, and—you guessed it—the hypothalamus. The insula is known to be involved in sensory processing, particularly of touch sensations. The cingulate cortex has been demonstrated in other studies to be involved in attentional processes and in guiding responsiveness to new environmental stimuli. Doubtless it was activated because of the men's attention to the erotic film.

Another study used fMRI to assess brain activation in both men and women while viewing erotic video segments (Karama et al., 2002). This study found brain activation in roughly the same regions as the study discussed previously. Almost all regions responded similarly in women and men. This study also found evidence of activation of the amygdala during sexual arousal. The amygdala is part of the limbic system, and as noted in this chapter, plays a role in sexual response. The amygdala is known to be involved in emotion, and its activation speaks to the strong emotions—sometimes positive, sometimes negative—that are evoked by sexual stimuli.

Research with women with spinal-cord injury indicates that they experience sexual arousal and orgasm as a result of genital stimulation (Komisaruk & Whipple, 2005). The neural signals do not travel up the spinal cord, which has been damaged, but rather pass up to the brain through the vagus nerves. fMRI scans indicate that the brain regions activated during arousal include the hypothalamus, amygdala, hippocampus, and the rest of the list of structures identified in fMRI research on people without spinal-cord injuries.

These studies are fascinating in themselves as they allow us to view the workings of the brain during sexual responding. As research advances, future studies will help us understand the brain regions and associated neurotransmitters involved in sexual dysfunction, which may lead to more effective treatments for these

castration or by illness, there is a dramatic decrease in sexual behaviour in some, but not all, cases. Sexual desire is rapidly lost if a man is given an anti-androgen drug. Thus, testosterone seems to have an activating effect in maintaining sexual desire in men. However, in cases of castration, sexual behaviour may decline very slowly and may be present for several years after the source of testosterone is gone; this points to the importance of experience and brain control of sexual behaviour in humans.

It has also been demonstrated that levels of testosterone are correlated with sexual behaviour in boys around the time of puberty (Udry et al., 1985). Boys in Grades 8, 9, and 10 filled out a questionnaire about their sexual behaviour and gave blood samples from which their level of testosterone was measured. Among the boys whose testosterone level was in the highest quartile (25 percent of the sample), 69 percent had engaged in sexual intercourse, whereas only 16 percent of the boys whose testosterone level was in the lowest quartile had. Similarly, of the boys with testosterone levels in the highest quartile, 62 percent had masturbated, compared with 12 percent for the boys in the lowest quartile. These effects were uncorrelated with age, so it wasn't simply a matter of the older boys having more testosterone and more sexual experience. The authors concluded that at puberty testosterone affects sexual motivation directly.

Figure 9.9 fMRI scans of the brain are opening up exciting opportunities to learn how the brain is involved in sexual response.

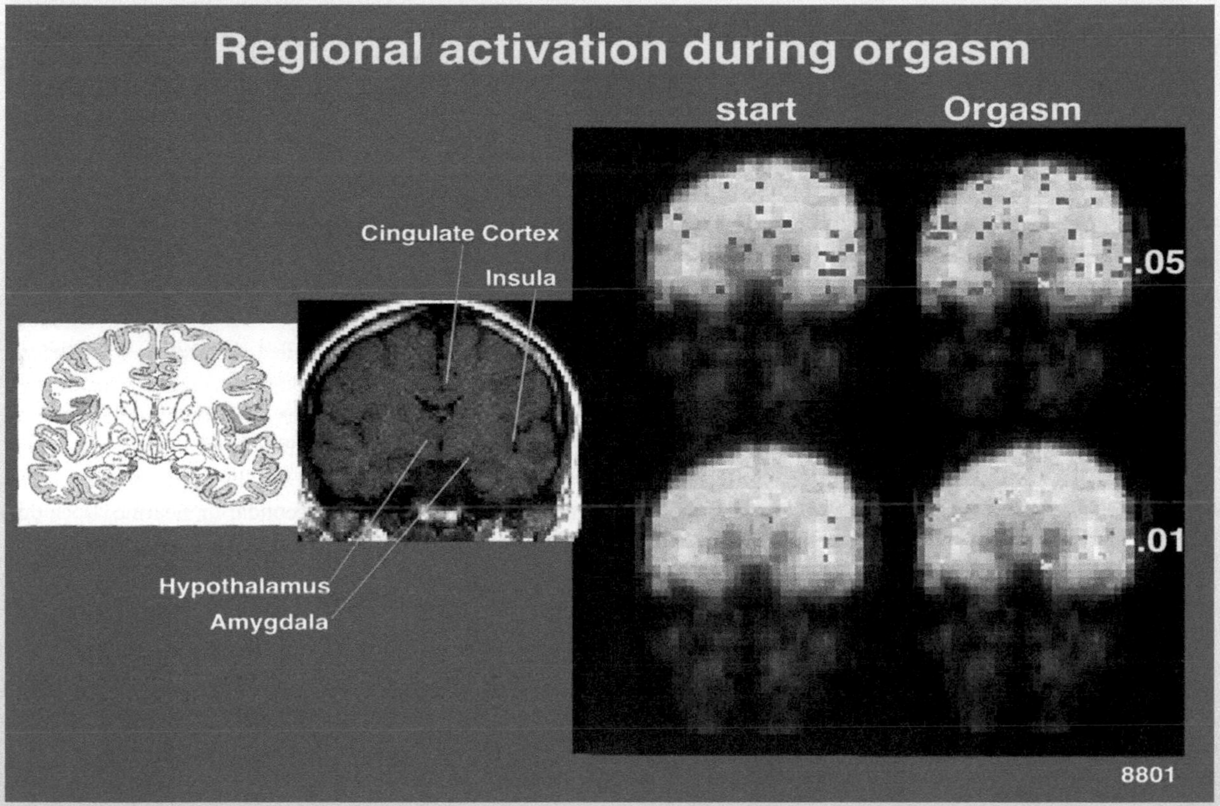

Regional activation during orgasm

start   Orgasm

Cingulate Cortex
Insula

Hypothalamus
Amygdala

© Dr. Barry Komisaruk

problems. They will also allow us to better understand and treat arousal problems, such as those suffered by pedophiles, who are aroused by completely inappropriate stimuli—children.

Sources: Arnow et al., 2002; Holstege et al., 2003; Karama et al., 2002; Komisaruk & Whipple, 2005; Schultz et al., 1999.

Research indicates that androgens are related to sexual desire in some women also (Bancroft & Graham, 2011).[3] If all sources of androgens (the adrenals and the ovaries) are removed, women lose sexual desire. Women who have undergone *oophorectomy* (surgical removal of the ovaries, typically because of cancer) report marked decreases in their sexual desire. If they are treated with testosterone, their sexual desire increases (Shifren et al., 1998; 2000). Androgen levels decline with age in women, and research shows that administration of DHEA (a pre-testosterone hormone) to women over age 60 may result in their having increased sexual desire (Baulieu et al., 2000; Spourk, 2002). However, the sexual desire of other women does not appear to be sensitive to levels of testosterone (Bancroft, 2010). Further, in premenopausal women, the level of testosterone is not related to their sexual desire (van Anders et al., 2009).

The complicating factor is that not only does testosterone have an effect on sexual desire and behaviour, but

---

[3] Lest the reader be distressed by the thought that women's considerably lower levels of testosterone might mean that they have lower sex drives, it should be noted that the sensitivity of cells to hormone levels is critical. Women's cells may be more sensitive to testosterone than men's are. Thus for women, a little testosterone may go a long way.

sexual behaviour also affects testosterone levels (van Anders, 2012). Masturbation, for example, increases testosterone levels. The effects are bi-directional—testosterone influences sex and sex influences testosterone.

L04

Pheromones

Scientists and laypeople alike are intrigued by the role that pheromones play in sexual behaviour (Cutler, 1999; McClintock, 2000). Pheromones are somewhat like hormones. Recall that hormones are biochemicals that are manufactured in the body and secreted into the bloodstream to be carried to the organs that they affect. **Pheromones**, in contrast, are biochemicals that are secreted outside the body. Through the sense of smell, they are an important means of communication between animals. Often the pheromones are contained in the animal's urine. The dog that does scent marking by urinating on trees is actually depositing pheromones.

Some pheromones appear to be important in sexual communication, and some have even been called *sex attractants.*

Much of the research on pheromones has been done with animals and demonstrates the importance of pheromones in sexual and reproductive functioning (Figure 9.10). For example, pheromones present in female urine have an influence on male sexual behaviour (Snowdon et al., 2006).

The sense of smell (olfaction) is essential for pheromone effects to occur. Removal of the olfactory bulbs, specifically a region called the *vomeronasal organ* (VNO), dramatically reduces the sexual behaviour of males from such species as mice and guinea pigs (Thorne & Amrein, 2003). The VNO, located inside the nose, is a chemoreceptor—that is, it is activated by chemicals, such as pheromones. Neuroscientists even recorded the activity of single neurons in the VNO of male mice and found that certain neurons fire when the animal comes into contact with another male, but different neurons fire when he comes into contact with a female (Luo et al., 2003). Activation of the VNO then activates cells in the hypothalamus (Keverne, 1999); as we have seen, the hypothalamus is crucial to sexuality. The VNO is a kind of second olfactory pathway, sometimes called the *accessory olfactory bulb,* that functions in addition to the main sense of smell.

What relevance does all this have for humans? Humans are not, by and large, scent animals. Olfaction is much less important for us than for most other species. We tend to rely mostly on vision and, secondarily, hearing. Does this mean that pheromones have no influence on our sexual behaviour?

pheromones (FARE-oh-mones): Biochemicals secreted outside the body that are important in communication between animals and that may serve as sex attractants.

(a) © Juniors Bildarchiv/Alamy

(b) © Brooke Fasani Auchincloss/Corbis

Figure 9.10 Pheromones. *(a)* Pheromones are a major means of communication between animals. *(b)* Are there human pheromones that are sex attractants?

New research may provide an answer to this question. Researchers have discovered that there is a long-overlooked cranial nerve, called nerve zero, that sprouts from the base of the brain, connects to parts of the brain controlling reproduction, and releases gonadotropin-releasing hormone (GnRH) into the blood (Fields, 2007). Nerve zero has been found in animals and humans. Nerve zero may sense pheromones even if they do not have an odour and thus may influence behaviour even though we are not conscious of them. More research is needed before the role of nerve zero in human sexual and reproductive behaviour is clear (Fields, 2007).

It is clear that human pheromones exist and may play an important role in sexuality (Wyatt, 2003). Indeed, pheromones may be exactly the "body chemistry" that attracts people to each other. Perfumes with musky scents have become popular and presumably increase sexual attractiveness, perhaps because they smell like pheromones. The perfume industry has eagerly tried to capitalize on pheromone research, making rather large claims for the effects of their products on attraction (e.g., "makes good girls go bad").

What scientific evidence is there regarding the existence and effects of pheromones in humans? First, the VNO—which, as noted, is related to olfaction and sexual behaviour in other species and essentially seems to function as a pheromone sensor—consists of just a few neurons in humans and seems to be nonfunctional (Georgiadis & Kringelbach, 2012). That said, there is evidence that when humans smell pheromones, a region of the hypothalams is activated, as is the amygdala. That is, our brains do respond to pheromones. Even though humans do not have a functional VNO, they have cells in the lining of the nose that contain pheromone receptors. Scientists have identified several genes in humans that code for these receptors (Wallrabenstein et al., 2015).

Second, it is clear that humans do secrete pheromones. Androstenol, an odorous steroid that is well documented as a pheromone in pigs, has been isolated in the underarm sweat of humans (Gower & Ruparelia, 1993). Short-chain fatty acids that are known to be sex-attractant pheromones to male rhesus monkeys have been isolated in human vaginal secretions (Cowley & Brooksbank, 1991).

Research provides important indications that pheromones may play a role in human sexuality. In one experiment, for example, a synthesized female pheromone was added to women's perfume in one group; a placebo was added to the perfume in the control group (McCoy & Pitino, 2002; Rako & Friebely, 2004). The women recorded their sexual behaviour over the next three months. Compared with the control group, pheromone-treated women showed a significantly greater frequency of intercourse, dates, sexual fondling, and kissing. They did not differ in frequency of masturbation. The researchers concluded that the pheromone had increased the women's attractiveness to men. In an imaging study, eight heterosexual men were exposed to women's perfume (Huh et al., 2008). Two reported "strong" arousal and three reported "moderate" arousal. All eight experienced brain activity in the insula, the gyrus, and the hypothalamus, areas we noted earlier are involved in arousal.

Classic research by Martha McClintock (1971) documented the existence of a phenomenon known as **menstrual synchrony**: the convergence, over several months, of the dates of onset of menstrual periods among women who are in close contact with each other (McClintock, 1998; Weller et al., 1995). This phenomenon is now thought to be due to pheromones produced by the women.

In perhaps the most dramatic experiment to date in humans, the results indicated that the timing of ovulation could be experimentally manipulated with human pheromones (Stern & McClintock, 1998). Odourless secretions from women's armpits were collected in the late follicular phase—that is, just before ovulation. Recipient women exposed to these secretions showed an accelerated appearance of the LH surge that triggers ovulation. Underarm secretions from the same donors collected later in the menstrual cycle had the opposite effect: They delayed the LH surge of recipients and lengthened the time to menstruation. In another study, men smelled T-shirts worn by (1) women near ovulation, (2) women far from ovulation, or (3) no one. Men exposed to the scent of an ovulating woman subsequently had elevated levels of testosterone (Miller & Maner, 2010).

Other pheromone research has found that preference for human body odours and brain responses to pheromones differ as a function of sexual orientation (Berglund et al., 2006; Martins et al., 2005). In one study, armpit secretions were collected from heterosexual men, heterosexual women, gay men, and lesbians (Martins et al., 2005). Odour evaluators then rated the pleasantness of these odours, not knowing the source of them. Heterosexual men, for example, gave the lowest pleasantness ratings to the pheromones from gay men. Gay men gave low ratings to the pheromones of heterosexual men. The researchers concluded that human *odour prints* may help us identify groups of people who are potential sexual partners.

If these speculations about the effects of pheromones on human sexual behaviour are correct, our hyperclean society may be destroying the scents that attract people to each other.

> **menstrual synchrony:** The convergence, over several months, of the dates of onset of menstrual periods among women who are in close contact with each other.

Sexual Techniques

In the earlier sections of this chapter, we discussed some of the wonderful things that happen to the body during sexual arousal and orgasm. How do we get to these marvellous states, both for ourselves and our partners?

We live in the era of sex manuals. Books like *Electrify Your Sex Life*, *The Illustrated Guide to Extended Massive Orgasm*, and *The Complete Guide to Sexual Fulfillment*, as well as feature articles and advice columns in many magazines and talk shows, give us advice on how to produce bigger and longer orgasms in ourselves and our partners. The sex manuals may also set up impossible standards of sexual performance that none of us can meet.

On the other hand, we live in a society that has a history of leaving the learning of sexual techniques to nature or to chance, in contrast to some other societies in which adolescents are given explicit instruction in methods for producing sexual pleasure. For human beings, sexual behaviour is a lot more than doing what comes naturally; we all need some means for learning about sexual techniques, and the sex manuals may help to fill that need. People with disabilities may need specific suggestions about how to adapt conventional ideas about sexual techniques to their own unique circumstances (see First Person for a discussion of sexuality and disability).

In the sections that follow, we consider techniques that bring people sexual pleasure. Of course, sexual techniques are not enough to build a satisfying sexual relationship with another person, so we also consider factors that contribute to "great sex" (Kleinplatz & Ménard, 2007). We discuss two of these components, loving attachment and communication, in Chapter 12.

Erogenous Zones

Although the notion of erogenous zones originated in Freud's work, the term is now part of our general vocabulary. It refers to parts of the body that are sexually sensitive; stroking them or otherwise stimulating them produces sexual arousal. The genitals and the breasts are good examples. The lips, neck, and thighs are generally also erogenous zones. But even some rather unlikely regions—such as the back, the ears, the stomach, and the feet—can also be erogenous. One person's erogenous zones can be different from another's. Thus, it is impossible to give a list of sure turn-ons. The best way to find out is to communicate with your partner, verbally and nonverbally (see Chapter 12).

 L05 ## One-Person Sex

It does not necessarily take two to have sex. People can create

autoeroticism: Sexual self-stimulation; for example, masturbation.

their own sexual stimulation. Sexual self-stimulation is called **autoeroticism**.[4] Two examples are masturbation and fantasy.

Masturbation

Here the term *hand–genital stimulation* will be reserved for stimulation of another's genitals and the term *masturbation* for self-stimulation, either with the hand or with some object, such as a pillow or a vibrator. Masturbation is a very common sexual behaviour; almost all men and the majority of women in Canada masturbate to orgasm at least a few times during their lives. In the National Survey of Sexual Health and Behavior, 72 to 84 percent of men (depending on age and other factors) ages 18 to 60 reported that they had masturbated in the preceding year, as did 54 to 65 percent of the women (Herbenick et al., 2010a, 2010b); 56 to 66 percent of the men and 26 to 52 percent of the women had masturbated in the previous month.

Although there are no national data on masturbation, our research has found that most Canadian university students (92 percent of the men and 72 percent of the women in one study) have masturbated at least once. Further, 65 percent of Canadians have positive attitudes toward masturbation. A study of German university students found that the percentage of students who report masturbating was not affected by whether they had a sexual partner; rather masturbation was seen as a sexual activity in its own right (Dekker & Schmidt, 2002).

The techniques used by men and women in masturbation are interesting in part because they provide information to their partners concerning the best techniques to use in lovemaking (Figure 9.11).

Most commonly women masturbate by manipulating the clitoris and the inner lips. They may rub up and down or in a circular motion, sometimes lightly and sometimes applying more pressure to the clitoris. Some prefer to rub at the side of the clitoris, while a few stimulate the glans of the clitoris directly. The inner lips may also be stroked or tugged. One woman described her technique as follows:

> I use the tips of my fingers for actual stimulation, but it's better to start with patting motions or light rubbing motions over the general area. As excitement increases I begin stroking above the clitoris and finally reach a climax with a rapid, jerky circular motion over the clitoral hood. Usually my legs are apart, and occasionally I also stimulate my nipples with the other hand. (Hite, 1976, p. 20)

Other techniques used by women in masturbation include breast stimulation, thigh pressure exerted by

---

[4] For those of you who are interested in the roots of words, *autoeroticism* does not refer to sex in the back seat of a car. The prefix *auto* means "self" (as in *autobiography*); hence, self-stimulation is autoeroticism.

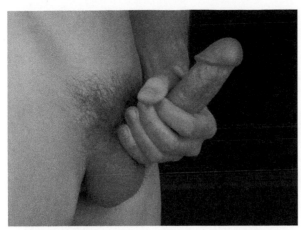

(a) © H.S. Photos/Alamy

(b) © Westend61 GmbH/Alamy

Figure 9.11   *(a)* Male masturbation using hand stimulation of the penis. *(b)* Female masturbation using clitoral stimulation.

crossing the legs and pressing them together rhythmically to stimulate the clitoris, and pressing the genitals against some object, such as a pillow, or massaging them with a stream of water while in the shower. A few women are capable of using fantasy alone to produce orgasm; fantasy-induced orgasms are accompanied by the same physiological changes as orgasms produced by masturbation (Whipple et al., 1992).

Almost all men report masturbating by hand stimulation of the penis. For those interested in speed, an orgasm can be reached in only a minute or two. Most men use the technique of circling the hand around the shaft of the penis and using an up-and-down movement to stimulate the shaft and glans. Because the penis produces no natural lubrication of its own, some men like to use a form of lubrication, such as soapsuds while showering. The tightness of the grip, the speed of movement, and the amount of glans stimulation vary from one man to the next. Most increase the speed of stimulation as they approach orgasm, slowing or stopping the stimulation at orgasm because further stimulation would be uncomfortable (Masters & Johnson, 1966). At the time of

ejaculation, men often grip the shaft of the penis tightly. Immediately after orgasm, the glans and corona are hypersensitive, and men generally avoid further stimulation of the penis at that time.

Some men and woman incorporate the use of mass media into their autoerotic activity. Some people masturbate as they view erotic images in magazines, on video or DVD, or on the Internet. For example, a New Brunswick survey found that 86 percent of male and 39 percent of female undergraduates had viewed sexually explicit materials online in the previous month, and most of these individuals had masturbated while doing so (Shaughnessy, Byers, & Walsh, 2011).

Fantasy

Sexual fantasy refers to any conscious mental imagery or daydream that includes sexual activity or is sexually arousing (Bivona & Critelli, 2009). Almost all men and women report that they have experienced sexual fantasies, often frequently (Kahr, 2008; Leitenberg & Henning, 1995). However, many people are uncomfortable with acknowledging that they deliberately think about sex and enjoy doing so (Renaud & Byers, 2001).

Researchers in New Brunswick studied the sexual thoughts and fantasies of heterosexual university students (Renaud & Byers, 1999). They found that although men think about sex more frequently than women do, for the most part, the content of their sexual fantasies is similar. The most common themes have to do with intimacy and romance. More than 90 percent of students had fantasies about having intercourse with a loved partner, kissing passionately, making love elsewhere than the bedroom (e.g., out of doors), and giving and receiving oral sex.

Some fantasies show gender differences in preferences. Compared with the women, the men's fantasies more often revolved around themes of anonymous or impersonal sex. The women had romantic fantasies and fantasies about playing a role during sexual activity—such as exposing themselves provocatively or tying their partner up—more often than the men did (Renaud & Byers, 1999). Other research has shown that men are more likely than women to fantasize about being masturbated by an unknown person, having anal sex, having interracial sex, and having sex with someone much younger (but legally) than they are. Women are somewhat more likely to have fantasized about engaging in same-sex sexual activity (Joyal et al., 2015). Women are also more likely than are men to have sexual fantasies in which they are desired sexually by someone else (Bogaert et al., 2015).

Gay men and lesbians tend to fantasize about sexual partners of the same gender, although at times they may fantasize about

sexual fantasy: Sexual thoughts or images that alter the person's emotions or physiological state.

First Person

Sex Toys and Physical Disability

All sorts of people use sex toys—people of all ages, abilities, genders, and sexual orientations. There is really no limit to who can benefit from the different sensations and types of stimulation that sex toys may provide. Sex toys can be especially enjoyable and helpful to people who have different abilities.

People with disabilities may experience multiple barriers to sexual pleasure. Some of these barriers are intangible. For instance, *ableism*, which is the oppression and stigmatization of people with disabilities, has worked to misconstrue people with disabilities as nonsexual. The historical medical model of disability posited people with disabilities as weak and infantile and in need of being cured or cared for. This ableist, socially constructed identity did not allow people with disabilities dignity, autonomy, or access to their sexual rights. As political awareness around the rights of people with disabilities grew in the 1970s, the social model of disability began to replace the medical model. The social model of disability views disability holistically and differentiates between an *impairment* and a *disability*. An impairment is a bodily difference, such as having a limp; a disability is the way that an impairment is viewed by society as something that makes that person less valuable simply because their body does not conform to a norm. This social model of disability has been beneficial in that it recognizes that people with disabilities are whole people who deserve full access to human rights (WHO, 1980). However, despite this positive change, historically rooted ideas of people with disabilities as being nonsexual still exist. It is

important for all of us to re-imagine such limited ideas of who is sexual and who has the right to sexual pleasure.

There are also other more tangible barriers to individuals with physical disabilities experiencing sexual pleasure, and these ones can be easier to counter. These barriers are physical ones, such as different degrees of sensation and mobility, muscle spasticity, erectile difficulties, and an absence of vaginal lubrication. Sex toys can play a revolutionary role in helping to overcome these physical differences. That is, they can allow people to experience all new bodily sensations and stimulations. What are some ways in which the sex toys described later in this chapter can be used to help overcome the physical barriers experienced by people with disabilities?

Limited Sensation

Many people with different disabilities experience limited degrees of sensation at different points of their body. For example, people with spinal cord injuries, MS, or cerebral palsy, or who are taking certain medications may lack sensation in their genitals. Here, vibrators can play a crucial role in allowing them to feel sexual stimulation. People who have limited sensation may want to use a very strong vibrator either externally against their genitals (the clitoris or the shaft of the penis, for example) or internally (inside the vagina or anus). There are a plethora of vibrators each designed to stimulate different parts of the body, making this a very versatile type of toy. Vibrators also range widely in shape, size, and control mechanisms. Some may be easier for people with disabilities to use

someone of the other gender (Price et al., 1985). Conversely, heterosexuals most often fantasize about sexual activities with someone of the other gender, but they also fantasize about someone of the same gender. Sexual fantasies often involve people, places (Disney World), or animals with which the person has no real-world connection (Kahr, 2008).

Where do sexual fantasies come from? The images may come from past experience, dreams, media portrayals, or stories someone told you. The activity may be dreamlike and sensuous, or explicit and vigorous. Like

all fantasy, sexual fantasies represent a fusion of mind, body, and emotions. Sexual fantasies may represent earlier or childhood experiences, pleasant or abusive (Maltz & Boss, 1997). They may be experienced as positive and pleasant or as negative and unwanted (Byers, Purdon, et al., 1998; Renaud & Byers, 1999).

Sexual fantasy can serve a variety of functions for the person doing the fantasizing (Maltz & Boss, 1997). These include enhancing self-esteem and attractiveness, increasing sexual arousal (e.g., during masturbation or partnered sex), and facilitating orgasm. In fact,

than others, depending on the person's strength, the ease of which the vibrator can be operated (small buttons versus a dial, for example), and how heavy it is.

Different Degrees of Mobility

Some people with disabilities experience different degrees of mobility. This may make it difficult to get into certain sexual positions or to be able to touch some parts of their body or their partner's body. Here again vibrators can be helpful. Vibrators that have a long handle may be able to reach these parts of the body without requiring difficult or painful bending.

Sex furniture can also be of use when it comes to getting into and maintaining different sexual positions. Sex furniture is essentially different designs of pillows and slings that, for example, can help lift up a person's bum, spread the legs, or reposition the neck. They can make it more comfortable to lie in different positions. The Intimate Rider is a piece of sex furniture created specifically for people with disabilities. It is intended to facilitate motion so as to allow for penetrative sex. It has two parts: a low-slung rocking chair (which can be easier to transfer into out of a wheelchair) and a cot positioned at the same height. One person sits in the rocking chair allowing them to thrust, while their partner lies on the cot in front of them.

Concerns Related to the Sexual Response

Some people experience erectile difficulties related to their physical disability. Medication such as Viagra, Levitra, or Cialis may be helpful to them (see Chapter 18). Other people choose to use a penis pump and a ring instead. A pump is a device that is placed over the shaft of the penis and then squeezed, drawing blood into the penis. When blood moves into the shaft it creates an erection. When the pump is removed, the blood could simply cycle back out of the penile shaft, causing the erection to end. This is where rings come in. If a silicone or jelly vinyl ring is pulled around the shaft and the testicles so that it presses against the base of the penis, this can stop blood from flowing out of the shaft. When the blood is trapped inside the shaft, an erection can be maintained.

Some women who have a physical disability have decreased vaginal lubrication, making penetrative sex painful. There are a variety of water-based or silicone-based lubricants that they (or their partner) can apply to the genitals to facilitate penetration and keep the vagina from being irritated. Water-based lubricants may be all natural and mimic natural vaginal lubrication well. Silicone-based lubes are not natural and they feel more like oil; however, they may last longer than a water-based lube because they do not absorb into the body.

Because sexual health is an important facet of human well-being, it is important that health care providers and support workers remember to consider the sexual health needs of persons with disabilities. Some important resources have been developed to help caregivers better support those needs. Two examples are the Sexuality and Access Project (http://sexuality-and-access.com/about-us/), an Ontario-based project, and the booklet titled *Supporting Sexual Health and Intimacy in Care Facilities: Guidelines for Supporting Adults Living in Long-Term Care Facilities and Group Homes in British Columbia, Canada.*

Sources: Silverberg & Odette, 2011; Vancouver Coastal Health Authority, 2009. Written by Kaleigh Trace

---

research has shown that people who engage in more frequent sexual fantasies tend to be better adjusted sexually (Renaud & Byers, 2001). A very important role is enabling the person to mentally rehearse future possibilities. Such rehearsal may enable the person to change behaviour, initiate communication with a partner, or change partners. Although many people use fantasy as part of sexual interactions, others may have no sexual contact with another person and rely exclusively on sexual fantasy and masturbation for their erotic pleasure (Kahr, 2008).

Sometimes sexual thoughts or fantasies can be experienced as negative—that is, unacceptable, upsetting, and unpleasant. In fact, research in New Brunswick found that 84 percent of university students had these types of thoughts (Byers, Purdon, et al., 1998). The negative images most frequently reported by men were of having sex in a public place, meeting naked people, and engaging in sex with a person having authority over them. Those most frequently reported by women were of having sex in a public place, having sex with a person having authority over them, and being sexually victimized. Students who have more frequent negative sexual thoughts and fantasies are not more poorly adjusted, although some people experience anxiety and guilt because of the thought (Byers, Purdon, et al., 1998; Renaud & Byers, 2001).

Here is the fantasy of one man when he masturbates:

I lie back on the bed completely naked, but without an erection. A lady dressed only in the sexiest lingerie ever climbs onto the bed, but does not undress or touch me yet with her hands. Slowly, she sits almost upon my face and she slips a hand into her panties and starts to masturbate herself and cums into her panties and just lowers herself enough to allow me to have the slightest taste of her juices with my tongue on her panties. She lowers herself further down my body and slowly gives me oral sex, flicking her tongue around my penis. She gives me slow lingering oral and then we continue to have slow passionate sex together. (Kahr, 2008, pp. 115–116)

Here is the fantasy of one woman:

This involves me as a doctor in a really sexy outfit. My partner is my patient strapped to the bed. I strip for him and make him watch since he can't touch me. I tease him with feathers and ribbons. I then mount him and have rough sex with him while he is tied up (Kahr, 2008, pp. 73–74).

Sex Toys

Various sexual devices, such as vibrators, dildos, cock (penis) rings, butt plugs, and lube (lubricant), are used as *sex toys* by some people in masturbation or by couples as they have sex together. Each type of sex toy comes in endless variations. Some people consider use of sex toys to be examples of *spicy sex*, meaning a change from the usual sexual script, which is sometimes called *vanilla sex* (Rye & Meaney, 2007a). Sex toys used to only be available in specialty sex stores or online. However, they have gone main stream and are now available in pharmacies and other mainstream stores. Here we describe a few of the more common sex toys, but there are many other devices that people can use to enhance their sexual pleasure.

Both male and female artificial genitals can be purchased. A **dildo** is a rubber, silicone, or plastic cylinder, often shaped like a penis; it can be inserted into the vagina or the anus. Dildos are used by some women in masturbation, by same-sex couples, and by heterosexual couples (Figure 9.12). Some couples use a dildo with a harness, often called a *strap-on*. Artificial vaginas, and even inflatable replicas of the entire body, male or female, can also be purchased.

A **vibrator** is a handheld device that vibrates and is used

dildo: A rubber or plastic cylinder, often shaped like a penis.
vibrator: A handheld device that vibrates and is used for massage or held against the body to provide sexual stimulation.

Figure 9.12   Vibrators and dildos, used for sexual stimulation.

© imagebroker.net/SuperStock

for massage or held against the body to provide sexual stimulation. Vibrators come in a variety of shapes and sizes (from small to large). They also vary in the intensity of the vibrations. Vibrators can be electric, with a cord that plugs into an electric socket, or cordless rechargeable or battery-powered models. Some vibrators are shaped like a penis but others are not. Women may use them to masturbate, stimulating the clitoral and mons area, or may insert them into the vagina. Men may use them during masturbation or during sex with a partner (Reece et al., 2009).

Vibrators designed for woman are not recent; they were invented in the 1880s and sold as a medical device (Maines, 1999). Physicians prescribed their use for the treatment of various female "maladies," especially hysteria.[5] Vibrators disappeared from medicinal use after they were used in pornographic films in the 1920s. Today they are back in full force, with women throwing Passion Parties or Slumber Parties, which are Tupperware-style home parties where you and your friends can buy sex toys from the local salesperson (Jefferson, 2005). Vibrators can also be purchased online or at a sex store. Vibrators provide more intense stimulation than can be provided by oral or manual stimulation and so can be particularly helpful to women who have difficulty reaching orgasm or just want to explore the full depth of their sexual potential and response—they are the easiest way for a woman to have an orgasm or multiple orgasms (see Chapter 18 for a discussion of orgasmic dysfunction).

How common is vibrator use? In one study more than half of women in the United States (53 percent)

---

[5] Some of you may have read *The Birth House*, a novel by Ami McKay set in Nova Scotia, which features a physician's use of a vibrator with his female patients.

reported that they had used a vibrator for sexual stimulation; about a fifth (20 percent) had used one in the previous month (Herbenick et al., 2009). Similar numbers of women reported using them during masturbation, intercourse, and sexual play with a partner. About half of men in the United States (45 percent) also report that they have used a vibrator, 10 percent in the previous month (Reece et al., 2009). Interestingly, in these studies the women and men who had used a vibrator engaged in more health-promoting behaviour and had better sexual functioning than those who had never used a vibrator.

Lubricant (lube) can make sex better. It can make sex—vaginal, anal, clitoral stimulation—more comfortable, especially for women who experience genital pain (Sutton et al., 2012). It can also increase stimulation. Lube can be water-based, which can be used with condoms and all sex toys. It can also be silicone-based, which lasts longer. Lubes come from thin to thick, unscented or in a variety of scents, and unflavoured or in a variety of flavours. Some are even organic. Sex stores sell many types of lubricants, but then so do most pharmacies these days.

Body oils are also popular for sexual use. In fact, their use has been encouraged by experts in the field; for example, sex therapists recommend them for the touching or sensate focus exercises that they prescribe for their patients in sex therapy (see Chapter 18). Oils have a sensuous quality that heightens erotic feelings. Furthermore, if you are being stroked or massaged for any extended period of time, the oil helps ensure that the part of your body that is being stimulated will not end up feeling like a piece of wood that has been sandpapered. Sex stores sell oils in a variety of exotic scents, but plain baby oil will also do nicely. Be aware that Vaseline and some other lubricants cause condoms to break.

LO6 Two-Person Sex

When many of us think of techniques of two-person sex,[6] the image that flashes across our mind generally reflects several assumptions. One assumption may be that one of the people is a male and the other a female—that is, that the sex is heterosexual. This reflects a belief that heterosexual sex is normative. We also tend to assume that the man is supposed to do certain things during the act and the woman is supposed to do certain other things, reflecting the sexual scripts of our culture. He, for example, is supposed to take the initiative in deciding what techniques are used, while she is to follow his

---

[6] Of course, some people choose to engage in sexual activities with two or more other persons at the same time. This is called a *threesome, group sex,* or *swinging* depending on who is involved. Swinging is discussed in Chapter 11.

lead. Although there is nothing particularly evil in these assumptions, they do tend to impose limitations on our own sexual expression and to make people think that their own sexual behaviour is not quite right. Therefore, we will attempt to avoid these assumptions in the sections that follow.

Kissing

Kissing (or what we might call, technically, *mouth-to-mouth stimulation*) is an activity that virtually everyone in our culture has engaged in. In simple kissing, the partners keep their mouths closed and touch each other's lips. In deep kissing (*French kissing*), both people part their lips slightly and insert their tongues into each other's mouths (somehow these clinical descriptions do not make it sound like as much fun as it is). There are endless variations on these two basic approaches, such as nibbling at the partner's lips or tongue or sucking at the lips; they depend only on your imagination and personal preference. There are also plenty of other regions of the body to kiss: the nose, the forehead, the eyelids, the earlobes, the neck, the breasts, the genitals, and even the feet, to give a few examples.

Touching

Enjoying touching and being touched is essential to sexual pleasure. Sensual touching is important to feelings of closeness and desire. In addition, caresses or massages, applied to virtually any area of the body, can be exciting. The regions that are exciting vary a great deal from one person to the next and depend on how the person is feeling at the moment; thus it is important to communicate what sort of touching is most pleasurable to you. (For specific exercises on touching and being touched, see Chapter 18.)

As noted earlier, one of the best ways to find out how to use your hands in stimulating the genitals of another person is to find out how that person masturbates (see Figure 9.11). Alex Comfort (1991), in *The New Joy of Sex,* recommends the following techniques:

> If he isn't circumcised, [you] will probably need to avoid rubbing the glans itself, except in pursuit of very special effects. [Your] best grip is just below the groove, with the skin back as far as it will go, and using two hands—one pressing hard near the root, holding the penis steady, or fondling the scrotum, the other making a thumb-and-first-finger ring, or a whole hand grip. [You] should vary this, and, in prolonged masturbation, change hands often. (p. 85)

One of the things that make hand stimulation most effective is for the man's partner to have a playful delight in, and appreciation of, the man's penis. Most men think their penis is pretty important. If the partner cannot honestly appreciate it and enjoy massaging it, hand stimulation might as well not be done.

The hands can be used to stimulate the woman's genitals to produce orgasm, as a preliminary method of arousing the woman before intercourse, or simply because it is pleasurable. Generally it is best, particularly if the woman is not already aroused, to begin with gentle, light stroking of the inside of the thighs and the inner and outer lips, moving to light stroking of the clitoris. As she becomes more aroused, the stimulation of the clitoris can become firmer. The clitoris is very sensitive and this sensitivity can be either exquisite or painful. Some care has to be used in stimulating it; it cannot be manipulated like a piece of Silly Putty. Generally, the clitoris should not—except, perhaps, for some light stroking—be rubbed while it is dry, for the effect can be abrasive. If the woman is already somewhat aroused, lubrication can be provided by touching the fingers to the vaginal entrance and then spreading the lubrication on the clitoris. If she is not aroused or does not produce much vaginal lubrication, saliva or a water-based lube works well too. Moisture makes the stimulation not only more comfortable but also more sensuous. Some women find direct stimulation of the clitoral glans to be painful in some states of arousal. These women generally prefer stimulation on either side of the clitoris instead.

With these caveats in mind, the clitoris can be stimulated with circular or back-and-forth movements of the finger. The inner and outer lips can also be stroked or rubbed. These techniques, if done with skill and patience, can bring the woman to orgasm. Another technique that can be helpful in producing orgasm is for the partner to place the heel of the hand on the mons, exerting pressure on it while moving the middle finger in and out of the vaginal entrance. If it isn't clear by now, the partner needs to have close-trimmed nails that do not have any jagged edges. This is sensitive tissue we are dealing with.

Many couples engage in sexual activities that do not involve penetration or hand stimulation but nonetheless allow one or both partners to receive genital stimulation (the slang term for two people rubbing their bodies, usually fully clothed, together for sexual stimulation is *dry humping*). For example, a woman may lie on top of her partner and rub her clitoris against her partner's genitals (when two women do this, it is sometimes called *tribadism*). Alternatively, a man may move his penis between the thighs of his partner, a technique that has been referred to as *interfemoral intercourse*.

The Other Senses

So far, this chapter has been focused on tactile (touch) sensations in sexual arousal. However, the other senses—vision, smell, and hearing—can also make contributions.

The things you see can contribute to your arousal. Men seem, in general, to be turned on by a variety of visual stimuli, such as an attractive person, or partially dressed or nude bodies. As we discussed earlier, both men and women respond with physiological, neural, and neurochemical arousal to portrayals of partnered sexual activity. Just as erotica may be used during autoerotic activity, viewing sexual activity on a video or on the Internet may contribute to partnered sexual activities. Some men, and a few women, have mild fetishes (see Chapter 15 for more detail) and like to see their partner wearing certain types of clothing, such as leather or rubber clothing, or schoolgirl dresses. A good rule here, as elsewhere, is to communicate with your partner to find out what he or she would find arousing.

Perhaps the biggest visual turn-on comes simply from looking at your own and your partner's body. According to the National Health and Social Life Survey, watching a partner undress is one of the most appealing sexual activities (Michael et al., 1994, Table 12).

Odours can be turn-ons or turn-offs. The scent of a body that is clean, having been washed with soap and water, is a natural turn-on. It does not need to be covered up with an "intimate deodorant."[7] In a sense, the scent of your skin, armpits, or genitals is your *aroma signature* and can be quite arousing.

Many people respond with arousal to specific musical stimuli, probably reflecting classical conditioning (see Chapter 2). Research in Ontario assessing genital arousal to audio narratives of sexual or neutral interactions with male and female strangers, friends, or a long-term partner found that men responded to stories involving women. Women responded to stories involving both men and women, and more strongly to stories involving friends or partners (Chivers & Timmers, 2012).

A body that has not been washed or a mouth that has not been cleaned or has recently been used for smoking cigarettes can be a real turn-off. Breath that reeks of garlic may turn a desire for closeness into a desire for distance. Ideally, the communication between partners is honest and trusting enough so that if one offends, the other can request that the appropriate clean-up be done.

Fantasy during Two-Person Sex

Fantasies can be done solo or can heighten the experience of sex with another person. Particularly in a long-term, monogamous relationship, sexual monotony can become a problem; fantasies are one way to introduce some variety and excitement without violating an agreement to be faithful to the other person. It is important

---

[7] With the increased popularity of mouth–genital sex, some women worry that the scent of their genitals might be offensive. The advertisements for feminine hygiene deodorant sprays prey on these fears. These sprays should not be used because they may irritate the vagina. Besides, there is nothing offensive about the scent of a vulva that has been washed; many people, in fact, find it arousing.

to view such fantasies in this way, rather than as a sign of disloyalty to, or dissatisfaction with, one's sexual partner.

Fantasies during two-person sex are generally quite similar to the ones people have while masturbating. In one study, 84 percent of men and 82 percent of women reported that they fantasized at least some of the time during intercourse (Cado & Leitenberg, 1990). This kind of fantasizing is quite common. Some sexual partners enjoy sharing their fantasies with each other. Describing a sexual fantasy to your partner can be a turn-on for both of you. Some couples act out all or part of a fantasy and find it very gratifying. One man says:

> I fantasized about being a fourteen-year-old girl. This is a long-lived fantasy of mine. The girl is pretty, with a petite body, probably five-one, five-two, cute ass, maybe light blond or dark brown pussy hair. Small to medium size breasts. Kind of sweet-looking, virginal. . . . Anyway, Sue got into it, like we were two girlfriends sleeping over and she was a couple years older and she was going to show me some things. I happen to be very sensitive around my nipples, so she'd say, "Oh, you have nice little nipples, you're going to have very pretty breasts." Then she'd massage my crotch like she was massaging a vagina: "Do you like it when I pet you down there?" And she'd show me what to do to pleasure her, how to masturbate her and go down on her. We played around with that for a few months. (Maurer, 1994, p. 231)

Positions of Penile–Vaginal Intercourse

One of the most common heterosexual techniques involves the insertion of the penis into the vagina; this is called **coitus**[8] or *sexual intercourse*. Ancient love manuals and other sources illustrate many positions of intercourse.

---

[8] From the Latin word *coire*, meaning "to go together."

Some authorities state that there are only four positions of intercourse. Personally, we prefer to believe that there are an infinite number. Consider how many different angles your arms, legs, and torso may be in, in relation to those of your partner, and all the various ways in which you can intertwine your limbs—that's a lot of positions. We trust that given sufficient creativity and time, you can discover them all for yourself. We would agree, though, that there are a few basic positions. One basic variation depends on whether the couple face each other (face-to-face position) or whether one partner faces the other's back (rear-entry position); if you try the other obvious variation, a back-to-back position, you will quickly find that you cannot accomplish much that way. The other basic variation depends on whether one partner is on top of the other or whether the couple are side by side. Let us consider four basic positions that illustrate these variations. As cookbooks often do, we'll give you the basic recipes and let you decide on the embellishments.

The face-to-face, *man-on-top* position (*missionary* position—see Figure 9.13) is probably the one used most frequently by mixed-sex couples in Canada. In this position the man and woman stimulate each other until he has an erection, she is producing vaginal lubrication, and preferably both are highly aroused. Then he moves on top of her as she spreads her legs apart, either he or she spreads the vaginal lips apart, and he inserts his penis into her vagina. He supports himself on his knees and hands or elbows and moves his penis in and out of the vagina (pelvic thrusting). Some men worry that their heavy weight will crush the poor woman under them; however, because the weight is spread out over so great an area, most women do not find this to be a problem at all, and many find the sensation of contact to be pleasurable.

coitus: Sexual intercourse; insertion of the penis into the vagina.

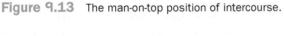

Figure 9.13 The man-on-top position of intercourse.

The woman can have her legs in a number of positions that create variations. She may have them straight out horizontally, a position that produces a tight rub on the penis but does not permit it to go deeply into the vagina. She may bend her legs and elevate them to varying degrees, or she may hook them over the man's back or over his shoulders. The last approach permits the penis to move deeply into the vagina. The woman can also move her pelvis, either up and down or side to side, to produce further stimulation.

The man-on-top position has some advantages and some disadvantages. It is the best position for ensuring conception, if that is what you want. The couple may feel better able to express their love or to communicate other feelings, since they are facing each other. This position, however, does not work well if the woman is in the advanced stages of pregnancy or if either she or the man is extremely obese. Sex therapists have also found that it is not a very good position if the man wants to control his ejaculation; the woman-on-top position is better for this.

For the *woman-on-top* position (see Figure 9.14), the woman kneels over the man, with one knee on either side of his hips. Then his hand or her hand guides the erect penis into the vagina as she lowers herself onto it. She then moves her hips to produce the stimulation. Beyond that, there are numerous variations, depending on where she puts her legs. She can remain on her knees, or she

Figure 9.14 The woman-on-top position of intercourse.

can straighten out her legs behind her, putting them outside his legs or between them. Or she can even turn around and face toward his feet.

This position has a number of advantages. It provides a lot of clitoral stimulation, and the woman can control the kind of stimulation she gets; thus many women find it the best position for them to have an orgasm. It is also a good position for the man who wants to delay his ejaculation, and for this reason it is used in sex therapy.

In the *rear-entry* position, the man faces the woman's back. One way to do this is to have the woman kneel with her head down; the man kneels behind her and inserts his penis into her vagina (see Figure 9.15). (This is sometimes called the *doggie position*, because it is the manner in which dogs and most other animals copulate.) Another possibility is for the woman to lie on her stomach, raising her hips slightly so that the man can insert his penis while kneeling over her. Rear entry can also be accomplished when the couple are in the side-to-side position. A small amount of air may enter the vagina when this position is used, producing interesting noises when it comes out.

In the *side-to-side* position, the man and woman lie beside each other, either face to face or in a rear-entry position (see Figure 9.16). The side-to-side position is good for leisurely or prolonged intercourse or if one or both of the partners are tired. It is also good for the pregnant and the obese.

Aside from the variations in these basic positions that can be produced by switching the position of the legs, there are many other possibilities. For example, the man-on-top position can be varied by having the woman lie on the edge of a bed with her feet on the floor while the man kneels on the floor. Or the woman can lie on the edge of a table while the man stands (don't forget to close the curtains first). Both of these positions produce a somewhat tighter vagina and therefore more stimulation for the penis. Or the man can sit on a chair and insert the penis as the woman sits on his lap, using either a face-to-face or a rear-entry approach. Or with both partners standing, the man can lift the woman onto his erect penis as she wraps her legs around his back, or she can put one leg over his shoulder (you have to be pretty flexible to manage this one, however). For even more advanced positions, see A Sexually Diverse World.

Mouth–Genital Stimulation

One of the most striking features of the sexual revolution of the last few decades is the increased popularity of mouth–genital, or oral–genital, techniques (Hunt & Curtis,

Figure 9.15 The rear-entry position of intercourse.

2006). There are two kinds of mouth–genital stimulation (*going down on* a partner): cunnilingus and fellatio.[9]

In cunnilingus or *eating* (from the Latin words *cunnus,* meaning "vulva," and *lingere,* meaning "to lick"), the woman's genitals are stimulated by her male or female partner's mouth. Generally, the focus of stimulation is the clitoris. The tongue stimulates it and the surrounding area with quick darting or thrusting movements, or the mouth can suck at the clitoris. A good prelude to cunnilingus can be kissing of the inner thighs or the belly, gradually moving to the clitoris. The mouth can also suck at the inner lips, or the tongue can stimulate the vaginal entrance or be inserted into the vagina. During cunnilingus, some women also enjoy having a finger inserted into the vagina or the anus for added stimulation. The

best way to know what she wants is through communication between partners, either verbal or nonverbal.

Many women are enthusiastic about cunnilingus and say that it is the best way, or perhaps the only way, for them to orgasm. Such responses are well within the normal range of female sexuality. As one woman put it:

> A tongue offers gentleness and precision and wetness and is the perfect organ for contact. And, besides, it produces sensational orgasms. (Hite, 1976, p. 234)

In one large, well-sampled study of Australians, respondents reported the specific sexual practices that were used in their most recent heterosexual encounter (Richters et al., 2006). If women had intercourse only, 50 percent had an orgasm, but when they had cunnilingus plus intercourse, 73 percent had an orgasm. In contrast, among men who engaged only in intercourse, 95 percent had an orgasm. It just isn't fair.

Cunnilingus (like fellatio, discussed next) can transmit

---

[9] Early marriage manuals in North America called cunnilingus and fellatio the *genital kiss*—definitely a more romantic term (Hunt & Curtis, 2006).

cunnilingus (cun-ih-LING-us): Mouth stimulation of the female genitals.

Figure 9.16   The side-to-side position of intercourse.

some sexually transmitted infections, such as gonorrhea. Oral sex can also result in the transmission of HPV and HSV from the genitals of an infected person to the mouth of the partner or vice versa. Some cases of oral cancers involve the HPV-16 strain, which may have been transmitted by oral sex (Herrero et al., 2003). Therefore, you need to be as careful about with whom you engage in mouth–genital sex as about with whom you would engage in intercourse. A small sheet of plastic, called a dental dam, can be placed over the vulva for those wanting to practise safer sex. Unlubricated condoms can also be cut open and used in place of a dental dam.

One other possible problem should be noted as well. Some women enjoy having their partner blow air forcefully into the vagina. While this technique is not dangerous under normal circumstances, when used on a pregnant woman it has been known to cause death (apparently as the result of air getting into the uterine veins), damage to the placenta, and embolism. Thus it should not be used on a pregnant woman.

In **fellatio**[10] (*sucking, a blow job*), the man's penis is stimulated by his partner's mouth. The partner licks the glans of the penis, its shaft, and perhaps the testicles. The penis is gently taken into the mouth. If it is not fully erect, an erection can generally be produced by stronger sucking combined with hand stimulation along the penis. After that, the partner can produce an in-and-out motion by moving the lips down toward the base of the penis and then back up, always being careful not to scrape the penis with the teeth. Or the tongue can be flicked back and forth around the tip of the penis or along the corona.

To bring the man to orgasm, the in-and-out motion is continued, moving the penis deeper and deeper into the mouth and perhaps also using the fingers to encircle the base of the penis and give further stimulation. Sometimes when the penis moves deeply toward the throat, it stimulates a gag reflex, which occurs anytime something comes into contact with that part of the throat. To avoid this, the partner should concentrate on relaxing the throat muscles while firming the lips to provide more stimulation to the penis.

When a couple are engaged in fellatio, the big question in their minds may concern ejaculation. The man may, of course, simply withdraw his penis from his partner's mouth and ejaculate outside it. Or he may ejaculate into it, and his partner may enjoy swallowing the ejaculate. The ejaculate resembles partially cooked egg white in texture; it does not have a very distinctive flavour but often leaves a salty aftertaste. Because some people have mixed feelings about having the semen in their mouths, it is probably a good idea for the couple to discuss ahead of time (or during the activity) what they plan to do, particularly because ejaculation into the mouth is an unsafe practice in the AIDS era (see Chapter 8).

Most men find fellatio to be a highly stimulating experience, which no doubt accounts for the high frequency with which prostitutes are asked to do it. Enjoyment of fellatio is certainly within the common range of male sexuality.

Both partners can perform mouth–genital stimulation simultaneously. This is often called **sixty-nining** because the numerals 69 suggest the position of the two

fellatio (fen-LAY-shoh): Mouth stimulation of the male genitals.
sixty-nining: Simultaneous mouth–genital stimulation; also called *soixante-neuf.*

---

[10] *Fellatio* is from the Latin word *fellare*, meaning "to suck." Partners should not take the sucking part too literally. The penis, particularly at the tip, is a delicate organ and should not be treated like a straw in an extra-thick milkshake.

bodies during simultaneous mouth–genital sex. Sixty-nining may be done either side to side or with one person on top of the other, each with the mouth on the other's genitals (Figure 9.17).

Simultaneous mouth–genital sex allows both people to enjoy the pleasure of that stimulation at the same time. It can give a feeling of total body involvement and total involvement between partners. Some couples, however, feel that this technique requires doing too many things at once and is more complicated than enjoyable. For example, a woman may be distracted from enjoying the marvellous clitoral stimulation she is receiving because she has to concentrate at the same time on using her mouth to stimulate her partner's genitals. If sixty-nine is done with one partner on top, the bottom partner may feel that he or she has no control over the movement and may be choked.

Anal Intercourse

In **anal intercourse** the man inserts his penis into his female or male partner's rectum. In legal circles, anal intercourse used to be called *sodomy* (although this term may also refer to other sexual practices such as intercourse with animals), and it is sometimes referred to as having sex *Greek style*.

Anal intercourse may be somewhat difficult because the rectum has no natural lubrication and because it is surrounded by fairly tight muscles. The man should therefore begin by moistening the partner's anus, either with saliva or with a sterile surgical lubricant such as K-Y Jelly (*not* Vaseline). He should also lubricate his penis. He then inserts it gently into the rectum and begins controlled pelvic thrusting. It is typically done in the rear-entry position or in the man-on-top position. The more the partner can relax and be in control, the more

pleasurable it is; if it is done properly, it need involve no pain. Although some couples are not interested in anal sex, others delight in it. Some women report orgasm during anal intercourse, particularly when it is accompanied by hand stimulation of the clitoris. Men also report orgasms from anal intercourse, primarily because of stimulation of the prostate.

There are some health risks associated with anal intercourse. It can lead to infections with various organisms. Of greatest concern, HIV can be transmitted through anal intercourse. Thus, safer sex consists of either refraining from engaging in anal intercourse, or using a condom if one does (or doing it only in a mutually monogamous relationship with an uninfected partner). Furthermore, for mixed-sex couples, the penis should never be inserted into the vagina after anal intercourse unless the penis has been washed thoroughly. The reason for this is that the rectum contains bacteria that do not belong in the vagina and that can cause a dandy case of vaginitis if they happen to get there. Also, sex toys or other objects inserted in the anus should be thoroughly washed following removal.

Another variation is **anilingus** (*rimming, rim job,* or *tossing the salad* in slang), in which the tongue and mouth stimulate the anus. The anus may also be stimulated by the hand, and some people report that having a finger inserted into the rectum near the time of orgasm provides a heightened sexual sensation. Anilingus carries with it the risk of HIV, hepatitis, or *E. coli* infections.

Sexual Scripts

The sexual scripts of heterosexual, gay, and lesbian couples are quite similar, and same-sex partners and mixed-sex

> **anal intercourse:** Insertion of the penis into the partner's rectum.
> **anilingus (ay-nih-LING-us):** Mouth stimulation of the partner's anus.

Figure 9.17 Simultaneous heterosexual mouth–genital stimulation in the sixty-nine position.

A Sexually Diverse World

What Is Tantric Sex?

Many people have heard of tantric sex, particularly after Sting boasted that he and his wife, Trudie Styler, were advocates of tantric sex and could make love for up to eight hours at a time. (By the way, he later clarified that this was a major exaggeration.) What exactly is tantric sex? The word *tantric* is thought to come from the Sanskrit *tantra*, which means "writing or a written text." Tantric texts, also known as tantric threads or fundamentals, are ancient texts that offer sexual instructions (Figure 9.18). They come down to us from a number of ancient spiritual traditions including the *Kama Sutra* and the *Ananga Rang* from South Asia, *The Perfumed Garden* from the Middle East, *The Tao of Sex* from the Far East, and other "pillow books."

What is tantric sex?

If tantric texts are simply old sex manuals, why does tantric sex seem to enjoy a kind of sexual mystique or reverence? Tantric texts have typically emerged from a spiritual approach to sex rather than biological, physiological, or empirical traditions. More than simple sexual how-to manuals, tantric texts often claim that adherents can not only have great sex but also, in so doing, can attain a greater spiritual awareness of themselves, their partner, and even the universe as a whole. Sexual "energy" is a recurrent theme in tantric writings. According to these texts, sexual energy can be stored and moved from one part of the body to another through energy channels or lines (sometimes referred as *chakras*), as well as to and from sexual partners. In some tantric traditions transfer between partners is seen as particularly important, because men and women are believed to possess complementary forms of energy. Adherents believe that people can learn the skills needed to gain control over and manipulate this sexual energy and then use it to intensify orgasm. Summoning and discharging sexual energy through orgasm is then used to attain a higher state of consciousness and becomes a tool to allow contact with universal energies or spirits. It is claimed that long-time practitioners of tantric sex can induce orgasmic responses simply through meditation, eliminating the need for a partner and his or her energies. Unfortunately, there is little scientific evidence to support any of these claims.

Ancient tantric writings assume that sex would occur between a man and a woman; they view the combining of male and female energies as necessary to reach greater enlightenment. More contemporary tantric writers dismiss this idea and claim, for example, that men or women engaging in the sixty-nine position with a same-sex partner can achieve this same type of enlightenment.

Tantric teachings advocate delaying ejaculation and orgasm: A prolonged period of sex without ejaculation or orgasm is believed to allow sexual energy to be built up, manipulated, and transferred to a partner. They suggest specific techniques, often considered mystical or secret, for both men and women to use to delay orgasm and increase their chances of having multiple orgasms. These include focusing on breathing patterns and learning how to coordinate breath, thrusting movements, and other sexual acts; attending to the emotional and sexual needs of the partner to facilitate buildup and transfer of sexual energy; and using all manner of sexual techniques and intercourse positions so that sexual activity remains exciting and playful.

Intercourse positions are frequently given metaphorical or mystical names. Sexual intercourse standing up is

---

partners mostly engage in the same behaviours (Holmberg & Blair, 2009). That is, for most couples—straight and gay—hugging, kissing, caressing, and snuggling are very important. These behaviours are often precursors to oral–genital sex (fellatio or cunnilingus), mutual masturbation, and (less frequently) anal intercourse. For most mixed-sex couples, lovemaking involves and often culminates in vaginal–penile intercourse. Among gay men, there appears to be a strong enjoyment or strong dislike of anal play, with significant numbers of men in each camp (Lever, 1994). Relative to anal sex, more gay men prefer giving and receiving oral sex (fellatio), masturbation, licking and sucking testicles, and sucking nipples. Female couples commonly engage in rubbing each other's genitals, and oral stimulation (cunnilingus). Further, many lesbians (and other couples) report using a

called Congress of the Monkey. The Large Bee position is a woman-on-top intercourse position where she leans back and, while supporting herself with her hands, twists her hips while the man is inside her. The Tail of the Ostrich intercourse position is achieved when she is on her back and he kneels between her legs. She then puts her legs over his shoulders and he lifts her up until only her head touches the ground. In the process, he enters her. The Wife of Indra, considered to be one of the most advanced positions, is achieved when, while in a sitting position, the woman puts her ankles behind her head. The man then enters her and pinches her nose, forcing her to breathe deeply from her diaphragm.

There are intriguing parallels between the advice given by sex therapists and some of the teachings in ancient tantric texts. For example, sex therapists often encourage people interested in experiencing more powerful orgasms to allow natural muscular tension or myotonia and vasocongestion to build up during sex play before orgasming. Higher levels of myotonia and vasocongestion before orgasm often feel more pleasurable and satisfying when released. Some of the tantric techniques are quite similar to the behavioural exercises used in contemporary sex therapy (see Chapter 18). For example, Eastern approaches emphasize mindfulness or the ability to focus on sexual stimuli and stay in the present in a nonjudgmental manner (Brotto et al., 2009). Sensate focus exercises used by sex therapists also have this goal. Sex therapists emphasize the importance for sexual satisfaction of relationship satisfaction, sexual communication, adopting a mutually enjoyable sexual script that is not routine and predictable, and not focusing on orgasm. Nonetheless, if stripped of its mysticism, colourful language, and secrecy, tantric sexual practices may augment what one would learn from a sex therapist (Brotto et al., 2009).

Figure 9.18 Erotic sculptures at the Temple of Kandariya Mahadevo, India, built in 1000 CE.

© Denis Dymov/Shutterstock

Sources: Craze (2003); Lacroix (2003); Tannahill (1980). Written by Dr. Guy Grenier

hand-held or strap-on dildo—43 percent of lesbians have used a hand-held dildo and 27 percent have used a strap-on dildo, according to one survey (Lever, 1995).

Masters and Johnson (1979), in their laboratory studies, made direct observations of the lovemaking techniques of lesbians (Figure 9.19) and gay men (Figure 9.20) and compared them with those of heterosexuals. They found no differences in masturbation techniques. However, in couple interactions there were some substantial differences. The major one was that gay men and lesbians took their time—that is, they seemed not to have any goal orientation. Similarly, Canadian researchers have shown that the sexual encounters of women in same-sex relationships are significantly longer than those of men or women in mixed-sex relationships or men in same-sex relationships (Blair &

Figure 9.19   Female-to-female sexual expression.

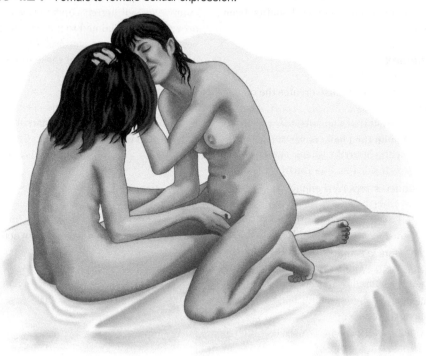

Pukall, 2014). Heterosexual couples, on the other hand, seemed to be performance-oriented—they seemed to strive toward a goal of orgasm for each partner. In the initial approach to stimulating the woman, heterosexuals and lesbians began with holding and kissing, but this lasted only about 30 seconds for the heterosexuals, who quickly moved on to genital stimulation. Lesbians, on the other hand, spent more time in holding and kissing and then went on to a long period of breast stimulation, which sometimes resulted in orgasm in the absence of genital stimulation. Lesbians also appeared to communicate more with each other. In the initial approach

to stimulating the man, gay men did extensive stimulation of the nipples, generally producing erection; such a technique was rare among heterosexuals (with only 3 of 100 couples). Gay men were also much more likely to stimulate the frenulum (the area of the penis on the lower side, just below the corona). They also used a *teasing technique* in which the man brings his partner near orgasm, then relaxes the stimulation, then increases the stimulation again, and so on, essentially prolonging the pleasure. Among heterosexuals, the man's most frequent complaint was that his partner did not grasp the shaft of the penis tightly enough. Masters and Johnson argued

Figure 9.20   Male-to-male sexual expression.

that heterosexuals can learn from gay men and lesbians; the technique of gay men and lesbians benefits from stimulating another body like their own.

Two-Person Cybersex

The Internet provides not only visual sexual images for people wanting to masturbate but also creates the opportunity for two-person cybersex. People report forming relationships on the Internet that they consider to be sexually intimate, even though they have never actually met the person face to face (Ross, 2005). Researchers in New Brunswick found that 25 percent of male students and 13 percent of female students reported engaging in online sexual activities with a partner in the previous month, although most did so infrequently (Shaughnessy, Byers, & Walsh, 2011). A more recent international study found that 31 percent of students in Canada, Germany, Sweden, and the United States had engaged in cybersex—there were no differences between the four countries (Döring et al., 2015). People engage in cybersex both with strangers and with people they know. Cybersex has also created a new sexual space that is somewhere between fantasy and action. Essentially, one can type sexual acts without actually doing them (Ross, 2005). In Chapter 11, we discuss data from a survey of persons who used the Internet to meet partners, and the activities that they engaged in. It is also possible to have cybersex using webcams, social networking sites, and avatars in virtual worlds. Indeed, the increasing integration of online communication into everyday life suggests that cybersex is likely to become more frequent and more common. These Internet activities challenge us to think more clearly about our definitions of sexual activity. For example, a woman accuses her partner of being unfaithful to her because he engaged in cybersex with another woman and he replies that he was only typing. Who is right?

L07 Aphrodisiacs

Is There a Good Aphrodisiac?

An **aphrodisiac** is a substance—such as a food, a drug, or a perfume—that excites sexual desire. Throughout history, people have searched for the surefire aphrodisiac. Before arousing your hopes, we should note that the search has been unsuccessful; there is no known substance that works well as an aphrodisiac.

A number of foods are thought to be aphrodisiacs, perhaps because they resemble the sex organs. These include oysters (which resemble the testes), elk antler velvet, seal penis, powdered rhinoceros horn, bananas, and asparagus (which resemble the penis). In addition, the current interest in nutrition and natural and organic foods and supplements has created a market for natural aphrodisiacs. According to one industry source, the popular herbs purchased for this purpose include yohimbe, cayenne, arginine, avena sativa, and damiana. Some companies sell herbal combinations, edible syrups, and brews that are claimed to increase sexual desire, sexual performance, sexual stamina, or all three. Again, there is no evidence that any of these foods or products affect sexual desire. However, with all these substances, the belief that they will be arousing may enhance sexual functioning. Perhaps this is why people continue to believe that they are aphrodisiacs.

What about various drugs? The effects of alcohol on sexual functioning will be discussed in Chapter 18. Briefly, drinking small quantities of alcohol may, for some people, decrease psychological inhibitions and therefore increase sexual desire. Moderate to large quantities, however, rapidly lead to an inability to function sexually.

Users of marijuana report that it acts as a sexual stimulant (McKay, 2005a). Probably this is due, in part, to the fact that marijuana produces the sensation that time is being stretched out, thus prolonging and intensifying sensations, including sexual sensations. There is no scientific documentation of the aphrodisiac effects of marijuana except for the reports of users. Possible negative effects of marijuana on sexual functioning are discussed in Chapter 18.

Unfortunately, some of the substances that are thought to enhance sexual functioning are quite dangerous. For example, cantharides (Spanish fly) has a reputation as an aphrodisiac, but it is poisonous and an irritant.

Amyl nitrite (*poppers*) is popular among some people. Because it relaxes the sphincter muscle of the anus, it is used by those engaging in anal intercourse (Taberner, 1985). Users report that it produces heightened sensations during orgasms (Everett, 1975). Probably it acts by dilating the blood vessels in the genitals. It may, however, have side effects, including dizziness, headaches, fainting, and, in rare cases, death; thus it can be dangerous (Taberner, 1985).

Butyl nitrite—sold under such trade names as Rush, Locker Room, and Climax—is a chemical relative of amyl nitrite. It is used to heighten sexual pleasure. Although no deaths have been reported from inhaling it, there are reported deaths from swallowing it (UPI, 1981).

In contrast to these street drugs, several prescription drugs have been approved by Health Canada for use in treating male sexual dysfunction. Viagra, Cialis, and Levitra are designed to increase the flow of blood to the penis and maintain the resulting erection. Note that none of these drugs increases desire. (For more information, see Chapter 18.) It is dangerous to combine these drugs with amyl nitrite. Although filbanserin (sold under the trade name Addyi) was recently approved for use in the U.S. to increase sexual desire in women, critiques argue that there is little evidence that it is effective and lots of evidence that it can have serious side effects.

aphrodisiac (ah-froh-DIZ-ih-ak): A substance that increases sexual desire.

Anaphrodisiacs

Just as people have searched for aphrodisiacs, so they have sought **anaphrodisiacs**—substances or practices that would diminish sexual desire. Cold showers are reputed to have such effects as does potassium nitrate (saltpeter). The latter contains nothing that decreases sexual drive, but it does act as a diuretic; it makes the person want to urinate frequently, which may be distracting enough so that he or she is not much interested in sex.

There has been some medical interest in finding drugs that would decrease sex drive for use in treating aggressive sexual offenders. One such drug is cyproterone acetate, which is an anti-androgen (for more information, see Chapter 16).

Other drugs that may lead to a loss of sexual functioning are discussed in Chapter 18.

Approaches to Lovemaking

As the old joke goes, sex is like pizza: When it's good, it's very, very good, and when it bad, it's still pretty good. Jokes aside, what differentiates *good sex* from *great sex?*

Sex as Work

Western culture has traditionally held the belief that intercourse is the important part of sex. The view that orgasm is the goal toward which both partners must strive is pervasive. This belief system is reflected in the term *foreplay*, which implies that activities like hand stimulation of the genitals, kissing, and mouth—genital sex—are only preliminaries that take place before intercourse, the last being "real sex." In reality all these activities and more can result in sexual pleasure (Rye & Meaney, 2007a). In short, our achievement drives now seem to be channelled into our sexual behaviours, and sex has become work—something at which we must work hard and become successful (Perel, 2006). As a result, our discussions of sex tend to focus on the physical aspects while ignoring our feelings about sex. Orgasm is the observable product, and we are concerned with how many orgasms we can produce or have, much as a plant manager is concerned with how many cans of soup are produced on the assembly line each day. Similar beliefs are reflected in the commonly used phrase *achieving orgasm*, as if orgasm were something to be achieved like a promotion on the job.[11] Viagra has only made this situation worse because it encourages people to reduce sexuality to an erection.

anaphrodisiacs (an-ah-froh-DIZ-ih-ak): Substances that decrease sexual desire.

[11] To avoid this whole notion, we never use the phrase "to achieve orgasm" in this book. Instead, we prefer "to have an orgasm" or simply "to orgasm." Why not turn it into a verb so that we will not feel we have to work at achieving it?

The emphasis on simultaneous orgasm expresses how clock-oriented we are. It is important to have things running on schedule and happening at exactly the right time, and so orgasms must be timed perfectly.

As sex therapist Esther Perel (2006) puts it,

> We are indeed a nation that prides itself on efficiency. But here's the catch: eroticism is inefficient. It loves to squander time and resources. . . . We glorify efficiency and fail to recognize that the erotic space is a radiant interlude in which we luxuriate, indifferent to demands of productivity; pleasure is the only goal. (p. 75)

The best approach is to enjoy all the various aspects of lovemaking for themselves, rather than as techniques for achieving something. We need to experience sex as a feast of the senses, rather than as an achievement competition. We need to broaden our view of sexual expression to recognize that a broad continuum of activities may provide sexual pleasure—a dream, a thought, a conversation, cuddling, kissing, sensual message, dancing, oral–genital stimulation, and intercourse (Chalker, 1995; Rye & Meaney, 2007a).

Couples who delight in the process of lovemaking also spend more time pleasing each other. In one New Brunswick study, 21 percent of men and 24 percent of women in long-term relationships complained that they and their partner spent too little time in foreplay before intercourse (MacNeil & Byers, 1997). How much longer do men and women want lovemaking to last? A study of 152 Canadian heterosexual couples in long-term relationships asked the men and women how long foreplay[12] and intercourse typically last in their relationship and how long they would ideally like each to last (Miller & Byers, 2004). The researchers found that on average the women wanted foreplay to last about eight minutes longer and the men wanted it to last about five minutes longer than it typically did. They also wanted intercourse to last longer—on average women wanted about 7 more minutes and men wanted about 11 more minutes of intercourse. In short, we need to think of sex as play, not as work.

Exceptional Sex

What are the ingredients for absolutely great sex? Sex researchers in Ontario interviewed a diverse sample of adults and asked them about the difference between very good sex and great sex, as well as about the characteristics of the best sexual experiences they had ever had

[12] We used the term *foreplay* in this study because it is easily understood by participants and has been used in other research. We don't use this term in this book, because it implies a rigid sexual script in which intercourse is the main event and other activities are merely warm-ups.

(Kleinplatz, 2010; Kleinplatz, Ménard, Paquet, et al., 2009). The components of great sex that emerged from these interviews were (for information on great sex in older adults, see Milestones in Sex Research in Chapter 11):

1. *Being fully present and focused:* Attention was focused intensely on the sexual interaction.

2. *Sense of connection, merger, being in synch:* The person felt a deep connection with the partner, even a sense of merging together for a time.

3. *Deep intimacy:* This refers to the kind of emotional and erotic intimacy with the partner that is discussed in Chapter 12.

4. *Extraordinary communication:* This quality goes far beyond the techniques of good communication discussed in Chapter 12 and involves a total sharing between partners, as well as a nonverbal component of touching with exceptional sensitivity to the other.

5. *Authenticity, being genuine, uninhibited:* The person felt totally uninhibited and unselfconscious.

6. *Exploration, interpersonal risk-taking, fun:* With a sense of humour and fun—not a dogged determination to perform well—the sexual interaction seemed like an adventure.

7. *Letting go and being vulnerable:* This refers to surrendering control and letting oneself be swept away by and vulnerable to the other person.

8. *Moments of transcendence and awe:* During these experiences, the person often experiences an altered mental state similar to the one achieved during meditation that are often growth-enhancing.

Interestingly, none of these participants felt that they had a natural talent for being a great lover. Rather, they learned the components of optimal sex over time. We could all learn something from these ideas.

Critical THINKing Skill

DEFENDING AGAINST EVERYDAY PERSUASIVE TECHNIQUES

Sexual functioning is important throughout life. We often become concerned if our performance doesn't live up to our (or others') expectations. Imagine that the last couple of times you attempted a sexual interaction, you weren't able to enjoy it. One day, your best friend casually inquires about your "love life." Since you have an open relationship and like him, you reply, "Well, it's not great these days." He says, "Well, I think you're just too tense. Next time, you should have a couple of stiff drinks before you try to get it on."

This is an example of everyday persuasion. A well-meaning friend or co-worker or roommate is trying to persuade you to solve a problem in the way they think will work. In this situation, many of us are tempted to follow the suggestion. They mean well; you like them; you don't want to be critical or start an argument. But is it a good idea? Your friend is suggesting that alcohol is an aphrodisiac. But is it? There is a lot of good evidence

on this point. We noted in this chapter that alcohol may reduce inhibitions, but it does not improve performance. In fact, two stiff drinks may inhibit sexual functioning. There is more information on alcohol and its effect on sexual functioning in Chapter 18.

As we suggest in Chapter 12, direct, honest communication is always preferred. If you aren't sure you want to try your friend's advice, you could say, "I appreciate your suggestion. I'll check it out." Then you can gather information about alcohol's effect on sexual functioning. If you conclude it isn't a good idea, you can ignore the advice. If the friend asks later on, you can say that you learned that alcohol isn't an aphrodisiac. That might lead to an interesting conversation!

You should, of course, also gather evidence about sexual dysfunctions if you want to address your concern. A good place to start is Chapter 18.

SUMMARY

William Masters and Virginia Johnson conducted an important program of research on the physiology of human sexual response. They found that two basic physiological processes occur during arousal and orgasm: vasocongestion and myotonia. The sexual response cycle occurs in three stages: excitement, orgasm, and resolution. Their research indicates that there is no physiological distinction between clitoral and vaginal orgasms in women, which refutes an early idea of Freud's. They also provided convincing evidence of the existence of multiple orgasm in women.

Criticisms of Masters and Johnson's model are that (1) they ignored cognitive and affective factors, and (2) their selection of research participants may have led to a self-fulfilling prophecy in their results.

According to Kaplan's cognitive-physiological model, three components are involved in sexual responses: desire, vasocongestion, and muscle contraction. According to the intimacy model, some people rarely experience spontaneous desire and desire for intimacy motivates them to engage in sexual activity. The dual control model holds that two basic processes—excitation and inhibition—are involved in sexual response, and that our responses to sexual stimuli are shaped by culture and early learning. Emotion is another important psychological aspect of sexual response.

The nervous system and sex hormones are important in sexual response. The nervous system functions in sexual response by a combination of spinal reflexes (best documented for erection and ejaculation) and brain influences (particularly of the limbic system). Hormones are important to sexual behaviour, both in their influences on prenatal development (organizing effects) and in their stimulating influence on adult sexual behaviour (activating effects). Testosterone is crucial for maintaining sexual desire in both men and women. Neurochemical changes during sexual response parallel arousal and inhibition.

Pheromones are biochemicals secreted outside the body that play an important role in sexual communication and attraction. Much of the evidence is based on research with animals, but evidence in humans is accumulating rapidly.

Sexual pleasure is produced by stimulation of various areas of the body called erogenous zones. Sexual self-stimulation, or autoeroticism, includes masturbation and sexual fantasies. Many people have sexual fantasies while masturbating or having sex with a partner.

Same-sex couples and mixed-sex couples mostly engage in the same sexual behaviours, with the exception of penile-vaginal intercourse. An important technique in two-person sex is hand stimulation of the partner's genitals. Touching other areas of the body and kissing are also important. The other senses—sight, smell, and hearing—can also be used in creating sexual arousal. Although there are infinite varieties in the positions in which one can have penile–vaginal intercourse, there are four basic positions: man on top (the missionary position), woman on top, rear entry, and side to side. There are two kinds of mouth–genital stimulation: cunnilingus (mouth stimulation of the female genitals) and fellatio (mouth stimulation of the male genitals). Anal intercourse involves inserting the penis into the rectum.

An aphrodisiac is a substance that arouses sexual desire. There is no known reliable aphrodisiac, and some of the substances that are popularly thought to act as aphrodisiacs can be dangerous.

People with disabilities have sexual needs and desires. However, they may experience multiple barriers to sexual pleasure. On such barrier is ableism, the oppression and stigmatization of people with disabilities.

We have a tendency in our culture to view sex as work and to turn sex into an achievement situation, as witnessed by expressions such as *achieving orgasm*. Such attitudes make sex less pleasurable and may set the stage for sexual failures or sexual disorders. These are quite different from the characteristics individuals identify as part of great sex, which including being fully present in the moment, having a deep sense of connection and feeling of intimacy with your partner, being totally uninhibited and unselfconscious, and extraordinary communication.

CHAPTER 10

Sexuality and the Life Cycle: Childhood and Adolescence

Jupiterimages/Stockbyte/Thinkstock

LEARNING OBJECTIVES

After studying this chapter, you will be able to

LO1 List examples of some problems associated with accurate sexuality data collection in infancy, childhood, and adolescence, and the sources of the information we have.

LO2 Describe sexual development in infancy and the preschool years.

LO3 Identify the types of sexual development in childhood.

LO4 Explain the process of the sexualization of children.

LO5 Describe sexual development in adolescence.

LO6 Illustrate the types of sexual development in late adolescence.

LO7 Describe how sexuality aids in development.

Are YOU Curious?

1. What is the sexualization of children and why is it a problem?
2. Do media portrayals of sex really affect my sexual attitudes and behaviours?
3. How many Canadian teens have engaged in sexual intercourse by Grade 11?
4. What should I consider before sexting?

Read this chapter to find out.

My son Jeremy . . . naively decided to wear barrettes to nursery school. Several times that day, another boy insisted that Jeremy must be a girl because "only girls wear barrettes." After repeatedly asserting that "wearing barrettes doesn't matter; being a boy means having a penis and testicles," Jeremy finally pulled down his pants as a way of making his point more convincingly. The boy was not impressed. He simply said, "Everybody has a penis; only girls wear barrettes."*

* Sandra L. Bem. (1989). Genital knowledge and gender consistency in preschool children. *Child Development, 60,* 649–662. Blackwell Publishing Ltd.

Stop for a moment and think of the first sexual experience you ever had (you will find examples of some youths' first sexual experience in First Person). Some of you will think of the first time you had sexual intercourse. New Brunswick researchers have shown that we tend to use the terms *having sex* and *sexual intercourse* synonymously (Byers et al., 2009; Randall & Byers, 2003). For example, Randall and Byers (2003) found that fewer than 15 percent of students thought that genital fondling and fewer than 25 percent thought that oral sex was having sex. Further, research in Alberta has shown that students are more likely to label a behaviour as having sex if it occurs in a mixed-sex relationship than in a same-sex relationship (Trotter & Alderson, 2007). Nonetheless, sex is more than just having heterosexual sexual intercourse. Others of you will think of earlier episodes, like playing doctor with the other kids in the neighbourhood, or your first passionate kiss, or orgasms with a partner through manual or oral stimulation. Unfortunately, some of you will think of abusive sexual experiences in childhood or adolescence. Child sexual abuse and sexual coercion and assault are discussed in Chapter 16.

Now think of the kind of sex life you had, or expect to have, in your early 20s. Finally, imagine yourself at 65 and the kinds of sexual behaviour you will be engaging in then.

Scientists think of human development, including sexual development, as a process that occurs throughout the lifespan. This process is influenced by biological, psychological, social, and cultural factors. This chapter and Chapter 11 are based on the contemporary approach to **lifespan development**, the study of sexuality throughout the course of our lives. The things you were asked to remember and imagine about your own sexual functioning in the paragraph above will give you an idea of the sweep of this approach to development. In Chapter 19 you will find a discussion of sex education across the lifespan as well as tips for parents who want to do a better job of talking to their children about sex.

lifespan development: Development from birth through old age.

Data Sources

What kinds of scientific data are available on the sexual behaviour of people during childhood and adolescence? Most of the data come from surveys in which adults are questioned about their pasts. Their responses form some of the data to be discussed in this chapter. As noted in Chapter 3, these are self-report data and thus may be subject to reporting biases, such as exaggeration and purposeful concealment. These responses may be even more problematic than some of the other kinds of data from self-report studies, though. For example, a 50- or 60-year-old man is asked to report on his sexual behaviour at age 10. How accurately will he remember things that happened 40 or 50 years ago? Surely there will be some forgetting. Thus, the data on childhood sexual behaviour may be subject to errors that result from faulty memory.

An alternative would be to interview children about their sexual behaviour or perhaps even to observe their sexual behaviour. Few researchers have done either, for obvious reasons. Such a study would arouse opposition from many parents, religious leaders, and politicians, who might argue that it is unnecessary or that it would harm the children who were studied. These reactions reflect in part the widespread beliefs that children are not yet sexual beings and should not be exposed to questions about sex. Such research also raises ethical issues: At what age can a child give truly informed consent to participate in such a study?

In a few studies, children have been questioned directly about their sexual behaviour. Kinsey interviewed 432 children, ages 4 to 14, and the results of the study were published after his death by Elias and Gebhard (1969). An innovation is the use of a "talking" computer to interview children (Romer et al., 1997). The computer is programmed to present the questions through headphones, and the child enters his or her answers by using the keyboard. This process preserves confidentiality, even when others are present, because only the child knows the

First Person

What Was Your First Sexual Experience?

Think about your first sexual experience. What was it like? Where and how did it happen? How old were you? Was it planned? Are you thinking of your first kiss? The first time you had sexual intercourse? The first time you engaged in oral sex? Was it with a boyfriend or girlfriend or someone you just met? Did the two of you talk about it beforehand or did it "just happen"?

We asked youth to tell us about their first sexual experience. As you will see, no two first sexual experiences are alike.

Kirsten from Saskatchewan

My first real sexual experience happened when I was 15. It was the long weekend in May, and a bunch of us from my high school were out drinking at a friend's cabin. There was this guy who was in the same grade as me, and he and I found ourselves walking on a gravel road alone. We sat down to "talk." We chatted awkwardly for a while, and it took him forever to slyly nudge closer to me, and finally we worked up the courage, aided in no small part by all the booze. We fooled around for a while until some friends of his came along and we jumped up (and zipped up) like frightened animals. I quickly scurried off to find the rest of the girls and tell them what had just happened. He and I couldn't look each other in the eye for months.

Trishia from Nova Scotia

My first sexual experience was with my best friend in Grade 6; we were 12 and 13 years old at the time. She had come for a sleepover and we were sharing my double bed. I do not recall much being said at the time, or how we both started kissing one another. It just happened, nothing ever discussed. As I recall we took turns kissing each other in various areas and moving around on top of one another. We never spoke of what happened that night.

Simon from Alberta

As a 16-year-old, the only thing I wanted to do was to have sex, because I heard it was a great experience. I also heard that it hurt a lot at the first time but you get used to it, and that I had to be very careful. I was also told that it would make me a man. On February 7th, I found my first boyfriend. He was some years older than me, but I didn't care at the time. We dated for one week, and I was so excited that I finally found a boyfriend, and I was so glad that I could finally have sex. So the moment finally happened and it did hurt for the first time. But I felt that I was finally a man.

Emily from New Brunswick

The first time I had sex was a very positive experience. I was 16 and had been with my boyfriend at the time for eight months and it was a great relationship. We were in love. We had discussed the desire to have sex for a few months and were well prepared. I went on birth control three months before we had intercourse. We wanted to make sure we were being safe. The opportunity arose one afternoon in July at my cottage; we brought blankets down to the beach and made love. It was comfortable and I felt like we were ready to go there in our relationship. I have very positive memories about the entire situation. We were together for the following two years.

Jeff from Alberta

I was 16 years old when I had my first sexual experience. I am gay and had not come out to many people at that point. I was attending a cross-Canada high school music festival away from home. I had my eye on one guy in particular but was too shy to do anything except exchange friendly pleasantries with him. On the very last night of the festival, however, everything changed. We had been drinking, and I found the courage to come out to a small group of friends. The guy that I liked overheard our conversation, and he cornered me later in the hallway, telling me he was gay too. I was a little scared. I had never discussed my sexuality with another gay man before. It was freeing, too, to be able to talk so openly. We slept together that night, and how it felt is hard to describe. It felt really good and right to be intimate with another man, but I still felt guilty and nervous at the same time. I was still very young. I threw up afterwards because I was so nervous. It was not the most romantic ending.

Paige from New Brunswick

I had hooked up with some guys but I had never had sex. Then I started dating Paul. The first time we had sex, we hadn't seen each other in like two weeks because of exams. We were hanging out at one of our mutual friends' birthday parties. We came back to my house from that. He had slept over before. He would sleep in the basement and I'd go upstairs. This time, I didn't go upstairs and it just kind of sort of happened. I'd been thinking about it for a little bit before then because we'd been together for a little bit and that was our month anniversary. There wasn't a lot of pre-planning involved.

question. In one study, this procedure was used to gather data from samples of high-risk youth ages 9 to 15 (Romer et al., 1997). More children reported sexual experience to the computer than in face-to-face interviews.

Many studies of adolescent sexual behaviour and attitudes have also been done. The Canadian Youth, Sexual Health, and HIV/AIDS Study (CYSHHAS; Boyce et al., 2003, 2006) and its predecessor, the Canada Youth and AIDS Study (King et al., 1988), are important national surveys. A series of surveys by sociologist Reginald Bibby (Bibby, 2001; Bibby et al., 2009) also provide some information about adolescent sexuality in Canada. We can have particular confidence in recent, well-sampled studies of adolescent sexuality.

The studies of child and adolescent sexual behaviour have mostly involved surveys that have used either questionnaires or interviews. Virtually no researchers have made systematic, direct observations of children's sexual behaviour (we know of only one), although some have asked parents to report on their children's sexual behaviour (de Graaf & Rademakers, 2011). Once children have learned that sexual behaviour has to be kept private or hidden, though, parents may not be able to report their children's behaviour very accurately.

Similar to conclusions drawn from cross-cultural research (see Chapter 1), the sexual attitudes and behaviour of children and adolescents in Canada are affected by culture. That is, children and youth from Canada's ethnocultural minority groups (for example, from Asian, South American, or Middle Eastern cultures) are influenced by the sexual attitudes, expectations, and parenting practices of their family and community. However, they are also influenced by the dominant Canadian culture and by the behaviour of their peers from the majority culture. This can and does cause conflict between parents and children. However, there has been little research on the sexual development of children and adolescents in Canada from these ethnocultural communities. Thus, some of the data reported here, particularly for older children and adolescents, may not conform closely to the attitudes and experiences of children and youth from some ethnocultural communities in Canada.

L02

Infancy and the Preschool Years (Birth to 4 Years)

Before 1890, it was thought that sexuality was something that magically appeared at puberty. Sigmund Freud first expressed the notion that children—in fact, infants— have sexual urges and engage in sexual behaviour.

The capacity of the human body to show a sexual response

is present from birth. Male infants, for example, get erections. Indeed, boy babies are sometimes born with erections. Ultrasound studies indicate that reflex erections occur in the male fetus for several months before birth (Masters et al., 1982). Vaginal lubrication has been found in baby girls in the 24 hours after birth.

The first intimate relationship most children experience is with their mother, and perhaps their father in families in which fathers participate equally in child rearing.[1] The mother–infant relationship involves a good deal of physical contact and typically engages the infant's tactile, olfactory, visual, and auditory senses (Frayser, 1994). Breast-feeding especially involves close physical contact, but other activities involved in caring for infants, such as diaper changing or bathing, involve intimate contact that can produce sensuous responses in the infant (Martinson, 1994; Figure 10.1).

Attachment

The quality of the relationship with the parents in infancy can be very important to the child's capacity for later sexual and emotional relationships. In psychological terms, an **attachment** (or bond) forms between the infant and the mother, father, or other caregiver. The bond begins in the hours immediately following birth and continues throughout the period of infancy (Coustan & Angelini, 1995). It is facilitated by cuddling

Figure 10.1 Some activities associated with nurturing an infant are potentially sensuous, because they involve pleasant physical contact.

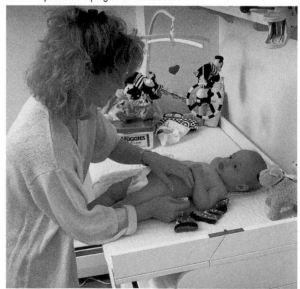

© Amy C. Etra/PhotoEdit

---

attachment: A psychological bond that forms between an infant and the mother, father, or other caregiver.

[1] According to the 2011 Canadian census, 65 percent of children live with married parents, 14 percent live with common-law parents, and 22 percent live with a lone parent (Bohnert et al., 2014).

and other forms of physical contact. Later, attachments form to other familiar people. These are the individual's earliest experiences with love and emotional attachment. The quality of these attachments—whether they are stable, secure, and satisfying or unstable, insecure, and frustrating—affects the person's capacity for emotional attachments in adulthood. Recent research (discussed in Chapter 12) indicates that adults' styles of romantic attachment are similar to the kinds of attachment they remember having with their parents in childhood.

Self-Stimulation

Infants are often observed fondling their own genitals (Figure 10.2). Generally the progression is that, between 6 and 12 months of age, infants discover their genitals by unintentionally touching them (de Graaf & Rademakers, 2006). They learn to walk, their coordination improves, and by 15 to 19 months, some boys and girls increase genital touching. A survey of Swedish parents of 3- to 5-year-olds found that 71 percent of boys and 43 percent of girls touched their genitals at home, and 28 percent of boys and 18 percent of girls masturbated with their hand (de Graaf & Rademakers, 2006). The comparable data for U.S. parents of 2- to 5-year-olds showed that 60 percent of boys and 44 percent of girls touched their genitals at home, and 17 percent of boys and 16 percent of girls masturbated with their hand. Early childhood educators in Ontario report observing many sexuality-related

Figure 10.2 Infant self-stimulation.

© Maya Barnes/The Image Works

behaviours in their day cares (Balter et al., 2016). These behaviours, then, are quite normal and do not indicate pathology. Orgasms from self-stimulation are possible even at this early age, although before puberty, boys are not capable of ejaculation.

Child–Child Encounters

Infants and young children are very self-centred. Even when they seem to be playing with another child, they may simply be playing alongside the other child, actually in a world all their own.

By the age of 4 or 5, though, children have become more social and some heterosexual play occurs. Boys and girls may hug each other or hold hands in imitation of adults. "Playing doctor" can be a popular game at this age. Research indicates that roughly 25 to 50 percent of children engage in this type of play (de Graaf & Rademakers, 2006). It generally involves no more than exhibiting one's own genitals, looking at those of others, and perhaps engaging in a little fondling or touching. One woman recalled,

> It was at the age of 5 that I, along with my three friends who were sisters and lived next door, first viewed the genitals of a boy. They had a male cousin who came to visit and we all ended up behind the furnace playing doctor. No matter what he would say his symptoms were, we were so fascinated with his penis that it was always the center of our examinations. I remember giggling as I punched it and dunking it in some red food-colored water that we were using for medicine. This seemed to give him great enjoyment. One girl put hand lotion and a bandage on his penis and in the process he had an erection. We asked him to do it again, but their [sic] was no such luck. (Martinson, 1994, p. 37)

Some children first learn about heterosexual behaviour by seeing or hearing their parents engaging in sexual intercourse—that is, witnessing the primal scene. Freud believed that this experience could inhibit the child's subsequent psychosexual development. What little data we have, though, suggest that the experience is not damaging. In surveys, about 20 percent of middle-class parents report that their child observed them when the child was 4 to 6 years of age, typically as a result of accidentally entering the parents' room. Parents report reactions such as curiosity ("Why are you bobbing up and down?"), amusement and giggling, or embarrassment and closing the door (Okami, 1995).

Sexual Knowledge and Interests

In the preschool years, children become interested in sexuality and begin to develop a simple understanding of some aspects of sexuality, although their knowledge is typically vague. For example, preschoolers are often interested in viewing people nude, and they may touch their mother's or other women's breasts (de Graaf & Rademakers, 2011; Kenny & Wurtele, 2012). They become interested in different postures for urinating, and some girls attempt to urinate while standing, just like boys do. Children at this age are very affectionate and enjoy hugging and kissing their parents. They may even propose marriage to the parent of the other gender.

By about the age of 5, children have formed a concept of marriage—or at least of its nongenital aspects. They know that a member of the other gender is the appropriate marriage partner, and they are committed to marrying when they get older. They practise marriage roles as they "play house."

Because, in Canada, children usually learn early that sex is taboo, they may turn to their peers for learning as they play games of "show" or "doctor." One young man recalled,

> One of my favorite pastimes was playing doctor with my little sister. During this doctor game we would both be nude and I would sit on her as if we were having intercourse. On one occasion, I was touching my sister's genital area and mother discovered us. We were sternly switched and told it was dirty and to never get caught again or we would be whipped twice as bad. So, we made sure we were never caught again. (Starks & Morrison, 1996)

In one study in Germany, the researcher interviewed children between the ages of 2 and 6 about their sexual knowledge (Volbert, 2000). When the children were shown a drawing of an unclothed child or adult, all 3- and 4-year-olds correctly identified whether it was male or female, but when asked to explain why, they generally gave answers based on characteristics such as hair. The 5- and 6-year-olds provided explanations based on the genitals. By age 4, 80 percent of the children knew some term for the genitals.

It is important to remember that children's sex play at this age is motivated largely by curiosity and is part of the general learning experiences of childhood.

Knowledge about Gender

By age 2½ or 3, children know what gender they are (see Chapter 13). This is the first step in developing a gender identity. Awareness of being a boy or a girl motivates them to be like other members of that group (Martin & Ruble, 2004). They know that they are like the parent of the same gender and different from the parent of the other gender and children of the other gender. At ages 4 to 6, ideas about gender are very rigid, as reflected in the opening vignette. As noted above, 3- and 4-year

olds typically do not understand the genital differences between males and females, but they acquire this knowledge by 5 or 6).

A small number of children, perhaps 1 or 2 out of 2000, do not identify with the gender assigned to them at birth. These children begin to exhibit *cross-gender behaviour* (Minter, 2012), wanting to dress, play, and be referred to or named in gender-atypical ways. These behaviours may be evident as early as age 2. The child's behaviour may range from tentative and playful to habitual and insistent, both inside and outside the home. Children who are adamant about their gender-atypical identification may be taken or referred to a clinician and be identified as experiencing *gender dysphoria* (see Chapter 13) or gender identity disorder (GID). Only a small percentage of children who display cross-gender behaviour in childhood are gender dysphoric in adolescence (Steensma et al., 2013).

L03

Childhood (5 to 11 Years)

Freud used the term *latency* to refer to the period of childhood following the resolution of the Oedipus complex (see Chapter 2). He believed that the sexual urges go "underground" during latency and are not expressed. The evidence indicates, however, that Freud was wrong and that children's interest in and expression of sexuality remain lively throughout this period (Figure 10.3). For many children, sexual awakening does not occur until adolescence, but for others it is a very real and poignant part of childhood.

Adrenarche, the maturation of the adrenal glands, occurs around 8 to 10 years of age (as early as 6 for some) and leads to increased levels of androgens in both boys and girls (Del Giudice et al., 2009). In short, some sex hormone action occurs in childhood, well before adolescence. Across several studies of adolescents and adults, the average age at which participants recalled first experiencing sexual attraction to another person was at age 10, probably linked to adrenarche and the rise in androgens (McClintock & Herdt, 1996).

Masturbation

During childhood, more and more children gain experience with masturbation. About 40 percent of university students recall masturbating before puberty (Bancroft et al., 2003). Generally, boys start masturbating earlier than girls, a trend that is even more pronounced in adolescence. About 40 percent of boys and 20 percent of girls report orgasms from masturbation by age 12 (Larsson & Svedin, 2002).

Boys and girls tend to learn about masturbation in different ways. Typically, boys are told about it by their male peers, they see their peers doing it, or they read about it; girls most frequently learn about masturbation through accidental self-discovery (Langfeldt, 1981).

Mixed-Sex Behaviour

There is generally little mixed-sex[2] sexual behaviour during childhood, mainly because boys and girls divide themselves into groups rigidly by gender. However, children commonly hear about penile–vaginal sexual intercourse for the first time during this period. For example, in a sample of adult women, 61 percent recalled having learned about intercourse by age 12 (Wyatt et al., 1988). Children's reactions to this new information are an amusing combination of shock and disbelief—particularly disbelief that their parents would do such a thing. A university woman recalled:

> One of my girlfriends told me about sexual intercourse. It was one of the biggest shocks of my life.

Figure 10.3 Between the ages of 3 and 7, children show a marked increase in sexual interest.

© Cassy Cohen/PhotoEdit

---

[2] We have chosen to use the rather unusual term *mixed-sex* instead of the more common term *opposite sex* because males and females are not opposites. In fact, as discussed in Chapter 13, males and females are more similar than they are different.

She took me aside one day, and I could tell she was in great distress. I thought she was going to tell me about menstruation, so I said that I already knew, and she said, "No, this is *worse!*" Her description went like this: "A guy puts his thing up a girl's hole, and she has a baby." The hole was, to us, the anus, because we did not even know about the vagina and we knew that the urethra was too small. I pictured the act as a single, violent and painful stabbing at the anus by the penis. Somehow, the idea of a baby was forgotten by me. I was horrified and repulsed, and I thought of that awful penis I had seen years ago. At first I insisted that it wasn't true, and my friend said she didn't know for sure, but that's what her cousin told her. But we looked at each other, and we knew it was true. We held each other and cried. We insisted that "my parents would never do that," and "I'll never let anyone do it to me." We were frightened, sickened, and threatened by the idea of some lusty male jabbing at us with his horrid penis. (From a student essay; Starks & Morrison, 1996)

There is some boy–girl contact (Figure 10.4). A study of Swedish high-school students asked them to recall consensual childhood sexual experiences with another child (Larsson & Svedin, 2002b). More than 80 percent reported having had at least one experience when they were between 6 to 12 years old, but most of this occurred at ages 11 or 12, the beginning of adolescence. Nonetheless, a substantial number (17 to 44 percent, depending on the behaviour) reported kissing and

Figure 10.4 Hanging out, group dating, and heterosexual parties emerge during preadolescence and may include making out.

Greg Ceo/Stone/Getty Images

hugging, showing their genitals, or another child touching their genitals, between ages 6 and 10. Turning to the gender of the partner, 57 percent of the boys reported such experiences with girls, 11 percent with another boy, and 33 percent with both boys and girls. For girls, the percentages were 31 with a boy, 29 with a girl, and 40 with both. Five percent of male adolescents and 1 percent of female adolescents in Canada report that they had engaged in sexual intercourse by the age of 12 (Maticka-Tyndale, 1997). Compared with their peers who first engage in intercourse during adolescence, Canadian youth who engage in intercourse during preadolescence are more likely to report having a poor relationship with their parents, having experienced pressure to engage in unwanted sex, having used drugs other than marijuana, and believing that they must break the rules to be popular (Boyce et al., 2008).

For some children, sexual activity occurs in a coercive relationship with a family member—whether a sibling, parent, stepparent, or other relative. This topic is discussed in detail in Chapter 16.

Same-Sex Behaviour

It is important to understand same-sex sexual activity as a normal part of the sexual development of children. In childhood, children have a **gender-segregated social organization**. That is, boys play separately from girls, and thus children spend most of their time with members of their own sex. Some of this social separation is actually comical; boys, for example, may be convinced that girls have "cooties" and that they must be very careful to stay away from them.

Given that children are spending time mainly with members of their own sex, sexual exploring at this age is likely to be with partners of the same sex. These activities generally involve masturbation, showing the genitals, and fondling others' genitals. Boys, for example, may engage in a *circle jerk*, in which they masturbate as a team. Girls are less likely to engage in such group activities, perhaps because the spectacle of them masturbating is not as impressive or perhaps because they already sense greater cultural restrictions on their sexuality. Nonetheless, girls have their own behaviours, as reported by one team of interviewers:

Fiona (first grade) said, "Chloe keeps kissing me in school!

gender-segregated social organization: A form of social grouping in which males play and associate with other males, and females play and associate with other females; that is, the genders are separate from each other.

heteronormativity: The belief that heterosexuality is the only pattern that is normal and natural.

sexualization: When a person is valued only for sex appeal or behaviour, is held to a standard that equates physical attractiveness with being sexy, or is sexually objectified, or when sexuality is inappropriately imposed on a person.

She kissed me on the back of the neck in line today." Chloe said, "I did, like this," and she crawled over to Fiona and kissed her on the back of her neck. Fiona said, "See!" Fiona was exasperated by these kisses, but she was also amused. Chloe was her best friend. And the kissing clearly entertained the whole group. (Myers & Raymond, 2010, p. 183)

A study of lesbian, gay, and bisexual youth found that the participants reported their first experience of same-sex sexual attraction at age 10 or 11 on average (Rosario et al., 1996). This age is comparable to that of first experiences of heterosexual attraction.

Sex Knowledge and Interests

Children learn very early that male–female pairings are the norm. That is, they learn **heteronormativity**, the belief that heterosexuality is the only pattern that is normal and natural. Intertwined with this view are beliefs that boys and girls are very different from each other, that boys should be attracted to girls, and that girls should be attracted to boys. A study of girls in kindergarten through Grade 5 used group interviews, which seem to be good for understanding children's experiences at these ages (Myers & Raymond, 2010). The girls' responses revealed well-learned heteronormativity. Even though they were initially embarrassed to talk about the topic, the girls revealed crushes on boys and then had excited discussions of their crushes. They used the term *hottie* for celebrity adolescent boys, such as *American Idol* contestants, and were excited about them as well. Yet despite all this talk, the girls thought that actual behaviours, such as kissing, were inappropriate: "Kissing is gross!"

LO4 Sexualization of Children

A major concern of some parents, educators, and researchers is the sexualization of girls and boys in Canadian society. **Sexualization**, as defined in an authoritative report from the American Psychological Association (2007), occurs when

- a person's value comes only from his or her sexual appeal or behaviour;
- a person is held to a standard that equates physical attractiveness with being sexy;
- a person is sexually objectified;
- sexuality is inappropriately imposed upon a person.

One example is beauty pageants for girls, such as in the television series *Toddlers and Tiaras*, in which girls as young as 4 are thrust into elaborate dresses and "dolled up" with sexy makeup and pouffy hairdos as they

Figure 10.5 The sexualization of children occurs in part through cultural messages in sexy clothing and sexy dolls. The Bratz dolls are a good example.

The McGraw-Hill Companies, Inc./Jill Braaten, photographer

compete in this beauty pageant for children. Another example is sexual harassment by peers, which will be discussed in more detail in Chapter 16. Sexualized products are involved as well, such as Bratz or Barbie dolls, books, and sexy clothing (Figure 10.5).

Boys are exposed to TV shows, video games, and movies that often teach messages that males should have "buff" bodies, that they should be physically powerful and always ready to fight, and that sex for men involves aggressive domination of beautiful women for the pleasure of the man (Levin, 2009, p. 79).

Sexualization also results when girls are treated like sexual objects by peers, family, teachers, or other adults. As a result of learning to view themselves as sexual objects, many girls and women engage in self-sexualization, leading them to purchase clothing because it is sexy and undergoing cosmetic surgery at a young age (American Psychological Association, 2007).

Experts are concerned that sexualization may lead to reduced self-esteem and body dissatisfaction because

the child does not meet the cultural standard of sexy appearance. Cognitive performance, such as math performance, can be impaired as well because of distracting thoughts resulting from sexualization (Gervais et al., 2011). Educational and career aspirations may be reduced. In adolescence, viewing oneself as a sexual object may lead young people to initiate sexual activity, to engage in unwanted sexual activity and relationships, and to engage in risky sexual behaviour, such as unprotected vaginal intercourse.

The APA report suggested many ways to counteract sexualization. Within the schools, we can provide media literacy programs, a broader range of athletic opportunities, and comprehensive sexuality education. Within the family, parents can watch TV and movies and navigate the Internet with their children, sharing their values about appropriate and inappropriate content. Youth can create alternative media including zines, blogs, and alternative magazines and books. Finally, parents, educators, and boys and girls can engage in activism and resistance, such as campaigning against companies that use sexualized images to sell products.

Why is the sexualization of children problematic?

LO5
Adolescence (12 to 18 Years)

Researchers today define adolescence as a bit more than the teenage years—that is, beginning at age 11 or 12 and extending through the college and university years, to age 21 or 22 (Steinberg, 2011). Here we use the category of adolescence for ages 12 to 18, through the end of high school. Then we devote a section to sex during the college and university years, often called emerging adulthood.

A tension exists in thinking about adolescent sexuality. On the one hand, sexuality is a normative part of adolescent development, and it plays an important positive role in growth and development (Halpern, 2010; Tolman & McClelland, 2011). Adolescent relationships, including sexual relationships, provide the context in which the individual develops the skills and learns the scripts needed to sustain long-term intimate relationships (O'Sullivan & Meyer-Bahlburg, 2003). The last section of this chapter is devoted to ways in which sexuality aids in psychological development. On the other hand, not all adolescent sex is good sex. Sometimes the person is too young, or the sex is coerced, or the sex is risky and unprotected. Quite frankly, researchers have focused much more of their energy on the second, negative aspect of adolescent sexuality than they have on the first, positive aspect. They have done so because of the enormous potential for negative consequences for the individual, the family, and the broader society when adolescent sex goes awry. In this chapter, though, we will focus mainly on the normative aspects of sexual development.

A surge of sexual interest occurs around puberty and continues through adolescence. This heightened sexuality may be caused by a number of factors, including bodily changes and an awareness of them, rises in levels of sex hormones, increased cultural emphasis on sex (see Milestones in Sex Research for a discussion of the effects of the media on adolescent sexuality), and rehearsal for adult gender roles. We can see evidence of this heightened sexuality particularly in the data on masturbation. But before examining those data, let's consider some theoretical ideas about how hormones and social forces might interact as influences on adolescent sexuality.

Udry (1988) has proposed a theoretical model that recognizes that both social and biological factors are potent in adolescent sexuality. He studied students in Grades 8, 9, and 10 (13 to 16 years old), measuring their hormone levels (testosterone, estrogen, and progesterone) and a number of sociological factors (e.g., whether they were in a two-parent family, their parents' educational level, the teenager's response to a scale measuring sexually permissive attitudes, and the teenager's attachment to conventional institutions, such as involvement in school sports and religious attendance). Overall, 35 percent of the boys and 14 percent of the girls had engaged in sexual intercourse.

For boys, testosterone levels had a strong relationship to sexual activity (including coitus, masturbation, and feeling sexually turned on). Sexually permissive attitudes, a social variable, also were related to sexuality among boys, although they had a smaller effect than testosterone did. For girls, there was a relationship between testosterone level and sexual activity, although it was not as strong as it was for boys—and it was testosterone that was related to sexuality, not estrogen or progesterone. Pubertal development (developing a curvy figure) had an effect, probably by increasing boys' attention. And the effects of testosterone were accentuated among girls in father-absent families. Permissive attitudes and religious attendance played a role as well.

The bottom line in this study is that it shows that testosterone levels have a substantial impact on the sexuality of adolescent boys and girls. Social psychological variables (permissive attitudes, father absence for girls, and religious attendance) then interact with the biological effects, in some cases magnifying them and in some cases suppressing them. Similarly, a study with gay and lesbian youth found that increases in hormone levels with puberty resulted in increases in homoerotic sexual feelings and behaviours (Savin-Williams, 1995).

Masturbation

According to the Kinsey data, there is a sharp increase in the incidence of masturbation for boys between the ages of 13 and 15, as illustrated in Figure 10.6. Note that the curve is steepest between the ages of 13 and 15, indicating that most boys begin masturbating to orgasm during that period. By age 15, 82 percent of the boys in Kinsey's study had masturbated. Many girls also begin masturbating in adolescence, but note that the curve on the graph is flatter for them, indicating that many girls do not begin masturbating until later. The increase in their masturbation behaviour is much more gradual for girls than for boys and continues past adolescence.

A study at the University of British Columbia asked students whether they had ever masturbated (Meston et al., 1996). Overall, 80 percent of the male students and 48 percent of the female students reported masturbating at least once. Asian students were significantly less likely to report having masturbated than were non-Asian students. Eighty-five percent of non-Asian males compared with 74 percent of Asian males reported that they had masturbated. The difference between non-Asian and Asian females was even greater—59 percent compared with 39 percent. A German study found that 94 percent of male university students and 74 percent of female students reported that they had masturbated in the previous year; interestingly, being in a satisfying sexual relationship did not affect how likely they were to report masturbating (Dekker & Schmidt, 2002). On average, female students reported masturbating about three times a month and male students about eight times a month.

More recent data indicate that children and adolescents begin to masturbate earlier today, and thus the Kinsey data need to be pushed back about a year. However, the general shape of the curves still holds (Bancroft et al., 2003).

Figure 10.6 Cumulative incidence of males and females who have masturbated to orgasm, according to Kinsey's data. Current data suggest that contemporary youth begin masturbating one or two years earlier.

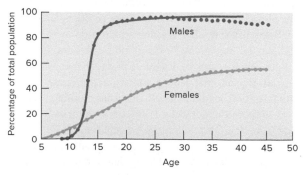

Attitudes toward Masturbation

Attitudes toward masturbation underwent a dramatic change in the twentieth century. As a result, adolescents are now given much different information about masturbation than were earlier adolescents, and this may affect both their behaviour and their feelings. For example, a popular handbook, *What a Boy Should Know,* written in 1913 by two doctors, advised its readers:

> Whenever unnatural emissions are produced. . . the body becomes "slack." A boy will not feel so vigorous and springy; he will be more easily tired. . . . He will probably look pale and pasty, and he is lucky if he escapes indigestion and getting his bowels confined, both of which will probably give him spots and pimples on his face. . . .

> The results on the mind are the more severe and more easily recognized. . . . A boy who practices this habit can never be the best that Nature intended him to be. His wits are not so sharp. His memory is not so good. His power of fixing his attention on whatever he is doing is lessened. . . . A boy like this is a poor thing to look at. . . .

> The effect of self-abuse on a boy's character always tends to weaken it, and in fact, to make him untrustworthy, unreliable, untruthful, and probably even dishonest. (Schofield & Vaughan-Jackson, 1913, pp. 30–42)

Masturbation, in short, was once believed to cause everything from warts to insanity.[3]

---

[3] In case you're wondering why boys' advice books were saying such awful things, there is a rather interesting history that produced those pronouncements (Money, 1986). Swiss physician Simon André Tissot (1728–1797) wrote an influential book called *Treatise on the Diseases Produced by Onanism,* taking the term from the biblical story of Onan (Genesis 38:9). In this work he articulated a degeneracy theory, in which loss of semen was believed to weaken a man's body; Tissot had some very inventive physiological explanations for his idea. The famous American physician of the nineteenth century Benjamin Rush was influenced by Tissot and spread degeneracy theory in North America. The theory became popularized by Sylvester Graham (1794–1851), a religious zealot and health reformer, who was a vegetarian and whose passion for health foods gave us the names for Graham flour and Graham crackers. To be healthy, according to Graham, one needed to follow the Graham diet and practise sexual abstinence. Then John Harvey Kellogg (1852–1943) of—you guessed it—cornflakes fame entered the story. He was an ardent follower of Graham and his doctrines of health food and sexual abstinence. While experimenting with healthful foods, he invented cornflakes. His younger brother, Will Keith Kellogg, thought to add sugar and made a fortune. John Harvey Kellogg contributed further to public fears about masturbation by writing (during his honeymoon, no less) *Plain Facts for Old and Young: Embracing the Natural History and Hygiene of Organic Life,* which provided detailed descriptions of the horrible diseases supposedly caused by masturbation. These ideas then found their way into the advice books for boys in the early twentieth century.

Attitudes toward masturbation are now considerably more positive, and today few people would subscribe to notions like those expressed earlier; most individuals see masturbation as normal (Morrison et al., 2008). Indeed, sex therapists recommend masturbation as a way for people to increase their awareness of their own sexual response and as a step in overcoming a number of sexual problems and concerns. As psychiatrist Thomas Szasz (1973, p. 10) said, the shift in attitudes toward masturbation has been so great that in a generation it has changed from a disease to a form of therapy. On the other hand, there is evidence that attitudes toward masturbation are not quite as positive as we might want to believe. For example, researchers in British Columbia did a content analysis (see Chapter 3) did a content analysis of how masturbation is portrayed in popular North American movies released between 2005 and 2010. They found that masturbation was generally depicted somewhat negatively, especially when engaged in by a male character, often leading to negative outcomes. How might such portrayals affect our attitudes toward masturbation and its outcomes?

Same-Sex Sexual Behaviour

Grade 9 and 11 students in the CYSHHAS were asked about their sexual attraction. About 5 percent of the girls reported being attracted to girls or to both boys and girls. Among the boys, 2 to 6 percent reported being attracted to boys or to both boys and girls. According to the National Survey of Family Growth, a large, nationally representative U.S. survey, 7 percent of girls and 2 percent of boys between the ages of 15 and 19 report having engaged in oral sex with a same-sex partner (Chandra et al., 2011). It seems that girls are more willing to engage in these behaviours than boys are.

Experts believe that adolescence is the period during which one's identities develop and become stabilized. As noted earlier, sexual minority youth report awareness of attraction to persons of the same gender as early as age 10. The process of self-identification as a sexual minority person typically occurs between 14 and 21 (O'Sullivan & Thompson 2014), and occurs at somewhat younger ages for boys. For example, a survey of students in Grades 7 through 12 in British Columbia found that 8 percent of the male students and 9 percent of the female students self-identified as bisexual, gay, lesbian, or not sure (McCreary Centre Society, 2007).

Adolescents are generally accepting of same-sex sexual behaviour (Figure 10.7). Alberta sociologist Reginald Bibby (Bibby et al., 2009) surveyed 5564 teenagers across Canada, ages 15 to 19. He found that only 44 percent approved of sexual relations between two people of the same sex; however, an additional 28 percent did not approve of it but nonetheless accepted it.

Nonetheless, many sexual minority adolescents experience prejudice and rejection within their families or

Milestones in Sex Research

What Impact Does Mass Media Have on Adolescent Sexuality?

A major developmental task of adolescence is learning how to manage physical and emotional intimacy in relationships with others. It is not surprising, therefore, that young people are curious about sex and seek information about it. Although most Canadian students identify school as their main source of information on human sexuality, an increasingly important source of information are the media—in particular, the Internet. In one study of youth ages 14 to 17, 54 percent of the participants identified television and 44 percent identified the Internet as a source for information about sex and sexual health (Canadian Association for Adolescent Health, 2006). Canadian youth are influenced by both the Canadian and American media. *Law & Order: SVU* provides information on sexual assault and the sexual abuse of children. *The Jersey Shore* features plenty of sexual images. But how much sexual content actually is there in the mass media? To what extent are children and adolescents exposed to it, and what is the impact of this exposure?

Do media portrayals of sex really affect my sexual attitudes and behaviour?

Media are a major part of adolescents' lives. On average, they have more than 11 hours of exposure per day, including TV, music, computers, video games, print media, and movies (Rideout et al., 2010). In analyzing how much sexual content there is in the mass media in the United States, sexual material is defined to include talk about sex, sexually suggestive behaviour, and explicit portrayals of sex. Using the methods of media content analysis (described in Chapter 3), a major project analyzed sexual material on television in 2004–2005 (Kunkel et al., 2005). The sample included more than 1000 programs on the four commercial U.S. networks, public television, four cable networks (including HBO), and one independent broadcaster. The sample included all types of programs broadcast between 6 a.m. and 10 p.m. Sexual material was carefully defined and these definitions were used by trained coders to analyze the content of each program. On prime-time television, 70 percent of the programs included sexual material; 4.6 scenes per hour included talk about sex, and 2 scenes per hour included sexual behaviour. These numbers represent substantial increases since the 1990s, when a similar

project was carried out. Portrayals of risks or responsibilities associated with sex were notably absent; only 4 percent of scenes carried such material.

Cable movie networks have the largest proportion of programs with sexual content (Fisher et al., 2004). The most frequent portrayals are of unmarried heterosexual intercourse, often in a context of alcohol and drug use. There are no safer sex messages here!

Many adolescents read books. A content analysis of the 40 best-selling books targeting youth ages 9 to 14+ found that they contain a great deal of sex-related information (Callister et al., 2012). One-third of the references were to behaviour, one-third to sexual talk and descriptions, and one-third to displays of sexual affection. Portrayals of sexual intercourse involved unmarried couples in uncommitted relationships. Health risks and safer sex practices were rarely mentioned.

How much of this sexual material are adolescents exposed to? In one study, adolescents (in Grades 8 to 10) completed questionnaires about their media "diets" (Schooler et al., 2009). The 25 most frequently viewed TV programs were then content-analyzed for sexual material. The results indicated that, in a typical hour of television viewing, these adolescents were exposed to an average of 17 references to sexual talk or behaviour.

The newer media, especially the Internet, also contain plenty of sexual content. In one study of U.S. adolescents (12–14 years old), 66 percent of boys and 39 percent of girls had seen at least one form of sexually explicit media (Internet sites, X-rated movies, adult magazines) in the past year (Brown & L'Engle, 2009). It would be a mistake, though, to think of adolescents as passive victims of an onslaught of media sex; research indicates that teens actively seek sexual content in their media choices (Bleakley et al., 2011). (Pornography is discussed in more detail in Chapter 17.)

There are some differences between Canadian and U.S. television shows. In particular, some topics can be introduced into Canadian television shows that would not be considered acceptable by the U.S. networks. For 30 years, *Degrassi* (and its predecessors *Degrassi: The Next Generation*, *Degrassi High*, and *Degrassi Junior High*) portrayed youth sexuality in diverse ways and used storylines to explore different sexual choices, such as the decision to engage in intercourse, as well as the realistic consequences of sexual behaviour (M. Byers, 2005). The results have often been groundbreaking and a source of discussion and controversy. For example, throughout the *Degrassi* series, some of the female characters became pregnant; some chose to parent, some placed their baby for adoption, and some obtained abortions. Although all these episodes were shown on the Canadian network carrying the show, the American cable station that carried it would not air the abortion episodes. American television explores pregnancy issues in shows such as *The Secret Life of the American Teenager, 16 and Pregnant,* and spinoff *Teen Mom,* all of which portray teens who are pregnant, parenting, or post-adoption, rarely discussing the option of abortion. Further, on American TV when abortion issues develop, it often turns out to be a false alarm, the character miscarries, or she has the baby. If the character does have an abortion, negative consequences follow—she is punished or experiences extreme guilt (M. Byers, 2005).

Some popular television programs and movies meant for adolescent audiences do explore teen sexuality in a more realistic and sex-positive way and encourage positive behaviour: Teens talk about sex and obtain consent from their partners for sexual activities; abstinence is respected as a choice; condoms are discussed and used; and youth obtain STI/HIV testing, use birth control, and discuss their pregnancy options with partners and health practitioners. Media representations of gay and lesbian adolescent characters have increased, giving gay, lesbian, bisexual, queer, and questioning youth more characters they can identify with. Popular prime-time U.S. television shows *Glee* and *90210*, and Canadian classic *Degrassi*, all present realities faced by these youth. Such portrayals of adolescent queer desire and empathetic views of queer and questioning youth experiences mean less isolation for these youth, as well as education for their heterosexual counterparts. *Degrassi* also introduced the first recurring transgender character and portrays the impact of transphobic bullying, coming out transgender, family relationships, and what the discovery of sexual and emotional desire can be like for a transgender youth.

Nonetheless, these examples of positive messages about sex and sexual health in the media are still in the minority, with the majority of portrayals of sex being confusing or negative. What effect do these portrayals have on adolescents? Experts say that these portrayals represent *sexual socialization* by the media (Wright, 2009). Youth may learn scripts that influence their later sexual decision-making and behaviour. For example, one team of researchers developed measures of a *heterosexual script* that includes guidelines for men's and women's behaviour (Kim et al., 2007). In this script, masculinity is defined, in part, by sexual conquest and experience, by taking the initiative in relationships and aggressively seeking sex, and by limiting emotional commitment. The script defines femininity as being chaste yet seductive, setting sexual limits, attaining power and status by sexually objectifying oneself, and seeking commitment. The researchers' analysis of prime-time network TV programs indicated that there were 15.5 portrayals of elements of this heterosexual script per hour.

One college student, recalling his first sexual intercourse, described it in relation to media portrayals:

Interviewer: What were you thinking at the time?

Michael: When I had sex with her? "Let's see if this is really as good as everyone says." And it wasn't. It was pretty bad actually. Just because there was like, no love, no passion, she wasn't like I thought she'd be. You know, you always have these sexual fantasy ideas—the movies, the magazines—you see all this stuff and you're like "Oh yeah! This is the way it is!" And then in real life it's like. . . . It was just not a good experience. (Albanesi, 2010, p. 124)

Many studies demonstrate correlations between the amount of sexual media consumption and adolescents' sexual attitudes and behaviour. For example, university students who view more reality-dating programs are more likely to endorse a sexual double standard and to believe that men are sex-driven, that appearance is important in dating, and that dating is a game (Zurbriggen & Morgan, 2006). In another study, university students with higher use of sexually explicit materials reported having more intercourse partners but lower sexual and relationship satisfaction (Morgan, 2011). The media may also influence standards of physical attractiveness and contribute to the dissatisfaction with their bodies that many, especially women, feel. For example, research has shown that viewing as little as 30 minutes of television can change women's perceptions of their bodies, which the authors term the "elastic body image" (Myers & Biocca, 1992). Of course, as we noted in Chapter 3, we

(continued)

(*continued*)

should not make causal inferences from correlational data. We cannot conclude, for example, that exposure to the reality-dating programs affected students' attitudes. Therefore, researchers have turned to other designs to test the effects of the media on sexuality—in particular, to longitudinal designs and experimental designs.

Several longitudinal studies have assessed adolescents' TV viewing at one time (baseline) and then followed them a year or more later to measure changes in their sexual behaviour (Ashby et al., 2006; Bleakley et al., 2008; Brown et al., 2006; Collins et al., 2004). Youth who view more sexual content at baseline are more likely to progress to more advanced sexual activities and to engage in first intercourse in the following year.

The effects of exposure to scenes of sexual behaviour in movies were studied by first coding the number of seconds of sexual content in several hundred top-grossing films. A sample of 6522 adolescents aged 10 to 14 were conducted by telephone over a seven-year period and asked which of the coded films they had seen. Participants over 18 were asked to report their sexual behaviour. Youth who had spent more time watching these films reported a younger age of first intercourse and more risky sexual behaviour, including more sexual partners and more frequent casual sex without a condom (O'Hara et al., 2012).

Experiments, too, indicate that the media have an impact on sexual attitudes and behaviour. For example, in one study youth exposed to four music videos with stereotypic male and female characters expressed more traditional views of gender and sexual relationships, compared with the control group (Ward et al., 2005).

The evidence is strong that media portrayals have an important impact on adolescents' sexual knowledge, attitudes, and behaviour (Wright, 2011). The problem lies in the fact that these portrayals are not realistic. For example, in sharp contrast to the high rates of nonmarital sex portrayed in the media, most sexual activity involves persons who are married or in long-term, committed relationships (see Chapter 11). Many couples in real life, whether married or not, are responsible users of birth control. Many adolescents and adults use condoms to prevent STIs. It is unfortunate that these realities are invisible in media portrayals of sexual behaviour. It is also unfortunate that the media have generally not taken advantage of their opportunity to provide positive sexuality education.

As a final note, most adolescents are not only exposed to sexuality in the mass media but are also increasingly exposed to sexual depictions in pornography, which they easily access over the Internet. Pornography is characterized by unrealistic body types (very thin women with large breasts, men with very large penises), unrealistic sexual expectations (for example, in terms of ejaculatory control), and unequal gender roles (women's roles typically being to satisfy men's needs). There is concern that viewing pornography at a young age can affect adolescents' views of the ideal male or female body or of the expected sexual script (Löfgren-Mårtenson & Månsson, 2010; Štulhofer et al., 2010). On the other hand, for the most part, young people believe that they can differentiate between the fantasy depicted in pornography and real life (Löfgren-Mårtenson & Månsson, 2010). (Pornography is discussed in more detail in Chapter 17.)

With updates and contributions from Erica Doty.

their schools (Saewyc, 2011). Calling someone *gay* is a common form of peer harassment in middle schools and high schools. Nonetheless, most sexual minority youth successfully navigate these difficulties and emerge at the end of adolescence with well-being comparable to their heterosexual peers (Saewyc, 2011). Having a gay–straight alliance in the school helps youth deal with these difficulties (see http://mygsa.ca for information on establishing a gay–straight alliance).

Adolescence is also the period during which gender identity, one's sense of being male, female, or in some other gender category, undergoes substantial development (Steensma et al., 2013). Most youth experience gender intensification—that is, further development and elaboration of the assigned gender in childhood. For a minority, this involves the further development of a gender-variant identity. There are several events or experiences in late childhood/early adolescence that may intensify youths' concerns about their gender. These include pubertal development, intensified cultural and peer pressure to conform to gender-role norms, and increased time spent in gendered social contexts. These may encourage the adolescent to explore the possibility that s/he is trangender.

Mixed-Sex Sexual Behaviour

In middle and late adolescence, more and more young people engage in sex with a member of the other gender, with more and more frequency. Thus mixed-sex sexual behaviour gains prominence and becomes the major sexual outlet. Many adolescents who go on to adopt gay, lesbian, or bisexual identities report having engaged in heterosexual activity during adolescence—74 percent of the females and 57 percent of the males in one study (D'Augelli, 2002). Only a small percentage of these youth engage in only same-sex activity and no other sex activity (Savin-Williams & Cohen, 2007). As noted above, the reverse is also true—many heterosexuals engage in same-sex experimentation during adolescence.

Generally there is a progression beginning with kissing, then breast and genital fondling, moving on to oral sex, and then to penis-in-vagina intercourse (Boyce et al., 2006; de Graaf et al., 2009). To use terminology introduced in Chapter 2, these behaviours tend to follow a sexual script. Variations on the normative sequence can occur based on factors such as social class and ethnicity. Initially there were claims that most of the oral sex involved girls "servicing" boys; however, research indicates a general pattern of gender equality in giving and receiving oral sex (Tolman & McClelland, 2011).

The progression in sexual behaviour is evident from data provided in Table 10.1 on the percentage of Canadian adolescents who have engaged in five different sexual behaviours. For example, in Grade 9, almost three times as many students had engaged in deep kissing and more than twice as many had engaged in touching below the waist than had engaged in sexual intercourse. Further, more students had engaged in oral sex than had engaged in sexual intercourse. The progression of sexual experience is also evident in the finding that the percentage of students who had engaged in each of the five sexual behaviours was greatest for Grade 11 students, intermediate for Grade 9 students, and lowest for Grade 7 students. As shown in Table 10.1, by Grade 11 almost half of students report that they have engaged in intercourse; about 10 percent had engaged in fellatio or

Figure 10.7 A crowd gathers on the street saluting gay youth celebrating their coming out.

© AP Photo/Michael Perez/CP Images

cunnilingus but not in intercourse (Boyce et al., 2006). Many sexually experienced youth have had two or more sexual partners (Fisher & Boroditsky, 2000). For example, almost half of the Grade 9 and 11 students surveyed in the CYSHHAS who had engaged in sexual intercourse had had two or more partners (Boyce et al., 2003). More recent data from the Canadian Community Health Survey in 2009–2010 found that 30 percent of 15- to 17-year-olds and 68 percent of 18- and 19-year-olds reported that they had engaged in intercourse (Roterman, 2012).

It is interesting to compare youth involvement in sexual activity in the CYSHHAS to the results from the Canadian Youth and AIDS Study conducted in 1988 (King et al., 1988). The percentage of students who reported having engaged in deep kissing and sexual touching changed very little over the 14 years between the two studies. However, somewhat fewer students reported having engaged in sexual intercourse in 2003 than in 1988. The earlier survey did not ask about oral sex. Other researchers have also found that the average age of first intercourse in

> **How many Canadian teens have engaged in sexual intercourse by Grade 11?**

Table 10.1 Percentage of Canadian Youth Who Have at Least Once Engaged in Various Sexual Behaviours

	Grade 7		Grade 9		Grade 11	
	Boys	**Girls**	**Boys**	**Girls**	**Boys**	**Girls**
Deep (open-mouth) kissing	49%	35%	65%	67%	81%	82%
Touching above the waist	46%	34%	67%	64%	81%	81%
Touching below the waist	33%	23%	57%	54%	75%	74%
Oral sex			32%	28%	53%	52%
Sexual intercourse			3%	19%	40%	46%

Boyce et al (2006). Sexual health of Canadian youth: Findings from the Canadian youth, sexual health and HIV/AIDS Study. *Canadian Journal of Human Sexuality, 15,* 59-68. Used with permission.

Canada is no longer decreasing and may even be increasing (Maticka-Tyndale, 2008; Rotermann, 2008). For example, research in British Columbia shows that from 1992 to 2003, the percentage of both male and female adolescents who have had intercourse decreased as did the percentage who engaged in intercourse before the age of 14 (Saewyc et al., 2008). However, this differs from one region of Canada to the next (Canadian Federation for Sexual Health, 2007). Teens in Quebec are most likely to report having engaged in sexual intercourse (Rotermann, 2008).

When Canadian high school students were asked the most important reason for engaging in sexual intercourse, 60 percent of female Grade 11 students but only 39 percent of male students gave love as the reason. Curiosity and experimentation was also an important reason given by 21 percent of males but only 14 percent of females (Boyce et al., 2006). In other research adolescents also identify relationship goals, such as increased intimacy, sexual pleasure (let's not forget that one!), and increased social status (Ott et al., 2006).

Adolescents also have a variety of reasons for not engaging in intercourse. In the CYSHHAS, the most common reasons were not feeling ready, not having had the opportunity, and not having met the right person (Boyce et al., 2006).

First intercourse is an important experience for many people. In many cultures, it is a symbol of having reached (reproductive) adulthood. In Canadian culture, it may also be a symbol of the young person's attractiveness and popularity. What do we know about people's first intercourse experiences? An Ontario study found that 60 percent of participants had their first intercourse experience with a serious dating partner, 20 percent with a casual dating partner, 16 percent with a friend or an acquaintance, and 4 percent with someone they just met (Reissing et al., 2011). Women were more likely than men to be in a serious relationship. The researchers also analyzed the participants' emotional reactions to first coitus. Almost all the men (91 percent) and three-quarters of the women (73 percent) overall had a positive emotional reaction to their first intercourse experience. Nonetheless, despite our culture's romanticized high expectations that the first intercourse experience will be like fireworks on Canada Day, it turns out to be much less thrilling than that for many people. The Ontario study found that only 6 percent of the women compared with 62 percent of the men experienced orgasm during their first experience (Reissing et al., 2011). In addition, research in Alberta found that only about half the women and men in their study reported being emotionally satisfied after their first intercourse experience, and only 40 percent rated the experience as very good or excellent (Tsui & Nicoladis, 2004). Researchers have found that an experience that was intentional (not spontaneous), involving people who were less committed to "traditional": gender roles (more committed to mutual pleasure?), and more satisfied with

their bodies produced more positive emotions (Smiler, et al. 2005). Other researchers have found that undergraduates who reported a more positive first experience were more emotionally and physically satisfied with their current sexual relationships, up to seven years later (Smith & Shaffer, 2013). These data suggest that carefully selecting the partner and setting for one's first experience will have more favourable long-term outcomes.

Many people assume that having penile–vagina intercourse for the first time equals losing one's virginity. However, research in Alberta has shown that students have a broader definition of what constitutes "having sex" than of "virginity loss" (Trotter & Alderson, 2007). Carpenter (2005) identified three different meanings of virginity to youth: a gift to be given to a committed partner, a stigma to be gotten rid of, or a state that one will inevitably transition out of. Canadian researchers found that 54 percent of adolescents who had experienced penile–vaginal intercourse were process-oriented, 38 percent were gift-oriented, and 8 percent were stigma-oriented at first coitus (Humphreys, 2013). Men are more likely to be stigma-oriented than were women (Eriksson & Humphreys, 2013). University students viewing it as a gift were more likely to delay intercourse and plan for their first experience, but not for contraceptive use at first intercourse (Humphreys, 2013).

Even though there has been a slight decline recently in the percentage of high school students who have engaged in intercourse, adolescents today are engaging in intercourse for the first time at younger ages compared with persons born 40 years ago. Figure 10.8 provides

Figure 10.8 Young people are engaging in first intercourse at younger ages than men and women 50 years ago.

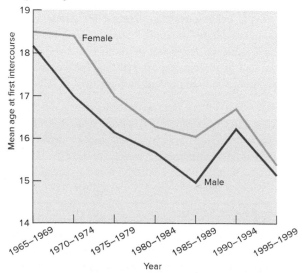

Brooke E. Wells & Jean M. Twenge, "Changes in young people's sexual behavior and attitudes, 1943-1999: A cross-temporal meta-analysis," *Review of General Psychology*, 9, 2005, 249–261 (Figure 2). Reprinted by permission of the American Psychological Association and the author.

data from studies conducted in the 1960s through the late 1990s in the United States and Canada (Wells & Twenge, 2005). The mean age of first intercourse for boys declined from 18 in the 1960s to 15 in 2000. Among girls, it declined from 18.5 to 15.5 across the same period. Similar declines in age of first intercourse have been reported in Australia (Smith et al., 2003). The majority of Canadians first engage in intercourse between the ages of 16 and 19 (Maticka-Tyndale, 1997).

These trends reflect, in part, the impact of the sexual revolution of the 1960s and 1970s, which encouraged greater openness about sexuality and acceptance of sex between unmarried people, particularly for women. For all age groups included in the National Population Health Survey, immigrants to Canada initiated intercourse at later ages than those born in Canada did. For example, for the age group that was between 20 and 24 at the time of the survey, 41 percent of immigrant men compared with 60 percent of Canadian-born men had engaged in intercourse by age 17. The difference was even larger for women; 18 percent of immigrant women between the ages of 20 and 24 and 58 percent of Canadian-born women in that age group had engaged in intercourse by age 17 (Maticka-Tyndale et al., 2000a).

Rates of sexual intercourse also differ substantially for adolescents who come from different ethnocultural backgrounds. For example, a study of adolescents of East Asian origin adolescents (grades 7 to 12) living in British Columbia found that less than 10 percent had engaged in sexual intercourse compared to the provincial rate of 22 percent (Homma et al., 2013). The East Asian adolescent were also less likely to have engaged in oral sex (11 percent versus 26 percent). The rates were similar for the boys and the girls. Students who reported speaking a heritage language at home were the least likely to have engaged in sexual intercourse. Youth who identified more strongly with their ethnic group were less likely to have engaged in sexual intercourse (Homma et al., 2014).

These ethnocultural differences mirror the substantial variations in patterns of adolescent intercourse in different cultures around the world, as the data in Table 10.2 indicate. Most of the data were collected by the Demographic and Health Surveys Program, which administers the same questions to people in different countries. Note that the time frames are different from the United States and Canada than for the other countries. Several interesting points emerge from the data. First, the percentage of young women who report intercourse is smaller in Latin and South American countries than in African nations, partly because of the greater influence of the Catholic Church in Latin America (Figure 10.9). Second, there is not much variation across nations in the average age of first intercourse; it is either 16, 17, or 18 in all but one country.

Figure 10.9 In South American nations, the percentage of unmarried young women who engage in premarital intercourse is lower than in North America owing to the strong influence of the Catholic Church.

© James Brunker / Alamy Stock Photo

In many countries around the world, the incidence of adolescent intercourse has risen in the last several decades. Around the globe, especially where modernization has been rapid, adolescents are less and less under the influence of family, community, and religion and more and more responsive to peers and the mass media (Liskin et al., 1985).

Too Early Sex

Although sex is a normative part of adolescent development, sometimes sex occurs too early. Experts agree that sex at age 15 or earlier is "early" sex and that it carries a number of risks (Price & Hyde, 2009). Those who engage in intercourse early are more likely not to use a condom and to have sex with more than one partner. The result is increased risk for teen pregnancies and sexually transmitted infections. According to the results of the Canadian Community Health Survey, 8.2 percent of female adolescents and 10.8 percent of male adolescents have engaged in sexual intercourse before the age of 15 (Rotermann, 2012). Another 25 percent had intercourse for the first time at age 15 or 16.

Researchers in Quebec have identified a number of factors that predict engaging in early sex, including (1) living in a single-parent family, (2) having more depressive symptoms, (3) displaying more antisocial behaviour, (4) having less self-disclosure to parents and more parent–child conflict, (5) having more other-sex friends and friends who use alcohol and drugs, and (6) having lower academic achievement (Boislard & Poulin, 2011). These same factors also tend to predict a higher number of sexual partners (Lansford et al., 2010). In contrast, Ontario researchers have shown that adolescents' perceptions that their parents would disapprove of them engaging in sexual intercourse are unrelated to their behaviour (Hampton et al., 2005).

Table 10.2 A Global Perspective on Female Adolescent Intercourse

Country and Year	Age of Respondents (years)	Percentage Having Had Intercourse (last four weeks)*	Median Age of First Coitus (years)
Africa			
Cameroon, 1998	15–19	33.7	16.3
Kenya, 1998	15–19	19.4	17.3
Nigeria, 1999	15–19	24.6	18.1
Tanzania, 1996	15–19	28.2	17.4
Zambia, 1996	15–19	26.9	16.6
Central America			
Mexico, 1985	15–19	13.0	17.0
Nicaragua, 1998	15–19	21.7	18.1
South America			
Bolivia, 1998	15–19	8.6	19.6
Brazil, 1996	15–19	21.5	18.7
United States, 2005	15–18	34.6**	17.4[†]
Canada, 2000	15–19	52.7***	16.0

* These percentages are of all women, so some of these women are married.

** Had intercourse in the last three months.

*** Had intercourse in the last 12 months.

[†] Mean age of first intercourse.

Source: Data for the United States are from the 2005 Youth Risk Behavior Survey conducted by the Centers for Disease Control and Prevention. The data for other countries are from the Demographic and Health Surveys Pro-gram, which collects comparable data from many countries around the world. The results are published in indi-vidual volumes for each country by Macro International, Inc., Calverton, MD. The typical reference is: Kenya: Demographic and Health Survey, 1998. Calverton MD: Macro International, 1999. The data for Canada are from the Canadian Community Health Survey, 2000–2001.

One college woman, reflecting back on her decision to have sex at age 14, said this:

Interviewer: And in junior high? What did you think about sex before you had sex?
Shari: I didn't like it much. It was more about feeling grown up and stuff. Plus everyone was doing it. Plus if I did it early maybe it would be better.
Interviewer: Why would it be better?
Shari: Because of all of my friends I would be the first one, so it would be kinda cool. That's what I thought.
Interviewer: So did you decide beforehand . . . or was it just something that happened?
Shari: I decided beforehand. (Albanesi, 2010, p. 23)

Research using the Add Health longitudinal data compared persons whose first intercourse experience occurred early (age 14 or younger) with persons who were on time (15 to 19), or later (20 or older) (Harden, 2012). Both men and women who had early sex were more likely to cohabit, and reported an increased number of sexual partners (considered a measure of "risky sex"). Women who reported early sex were less likely to be married 10 to 12 years later.

It is sometimes assumed that once an adolescent has initiated sexual activity, they will thereafter engage in sexual activity if given the opportunity. However, researchers in New Brunswick found that 36 percent of sexually experienced female adolescents and 16 percent of sexually experienced male adolescents report that they had purposely avoided sexual activity for a period of time, most for a few months or longer (Byers et al., 2016).

Adolescent Romantic Relationships

Most Canadian teens say that they have had a boyfriend or girlfriend, although some of these are likely short-lived (Price et al., 2000). These relationships are a context in which sexual activity typically occurs (Collins et al., 2009; Giordano et al., 2010).

Experts believe that these relationships can contribute to psychological development, but they can also have negative outcomes, such as dating violence (Collins et al., 2009). Low-quality relationships are characterized by antagonism, high levels of conflict, and controlling behaviour; they have been linked to lower academic performance and poor emotional health. High-quality relationships are marked by qualities such as supportiveness and emotional intimacy, and relationships such as these can contribute to an adolescent's feelings of self-worth.

On the other hand, break-ups are difficult and distressing for adolescents, and many individuals have difficulty letting go of the relationship (Lee & O'Sullivan, 2014). New Brunswick researchers found that, in their most recent break-up, three quarters of individuals tried to re-establish contact with their former partner or to monitor their whereabouts or activities—there were no gender differences. They used both online and offline means to do so. On the other hand, few individuals reported engaging in behaviours that might be characterized as stalking or cyberstalking. Some adolescents avoid romantic and/or sexual involvement for a period of time after the break-up (Byers et al., 2016).

Adolescent relationships provide the context in which the individual develops the skills and learns the scripts needed to sustain long-term intimate relationships (O'Sullivan & Meyer-Bahlburg, 2003). Relationships with romantic partners provide opportunities to explore identity, develop future goals, learn communication and conflict resolution skills, and learn how to enhance intimacy and sexuality. On the negative side, these relationships increase the likelihood of experiencing negative emotions—anxiety, jealousy, and depression, perhaps increasing the risk of suicide (Kerpelman, 2014).

Research indicates that the process begins around ages 9 to 12 with a first boyfriend or girlfriend; often there is little direct interaction between the two, but the relationship does provide an opportunity to play an "adult" role. Later comes group dating and perhaps mixed-sex social events at school. These situations provide an opportunity for conversation and for peers to observe and instruct the person in sexual scripts. In mid- to late adolescence, youth begin to spend time in mixed-sex, unsupervised interaction, which provides an opportunity for more sexual expression.

We can apply symbolic interaction theory, explained in Chapter 2, to understanding adolescents' romantic relationships (Giordano et al., 2010). The meaning of an adolescent romantic relationship to the individuals depends very much on the communication between them. Intimate self-disclosure (see Chapter 12) heightens feelings of emotional intimacy, for example. Power dynamics can be involved as well, as the romantic partner becomes an important influence on behaviour and attitudes.

A Quebec study asked 6961 adolescents between 14 and 19 years of age to describe their ideal romantic experience. Their responses represented six dominant themes, including fidelity and respect; sensuality

(kissing and hugging); connecting through spending time together and engaging in joint activities; passion, magic, and (especially for boys) pleasure; shared future plans; and creating tangible memories.

Most lesbian and gay youth do not date those they are most attracted to out of very real fear of harassment from their peers. Further, gay and lesbian youth in Canada are more likely to be the victims of harassment and violence than are their heterosexual peers (D'Augelli, 2006; McCreary Centre Society, 2007). Many date partners of the other gender to conform to societal expectations (Savin-Williams, 1995).

Adolescents also engage in extradyadic sexual activity. New Brunswick researchers found in their sample of 15- to 19-year-olds, 21 percent reported having kissed someone romantically other than their boyfriend or girlfriend while in a romantic relationship (O'Sullivan & Ronis, 2013). Even more adolescents (26 percent) reported kissing someone romantically who they knew was in a relationship with someone else. The same percentage of male and female adolescents reported engaging in these behaviours.

Internet Use, Risk, and Sexting

Adolescence is the time when most young people are learning about their bodies and sexuality, and developing their gender and sexual identities (Smahel & Subrahmanyam, 2014). New technologies have had a major impact on the ways in which these developments occur. One popular technique is the use of social networking sites, such as Facebook. Roughly 90 percent of teens and young adults have a profile on such a site (National Campaign to Prevent Teen and Unplanned Pregnancy, 2009).

One purpose of maintaining an online profile is to keep up with friends; about 85 percent of adolescents use social networking sites for this purpose (Valkenburger & Peter, 2009). This kind of online communication stimulates self-disclosure. This may be because other people are not actually present, thereby reducing concerns about how others will react and leading to self-disclosure of more personal information. Research indicates that self-disclosure enhances relationship quality, and high-quality peer relationships improve personal well-being (see Chapter 12). So rather than leading to reduced social integration and connection, these online exchanges can increase it.

Another purpose is to meet people or make new friends. Users often self-disclose via text or pictures in the hope of attracting certain kinds of people. In this context, personal information can put the poster at risk. A content analysis of 500 web profiles of 18-year-olds considered references to sexual behaviour, substance (alcohol or other drugs) use, and violence to be risky (Moreno et al., 2009). Whether true or not, such references attract others who may want to take advantage of or exploit the poster. Of the profiles that were analyzed, 54 percent contained risk-behaviour information; 24 percent referred to risk behaviour related to sex, 41 percent to substance use, and 14 percent to violence. The researchers suggested many youth should be more cautious about what they post on their profiles.

Sexting, sending sexually charged messages or images by cellphone or other electronic media, has gained national attention (Figure 10.10). According to a New Brunswick survey of 15- to 19-year-olds, 15 percent reported having sent a nude or semi-nude photograph of themselves over the Internet, and 30 percent reported having received such a photograph (O'Sullivan, 2011). Young men reported receiving photos more than young women, but there were no differences found in their reports of sending photos. Therefore, it is far from true that all adolescents are involved in sexting. However, sexting is more prevalent among young adults—a B.C. study found that 26 percent had sent an explicit word-based message, and an additional 51 percent had sent a nude or semi-nude photo or video of themselves.

In one innovative study, the BlackBerry Project, 15-year-olds were each given a BlackBerry device with a prepaid plan; their text messages were then stored and content-analyzed (Underwood et al., 2011). Roughly 7 percent of the messages contained sexual themes, again indicating that sending sexual messages is not a normative behaviour for adolescents.

A survey of 11- to 16-year-olds in 20 European countries investigated the prevalence and correlates of sexting (Baumgartner, Sumter, Peter, et al., 2014). In most countries, between 1 and 5 percent of boys and 1 and 4 percent of girls reported sexting. Older youth, those scoring higher in sensation seeking, and more frequent Internet users were more likely to sext. The only variation across countries was that girls in societies with more traditional values were less likely to sext.

A longitudinal study of an ethnically diverse sample of high school students found that the specific act of having sent a nude picture of oneself predicted engaging in "sex (intercourse)" in the following year. The relationship was found among both male and female youth. Sending a nude photo was not related to risky sex in the following year—that is, having more sexual partners or reporting alcohol or drug use before sex (Temple & Choi, 2014).

Nonetheless, the consequences can be serious for those who do engage in sexting. The *Criminal Code of Canada* defines nude photos and videos of persons under 18 as child pornography. In 2001, a ruling by the Supreme Court of Canada established what has been called the intimate photo exception. It ruled that if the photo or video was taken by one of the people involved, was consensual, and is kept private, the image is not child pornography even if the person is under 18. However, if the photo is nonconsensual or was distributed without permission or maliciously, child pornography charges can be laid. In 2014, the federal government passed legislation that makes it illegal to knowingly circulate intimate images of another person of any age who did not give their consent.

A study of youth Internet victimization found that in 2010, 23 percent of adolescents reported unwanted exposure to pornography, and 9 percent of adolescents had received an unwanted sexual solicitation via the Internet (Jones et al., 2012). These rates actually represent a decline from 2000, suggesting that various protective measures for the online environment (for example, Internet education programs, spam filters for e-mail) have been at least partially successful.

Based on concerns about negative consequences for both those who send and those who receive sexual messages or images, a discussion of five things to think about before pressing send was developed by the U.S. National Campaign to Prevent Teen Pregnancy (see Table 10.3).

When stories about incidents of sexting became public, the phenomenon quickly became the subject of a media circus. Most major media outlets publish or broadcast sensationalized stories based on one or two incidents, sometimes citing questionable survey results to enhance the apparent magnitude of the problem (Best & Bogle, 2014). Headlines sometime include red flag terms such as "sex," "child porn," "danger," and "suicide." The result is increasing public concern, leading to school administrators, law enforcement officials, and politicians weighing in on the latest threat to children and youth. The result is a **moral panic**, an extreme social response to the belief that the moral condition of society is deteriorating at a rapid pace (Crossman, 2015). Moral panics lead to all sorts of new regulations and laws, often duplicating or fine-tuning ones that already exist.

> **What should I consider before sexting?**

sexting: Sending sexually charged messages or images by cellphone.
moral panic: An extreme social response to the belief that the moral condition of society is deteriorating at a rapid pace.

Figure 10.10   Sexting: Think carefully about the potential consequences.

© Paul Viant/Photographer's Choice/Getty Images

Table 10.3 Five Things to Think About before Pressing Send

Don't assume anything you send or post is going to remain private.

Your messages and images will get passed around, even if you think they won't: 40 percent of teens and young adults say they have had a sexually suggestive message (originally meant to be private) shown to them and 20 percent say they have shared such a message with someone other than the person for whom it was originally meant.

There is no changing your mind in cyberspace—anything you send or post will never truly go away.

Something that seems fun and flirty and is done on a whim will never really die. Potential employers, college recruiters, teachers, coaches, parents, friends, enemies, strangers, and others may all be able to find your past posts, even after you delete them. And it is nearly impossible to control what other people are posting about you. Think about it: Even if you have second thoughts and delete a racy photo, there is no telling who has already copied that photo and posted it elsewhere.

Don't give in to the pressure to do something that makes you uncomfortable, even in cyberspace.

More than 40 percent of teens and young adults (42 percent total, 47 percent of teens, 38 percent of young adults) say "pressure from guys" is a reason girls and women send and post sexually suggestive messages and images. More than 20 percent of teens and young adults (22 percent total, 24 percent teens, 20 percent young adults) say "pressure from friends" is a reason guys send and post sexually suggestive messages and images.

Consider the recipient's reaction.

Just because a message is meant to be fun doesn't mean the person who gets it will see it that way. Four in ten teen girls who have sent sexually suggestive content did so "as a joke" but many teen boys (29 percent) agree that girls who send such content are "expected to date or hook up in real life." It's easier to be more provocative or outgoing online, but whatever you write, post or send does contribute to the real-life impression you're making.

Nothing is truly anonymous.

Nearly one in five young people who send sexually suggestive messages and images do so to people they only know online (18 percent total, 15 percent teens, 19 percent young adults). It is important to remember that even if someone only knows you by screen name, online profile, phone number, or e-mail address, that they can probably find you if they try hard enough.

The National Campaign to Prevent Teen and Unplanned Pregnancy, 2009. Reprinted with permission.

They may also result in cash-strapped school boards and legislatures authorizing millions of dollars for new and often untested "prevention" programs.

Time for some critical thinking! We have just reviewed the data indicating that few "middle schoolers" or teens sext. Of those who do, only a minority engages in risky sex, and only a handful commit suicide. This is not to suggest that these outcomes are not serious, only that they are very uncommon, much less so than the media hype suggests. Using data to understand the real magnitude of the problem provides a much better basis for developing prevention programs that are likely to work. Moral panics are undesirable because they create unnecessary fears which often lead to attempts to control people's behaviour (reduce their freedom?) and divert attention from more serious social problems.

Contraceptive and Condom Use

Research indicates that adolescents are not consistent in using contraceptives and condoms to prevent pregnancy and STIs. As a consequence about 2.8 percent of all Canadian teenage girls became pregnant in 2010, and adolescents and young adults were disproportionately likely to be diagnosed with an STI. The rates of teen pregnancy and contracting an STI vary considerably across provinces and territories, however (McKay, 2012).

The Canadian Community Health Survey found that 76 percent of 15- to 19-year-olds used a condom the last time they had intercourse. Fewer adolescents use a condom every time they have intercourse (Calzavara et al., 1998; King et al., 1988; Langille et al., 1994). Condoms are used most frequently at the beginning of relationships or in casual encounters, and adolescents in mixed-sex relationships are likely to stop using condoms and switch to the birth control pill as they get to know a partner better (Bolton et al., 2010; Fisher & Boroditsky, 2000; McMahon et al., 2004). One factor that may interfere with condom use is that adolescents feel embarrassed and concerned about being exposed ("Everyone is thinking 'I know what they are doing tonight'") when purchasing condoms (Ronis & LeBouthillier, 2013). This study found that adolescents who were less religious, had more positive attitudes toward birth control, were lower in neuroticism, and had engaged in more extensive discussions of sexuality with their parents were more comfortable purchasing condoms.

Research by Ontario sociologist Eleanor Maticka-Tyndale (1992) identified two beliefs that account for why young people do not perceive themselves to be at risk to contract an STI. First, teenagers minimize the seriousness of contracting an STI, such as HIV, through their beliefs that medical science will find a cure in time should they need one. Second, they believe that by choosing partners who are like themselves and their peers, they can ensure that their partners are not infected. In addition, the sexual script for an affectionate, trusting relationship does not fit with the idea that a partner can be infected and either not know it or not disclose such information, and so it does not include continued condom use (Bolton et al., 2010; Hynie et al., 1998). Teenagers are particularly likely to underestimate their cumulative risk (risk from repeated unprotected sex) of becoming infected with an STI from a partner if they are familiar with them (even if they are a new partner), are committed to them, or find them particularly appealing (Knäuper et al., 2005; Sparling & Cramer, 2015). Finally, teenagers are more likely to use condoms when they have the motivation (e.g., positive attitudes toward condoms and the perception that their peer group supports condom use with romantic partners) and skills (e.g., ideas about how easy or hard it would be to use them, confidence that they can do so, negotiation skills) to do so (Camilleri et al., 2015; Fazekas et al., 2001; Fullerton et al., 2013; Ploem & Byers, 1997; Tremblay & Frignon, 2004). The information–motivation–behavioural skills model described in Chapter 7 (Fisher & Fisher, 1998) provides a framework to design effective interventions to increase condom use among adolescents.

The rate of teenage pregnancy in Canada is less than half that in the United States and United Kingdom but significantly higher than in France, Germany, and some northern European countries (Maticka-Tyndale, 2001; McKay, 2012; Singh & Darroch, 2000). The levels of sexual activity or the ages at which teenagers start engaging in sexual intercourse do not differ across Western countries, so what accounts for the differences in teenage pregnancy rates?

To answer this question, a team of researchers from Sweden, France, Canada, Great Britain, and the United States conducted a large-scale investigation into factors that account for the differences in teenage pregnancy rates in their five countries (Darroch et al., 2001). Of these countries, the lowest rates are in Sweden and France; Canada and Great Britain have intermediate rates; and the United States has the highest rate. The authors concluded that there are five primary factors that contribute to these differences:

1. The rates are higher in countries in which teenagers are less likely to use effective contraception.

2. Teenagers from poor and disadvantaged families are less likely to use contraception.

3. National programs that support the transition to adult economic roles and parenthood provide young people with greater incentives and means to delay child-bearing.

4. Countries with lower rates have greater societal acceptance of sexual activity among young people.

5. Teenagers are more likely to use contraceptives if they know where to obtain information and services; can reach a provider easily; are assured of receiving confidential, nonjudgmental services; and can obtain contraceptive supplies at little or no cost.

Canada's scores on these five factors were mixed— we scored high on some and intermediate on others compared with the other four countries. Within Canada there are differences in adolescent pregnancy rates across provinces, territories, and communities (McKay, 2012; McKay & Barrett, 2010).

The teenage pregnancy rate has dropped substantially in the past ten years, especially among younger teenagers, probably because of teens' increasingly consistent use of contraceptives and teens increasingly choosing to delay sexual activity to later ages (McKay, 2012; McKay & Barrett, 2010). So why is teenage pregnancy considered a major social problem in Canada? The reason is that 45 percent of teenagers who get pregnant give birth to a child, and infants born to teenagers are more likely to have health problems. Most of these births are to single mothers from low-income homes, so having a baby as a teenager may limit the mother's economic and education opportunities (Rotermann, 2007b). However, some ethnocultural communities, including northern Aboriginal and First Nations communities, are accepting of teenage girls having babies (SIECCAN, 2004).

A Nova Scotia study that followed pregnant women for up to ten years after they gave birth gives us important information on the effects of teenage pregnancy on the mother and the child (Bissell, 2000; Nova Scotia Department of Community Services, 1991) This study compared 403 unmarried women with 416 married women, dividing these women into teenage mothers (19 years old or younger) and nonteenage mothers (20 or older). The study also included psychological and educational testing with the children. Unmarried mothers of all ages were most dissatisfied with their educational achievement. Women who were still in school before the pregnancy were most likely to return to school after the birth. Fifty-two percent of the single teenage mothers lived in poverty, but so did 54 percent of the older unmarried women and 29 percent of the teenage married women. The young unmarried mothers made the most economic gains over the ten years, but they never caught up to the older married group. Eighty-seven percent subsequently married. There were few differences in their children's educational achievement. There were also no differences in the ways in which teenage mothers and older mothers dealt with their children's behaviour.

In short, the negative consequences associated with teenage pregnancy are largely a result of the fact that teenage mothers have less education and lower incomes rather than with the age of the mother (Bissell, 2000; Hardwick & Patychuk, 1999; Luong, 2008; Maticka-Tyndale, 2001; Singh et al., 2001). Two critical factors for successful outcomes for adolescent mothers are finishing high school (and preferably going for even more education; Figure 10.11) and postponing other births (Furstenberg, 1987; Luong, 2008). Teenage mothers are more likely to marry in their teens, on average have more children, and have lower incomes than women who were adult mothers (Luong, 2008). Thus, it is important to have social programs to assist adolescent mothers in finishing high school (such as school-based daycare), as well as effective sex education programs and access to contraception. See First Person for a success story: one woman's challenging but empowering experience of being a teen mother.

Late Adolescence (19 to 22 Years)

As noted earlier, adolescence researchers now classify traditional-age university and college students (ages 19 to 22) as late adolescents, although some refer to them as emerging adults. Whatever the terminology, the college or university years are now seen by students as a time for sexual experimenting with little or no responsibility (Bogle, 2008). Adult commitments are seen as being

Figure 10.11 An important factor in life success for a pregnant teenager is the existence of special programs that allow her to complete high school.

© PureStock/Punchstock

a long way away in the future. Almost all the research on the sexual behaviour of people in this age range has been conducted with university students, so we know little about the nonuniversity population.

Masturbation

Typically about 98 percent of the men and 80 percent of the women in our undergraduate human sexuality classes report that they masturbate. These numbers may be a bit higher than one would see in the general university population because students who choose to take a sexuality course tend to be somewhat more sexually liberal than average. Nonetheless, it seems likely that almost all university men and the great majority of university women do masturbate.

Undergraduates report that they have learned that masturbation is somewhat taboo, yet at the same time it is a source of great pleasure (Kaestle & Allen, 2011). Most men resolve this contradiction in favour of pleasure, whereas women are more likely to struggle with the contradiction.

Patterns of Mixed-Sex Behaviour

One study of new students found that by the summer before starting university, 44 percent had already engaged in intercourse (Patrick & Lee, 2010). An additional 11 percent began engaging in intercourse over the next six months, and 48 percent still had not engaged in intercourse six months into their first year. Another study showed that by ages 20 to 24 (a sample a bit older than those in the first study), 85 percent had engaged in sexual intercourse (Chandra et al., 2011). Research in Ontario has shown that most sexual encounters involve oral sex: More than two-thirds of university students report that their last sexual encounter involved giving and/or receiving oral sex (Wood et al., 2016). More men than women reported receiving oral sex, and more women than men reported giving oral sex to their partner. However, the most common pattern was both giving and receiving. Most participants found receiving oral sex to be very pleasurable, but more so with committed than with casual partners. Interestingly, in contrast to many media depictions, researchers in New Brunswick have shown that most oral sex encounters occur within a committed relationship that typically also includes intercourse (Vannier & O'Sullivan, 2012).

Some young adults engage in multi-person sex. A New Brunswick study of mixed-gender threesomes (two men and one woman or two women and one man), showed that 24 percent of the men and 8 percent of the women reported having experienced a mixed-gender threesome. Almost two-thirds (64 percent) reported some interest in doing so, although the level of interest was low and

First Person

Becoming a Teen Mother: An Indigenous Woman's Story

I am a 46-year-old First Nations mother of four sons and one daughter. I also identify as a fourth-generation Indian Residential School (IRS) survivor. My *Kohkum* and *Moosum* attended Marieval (Cowesess, Crooked Lake), Grayson, Saskatchewan IRS and all of their children did as well, including my mother, who attended Lebret IRS (Qu'Appelle, Whitecalf, St. Paul's High School), Lebret, Saskatchewan. This was mandatory for all First Nations families across Canada, so they had no choice about whether their children would go. Thankfully, when I was a child, the *Indian Act* had changed and I was not forced by my parents or the government to attend residential school. However, IRS not only had a direct impact on my parents and grandparents, it also has directly affected my life. I firmly believe the legacy of their experiences attending residential school is one of the reasons why I became a teen mother at the age of 15. IRS took away the way of life which my relatives had for generations, where teachings of becoming a young woman or man were celebrated, not shamed.

I am the youngest of my four sisters and have a younger brother. Growing up, sexuality was not a topic of conversation at any time in my family—it was NEVER discussed. My siblings and I have built life strategies in a hope of stopping the cycle of limited parenting skills and ability to express emotions. These are the results from IRS that directly impacted my family members who attended. This impact continues to affect generation after generation where sexuality was shamed and not encouraged. I am writing this in hopes of sharing my life experiences to break the silence in our First Nation/Indigenous communities about sexual health. I was successful in breaking the silence and have had four children make it into adulthood without becoming a teen parent. I continue to educate my own children and our nieces and nephews about sexual health, and provide them with options for birth control methods and options for practising safe sex. We want to make sure that the next generations can continue to make healthy choices about their sexuality, practise safe sex if they choose to have sex, and plan when they would like to become parents. I am a Kohkum now, and my granddaughters were born to parents who were mature and ready to become parents in their 20s.

My older sisters and I experienced our moon time (menstruation) without the traditional supports and information required when experiencing the gift from the Creator of coming of age and becoming a First Nations woman. Our grandmothers were not there to share the teachings of becoming women, as they were shamed through IRS to not discuss sexuality. They did not have the teachings to share about our moon time and the traditional teachings that were passed on in previous generations when a girl becomes a woman. I was not educated about my moon time, womanhood, or sexuality. Most importantly, I did not know what to do or that when woman experiences her moon time she can conceive a child and can become pregnant if sexually active. IRS prevented many generations of women, like myself and my siblings, from learning about our bodies, sexuality, and our moon time. It is quite disappointing to reflect on this loss of knowledge that was not passed down as it had been historically in our Indigenous communities before contact. This resulted in me not being informed or taught about sexuality, sexual health, or pregnancy at home, at school, or by my peers.

I twice became a teen mother in the mid-1980s, a time when sexuality as a First Nations urban young woman

was influenced by what other people were involved (Thompson & Byers, 2016).

Different students show very different patterns of sexual behaviour. One study aimed at characterizing these different patterns in a sample of 20- to 21-year-olds, 69 percent of whom were attending university and the remainder of whom were not (McGuire & Barber, 2010). At that point, 8 percent were married and an additional 8 percent were engaged or cohabiting; 12 percent had children. Eighty-six percent had engaged in sexual intercourse. Those who were engaging in intercourse fell into several distinct clusters. One group was called Active Unprotected—they had a relatively high frequency of sex and were moderately satisfied with their sex lives, but they did not practise safer sex. The Satisfied group were very satisfied with their sex life while placing low importance on having regular sex; they also scored high in risk reduction, both in terms of using contraceptives and limiting their number of partners. Those in the Inactive group had a low frequency of sex

was a taboo subject. I recall my first pregnancy with my son; I was very ill and nauseous while visiting my boyfriend on the reserve. While he went to town with his mother, I had a discussion with one of his older brothers. I mentioned that I was not feeling well and he grabbed a book called *The Book of Home Remedies*. After consulting this book, he told me that he believed I was pregnant. I was quite confused and honestly did not understand how this happened. I later visited a doctor who confirmed that I was indeed pregnant. That day my life changed forever. From the moment I knew I was carrying a child, I changed the direction of my life. My child is the reason why I am where I am today. I realized that I wanted to live for the future and provide for my child's needs in every way—physically, mentally, emotionally, and spiritually.

At the time I became pregnant, I was attending a high school in a small town. I experienced stigma and discrimination and was shunned by many of the educators at my high school because I was pregnant. To make matters worse, I was not just a teen mom; I was an urban First Nations pregnant teenager. That title alone carried a tremendous amount of stigma. The way I was treated was very stressful for me. I made the choice that it was important for me to continue my education if I was to provide the needs for my unborn child. Therefore, I returned to Regina, where I had grown up, to complete high school. When the high school in Regina learned that I was pregnant, they called a meeting with the principal, the vice principal, and the student support counsellors. They informed me that I would not be able to attend school there any longer and that I would have to transfer to the pregnant mothers' program located in a basement of a school, out of sight and out of mind. When I left the meeting I felt disappointed and disrespected. However, soon my disappointment turned to anger and then to the drive and dedication to not leave that high school. I fought to

remain there. I was informed that being a pregnant teen would affect all adolescents in the school, and this might become "contagious" among my peers. Thankfully, in the end, I won the right to continue to attend this high school. The teen mom program that the school wanted me to attend did not provide the same level of education as I got in the regular high school, and I felt I had a right to choose where I attended school.

Becoming a teen mother was a challenge, yet it was also an empowering experience. I welcomed my son, Raymond, into the world on January 16, 1986. I was in labour for over 36 hours and started to have numerous complications, so Raymond was delivered by Caesarean section. I brought my son home with the passion to provide for his needs the best that I could. Twenty months later, I became a teen mother again. On May 2, 1988, Rowan joined our family, and I was a single teen mom determined to provide for both of my sons as well as to achieve all of my dreams. Having two children assisted me to make the right choices, to complete my high school education, and to work hard to follow my dreams. I successfully completed my PhD in clinical psychology, registered as a psychologist, and have my own private practice. I was a professor at the First Nations University of Canada from 2005 to 2012, when I chose to open my own practice and work within our community as a psychologist. I am living my dreams to the fullest and would not change anything in my life. My journey has been tremendously hard at times, especially as a single teen mom of two young sons, but it has been so worth it!

Kim McKay-McNabb, MA, who is originally from Sakimay First Nation. Her husband Patrick is from George Gordon First Nation.

and gave low ratings to the importance of a sexual relationship, but their satisfaction was also low. The Pressured group reported more frequently being pressured or coerced into sex, and their satisfaction was low. The stories we hear in the mass media tend to characterize all university students as alike in their sex lives—as happy hooker-uppers. Certainly there is a hookup culture at most universities today, but this study shows how very diverse the patterns of sexuality can be for people of this age.

Casual Sex

Young adults have engaged in casual sex for decades. In recent years, many single men and women, particularly on university campuses, have begun to use the term "hooking up" to refer to it, a term rapidly picked up by the mass media (Figure 10.12). **Hooking up** is a generic term referring to a sexual encounter that involves

> **hooking up:** A sexual encounter that involves people who are strangers or brief acquaintances, without an expectation of forming a committed relationship; the behaviour itself may range from making out to oral sex or intercourse

Figure 10.12 Hooking up has become common on post-secondary campuses.

© Jules Frazier/Getty Images

people who are strangers or brief acquaintances, without an expectation of forming a committed relationship. Research asking students what happens when they "hook-up" finds that the behaviour may range from making out to oral sex or intercourse (Bogle, 2008; Heldman & Wade, 2010).

An unfortunate reality is that much hookup sex is bad sex, whether because it is not pleasurable or because it is actually coercive (Heldman & Wade, 2010). In one study of university students, 78 percent of coerced sex occurred while hooking up (Flack et al., 2007). Another factor contributing to the bad sex is that there is an "orgasm gap," with women being much less likely to orgasm in such encounters than men are. Happily, though, women of the same age are much more likely to have orgasms when the sex occurs in the context of a committed relationship (Armstrong et al., 2012). In addition, women often appreciate receiving cunnilingus, but it is not part of the hookup script—although it is part of the script in committed relationships (Backstrom et al., 2012).

Hookups typically occur in the context of parties, whether residence-hall or off-campus (Bersamin et al., 2012). Alcohol use is frequently associated with hooking up. A survey of over 800 university students found that women who were drinking prior to their most recent hookup and who met the partner while drinking were

more likely to be unhappy about the decision to hook up. About 30 percent of the men and women who hooked up while drinking reported they would not have hooked up with the partner had they not been drinking. Finally, a greater number of drinks was associated with engaging in vaginal or anal sex (LaBrie, Hummer, Ghaidarov, et al., 2014).

Some students are enthusiastic about their experiences with hooking up, but others report emotional distress (Heldman & Wade, 2010; Owen & Fincham, 2011b). Often there is a discrepancy between what students want and what they get in such encounters, and the lack of emotional connection can leave some feeling lonely. One study found that hookups that involved oral, vaginal, or anal sex increased psychological distress for female students but not for male students (Fielder & Carey, 2010).

Does a double standard exists in hookup culture? Recent research in Ontario did not find so in explicit attitudes towards men or women engaging in casual sex and/or having many partners (Sakaluk et al., 2014). Similarly, researchers in Nova Scotia asked university students to judge a person (male or female) engaging in recurring sexual activity between friends who are not romantically involved (Weaver et al., 2013). They also did not find evidence of a double standard; that is, the gender of the person in the scenario did not affect how they were judged. However, they did find that participants expected that a woman would be judged more harshly than a man would; that is, they likely perceived that there is a double standard. On the other hand, it may be that people still hold these (implicit) attitudes (for a discussion of implicit attitudes, see Chapter 3), but just do not express them. On the surface, hooking up is equally acceptable for women and men, but in reality, men gain status from having many partners but women can come to be labelled as a slut (Bogle, 2008).

Some researchers have recently recognized that there are specific varieties of casual sex, within the generic category (Rodrigue et al., 2015; Wentland & Reissing, 2011). Researchers in Ontario asked students about the implicit and explicit rules that guide different four types of casual sex relationships; the one-night stand (or hookup), friends with benefits (FWB), fuck buddy, and booty call (Wentland & Reissing, 2011). They found that the four types could be differentiated based on five characteristics: frequency of contact, type of contact, personal disclosure, discussion of the relationship, and friendship. Figure 10.13 describes these four types of casual sexual relationships as well as committed relationships on each of these dimensions. When provided with these definitions, most emerging adults can accurately apply the corresponding label (Wentland & Reissing, 2014).

Friends with benefits (FWB) refers to a situation in which two people who are friends (not romantic partners) occasionally have sex with each other. In one study of university students, 54 percent of the men and 43 percent

Figure 10.13 Four types of casual sexual relationships can be differentiated based on frequency of contact, type of contact, personal disclosure, discussion of the relationship, and friendship.

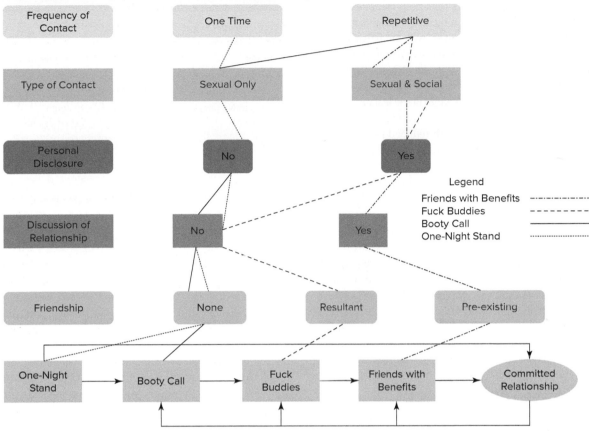

Wentland, J. J., & Reissing, E. D. (2011). "Taking casual sex not too casually: Arriving at consensus definitions for different types of casual sexual relationships." *Canadian Journal of Human Sexuality, 20,* 75–91, 2011. Used with permission.

of the women reported at least one FWB relationship (Owen & Fincham, 2011a). Unlike hookups, FWB relationships involve just that—a relationship, which involves support, companionship, and common activities. Yet the sex occurs without the expectation that the relationship will become romantic. A Nova Scotia study demonstrated that late adolescents who have engaged in FWB relationships agreed on what the unstated rules are about these types of relationships. They also identified some downsides (such as unreciprocated feelings) as well as a range of benefits (Weaver et al., 2011). As one man explained:

> You want to experience sexual things and you'd rather do it with a best friend and have no attachments than figure out later on, like when you're in a relationship and don't want to do things for the first time because it might ruin your relationship . . . we were exploring, I guess. You know, just figuring things out. (Weaver et al., 2011, p. 47)

A **fuck buddy** refers to a partner with whom one regularly engages in sexual activity but not other types of activity and is not a friend. Thus, there is ongoing interaction over time but not the support and companionship associated with a friendship with benefits. Some refer to such a relationship as "just sex." One study found that

men are more likely to use FWB and fuck buddy interchangeably, which may send confusing signals to their female friend and partners (Wentland & Reissling, 2014).

Yet another variation is the **booty call**, which refers to a communication to a person who is not a relationship partner but is an acquaintance, conveying an urgent request for sexual activity, perhaps including intercourse (Jonason et al., 2009; Jonason et al., 2011). Most often the message is delivered by phone (thus booty *call*), but it also may be delivered by texting or online chatting. In contrast to hooking up, the people are not in the same room with each other, at least not initially. Men are more likely to initiate booty calls, and women are more likely to receive them. Reasons for agreeing to the request include the physical attractiveness of the other person and having time for it. Two people can have a booty-call relationship, in which they engage in booty calls repeatedly over time; therefore, this kind of relationship is different from a one-night stand. Behaviours in a booty-call

friends with benefits (FWB): Two people who are friends (not romantic partners) who occasionally have sex with each other.
fuck buddy: A partner with whom one regularly engages in sexual activity but not other types of activity and is not a friend.
booty call: A communication to a person who is not a relationship partner, conveying an urgent request for sexual activity, perhaps including intercourse.

relationship show some signs of intimacy, such as kissing, but they also are characterized by such behaviours as leaving immediately after sex that keep the relationship from evolving into a long-term romantic relationship.

Casual sex can be associated with negative mental health outcomes. Researchers surveyed more than 3900 undergraduates across the U.S. Participants reported whether they had had casual sex (sex with someone they had known for less than seven days) in the last month, and completed several measures of mental health. Engaging in casual sex was associated with reduced psychological well-being and increased psychological distress among both men and women (Bersamin et al., 2014). However, the after-effects of engaging in casual sex may depend on the circumstances in which it occurs. A longitudinal study of 528 undergraduates surveyed them at the beginning and end of the academic year (Vrangalova, 2015). Among students who reported hookups involving genital sex during the year, men and women who reported they engaged in it due to pressure from self or others, alcohol, or unintentionally ("I didn't want to") experienced lower self-esteem, and more depression and anxiety, and more physical symptoms. Men and women who reported autonomous motivations/agency—I wanted to, I believe it is an important experience—did not experience negative outcomes.

Same-Sex Sexual Behaviour

Well-sampled research in the U.S. shows that among 20- to 24-year-olds, 16 percent of women have engaged in same-sex sexual behaviour and 6 percent of men have (Chandra et al., 2011). At these ages, people can show distinct changes in their sexual identity, attractions, and behaviour over time, a point discussed in more detail in Chapter 13.

How Sexuality Aids in Development

Erik Erikson postulated a model of psychosocial development according to which we experience crises at each of eight stages of our lives (Erikson, 1950, 1968). Each crisis may be resolved in one of two directions. Erikson emphasized the idea that social influences are particularly important in determining the outcomes of these crises.

The stages postulated by Erikson are listed in Table 10.4. Notice that the outcomes of several of them may be closely linked to sexuality. For example, in early childhood there is a crisis between autonomy and shame, and later between initiative and guilt. The child who masturbates at age 5 is showing autonomy and initiative. But if the parents react to this activity by severely punishing the child, their actions may produce shame and guilt. Thus they may be encouraging the child to feel ashamed and consequently to suffer a loss of self-esteem.

Table 10.4 Erikson's Stages of Psychosocial Development

Approximate Stage in the Life Cycle	Crisis
Infancy	Basic trust versus mistrust
Ages 1½ to 3 years	Autonomy versus shame and doubt
Ages 3 to 5½ years	Initiative versus guilt
Ages 6 to 12 years	Industry versus inferiority
Adolescence	Identity versus role confusion
Young adulthood	Intimacy versus isolation
Adulthood	Generativity versus stagnation
Maturity	Ego integrity versus despair

In adolescence, the crisis is between identity and role confusion. Gender roles are among the most important; in later adolescence, the person may emerge with a stable, self-confident sense of manhood or womanhood or, alternatively, may feel in conflict about gender roles. A choice of career is important in this developing sense of identity, and gender roles influence career choice. A sexual identity also emerges—for example, heterosexual, gay, lesbian, bisexual, or asexual.

In young adulthood, the crisis is between intimacy and isolation. Sexuality, of course, can function in an important way as people develop their capacity for intimacy. Researchers in Nova Scotia have demonstrated that an individual's sexual behaviour can be understood within an attachment framework (Szielasko et al., 2013).

Furman (2002), a developmental psychologist, proposed that the behavioural sequence from adolescence through emerging adulthood parallels a developmental one. Early relationships reflect simple interest. Subsequent ones fulfill primarily affiliative and sexual needs as young people explore their sexual feelings. As the person moves into late adolescence and early adulthood, longer-term relationships fulfill needs for attachment and mutual caring. One important consequence of this process is the development of a sexual identity with regard to both sexual orientation and the sense of one's own sexual attractiveness. The timing of this process varies from one person to another, one influence being culture with some cultures insisting on more parental control over adolescents. Furman points out that many social and cultural arrangements facilitate the emergence of mixed-sex relationships and at the same time deter same-sex relationships.

Clearly, sexuality is an integral part of adolescent development.

DECISION MAKING AND PROBLEM SOLVING

In making good decisions, it helps to (1) identify your goal(s) in the situation, (2) list at least two possible solutions to the problem, and (3) evaluate the quality of each solution (Does it help you meet your goal? Does it have any negative aspects?) and decide on the best one. Consider the following scenario.

Britney, an undergraduate student, has been seeing Craig for a month. At a party in a campus house, she sees Shelley flirting with Craig and starts to worry that Shelley will steal him from her. Back at her own apartment the next day, she tries to decide what to do to keep Craig. They have not had intercourse yet but have done just about everything else sexually. She thinks maybe the thing to do is sext him a nude picture of herself to get his interest and make herself seem hot to him.

What should Britney do? Apply the techniques listed above to consider what her best decision is. (1) What is her goal? (2) What are at least two possible solutions? (3) Evaluate each solution in terms of whether it helps her meet her goal and whether it has any negative aspects. Do this before you read the next paragraph.

Britney's goal is to keep Craig. One solution is to send him the nude photo. Another is to do nothing. Did you think of a third or fourth solution? A third solution would be to text him a positive, enthusiastic message without a nude photo. A fourth solution would be to make sure that she bumps into him before class that day so that she can be friendly and flirt. If Britney is feeling emotional and desperate, it would be best to take out a piece of paper and write down her goal and the possible solutions.

Here are evaluations of each solution:

1. *Send Craig the nude photo:* If her goal is to keep Craig, it might help her achieve her goal but it might not, for example if the result is that Craig forms a negative impression of her because of the photo (this is an application of the point "consider the recipient's reaction" in Table 10.3). As for negative aspects, as explained in Table 10.3, Britney cannot assume that Craig will keep the photo private. He might decide to send it to everyone in his fraternity, with the result that she is highly embarrassed.

2. *Do nothing:* This strategy does nothing to help Britney achieve her goal of keeping Craig; however, it also carries no risks.

3. and 4. *Send a positive text or be sure to see him in person:* Both of these solutions are similar; they differ only in whether it's electronic contact or in-person contact. Both of them make use of social psychological research findings discussed in Chapter 13, which point to the importance of frequent contact with another person to promote attraction, as well as the importance of positive contact (in contrast to negative contact, such as sending him a nasty message about what a jerk he was to flirt with Shelley). Either one of them could help her achieve the goal. And best of all, neither one of them seems to have a negative aspect.

Overall, then, in making good decisions, it's important to think first! Be clear about the goal (this is sometimes difficult to do). Think of multiple solutions and don't stop with the obvious ones. Then carefully evaluate each possible solution to identify the one that seems likeliest to help you achieve your goal and has few or no negative aspects.

SUMMARY

Data on sexuality in childhood are often based on surveys of adults, asking them to recall their childhood behaviour. In addition, parents are sometimes asked about their children's sexual behaviour. Much more data are available on adolescents' sexual behaviour based on direct information from adolescents.

A capacity for sexual response is present from infancy. Attachment processes are important in infancy and may have an impact on the person's capacity for adult romantic relationships. Parents of 2- to 5-year-olds report that about 17 percent of boys and girls masturbate with their hand. Children also engage in some sex play, with games of doctor. Preschoolers are interested in learning about sexuality, although they often have misunderstandings.

Adrenarche causes increased levels of androgens and occurs around 8 to 10 years of age. More children begin to masturbate in this age range. Children have a gender-segregated social organization, so their sex play tends to occur with same-gender peers. Children also quickly learn heteronormativity. Many experts are concerned about the sexualization of children.

A tension exists between thinking about adolescent sexuality as a normative, growth-promoting part of development and thinking that much adolescent sexuality is risky. According to one theory, the increase in sexual activity in adolescence is influenced by the interaction of biological factors (increasing testosterone levels) and social and psychological factors (for example, sexually permissive attitudes). By age 15, most boys have masturbated, but girls tend to begin masturbating somewhat later than boys and fewer of them do masturbate.

The research evidence indicates that the media have an impact on adolescent sexuality. Some girls and boys engage in same-sex sexual behaviour in adolescence, and about 43 percent of high school students have engaged in penile–vaginal intercourse. Sex that occurs too early (age 15 or before) is more likely to be risky sex and is a cause for concern. Social networking through sites such as Facebook is a popular way for adolescents to communicate. Sexting is not as common as media reports suggest, but it can be serious for those involved.

Patterns of mixed-sex sexual behaviour for university students can be quite varied. Casual sex involving hook-ups, friends with benefits, fuck buddies, and booty calls is one pattern. Other students engage in same-sex sexual behaviour or bisexual behaviour.

Following Erik Erikson's theory, experiences with sexuality can serve important functions in a person's psychological development. They may be important, for example, in the process of developing an identity and in developing a capacity for intimacy.

CHAPTER 11

Sexuality and the Life Cycle: Adulthood

Masaaki Toyoura/The Image Bank/Getty Images

Are **YOU** Curious?

1. Do young single adults go to bars to hook up?
2. Do single people have sex more frequently than married people?
3. What happens to sex in long-term relationships over time?
4. How does sex change for older adults?

Read this chapter to find out.

LEARNING OBJECTIVES

After studying this chapter, you will be able to

LO1 Describe the continuing sexual development that occurs throughout young adulthood.

LO2 Identify the various never-married groups and describe the single lifestyles.

LO3 Describe the rates of and influences on cohabitation, as well as the sexual lives of people who live together.

LO4 Describe sex in marriage.

LO5 Differentiate the qualities seen in happy versus unhappy couples.

LO6 Define the different kinds of extradyadic sex and their prevalence, acceptance, and causes among Canadians.

LO7 Describe the sexual lives of divorced and widowed men and women.

LO8 Describe the physical, psychological, and behavioural effects of aging on sexuality and how these compare with attitudes toward sexuality and aging.

Grow old along with me!
The best is yet to be.*
Life begins at forty.**

---

* Robert Browning. (1864). *Rabbi Ben Ezra.*
** Attributed to Sophie Tucker.

This chapter continues to trace the development of sexuality across the lifespan. We will look at various aspects of sexuality in adulthood: sex and the single person, cohabitation, common-law and marital sexuality, nonmonogamous sexuality, sex in a second long-term relationship, and sex among older adults. Each lifestyle is an option, reflecting the diversity of choices available in Canada today. We have incorporated information about both same-sex and mixed-sex couples into this chapter, although we consider lifestyles specific to same-sex partners in more detail in Chapter 14.

The fact that these lifestyles are options today represents a huge social change from 1960, when three-quarters of all adults were married. In a major report, the Pew Research Center (2010) summarizes this change as "the decline of marriage and the rise of new families." Several new relationship and family forms have emerged, as we will see.

LO1

Sex and the Single Person

Sexual Unfolding Development

The process of sexual development discussed in Chapter 10 continues into adulthood. There remains a need to define one's sexual identity and orientation.

Heterosexuality is the norm in our society, and some people slip into it easily. Others sense that they are different. Some sense that their orientation is gay or lesbian and must struggle with society's **heterosexism** and negative messages about these groups. Others sense that they are attracted to both men and women and may experience sexual fluidity (see Chapter 14). These struggles over sexual orientation seem to be more difficult for men than for women because heterosexuality is such an important cornerstone of the male role in many societies, including ours (see Chapter 13).

Another step toward maturity is identifying our sexual likes and dislikes and how they vary across situations. Learning what they like and dislike may occur naturally as individuals experience various behaviours over time. Alternatively, some people intentionally seek opportunities to engage in novel behaviours or in sexual intimacy with novel partners. Of course, it is not enough to know our likes and dislikes; we must also learn to communicate them to a partner. Learning to communicate with sexual partners is difficult for many persons, perhaps because there are few role models in our society showing us how to engage in direct, honest communication. Effective sexual communication is described in Chapter 12.

Two more issues are important in achieving sexual maturity: becoming responsible about sex, and developing a capacity for intimacy. Taking responsibility includes being careful about contraception and sexually transmitted infections, and being responsible for yourself and for your partner. Intimacy (see Chapter 12) involves a deep emotional sharing between two people that goes beyond casual sex or manipulative sex.

The media influence our ideas of what constitutes mature sexuality. Most television shows promote a rather stereotyped and heterosexist view of sex and the single person. Recently, there has been an increase in the number of television programs that have sexuality as a major focus, and some of them are tackling topics that never used to be discussed on television. For example, in the early 1990s, the main characters in *Seinfeld* had a competition to see who could go the longest without masturbating. In an episode of *Friends*, Rachel and Monica struggle over who gets the last condom and, by implication, which one of them gets to have sex. *Queer as Folk* and *The L Word* introduced gay men and lesbians as central characters. In fact, *Queer as Folk* was one of the first television shows about the lives of gays and lesbians. It also regularly featured scenes of explicit same-sex sexual activity, often emphasizing the use of condoms. More recently *Orange Is the New Black* has a female character who doesn't define her sexual identity. For example, she says, "I like hot girls, I like hot boys, I like hot people." *Sex and the City* introduced single female characters who were not only comfortable with their sexuality but actively pursued sex for pleasure and talked openly about it. Of course, most single television characters still fit societal stereotypes and, even in the more progressive shows, characters tend to fit

heterosexism: The belief that heterosexuality is the only legitimate, acceptable, and healthy way for people to be; homosexuality is denigrated.

the media ideal of young, thin, and attractive. Nonetheless, even though they are isolated examples, these shows expose and challenge the hidden and explicit media messages about sexuality and the single person.

The Never-Married

The term *never married* refers to adults who have never been legally married. This group includes those who intend to marry someday and those who have decided to remain single, perhaps living in a long-term common-law relationship. People are also waiting longer to get married. In the 2016 census, 96 percent of people ages 20 to 24 and 77 percent of those ages 25 to 29 were never married, compared with 56 percent and 21 percent, respectively, in the 1971 census. About 24 percent of these never-married individuals are in a common-law relationship. Most Canadians (91 percent) expect to have children (Stobert & Kemeny, 2003).

Most adults in Canada (up to 95 percent) do marry. The average age of first marriage in 2011 was 28 for women and 31 years for men, so the typical person who marries spends several adult years in the never-married category. Canadians are older at the age of first marriage now than in the past, largely because most live together first and delay getting married. Some of these men and women spend this entire time in one relationship that eventually leads to marriage. According to the National Health and Social Life Survey (NHSLS), among married persons 20 to 29 years old, 46 percent of the men and 65 percent of the women are in this category (Laumann et al., 1994). Other young adults continue the pattern of *serial monogamy*, which (as we saw in Chapter 10) characterizes adolescent intimate relationships; they are involved in two or more sexually intimate relationships before marriage. According to the NHSLS, among married persons 20 to 29, 40 percent of the men and 28 percent of the women had two or more sexual partners before they married.

Many never-married individuals are in a romantic relationship. Some of these individuals are cohabiting. Others choose to live in a different residence than their partner (sometimes called *living apart together* or LAT relationship). This may be because they want to maintain their independence or keep their own residence, or because they are caring for children or aging parents (Levin & Trost, 1999).

Increasing numbers of these relationships are long distance, particularly among young adults (Arnett & Tanner, 2011; Larsen et al., 2006). Geographical separation can be stressful, and some investigators have found that individuals in long-distance relationships (LDRs) report lower relationship quality compared to those in geographically close relationships (Aylor, 2003; Cameron & Ross, 2007; Ficara & Mangeau, 2000). However, despite the difficulties associated with being physically separated, other researchers have found that individuals in LDRs report similar relationship satisfaction and stability, as well as sexual satisfaction, as do individuals in geographically close relationships (Dargie et al., 2015; Kelmer et al., 2013; Roberts & Pistole, 2009; Stafford & Merolla, 2007). What factors predict whether an LDR will survive or end? Research has shown that LDRs are less likely to end if people have more trust and faith in their partner's commitment, expect more support from their partner, are more optimistic about the future of the relationship, and engage in high rates of positive behaviours aimed at maintaining the relationship (Cameron & Ross, 2007; Merolla, 2012; Ogolsky & Bowers, 2012). People in LDRs are also happier and the relationship is more stable when they see their partner in an idealized rather than in a realistic way. People who see each other less frequently are more likely to maintain their idealization notions (Stafford & Merolla, 2007).

The attitudes of singles about their status vary widely. Some young men and women decide to live both single and sexually celibate or **chaste** (abstaining from sexual intercourse). Little research has been done on celibacy, and published studies often do not distinguish voluntary from involuntary celibates. Research using a questionnaire posted on the Internet (Donnelly et al., 2001) identified three types of involuntary celibates. *Virgins* had never had intercourse, had rarely dated, and often had not engaged in any partnered sexual intimacy. Some had not made the developmental transitions discussed earlier; others had chosen not to engage in intercourse before marriage. *Singles* had sexual experience but often reported that it was not satisfying; they were unable to find and maintain long-term relationships. Both their residential and work arrangements made it difficult for persons in either group to meet potential partners. The third type are *partnered* persons in sexless relationships. Typically the relationship had included sex in the past but the frequency gradually declined over time.

Some people plan to remain single but not chaste. They find the single lifestyle exciting and enjoy their freedom. Other men and women are searching for a spouse. According to a recent online survey, about 61 percent of the straight women and 66 percent of the straight men not in a relationship wished they were in one ("Sex Survey," n.d.). The search for a spouse affects some people with increasing desperation as the years go by. According to one researcher, their desperation is fuelled by **singleism**, the stigmatizing and stereotyping of people who are not in a socially recognized couple relationship (DePaulo, 2006). They may adhere to the *committed relationship ideology*, which is the view that individuals with a partner are better than single

> **chaste:** Abstaining from sexual intercourse; sexually celibate.
> **singleism:** The stigmatizing and stereotyping of people who are not in a socially recognized couple relationship.

individuals and that a committed romantic relationship is seen as more important than other relationship types (Day et al., 2011). However, singles can and do live "happily ever after."

How do never-married Canadians over 30 years old who expect to marry differ from those who do not expect to ever marry? The "won't marry" group are more likely to be single parents, have lower incomes, and have less education. They also view love, marriage, and family as less important (Crompton, 2005).

Being Single

The person who passes age 30 without getting married gradually enters a new world in terms of finding ways to meet potential partners. At one extreme, there is the *singles scene*. It is institutionalized in such forms as singles apartment complexes and singles bars. Fitness centres, religious groups, and parties provide opportunities for meeting others (Figure 11.1). A recent innovation, intended for the busy urban professional, is *speed dating*. Singles attend a dating event involving 15 to 25 other singles. They are given a sticker with a number on it and then speak to each of the other attendees for a short and fixed time that often depends on the number of attendees, but typically ranges between four and ten minutes. At the end of the evening, they indicate their interest in seeing each individual again (yes or no) on a form and wait to see whether there is a match. This process is not without its anxieties. Attendees may find it difficult to remember the characteristics and qualities of the many people they meet, worry about finding something interesting to say in the short time allotted, and feel disappointed and despondent if none of the attendees they were interested in indicated reciprocal interest in them.

> **Do young single adults go to bars to hook up?**

Figure 11.1 Fitness clubs are one current alternative to singles bars for some people who are hoping to meet that special someone.

© Bojan Milinkov/Shutterstock

The urban bar provides a visible display of the singles scene (Grazian, 2008). Young men and women, most of them single, engage in *sporting rituals*, game-oriented cultural scripts for nightlife participation. These rituals involve elaborate preparations for all genders: careful attention to grooming, to clothing choice, and to adornment; stiletto heels are required and young women want to be "alluring" and to display (not too much) skin. There is usually drinking in advance at home, both to jump-start the alcohol and to save money. The number and type of companions are also often chosen to reflect the night's purpose; a group of five or six often goes out to have fun, flirt, be seen, dance, and perhaps collect some phone numbers. If the purpose is to find a sexual partner, a pair usually works better. Public behaviour in the bars is intended to display traditional masculinity and femininity. The "pickup" is usually not the purpose according to Grazian; most participants know it is unlikely but when it is the purpose, it has its own elaborate rituals. For example, researchers in Ontario have shown that most women prefer to be approached in a nonsexual manner. Researchers also observed behaviour in dance clubs, pubs, and lounges. They found that use of sexual overt approach behaviours is common in the sexualized atmosphere on the dance floor (Huber & Herold, 2006). The most common overt behaviour was grinding, which was sometimes initiated by men and sometimes initiated by women. For example, the researchers observed the following interaction:

> A female wearing jeans and a white button-down shirt, approached a seemingly unacquainted man to grind from behind. The man smiled and continued dancing with her. A moment later, a second woman, a friend of the first, approached the man to grind pelvis-to-pelvis, forming a "sandwich." After approximately 10 seconds, the group spontaneously dispersed. (Huber & Herold, 2006, p. 139)

Many singles, however, do not go to singles bars. Some are turned off by the idea; some feel that they cannot compete, that they are too old or not attractive enough; and some live in rural areas where they have no access to such places.

Technology has expanded the ways in which singles can meet. *Tinder, Grinder,* and a number of similar apps enable men and women to find potential partners using their cellphone in a process that takes seconds. For many singles in major metropolitan areas like Vancouver, Toronto, and Montreal, these apps have replaced cruising the bars and clubs.

> . . .[this is the] technologized dating scene. Except for ordering their drinks, none of the people I was with that night spoke to any other actual human beings. Their erotic energy was focused on the touchscreens of their smartphones. (Feuer, 2015, MB1)

Of course, there are also hundreds of websites—for example, Zoosk, Match.com, and Lavalife.com—where one can create profiles and search the profiles of thousands of others. Numerous sites specialize in the types of persons profiled: religious singles, Jewish singles, vegetarian singles, pet lovers, and the list goes on. Contacts made online can lead to one-night stands, dates, or continuing relationships. Researchers in Ontario have shown that, compared with Internet users who are not online daters, Internet daters are more likely to be male, single, divorced, employed, and urban, and have higher incomes (Brym & Lenton, 2003). The online daters were not socially isolated, as has sometimes been assumed. They belonged to clubs, socialized with family and friends, and saw themselves as self-confident. Internet dating sites are particularly important in reducing the isolation experienced by some sexual and gender-minority individuals—that is, gay, lesbian, intersex, and transgender individuals.

Some contacts may evolve to include **cybersex**, in which participants engage in sexual talk online for the purpose of sexual pleasure. It may or may not involve masturbation. It may also include real-time videos or webcams (Daneback et al., 2004; Shaughnessy, Byers, & Thornton, 2011).

Cellphones not only play a key role in meeting and screening potential partners, but they are a major means by which relationships are maintained, and terminated (Bergdall et al., 2012). Researchers collected data for five weeks on the sexual and relationship behaviours of a sample of 18- to 25-year-old American men and women. Use of cellphones to maintain relationships included making plans, assessing the partner's interest by frequency and type of contact, discussing difficult topics, and checking the partner's phone and e-mail for evidence of other partners. Participants reported concealing multiple partners by deleting data. They also used their cellphones to terminate relationships, including reducing frequency of contacts, ending the relationship with a call, and restoring data from other/former partners.

The visibility of online dating, singles bars, singles tours, and other activities geared toward single adults suggests a fun-loving lifestyle with frequent sexual activity. Undoubtedly, some single persons live such a life. As Figure 11.2 indicates, among 18- to 24-year-old Americans, 10 percent of the men and 13 percent of the women who completed the National Survey of Sexual Health and Behavior (NSSHB) online survey reported having vaginal intercourse two or more times per week. Among singles ages 30 to 39, 41 percent of the men but only 4 percent of the women reported vaginal intercourse that often. The reality is different for other singles; among 18- to 24-year-olds, 57 percent of the men and 51 percent of the women did not have vaginal intercourse in the preceding year. Among those 30 to 39, single men were much more likely to experience intercourse than their younger counterparts, but three-fourths of the single women had not had intercourse in the past year. Bibby (2006) has shown that 42 percent of single Canadians engage in sexual intercourse on a weekly basis or more often.

Single adults engage in a variety of relationships, including "booty calls," "friends with benefits" (see Chapter 10), and casual dating, or in relationships reflecting serious involvement, "seriously dating," or engaged. Do these vary in their quality and the satisfaction the person experiences? Two Nova Scotia researchers compared sexual satisfaction in five relationship types: friends with benefits, casual dating, exclusive dating, engaged, and married (Birnie-Porter & Hunt, 2015). Engaged individuals reported higher sexual satisfaction than all other relationship types except exclusively dating. There were no differences in the sexual satisfaction of individuals in friends with benefits, casual dating, or marital relationships.

On the border between single and cohabiting is LAT—*living apart together*—intimate relationships involving unmarried persons who live in separate residences but consider themselves a couple (Strohm et al., 2009). In the U.S., about 7 percent of men and women are in this type of relationship; their average age is mid-30s. Some of these couples involve two men or two women. They are less likely than cohabiters to expect to marry the partner. A study in the U.K. found that two-thirds of the LAT couples lived within 10 miles of each other (Duncan et al., 2013). Asked why they were living apart, one third said it was "too early" to live together, one-third preferred to live alone (in some cases to prioritize their children), and the remainder felt constrained by lack (potential loss) of income, or work or living arrangements.

> **Do single people have sex more frequently than married people?**

LO3

Cohabitation

In early adulthood, it is common for couples to experiment with various levels of commitment, such as an exclusive dating relationship or living together. Even when living together, there are different levels of commitment, from "living together apart" to "some days and nights" to "all the time." Living together is an important turning point not only because it represents commitment but also because it is a public declaration of a sexual relationship. It is rare for two people who are going out to live together just because it will save on rent. Cohabiting is an opportunity to explore a more serious commitment, at least to some extent. Forty-two percent of Canadians have lived with a nonmarital partner; this percentage is even higher for people under 40 years old (Bibby, 2006). Most of these individuals indicate that they want to be married at some point in their

cybersex: Online sexually oriented communication, activities, or exchanges with a partner.

Figure 11.2 Frequency of sexual activity is closely related to marital status. Note that there is substantial variability in frequency within each status as well. Frequency also varies by age, within each status.

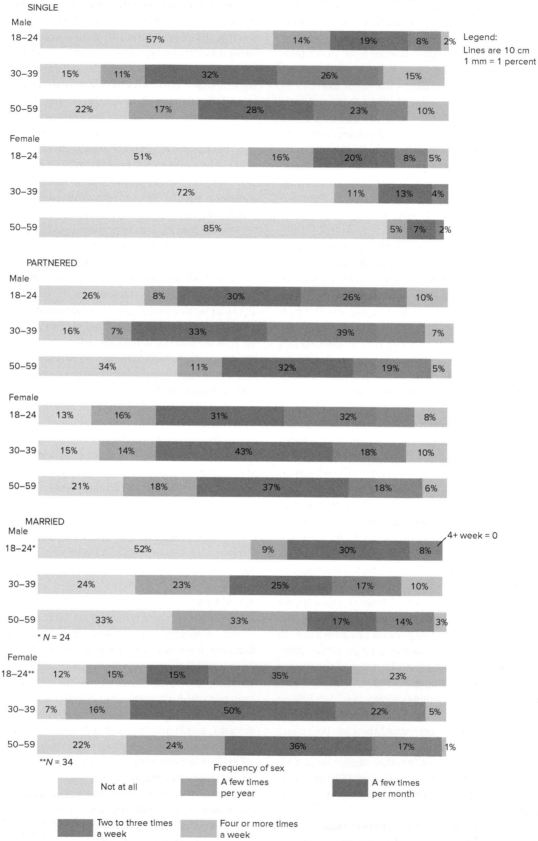

Source: Herbenick et al., 2010; Reece et al., 2010

lives. Increasingly, middle-aged and older individuals are living common law (Statistics Canada, 2007).

Cohabitation has become an increasingly common alternative to marriage, particularly in Quebec (see Chapter 1 for discussion of Quebec as a distinct society sexually), and most Canadians (93 percent) accept people living together without being married (Bibby, 2006; Le Bourdais & Lapierre-Adamcyk, 2004). According to the 2011 Canadian census, the number of common-law couples had grown four times as fast as the number of married couples since 2006. Under federal law, when two people live together as a couple for 12 continuous months but are not legally married to each other, they are in a **common-law relationship**. People in a common-law relationship are entitled to most but not all of the rights of people who are married. According to the 2016 census, 21 percent of Canadians were living in common-law relationships, up from 17 percent in 2011 and 6 percent in 1981. The rate of common-law relationships is higher among same-sex couples—in the 2016 Census 67 percent of same sex couples were living common law. The rate is highest in Quebec and in the Nunavut, where 40 and 50 percent of couples, respectively, are living common law. Common-law relationships are most common among people ages 20 to 24. Interestingly, the rate of cohabitation in Canada considerably higher than in the United States where only 6 percent are in non-marital cohabiting unions.

Slightly more than half of couples living together eventually marry, although this percentage is lower in Quebec. That is, in most of Canada cohabitation is typically seen as a relationship stage preceding marriage (Le Bourdais & Lapierre-Adamcyk, 2004). Two-thirds of cohabiting couples that marry do so within two years of starting to live together. However, common-law relationships break up more often than marriages do. About 60 percent of people who end common-law relationships do so before the age of 30; most of these couples do not have children (Statistics Canada, 2007). Common-law relationships that end do so, on average, after four years, compared with marriages that end, which do so after an average of 14 years. However, in Quebec, cohabitation is more often seen as replacing marriage rather than as a stage preceding marriage and as an appropriate relationship within which to have and raise children (Le Bourdais & Lapierre-Adamcyk, 2004). According to Le Bourdais and Lapierre-Adamcyk (2004), the higher rate of common-law relationships in place of marriage in Quebec has to do with stronger acceptance of egalitarian roles for men and women in Quebec than elsewhere in Canada. It is also in keeping with the more liberal attitudes toward sexuality held by Quebecers (see Chapter 1 for a discussion of other differences between Quebec and the rest of Canada).

Does living together before marriage make it less likely that the marriage will end in divorce? Contrary to what many people think, marriages that are preceded by cohabitation are more (not less) likely to end in separation than marriages that are not preceded by cohabitation (Clark & Crompton, 2006; Le Bourdais & Lapierre-Adamcyk, 2004; Rhoades et al., 2009). Does this mean that cohabiting causes divorce? If so, it might be because some couples who live together get married even though they would not have gotten married had they not lived together, perhaps because of inertia (Stanley et al., 2006). In keeping with this view, a longitudinal study compared couples who cohabited before they were engaged, couples who cohabited after engagement/before marriage, and couples who did not live together until after marriage (Kline et al., 2004). Couples were assessed twice, following engagement and after ten months of marriage. At both times, couples who lived together before engagement had more negative interactions (e.g., criticizing their partner), lower commitment, and lower relationship quality. Thus, the seeds of divorce were sown in the pre-engagement relationship. A related study found that men in pre-engagement cohabiting relationships were less committed to the partner than those who were not cohabiting (Rhoades et al., 2006). However, other researchers have found that cohabitation has little effect on divorce rates after taking personal and cultural characteristics of individuals into account (Woods & Emery, 2002). Taken together, these data suggest that living together does not cause divorce, even though the rate of divorce is higher for couples who have lived together before marriage.

The popular image of cohabitation is that it involves young, never-married couples without children. However, in the 2016 Census, 44 percent of common-law couples had children living in the home. Canadians whose first marriage has dissolved often choose common-law over remarriage. This accounts for more than one-quarter of common-law relationships in Canada and is especially true of people in their 30s and 40s. People living in common-law relationships of some permanence are entitled to most of the same legal rights as married individuals.

With respect to sexual behaviour, Bibby (1995) found that 60 percent of married persons reported having sexual intercourse once a week or more, whereas 71 percent of cohabiting persons had sexual intercourse with that frequency (see Figure 11.2b). Similarly, an analysis of data from a large, representative sample of adults in the United States found that married persons reported having intercourse 8 to 11 times a month, whereas cohabiters reported a frequency of 11 to 13 times per month (Call et al., 1995). The NHHSB found that partnered men reported more frequent sex than did married men (see Figure 11.2). However, notice the wide variation; some

common-law relationship: Two people who have lived together as a couple for 12 continuous months but are not legally married to each other.

partnered men and women report having sex only a few times per year. It is interesting that, on average, cohabiting couples have sex more often than married couples do. Some cohabitors are concerned about the stability of the relationship (Bumpass et al., 1991); they may have sex more frequently in the hope that it will strengthen the relationship (Blumstein & Schwartz, 1983).

Although 25 to 30 percent of gay men and lesbians live with a same-sex partner, there has been little research on sexuality within committed same-sex relationships (Peplau et al., 2004). Among both gay men and lesbians, there is considerable variability in the frequency with which couples have sex. For example, New Brunswick researchers asked women in a same-sex relationship about their frequency of genitally focused and non–genitally focused sexual activity in the previous month (Cohen & Byers, 2014). They found that, on average, these women reported engaging in non-genital sexual activity every day and genital sexual activity between one and three times per week. Generally, the longer couples have been together, the less frequently they have sex. Most individuals in a same-sex relationship report being sexually satisfied. Sexual exclusiveness or monogamy tends to be the norm for lesbians whereas many gay men are in relationships that are, by agreement, sexually open (Peplau et al., 2004).

LO4
Marriage

In 2000 the Supreme Court of Canada ruled that, for the most part, under the equality provision of the *Charter of Rights and Freedoms,* same-sex couples (and heterosexual common-law couples) have the same rights and responsibilities as heterosexual married couples (the situation in Quebec is somewhat different because they operate under civil law not common law). In 2005 the federal government passed legislation that ensured that all Canadians have the right to marry, regardless of whether the person is the same or other sex. According to the 2016 census, there were 14 370 same-sex married couples in Canada (one-third of all same-sex couples); that is more than three times as many same-sex married couples as in 2006 (Statistics Canada, 2016). Female couples (36 percent) are somewhat more likely to be married than are male couples (31 percent). Same-sex weddings in Canada are now sufficiently mainstream that they have even spawned a prime-time reality television show, *My Fabulous Gay Wedding.* However, it will probably be a number of years before we have research on sexuality within same-sex marriages. Therefore, the following sections focus on sex in heterosexual marriages.

Given that common-law couples have many of the same rights and responsibilities as married couples, why do people want to marry? Marriage is a psychological turning point for many people (Figure 11.3). The decision to get married is a real decision these days, in contrast to previous decades when everyone assumed that they would marry and the only question was to whom. Today, most couples have had a full sexual relationship, sometimes for years, before they marry. The three most important reasons Canadians give for getting married are that it signifies their commitment, is consistent with their moral values and beliefs, and reflects their belief that children should have married parents (Bibby, 2006).

Married and engaged lesbian, gay, or bisexual (LGB) individuals also identify demonstrating their commitment as a reason for getting married (Alderson, 2004). Other reasons include the legal protection that marriage provides, the further cementing of the relationship, the political fight for equality and public acknowledgement of same-sex

Figure 11.3 Sexual turning points. *(a)* Marriage and the commitment it represents is a major turning point. *(b)* The birth of a baby is a turning point that can have a negative impact on sexual aspects of the relationship, but couples who are aware of this possibility can work to overcome these problems and keep the romance going.

(a) © Hill Street Studios/Stockbyte/Getty Images   *(b)* © Paul Vozdic/The Image Bank/Getty Images

relationships, and the importance of being able to use the language of marriage (e.g., spouse, wife, husband, daughter-in-law) (Alderson, 2004; MacIntosh et al., 2010).

Some psychological pressures seem to intensify with marriage, and these pressures may result in problems where there were none previously. For many people, marriage is a tangible statement that one has left the family of origin (the family in which you grew up) and shifted to creating one's own family (in which many people become the parents rearing children); for some, this separation from parents is difficult. The pressure for sexual performance may become more intense once people are married, as sexual dissatisfactions that were easy to overlook in the early, rose-coloured-glasses phase of the relationship have more and more impact on each individual's sexual satisfaction. Finally, marriage still carries with it an assumption of a lifelong commitment to fidelity or faithfulness, a promise that is hard for some to keep.

In any long-term relationship, there is a need to work out issues of roles. Who will do what? Some of the decisions are as tame as who cooks supper. However, who initiates sex is far more sensitive, and who has the right to say no to sex is even more so.

This is the era of two-career couples, or at least dual-earner couples. There are issues here of finding time for sex and for just being with each other.

As a relationship progresses, it cannot stay forever as blushingly beautiful as it seemed when it began. The nature of love changes (see Chapter 12), and for some couples there is a gradual disenchantment with sex. Couples need to take steps to avoid boredom in the bedroom. Sexual disorders (see Chapter 18) occur in many long-term relationships, and couples need to find ways to resolve them.

Frequency of Intercourse

According to the 2006 census, 90 percent of Canadians ages 50 to 69 are or have been legally married. However, it is expected that only 73 percent of men and 78 percent of women ages 30 to 39 will marry. About a third of first marriages end in divorce; the rate is somewhat higher for remarriages (Ambert, 2009). Of those who divorce, 70 percent of the men and 58 percent of the women remarry (Ambert, 2009). In our society, marriage is also the context in which sexual expression has the most legitimacy. Therefore, sex in marriage is one of the commonest forms of sexual expression for adults.

Research in the United States shows that the average married heterosexual couple has coitus two to three times per week when they are in their 20s, with the frequency gradually declining as they get older (there is no data on sexual frequency in same-sex marriages). The data on this point from three studies is shown in Table 11.1. Several things can be noted from the table. First, the frequency of marital sex remained about the same from the 1940s to the 2000s. In each survey, people in their 20s reported having intercourse about every three days. Second, the frequency of intercourse declines with age; however, in 2003, among couples in their 50s, the frequency was still once per week. A survey of 19 307 Australians reported similar results (Rissel et al., 2003a, 2003b). Social characteristics such as race, social status, and religion are generally not related to marital sexual frequency (Christopher & Sprecher, 2000).

Two general explanations have been suggested for the age-related decline in frequency: biological aging and habituation to sex with the partner (Call et al., 1995). With regard to aging, physical factors may be associated with age that affect sexual frequency, such as a decrease in vaginal lubrication in women or increased likelihood of poor health. The habituation explanation states that we lose interest in sex as the partner becomes more and more familiar. Recent data indicate a sharp decline in frequency after the first year and a slow, steady decline thereafter. The decline after the first year may reflect habituation (Call et al., 1995). It is often assumed that this decline in frequency reflects a loss of interest in sex,

> **What happens to sex in long-term relationships over time?**

Table 11.1 Marital Coitus: Frequency per Week (Male and Female Estimates Combined), 1938–1949, 1970, and 2003

1938–1949 (Kinsey)		1970 (Westoff)		2003 (Smith)	
Age	**Median Frequency per Week**	**Age**	**Mean Frequency per Week**	**Age**	**Mean Frequency per Week**
16–25	2.45	20–24	2.5	18–29	2.1
26–35	1.95	25–34	2.1	30–39	1.7
36–45	1.40	35–44	1.6	40–49	1.4
46–55	0.85			50–59	1.0
56–60	0.55			60–69	0.6
				70+	0.3

meaning a decline in quality. However, there is an alternative possibility: learning about your partner's sexual desires, preferences, and habits may result in increased marital sexual quality, if not frequency (Liu, 2003). But analysis of the data on satisfaction with the marital sexual relationship from the NHSLS found a significant decline with length of marriage, controlling for age, consistent with the habituation hypothesis. A third factor is the arrival of children, as discussed later.

It is important to note that there is wide variability in these frequencies. For example, 2 percent of couples in their 20s report not engaging in intercourse at all; 6 percent of married couples had not had sex in the 12 months before the interview (Smith, 2003). Research on a sample of 6029 married couples found that sexual inactivity was associated with unhappiness with the marriage, lack of shared activity, the presence of children, increased age, and poor health (Donnelly, 1993). In contrast, a married couple in Seattle have claimed the world record, having had intercourse more than 900 times in 700 days! Data from the NHSLS and Bibby (1995) also confirm this wide variability, as was shown in Figure 11.2.

Sexual Techniques

The NHSLS (Laumann et al., 1994) asked respondents to estimate the duration of their last sexual interaction. Sixteen percent of their married participants reported that sex lasted 15 minutes or less; 9 percent re-ported that it lasted one hour or more. Participants in the *Maclean's/CTV* poll (1994) reported on the average length of their sexual encounters: 12 percent reported that their sexual encounters lasted 15 minutes or less; 25 percent reported that they lasted more than an hour. A New Brunswick study found that, on average, sexual encounters lasted about 20 minutes (Miller & Byers, 2004).

Mouth–genital techniques are very common in long-term relationships. In the NHSLS data, 74 percent of women reported that their partners had stimulated their genitals orally, and 70 percent of them had stimulated their partner orally. Similarly, a Montreal study found that almost 80 percent of married and cohabiting respondents had stimulated their partner's genitals orally and that on average this occurred once a week (Samson et al., 1993). Younger respondents were most likely to include oral sex in their sexual repertoires. For example, 90 percent of people ages 18 to 34 had stimulated their partner orally, compared with only 40 percent of people in the 55 and older age group. People with higher levels of education and incomes were more likely to report engaging in oral sex, showing that there are some social-class differences.

According to the NHSLS data, 27 percent of the married men and 21 percent of the married women reported having engaged in anal intercourse (Laumann et al., 1994).

Negotiating Sex

Before executing any of these techniques, there is typically a "mating dance" between partners. Sexual scripts are played out in established and in new relationships, as in other aspects of sex (Gagnon, 1977, pp. 208–209). How do married people talk about sex? Researchers created a list of 44 diverse words/phrases that refer to various sexual activities, and male and female body parts related to sexual activity. A sample of about 300 married men and women ages 20 to 73 rated how often they used each word/phrase in interactions with their spouse. A cluster analysis assessing which words were likely to be used together identified three different vocabularies: *clinical* (coitus, cunnilingus, fellatio), *erotic* (intercourse, have sex, oral sex), and *slang* (fuck, blow job). Participants were least likely to report using clinical language; both men and women reported more frequent use of words in the other categories. Participants also rated their satisfaction with their sexual communication with their spouse, their relational satisfaction, and their closeness. The more often they reported using sexual language, the greater their satisfaction on both measures and their reported closeness (Hess & Coffelt, 2012).

Some scripts involve direct verbal statements. For other couples, deciding to make love involves preliminary negotiations, which are phrased in indirect or euphemistic language, in part so that the person's feelings can be salvaged if her or his partner is not interested. For example, an individual may say, "I think I'll go take a shower" or "I think I'll go take a nap" (that means, "I want to, do you?"). The partner might respond with, "I think I'll take one too" or "The kids will be home any moment" or "I have a report to finish for tomorrow." Conversely, the individual may kiss his or her partner a bit more passionately than usual after work (that is the offer). The partner may respond with, "I had an exhausting day at work" or "I'll meet you upstairs." Although in these latter examples, the partner never says "yes" or "no," the meaning is clear. To avoid some of the risk of rejection inherent in such negotiations, some couples ritualize sex so they both understand when it will and when it will not occur—Thursday night may be their time or perhaps Sunday afternoon.

Which of these strategies do heterosexual couples use most frequently? A New Brunswick study found that people most frequently use a direct verbal statement to initiate sex (Byers & Heinlein, 1989). The second most frequent strategy is more ambiguous—kissing passionately without saying anything. This study also examined the stereotype that men are more interested in sex than women are. They had people in long-term mixed-sex relationships keep track of sexual initiations by the man and sexual initiations by the woman over a one-week period. On average the men initiated sex almost twice as often as the women did—about twice a week for the men compared with once a week for the women. Interestingly, the men and the women were equally likely to respond positively to the initiation—about three-quarters of the time. Thus, traditional gender roles persist in some areas, with men more often having the initiating role. There was also some evidence of converging gender roles. Women initiated sex regularly (and in some couples were the usual initiator) and usually were interested in engaging in sex when their partner suggested it. Contrary to the male stereotype, the men were not always interested in sex and the men and the women were equally likely to refuse their partner's initiations. There may be differences in how men and women respond when their partner refuses their initiation. According to traditional stereotypes, a woman's refusal can be attributed to her lesser sexual appetite. However, refusals by men go against traditional views of male sexuality. Therefore, a woman may conclude that the man's refusal means that he is not interested in her. Nonetheless, most of the time couples are satisfied with how they resolve disagreements about whether to have sex (Byers & Heinlein, 1989).

Researchers in Ontario have studied characteristics of couples in long-term relationships who remain satisfied despite differences in their levels of sexual desire (Muise & Impett, 2015). They found that a key is how high they are in **sexual communal strength**, or the extent to which they are motivated to meet their partner's sexual needs without expecting direct reciprocity. People high in sexual communal strength tend to engage in sexual activity for positive reasons (called *approach goals*) rather than for negative reasons (called *avoidance goals;* e.g., to avoid guilt or conflict). Engaging in sexual activity for approach goals, in turn, tends to result in higher sexual desire and relationship and sexual satisfaction on their part (Day et al., 2015; Muise et al., 2012, 2016). People also are more satisfied and committed to the relationship when they perceive that their partner is more responsive to their sexual needs (Muise & Impett, 2014). This does not, of course, mean that partners should always meet their partner's sexual needs. Always meeting a partner's needs without concern for one's own needs is associated with negative outcomes such as decreased desire and satisfaction (Impett et al., 2015; Muise et al., 2013). Thus, couples need to find the right balance between being responsive to each other's sexual needs and being assertive about their own needs.

Masturbation

Many adults continue to masturbate even though they are married and have ready access to sexual activity with a partner. For example, the NSSHB found that 41 to 61 percent of married men and 44 to 55 percent of married women ages 18 to 49 reported solo masturbation in the preceding 90 days (Herbenick et al., 2010b; Reece et al., 2010b). This behaviour is perfectly normal, although it sometimes evokes feelings of guilt and may be done secretly. According to the NHSLS, married people were more likely to report that they masturbated than were single people (Michael et al., 1994). Masturbation can serve very legitimate sexual needs in long-term relationships. It feels good whether one is living with a partner or not. It can provide sexual gratification while allowing the partner to remain faithful to a spouse when they are separated or cannot have sex for some reason such as illness.[1] Masturbation can also be a pleasant adjunct to relationship sex. According to a 49-year-old man:

> One of the other things we do a lot is masturbation. We have it developed to a fine art. We rent a porno movie, take a bath, rub each other down with baby oil. My wife and I not only masturbate each other at the same time, but we get pleasure watching each other masturbate individually as well. It's a terrifically exciting thing. (Janus & Janus, 1993, p. 383)

Sexual Satisfaction

Sexual satisfaction is an important aspect of most people's lives (Byers & Rehman, 2013; Rehman et al., 2013). Sexual satisfaction is not just physical pleasure, nor is it simply the absence of dissatisfaction or problems. In fact, couples with sexual difficulties may feel sexually satisfied, and couples with no sexual problems may not feel satisfied at all (MacNeil & Byers, 1997). Rather, sexual satisfaction is the overall feeling we are left with after considering the positive and negative aspects (or sexual rewards and costs) of our sexual relationship. Of course, one person's reward may be another person's cost. For example, having sex every day might be a reward for someone who desires sex frequently. It may be a cost for someone who prefers to have sex less frequently, say twice a week. A New Brunswick study found that for men in long-term relationships, the most frequently identified sexual rewards were feeling comfortable with their partner, feeling good about themselves during and after sex, and having fun during sexual activity. For women the most frequent rewards were being treated well by their partner during sex, feeling comfortable with their partner, and having sex in the context of a long-term relationship (Lawrance & Byers, 1995).

Canadian psychologists Kelli-an Lawrance and Sandra Byers (one of the authors of this textbook) developed the

> **sexual communal strength:** The extent to which people are motivated to meet their partner's sexual needs.

---

[1] As an old navy saying has it, "If your wife can't be at your right hand, let your right hand be your wife." This saying probably should be updated to refer to both men and women.

interpersonal exchange model of sexual satisfaction, which identifies four distinct aspects of relationships that influence sexual satisfaction (Lawrance & Byers, 1995). According to this model, we are more sexually satisfied if (1) we perceive ourselves to be getting many sexual rewards and few sexual costs, (2) we perceive that we are getting more rewards and fewer costs than we expect to get, (3) we perceive our own and our partner's rewards and costs to be relatively equal, and (4) we are happy with the nonsexual aspects of the relationship. A longitudinal study of 244 heterosexual New Brunswick adults living with a partner found that these four components measured at Time 1 predicted sexual satisfaction three months later. Studies involving Canadian dating couples, married individuals living in China and Spain, and individuals with autism spectrum disorder found similar results (Byers et al., 1998a; Byers & Nichols, 2014; Renaud et al., 1997; Sánchez-Fuentes et al., 2015). As you might expect, we are also more sexually satisfied if our partner also experiences high sexual rewards and low sexual costs (Byers & MacNeil, 2006). Clearly, our assessment of the rewards and costs in our intimate relationships are associated with our feelings of sexual satisfaction. One factor that is important in ensuring that couples experience high sexual rewards and low sexual costs is having good sexual communication skills (Byers & Rehman, 2013; Rehman et al., 2013). Sexual communication is discussed in Chapter 12.

How we get along outside the bedroom and how we perceive the overall relationship also affects our sexual satisfaction (Byers & Rehman, 2013; Rehman et al., 2013). For example, married men and women are significantly more satisfied than are cohabiting or single men and women in a continuing relationship (Waite & Joyner, 2000). This suggests that the stronger emotional commitment and sexual exclusivity associated with marriage result in higher sexual satisfaction. Conversely, sexual satisfaction is an important contributor to marital quality and stability (Yeh et al., 2006). Thus, sex and relational education programs that increase sexual satisfaction for both partners have the potential to lower the divorce rate.

In-depth interviews with 52 people (ages 12 to 69; straight, gay, lesbian, and bisexual) identified four factors that differentiate people who are happy with their sex lives (Maurer, 1994). First, there is a sense of calm about, and acceptance of, their sexuality. Second, happy people delight in giving their partners sexual pleasure. Third, these people *listen* to their partners and are aware of the partner's quirks, moods, likes, and dislikes. Fourth, they *talk*, both in and out of bed, even though it is often difficult. These interviews remind us that good communication is essential to a satisfying relationship (see Chapter 12). People who view themselves more positively as a sexual person also tend to report higher sexual satisfaction (Mueller et al., 2016).

Sexual Patterns

The level of sexual desire experienced by each person influences sexual patterns in marriage. A study of 24 married couples obtained daily ratings of relationship affect (positive or negative), relationship status (closeness, equality of power), and lust from each partner (Ridley et al., 2006). Researchers identified four patterns in ratings of desire: (1) stable and low, (2) slight fluctuations (1 point on a 1-to-5 scale) and low, (3) moderate fluctuations, and (4) highly fluctuating. On days when positive affect toward the spouse was high, lust was high; when negative affect was high, lust was low. Interestingly, on days when people reported high closeness to their spouse, the link between positive (negative) affect and lust was stronger. Finally, there was a significant positive association between own lust and partner's lust each day.

Sexual patterns can change during the course of a marriage. After ten years of marriage they may be quite different from what they were during the first year. One stereotype is that sex becomes duller as time goes on, and certainly that happens in some marriages. In a survey of adults in the United States, 23 percent of the sexually active men and women reported that their sexual relationship was often or always "routine"; 38 percent said it was never or hardly ever routine (Kaiser Family Foundation, 1998). A boring sexual relationship can be spiced up by telling each other what you really want to do and then doing it, by consulting a how-to manual or watching videos about improving your sex life, or by acting out fantasies (see Table 11.2). There are also relationships in which the sex remains very exciting. A 36-year-old engineer said:

> [Though my wife's career] is tremendously important to her, she manages to look attractive, and to dress chicly, and though she is not what many would call a beautiful woman, she is, to me, a handsome woman. In bed, she is the hottest, most exciting woman I have ever known. We have been married seven years. . . . When we get to bed, and she lets herself go, we get wild together. (Janus & Janus, 1993, p. 191)

Having a baby—what researchers call the transition to parenthood—has an impact on the sexual relationship of the couple. According to one 44-year-old mother of three children, "There's the passionate period when you can't get enough of each other, and after a few years it wanes, and after kids it really wanes" (Maurer, 1994, p. 403). Trying to get pregnant and the threat of infertility, which are so much publicized, can be potent forces on people's identity as sexual beings (Daniluk, 2001a). Pregnancy itself can influence a couple's sexual interactions, particularly in the last few months (see Chapter 6). For the first few weeks after the baby is born, intercourse is typically uncomfortable for the woman. While

Table 11.2 Frequency of Activities to Enhance Sexual Interactions Reported by Adults[*]

	Very Often	Often	Sometimes	Hardly Ever	Never	Don't Know
Do romantic things like eat by candlelight	8%	18%	35%	30%	6%	3%
Act out fantasies together	4	10	28	39	12	7
Wear sexy lingerie (women[**])	9	10	28	35	12	6
Try different sexual positions	11	19	35	23	4	8
Read books or watch videos about improving your sex life	2	3	14	52	26	3
Go out on special evenings or dates or go away on weekends alone	11	22	37	22	5	3

[*] Number of respondents = 1109

[**] Number of female respondents = 564

Source: Kaiser Family Foundation (1998).

estrogen levels are low—which lasts longer when breast-feeding—the vagina does not lubricate well. Then, too, the parents (including nonbiological parents) feel exhausted with 2 a.m. feedings. The first few months after a baby is born are usually not the peak times in a sexual relationship, and so that, too, must be negotiated between partners. A follow-up study of parents six months and four years after the birth of their first child found that sexual frequency did not change significantly, but it remained low (Ahlborg et al., 2008).

Of course, not all couples have children. Data from the 2001 General Social Survey (GSS) indicate that 26 percent of Canadian women ages 30 to 34 do not have children (Stobert & Kemeny, 2003). Some of these women were delaying child-bearing while they completed their education and established their careers; 20 percent of women in the 30-to-34 age group do not have children but intend to have a child. There is a tendency for women to delay having their first child. For example, in 2012, 29 percent of first births were to women aged 30 to 34, and 13 percent were to women aged 35 to 49. This compares to 19 percent and 6 percent, respectively, in 1992 (Statistics Canada, 2017). There is some risk in this strategy; fertility declines with age, so some of these women may be unable to have a child if they want to. Other women have made a decision to remain childfree. According to the GSS, 5 percent of women do not expect to have children. A third group of women are those who choose to adopt; adopting an infant probably has effects on relationships and sexual activities similar to those of having a baby.

Some people will experience fundamental changes in their sexual experience at least once over the course of the marriage. The change may result from developing a capacity to give as well as receive sexual pleasure and to expand our sexual scripts beyond traditional expectations for men and women. A man may outgrow

performance anxiety and enlarge his focus to include his partner. A woman may learn that she can take care of her own sexual needs as well as her partner's. Aging may produce change in sexual experience, a topic we consider later in this chapter. There are changes caused by illness, which can lead to sexual disaster or triumph depending on how the couple copes with it.

Sex and the Two-Career Family

In our busy, achievement-oriented society, do work commitments interfere with a couple's sex life? One couple, both of whom are professionals, commented to us that they actually have to make an appointment with each other to make love.

Research with married couples shows that there is little cause for concern (Figure 11.4). A longitudinal study followed 570 women and 550 of their husbands for one year following the birth of a baby (Hyde et al., 1998). The women were categorized according to the number of hours worked per week: homemakers, employed part time (6 to 31 hours/week), employed full-time (32 to 44 hours), and employed high full-time (45 or more hours). There were no significant differences among the four groups in frequency of sexual intercourse, sexual satisfaction, or sexual desire. It was not the number of hours of work outside the home, but rather the quality of work that was associated with sexual outcomes. Women and men who had satisfying jobs reported that sex was better compared with people who expressed dissatisfaction with their jobs. For women, fatigue was associated with decreased sexual satisfaction, but that was true for both homemakers and employed women; homemakers reported the same level of fatigue as employed women.

Research using data from the National Survey of Families and Households analyzed the relationship between hour per week spent in housework, hours

Figure 11.4   Sex and the two-career family. *(a)* Research indicates that sexual relationships do not suffer if the woman works outside the home. *(b)* However, for those working 60 or more hours per week, some experts are concerned because these workaholics literally take their work to bed with them.

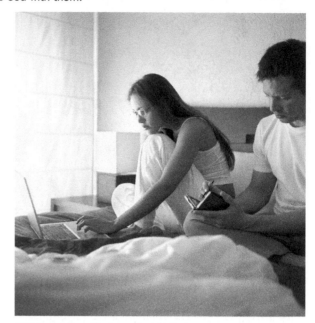

(a) Ariel Skelley/Blend Images/Getty Images

(b) © Jerome Tisne/The Image Bank/Getty Images

per week spent in paid work, and frequency of sexual intercourse (Gager & Yabiku, 2010). Results from 6877 married men and women indicate that the more hours of housework and paid work per week, the more frequently the person reported sexual activity. Clearly, there is not a trade-off between work/career and sexual frequency. Further, the presence of young children did not change the relationship between work and sex.

Keeping Your Mate

Most couples who establish a long-term relationship intend to stay together. However, we all know that not all couples succeed in this. What makes men and women susceptible to infidelity? A study of 107 couples married less than one year asked each partner how likely he or she was to be unfaithful in the next year (Buss & Shackelford, 1997b). Each was asked the likelihood that she or he would flirt, kiss passionately, and have a romantic date, a one-night stand, a brief affair, or a serious affair with someone of the other sex. Thirty-seven percent of the men and 38 percent of the women predicted they would flirt, while 5 percent of the men and 7 percent of the women said they would kiss. Two percent (of men and of women) predicted a one-night stand, and less than 1 percent (of men and women) thought they would have a serious affair. In addition, researchers measured a variety of personality, mate value, and relationship characteristics. Among the personality variables, high scorers on narcissism and impulsiveness gave a higher

probability of infidelity. Characteristics of the relationship associated with greater likelihood of infidelity included reports of conflict, especially that the partner sexualized others, engaged in sexual withholding, and abused alcohol. Finally, among both men and women, dissatisfaction with the marriage and with marital sex was associated with susceptibility to infidelity.

Our awareness of the possibility of infidelity sometimes leads us to engage in behaviours designed to preserve the relationship, or *mate retention tactics* (Buss & Shackelford, 1997a). Such tactics may be elicited by our own fear that the partner is losing interest or is dissatisfied, or because we observe some cues to infidelity.

In a study, 355 Canadians in same-sex and mixed-sex relationships were asked about their use of 19 different mate retention tactics (VanderLaan & Vasey, 2008). There were marked gender differences in the reported actions. Men in mixed-sex relationships reported greater use of resources display (e.g., giving her money). Women in mixed-sex relationships reported more frequent use of monopolizing their partner's time, punishing threats of infidelity, saying derogatory things about competitors, providing sexual inducements, and enhancing their appearance or attractiveness. The tactics used by men in same-sex relationships were similar to those used by men in mixed-sex relationships, with the exception that gay men tended to use resource display more frequently. In contrast, women in a same-sex relationship tended to use tactics that were more similar to those of men than to those of women in a mixed-sex relationship. Thus, the most frequent mate retention strategies of men and women in mixed-sex relationships, but not women in same-sex relationships, tend to fall along traditional gender lines. Unfortunately, these strategies do not address the problems typical of distressed couples just listed so they are unlikely to affect relationship satisfaction.

LO5 Maintaining a Long-Term Relationship

Most couples who establish a long-term relationship intend to stay together. However, we know that not all couples succeed. In Canada, about 40 percent of marriages end in divorce; this rate is considerably lower than in the United States (Roterman, 2007a). The rate of breakup is even higher for common-law relationships. Further, the end of a relationship is often associated with depression and other psychological distress (Goldfarb et al., 2007; Roterman, 2007a). What differences have researchers found between nondistressed (happy) couples and distressed (unhappy) couples?

1. Nondistressed couples have good listening and communication skills. Suggestions for enhancing communication skills are outlined in Chapter 12.

2. Nondistressed couples have effective problem-solving skills. In contrast, distressed couples may discuss problems, but they rarely resolve them. As a result, the same problems tend to come up repeatedly.

3. Nondistressed couples have many positive interactions and few negative interactions. For example, they have many enjoyable shared leisure-time activities, are affectionate with each other, and feel good about their communication. In fact, Gottman (1994) found that nondistressed couples have five times as much positive interaction as negative interaction.

4. Nondistressed couples tend to have realistic expectations about what relationships should be like. In contrast, distressed couples may believe that disagreements are destructive, that one must be a perfect sexual partner at all times, or that people who are in love feel intensively passionate about their partner at all times. None of these expectations is realistic.

5. Nondistressed couples tend to interpret their partner's behaviour and the causes of that behaviour positively. For example, if the woman is late for dinner, her partner is likely to assume that it was due to something beyond her control, such as heavy traffic. A distressed partner is more likely to see this as an example of her being thoughtless.

6. Nondistressed couples are more likely to share a common view of roles and responsibilities within the relationship. Unhappy couples may disagree on how the relationship should work; for example, they may have different ideas about financial decision-making or how involved each should be with taking care of the children.

These research findings have implications for maintaining a satisfying long-term relationship. That is, couples with good communication and problem-solving skills, many positive and few negative interactions, and realistic expectations about their relationship; who do not engage in blaming; and who share a common view of relationships are likely to have happy and stable relationships. Of course, feelings of love and intimacy are also important to maintaining a long-term relationship (see Chapter 12 for a discussion of love in long-term relationships). These feelings often are what motivate couples to work through the problems that inevitably come up. Feelings of equity in the relationship (discussed later in this chapter) are also important.

Relationship satisfaction is one of the key elements contributing to sexual satisfaction, so many of these factors also contribute to sexual satisfaction and optimal sexual experiences (Kleinplatz et al., 2013; Lawrance & Byers, 1995). Further, dissatisfaction with the relationship and conflict between spouses are associated with susceptibility to extradyadic sexual activity, which is discussed next (Buss & Shackelford, 1997b). For example, one woman used her dissatisfaction with her relationship to explain her serious affair: "I'm definitely not looking for more sex. The affair I'm having is for emotional reasons. Freddie [her husband] is very self-centered. He's not an emotional support. He's distant, and we have nothing in common" (Maurer, 1994, p. 391).

LO6

Nonmonogamous Relationships

People in Canada who marry usually make a public vow to be (sexually) faithful to the partner, to be monogamous. In the past, those who found it impossible to keep the vow engaged in *adultery*, sex with someone other than the spouse, and usually tried to hide the activity, sometimes going to great lengths to do so. Similarly, most people entering into cohabiting, or even committed ("exclusively dating"), relationships expected themselves and the partners to be sexually faithful. But there has been a decline in marriage and the rise of alternative relationship forms in the recent past. Accompanying this change has been a decline in fidelity, with as many as one-third of people dating, cohabiting, and in marriages reporting one or more instances of having sex with someone other than the partner while in the relationship.

Within committed or marital relationships, several new relationship forms have developed. One is Internet infidelity, which, like adultery, is often kept secret. Two others, swinging and polyamory, however, are done with the knowledge and often participation of the long-term partner. These are quite different, reflecting a process of negotiation involving not only the partners but others as well. We need a new term to incorporate all of these, and *nonmonogamous relationships* seems appropriate. Following the lead of researchers (Frank & DeLamater, 2010), we will distinguish between secret nonmonogamy, sexual activity involving a person in a committed relationship with a third person without the knowledge of the partner, and open nonmonogamy, sexual activity involving a person in a committed relationship with a third (or multiple) person(s) with the consent of the partner.

Most of the research in this area has focused on extra-marital sex, and has assumed that it is kept secret from the partner, so adultery and Internet infidelity will be treated as secret. Negotiated nonmonogamy (e.g., every other Friday from 7 p.m. to midnight), swinging, and polyamory will be discussed as open nonmonogamy.

Extra-Relationship Sex

Extra-relationship sex refers to sexual activity involving a person in a long-term committed relationship (exclusive dating, LAT, cohabiting, common-law, or married) and someone other than the person's long-term partner. When a person who is married engages in extra-relationship sex, we call it **extramarital sex**. Many people refer to extra-relationship sex, married or not, as cheating.

How Many People Engage in Extra-Relationship Sex?

A survey of 783 adults ages 18 to 59 asked them whether they had concurrent sexual partners (two or more partners simultaneously) during their current/most recent relationship (Paik, 2010). Half reported on a marital relationship, 15 percent on a cohabiting relationship, and the rest on a non-residential partnership. Seventeen percent of the men and 5 percent of the women reported a concurrent sexual partner.

Extra-marital sexual activity is not as common as many people believe. According to the National Survey of Family Growth (NSFG), 7.6 percent of married men and 5.8 percent of married women ages 15 to 44 reported more than one sexual partner in the preceding 12 months (Mosher et al, 2005). The comparable percentages were 4.9 and 2.9 in an Australian survey (Rissel et al., 2003c).

The Kinsey Institute posted an online survey that included questions about infidelity in couples, and 918 respondents said they were heterosexual and in a committed relationship. Among

extra-relationship sex: Sexual activity between a person in a long-term committed relationship and someone other than that person's partner; adultery, cheating.
extramarital sex: Sexual activity between a married person and someone other than that person's spouse.

married respondents, 26 percent of men and 23 percent of women reported "engaging in sexual interactions with someone other than the primary partner" that could harm the relationship. Among the not-married (single and cohabiting), the results were 19 percent of men and 16 percent of women. The questionnaire included the sexual inhibition scale (SIS) and sexual excitation scale (SES; see Chapter 9). Men and women who reported cheating had higher scores on sexual excitation, and lower scores on sexual inhibition; the women also reported lower happiness in their relationships (Mark et al., 2011).

The incidence of extradyadic sex varies from one group to another and one region to another. As noted in Chapter 1, the rate of extradyadic sexual activity is highest in Quebec.

There is no indication that extramarital sex is casual or frequent. In one Canadian survey, of the respondents who had had extramarital sex, 40 percent had done so with only one partner (Gallup, 1988).

Influences on Extra-Relationship Sex

Why do people in committed relationships cheat? Research on a sample of unmarried men and women ages 18 to 35 in opposite-sex relationships collected data from 933 participants; the survey included demographic questions about the participant and the partner, and questions about the relationship, communication patterns, and substance use (Shaw et al., 2013). Twenty months later, participants completed a second survey that included questions about extra-relationship sexual involvement. The results indicated that relationship dissatisfaction at Time 1, negative communication patterns (e.g., agreeing that "little arguments escalate"), and lower commitment to the relationship predicted involvement in extra-relationship sex between the first and second survey.

Dutch researchers invited readers of a magazine targeting professionals to complete an online survey (Lammers et al., 2011). Of the 1561 respondents, 1275 (46 percent women, average age 39) were in a current relationship. The survey assessed the respondent's power by asking him/her to indicate on a vertical line his/her power in their organization. They also measured extra-relationship sex by asking how often the person had secretly had sex with another person. Twenty-six percent reported having done so at least once. As predicted, power was strongly correlated with extra-relationship sex; power was positively associated with the person's confidence that s/he could seduce someone. The results were the same for men and for women. The authors explicitly link their research to cases of high-profile American politicians and CEOs who have cheated on their wives.

A longitudinal study followed 1270 married respondents over a 20-year period (DeMaris, 2009). At the initial survey, none had been involved in extra-marital sex. By the end of the follow-up period, 99 men and women

(8 percent) reported problems in the marriage due to a sexual relationship with a third person. The strength of the relationship bond was the principal predictor; respondents who had experienced a trial separation, reported violence in the relationship, and spent less time in activities with the spouse were more likely to report problems due to extra-relationship sex.

Most people in Canada disapprove of extra-relationship sex. According to a series of well-sampled surveys conducted by Bibby and his associates (1995), in 1975, 50 percent of Canadian adults felt that it is always wrong to have sex with someone other than the spouse. In 1995, this figure had risen to 60 percent. A 2005 COMPAS poll found that most Canadians feel that extra-relationship sexual activity by their partner would probably (27 percent) or definitely (41 percent) mean the end of a relationship.

Attitudes toward extra-relationship sex are not very good predictors of extra-relationship sexual behaviour. That is, the person who disapproves of extra-relationship sex is no less likely to engage in extra-relationship sex than the person who does not disapprove of it. Several other factors are related to attitudes toward sex outside the primary relationship, including gender, education, and social class—men, people with more education, and people who are upper-middle-class are more tolerant of it (Willetts et al., 2004).

Because our society condemns extra-relationship sex, the individual who engages in it typically has confused, ambivalent feelings. A young married woman describes her feelings:

> I don't like the illicit part of the affair. Mostly, it's a nuisance, because it's very difficult to find time, and I don't like lying to Freddie and sneaking around. If he wouldn't mind, I'd tell him. I don't think he would go for that. He'd show up with a gun. (Maurer, 1994, p. 393)

Internet Infidelity

The proliferation of websites designed to connect people looking for romantic or sexual partners, along with chat rooms and other forms of digital communication, has created new opportunities for people in committed relationships to engage in sexual activity with people other than their partner (see Milestones in Sex Research). A **cyberaffair** is a romantic or sexual relationship initiated by online contact and maintained primarily via online communication (Young et al., 2000). A new twist on cyberaffairs occurs when two people's avatars engage in sexual activity in virtual reality worlds, such as Second Life. After establishing a relationship online, contacts can turn into mutual erotic dialogue, which may be accompanied by masturbation. In some cases, the participants arrange to meet face to face and may then engage in sexual intimacy. Most people think that people

are unfaithful if they engage in cybersex with someone other than their partner, even if the two individuals never physically meet (Randall & Byers, 2003).

An online survey collected data about the seeking of online sex from 15 246 men and women with an average age of 38 years who varied in their marital status and sexual identity. The results provide a statistical snapshot of the phenomenon (Albright, 2008). However, given that participants were recruited online for a "Cybersex Survey," the percentages are likely higher than would be found in the general population. As shown in Table 11.3, there were no differences in the percentage of men and women who had accessed a personals site. However, more LGB individuals than straight individuals had done so. Divorced individuals were more likely to go on personal sites than were never-married or married individuals. Of those who had accessed an online site, most in all groups went on to post a profile; straight individuals and married individuals were least likely to have posted a profile. What about the married individuals—that is, the ones who were engaging in cyberaffairs? Of the married individuals who had accessed a site, 36 percent had sent one e-mail and 27 percent had sent two or more e-mails; similar percentages had met one or more contacts in person. Married individuals were five times as likely to be seeking a serious relationship than were singles and were also more likely than singles to go on a date as a result of being on a sex-related site. Albright uses equity theory (next section) to suggest that married people who go online seeking sex may be dissatisfied with their relationship—that is, perceive their marriages

> **cyberaffair:** A romantic or sexual relationship initiated by online contact and maintained primarily via online communication.

Table 11.3 Accessing Personal Sites Online

	Accessed Online Personal Ads	Created a Profile (of those who had accessed a site)
Gender		
Men	58%	75%
Women	55	72
Sexual identity		
Straight	54%	71%
Bisexual	78	82
Gay	87	87
Marital status		
Never married	69%	80%
Married	42	61
Divorced	81	83

Based on data from Albright, J. M. (2008). Sex in America online: An exploration of sex, marital status, and sexual identity in Internet sex-seeking and its impacts. *Journal of Sex Research, 45*(2), 175–186.

Milestones in Sex Research

Sex on the Internet

When people think about sex, they generally think about two people engaging in face-to-face bodily contact. The Internet introduces all kinds of other possibilities when it comes to sexual expression. Online sexual activities (OSA) range from using the Internet for sexual information to finding and connecting with prospective dating or sex partners to accessing or producing sexually explicit materials. These activities are often referred to as solitary-arousal OSA because they do not involve a partner. Most people would not see any of these activities as "having sex" (Randall & Byers, 2003).

People also engage in interactive, interpersonal sexual experiences—that is, activities that involve another person—online through text, words, or images. For example, people describe in detail sexual activities or a sexual scene back and forth with another person as if it were happening, create a story based on sexual fantasies where each person adds to the story as it goes, or behave (or watch someone behave) sexually for another person to watch. All these are examples of interpersonal sexual activity online. These interactions can and do occur through a variety of forums and formats including e-mails, instant messaging, social networking sites, and video chat. These activities are referred to as *partnered-arousal OSA* because they require that at least two people be involved and are generally geared around sexual arousal. Pop culture has also provided us with terms that capture these kinds of sexual interactions, such as *cybering* or *cybersex*. However, people do not agree on exactly which activities constitute cybersex (Shaughnessy, Byers, & Thornton, 2011). The term *sexting* is generally used to refer to sexual

interaction that occurs through text messaging or picture messaging on cellphones or smartphones.

Another venue for cybersex is in virtual worlds. In virtual worlds, people can visually re-create sex by having their avatars engage in sexual activities with other avatars. Second Life is a free 3D virtual world designed for online social interaction, connection, and creation. It essentially focuses on re-creating the "real world" in a virtual forum. In Second Life, online sexual interaction can occur in all the contexts that it occurs in the real world—with virtual romantic partners, virtual friends, virtual hookups, virtual sex work, and so on. However, Second Life is not specifically designed for sexual purposes. Some virtual worlds, such as Red Light Center, are for adults only and are designed specifically for avatars to engage in sexual activities. As technologies continue to advance, the possibilities of sexual interaction increase. Recently, for example, developers in Japan have been working on a device that would simulate kissing across Internet connections.

Given the range of interpersonal sexual behaviours that can occur online and the fact that new possibilities emerge with each advance in technology, it is important to have a definition of what constitutes cybersex. According to Shaughnessy, Byers, and Thornton (2011), cybersex is

> a real-time communication with another person that occurs through a device connected with the Internet (e.g., computer, cellphone, smart phone) in which one or both of you describe or share in other ways sexual activities, sexual behaviours, sexual fantasies, or sexual desires that may lead to feelings of sexual pleasure or physical intimacy. You and/or your partner

as inequitable; the Internet provides literally tens of thousands of potential alternative partners.

There has been little empirical study of cyberaffairs. Professionals engaged in relationship and sexual counselling report working with couples whose problems include loss of trust by one person over another's online relationships. Some partners define such a relationship as infidelity even if it did not involve sexual conversation or activity.

Note that these can be mixed-sex or same-sex couples who are married, cohabiting, or committed to each other.

Equity and Extra-Relationship Sex

Social exchange theories are a type of social-psychological theory that have been used to explain sexuality in close relationships. Unlike most theories that focus on the individual, the social exchange perspective

may or may not be stimulating yourself/himself/herself sexually during this conversation.

How common is cybersex? At the turn of the twenty-first century, between 8 and 13 percent of undergraduate men and women reported having had an online sex partner, visiting and participating in a sexual chat room, or having cybersex with an online partner (Boies, 2002; Goodson, McCormick, & Evans, 2001). Shaughnessy, Byers, and Walsh (2011) found that 23 percent of their student sample reported engaging in cybersex. More recently, Shaughnessy and Byers (2013) found that 75 percent of students and 53 percent of an online community sample reported participating in at least one of these specific cybersex activities. These recent figures suggest that cybersex, or at least some specific types of cybersex, are becoming more common.

Is there something wrong with engaging in cybersex? Media discussions of cybersex usually focus on problematic activities online highlighting stories of cybersex addicts, cybersex infidelity, and illegal forms of cybersex. This suggests that people who engage in cybersex have a problem. Similarly, most early research on cybersex focused on cybersex addiction. However, researchers have consistently found that less than 10 percent of survey respondents report levels of cybersex and OSA experience that can be considered compulsive or addictive (Cooper et al., 2004; Daneback, Cooper, & Månsson, 2005). This means that many more people participate in recreational cybersex. People who engage in recreational cybersex spend only a few hours online per week or less participating in cybersex, and report few, if any negative outcomes. They also report few positive outcomes of cybersex, suggesting that the effects of recreational cybersex are fairly neutral (Shaughnessy & Byers, 2013).

Why do people participate in cybersex? Just like with offline sex, people who participate in cybersex do so for a variety of reasons and with partners, acquaintances, or strangers. Having cybersex can be a source of sexual/physical excitement, arousal, pleasure, or release. It can be a way to relieve stress or anxiety, or a distraction from offline life—such as a break from work, housework, or boredom. Some people use cybersex (whether with their offline partner or someone else) as a way to avoid problems in their offline life or relationship. For example, some people engage in cybersex because they do not want the complexities of having an offline relationship, or to avoid the risks associated with offline sex, such as STIs and pregnancy. Others use cybersex to help address problems in their sexual relationship with their partner, for example, by alleviating anxiety or creating a space to communicate about unexpressed sexual desires. Some people use cybersex to feel a sense of emotional connection or intimacy with another person. For partners who are geographically separated for a period, cybersex can be an important part of maintaining sexual intimacy while apart. Finally, for some people the Internet provides a safe space to explore or express aspects of their sexual selves that they are not comfortable exploring or expressing offline. This can be especially important to people who are members of sexual minorities.

The commonality and impact of cybersex has evolved along with technological developments and the increased pervasiveness of the Internet. Just as online social connections have become part of regular life, online sexual interactions have become increasingly mainstream. Thus, it is likely that cybersex will become a regular part of adult sexual experience in the future.

Written by Krystelle Shaughnessy

takes the interpersonal context in which most sexual activities occur into account (Byers & Wang, 2004). One such theory, **equity theory**, has been used to predict patterns of extradyadic sex (Hatfield, 1978).

The basic idea in equity theory is that in a relationship, people mentally tabulate their inputs to it and what they get out of it (benefits or rewards), and then they calculate whether these are equitable or not.

According to equity theory, if individuals perceive a relationship as inequitable (if they feel they are not getting what they put in), they become distressed. The more inequitable the relationship, the more distressed they feel. To relieve the

equity theory: A social exchange theory that states that people mentally calculate the benefits and costs for them in a relationship; their behaviour is then affected by whether they feel there is equity or inequity, and they will act to restore equity if there is inequity.

distress, they attempt to restore equity in the relationship. For example, people who feel they are putting too much into a relationship and not getting enough out of it might let their appearance go, or not work as hard to earn money, or refuse to have sex or contribute to conversations. The idea is that such actions will restore equity (Figure 11.5).

If these equity processes do occur, they might help to explain patterns of extra-relationship sex; that is, engaging in extra-relationship sex would be a way of restoring equity in an inequitable relationship. Social psychologist Elaine Hatfield (1978) tested this notion with married individuals. Her prediction was that people who felt underbenefited in their marriages (that is, they felt that there was an inequity and that they were not getting as much as they deserved) would be the ones to engage in extramarital sex. Confirming this notion, people who felt they were underbenefited began engaging in extramarital sex earlier in their marriages and had more extramarital partners than did people who felt equitably treated or overbenefited. (As an aside, equitable marriages were rated as happier than inequitable ones.)

Equity theory includes rewards and costs of all kinds, as indicated by our examples. However, as noted earlier in this chapter, our perceptions of our *sexual* rewards and costs and the extent to which they are equal to our partner's sexual rewards and costs have a particular impact on our satisfaction (Lawrance & Byers, 1995). Researchers in Quebec developed a scale to assess sexual equity and equality (Schoeb et al., 2013). Their results show that people who see their sexual relationship as more equitable are more satisfied with both their overall and their sexual relationship.

Clearly, both our perceptions of equity and equality in our intimate relationships, both sexual and nonsexual, may affect our satisfaction with those relationships and the likelihood that we will become involved in extramarital (or extra-partner) sexuality.

Evolution and Extra-Relationship Sex

Extra-relationship sex is not unique to Canada. In fact, it occurs in virtually every society. When evolutionary psychologists observe a behaviour that occurs in all societies, they are inclined to explain that behaviour in terms of evolutionary processes. That is, some people engage in extra-relationship sex because they carry in their genetic makeup something that motivates them to do so.

Why would some people carry these types of genes? From an evolutionary perspective, the genes that enable

Figure 11.5 Equitable sharing of household tasks—such as budgeting and paying bills—in a marriage. According to equity theory, if a person perceives that the relationship is inequitable and feels underbenefited, he or she is more likely to engage in extra-relationship sex.

© Ryan McVay/Getty Images

their bearers to produce larger numbers of offspring are more likely to survive from one generation to the next than genes that do not. A man who mates with one woman for life may produce a maximum of 6 to 12 offspring, depending on the length of time infants are breastfed, postpartum sex taboos, and so on. If that same man occasionally has sex with a second woman (or a series of other women), he could produce 12 to 24 offspring. We think you get the picture. Historically, men who sought out other women produced more offspring, who in turn produced more offspring carrying the genetic makeup that leads to extradyadic liaisons (Fisher, 1992). One study reported an association between a dopamine receptor gene (DRD4) and reports of extra-relationship sexual experiences (Garcia et al., 2010).

What about women? They cannot increase the number of their offspring by increasing the number of their sexual partners. However, there are ways in which having more than one sexual partner might have been biologically adaptive for women. First, sexual liaisons with other men might have enabled a woman to acquire extra goods and services, which enhanced her offspring's chances for survival. Second, having another partner could serve as "insurance"; if her husband died, she would have another man to turn to for food, shelter, and protection. Third, a woman married to a timid, unproductive hunter could "upgrade her genetic line" by mating with another man. Finally, having children with multiple partners increases the genetic diversity of one's offspring, increasing the chances that some of them will survive. Research on this point with animal populations reports mixed results. In some cases, offspring of extra-pair matings are more fit (Gerlach et al., 2012), in others not (Sardell et al., 2012). In the latter study, extra-pair offspring were less likely to hatch!

According to this sociobiological perspective, then, extra-relationship sex occurs because some men and women carry in their genetic makeup something that motivates them to be unfaithful. If there are environments in which extra-relationship sex is adaptive in contemporary society, people with those genes would have a selective advantage. Yet more and more societies that at one time allowed polygyny have moved to monogamy. Why might this be? Researchers in British Columbia concluded that monogamy has evolutionary advantages at the societal level for two primary reasons (Henrich et al., 2012). It reduces competition between men, resulting in less crime. It also increases paternal investment in each child, resulting in lower rates of child neglect and abuse and improving child outcomes.

Open Nonmonogamous Relationships

There are several types of open or consensually nonmonogamous relationships, in which all partners explicitly agree that the partner(s) may have other partners (Rubel & Bogaert, 2014). One type are agreements that partners can have other relationships within clearly defined limits, such as every other Friday night, or "while I am travelling." There may also be rules limiting behaviours that can occur, or locations ("not in our bed").

Swinging

Another form of open nonmonogamy is **swinging**, in which married couples exchange partners with other couples, or engage in sexual activity with a third person, with the knowledge and consent of all involved.[2]

---

[2] Swinging was originally called "wife-swapping." However, because of the sexist connotations of that term and the fact that women were often as eager to swap husbands as men were to swap wives, the more equitable "mate-swapping" or "swinging" was substituted.

Swingers may find their partners in several ways. Often they advertise in tabloid newspapers, in "lifestyle" magazines such as *Maritime Connection,* or on specialized bulletin boards and websites on the Internet. The following is an example:

> We are engaged bicouple lookin to meet bim, bif and bicouples for friendship and fun . . . we are into nudism, motorcycling, fishin, volleyball, pool and campin . . . she is 22 5′5″ 180# 38-d blond blue . . . he is 24 5′10″ 145# blond green 7″ and very thick. email: (www. . ./~gnkfoxx/nefriend.htm)

Swingers may also meet potential partners at swingers' clubs, parties, or resorts. Many of these places advertise in swingers' magazines and newsletters and are listed on specialized websites.

Several organizations and many local groups or couples sponsor parties. The date and general location of the party are publicized in magazines and on the Internet. Interested persons call or e-mail a contact person who screens them. If they pass, they are told the exact location of the party, often a private home or a hotel. A fee per couple may be charged for membership or entry to the party. One website lists 41 swinger clubs across Canada, including clubs in seven provinces. In 1998, police raided a members-only swing club in Montreal and charged the owner with running a common bawdy house—that is, a place "for the purpose of prostitution or the practice of acts of indecency" (Figure 11.6). The Supreme Court eventually ruled that swinging is legal in Canada as long as it takes place in private and that "consensual sexual conduct behind code-locked doors can hardly be supposed to jeopardize a society as vigorous and tolerant as Canadian society." A CROP poll (Gallant, 2003) found that 64 percent of Canadians (76 percent of Quebecers) were accepting of swingers clubs; that is, swinging passes the community standards of tolerance test (see Chapter 17).

A man who frequently hosts parties describes what happens:

> A lot of people have the idea that swinger parties are big orgies, where everybody jumps on everybody else. It isn't that way. People are selective, like they are anyplace else. [It starts with the eyes.] So if the interest continues from eye contact to talking, and to desire, there's touching. You just go with it. So you go from talking to touching, and at a swinging party you can go from touching to bed. (Maurer, 1994, p. 120)

Swinging may be closed or open. In *closed swinging,* the couples meet and exchange partners, and each pair goes off separately to a private place to have sex, returning to the meeting place at an agreed time. In *open swinging,* the pairs get together for sex in the same room for at least

swinging: A form of extradyadic sex in which married couples exchange partners with each other.

Figure 11.6 A mannequin hangs from the ceiling of this members-only swingers' club in Montreal, which the police shut down in 1998. It later reopened after the Supreme Court ruled that swinging is legal in Canada as long as it takes place in private.

© Ryan Remiorz/CP Images

part of the time. Many swingers start with *soft swinging,* which involves watching another couple engage in sexual activity, and sometimes participating in kissing, fondling, or oral sex, but not intercourse.

What kind of people are swingers? A review of 15 published studies, most of them involving small, convenience samples, concluded that the majority are upper or middle class, above average in education and income, and employed in the professions and in management (Jenks, 1998). Although one might expect them to be politically liberal, in one study only 27 percent described themselves as politically liberal—the rest were moderate or conservative (Jenks, 1985). The evidence indicates that at least two-thirds were raised in a religious home, but as adults they did not attend services and were not affiliated with a denomination. Swingers tend to report high marital satisfaction and that swinging improved their relationship (Bergstrand & Williams, 2000).

polyamory: The "non-possessive, honest, responsible and ethical philosophy and practice of loving multiple people simultaneously" (Ve Ard & Veaux, 2003); often referred to as poly.

Swinging appears to involve a small minority of people. Published estimates range from less than 1 to 2 percent, although none of these is current.

Polyamory

Polyamory (often referred to as *poly*) is "the non-possessive, honest, responsible, and ethical philosophy and practice of loving multiple people simultaneously" (Ve Ard & Veaux, 2003). You will notice that the focus in the definition is on love (*amory*) rather than on sex, although polyamorous relationships typically are also sexual relationships. There are several forms of such relationships, including the *intentional family,* involving three or more persons; the *group relationship,* with committed, loving relationships involving three or more partners; and *group marriage,* involving three or more persons. One specific type of *group relationship* is a triad involving a married couple and an additional man or woman, all of whom share sexual intimacy; the third person and one or both members of the couple may be bisexual. Other arrangements involve two or more men and two or more women. Unlike the extradyadic affair, there is (ideally) full disclosure of the network of relationships to all participants. Unlike swinging, the emphasis is on long-term intimate relationships. Unlike polygyny, both men and women can have multiple partners. Thus, individuals in polyamorous relationships would not consider themselves to be uncommitted or unfaithful (Ritchie & Barker, 2006). Such arrangements have even made it to popular television; you may be familiar with the television show *Big Love,* which depicts a man with three wives.

The legality of polygamy was tested in the B.C. Supreme Court. In 2010, based on polygamist marriages in the Fundamentalist Church of Jesus Christ of Latter Day Saints located in Bountiful, British Columbia, the B.C. government asked the court to rule on whether the federal law banning polygamy violated the *Charter of Rights and Freedoms.* The court ruled that the ban against polygamy is constitutional. The judges ruled that even though the law violates religious freedom of fundamentalist Mormons, the harm against women and children outweighed that concern.

What do Canadians think about people being able to have more than one marital partner at a time? Only 4 percent approve of it; an additional 16 percent do not approve but are willing to accept it (Bibby, 2004). That is, overall 80 percent of Canadians do not accept being married to more than one person; this figure is slightly lower, although still overwhelmingly negative, for younger Canadians.

British Columbia researchers investigated the relationship satisfaction of 1093 polyamorous individuals (57 percent women, 38 percent men, 3 percent gender queer, 1.4 percent transgender or other) in Canada, the U.S., Australia, the U.K., and New Zealand

(Mitchell et al., 2014). Participants were 37 years old on average and were highly educated. Most identified as white, and 44 percent had children. Participants had been in their primary relationship an average of 8.8 years and in their other relationship an average of 2.6 years. They rated their primary relationship higher than their other relationship in terms of relationship satisfaction, commitment, and overall need fulfillment but lower in terms of sexual need fulfillment. Need fulfillment was high with both partners across a wide range of needs; that is, the two relationships were fairly independent of each other, and participants did not appear to be in two relationships because their primary relationship was not fulfilling important needs.

Women involved in polyamory report expanding their familial, gender, and sexual roles. For example, some of these women rejected monogamy in favour of a network of intimate partner relationships. With respect to gender roles, the women adopted a much more assertive style in their relationships with men. In the realm of sexuality, the women often recognized their high sex drive, the emotional and sexual value of intimacy with other women, and their bisexual interests or identities. Moving away from traditional roles was reported to be both liberating and frightening; creating new roles was often difficult.

In multiethnic settings, such as Hong Kong, polyamorous relationships may cross ethnic, racial, and social-class boundaries (Sik Ying Ho, 2006). For example, a 37-year-old woman described concurrent sexual relationships with both men and women, of different races and social classes. Such relationships provide novel experiences that may both be anxiety provoking and expand one's understanding of sexual diversity.

Interestingly, research in British Columbia has shown that compared with people in other types of relationships, men and women in polyamorous relationships have higher testosterone levels (van Anders et al., 2007).

Consequences of Nonmonogamous Relationships

What are the consequences of nonmonogamy for the primary relationship? Ontario psychologists reviewed the limited published research looked at the consequences for psychological well-being, as measured by personality tests, and measures of anxiety and depression (Rubel & Bogaert, 2014). In most comparisons, monogamists and consensual nonmonogamists (CN) did not differ significantly. A few studies found the CNs were more likely to report present and past psychological distress, suggesting that poorer well-being predates participation in CN relationships. Turning to measures of relationship quality—adjustment, satisfaction, sexual frequency, jealousy—the authors conclude "there is an absence of

evidence that consensual nonmonogamists differ from monogamists in these domains" (p. 19). There is also little evidence that consensual nonmonogamy leads to higher rates of separation and divorce. Of course, these alternative relationship forms are relatively new. As more research is carried out on more diverse samples and over longer time periods, the results may differ.

What about the effects of secret nonmonogamy on the primary relationship? In a sample of 539 women students, 36 percent reported an extra-relationship sexual or romantic relationship in the preceding two months (Negash et al., 2014). Both emotional and sexual cheating was related to the termination of the primary relationship. Especially interesting is the finding that women who reported cheating on a high-quality relationship were more likely to report that the relationship ended. Relative to married respondents, persons who report extramarital sex are two to five times more likely to report being separated or divorced (Allen & Atkins, 2014). The question remains, who leaves in response to an affair? Researchers studied ex-spouses' reports of who (if either) was having an affair, and who wanted the divorce more (England et al., 2014). The results indicated that the spouse having the affair was more likely to want the divorce more. There was no gender difference in who had the affair. The results may reflect either the fact that the person who has decided to get divorced initiates an affair, or that an affair leads to the decision to divorce.

L07

Postrelationship Sex

From the point of view of developmental psychologists, the sexual relationship in a second union, perhaps following a divorce or the death of one's partner, is especially interesting. In what ways is it the same, and how does it differ, from the sexual relationship in the first long-term relationship? It represents the blending of things that are unique and consistent about the person with things that are unique to the new situation and new partner. As we develop sexually throughout the lifespan, these two strands continue to be intertwined—the developmental continuities (the things that are us and always will be) and the developmental changes (things that differ at various times in our lives, either because we are older or have experienced more, or because our partner or the situation is different).

Almost all Canadians agree that ideally their marriage should last for the rest of their life (Bibby, 2006). Nonetheless, about 40 percent of Canadian marriages will end in divorce, on average when people are in their 40s (Roterman, 2007a). The younger people are when they marry, the more likely they are to divorce (Clark & Crompton, 2006). Most divorced individuals say that they do not intend to remarry—64 percent of the women compared to 58 percent of the men (Beaupré, 2008). However, some of these individuals are living in common-law relationships, indicating that they are interested in being in a long-term relationship, just not in marriage.

People who are divorced or widowed are in a somewhat unusual situation in that they are used to regular sexual expression and suddenly find themselves in a situation in which they no longer have a regular sexual partner. Partly recognizing this dilemma, our society places few restrictions on postrelationship sexual activity. However, among heterosexuals, divorced and widowed Canadians are least likely to be satisfied with their sex life; 51 percent are satisfied, compared with 79 percent of people living with a partner and 75 percent of never-married individuals. An increasing concern is that many of these individuals do not practise safer sex (Idso, 2009), and thus are at risk for sexually transmitted infections (STIs).

Table 11.4 presents data on the number of sexual partners in the past year by a person's current marital status (Fryar et al., 2007). Among women, more than 26 percent of the widowed, divorced, or separated reported two or more (male) partners; more than one-third of the men in this status report more than two (female) partners. Note that never-married persons are 6 and 9 percent less likely to report this many partners. It is interesting that cohabiting women and men were more than twice as likely as married women and men to report this many partners. We noted earlier that the greater extra-relationship sexual activity of cohabiting individuals is thought to reflect their lower commitment, compared with married persons. Finally, note that in every category, men reported a larger number of partners than did women.

Table 11.4 Number of Heterosexual Partners in the Past Year, Adults 20–59, United States

	None	1	2 or more
Women			
Married	6%	91%	3%
Widowed, divorced, or separated	32	42	26
Never married	47	36	17
Cohabiting	11	81	8
Men			
Married	7%	86%	7%
Widowed, divorced, or separated	25	39	36
Never married	41	30	30
Cohabiting	5	80	15

Source: Fryar et al., 2007, Tables 8 and 10.

Most divorced women, but fewer widowed women, return to an active sex life. The NHSLS found that 46 percent of divorced and widowed men and 58 percent of divorced and widowed women had sex a few times per year or not at all (Laumann et al., 1994). In another study, 77 percent of the widowed had not engaged in intercourse in the last year, compared with 29 percent of the divorced (Smith, 2003).

The lower incidence of postmarital sex among widows, compared with divorced women, is due in part to the fact that widows are, on average, older than divorced women; however, even when matched for age, widows are still less likely than divorcees to engage in postmarital sex. One likely reason for this is that widows have the continuing social support system of in-laws and friends, and so they are less motivated to seek new friendships.

Widowed and divorced women who have postmarital sex often begin a relationship within one year of the end of the marriage. Evidence from an American survey suggests that these are long-term relationships (Stack & Gundlach, 1992). The average frequency of intercourse was twice a month.

Divorced women face complex problems of adjustment (Lichtenstein, 2012). These problems may include reduced income, a lower perceived standard of living, and reduced availability of social support. Some divorced men face similar problems. These problems may increase the motivation to establish a new long-term relationship. Single parents face a trade-off between parenting their children and devoting resources to establishing a new relationship (Gray et al., 2015). The conflicts may be more intense for mothers since they tend to provide more custodial care than fathers, and for parents of young children who are most dependent on adults. Analyses of data from a survey of 5481 single persons found that among single mothers, as number of children under two increased, the number of persons dated in the past three months increased. The researchers suggest this may reflect a more intensive search for a new partner to share the workload of caring for young children. Compared to parents of children over 5, parents of children under 5 reported greater frequencies of sexual activity and first dates.

Earlier in this chapter, we noted that substantial numbers of men and women cohabit. Like marriages, these relationships break up. What are the similarities and differences between formerly married and formerly cohabiting men and women? To answer this question, Wade and DeLamater (2002) used the NHSLS data to analyze the rate of acquisition of new partners following the dissolution of a relationship. The results indicate that these newly single men and women do not acquire new sexual partners at a high rate, and there were no significant differences between formerly married and formerly cohabiting men and women. Newly single persons acquire new partners at a significantly higher rate than single, never-married persons in the year following a breakup. Men with custody of children and men and women with low incomes have higher rates of new-partner acquisition, perhaps reflecting the impact of familial and economic instability associated with the dissolution. The results suggest that the postdissolution experience is similar across various demographic groups; given the high rates of breaking up in Canada and the United States, dissolution may, we suggest, be considered a significant life stage with its own specific characteristics.

Researchers interviewed 45 people age 60 to 92 who were experiencing or had recently experienced a romantic relationship that began late in life (Malta & Farquharson, 2012). All reported that they were seeking a long-term relationship. Twenty reported that they had experienced a casual relationship that lasted less than 12 months; reasons for the relationship ending included that the partner was not who they were looking for, or was not willing to be flexible. Twenty-five developed a long-term relationship: Six married or cohabited, and the other 19 established LAT relationships. These men and women desired romantic and sexual equality, and generally valued their independence.

As more men and women leave long-term relationships and initiate new ones in later life, a new problem has emerged: increasing rates of STIs, including HIV and AIDS, among older persons (see Chapter 8). In 2015, 13.5 percent of the new cases of HIV infection in Canada were among men and women 55 and older. Newly single older persons grew up at a time when there was less concern and publicity about STIs. An important tool in preventing STIs in this population is sex education geared toward them. Programs serving senior citizens in major cities are offering classes for "sexy seniors," often in senior centres and residential facilities.

Sex in Later Life

When Freud suggested that young children, even infants, have sexual thoughts and feelings, his ideas met with considerable resistance. When, 50 years later, researchers began to suggest that senior men and women also have sexual thoughts and feelings, there was similar resistance. This section deals with the sexual behaviour of older men and women, the physical changes they undergo, and the attitudes that influence them.

Physical Changes in Women

Biological Changes

The *climacteric* is a period lasting about 15 or 20 years (from about ages 45 to 60) during which a woman's body makes the transition from being able to reproduce to not being able to reproduce; the climacteric is marked particularly by a decline in the functioning of the ovaries. However, climacteric changes occur in many other body tissues and systems as well. This period is often called **perimenopause**. The woman knows that she is in the early perimenopausal stage when she either has skipped a menstrual period or has periods that are more irregular by more than seven days (Brotto & Luria, 2008). **Menopause** (the *change of life*, the *change*) refers to one specific event in this process: the cessation of menstruation; this occurs, on average, at around age 51 (with a normal menopause occurring anywhere between the ages of 40 and 60).

Biologically, as a woman grows older, the pituitary continues a normal output of FSH (follicle-stimulating hormone) and LH (luteinizing hormone); however, as the ovaries age, they become less able to respond to the pituitary hormones. In addition, the brain—including the hypothalamus-pituitary unit—ages (Lamberts et al., 1997). With the aging of the ovaries, there is an accompanying decline in the output of their two major products: eggs and the sex hormones estrogen and progesterone (see Figure 11.7). Androgen levels also decline during perimenopause (Brotto & Luria, 2008).

There are a number of physical symptoms that may accompany menopause. Research has identified two broad groups: vasomotor symptoms, especially hot flashes and night sweats, and psychosomatic symptoms, including feeling tense, irritable, and depressed (Richard-Davis & Wellons, 2013). The hot flash is probably the best known of the symptoms. Typically it is described as a sudden wave of heat from the waist up. The woman may get red and perspire a lot; when the flush goes away, she may feel chilled and sometimes shiver. The flashes may last from a few seconds to half an hour and occur several or many times a day. They may

perimenopause: The time before menopause and the first year after the last menstrual period.
menopause: The cessation of menstruation that usually occurs in middle age.

Figure 11.7 Levels of estrogen production in women across the lifespan.

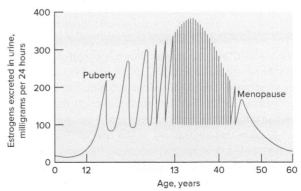

also occur at night, causing insomnia; the resulting perspiration can actually soak the sheets. Two other possible effects of the decline in estrogen levels are vaginal dryness, and *osteoporosis* (porous and brittle bones). Research in Ontario also showed that women have poorer working memories after menopause. This appears to be due to decreased levels of estrogen; estrogen levels did not affect passive recall (Duff & Hampson, 2000).

How many women experience symptoms? It depends on the woman's socio-cultural environment—that is, symptoms vary considerably from one culture to the next (Brotto & Luria, 2008). Diet, smoking, exercise, attitude, marital status, and socio-economic status also are potential influences (Richard-Davis & Wellons 2013). Controlling for a number of these variables, white women report significantly more psychosomatic symptoms (40 to 56 percent), while black women are more likely to report vasomotor symptoms (32 to 40 percent). Japanese and Chinese women are less likely than other groups to report any symptoms. This variation is evidence against the idea that there is a universal menopausal experience. Furthermore, many women who experience symptoms such as hot flashes and night sweats report that they are not bothered by them (Avis & McKinlay, 1995; McKinlay et al., 1992). A study of midlife women assessed their daily stress levels and several potential causes (Woods et al., 2009). The experience of menopausal symptoms by itself was not associated with increases in stress.

There are four approaches to the treatment/management of symptoms of menopause: hormone therapy, medications to relieve specific symptoms, complementary or alternative treatments, and seeking advice from friends and family. The current guidelines for the use of hormone therapy were drawn up jointly by 15 top medical societies in North America in 2012 (Manson, 2012); similar guidelines have been adopted by the British Menopause Society (Panay et al., 2013). Hormone therapy (HT) using oral estrogen is recommended to treat moderate to severe vasomotor symptoms; it is best to start it in early menopause (within ten years of onset). HT is also recommended to prevent osteoporosis in high-risk women, including those with low bone mineral density. If the only bothersome symptoms are genitourinary or vaginal dryness, this should be treated with vaginal estrogen or a lubricant, not a systemic medication. Current recommendations are to use the lowest dose of HT for the shortest period that allows successful treatment (Pinkerton et al., 2009; SOGC, 2006). The use of estrogen-progesterone therapy is associated with increased risk of venous thrombosis and stroke, though the absolute risk in younger, recently menopausal women is low.

A major health concern is the use of "bioidentical" compounded menopausal hormone therapy products. These products are compounds of various hormones that are described as "customized" for the patient, and prescribed by various types of physicians. None of these have been approved by Health Canada and they have not been tested for safety or effectiveness. These products are estimated to make up 40 percent of all menopausal hormone treatments used in the U.S, and 86 percent of the women taking them have no idea what they are taking (Tucker, 2014).

There are a variety of medications that can be used to treat specific symptoms, such as headaches, depression, and muscular soreness. Some require a prescription and some are sold over the counter. There are numerous complementary and alternative treatments for menopause, including black cohosh and red clover, that may be effective in treating mild menopausal symptoms (SOGC, 2006). Researchers have shown that most Canadian women have tried one or more of these complementary therapies to deal with menopausal symptoms (Lunny & Fraser, 2010; Paksad et al., 2007). Treatments include acupuncture, herbal remedies, various spices, and other compounds. Finally, some ethnic minority women seek advice from elders and close friends as the primary means of managing menopause. Most white women prefer to consult a physician. Japanese women believe menopause is part of normal aging and do not seek advice.

Sexuality and Menopause

Physical changes occur in women's genitals during perimenopause. The decline in estrogen causes the vagina to become less acidic, which leaves it more vulnerable to infections. Estrogen is also responsible for maintaining the mucous membranes of the vaginal walls. As a result of decreased estrogen, the walls of the vagina become thin and inelastic. The vagina and labia majora shrink, and there is a decline in vaginal lubrication during arousal. These changes may make intercourse somewhat more difficult and painful for the woman. Several remedies are available, including use of artificial lubricants or local estrogen therapy (SOGC, 2006). On the other hand, some women report that sex is even better after menopause, when fear of pregnancy no longer inhibits them. Furthermore, women have the same physical capacity for arousal and orgasm at 80 as they did at 30. For example, researchers in British Columbia examined premenopausal and postmenopausal women's physiological and subjective arousal to an erotic film and found no differences between the two groups (Brotto & Gorzalka, 2002).

Experts reviewing the research on women's sexuality during and after menopause have reached the following conclusions (Dennerstein et al., 2003; McCoy, 1996, 1997):

1. The majority of women with partners continue to engage in sexual activity and most enjoy it both during and after menopause.
2. There is some decline in sexual functioning, on average, during perimenopause and particularly after the last period.

3. Estrogen is related to the decline in sexual functioning, in part because low estrogen levels cause vaginal dryness. There is some evidence that higher estrogen levels are associated with better sexual functioning.

4. Testosterone is also important; a woman's sexual desire may decline as her levels of ovarian testosterone decline.

One study analyzed the data from an American Association of Retired Persons (AARP) survey of persons aged 45 and older (DeLamater & Moorman, 2007). The AARP survey included questions about various factors that might affect the frequency of sexual behaviour, including physical limitations, such as prior stroke and arthritis; emotional problems, such as depression; and use of various medications. Although some men and women reported these conditions, they were relatively uncommon and were not significantly related to the frequency of oral sexual activity or vaginal intercourse. The factors that were significantly related were high scores on an index of sexual desire (frequent sexual thoughts, desire), positive attitudes toward sex for oneself, and the presence of a partner with no limitations related to sexuality. Men and women who reported that their partner had limitations that interfered with sexual expression were significantly more likely to report masturbating.

Some people believe that having a hysterectomy means the end of a woman's sex life. In fact, sex hormone production is not affected as long as the ovaries are not removed (surgical removal of the ovaries is called **oophorectomy** or ovariectomy). The majority of women report that a hysterectomy has no effect on their sex lives. However, approximately one-third of women who have had hysterectomies report problems with sexual response (Zussman et al., 1981). There are two possible physiological causes for these problems. If the ovaries have been removed, hormonal changes may be responsible; the ovaries produce androgens, and they may play a role in sexual response. The other possibility is that the removal of the cervix, and possibly the rest of the uterus, is an anatomical problem if the cervix serves as a trigger for orgasm or if contractions of the uterus contribute to sexual pleasure.

Androgen therapy may improve sexual functioning and sexual well-being in women who had both ovaries removed and are experiencing androgen insufficiency syndrome (Chu & Lobo, 2004).

Changes in Men

Physical Changes

Although people use the term *male menopause*, in the technical sense men do not experience a menopause; never having menstruated, they can scarcely cease menstruating. However, men do experience a very gradual decline in the manufacture of both testosterone and sperm by the testes (see Figure 11.8). Some refer to this time of life as *andropause*, likening the declining levels of androgens to the climacteric in women (Lamberts et al., 1997). Drug manufacturers discovered this a few years ago and started massive advertising campaigns to persuade men to use prescription androgen/testosterone supplements. An advisory panel states that the only clear indicator of need for such supplements is in men with congenital or acquired primary hypogonadism, a condition requiring medical diagnosis (Tucker, 2014). Men who do not have low levels of testosterone confirmed by hormonal assay should not take these drugs.

Vascular diseases, such as hardening of the arteries, are increasingly common with age in men, which may cause erection problems because good circulation is essential to erection (Riportella-Muller, 1989). A major change is that erections occur more slowly. It is important for men to know that this is a perfectly natural slow-down so that they will not jump to the conclusion that they are developing an erection problem. It is also important for partners to know about this so that they will use effective techniques of stimulating the man and will not mistake slowness for lack of interest.

The refractory period lengthens with age; thus for an older man, it may be 24 hours after an orgasm before he can get an erection again. (Note that women do not undergo a similar change; most women do not enter into a refractory period and are still capable of multiple orgasms at

oophorectomy (OH-uh-fuh-REK-tuh-mee): Surgical removal of the ovaries.

Figure 11.8 Levels of testosterone production in men across the lifespan.

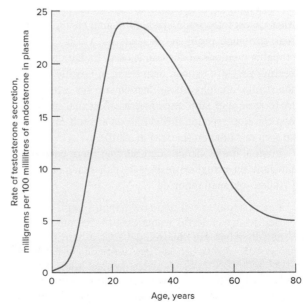

age 80.) Other signs of sexual excitement—the sex flush and muscle tension—diminish with age.

The volume of the ejaculate gradually decreases, and the force of ejaculation lessens. The testes become somewhat smaller, but even very old men produce viable sperm. Ninety-year-old men have been known to father children.

One advantage is that middle-aged and older men may have better control over orgasm than young men may; thus, they can prolong sexual intercourse and may be better sexual partners.

A study of healthy men, ages 45 to 74, all married, assessed their biological, psychological, and behavioural functioning (Schiavi et al., 1994). Erectile problems, low sexual information, and low marital adjustment were associated with lower general satisfaction. Accurate information is important because it may result in more realistic expectations for sexual performance.

One of the most common physical problems for middle-aged and older men is noncancerous enlargement of the prostate gland, which is believed to be related to changes in hormone levels. Enlargement of the prostate causes urination problems; there is difficulty in voluntarily initiating urination, as well as frequent nocturnal urination. Surgery to remove the part of the gland pressing against the urethra usually remedies these symptoms. Unfortunately, complications of the surgery include retrograde ejaculation in about 65 percent of men and erection problems in about 10 percent (American Urological Association Practice Guidelines Committee, 2003). New treatments have recently been developed to avoid these problems, including anti-androgen drugs and laser treatments.

Some people believe that prostate surgery or removal of the prostate (**prostatectomy**) means the end of a man's sex life. It is true that the volume of the ejaculate will decrease. Prostatectomy can cause damage to the nerves supplying the penis, creating erectile problems. In other cases, retrograde ejaculation may result. Whether there are such problems depends on which of several available methods of surgery is used. Radiation, used in treating prostate cancer, may result in erectile dysfunction. Unfortunately, many men equate sex with sexual intercourse and stop engaging in all sexual activity if they develop erection difficulties as a result of prostate surgery or radiation (Letts et al., 2010).

In sum, the evidence suggests that there need be no time limit on sexual expression for either men or women. A 73-year-old man reported:

> I can't begin to tell you how happy I am. I am married to a wonderful woman who loves me as much as I love her. My children gave me a hard time of it at first, especially because she is a bit younger than me. [My son] was telling me that marrying again and trying to have a lot of sex—imagine that, saying to me trying to have sex—could be dangerous to the marriage. So, I said to him with a straight face, "Do you think she'll survive it?" He was so shocked, he laughed. (Janus & Janus, 1993, p. 8)

Attitudes about Sex and Older Adults

Our society has a negative attitude toward sexual expression among older adults. People are uncomfortable with the idea of two 70-year-old people having sex with each other and even more uncomfortable with the thought of a 70-year-old masturbating. These negative attitudes become particularly obvious in assisted living and care facilities, where staff members may frown on sexual activity among the residents. Somehow, what is virility at 25 becomes lechery at 75. Attitudes toward sexual expression in gay, lesbian, and bisexual individuals may be even more negative, given that they face stigma associated with both their sexual orientation and their age (Figure 11.9). Similarly, because we tend to think of people with disabilities as asexual and uninterested in sex, attitudes towards sexual expression in older people with physical or other disabilities such as autism may be particularly negative (Nichols & Byers, 2016).

Researchers in New Brunswick assessed young people's explicit (self-report) and implicit attitudes (involuntary and effortless responses occurring outside of conscious awareness) toward the sexuality of older adults (see Chapter 3 for a description of how implicit attitudes are assessed) (Thompson et al., 2014). They found that their participants reported positive explicit attitudes; that is, they said that they were accepting of sexuality in older adults. However, their implicit attitudes told a different story and showed negative implicit attitudes regarding the sexual lives of older adults.

Figure 11.9 Affection, romance, and sex are not just for the young.

© threerocksimages/Shutterstock

prostatectomy (pros-tuh-TEKtuh-mee): Surgical removal of the prostate.

Cross-cultural research indicates that the sexual behaviour of older adults is related to these cultural expectations (Winn & Newton, 1982). Older adults continue to be sexually active in 70 percent of societies and in precisely those societies where they are expected to be sexually active. Indeed, in 22 percent of societies, women are expected to become more uninhibited about sexuality when they become older.

Why does our society have such negative attitudes toward sex among older adults? In part, these attitudes stem from the fact that ours is a youth-oriented culture. We value youth, and the physical characteristics that are considered sexy are youthful ones, such as a trim, firm body and smooth skin. It is therefore hard to believe that someone with old, wrinkled skin could be sexually active. According to one youthful-looking 59-year-old woman:

> No one looks at me today with any kind of sexual interest. I mean, I don't even get the time of day from any man. I'm an older woman. I want men to be aggressive now. I'm not going to approach a man, because I'm afraid to be rejected. So I've just given up. (Maurer, 1994, p. 475)

A study of heterosexual, mid-life women assessed menopausal status, self-rated attractiveness, sexual desire, and frequency of sexual intercourse (Koch et al., 2005). Regardless of menopausal status, women who perceived themselves as less attractive than ten years earlier reported a decline in both sexual desire and sexual behaviour. Women who perceived themselves as more attractive reported an increase in sexual desire, frequency of sex, and frequency of orgasm. This study demonstrates a link between feelings of attractiveness and sexual behaviour. Of course, because these data are correlational, it is not known whether changes in feelings of attractiveness caused the decline in sexual desire and behaviour.

Our negative attitudes may be a holdover from the belief that sex was for reproductive purposes only—and those past the age of reproduction should therefore not engage in it. Also, we tend to identify older people with our parents or grandparents and find it hard to think of them as sexual beings. This attitude is encouraged by the fact that many parents take great pains to hide their sexual activity from their children.

These attitudes affect the way older people are treated, and older adults, whether gay or straight, may hold such attitudes themselves (Badeau & Bergeron, 1997). The current generation of older people was raised in a time in which they had little access to accurate sex information and myths about sexuality in older adults were common. Thus, older people today may be particularly affected by their own negative attitudes. For example, a Montreal study found that older men had less tolerant views about sexual expression in older

people than did middle-aged men (Libman, 1989). One remedy that has been proposed for these negative attitudes is a "coming out of the closet"; as one 67-year-old commented:

> The common view that the aging and aged are nonsexual, I believe, can only be corrected by a dramatic and courageous process—the *coming out of the closet* of sexually active older women and men, so that people can see for themselves what the later years are really like. (Brecher, 1984, p. 21)

Various specific misunderstandings may influence sexuality. For example, a man might believe that sex will precipitate a heart attack or, if he has already had a heart attack, that it will bring on another one. Although heart rate accelerates during sexual intercourse, the mean heart rate during orgasm is only 117 beats per minute, which is about that attained during many common forms of daily exercise. This rate is about the equivalent of climbing two flights of stairs at a moderate pace. Thus, the demands of sex on the heart are not unreasonable (Jackson, 2009). A study of patients who had had a heart attack questioned them about their activities immediately before the attack and in the year before the attack (Muller et al., 1996). The results indicate that the increase in risk caused by sexual activity is one chance in a million for a healthy individual. Furthermore, the relative risk is no greater in patients with a history of cardiac disease.

Ideas such as this, as well as such factors as illness or hospitalization, may lead to a period of sexual inactivity. However, being sexually inactive is one of the most effective ways of diminishing sexuality. Masters and Johnson emphasized that two factors are critical in maintaining sexual capacity in old age:

1. *Good physical and mental health:* An excellent study confirms this notion (Persson, 1980). A representative sample of 70-year-olds in one town in Sweden was selected, and 85 percent agreed to participate in the detailed interviews. For both men and women, those who continued to have sexual intercourse had better mental health as rated by a psychiatrist and more positive attitudes toward sexual activity among older adults.

2. *Regularity of sexual expression:* As was noted earlier, there is evidence that some physical changes of the sex organs in old age are related to sexual inactivity. As the saying goes, "Use it or lose it." In fact, the results of a longitudinal study suggest that, for men, frequency of orgasm is positively associated with longevity. The study involved men ages 45 to 59. At the beginning of the study, the men completed a standard medical history and a questionnaire that assessed sexual behaviour. Ten years

later, the researchers found out who had died, and compared their questionnaire answers with those of the survivors. Men who reported fewer than one orgasm per month at the beginning of the study were more than twice as likely to die as the men who reported two orgasms per month (Smith et al., 1997). Of course, these data are correlational (see Chapter 3), so we cannot conclude that more frequent sexual expression causes men to live longer.

Apparently, some older people have caught on to this fact. As one 80-year-old husband said of his relationship with his 75-year-old wife:

> My wife and I both believe that keeping active sexually delays the aging process . . . if we are troubled with an erection or lubrication, we turn to oral methods or masturbation of each other. We keep our interest alive by a great deal of caressing and fondling of each other's genitals. We feel it is much better to wear out than to rust out. (Brecher, 1984, p. 33)

How does sex change for older adults?

Reformers urge us to change our attitudes about sex and older adults. Nursing homes particularly need to revise their practices, and staff need to become more comfortable discussing sexuality with residents (Figure 11.10). Changes such as knocking before entering a resident's room would help (people masturbate, you know). Other reforms would include making provisions for partners to stay overnight

Figure 11.10   Romance is important for many nursing-home residents.

© Ryan McVay/Getty Images

and allowing couples—married or unmarried—to share a bedroom.

The introduction of Viagra© in 1998 ushered in a "new era" that some refer to as the *biomedicalization* of sex in later life (Marshall, 2012). The marketing of Viagra and related medicines conveys the message that declining sexual function is a medical problem, not an aspect of normal aging to be accepted. This is leading to changing attitudes about sex in later life, perhaps creating the belief that everyone should be sexually active until they die and there is something wrong with you if you aren't. That is as false as the belief that everyone loses sexual desire and function sometime after age 50. Clearly, each person/couple needs to determine the amount and kind of sexual expression that best fits their health, relationship status, living situation, and desires.

Sexual Behaviour

Although sexual desire and sexual behaviour do decline somewhat with age, substantial numbers of older men and women have active sex lives. The National Social Life, Health and Aging Project (NSHAP) interviewed 3000 women and men ages 57 to 85 in 2005–2006 (Tessler Lindau et al., 2007). Among men ages 75 to 80, more than 40 percent had frequent sexual thoughts, 30 percent had masturbated in the preceding year, and 45 percent had had sexual intercourse. Among women ages 75 to 80, the percentages were about 10, 18, and 20, respectively (Das et al., 2012). There does not seem to be any age beyond which all people are sexually inactive. Research has identified some factors associated with how frequently older adults engage in sexual activity (Bell et al., 2016). More frequently, past sexual activity and having a partner who is more interested in sexual activity are associated with more frequent sexual activity.

Some older people do, for various reasons, stop having intercourse after a certain age. For example, a Montreal study found that 27 percent of men and women over 60 reported that sex did not interest them very much, whereas only 5 percent of participants under 60 responded this way (Trudel, 2002). Analyses of the data from NSHAP (men and women ages 57 to 72) and NHSLS (men and women ages 44 to 59) found that, for both men and women, frequency of intercourse declined with age. Among men, declining frequency was also associated with declining happiness in the past year and declining physical health. The relationship between frequency and happiness was stronger among younger men. Among women, declining frequency was associated with happiness and especially with widowhood (Karraker et al., 2011). Subsequent analyses of NSHAP data indicate that, among men and women ages 57 to 85 who are married, overall two-thirds remain sexually active; when sexual activity within a marriage stops, it is primarily because of declining health and sexual dysfunction (Bell et al., 2016; Karraker & DeLamater, 2013).

Further, researchers in Ontario found that some older adults reported that sex improved with age, maturity, and experience (Kleinplatz et al., 2009). They counter the stereotype that aging leads to loss of sexual well-being by showing that older adults can and do experience "great sex" (see Milestones in Sex Research for more information about what the researchers found). Indeed, many older adults would like to engage in sexual activity more often than they do (Ginsberg et al., 2005).

One of the most important influences on sexuality in older adults is that there are far more older women than older men. Because of men's earlier mortality as well as their preference for younger women, older women are more likely to be living alone and to have less access to sexual partners. Men ages 65 and older are much more likely to live with a spouse or partner than are women in that age group. For example, in the 2016 Canadian census, overall 75 percent of the men but only 49 percent of the women ages 65 and older were living with a spouse or common-law partner. The discrepancy is even larger in older age groups. For example, for those ages 85 and over, 58 percent of the men and only 16 percent of the women were living with a partner. Some innovative solutions have been proposed, such as senior women forming same-sex relationships. Of course, some widowed women remarry. A British Columbia study of remarried older women found that many of them described strong sexual chemistry and a passionate sex life with their second husband that was often better than their early sexual experiences. As one woman who remarried at the age of 72 said:

> There was an incredible chemical reaction with my second husband, for both of us. Quite different from the first marriage which evolves . . . there was an absolute click. Absolutely incredible! I mean, at that age. It was like a couple of teenagers. I can't tell you. Um, oh, we had a lot of fun. (Clarke, 2006, p. 132)

Lesbians do not face the same problem of lack of suitable partners that heterosexual women face because they tend to be attracted to women of their own age (Garnets & Peplau, 2006).

A Montreal study of 144 married men ranging in age from 51 to 80 and 71 of their female spouses provides some data on how age affects sexual expression (Libman, 1989). All participants were in good health and all the men had previously undergone one of two non-life-threatening surgical procedures. The sample was divided into younger (under 65) and older (age 65 and older) groups. The two groups did not differ in their frequency of sexual activity or in their satisfaction with their sex lives—both groups were generally satisfied. However, the older men and women experienced a desire for sex less often, and the older men had more concerns about erectile difficulties (erectile difficulties themselves were infrequent in both male age groups, about 15 percent of the time).

A large representative survey on the sexuality of older adults living in the community was conducted in the United States in 2004 (Tessler Lindau et al., 2007). The researchers interviewed 3005 adults between the ages of 57 and 85. Because older adults who are sick or in care facilities are unlikely to have completed the survey, we must regard this as a survey of older adults who are above average in health and who are doubtless more sexually active than some older adults. In addition, few gay men and lesbians completed the survey, so the data apply only to heterosexual individuals. Indeed, there is little research on the effects of aging on same-sex sexual relationships. Nonetheless, this survey is a very important source of information about sex in later life.

Some statistics from the survey, presented by age group, are included in Table 11.5. Note that women over 60 are much less likely to have a sexual partner available, so the women reported much lower frequencies of partnered activities than the men did. For both men and women, the likelihood of having engaged in sexual activity with a partner declined with age. Of those in the 64-to-74 age group who had engaged in sexual activity, about two-thirds had engaged in intercourse at least weekly and half had engaged in oral sex. Among individuals who had engaged in sexual activity, the frequency of sex was lower among those who were 75 to 85 years of age, and one-third had engaged in oral sex. The frequency of masturbation also decreased with age, and was higher for men than for women. Having a current partner did not affect the likelihood of having masturbated in the previous 12 months.

About half of the respondents reported having at least one bothersome sexual problem. Erectile difficulties, reported by 37 percent of the men, were the most common problem for men. Low desire, reported by 43 percent of the women, was the most common problem reported by women. As shown in Table 11.5, about one-quarter of the men also reported a lack of interest in sex. Most men and women described sexual activity as an important part of their life.

We see, then, that many older people who are healthy engage in a range of sexual activities with a partner and consider sex an important part of their life.

Milestones in Sex Research

Older Adults Who Have Optimal Sexual Experiences

There are many stereotypes of sexuality and older adults, and most of these are negative. That is, the common view is that extraordinary sex is for the young and that older adults, if they have sex at all, must settle for infrequent boring sex fraught with sexual problems. But is this necessarily the case? Can sex get even better as we get older? As part of a larger investigation into the nature and contributors to optimal sexuality, Dr. Peggy Kleinplatz and her colleagues conducted in-depth interviews with individuals over the age of 60 who had been in relationships for 25 years or more about their recent experiences of optimal sexuality. They ranged in age from 60 to 84. What could be learned about optimal sexuality by studying those who have made it last a lifetime? Six lessons emerged:

1. *Great lovers are made—not born.* None of the participants in this study felt that his/her facility for optimal sexuality was a natural talent that had suddenly appeared in youth. Participants identified the beginnings of "great" sex with clear and distinct improvement in their sex lives as they reached emotional maturity in mid-life. As one man put it, "It's like, there's not a goal, and I think before one of the differences was . . . it was like reaching a peak and ejaculating or something and that was the end product and I don't think of it that way, I think of it more as riding a wave and trying to stay on the crest as long as you can. It seems now silly to focus on the end, on an end state, on any end state as if that's what you've got to do. It just seems silly and counterproductive and just inconsequential [laughing] to the experience. But that's been a big change for me." For those who choose to expend the effort, the heights of sexual relations could grow given time, experience and the commitment to making sex extraordinary.

2. *Developing optimal sexuality required jettisoning normative sex scripts.* Ironically, most stated that a prerequisite for developing the capacity to experience great sex was unlearning everything they had learned about sex growing up. They emphasized the necessity of overcoming conventional sexual scripts and the shame with which they had been raised, letting go of concerns about body image, performance expectations, and the idea that sex should be "natural and spontaneous." One woman stated, "For the first few times I just assumed I had to lie there and the guy would do all the work, and somehow I was supposed to be in ecstasy and I learned that no, I had to be an active participant . . ." To become great lovers, they had to reject old one-size-fits-all norms that had never actually fit at all.

3. *Be less willing to settle.* With experience, many found that they were less willing to settle for anything less than what they really wanted. Participants emphasized the importance of sex between equals, which entailed going beyond conventional gender role norms to seek lovers who would be full partners with equal input in sexual relations. As one man stated, "The older I've gotten, the more particular I have been in my choice of partners. . . . And I'm willing to make fewer compromises about what I want sexually as I get older."

4. *"Great sex" takes a lot of time, devotion, and intentionality.* A major lesson from these interviews was that sex of this calibre does not simply "happen" but requires considerable planning, prioritizing, being deliberate, and intentionality. All the participants emphasized devoting a lot of time to sex. One man stated, "We'll play for six hours until maybe eleven at night or twelve at night." Many described the importance of creating an environment suited to the

couple's sexual inclinations. The details of such an environment might vary but the intent was invariant: "The most important thing is that it not interfere with whatever kind of sex you wanted to have that day. So it could be quiet and private and comfortable with no interruptions for about four days or it could be that the participants lose themselves in a room with other people in it or nearby. It depends what you want" (as described by a woman).

5. *Exploration and familiarity both have advantages.* Participants spoke about the opportunity for self-exploration afforded in truly intimate relationships. This was not about trying out new activities or novelty for its own sake so much as a chance for revealing themselves and one another anew and in ever-deeper ways. As one participant described it, "The better we are, the more I am dazzling and dazzled by you." The role of familiarity often is overlooked but together, exploration and familiarity create an atmosphere rich with "anticipated surprise." For these participants, a balance was required between discovery and trust. "It's the thing that makes me feel freest . . . when I feel safe" (as stated by a man). As described by another man, "You've been through so many ups and downs that you know you're going to come out of it OK."

6. *Aging, chronic illness, and disability are not necessarily obstacles to optimal sexuality.* Almost all of the participants believed that sex improved with increasing age, personal growth, and maturity. As one older man put it, "Young people are more performance and . . . they're just too anxious. Older people have more understanding for what it takes. . . . Sex comes with maturity. Sex becomes better and better with time," or as another noted, "We can still revel in sexuality." Many participants saw aging, chronic illness, and disability as assets towards optimal sexual development. "You can always have sex in

a new form," said one older woman. Another older woman who had survived breast cancer spoke of never having enjoyed sexuality or her body and body image more than since her mastectomy, which had freed her to move beyond conventional ideas of sexiness. An older man stated, "Someone who looks on themselves as being somehow broken . . . need not map to any kind of externally defined disability. . . . It never struck me as being a defining issue in terms of sexual engagement, sexual passion. . . . If there were a disability that restricts one's access to sexual fulfillment, I would say it was a disability of the energy or the imagination." Or as another participant reflected, "A lot of barriers to great sex [exist] for able-bodied people as they hold themselves to standards that get in the way of open-mindedness and experimentation."

A variety of implications emerge from these findings: It may be necessary to redefine and reconceptualize how we define "sex" and dispense with the notion that sex is supposed to be "natural and spontaneous." Older people who self-identify as having "great sex" demonstrate that sexual functioning and optimal sexuality are very different phenomena: Being sexually functional is neither *necessary* nor *sufficient* for optimal sexual experiences. Aging may be an asset for optimal sexual development. Among those having extraordinary sex, the capacity was acquired and developed rather deliberately, thus allowing for the prospect that others who might value optimal sexuality could cultivate the ability as they mature, too.

Based on: Kleinplatz, P., Menard, A. D., Paquet, M.-P., et al. (2009). The components of optimal sexuality: A portrait of "great sex." *Canadian Journal of Human Sexuality, 18*(1–2), 1–13.

Written by Dr. Peggy Kleinplatz, Department of Psychology, University of Ottawa.

Table 11.5 Sexual Activity in a Sample of Persons Ages 57 to 85

Women	57–64 (492)	65–74 (545)	75–85 (513)
Sexual activity with partner in previous 12 months	61.6%	39.5%	16.7%
Have sexual activity at least once a week*	62.6	65.4	54.1
Vaginal–penile intercourse*	86.8	85.4	74.4
Oral sex*	52.7	46.5	35.0
Masturbate in last 12 months	31.6	21.9	16.4
Lack of interest in sexual activity in last 12 months	44.2	38.4	49.3
Men	**(528)**	**(547)**	**(380)**
Sexual activity with partner in previous 12 months	83.7%	67.0%	38.5%
Have sexual activity at least once a week*	67.5	65.4	54.2
Vaginal–penile intercourse*	91.1	78.5	83.5
Oral sex*	62.1	47.9	28.3
Masturbate in last 12 months	63.4	53.0	27.9
Lack of interest in sexual activity in last 12 months	28.2	28.5	24.2

*Of people who had engaged in sexual activity within the preceding 12 months.

Source: Lindau et al., 2007

Critical THINKing Skill

THINKING AS HYPOTHESIS TESTING

In many of our everyday interactions, we function like intuitive scientists. Events occur and we want to explain and then perhaps control them. To do so, we use the same skills as a scientist testing a hypothesis: (1) We accumulate observations; (2) we formulate hypotheses or explanations; and (3) we use the information to see if it confirms or disconfirms the hypothesis.

A common event in a long-term relationship is a decline in the frequency of sexual activity. It can be upsetting, because (1) you enjoy sex, (2) it symbolizes the bond between you, (3) it asserts your power, and (4) _____. So one morning, you think, "We haven't had sex for a week; we're having sex a lot less than we did at first." You get upset. You search for a reason and think that your partner is having an affair and is therefore less interested in sex with you. Before you leap to the conclusion that your partner is having an affair, use critical thinking skills. Accumulate observations and track frequency for some period of time. It may be that your initial observation was just about one week and coincided with a string of 12-hour days at work, a visit by the parents, or some other unusual occurrence. If indeed, over time, sex is infrequent, then try to recall accurately how often you did have sex "at first."

If your observations are consistent with the hypothesis of decline, consider possible explanations. An affair is one possibility, but this chapter has suggested several others. Some are job-related; one of you switched to a more demanding job six months ago. You had or adopted a baby eight months ago (look at the data in Table 6.3). You are getting older (look at the data in Table 11.2). Now you have four plausible hypotheses. You can make observations about work, the baby, fatigue and problems related to age, and odd absences by the partner, and assess the evidence for each of these.

This process will take some time. At some point, you will want to involve your partner by discussing your concerns, your observations, and perhaps your hypotheses. When you do, use the principles of good communication discussed in Chapter 12. With good communication skills, the odds are higher that the result will be that both of you become positively engaged in the process.

SUMMARY

Sexuality continues to develop throughout the lifespan. It may be expressed in being single, cohabitation, common-law relationships, marriage, nonmonogamous relationships, relationships following divorce, or a variety of contexts as the individual ages.

Young adults grow toward sexual maturity. Many do so in the context of a single relationship that results in marriage. Others are involved in two or more relationships before they begin to live with or marry someone. Never-married people over 30 may find themselves part of the singles scene.

Cohabitation is a stage that up to 40 percent of people experience. Sixty percent of cohabiting couples marry. Some cohabiting couples have children, either together or with previous partners. Men and women who are living together engage in sexual activity more often, on average, than those who are married or dating.

Marriage represents a major turning point as couples face new responsibilities and problems and try to find time for each other. Married mixed-sex couples in their 20s engage in sexual intercourse two or three times per week on average, with the frequency declining to two or three times per month among couples over age 60. Perhaps the most dramatic change in marital sex practices in recent decades is the increased popularity of oral–genital sex. Many married people continue to masturbate. Most people today—both women and men—express general satisfaction with their marital sex life. Sexual patterns in marriage, however, show great variability. There are no data on the sexual activity of married same-sex couples.

Up to one-third of people who commit to a monogamous relationship engage in extra-relationship sex at some time, including between 14 and 25 percent of married men and between 7 and 15 percent of married women. Our society disapproves of extramarital sex, and it is generally carried on in secrecy. In some couples, it is agreed that both partners can have extra-partnership sex, as in negotiated nonmonogamy, swinging, and polyamory. Equity theory and the sociobiological perspective may be helpful in understanding patterns of extramarital sex.

Virtually all widowed and divorced men return to an active sex life, as do most divorced women and about half of widowed women.

Although sexual activity declines somewhat with age, many people remain sexually active into their 80s and 90s. Problems with sex or the cessation of intercourse may be related to physical factors. In women, declining estrogen levels associated with menopause result in a thinner, less elastic vagina and less lubrication; in men, there is lowered testosterone production and increased vascular disease, combined with slower erections and longer refractory periods. Psychological factors can also be involved, such as the belief that older adults cannot or should not have sex. Masters and Johnson emphasized that two factors are critical to maintaining sexual capacity in old age: good physical and mental health, and regularity of sexual expression. A recent survey indicates that most older people who are healthy engage in sexual activity with a partner and consider it an important part of their life.

CHAPTER 12

Attraction, Love, and Communication

Brand X/Punchstock

Are YOU Curious?

1. Do opposites really attract?
2. How do Internet dating sites match people?
3. How important is emotional intimacy in relationships?
4. Why do people get jealous?

Read this chapter to find out.

LEARNING OBJECTIVES

After studying this chapter, you will be able to

LO1 Describe the factors that influence attraction.

LO2 Describe and evaluate the role of the Internet in dating.

LO3 Explain the nature and the value of emotional intimacy in relationships.

LO4 Describe the four views of love.

LO5 Describe jealousy.

LO6 Describe and evaluate the two-component theory of love.

LO7 Describe how culture influences love and marriage.

LO8 Describe the outcomes and characteristics of effective communication.

The intimacy in sex is never only physical. In a sexual relationship we may discover who we are in ways otherwise unavailable to us, and at the same time we allow our partner to see and know that individual. As we unveil our bodies, we also disclose our persons.*

* Dr. Thomas Moore, "Soul Mates," *Psychology Today*, March–April 1994, downloaded from http://faculty.uccb.ns.ca/pmacintyre/psych365/quotes.htm.

Many people believe that there is (or should be) a close connection between love and sex. The primary sexual standard of today for many is that sex is appropriate if we love the other person. Of course, sex and love do not necessarily go together. Some people have satisfying sexual relationships without emotional involvement; other people are in love with a person with whom they do not have a sexual relationship. Nonetheless, for most people emotional passion and sexual passion are closely linked—without the sexual passion, we might be more likely to think of the person as a friend. People want to express their loving feelings to their romantic partner in a sexual way. Lovemaking, in turn, contributes to their feelings of love. In short, sex is an important part of most romantic relationships. Therefore, it is important in a text on sexuality to spend some time considering the emotion we link so closely to sex: love.

This chapter is organized in terms of the way relationships usually progress—if they progress. We begin by talking about attraction, what brings people together in the first place. Then we consider intimacy, which develops as relationships develop. Next, we look at four different views of what love is. We discuss some of the research on love, including cross-cultural research. Finally, we conclude with one of the requirements for fulfilling, long-term relationships: good communication.

Attraction

What causes you to be attracted to another person? Some people are attracted only to men, some only to women, some to both, and some to neither, so gender is an important component of attraction for many, although not all, people. Sexual orientation, including its causes, is discussed in Chapter 14, so it is not discussed here. Social psychologists have done extensive research on interpersonal attraction. We consider the major results of this research in this section. Unfortunately, much of the research on attraction has been restricted to studying male–female relationships and has not included same-sex relationships.

The Girl Next Door

Geography and time limit our opportunities to meet people. You may meet that attractive person sitting two rows in front of you in human sexuality class, but you are unlikely to meet the wealthy, brilliant engineering student who sits in your seat two classes later. You are much more likely to meet and be attracted to the boy or girl next door than the one who lives across town.

In a longitudinal survey of more than 4000 adults, 3009 had a spouse or romantic partner. Each was asked where they met their partner (Rosenfeld & Thomas, 2012). Of the mixed-sex couples who met between 2005 and 2010, 30 percent met through friends, 20 percent in (primary or secondary) school, 20 percent online, 10 percent in university and about 5 percent each through family, at work, in church, and in bars. In pre-Internet days (1980–1990), more couples met through family and in school. Of the same-sex couples who met between 2005 and 2010, almost 70 percent met online, 20 percent in bars, and 10 percent through friends. From 1980 to 1990, same sex-couples were more likely to meet through friends and in bars.

Among those with whom we work or take the same class, we tend to be more attracted to people we have had contact with several times than we are to people with whom we have had little contact. This tendency has been demonstrated in laboratory studies in which the amount of contact between participants was systematically varied. At the end of the session, people gave higher "liking" ratings to those with whom they had had much contact and lower ratings to those with whom they had had little contact (Saegert et al., 1973). This is the **mere-exposure effect**; repeated exposure to any stimulus, including a person, leads to greater liking for that stimulus (Bornstein, 1989). For this reason, the chance of a boy falling in love with the girl or boy next door is greater than the chance of falling in love with someone he seldom meets.

mere-exposure effect: The tendency to like a person more if we have been exposed to him or her repeatedly.

Birds of a Feather

We tend to like people who are similar to us. We are attracted to people who are approximately the same as we are in age, ethnicity, background, and economic and social status. Similarity on these social characteristics is referred to as **homophily**, the tendency to have contact with people equal in social status. When a person marries someone with whom they share important characteristics (i.e., with whom they are homophilous), it is called *homogamy*. Table 12.1 displays data on homophily from the National Health and Social Life Survey (NHSLS). Note that the greatest homophily is by race/ethnicity, followed by education and age. In Canada, although this percentage has been increasing, only 3.9 percent of couples are in "mixed unions"; mixed unions refer to relationships in which one member of the couple is from a visible minority group and the other is not, or each member is from a different visible minority group (Milan et al., 2010). Couples are least likely to be the same on religion. It is interesting that short-term partnerships are as homophilous as marriages and common-law relationships. These data take a somewhat liberal view of educational homophily. However, educational homophily has been increasing, and currently 54 percent of Canadian couples have the same educational level (Hou & Myles, 2007). How important is homophily to Canadians? Almost one-half (46 percent) prefer a spouse who shares their religious views, and about a third (34 percent) prefer a spouse who shares their ethnic background (Compas Inc., 2005). One of the reasons for homophily by ethnicity is that persons from ethnocultural minorities have tended to live in socially and economically separate communities. In communities where different racial groups have coexisted for generations, such as Nova Scotia, there tend to be more interracial relationships.

Do opposites really attract?

homophily: The tendency to have contact with people who share our social characteristics.

Social psychologist Donn Byrne (1971) did numerous experiments demonstrating that we are attracted to people whose attitudes and opinions are similar to ours. In these experiments, Byrne typically has people fill out an opinion questionnaire. They are then shown a questionnaire that was supposedly filled out by another person and asked to rate how much they think they would like that person. In fact, the questionnaire was filled out to show either high or low agreement with the participant's responses. Participants report more liking for a person whose responses are similar to theirs than for one whose responses are quite different. The relationship between similarity and liking may also work in the opposite direction. Research in Manitoba showed that the more satisfied that individuals are with their relationship, the more they assume the other person is similar to them (Morry, 2007).

Folk sayings are sometimes wise and sometimes foolish. The interpersonal-attraction research indicates that the saying "Birds of a feather flock together" contains some truth.

Despite the saying that "opposites attract," dissimilar attitudes tend to cause disliking, not liking (Pilkington & Lydon, 1997). Nonetheless, we may be attracted to people whose interpersonal styles are dissimilar to our own. In one study, dominant people paired with submissive people reported greater satisfaction with their relationship than dominant or submissive people paired with a similar partner (Dryer & Horowitz, 1997).

People vary on a large number of characteristics. Perhaps similarity on some is important to attraction and relationship success, while similarity on others is not. Attitudes are one set of characteristics, personality traits are another, and attachment style is another. The research discussed so far argues that similarity in attitudes is important, but similarity in personality is not.

These predictions were tested in research involving newly married mixed-sex couples (Luo & Klohnen, 2005). The average participant was 28 years old, white, fairly well

Table 12.1 Percentage of American Relationships That Are Homophilous, by Type of Relationship

	Type of Relationship			
Type of Homophily	**Marriages**[*]	**Cohabitations**[*]	**Long-Term Partnerships**	**Short-Term Partnerships**
Racial/ethnic	93%	88%	89%	91%
Age[†]	78	75	76	83
Educational[‡]	82	87	83	87
Religious[§]	72	53	56	60

[*] Percentages of marriages and cohabitational relationships that began in the ten years before the survey.

[†] Age homophily is defined as a difference of no more than five years in partners' ages.

[‡] Educational homophily is defined as a difference of no more than one educational category. The educational categories used were less than high school, high school graduate, vocational training, four-year college, and graduate degree.

[§] Cases in which either partner was reported as "other" or had missing data are omitted.

Edward O. Laumann, et al., *The Social Organization of Sexuality: Sexual Practices in the United States*, pp. 82, 98, 177, 305, 458. Copyright © 1994 University of Chicago Press. Reprinted with permission.

educated, and Christian. The researchers calculated couple similarity scores on numerous measures in the three domains. They compared these real-couple scores with the mean scores of randomly paired couples. As predicted, real couples were significantly more similar on values, religiosity, and political attitudes but no more similar than random couples on personality. The NHSLS found that couples are similar in age, race, and education. Could this homophily account for similarity in attitudes? Researchers tried to predict similarity in attitudes and personality from similarity in background characteristics but could not.

Finally, what is the relationship between similarity and quality of relationship? Among these couples, similarity on attachment styles was associated with indicators of marital satisfaction, but similarity in attitudes was not. Perhaps we need to revise the adage to "Birds of a feather (attitudinal similarity) flock, but may not stick, together."

Physical Attractiveness

A great deal of evidence shows that, given a choice of more than one potential partner, gay, lesbian, and straight individuals prefer the one who is more physically attractive (Bailey et al., 1997; Fisher & Cox, 2009; Hendrick & Hendrick, 1992). Research in Ontario has shown this phenomenon in children as young as 3 to 6 years of age; even young children are more attracted to children with attractive faces (Dion, 1973, 1977).

Physical attractiveness is one aspect of sex appeal; in fact, young men and women typically rate physical appearance as most important (Regan, 2004). Other aspects include general body size (measured in various ways) and certain facial features. Much of the research on attractiveness uses data from samples of white persons. One exception is research on the impact of lightness of skin on ratings of attractiveness among African Americans. Skin tone was strongly associated with the attractiveness ratings given female respondents by both male and female interviewers (Hill, 2002). Light skin was rated as more attractive, perhaps reflecting the use of white skin as the standard.

In general, then, we are most attracted to good-looking people. However, among heterosexuals, this effect depends on gender to some extent; physical attractiveness is more important to men evaluating women than it is to women evaluating men (Feingold, 1990). Also, our perception of attractiveness or beauty of another person is influenced by our evaluation of their intelligence, liking, and respect (Kniffin & Wilson, 2004), as well as by our own objective attractiveness (Montoya, 2008). In addition, this phenomenon is somewhat modified by our own feelings of personal worth, as we will discuss later in the chapter. The good news is that although Canadians on average give themselves a 6.7 out of 10 in physical attractiveness, they rate their partner significantly higher, giving their partner an 8.0 out of 10 (Harris/Decima, 2007).

Similar results have been found among gay men and lesbians (Swami, 2009). As a final note, a 2001 Compas survey asked 400 Canadians to choose whether their perfect partner would have an ordinary face and an extraordinary body or an extraordinary face and an ordinary body. Twice as many women as men chose the extraordinary face—57 percent to 29 percent (Anderson, 2001).

The Interpersonal Marketplace

Although this may sound somewhat callous, whom we are attracted to and pair off with depends a lot on how much we think we have to offer and how much we think we can "buy" with it. That is, people seek relationships in which there is equity and both partners receive the same balance of rewards and costs (see Chapter 2 for a discussion of social exchange theory). This tendency for men and women to choose as partners people whose social worth matches their own is called the **matching phenomenon**. Generally, the principle seems to be that women's worth is based on their physical beauty, whereas men's worth is based on their success. There is a tendency, then, for beautiful women to be paired with wealthy, successful men (Figure 12.1).

> **matching phenomenon:** The tendency for men and women to choose as partners people who match them—that is, people who are similar in attitudes, intelligence, and attractiveness.

Figure 12.1 Historically, women's worth has been based on their beauty, whereas men's worth has been based on their success, as exemplified in this photo of the late Hugh Hefner and his young wife.

© WENN Ltd / Alamy Stock Photo

Data from many studies document this phenomenon in mixed-sex relationships. In one study, high school yearbook pictures were rated for attractiveness (Udry & Eckland, 1984). These people were followed up 15 years after graduation, and measures of education, occupational status, and income were obtained. Females rated the most attractive in high school were significantly more likely to have husbands who had high incomes and were highly educated.

Research showing that attractive women marry successful men began in the 1970s when many women did not work, and did not have an occupation or income, and so it seemed as if they were exchanging beauty for money and status. Also, researchers rarely assessed the man's attractiveness. Homophily, of course, would predict that physically attractive people marry each other. By 2010, many men and women each possess physical attractiveness, educational achievement, occupational status, and income. A study of a probability sample of young mixed-sex couples (average age 22 to 23; 500 dating, 500 cohabiting, 500 married) used Add Health data, which contains all of these measures (McClintock, 2014). In fact, for both men and women, the person's physical attractiveness was highly correlated with his/her education, income, and measure of social status. In couples, his/her attractiveness and success was highly correlated with her/his attractiveness and success. Sophisticated analyses of the data provide little support for the idea that either gender exchanges beauty for status. Instead, the results are consistent with the hypothesis that people select mates who match them on these characteristics, and that matching on any one of them will lead to a match on the others.

The question becomes, why is there such a high correlation between a person's physical attractiveness and his/her educational achievement and socio-economic success? A multi-method research project combined analysis of the Add Health data on students in grades 7 to 12 with observations, interviews, and school records from a large high school in Texas (Gordon et al., 2013). The results show that attractiveness in high school is associated with greater social integration and favourable treatment by teachers and classmates. This, in turn, predicts education, work, and mental health outcomes as the person becomes an adult.

From the Laboratory to Real Life

The phenomena discussed so far—feelings of attraction to people who are similar to us and the choosing of partners whose social worth matches our own—have been demonstrated mainly in psychologists' laboratories. Do these phenomena occur in the real world?

perceived similarity: The extent to which an individual believes his or her partner is similar on important characteristics.

With respect to similarity, much of the research has focused on actual similarity. It is relatively easy to do this in the laboratory. We reviewed several studies where researchers measured some characteristic and then paired participants based on (dis)similarity of scores. When we move into the everyday world (the field), researchers generally cannot manipulate degree of similarity, so they measure the existing (dis)similarity among couples of various types and correlate it with various outcomes (e.g., attraction). We cannot draw causal conclusions from such data; for that reason, researchers prefer laboratory work to test the theory. Also, as research on the topic expanded, some suggested that what is important is **perceived similarity**, the extent to which the individual believes his or her partner is similar on important characteristics. This research is usually done in field settings.

A meta-analysis assessed the importance of actual and perceived similarity as measured in laboratory and field settings (Montoya et al., 2008). In addition, researchers coded the amount of interaction participants experienced: no interaction, short interaction (e.g., five to ten minutes), and existing relationship. The results indicated that both actual and perceived similarity are associated with interpersonal attraction; the associations were significant and large. Actual similarity was important in studies involving no or short interaction—that is, in the laboratory—but it was not related to attraction in existing relationships. Perceived similarity was associated with attraction in all three settings. In this case, extending the research into everyday life resulted in an important modification of the theory.

With respect to the matching hypothesis, a series of studies combining data from the laboratory and an online dating site (everyday life) found that the nature and importance of matching varies as relationships develop (Taylor et al., 2011). In predicting whom individuals would choose from a set of potential partners, researchers found that each individual's rating of self-worth predicted the level of physical and social attractiveness of the choice. In predicting whom individuals would communicate with in online dating, matching occurred on popularity rather than physical or social attractiveness. Importantly, as the theory predicts, individuals who rated their self-worth low voluntarily selected less desirable partners. Thus, in a somewhat revised form, the importance of similarity and matching principles apply in everyday life as well as in the psychological laboratory.

Some researchers have investigated the qualities that initially attracted an individual to a person with whom they ultimately formed a romantic relationship. For example, one study asked 120 individuals in same-sex relationships the extent to which a number of qualities had initially attracted them to their partner (Felmlee et al., 2010). Qualities related to agreeableness (e.g., kindness, supportiveness, consideration, understanding) were rated as most important. The least important qualities related to status (e.g., potential for a good job, security, success). Physical attractiveness fell between agreeableness and status. Another important finding was there were no gender differences in ratings of any of these qualities.

Numerous published studies have reported that in everyday life, the type of man that women find attractive is influenced by hormonal fluctuations related to the menstrual cycle. These studies find that near ovulation, women are more likely to prefer men who are of higher genetic quality—masculine (in voice, appearance); dominant (in appearance, reputation), that is "cads"; and healthy—than men who are kind, especially if they are interested in a short-term relationship (i.e., a one-night stand). As a result, they dress in ways that enhance their sex appeal, expose more skin, and choose social events more likely to result in a hook-up around ovulation. Other studies have failed to replicate these results. A meta-analysis (see Chapter 3) identified 45 published studies and 13 unpublished ones (Wood et al., 2014). These studies varied in 1) how they defined where a woman was in relation to her cycle (hormone fluctuation), 2) what masculine traits they measured a preference for and 3) how they measured them, and 4) whether they specified a long-term versus a short-term relationship in the measure. The authors conclude, "Fertile women did not especially desire sex in long-term relationships with men purported to be of higher genetic quality" (p. 229). The effect was not significant in more recent studies or in studies that used precise definitions and measures of the fertile phase.

L02 Attraction Online

Technology has created a new way to meet potential partners: online (Figure 12.2). Indeed, there are now more than 800 different online dating websites (Marsan, 2008). Some websites, such as Toronto-based Lavalife, have more than a million members. Both Lavalife (www .lavalife.ca) and PlentyOfFish (www.pof.com) claim hundreds of thousands of hits per day. There are also ethnocultural-specific dating sites for individuals looking for a partner who is, for example, Jewish, South Asian, or black. Most of these sites also have apps, so now you can get messages right to your phone.

What accounts for the remarkable growth of this phenomenon? According to a Canadian study (Brym & Lenton, 2001), four social forces are at work. First, a growing proportion of the population is single, so more people are looking. Second, career and time pressures lead people to seek more efficient ways to look. Third, single people are highly mobile, increasing the difficulty

of meeting people. Fourth, workplace romance is less acceptable because of concerns about sexual harassment (see Chapter 16).

Online dating has become increasingly common and socially acceptable. There is no longer stigma associated with meeting a partner online, and people feel free to tell their friends and family that they are using online dating (Sritharan et al., 2010; Stephure et al., 2009). Indeed, a recent survey found that, in the United States, 74 percent of the single Internet users looking for a romantic partner had used the Internet to try to meet someone (Madden & Lenhart, 2006). As is the case offline, research in Ontario has shown that physical attractiveness has a strong influence on initial evaluations of potential online partners (Sritharan et al., 2010).

The Internet also provides a mechanism for lesbian, gay, and bisexual individuals to meet people who share their sexual orientation. This is particularly important for youth or individuals in small communities who choose not to be open about their sexual orientation or do not want to risk experiencing rejection from an offline potential partner. Indeed, gay men and lesbians of all ages are more likely than heterosexuals are to meet and form an offline relationship with someone they met online (Lever et al., 2008). In addition, the Internet allows individuals who have specific sexual interests, such as bondage and discipline (see Chapter 15), to meet romantic partners who share their sexual interests rather than risk rejection.

Surveys suggest that the people seeking partners online are educated, affluent, 20- to 40-year-olds who do not have the time or the taste for "singles bars." Telephone interviews in 2005 with a sample of adults found that 11 percent of Internet users had visited an online

Figure 12.2 Technology has created a new way to meet potential partners: online.

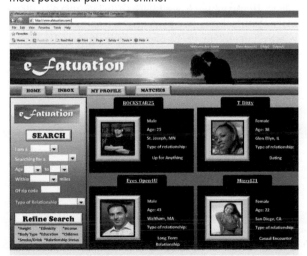

dating site. Homophily may come into play here if people choose to visit a website specifically for people who share their ethnocultural background.

Advantages and Disadvantages of Online Dating

Users say that one advantage of meeting online is that the technology forces you to focus on the person's interests and values. This focus may facilitate finding a person with whom you have a lot in common; however, individuals who are in relationships that started online report lower relational intimacy than those who are in relationships that started face to face (Scott et al., 2006). Online, you do not have access to body language, facial expressions, posture, and other cues that provide information. As a result, imagination heavily influences impressions, which can create a powerful attraction to the other (Ben-Ze'ev, 2004).

The relative lack of (reliable) information about the person you are chatting or exchanging e-mails with is the downside of meeting online. She or he may not be all they claim to be or how you imagine the person in your mind. In fact, research suggests that one-quarter of Canadian online daters admit to having misrepresented themselves online (Brym & Lenton, 2001). Kaufmann (2012) analyzed love online by studying blog posts of men and women about their experiences. (We have little information about the sample; as computer users, they are probably younger, better educated, and white.) He found that the appeal of online dating was the hundreds of prospects available with a few clicks, giving the user a great sense of control. However, he also found that if you arrange a date, anything can happen; you have doubts about whether to go. The person doesn't show up. Disillusionment occurs at first glance; the person doesn't match the photo, the description, or your fantasy. The person has annoying habits, bad body odour, or poor manners. The person talks incessantly about exes. Indecision about kissing or going to one of your places ruins the date. Mediocre or disastrous sex takes place. You feel like you paid or were paid for sex. (This is especially likely after an expensive dinner.) The result according to Kaufmann? Most of those first dates are last dates. Kaufmann argues that this tremendous variety of outcomes, including many that neither party wanted, reflects the lack of scripts for these dates. In part, the lack of scripts reflects the newness of the phenomenon, but in part it reflects the difficulty of devising scripts for diverse types of users with diverse types of motives.

How do Internet dating sites match people?

The "Science" of Online Dating

In recent years, online dating sites have enlisted the help of researchers in developing a "scientific" approach to pairing clients (Gottlieb, 2006). The most renowned is eHarmony, thanks to its outgoing founder, Neil Clark Warren. Similar sites include Chemistry.com, whose chief adviser is sociobiologist Helen Fisher, and PerfectMatch.com, whose system was developed by Dr. Pepper Schwartz, a sociologist. Each site uses clients' responses to an online questionnaire to match them.

How do they differ? Each site has its own matching strategy. Following the research on attraction, eHarmony uses a 436-question survey to assess a broad range of attitude, value, and personality domains. Couples are matched based on relative similarity on each domain. Chemistry.com focuses on pairing adults who will experience a "spark" when they meet. Fisher argues that testosterone, dopamine, oxytocin, and vasopressin are the basis of romance (Fisher et al., 2006). Genes associated with these hormones are associated with traits such as calmness, popularity, rationality, and sympathy. Chemistry.com uses a 146-item survey to measure these traits and infers the clients' "chemistry."

PerfectMatch.com uses the Duet system, based on 48 questions assessing eight domains. Schwartz believes that a well-matched couple should be similar on romantic impulsivity, personal energy, outlook, and predictability, and different on flexibility, decision-making style, emotionality, and self-nurturing style. What do you think?

How successful are Internet dating sites at helping people form long-term relationships? First, in one study of Canadian online daters, only two-thirds of people using online dating services met even one person face to face. Of those who did meet someone face to face, 27 percent formed a romantic relationship with a person they met online, but only 3 percent had married someone they met online (Brym & Lenton, 2001). Several researchers assessed online dating from the perspective of relationship science and considered the degree to which online dating algorithms and practices fit with what we know scientifically (Finkel et al., 2012). Online dating sites claim to produce outcomes superior to traditional methods of meeting, dating, and developing a committed relationship; is that likely? Research over the past 40 years has identified three classes of influence on relationship success: personal characteristics, individual change, and external, uncontrollable events (e.g., unemployment, infertility, chronic illness, natural disasters). Online dating sites can measure and provide information only about variables in the first group. Research indicates that variables in that category account for only a small part of the long-term outcome. Bottom line? Claims by these sites to produce superior outcomes are impossible to justify. If a long-term intimate relationship is your goal, online dating is not more likely to get you there.

Explaining Our Preferences

The research data are quite consistent in showing that we select as potential partners people who are similar to us in social characteristics—age, race, education—and who share our attitudes and beliefs. Moreover, both men and women prefer physically attractive people, although heterosexual women place greater emphasis on a man's social status or earning potential (Sprecher et al., 1994). The obvious question is, Why? Two answers are suggested, one drawing on reinforcement theory and one drawing on sociobiology (see Chapter 2 for discussions of these theories).

Reinforcement Theory: Byrne's Law of Attraction

A rather common-sense idea—and one that psychologists agree with—is that we tend to like people who give us reinforcements or rewards and to dislike people who give us punishments (Figure 12.3). Social psychologist Donn Byrne (1997) formulated the law of attraction. It says that our attraction to another person is proportionate to the number of reinforcements that person gives us relative to the total number of reinforcements plus punishments the person gives us. Or, simplified even more, we like people who are frequently nice to us and seldom nasty.

According to this explanation, most people prefer to interact with people who are similar to them because interaction with them is rewarding. People who are similar in age, ethnic background, and education are likely to have similar outlooks on life, prefer similar activities, and like the same kinds of people. These shared values and beliefs provide the basis for smooth and rewarding interaction. It will be easy to agree about such things as how important schoolwork is, what TV programs to watch, and what to do on Friday night. Disagreement about such things would cause conflict and hostility, which are definitely not rewards (for most people, anyway). We prefer pretty or handsome partners because

Figure 12.3 According to Byrne's law of attraction, our liking for a person is influenced by the reinforcements we receive from interacting with them. Shared activities provide the basis for smooth and rewarding interaction.

© Fuse/Getty Images

we are aware of the high value placed on physical attractiveness in Canadian society; we believe others will have a higher opinion of us if we have a good-looking partner. Finally, we prefer someone with high social status or earning potential because all the material things that people find rewarding cost money.

These findings have some practical implications (Hatfield & Walster, 1978). If you are trying to get a new relationship going well, make sure you give the other person lots of positive reinforcement. Also, make sure that you have some good times together so that you *associate* each other with rewards. Do not spend all your time stripping paint off old furniture or cleaning out the garage. And do not forget to keep the positive reinforcements (or "strokes," if you like that jargon better) going in an old, stable relationship.

A variation of the reinforcement view comes from the implicit egotism perspective (Jones et al., 2004). It states that we are attracted to persons who are similar to us because they activate our positive views of ourselves. For example, archival research found that men and women are more likely to marry people whose names resemble their own.

Sociobiology: Sexual Strategies Theory

Sociobiologists view sexual behaviour within an evolutionary perspective and thus focus on heterosexual relationships. Historically, the function of mating has been reproduction. Men and women who selected mates according to some preferences were more successful than those who chose them based on other preferences. The successful ones produced more offspring, who in turn produced more offspring, carrying their mating preferences to the present.

Men and women face different adaptive problems in their efforts to reproduce (Buss & Schmitt, 1993). Since women bear the offspring, men need to identify reproductively valuable women. Other things being equal, younger women are more likely to be fertile than older women—hence heterosexual men's preference for young women. Also, sociobiologists assert that men want to be certain about the paternity of offspring; hence, they want a woman who will be sexually faithful.

Sociobiologists argue that, other things being equal, a physically attractive person is more likely to be healthy and fertile than someone who is not physically attractive—thus the preference for good-looking partners. If attractiveness is an indicator of health, we would expect it to be more important in societies where chronic diseases are more prevalent. Gangestad and Buss (1993) measured the prevalence of seven pathogens, including those that cause malaria and leprosy, in 29 cultures and also obtained ratings of the importance of 18 attributes of mates. They found that physical attractiveness was considered more important by residents in societies that had a greater prevalence of pathogens. However, one study found that there was no relationship between rated facial attractiveness (based on a photograph) and a clinical assessment of health in a sample of adolescents, suggesting that the assumed link between attractiveness and health is not there. At the same time, the raters ranked more attractive persons as healthier (Kalick et al., 1998).

Some evolutionary analysts have argued that the critical feature of an attractive face is symmetry, having features on one side of the nose that are mirror images of features on the other side. **Fluctuating asymmetry**, asymmetry of bilateral features that are on average symmetrical in the population, are said to reflect developmental instability (DI), the inability of the developing body to buffer itself against random perturbations (Van Dongen & Gangestad, 2011). Visible asymmetry in the face would reflect DI, which could have caused other anomalies that could impair reproductive success. Thus, attractiveness might be an important indicator of fertility, fetal survival, and normal growth. There have been dozens of studies of the relationship between symmetry and numerous features, including measures of health, fetal outcomes, hormonal functioning, facial attractiveness, and reproduction (number of sexual partners). They indicate that the correlation between symmetry and health and fitness is small (Van Dongen & Gangestad, 2011).

Women must make a much greater personal investment than men to reproduce. They will be pregnant for nine months, and after the birth they must care for the infant and young child for many years. Thus, women want to select as mates men who are reproductively valuable—hence the preference for good-looking mates. They also want mates who are able and willing to invest resources in them and their children. Obviously, men must have resources to invest them, so women prefer men with higher incomes and status. Among young people, women will prefer men with greater earning potential—thus, the preference for men with greater education and higher occupational aspirations. The matter of resources is more important than the problem of identifying a reproductively valuable male, so women rate income and earning potential as more important than good looks.

Note that these arguments assume that women have limited access to resources, forcing their reliance on men. But today, women are increasingly working and controlling their own earnings. These women may place less emphasis on a man's resources in selecting a mate. Analysis of survey data from women ages 18 to 35 (44 percent in a relationship) found that wealthier women prefer older men, and resource control predicted a preference for physical attractiveness over financial prospects (Moore et al., 2006). In effect, wealthier women have more to offer in the relationship marketplace.

Sexual strategies theory asserts that gender differences in mate preferences reflect genetic predispositions based on universal biological roles of men and women in reproduction. An alternative view is that preferences reflect current sex roles in a specific culture. In cultures where women are forced to rely on men for resources and protection, the roles and, therefore, preferences will be differentiated. In cultures where there is equal access to resources and gender equity, the sex role perspective suggested that gender differences in preferences will be weakened or disappear. To test this hypothesis, an online questionnaire assessed the preferences of more than 2000 women and 1000 men from ten nations for eight characteristics used in prior research that found differences. The Global Gender Gap Index (developed by the World Economic Forum) provided the measure of gender equity for each country. The ten countries included three with low gender parity, three with medium parity, and four with high parity. The results indicated that gender differences in mate preferences declined as gender parity increased (Zentner & Mitura, 2012).

These two explanations—reinforcement theory and sociobiology—are not inconsistent. We can think about reinforcement in more general terms. Reproduction is a major goal for most adults in every society. Successful reproduction—that is, having a healthy child who develops normally—is very reinforcing. Following the sexual strategies that we have inherited is likely to lead to such reinforcement. Of course, sexual strategies theory is not a good explanation for same-sex attraction.

L03

Intimacy

What is intimacy? Intimacy is a major component of any close or romantic relationship. Today, many people are seeking to increase the intimacy in their relationships. And so, in this section we will explore intimacy in more detail to try to gain a better understanding of it.

Kaufmann (2012), in his analysis of love online, suggests that many online daters are searching for a long-term intimate relationship. Intimate relationships are important to us for two reasons. The first is the desire to someday have children and the awareness that raising a child is a lot easier with two people. The other is to obtain the benefits of mutual trust and reciprocal recognition by another person. This benefit is increasingly important in an impersonal and sometimes cruel world that is very stressful for some people. Indeed, stress

fluctuating asymmetry: Asymmetry of bilateral features that are on average symmetrical in the population.

researchers have long recognized the need for interpersonal support to successfully cope with stress.

Defining Intimacy

Psychologists have offered a number of definitions of intimacy. For example, Perlman and Fehr (1987) propose that the defining features of intimacy include "openness, honesty, mutual self-disclosure; caring, warmth, protecting, helping; being devoted to each other, mutually attentive, mutually committed; surrendering control, dropping defenses; becoming emotional, feeling distressed when separation occurs" (p. 17). Prager (1997) expanded on this definition by making a distinction between intimate interactions and intimate relationships.

Intimate interactions include both intimate experiences and intimate behaviours. **Intimate experiences** are the meaning a person gives to their interactions with another person. Intimate experiences are usually associated with positive emotions. For example, you might perceive meeting your partner's family as an intimate experience because it symbolizes your partner's desire to include you in his or her life. Intimate behaviours are more concrete than intimate experiences. Intimate behaviours can be nonverbal, and include behaviours such as eye contact, smiling, physical closeness, or sexual activity. However, the most common type of intimate behaviour is verbal self-disclosure, which includes the sharing of information about one's self with a partner. Self-disclosure is discussed in more detail in the next section.

As you interact with an individual over time, you may develop an intimate relationship. **Intimate relationships** are the result of many intimate interactions with an individual and are typically characterized by love, affection, trust, sharing, and reciprocity. However, intimate interactions can also occur outside the context of an intimate relationship. For example, it is possible to disclose your feelings to a stranger without having an intimate relationship with that person.

Another definition of **intimacy** in romantic relationships is "the level of commitment and positive affective, cognitive, and physical closeness one experiences with a partner in a reciprocal (although not necessarily symmetrical) relationship" (Moss & Schwebel, 1993, p. 33). The emphasis in this definition is on closeness or sharing (intimate behaviour) and on partner responsiveness, which has three dimensions—affective (emotional), cognitive, and physical. Note, too, that whereas intimacy must be reciprocal, it need not be equal. Many people have had the experience of feeling closer to another person than that person seems to feel toward them. Finally, note that although intimacy has a physical dimension, it need not be sexual. Interestingly, although Canadians of European descent and those of Asian descent both conceptualize intimacy in this way, the Asian-Canadian

daters reported significantly less intimacy in their relationships (Marshall, 2008). This is problematic because, for both groups, lower intimacy was related to a higher likelihood that the relationship would end.

> **How important is emotional intimacy in relationships?**

In one study, university students were asked to respond to an open-ended question asking what they thought made a relationship one of intimacy (Roscoe et al., 1987). The qualities that emerged, with great agreement, were sharing, sexual interaction, trust in the partner, and openness. Notice that these qualities are quite similar to the ones listed in the definitions just given.

Intimacy and Self-Disclosure

One of the key characteristics of intimacy appearing in psychologists' and university students' definitions is self-disclosure (Prager, 1997). **Self-disclosure** involves telling your partner personal things about yourself. It may range from telling your partner about something embarrassing that happened to you at work today, to disclosing a very meaningful event that happened between you and your parents 15 years ago, to sharing your innermost thoughts, feelings, and fantasies. Note that self-disclosure does not mean that partners should be saying anything they want to each other without consideration for the other person's feelings. As discussed in the section on communication, even in an open and self-disclosing relationship, it is important that people censor some (not all) thoughts and feelings that would be deliberately hurtful to their partner.

Research consistently shows that self-disclosure leads to reciprocity (Berg & Derlega, 1987; Hendrick & Hendrick, 1992). In other words, if one member of the couple self-discloses, this act seems to prompt the other partner to self-disclose also. Self-disclosure by one member of the couple can essentially get the ball rolling.

Why does this occur? Psychologists have proposed a number of reasons (Hendrick & Hendrick, 1992). First, disclosure by our partner may make us like and trust that person more. Second, as social learning theorists would argue, simple modelling and imitation may occur. That is, one partner's self-disclosing serves as a model for the other partner. Norms of equity may also be involved (see Chapter 11 for a discussion of equity theory). After one partner has self-disclosed, the other person may follow suit to maintain a sense of balance or equity in the relationship.

intimate experiences: The meaning a person gives to their interactions with another person.

intimate relationships: Relationships in which intimate interactions occur on a regular and predictable basis; relationships characterized by affection between partners, mutual trust, and partner cohesiveness.

intimacy: A quality of relationships characterized by commitment, feelings of closeness and trust, and self-disclosure.

self-disclosure: Telling personal things about yourself.

Self-disclosure relates closely to satisfaction with the overall relationship and, as discussed later in the chapter, with the sexual aspects of the relationship. That is, couples that engage in more self-disclosure are more satisfied with their relationship (MacNeil & Byers, 2005, 2009). Patterns of self-disclosure can actually predict whether a couple stays together or breaks up. Research in which couples are followed for periods ranging from two months to four years shows that the greater the self-disclosure, the greater the likelihood that the relationship will continue, and the less the self-disclosure, the greater the likelihood of breakup (Hendrick et al., 1988; Sprecher, 1987).

Self-disclosure promotes intimacy in a relationship and makes us feel close to the other person. It also is important for the partner to be accepting in response to self-disclosure. If the acceptance is missing, we can feel betrayed or threatened, and we certainly will not feel on more intimate terms with the partner.

A study of naturally occurring interactions examined the relationships between self-disclosure, perceived partner disclosure, and the degree of intimacy experienced (Laurenceau et al., 1998). Young people recorded data about every interaction lasting more than 10 minutes, for 7 or 14 days. Data were analyzed for more than 4000 dyadic (that is, two-person) interactions recorded by 158 participants. Both self-disclosure and partner disclosure were associated with the participant's rating of the intimacy of the interaction. Self-disclosure of emotion was more closely related to intimacy than was self-disclosure of facts.

Self-disclosure and intimacy, then, mutually build on each other (Figure 12.4). Self-disclosure promotes our feeling that the relationship is intimate, and when we feel that it is, we feel comfortable engaging in further self-disclosure. However, self-disclosure and intimacy do not necessarily increase consistently over time. In some

relationships, the pattern may be that an increase in intimacy is followed by a plateau or even a pulling back (Collins & Miller, 1994).

Self-disclosure of personal attitudes, experiences, and motives increases one's vulnerability. There is a risk that the partner will evaluate you negatively for disclosing some information or past behaviours. People who are anxious about how others evaluate them may engage in less self-disclosure or avoid it all together. According to the ideas laid out above, this should reduce intimacy. Other research finds that greater intimacy is associated with greater relationship and sexual satisfaction. Research testing these relationships analyzed data from 105 undergraduate, mixed-sex couples who had been in a committed relationship for at least three months (Montesi et al., 2013). Participants earning high scores on a social anxiety scale reported difficulty communicating openly about sex, which in turn predicted sexual dissatisfaction.

Measuring Intimacy

Psychologists have developed some scales for measuring intimacy that can give us further insights. One such scale is the Personal Assessment of Intimacy in Relationships (PAIR) Inventory (Schaefer & Olson, 1981). It measures emotional intimacy in a relationship by using items such as the following:

1. My partner listens to me when I need someone to talk to.
2. My partner really understands my hurts and joys.

Another scale measuring intimacy in a relationship includes items such as these (Miller & Lefcourt, 1982):

1. How often do you confide very personal information to him or her?
2. How often are you able to understand his or her feelings?
3. How often do you feel close to him or her?
4. How important is your relationship with him or her in your life?

If you are currently in a relationship, answer these questions for yourself and consider what the quality of the intimacy is in your relationship.

In summary, an intimate relationship is characterized by commitment, feelings of closeness and understanding, and self-disclosure. We can promote intimacy in our relationships by engaging in self-disclosure and being accepting of the other person's self-disclosure. However, we are unlikely to be willing to self-disclose unless we trust our partner.

Figure 12.4 Intimacy occurs in a relationship when there is warmth and mutual self-disclosure.

© Thinkstock

LO4

Theories of Love

At the beginning of this chapter, we noted that there is a connection between love and sex in our society. In everyday life and in theories of love, this connection lies along a continuum (Hendrick & Hendrick, 2004). At one end are *hookups*, short-term sexual relationships on a Saturday night, spring break, or a singles cruise, with little romance (Grello et al., 2006; Lambert et al., 2003; Maticka-Tyndale et al., 2003). In theories of love, this is the "love is really sex" view found, for example, in evolutionary theory. At the other end are romantic love relationships in which sex is nonexistent or incidental, as for example in a nonsexual affair. In theories, this is the view found, for example, in the theory of love as a story. Toward the middle is the "sex is really love" view, as in the theory of passionate love. In the centre is a relationship that balances the two and theories that recognize both, such as the triangular theory.

In the following sections, we will consider four views of love: the triangular theory, the attachment theory, the love-as-a-story perspective, and the theory of passionate love. We also consider the neuroanatomy and neurochemistry of love.

Triangular Theory of Love

Robert Sternberg (1986) has formulated a triangular theory of the nature of love. According to his theory, love has three fundamental components: intimacy, passion, and commitment. He calls it a triangular theory because he depicts these three components graphically in a love triangle.[1] As shown in Figure 12.5, the top point is intimacy, the left point is passion, and the right point is decision or commitment.

Three Components of Love

Intimacy is the emotional component of love. It includes our feelings of closeness or bondedness to the other person. The feeling of intimacy usually involves a sense of mutual understanding with the loved one; a sense of sharing one's self; intimate communication with the loved one, involving a sense of having the loved one hear and accept what is shared; and giving and receiving emotional support to and from the loved one. Intimacy, of course, is present in many relationships besides romantic ones. Intimacy here is definitely not a euphemism for sex (as when someone asks, "Have you been intimate with

Figure 12.5 The triangle in Sternberg's triangular theory of love.

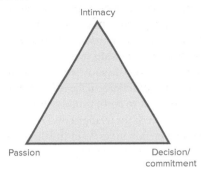

him?"). The kind of emotional closeness involved in intimacy may be found between best friends and between parents and children, just as it is between lovers.

Passion is the motivational component of love. It includes physical attraction and the drive for sexual expression. Physiological arousal is an important part of passion. Passion is the component that differentiates romantic love from other kinds of love, such as the love of best friends or the love between parents and children. Passion is generally the component of love that is faster to arouse, but in a long-term relationship, it is also the component that fades most quickly.

Intimacy and passion are often closely intertwined. In some cases passion comes first, when a couple experiences an initial, powerful physical attraction to each other; emotional intimacy may then follow. In other cases, people know each other only casually, but as emotional intimacy develops, passion follows. Of course, there are also cases where intimacy and passion are completely separate. For example, in cases of casual sex, passion is present but intimacy is not.

Decision or commitment is the third component and is the cognitive component. This component actually has two aspects. The short-term aspect is the decision that one loves the other person. The long-term aspect is the commitment to maintain that relationship. Commitment is what makes relationships last. Passion comes and goes. All relationships have their better times and their worse times, their ups and their downs. When the words of the traditional marriage ceremony ask whether a person promises to love his or her partner "for better or for worse," the answer "I do" is the promise of commitment.

The Triangular Theory

According to Sternberg, people who have high levels of all three components—intimacy, passion, and commitment—experience consummate love. What term would you use to describe a person who only experiences commitment and intimacy, for example, but not passion? What about someone who has high commitment but low intimacy and passion?

---

[1] This terminology should not be confused with the popular use of the term *love triangle* , which occurs when three people are involved in love, but the love is not reciprocated, and things don't work out quite right. For example, A loves B, B loves C, and C loves A, but A doesn't love C and B doesn't love A. Alas.

Sternberg's (1986) triangle metaphor allows us to show how the two people in a couple can be well matched or mismatched in the love they feel for each other. Sternberg's research indicates that when there is a good "match" between the two partners' love, both tend to feel satisfied with the relationship. When there is a mismatch in the triangles, they feel dissatisfied with the relationship.

Thinking about practical applications of the theory, if a relationship seems to be in trouble, it may be because there is a mismatch of the triangles. We could analyze the love in the relationship in terms of the three components (intimacy, passion, and commitment) to see where the partners are mismatched. It could be that they are well matched for passion but that one feels and wants more intimacy or commitment than the other person does.

Sternberg also argues that each of the three components of love must be translated into action. The intimacy component is expressed in actions such as communicating personal feelings and information, offering emotional (and perhaps financial) support, and expressing empathy for the other. The passion component is expressed in actions, such as kissing, touching, and making love. The decision or commitment component is demonstrated by actions such as saying "I love you," getting married, and sticking with a relationship through times when it is not particularly convenient.

Evidence for Sternberg's Triangular Theory of Love

What kind of support is there for Sternberg's theory? Sternberg has developed a questionnaire, the Sternberg Triangular Love Scale (STLS), to measure the three components in his theory. Several studies have been done on the characteristics of the scale itself (e.g., Sternberg, 1987, 1997; Whitley, 1993). The scale provides good measures of the components, especially of passion and commitment. Scores for the same relationship are stable for up to two months.

Sternberg makes several predictions about how scores ought to change over time. Acker and Davis (1992) recruited 204 adults, ages 18 to 68; 65 percent were married. The average length of the relationship was 9.5 years. As predicted, commitment scores increased as relationships progressed from dating to marriage. Sternberg expects intimacy behaviours to decrease over time as familiarity with the partner increases; sure enough, behavioural intimacy (sharing inner feelings, trying to understand the partner) decreased as predicted. Similar results were reported in a study of 446 people who were casually dating, exclusively dating, engaged, or married (Lemieux & Hale, 2002). A study of a sample of German adults assessed the relationship between the three components and sexual activity and satisfaction (Grau & Kimpf, 1993). The theory predicts that the amount of passion should be most closely related to sexual activity, but the results indicated that intimacy was most closely related to sexual behaviour and sexual satisfaction.

Qualitative research also provides support for the theory. In-depth interviews with eight heterosexual women focused on what they considered important and positive aspects of romantic love. The women identified intimacy, passion, and commitment (Schafer, 2008).

Attachment Theory of Love

In Chapter 10 we discussed the earliest attachment that humans experience, the attachment between infant and parent. One hypothesis is that the quality of this early attachment—whether secure and pleasant or insecure and unpleasant—profoundly affects us for the rest of our lives, and particularly affects our capacity to form loving attachments to others when we are adults.

The *attachment theory of love* is based on these ideas (Hazaen & Shaver, 1987; Simpson, 1990). According to the most recent formulation proposed by British Columbia psychologist Kim Bartholomew, adults are characterized in their romantic relationships by one of four attachment styles (Bartholomew & Horowitz, 1991). These attachment styles are based on our perceptions of ourselves and on our expectations of how others will respond to us. As shown in Figure 12.6, we either see ourselves in a positive way as worthy of love and support, or we see ourselves in a negative way, as unworthy of love. People with a positive model of self are self-confident; people with a negative model of self are anxious about relationships. Similarly, either we see other people in a positive way as trustworthy and available, or we see them in a negative way as unreliable and rejecting. People with a positive model of others seek others out; people with a negative model of others avoid intimacy.

Secure lovers have a sense of their own lovability and the expectation that other people are generally accepting and responsive. *Preoccupied lovers* have a sense of their own unlovability but a positive evaluation of other people. They try to achieve self-acceptance by gaining the acceptance of people they value. They want desperately to get close to a partner but are so worried that the partner does not love them that they may scare them away. *Fearful lovers* have a negative expectation of both themselves and other people. They expect to be rejected by others and avoid romantic relationships. They are uncomfortable feeling close to, trusting, or depending on another person or having that person feel close to them. Finally, *dismissing lovers* feel themselves to be worthy of love but have negative views of other people. These people may protect themselves against disappointment by avoiding close relationships and maintaining a sense of independence.

Dismissing and fearful lovers are similar in that both avoid intimacy. Preoccupied and fearful lovers are alike in that both depend on acceptance from others to feel good about themselves. Research shows that about 49 percent of adults have a secure attachment style, 12 percent a preoccupied style, 21 percent a fearful style, and 18 percent a dismissing style (Bartholomew & Horowitz, 1991). The research also shows that separation from parents in childhood—perhaps because of divorce or death—is not related to adult attachment styles (Hazaen & Shaver, 1987). That is, children of divorced parents are no more or less likely to be secure lovers than are children from intact marriages (a finding that is probably fortunate, given the high divorce rate in Canada). What does predict adult attachment style is the person's perception of the *quality* of the relationship with each parent. The quality of friendships in childhood and adolescence also affects adult attachment styles. For example, research using a sample of 191 gay and bisexual men in Vancouver found that both the quality of parental relationships (particularly relationships with fathers) and the quality of peer relationships were associated with adult attachment style (Landott et al., 2004).

Longitudinal research has identified pathways by which attachment in early life relates to adult attachment styles and relationships. A longitudinal study of 707 children from birth through age 18 found that the quality of caregiving in childhood, social competence as rated by mothers and teachers, and quality of best friendship were related to differences in attachment style at age 18 (Fraley et al., 2013). Another study found that children identified as securely attached at 12 months were rated more socially competent by teachers in elementary school. Social competence predicted more secure friendships at age 16, which in turn predicted more positive daily emotional experiences in relationships at ages 20 to 23 (as reported by self and partner) (Simpson et al., 2007).

This research has important implications. First, it helps us understand that adults bring to any particular romantic relationship their own personal history of love and attachment. The forces of that personal history can be strong, and one good and loving partner may not be able to change a dismissing lover into a secure lover. This does not mean that people who have insecure attachment relationships with their parents cannot have a secure attachment relationship with their romantic partner. Research in New Brunswick has shown that although many people form a particular type of attachment relationship with all the important people in their lives, some people with insecure attachment relationships with family have secure attachment relationships with their romantic partner (Caron et al., 2012; Ross & Spinner, 2001). This is sometimes called *earned-secure attachment*. Second, it helps us understand that conflict in some relationships may be caused by a mismatch of attachment styles. A secure lover who wants a close, intimate relationship is likely to feel frustrated

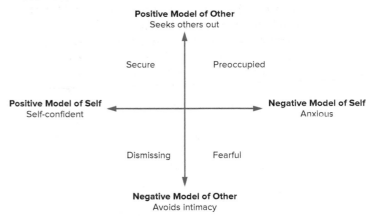

Figure 12.6   Bartholomew's four-category, two-dimensional model of adult attachment.

Source: Henderson et al., 2005.

and dissatisfied with a dismissing or fearful lover who is uncomfortable with feeling close. Attachment theory suggests that an important form of similarity is similarity in attachment style (Latty-Mann & Davis, 1996). Third, this theory provides some explanation for jealousy (see Milestones in Sex Research), which is most common among preoccupied lovers (although present among the others) because of their early experience of feeling anxious about their attachment to their parents. Finally, attachment style may help to explain high-risk sexual behaviour. Research in Ontario showed that women who have insecure attachment styles tend to engage in sexual intercourse at a younger age and have more sexual partners than do women with secure attachment styles (Bogaert & Sadava, 2002). Similarly, researchers in Quebec found that adolescents and young adults with insecure attachment engaged in more risky sexual behaviour (Lemelin et al., 2014).

Attachment style affects relationships by affecting the way the partners interact. A study of 128 established couples (average length of relationship 47 months) assessed attachment style, patterns of accommodation, and satisfaction with the relationship (Scharfe & Bartholomew, 1995). Individuals with a secure attachment reported responding constructively to potentially destructive behaviour by the partner, for example, with efforts to discuss and resolve the problem. People who were fearful of attachment to another responded with avoidance or withdrawal. This may affect relationship satisfaction. Research in Nova Scotia has shown that when individuals with an avoidant attachment style enter into new relationships, they expect that their partner will not engage in behaviours that signify commitment (e.g., honesty, spending more time together) and will engage in behaviours that signify the absence of commitment (e.g., infidelity, unequal give and take). This expectation leads them to assume the relationship will end (Birnie et al., 2009). A longitudinal study of university students

Milestones in Sex Research

What Is Jealousy? L05

Jealousy—the green-eyed monster—is an unpleasant emotion often associated with romantic and sexual relationships. Intense cases of jealousy may result in violence, including partner abuse, assault, and homicide. As a result, it has been the focus of considerable scholarly work. Several perspectives contribute to our understanding of this emotion.

Jealousy is a cognitive, emotional, and behavioural response to a threat to an interpersonal relationship (Guerrero et al., 2004). The cognitive appraisal perspective suggests that jealousy occurs when an individual *interprets* some stimulus as representing a threat to a valued relationship; in reality, there may or may not be a threat to the relationship. A variety of behaviours by the partner may be interpreted as a threat; in one study, individuals in dating relationships said that having their partner just spend time with another person was one of the top three acts of betrayal (Roscoe et al., 1988). Interaction with someone via the Internet, behaviour or remarks by third parties, or coming home late may arouse suspicion and elicit jealousy from a partner.

✳Two types of jealousy may occur together or separately: emotional and sexual. *Emotional jealousy* occurs when one person believes or knows that the partner is emotionally attached to or in love with another. *Sexual jealousy* occurs when the person believes or knows that the partner wants to engage in or has engaged in sexual intimacy with another. These two can occur together or separately. A study of heterosexual and sexual minority adults found that although

> **Why do people get jealous?**

both women and men are concerned about both types of infidelity, they are more concerned about the emotional infidelity of a partner (Harris, 2002). Which would concern you more, emotional infidelity or sexual infidelity?

Psychologists Gregory White and Paul Mullen (1989) see jealousy as a constellation including thoughts, emotions, and actions. Two situations, according to their research, activate jealousy. One occurs when there is a threat to our self-esteem. In a good relationship, our romantic partner helps us feel good about ourselves—makes us feel attractive or fun to be with, for example. If a rival appears and our partner shows interest, we may think things like "He finds her more attractive than me" or "She finds him more fun to be with than me." We then feel less attractive or less fun to be with—that is, our self-esteem is threatened. Two experiments report evidence that support the hypothesis that it is threats to the self that cause jealousy (DeSteno et al., 2006).

The second situation that activates jealousy is a threat to the relationship (Figure 12.7). If a rival appears on the scene, we may fear that our partner will separate from us and form a new relationship with the rival. Jealousy is activated because of our negative thoughts and feelings about the loss of a relationship that has been good for us and the loss of all the pleasant things that go along with that relationship, such as companionship and sex.

According to White and Mullen (1989), we go through several stages in the jealousy response, sometimes very quickly. The first is cognitive, in which we make an initial appraisal of the situation and find that there is a threat to our self-esteem or to the relationship. Next we experience

---

in Ontario showed that, over a four-month period, participants with a secure attachment style did not change their feelings about the relationship. In contrast, participants with one of the insecure attachment styles reported lower levels of satisfaction and commitment over time (Keelan et al., 1994).

Research in Ontario and Quebec has shown that when either partner in a couple has an avoidant attachment style, the partners engage in sex less frequently and have lower sexual satisfaction (Brassard et al., 2007; Butzer & Campbell, 2008). Researchers in Quebec have shown

that having an insecure attachment style is related to lower sexual satisfaction, lower sexual self-esteem, more sexual problems, and higher sexual anxiety for the individual and/or their partner (Brassard et al., 2015; Péloquin et al., 2013, 2014). This happens because insecure attachment interferes with effective sexual communication, which, in turn, negatively affects sexual satisfaction (Davis et al., 2006). However, perceptions that one's partner is supportive may counter some of the negative effects of insecure attachment (Péloquin et al., 2014). Individuals with avoidant attachment styles are also

an emotional reaction that in itself has two phases. The first is a rapid stress response, the "jealous flash." To use the terminology of the two-component theory of love discussed later in this chapter, this stress response is the physiological component of the jealous emotion. The second phase of emotional response occurs as we reappraise the situation and decide how to cope with it. In the reappraisal stage, we may shift from seeing the situation as a threat to seeing it as a challenge, for example. The intense initial emotions quiet down and may be replaced by feelings of moodiness.

Attempts to cope with jealousy lead to a variety of behaviours. Some of these are constructive, such as effective communication with one's partner. Such communication may lead to an evaluation of the relationship and attempts to change some of the problematic aspects of it. If the problems seem sufficiently serious, a couple may seek help from a mediator or therapist. Other behavioural responses to jealousy are destructive. The threat to one's self-esteem may lead to depression, substance abuse, or suicide. Aggression may be directed at the partner, the third person, or both, and may result in physical or sexual abuse or even murder.

Research suggests that a person's attachment style may be an important influence on how he or she responds to jealousy (Sharpstein & Kirkpatrick, 1997). Undergraduates were asked how they had reacted in the past to jealousy. Those with a secure attachment style reported that they had expressed their anger to the partner and maintained the relationship. Those with a preoccupied or anxious style reported the most intense anger, but they were most likely to say they did not express that anger. People with a fearful or avoidant style were more likely to direct their anger toward the third person. More recent research suggests that people with a preoccupied attachment style

Figure 12.7 One situation that activates jealousy is a perceived threat to the relationship.

© Digital Vision RF

are most likely to be angry and vengeful in response to a relationship breakup (Davis et al., 2003).

Sources: Fisher, 1992; Guerrero et al., 2004; Reiss, 1986; White & Mullen, 1989.

more likely to engage in extradyadic sexual activity (Frías et al., 2014).

Love as a Story

When we think of love, our thoughts often turn to the great love stories: *Romeo and Juliet,* Cinderella and the Prince (Julia Roberts and Richard Gere), King Edward VIII and Wallis Simpson, and *Pygmalion/My Fair Lady.*[2]

According to Sternberg (1998), these stories are much more than entertainment. They shape our beliefs about love and relationships, and our beliefs in turn influence our behaviour:

> Zach and Tammy have been married 28 years. Their friends have been predicting divorce since the day they were married. They fight almost constantly. Tammy threatens to leave Zach; he tells her that nothing would make him happier. They lived happily ever after.

---

[2] Notice that all these stories are about heterosexuals.

Valerie and Leonard had a perfect marriage. They told each other and all of their friends that they did. Their children say they never fought. Leonard met someone at his office and left Valerie. They are divorced. (Adapted from Sternberg, 1998)

Wait a minute! Aren't those endings reversed? Zach and Tammy should be divorced, and Valerie and Leonard should be living happily ever after. If love is merely the interaction between two people, how they communicate and behave, you are right; the stories have the wrong endings. But there is more to love than interaction; what matters is how each partner *interprets* the interaction. To make sense out of what happens in our relationships, we rely on our love stories.

A **love story** is a story about what love should be like; it has *characters*, a *plot*, and a *theme*. Every love story has two central characters who play roles that complement each other. The plot details the kinds of events that occur in the relationship. The theme is central; it provides the meaning of the events that make up the plot and gives direction to the behaviour of the principals.

The story guiding Zach and Tammy's relationship is the *war story*. Each views love as war; a good relationship involves constant fighting. The two central characters are warriors, doing battle, fighting for what they believe. The plot consists of arguments, fights, and threats to leave—in other words, battles. The theme is that love is war. One may win or lose particular battles, but the war continues. Zach and Tammy's relationship endures because they share this view and because it fits their temperaments. (Can you imagine how long a conflict avoider would last in a relationship with either of them?)

According to this view, *falling in love* occurs when you meet someone with whom you can create a relationship that fits your love story. Further, we are satisfied with relationships in which our partner and we match the characters in our story (Beall & Sternberg, 1995). Valerie and Leonard's marriage looked great on the surface, but it did not fit Leonard's love story. He left when he met his "true love"—that is, a woman who could play the complementary role in his primary love story.

Where do our stories come from? Many of them have their origins in culture, folktales, literature, theatre, films, and television programs. The cultural context interacts with our personal experience and characteristics to create the stories that each of us has (Sternberg, 1996). As we experience relationships, our stories evolve, taking into account unexpected events. Each person has more than one story; the stories often form a hierarchy. One of Leonard's stories was *house and home*, where home was the centre of the relationship, and

he (in his role of caretaker) showered attention on the house and kids (not on Valerie). But when he met Sharon, with her aloof air, ambiguous past, and dark glasses, he was hooked—she elicited the *love is a mystery* story, which was more salient to Leonard. He could not explain why he left Valerie and the kids; like most of us he was not consciously aware of his love stories.

You can see from these examples that love stories derive their power from the fact that they can be self-fulfilling. Our love story affects the way we think about and behave in our relationship. That is, we create in our relationships events according to the plot and then interpret those events according to the theme. Our love relationships are literally social constructions. Because our love stories are self-confirming, they can be very difficult to change. As noted, many people are not aware of their love story (Sternberg et al., 2001).

Sternberg and his colleagues have identified 25 common love stories found in North American culture (Sternberg et al., 2001). They have also developed a series of statements that reflect the themes in each story. People who agree with the statements "I think fights actually make a relationship more vital," and "I actually like to fight with my partner" are likely to believe in the *war story*. Sternberg and Hojjat (cited in Sternberg, 1998) studied samples of 43 and 55 couples. They found that couples generally believed in similar stories. The more discrepant the stories of the partners, the less happy the couple was. Some stories were associated with high satisfaction, such as the *garden story*, in which love is a garden that needs ongoing cultivation. Two stories associated with low satisfaction were the *business story* (especially the version in which the roles are employer and employee), and the *horror story*, in which the roles are terrorizer and victim. If you watch *The Simpsons*, what do you think Marge and Homer's love story is?

If love stories are influenced by culture, different stories should be prevalent in different cultures. Researchers recruited dating and married couples in the United States and in China. All participants completed parts of Sternberg's love stories scale. There were several components common to both cultures: objectification-threat (my partner is unpredictable, strange), nurturing-caring (I think about moments we share, nurturing a relationship is important), pornography (I like when we use bizarre sexual techniques; I do what my partner wants sexually even if it is degrading), and pragmatism (there is a recipe for success; I am following the rules). However, there were also components that were unique to each culture. Components unique to Americans were "love as war" and "love as a fairy tale." Unique components for Chinese were "love as current tending" and "the incomprehensibility of a lover" (Jackson et al., 2006).

love story: A story about what love should be like, including characters, a plot, and a theme.

Passionate and Companionate Love

The three theories considered so far define love as a single phenomenon. A fourth perspective differentiates between two kinds of love: passionate love and companionate love (Berscheid & Hatfield, 1978). **Passionate love** is a state of intense longing for union with the other person and of intense physiological arousal. It has three components: cognitive, emotional, and behavioural (Hatfield & Sprecher, 1986). The cognitive component includes preoccupation with the loved one and idealization of the person or of the relationship. The emotional component includes physiological arousal, sexual attraction, and desire for union. Behavioural elements include taking care of the other and maintaining physical closeness. Passionate love can be overwhelming, obsessive, and all consuming.

Passionate love can also lead to overly optimistic predictions about the likelihood that the relationship will last. Researchers in Ontario asked university students who were in a dating relationship of between one month and one year, their roommates, and their parents to predict how long the students' dating relationships would last (MacDonald & Ross, 1999). The students described their relationship more positively than did the other two groups, because they tended to focus on the strengths and minimize the negative aspects of the relationship. Students predicted that the relationship would last longer than did parents and roommates. Who was right? The results indicated that roommates were the most accurate about whether the couple would still be together one year later; the students were the least accurate.

By contrast, **companionate love** is a feeling of deep attachment and commitment to a person with whom one has an intimate relationship (Hatfield & Rapson, 1993b).

Passionate love is hot; companionate love is warm. Passionate love is often the first stage of a romantic relationship. Two people meet, fall wildly in love, and make a commitment to each other. But as the relationship progresses, a gradual shift to companionate love takes place (Cimbalo et al., 1976; Driscoll et al., 1972). The transformation tends to occur when the relationship is between 6 and 30 months old (Hatfield & Walster, 1978).

Some may find this perspective a rather pessimistic commentary on romantic love because it does not fit the societal love story in which people see stars and hear bells when they fall in love and continue to do so forever after. But it may actually describe a good way for a relationship to develop. Passionate love may be necessary to hold a relationship together in the early stages, while conflicts are being resolved. But past that point, most of us find that what we really need is a friend—someone who shares our interests, who is happy when we succeed, and who empathizes when we fail—and that is just what we get with companionate love. However, even when

passionate love has evolved to companionate love, it helps to continue to see our partner and our relationship in somewhat idealized ways. An Ontario study found that couples with these positive relationship "illusions" were more satisfied with their relationship (Murray & Holmes, 1997; Murray et al., 1996). Of course, illusions are not sufficient to maintain a relationship if they are not based on common needs and goals.

Sexual desire and romantic love may often be independent processes (Diamond, 2004). Sexual desire is a motivational state leading to a search for opportunities for sexual activity. It motivates proximity seeking and contact, and it leads to feelings of passion (passionate love). As we have seen, sexual desire responds to reproductive cues, such as physical attractiveness and high status. Romantic love is a motivational state leading to attachment and commitment. It promotes self-disclosure and intimacy, leading to long-term relationships (companionate love).

Research involving observation of romantic couples identified distinctive nonverbal displays of affiliation (smiling, leaning toward partner) and of sexual cues (licking the lips, lip puckering) (Gonzaga, et al., 2006). Displays of affection were associated with subjective reports of feeling love and of happiness. Displays of sexual cues were associated with subjective reports of sexual arousal and desire.

From an evolutionary perspective, successful reproduction requires mating and the establishment of a pair bond to ensure parental care of offspring (see Chapter 2). Fisher and colleagues (2006) propose that there are three internal systems involved in this process: desire to mate, pairing (mating), and parenting. They believe that each system involves reward pathways in the brain and associated hormonal changes. The sex drive motivates a person to seek a partner. Processes of attraction lead to pairing, a focusing of energies on a specific partner. Processes of attachment lead to long-term relationships that facilitate parenting. Research indicates that *priming* (subliminal exposure to) sex-related pictures and words led to outcomes associated with forming and maintaining close relationships (Gillath et al., 2008). These included willingness to self-disclose among women and willingness to sacrifice for one's partner and a preference for positive conflict resolution strategies among men and women.

The Biology of Love

What causes the complex phenomena of passionate and companionate love? Where does the rush of love at first sight come from? Research suggests that it is caused by bodily chemistry

passionate love: A state of intense longing for union with the other person and of intense physiological arousal.
companionate love: A feeling of deep attachment and commitment to a person with whom one has an intimate relationship.

and neural activity in the brain (see also Chapter 9). For example, animal studies suggest that dopamine is associated with pair bonding (Curtis & Wang, 2003). Dopamine is also likely important to human experiences of love and is associated with euphoria and craving. A surge of dopamine in the human body can produce increased energy, focused attention, and reduced need for food and sleep; these are common experiences of people in the early stages of love.

The frequent presence of the loved one, produced initially by passionate love, triggers the production of two other chemicals: prolactin and oxytocin. The levels of prolactin rise following orgasm in humans and are also related to pair bonding in voles.

Oxytocin may contribute to long-term relationships. It has been shown to play an important role in pair bonding in some animals (McEwen, 1997). In humans it is stimulated by touch, including sexual touching and orgasm, and produces feelings of pleasure and satisfaction. Research indicates that levels of interpersonal trust correlate positively with oxytocin as well (Zak et al., 2004). In an experiment, researchers administered either oxytocin or a placebo to young men through the nose. Compared with the men who received a placebo, the men who received oxytocin were more likely to take social risks during interactions with another person but not other types of risks (Kosfeld et al., 2005).

The newest research with humans involves the use of magnetic resonance imaging (MRI) to study brain activity related to love. Bartels and Zeki (2004) recruited young men and women who were in love. While their brain activity was being measured, each participant was shown photos of the romantic partner and of a close friend. The picture of the partner activated specific areas of the brain. Which ones? The areas rich in dopamine pathways were enervated, lending weight to the neurochemical findings that suggest dopamine is important in the experience of love. Furthermore, when measures of levels of brain activity in response to the picture of the lover were correlated with scores on the Passionate Love Scale (discussed shortly), the scores were positively correlated.

Visual stimuli associated with the lover stimulate subcortical activity in the ventral tegmental area, caudate nucleus, and putamen (Cacioppo et al., 2012b). As noted above, this area is rich in dopamine pathways. More generally, these are the areas associated with motivation, reward, and euphoria. Activity also occurs in areas associated with complex cognitive processing, including segments of the gyrus and the occipital cortex, such as memory and self-representation. Interestingly, activity in these areas does not vary by length of the love relationship. A study

of 21 men and women, married an average of 21 years, found that photos of the spouse triggered activity in these areas but also in areas associated with maternal attachment, such as the thalamus and anterior and posterior cingulate (Acevedo et al., 2011).

Little work has been done with humans to identify neural correlates of companionate love. Animal research suggests that it is associated with oxytocin and vasopressin, and neural activity in the nucleus accumbens and ventral palladium (Cacioppo et al., 2012b).

Is there a difference between passionate love and sexual desire in the brain? (Is love just sex?) Both passionate love and sexual desire activate the same reward-related and higher-order cortical areas in the brain. However, love is associated with reduced activity in the hypothalamus, amygdala, and somatosensory cortex compared with sexual desire. These differences are consistent with the view that sexual desire is a motivation with a specific goal, whereas love is an abstract, behaviourally complex phenomenon not dependent on the physical presence of the object (Cacioppo et al., 2012a). The answer? Love is more than sex (neurally speaking).

Researching Love

You can see that various theorists—Sternberg, Bartholemew, Berscheid, and Hatfield—mean different things when they use the term *love*. One way psychologists and sociologists define terms is by using an **operational definition**. In an operational definition, a concept is defined by the way it is measured. Operational definitions are very useful because they are precise and because they help clarify exactly what a scientist means by a complex term, such as love.

Measuring Love

We introduced the concept of *passionate love* earlier. Hatfield and Sprecher (1986) developed a paper-and-pencil measure of passionate love. They wrote statements intended to measure the cognitive, emotional, and behavioural components of passionate love. The respondent rated each statement on a scale from 1 (not true at all) to 9 (definitely true of him or her). If you feel that you are in love with someone, think about whether you would agree with each of the following statements, keeping that person in mind.

1. *Cognitive component:*
   Sometimes I feel I can't control my thoughts; they are obsessively on _____.
   For me, _____ is the perfect romantic partner.

operational definition: Defining some concept or term by how it is measured–for example, defining intelligence as those abilities that are measured by IQ tests.

2. *Emotional component:*

I possess a powerful attraction for _____.

I will love _____ forever.

3. *Behavioural component:*

I eagerly look for signs indicating _____'s desire for me.

I feel happy when I am doing things to make _____ happy.

Hatfield and Sprecher (1986) administered their questionnaire along with some other measures to students who were in relationships ranging from casually dating to engaged and living together. The results indicated that scores on the Passionate Love Scale (PLS) were positively correlated with other measures of love and with measures of commitment to and satisfaction with the relationship. These correlations give us evidence that the PLS is valid—in other words, it measures what it is supposed to measure. The findings confirm that the scale measures passion. For example, students who got high scores on the PLS reported a stronger desire to be with, held by, and kissed by the partner, and said that they were sexually excited just thinking about their partner. These findings confirm that the scale is measuring passion. Finally, the passionate love scores increased as the nature of the relationship moved from dating to dating exclusively. Hatfield and Sprecher's research is a good example of how to study an important but complex topic, such as love, scientifically.

L06 Love and Adrenaline

✈ Two-Component Theory of Love

Social psychologists Ellen Berscheid and Elaine Walster (1974) proposed a **two-component theory of love**. According to their theory, passionate love occurs when two conditions exist simultaneously: (1) the person is in a state of intense *physiological arousal*, and (2) the situation is such that the person applies a particular label—*love*—to the sensations being experienced. Their theory is derived from an important theory developed by Stanley Schachter (1964).

Suppose that your heart is pounding, your palms are sweating, and your body is tense. What emotion are you experiencing? Is it love—has reading about passionate love led to obsessive thoughts of another person? Is it fear—are you frantically reading this text because you have an exam tomorrow morning? Is it sexual arousal—are you thinking about physical intimacy later tonight? It could be any of these, or it could be anger or embarrassment. A wide variety of emotions are accompanied by the same physiological states: increased blood pressure, a higher heart rate, increased myotonia (muscular tension), sweating palms. What differentiates these emotions? The key is the way we interpret or label what we are experiencing.

Schachter's (1964) two-component theory of emotion says exactly that; an emotion consists of a physiological arousal state plus the label the person assigns to it (for a critical evaluation of this theory, see Reisenzein, 1983). Berscheid and Walster (1974) have applied this to the emotion of love. They suggest that we feel passionate love when we are aroused and when conditions are such that we identify what we are feeling as love.

Evidence for the Two-Component Theory

Several experiments provide evidence for Berscheid and Walster's two-component theory of love. In one study, male research participants exercised vigorously by running in place; this produced the physiological arousal response of pounding heart and sweaty palms (White et al., 1981). Afterward, they rated their liking for an attractive woman, who actually was a confederate of the experimenters. Men in the running group said they liked the woman significantly more than did men who were in a control condition and had not exercised. This result is consistent with Berscheid and Walster's theory (1974). The effect is called the **misattribution of arousal**; that is, in a situation like this, the men misattribute their arousal—which is actually due to exercise—to their liking for the attractive woman (Figure 12.8). An analysis of 33 experiments found that arousal

> **two-component theory of love:** Berscheid and Walster's theory that two conditions must exist simultaneously for passionate love to occur: physiological arousal and attaching a cognitive label (*love*) to the feeling.
>
> **misattribution of arousal:** When a person in a stage of physiological arousal (e.g., from exercising or being in a frightening situation) attributes these feelings to love or attraction to the person present.

Figure 12.8 The misattribution of arousal. If people are physically aroused (e.g., by jogging), they may misattribute this arousal to love or sexual attraction, provided the situation suggests such an interpretation.

© Bill Aron/Photo Edit

affects attraction even when the source of the arousal is unambiguous (Foster et al., 1998).

A study conducted in North Vancouver suggests that fear can increase a man's attraction to a woman (Dutton & Aron, 1974). An attractive female interviewer approached male passers-by either on a fear-arousing bridge (you may be familiar with the Capilano Bridge) or on a non-fear-arousing bridge. The fear-arousing bridge was constructed of boards attached to cables and had a tendency to tilt, sway, and wobble; the handrails were low, and there was a 70-metre drop to rocks and shallow rapids below. The control bridge was made of solid cedar; it was firm, and there was only a 3-metre drop to a shallow rivulet below. The interviewer asked subjects to fill out questionnaires that included projective test items. These items were then scored for sexual imagery.

The men in the suspension-bridge group should have been in a state of physiological arousal, whereas those in the control-bridge group should not have been. In fact, there was more sexual imagery in the questionnaires filled out by the men in the suspension-bridge group, and these men made more attempts to contact the attractive interviewer after the experiment than the men on the control bridge. Intuitively, this result might seem to be peculiar: that men who are in a state of fear are more attracted to a woman than men who are relaxed. But in terms of the Berscheid and Walster two-component theory, it makes perfect sense. The fearful men were physiologically aroused, while the men in the control group were not. And according to this theory, arousal is an important component of love or attraction.[3]

Now, of course, if the men (most of them heterosexuals) had been approached by an older man or a child, probably their responses would have been different. In fact, when the interviewer in the experiment was male, the effects discussed above did not occur. Society tells us what the appropriate objects of our love, attraction, or liking are. That is, we know for what kinds of people it is appropriate to have feelings of love or liking. For these heterosexual men, feelings toward an attractive woman could reasonably be labelled as love or attraction, whereas such labels would probably not be attached to feelings for a man.

The physical arousal that is important for love need not always be produced by unpleasant or frightening situations. Pleasant stimuli, such as sexual arousal or praise from the other person, may produce arousal and feelings of love. Indeed, Berscheid and Walster's theory does an excellent job of explaining why we seem to have such a strong tendency to associate love and sex. Sexual arousal is one method of producing a state of physiological arousal, and it is one that our culture has taught us to label as love. Thus both components necessary to feel

---

[3] According to the terminology of Chapter 3, the Dutton and Aron study is an example of *experimental* research.

love are present: arousal and a label. On the other hand, this phenomenon may lead us to confuse lust with love, an all-too-common error.

LO7 Cross-Cultural Research

In the past two decades, researchers have studied people from various ethnic or cultural groups to see whether they experience attraction, intimacy, and love in similar ways. Three topics that have been studied are the impact of culture on how people view love, on whom people fall in love with, and on the importance of love in decisions to marry.

Cultural Values and the Meaning of Love

Cross-cultural psychologists have identified two dimensions on which cultures vary (Hatfield & Rapson, 1993a). The first is individualism–collectivism (Figure 12.9). *Individualistic cultures*, like those of Canada, the United States, and Western European countries, tend to emphasize individual goals over group and societal goals and interests. *Collectivist cultures*, like those of China, Africa, and Southeast Asian countries, emphasize group and collective goals over personal ones. Several specific traits have been identified that differentiate these two types of societies (Triandis et al., 1990). In individualistic cultures, behaviour is regulated by individual attitudes and cost–benefit considerations; emotional detachment from the group is accepted. In collectivist cultures, the self is defined by group membership; behaviour is regulated by group norms; attachment to and harmony within the group are valued.

The two types of cultures have different conceptions of love. The majority group in Canadian society, for example, emphasizes passionate love as the basis for marriage (Dion & Dion, 1993b). Individuals select mates on the basis of such characteristics as physical attractiveness, similarity (compatibility), and wealth or resources. We look for intimacy in the relationship with our mate. In Chinese society, by contrast, many marriages are arranged; the primary criterion is that the two families be of similar status. The person finds intimacy in relationships with other family members.

The second dimension on which cultures differ is independence–interdependence. Many Western cultures view each person as independent and value individuality and uniqueness. Many other cultures view the person as interdependent with those around him or her. The self is defined in relation to others. Canadians value standing up for one's beliefs. The people of India value conformity and harmony within the group.

Dion and Dion (1993a) studied university students in Toronto from four ethnocultural groups. Students from Asian backgrounds were more likely to view love as companionate, as friendship, in contrast to those from English and Irish backgrounds. This tendency is consistent with the collectivist orientation of Asian cultures.

Figure 12.9 Whether a culture is individualistic or collectivistic determines its views on love and marriage. In Canada, which is an individualistic culture, individuals choose each other and marry for love. In India, a collectivistic culture, marriages are arranged by family members to serve family interests.

© Jerry Cooke/Science Source

Cultural Influences on Mate Selection

Buss (1989) conducted a large-scale survey of 10 000 men and women from 37 societies. The sample included people from four cultures in Africa, eight in Asia, and four in eastern Europe, in addition to twelve Western European and four North American ones. Each respondent was given a list of 18 characteristics one might value in a potential mate and asked to rate how important each was to him or her personally. Regardless of which society they lived in, most respondents, male and female, rated intelligence, kindness, and understanding at the top of the list; note that these are characteristics of companionate love. Men worldwide placed more weight on cues of reproductive capacity, such as physical attractiveness; women rated cues of resources as more important. The results support the sociobiological perspective and suggest that there are not large cultural differences in mate selection.

Many people prefer mates who are physically attractive. We often hear that "beauty is in the eye of the beholder." This saying suggests that standards of beauty might vary across cultures. In one study, researchers had students from varying cultural backgrounds rate 45 photographs of women on a scale ranging from very attractive to very unattractive (Cunningham et al., 1995). The photographs portrayed women from many different societies. Overall, Asian, Hispanic, and white students did not differ in their ratings of the individual photographs. However, Asian students' ratings were less influenced by indicators of sexual maturity (such as facial narrowness) and expressivity (such as the vertical distance between the lips when the person smiled).

Love and Marriage

We noted earlier that individualistic cultures place a high value on romantic love, while collectivist cultures emphasize the group. The importance of romantic love in North American society is illustrated by responses to the question "If a man (woman) had all the other qualities you desired, would you marry this person if you were not in love with him (her)?" Over time, increasing percentages of North American men and women answer no. The change has been greater for women.

Researchers asked this question of men and women in 11 different cultures (Levine et al., 1995). We would predict that members of individualistic cultures would answer no, whereas those in collectivist cultures would answer yes. Research has shown that, as predicted, many—about half of Indians and Pakistanis—would marry even though they didn't love the person (Levine et al., 1995). In Thailand, which is also collectivist, 19 percent said yes. In the individualistic cultures of Australia, England, and the United States, less than 7 percent of people would marry someone they did not love.

When we look at the findings of the cross-cultural research on love, attraction, and marriage, the pattern that emerges is one of *cross-cultural similarities and cross-cultural differences*, a theme we introduced in Chapter 1. That is, some phenomena are similar across cultures; for example, valuing intelligence, kindness, and understanding in a mate. Other phenomena differ substantially across cultures; for example, whether love is a prerequisite for marriage. However, even in Asian (collectivist) societies, young people are increasingly seeing love as a basis for marriage (Dion & Dion, 1993a). But they may also see love as developing after marriage rather than as a prerequisite for marriage.

What happens when an individual from a collectivist culture is raised in Canada? First Person tells the story of a Canadian man's decision to enter into an arranged marriage.

First Person

Why I Chose to Have an Arranged Marriage

O n my wedding day, I remember thinking that my choice of wanting an arranged marriage was rare for someone living in the West. I later realized that having an arranged marriage is not atypical for many individuals in North America and around the world.

I was born in Fiji Islands and immigrated at the age of seven to Vancouver with my parents and younger brother. Though I was raised in a traditional, Muslim home, I was nonetheless still affected by Western social ideals. The clash of cultures became more apparent as I matured.

My mother, a strong member of our religious community, travels the world in her efforts to spread Islam. Ever since I turned 18, she had been sending me photographs and "résumés" of girls (i.e., potential wives) she had met during her journeys. I would return the photos to my mother, with a lengthy explanation of what I considered to be the many limitations to an arranged marriage and how I would marry a girl I fall in love with and have known for some time.

Luckily for me, my denials and many "rejections" fell on deaf ears. In the spring of 1997, my mother sent me a package. It contained some souvenirs from her recent visit to Pakistan and four pictures of Ayesha, a young woman from Peshawar. As I looked carefully at the photos of this person, studying the softness of her complexion, the welcoming nature of her smile, the innocence of her gaze, something inside me wanted to know more about her.

I telephoned my mother and began asking her about the mysterious woman in the photos. At my very utterance of Ayesha's name, my mother let out a slightly audible sigh, one, which if given words to, would say, "Yes! I finally got him!"

This was one of the longest phone conversations I had with my mother. I learned that Ayesha was a caring, loving, and family-oriented person (qualities I admire), who, like me, also majored in English literature and psychology. The more I heard, the more I liked.

Of course, being raised in Canada, in a society where mothers and sons do not always prefer the same girl, I had to find out for myself. I asked my mother for Ayesha's phone number but was met with resistance: "Her parents will not allow a strange man to speak with her on the phone." I thought, is this for real? Do the parents really expect me to marry their daughter without getting to know her? At this point I felt like abandoning this whole fantasy I had of meeting this "Pakistani Princess."

My mother then suggested that I fly to Peshawar to meet Ayesha and her family. Trusting my mother's good intentions and my own inner voice, I took time off from my practice and flew to Pakistan. Somewhere over the Atlantic Ocean, I remember thinking about stories I had heard of other men travelling overseas to meet women. The stories were similar. When they visited the home of the women, these women were adorned in their finest clothes, wore copious amounts of makeup and even cooked the meal, behaviour aimed at impressing their potential husbands.

I was no doubt surprised, then, when I met Ayesha, who greeted me with not a speck of makeup on. She had on clothes, which, while pleasant-looking, were not anything extraordinary. And she did not cook, nor help, with dinner. Ayesha was different from the rest. She was unique and real. In trying not to pique my interest, she did just that.

L08

✱ Communication

Consider the following situation involving Chris and Donna. (We have purposely left Chris's gender ambiguous—Chris and Donna could be a same-sex or a mixed-sex couple.)

Chris and Donna are undergraduate students who have been living together for about three years. Donna had had sex with only one other person before Chris, and she had never masturbated. Since they've been together, she has had orgasms only twice during lovemaking, despite the fact that they make love

Our interest in each other developed with our first conversation. I didn't want to tell Ayesha of my academic or professional achievements and question her on her domestic acumen (as is the typical queries in such meetings). I wanted to know about her interests, her passions, about her. As we felt more comfortable with each other, I asked her what types of books she liked to read, to which she responded with every relationship therapist's idea of romance—"love stories," she said, modestly looking at me for a response. I accepted Ayesha's openness and courage with an appreciative smile.

Realizing that my mother had told Ayesha's family that I was a psychologist, it was important for me that Ayesha know of my specialization. In telling her that I am a clinical sexologist, not only did she not judge me, she in fact grew curious about my career and later shared that I must be helping many people in need.

It was obvious to us that we had already begun to satisfy each other's needs. That night, the night of our first meeting, I shared with my mother my intentions of wanting to marry Ayesha. The next morning, my mother took a formal proposal to Ayesha's mother, who discussed the proposal with Ayesha. Ayesha accepted the proposal and we were wed ten days later.

I returned to Canada shortly after our wedding (our Nikka) and began the sponsoring process. Ayesha and I talked almost every day for about one year. In fact, we dated by phone and fell in love, long-distance, after we got married. Imagine that.

On May 2, 2007, Ayesha and I, along with our two beautiful daughters, Malaika and Alishba, celebrated our tenth year of wedded bliss. So, is having an arranged marriage the secret to our happiness? Maybe and maybe not. Our relationship is based on six key qualities: love, openness, a non-judgmental attitude, respect, commitment, and

trust (I, till this day, have never broken a promise to her). When you consider that these same qualities also result in happy non-arranged marriages, it makes us wonder about the deeper meaning of the institution of marriage, regardless of how the individuals meet.

Her Perspective

I come from a traditional, yet open-minded family. Since it is typical for parents in Pakistan to arrange a marriage for their children, when my parents asked me if they could do the same for me, I had no objections. I trusted my parents and put my faith in God to find the "right" person for me.

When my parents told me that a family from Canada was coming to visit us, I sensed that they would be special because my parents had never asked me to meet any other families who were also interested in meeting me.

When I first met Faizal, I didn't even clearly see his face because it is a custom for women to not make eye contact with a man who is not related to them. However, from the way he spoke, I could sense his gentle personality and caring ways. Though we talked alone for an hour, I remember time just flying by—it was so easy and so much fun to talk to him that I could imagine my married life with him being full of love and happiness.

I hardly knew Faizal when we first got married. Soon afterward, I began to slowly fall in love with him, and ever since I am falling more and more in love with him every day.

Faizal Sahukhan, Ph.D., couples counsellor, sex therapist, university instructor, advice columnist, author. www.multiculturalromance.com.

three or four times per week. She has been reading some magazine articles about female sexuality and is beginning to think that she should be experiencing more sexual satisfaction. As far as she knows, Chris is unaware that there is any problem. Donna feels lonely and a bit sad.

What should Donna do? She needs to communicate with Chris. They apparently have not communicated much about sex in the last three years, and they need to begin. The following sections will discuss the relationship between sex, communication, and relationships, and provide some suggestions on how to communicate effectively.

✦ Communication and Relationships

A good deal of research has looked at differences in communication patterns between nondistressed (happy) couples and distressed (unhappy, seeking relationship counselling) heterosexual couples. This research shows, in general, that distressed couples tend to have communication deficits (Gottman, 1994). Further, research in Quebec has shown that heterosexual, gay male, and lesbian couples do not differ in their communication skills or in the contribution of communication deficits to their relationship adjustment (Julien et al., 2003). Research also shows that couples with sexual problems have poorer sexual and nonsexual communication than couples without sexual problems (Kelly et al., 2006). Of course, many other factors contribute to relationship conflict or sex problems, but poor communication patterns are certainly among them. Good communication skills are particularly important in negotiating the challenges of adjusting to life changes, positive or negative, such as a new job, the birth of a baby, parenting responsibilities, job loss, or retirement. The problem with this research is that it is correlational (see Chapter 3 for a discussion of this problem in research methods); in particular, we cannot tell whether poor communication causes unhappy relationships or whether unhappy relationships create poor communication patterns.

An elegant longitudinal study designed to meet this problem provides evidence that unrewarding, ineffective communication precedes and predicts later relationship problems (Markman et al., 2010). Couples who were planning to marry were recruited for the research. Each person completed a questionnaire, including a rating of the negativity (e.g., she or he criticizes, belittles me) of their communication. Each couple participated in a videotaped interaction, discussing the top problem in their relationship. Trained coders rated each person's communication during the discussion on ten dimensions, including positive (e.g., problem solving skills, support, validation) and negative (e.g., denial, dominance, withdrawal). A composite positive score and negative score was calculated for each. Some 200 couples married, and were assessed near their fifth anniversary; at the time they were recruited, they averaged 26 years of age and 16 years of education, and most were white (84 percent). Couples who divorced before the fifth year had rated their communication as significantly more negative at baseline. Among those who remained married, both observed and self-reported negative communication predicted lower marital adjustment at year five. Researchers considered couples with adjustment scores less than 100 distressed. These couples experienced significantly less decline in negative communication and

significantly greater decline in positive communication over five years, compared with nondistressed couples.

On the basis of this notion that communication deficits cause communication problems, relationship counsellors and therapists often work on teaching couples communication skills. Research suggests that distressed couples do not always differ from nondistressed couples in their communication skills or ability; rather, some distressed couples use their skills as weapons, to send negative messages (Burleson & Denton, 1997; Gottman & Notarius, 2002). These results suggest that therapists should focus on the intent of the partners as they communicate with each other, not just on techniques.

But what are these negative messages? Gottman (1994) used audiotape, videotape, and monitoring of physiological arousal to answer this question. He identified four destructive patterns of interaction: criticism, contempt, defensiveness, and withdrawal. *Criticism* refers to attacking a partner's personality or character: "You are so selfish; you never think of anyone else." *Contempt* is intentionally insulting or orally abusing the other person: "How did I get hooked up with such a loser?" *Defensiveness* refers to denying responsibility, making excuses, replying with a complaint of one's own, and other self-protective responses, instead of addressing the problem. *Withdrawal* involves such activities as responding to the partner's complaint with silence, turning on the TV, or walking out of the room in anger. You can probably see that these types of communication are likely to lead to an escalation of the hostility rather than to a solution to the problem. In fact, a Quebec study found that a pattern of withdrawal was associated with a decrease in relationship adjustment (Guay et al., 2003).

On the other hand, positive communication is important in developing and maintaining intimate relationships (see First Person, "Sexuality and Disability: Constructing a Sexual Blueprint"). In the following discussions, we describe some of the skills involved in positive sexual communication.

Sexual Self-Disclosure

As discussed earlier in this chapter, one of the keys to building a good relationship is self-disclosure. One of the keys to building a satisfying *sexual* relationship is *sexual* self-disclosure. **Sexual self-disclosure** involves telling personal sexual things about yourself. It may range from sharing your sexual likes and dislikes to disclosing about an unwanted sexual experience you had with a previous partner.

Unfortunately, most romantic partners have difficulty telling each other what pleases and displeases them sexually (Byers, 2011). How much do couples self-disclose about their preferences? In a survey of more than 3000 Canadian men and women, 97 percent said that

sexual self-disclosure: Telling personal sexual things about yourself such as your sexual likes and dislikes.

they were sometimes or always able to discuss sex with their partner openly; however, only 28 percent had had one or more serious discussions in the past year (Auld & Brock, 2002). According to one New Brunswick study of individuals in mixed-sex dating relationships, although people do talk to their dating partner about their sexual likes and dislikes, they do not fully reveal their personal feelings about them (Byers & Demmons, 1999). Both the men and the women in this study revealed more to their partner about their nonsexual feelings than about their sexual feelings and more about what they liked sexually than about what they didn't like. However, the more that one member of the couple self-disclosed sexually, the more they reported that their partner did so too. That is, the sexual self-disclosure by one partner was reciprocated by the other partner, perhaps because self-disclosure by a partner assures us that he or she is comfortable talking about sex and shares similar values (Herold & Way, 1988). Researchers in Nova Scotia have shown that heterosexual, gay male, and lesbian couples do not differ in their levels of sexual self-disclosure (Holmberg & Blair, 2009).

Sexual self-disclosure leads to sexual satisfaction in two ways (MacNeil & Byers, 2005, 2009). First, it increases intimacy between partners. Talking about sexual likes and dislikes allows partners to feel closer to each other and see themselves as compatible (Offman & Matheson, 2005). Feeling closer and more satisfied with the nonsexual aspects of the relationship leads to higher sexual satisfaction. Researchers in Nova Scotia have shown that there is a strong link between relational closeness and well-being and sexual satisfaction in both mixed-sex and same-sex relationships (Holmberg et al., 2010). Second, sharing what pleases and displeases us sexually with our partner allows him or her to learn about our sexual preferences. This kind of understanding helps partners to negotiate mutually enjoyable sexual interactions. That is, by telling our partner what we like and don't like sexually, we receive more of what we want and less of what we don't want during sexual interactions (Byers & Demmons, 1999; MacNeil & Byers, 1997; Purnine & Carey, 1997). In turn, having more pleasing sexual interactions leads to enhanced sexual satisfaction.

Sexual self-disclosure is especially important for maintaining sexual satisfaction in long-term relationships. In contrast, early in a relationship, sex is new and exciting and may feel satisfying even though our partner is not fully aware of what pleases and displeases us sexually (Byers, 1999).

✶ Being an Effective Communicator

Back to Donna and Chris: One of the first things to do in this type of situation is to decide to talk to one's partner, admitting that there is a problem. Then the issue is to resolve to communicate and particularly to be an *effective* communicator. Suppose Donna begins by saying,

You're not giving me any orgasms when we have sex.(1)

Chris gets angry and walks away or gets upset. Donna meant to communicate that she wasn't having any orgasms, but Chris thought she meant that Chris was a lousy lover.

It is important to recognize the distinction between **intent** and **impact** in communicating (Gottman et al., 1976; Purnine & Carey, 1997). Intent is what you mean. Impact is what the other person thinks you mean. An **effective communicator** is one whose impact matches her or his intent. Donna wasn't an effective communicator in the above example because the impact on Chris was considerably different from her intent. Notice that effectiveness does not depend on the content of the message. One can be as effective at communicating contempt as communicating praise.

Many people value spontaneity in sex, and this attitude may extend to communicating about sex. It is best to recognize that to be an effective communicator, you may need to plan your strategy. It often takes some thinking to figure out how to make sure that your impact will match your intent. Planning also allows you to make sure that the timing is good—that you are not speaking out of anger, or that your partner is not tired or preoccupied with other things.

In the last few decades public communication about sex has become relatively open, but private communication remains difficult (Crawford et al., 1994). This doesn't mean that Donna can't communicate. But she shouldn't feel guilty or stupid if it is difficult for her. And she will be better off if she uses some specific communication skills and has some belief that they will work. The sections that follow suggest some skills that are useful in being an effective communicator and how to apply these to sexual relationships.

Good Messages

Every couple has problems. The best way to voice them is to complain rather than to criticize (Gottman, 1994). Complaining involves the use of **"I" language**, in which you speak about your own thoughts and feelings rather than about your partner. In contrast, "you" messages tend to be criticisms of the other person. Research has shown that nondistressed couples are more likely to self-disclose thoughts and feelings during problem-solving than to criticize their partner (Gottman & Notarius, 2002). When you use "I" language, your partner

intent: What the speaker means.
impact: What someone else understands the speaker to mean.
effective communicator: A communicator whose impact matches his or her intent.
"I" language: Speaking about yourself, using the word "I"; not mind reading.

Sexuality and Disability: Constructing a Sexual Blueprint

F or most people, coming out as a sexual being is just assumed. It isn't something they have to declare and take a stand for—that is, unless they live with a disability like I do. Whenever I talk about sexuality and disability, the "elephant in the room" that tends not to get named but is so very much part of the conversation is that sex for people with a disability is somehow not the "real thing" or that we really don't have the same feelings when we're kissed, touched, or fucked. I'm here to tell you that we do have the same sensations, wants and desires as anyone else, kink, vanilla, or otherwise. And when you have a disability and declare that you're queer, well, that's a whole other story!!

Part of my work in the community is that of a sexual health educator, and I have been educating people about sexuality and disability for more than ten years. I began to do this work because of my own journey discovering how to be sexual in a world that overtly says that people with disabilities shouldn't have sex, relationships, and all the trimmings or "trappings" that go with them. My interest in talking to groups about sexuality and disability is

personal—it's important to me to remove the mystery and misconceptions that people have about what sex is like for disabled folks. I want to connect with people on a very real level that acknowledges the fragility of the body and that disability or difference is something that can enter into anyone's life whether through aging, illness, or accident. People with disabilities actually have lots to teach about pushing the boundaries surrounding conventional ideas about sex, how to make love, and notions of intimacy with oneself and with another person. I felt that it was so important to get the message out that I also coauthored a book on sexuality and disability entitled *The Ultimate Guide to Sex and Disability*.

In my own journey of sexual discovery, I experimented sexually with my male and female friends, all of whom lived with disabilities. My first sexual relationship was with a man when I was 18. We both lived with physical disability. Negotiating a sexual relationship was challenging but most of all it was fun, exciting, and very hot. I later had relationships with other men, some living with some form of physical disability and others not. I had to

is less likely to become defensive. "I" language uses soft emotions, such as feelings of unhappiness or concern, rather than hard emotions such as anger. (Note that saying something like "I think you are a lousy lover" or "I feel that you're only interested in your own pleasure" are actually "you" messages not "I" language, even though they contains the word "I".) Thus, if Donna were to use this technique, she might say,

> I feel a bit unhappy because I don't have orgasms very often when we make love. (2)

Notice that she focuses specifically on herself. There is less cause for Chris to get angry, upset, or defensive than there was in message 1.

mind reading: Making assumptions about what your partner thinks or feels.

One of the best things about "I" language is that it avoids mind reading (Gottman et al., 1976). Suppose Donna says,

> I know you think I'm not much interested in sex, but I really wish I had more orgasms. (3)

She is engaging in **mind reading**. That is, she is making certain assumptions about what Chris is thinking. She assumes that Chris believes she is not interested in sex or having orgasms. Research shows that mind reading is more common among distressed couples than among nondistressed couples (Gottman et al., 1977). Worse, Donna doesn't *check out* her assumptions with Chris. The problem is that she may be wrong, and Chris may not think that at all. "I" language helps Donna avoid this by focusing on herself and what she feels rather than

learn to create opportunities for communication because each sexual experience forced me and my partner to confront our assumptions. This meant that both of us had to ask questions about our desires as well as about what felt pleasurable and what didn't. Communication is important, although not easy, for everyone but particularly for people with a disability.

In one of the chapters of *The Ultimate Guide to Sex and Disability*, we wrote:

> Despite what people actually experience, many still view sex as something that is the same for everybody "normal," and inferior for the rest of us. Every person needs to discover what sex is to her/him, how it feels, what she/he respond to. Constructing a sexual blueprint, an understanding of where you have more or less sexual sensation, what your body looks like (inside and out), its textures and rhythms, leads to a healthier sexuality for anyone.

Whether my partner is someone living with disabilities or not, I am reminded that I can't rely on what I know from previous experiences. I have to be open to really exploring what's pleasurable and hot with this new person.

In my 20s through to my late 30s, my primary sexual relationships were with men. When I was 37, I fell in love and fell hard for a woman younger than myself. Although we were only together for a short period of time, I had previously never felt the depth of emotional and physical connection in a relationship that I had with her. I felt that I really had found where I belonged. Since then, my primary relationships have been with women, again some living with disability and others not. It really doesn't matter to me whether they have a disability. What does matter is how we feel together: whether the chemistry is there; whether we can make each other laugh; and what we each bring to the relationship that keeps it alive, interesting, and hot.

The bottom line is that people with disabilities, straight or queer, *are* sexual—and as often as possible.

Source: Fran Odette is program manager of the Women with Disabilities and Violence Program at Springtide Resources (formerly Education Wife Assault) in Toronto.

---

on what Chris is doing or failing to do. Another important way to avoid mind reading is by giving and receiving feedback, a technique discussed in a later section.

Documenting is another important component of giving good messages (Brenton, 1972). In documenting you give specific examples of the issue. This is not quite so relevant in Donna's case, because she is talking about a general problem; but even here, specific documenting can be helpful. Once Donna has broached the subject, she might say,

> Last night when we made love, I enjoyed it and it felt really good, but I didn't have an orgasm, and then I felt disappointed. (4)

Now she has gotten her general complaint down to a specific situation that Chris can remember.

Suppose further that Donna has some idea of what Chris would need to do to bring her to orgasm: she would like more sensual touching or more oral stimulation of her clitoris. Then she might do specific documenting as follows:

> Last night when we made love, I enjoyed it, but I didn't have an orgasm, and then I felt disappointed. I think what I needed was for you to stimulate my clitoris with your mouth a bit more. You did it for a while, but it seemed so brief. I think if you had kept doing it for two or three minutes more, I would have had an orgasm. (5)

Now not only has she documented to Chris exactly what the problem was, but she has

documenting: Giving specific examples of the issue being discussed.

given a specific suggestion about what could have been done about it, and therefore what could be done in the future.

A study of mixed-sex dating couples found that open communication about sex ("I tell my partner when I am especially sexually satisfied") was positively associated with satisfaction with sex and the relationship (Montesi et al., 2010).

Levelling and Editing

Levelling means telling your partner what you are feeling by stating your thoughts clearly, simply, and honestly—that is, self-disclosing your feelings (Gottman et al., 1976). This is often the hardest step in communication (Figure 12.11), especially when the topic is sex. It is especially difficult for adults to reach shared understandings about sex, since there is great secrecy about it in our society (Crawford et al., 1994). In levelling, keep in mind that the purposes are as follows:

1. To make communications clear
2. To clear up what partners expect of each other
3. To clear up what is pleasant and what is unpleasant
4. To clear up what is relevant and what is irrelevant
5. To notice things that draw you closer or push you apart (Gottman et al., 1976)

When you begin to level with your partner, you also need to do some editing. **Editing** involves censoring (not saying) things that would be deliberately hurtful to your partner or that would be irrelevant. You must take responsibility for making your communication polite and considerate. For example, details about past sexual relationships and comparison with past sexual partners are unnecessary and may be hurtful to your partner. Levelling, then, should not mean a "no-holds-barred" approach. Ironically, research indicates that married people are ruder to each other than they are to strangers (Gottman et al., 1976). This is likely also true of all partners in long-term relationships.

Donna may be so disgruntled about her lack of orgasms that she's thinking of having sex with someone else to jolt Chris into recognizing her problem or perhaps to see if another partner would stimulate her to orgasm. Donna is probably best advised to edit out this line of thought and concentrate on the specific problem: her lack of orgasms. Having sex with someone else is not likely to magically solve her problem. If she and Chris can work it out together, not only will Donna be more sexually satisfied, but their relationship also will be stronger.

The trick is to balance levelling and editing. If you edit too much, you may not level at all, and there will be no communication. If you level too much and don't edit, the communication will fail because your partner will respond negatively, and things may get worse rather than better.

Listening

Up to this point, we have been concentrating on techniques for you to use in sending messages about sexual relationships. But, of course, communication is a two-way street, and you and your partner will exchange responses. It is therefore important for you and your partner to gain some skills in listening and responding constructively to messages. The following discussion will suggest such techniques.

One of the most important things is that you must really *listen*. This means more than just removing the headphones from your ears. It means actively trying to understand what the other person is saying. Often people are so busy trying to think of their next response that they hardly hear what the other person is saying. Good listening also involves positive nonverbal behaviours, such as maintaining eye contact with the speaker and nodding one's head when appropriate. Be a *nondefensive listener*; focus on what your partner is saying and feeling, and don't immediately become defensive or counterattack with complaints of your own.

The next step, after you have listened carefully and nondefensively, is to give *feedback*. This often involves giving brief vocalizations—"Uh-huh," "Okay"—nodding your head, or making facial movements that indicate you are listening (Gottman et al., 1998). It may involve the technique of **paraphrasing**—that is, repeating in your own words what you think your partner meant. Suppose, in response to Donna's initial statement, "You're not giving me any orgasms when we have sex," Chris hadn't gotten upset and instead had tried to listen and then gave her feedback by paraphrasing. Chris might have responded,

> I hear you saying that I'm not very good at making love to you, and therefore you're not having orgasms. (6)

At that point, Donna would have had a chance to clear up the confusion she had created with her initial message, because Chris had given her feedback by paraphrasing. She could have said, "No, I think you're a good lover, but I'm not having any orgasms, and I don't know why. I thought maybe we could figure it out together." Or perhaps she could have said, "No, I think you're a good

levelling: Telling your partner what you are feeling by stating your thoughts clearly, simply, and honestly.

editing: Censoring or not saying things that would be deliberately hurtful to your partner or that are irrelevant.

paraphrasing: Saying in your own words what you think your partner meant.

lover. I just wish you'd do more of some of the things you do, like going down on me and stimulating my clitoris with your tongue."

It's also a good idea to *ask for feedback* from your partner, particularly if you're not sure whether you're communicating clearly.

Body Talk: Nonverbal Communication

Just as it is important to be a good listener to your partner's verbal messages, so too is it important to be good at reading your partner's nonverbal messages (Figure 12.10). Often the precise words we use are not as important as our **nonverbal communication**—the way we say them. Tone of voice, expression on the face, position of the body, whether you touch the other person—all are important in conveying the message. In fact, when verbal and nonverbal messages conflict, we tend to believe the nonverbal message (e.g., saying "I'm listening" while continuing to stare at the computer screen).

As an example, take the sentence "So you're here." If it is delivered as "So *you're* here" in a hostile tone of voice, the message is that the speaker is very unhappy that you're here. If it is delivered as "So you're *here*" in a pleased voice, the meaning may be that the speaker is glad and surprised to see you here in Newfoundland, having thought you were in Europe. "So you're here" with a smile and arms outstretched to initiate a hug might mean that the speaker has been waiting for you and is delighted to see you.

Suppose that in Donna and Chris's case, the reason Donna doesn't have more orgasms is that Chris doesn't stimulate her firmly enough or in the spot that feels best to her. During sex, Donna is worried that it is taking her too long to reach orgasm and that Chris is getting tired or bored stimulating her. (Notice that Donna is mind reading again.) As a result, Donna does not enjoy the stimulation she does get as much as she could, and her body language communicates that she's not really into it. Chris already believes that Donna does not really like sex and the response (or rather nonresponse) of her body confirms these assumptions. Chris reads Donna's body language as communicating that she's not really enjoying having her clitoris stimulated. Although she would like to have an orgasm and for Chris to keep stimulating her, her body is saying, "I'm not into this. Let's get it over with." And that's exactly what Chris does.

To correct this situation, Donna might adopt a more active, encouraging approach. She might take Chris's hand and guide it to her clitoris, showing exactly where and how firmly she likes to have it rubbed. She might give Chris verbal feedback, saying "That's good" when Chris touches her in a way that she likes, or "Please don't stop" if she wants oral stimulation to continue.

Figure 12.10 (*a*) A couple with good body language (good eye contact and body position); (*b*) A couple with poor body language (poor eye contact and body position).

(a) © Digital Vision/PunchStock

(b) Bruce Ayres/Tony Stone/Getty Images

The point is that in communicating about sex, we need to be sure that our nonverbal signals help to create the impact we intend rather than one we do not intend. It is also possible that nonverbal signals are confusing communication and need to be straightened

nonverbal communication: Communication not through words but through the body (e.g., eye contact, tone of voice, touching).

out. "Checking out" is a technique for doing this that will be discussed in a later section.

Interestingly, research shows that distressed couples differ from nondistressed couples more in their nonverbal communication than in their verbal communication (Gottman et al., 1977; Vincent et al., 1979). For example, even when a person from a distressed couple is expressing agreement with his or her partner, that person is more likely to accompany the verbal expressions of agreement with negative nonverbal behaviour. Distressed couples are also more likely to be negative listeners—while listening, the individuals are more likely to display frowning, angry, or disgusted facial expressions or tense or inattentive body postures. Contempt is often expressed nonverbally, by sneering or rolling the eyes, for example. In contrast, harmonious relationships are characterized by closer physical distances and more relaxed postures than are found in distressed couples (Beier & Sternberg, 1977). Once again, it is not only what we say verbally but also how we say it, and how we listen, that makes the difference.

Validating

Another good technique in communication is **validation** (Gottman et al., 1976), which means telling your partner that, given his or her point of view, you can see why he or she thinks a certain way. It doesn't mean that you agree with your partner or that you're giving in. It simply means that you recognize your partner's point of view as legitimate, given his or her set of assumptions, which may be different from yours.

It is important to recognize that all couples have disagreements. What is important is how you handle these disagreements. If they lead to fights because one partner thinks the other is wrong, these will likely damage the relationship. It is much better to try to understand the other person's viewpoint. In a study of 76 couples, understanding of the partner's preferences for such things as sexual techniques, use of erotica, and use of contraception (not agreement with them) was associated with satisfaction with the sexual aspects of the relationship (Purnine & Carey, 1997).

Suppose that Donna and Chris have gotten into an argument about cunnilingus. Donna thinks it would bring her to orgasm. Chris doesn't want to do it and feels very uncomfortable with the idea. If Donna tried to validate Chris's feelings, she might say,

> I can understand the way you feel about going down on me, especially given the way you were brought up to think about sex. (7)

Chris might validate Donna's feelings by saying,

> I understand how important it is for you to have an orgasm. (8)

validation: Telling your partner that, given his or her point of view, you can see why he or she thinks a certain way.

Validating hasn't solved their disagreement, but it has left the door open so that they can now make some progress.

Drawing Your Partner Out

Suppose it is Chris who initiates the conversation rather than Donna. Chris has noticed that Donna doesn't seem to get a lot of pleasure out of sex and would like to find out why and see what they can do about it. Chris needs to draw Donna out and might begin by saying,

> I've noticed lately that you don't seem to be enjoying sex as much as you used to. Am I right about that? (9)

That much is good because Chris is checking out an assumption. Unfortunately, the question leads to a "yes" or "no" answer, and that can stop the communication. So, if Donna replies "yes," Chris had better follow it up with an *open-ended* question like

> What can I do to help you enjoy it more? (10)

If Donna can give a reasonable answer, good communication should be on the way. One of the standard—and best—questions to ask in a situation like this is

> What can we do to make things better? (11)

Accentuate the Positive

We have been concentrating on negative communications —that is, communications in which some problem or complaint needs to be voiced. It is also important to communicate positive things about the relationship in general and sex in particular (Gottman & Notarius, 2002). If that was a great episode of lovemaking, or the best kiss you've ever experienced, say so. A learning theorist would say that you're giving your partner some positive reinforcement. As discussed earlier in this chapter, social psychologists' research shows that we tend to like people better who give us positive reinforcements. Recognition of the strengths in a relationship offers the potential for enriching it (e.g., Miller et al., 1975). And if you make a habit of positive communications about sex, it will be easier to initiate the negative ones, and they will be better received.

Most communication during sex is limited to muffled groans, or "Mmm," or an occasional "Faster, John" or "Did you, Michèle?" It might help your partner greatly if you gave frequent verbal and nonverbal feedback, such as "That was great" or "Let's do that again." This would make the positive communications and the negative ones far easier.

Research shows that nondistressed couples make more positive and fewer negative communications than distressed couples (Billings, 1979). In fact, Gottman's

(1994) research with married couples found that there is a *magic ratio* of positive to negative communication. In stable marriages, there is five times as much positive interaction—verbal and nonverbal, including hugs and kisses, as there is negative. Not only do happy couples make more positive communications, they are also more likely to respond to a negative communication with something positive (Billings, 1979). Distressed couples, on the other hand, are more likely to respond to negative communication with more negative communication, escalating into conflict. We might all take a cue from the happy couples and make efforts not only to increase our positive communications but even to make them in response to negative comments from our partner.

Fighting Fair

Even if you use all the techniques just described, you may still get into arguments with your partner. Arguments are a natural part of a relationship and are not necessarily bad. Given that there will be arguments in a relationship, it is useful if you and your partner have agreed to a set of rules called **fighting fair** (Bach & Wyden, 1969) so that the arguments may help and won't hurt (Figure 12.11).

Here are some of the basic rules for arguing that may be useful to you (Brenton, 1972; Creighton, 1992). Many of them relate to the four destructive communication patterns identified by John Gottman (Gottman & Silver, 1999).

1. Edit what you say. Don't make sarcastic or insulting remarks about your partner's sexual adequacy. This generates resentment, opens you to counterattack, and is just a dirty way to fight.

Figure 12.11 Arguments are not necessarily bad for a relationship, but it is important to observe the rules for fighting fair.

© Bill Aron/Photo Edit

2. Don't bring up the names of former partners, lovers, boyfriends, or girlfriends to illustrate how all these problems didn't happen with them. Stick to the issue: your relationship with your partner.

3. Don't play amateur psychologist. Don't say things like "The problem is that you're a compulsive personality" or "You acted that way because you never resolved your Oedipus complex." You really don't have the qualifications (even after reading this book) to do so. Even if you did, your partner is likely to think you are biased and would not be apt to recognize your expertise in the middle of an argument.

4. Don't engage in dumping. Don't store up gripes for six months and then dump them on your partner all at one time.

5. Don't hit and run. Don't bring up a serious negative issue when there is no opportunity to continue the discussion, such as when you're on the way out the door going to work or when guests are coming for dinner in five minutes.

6. Don't focus on who's to blame. Focus on looking for solutions, not on who's at fault. If you avoid blaming, it lets both you and your partner save face, which helps both of you feel better about the relationship.

Checking Out Sexy Signals

One of the problems with verbal and nonverbal sexual communications is that they are often ambiguous. This problem may occur more often with couples who don't know each other well, but it can cause uncertainty and misunderstanding in couples in long-term relationships as well.

Some messages are very direct. Statements like "I want to have sex with you" are not ambiguous at all. Unfortunately, such directness is not common in our society. Two New Brunswick studies show that only a minority of people in mixed-sex relationships—22 percent in dating relationships and 41 percent in long-term relationships—use a direct verbal statement to initiate sex (Byers & Heinlein, 1989; O'Sullivan & Byers, 1992). The rest use ambiguous verbal or nonverbal messages. Similarly, Ontario researchers found that men and women in same-sex relationships are more likely to initiate sex by using nonverbal than by using verbal behaviours (Beres et al., 2004). Consider George, who stands up, stretches, and says, "It's time for bed." Does he mean he wants to engage in sexual activity or to go to sleep?

fighting fair: A set of rules designed to make arguments constructive rather than destructive.

Ambiguous messages can lead to feelings of hurt and rejection or to unnecessary anger and perhaps complaints to third parties. If George wants to have sex but his partner interprets his behaviour as meaning that George is tired, George may go to bed feeling hurt, unattractive, and unloved. A woman who casually puts her arm around the shoulders of a co-worker and gives him or her a hug may find herself explaining to her supervisor that it was a gesture of friendship, not a sexual proposition.

Ideally, each of us should be effective communicators, making sure our message clearly matches our intent. It helps to be clear yet also subtle and seductive as messages that are too direct or too polite may be a turnoff (Graham et al., 2004). As recipients of ambiguous messages, we need to make an effort to clear them up. In response to an invitation to a woman's apartment for coffee, a man might reply, "I would like some coffee, but I'm not interested in sex this time." Or he might draw her out with a question: "I'd like some coffee; is that all you have in mind?" Check out sexy signals. Don't make any assumptions about the meaning of ambiguous messages.

Gender Differences in Communication

Some authors argue that men and women have radically different verbal communication styles (Tannen, 1991). We should not be led astray by flashy claims that men and women are so different that they belong to different linguistic communities. Research generally has shown that there are some gender differences in communication. For example, as discussed in Chapter 13, women tend to self-disclose personal information about themselves and talk about their feelings more than men do, and women are generally better at reading another person's emotions and nonverbal behaviour (Hall, 1998; MacNeil & Byers, 2005). However, in general these differences are small and, contrary to gender stereotypes, both men and women place the highest value on communication that provides emotional support (Burleson, 2003). So whether an individual is in a relationship with a partner of the same gender or of the other gender, with a little effort couples should be able to engage in clear, accurate sexual communication. However, as noted earlier, for some couples poor communication leads to relationship distress or low sexual satisfaction. Not all these couples are able to improve communication on their own. For these couples, relationship or sexual therapy can be an effective way to improve communication and enhance relationship and sexual satisfaction.

Relationship Education

Recognizing the importance of good communication to reducing conflict, and with an eye toward the high divorce rate in the North America, relationship or marital education programs were developed in the 1980s. There are a substantial number of these programs today; many now have web pages and some can be taken entirely online. The best known include The Art and Science of Love, Better Marriages, Couple Communication, Marriage Encounter, and PAIRS (Practical Application of Intimate Relationship Skills). Although there is variation in content and curriculum, most of these programs are psychoeducational (not therapeutic). Most focus primarily on developing better communication and problem solving skills, and include much of the material covered in this section, with classroom sessions and many activities designed to encourage practice. A secondary focus may be on information and skills to improve a couple's ability to manage finances, raise children, cope with stress, etc.

A meta-analysis of evaluations of these programs found that they on average are somewhat effective, with larger effects for communication skills than marital quality. Programs lasting 9 to 20 hours were more effective than were shorter programs. (Hawkins et al., 2008). Another meta-analysis found that program effects lasted longer for initially well-functioning couples than distressed ones (Blanchard et al., 2009)—not surprising, since these programs are not intended to be therapeutic and usually are not led by therapists. Most participants in these evaluations were white, middle class, primarily married couples. A separate meta-analysis identified 15 evaluation studies of programs targeting low-income couples. The curricula used were adapted to the needs and circumstances of lower-income couples. The programs had small to moderate positive effects on both communication skills and relationship quality (Hawkins & Fackrell, 2010).

Thus, relationship education does work for some couples. The next steps are to find out for which couples, and to identify the specific aspects of these programs that produce changes in communication skills and relationship quality (Wadsworth & Markman, 2012). Of course, it is also important to develop new approaches for the couples for whom they do not work.

Critical THINK *ing Skill*

UNDERSTANDING THE IMPORTANCE OF CLEAR COMMUNICATION

Our lives consist of our relationships with other people—parents or caregivers, siblings, lovers, children, friends, supervisors, co-workers. The quality of our lives rests on the quality of those relationships. And what does a relationship depend on? Communication. In this chapter we argued that an essential aspect of developing a relationship is self-disclosure leading to intimacy. This is true not only in romantic relationships, but in many areas of life. Self-disclosure involves telling the other person personal things about yourself—that is, communicating.

For many people, good, satisfying relationships are those in which we get some of our needs met, whatever the needs may be. In order for that to happen, the other person needs to know what our needs are and how to satisfy them. We often wish that person would know without our having to tell them; we wish they could read our minds. Or we think, "If you really loved me, you would know what I want." Some reflection or critical thinking will reveal these to be false beliefs. Mind reading usually doesn't work, as we discuss in this chapter; and love does not bestow the superpower of reading another's mind. So we are left with the need to communicate.

In order for another person to meet our needs, we must communicate clearly and honestly. This can be harder than it sounds. Our communication often follows well-rehearsed scripts, as in ordering food in a restaurant, or flirting at a party or club, or engaging in sex. We rely on social conventions, but these may not clearly communicate about who we are as individuals and what we want. That's why in this chapter we encourage using "I" language. We advise asking direct questions, paraphrasing what we hear, and checking out sexy signals. These communication techniques help to reduce ambiguity and misunderstanding.

Communication involves not only words, but also the way one speaks—warmly, coldly, with hostility; loudly or softly, fast or slow. Specialists believe that these cues are especially likely to convey the speaker's emotional state. Perhaps you have been in conversations where the words didn't match the person's mood. There are some interesting issues here. When your partner asks if you are mad that he is late for dinner, a date, or work, you may say "No!" but your tone, the loudness of your voice, may give you away. Your effort to avoid clear, honest communication may not work.

Communication also involves nonverbal behavior and body language. A tense body, arms folded across the chest and avoidance of eye contact, may indicate anxiety, anger, or withdrawal from the conversation. On the other hand, a smile, relaxed posture, and a nodding head indicate engagement and desire to communicate.

Clear communication requires effort and critical thinking. First, you need to understand yourself. What do you want to say? Once you can identify your intention, think about how best to communicate it. Choose the time and place. And be aware that social scripts and conventions may not provide the means for clear, honest communication. Use "I" language, be honest, and try to match your verbal and nonverbal cues.

SUMMARY

For most people—heterosexual, gay, and lesbian—emotional passion and sexual passion are closely linked. Unfortunately, much of the research on love has been restricted to heterosexuals and has not included gay men, lesbians, or bisexuals.

Research indicates that mere repeated exposure to another person facilitates attraction. We tend to be attracted to people who are similar to us socially (age, race or ethnicity, economic status) and psychologically (attitudes, interests). In first impressions, we are most attracted to people who are physically attractive; we also tend to be attracted to people whom we believe to be within our reach, depending on our sense of our own attractiveness or desirability.

According to reinforcement theory, we are attracted to those who give us many reinforcements. Interaction with people who are similar to us is smooth and rewarding; they have similar outlooks and like the same things we do. According to sexual strategies theory, we prefer young, attractive people because they are likely to be healthy and fertile. Men prefer women who are sexually faithful; women prefer men with resources who will invest in them and their children.

Intimacy is a major component of a romantic relationship. It is defined as a quality of a relationship characterized by commitment, feelings of closeness and trust, and self-disclosure.

According to the triangular theory, love has three components: intimacy, passion, and decision or commitment. Love is a triangle, with each component as one of the points. Partners whose love triangles are substantially different are mismatched, and they are likely to be dissatisfied with their relationship.

According to the attachment theory of love, adults vary in their capacity for love as a result of their love or attachment experiences in infancy. The theory says that there are four types of lovers: secure lovers, preoccupied lovers, fearful lovers, and dismissing lovers.

Love can also be viewed as a story, with characters, a plot, and a theme. People use their love stories to interpret experiences in relationships. Falling in love happens when a person meets someone who can play a compatible role in his or her story.

Love may have a neurochemical component. Passionate love, a state of intense longing and arousal, may be produced by dopamine. Like all chemically induced highs, passionate love eventually comes to an end. It may be replaced by companionate love, a feeling of deep attachment and commitment to the partner. This type of love may be accompanied by elevated levels of prolactin and oxytocin, which may be produced by physical closeness and touch.

Passionate love is associated with brain activity in areas associated with reward and complex cognitive processing. Long-term love relationships are associated with brain areas related to maternal attachment. Brain activation by looking at photos of lovers differs from the activity associated with objects of sexual desire.

Hatfield and Sprecher have constructed a scale to measure passionate love. Such scales make it possible to do scientific research on complex phenomena like love. Scores on this scale were correlated with measures of commitment to and satisfaction with romantic relationships.

Researchers have hypothesized that there are two basic components of romantic love: being in a state of physiological arousal and attaching the label *love* to the feeling. Several studies report evidence consistent with the hypothesis.

Cross-cultural research indicates that individualistic cultures like that of Canada emphasize love as the basis for marriage and encourage intimacy between partners. Collectivist cultures emphasize intergroup bonds as the basis for marriage and discourage intimacy between partners. Culture influences the importance of various characteristics in choosing a mate; it also affects our standards of beauty and the likelihood of marrying someone we don't love.

Research reveals clear differences in communication patterns between happy, nondistressed couples and couples who are unhappy, seeking counselling, or headed for divorce. Destructive patterns of interaction include criticism, contempt, defensiveness, and withdrawal. The key to building a good relationship is reciprocal self-disclosure. The key to maintaining a good relationship is being a good communicator.

Specific tips for being a good communicator include using "I" language, avoiding mind reading, documenting your points with specific examples, levelling and editing, being a nondefensive listener, giving feedback by paraphrasing, being aware of your nonverbal messages, validating the other's viewpoint, drawing your partner out, and engaging in positive verbal and nonverbal communication. When you do fight, fight fair. Finally, it is important to check out ambiguous sexy signals to find out what they really mean.

CHAPTER 13

Gender and Sexuality

© Yao Yongqiang/ChinaFotoPress/Getty Images

Are YOU Curious?

1. What are some major ways in which men and women differ in their sexuality?
2. When heterosexual men report more sexual partners than heterosexual women do, is this accurate? How can this be?
3. How do surgeons create a penis or a vagina when they do gender-reassignment surgery?

Read this chapter to find out.

The majority of women (happily for them) are not very much troubled with sexual feelings of any kind. What men are habitually, women are only exceptionally.*

The root of all men's desire is to have sex. When you brush your teeth, it's to have sex. When you eat, it's, well, I gotta have energy to have sex. When you get dressed, you think, oh, maybe if I wear these jeans I'll be more likely to have sex.**

* Dr. William Acton. (1857). *The functions and disorders of the reproductive organs.*
** Seth Rogen (2008).

When a baby is born, what is the first statement made about it? "It's a boy" or "It's a girl," of course. Children learn what gender they are early in development—by age 2½, most children can correctly identify their own gender (Campbell et al., 2002; Thompson, 1975). Sociologists tell us that gender is one of the most basic of status characteristics. That is, in terms of both our individual interactions with people and the position we hold in society, gender is exceptionally important. Many people experience consternation when they are uncertain of a person's gender or when the individual is intersex and the eight variables of gender outlined in Chapter 5 are not all in agreement. They may not know how to interact with the person and may feel flustered, not to mention curious, until they can ferret out some clue as to whether the person is a man or a woman. In this chapter we explore gender roles and the impact they may have on sexuality. As depicted in the quotes above, we have clear stereotypes about male and female sexuality. But just how accurate are these stereotypes? We also discuss the phenomenon of transgender, which includes several variations on typical gender.

This happens because not all cultures define gender as a male–female dichotomy; some cultures have three or even four genders. Examples are the *two-spirit people* among Native North Americans, the *acault* from Burma, *hijras* and *jo-gappa* from India, *xaný-th* from Oman, *bantut* from the Phillipines, *kathoey* from Thailand, and *fa'afafine* from Samoa (Poasa et al., 2004). (See Milestones in Sex Research for a discussion of the *fa'afafine*). Australia and some other jurisdictions now allow people to choose a third gender (X) on their passport instead of having to choose either male or female.

The consternation that people experience when they are uncertain of another person's gender is rooted in the **gender binary**, which is the classification of people into one of two categories, male and female, and excludes people who fall outside traditional conceptions

of masculinity or femininity. The dominant culture in Canadian society adheres to this rigid two-gender system. Today we know that there are more possibilities. For example, some people see themselves as genderqueer and outside the gender binary. The psychological research on gender stereotypes and gender differences has all been based on the assumption of a gender binary. In the last section of this chapter, we consider transgender, which goes beyond the gender binary.

 LO1

Gender Roles and Stereotypes

One of the basic ways in which societies codify this emphasis on gender is through gender roles.[1] A **gender role** is a set of norms, or culturally prescribed expectations, that define how people of one gender ought to behave. A closely related phenomenon is a **stereotype**, which is a rigid set of beliefs about a group of people (e.g., men) that distinguishes those people from others (e.g., women) and is applied to all members of that group. Research shows that even in modern North American society, and even among university students, there is a belief that males and females do differ psychologically in many ways, and the stereotypes have not changed much since 1972 (Bergen & Williams, 1991).

Children as young as 6 are aware of these stereotypes. Researchers in Nova Scotia showed children pictures containing a man and a woman and told them brief stories about the pictures. Each story described a gender stereotype. The researchers then asked the children which person in the picture the story was about. The children responded with the appropriate stereotype most of the time. More than 85 percent of 8-year-olds identified the woman in the picture as appreciative, gentle, weak, soft-hearted, sentimental, emotional, excitable, and meek and mild. They identified the man in the picture as aggressive, strong, coarse, cruel, loud, and ambitious.

[1] The distinction between sex and gender will be maintained in this chapter. Male–female roles–and thus gender roles–are being discussed here.

gender binary: The classification of people into one of two categories, male or female.

gender role: A set of norms, or culturally defined expectations, that define how people of one gender ought to behave.

stereotype: A rigid set of beliefs about a group of people (e.g., men) that distinguishes them from others (e.g., women) and is applied to all members of that group.

Heterosexuality is viewed as an important part of gender roles (Hyde & Jaffee, 2000). The "feminine" woman is expected to be sexually attractive to men and in turn to be attracted to them. Women who violate any part of this role—for example, lesbians because they are not attracted to men—are viewed as violators of gender roles and are considered masculine. Heterosexuality is equally important in the male role.

Gender Schema Theory

In Chapter 2 we discussed gender schema theory, a cognitive approach to understanding gender stereotypes. Recall that according to that theory, a gender schema is the set of ideas (about behaviours, personality, appearance, and so on) that we associate with males and females (Bem, 1981; Martin et al., 2002). Our gender schema influences how we process information. It causes us to tend to dichotomize information based on gender. It also leads us to distort or fail to remember information that is stereotype inconsistent. As a result, it is relatively difficult to change people's stereotyped notions because we tend to filter out information that contradicts stereotypes. Of course, people do not process information by using gender schema in every situation. Research in Ontario has shown that both our own gender roles (i.e., how traditional we are) and the situation we are in affect how likely we process information in terms of gender schema (McKenzie-Mohr & Zanna, 1990). In this study the researchers found that traditionally masculine men who were exposed to a nonviolent erotic film treated the female confederate in a *more sexist way* than did nontraditional men or men who saw a control film, suggesting that the erotic film activated a traditional gender schema for this group of men.

The Traditional Sexual Script

Scripts are cognitive frameworks for how people are expected to behave in social situations. The sexual script that is most pervasive in North America is a heterosexual script, termed the *traditional sexual script* (TSS). The TSS specifies how men and women are expected to behave in (heterosexual) sexual situations (Byers, 1996; Gagnon & Simon, 1973; Striepe & Tolman, 2003). Although young people often state that things have changed and that the gender roles are now egalitarian, research suggests that the traditional script is still the most common dating script (Laner & Ventrone, 2000). The following are some aspects of the TSS and the underlying gender schema:

1. Men are "oversexed" and women are "undersexed." As such, men are seen as having strong sexual needs and being highly motivated to engage in sexual activity at any opportunity. Women are depicted as being sexually reluctant, slow to arouse, and interested in sex only in the context of love and commitment.

2. High sexual experience enhances men's but decreases women's perceived status. That is, for men, sexual experience is perceived as reflecting positive characteristics, such as masculinity and attractiveness. In women, high sexual experience is attributed to undesirable characteristics, such as nonselectivity and lack of values. Think of the differences in the values attached to the words used to describe the highly sexually experienced man (*macho, stud*) compared with those used for the highly sexually experienced woman (*slut, whore*).

3. Men are expected to be "sexperts" and to take responsibility for both their own and their female partner's sexual pleasure and orgasm. Women are expected to be sexually naive. Thus, they may be afraid to share their sexual preferences with their partner out of fear that he will take this as evidence that they have had many sexual partners (something that is evaluated negatively in women). They also may fear that their partner will think they are criticizing him for not being the sexpert he is supposed to be.

4. Men, because of their greater sexual interest, are supposed to be the initiators in sexual situations.

5. To avoid being judged negatively by being too sexually available, women are expected to be sexual gatekeepers and place limits on sexual activity, particularly with a new partner. Thus, even when they are interested in engaging in sexual activity, females are expected to offer at least initial token resistance to their partner's sexual advances.

A group of Canadian research have demonstrated that young adults still identify all of these elements as part of the heterosexual sexual script (Sakaluk et al., 2016). For example, in a focus group study, participants endorsed many aspects of the TSS. For example, they indicated that men are always ready for sex whereas women inhibit their sexual expression. As another example, they indicated that men have a physical approach to sex whereas women have an emotional/relational approach to sex. They also developed a scale to assess the extent to which individuals endorse the TSS.

How much evidence is there that heterosexuals follow the TSS? Research conducted in New Brunswick sheds some light on this question (Byers, 1996). Participants in two studies (one of dating relationships, the other of long-term relationships) kept a diary in which they recorded sexual initiations and responses to initiations in their relationships (Byers & Heinlein, 1989; O'Sullivan

& Byers, 1992). The results indicated that men initiate sex more often than women do in both mixed-sex dating and long-term relationships. This is consistent with the TSS. However, men are not always the initiators—on average, women initiated sex more than once a week. Responses to initiations also did not follow the TSS. The research showed that men and women are equally likely to accept or refuse an initiation—they respond positively about 83 percent of the time in dating relationships and about 74 percent of the time in long-term relationships. Recent research also conducted in New Brunswick has found similar results (Simms & Byers, 2013; Vannier & O'Sullivan, 2011). Further, when one partner is reluctant to engage in sexual activity, men and women use the same strategies to try to change their partner's mind—most often flirting or touching and stroking the partner (O'Sullivan & Byers, 1996).

These results indicate that some aspects of the TSS, such as the expectation that it is the male role to initiate sex, continue to characterize heterosexual relationships. However, women regularly initiate sexual activity, albeit less frequently than their male partners. Further, research does not support other aspects of the TSS. Women are no more reluctant to engage in sexual activity than men are. To this extent, men's and women's roles in mixed-sex sexual interactions appear to be converging. Nonetheless, as discussed in Chapter 16, adherence to the TSS may be a cause of some men's use of sexually coercive behaviour with women (Byers, 1996).

✶ L02 Socialization

Many adult women and men do behave as gender roles say they should. Why does this happen? Psychologists and sociologists believe that it is a result of gender-role socialization. **Socialization** refers to the ways in which society conveys to the individual its

socialization: The ways in which society conveys to the individual its norms or expectations for his or her behaviour.

norms or expectations for his or her behaviour. Socialization occurs especially in childhood, as children are taught to behave as they will be expected to in adulthood. Socialization involves several processes. Children may be rewarded for behaviour that is appropriate for their gender ("What a brave little man he is"), or they may be punished for behaviour that is not appropriate to their gender ("Nice young ladies don't do that"). The adult models they imitate—whether these are parents of the same gender, teachers, or women and men on television—also contribute to their socialization (Figure 13.1). In some cases, simply telling children what is expected of boys/men and girls/women may be sufficient for role-learning to take place. Children also engage in *self-socialization*, which operates in two ways. The more children come to identify with a particular gender (i.e., have a male or female gender identity), the more they are motivated to incorporate attributes associated with that gender into their self-concept. Conversely, seeing themselves as matching the stereotypes for their own gender strengthens children's gender identity (Tobin et al., 2010). Socialization continues in adulthood, as society conveys its norms of appropriate behaviour for adult women and men. These norms extend from appropriate jobs to who initiates sexual activity.

Gender socialization comes from multiple sources, including parents, peers, and the media (Leaper & Friedman, 2007). Certainly parents have an early, important influence, from buying dolls for girls and footballs or baseball bats for boys, to giving boys more freedom to explore. Research indicates that parents treat girls and boys similarly in many ways, with the exception that parents strongly encourage gender-typed activities (Blakemore et al., 2009).

The peer group also can have a big impact on socializing for gender roles. In an Ontario experiment, children in Grades 3 to 6 read stories about boys and girls who engaged in traditionally masculine, traditionally feminine, or a combination of masculine and feminine

Figure 13.1 Children are very interested in imitating adult behaviour that entails gender.

© Anne Flinn Powell/Photolibrary/Getty Images

© ESB Professional/Shutterstock

behaviours (Zucker et al., 1995). The boys preferred to be friends with the exclusively masculine boy, and girls preferred the exclusively feminine girl. Teenagers may be particularly effective at exerting pressure for gender-role conformity (Maccoby, 2002).

The media are also important socializing agents. Many people assume that things have changed a lot in the last 30 years and that gender stereotypes are a thing of the past. On the contrary, various media—from television to teen magazines—continue to show females and males in stereotyped role. An analysis of G-rated films, for example, showed that male characters outnumbered female characters by 2.5 to 1, a pattern that had not changed in 15 years (Smith et al., 2010). Both males and females were shown mainly in gender-stereotyped occupations. And music videos show females as subordinate and males as aggressive (Wallis, 2011).

An analysis of advertising on the major television networks found that the "voice of authority"—the voice-over—is male in 71 percent of ads (Messineo, 2008). In these commercials, men are more likely to be portrayed as assertive and employed, and women are more likely to be shown as parents and as sex objects.

Dozens of studies show that gender stereotypes shown on television affect children's stereotyped ideas (Ward & Harrison, 2005). For example, in one study children in Grades 1 and 2 were exposed to television commercials in which all boys were playing with a gender-neutral toy (traditional condition), all girls were playing with it (nontraditional condition), or the commercials were not about toys (control) (Pike & Jennings, 2005). Afterward, children were asked to sort six toys into those that were for boys, those that were for girls, or those that were for both boys and girls. Among the six toys was the toy they had seen in the commercial. Children in the traditional condition were more likely to say that the toy was for boys, whereas children in the nontraditional condition were more likely to say that it was for both boys and girls. These results show not only the power of stereotyped television images but also that children can respond positively to nonstereotyped messages.

But picture books and TV are old-fashioned media. One might expect the new media to be less stereotyped; to the contrary, however, video games show patterns of extreme gender stereotyping. In *Grand Theft Auto*, the men are violent and the women are hookers (Chong et al., 2012). Adolescents average more than an hour a day playing video games (Rideout et al., 2010). In short, adolescents' exposure to these games and their gender stereotypes is massive.

Although gender roles themselves are universal (Rosaldo, 1974)—that is, all societies have gender roles—the exact content of these roles varies from one culture to the next, from one ethnic group to another,

and from one social class to another. Gender roles in the major ethnocultural Canadian communities are described next.

 ## **LO3** Gender Roles and Ethnicity

Ethnicity refers to a sizable group of people who share a common and distinct racial, national, religious, linguistic, or cultural origin or heritage. Although people of British and French backgrounds make up the largest ethnic groups in Canada, only 12 percent of Canadians report only British or French origins (Statistics Canada, 2008b). More than one in five (20.6 percent) Canadians were not born in Canada, and about two thirds of these individuals (63 percent) live in Toronto, Montreal, or Vancouver. Indeed, between 23 and 46 percent of the population in Toronto, Vancouver, and Montreal were born outside Canada (Statistics Canada, 2013). Changing immigration patterns since the 1980s have increased the ethnocultural diversity of Canada and have introduced a wide range of attitudes and traditions surrounding gender roles.

As we consider variations in gender roles across variations in ethnic groups, it is crucial to understand how these gender roles are a product of *culture*. In the sections below, we consider some aspects of the culture of four ethnic groups and their relevance to gender roles and sexuality.

First, though, we will consider a key concept, **intersectionality**, which can be defined as an approach that simultaneously considers the meaning and consequences of multiple categories of identity, difference, and disadvantage (Cole, 2009). That is, according to this approach, we should not consider the effects of gender in isolation. Instead, we should consider the effects of gender, race, social class, and sexual orientation simultaneously. When we talk about the category "women," for example, we are talking about a complex group that differs by ethnicity, social class, sexual orientation, and many other identities, such as religion.

Within this framework, it becomes clear that some groups experience multiple disadvantages, such as poor Aboriginal women or lesbian women of colour. Others may be part of a disadvantaged group but also part of a privileged group, such as a middle-class Aboriginal person. In the sections that follow, we will look at the intersection of gender and ethnicity. In Chapter 14, we will also examine the intersection of gender, ethnicity, and sexual orientation. For example, Ontario researchers have shown that acceptance and experience of intimate cross-gender relationships of second-generation South Asians living in Toronto varied depending on their religion, religiosity, ethnic identity, and gender (Zaidi et al., 2014).

intersectionality: An approach that simultaneously considers the consequences of multiple group membership, such as the intersection of gender and ethnicity.

In some ways, the gender roles of members of Canadian ethnocultural communities reflect the values and norms of their country of origin. However, gender roles are also influenced by the majority Canadian culture through the process of **acculturation**—the process of incorporating the beliefs and customs of a new culture. For example, in keeping with traditional values, immigrant parents may allow their sons but not their daughters to engage in unsupervised dating. However, the same parents may encourage their daughters to obtain professional degrees and take up careers even though women in their culture traditionally do not work outside the home (Mackie, 1991). Second-generation youth may feel caught between two cultures. On the one hand, the norms of the country of origin and within their family may forbid cross-gender relationships. On the other hand, they may feel pressure to conform to their peer group and behave differently inside and outside of their home (Zaidi et al., 2014).

The study titled Ethnocultural Communities Facing AIDS examined sexuality within six Canadian ethnocultural communities (see Chapter 1 for a description of this study). Groups were chosen based on ethnicity, not race.

acculturation: The process of incorporating the beliefs and customs of a new culture.

The researchers chose large, cohesive communities with a large proportion of young people and people who had immigrated to Canada since 1986 (Cappon et al., 1996). They found a number of cross-cultural similarities in gender roles. Generally, men and women in these communities are seen as having distinct roles in that men are expected to be the head of the family, and women are expected to be the caregivers. However, economic realities often mean that women must work outside the home, and these role changes often create conflict within the family. There tends to be a double standard with respect to sexual behaviour. Dating and premarital sex are accepted and often encouraged in sons but not tolerated in daughters. Men are expected to be active in sexual relationships, whereas women are expected to be passive and to meet men's needs (Manson Singer et al., 1996).

There also are differences in gender role expectations between various ethnocultural groups (Figure 13.2), as the following descriptions of the Chinese, South Asian, and Caribbean communities in the aforementioned study demonstrate (Baxter et al., 1993a, 1993b; Brabazon et al., 1993a, 1993b; Gunter et al., 1993a, 1993b). As you will see, gender roles in Canada are not uniform. Different ethnic groups define gender roles differently. As with the majority Canadian culture, there also are variations

Figure 13.2 Gender roles in Canada's ethnocultural communities reflect aspects of the majority culture and aspects of the minority culture, such as this arranged Hindu marriage in Montreal.

© The Canadian Press Images/Montreal Gazette

in gender roles within each ethnocultural community. The following descriptions refer to the dominant views within these cultures.

The South Asian Communities

In 2006 there were 1 316 700 people who identified themselves as South Asian (e.g., Indians and Pakistanis) living in Canada, the second-largest visible minority group in Canada. In South Asian communities, religion is a major focus of community life. Hard work, education, and achievement are seen as important. Respect for traditional values, which in some cases includes arranged marriages even for people born in Canada, is also highly valued (see First Person in Chapter 12). South Asian men and women tend to be assigned different roles, and women are expected to be submissive to men. Boys tend to be given privileges and freedom, dating is allowed, and it is expected that they will have some sexual experience. However, girls may not be allowed to date because female virginity before marriage is highly valued. Men are expected to take the lead in the sexual encounter; women are expected to be passive, submissive, and uninformed about sex. As a result of women's prescribed sexual passivity, some men visit sex workers for casual sex before and during marriage. The women are not supposed to question the behaviour of their husbands or to complain about extramarital sexual activity.

The Chinese Community

In the 2006 census, 1 346 510 people in Canada identified themselves as Chinese Canadians, the largest visible minority group in the country. Chinese culture emphasizes responsibility to the family and the community over self-fulfillment and individualism as in the majority Canadian culture. Marriage is highly valued, so couples are reluctant to separate or divorce even when experiencing significant marital problems. In most families, the man is considered the head of the household; the woman is the primary caregiver and is expected to adopt a submissive role with her male partner. It is not acceptable for women to engage in premarital or extramarital sexual activity, and premarital sex is also discouraged for men. However, extramarital sexual activity by men may be accepted, particularly in "astronaut families" in which the man works away from home, for example, in Hong Kong or Taiwan. Today, gender roles within the community are becoming more diverse as people move away from their traditional roles. Because achievement and education are important within the Chinese community, women who pursue their education in Canada may experience conflict between the traditional gender roles of Chinese culture and those of Canadian culture, which increasingly prizes independence and assertiveness in women (Figure 13.3). Men may also experience conflict between family values and individual achievement.

Figure 13.3 Gender roles in Canada's Asian community are becoming more diverse as people move away from their traditional background.

Jim Zukerman/Alamy

English-Speaking Caribbean Communities

In 2006 there were 783 800 individuals in Canada who identified themselves as black, most with roots in the Caribbean. English-speaking Caribbean (e.g., Jamaican) communities have a strong sense of family and community. Traditionally, the man was expected to be the provider and the woman was expected to care for the children and the household while also working outside the home. Today there are many single-parent families in the Caribbean communities, usually headed by women. More restrictions are placed on girls than on boys, in part as an attempt to prevent adolescent pregnancy. In adolescence and into adulthood, women's focus is on developing relationships, and they may engage in serial monogamy. Both having a male partner and having a child are considered important aspects of the female role and indicators of success. In contrast, young men are more likely to want to have many sexual partners. It also is not uncommon for married and cohabiting men to have multiple partners.

Aboriginal Communities

In the 2006 Canadian census, 1 678 235 people reported First Nations ancestry (Statistics Canada, 2008b). The Indigenous peoples constitute important ethnocultural minority groups in Canada. Before contact with Europeans, at least some of the Indigenous peoples in North America had relatively egalitarian gender roles (Kinsman, 1996; LaFromboise et al., 1990). That is, their roles were more egalitarian than those of the European culture of the same period. The process of acculturation and adaptation to the majority culture seems to have resulted in increased male dominance among North American Indigenous peoples.

Among the more than 200 Indigenous languages spoken in North America, at least two-thirds have a term

Milestones in Sex Research

Sex, Gender, and Sexual Orientation in Samoa

Canadians live in a culture that recognizes two genders: male and female. But, there are many places in the world where three or more genders are recognized. When I first learned about such places, my mind did somersaults. How was it possible that someone could be neither male nor female? It took me a while to realize that while male and female bodies are certainly grounded in biological reality, how these bodies are "gendered" varies historically and cross-culturally. If two gendered categories of personhood, such as "male" and "female," can be socially constructed, why not three . . . or more?

Since 2003, I have worked in Samoa, a culture where persons can be one of three genders: men, women, and *fa'afafine*. In the Samoan language, *fa'afafine* means "in the manner of a woman." Like men, *fa'afafine* are biological males. They differ from Samoa men, however, in that they are very feminine. From a Canadian perspective, many would be considered transgender. *Fa'afafine* are recognized in childhood, by their families and the members of their community, based on their tendencies to engage in feminine activities (e.g., playing with girls) and their aversion toward masculine activities (e.g., rough-and-tumble play) (Bartlett & Vasey, 2006). This

process of recognition does not mean that boys are made into *fa'afafine*. Rather, in Samoan culture, boyhood femininity is interpreted to mean that individuals simply are *fa'afafine*, and it is understood that such individuals will not grow up to be "men." Some families react negatively to the presence of a *fa'afafine* child, with corporal punishment. However, the majority have a laissez-faire attitude, some even facilitate the child's feminine behaviour—sewing "him" dresses, for example (Vasey & Bartlett, 2007).

In Samoa, *fa'afafine* enjoy a high level of social acceptance that, while not absolute, stands in stark contrast to the overt discrimination experienced by Western trans-women. Indeed, *fa'afafine* are highly visible, active, and productive members of Samoa society. They occupy all manner of positions from stay-at-home caregivers to assistant chief executive officers in the government. The prime minister of Samoa, the Honourable Tuilaepa Sailele Malielegaoi, is Patron of the National Fa'afafine Association and has spoken publicly on many occasions about the value of *fa'afafine* for Samoan society.

My Samoan research has afforded me the opportunity to examine how human sexuality is expressed in a cultural system that recognizes two sexes and three

that refers to a third (or third and fourth) gender beyond male and female (Tafoya & Wirth, 1996). European anthropologists termed this additional category *berdache*, a term rejected by many Indigenous peoples who prefer the term *two-spirit* (Jacobs et al., 1997). These same anthropologists concluded that the people were homosexuals, transsexuals, or transvestites, none of which are accurate from an Indigenous point of view (Kinsman, 1996). A man might be married to a two-spirit male, but the marriage would not be considered homosexual because the two are of different genders (Tafoya & Wirth, 1996).

There was also a role of the "manly hearted woman," a role that a woman who was exceptionally independent and aggressive could take on (Figure 13.4). There

was a "warrior woman" role among the Apache, Crow, Cheyenne, Blackfoot, Pawnee, and Navajo tribes (e.g., Buchanan, 1986; House, 1997). In both cases, women could express masculine traits or participate in male-stereotyped activities while continuing to live and dress as women.

 LO4

Gender Differences in Psychological Functioning

Psychologists have extensively studied gender differences in personality and behaviour (e.g., Hyde &

genders. In adulthood, the vast majority of *fa'afafine* are androphilic (i.e., sexually attracted and aroused to adult males). This fact might lead many to conclude, "Oh well, they're just gay, but in a different culture." I believe that would be a mistake. Remember, *fa'afafine* are identified in childhood, long before they have engaged in sexual activity. Moreover, *fa'afafine* do not consider themselves to be gay. At first, this was also difficult for me to grasp until I realized that "gay" is yet another culturally specific identity category with its own code of conduct. "Gays" as one of my *fa'afafine* friends pointed out to me, "have sex with other gays." "OK," I thought, "I'm with you on that one." "But," my friend continued, "*fa'afafine* don't have sex with each other. They have sex with straight men." Huh? More mental somersaults. If *fa'afafine* have sex with "straight men," how could those men be "straight"? My *fa'afafine* friend regarded me as if I was a bit thick.

It took me a while to grasp that Samoans were obviously stretching the definition of the term "straight man" beyond its more narrow meaning as understood by most Canadians. In a Samoan cultural context, regardless of sexual orientation, "straight man" means a man who is masculine and who self-identifies as a "male" and as a "man." Some "straight men" in Samoa are gynephilic (i.e., sexually attracted and aroused to adult women) and only have sex with women. However, other gynephilic Samoan men have sex with *fa'afafine* when they are unable to access their preferred sexual partners (i.e., adult females). The majority of men who have sex with *fa'afafine* likely fall into this latter group. Other men who have sex with *fa'afafine* appear to be attracted specifically to *fa'afafine*, to be bisexual, or to be androphilic (i.e., attracted to adult men). In short, the Samoan category of "straight man" is a very heterogeneous one with respect to sexual attraction and sexual orientation. All of this underscores the complex ways that sex, gender, and sexual orientation interact and how the pattern of interactions can vary from one culture to the next.

Much of the research I have conducted in Samoa involved interviewing *fa'afafine* about their behaviour in childhood (Bartlett & Vasey, 2006; VanderLaan et al. 2011; Vasey & Bartlett, 2007; Vasey et al., 2011). I have used this information to critically examine how Western psychologists characterize the mental health of gender-variant children. *Fa'afafine* don't grow up being constantly bombarded with the message that they're sick or that there is something wrong with them. Samoans simply acknowledge that "transgender" males are part of the cosmos and they move on. They don't try to "fix" them medically and, as a consequence, the society benefits as a whole. What a lesson Canada has to learn from these tiny islands.

Prof. Paul Vasey, University of Lethbridge

Else-Quest, 2012). Here we will focus on gender differences in two areas that are particularly relevant to gender and sexuality: aggressiveness and communication styles.

Males and females differ in *aggressiveness*. Males are generally more aggressive than females, and this difference is found cross-culturally (Best, 2001). This is true for virtually all indicators of aggression (physical aggression, such as fighting; verbal aggression; and fantasy aggression) (Archer, 2004). It is also true at all ages; as soon as children are old enough to perform aggressive behaviours, boys are more aggressive and men dominate the statistics on violent crimes. Researchers have found that there are some differences between men and women in their style of communicating, both verbally and nonverbally (Leaper & Ayres, 2007). Of particular relevance to sexuality, social psychologists have found gender differences in self-disclosure. Within dating relationships, women tend to self-disclose more than men do about both sexual and nonsexual issues (Byers & Demmons, 1999; MacNeil & Byers, 2005), and adolescent girls self-disclose to friends more than adolescent boys do (Rose & Rudolph, 2006).

Today, of course, males and females do much of their self-disclosure online. In one study of adolescents, girls' online self-disclosure increased greatly between ages 10 and 13; boys displayed a similar increase, but it started about two years later (Valkenburg et al., 2011). Girls engaged in more online self-disclosure than boys did at all ages. Another study examined college students'

Figure 13.4 Among some First Nations there are three gender roles, the third being known as a "manly hearted woman" or "warrior woman." Chiricahua Tah-des-te was a messenger and warrior in Geronimo's band. She participated in negotiations with several U.S. military leaders and surrendered with Geronimo in 1886.

© F.A. Rinehart for B.A.E./Smithsonian Institute

self-disclosure on their Facebook pages (Special & Li-Barber, 2012). For both the male and female students, the top motive for using Facebook was maintaining relationships—that is, motives displayed gender similarities. Moreover, there was no gender difference in disclosure of personal information in this particular medium.

Norms about self-disclosure are changing, though. Traditional gender roles favoured emotional expressiveness for women but emotional repressiveness and avoidance of self-disclosure for men. There is a contemporary ethic, though, of good communication and openness that demands equal self-disclosure from males and females (Rubin et al., 1980). Research with university students in New Brunswick indicates that traditional gender roles persist in that women are more emotionally expressive than men are in both nonsexual and sexual situations (Lawrance et al., 1996). However, this research also shows that we are moving toward a norm of greater emotional expressiveness for men. Men were described as ideally equally as expressive as women in sexual situations. Thus,

> **What are some major ways in which men and women differ in their sexuality?**

the traditional expectation that men should not express their feelings seems to be gradually shifting toward the expectation that they be open and communicative.

There are gender differences in people's ability to understand the nonverbal behaviours of others. The technical phrase for this is "decoding nonverbal cues"—that is, the ability to read others' body language correctly. It might be measured, for example, by one's accuracy in interpreting facial expressions. Research shows that women are better than men are at decoding such nonverbal cues and at discerning others' emotions (Hall, 1998). Certainly, this is consistent with the gender-related expectation that women will show greater interpersonal sensitivity.

What are the implications of these gender differences in communication styles for sexuality? For example, if men are less able to disclose personal information about themselves, might this hamper their ability to communicate their sexual needs to their partners?

✷ Gender Differences in Sexuality

In this section, the discussion will focus on areas of sexuality in which there is some evidence of male–female differences. As we will point out, differences do exist, but they are in a rather small number of areas—masturbation, attitudes about casual sex, arousal from erotica, consistency of orgasm during sex, and sex drive. There is a danger in focusing on these differences to the point of forgetting about gender similarities. Keep in mind that men and women are in many ways quite similar in their sexuality—for example, in the physiology of their sexual response (Chapter 9)—as you consider the evidence on male–female differences that follows.

Masturbation

A review of 730 studies of gender differences in sexuality found that one of the largest gender differences was the incidence of masturbation (Petersen & Hyde, 2010).

Recall that in the Kinsey data, 92 percent of the men had masturbated to orgasm at least once in their lives, as compared with 58 percent of the women. Not only did fewer women masturbate but, in general, those who did masturbate had begun at a later age than the men. Virtually all men said they had masturbated before age 20 (most began between ages 13 and 15), but substantial numbers of women reported masturbating for the first time at age 25, 30, or 35. This gender difference still appears in recent studies. For example, for adults between 25 and 29 in the National Survey of Sexual Health and Behavior (NSSHB), 94 percent of the men had masturbated at least once in their lives, compared with 85 percent of the women (Herbenick et al., 2010a).

And 20 percent of the men masturbated four or more times per week, compared with 5 percent of the women (Herbenick et al., 2010b; Reece et al., 2010b). Similarly, 80 percent of male students but only 48 percent of female students at the University of British Columbia reported masturbating at least once (Meston et al., 1996). The data suggest, then, that there is a gender difference in the incidence of masturbation, with men more likely to have masturbated than women.

Attitudes about Casual Sex

In the review just mentioned, another substantial gender difference was in attitudes toward casual sex—that is, sexual intercourse in a situation, such as a one-night stand, in which there is no emotionally committed relationship between the partners (Petersen & Hyde, 2010; Yost & Zurbriggen, 2006). Men are considerably more approving of such interactions, and women tend to be disapproving (Figure 13.5). Many women feel that sexual intercourse is ethical or acceptable only in the context of an emotionally committed relationship. For many men, that is a nice context for sex, but it isn't absolutely necessary.

One study has gained legendary status as an illustration of men's greater interest in casual sex. Clark and Hatfield (1989) had female and male research assistants,

Figure 13.5 In pickup situations, men are likely to be more interested in having the interaction lead to casual sex than women are.

© sirtravelalot/Shutterstock

who were confederates of the experimenters, approach people of the other gender and invite them to engage in casual sex. No women agreed to such a sexual encounter, whereas 70 percent of men agreed (see also Guéguen, 2011). Evolutionary theorists see these results as evidence of men's selection to have sex with many partners and women's selection to be choosy (Chapter 2). However, socialization explanations are equally plausible (Conley, 2011). Girls are socialized to perceive risk in the environment and, in particular, to be sensitive to the possibility of sexual assault. Boys, in contrast, are encouraged to ignore risk. Moreover, it may be more about the proposer than about the person receiving the proposal. Male proposers may be perceived as dangerous and female proposers as harmless. Then there is the issue of sexual pleasure. Doubtless men anticipate sexual pleasure from the encounter, whereas women would be less likely to think that the male proposer would give them pleasure. Several clever laboratory experiments support these socialization explanations (Conley, 2011).

In Canada, 68 percent of male adolescents but only 48 percent of female adolescents approve of having sex before marriage with someone you like (Bibby, 2001). Further, adolescent females are more likely to believe that sex without love is not satisfying. Gender differences in attitudes toward casual sex were even greater; in the Canada Youth Sexual Health and HIV/AIDS Study, 66 percent of Grade 11 boys but only 32 percent of Grade 11 girls agreed that it was all right to have casual sex (Boyce et al., 2003).

One study asked male and female university students about their motives for having sex (Meston & Buss, 2007). Participants identified 237 reasons for having sex, ranging from wanting to experience physical pleasure to wanting to express love for the person, feel closer to God, improve their sexual skills, or make their partner happy. Twenty of the top 25 reasons were the same for the men and the women. However, consistent with traditional gender roles, the men were more likely to have sex because of the physical desirability of their partner (e.g., "The person had a desirable body"), opportunity (e.g., "The person was available"), physical pleasure (e.g., "I wanted to achieve an orgasm"), and insecurity (e.g., "I felt obligated to"). Contrary to stereotypes, for the most part, the women were not more likely than the men were to endorse emotional and commitment motives for having sex, although the women were more likely to say that they had sex to express their love for their partner. However, motives for having sex may be different with a casual compared to a committed partner. For example, researchers in Ontario have shown that women are more likely to endorse physical reasons as compared to emotional reasons for having sex with a casual partner; the reverse was true for sex in a committed relationship (Armstrong & Reissing, 2015).

Use of Pornography

The third substantial gender difference found in the review noted above was in the use of pornography (Petersen & Hyde, 2010). Men were considerably more likely to report using porn than women were. Further, research in New Brunswick has shown that men are more likely to go online to view pornography than are women; they are also more likely to go online to engage in sexual activity with a partner (Shaughnessy, Byers, & Walsh, 2011). The gender difference in pornography use, in turn, is probably connected to the topic discussed next.

Arousal from Erotica

Traditionally in our society, most erotic material—sexually arousing pictures, movies, or stories—has been produced for a male audience. The corresponding assumption presumably has been that women are not aroused by such things. Does the scientific evidence bear out this notion?

Laboratory research shows that men are more aroused by erotic materials, but the gender difference is not large (Murnen & Stockton, 1997). A classic study by psychologist Julia Heiman (1975) provides a good deal of insight into the responses of men and women to erotic materials. The participants were sexually experienced university students, and Heiman studied their responses as they listened to tape recordings of erotic stories. Not only did she obtain the participants' self-ratings of their arousal, as other investigators have done, but she also got objective measures of their physiological levels of arousal. To do this, she used two instruments: a penile strain gauge and a vaginal photoplethysmograph (see Figure 13.6). The **penile strain gauge** (which our students have dubbed the "peter meter"), or *plethysmograph*, is used to get a physiological measure of arousal in men; it is a flexible loop that fits around the base of the penis. The vaginal **photoplethysmograph**, or *photometer*, measures physiological arousal in the female; it is an acrylic cylinder, about the size of a tampon, that is placed just inside the entrance to the vagina. Both instruments measure vasocongestion in the genitals, which is the major physiological response during sexual arousal (see Chapter 9). A problem with these devices is that they are intrusive and neither can be used with both women and men. New technology has come to the rescue. Researchers in Quebec have shown that **thermal imaging** technology (i.e., changes in the temperature of the genital area

penile strain gauge: A device used to measure physiological sexual arousal in the male; it is a flexible loop that fits around the base of the penis.

photoplethysmograph (foh-toh-pleth-ISS-moh-graf): An acrylic cylinder that is placed inside the vagina to measure physiological sexual arousal in the female; also called a photometer.

thermal imaging: A method of detecting genital arousal by using a remote camera focused on the genital region to measure its temperature.

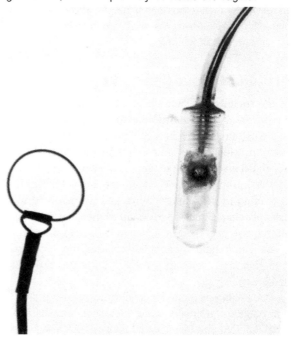

Figure 13.6 Two devices used to measure physiological sexual response in males and females. The penile strain gauge (left) consists of a flexible band that fits around the base of the penis. The photoplethysmograph (right) is an acrylic cylinder containing a photocell and a light source, which is placed just inside the vagina.

Courtesy of J.R. Heiman

because of sexual arousal detected by a remote camera focused on the genital region) may be useful in assessing physiological genital arousal in both women and men (Kukkonen et al., 2007, 2010). Researchers in Ontario, are investigating the utility of a *clitoral photoplethysmograph* that is positioned externally between the labia and measures blood flow to the clitoris (Suschinsky et al., 2015).

In the Heiman (1975) study, research participants heard one of four kinds of tapes depicting heterosexual couples to test the stereotype that women are more turned on by romance, whereas men are more aroused by "raw sex." The tapes varied according to which of these kinds of content they contained. The first group of tapes was *erotic;* they included excerpts from popular novels giving explicit descriptions of heterosexual sex. The second group of tapes was *romantic;* a couple was heard expressing affection and tenderness for each other, but they did not actually engage in sex. The third group of tapes was *erotic-romantic;* they included erotic elements of explicit sex but also romantic elements. Finally, the fourth group of tapes served as a control; a couple were heard engaging in conversation but nothing else. The plots of the tapes also varied according to whether the man or the woman initiated the activity and whether the description centred on the woman's physical and psychological responses or on the man's. Thus, the tapes were either male-initiated or female-initiated and either female-centred or male-centred. Three important results emerged from the study:

1. Explicit mixed-sex (the erotic and erotic-romantic tapes) was most arousing, both for women and for men. The great majority of both men and women responded most strongly, both physiologically and in self-ratings, to the erotic and erotic-romantic tapes. Women, in fact, rated the erotic tapes as more arousing than men did. Neither men nor women responded—either physiologically or in self-reports—to the romantic tapes or to the control tapes (except for a couple of men who were aroused by a discussion of the relative merits of an anthropology major versus pre-med—ah, well).

2. Both men and women found the female-initiated, female-centred tape to be most arousing. Perhaps the female-initiated plot was most arousing because of its somewhat forbidden or taboo nature.

3. Women were sometimes not aware of their own physiological arousal. Generally there was a high correlation between self-ratings of arousal and objective physiological measures of arousal for men. When men were physically aroused, they never made an error in reporting this in their self-ratings—it is pretty hard to miss an erection. But when the women were physically aroused, about half of them did not report arousal in their self-ratings. (One might assume that women who were sophisticated enough to volunteer for an experiment of this nature and who were willing to insert a photoplethysmograph into their vagina would not suddenly become bashful about reporting their arousal; that is, it seems likely that these women honestly did not perceive themselves to be aroused.)

In sum, then, Heiman's study indicates that women and men are quite similar in their responses to erotic materials but that women can sometimes be unaware of their own physical arousal. Researchers in New Brunswick measured men's and women's implicit attitudes (see Chapter 3) toward romantic and sexual stimuli and also found that men and women are similar in that both show a preference for romantic over sexual stimuli (Thompson & O'Sullivan, 2012). However, the women's preference was stronger than was the men's.

In statistical terms, Heiman found a low correlation between women's self-reports of arousal and the physiological measures of their arousal, a pattern that is still found in contemporary studies (Chivers et al., 2010; Suschinsky et al., 2009, 2011). In an interesting follow-up study, one group of women was instructed to attend to their genital signs of sexual arousal ("While rating these slides, I would like you to attend to various changes that may occur in your genital area, such as vaginal lubrication, pelvic warmth, and muscular tension"), and a second group was told to attend to nongenital signs of arousal ("While rating these slides, I would like you to attend to various changes that may occur in your body. These are heart rate increase, nipple erection, breast swelling, and muscular tension"), while a control group was given no instructions (Korff & Geer, 1983). Both experimental groups showed high correlations between self-reports and physiological measures of arousal, while the control group showed the same low correlation that Heiman found. This shows that women can be quite accurate in realizing their physical arousal if they are simply told to focus their attention on it. The broader culture, of course, does not give women such instructions but rather tells them to focus on the environment outside themselves—the love, romance, partner—so that many women have not learned to focus on their body. However, the experiment described here shows quite clearly that they can. A number of Canadian studies have also shown that there is better correspondence between women's subjective and physiological sexual arousal when blood flow is measured externally than when it is measured internally, but there is still a disconnect between subjective and physical arousal for some women (Kukkonen et al., 2007; Payne & Binik, 2006; Waxman & Pukall, 2009).

Heiman studied sexual arousal to preferred sexual stimuli. Recent Canadian research has shown that physiological sexual arousal is category specific in men but not in women. That is, heterosexual men are more physiologically aroused by stimuli depicting male–female sexual activity than by stimuli depicting male–male sexual activity, whereas the reverse is true for gay men. In contrast, both heterosexual women and lesbians show similar arousal to male and female stimuli (Chivers, 2005; Chivers et al., 2004). This does not necessarily mean that women are inherently bisexual, just that there are a wide range of stimuli that can turn women on. In contrast, subjective arousal for both women and men was greatest in response to their preferred type of partner. However, when men and women are presented with stimuli that show only one person (rather than two partners), only women who are attracted to men (and not women who are primarily attracted to women) show this nonspecific response (Dawson & Chivers, 2014).

Researchers have used fMRI brain scans to examine gender differences in response to erotic materials (Rupp & Wallen, 2008). The results show that the brain regions that fire, mostly in the limbic system, are the same in women and men. However, only men show increased activation in the hypothalamus, which, as we have seen in earlier chapters, is important to the release of testosterone.

Orgasm Consistency

Men are more consistent than women at having orgasms during sex. For example, according to the NSSHB, 91 percent of men but only 64 percent of women always have an orgasm during sex with their partner (Herbenick et al., 2010c). The gap is narrower for orgasm consistency during masturbation, but even here men seem to be more consistent: 80 percent of men, compared with 60 percent of women, report that they usually or always have an orgasm when masturbating (Laumann et al., 1994).

Sex Drive

Evidence from a number of sources indicates that men, on average, have a stronger sex drive than women do (Baumeister et al., 2001; Peplau, 2003). This is true for both individuals in mixed-sex and those in same-sex relationships (Holmberg & Blair, 2009). That is, men think about sex more often and have more frequent and varied fantasies than women do (Renaud & Byers, 1999). Further, compared with women, men desire more sexual partners and a greater frequency of intercourse. In a study across 52 nations, the gender difference in the preferred number of partners was found in all regions of the globe (Schmitt, 2003). It is important to remember, of course, that these are average differences. For a particular mixed-sex couple, it is quite possible that the woman's level of sexual desire would be higher than the man's.

Do men have sex on the brain? Do they think about sex constantly as the TSS suggests? And do women never think about sex? Flashy media reports suggest that this is true. However, a clever study indicates otherwise. Undergraduates were given golf tally counters and tallied their thoughts about sex for one week (Fisher et al., 2012). Men thought about sex on average 19 times a day, compared with 10 times a day for women, so men thought about sex more but not anything like 100 times per day. Moreover, other students tallied their thoughts about food and about sleep, and men thought about both food and sleep more than women did, so it isn't just sex on their brains. Also, the range was enormous among men: one man thought about sex only once a day and, at the other end of the spectrum, another thought about it 388 times per day. One woman thought about sex 140 times per day. The differences from one man to the next, or from one woman to the next, are far greater than the average difference between women and men.

L05

Why the Differences?

The previous section reviewed the evidence on differences in male and female sexuality. Four differences—the lower percentage of females, compared with males, who masturbate; women's more disapproving attitudes toward casual sex; women's lesser orgasm consistency; and men's greater sex drive—are fairly well documented. Thus, we need to explain them. What factors lead to these differences? Many possible explanations have been suggested by a wide variety of scholars. Before considering factors that may have resulted in gender differences, it is important to remember that these are differences in the average scores, and there is considerable variation among women and among men. Thus, these gender differences do not apply to all women and all men. For example, research in Ontario has identified a group of highly sexual women who report a high sex drive, high sexual desire, more frequent sexual thoughts and fantasies, and more positive attitudes toward casual sex and pornography (Wentland et al., 2009).

Are the Differences Bogus?

One possibility is that many of these gender differences, typically documented by self-report, are not true differences. Instead, it could be that people report what is expected of them, shaped by gender norms and societal expectations. Men are expected to want lots of sex, so they exaggerate their desire in self-reports, or women minimize theirs, knowingly or due to faulty memory (Dawson & Chivers, 2014); see Chapter 3 for a discuss of biases associated with self-report).

A clever study used the bogus-pipeline method to investigate this possibility (Alexander & Fisher, 2003; see also Conley et al., 2011; Jonason & Fisher, 2009). University students were brought to the lab to fill out questionnaires about their sexual attitudes and behaviours. They were randomly assigned to one of three experimental conditions. In the *bogus-pipeline condition*, the student was hooked up to a fake polygraph or lie-detector machine and told that the machine could detect false answers. People should respond very honestly in this condition. In the anonymous condition, the student simply filled out the questionnaire anonymously, as is typical of much sex research, and placed the questionnaire in a locked box when finished. In the exposure threat condition, respondents were instructed to hand their completed questionnaires directly to the experimenter, who was an undergraduate peer, and the experimenter sat in full view while the respondents completed their questionnaires, serving as a reminder that this other person would easily be able to see their answers. Figure 13.7 shows the results for reports of the number of sexual partners the respondents had had.

When people were in the bogus-pipeline condition and gave the most honest reporting, men's and women's reports of their number of partners were nearly identical—in fact, women's were slightly higher than

Figure 13.7 Mean number of sexual partners reported by men and women in the Bogus Pipeline Study (see text for further details).

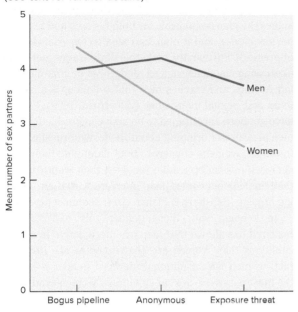

contrast, are hidden. The nude woman looks down and sees nothing except pubic hair (which really is not very informative); she looks in a full-length mirror and sees the same thing. Only by using a hand-held mirror can she get a good view of her own genitals. To make matters worse, the word *clitoris*—but not *penis*—is often missing from books about sexuality, from parents' talk about sex, and from students' knowledge about sexuality (Ogletree & Ginsburg, 2000). Furthermore, women's genitals do not have an obvious arousal response like the male's erection. As a result, women may be less aware of their own arousal, a notion that is supported by Heiman's research.

The anatomical explanation, then, is that because the woman's genitals are not in plain view and because their arousal response is less obvious than that of the man's genitals, she is less likely to masturbate and less likely to be fully aware of her own sexual response (Baldwin & Baldwin, 1997). If this explanation is correct, or at least part of the answer, could steps be taken to help women become more aware of their own sexuality? Perhaps parents can help their daughters to become more aware of their own sexual organs by naming the parts of their genitals including their clitoris and encouraging them to look at their genitals in the mirror. And parents might want to discuss the idea of masturbation with their daughters.

men's. In the standard conditions of anonymity used in most sex research, women reported fewer partners than men did. Under a threat that responses would be made public, the largest gap between women and men appeared. In the anonymous condition and the exposure threat condition, differences emerged that were consistent with gender roles. Women confirmed the expectation that they have fewer partners.

What are the implications of this study? Does it mean that all the differences described in the previous section are bogus? Probably not, but it means that findings of gender differences obtained by self-reports are probably exaggerations of the truth. And it is important to note that findings obtained from physiological measures, such as those used in Heiman's study, are not vulnerable to these reporting biases.

Let's assume that the gender differences discussed in the previous section are real, although perhaps not as dramatically large as the research suggests. How can these differences be explained?

Biological Factors

Gender differences in sexuality might be created, in part, by two biological factors: anatomy and hormones.

Anatomy

Men's sexual anatomy is external and visible and has a very obvious response: erection. While a man is nude, he can easily see his sexual organs, either by looking down or by looking in a mirror. The female sexual organs, in

Hormones

The hormonal explanation rests on the finding that testosterone is related to sexual behaviour. This evidence was reviewed in Chapter 9. Basically, the evidence comes from studies in which male animals are castrated (and thus lose their natural source of testosterone), with the result that their sexual behaviour disappears, presumably reflecting a decrease in sex drive. If replacement injections of testosterone are given, the sexual behaviour returns.

Females generally have lower levels of testosterone in their tissues than males do. Women, for example, have about one-tenth the level of testosterone in their blood that men do (Janowsky et al., 1998).

The hormonal explanation, then, is that if testosterone is important in activating sexual behaviour and if women have only one-tenth as much of it as men have, this might result in a lower level of sexual behaviour such as masturbation in women or a lower sex drive.

There are at least two problems with this logic. First, it may be that cells in the hypothalamus or the genitals of women are more sensitive to testosterone than the comparable cells in men; thus a little testosterone may go a long way in women's bodies. Second, we must be cautious about making inferences to humans from studies done on animals. Although some recent studies have demonstrated the effects of testosterone on sexual interest and behaviour in humans, the effects are less consistent and more complex than in other species (Chapter 9).

Cultural Factors

Our culture has traditionally placed tighter restrictions on women's sexuality than it has on men's, and vestiges of these restrictions linger today. It seems likely that these restrictions have acted as a damper on female sexuality, and thus they may help to explain why some women do not masturbate, why some women have difficulty having orgasms, and why some women are wary about casual sex.

One of the clearest reflections of the differences in restrictions on male and female sexuality is the double standard. As we saw in Chapter 10, the double standard says that the same sexual behaviour is evaluated differently, depending on whether a male or a female engages in it. The sexual double standard gives women less sexual freedom than men (Crawford & Popp, 2003). An example is casual sex, which has been more acceptable for men than for women. Indeed, casual sex with multiple partners might be a status symbol for a man but a sign of undesirable characteristics for a woman. The sexual double standard is alive and well on prime-time television, where negative consequences (e.g., rejection or humiliation) are more common in scenes in which female characters initiate sex than scenes in which male characters initiate (Aubrey, 2004). In teen magazines, negative consequences of sex are associated more often with girls than with boys (Joshi et al., 2011).

Generally, there seems to be less of a double standard today than in the past, at least in terms of people's explicit attitudes—that is, the attitudes they self-report on questionnaires. The decline of the double standard may help to explain why some of the gender differences found in older studies of sexual behaviour have disappeared in more recent studies. When cultural forces do not make such a distinction between men and women, men and women become more similar in their sexual behaviour. Yet traces of the double standard remain today in regard to casual sex (Bogle, 2008). For example, a Quebec study showed that university women rate women who have sex in an uncommitted relationship more negatively and believe male partners will see them more negatively if the women supply the condom than if the men supply the condom (Hynie & Lydon, 1995; Hynie et al., 1997). Also, students in Saskatchewan saw it as less normal for a man than a woman to be disinterested in sex, engage in same-sex sexual fantasies, and engage in sexual activities reflecting submission (Morrison et al., 2008). These results suggest that there is still a double standard in at least some areas of sexual behaviour.

Gender roles, particularly as prescribed by the traditional sexual script described earlier in this chapter, also contribute to differences in male and female sexuality (Sanchez et al., 2012). For example, the expectation is that in mixed-sex relationships men are the initiators and women are the passive objects of men's advances. This makes the man responsible for both his own and his partner's response, and it may lead men to experience a lot of pressure. Further, the male role discourages men from expressing emotions such as tenderness or communicating feelings and teaches men that touching is a means to an end: sexual intercourse (Zilbergeld, 1999). Women have not been encouraged to be active in producing their own pleasure or bringing about their own orgasms. Furthermore, women's concerns about damaging their partner's self-esteem by asking for what they want (part of the female gender role), may interfere with them reaching orgasm (Salisbury & Fisher, 2014; Séquin et al., 2015).

In keeping with these gender role expectations, research has shown that men are more active in sexual situations than women are (Lawrance et al., 1996). In fact, women with traditional views of gender roles are the most passive in sexual situations. Women (and men) who are sexually passive have more difficulty becoming aroused and report lower sexual satisfaction (Kiefer & Sanchez, 2007; Sanchez et al., 2006).

Research in New Brunswick has shown that the cultural sexual script affects perceptions of a partner's sexual preferences (Miller & Byers, 2004). The researchers had 152 heterosexual couples report their actual and ideal duration of foreplay and intercourse, as well as their perceptions of their partner's desired duration of foreplay and intercourse. They found that men's estimates of their partner's ideals were more similar to their estimates of what the average woman would want than they were to the actual preferences stated by their partner. Similarly, women's estimates of their partner's ideals were more similar to their estimates of what the average man would want than they were to their partner's stated preferences. This suggests that people use stereotypes to guide their understanding of their partner's sexual preferences (and possibly the way they make love) more than they use explicit or implicit information provided by the partner. This is more evidence for the need for better sexual communication (see Chapter 12 for a discussion of good sexual communication).

Relationship and family roles may play a part. When children are born, they can act as a damper on the parents' sexual relationship. The couple lose their privacy when they gain children. They may worry about their children bursting through an unlocked door and witnessing them making love. Or they may be concerned that their children will hear the sounds of lovemaking. Generally, the woman is assigned the primary responsibility for child-rearing, so she may be more aware of the presence of the children in the house and more concerned about the effects on them of witnessing their parents engaging in sex. Once again, her worry and anxiety do not contribute to her having a satisfying sexual experience.

Body image issues also contribute to gender differences in sexuality and, in particular, to women's sexual functioning (Woertman & van den Brink, 2012). Canadian researchers have shown that there are gender differences in body image; compared with men, women feel more dissatisfied with their bodies, are more self-conscious about their bodies, and are more likely to let their appearance influence their behaviour (Milhausen et al., 2014). And sex is all about bodies. Research shows that women who are dissatisfied with their bodies report lower levels of sexual desire and arousal and more avoidance of sex (La Rocque & Cioe, 2011; Weaver & Byers, 2006, 2013). Men with poorer body image report lower sexual satisfaction (Milhausen et al., 2014). In part this is due to a kind of self-conscious monitoring of how one's body looks during sex. These are distracting thoughts and, as we will see in Chapter 18, distracting thoughts contribute to reduced enjoyment of sexual experiences. Why are women more dissatisfied with their bodies, and why do they monitor their appearance more? The major factor appears to be the media, which portray skinny women with airbrushed features that real women can't live up to, making them feel bad about their bodies (Grabe et al., 2008). Positive and negative messages from a partner about one's body, as well as concerns that their body does not match their partner's ideals also affect sexual well-being (Goldsmith & Byers, 2016; Weaver & Byers, 2013). Interestingly, researchers in Ontario have shown that women who focus more on appearance and who feel more pressure to fit the media ideal are more likely to consent to unwanted sexual advances rather than to use strategies to get out of the situation (Kennett et al., 2012).

Other Factors

A number of other factors, not easily classified as biological or cultural, may also contribute to differences between male and female sexuality.[2]

Many Canadian adolescent girls who are sexually active do not use contraceptives or do not use them consistently—32 percent in one study (Fisher et al., 1999a; Levy et al., 1992). A woman who is worried about whether she will become pregnant—and, if she is single, about whether others will find out that she has been engaging in sexual activity—is not in a state conducive to the enjoyment of sex, much less the experience of orgasm (although this scarcely explains why fewer women than men masturbate).

Ineffective techniques of stimulating the woman may also be a factor, particularly in heterosexual relationships. The heterosexual techniques of intercourse, with the penis moving in and out of the vagina, may provide good stimulation for the man but not the woman, since she may not be getting sufficient clitoral stimulation. Perhaps the problem, then, is that women are expected to orgasm as a result of intercourse, when that technique is not very effective for producing orgasms in women. Although some lesbians also use ineffective techniques, Masters and Johnson (1979) found that lesbians benefited from stimulating another body like their own.

A relationship probably exists between the evidence that fewer women than men masturbate and gender differences in orgasm consistency. Childhood and adolescent experiences with masturbation are important early sources of learning about sexuality. Through these experiences we learn how our bodies respond to sexual stimulation and what the most effective techniques are for stimulating our own bodies. This learning is important to our experience of adult, two-person sex. For example, Kinsey's data suggested that women who masturbate to orgasm before marriage are more likely to orgasm in intercourse with their husbands;[3] 31 percent of the women who had never masturbated to orgasm before marriage had not had an orgasm by the end of their first year of marriage, while only 13 to 16 percent of the women who had masturbated had not had orgasms in their first year of marriage (Kinsey et al., 1953, p. 407).

Women's relative inexperience with masturbation may not only lead to a lack of sexual learning, but it also may create a kind of "erotic dependency" on men. Typically, boys' earliest sexual experiences are with masturbation, which they also hear about from other boys. More important, they learn that they can produce their own sexual pleasure. Girls typically have their earliest sexual experiences in mixed-sex touching and fondling. They therefore learn about sex from boys, and they learn that their sexual pleasure is produced by the male. As sex researcher John Gagnon (1977) commented:

> Young women may know of masturbation, but not know *how* to masturbate—how to produce pleasure, or even what the pleasures of orgasm might be. . . . Some young women report that they learned how to masturbate after they had orgasm from intercourse and petting, and decided they could do it for themselves. (p. 152)

Numerous factors that may contribute to shaping male and female sexuality have been discussed. Our feeling is that a combination of several of these factors

---

[2] Other possible causes of orgasm problems in women are discussed in Chapter 18.

[3] Note that this is in direct contradiction to the old-fashioned advice given in manuals that suggested that "getting hooked" on masturbation might impair later marital sexuality; if anything, just the reverse is true.

produces the differences that do exist. The early differences in experiences with masturbation are very important. Although these differences may result from differences in anatomy, they could be eliminated by giving girls information on masturbation. Women may enter into adult sexual relationships with a lack of experience in the bodily sensations of arousal and orgasm, and they may be unaware of the best techniques for stimulating their own bodies. Put this lack of experience together with various cultural forces, such as the double standard and ineffective techniques of stimulation, and it is not too surprising that there are some gender differences in sexuality.

Beyond the Young Adults

One of the problems with our understanding of gender differences in sexuality is that so much of the research has concentrated on heterosexual university students or other groups of young adults (as is true of much behavioural research). This provides a very narrow view of male–female differences as female and male sexuality change in their nature and focus across the lifespan, and differences may decrease as people age.

For example, psychiatrist Helen Singer Kaplan advanced an interesting view of differences between male sexuality and female sexuality across the lifespan (Kaplan & Sager, 1971). According to her analysis, the male teenager's sexuality is intense and almost exclusively genital in its focus. As a man approaches age 30, he is still highly interested in sex but not as urgently. He is also satisfied with fewer orgasms compared with when he was an adolescent. By the age of 50, he is typically satisfied with two orgasms a week, and the focus of his sexuality is not so completely genital; sex becomes a more sensuously diffuse experience and has a greater emotional component.

In women, the process is often quite different. Their sexual awakening may occur much later; they may, for example, not begin masturbating until age 30 or 35. While they are in their teens and 20s, their orgasmic response often is slow and inconsistent. However, by the time they reach their mid-30s, their sexual response has become quicker and more intense, and they orgasm more consistently than during their teens and 20s. They initiate sex more frequently than they did in the past. Vaginal lubrication takes place almost instantaneously in women in this age group.

Most men, then, seem to begin with an intense, genitally focused sexuality and only later develop an appreciation for the sensuous and emotional aspects of sex. Most women have an early awareness of the sensuous and emotional aspects of sex and develop the capacity for intense genital response later. To express this in another way, we might use the terminology suggested by Ira Reiss: **person-centred sex** and **body-centred sex**. Adolescent male sexuality is body-centred, and the person-centred aspect is not added until later. Adolescent female sexuality is person-centred, and body-centred sex comes later.

It is important to remember, though, that these patterns may be culturally, rather than biologically, produced. In some other cultures—for example, the Mangaia in the South Pacific (see Chapter 1)—all females reportedly have orgasms during coitus, even when they are adolescents.

 L06

Transgender

Many textbooks cover transgender issues and identity in the chapter on sexual variations or deviations. However, we have included it in our chapter on gender because it is fundamentally an issue of gender and, more specifically, a major part of the discussion on gender identity.

The term **transgender** is broad, encompassing people whose gender identity does not match their gender assigned at birth or the appearance of the genitals (natal gender). Some have an identity that is not male or female, but instead a third category, *genderqueer*. That is, they see themselves as falling outside the gender binary, and some use the term "non-binary." Others do not wish to be categorized. And still others are **transsexuals**, whose gender identity does not match their natal gender—for example, a person born with a male body who has a female identity; typically this term is reserved for those who choose to undergo medical treatments, such as surgery and hormone therapy, so that the gender of their body is consistent with their gender identity. A **male-to-female transsexual (MtF)**, or *transwoman*, is someone whose natal gender was male and whose gender identity is female, and a **female-to-male**

---

person-centred sex: Sexual expression in which the emphasis is on the relationship and emotions between the two people.

body-centred sex: Sexual expression in which the emphasis is on the body and physical pleasure.

transgender: A term encompassing a broad range of individuals whose gender identity does not match their gender assigned at birth (natal gender); includes those who identify as genderqueer, genderfluid, gender nonconforming, and transsexual.

transsexuals: Persons who believe that they were born with the body of the other gender—for example, a person born with a male body who has a female identity. These individuals often see medical gender reassignment procedures.

male-to-female transsexual (MtF): A transsexual whose natal gender is male and whose identity is female; also referred to as *transwoman*.

female-to-male transsexual (FtM): A transsexual whose natal gender is female and whose identity is male; also referred to as *transman*.

transsexual (FtM), or *transman,* is someone whose natal gender was female, who has a male identity. Most of these individuals identify closely with the gender to which they had transitioned to—that is, their felt gender (Dargie et al., 2014). Although they identified more with the gender roles of their felt gender, many also identified with some aspects of the gender roles of the gender they were assigned at birth.

The term **trans** is even broader, and includes people who identify as transsexual, transgender, cross-dressing, gender nonconforming, gender fluid, genderqueer, and other gender-variant people (Devor & Dominic, 2015). Some people add an asterisk to the term (trans*) to signal how broad it is, but we'll keep it simple and just use trans for the purposes of this discussion. Trans-identified people constitute about 0.5 to 1 percent of the population in Western societies (Conron et al., 2012). The terms for various expressions of gender variance have developed rapidly in the last few years and show every sign of continuing to change, so stay tuned for new developments!

What are we to call everyone else, those who are not transgender? It might be tempting to call them "normal," but a more equitable term has been introduced: **cisgender** (named after *cis* and *trans* isomers in organic chemistry). An interesting study conducted by New Brunswick researchers asked cisgender individuals whether they would choose to be reincarnated as a man or a woman and whether they would choose to experience being the other gender on a temporary basis (Byers et al., 2016). They found that 30 percent indicated that they would choose to be the other gender if they were reincarnated, 56 percent for a week, 67 percent for a day, and 65 percent for an hour. Some of the participants' reasons for their choices reflected openness (or not) to the new experience or perspective of being the other gender.

Gender dysphoria refers to psychological distress about a mismatch between a person's gender identity and natal gender, and is the term used in the American Psychiatric Association's *Diagnostic and Statistical Manual* (DSM-5, American Psychiatric Association, 2013). Gender dysphoria can appear in childhood and is characterized by a strong desire to be the other gender, substantial distress about the situation, a resistance to wearing clothing typical for the natal gender, a preference for toys and games typical of the other gender, and a desire for their genitals to match their gender identity. Gender dysphoria can also appear in adolescence or adulthood and is then called late-onset gender dysphoria.

An interesting study of transgender children aged 5 to 12 used the IAT (implicit attitudes test), discussed in Chapter 3, to measure their mental gender associations (Olson et al., 2015). The results indicated that the transgender children displayed response patterns consistent with their gender identity, not their natal gender. Their responses differed significantly from the cisgender control group of their natal gender and did not differ significantly from the cisgender group of their gender identity. That is, for example, the children born boys who had a female identity showed responses—even subconscious, implicit ones—that were the same as cisgender girls. These results indicate that, at some deep level, these natal boys are like girls psychologically.

In another new study, children and adolescents with gender dysphoria were given a scent of androstadienone, a pheromone that activates the hypothalamus differently in males and females; their hypothalamic response was then monitored using MRI (Burke et al., 2014). Among the adolescents, their hypothalamic response resembled that of the control group matching their gender identity, not their natal gender. Thus their brains functioned more like a person of their gender identity rather than a person of their natal gender. The researchers suggested that this pattern reflects prenatal brain differentiation in the direction of the gender identity. The children with gender dysphoria showed more complicated results, which may be explained by the data presented in the next paragraph.

Gender dysphoria in childhood does not always persist into adulthood, making it difficult to know how much it should be treated. In studies of children with gender dysphoria, only about 20 percent continue to experience gender dysphoria in adulthood; more often, those who were natal males identify as gay men in adulthood (Coleman et al., 2011). As a result, the question of how to treat children with gender dysphoria has been very controversial. Based on the experiences of adult transsexuals who often suffered from not being accepted as their felt gender, some argue that we should help children transition, at least socially, even at a young age. Others argue that in order to allow for developmental changes in children's views of themselves, we should support children's desire to engage in cross-gender behaviour (i.e., not make them conform to the other gender); we should also help them become more comfortable with their natal gender. Still others argue that we should regard such children as simply not fitting into the gender binary and encourage them to define their own gender (Bartlett et al., 2000). Alberta researchers studying the *fa'afafine* in Samoa found

trans: A broad term encompassing those identifying as transgender, transsexual, agender, and other gender-variant people.

cisgender: A person whose natal gender and gender identity match—for example, a person born with female genitals whose identity is female.

gender dysphoria: Psychological distress about a mismatch between a person's gender identity and natal gender.

that cross-gender behaviours or identities do not cause distress in children who are raised in cultures where they are accepted as members of a third gender (Vasey & Bartlett, 2007). Clearly, all sides are concerned with the welfare of the child. The key question appears to be about how parents should respond to their children who experience gender dysphoria. Gender dysphoria in adolescence is much more likely to persist into adulthood. The website gendercreativekids.ca provides resources for gender creative kids and their families, communities, and schools.

Transgender is not a new phenomenon. References are found throughout much of recorded history, although that modern term is not used (Devor, 1997). In the early centuries of Christianity, a number of women transformed themselves into men. One example is Pelagia, a woman who refused to marry and fled, dressing as a man and entering a monastery. She became Pelagius, a man, and was later elected prior of a convent. A woman at the convent became pregnant and accused Pelagius of being the father. Nothing, of course, could have been further from the truth, but Pelagius was not in a position to offer the strongest defence. He was expelled from the convent and died in disgrace. When he died, it was discovered that he had a female body. The Transgender Archives at the University of Victoria holds the world's largest collection of materials documenting the lives of trans individuals, focusing on the contributions of activists and researchers (Devor, 2015). It includes business records, audio histories, posters, scholarly books, conference programs, pornography, medical textbooks, and newsletters.

The Experiences of Trans Individuals

Transphobia and anti-trans prejudice are terms that parallel the terms homophobia and anti-gay prejudice (see Chapter 14). **Transphobia** refers to a strong, irrational fear of trans people. **Anti-trans prejudice**, which is the more scientific term, refers to negative attitudes and behaviours toward trans individuals (Tebbe, Moradi, & Ege, 2014). See Milestones in Sex Research for an explanation of how these attitudes are measured by researchers. Importantly, the *Canadian Human Rights Act* now makes it illegal to discriminate on the basis of gender identity or gender expression; most provinces and territories have similar legislation.

There is research demonstrating that the rates of discrimination against trans people are high. The Trans PULSE Project assessed rates of violence among trans individuals in Ontario (Bauer & Scheim, 2015). It found that 20 percent had

transphobia: A strong, irrational fear of trans individuals.
anti-trans prejudice: Negative attitudes and behaviours toward trans individuals.

been physically or sexually assaulted for being trans, and 34 percent had been verbally threatened or harassed but not assaulted. In addition, 18 percent reported being turned down for a job, and 13 percent reported being fired for being trans; 40 percent reported discrimination in a doctor's office or hospital. Yet respondents also demonstrated remarkable resilience. As one trans person commented (Grant et al., 2011):

> My mother disowned me. I was fired from my job after 18 years of loyal employment. I was forced onto public assistance to survive. But still I have pressed forward, started a new career, and rebuilt my immediate family. You are defined not by falling, but how well you rise after falling. I'm a licensed practical nurse now and am studying to become an RN. I have walked these streets and been harassed nearly every day, but I will not change. I am back out there the next day with my head up. (Grant et al., 2011)

Focusing on adolescents specifically, an American survey of youth between the ages of 13 and 18 compared the bullying experiences of gender minority (trans, gender-nonconforming) youth to cisgender youth

Figure 13.8 Brandon Teena, an MtF who was murdered because of the ignorance and prejudice of those around him.

AP Photo

Milestones in Sex Research

Measuring Anti-Trans Prejudice

Elliot Tebbe, Bonnie Moradi, and Engin Ege (2014) developed a Genderism and Transphobia Scale. Here are some of the items. Each is rated on a scale from 1 (*strongly agree*) to 7 (*strongly disagree*). How would you rate the items?

1. If I found out that my best friend was changing their sex, I would freak out.
2. Women who see themselves as men are abnormal.
3. A man who dresses as a woman is a pervert.
4. Sex change operations are morally wrong.
5. I have behaved violently toward a man because he was too feminine.

Source: Tebbe, E.A., Moradi, B., & Ege, E. (2014). Revised and abbreviated forms of the Genderism and Transphobia Scale: Tools for assessing anti-trans prejudice. *Journal of Counseling Psychology, 61,* 581–592.

(Reisner et al., 2015). Among cisgender youth, 58 percent had experienced bullying in the past 12 months, compared with 83 percent for gender minority youth. Perhaps as a result, Canadian researchers have shown that transgender youth have a higher risk of reporting psychological distress, self-harm, depression, and suicidal behaviour (Veale et al., 2016).

In one extreme case, Brandon Teena, an American MtF, was raped and murdered in Humboldt, Nebraska, when his trans identity was revealed (see Figure 13.8). His life and death inspired the 1993 documentary *The Brandon Teena Story* and the 1999 Academy Award winning film *Boys Don't Cry.* Teena's murder shed light on transgender discrimination and how these attitudes and prejudices in the legal and medical communities contributed to his violent death.

These experiences of prejudice and sometimes outright violence can take a toll on the mental and physical health of trans individuals, even for those who are fortunate to survive. In one Canadian study, 26 percent of transgender adults had attempted suicide, and 24 percent had often thought of suicide in the previous year (Moody & Smith, 2013). Individuals who have more experiences with people not affirming their gender identity report more symptoms of depression (Testa et al., 2015). In one sample, trans individuals who had experienced violence were about four times as likely to have attempted suicide (Testa et al., 2012). Having more social support, being in a happy romantic relationship, reduced transphobia,

and changes in personal identification documents are protective factors in that they are associated with less depression, stress, anxiety, and suicidal behaviour (Bauer et al., 2015; Dargie et al., 2014; Moody & Smith, 2013). Many communities have organizations designed to provide a supportive and nonjudgmental environment for people to express their gender identity. One such organization is Gender Mosaic in Ottawa (www.gendermosaic.com).

Additionally, pronouns can be an issue for trans individuals. One of the problems is misgendering by others—that is, being called by pronouns that indicate a gender different from one's identity. Those who identify with one of the two gender binary categories, male or female, prefer to be called by the pronouns that match their gender identity. Those whose identity falls outside those two categories, such as those whose identity is genderqueer, may prefer to be called by gender-neutral pronouns. Table 13.1 shows a list of traditional pronouns in the first two rows, and then two alternatives for gender-neutral pronouns. The first involves "they"—that is, using plural pronouns to refer to an individual. The second alternative, shown in the bottom row, is a new set of pronouns. "Ze," for example, is substituted for "he or she." It is important, when interacting with people who have told you they are trans, to ask what pronouns they prefer. It's interesting to note that in the case of Brandon Teena, he was interred in Nebraska with his natal gender on his headstone. Even in death, he was not referenced in the gender he identified with.

Table 13.1 An Alternate Set of Gender-Neutral Pronouns for Trans People

Some trans individuals do not wish to be called by traditional pronouns based on the gender binary.

	Subject	Object	Possessive	Possessive Pronoun	Reflexive
He	*He* laughed	I called *him*	*His* dog barked	That is *his*	He likes *himself*
She	*She* laughed	I called *her*	*Her* dog barked	That is *hers*	She likes *herself*
They	*They* laughed	I called *them*	*Their* dog barked	That is *theirs*	They like *themselves*
Ze	*Ze* laughed ("zee")	I called *hir* ("heer")	*Hir* dog barked ("heer")	That is *hirs* ("heers")	Ze likes *hirself* ("heerself")

Sexual Orientation and Transgender Identity

Gender identity is a separate issue from sexual orientation. With people undergoing gender transitions, terminology becomes confusing. For example, if a trans individual is straight, does that refer to attractions based on natal gender or gender identity? Therefore, Ontario psychologist Ray Blanchard proposed that we use the terms *gynephilic* and *androphilic* (Blanchard et al., 1985; Smith et al., 2005). Those who are gynephilic are sexually attracted to women and those who are androphilic are sexually attracted to men. For example, if we think of an FtM, he would be classified as androphilic if he is attracted to men and as gynephilic if he is attracted to women. Among FtMs, those who are gynephilic are typically more interested in surgery to construct a penis, compared with those who are androphilic (Chivers & Bailey, 2000). Some transsexuals, too, are bisexual. In a large sample of MtFs, 23 percent said they were attracted to men, 29 percent to women, and 31 percent to both (Grant et al., 2011). In that same study, among FtMs, 25 percent were attracted to women, 13 percent were attracted to men, 13 percent were attracted to both, and 46 percent identified as queer.

Trans Health

Trans individuals need health care for a variety of the same conditions and problems that cisgender people have: tobacco use, alcohol abuse, reproductive health, cancer, and mental health issues. Programs in Montreal, Toronto, and Vancouver offer a range of services to transgender individuals; most of the gender-reassignment surgery is conducted at a private clinic in Montreal. Sex-reassignment surgery is either partially or fully funded in all provinces; however, there are big differences in what is covered from province to province. The Canadian Professional Association for Transgender Health provides detailed information about what procedures are covered in each province (www.cpath.ca).

Nonetheless, health care provided to trans individuals in Canada needs substantial improvement. For example, all of the medical interventions described in the next section should be covered by Medicare in all provinces just as they would be for anyone else who needed hormone therapy or surgery. And as noted above, many trans people report experiencing discrimination from health care providers, so more education of providers is needed.

Many services should be available for trans individuals short of medical transition treatments (Coleman et al., 2011). These include (1) voice and communication therapy, to help the person speak in the range typical for their gender identity and communicate nonverbally in ways that match their gender identity; (2) supportive therapy and peer support to reduce stress; and (3), for natal males, facial hair removal by electrolysis or other methods. Supportive therapy for the family is important, as well.

The Medical and Surgical Transition Process

Typically transsexuals have a gender binary identity (e.g., their natal gender is male but their gender identity is female or vice versa) and wish to undergo medical treatments so that their body matches their identity. Some refer to this as *gender-confirming therapy*. A range of medical interventions are possible, and different individuals will choose different interventions. The World Professional Association for Transgender Health (WPATH) has set standards of care for transsexuals, including standards for medical treatment (Coleman et al., 2011; see also the Endocrine Society, 2009). An assessment and referral by a mental health professional are required before medical treatments can occur.

Medical treatments include the following (Coleman et al., 2011):

- Hormone therapy to accomplish *pubertal suppression* in early adolescents with strong gender dysphoria: This treatment is helpful in buying some time for the adolescent to mature and make a well-informed decision about whether to go through additional medical interventions. Pubertal suppression treatments are reversible if the adolescent decides not to pursue a transition. But if the adolescent decides to transition, it will be a simpler process. For example, for a trans man, it will not be necessary to perform a mastectomy, because the breasts did not develop under pubertal suppression. Pubertal suppression is a relatively new technique; preliminary evaluations of it indicate that, in young adulthood, transgender individuals treated in this manner function as well psychologically as cisgender individuals, in contrast to the strong gender dysphoria they had before treatment (de Vries et al., 2014).

- *Hormone therapy* to feminize or masculinize the body: This type of therapy is only partially reversible and is typically applied only with older adolescents and adults who are capable of making a definite decision about wanting to transition. In FtMs, hormone therapy can lead to a deeper voice, growth in facial hair, growth of the clitoris, and a decrease in percent body fat. In MtFs, hormone therapy results in breast growth, fewer erections, and increased body fat that creates feminine curves. Surgical treatments are irreversible and should be chosen only by a mature adolescent over the legal age of consent or an adult. The typical requirement is that the individual has to have lived as a member of the gender with which they identify for at least 12 months, to ensure that the transition is truly workable and desirable.

- *Chest surgery:* Removal of breasts for FtMs and breast augmentation for MtFs. This is sometimes referred to as "top surgery."

- *Genital surgery:* For MtF transsexuals, this can include penectomy (removal of the penis), orchiectomy (removal of the testes), vaginoplasty (creation of a vagina from the skin of the penis), clitoroplasty (creation of a clitoris), and vulvoplasty (other surgery to create a female-appearing vulva). The results of this type of genital surgery are shown in Figure 13.9.

- *Genital surgery:* For FtM transsexuals, this can include removal of the uterus (hysterectomy), fallopian tubes, and ovaries; metoidioplasty or phalloplasty (to create a penis); and insertion of artificial testes. Metoidioplasty involves releasing the clitoris, which enlarges with hormone therapy, to create a small penis (see Figure 13.10), whereas phalloplasty involves creation of a penis from

tissue such as the forearm (see Figure 13.11). These penis-creating surgeries are difficult and often not completely successful, so many FtMs decide against them.

> **What are some of the medical treatment options for trans individuals?**

According to research, the adjustment of transsexuals who seek surgery is significantly better following

Figure 13.9 *(a)* The appearance of the genitals following MtF surgery. *(b)* Breast augmentation for the MtF transsexual.

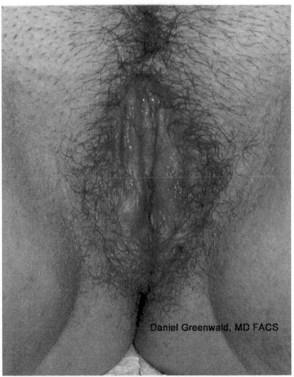

(a) Courtesy of Dr. Daniel Greenwald

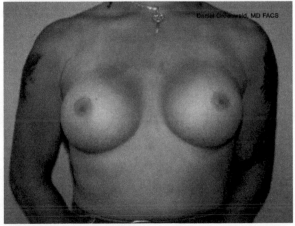

(b) Courtesy of Dr. Daniel Greenwald

surgery. In one study, 86 percent of MtFs were satisfied with their surgery to create a vagina, and 89 percent of FtMs were satisfied with their surgery to create a penis (De Cuypere et al., 2005). And in a study of MtFs and FtMs, none expressed regret at having had the surgery (Johansson et al., 2010). In that sense, then, gender transition surgeries are successful and many go on to live fulfilling and successful lives in their new gender (see Figure 13.12; see also First Person).

The Trans PULSE research project provides information about the extent to which transgender individuals living in Ontario undergo medical interventions (Scheim & Bauer, 2015). They found that 30 percent were living their day-to-day lives in their birth gender and 23 percent were living in their felt gender with no medical interventions. In all, 42 percent were using hormones; 15 percent of transwomen and less than 1 percent of transmen had undergone genital surgery. That is, in many cases trans individuals do not seek these medical interventions.

Psychotherapy can be very helpful for people with gender dysphoria, and medical interventions may not

Figure 13.10   FtM surgery. *(a)* Skin on the forearm marked before transfer to the groin. *(b)* The penis is constructed (blood vessels and nerves shown on the left). *(c)* An inflatable prosthesis, wrapped in Goretex and ready for insertion. *(d)* Penis before insertion of the implant. *(e)* Erect penis.

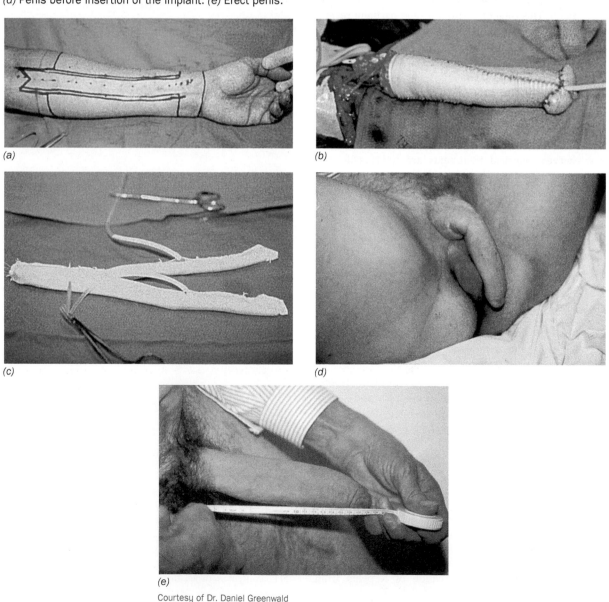

(a)

(b)

(c)

(d)

(e)

Courtesy of Dr. Daniel Greenwald

Figure 13.11   Metiodoplasty, one technique for female-to-male transsexual surgery.

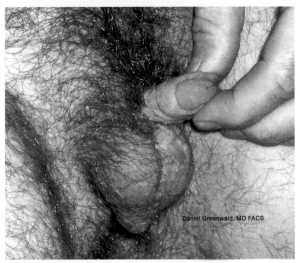

Courtesy of Dr. Daniel Greenwald

Figure 13.12   Jenna Talackova is a transgender woman who competed in Miss Universe Canada.

MARK BLINCH/Reuters /Alamy

be necessary or desired. For some, a social transition seems to be all that is needed or wanted. In addition, to the extent that people do not feel forced to fit into one of the two gender binary categories, they may not feel the need for surgery.

LO8 What Causes Gender Variance?

Almost all of the research on causes of various kinds of gender variance has been done on transsexuals. There are some inklings of biological factors. One line of thought is that processes in prenatal development are involved, in which the genitals differentiate toward those of one gender and identity differentiates toward the other gender. Two studies have found differences between MtFs and typical men in the bed nucleus of the stria terminalis (BST), which is part of the limbic system (Kruijver et al., 2000; Zhou et al., 1995). As noted in earlier chapters, the limbic system is important in sexuality.

In other MRI studies, FtMs display brain regions that are intermediate between cismales and cisfemales (Rametti et al., 2011).

Other research has identified several genes associated with transsexualism, and the genes are different for MtFs and FtMs (Bentz et al., 2008; Hare et al., 2008; Henningsson et al., 2005). MTFs, for example, are more likely than control males to have a mutation in the androgen receptor gene. However, not all MTFs carry this mutation.

The bottom line is that, right now, we do not know the exact causes of transsexualism or other kinds of gender variance.

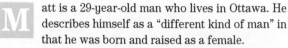

Matt: A Transman's Story

Matt is a 29-year-old man who lives in Ottawa. He describes himself as a "different kind of man" in that he was born and raised as a female.

Matt grew up in a small town in Southern Ontario. Unlike his sisters, Matt was not interested in being a Brownie or taking ballet. He had short hair and wore mainly T-shirts. He recalls feeling little pressure to behave like a girl until Grades 7 and 8, when he started to feel a need to conform to what was expected of him. Matt remembers thinking that he looked better as a boy than as a girl yet knowing that he would need to change to fit in. He started wearing more feminine clothing and grew his hair. As a teenager, Matt knew he was not interested in boys, yet living in a small town he had no idea of what it meant to be gay.

At 20, Matt moved to Ottawa to attend university. He became involved in the queer community and gradually began to change how he presented himself. He cut his hair, wore more masculine clothing, and expressed himself in more masculine ways. He felt comfortable with this gender presentation. More and more often, Matt was perceived and responded to as male. He recalled that one year he had two jackets. When he wore one of them, he would be perceived as female; when he wore the other, he would be perceived as male. It felt like society was presenting the idea of transitioning to him.

The decision to transition was very difficult for Matt. On the one hand, he did not find being a woman aversive and was concerned about the social consequences of not conforming to his biological gender and the physical consequences of taking testosterone. On the other hand, Matt felt more comfortable presenting as male. There was also the matter of how others responded to his gender presentation. Most often, people would initially perceive him as male, but then—often after noticing that Matt had breasts—see him as female. Some people were apologetic, which could be uncomfortable for Matt; others were hostile and, in many cases, verbally insulted him. He found public washrooms to be particularly difficult because of how others would respond to him. It was the fear for his physical safety and the stress associated with

these daily interactions that prompted Matt to transition: "It took up so much energy not to conform to society's expectation that I present as one gender or the other. I had to choose."

At 25, Matt started taking testosterone. So that the changes would be gradual, he started on a low dose and slowly increased it. He grew facial hair and his voice deepened. Taking the testosterone enabled Matt to be more confident in his interactions with others. He did not have to be constantly vigilant about his personal safety or be concerned about how others would respond to him. Matt has since had a hysterectomy and a double mastectomy and now feels very happy with his body.

Matt feels like his family transitioned with him. Initially, they were concerned that he was transitioning only because he had been influenced by a friend's example. They worried that he would have difficulty establishing a career, finding a long-term partner, and having a secure and happy future. However, when they recognized that Matt was becoming happier and healthier as he transitioned, they became less concerned. Matt feels his relationship with his parents is much closer than before he transitioned because they have become much more open with each other.

At present, Matt is completing the last year of an accounting diploma. He is in a four-year relationship with a woman, in which he is very happy. He feels that because of his experiences he is much more critical of society's messages about gender and other social categories. He has also developed much closer relationships with others as a result of his personal experiences of discrimination. Matt regards being trans and his decision to alter his body as a function of societal pressure to act in certain ways based on sex. He believes that we would all benefit from treating people in accordance with their personality, not their gender presentation.

Source: Based on an interview with Jacqueline Cohen.

UNDERSTANDING STEREOTYPING

Books like John Gray's *Men Are from Mars, Women Are from Venus* have sold millions of copies. In that book, Gray argues that men and women are so different, it's like they are from differerent planets, and communication between the two is as difficult as communication between a Canadian person and a Japanese person. The scientific data, however, show a very different picture. Men and women are actually quite similar on most, though not all, psychological characteristics, including behaviours such as math performance and leadership (Hyde, 2005). If men and women are so similar, why do people like to believe that they are so different?

The answers lie in *stereotypes* and *motives for stereotyping*. As we noted earlier in the chapter, a stereotype is a generalization about a group of people (e.g., men) that distinguishes those people from another group (e.g, women). Gender stereotypes abound. Women are the talkers while men are strong and silent. Women are emotional and men are unemotional. When we collect rigorous scientific data, it turns out that some stereotypes are fairly accurate and some are not. For example, it turns out that the difference between boys and girls in talkativeness is tiny (Leaper & Smith, 2004). Girls are stereotyped as being bad at math, but in fact girls perform equally to boys on standardized math tests (Hyde et al., 2008).

If so many stereotypes turn out not to be accurate, why do people continue to stereotype? Social psychologists have uncovered two basic motives for stereotyping (whether gender stereotyping, racial stereotyping, or other kinds of stereotyping): comprehension goals and self-enhancement goals (van den Bos & Stapel, 2009). As for the *comprehension goal,* when we meet a new person, we tend to fill in a lot of assumed information about that person so that we can understand him or her, until we have more actual information. For example, breadwinner is a key aspect of the male role. When we meet a man, we are likely to invoke that stereotype and ask an opening question such as "What kind of work do you do?" Our first question is not, "Do you stay home full-time with the kids?" When people stereotype for comprehension purposes, the stereotypes can be positive or negative.

In contrast, when we stereotype for *self-enhancement* purposes, the stereotypes tend to be negative. We make ourselves feel better by denigrating people from another group. For example, if we say or think, "Teenagers are so irresponsible," by implication we, as adults, are much more responsible.

Using these principles, why do people engage in gender stereotyping? Answer this question before you proceed to the next paragraph.

When people engage in gender stereotyping, sometimes it is for comprehension goals, as in the example above in which we might assume that a man is employed, so we can ask him about his work. Sometimes, though, people engage in gender stereotyping for self-enhancement purposes. A man might say, "You women are so emotional," which makes him feel emotionally in control and manly. Or a woman might say, "Men are just clueless about how other people feel," which makes her feel good about her skills at reading others' emotions.

Good critical thinking involves understanding why people stereotype and that gender stereotypes are often not accurate. The next time you hear someone (or yourself) making a gender stereotyped comment, ask yourself two questions: (1) What is this person's goal in stereotyping? and (2) Is this an accurate stereotype that is supported by scientific data?

SUMMARY

A gender role is a set of norms, or culturally defined expectations, that specify how people of one gender ought to behave. Children are socialized into gender roles first by parents and later by other forces, such as peers and the media.

Gender roles are not uniform in Canada. They vary according to ethnic group and other factors, using the concept of intersectionality. Gender roles in ethnocultural communities, such as the Chinese, South Asian, and Caribbean communities, tend to reflect the traditional values of the country of origin. Although most Aboriginal people have adopted gender roles similar to those of the majority Canadian culture, some Aboriginal peoples traditionally had more egalitarian gender roles in comparison with European culture.

The traditional sexual script specifies how men and women are expected to behave in sexual situations. Research suggests that male and female roles in sexual situations differ in some respects but are converging.

Psychological gender differences have been documented in aggressiveness and communication styles, both of which have implications for sexuality.

Three substantial gender differences in sexuality are in the incidence of masturbation (men having the higher incidence), attitudes about casual sex (women being more disapproving), and the use of pornography (men reporting more use). Heiman's study of arousal from erotic materials illustrates how men and women are in some ways similar and in others different in their responses. Men are more consistent at having orgasms, especially during heterosexual intercourse, than women are, and men have a somewhat stronger sex drive.

One question is whether some of these gender differences, obtained through self-report, are accurate or whether they are the result of response biases, for example, with men exaggerating and women minimizing. Although some of the gender differences in sexuality may be due to biased reporting, some differences remain.

Three sets of factors have been proposed to explain gender differences in sexuality: biological factors (anatomy, hormones), cultural factors (gender roles, the double standard, body image), and other factors (fear of pregnancy, differences in masturbation patterns creating other gender differences).

Most research on gender and sexuality has been done with university-age samples. There is reason to believe that patterns of gender differences in sexuality change in middle age and beyond.

Transgender is a broad category of people whose gender identity does not match their anatomy. Transgender individuals respond in different ways, including some who seek surgery (transsexuals) and those who do not seek surgery or who see themselves as being in a third gender category. Generally, the adjustment of transsexuals following gender reassignment is a successful one.

CHAPTER 14

Sexual Orientation and Identity: Gay, Lesbian, Bi, Straight, or Asexual?

© Thinkstock

Are **YOU** Curious?

1. What percentage of people are gay, lesbian, bisexual, or asexual?
2. How does growing up with two parents of the same gender affect children psychologically?
3. What causes people to be gay or heterosexual?
4. Are men or women more likely to be attracted to both genders?

Read this chapter to find out.

LEARNING OBJECTIVES

After studying this chapter, you will be able to

LO1 Discuss the meanings of the various terms used to describe sexual identity.

LO2 Describe and evaluate the various ways in which sexual orientation can be defined and measured.

LO3 Describe the attitudes toward and stereotypes of gay men, lesbians, and bisexuals, and discuss the extent to which research supports these stereotypes.

LO4 Discuss the consequences of homonegativity.

LO5 Provide a brief history of the Canadian laws surrounding homosexuality.

LO6 Describe the life experiences of LGB individuals.

LO7 Evaluate the research on the mental health of LGB individuals and the success of therapies used to change a person's sexual orientation.

LO8 Evaluate the various theories used to explain sexual orientation.

LO9 Describe how culture affects attitudes toward and expression of sexual orientation.

The state has no business in the bedrooms of the nation.[*]

Jeffrey and I met when he responded to an online message I posted, seeking gay teenagers willing to discuss their online lives. . . . He made it clear that he could allow no overlap between his online gay life and the life he led in the "real world." . . . He feared that if word of his sexual orientation were to reach his parents, they might refuse to support him or pay for college. From his peers at school he dreaded violence.[**]

[*] Pierre Trudeau, 1967, when defending his bill to overhaul the *Criminal Code of Canada*, including statutes that had criminalized consensual same-sex sexual activity.

[**] Jennifer Egan. (2000). Lonely gay teen seeking same. *The New York Times Magazine*, December 10, 2000, p. 113.

Every summer, cities across North America hold a Gay Pride Day, usually including a parade (called *pride parade* or *pride festival*) to celebrate gay, lesbian, bisexual, and transgender culture. These events also commemorate the first time that gay, lesbian, and transgender individuals openly fought back against police harassment; this occurred in June 1969 in the Stonewall, a gay bar in New York City's Greenwich Village. Gay liberation was born. The first gay liberation group in Canada was formed in Vancouver in 1970 (Kinsman, 1996). Eight months later, 200 protesters on Parliament Hill demanded equal rights for gays and lesbians (Smith, 1999). In 1981, 3000 people rallied in Toronto to protest the arrest of 300 men during police raids on gay bathhouses (Kinsman, 1996).

LO1 The purpose of this chapter is to try to provide a better understanding of people's sexual orientations, whether to their own gender, the other gender, both genders, or neither gender. Note that both *cisgender* and *transgender* individuals (see Chapter 13) can be attracted to people of their own gender or of the other gender. First, though, several concepts need to be clarified. A distinction has already been made between sex (sexual behaviour) and gender (being male or female)[1] and between gender identity (the psychological sense of maleness or femaleness) and sexual orientation (heterosexual, gay, bisexual, or asexual). To this, the concept of **sexual identity** should be added; this refers to one's self-label or self-identification as heterosexual, gay, lesbian, bisexual, asexual, or perhaps something

sexual identity: One's self-identity as gay, heterosexual, bisexual, or asexual.

sexual orientation: A person's erotic and emotional orientation toward members of his or her own gender or members of the other gender.

homosexual: A person whose sexual orientation is toward members of the same gender. Use of the terms gay or lesbian to refer to individuals is preferable.

heterosexual: A person whose sexual orientation is toward members of the other gender.

bisexual: A person whose sexual orientation is toward both men and women.

asexual: A person who is not attracted to men or women.

lesbian: A woman whose sexual orientation is toward other women.

else. (For a discussion of transgender, which refers to gender identity, not sexual identity or sexual orientation, see Chapter 13.)

There may be contradictions between people's sexual identity and their actual choice of sexual partners (Mathieson & Endicott, 1998). For example, a woman might identify herself as a lesbian yet occasionally have sex with men. Objectively, her choice of sexual partners is bisexual, but her identity is lesbian. More common are persons who think of themselves as heterosexuals but who engage in sex with both male and female partners. A good example of this is the tearoom trade—the successful, heterosexual married men who occasionally stop off at a public restroom to engage in oral sex with another man. Once again, the behaviour is objectively bisexual, in contradiction to the heterosexual identity. Another example is the group of women who report having bisexual identities but who have experienced only sex with men. These women claim bisexuality as an ideal they are capable of attaining at some later time. Once again, identity contradicts behaviour. Finally, some individuals identify as asexual but occasionally have sex with men or women.

Given these contradictions, **sexual orientation** is best defined by whom we are emotionally, romantically, and sexually attracted to (American Psychological Association, 2008). Thus a **homosexual** or gay person's sexual orientation is toward members of her or his own gender; a **heterosexual** person's sexual orientation is toward members of the other gender; a **bisexual** person's sexual orientation is toward both genders; and an **asexual** person does not have a sexual orientation toward either men or women (see Milestones in Sex Research). Again, however, a person's attraction may not match his or her behaviour or sexual identity. The word *homosexual* is derived from the Greek root *homo*, meaning "same" (not the Latin word *homo*, meaning "man"). The term *homosexual* may be applied in a general way to people of both genders or specifically to men. The term **lesbian**, which is used to refer to women, can be traced to the great Greek poet Sappho, who lived on the island of Lesbos (hence

[1] As discussed in Chapter 13, these two gender categories do not fit for some people who would identify as transgender.

Figure 14.1 Homosexuality has been found in many cultures and historical eras. Here we see male–male couples at a banquet in Roman art from the fifth century BCE.

© Scala/Art Resource, NY

"lesbian") around 600 BCE (Figure 14.1). She is famous for the love poetry that she wrote to other women.

Use of the term *homosexual* to refer to lesbians and gay men is problematic for three main reasons (American Psychological Association, 2009). First, in the past it has been associated with negative stereotypes,[2] such as deviance, mental illness, and criminal behaviour, and thus can be used as a derogatory label. Second, it emphasizes sexual behaviour rather than sexual identity. As discussed later in this chapter, many women and men engage in same-sex[3] behaviour, yet do not consider themselves to be lesbian, gay, or bisexual. Third, it is ambiguous because even though it is a general term, it has often been used to refer exclusively to gay men. For these reasons, it is preferable to use the terms lesbians, gay men, bisexual women, and bisexual men. A heterosexual is then referred to as **straight**.

In recent years, some members of the gay, lesbian, and bisexual communities have reclaimed terms that have historically been used as derogatory terms. Examples of such terms include *dyke, fairy, fag* or *faggot,* and *queer.* For example, the term **queer** has now been taken back by gay and lesbian activists and scholars, who use it as a proud term encompassing gay men, lesbians, and transgender persons—that is, all people who identify

as outside the social norm with respect to gender and/or sexuality. As an umbrella term, it has the advantage of not forcing people to adopt a narrow, societally defined label that may not reflect their experience or the fluidity of sexual identity (Bower et al., 2002). Queer theory, explained in Chapter 2, is prominent in lesbian-gay-bisexual (LGB) studies.[4]

Another term that rejects societally imposed labels for sexual attraction and sexual orientation is *pansexual* (sometimes referred to as *omnisexual* or *polisexual*). Pansexual individuals are open to relationships with people of any sex, gender, or gender identity—that is, men, women, transgender, and intersex individuals. However, although some people are comfortable using these terms to refer to themselves, other people are not, perhaps because the terms have been used to belittle them in the past. Thus, while LGBs may use these terms themselves, it is probably not a good idea to impose these terms on them. *Sexual minority* is another term that encompasses all people who do not identify as heterosexual, regardless of their specific identity.

In this chapter, we will use the abbreviation "LGB" for lesbians, gay men, bisexual women, and bisexual men whenever possible because it is awkward to repeat the phrase "gay men and lesbians," and even that phrase omits bisexuals. Further, it omits the terms some individuals use to refer to themselves, such as queer,

> **straight:** Heterosexual.
> **queer:** A self-label used by some LGBs and by some heterosexuals who want to identify as outside the social norm with respect to gender or sexuality.

---

[2] A stereotype is a rigid set of beliefs about a group of people that distinguishes them from others and is applied to all members of the group.

[3] To be consistent with the definitions of gender and sex adopted in this book, we should use the terms "same-gender" or "other gender" when describing sexual behaviour or relationships. However, we have used the term "same-sex" because it is the term most people use–for example, there has been considerable public debate about same-sex marriage.

[4] You are probably familiar with the acronym LGBT, which stands for lesbian, gay, bisexual, and transgender. In this chapter, we focus on sexual minorities or LGBs. Transgender is covered in Chapter 13.

questioning, undecided, asexual. Of note, many organizations use more comprehensive abbreviations, such as LGBT or LGBTQ to represent all sexual and gender minorities.

LO2

How Many People Are Gay, Lesbian, Bi, Straight, or Asexual?

Most people believe that homosexuality is rare. What percentages of people in North America are gay, lesbian, or bisexual? As it turns out, the answer to this question is complex. Basically, it depends on the definition we use. Determining how best to define and measure sexual orientation, particularly among adolescents, is quite complicated. Do we ask people about their attraction, identity, or behaviour? This is important because the three do not always go together (Saewyc, 2011).

> **What percentage of people are gay, lesbian, bisexual, or asexual?**

Several well-sampled surveys in Canada, the United States, the United Kingdom, and France have given us estimates regarding sexual identity (Savin-Williams, 2006). Data from the (American) National Survey of Family Growth (NSFG) and the Canadian Community Health Survey (CCHS) are shown in Table 14.1. The 2003 and 2005 CCHS surveyed adults ages 18 to 59 and asked respondents to indicate whether they considered themselves to be homosexual, bisexual, or heterosexual; that is, it assessed sexual identity. Of the men surveyed, 1.4 percent considered themselves to be homosexual, 0.7

percent to be bisexual. Of the women surveyed, 0.8 percent self-identified as homosexual, 0.9 percent as bisexual.

People's sexual identities can change (Saewyc, 2011). For example, one longitudinal study followed, over ten years, women who initially said that they were lesbian, bisexual, or "unlabelled" in their sexual orientation (Diamond, 2008b). At the start of the study, the women ranged in age between 18 and 25. Many women changed their identity over time, often in response to relationship experiences. These changes occurred in all directions and thus were not just a result of a coming-out process. Another study followed men and women in New Zealand from age 21 to 26 (Dickson et al., 2003). Women were more likely to report changes in their pattern of attraction than men were, but some men also reported changes in their attractions. Again, especially for women, attractions seemed to change in all possible directions, likely because women are more greatly influenced by relationship experience than are men when it comes to sexual identity.

The statistics from the NSFG are more complex because the survey asked several questions about sexual orientation, and much depends on how *gay, lesbian,* and *bisexual* are defined. Should the definition be based on self-identification alone or also on behaviour? This is particularly important for adolescents who may not yet be involved in sexual relationships (Saewyc, 2011). In terms of behaviour, does the definition of gay or lesbian require someone to have had exclusively same-sex sexual experiences, or just some same-sex experiences, or perhaps just to have experienced sexual attraction to members of his or her own sex without ever acting on it? We will return to this point. What we can say here is that, according to the NSFG, 5 percent of men and 12 percent of women have had

Table 14.1 The NSFG and CCHS Statistics on Same-Sex Behaviour, Identity, and Attraction

	NSFG		CCHS	
	Men	**Women**	**Men**	**Women**
Behaviour				
Ever had sexual contact with same-sex partner	5.2%*	12.5%		
Sexual Identity				
Heterosexual	97.0	94.8	96.9%	98.3%
Bisexual	1.1	3.5	0.7	0.9
Homosexual/lesbian/gay	1.7	1.1	1.4	0.8
Something else**	0.2	0.6		
Sexual Attraction				
Only or mostly to same gender	1.9	1.4		
Equally to both	0.5	2.8		
Mostly to opposite sex	3.7	11.9		

* Different questions were used for men and women, and men's questions were narrower, so this percentage is an underestimate.

** The "something else" category may include people identifying as queer, questioning, and so on.

Sources: Chandra et al., 2011; Tjepkema, 2008.

at least one same-sex sexual experience in adulthood, and about 4 percent of both men and women experience sexual attraction to members of their own sex. Roughly 2 percent of men and 1 percent of women have a gay identity.

Estimates based on the NSFG may not be perfectly accurate, however. We can expect underreporting on any kind of sensitive topic like sexual orientation, and the NSFG asked nonequivalent questions on behaviour to men and women, making gender comparisons inaccurate. The NSFG statistics are comparable to those found in a well-sampled international survey, which included the United Kingdom and France (Sell et al., 1995). So these results likely also apply to Canada.

Recently researchers have also started to assess how many people consider themselves to be asexual. According to a large British study, 1 percent of people reported that they have no sexual attraction to men or women, although some did engage in a low level of sexual activity with a partner (Bogaert, 2004). In another study completed on the Internet, 3.6 percent of respondents chose to identify themselves as having an asexual sexual orientation (Prause & Graham, 2007). These persons reported less desire for partnered sex but not necessarily no desire for sex. British Columbia researchers have shown that many asexual individuals (40 percent) but very few other individuals report never having had a sexual fantasy (Yule et al., 2014). (See Milestones in Sex Research in this chapter for more on asexuality.)

What about youth? The CYSHHA survey asked Grade 7, 9, and 11 students whether they were attracted to males, to females, to both males and females, or to no one. Somewhat fewer than 3 percent indicated that they are attracted to members of their own gender. Interestingly, 9 percent of Grade 7 students but fewer than 2 percent of Grade 9 and 11 students said they were attracted to no one.

After reading these statistics, though, you may still be left wondering how many people are gay, lesbian, bisexual, and asexual. As Kinsey soon realized in trying to answer this question, it depends on how you count. A prevalent notion is that like the difference between the colours black and white, homosexual and heterosexual are two quite separate and distinct categories. This is what might be called a *typological conceptualization* (see Figure 14.2). Kinsey made an important scientific breakthrough when he decided to conceptualize mixed-sex and same-sex behaviour not as two separate categories but rather as variations on a continuum (Figure 14.2, section 2). The black and white extremes of heterosexuality and homosexuality have many shades of grey in between: people who have had some other-sex and some same-sex experience, in various mixtures. To accommodate all this variety, Kinsey constructed a scale running from 0 (*exclusively heterosexual experience*) to 6 (*exclusively homosexual experience*), with the midpoint of 3 indicating equal amounts of heterosexual and homosexual experience (see Figure 14.2 for the complete scale).

One problem with Kinsey's scale is that it refers only to behaviour and not to attraction. As discussed later in this chapter, some people engage in sexual activity with a person of the same gender or of the other gender because of circumstances rather than out of attraction. Conversely, some people do not engage in sexual activity with people of the same gender because of societal or their own negative attitudes. In addition, some theorists have suggested that Kinsey's one-dimensional scale is too simple (Sell, 1997; Storms, 1980). The alternative is to form a two-dimensional scheme. The idea here is to

Figure 14.2 Three ways of conceptualizing homosexuality and heterosexuality.

1. The typology

Heterosexual		Homosexual

2. Kinsey's continuum

0	1	2	3	4	5	6
Exclusive heterosexual	Mostly heterosexual with incidental homosexual experience	Heterosexual with substantial homosexual experience	Equal heterosexual and homosexual experience	Homosexual with substantial heterosexual experience	Homosexual with incidental heterosexual experience	Exclusive homosexual

3. Two-dimensional scheme (Storms, 1980)

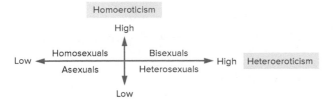

Milestones in Sex Research

Asexuality: A Sexual Dysfunction, a Sexual Orientation, or Something Else?

A lthough we generally think about the categories of heterosexual, homosexual, and bisexual when we consider a person's sexual orientation, more recently people have started identifying themselves as asexual. For example, in Kinsey's work that led to the development of the "Kinsey Scale." He found that 1.5 percent of the men sampled fit into the category described as "Asexual, Non-Sexual" and defined as individuals with "no socio-sexual contacts or reactions" (Kinsey, 1948). This figure was replicated nearly 60 years later when Anthony Bogaert (2004), a Canadian psychologist, examined data collected as part of a British national probability sample of 18 000 men and women. He found that 1.05 percent of people agreed with the following statement about sexual attraction: "I have never felt sexually attracted to anyone at all." This group had fewer sexual partners, a later debut of sexual activity (if it ever occurred), and less frequent sexual activity with a current partner.

Opinions differ about what exactly asexuality is. One view is that asexuality is about behaviour (or lack thereof). People who hold this view conclude that the lifelong lack of interest in sexual activity indicates that asexuality is really a sexual dysfunction related to a lack of sexual desire. Others conceptualize asexuality within the broader domain of sexual attraction. For them, asexual individuals' experience of not having sexual attraction raises many questions about whether sexual attraction indeed is evolutionarily hard-wired; it is usually assumed that there is such a mechanism that drives procreation. The observation that asexual individuals often retain "romantic attraction"—or in other words, a desire to have a meaningful, committed, emotionally fulfilling relationship with a partner—also suggests that the processes underlying romantic attraction and sexual attraction may become uncoupled. Bogaert's study of the British probability sample found that 44 percent of the asexual sample had been or were currently in a serious relationship.

Asexuals themselves prefer to understand their asexuality from the perspective of it being a sexual

identity/sexual orientation. This view holds that asexuality is genetic, lifelong, and not amenable to "treatment" in the same way that other sexual orientations (e.g., homosexuality) are not amenable to treatment. There is evidence to support this view that asexuality is likely biologically based. For example, Bogaert found that asexual individuals had a later onset of menarche, and were shorter and weighed less. This led him to conclude that asexuality was likely at least partly biologically based and determined before birth.

Although the Asexuality Visibility and Education Network (AVEN) online community had been established in 2001 (www.asexuality.org), the publication of Bogaert's paper led to a massive media blitz spotlighting asexuality. Critics doubted the possibility that people could be apathetic about sex—a basic biological drive necessary for the survival of our species. Moreover, the finding that almost half of asexual individuals were in committed relationships raised skepticism about the conclusion that romantic attachment can be preserved despite sexual attraction being deficient. Furthermore, the finding that many asexual individuals continued to masturbate also raised doubt that asexuality could even exist. That is, how could it be that, on the one hand, asexual individuals declared no interest in sex, yet on the other, they engaged in sexual acts with themselves?

What Does the Research on Asexuality Suggest?

Prause and Graham (2007) provide research evidence that supports the view that asexuality might be best construed as a sexual dysfunction. They conducted semi-structured individual interviews with four asexual individuals followed by online questionnaire completion by 1146 individuals, 41 of whom self-identified as asexual. The asexual individuals reported lower sexual desire and arousability than did the rest of the sample. However, they expressed no desire to speak to a health professional about their asexuality. The researchers also found that asexual individuals had lower excitatory processes but not necessarily higher inhibitory processes when compared with the sexual sample (see Chapter 9 for a discussion of excitatory and inhibitory processes in sexual response). Their low levels of sexual responding on validated questionnaires seemed to lead to the conclusion that asexuality might be a disorder of sexual response.

In 2010, Lori Brotto, a Canadian psychologist, and colleagues conducted a study of asexual men and women recruited from AVEN that sheds further light on this question. As would be expected, rates of sexual desire were low among the men and women in this study. However, they were not distressed about this. Because "distress or interpersonal impairment" is a fundamental component of the criteria for diagnosing a sexual disorder (see Chapter 18), asexual individuals do not meet the *DSM-5* definition of any sexual disorder. Further, follow-up in-depth interviews with 15 of the participants found that they strongly resisted the characterization of themselves as sexually dysfunctional. Rather, they sought to educate the public that asexuality may be better conceptualized as a sexual orientation or sexual identity (akin to homosexuality).

Is Asexuality Caused by Problems with Physiological Arousal?

Brotto and colleagues (2010) found that asexual individuals were as likely to masturbate as the general population. They rationalized their masturbation behaviour as an attempt to "clean out the plumbing" or as means of getting to sleep, rather than stemming from any intrinsic sexual need. This suggests that sexual arousal and ability to experience orgasm might be no different in asexual individuals than in the rest of the population. To explore this further, and to examine the critical position that suggests that asexuality is nothing more than an extreme sexual dysfunction, Brotto and Yule (2011) conducted a sexual psychophysiological study of asexual women. Equal numbers of asexual, heterosexual, bisexual, and homosexual women had their genital arousal measured with a vaginal photoplethysmograph while they watched an explicit film in a private room. Not surprising to the researchers, ratings of sexual attraction during the erotic film were lower in the asexual women compared with the other three groups (which did not differ from each other). However, there were no significant group differences in genital sexual arousal, indicating that the asexual women became just as genitally engorged to the erotic film as did women in the sexual groups. The authors interpreted this finding as supporting their position that asexuality should not be characterized as a disorder of sexual response, given that, in the face of potent sexual stimuli, asexual individuals' bodies reflexively responded sexually in the same way as did sexual women.

Should Asexuality Be Considered a Sexual Orientation?

Much more research is needed before we can conclude that asexuality is a sexual orientation. One means of exploring this further is through the use of genetic marker and biological studies. These will allow us to test for the possibility that asexuality is associated with prenatal developmental factors and is not an adaptive response to early childhood trauma or extreme religiosity (as has been speculated by some). Yule (2011) studied 1200 men and women (315 of whom were asexual) and examined biological markers previously found to be associated with homosexual orientation. They found that the asexual individuals were significantly more likely than their heterosexual counterparts to be left-handed, and asexual men were significantly more likely to have older brothers than sexual men, but there were no significant group differences in their 2D:4D digit ratios (discussed later in the chapter). These data provide preliminary evidence of a neurodevelopmental basis to asexuality similar to the research found with homosexuality. Of course, more research is necessary.

Asexuality research may shed new light on the pathways toward the development of sexual and romantic attraction, potentially leading to new theories. This research may also lead to a better understanding of who is best suited for treatment of sexual difficulties versus those individuals who fully identify as asexual and are, essentially, not motivated to change.

Written by Dr. Lori Brotto, University of British Columbia.

have one scale for heteroeroticism (the extent of one's attraction to members of the other gender), ranging from low to high, and another for homoeroticism (the extent of attraction to members of one's own gender), ranging from low to high (see Figure 14.2, section 3). Thus if one is high on both heteroeroticism and homoeroticism, one is a bisexual; the person high on heteroeroticism and low on homoeroticism is heterosexual; the person high on homoeroticism and low on heteroeroticism is gay; and the person low on both scales is asexual. This two-dimensional scheme fits well for individuals who define themselves as asexual. Asexual individuals define asexuality in terms of a lack of attraction to men or women, not in terms of behaviour or desire (Brotto et al., 2010).

The answer to the original question—How many people are gay, lesbian, bisexual, and asexual?—is complex. Probably about 90 percent of men and 90 percent of women are exclusively heterosexual. About 10 percent of men and women have had at least one same-sex sexual experience in adulthood. About 2 percent of men and 1 percent of women identify themselves as gay; about 1 to 2 percent identify themselves as bisexual. These figures are based on the NSFG and the NHSLS but adjusted somewhat to allow for concealment by some respondents. About 1 percent of people identify as asexual.

Another group that is being recognized today is the *mostly heterosexuals*— that is, people who are not exclusively heterosexual, but also not quite bisexual (Savin-Williams & Vrangalova, 2013). Kinsey might have called them a 1 on his scale. They have a small amount of same-sex sexual attraction and they engage in same-sex sexual behaviour only occasionally. Research on mostly heterosexuals challenges the idea that sexual orientation can be understood as two—or maybe three—distinct categories. Instead, it supports the idea that sexual orientation exists along a continuum.

Attitudes

Your sexual orientation has implications for the attitudes people have toward you. In Canadian culture, the assumption typically is that a person is heterosexual, that heterosexuality is the norm. Furthermore, just as there are stereotypes about other minority groups, there are stereotypes (usually negative) about gay men and lesbians. These stereotypes and negative attitudes lead to discrimination and hate crimes against gay men and lesbians. In this section we will examine some of the scientific data on these negative attitudes.

homophobia: A strong, irrational fear of gay men and lesbians; negative attitudes and reactions to gay men and lesbians.

homonegativity: Negative attitudes and behaviours toward gay men and lesbians; sometimes called antigay prejudice or sexual prejudice.

antigay prejudice: Negative attitudes and behaviours toward gays and lesbians. Also termed sexual prejudice.

Attitudes toward Gay Men and Lesbians

What are Canadians' attitudes toward gay men and lesbians? Today, the vast majority of Canadians (80 percent) say that society should accept gays and lesbians (Pew Research, 2013). Note that the attitudes of Canadians toward gay men and lesbians are becoming increasingly accepting; for example, six years earlier only 70 percent of Canadians had this view. As shown in Table 14.2, most Canadians are also accepting of same-sex marriage and the rights of same-sex couples to adopt children, although women are more accepting than are men, and younger people are more accepting than are older people (Ipsos, 2013). Canadians also are more accepting of same-sex relationships than Americans are. For example, whereas 80 percent of Canadians say that society should accept gays and lesbians only 60 percent of Americans do. Similarly, whereas 76 percent of Canadians are accepting of same-sex marriage, only 65 percent of Americans are (Ipsos, 2013). The percentage for people living in the United Kingdom who favour same-sex marriage is about the same as in Canada. It's important to note that many Canadians accept same-sex relationships, same-sex marriage, and adoption by same-sex couples even if they are not "in favour" of them. For example, 13 percent of Canadians are in favour of some sort of legal recognition for same-sex couples, just not marriage.

Homophobia may be defined as a strong, irrational fear of gay individuals and, more generally, as fixed negative attitudes and reactions to gay men and lesbians. Some scholars dislike the term *homophobia* because, although certainly some people have anti-gay feelings so strong that they could be called a phobia, what are more common are negative attitudes and prejudiced behaviours. Therefore, some prefer the terms **homonegativity**, **antigay prejudice**, or sexual prejudice (Herek, 2000; Morrison & Morrison, 2002). Interestingly, Canadian researchers have shown that traditional, or old-fashioned, homonegativity is less prevalent among Canadian students than is modern homonegativity (Morrison et al., 2009; Rye & Meaney, 2010). Traditionally, homonegativity was based on moral and religious views or beliefs that homosexuality is not "normal." Modern homonegativity reflects beliefs that gay men and lesbians exaggerate the importance of their sexual orientation or make unnecessary demands for social change. Research suggests that Canadian university students do not hold negative views toward homosexuality, although men's attitudes are more negative than are women's (Meaney & Rye, 2010). Furthermore, research in Saskatchewan still found that a substantial percentage of undergraduate students engaged in covert antigay behaviours (Jewell & Morrison, 2010). For example, 43 percent reported that they had yelled insulting comments at gay men and 43 percent reported that they had told an antigay joke.

Table 14.2 The Global Divide on Homosexuality

In response to the question, **Should society accept homosexuality?**

	Percent Saying "Yes"
North America	
Canada	80%
U.S.	60%
Europe	
Spain	88%
Germany	87%
Britain	76%
Russia	16%
Middle East	
Israel	40%
Egypt	3%
Asia/Pacific	
Philippines	73%
S. Korea	39%
China	21%
Latin America	
Mexico	61%
Brazil	60%
Africa	
Kenya	8%
Uganda	4%

Source: Pew Research (2013), www.pewglobal.org

A related term is heterosexism. **Heterosexism** is the belief that being heterosexual is "normal" and that heterosexuality is the only legitimate, acceptable, and healthy way for people to be; gay people and behaviours are denigrated (Berkman & Zinberg, 1997). It is closely connected to **heteronormativity**, the belief that heterosexuality is the norm. Some LGBs experience multiple forms of prejudice. Lesbians may face sexism as well as homonegativity. LGBs from visible minority groups may face racism as well as antigay prejudice. (See Chapter 13 for a discussion of intersectionality.)

Media and LGB Attitudes

What role do the media play in homonegativity/antigay attitudes? In previous decades there were almost no portrayals of gay men or lesbians, so they were invisible in the mass media. Current research, however, now finds more representations of sexual minorities in the media. In one study of television programming, content associated with sexual minorities occurred in 15 percent of programs overall, most of it in movies and sitcoms (Fisher et al., 2007).

So gays are now more visible in the media, but are they portrayed positively or negatively? Some argue that even successful programs increase stereotypes because they present the LGB characters in stereotypic ways, including lacking a stable relationship, being preoccupied with their sexuality, and being laughable (Calzo & Ward, 2009). Others, though, argue that there are some programs that are positive because they use humour to expose and challenge stereotypes. For example, in shows such as *Glee* and *Modern Family*, sexual orientation still seems to be the defining feature of LGB characters or why they are funny. *The L Word* is a lesbian-centric show that is fairly realistic. And the main character in *Orange Is the New Black* is a queer character who does not define her sexuality.

These shows are doing a better job of addressing heterosexism and stereotypes head on as part of the plot lines. Research on the actual effects of the media on attitudes is very new and paints a complex picture (Calzo & Ward, 2009). For example, reading popular magazines is associated with more positive attitudes toward LGBs, but reading teen magazines is associated with less positive attitudes, probably because teen magazines tend to be conservative about sexuality.

 LO4 ### Consequences of Homonegativity and Heterosexism

Homonegativity and heterosexism can have serious emotional and health consequences for LGB individuals (Maticka-Tyndale, 2008; Wells, 2009). This may be a particular problem for adolescents establishing their sexual identity. Antigay bullying and overt acts of antigay prejudice can cause significant pain and suffering. Sometimes the prejudice is subtle. The prevalence of antigay humour and the widespread insult "that's so gay" are hurtful to LGB youth who may be listening (go to www.thinkb4youspeak.com for a media campaign against this expression and others). The message is that there is something really bad about acting in any way that might suggest being gay (Adam, 2007). Some—but not all—LGB youth adopt the negative attitudes they see around them, called *internalized homonegativity,* and this may make it difficult for them to accept their sexual orientation. Cultural homonegativity, as well as internalized homonegativity, may also affect some LGB individuals' self-esteem (Blais et al., 2014). In some cases, LGB youth so devalue their self-worth that they contemplate or attempt suicide (D'Augelli, 2006). It may also affect their willingness to be open about their sexual identity (Figure 14.3).

The most extreme expressions of antigay prejudice occur in *hate crimes* against LGBs. One horrifying case occurred in

heterosexism: The belief that heterosexuality is the only legitimate, acceptable, and healthy way for people to be; homosexuality is denigrated.

heteronormativity: The belief that heterosexuality is the only pattern that is normal and natural.

Figure 14.3   Camp fYrefly is a summer leadership camp for LGBTQ youth in Canada.

Camp fYrefly - University of Alberta

Vancouver. In 2001, Aaron Webster, a prominent photographer and a gay man, was beaten to death by four men wielding baseball bats, a golf club, and a pool cue after they found him naked in an area widely known as a stroll for gay men looking for casual sex.

A survey of Canadian LGBs found high rates of violence (Faulkner, 1997). Seventy-eight percent had experienced verbal assaults, 21 percent had been physically assaulted, 21 percent reported harassment by the police, and 7 percent had been assaulted with a weapon. A study of LGBs in Vancouver found similar results: 74 percent had been verbally abused, 32 percent had been physically assaulted, and 9 percent had been physically and sexually assaulted. Indeed, according to Statistics Canada (Beauchamp, 2008), Canadians over the age of 15 who identify themselves as gay or lesbian are 2.5 times as likely to be victims of violent victimization as are heterosexual Canadians.

A survey of homophobia, biphobia, and transphobia in Canadian schools found that 55 percent of the sexual minority students had been verbally harassed and 21 percent had been physically harassed or assaulted about their gender expression or perceived sexual orientation (Taylor et al., 2011). The rates were even higher for trans youth (see Chapter 13 for a discussion of antitrans prejudice). About a third of youth with LGBT parents (37 percent) also reported being harassed about their parents' sexual orientation or gender identity. More than 70 percent of participating students (LGBT and heterosexual) reported hearing homophobic expressions such as "that's so gay" *every day* in school; 48 percent heard the use of terms such as *faggot, lesbo,* and *dyke* as insults *every day* in school. The rates were higher among sexual minority students. Very few students had never heard these comments made at school. Sexual minority youth in Canada are more likely than their heterosexual counterparts to experience physical and sexual victimization, verbal harassment, cyberbullying, prejudice, and discrimination (Blais et al., 2013; Cénat et al., 2015; McCreary Centre Society, 2007; Taylor et al., 2008). These studies show that hate crimes against and harassment of LGB youth are not rare, isolated incidents. These incidents exact a psychological toll and can affect adolescents' health, mental health, self-esteem, and development (Blais et al., 2014, 2015; Saewyc, 2007, 2011). LGB youth are less likely to feel safe at school. Alarmingly, one study of students in Saskatchewan found that teachers and students never or rarely intervened when they heard homonegative speech despite its prevalence (Morrison et al., 2014).

But we should also recognize the other side of the coin. As we can see from the statistics in Table 14.2, most Canadians are tolerant or supportive of LGB individuals. For example, 67 percent of Canadians approve of overt gay and lesbian teachers in middle school, and 86 percent approve of openly gay MPs (Figure 14.4). Thus while some Canadians are bigots on the issue of homosexuality, most Canadians are not.

Attitudes toward Bisexuals

Bisexuals experience a different kind of stigma than do lesbians and gay men. If you are asked to imagine a lesbian or gay couple, you can likely come up with a mental image—two women kissing or two men holding hands or dancing together are easily recognizable as a lesbian or gay couple. Now what do you imagine when you are asked to think of a bisexual couple? The point is that we have few cultural images of bisexuality (Trynka & Tucker, 1995). As such, bisexuality is rarely even recognizable. A study of 22 self-identified bisexual Canadian women found that all participants felt that bisexuality was misunderstood by straight, lesbian, and gay communities (Bower et al., 2002).

There are a great many negative stereotypes about bisexuals (Herek, 2002). Bisexuals are often thought of as internally conflicted or psychologically immature (Rust, 2000a). They are stereotyped as nonmonogamous, needing both same-sex and other-sex partners to satisfy both the gay/lesbian and heterosexual sides of their sexualities (Yost & Thomas, 2012). Perhaps as a result, researchers in Ontario have found that people have negative attitudes towards entering a committed relationship with a bisexual partner (Armstrong & Reissing, 2014). They worried that the person was actually gay, that they wouldn't be able to fulfill their sexual needs, that they would engage in extra-relationship sex, and that they would be suspicious of their partner's friendships. In contrast, research has found that few bisexuals have both female and male partners at the same time (although

Figure 14.4 Kathleen Wynne, premier of Ontario, made history when she became the first openly gay premier in Canada.

MARK BLINCH/Reuters /Alamy

some do), and bisexuals do not differ from lesbians and gay men in their relationship status and length (Balsam, 2004; Rust, 2000b). Further, few bisexuals report that they "need" both male and female partners to think of themselves as bisexual (Rust, 2001). They can also be stereotyped as confused and untrustworthy (Zivony & Lobel, 2014).

Similarly, bisexuals may be viewed with suspicion or downright hostility by the gay and lesbian communities (Bower et al., 2002; Rust, 2002). Bisexual-identified women are often told they are denying their true identity, which must be lesbian or heterosexual. Young women who have sexual involvements with other women are often regarded as heterosexuals who are merely experimenting with women because lesbianism is chic (Rust, 2000a). Bisexual women who are involved in lesbian communities may be told they are really lesbians who have not yet realized it. Bisexuality is sometimes seen as fence-sitting, a way to get the best of both worlds without having to commit to a particular identity. Some gay men and lesbians even argue that there is no such thing as a true bisexual (Rust, 2002).

In contrast, proponents of bisexuality argue that it has some strong advantages. It allows more variety in

one's sexual and human relationships than does exclusive heterosexuality or exclusive homosexuality. The bisexual does not rule out any possibilities and is open to the widest variety of experiences.

On the question of whether there are true bisexuals, the emerging scientific evidence increasingly indicates that there really are individuals who are attracted to both women and men. For example, in one study the researchers recruited self-identified bisexual women and men, as well as heterosexual women and men (Lippa, 2013). The participants then viewed multiple photos of male and female swimsuit models and rated their sexual attractiveness. Meanwhile, their viewing times for each photo were measured unobtrusively. As might be expected, the heterosexual men rated the female models as very attractive and the male models as not attractive. Similarly, the heterosexual women rated the male models as attractive and the female models as less attractive. The bisexual men found both male and female models to be attractive, as did the bisexual women; that is, the bisexuals really did show a pattern of attractions that was distinct from the heterosexuals. Even more interesting, though, were the findings for the unobtrusive behavioural measure of looking times. The bisexual women and men spent about equal amounts of time looking at the male and the female models, in contrast to heterosexuals whose looking times were quite skewed toward models of the other sex. Other research, using physiological measures of arousal, shows similar results (Cerny & Janssen, 2011). In short, bisexual people, with bisexual patterns of attraction, really do exist.

Attitudes toward Asexuals

Asexual individuals may experience many of the challenges faced by LGB individuals (Bogaert, 2015). Just as many Canadians assume that heterosexuality is the norm, most also assume that everyone is sexual (i.e., that sexuality is the norm). They see not being attracted to men or women is a sign that the individual has a sexual problem. In fact, they tend to view asexual people more negatively than they view gays and lesbians (MacInnis & Hudson, 2012). In this study, some people characterized asexual individuals as "less than human." In addition, many people hold to a *committed relationship ideology* (i.e., being in a committed relationship is superior to being single) (Day et al., 2011). This may also result in prejudice against asexual individuals who choose to remain single.

LO5 LGBs and the Law

Same-sex sexual activity used to be illegal in Canada. For example, in 1967 Everett Klippert was sent to prison as a "dangerous sex offender" after he told police that he had

had sex with men over a 24-year period and was unlikely to change. However, consensual same-sex activity was decriminalized in 1969 when, under Prime Minister Pierre Trudeau, Parliament passed a bill introducing widespread changes to laws regulating sexual behaviour in the *Criminal Code of Canada*. Before 1969, "homosexual offences" included some outdated and derogatory terms, such as "buggery (anal intercourse), attempted buggery, indecent assault on a male by a male or female on a female, acts of gross indecency between men, procuring and attempting to procure acts of gross indecency between males" (Lahey, 1999, p. 135). These changes to the *Criminal Code* were a turning point in the recognition and increasing acceptance of LGBs in Canada. However, at that time, the offence of anal intercourse was added to the *Criminal Code*. Anal sex is illegal only if it involves children or is not done in private. However, currently the age of consent for anal sex is 18, whereas the age of consent for vaginal intercourse is 16. Further, anal sex is deemed not to be done in private (and therefore is illegal) if more than two persons are present. There is no similar provision for vaginal intercourse. This puts gay (and straight) youth who want to experiment sexually with anal intercourse (many gay males do not engage in anal intercourse) in a difficult situation. Thus, at the time this book went to press, the *Criminal Code* still discriminated against gay men in this way. However, several court rulings suggested that the higher age of consent for anal intercourse violates the equality provisions of the *Charter of Rights and Freedoms* and the government has introduced a bill to repeal this unconstitutional section of the *Criminal Code*.

Activists also argue that there has been more vigorous enforcement of the bawdy-house and obscenity laws (see Table 2.1 for a list of Canadian laws related to sexuality) against LGBs and same-sex erotic materials. For example, following the 1969 changes to the *Criminal Code*, police continued to lay "indecent act" and "bawdy-house" charges against men for engaging in consensual sex with other men. Nor were gay men and lesbians legally protected from discrimination (Kinsman, 1996). Before the *Charter of Rights and Freedoms*, virtually no human rights complaints by gay men and lesbians were successful (Lahey, 1999; Smith, 1999). For example, before 1992, homosexuality was grounds for dishonourable release from the military (Gouliquer, 2000). In the early 1980s, men and women who were suspected of being gay or lesbian were investigated, interrogated, and sometimes released by the military. However, in 1992 Canadian Forces policy concerning sexual orientation was found to violate the *Charter of Rights and Freedoms*. LGBs can no longer be denied the right to serve in the military.

In 1995, Parliament passed a hate crimes sentencing bill, which specifies longer sentences for hate-motivated crimes—that is, crimes motivated by hate, bias, and prejudice against specific groups. The list of unacceptable hate crimes includes those committed against gay men and lesbians. In 2004, Parliament passed a private member's bill introduced by former MP Svend Robinson that bans hate propaganda that targets gay men and lesbians. Although this is a step in the right direction of providing some legal protection to LGBs, it may seem like cold comfort to a person who has been the victim of such a crime. Further, police have some discretion in what charges are laid and do not always identify assaults against LGBs as motivated by hate.

Recent decisions by the Supreme Court of Canada recognize that the equality rights guaranteed in the Canadian *Charter of Rights and Freedoms* include sexual orientation and that provincial human rights codes must recognize sexual orientation as a prohibited ground for discrimination. In 1996, Parliament amended the *Human Rights Act* to specifically prohibit discrimination based on sexual orientation. The act already prohibited discrimination based on other characteristics, such as gender, race, and disability. (In 2017 they added gender identity and gender expression). The act also bans "hate speech" against gay men and lesbians. This means, among other things, that gay men and lesbians cannot be fired because of their sexual orientation, they cannot be refused housing, and they are entitled to adopt children. In fact, Parliament recently passed the *Modernization of Benefits and Obligations Act,* which amended existing federal statutes to ensure that they apply equally to couples in same-sex and mixed-sex relationships. The majority of Canadians support such entitlement (refer to Table 14.2). In contrast, in the United States, gay men and lesbians do not have legal protection against discrimination, and fewer Americans support equal rights for gay men and lesbians.

The most recent area in which gay men and lesbians have attained equal rights is marriage. In 2003, courts in Ontario and British Columbia were the first to legalize same-sex marriage, ruling that federal laws restricting marriage to one man and one woman violated the *Charter of Rights and Freedoms* (Figure 14.5). In 2004, courts in Quebec, Manitoba, Nova Scotia, Saskatchewan, Newfoundland and Labrador, and Yukon made the same ruling. On June 28, 2005, the House of Commons passed a bill ensuring that marriage is a right for all Canadians regardless of sexual orientation so that all Canadians are treated as equal under the law; the bill was given royal assent and became law less than a month later, on July 20, 2005. Marriage is now defined as "the union of two people to the exclusion of all others." Canada was the fourth country in the world to legalize same-sex marriage; by 2017 a total of 20 countries had done so; many additional countries have other legal statuses for same-sex partnership, although not marriage. In 2007, the

Ontario Court of Appeal ruled that a child can have three parents—in this case, a biological mother and father and the mother's same-sex partner.

Gay Men, Lesbians, and Bisexuals as a Minority Group

From the foregoing discussion, it is clear that LGB people are the subject of many negative attitudes and stereotypes, just as other minority groups are (Meyer, 2003). Like members of other minority groups, they can experience discrimination, for example, in employment and housing, even though this is illegal in Canada. Only fairly recently have their rights been protected by law.

Discrimination goes hand in hand with stereotypes. One such stereotype is that gay men are child molesters. As with many stereotypes, this one is false. Research shows that the vast majority of child abusers have a heterosexual orientation; only 2 to 3 percent are gay (Jenny et al., 1994).

There is an important way in which LGBs differ from other minority groups, though. In the case of most other minorities, appearance is a fairly good indicator of minority-group status. It is typically easy to recognize a Chinese Canadian or a woman, for example, but one cannot tell simply by looking at a person what his or her sexual orientation is (see Milestones in Sex Research). Thus LGBs, unlike other minorities, can hide their status. There are certain advantages to this. It makes it fairly easy to get along in the heterosexual world—to "pass." However, it has the disadvantage of encouraging the person to conceal her or his true identity to avoid homonegativity; this hiding may be psychologically stressful (Meyer, 2003). Concealing a stigma—whether it is one's sexual orientation, mental illness, illiteracy, or history of child sexual abuse—exacts a psychological, and sometimes physical, toll (Pachankis, 2007).

We shouldn't leave this discussion of discrimination and prejudice against LGBs without asking a crucial question: What can be done to prevent or end this prejudice? Change must occur at many levels: the individual, the interpersonal, and the organizational levels (e.g., corporations, educational institutions), as well as society as a whole and its institutions (e.g., the federal government). At the individual level, all of us must examine our own attitudes toward LGBs to see if they are consistent with basic values we hold, such as a commitment to equality and justice. Some people may need to educate themselves or attend workshops to examine their attitudes. Research in Ontario has shown that workshops for university students that include imagery exercises, coming out stories, and discussion significantly reduce homonegativity and increase comfort with sexual matters (Rye & Meaney, 2009). These attitudes, though, were formed as we grew up—influenced by our parents, our peers,

Figure 14.5 Michael Stark and Michael Leshner of Toronto. Together for more than 20 years, this couple was instrumental in getting Ontario courts to recognize same-sex marriage. The federal government legalized same-sex marriage in June 2005.

© Frank Gunn/CP Images

and the media. Parents must consider the messages they convey to their children about sexual minority groups. The adolescent peer group is strongly homophobic. What can be done to change it? How can the media change so as not to promote antigay prejudices and stereotypes? At the interpersonal level, people must recognize that LGBs are often a hidden minority. Eric, for example, just told a joke that ridiculed gay men. What he didn't know was that one of his three listeners is gay—just not "out" with Eric (for obvious reasons). We must examine our interactions with other people, recognizing the extent to which many of us assume that everyone is heterosexual until proven otherwise.

At the institutional level, how can education be changed to reduce antigay discrimination? A strong program of sex education across the grades, with open discussion of sexual orientation, would be a good start (see Chapter 19). In fact, schools have a responsibility to ensure that homophobic harassment and name-calling does not occur. Azmi Jubran filed a complaint against his school with the B.C. Human Rights Commission. Year after year he had been harassed verbally and physically by his school peers because they believed he was gay. In 2005, the B.C. Court of Appeal ruled that it is not enough for schools to discipline the offending students. Schools must provide preventive anti-homophobic education to prevent this kind of harassment. In addition, gay–straight alliances (GSAs) can work to combat heterosexism and antigay prejudice in organizations (see http://mygsa.ca for resources to support GSAs in Canadian schools). Such alliances have been established at many

Figure 14.6 In a number of Canadian communities and institutions, Safe Spaces supports gay, lesbian, bisexual, transgender, two-spirit, and questioning individuals and their allies.

Funded by the Ministry for Children and Family Development (MCFD).

high schools and universities across Canada. They are open to all students and staff who want to work toward a more inclusive and supportive environment for LGB and trans students. A number of Canadian universities also have a Safe Spaces Projects (Figure 14.6), which involves supportive faculty, staff, and students displaying a sticker on their door to indicate that their space is open to and supportive of people with all sexual orientations and gender identities and that they will not tolerate homophobic or transphobic comments or jokes. It serves as a visible statement to sexual minority individuals that support is around them and provides an opportunity for education and discussion.

Scientists have tested a number of interventions designed to reduce antigay prejudice (Bartos et al., 2014). Education designed to reduce prejudice is effective, as is inter-group contact—that is, getting to know gays and lesbians. Inter-group contact has a long history as a social psychological intervention and was initially designed to reduce racial prejudice. Prejudice can also be reduced if tolerance is conveyed to be the norm, either by an expert or by one's peers. There are many possibilities, then, for systematic efforts to reduce anti-gay prejudice.

Life Experiences of LGB Individuals

In understanding the lives of LGBs, it is important to recognize that there is a wide variety of experiences. An important aspect of this variability is whether the person is a **covert homosexual** (in the closet) or an **overt homosexual** (out of the closet) about his or her sexual identity. As

covert homosexual: A gay man or lesbian who is "in the closet," who keeps his or her sexual orientation a secret.

overt homosexual: A gay man or lesbian who is "out of the closet," who is open about his or her sexual orientation.

discussed earlier, some people may be in a mixed-sex marriage and have children but spend a few hours a month engaging in secret same-sex sexual behaviour or sexual fantasies.[5] Other gay men and lesbians may live almost entirely within an LGB community, particularly in a large city like Toronto or Vancouver where there is a large gay subculture. There are also various degrees of overtness (being "out") and covertness. Many lesbians and gay men are out with trusted friends but not with casual acquaintances, or in some situations but not in others. The lifestyle of gay men differs from that of lesbians, perhaps as a result of the different roles assigned to men and women in our society and the different ways that boys and girls are reared. In addition, there is different discrimination against gay men than there is against lesbians. For example, it is considered quite natural for two women to share an apartment, but if two men over a certain age do so, eyebrows may be raised.

The lifestyles of LGBs are thus far from uniform. They vary according to whether one is male or female and overt or covert about one's sexual identity, and according to social class, occupation, personality, and a variety of other factors.

LGB Development

Some experts believe that sexual orientation is determined by age 5 or 6 or even prenatally, whereas others say that it is determined by age 10 or 12. Scientists don't have exact answers to this question, but without doubt it depends on the individual in ways that are discussed in the section that follows.

Some evidence indicates that gender variance in childhood predicts later LGB orientation (Steensma et al., 2012). That is, children who are rated by their parents as having characteristics such as "behaves like the opposite sex" and "wishes to be the opposite sex," at least somewhat, are more likely, in adulthood, to have same-sex attractions and behaviours. However, this prediction is far from perfect. In one study, the prevalence of homosexuality was 10 to 12 percent in adulthood among those who displayed gender variance in childhood, compared with 1 to 2 percent among those who did not display gender variance in childhood (Steensma et al., 2012). In fact, then, the majority of gender variant children did not turn out to be gay.

Sexual minority women report their first same-sex romantic attraction on average at age 12 and sexual minority men at age 11, but there is lots of variability around those averages (Katz-Wise, 2012). First questioning of one's sexual orientation occurs on average at age 12 for males and age 15 for females, and self-labelling as

---

[5] Men who secretly have sex with other men while in a sexual relationship with a woman are sometimes said to be on the "down low" or "d" for short.

Milestones in Sex Research

Does Gaydar Exist?

An idea has become part of pop culture, the idea that people have *gaydar*, a kind of sixth sense that allows them to detect who is gay. Some research appears to support the existence of gaydar, but the latest research disputes it.

In one set of studies, researchers found that there are visibly perceptible differences between gay and straight men's faces, and between lesbian and straight women's faces, and that people can accurately identify sexual orientation based on photos of faces (Rule & Ambady, 2008; Rule et al., 2008; Rule, Ambady, & Hallett, 2009). The researchers also argue that gaydar is found in other cultures as well (Rule et al., 2011).

How do scientists go about studying gaydar? In one typical experiment, researchers captured photos posted on dating websites (Rule et al., 2008). The photos were cropped to show just the face and hair and all were grey-scaled, to remove extraneous cues. The researchers assessed sexual orientation by whether the individuals were seeking same-gender or other-gender partners. The photos (81 of them, some of gay men, some of straight men) were then shown to undergraduates, who rated each photo on a scale with labels *very gay, somewhat gay, somewhat straight, straight*. The researchers calculated the correlation between participants' ratings of the photos and whether the photo was actually of a gay or straight person. If participants were completely inaccurate so that their responses were random, the correlation between ratings and actual sexual orientation would be 0. The correlation was $r = 0.31$, which is significantly greater than 0, but it isn't exactly a perfect correlation of 1.0 either. Therefore, participants did better than chance, but they certainly were not perfect in identifying who was gay and who was straight. The researchers also repeated their experiments using stimuli that were photos of lesbian and straight women and obtained similar results (Rule, Ambady, & Hallett, 2009). It is studies like these that people use as evidence for gaydar.

Another research team has challenged the gaydar research (Cox et al., 2015). They argue that gaydar is just a slick-sounding term for the practice of using stereotypes to identify a person's sexual orientation. Many people might reason as follows: A man who is sitting around drinking beer, wearing a dirty T-shirt—well, he must be straight. A man who is carefully groomed and wearing a fashionable shirt—he must be gay. Both of those are stereotypes about gay men and straight men, but it doesn't mean that we are right about either person. But how could plain pictures of faces, without all the extra cues, be judged using stereotypes? When the Cox research team tried to replicate the earlier research by the Rule team, they found that there was a confound in the stimuli. The gay men's pictures were higher quality than the straight men's. The same was true of pictures of lesbian women compared with straight women. The Cox team corrected this problem by choosing pairs of straight and gay men's faces that were matched for rated quality. The results indicated that, when photos were matched for quality, participants judged photos as gay at the same rate for photos of actual gay men and actual straight men—that is, they couldn't tell the difference. Additionally, the researchers created a 2×3 experimental design, in which each face was randomly paired with a stereotypic gay or straight statement, such as "He is a hairdresser" or "He drives a pick-up truck," or a neutral statement, such as "He likes spaghetti." So, a respondent might see a gay man's face with a statement that he is a hairdresser or a statement that he drives a pick-up truck or a statement that he likes spaghetti. The results indicated that, whether the photo was of a gay man or a straight man, he was judged as gay 57 percent of the time if the photo had been paired with a gay-stereotyping statement, but he was judged as gay only 20 percent of the time when paired with a straight-stereotypic statement. Stereotypic information about the people, then, guided subjects' judgments, not the photos of faces. This study argues against gaydar.

In another experiment by this same team, participants were randomly assigned to one of three conditions: (1) they were told that gaydar is real; (2) they were told that gaydar is not real and is just another term for stereotyping; or (3) a control group that was told neither (Cox et al., 2015). As in the study described previously, participants made judgments about fictitious men who were described with gay-stereotypic, straight-stereotypic, or neutral statements. The results indicated that those who had been told that gaydar is real relied more on stereotypes in making their judgments, compared to those in the control group. Those who had been told that gaydar is merely another term for stereotyping, however, stereotyped less than the control group. Popular claims about gaydar, then, could be harmful insofar as they lead people to rely on stereotypes more. And yet, by pointing out that gaydar is not real and that it is just a kind of stereotyping, we can actually reduce people's stereotyping.

Overall, then, the evidence for gaydar is not strong. The Cox research shows that gaydar is a folk concept that perpetuates stereotyping.

LGB occurs on average at age 16 for men and 17 or 18 for women. As we discussed in Chapter 10, a crucial task of adolescence is identity development, and sexual orientation is one important aspect of development that occurs over the adolescent years. Related to identity development is **coming out**, which involves acknowledging to oneself, and then to others, that one is gay or lesbian. Although many youth do not disclose their sexual orientation to their parents, if they do, they are more likely to tell their mothers than their fathers. Mothers also tend to react more positively to the disclosure than do fathers. Nonetheless, a study of 542 gay, lesbian, and bisexual youth found that 24 percent of mothers and 37 percent of fathers were intolerant or rejecting when they found out about their child's sexual orientation. Only 48 percent of mothers and 35 percent of fathers were accepting (D'Augelli, 2002). Whether the person experiences acceptance or rejection from family, friends, and others to whom he or she comes out can be critical to self-esteem and mental health. The Internet can also have a positive impact on the coming out process. For teenagers who are just realizing that they are gay or lesbian, the Internet provides boundless information and the opportunity to "chat" with others while remaining safe at home and not acknowledging the identity publicly in ways that could be embarrassing or even dangerous. Interactions with others on the Internet can foster a positive identity and self-acceptance (Schneider, 1991).

These developmental processes are complicated by the negative climate for sexual minority youth that exists in middle school, high school, and college or university. Many LGB youth report harassment by peers, especially in middle school (Robinson & Espelage, 2011). Indeed, as noted earlier, Canadian researchers found that 70 percent of students reported hearing expressions such as "that's so gay," and words like *faggot, lesbo,* and *dyke* every day at school. The use of homophobic epithets (name-calling) is common in middle school and high school (Poteat et al., 2012). Boys engage in this name-calling to each other more than girls do, and the frequency for boys actually increases from Grade 7 to Grade 12. Homophobic epithets are, in reality, a form of bullying and, among boys, they enforce the rules of masculinity (Poteat et al., 2011). Ironically, those who dish them out are also the most likely to receive them. And today, cyberbullying also occurs, often allowing perpetrators to remain anonymous and facilitating the "outing" of LGB adolescents to hundreds of peers with just a click (Robinson & Espelage, 2011). Harassment can lead sexual minority youth to skip school, which creates another set of problems. One Canadian high school student described one of his experiences of harassment in this way:

> At school I was attacked a couple of times in the hallway. Once I was walking down the hallway and a guy jumped on me and pretended to fuck me. It was a big joke for him and his friends. After throwing him off me, I collapsed. I couldn't

> believe that I had been violated in such a sexual way in front of the school. I had to deal with the students going around and saying I was going to take him to court. I had to deal with total strangers coming up to me and saying, "What are you doing to my friend? How come you are taking him to court?" These people didn't even recognize that I was the victim. I was not the one at fault. (Grace & Wells, 2007, p. 7)

Even at the undergraduate level, peer harassment can be intense (Figure 14.7), and this harassment has been linked to suicidal thoughts and suicide attempts (Robinson & Espelage, 2011). One much publicized example is the case of Tyler Clementi, a Rutgers University student, whose roommate used a webcam to record him kissing another man in the privacy of his room. The roommate then urged many others to view another encounter, and Clementi discovered what was happening. The next day, Clementi killed himself by jumping off the George Washington Bridge.

Support from adults, especially parents and adults at school, is crucial as sexual minority youth weather these storms (Darwich et al., 2012; Heatherington & Lavner, 2008). Often schools fail to address individual incidents and lack proactive policies to reduce negative climates. The case of Azmi Jubran, a B.C. high school student, described earlier, established that legally schools must provide preventive anti-homophobic education to prevent this kind of harassment. In addition, schools should

Figure 14.7 Peer harassment, such as spreading rumours, can be part of the school climate for LGB youth.

© Tetra Images/Getty Images

coming out: The process of acknowledging to oneself, and then to others, that one is gay or lesbian.

First Person

Sexual Fluidity and Questioning

This case is taken from a series of interviews conducted by psychologist Lisa Diamond, author of *Sexual Fluidity* (2008).

At the very first interview, Eleanor described herself as "questioning." She has an outgoing, vivacious demeanour, with a broad, engaging smile and a self-deprecating sense of humour.

Eleanor flatly refused to characterize her same-sex attractions on a 0–100 percent scale. She threw up her hands and exclaimed, "I can't make any sense of that at all! There are too many variables involved when I'm attracted to someone, so there's no way for me to divide it up that way." Eleanor was 20 years old and had first begun to question her sexuality about a year earlier, when her boyfriend told her that he was bisexual. She had been aware of sporadic same-sex attractions since the age of 13, and, in her words, "they scared the hell out of me." Yet the attractions had always confused her. Most of her "gut level" urges were in response to men, but she found women more aesthetically and emotionally desirable. As she put it:

> I prefer to make out with men, but the idea of having sex with a man utterly repulses me. I would, however, like to marry a woman, and that's who I want to make a long-term commitment to. . . . When people ask me if I'm straight and I say yes, I know I'm being dishonest, and I can't tolerate that dishonesty. But if somebody asked me if I was a lesbian, I'd also feel dishonest saying yes. I guess I might be bisexual. I'm annoyed by the uncertainty. I know I'm not straight, it's just a matter of defining my not-straightness. . . .

By the second interview Eleanor had settled on the compromise of a bisexual identification, despite the fact that her feelings for women remained relatively ambiguous. She was eager for more certainty about her sexuality:

I still go through this whole explanation when I tell people I'm bisexual, because the truth is that my attraction to women isn't really all that sexual. It's more aesthetic. Women are just so much better looking than men. I guess I find women magnetic. That's not quite the same as a sexual attraction. . . . I thought that things would resolve themselves. I expected that over time I'd either feel clear sexual attractions and I'd identify as bisexual or I wouldn't feel them at all and I'd identify as heterosexual. But now I realize that won't happen—I still feel the same and I've accepted that.

At the third interview, at age 25, Eleanor had finally reconciled with the fact that her emotional and aesthetic appreciation for women did not really qualify as sexual attraction. Yet contrary to the notion that this might just be a rationalization for not identifying as lesbian or bisexual, Eleanor actually expressed great disappointment that she was not gay:

> I've kind of straightened out! I still call myself bisexual but I'm on the edge of heterosexual, which I'm not pleased about. . . . I never really wanted to be heterosexual but I don't have much choice in the matter. . . . I think sexuality definitely changes, because it's not that I'm just more aware of the straight parts of me, I've actually become more straight, but I don't have any idea what causes those changes.

Eleanor reported the same basic perspective at the eight-year and ten-year follow-up interviews, when she characterized herself as "reluctantly heterosexual." At the time of the ten-year interview, she described her emotional attraction as 70 percent to women, but her physical attraction as only 5 percent to women.

Lisa M. Diamond in Sexual Fluidity: Understanding Women's Love and Desire, pp. 155-158. Copyright © Harvard University Press. Reprinted with permission.

provide professional development opportunities on LGB issues for all school staff. Schools can also host gay–straight alliances, Safe Spaces programs, and wellness programs for sexual minority youth.

To this point, we have discussed sexual identity as something that develops during adolescence and then is fixed. That may be true for many people, but psychologist Lisa Diamond (2005, 2008a) has documented what she calls **sexual fluidity**, which refers to changes over time in sexual attractions, identity, or behaviour, which can occur with people in their 20s, 30s, or later (see First Person). Her research involved young women, followed longitudinally, over eight years. The women's attractions and identity shifted in all directions, for example,

> **sexual fluidity:** Changes over time in a person's sexual attractions, identity, or behaviour.

from bisexual to lesbian or from lesbian to heterosexual. Similar patterns have been documented in men as well (Katz-Wise, 2012). Some of these people report that they are attracted to the person, not the gender. As one man said,

> I find gender matters, but it's definitely not the first priority on the list for me. . . . In terms of attraction, I just like beautiful things, and I don't really classify those in men or women. I find both of them beautiful. (Katz-Wise, 2012, p. 122)

For some people, then, patterns of attraction and behaviour can continue to develop and evolve well past adolescence.

Today, North American culture has a much wider variety of possible self-labels so that people don't have to fit themselves into just one of two boxes: heterosexual or homosexual. People can be bisexual, queer, questioning, or unlabelled. In one well-sampled American survey, 86 percent of women and 92 percent of men said that their sexual attractions were only to members of the opposite sex, but 10 percent of women and 4 percent of men said that their sexual attractions were "mostly" to the opposite sex (Chandra et al., 2011). They don't fit neatly into the heterosexual box or into the homosexual box.

Bisexual and Assexual Identities

Bisexual men and women generally begin to think of themselves as bisexual in their early to mid-20s (Fox, 1995; Weinberg et al., 1994). There are some gender differences in the sequence of behaviours, though. Bisexual women typically have their first other-sex attraction and sexual experiences before their first same-sex ones. Bisexual men, in contrast, are more likely to have same-sex experiences first, followed by mixed-sex ones. What do bisexuals base their identity on? Sexual behaviour, feelings of attraction, or something else?

Research has shown that most bisexual men and women base their sexual identity on their feelings of sexual attraction or capacity to fall in love with either women or men regardless of whether they have expressed these feelings through sexual behaviour (Rust, 2001). Many describe their sexual attractions to women and men as different from each other. Those respondents who have had sexual experiences with both women and men generally report having these experiences serially over time, often including lengthy monogamous relationships. They indicate that they do not cease being bisexual when they became monogamously involved with either a woman or a man, just as heterosexuals do not cease being straight during a period of celibacy (Rust, 2000a). Some individuals adopt bisexual identities to reflect their politics. They may see bisexuality as a challenge to the importance of

gender in defining sexuality, viewing their bisexual identity not as a combination of their attractions to women and men, but an attraction to specific people regardless of their gender.

Asexual individuals often experience the same issues with respect to identity and development as bisexual individuals do (Bogaert, 2015).

Lesbian, Gay, and Bisexual Communities

A loose network of lesbian, gay, and bisexual communities extends around the world. As one woman put it,

> I have seen lesbian communities all over the world (e.g., South Africa, Brazil, and Israel) where the lesbians of that nation have more in common with me (i.e., they play the same lesbian records, have read the same books, wear the same lesbian jewellery) than the heterosexual women of that nation have in common with heterosexual women in North America. (E. D. Rothblum, personal communication, 2007)

These links have been cemented in the past decade by increases in international travel, globalization, and the international reach of the Internet (Puar, 2001).

Distinct LGB communities became visible in Canada in the 1970s in Toronto, Vancouver, and Montreal (Kinsman, 1996). During this period, there was a flourishing of businesses catering to a gay clientele including bars, clubs, bathhouses, restaurants, bookstores, theatres, and social organizations. Many of these establishments also cater to a lesbian and bisexual clientele, although generally there are fewer businesses geared specifically toward lesbians. The lesbian community in particular has been involved in creating a lesbian culture, expressed in music and literature, and celebrated at festivals and women's sporting events. LGB residential areas grew up close to these commercial establishments, creating LGB neighbourhoods in these cities, although most gay men and lesbians do not live in these "gay villages" (Kinsman, 1996).

LGBs tend to be less visible in smaller Canadian communities, but they nonetheless tend to have strong social networks. Some people move to large urban centres seeking greater anonymity, acceptance, and perhaps distance from their families.

Several symbols are used as representations of gay, lesbian, and bisexual pride. That is, they are used to indicate that being gay is something to be proud of, not to hide. An upside-down pink triangle, which is what the Nazis used to label gay men, has been reclaimed by the gay community. The lowercase Greek letter lambda is also used. However, perhaps the most easily recognizable symbol is the rainbow flag, used by the gay community since 1978 and a representation of diversity and multiculturalism. A pink, purple, and blue striped flag is used to symbolize bisexual pride, with the pink representing attraction to members of the same gender, the blue representing attraction to people of the other gender, and the purple (the middle stripe) representing attraction to both men and women. Pride celebrations, which celebrate the anniversary of the Stonewall rebellion mentioned earlier, take place in various cities across Canada each summer. The Pride Parade, in particular, is considered an important celebration of what it means to be gay, lesbian, or bisexual (Figure 14.8). The use of slang is another sign of solidarity among LGBs.

Gay bars are one aspect of the LGB social life. These are gay-friendly clubs in which drinking, perhaps dancing, talking, socializing with friends, and, sometimes, the possibility of finding a romantic or sexual partner are important elements. In large cities, some gay bars cater to either gay men or lesbians. However, many gay bars, particularly in smaller Canadian cities, are mixed gender and mixed orientation. This means that they cater to both gay men and to lesbians, as well as to gay-positive heterosexuals. What makes them gay bars is not that they are different from other bars but that they are accepting of same-sex relationships. Thus, patrons can be open about their sexual orientation and feel free to socialize and dance with whomever they want without fearing verbal or physical harassment from other customers. Some gay bars look like any other bar from the outside, while others may have names—for example, The Open Closet—that indicate to the alert that they are gay bars. LGB-community dances and parties are other important avenues for socializing, particularly in small centres.

Gay baths are another aspect of some gay men's social and sexual lives (note that bathhouses, particularly in Toronto, were where the police raids took place that sparked numerous protests in the 1970s and 1980s). The baths are clubs with many rooms in them, generally including a swimming pool or whirlpool, as well as rooms for dancing, watching television, and socializing; most areas are dimly lit. Once a man has found a sexual partner, they go to one of a number of small rooms furnished with beds, where they can engage in sexual activity. The baths feature casual, impersonal sex, since a partner can be found and the act completed without the two even exchanging names, much less making any emotional commitment to each other.

In many parts of Canada, there are no or relatively few bathhouses (Myers et al., 1993). However, there are about six in each of Montreal, Toronto, and Vancouver. There is some controversy in the gay community about whether they encourage risky sexual practices. Some

Figure 14.8 Today many Canadian cities have an annual Pride Parade as part of Gay Pride Week, such as this parade in Toronto. In the early 1990s, mayors of Fredericton, Hamilton, London, and Saskatoon refused to declare Gay Pride Week. In each case, the provincial Human Rights Commission found the mayors at fault, fined them, and ordered them to issue gay pride proclamations.

© Ian Willms/CP Images

see the baths as an aspect of gay culture that spreads HIV and will continue to do so, killing thousands; they believe the baths must be closed and the destructive practices they encourage should stop (Rotello, 1997; Signorile, 1997). Others celebrate the liberated sexuality fostered by the baths and see it as an essential part of gay men's lifestyle. Today many bathhouses emphasize safe sex—for example, by supplying condoms and handing out safer sex information.

In keeping with the increased use of online dating websites by single individuals, a major way for LGB individuals to meet each other is through the Internet. Cyberspace is also a place where gay men and lesbians can find community when, geographically, they do not live in a place that has a gay community (Brown et al., 2005). Gay-related websites provide chat rooms and have ways for LGBs to form online relationships and perhaps find partners for casual sex or a long-term relationship (Brown et al., 2005; Ross et al., 2007).

Certainly, in the last three decades the *gay liberation movement* has had a tremendous impact on the gay lifestyle and community. In particular, it has encouraged LGBs to be more overt and to feel less guilty about their behaviour. The gay liberation movement has given rise to a number of provincial and

gay bars: Gay-friendly bars or clubs frequented by lesbians and gay men.
gay baths: Clubs where gay men can socialize; features include a swimming pool or whirlpool and access to casual sex.

national organizations committed to ending discrimination against LGBs. For example, EGALE (Equality for Gays and Lesbians Everywhere) is a national organization committed to advancing equality and justice for lesbian, gay, bisexual, and transgender individuals and their families across Canada. The organization does so by fighting for justice in the courts as well as by building communication and action networks. There are also many LGB organizations at the provincial and local levels. Some address social justice issues; others provide community service and education. For example, large Canadian cities and most Canadian universities have pride centres. The Canadian Lesbian and Gay Archives serves as a central clearinghouse for LGB information.

There are thus many places for LGBs to socialize besides bars, including the Metropolitan Community Church (a network of gay and lesbian churches with three churches in Ontario), gay athletic organizations, and gay political organizations.

Among other accomplishments, members of the gay liberation movement have founded numerous gay newspapers, magazines, and Internet sites. These have many of the same features as other media: forums for political opinions, human-interest stories, and fashion news. Today there are many regional Canadian LGB publications; most of them are web-only including *Wayves, Fugues, Outwords Inc. Outlooks* and *Xtra*. There are also several publications that list gay-owned or gay-friendly businesses, including information about bars, accommodations, shops, services, and tours. There is also a national GLB television station in Canada, OUTtv (Figure 14.9). The Canadian Gay, Lesbian, and Bisexual Resource Directory distributes information relevant to LGB communities across Canada.

Figure 14.9 The television comedy series *Modern Family* is an example of a mainstream show that often deals with gay-friendly storylines.

© AP Photo/Chris Pizzello/CP Images

Same-Sex Relationships

Contrary to stereotypes, a substantial number of lesbians, gay men, and bisexuals form long-term relationships. Some bisexuals are in a relationship with a person of the other gender; others are in a relationship with someone of their same gender. Across numerous surveys, between 8 and 21 percent of lesbian couples had been together for 10 years or more, as had between 18 and 28 percent of the gay male couples (Kurdek, 2005) (Figure 14.10).

In the 2016 census, there were 24 370 same-sex married couples and 48 510 same-sex common-law couples in Canada (Statistics Canada, 2017). This is an increase of 61 percent since 2006. Of these, 52 percent were male couples and 48 percent were female couples. About 12 percent of same-sex couples had children living with them; female couples were four times as likely to have children living with them than male couples. One study asked same-sex Canadian couples why they wanted to be married (Alderson, 2004). For some, it was important to publicly declare their lifelong commitment to each other. For others, marriage was part of a spiritual journey, including feeling that marriage brings greater depth to a relationship. Some felt that the legal protection provided by marriage (e.g., if their partner got sick) was important. Finally, for some it was about equality rights and making things better for gay and lesbian youth in the future. For example, here's what one 41-year-old woman said:

> You can't represent the essence of it and that's the spiritual part that I'm talking about—that indescribable experience of being a family. And now that we're being recognized by the outside state as a family. It's very powerful to be recognized. (Alderson, 2004, p. 113)

All couples—gay or straight—must struggle to find a balance that suits both persons. Three aspects of the relationship typically have to be negotiated and can be sources of conflict: money, housework, and sex (Solomon et al., 2005).

What is striking about all the research on gay and lesbian relationships is how similar all relationships are, regardless of sexual orientation, in their satisfactions, loves, joys, and conflicts (Holmberg & Blair, 2009; Patterson, 2000) (see First Person). For example, in a Quebec study, gay, lesbian, and heterosexual couples were brought to the laboratory and told to discuss a problem (Julien et al., 2003). Each couple's interactions were videotaped and later coded for both positive and negative behaviours by each partner. The results showed no differences among lesbian, gay, and heterosexual couples on any of the interaction measures. Similarly, research in Alberta assessed the similarities and differences of the experiences of women who were currently in a same-sex relationship but had been married to a man in the past (Boon & Alderson, 2009). The women reported that many

Figure 14.10 Many lesbians and gay men report currently being in a steady romantic relationship.

© Image Source/Getty Images

of the issues they faced in the two relationships were similar. However, they also identified some differences including in the level of intimacy, communication style, and sharing of responsibilities. In addition, experiences of antigay prejudice, heterosexism, and homonegativity can affect same-sex relationships (Boon & Alderson, 2009; Cohen et al., 2008). Nonetheless, couples in which the partners were more out to the world tended to report higher relationship satisfaction (Clausell & Roisman, 2009). Furthermore, sexual minority individual who are in a happy relationship report better sexual functioning across a range of domains (Cohen & Byers, 2015).

Lesbian and Gay Families

Increasingly, gay and lesbian couples are creating families that include children (Bowe, 2006). In the past, the courts tended to grant custody to the nongay or nonlesbian parents and have often restricted visitation by the gay or lesbian parent (Barrett et al., 1997). However, legislation in most provinces allows same-sex adoption either by the partner of a parent or of an unrelated child. In provinces where there has not been such legislation, the courts have ruled that provincial acts that prevent same-sex couples from applying to adopt are unconstitutional. The Canadian *Charter of Rights and Freedoms* prohibits discrimination based on sexual orientation, and this applies to adoption, custody, and access

(Figure 14.11). This legislation appears to recognize the result of research on the effects on children of living in a gay or lesbian family, which is reviewed below.

Of course, these families are not all the same. In some, the children were born to one partner in a previous mixed-sex relationship. In others, the children were adopted or, in the case of lesbian couples, born by means of assisted insemination. There is some preliminary evidence that use of donor sperm by lesbians in Canada has increased significantly since the legalization of same-sex marriage (Moskovtsev et al., 2013). Some are single-parent families, with, for example, a lesbian mother rearing her children from a previous mixed-sex marriage.

> **How does growing up with two parents of the same gender affect children psychologically?**

Heterosexuals often make the assumption, based on their homonegativity, that it is better for children to grow up in heterosexual families than in families with two parents of the same gender. For example, researchers in Saskatchewan found that undergraduates, particularly those higher in homonegativity, rated possible outcomes for an adoptive child significantly more negatively if the adoptive parents were a same-sex couple than if they were a mixed-sex couple (McCutcheon & Morrison, 2015). Based on this assumption, people raise three questions about how children fare. First, will they be less healthy psychologically than children who grow up with two heterosexual parents? Second, will they have difficulties

Figure 14.11 Lesbian and gay parents and their children. It is illegal to discriminate against gay men or lesbians in adoption, custody, or access decisions.

(a) © Geoff Manasse/IPN/Aurora

(b) © Colin McPherson/Corbis SYGMA

in relationships with their peers, perhaps being stigmatized or teased because of their unusual family situation? Third, will they show "disturbances" in gender identity or sexual identity? Will they become gay or lesbian? (Note the assumption that it would be better if they didn't.) What has research found?

Research on children growing up in lesbian or gay families, compared with those growing up in heterosexual families,

medical model: A theoretical model in psychiatry in which mental problems are thought of as sickness or mental illness; the problems in turn are often thought to be due to biological factors.

dismisses these assumptions. For example, the adjustment and mental health of children in lesbian and gay families are no different from those of children in heterosexual families (Farr et al., 2010; Gartrell et al., 2005; Patterson, 2006). They fare about as well in terms of social skills and popularity as children growing up in heterosexual families (Patterson, 2009). This may be because, as shown by research in Quebec, the quality of the mother–child relationship is the same for heterosexual, lesbian, and bisexual mothers (Julien et al., 2008). Finally, the overwhelming numbers of children growing up in lesbian or gay households have a heterosexual orientation (Allen & Burrell, 2002).

In conclusion, although some people have raised concerns about children growing up in lesbian and gay families based on their negative assumptions, research consistently shows no difference between these children and those in heterosexual families in psychosocial development, gender identity, or sexual orientation (Canadian Psychological Association, 2003). Children need at least one loving, supportive parent and that can be found in many types of families. Nonetheless, these children may have to deal with the homonegativity of their peers. For example, a Canadian study found that 37 percent of youth with LGBTQ parents reported being verbally harassed about the sexual orientation of their parent (Taylor & Peter, 2011).

LO7

LGB Sexual Orientation and Mental Health

Some Canadians believe that homosexuality is a kind of mental illness. Is this really true? Do psychologists and psychiatrists agree that LGBs are poorly adjusted or deviant?

Sin and the Medical Model

The belief that homosexuality is a form of mental illness is something of an improvement over previous beliefs about homosexuality. Before the last century, the dominant belief in Europe and North America was that homosexuality was a sin or a heresy. During the Inquisition, people who were accused of being heretics were also frequently accused of being homosexuals and were burned at the stake. Indeed, in those times, all mental illness was regarded as a sin. In the twentieth century, this view was replaced by the **medical model**, in which mental disturbance, and homosexuality in particular, is viewed as a sickness or illness.[6]

[6] As one gay comedian quipped, "If homosexuality is an illness, hey, I'm going to call in queer to work tomorrow."

First Person

Carolyn and cj: A Same-Sex Couple

Carolyn is 29 and cj is 31. They have been together for eight years. They live in Ottawa, where Carolyn works for the federal government, and cj works as a researcher for an online activist organization.

Carolyn has always had close relationships with her parents and younger sister. They were her best friends when she was growing up, and she has many fond memories of working on family craft activities. In school, she was active in almost every nonsports extracurricular club. In middle school she wanted to have a boyfriend, mainly for the social status. In Grade 12, she had an impassioned relationship with a young man, and his openness about sexual identity influenced her own ideas on the subject. After this relationship, Carolyn wanted to balance her romantic experiences by having a relationship with a woman. She dated two women before cj and found that she was more able to be herself with women. Carolyn's nuclear family was supportive when she came out to them; they indicated that the gender of her partner was not an issue. She delayed coming out to her extended family, fearing that they would be less supportive. Carolyn identifies as a dyke: For her, the term *lesbian* assumes an attraction to women only, whereas the term *dyke* does not negate her past relationship with a man and recognizes her attraction to trans people.

cj's family is also close. She has two brothers and a sister. She had an active childhood and adolescence, spending much of it horseback riding and at the family cottage. Classism was a particular challenge for cj in school. She felt that there were certain expectations of her because she was from an upper-middle-class home. She rejected these expectations and purposefully sought out like-minded friends. Although cj had boyfriends in high school, including a couple of long-term relationships, she now recognizes that she was always attracted to women. In first-year university, cj had crushes on some of the women in her classes yet did not know how to act on her feelings. She dated one woman before Carolyn.

When cj came out to her family, her father was immediately accepting. Her mother found it harder to come to terms with cj's sexual identity. Her minister and cj's sister were instrumental in helping her accept her daughter's identity. cj identifies as pansexual—that is, she is not exclusively attracted to women; rather, she is attracted to people regardless of their gender.

cj and Carolyn were both raised in Fredericton, where they attended the same high school. Although they knew each other by name, they travelled in different circles. When cj returned to Fredericton after university, she and Carolyn kept running into each other and had some awkward flirtatious moments. Yet they were not certain of each other's sexual identity or their mutual attraction until they saw each other at an LGBT event. Following this, they went on a coffee date, and within a few months were dating exclusively. Approximately 18 months later, they moved to Ottawa together so that Carolyn could complete a degree in art history and cj could do a master's degree in legal studies.

In spring 2000, three years before same-sex marriage was legalized in Ontario, Carolyn and cj applied for a marriage licence. Although they do not regard marriage as necessary to affirm their relationship, it was important for them to have the legal benefits and protections associated with marriage. They wanted to buy a house together and did not want to wait until same-sex marriage was legalized. So they took the necessary steps to ensure they would have as close to a legal equivalent to marriage as possible.

Most of Carolyn and cj's disagreements relate to household chores. Important aspects of their relationship are having similar politics and values, enjoying discussing such issues, and finding each other interesting. Their trust that the other person will be there to support them is also very important to them.

Source: Based on an interview by Dr. Jacqueline Cohen.

Research Evidence

What do the scientific data say? Early research compared a group of gay men and lesbians in therapy with a group of randomly chosen heterosexuals not in therapy.

Not surprisingly, these studies tended to find more problems of adjustment among the gay and lesbian group than among the heterosexual group (Rosen, 1974). However, the reasoning was circular in assuming that LGBs were abnormal (in therapy) and that heterosexuals were normal (not in therapy), and then finding exactly that.

A major breakthrough came with the next group of studies, which involved nonpatient research. In these studies, a group of gay men and lesbians not in therapy (nonpatients) were compared with a group of heterosexuals not in therapy. The nonpatient gay men and lesbians were generally recruited through LGB organizations, advertisements, or word of mouth. Such nonpatient research has found no differences between the groups (Ross et al., 1988; Rothblum, 1994). That is, gay men, lesbians, and heterosexuals are equally well adjusted, a finding that is quite remarkable in view of the negative attitudes that some members of the general public tend to hold toward LGBs (Gonsiorek, 1996). This position has received official professional recognition by the American Psychiatric Association (APA). Before 1973, the APA had listed homosexuality as a disorder in its authoritative *Diagnostic and Statistical Manual of Mental Disorders* (which Canadian psychiatrists also use). In 1973, the APA voted to remove homosexuality from that listing so that it was no longer considered a psychiatric disorder by the APA or by the Canadian Psychiatric Association. Other countries were slower to make these changes. Homosexuality was removed from the list of mental disorders by the World Health Organization only in 1993, by Japan in 1995, and by China in 2001.

More recently, a new set of studies has emerged using even better designs that, for example, obtain a random sample of the general population and then compare the gay men and lesbians and the heterosexuals in the sample on indices of mental health (Cochran et al., 2003; Meyer, 2003; Roberts et al., 2010; Wichström & Hegna, 2003). These studies find higher rates of depression, anxiety, and post-traumatic stress disorder among gay men and lesbians compared with heterosexuals, and suicide attempts are more common among LGB youth than among heterosexual youth (King et al., 2008; Mustanski et al., 2010; Roberts et al., 2010).

However, scientists vigorously debate the meaning of the statistics. One controversy concerns how big or meaningful the differences are. For example, in one study, 9.1 percent of LGB adolescents had made a suicide attempt, compared with 3.6 percent for heterosexual adolescents (Wichström & Hegna, 2003). We could focus on the fact that LGB youth were nearly three times as likely to attempt suicide. Alternatively, we could say that it's a gap of less than 6 percentage points and 90.9 percent of the LGBs had *not* attempted suicide (Savin-Williams, 2001; Savin-Williams & Ream, 2003). Should we view the glass as half full or half empty?

Beyond that, scientists agree that higher rates of depression and suicide among LGBs do not mean

that homosexuality per se indicates mental illness. Rather, the higher rates reflect the following: (1) the exposure of LGBs to maltreatment and violence (Dunbar, 2006; Roberts et al., 2010); (2) the lack of support or downright rejection by family and friends that some LGBs experience (Ryan et al., 2009; Ueno, 2005); and (3) the stress of concealing their true identity (Meyer, 2003).

Resilience in Sexual Minority Individuals

To this point we have focused on negative psychological outcomes such as depression and suicide attempts. A major trend in psychology today is positive psychology, which focuses on people's resilience and factors that contribute to resilience. What is perhaps more striking than the negative outcomes is the resilience that most LGB people display in the face of stigma. Factors that promote resilience in LGBs include social support, especially support for the person's sexual orientation, and personal traits of hope and optimism. These help LGBs maintain their psychological health even when they encounter prejudice (Fenaughty & Harré, 2003; Kwon, 2013; Russell & Richards, 2003).

Can Sexual Orientation Be Changed by Psychotherapy?

Conversion therapy or **reparative therapy**— treatments designed to change LGBs into heterosexuals— have been around for more than 100 years (Haldeman, 1994; Shidlo et al., 2001). The latest versions come from far-right religious groups. Many earlier techniques were downright inhumane. They included crude behaviour therapy that involved giving gay men electrical shocks while they viewed slides of nude men, as well as surgeries ranging from castration to brain surgery. All these treatments rested on the assumption that homosexuality was an illness that should and could be cured.

Investigations of reparative therapies today reveal that many individuals undergoing reparative therapy do so because of pressures from their family. They also identify the personal agonies that people experience as they are forced into changing, or perhaps choose to change, their orientation. One man, who is now a psychologist, quoted from his diary:

> I am going to meet with the counselor tomorrow. I don't really know what to think. I feel that I need help but I also feel that I'm trying to do away with a part of myself. I know I should look at it as sinful and ugly, like a wart that needs to be burned off. Is it possible that those emotions are what allow me to be a sensitive caring male? Is it possible that God has allowed this in my life to build certain characteristics? Is it really ugly and sinful that I want to hold and be held by a man and that I want to have a relationship with a man that includes sex? It sure sounds ugly on paper. I don't like admitting these things. I really don't. What

conversion or reparative therapy: Any one of a number of treatments designed to turn LGBs into heterosexuals.

is it that causes me to think and feel this way? Is it Satanic? Am I possessed? (Ford, 2001, p. 77)

The consequences of reparative therapies can be ugly because they do not actually change people's sexual orientation but do make them feel awfully guilty about it. Thus, reparative therapy itself can create mental health problems. As a result, some gay men and bisexuals seek psychotherapy to help them recover from conversion therapies (Haldeman, 2001).

Given the evidence discussed earlier in this section supporting the argument that LGBs do not have a mental illness, reparative therapies make no sense. In addition, they do not work. Ethical issues are raised as well: Should a person be changed from gay to straight against his or her will? Why do we only try to change people from gay to straight and not the reverse? By 2000, the scandals associated with conversion therapies had become so great that the American Psychiatric Association issued an official position statement opposing them (American Psychiatric Association, 2000b).

LO8

What Determines Sexual Orientation?

A fascinating psychological question is, Why do people become homosexual, heterosexual, or bisexual? Several theoretical answers to this question, as well as the relevant evidence, are discussed in this section. You will notice that the older theorists and researchers considered it their task to explain homosexuality by reflecting a heteronormative approach; more recent investigators, realizing that heterosexuality needs to be explained as well, are more likely to consider it their task to understand the developmental pathways for all orientations, including heterosexuality.

Biological Theories

A number of scientists have proposed that sexual orientation is caused by biological factors. Interestingly, this is also the view of the majority of Canadians—54 percent believe that homosexuality is something a person is born with and an additional 8 percent believe that it results from a combination of biological factors and environment (Mazzuca, 2004). The likeliest candidates for these biological causes are genetic factors, prenatal factors, differences in brain structure, and an endocrine imbalance.

Genetic Factors

One study recruited gay and bisexual men who had a twin brother or an adopted brother (Bailey & Pillard, 1991). Among the 56 gay men who had an identical twin brother, 52 percent of the co-twins were themselves gay

(in the terminology of geneticists, this is a 52 percent concordance rate). Among the 54 gay men who had a nonidentical twin brother, 22 percent of the co-twins were themselves gay. Of the adoptive brothers of gay men, 11 percent were gay. The same research team later repeated the study with lesbians (Bailey et al., 1993). Among the 71 lesbians who had an identical twin, 48 percent of the co-twins were also lesbian. Among the 37 lesbians who had a nonidentical twin sister, 16 percent of the co-twins were lesbian. Of the adoptive sisters of lesbians, 6 percent were lesbian. The statistics for women were therefore quite similar to those for men. Later studies using improved methods have found similar results (Kendler et al., 2000; Kirk et al., 2000).

> **What causes people to be gay or heterosexual?**

The fact that the rate of concordance is substantially higher for identical twins than for nonidentical twins argues in favour of a genetic contribution to sexual orientation. If genetic factors absolutely *determined* sexual orientation, however, the concordance rate would be 100 percent for the identical twin pairs, and the rates are far from that. The implication is that factors other than genetics also play a role in influencing sexual orientation.

A milestone came in 2005 with the first full genome scan for sexual orientation in men, using modern genotyping methods (Mustanski et al., 2005). The sample consisted of 456 individuals from 146 different families, all of whom had two or more gay brothers. It included many heterosexual siblings and parents from those families, as well as the gay siblings. This design is ideal for spotting regions of DNA that are the same for two gay brothers but that differ from the heterosexual siblings or parents. The findings indicated possible influence by three genes, found on chromosomes 7, 8, and 10. It seems likely that multiple genes contribute to sexual orientation. This research is still in its infancy but should yield important findings in the next decade.

Prenatal Factors

Another possible biological cause is that homosexuality develops as a result of factors during the prenatal period. As we suggest in Chapter 5, exposure to inappropriate hormones during fetal development can lead a genetic female to have male genitals or a genetic male to have female genitals. It has been suggested that a similar process might account for homosexuality (and also for transgender—see Chapter 13).

According to one theory, homosexuality is caused by a variation in prenatal development. There is a critical time of fetal development during which the hypothalamus differentiates and sexual orientation is determined (Ellis & Cole-Harding, 2001). According to this theory, any of several biological variations during this period will produce homosexuality.

One line of animal research that supports this theory has found evidence that severe *stress to a mother* during pregnancy tends to produce homosexual offspring. For example, exposing pregnant female rats to stress produces male offspring that assume the female mating posture, although their ejaculatory behaviour is typical for males (Ward et al., 2002). The stress to the mother reduces the amount of testosterone in the fetus, which is thought to produce homosexual rats. Research with humans designed to test the prenatal stress hypothesis reports mixed results. Some studies find effects like those in the rat studies, and others do not (Bailey et al., 1991; Ellis & Cole-Harding, 2001).

Canadian researchers have been leaders in examining prenatal factors that may determine a person's sexual orientation. For example, Ontario psychologists Ray Blanchard and Anthony Bogaert studied the birth order of gay men. Their research shows that consistently, across many samples in a number of countries, compared with heterosexual men, gay men are more likely to have a late birth order and to have more older brothers but not more older sisters (Blanchard, 2004; Bogaert, 2003). This is termed the fraternal birth order effect. The researchers find no birth order or sibling effects for lesbians compared with heterosexual women. They believe that they have uncovered a prenatal effect, hypothesizing that, with each successive pregnancy with a male fetus, the mother forms more antibodies against an antigen (H-Y antigen) produced by a gene on the Y chromosome (Bogaert & Skorska, 2011). Because H-Y antigen is known to influence prenatal sexual differentiation, the hypothesis is that the mother's antibodies to this antigen may affect sexual differentiation in the developing fetal brain and subsequent sexual attraction. These researchers estimate that between 15 and 30 percent of gay men had their sexual orientation created in this manner (Blanchard & Bogaert, 2004; Cantor et al., 2002).

Other researchers have documented an odd but potentially important pattern concerning the 2D:4D finger-length ratio. This refers to the ratio of the length of the index finger (2D) to the length of the ring finger (4D). In general, men have lower 2D:4D ratios than women; that is, men's index fingers are relatively shorter than their ring fingers, compared with women's. Lesbians have a lower 2D:4D ratio than heterosexual women. There are no differences between gay men and heterosexual men (Grimbos et al., 2010). It is thought that the 2D:4D ratio is an indicator of prenatal androgen exposure, so these results suggest possible prenatal effects on women's sexual orientation. Ontario researcher Martin Lalumière has found that gay men and lesbians are more likely to be left-handed than are heterosexuals; gay men are about 40 percent more likely than straight men to be left-handed, and lesbians are nearly twice as likely as heterosexual women to be left-handed (Lalumière et al., 2000). Both

patterns suggest some kind of prenatal hormone effect on the developing brain.

Recently researchers in B.C. investigated whether the fraternal birth order, increased non-right-handedness, and 2D:4D finger-length ratio effects are also found in asexual individuals (Yule et al., 2014). They conducted an online study of asexual, heterosexual, and sexual minority individuals. They found that the asexual men and women were 2.4 and 2.5 times more likely to be non-right-handed than were the heterosexual individuals. They also found that asexual men tended to be later born than were heterosexual men. There were no differences in the 2D:4D ratio. This may mean that there is an underlying neurodevelopmental basis to asexuality.

Recall that in Chapter 5 we introduced the concept of epigenetics and ways in which epigenetic factors may shape prenatal sexual differentiation. Yet another group of researchers has hypothesized that same-sex sexual orientation results from epigenetic factors during prenatal development that make the fetus more or less sensitive to androgens (Rice et al., 2012).

These theories of prenatal influence are intriguing, but none right now have enough scientific evidence behind them to be completely accepted (Gooren, 2006).

Brain Factors

Another line of theorizing argues that there are anatomical differences between the brains of gays and straights that produce the differences in sexual orientation. A number of studies have pursued this possibility, all looking at somewhat different regions of the brain (Swaab, 2005). A highly publicized study by neuroscientist Simon LeVay (1991) is an example. LeVay found significant differences between gay men and straight men in certain cells in the anterior portion of the hypothalamus. However, the study had a number of flaws. Other scientists who looked for this effect found no differences in this region of the hypothalamus as a function of the person's sexual orientation (Byne et al., 2000; Swaab, 2005). Yet animal researchers believe that they have identified a similar region in the hypothalamus of the rat that does seem to be involved in sexual behaviour (Swaab, 2005).

Using modern functional brain scanning methods, researchers exposed gay men, heterosexual men, and heterosexual women to human pheromones and recorded their brain responses (Savic et al., 2005). One of the pheromones, AND, is a "male" pheromone and is found in male sweat. The other, EST, is a "female" pheromone and is found in female urine. Gay men and heterosexual women showed activation of a region of the hypothalamus (the medial preoptic area, MPOA, of the anterior hypothalamus) in response to AND, whereas heterosexual men did not show the brain response to AND. As a control, the participants were also exposed to common odours, such as lavender oil; these odours did not activate the hypothalamus. In a second experiment, the researchers repeated the study with lesbians and found that EST stimulated their hypothalamus, as it does with heterosexual men (Berglund et al., 2006). What do these studies mean? They definitely don't mean that gay men have female brains and lesbians have male brains. What they do show is that both heterosexual men and lesbians are turned on (in their brains) by women's pheromones, and that gay men and heterosexual women are turned on by male pheromones.

Hormonal Factors

Investigating the possibility that endocrine factors are the cause of homosexuality, many researchers have tried to determine whether the testosterone levels of gay men differ from those of straight men. These studies have not found any hormonal differences between the two groups (Gooren, 2006).

Despite these results, in past decades some clinicians attempted to cure male homosexuality by administering testosterone therapy (Glass & Johnson, 1944). This therapy failed; indeed, it seems to result in even more same-sex sexual activity than usual. This is not an unexpected result, since, as we saw in Chapter 9, androgen levels seem to be related to sexual responsiveness. As a clinician friend of the authors replied to an undergraduate male who was seeking testosterone therapy for his homosexuality, "It won't make you heterosexual; it will only make you horny."

In conclusion, of the biological theories, the genetic theory has the best supporting evidence, but much more research is needed.

Learning Theory

Behaviourists emphasize the importance of learning in the development of sexual orientation. They note the prevalence of bisexual behaviour both in other species and in young humans, and they argue that rewards and punishments shape the individual's behaviour into predominant homosexuality or predominant heterosexuality. The assumption, then, is that humans have a relatively amorphous, undifferentiated pool of sex drive that, depending on circumstances (rewards and punishments), may be channelled in any of several directions. In short, people are born sexual, not heterosexual or homosexual. Only through learning does one of these behaviours become more likely than the other. For example, if early sexual experiences are with a same-sex partner and pleasant, the person may become gay. Same-sex sexual activity has essentially been rewarded and therefore becomes more likely.

Another possibility, according to a learning-theory approach, is that a person who has early heterosexual experiences that are very unpleasant might develop toward homosexuality. Heterosexuality has essentially been punished and therefore becomes less likely. This might occur, for instance, in the case of a girl who is sexually assaulted by a man at an early age; her first experience with a male was extremely unpleasant, so she avoids it and turns to homosexuality.

The learning-theory approach treats same-sex sexual activity as a normal form of behaviour and recognizes that both heterosexuality and homosexuality are not necessarily inborn but must be learned.

The evidence on learning-theory's explanation of sexual orientation is mixed. Sexual minority women are significantly more likely to experience sexual assault in both childhood and adulthood than are heterosexual women (Balsam et al., 2005, 2011; Descamps et al., 2000; Hughes et al., 2001; Moracco et al., 2007; Stoddard et al., 2009). Nonetheless, most women who have experienced sexual assault identify as heterosexual. In addition, research using an animal model does point to the importance of early learning. Zebra finches are small birds that are monogamous, mate for life, and are almost invariably heterosexual. If the fathers are removed from the cages, though, so that the young birds grow up without adult males or male–female pairs, in adulthood these birds pair with either males or females (Adkins-Regan, 2002). That is, their behaviour, which is bisexual, is a result of early experience.

In contrast to the bird research, research with humans indicates that the great majority of children who grow up with a gay or lesbian parent identify themselves as heterosexual (Allen & Burrell, 2002; Gartrell et al., 2011; Patterson, 2006). In this sense, then, sexual orientation is not "learned" from one's parents.

Interactionist Theory

Psychologist Daryl Bem (1996) proposed a theory of the development of sexual orientation that encompasses the interaction of biological factors and experiences with the environment best described as the exotic becomes erotic. Bem's theory is diagrammed in Figure 14.12.

The theory begins with biological influences, relying on the evidence discussed earlier about biological contributions to sexual orientation (box A in Figure 14.12). However, Bem does not believe that genes and other biological factors directly and magically determine a person's sexual orientation. Rather, he theorized that biological factors exert their influence on sexual orientation through their influence on temperament in childhood (box A to box B). Psychologists have found abundant evidence that two aspects of temperament have some biological basis: aggression and activity level. Moreover, these two aspects of temperament show reliable gender differences. According to Bem, most children show levels of aggression and activity that are typical of their

Figure 14.12 Daryl Bem's theory of the development of sexual orientation: the exotic becomes erotic.

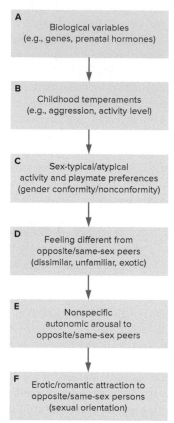

gender; boys are generally more aggressive and more active than girls are. These tendencies lead children to engage in gender-conforming activities (boxes B to C). Most boys play active, aggressive sports, and most girls prefer quieter play activities. These play patterns also lead children to associate almost exclusively with members of their own gender. The boy playing tackle football is playing in a group that consists either entirely or almost entirely of boys. This chain of events will eventually lead to a heterosexual orientation in adulthood.

A minority of children, however, have temperamental characteristics that are not typical of their gender: some boys are not particularly active or aggressive and some girls are. These children are then gender-nonconforming in their play patterns. The boys prefer quieter, less active play and have more girls as friends, and the gender-nonconforming girls prefer aggressive sports and have more boys as friends.

These experiences with childhood play and playmates create a feeling in children that certain other children are different from them and therefore are exotic (boxes C to D). For the boy who spends most of his time playing active, aggressive sports with other boys, girls are different, mysterious, and exotic. For the

gender-nonconforming girl who plays active sports with boys, most girls, too, seem different and exotic to her.

The presence of an exotic other causes a person to feel generalized arousal, whether in childhood, adolescence, or adulthood (boxes D to E). Those of you who are heterosexual certainly remember many instances in your past when you felt ill at ease and nervous in the presence of a member of the other gender.

In the final link of the model, this generalized arousal is transformed into erotic or romantic attraction. Essentially, the exotic becomes erotic. This transformation may be a result of processes described in Berscheid and Walster's (1974) two-component theory of arousal, discussed in Chapter 12. Generalized arousal can easily be transformed into sexual arousal and attraction if the conditions are right. For heterosexual persons, the exotic people are members of the other gender, with whom they had less contact in childhood and who have become eroticized. For gay men and lesbians, the exotic people are members of their own gender, from whom they felt different in childhood and who have become eroticized. For most individuals, then, members of the other gender are exotic. Thus, one virtue of the theory is that it is designed to explain both gay and heterosexual sexual orientations.

One body of evidence that is consistent with Bem's theory indicates that gay men and lesbians, on average, are more likely than heterosexuals are to have had a childhood history of gender nonconformity. In one intriguing study, researchers recruited gay men, lesbians, heterosexual men, and heterosexual women (Rieger et al., 2008). They asked the participants for home movies or videos taken of them when they were children. The videos were then coded by trained raters who were unaware of the adult sexual orientation of the child shown in the video. For each video, they rated the child's behaviour on a seven-point scale ranging from more masculine to more feminine. The results showed that, as early as age four, the "pre-homosexual" children differed significantly from the "pre-heterosexual" children. The pre-homosexual children were less gender conforming; that is, the boys were, on average, more feminine in their behaviour than the pre-heterosexual boys were, and the pre-homosexual girls were more masculine, on average, than the pre-heterosexual girls were. It is fascinating that gender nonconformity can be detected at such an early age, and the study provides support for Bem's theory, although it is also consistent with the biological theories.

At the same time, Bem's theory and evidence have been criticized (Peplau et al., 1998; for Bem's response, see Bem, 1998). Two criticisms have been raised: (1) Evidence not discussed by Bem contradicts some central propositions of the theory, and (2) the theory reflects male experience and neglects female experience.

Regarding the evidence, Bem noted that, in one major study, lesbians (70 percent) were significantly more likely than were heterosexual women (51 percent) to recall feeling somewhat or very different from other girls their age (Bell et al., 1981). The difference is significant but perhaps more important is the finding that a majority of heterosexual women also felt different from other girls. Other girls seemed different or exotic to them. Why didn't they become lesbian, then?

Sociological Theory

Sociologists emphasize the effects of *labelling* in explaining homosexuality. The label "homosexual" has a big impact in our society. For example, one of the biggest insults used by middle school students is calling a classmate a "fag" (McFarland, 2001). The label "homosexual" often has derogatory connotations, reflecting our society's predominantly negative attitudes toward homosexuality.

But the label "homosexual" might also act as a self-fulfilling prophecy. Suppose that a young boy—possibly because he is gender nonconforming or poor in sports, or for no reason at all—is called "gay." He reacts strongly and becomes more and more anxious and worried about his problem. He becomes painfully aware of the slightest same-sex attraction in himself. Finally, he convinces himself that he is gay. He begins engaging in same-sex sexual activity and associates with a gay group. In short, a gay man has been created through labelling.

Recognizing the need to explain cross-cultural differences in sexual patterns, Reiss (1986) argued that male-dominant societies with a great rigidity of gender roles produce the highest incidence of homosexuality. In such societies, there is a rigid male role that must be learned and conformed to, but young boys have little opportunity to learn it from adult men precisely because the gender roles are rigid: Women take care of children, and men have little contact with them. It is therefore difficult to learn the heterosexual component of the male role. In addition, because the male role is rigid, there will be a certain number of males who dislike it and reject its heterosexual component. Cross-cultural studies support his observations. Societies that have a great maternal and low paternal involvement with infants and that have rigid gender roles are precisely those that have the highest incidence of same-sex sexual behaviour in males.

This pattern describes the negative pathway to becoming gay or lesbian. Reiss argues that there is also a positive pathway. It exists in less gender-rigid societies with more permissiveness about sexuality. In such societies, individuals feel freer to experiment with same-sex behaviour and may find it satisfying. Examples are provided by several First Nations peoples in which three gender roles have been recognized (see Chapter 13).

The Bottom Line

We have examined a number of theories of sexual orientation and the evidence supporting or refuting them. What is the bottom line? Which theory is correct? The answer is, we don't know yet. We do not know what causes sexual orientation. Several theories have strong evidence supporting them, but no one theory accounts for all cases. We believe that a good lesson can be learned from this conclusion.

It has generally been assumed not only that LGBs form a distinct category (which, we have already seen, is not very accurate) but also that they form a homogeneous category; that is, that all LGBs are fairly similar. Not so. Probably there are many different kinds or types of gay men, lesbians, bisexuals, and heterosexuals. If this is the case, then one would not expect a single cause of sexual orientation but rather many causes, each corresponding to its type. The next step in research, then, should be to identify the various types of LGBs and heterosexuals and the different pathways of development that lead to each.

Differences between Gay Men and Lesbians

Although gay men and lesbians are commonly lumped together in one category based on their attraction to individuals of their same gender, evidence from a number of sources indicates that there are some important differences between the two groups that go beyond one group being male and the other female.

Women are more likely to be bisexual and less likely to be exclusively homosexual than men are. In the NSFG data set, 2.8 percent of women and 0.5 percent of men indicated that they were sexually attracted to both women and men (Chandra et al., 2011).

In related research, among both individuals who identify as straight and gay, women show more flexibility or change over time in their sexual orientation (Kinnish et al., 2005). As noted earlier in this chapter, this is what Diamond (2008a) called *sexual fluidity*. In laboratory research, men are specific in their sexual arousal whereas women tend not to be (Chivers et al., 2004). That is, heterosexual men tend to be aroused, physiologically, by female stimuli and not male stimuli, and gay men show the reverse pattern. Women, however, whether lesbian or heterosexual, show arousal to both male and female stimuli.

Are men or women more likely to be attracted to both genders?

One controversial issue is whether sexual minority women are less sexual than are sexual minority men and heterosexual men and women. Early research suggested that sexual-minority women experienced lower sexual desire and engaged in sex less frequently than did individuals in other relationship types (Cohen & Byers, 2014). Indeed, this was thought to be so pervasive that it has been labelled "lesbian bed death." However, recent research has challenged this view. For example, researchers in New Brunswick found that sexual minority women reported experience their sexuality positively including experiencing moderate to high sexual desire, sexual satisfaction, and sexual self-esteem and low sexual anxiety (Cohen & Byers, 2014). They also found that even in long-term relationships, most of the women reported an active sex life with their partner, engaging in sexual activity once a week or more. Few reported that they had not engaged in sexual activity in the previous month. Researchers in Ontario questioned the assumption that frequency is a good measure of how sexual a couple is and argued that another important dimension is the duration of the sexual encounter Blair & Pukall, 2014). They found that, compared to other couple types, women in a same-sex relationship were less likely to report engaging in sexual activity more than twice a week but that the duration of sexual encounters was longer. The groups did not differ in their sexual satisfaction.

Some of the theories discussed earlier in this chapter seem to work for gay men or for lesbians but not for both. For example, the fraternal birth order effect has been found repeatedly; compared with heterosexual men, gay men are more likely to have a late birth order and an excess of older brothers. Lesbians, however, are no more or less likely to have a late birth order compared with heterosexual women (Blanchard, 1997; Bogaert, 2003).

We will almost certainly need somewhat different theories to explain the development of sexual orientation in women and in men (Hyde & Jaffee, 2000). This does not mean that any one theory will apply to all gay men or all lesbians; we likely will need different theories to explain development of sexual orientation within each gender as well.

 LO9

Sexual Orientation in Multicultural Perspective

Different cultures around the world hold different views of homosexuality and same-sex sexual behaviour. For example, as described in the A Sexually Diverse World box in Chapter 2, among the Melanesians of the southwest Pacific, same-sex behaviour is ritualized such that boys are expected to engage in exclusively same-sex sexual activity for about ten years but then marry women and become exclusively heterosexual. As one anthropologist observed about the Sambia of Papua New Guinea:

Semen is also necessary for young boys to attain full growth to manhood. . . . They need a boost, as it were. When a boy is eleven or twelve years old, he is engaged for several months in homosexual intercourse with a healthy older man chosen by his father. (This is always an in-law or unrelated person, since the same notions of incestuous relations apply to little boys as to marriageable women.) Men point to the rapid growth of adolescent youths, the appearance of peach fuzz beards, and so on, as the favorable results of this child-rearing practice. (Schieffelin, 1976, p. 124)

As shown in Table 14.2, earlier in this chapter, variations in attitudes toward homosexuality vary so much that it has been called a global divide. Some nations, such as Canada, Spain, and Germany, express high levels of acceptance. Others, such as Mexico and Israel, are intermediate. And in others, such as Kenya and Egypt, acceptance is rare (Pew Research, 2013).

Similarly, various Canadian ethnic minority groups differ in their cultural definitions for same-sex behaviours. Generally, members of Canadian ethnocultural communities have less tolerance for homosexuality than members of the majority culture do. There tends to be a stigma attached to being a gay man, a denial of the existence of homosexuality within the community, and considerable pressure to conform to community norms. As a result, many LGBs feel forced to stay in the closet with respect to their sexual orientation to be accepted within their family and community (Manson Singer et al., 1996). Thus, ethnic minority LGBs have a double minority status and may experience racism within the gay community, as well as antigay prejudice within their ethnic group (Ibañez, et al., 2009). Perhaps as a result, in the Canadian Community Health Survey, members of ethnocultural minorities were less likely to identify themselves as homosexual than were Canadians from the majority culture (Tjepkema, 2008).

For example, in both the Caribbean and African communities in Canada, gay and bisexual men may keep their activities secret for fear of being ostracized if they are open about their sexual orientation (Health Canada, 1994a, 1994b). Similarly, because of strong negative attitudes in the community, many gay and bisexual men in the South Asian community keep their same-sex relationships hidden. They may comply with family pressure to get married to avoid causing conflict in the family. South Asian men who were born in Canada are more likely to be open about their sexual orientation (Health Canada, 1994c).

Members of some ethnic groups, including men from the Caribbean and Latin American communities, may engage in extensive same-sex sexual behaviour while still considering themselves to be heterosexual (Manson Singer et al., 1996). An interesting example of these different cultural definitions comes from a study of Mexican and Mexican-American men (Magaña & Carrier, 1991). In Mexico, there is a dichotomizing of same-sex sexual behaviours that parallels traditional gender roles. Anal intercourse, because it most resembles penis-in-vagina intercourse, is the preferred behaviour, and fellatio is practised relatively little. A man adopts the role of either receptive partner or inserting partner and does this exclusively. Those who take the receptive role are considered unmanly, feminine, and homosexual. Those who take the inserting role are considered masculine, are not labelled as homosexual, and are not stigmatized. Research with Latin American men living in Montreal also found that men who take the inserting role during anal intercourse with men often consider themselves to be heterosexual (Health Canada, 1994d). In contrast, men who take the receptive role are considered gay and are marginalized in the community. This approach differs substantially from that in the gay Canadian majority, where men commonly switch roles and both are considered gay.

Such different definitions of homosexuality are not limited to Latin American cultures. One researcher described the scene in contemporary Egypt as follows:

> In Egypt, because there was so little sense of homosexuality as an identity, what position you took in bed defined all. Between men, the only sex that counted was anal sex. . . . In the minds of most Egyptians, "gay," if it meant anything at all, signified taking the receptive position in anal sex. On the other hand, a person who took the insertive role—and that seemed to include virtually all Egyptian men, to judge by what my acquaintances told me—was not considered gay. . . . Many of the insults in the Arabic language concern being penetrated anally by another man. (Miller, 1992, p. 76)

As for lesbians, Latin American women and Caribbean women experience conflicts in the complexities of ethnicity and sexual orientation (Espin, 1987; Gonzalez & Espin, 1996; Silvera, 1990). In both cultures, emotional and physical closeness among women is considered acceptable and desirable. However, attitudes toward lesbianism are extremely restrictive (Figure 14.13).

Figure 14.13 Ethnicity and sexual orientation. Among Latin American and Caribbean women, warmth and physical closeness are very acceptable, but there are strong taboos against female–female sexual relationships.

© Jeff Greenberg/PhotoEdit

Familism, the special emphasis on family—defined as mother, father, children, and grandparents in Latin American cultures—and the emphasis on attracting a man and bearing a child in Caribbean cultures makes the lesbian even more of an outsider. Women who are openly lesbian may be stigmatized and ostracized in these communities.

Among Asian communities in Canada, two features of the culture shape attitudes toward homosexuality and its expression: (1) a strong distinction between what may be expressed publicly and what should be kept private, and (2) a stronger value placed on loyalty to one's family and on the performance of family roles than on the expression of one's own desires (Chan, 1995; Cochran et al., 2007). Sexuality is something that must be expressed only privately, not publicly. And having an identity, much less a sexual identity or a gay lifestyle, apart from one's family is almost incomprehensible to traditional Asians. As a result, a relatively small proportion of LGB members of the Asian communities in Canada are "out" in their community. Nonetheless, there is an active gay Asian community in Vancouver. However, these individuals often remain in the closet within Asian communities because of fear of bringing shame to their families (Health Canada, 1994e). As with other ethnocultural communities in Canada, members of Asian communities who are out tend to be more acculturated—that is, influenced by Canadian culture.

In sum, when we consider sexual orientation from a multicultural perspective, two main points emerge. First, the very definition of homosexuality is set by culture. In Canada, we would say that a man who is the inserting partner in anal intercourse with another man is engaging in homosexual behaviour, but other cultures (such as Mexico and Egypt) would not agree. Second, many ethnocultural communities are more disapproving of homosexuality than is the majority Canadian culture. In those cases, LGBs feel conflicts between their sexual identity and loyalty to their ethnic group. That said, some researchers believe that coping skills can helpfully transfer from one minority status to the other (Kuper et al., 2014). For example, learning coping skills to deal with racial prejudice might also help the person cope with antigay prejudice and vice versa.

A Final Note

As we have seen in this chapter, most theory and research rests on the assumption that sexual orientation is determined by conditions in childhood or by prenatal or genetic factors. We have also seen that many people exhibit sexual fluidity–that is, their sexual identity is not fixed and evolves over time in adulthood (Diamond, 2003). This contradicts some scientists' assertion that sexual orientation is determined before adolescence (Bell et al., 1981). We think that when sexual orientation is determined is still an open question. For some it may be determined by genetic factors or experiences early in life, but for others it may be determined in adulthood or continue to be fluid.

A question is raised as to whether heterosexuality is really the "natural" state. The pattern in some theories has been to try to discover the pathological conditions that cause a person to become gay (e.g., a father who is an inadequate role model or an unusual dose of prenatal hormones)—all on the basis of the assumption that heterosexuality is the natural state and that homosexuality must be explained as a deviation from it. As we have seen, this approach has failed; there appear to be multiple causes of homosexuality, just as there may be multiple causes of heterosexuality. The important alternative to consider is that bisexuality is the natural state, a point acknowledged by Freud, the learning theorists, and sociological theorists (Weinberg et al., 1994). This chapter will close, then, with some questions. Psychologically, the real question should concern not the conditions that lead a person to become gay but rather the causes of exclusive attraction to members of one's own gender or to members of the other gender. Why do we eliminate some people as potential sex partners simply based on their gender? Why isn't everyone bisexual?

Critical **THINK** *ing Skill*

INTERPRETING RESEARCH FINDINGS

Earlier in this chapter, we saw that the rate of suicide attempts is higher among sexual minority youth (9.1 percent) than it is among heterosexual youth (3.6 percent). That is the statistical research result, but how should it be interpreted? What does it mean?

In interpreting research results, it is important to consider two questions: (1) Is the difference big enough to care about? and (2) What factor(s) could cause such an effect?

First, then, is the difference big enough to be important? For example, sometimes we hear a proclamation in the news that the unemployment rate is up, followed by the specifics that it is up from 7.8 percent in January to 7.9 percent in February. True, 7.9 is greater than 7.8, but the difference is tiny and not important. In the case of sexual minority youth, is the difference in suicide attempts big enough to be important? If you have had a statistics course, you will know that one way to evaluate a difference between two groups involves testing whether the difference is statistically significant. Therefore, statistical tests of significance are one way to decide whether a difference is big enough to be important. Another way to think about how big the difference is, especially when the data are given in terms of percentages, is to evaluate the percentages directly. Is it disturbing that the suicide attempt rate is more than twice as high among gay youth as straight youth? Or is a rate under 10 percent for gay youth still low and not cause for concern? We might add to that an evaluation of the cost of the behaviour. True, a suicide attempt rate of 9.1 percent represents just a small minority, but some suicide attempts foreshadow actual suicides and the death of a person, so a rate of 9.1 percent might be unacceptably high. Perhaps even the 3.6 percent rate for straight youth is unacceptably high. Statistical tests of significance cannot answer these questions, which rest much more on personal values.

Assuming that our answer to the first question is yes, there is a big enough difference between sexual minority and straight youth to be important, then we can ask what factor or factors cause the difference? Don't stop with generating just one cause, but think of several, and then ask, might more than one of them be important? It is not always necessary to choose between one cause and another. Think of some possible causes before continuing to the next paragraph.

Some possible causes, not all of them supported by research, include the following: Perhaps there are genetic factors that cause homosexuality, and those same genetic factors also cause depression and suicide attempts. Another possible interpretation might be that homosexuality is a mental illness and therefore more suicide attempts occur among LGB youth. A third possible interpretation involves thinking about what might cause suicide attempts in general, not just among LGB youth. A leading cause is serious stress, so a possible cause of the difference is that sexual minority youth experience more stress—such as bullying—than straight youth do, and that accounts for the higher rates of depression and suicide attempts.

Notice that the way that we interpret the research findings in this case could lead to very different conclusions and implications. One person might conclude that the research provides confirmation that homosexuality is a mental illness. Another person might conclude from the same findings that sexual minority youth face intolerable levels of stress and that we should institute social programs in schools and families to reduce the stress. For a person who wanted to pursue this question more, the important next step would be to consider what other research evidence would be needed to decide among these conclusions and then find out what the research says.

SUMMARY

Sexual orientation refers to a person's erotic and emotional attraction toward members of his or her own gender, toward members of the other gender, both, or neither.

Well-sampled surveys indicate (when corrected for some underreporting) that about 2 percent of men and 1 percent of women have a gay identity. Kinsey devised a scale ranging from 0 (exclusively heterosexual experience) to 6 (exclusively homosexual experience) to measure this diversity of experience. A person's sexual identity may be discordant with his or her actual behaviour.

Although some Canadians believe that homosexuality is wrong, the vast majority are in favour of equal rights for LGBs, and most favour same-sex marriage. In some cases homonegativity and antigay prejudice may be so strong that they result in maltreatment and harassment.

Lesbian, gay, and bisexual communities can be found around the world. These communities are defined by a common culture and social life and by rituals, such as pride marches. In surveys, the majority of gay men and lesbians report being in a steady romantic relationship. Although people with negative attitudes toward LGBs have voiced concerns about the psychological well-being of children who grow up in lesbian and gay families, these concerns are unfounded, according to the available studies.

Well-conducted research indicates that homosexuality per se is not a sign of poor adjustment. Research does show somewhat elevated rates of depression and suicide among LGBs, mainly because of exposure to prejudice and hate crimes and the failure of family and friends to support the person. Although some groups claim success in reparative therapy to change the sexual orientation of LGBs, there is no scientific evidence that one's sexual orientation can be changed and many indications that these therapies are psychologically harmful. Most therapists believe that it is impossible to change a person's sexual orientation (that is, their erotic and emotional attraction), although people can and do change their sexual identity.

In regard to the causes of sexual orientation, biological explanations include genetic factors, hormone imbalance, prenatal factors, and brain factors. The genetic explanation has some support from the data. Learning theorists stress that the sex drive is undifferentiated and is channelled, through experience, into heterosexuality or homosexuality. Bem's interactionist theory proposes that homosexuality results from the influence of biological factors on temperament, which in turn influences whether a child plays with boys or girls; the less familiar (exotic) gender becomes associated with sexual arousal. Sociologists emphasize the importance of roles and labelling in understanding homosexuality. Available data do not point to any single factor as a cause of sexual orientation but rather suggest that there may be many types of homosexuality and heterosexuality with corresponding multiple causes.

Gay men and lesbians differ in some important ways. Women are more likely to be bisexual, and theories that are effective in explaining men's sexual orientation are not supported for women. Bisexuality may be more "natural" than either exclusive heterosexuality or exclusive homosexuality.

Different ethnic groups in Canada, as well as different cultures around the world, hold diverse views of same-sex sexual behaviours.

CHAPTER 15

Variations in Sexual Behaviour

© Digital Vision/PunchStock

Are YOU Curious?

1. How can I tell if sexual behaviour is problematic?
2. Are men or women more likely to engage in problematic sexual behaviour?
3. What is kinky sex?
4. Is my online sexual activity compulsive?

Read this chapter to find out.

LEARNING OBJECTIVES

After studying this chapter, you will be able to

LO1 Differentiate between normal and abnormal sexual behaviour.

LO2 Define and describe sexual addictions and compulsive sexual behaviour, and apply these concepts to online sexual activity.

LO3 Discuss the different forms of fetishism and the mechanism by which they develop.

LO4 Define transvestism and the four possible motivations for it.

LO5 Define and compare the various components of BDSM.

LO6 Define and describe the similarities and differences between voyeurism and exhibitionism, and outline possible causes of these behaviours.

LO7 Describe hypersexuality and its relationship to other paraphilias.

LO8 Identify and define some of the less common sexual variations.

LO9 Describe the ways in which harmful sexual variations can be prevented and treated.

Variety's the spice of life
That gives it all its flavor.*

* William Cowper (1785).

Most laypeople, as well as most scientists, have a tendency to classify behaviour as normal or abnormal. There seems to be a particular tendency to do this with regard to sexual behaviour. Many terms are used for abnormal sexual behaviour, including *sexual deviance, perversion, sexual variance,* and *paraphilia.* The term *sexual variations* will be used in this chapter because it is currently favoured in scientific circles.

This chapter will deal with some behaviours that many people consider to be abnormal, so it seems advisable at this point to consider exactly when a sexual behaviour is abnormal. Which of the following would you consider abnormal? A man has difficulty getting aroused unless he is wearing women's panties. A woman enjoys being tied up as part of sex play. A man gets turned on watching someone undress without that person's knowledge.

When Is Sexual Behaviour Abnormal?

Defining Abnormal

As we saw in Chapter 1, sexual behaviour varies a great deal across cultures. There is a corresponding variation in what is considered to be "abnormal" sexual behaviour. Given this great variability, how can anyone come up with a reasonable set of criteria for what is abnormal?

One approach is to use a *statistical definition.* According to this approach, an abnormal sexual behaviour is one that is rare or not practised by many people. Following this definition, then, standing on one's hands while having intercourse would be considered abnormal because it is rarely done, although it does not seem very abnormal in other ways. This definition, unfortunately, does not give us much insight into the psychological or social functioning of the person who engages in the behaviour.

In the *sociological approach,* the problem of culture dependence is explicitly acknowledged. A sociologist might define a sexual behaviour that violates the norms of society as a deviant (or abnormal) sexual behaviour. Thus, if a

paraphilia (par-uh-FILL-ee-uh): Intense and persistent unconventional sexual interest.

society says that a particular sexual behaviour is deviant, it is—at least in that society. This approach recognizes the importance of the individual's interaction with society and of the problems that people face if their behaviour is labelled "deviant" in the culture in which they live.

A *psychological approach* was stated by Arnold Buss in his text entitled *Psychopathology* (1966). He says, "The three criteria of abnormality are discomfort, inefficiency, and bizarreness." The last of these criteria, bizarreness, has the problem of being culturally defined; what seems bizarre in one culture may seem normal in another. However, the first two criteria are good in that they focus on the discomfort and unhappiness sometimes felt by the person with a truly abnormal pattern of sexual behaviour and on inefficiency. For example, a male supermarket clerk was having intercourse with willing shoppers in their cars several times a day. This apparently compulsive behaviour led to his being fired. This is an example of inefficient functioning, a behaviour that can reasonably be considered abnormal.

The *medical approach* is exemplified by the definitions included in the *Diagnostic and Statistical Manual of Mental Disorders* (*DSM-5*) (American Psychiatric Association, 2013a). It recognizes eight specific paraphilic disorders: voyeuristic disorder, exhibitionist disorder, frotteuristic disorder, sexual masochism disorder, sexual sadism disorder, pedophilic disorder, fetishistic disorder, and transvestic disorder. The general definition of a **paraphilia** is

> any intense and persistent sexual interest other than sexual interest in genital stimulation or preparatory fondling with phenotypically normal, physically mature, consenting human partners. In some circumstances, the criteria "intense and persistent" may be difficult to apply. . . . There are also specific paraphilias that are better described as *preferential* sexual interests.

Canadian psychologist Peggy Kleinplatz and her colleague Charles Moser argue that because there is no agreed-on definition of healthy sexuality, it is difficult to be clear about what behaviours should be classified as paraphilic. They believe that behaviours that involve unusual sexual interests but not coercion, such as sexual sadism and sexual masochism, may be healthy expressions of sexuality for some individuals. They argue that the fact that they are labelled as paraphilias is due to socio-political and historical factors (Moser & Kleinplatz, 2005).

Paraphilias are atypical sexual interests. They are not mental disorders and may not require intervention. The *DSM-5* distinguishes between paraphilias and paraphilic disorders. In order to qualify as a **paraphilic disorder** the person must

> feel personal distress about their interest, not merely distress resulting from society's disapproval; or have a sexual desire or behaviour that involves another person's psychological distress, injury, or death, or a desire for sexual behaviours involving unwilling persons or persons unable to give legal consent.

Additional diagnostic criteria are stated for each of the specific disorders; these generally include that (a) the fantasies, urges, or behaviours have occurred over a period of at least six months, and (b) they cause "clinically significant distress or impairment in social, occupational, or other important areas of functioning." These definitions are very influential and may be used in many situations to determine who receives treatment.

Note that some paraphilias and most atypical sexual behaviours are not against the law (e.g., fetishism and sexual masochism). However, some are. For example, pedophilia, the most serious paraphilia, is against the law because it involves exploitation and force. It is discussed in Chapter 16. Other behaviours do not involve exploitation or force but do violate community standards of taste. In this area we find laws against **indecent exposure**, voyeurism, indecent acts in a public place, and public nudity (refer to Table 2.1 for a list of sex crimes contained in the *Criminal Code of Canada*).

An interesting case that demonstrates how community standards of taste can affect our legal system arose when Gwen Jacobs walked topless through the city of Guelph in Ontario in 1991. She was charged with committing an indecent act in a public place. However, in 1996, the Ontario Court of Appeal ruled that women have a right to go topless as long as it is not for commercial gain or sexual purposes. What are the attitudes of Canadians toward women going topless? One study found that 72 percent of Canadians think it should be illegal for women to go topless on city streets, and 48 percent think it should be illegal for them to go topless on a public beach (Fischtein et al., 2005). This does not necessarily mean they think it constitutes abnormal behaviour, however.

In this chapter we discuss a number of atypical sexual behaviours, including seven of the paraphilias—all except pedophilia, which is discussed in Chapter 16. We also discuss several other atypical sexual behaviours, including hypersexuality, asphyxiophilia, and compulsive online sexual activities.

The Normal–Abnormal Continuum

Each approach just described provides criteria that attempt to distinguish what is "normal" from what is "abnormal." Although such distinctions may be made in theory, they are often difficult to make in reality. For example, lingerie is often sexually arousing for both men and women (Figure 15.1). For a woman who is wearing a low-cut bra and silk thong panties, the sensuous feel of the material against her skin may be arousing; for a man it might be the sight of the woman wearing the lingerie. At the same time, lingerie is a common sexual fetish object. This is an excellent example of the continuum from normal

paraphilic disorder: A paraphilia that causes distress or impairment to the individual or that harms or would harm other people.
indecent exposure: Showing one's genitals in a public place to passersby; exhibitionism.

Figure 15.1 Wearing lingerie is an excellent example of sexual behaviour that falls on a continuum from normal (sexually arousing for both men and women) to abnormal (being a common sexual fetish object).

© Daniel Dash/Shutterstock

Figure 15.2 The continuum from normal to abnormal behaviour in the case of fetishes.

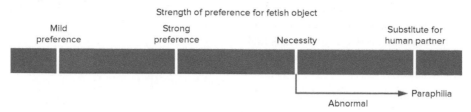

to abnormal sexual behaviour; that is, normal sexual behaviour and abnormal sexual behaviour—like other normal and abnormal behaviours—are not two separate categories but rather gradations on a continuum. Many people have mild fetishes, finding such things as silk underwear arousing, and that is well within the range of normal behaviour; only when the fetish becomes extreme is it abnormal. Indeed, in one sample of university men, 42 percent reported that they had engaged in voyeurism and 35 percent had engaged in *frottage* (sexual rubbing against a woman in a crowd) (Templeman & Stinnett, 1991). But the point is that many of these behaviours are common even in "normal" populations.

This continuum from normal to abnormal behaviour might be conceptualized by using the scheme shown in Figure 15.2. A mild preference, or even a strong preference, for the fetish object (say, silk panties) is within the normal range of sexual behaviour. When the silk panties become a necessity—when the man cannot become aroused and engage in sexual activity unless they are present—we have crossed the boundary into abnormal behaviour. When the man becomes obsessed with white silk panties and shoplifts them at every opportunity so that he will always have them available, the fetish has become a paraphilia. In extreme forms, the silk panties may become a substitute for a human partner, and the man's sexual behaviour consists of masturbating with the silk panties present. In these extreme forms, the man may commit burglary or even assault to get the desired fetish object, which would certainly fit our definition of abnormal sexual behaviour.

How can I tell if sexual behaviour is problematic?

The continuum from normal to abnormal behaviour holds for many of the sexual variations discussed in this chapter, such as voyeurism, exhibitionism, and sadism. Researchers in Ontario, using a large nonclinical online sample, found that many of the individuals in their sample reported some arousal to engaging in one or more sexual variation (Dawson et al., 2016). So when does a behaviour become abnormal? Putting it simply, a sexual behaviour is likely to fall on the abnormal end of the continuum when it interferes with having healthy relationships or completing day-to-day activities or causes harm to other people.

L02

Sexual Addictions and Compulsions

Patricia (not her real name), a divorced mother and self-described "soccer mom," described being preoccupied with finding and meeting male partners for sex—she had sex with more than 30 men in four years without using condoms. Benoit (real name) drove for three hours to meet a stranger for sex in a deserted grocery store parking lot at 1:00 a.m. Both of these individuals eventually entered treatment for "sex addictions." There are many other people with stories just like these; that is, they report intense desire and craving for sexual activity, and eventually experience impairment in work, family, or the social functioning of their daily lives.

The theory of sexual addiction was popularized by Patrick Carnes in his book *The Sexual Addiction*. He proposed that many cases of atypical sexual behaviour are a result of an addictive process much like alcoholism. According to Carnes' analysis, each episode of sexually addictive behaviour goes through a four-step cycle, which intensifies each time it is repeated.

1. *Preoccupation:* The person can think of nothing other than the sexual act to which he or she is addicted.
2. *Rituals:* The person enacts certain rituals that have become a prelude to the addictive act.
3. *Compulsive sexual behaviour:* The sexual behaviour is enacted and the person feels that he or she has no control over it.
4. *Despair:* Rather than feeling good after the sexual act is completed, the addict falls into a feeling of hopelessness and despair.

For example, consider the true story of a man who engaged in exhibitionism—let's call him Sam. Often, after a stressful interpersonal event, Sam would become preoccupied with (unrealistic) thoughts of women's positive reactions if he exposed himself. He would then put on certain clothes, go for a walk, "just happen" to walk by a coffee shop, and "just happen" to stop for coffee, all without acknowledging to himself that he intended to expose himself. Sam would look around until he identified a woman who did some small thing that he could misinterpret as indicating that she was interested in him sexually. He would follow her out to the parking lot and expose himself, feeling he had no control over the behaviour. He would feel good at the time but shortly after would feel bad about himself and about his lack of control over his behaviour. Interestingly, there is often a history of alcoholism or other types of addictions in the families of people with compulsive sexual behaviour. Sometimes, too, there is a family history of the same compulsive sexual behaviour.

One definition of alcoholism or other drug dependency is that the person has a pathological relationship with the mood-altering substance. In the case of sexual addiction, the person has a pathological relationship to a sexual event or process, substituting it for a healthy relationship with others. However, there are some differences between chemical addictions that create a physiological dependency and sexual "addictions." For example, if a person suddenly abstains from an addictive sexual behaviour, there are no physiological withdrawal symptoms as there are from abstaining from using alcohol. A basic criticism is that the concept of addiction is a social construction that provides a "scientific" term for behaviour we don't like and may become an excuse for illegal, destructive behaviour. For example, a sex offender might say, "I'm sexually addicted to forced sex and can't stop myself." High-profile celebrities who are caught behaving badly blame their behaviour on a sexual addiction. The term obviously also reflects *medicalization*, in this case of sexual functioning.

Compulsive Sexual Behaviour

Because of these problems with the term sexual addiction, some experts recommend that we use the term *compulsive sexual behaviour* instead of *sexual addiction* (e.g., Coleman, 1991). **Compulsive sexual behaviour**

is a disorder in which the individual experiences intense sexually arousing fantasies, urges, and associated sexual behaviors that are intrusive, driven, and repetitive. Individuals with this disorder (a) are lacking in impulse control, (b) often incur social and legal sanctions, (c) cause interference in interpersonal and occupational functioning, and (d) create health risks. (Coleman et al., 2001, p. 326)

A sexual compulsion can be paraphilic (i.e., involve the sexual behaviours listed in the *DSM-5*) or nonparaphilic (involve conventional sexual behaviours, such as compulsive masturbation or compulsive use of the Internet for sexual purposes) (Coleman et al., 2003). Note that this perspective differs from the addiction approach in emphasizing that the person may experience social and legal sanctions and take health risks. Coleman and colleagues (2003) estimate that approximately 5 percent of the population—more men than women—suffer from compulsive sexual behaviour.

The chief distinguishing feature of sexual compulsions is that the person has lost control over the behaviour. Thus, not all sexual variations are addictions or compulsions. Some people have intense urges to engage in behaviours, such as masturbation or online sexual activity, that in and of themselves are normal. Thus, for example, the man who masturbates every day in the privacy of his own home while looking at pornography on the Internet is probably not experiencing a sexual compulsion and the behaviour is well within the normal range. However, the married man who (and this is based on a real person) rushes from his desk at work several times a day to lock himself in the supply closet to masturbate and can think of little else than the next time he will masturbate, probably does have a sexual compulsion or addiction. The key is the compulsiveness, the lack of control, the obsession (constant thoughts of the sexual scenario), and the obliviousness to danger or harmful consequences.

Several studies have used a ten item sexual compulsivity scale (Kalichman & Rompa, 1995) in research on persons at risk for HIV/AIDS. High scorers on the Kalichman Sexual Compulsivity Scale (KSCS) report more sexual partners and more one-time or casual partners (Kalichman & Cain, 2004). Similarly, university students with high scores report more sexual partners and are more likely to report unprotected oral, anal, and vaginal intercourse, and engaging in sex in public places (Dodge et al., 2004).

Some researchers emphasize the out-of-control aspects of problematic sexual behaviour (Bancroft & Vikadinovic, 2004; Figure 15.3). Whereas most people lose interest in sex when anxious or depressed, a minority experience increased sexual interest. When coupled with low sexual inhibition (self-control) (see Chapter 9), the person may engage in compulsive sexual behaviour in an attempt to improve or escape from the negative mood. This intensive study of 31 self-defined "sex addicts" provided evidence supporting this perspective. The person's motive is to escape from the negative mood; sexual

compulsive sexual behaviour: A disorder in which the person experiences intense sexually arousing fantasies, urges, and associated sexual behaviour.

Figure 15.3 Tiger Woods, who was linked in media reports with at least 15 women, several of them claiming long-term affairs with him, entered treatment for sex addiction in 2010.

© Eric Gay-Pool/Getty Images

behaviour and gratification are one vehicle but alcohol and substance use, pornography use, gambling, or shopping could all provide the same escape.

A study of sexually compulsive men in New York City who identified as gay or bisexual also found that depression, low self-esteem, a need for validation and affection, and stress release were associated with their behaviour (Parsons et al., 2008). The men also pointed to relationship issues, the ready availability of male sex partners in New York City (bars, bathhouses, meeting areas) and on the Internet, and childhood sexual abuse. Other studies report that the percentage of people with sexual compulsivity who have been sexually abused ranges from 30 to 78 percent, suggesting it is an important factor.

People who have sexual compulsions often hold faulty beliefs that can contribute to the problem because they involve a denial or distortion of reality. These beliefs allow these people to justify their behaviour before engaging in it. For example, they may deny the possibility of contracting a sexually transmitted infection. They also engage in self-justification, such as "If I don't have it every few days, the pressure builds up." Like alcoholism, the compulsive behaviour leads to many self-destructive behaviours. The person with a sexual compulsion may spend money that he or she doesn't have (e.g., to pay prostitutes), may neglect work or family to engage in the behaviour (e.g., by spending many hours on the Internet), or may risk arrest (e.g., for indecent exposure).

fetishism: A person's sexual fixation on some object other than another human being and attachment of great erotic significance to that object.
media fetish: A fetish whose object is anything made of a particular substance, such as leather.
form fetish: A fetish whose object is a particular shape, such as high-heeled shoes.

Fetishism

Fetishism refers to a sexual fixation on some object other than another human being and attachment of great erotic significance to that object. A common fetish in Canada is for clothing made of leather (Figure 15.4). A fetishistic disorder is characterized by sexual fantasies, urges, or behaviours involving the use of nonliving objects to produce or enhance sexual arousal with or in the absence of a partner, over a period of at least six months and causing significant distress. In extreme cases, the person is incapable of becoming aroused and having an orgasm unless the fetish object is present. Typically, the fetish item is something closely associated with the body, such as clothing. Inanimate-object fetishes can be roughly divided into two subcategories: **media fetish** and **form fetish**.

An online survey that recruited women at "kink" community events and online forums assessed whether they had ever participated in 126 specific sexual activities (Rehor, 2015). The mean age of the 1580 women who completed the survey was 35.5; 55 percent were in a committed relationship, and some were professional sex services providers. Thus the results overestimate the prevalence of these activities in the population. Seventy-five percent of the women reported being sexually aroused by an object (a fetish behaviour). Items of clothing (such as lingerie, shoes, and corsets), specific body parts, and fabrics (such as leather, rubber, and vinyl) were the three most frequently mentioned categories of objects (see First Person).

Figure 15.4 A common fetish is for leather, often in association with sexual sadism and masochism. This store caters to clientele interested or involved in those activities.

© Julian Wasser/Getty Images

Why Do People Develop Fetishes?

Psychologists are not sure what causes fetishes to develop. Here we will consider three theoretical explanations: learning theory, cognitive theory, and the sexual addiction model. These theories can be applied equally well to explaining many of the other sexual variations in this chapter.

According to learning theory (e.g., McGuire et al., 1965), fetishes result from classical conditioning, in which a learned association is built between the fetish object and sexual arousal and orgasm. In some cases, a single learning trial might serve to cement the association. For example, one adult male recalled:

> I was home alone and saw my uncle's new penny loafers. I went over and started smelling the fresh new leather scent and kissing and licking them. It turned me on so much that I actually ejaculated my first load into my pants and have been turned on ever since. (Weinberg et al., 1995, p. 22)

In this case, shoes were associated with sexual arousal as the result of an early learning experience. Another example of a shoe fetishist is described in First Person. This case clearly exemplifies the *DSM-5* criteria for paraphilia. The youth/man experienced sexual fantasies and urges associated with women's shoes for years, experienced arousal and ejaculation only when they were present, and experienced significant impairment in his academic and social life as a result. In an experiment, it was even demonstrated that men could, in the laboratory, be conditioned to become sexually aroused when viewing pictures of shoes (Rachman, 1966).

A second possible theoretical explanation comes from cognitive psychology, discussed in Chapter 2

(Walen & Roth, 1987). According to cognitive theorists, people with fetishes (or other paraphilias) have a serious cognitive distortion in that they perceive an unconventional stimulus—such as black leather boots—as erotic. Further, their perception of arousal is distorted. They feel driven to the sexual behaviour when aroused, but the arousal may actually be caused by feelings of guilt and self-loathing. Thus, there is a chain in which there are initial feelings of guilt at thoughts of the unconventional behaviour, which produces arousal, which is misinterpreted as sexual arousal, which leads to a feeling that the fetish ritual must be carried out; it is, and there is orgasm and temporary feelings of relief, but the evaluation of the event is negative, leading to further feelings of guilt and self-loathing, which perpetuates the chain.

A third theory that has been advanced to explain some sexual variations, especially those that seem compulsive, is the theory of sexual addiction, discussed earlier in this chapter.

Whatever the cause, fetishism typically develops early in life. In one sample of foot or shoe fetishes, the mean age at which respondents reported first being sexually aroused by feet or shoes was 12 years (Weinberg et al., 1995).

 LO4

Cross-Dressing

Cross-dressing refers to wearing clothes stereotypically associated with the other gender. Cross-dressing may be done by a variety of people for a variety of reasons. As discussed in Chapter 13, transgender individuals

First Person

A Case History of a Shoe Fetishist

The following case history is taken directly from the 1886 book *Psychopathia Sexualis*, by Richard von Krafft-Ebing, the influential early investigator of sexual deviance. It should give you the flavour of his work.

Case 114. X., aged twenty-four, from a badly tainted family (mother's brother and grandfather insane, one sister epileptic, another sister subject to migraine, parents of excitable temperament). During dentition [teething] he had convulsions. At the age of seven he was taught to masturbate by a servant girl. X. first experienced pleasure in these manipulations when the girl happened to touch his member [penis] with her shoe-clad foot. Thus, in the predisposed boy, an association was established, as a result of which, from that time on, merely the sight of a woman's shoe, and finally, merely the idea of them, sufficed to induce sexual excitement and erection. He now masturbated while looking at women's shoes or while calling them up in imagination. The shoes of the schoolmistress excited him intensely, and in general he was affected by shoes that were partly concealed by female garments. One day he could not keep from grasping the teacher's shoes—an act that caused him great sexual excitement. In spite of punishment he could not keep from performing this act repeatedly. Finally, it was recognized that there must be an abnormal motive in play, and he was sent to a male teacher. He then revelled in the memory of the shoe scenes with his former school mistress and thus had erections, orgasms, and, after his fourteenth year, ejaculation. At the same time, he masturbated while thinking of a woman's shoes. One day the thought came to him to increase his pleasure by using such a shoe for masturbation. There after he frequently took shoes secretly and used them for that purpose.

Nothing else in a woman could excite him; the thought of coitus filled him with horror. Men did not interest him in any way. At the age of eighteen he opened a shop and, among other things, dealt in ladies' shoes. He was excited sexually by fitting shoes for his female patrons or by manipulating shoes that came for mending. One day while doing this he had an epileptic attack, and, soon after, another while practicing onanism in his customary way. Then he recognized for the first time the injury to health caused by his sexual practices. He tried to overcome his onanism, sold no more shoes, and strove to free himself from the abnormal association between women's shoes and the sexual function. Then frequent pollutions, with erotic dreams about shoes occurred, and the epileptic attacks continued. Though devoid of the slightest feeling for the female sex, he determined on marriage, which seemed to him to be the only remedy.

He married a pretty young lady. In spite of lively erections when he thought of his wife's shoes, in attempts at cohabitation he was absolutely impotent because his distaste for coitus and for close intercourse in general was far more powerful than the influence of the shoe-idea, which induced sexual excitement. On account of his impotence the patient applied to Dr. Hammond, who treated his epilepsy with bromides and advised him to hang a shoe up over his bed and look at it fixedly during coitus, at the same time imagining his wife to be a shoe. The patient became free from epileptic attacks and potent so that he could have coitus about once a week. His sexual excitation by women's shoes also grew less and less.

Source: Von Krafft-Ebing, 1886.

---

cross-dress to express a more feminine or masculine side of themselves and to live as the other gender as part of transitioning. Some gay men—**drag queens**—dress up as women, and some lesbians dress in masculine clothes (drag kings); these practices, though, are basically caricatures of traditional gender roles. **Female impersonators** are men who dress as women, often as part of their jobs as

drag queens: Gay men who dress in women's clothing.
female impersonators: Men who dress up as women as part of a job in entertainment.

entertainers (Figure 15.5). For example, Robin Williams in *Mrs. Doubtfire* and Dustin Hoffman in *Tootsie* won praise from critics and big box-office profits for their impersonations of women. Some, perhaps many, adolescent boys cross-dress, usually only once or a few times (Green, 1975).

Stephen, a professor at Harvard, explains his cross-dressing:

I enjoy dressing up as a woman and being called Stephanie . . . When I present myself as a woman (or a girl), I often feel better than my usual self, more present in my body . . . I am more at home in the physical world as well as excited by the relative novelty of what I get to wear, from silver flats to ruffly Swiss dot tops. While I enjoy being Stephanie—I'd hate to give it up—I am not unhappy enough about my male body, my life as a guy to spend the energy, time, and money required to live as a woman form day to day. (Burt, 2014)

In contrast to people who engage in cross-dressing for the reasons just discussed, some men regularly dress in female clothing to produce sexual arousal and experience sexual excitement. When this behaviour persists for at least six months and causes clinically significant distress, it is referred to as **transvestic disorder** (American Psychiatric Association, 2013). The cross-dressing is often done in private, perhaps by a married man without his partner's knowledge. An online article tells the story of a married man who has cross-dressed in women's satin lingerie for 19 years (Clark-Flory, 2011). He reports that it mentally brings a sense of relief and arousal.

Cross-dressing is almost exclusively a male sexual variation; it is essentially unknown among women. There may be a number of reasons for this difference, including our culture's tolerance of women who wear masculine clothing and intolerance of men who wear feminine clothing. Also, traditionally women's clothing is by design sensual and erotic, whereas men's clothing is functional (Wheeler et al., 2008). The phenomenon illustrates a more general point—namely, that many sexual variations are defined for, or practised almost exclusively by, members of one gender; the parallel practice by members of the other gender is often not considered deviant. Most sexual variations are practised mainly by men.[1]

A survey of a national sample in Sweden asked each participant whether she or he had ever dressed

Figure 15.5 Michelle Ross at the Carlu.

© The Canadian Press/Michael Hudson

in clothing of the other gender and experienced sexual arousal (Långström & Zucker, 2005). Almost 3 percent of men and 0.4 percent of women reported at least one such experience. Among men, this behaviour was associated with being easily sexually aroused (in general, not just by cross-dressing), more frequent masturbation, and same-sex sexual experience.

A common means of studying persons with atypical sexual behaviour patterns is to place ads in specialty newsletters and magazines, and to solicit participants at meetings and conventions attended by such persons. Using these procedures, researchers gathered survey data from 1032 cross-dressers (Docter & Prince, 1997). The sample did not include drag queens or female impersonators. The vast majority of the men (87 percent) were heterosexual, 60 percent were married, 65 percent had a university education, and 76 percent reported being raised by both parents through age 18. Sixty-six percent reported that their first cross-dressing experience occurred before age 10. About 40 percent reported that they often or always associated sexual excitement and orgasms with cross-dressing. This indicates that this sample included men who cross-dress for a variety of reasons—not just men who do so to enhance sexual arousal. Almost all (93 percent) preferred complete cross-dressing, but only 14 percent frequently went out in public dressed as a woman.

Another survey was conducted by mailing questionnaires to 1200 members of a U.S. cross-dressing organization (Bullough & Bullough, 1997). There were 372 questionnaires returned. The median age at which the men began to cross-dress was 8.5; 32 percent reported that they first dressed as a female before they were six. Most of them reported cross-dressing as children, and 56 percent said they were never caught.

> **Are men or women more likely to engage in cross-dressing?**

transvestic disorder: The practice of dressing as the other sex in order to experience sexual excitement which causes emotional distress or impairs social or interpersonal functioning.

---

[1] Several theories have been proposed to explain why there are so many more men than women with paraphilias (Finkelhor & Russell, 1984). Sociobiologists believe that the difference lies in the evolutionary selection of males to inseminate many partners and to be aroused by sexual stimuli devoid of emotional content (Wilson, 1987). Sociologists point to gender role socialization, which teaches males to be instrumental and to initiate sexual interactions. Females, on the other hand, are taught to be nurturing and to empathize with others; for example, with the vulnerability of children (Traven et al., 1990). Psychoanalytic theory (see Chapter 2) suggests that paraphilias result from castration anxiety, which is relieved by a forceful sexual act; because women do not fear castration, they are not subject to paraphilias. Moser and Kleinplatz (2005) argue that diagnosis of certain paraphilias, such as transvestism, results from the tendency in our culture to define masculinity very narrowly and to pathologize unconventional behaviour. The social construction perspective suggests that because we consider paraphilias a male phenomenon, a woman with the same behaviours (e.g., compulsive extradyadic sex) will not consider herself to have a paraphilia or an addiction. If she is concerned about her behaviour, she will define it as a relationship problem.

How do the partner and children of the cross-dresser react to his unusual behaviour? In one sample of 50 heterosexual cross-dressers, 60 percent of the wives were accepting of their husband's cross-dressing (Tala-mini, 1982). Most of these women commented that he was a good husband. Some of the wives felt fulfilled being supportive of the husband, and some even helped him in dressing and applying makeup. In the same sample, 13 of the couples had told their children about the cross-dressing. They claimed that the relationship with the children was undamaged and that the children were tolerant and understanding. However, given societal attitudes toward cross-dressing and gender roles, the partner may have problems with it—particularly if she did not know about the cross-dressing before they became involved.

Occasional cross-dressing is one of the harmless, victimless sexual variations. Like other forms of atypical behaviour, it is a problem only when it becomes so extreme that it is the person's only source of erotic gratification or when it becomes a compulsion the person cannot control and therefore causes distress in other areas of the person's life.

LO5

BDSM

Definitions

A **sexual sadist** is a person who derives sexual excitement and satisfaction from inflicting pain, suffering, or humiliation on another person. The term *sadism* derives from the name of the Marquis de Sade, who lived around the time of the French Revolution. Not only did he practise sexual sadism—several women apparently died from his attentions (Bullough, 1976)—but he also wrote novels about these practices (the best known is *Justine*), thus assuring his place in history.

A **sexual masochist** is a person who is sexually aroused by fantasies, urges, or behaviours involving being beaten, humiliated, bound, or tortured to enhance or achieve sexual excitement. This variation is named after Leopold von Sacher-Masoch (1836–1895), who was himself a masochist and who wrote novels expressing masochistic fantasies. Notice that the definitions of these variations make specific their sexual nature; the terms are often loosely used to refer to people who are cruel or to people who seem to bring misfortune on

sexual sadist: A person who derives sexual satisfaction from inflicting pain, suffering, or humiliation on another person.
sexual masochist: A person who derives sexual satisfaction from experiencing pain.
bondage and discipline: The use of physical or psychological restraint to enforce servitude, from which both participants derive sensual pleasure.
dominance and submission: The use of power consensually given to control the sexual stimulation and behaviour of the other person.

themselves, but these are not the meanings used here. These two are often referred to as a pair since the two behaviours or roles (giving and receiving pain) are complementary.

There are two styles of interaction that are related to sadism-masochism (S-M). These are bondage and discipline (B-D) and dominance and submission (D-S) (Ernulf & Innala, 1995). **Bondage and discipline** refers to the use of physically restraining devices or psychologically restraining commands as a central aspect of sexual interactions. These devices or commands may enforce obedience and servitude without inducing any physical pain. **Dominance and submission** refers to interaction that involves a consensual exchange of power; the dominant partner uses his or her power to control and sexually stimulate the submissive partner. Both B-D and D-S encompass a variety of specific interactions that range from atypical to paraphilic (see First Person for one man's account of BDSM).

There is considerable overlap between these variance terms. Thus, collectively they are often referred to as BDSM. That is, B and D, interpreted together, refer to bondage and discipline, D and S together refer to dominance and submission, and S and M together refer to sadism and masochism.

Sexual Sadism and Masochism

Sadomasochism (S-M) is a rare form of sexual behaviour, although in its milder forms it is probably more common than many people think. In fact, discussion of spanking and use of handcuffs during sexual activity has made it to such prime-time television shows as *Friends*, *Sex and the City*, and *Seinfeld*. Kinsey found that about one-quarter of both males and females had experienced definite or frequent erotic response as a result of being bitten during sexual activity (Kinsey et al., 1953). Sadistic or masochistic sexual fantasies are more common; a New Brunswick study found that 65 percent of university students have sexual fantasies of being tied up and 62 percent have fantasies of tying someone up (Renaud & Byers, 1999).

Another study administered questionnaires to 130 men and 52 women who responded to ads placed in S-M magazines (Breslow et al., 1985). Thirty-three percent of the men and 28 percent of the women preferred the dominant role; 41 percent of the men and 40 percent of the women preferred the submissive role; and 26 percent of the men and 32 percent of the women were versatile. The majority of these S-M respondents were heterosexual. Men involved in S-M frequently report having been interested in such activity since childhood; women are more likely to report having been introduced to the subculture by someone else (Weinberg, 1994). Women prefer bondage, spanking, and master-and-slave role-playing

(Levitt et al., 1994). A review of several studies concluded that 13 to 30 percent of the participants are women (Hucker, 2008).

The online survey of women recruited through the "kink" community described earlier (Rehor, 2015) included 62 "BDSM-related" behaviours; the author acknowledges that classification of some behaviours is arbitrary. Many participants (75 to 85 percent) reported behaviours that cause pain, including breast play (slap, clothespins), paddling, flogging, genital play (slap, kick, clothespins), and whipping and caning. The use of bondage toys for sensual or erotic pleasure was reported by 85 percent as well. By contrast, a telephone survey of 19 307 adults in Australia asked about participants' involvement in BDSM activities; only 2.2 percent of men and 1.3 percent of women reported involvement in the year prior to the survey (Richters et al., 2008). Notice the difference; in the first survey, women are reporting whether they have ever engaged in the behaviour in their lives; in the second they are reporting behaviour in the past year.

A good example of an atypical preference that seems benign is the activity at a Strictly Spanking party in New York City (David, 2011). These bimonthly parties attract men and women who like to be spanked, and spankings are the main activity. People wear coloured nametags noting whether they are a top, a bottom, or switch. At one party, most of the participants were over 45, and ordinary-looking people from many walks of life. Most were straight. "Spankos" talk about being fascinated by spanking from a young age and that it is not sexual; people do not pair off and have sex during or after the party. For a few participants, spanking becomes a central focus of their lives; they cultivate daddy–daughter relationships, and may live together. Spanking is also an activity that may be part of disciplinary or bondage scenes, but it has a different meaning in those settings.

Thus, a spectrum of activities constitute S-M. People who become involved in it often have tried a variety of these behaviours and find only some of them satisfying. They develop a script of activities (recall the concept of scripts in Chapter 2) that they prefer to enact each time they engage in S-M. One group of researchers (Santilla et al., 2002) identified 29 individual sexual behaviours associated with S-M. They administered questionnaires to 184 Finnish men and women who were members of S-M clubs. Each participant was asked which of the behaviours he or she had participated in during the preceding year. Four clusters or themes were identified: hypermasculinity (e.g., dildo, enema), administering and receiving pain (e.g., clothespins attached to nipples, caning, hot wax), physical restriction (e.g., handcuffs, straitjackets), and humiliation (e.g., verbal humiliation, face slapping). Further analyses of participation in the behaviours within each cluster identified a continuum in frequency from very common to very rare, with the order of the behaviours suggesting that this continuum reflects a dimension from least to most intense. For example, the humiliation continuum ranges from flagellation (reported by 81 percent; least intense) to verbal humiliation (70 percent) to gagging (53 percent) and face slapping (37 percent) to using knives to make surface wounds (11 percent; most intense). The results suggest that the S-M activities within each cluster are *scripted*, with the less intense behaviours being much more common.

Some observers note that S-M is about play, as in the theatre. S-M sexual activities are organized into *scenes*; one *plays* with one's S-M partners. In addition to the activities such as those just discussed, roles, costumes, and props are an important part of each scene. The roles include slave and master, maid and mistress, and teacher and pupil. The costumes range from simple to elaborate. The props may include tight leather clothing, pins and needles, ropes, whips, and hot wax. In S-M clubs, which may be heterosexual or homosexual, there are often rules governing the social and S-M interaction, particularly the creation and enactment of scenes. According to one website, the rules include no touching of another's body without consent, giving players the room they need to enact a scene, not intruding physically or verbally on a scene in progress, and sometimes no sexual penetration.

As you might expect, Canadian researchers have shown that male sexual sadists show greater subjective and genital arousal to sexual stimuli involving mutually consenting violence and injury than do other men (Seto et al., 2012). Nonetheless, sexual sadists and masochists do not consistently find experiencing pain and giving pain to be sexually satisfying. For example, the masochist who smashes a finger in a door will yell and be unhappy just like anyone else. Pain is arousing for such people only when it is part of a carefully scripted ritual. As one woman put it,

> Of course, he doesn't *really* hurt me. I mean quite recently he tied me down ready to receive "punishment," and then by mistake he kicked my heel with his toe as he walked by. I gave a yelp, and he said, "Sorry love—did I hurt you?" (Gosselin & Wilson, 1980, p. 55)

Causes of Preference for Sexual Sadomasochism

Most experts view sexual sadomasochism as a variation on other forms of healthy sexuality. The reasons why people come to prefer sexual activities that involve sexual sadism and masochism (and equally most other sexual preferences) are not precisely known. The theories in our discussion of fetishes can be applied here as well. For example, learning theory points to conditioning as an explanation. A little boy is being spanked

First Person

The Pleasure of Kinky Sex: Trevor Jacques, a BDSM Practitioner and Advocate

Trevor Jacques is 52 years old, is single, and lives in Toronto. He was born in England, the eldest of four children of middle-class parents. As a child, he was the "good son," even serving as an altar boy for a while. His parents raised him to ask questions and "do the right thing." This allowed him to chart his own course in life, both in his career and, in his words, his "kink."

In terms of his career, Trevor is a physicist who became an engineer. He worked on avionic missile systems in Great Britain, on infrared surveillance technology for the Canadian and U.S. navies, and as a database consultant. However, he identifies a strong passion for educating people about safer BDSM and conducting research about the experiences of members of the BDSM community. (Note how Trevor uses "safer" rather than "safe," in that nothing, even breathing, is entirely safe.)

What is kinky sex?

Trevor uses the term BDSM to describe the practices of the community because it encompasses multiple meanings and roles, and is almost free of the baggage that comes with words used in clinical diagnosis. Trevor also subscribes to the term *kinky*, because he feels it describes what BDSM practitioners like to do, while making it clear that they only are interested in consensual partners and do not want to hurt anyone who does not clearly want and consent to it. For Trevor, "hurt" refers to the application of intense stimulation, which may or may not include pain but does not entail injury.

Trevor does not recall being particularly interested in girls and sex as an adolescent, yet his father assured him "it would come." He had his first sexual experience when he was 21, with a woman. He describes it as conventional and very enjoyable, yet "missing something." Trevor came out as gay at 26. He also realized that he was attracted to more than conventional sex when he found himself gravitating toward erotica that depicted hypermasculine men and men representing or engaged in BDSM activities. He describes coming out as kinky as a far faster process than coming out as gay, because he had already been through the coming out process once. He realized that being kinky was "simply who he is and how he was born," in the same way he is gay.

Since openly identifying as kinky, Trevor has been very active in the BDSM community, which he regards as one of his two chosen families (the other being his "LGBTIQ" family). He finds "vanilla" (non-BDSM) sex enjoyable yet also looks for opportunities for BDSM play. He particularly enjoys social events organized by and for the BDSM community. Many of these are social functions that raise money for local charities. Some are similar to any other reception or dinner; others have people "dressed to the gills in leather/rubber/PVC or other role-playing clothes and accessories." There are other categories of BDSM gatherings that he likes, including BDSM conferences and sex events—the former referring to open public events, and the latter being very private events, limited to self-identified members of BDSM organizations.

over his mother's knee; in the process, his penis rubs against her knee, and he gets an erection. Or a little girl is caught masturbating and is spanked. In both cases, the child has learned to associate pain or spanking with sexual arousal, possibly setting up a lifelong career as a masochist.

A related theory points to childhood sexual abuse that causes sadistic fantasies, for example, of revenge, as the root of at least sadistic violence. For the child experiencing abuse, these fantasies are functional, helping them cope with the abuse. If sexual arousal is paired

with the fantasies, they may influence sexual behaviour (MacCulloch et al., 2000).

Another psychological theory has been proposed to explain sexual masochism specifically, although not sadism (Baumeister, 1988a, 1988b). According to the theory, the masochist is motivated by a desire to escape from self-awareness. That is, the masochistic behaviour helps the individual escape from being conscious of the self in the same way that drunkenness and some forms of meditation do. In an era dominated by individualism and self-interest, why would anyone want

What does Trevor like about these events? He enjoys the opportunity to meet new people who share his interests. He does not feel a need to have sex or BDSM play during (in the case of the private sex/BDSM events) or after the event, although he certainly enjoys it when it does happen. He also enjoys being able to express what he refers to as the "exhibitionist" and "voyeuristic" parts of himself at these events. Note that what he is referring to as exhibitionism is the desire to show off and be admired by other men when he is dressed up in his BDSM gear and, potentially, showing off his kinky prowess (e.g., by flogging a consenting partner). This is very different from exhibitionism that involves displaying one's genitals, for example, to a *non*consenting person in a public venue. (All of Trevor's teaching of BDSM strongly stresses consent and the avoidance of harm. He practises what he teaches.) Similarly, Trevor enjoys being able to see and watch other men, who know they are being watched, dressed up and engaging in the activities that turn him on.

Trevor describes himself as a "fetishistic switch." This means that he has a fetish for specific clothing/gear—in his case, leather, rubber, and other clothing—and that he likes to switch between being the top (the dominant/disciplining/sadistic partner) and the bottom (the submissive/receiving/masochistic partner). Pain may be part of his play; however, it is not essential. Indeed, he is very uncomfortable with the myth that "BDSM necessarily equals pain," and that all pain is undesired (e.g., stubbing one's toe during a heavy flogging is a good example of unwanted pain during desired pain). He enjoys many kinky pleasures, such as bondage, "artfully applied pain" for sexual pleasure, fetishes, control, and so on. However, consistent with the basic tenets of safer BDSM play, his limits extend to the agreed play, respect for his partner(s), and the assurance that harm does not occur. Like most BDSM practitioners, he is a proponent of what is termed safe, sane, and consensual (SSC) play. What Trevor enjoys at any point in time depends, among other factors, on the person with whom he's playing, how he and the person(s) feel at the time, and what his day has been like. One of the things he likes about BDSM is that he becomes immersed in the play and that his brain switches off the minutiae of daily life.

In 1991, Trevor and his co-authors of the bestselling *On the Safe Edge: A Manual for SM Play* designed and began to deliver a series of seminars on SM safety, under the auspices of the AIDS Committee of Toronto (ACT). Since that time, more than 3500 people have attended these courses. He also is frequently invited to talk about BDSM on television and radio and to university classes. One of his main messages is that people need to be honest with themselves and others about their practices and the pleasure they get from them: they should not let other people define them. Otherwise, they may miss out on years of pleasure and enjoyment. Further, people interested in BDSM need to learn what is safe. And they need informed consent while having their own kind of fun.

Source: As told to Sandra Byers.

---

to escape from the self? Probably because high levels of self-awareness can lead to anxiety as a result of a focus on pressures on the self, added responsibilities, the need to keep up a good image in front of others, and so on. Sexual masochistic activity allows the person to escape from being an autonomous, separate individual. Sexual masochism may be an unusually powerful form of escape because of its link to sexual pleasure. This theory can also explain why sexual masochism is more common among men than among women (Baumeister, 1988b). According to the theory, the male role is especially burdensome because of the heavy pressures for autonomy, separateness, and individual achievement. Sexual masochism accomplishes an escape from these aspects of the male role, explaining why masochism is more common among men than among women. Some men cross-dress while engaging in sexual masochistic activity, a finding that tends to support this theory (Chivers & Blanchard, 1996).

Whatever the original cause, researchers in Nova Scotia found that all of the practitioners they interviewed indicated that BDSM play had improved their roles. They identified a number of specific benefits of engaging in BDSM including physical pleasure and arousal, pleasure from pleasuring others, fun and experimentation, variety, personal growth, improved romantic relationship, community, psychological release, freedom from day-to-day roles, and being yourself. They also identified a number of challenges including risks of stigma, relationship problems, and self-acceptance as well as some challenges that were unique to each role.

Bondage and Discipline

Sexual bondage, the use in sexual behaviour of restraining devices that have sexual significance, has been a staple of erotic fiction and art for centuries. Current mainstream and adult films and videos portray this activity. In some communities, individuals interested in B-D have formed clubs. There are many B-D sites on the Internet that may also advertise BDSM "play parties," as well as BDSM *munches.* A BDSM munch is an informal gathering of people who are interested in BDSM, often at a restaurant (hence the term *munch*), so they can eat, socialize, and meet other people with similar interests.

We noted earlier the difficulty of gathering data on participation in variant forms of sexual expression. One innovative study downloaded all the messages about bondage mailed to an international computer discussion group (Ernulf & Innala, 1995). Of the messages in which senders indicated their gender, 75 percent were men. Of those indicating a sexual orientation, most were heterosexual; 18 percent said they were gay, and 11 percent said they were lesbian. The messages were coded for discussion of what the person found sexually arousing about B-D. Most frequently mentioned (12 percent) was play: "sex is funny, and sex is lovely, and sex is PLAY." Next was the exchange of power (4 percent): "It is a power trip because the active is responsible for the submissive's pleasure." The next most common themes were intensified sexual pleasure, tactile stimulation associated with the use of ropes and cuffs, and the visual enjoyment experienced by the dominant person.

There is a marked imbalance in preferences for the active ("top") and passive ("bottom") roles. Most men and women, regardless of their sexual orientation, prefer to be "bottom." This may be the reason why there are an estimated 2500 professional dominatrices in the United States. Researchers in Nova Scotia have documented differences between BDSM practitioners who prefer to take the top/dominant role and those who prefer to take the bottom/submissive role (Hébert & Weaver, 2014). Compared to submissives, dominants had a greater desire for control, were more extraverted, had higher self-esteem, were more satisfied with their lives, and were less

emotional. BDSM practitioners describe ways in which their over all personalities are similar to their BDSM role as well as ways in which their personality and BDSM role are dissimilar (Hébert & Weaver, 2015).

Dominance and Submission

Sociologists emphasize that the key to S-M is not pain but rather dominance and submission (D-S) (Weinberg, 1987). Thus it is not an individual phenomenon but rather a social behaviour embedded in a subculture and controlled by elaborate scripts.

Sociologists feel that to understand D-S, one must understand the social processes that create and sustain it (Weinberg, 1987). There is a distinct D-S subculture, involving DVDs, clubs, and bars. It creates culturally defined meanings for D-S acts. Thus a D-S act is not a wild outbreak of violence but rather a carefully controlled performance with a script. One woman reported,

> We got into dominance and submission. Like him giving me orders. Being very rough and pushing me around and giving me orders, calling me a slut, calling me a cunt. Making me crawl around . . . on all fours and beg to suck his cock. Dominance-submission is more important than the pain. I've done lots and lots of scenes that involve no pain. Just a lot of taking orders, being humiliated. (Maurer, 1994, pp. 253, 257)

Within the play, people take on roles such as master, slave, or naughty child. Thus men can play the submissive role in D-S culture, even though it contradicts the male role, because it is really not they who are the naughty child, just as an actor can play the part of a murderer and know that he is not a murderer (Figure 15.6).

One interesting phenomenon, from a sociological point of view, is the social control over risk taking that exists in the D-S subculture (Weinberg, 1987). That is, having allowed oneself to be tied up or restrained and then whipped, one could be seriously injured or even murdered, yet such outcomes are rare. Why? Research shows that complex social arrangements are made to reduce the risk (Lee, 1979). First, initial contacts are usually made in protected territories, such as bars or meetings, which are inhabited by other people involved in D-S who play by the same rules. Second, the basic scripts are widely shared so that everyone understands what will and will not occur. When the participants are strangers, the scenario may be negotiated before it is enacted. Third, as the activity unfolds, very subtle nonverbal signals are used to control the interaction (Weinberg, 1994). By using these signals, the person playing the submissive role can influence what occurs. Thus, as two people enact the master and slave script, the master is not in

Figure 15.6 Sexual bondage involves restraining devices and discipline, such as in this scene.

PBNJ Productions/Blend Images/Getty Images

complete control and the slave is not powerless. So it is the *illusion* of control, not actual control, that is central to D-S activity for both the master and the slave.

L06

Voyeurism and Exhibitionism

Voyeurism and exhibitionism are often discussed together because they seem complementary. However, they are rather different, and a voyeur would not find watching an exhibitionist arousing.

Voyeurism

A **voyeur** is a person who experiences intense sexual arousal from watching an unsuspecting person who is naked, in the process of undressing, or engaging in sexual activity, as manifested by fantasies, urges, or behaviours (American Psychiatric Association, 2013). Voyeurs are often referred to as "peeping toms."[2] The *DSM-5* states, "Voyeuristic acts are the most common of potentially law-breaking sexual behaviors." It estimates the lifetime prevalence of voyeuristic disorder at 12 percent of men and 4 percent of women. Thus, voyeurism appears to be much more common among men than among women. The most recent strategy of people who engage in voyeurism is to install small video cameras secretly so that they can observe women using the washroom or changing their clothes. Surreptitiously observing or recording

a naked person who is in a private place are both criminal offences (see Table 2.1).

Voyeurism provides another good illustration of the continuum from normal to abnormal behaviour. For example, many men and women find it arousing to watch a man or woman undress and "dance"—otherwise, there would be no strip clubs—and this is certainly well within the normal range of behaviour.

The appeal of watching is illustrated by an Ontario study that asked university students whether they would watch an attractive person undress and an attractive couple having sex (Rye & Meaney, 2007b). The likelihood of being caught was specified as 0, 10, or 25 percent. Two-thirds said they would watch someone undress; 45 percent said they would watch the couple. The likelihood of watching the person undress increased as the risk decreased; the likelihood of watching the couple did not vary by risk. There were no differences between the men and the women in the study.

Voyeurism becomes voyeuristic disorder when the fantasies, urges or behaviours continue for at least six months

> **voyeur:** A person who experiences sexual arousal from viewing unsuspecting person(s) who are nude, undressing, or having sex.

---

[2] Voyeur comes from the French word *voir*, meaning "to see." "Peeping Tom" comes from the story of Lady Godiva; when she rode through town nude to protest the fact that her husband was raising his tenants' taxes, none of the townspeople looked except one, Tom of Coventry.

and cause marked distress and interpersonal difficulty (American Psychiatric Association, 2013).

People who engage in voyeurism are typically men who want the woman they view to be a stranger and do not want her to know what they are doing. The element of risk is also important; while one might think that a nudist camp would be heaven to a voyeur, it is not, because the elements of risk and forbiddenness are missing (Sagarin, 1973).

A survey of randomly selected 18- to 60-year-old Swedes found that almost 8 percent reported one or more experiences of having been sexually aroused by watching others have sex. About three-quarters of them were men. Note that this is a very broad question and could include watching consenting others. People who reported these experiences tended to report more psychological problems and alcohol and drug use, as well as greater sexual interest, activity, and novelty-seeking (Långström & Seto, 2006).

A study of 561 men who sought treatment for paraphilias included 62 voyeurs (Abel & Rouleau, 1990). One-third reported that their first experience occurred before they were 12 years old. One-half said they recognized their interest before age 15. These men estimated that, on average, they had peeped at 470 persons.

This study points out one of the major problems with the research on sexual variations: Much of it has been done only on people who have been arrested for their behaviour or sought treatment. One analyst suggests that only a small minority of people who engage in voyeurism are distressed by their behaviour and thus likely to seek treatment (Lavin, 2008). The "respectable" person with a paraphilia who has the behaviour under somewhat better control or who is skilled enough or can pull enough strings not to get caught is not studied in such research. Thus, the picture that research provides for us of these variations may be very biased.

Exhibitionism

The complement to voyeurism is exhibitionism (*flashing*), in which the person derives sexual pleasure from exposing his genitals to an unsuspecting person (Figure 15.7). In the *Criminal Code of Canada,* this is referred to as indecent exposure. The pronoun "his" is used advisedly, since **exhibitionists** are usually men. The woman who wears a dress that reveals most of her breasts is likely to be thought of as attractive rather than abnormal. Here again, whether a sexual behaviour is considered abnormal depends greatly on whether the person doing it is a male or a female. (Recall our discussion of the social constructionist view of paraphilias and gender.) A man exposing himself

exhibitionists: Persons who derive sexual gratification from exposing their genitals to an unsuspecting person.

Figure 15.7 Exhibitionism.

© Jutta Klee/Flirt/Corbis

to another man is also quite rare, so the prototype we have for exhibitionism is a man exposing himself to a woman. Research in New Brunswick found that in 1996, 6 percent of male sex offenders were convicted of indecent exposure (Byers et al., 1997). Many of the men convicted of indecent exposure, 48 percent in one Canadian study, commit another similar offence within the next few years (Marshall et al., 1991). In addition, 6 percent of the exhibitionists in an Ottawa study were subsequently convicted of a hands-on sexual offence, such as sexual touching or sexual assault (Greenberg et al., 2002). According to one survey, 33 percent of university women have been the objects of indecent exposure (Cox, 1988).

When fantasies, urges, or behaviour involving surprise exposing of the genitals to a stranger lasts at least six months and causes distress or difficulty, it is a paraphilic disorder (American Psychiatric Association, 2013).

According to the benchmark study of men seeking treatment for paraphilias (Abel & Rouleau, 1990), 15 percent of the exhibitionists had exposed themselves at least once by age 12; half had done so by age 15.

According to other research (Blair & Lanyon, 1981), exhibitionists generally recall their childhoods as being characterized by inconsistent discipline, lack of affection, and little training in appropriate forms of social behaviour. An analysis of ten studies of the social skills of sexual offenders (rapists, child molesters, incest offenders, pedophiles, and exhibitionists) found that sexual offenders possess fewer social skills than nonoffenders (Emmers-Sommer et al., 2004).

The study of Swedish adults found that 3 percent reported ever being aroused by exposing their genitals to a stranger; about two-thirds were men. The same variables associated with reports of watching others were associated with exhibitionism (Långström & Seto, 2006).

The exact causes of exhibitionism are not known, but a social learning–theory explanation offers some possibilities (Blair & Lanyon, 1981). According to this view, the parents might have subtly (or perhaps obviously) modelled such behaviour to the person when he was a child. In adulthood, there may be reinforcements for the exhibitionistic behaviour because the man gets attention when he performs it. In addition, even if he is married, the man may lack the social skills to form an intimate adult relationship (Marshall et al., 1991). As a result he receives little reinforcement from interpersonal sex.

Many women, understandably, are alarmed by exhibitionists. But since the exhibitionist's goal is to produce shock or some other strong emotional response, the woman who becomes extremely upset is gratifying him. Probably the best strategy for a woman to use in this situation is to respond calmly and walk away.

A study of female sex offenders in Great Britain identified five women who had exhibited themselves (O'Connor, 1987). For example, one 21-year-old woman stripped off her clothes and masturbated in public on several occasions. All five women had histories of unusual behaviour and had been diagnosed with alcohol or psychiatric problems. A study in Ontario of persons seeking treatment for paraphilias included three women who were diagnosed with exhibitionistic paraphilia (Federoff et al., 1999). In all eight cases, their atypical sexual behaviours appear to reflect other problems rather than sexual motivations.

Extended online interviews with six women who exhibited themselves found that they rejected the paraphilic, deviant characterization of their behaviour (Hugh-Jones et al., 2005). Instead, they promoted and normalized it, saying that it provided self-confidence, that they were sensitive to the audience and would not exhibit to seniors or children, and that they received positive support from family, friends, and co-workers (consistent with learning theory). Four of the six women exhibited by posting nude photos online; it is not clear that any exposed themselves to unsuspecting strangers.

The term *exhibitionism* is also used to refer to people who get sexually aroused by having other people watch them engage in sexual activity, although this is not the way the term is used in the *DSM-5*. Conversely, *voyeurs* are turned on by watching people engaging in sexual activity. Thus, this is a consensual activity between exhibitionists and voyeurs and may occur in a private home or in an outdoor location. In Britain, the term used to describe all kinds of outdoor sexual activity watched by others is *dogging*.

Notice that both voyeurism and exhibitionism are considered problematic behaviour (and illegal) when the other person involved is an unwilling participant. A man who derives erotic pleasure from watching his partner or a willing participant (e.g., on the Internet) undress or a woman who is aroused by exhibiting her body in new lingerie to her partner is not engaging in criminal or paraphilic behaviour.

Hypersexuality

We turn now to several variations that are not explicitly listed in the *DSM-5;* however, each of these also may vary from atypical through compulsive to paraphilic, depending on their frequency, duration, and consequences.

Hypersexuality is when there is an extraordinarily high level of sexual activity and sex drive; the person is apparently insatiable, and at the extreme, sexuality overshadows all other concerns and interests. When it occurs in women, it is called **nymphomania**; in men, it is called **satyriasis**[3] (or Don Juanism; Figure 15.8). Although this definition seems fairly simple, in practice it is difficult to say when a person has an abnormally high sex drive. As we saw in Chapters 10 and 11, there is a wide range in the frequencies with which people engage in sexual activity; therefore, the range we define as "normal" should also be broad. In real life, nymphomania or satyriasis is often defined by the partner who thinks his or her partner wants sex too frequently. In particular, our society is not accepting of highly sexual women, and they are likely to be labelled in negative ways (Blumberg, 2003).

Because these two terms are imprecise, some researchers prefer the term hypersexuality.

> **nymphomania (nimf-oh-MANE-ee-uh):** An excessive, insatiable sex drive in a woman.
> **satyriasis (sat-ur-EYE-uh-sis):** An excessive, insatiable sex drive in a man.

---

[3] *Satyriasis* is named for the satyrs, who were part-human, part-animal beasts in Greek mythology. A part of the entourage of Dionysus, the god of wine and fertility, they were jovial and lusty and have become a symbol of the sexually active male.

Figure 15.8 Historical painting of a satyr, which gives the name to satyriasis, a sexual variation in which a man has an excessive, insatiable sex drive.

© Peter Horree / Alamy

Hypersexuality refers to an excessive, insatiable sex drive in either a man or a woman—not just to a high level of sexual desire or of sexual activity. It leads to compulsive sexual behaviour in the sense that the person feels driven to it even when there may be very negative consequences (Goldberg, 1987). The person is also never satisfied by the activity, and she or he may not be having orgasms, despite all the sexual activity. Such cases meet the criteria for abnormal behaviour discussed at the beginning of this chapter. The compulsiveness of the behaviour leads it to become extremely inefficient, with the result that it impairs functioning in other areas of the person's life.

A central debate among experts is whether hypersexuality is truly a disorder, or simply a medically constructed label for someone with high desire (in and of itself, not a disorder). Researchers posted an online survey containing measures of sexual desire, sexual activity, perceived control over one's sexuality, and a variety of potential negative outcomes (Carvalho, Stulhofer, Vieira & Jurin, 2015). Over 4500 men and women ages 18 to 60 completed the survey. The data were analyzed using cluster analysis, which identifies meaningful clusters based on scores on the various scales. The analyses identified two clusters, one reflecting problematic sexuality—lack of control and experiencing negative outcomes—and the other reflecting high desire and frequent activity. Comparing persons in the two clusters on other variables, persons in the hypersexuality cluster reported more psychopathology. Thus,

hypersexuality: An excessive, insatiable sex drive in either men or women.

hypersexuality properly defined/measured appears to be distinct from high desire.

One study recruited women from volunteers at presentations about highly sexual women and via newspaper ads in alternative newspapers (Blumberg, 2003). The authors used the term *highly sexual* to refer to women who desire sexual stimulation to orgasm six or seven times per week or who think of themselves as highly sexual and their sexuality frequently strongly affects their lives. Forty-four women were interviewed, ranging in age from 20 to 82, from such diverse occupations as janitor and corporate CEO. The preferred weekly frequency of sexual episodes—not orgasms—ranged from 3 to 70. The women reported that the internal demand for sexual excitement and satisfaction was too strong to be ignored; for many of them, it shaped their daily lives. This demand led to challenges in their feelings about themselves, their relationships with partners, and their relationships with female friends. Some of the women found it impossible to form a single relationship that could fulfill their needs, leading to multiple partners or the frequent forming of new relationships. The researcher believed that neither the term *sexual addiction* nor *compulsive sexual behaviour* should be applied to this behaviour. These women did not feel that their behaviour was out of control, and they did not report an increase in frequency of behaviour or the impact of it on their lives over time.

Researchers have developed a scale to assess hypersexuality, the Hypersexuality Behavior Inventory, or HBI (Reid et al., 2011). The scale includes 19 items asking respondents to report the relative frequency of a variety of experiences related to sexuality during the past 90 days. The scale was validated by using two samples of male outpatients drawn from several states, including men reporting compulsive masturbation, habitual solicitation of commercial sex workers, extramarital affairs, and multiple anonymous partners. Analyses indicate three underlying factors: control ("My attempts to change my sexual behaviour fail"), consequences ("My sexual activities interfere with . . . work or school"), and coping ("I use sex . . . [to] deal with my problems"). They propose the use of the HBI as an objective diagnostic tool compared with, for example, number of orgasms per week. The HBI is highly correlated with measures of compulsive sexual behaviour discussed earlier in this chapter.

A study of hypersexuality in women used data from an online survey that included the HBI and measures of present and past sexual activity (Klein, Rettenberger, & Briken, 2014). The survey was completed by 988 German women, about 90 percent of them college students. High-scoring women on the HBI reported significantly more frequent consumption of pornography (more than

30 times per month) and masturbation (more than 6 times per week). HBI score was unrelated to the number of sexual intercourse partners in the past six months. The researchers conclude that hypersexuality in women is associated with impersonal sexual activity.

Online surveys give us some idea of the prevalence of behaviours among persons in a population. Presumably many of those who attain high scores on a measure like the HBI are not experiencing significant impairments in their daily lives. On the other hand, recent research in Ontario with emerging adults has raised questions about whether the HBI and other similar scales are actually assessing hypersexuality (Levaque et al., 2016).

An alternative approach is to examine the characteristics of those who seek treatment for a condition or disorder. The Sexual Behaviours Clinic in Toronto sees a large number of patients every year. Researchers reviewed referrals and consultation requests for "hypersexualty" (Cantor et al., 2013), and identified six types. About one-third of the persons referred exhibited *paraphilic hypersexuality*, extremely high frequencies of behaviours such as adultery, pornography consumption, or very frequent solicitation of paid partners, and various additional paraphilic interests (fetishes, voyeurism, etc.). A second type is *avoidant masturbation*, men who spend a great deal of time viewing pornography and several hours per day masturbating, often leading to school failure, job loss, or social isolation. A third type, and the one most frequently publicized in the media, is *chronic adultery*, persons who chronically cheat on spouses, but have few paraphilic interests and do not spend large amounts of time pursuing sexual gratification. Men in this category often report a desire for daily sex and that sex with their wives is infrequent or does not occur, due to her dyspareunia, very low libido, or past sexual abuse. The fourth type is *sexual guilt*, men and women whose sexual activity is within the normal range but they feel extremely guilty about it. People in this group are often self-referrals, and more likely to be women than persons in the first three groups. The fifth type is the *designated patient*, someone referred by their romantic partner; the partner has very restrictive beliefs about sex and discovers some activity by the patient that s/he disapproves of. The patient shows no signs of behavioural extremes/paraphilic disorder. The last type is the person who is diagnosed as exhibiting a non-sexual condition—personality disorders, hypomania, or developmental delays. Sometimes their symptoms are related to medications they are taking. Notice that persons in three of these categories are not exhibiting signs of atypical or disordered sexuality, reminding us that we need to be very careful in applying diagnostic labels (such as hypersexuality) to people. Subsequent research by this group showed that there are differences in the sexual and mental health histories of individuals in each of these subtypes (Sutton et al., 2015).

Experts on hypersexuality have concluded that there is no specific, agreed-on definition or diagnosis (Kaplan & Krueger, 2010). This condition has been linked to a wide variety of behaviours and frequencies of behaviours. Therefore, it was not included in the *DSM-5*.

Online Sexual Activity Use and Abuse

Online sexual activity (OSA) refers to the use of the Internet for any activities of a sexual nature (Cooper & Griffin-Shelley, 2002; Shaughnessy, Byers, & Walsh, 2011). For some people this involves solitary activities; for other people this involves sexual activity with a partner, which is also called *cybersex* (Shaughnessy, Byers, & Thornton, 2011). A major concern in recent years, particularly in the media, has been whether the use of the Internet to access sexually oriented materials, chat rooms, and bulletin boards (Figure 15.9) can become compulsive, addictive, or paraphilic. Recall that compulsive behaviour involves (1) a lack of impulse control, (2) a tendency to lead to social and legal sanctions, (3) interference in interpersonal and occupational functioning, and (4) the creation of health risks. This concern has been raised by therapists and clinicians, who report cases of Internet use leading to job loss, relationship difficulties leading to divorce, and other adverse consequences (Galbreath et al., 2002).

If we think about Internet sexual behaviour as falling on a continuum from healthy and normal to unhealthy and abnormal, most

> **Is my online sexual activity compulsive?**

people who engage in OSA are recreational users, not abusers, addicts, or compulsives (Cooper et al., 1999a, 1999b). Indeed, a study in New Brunswick found that university students who engage in OSA did so infrequently, on average less than once a week (Shaughnessy, Byers, & Walsh, 2011). However, the Internet is thought to be especially likely to lead to addictive or compulsive behaviour because it is characterized by the three As: anonymity, accessibility, and affordability. Unlike in face-to-face behaviours, such as cruising for a partner or buying or renting X-rated DVDs, Internet users are anonymous. The Net is available 24/7, and its use is relatively cheap—you can download almost any kind of sexual material, often for free.

> **online sexual activity (OSA):** Use of the Internet for any activities of a sexual nature, including sexual activities with a partner, called cybersex.

Figure 15.9   Advertising for partners with similar kinky interests. Many websites, newspapers, and magazines carry such personal ads.

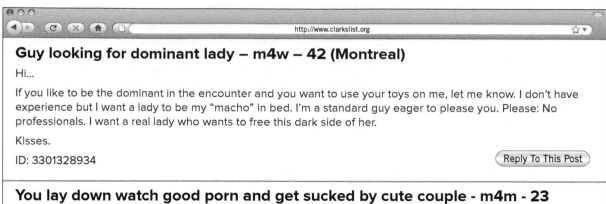

Guy looking for dominant lady — m4w — 42 (Montreal)

Hi...

If you like to be the dominant in the encounter and you want to use your toys on me, let me know. I don't have experience but I want a lady to be my "macho" in bed. I'm a standard guy eager to please you. Please: No professionals. I want a real lady who wants to free this dark side of her.

Kisses.

ID: 3301328934   Reply To This Post

You lay down watch good porn and get sucked by cute couple - m4m - 23 (Vancouver)

We are a cute couple of to guys 25 and 21. You lay down, watch good porn and get sucked by us. We are cute clean and serious. Please under 35 and send a facepic in first email.

ID: 2644997727   Reply To This Post

Girl for girl if my bf can watch - 18 (Calgary)

I'm young white, sexy, in shape c cup but I'm small and skinny, dark hair blue eyes, I'm looking for a girl to fool around with while my bf watches, must be clean.

ID: 2583531178   Reply To This Post

Looking for feminine boy who i can dress up and put makeup on - w4m - 22 (Halifax)

I want a skinny pretty boy who I can dress in my clothes and completely makeover in to a girl. I'd like to get fucked while both of us are wearing skirts. I'm not a crossdresser or a tv but a real girl so you have to be attracted to women for this to work. You also can't be over a size 5 in women's clothes unless you want to buy your own. I have a thing for nail polished fingers and toes so please don't have extremely hairy hands unless you're willing to wax. Send a picture so I can see what I'm going to be working with.

ID: 2600447786   Reply To This Post

Bi-ker Babe (Regina)

Wanted! Couple 30s, who like to ride. She's: sensuous, lewd. He's: fine, driving and lasting, You're: lovely in leather or lace. On bikes, bars, or candlelight dining, friends sharing what we like best. We're open!

ID: 6256001766

Reply To This Post

Internet "abuse" has been variously characterized as paraphilic, compulsive, or addictive. As noted elsewhere in this chapter, intense and persistent use of the Internet for at least six months in ways that significantly impair daily life or cause distress may constitute hypersexuality. The research reviewing referrals to the Sexual Behaviours Clinic in Toronto identified extremely high frequencies of pornography consumption as paraphilic hypersexuality. Men who spend a great deal of time viewing pornography and several hours per day masturbating were identified as a second group within the hypersexual category. It is likely that only a small number of men and women access sexually explicit materials in ways that fit the definition of a paraphilic disorder.

The most common characterization of problematic Internet use involving sexually explicit materials is *porn(ography) addiction*. A search for this term on

Yahoo! returned 35 million hits, including popular media articles, ads for treatment programs and centres, self-help and professional books, thousands of folk remedies, and too many porn sites to count. We discussed the concept of sexual addiction earlier in the chapter. The concept of addiction was developed to explain substance abuse. The craving for the substance and the inability to control its use result from neurophysiological changes due to repeated use; such changes have been documented. Advocates of the application of addiction to pornography argue that repeated exposure to pornographic images has similar or "parallel" effects. They point to some reported cases where excessive use leads to impairment in occupational or personal functioning or relationships. They also point to cases where men with histories of excessive exposure experience erectile dysfunction as evidence of "addiction." Critics respond that similar neurophysiological changes have not been documented in response to visual stimuli of any kind (Ley et al., 2014). Clearly various responses can become conditioned to viewing online porn (or any visual stimulus for that matter) (see Chapter 2). Conditioning and the desire to experience sexual gratification may account for repeated activity. Whether the user really cannot control the behaviour is the key question, but may not be answerable with empirical data. As we pointed out earlier, addiction provides a plausible reason (excuse?) for behaviour that results in pressure from others to change. Note that the review of referrals for hypersexuality identified one group as "designated patients," persons whose partners brought them in for treatment for "addiction."

Research on Internet use has used convenience samples of persons who respond to invitations on websites and agree to complete an online questionnaire. Obviously, such samples consist of persons with access to computers who possess basic online skills. Thus, these samples may underrepresent lower-income persons and those from minority groups, although they may be representative of people engaging in OSA. Of concern is the 8 percent of participants who report spending 11 or more hours per week in OSA (Cooper et al., 1999b). These heavy users were more likely than were recreational users to go online both at home and at work and to report that their online sexual behaviour interfered with their lives. A study based on more than 40 000 users assessed the relationship between the frequency and duration of Internet use and mental health. The results indicated that the number of months that had passed since participants first went online and the number of hours per week online were associated with a history of mental health problems and treatment (Mathy & Cooper, 2003).

A Swedish study focused on cybersex, or online sexual activity (OSA), which is two or more persons engaging in sexual talk for the purpose of sexual pleasure (Daneback et al., 2005). Researchers placed a banner soliciting participation on a web portal. The banner appeared randomly during a two-week period; 1835 persons completed the survey. Almost one-third reported cybersex; the most common location was in a chat room. Participants in OSA were young; gay men were four times more likely to report OSA than heterosexual men. Those who reported cybersex spent more time online and reported more offline sex partners.

Research using a sexual compulsivity scale sought to determine what percentage of OSA users were compulsive users (Cooper et al., 2000). The study found that 83 percent of the participants were not problematic users. Eleven percent attained moderate scores on the scale, 4.6 percent were sexually compulsive, and 1 percent were OSA compulsives; that is, they attained the highest scores on compulsivity and spent more than 11 hours per week in online sexual pursuits. Persons in the OSA compulsive group were more likely to be male, to be single and dating, and to report that they were bisexual; they reported spending 15 to 25 hours per week in OSA. Twenty-one percent of the respondents reported that their online activities had jeopardized at least one area of their life, the most common being personal relationships. The researchers concluded that bisexuals, and perhaps other sexually marginalized groups, may be especially at risk for online sexual compulsivity.

The research also suggests high rates of co-occurrence with other disorders; people whose Internet use is problematic are more likely to be depressed (by standard measures), report sleep disturbances, and report alcohol and drug abuse. The question is which came first: the Internet use, which then led to depression and substance abuse (because the Internet use was causing problems), or the depression and substance abuse, which led to the person finding escape online? A meta-analysis of studies of Internet "addiction" also noted the inconsistent criteria and indicated that online samples may result in biased estimates of the prevalence of the problem (Byun et al., 2009).

LO8

Other Sexual Variations

A review of the literature identified more than 100 sexual variations (Federoff, 2007). Some of these just describe unusual sexual interests; the individual involved may not actually have a paraphilia. Participation in others may be fatal (e.g., asphyxiophilia) or against the law (e.g., frotteurism, zoophilia). Most of the paraphilias are too rare to have had much research devoted to them.

Nonetheless, some of them are described here. The Internet provides an avenue for individuals with even rare sexual interests to find like-minded individuals.

Asphyxiophilia

Asphyxiophilia or *hypooxyphilia* is the desire to induce in oneself a state of oxygen deficiency to create sexual arousal or to enhance sexual excitement and orgasm (Zaviačič, 1994). A variety of techniques are used, including temporary strangulation by a rope around the neck, a pillow against the face, or a plastic bag over the head or upper body. Obviously, this is very dangerous behaviour; a miscalculation can lead to death.

Little is known about asphyxiophilia. Most of the deaths attributed to the practice involve men, about three men for every woman (Sauvageau & Racette, 2006). There were 118 recorded deaths from asphyxiophilia in Alberta and Ontario (the only provinces that record this information) between 1974 and 1987; only one was female (Hucker & Blanchard, 1992). The average age of death was 26 but ranged from 10 to 56 years. Such cases are often obvious to the trained investigator. Characteristics that distinguish these deaths from intentional suicides include a male who is nude, cross-dressed, or dressed with genitals exposed, and evidence of sexual activity at the time of death (Hucker & Blanchard, 1992). Pornography or other props, such as mirrors, are often present (Zaviačič, 1994).

Some cases have been identified involving women (Byard et al., 1993). A review of eight fatal cases among women found that only one involved unusual clothing, and none involved pornography or props. Two of the cases were initially ruled homicide, one suicide, and five accidental death. The investigators suggest that death from asphyxiophilia may be much more common among women than we realize, because these deaths are less often recognized for what they are.

Men and women engage in asphyxiophilia in the belief that arousal and orgasm are intensified by reduced oxygen. There is no way to determine whether this is true. If the experience is more intense, it may be due to heightened arousal created by the risk rather than by reduced oxygen. Some believe that certain women may experience an orgasm accompanied by urethral ejaculation; this belief has been identified as one reason women engage in asphyxiophilia. Again, there is no evidence.

An online survey collected data from practitioners and found that 71 percent reported masochistic activities, and 31 percent reported sadistic ones. Sixty-six percent

reported using bondage, and 14 percent reported using electrical stimulation. Forty-one percent engaged in it alone (Hucker, 2008).

Zoophilia

Zoophilia is sexual contact with an animal; this behaviour is also called *bestiality* (the term used in the *Criminal Code of Canada*). About 8 percent of the men in Kinsey's sample reported having had sexual experiences with animals. Most of this activity was concentrated in adolescence and probably reflected the experimentation and diffuse sexual urges of that period. Not surprisingly, the percentage was considerably higher among boys on farms; 17 percent of boys raised on farms had had animal contacts resulting in orgasm. Kinsey found that only about 3 to 4 percent of all women have had some sexual contact with animals. Contemporary therapists report cases of men and women engaging in sexual activity with household pets. Activities include masturbating the animal, oral–genital contact, and intercourse.

Researchers posted a questionnaire online and recruited participants through a letter to members of a network of people with sexual interests in animals (as we said, you can find anything on the Internet—that's accessibility). Those who volunteered were asked to refer others who had interests similar to those assessed by the questionnaire (Williams & Weinberg, 2003). Data were obtained from 114 men, all white, with a median age of 27; 64 percent were single, never married, and 83 percent had at least some university education. These characteristics undoubtedly reflect in part the fact that the sample was obtained via the Internet. Ninety-three percent defined themselves as "zoophiles" and said this identity involved a concern for the animal's welfare and an emphasis on consensual sexual activity. They compared themselves favourably with "bestialists," whom they said were not concerned about an animal's welfare. Given a list of possible reasons for sexual interest in animals, the two most common were a desire for affection and pleasurable sex. The type of sexual contact reported by the men varied by the type of animal. Receiving oral sex and receiving anal intercourse were the most frequent activities with dogs, whereas performing vaginal and anal intercourse were most frequent with horses. Only one man preferred sheep. Many of the men had not had a human partner of either sex in the preceding year. The researchers suggest that a preference for sexual activity with animals can be explained by learning theory in that the rewards offered by sex with animals are immediate, easy, and intense, and thus extremely reinforcing. They suggested that the respondents' choice of animal is explained by

asphyxiophilia: The desire to induce in oneself a state of oxygen deficiency to create sexual arousal or to enhance excitement and orgasm.
zoophilia: Sexual contact with an animal; also called bestiality or sodomy.

their early conditioning; most men preferred the type of animal they first had sex with.

Zoophilic disorder is defined as sexual fantasies, urges, or behaviours involving nonhumans, lasting more than six months, causing marked distress or interpersonal difficulty. It appears to be rare, with onset in adolescence (Milner et al., 2008).

Other Variations

Frotteurism is the seventh paraphilia identified by the *DSM-5*. It is defined as sexual fantasies, urges, or behaviours involving touching or rubbing one's genitals against the body of a nonconsenting person, usually in a crowded public place (Figure 15.10). When the behaviour is intense and occurs over a period of at least six months, causing clinically significant distress or impairment in functioning, it constitutes *frotteuristic disorder*. A man may approach a woman from the rear and press his penis against her buttocks, or a woman may approach a man from the side and rub her genitals against his leg or hip. The target may be unaware of it, if it occurs in a crowded elevator or subway train or in the crush of a crowd at a sports event or concert. We noted earlier that 35 percent of a sample of university men reported having engaged in this activity.

Limited evidence from clinical samples suggests that about 10 percent of persons with a history of paraphilia or paraphilic-related behaviour have engaged in acts of frotteurism. These activities tend to start in early adulthood (Lussier & Piché, 2008).

Saliromania is a variation found mainly in men; there is a desire to damage or soil a woman or her clothes or the image of a woman, such as a painting or statue. The man becomes sexually excited and may ejaculate during the act.

Coprophilia and **urophilia** are both variations having to do with excretion. In coprophilia, the feces are important to sexual satisfaction. In urophilia, it is the urine that is important. The urophiliac may want to be urinated on as part of the sexual act. Insiders refer to urination as "golden showers."

Necrophilia is sexual contact with a dead person. It is a very rare form of behaviour and is considered by experts to be psychotic and extremely deviant. Necrophiliacs derive sexual gratification from viewing a corpse or actually having intercourse, fellatio, or cunnilingus with it; the corpse may be mutilated afterward (Cantor & Sutton, 2014). Many individuals with necrophilia also have other paraphilias (Brankley, Goodwill, & Abracen, 2016). Interfering with or offering any indignity to a corpse is illegal in Canada.

Feederism consists of the eroticization of weight gain and feeding (Terry & Vasey, 2010). Individuals can

Figure 15.10 Frotteurism may involve touching or rubbing one's genitals against the body of a nonconsenting person, usually in a crowded public place.

Chris Turner/Stone/Getty Images

be either *feeders,* becoming sexually aroused by feeding their partner and encouraging them to gain weight, or *feedees,* becoming sexually aroused by eating, being fed, and the idea or act of gaining weight. Feeders are more often men, and feedees are more often women (Terry & Vasey, 2010).

Sexsomnia, or sleep sex, refers to automatic, unintentional sexual behaviours during sleep (Williams & Lettieri, 2012); the term was introduced in 2003 (Shapiro et al., 2003). The behaviour occurs during non-rapid eye movement sleep, usually in the first hours of sleep, and is related to an abnormal transition between sleep and wake states. It typically arises from slow-wave sleep, which is characterized by reduced cortical control by the brain leading to uninhibited behaviour. The person is unaware of the behaviour or his or her surroundings, and if awakened has no memory of what happened.

The range of reported sexual behaviours is broad, from sexual sounds like moaning to fondling, masturbation, cunnilingus, sexual intercourse with or without orgasm, and sexual assault (Schenck et al., 2007). About 80 percent of the reported cases involve men. Partnered behaviours typically involve another person in the same bed. Partners may experience physical injuries. Both the actor and the partner report various negative psychosocial after-effects, including guilt, shame, embarrassment, alarm, and low self-esteem.

frotteurism: Rubbing one's genitals against the body of a nonconsenting person.

saliromania: A desire to damage or soil a woman or her clothes.

coprophilia (cop-roh-FILL-ee-uh): Deriving sexual satisfaction from contact with feces.

urophilia (YUR-oh-fill-ee-uh): Deriving sexual satisfaction from contact with urine.

necrophilia: Deriving sexual satisfaction from contact with a dead person.

feederism: Deriving sexual pleasure from weight gain or feeding.

sexsomnia: Automatic, unintentional sexual behaviours during sleep; also called sleep sex.

Sexsomnia obviously may cause relationship problems. Sexsomnia has features in common with other sleep somnias (sleepwalking, sleep eating); the distinguishing feature is persistent sexual arousal—erection, lubrication, ejaculation—during the episode.

Causes or contributing features include things that can disrupt normal sleep cycles including sleep apnea, sleep deprivation, stress, alcohol use or abuse, and some medications. Sexsomnia is considered a sleep disorder rather than a paraphilia, but some reported cases involve paraphilic behaviour (e.g., genital fondling of a minor) repeated over a long time. Other sexual behaviours are also related to sleep disorders, for example, sexual acts related to seizures during sleep.

LO9

Prevention and Treatment of Paraphilic Disorders

For many of the variations discussed in this chapter, there is a continuum from normal to abnormal. People whose behaviour falls at the normal end enjoy these activities at no expense to themselves or others. Some may need reassurance that there is nothing wrong with engaging in these behaviours but do not need treatment to change their behaviour. They may, however, benefit from treatment aimed at helping them accept themselves and question pressure by family members or society to fit a narrow definition of normality. It is important that therapists are able to accept that there are a range of normal sexual behaviours. Individuals with atypical sexual interests may be reluctant to see a therapist out of fear that their interests will be pathologized. As a result, some therapists in Canadian cities are advertising themselves as "kink friendly" or "kink positive" to communicate their accepting attitudes.

However, some people engage in behaviours that fall at the abnormal end. Some people engage in sexual variations that they find highly distressing, causing them significant unhappiness. Their sexual interests (e.g., in the case of a person with a sexual compulsion or addiction) may interfere with having healthy relationships or completing their day-to-day responsibilities. Yet they may find these sexual interests extremely difficult to change or control. Other sexual variations—for example, pedophilia—cause significant harm to other people. However, some pedophiles do not see their behaviour as harmful. Thus, the issue of whom to treat is extremely complex. Nonetheless, it is important to develop programs to prevent and treat these types of abnormal or harmful sexual variations.

Prevention of Paraphilic and Nonparaphilic Disorders

In preventive medicine, a distinction is made between primary prevention and secondary prevention. Applied to the sexual variations, primary prevention would mean intervening in home life or in other factors during childhood to help prevent problems from developing or trying to teach people how to cope with crises or stress so that problems do not develop. In secondary prevention, the idea is to identify people who are at high risk to develop a problem as early as possible, so that difficulties are minimized.

It would be highly advantageous to do primary prevention of harmful or distressing sexual variations—that is, to head them off before they even develop. Unfortunately, this method is proving to be difficult, for a number of reasons. One problem is the diagnostic categories. The categories for the diagnosis of sexual variations are not nearly as clear-cut in real life as they may seem in this chapter, and multiple diagnoses for one person are not uncommon. If it is unclear how to diagnose sexual variations, it is going to be rather difficult to figure out how to prevent them. Further muddying the waters is the co-occurrence of paraphilia and other psychiatric conditions. A study of 120 men (88 diagnosed with paraphilias, 38 with paraphilia-related disorders) systematically assessed co-occurrence (Kafka & Hennen, 2002). More than two-thirds had mood disorders, such as major depression; 38 percent had anxiety disorders; and 34 percent abused psychoactive substances. Men with paraphilias were significantly more likely to abuse cocaine. One-third of the men had retrospectively diagnosed attention-deficit hyperactivity disorder.

An alternative approach that seems promising—rather than figuring out ways to prevent each separate variation—is to analyze the *components of sexual development*. Disturbance in one or more of these components in development might lead to different sexual variations. Two such components are arousal to appropriate stimuli and formation of relationships with others (Bancroft, 1978). Thus, for example, a disturbance in attachment relationships in childhood might lead to exhibitionism or to compulsive OSA. The idea would then be to try to ensure that as children grow up, their development in each component is healthy (primary prevention). We might have specific programs for children who demonstrate characteristics or behaviour that is known to lead to abnormal or harmful sexual variations (secondary prevention). Ideally, these types of sexual variations would then not occur. However, this task is made more difficult by the fact that we have little scientific knowledge about either what constitutes unusual sexual behaviours among children or what components of development lead to abnormal or harmful sexual variations (Moser et al., 2004).

The review presented in this chapter makes it clear that childhood sexual abuse is a risk factor for paraphilic behaviour and paraphilias later in life. Indeed, individuals with paraphilias are more likely to have experienced both sexual and nonsexual abuse in childhood, as well as neglect and disturbed family relationships (Brotto & Klein, 2007). It is obvious that adults are responsible for sexual violence against children, so prevention (and treatment) must be targeted at adults and at preventing child sexual abuse.

Two factors have increased interest in developing prevention programs targeting children. First, paraphilias often first occur when individuals are in their mid-teens, although for other individuals they occur in their mid-20s (Brotto & Klein, 2007). Second, each year a number of youth are charged with sexual offences. For example, in 2014 in Canada, 630 youth (mostly boys) were convicted of sexual assault, and 655 were convicted of other sexual offences. Of note, many more youth were charged with other crimes, such as physical assault and theft, than were charged with sexual offences. Research with 45 adolescent sex offenders in Toronto indicated that 42 percent showed equal or greater arousal to film clips of children than to film clips of adults; that is, they had pedophilic interests (Seto et al., 2003). One study of American adolescents incarcerated for sexual offences found that 46 percent committed their first offence before the age of 12 (Burton, 2000). Childhood victimization was positively associated with later sexual aggression by the youth, suggesting that social learning can help explain the development of sexual offending. Of course, most individuals who have experienced childhood abuse do not develop paraphilias. Nonetheless, if we reduce childhood abuse we may help to prevent abnormal or harmful sexual variations.

Treatment of Paraphilic and Nonparaphilic Disorders

Some of the sexual variations discussed in this chapter, such as the mild fetishes, regular masturbation, or viewing erotic materials are well within the normal range of sexual expression. There is no need for treatment. Others, however, fall into the abnormal range, causing personal anguish to the individual and possibly harming unwilling victims. Treatments are needed for these variations, particularly those that are paraphilic disorders as defined by the *DSM-5*. Various types of treatments have been tried, each based on a different theoretical understanding of the causes of sexual variations. We now look at four categories of treatments: medical treatments,

cognitive–behavioural therapies, skills training, and AA-type 12-step programs. We will also review research on the effectiveness of each.

Medical Treatments

Inspired by the notion that sexual variations are caused by biological factors, several medical treatments for sexual variations have been tried over the last century. Some of them look today like nothing other than cruel and unusual punishment. Nonetheless, people would love to have a "pill" that would cure some of these complex and painful or dangerous paraphilias, so the search for such treatments continues.

Surgical castration has never been commonly used in Canada as a treatment for various kinds of uncontrollable sexual urges, although it was used extensively in Europe and the United States. However, a few sex offenders in Canada do voluntarily undergo surgical castration. Indeed, a study of 134 men interested in castration found that 41 percent of them indicated that the reason that they wanted to be castrated was to have more control over their sexual urges (Wassersug et al., 2004). Such treatments are based on the notion that removing a man's testosterone by removing the testes will lead to a drastic reduction in sex drive, which will in turn erase urges to commit sex offences. However, as we saw in Chapter 9, a reduction in testosterone levels in humans does not always lead to a reduction in sexual behaviour (Federoff & Moran, 1997). Surgical castration cannot be recommended as a treatment for sex offenders either on ethical grounds or on grounds of effectiveness.

Hormonal treatment involves the use of drugs to reduce sexual desire. Sexual arousability is heavily dependent on maintaining the level of androgen in the bloodstream above a given threshold. Two ways to reduce this level are to administer (1) drugs that reduce the production of androgen in the testes (*chemical castration*), or (2) anti-androgens that bind to androgen receptors in the brain and genitals, blocking the effects of androgen. The use of either should produce a sharp decline in sexual desire. Several drugs have been tried in the past 50 years, typically with adult male offenders arrested for sexual contact with children or indecent exposure. The drug medroxyprogesterone acetate (MPA), which binds to androgen receptors, was commonly used in Canada for some years. However, the drug has serious, adverse side effects, and its use has been discontinued in Europe (Thibaut et al., 2010). Moreover, limited evidence suggests it did not reduce the likelihood of reoffending. Cyproterone acetate (CPA) is replacing MPA; it acts as both a progestin and an anti-androgen. It binds to all androgen receptors, including those in the brain, and blocks testosterone uptake. It is taken daily as a tablet (the usual dosage is 100 mg) or injected weekly or biweekly. In studies involving 900 men, its use was associated with significant decreases in sexual fantasy, activity, and masturbation. Problematic sexual behaviour disappeared in 80 to 90 percent of the men in 4 to 12 weeks. One study reported efficacy for up to eight years. One problem associated with CPA in pill form is poor compliance by patients.

Clinicians also use leuprolide acetate (LA), a synthetic analogue of gonadotropin-releasing hormone (GnRH; see Chapter 5); its continued use suppresses androgen production and reduces sexual fantasies and sex drive. One study reported the use of LA with 12 adults with paraphilic or other sexual disorders, with follow-up periods of six months to six years (Krueger & Kaplan, 2001). LA resulted in significant suppression of deviant sexual interests and behaviour. Similar results were found in a study of six young juveniles/young adults (Saleh et al., 2004). A review of research concluded that GnRH analogues may be needed for paraphilias that involve intense and deviant sexual desire and arousal or predispose the person to severe abnormal behaviour (Thibaut et al., 2010).

The use of alternative *psychopharmacological treatment* increased dramatically in frequency in the 1990s. Here, psychotropic medications, like antidepressants such as Prozac, are administered to offenders. These medications influence patients' psychological functioning and behaviour through their action on the central nervous system. Antidepressants are being used with individuals with paraphilias who are also diagnosed with obsessive-compulsive disorder or depression. These drugs appear to change the obsessive-compulsive behaviour rather than sexual desire (Federoff, 1995; Gijs & Gooren, 1996). There is a great deal of interest in the use of the newer antidepressants known as selective serotonin reuptake inhibitors (SSRIs). Case reports indicate that SSRIs reduce paraphilic fantasies and urges (Raymond et al., 2002). Their success with persons exhibiting paraphilic disorders suggests that these conditions may be a type of obsessive-compulsive disorder (Miner & Coleman, 2001). A review of effectiveness research suggests that SSRIs may be most effective with juvenile offenders (Thibaut et al., 2010).

Both hormonal and psychopharmacological treatment should be used as only one element in a complete program of therapy, which would include therapy and treatment for other emotional and social deficits (Saleh & Berlin, 2003). The best results are obtained with men who are highly motivated to change their behaviour and therefore comply with the prescribed treatment regimen. If the man with the paraphilia stops taking the drug or stops participating in other aspects of treatment, the program will fail. Unfortunately, one of the limitations of research on the effectiveness of these treatments is the high dropout rate, which was 46 percent in one study.

Cognitive-Behavioural Therapies

Compared with other therapeutic approaches, cognitive-behavioural therapy (CBT) is effective at reducing recidivism among sex offenders (Hanson et al., 2002; Marshall et al., 1991, 2006). Comprehensive programs target offender needs and risk factors. However, they also aim to reduce the need to reoffend by helping the offender attain the skills and self-beliefs (including self-esteem) needed to attain a "good life" (Marshall et al., 2006). As such, most programs include:

1. Behaviour therapy to reduce inappropriate sexual arousal and enhance appropriate arousal

2. Learning more effective ways of coping and managing moods

3. Social skills training to increase skills that are needed to form satisfying and effective interpersonal relationships

4. Modification of distorted thinking and challenging the rationalizations that the person uses to justify the undesirable behaviour

5. Relapse prevention—helping the person identify and control or avoid whatever triggers the behaviour and to identify sources of support

6. A search for other, less problematic ways of meeting the needs and desires fulfilled by the behaviour

CBT is used extensively to treat incarcerated sex offenders (Byers et al., 1997). An evaluation of the effectiveness of programs for adult offenders reports that high-quality CBT programs for sex offenders in prison reduce recidivism 15 percent; for offenders on probation, the reduction is 31 percent (Aos et al., 2006). Note that many persons do not reoffend following release. If the rate of re-offence for untreated persons is 30 percent, a 15 percent reduction would be about 5 persons per 100 released offenders. The Regional Treatment Centre in British Columbia is a secure, prison-based treatment facility; it provides high-risk offenders with an individualized, CBT-based program targeting criminal thinking patterns, criminal associates, deviant arousal, and other elements of the personality. Offenders are typically persons diagnosed with paraphilic disorders, including sexual interactions with children, exhibitionism and sexual sadism. The program typically lasts seven months. About 250 released offenders were followed for 2½ years post-release; only 5.5 percent (14 persons) reoffended in that period (Wilson et al., 2013).

One program designed for female offenders combined CBT with psychodynamic techniques and relied on one-on-one rather than group therapy (Traven et al., 1990). Male offenders typically deny responsibility for their behaviour, so the initial stage of treatment may focus on acknowledging his behaviour and its consequences. Women in this program readily acknowledged what they had done and were overwhelmed by guilt and shame, so the initial stage focused on self-esteem. Thus, different treatment programs may be needed for men and women with a paraphilic disorder. A meta-analysis found that recidivism rates for women convicted of sexual offences (only some of which were paraphilic) were much lower than rates for men (Cortini et al., 2010).

More youth are being identified as sex offenders. A therapeutic program targeting this group using CBT and skills training has been shown to be effective (LeTourneau et al., 2009). The program, multisystemic therapy (MST), involves family therapy, behavioural parent (skills) training, and CBT. The intervention is individualized to the specific offender and his or her caregivers and is presented in home and school. It addresses youth and caregiver denial about the offence, minimizing the youth's access to potential victims, and promoting age-appropriate and normative social experiences with peers. Youth (median age 14; all but three male) were randomly assigned to MST or the usual treatment prescribed for juvenile offenders in that jurisdiction, one weekly group treatment session following a standard protocol. At 12-month follow-up, youth in MST showed significant reductions in problematic sexual behaviour (77 percent versus 0 percent decline), delinquency (60 percent versus 18 percent), and substance abuse (50 percent versus 65 percent increase). A review of literature on treatment of sex offenders reports that such programs are more effective with youth than adults, and most effective with high-risk juvenile offenders, those with prior arrests (Ward et al., 2008).

Skills Training

According to yet another theoretical understanding, persons with paraphilias engage in their behaviour because they have great difficulty forming relationships and so do not have access to appropriate forms of sexual gratification. This perspective is consistent with data on IQ differences between sex offenders and controls. A meta-analysis of 75 studies found that adult men who committed sex offences scored significantly lower on IQ than nonoffenders did and lower than those who committed nonsexual offences (Cantor et al., 2005). Among sex offenders, the younger the age of the victims, the lower the IQ score of the offender.

Many of these people do not have the skills to initiate and maintain conversation. They may find it difficult to develop intimacy (see Chapter 12) (Keenan & Ward, 2000). Such people may benefit from a treatment program that includes social skills training. Such training may include how to carry on a conversation, how to develop intimacy, how to be appropriately assertive, and how to identify irrational fears that are inhibiting the person (Abel et al., 1992). These programs may also include basic sex education.

If a person needs to learn and practise sexual interaction skills, one approach would be to have him interact with a trained partner. This is the basis for a controversial practice: the use of *sex surrogates* as part of a treatment program.[4] The surrogate works with the therapist, interacting socially and sexually with the client to provide opportunities for using the newly acquired information and skills. Some therapists believe that the use of surrogates is ethical, but others see it as a type of commercial sex work (see Chapter 17). Just as the definition of abnormal depends on one's point of view, so does the definition of sex therapy.

AA-Type 12-Step Programs

As discussed earlier in this chapter, sexual addictions theory argues that many people who engage in compulsive, inappropriate sexual patterns are addicted to their particular sexual practice. The appropriate treatment, according to this approach, is one of the 12-step programs modelled on Alcoholics Anonymous (AA). Treatment programs based on this approach have become very common in the last 30 years. They include Sexaholics Anonymous (SA), Sexual Addicts Anonymous (SAA), Sexual Compulsives Anonymous (SCA), and Sex and Love Addicts Anonymous (SLAA). These programs are run by group members, and are generally free to participants. These groups can usually be found by calling the local phone number for Alcoholics Anonymous or by looking up their websites on the Internet. Perhaps because they are free, it is estimated that 5 million people attend AA-based groups in the U.S. every year (Dodes & Dodes, 2014). Most of the recovery or "rehab" centres for sexual addictions utilize groups based on AA principles, led by a professional staff member, as the core of their programs.

Twelve-step programs combine cognitive restructuring, obtaining support from other members who have

---

[4] The 2012 film, *The Sessions*, presents a sensitive portrayal of a sex surrogate–patient relationship, based on a true story.

Figure 15.11   The centrepiece of 12-step programs such as Sex Addicts Anonymous are group meetings in which participants confront their addiction with the support of other group members.

David Harry Stewart/The Image Bank/Getty Images

the same or similar problem behaviours, and enhancing spirituality (Figure 15.11). This last aspect involves increasing one's awareness of a "higher power" who can be relied on to help one recover. Twelve-step programs for alcohol or drug addiction demand that the addict abstain from contact with the substance. Similarly, 12-step programs for sexual addicts adopt a definition of "sexual sobriety." They cannot adopt an abstinence model, however, because sexual expression is a basic human need. Thus, they attempt to differentiate addictive sexual behaviour from healthy sexual behaviour. For some groups, although not all, only marital sex (and not other partnered sex or masturbation) is considered to fit the definition of sexual sobriety.

Given their popularity, the obvious question is whether they are effective. AA-based groups in the community are generally unwilling to cooperate with researchers, believing that to do so would prevent group members from concentrating on recovery. As a result, little research data exist on these programs. The major treatment centres do not report effectiveness data. AA-type programs are serving men and women who spontaneously seek help for their problems, compared to correctional facilities, which treat convicted offenders who live in the facility. So AA programs may be more effective, because participants are there voluntarily. On the other hand, community participants can easily stop attending, unlike the prisoner.

What Works?

Meta-analyses of the effectiveness of treatment programs for sex offenders consistently find that some programs are more effective than others. A systematic review of controlled outcome evaluations of psychosocial and hormonal treatment programs found that, overall, such programs reduced sexual recidivism by 37 percent compared with those in control groups (Schmucker & Losel, 2008). Classical behavioural programs, including skills training, were associated with the smallest significant effect. A review of all types of treatment programs concluded that only CBT-based programs are consistently shown to be effective (Thibaut, et al. 2010). Among programs treating incarcerated offenders, the rate of reoffending 20 years following treatment is estimated at 27 percent. As noted earlier, the intensive multifocal program of the Regional Treatment Centre reported a reoffending rate of 5.5 percent 2½ years following treatment. Programs are also more effective with some types of offenders than others. The programs have the largest effect with rapists, the second largest with exhibitionists, and the smallest significant effect with intrafamily child sex offenders.

An analysis focused specifically on programs to treat sexual abusers of children concluded that available evidence does not conclusively show that either pharmacotherapy or psychological treatments are effective with adults. There is evidence that multisystemic therapy prevents re-offence by youth (Langstrom et al., 2013). Finally, as suggested earlier, the programs were only effective when participation was voluntary.

The prestigious Cochrane Collaboration conducted one of the few systematic reviews of AA and other 12-step approaches to the treatment of alcohol use/abuse (Ferri, Amato, & Davoli, 2009). The review concludes, "No experimental studies unequivocally demonstrate the effectiveness of AA or TSF approaches for reducing alcohol dependence or problems." In short, although these groups are no doubt helpful for some individuals, there is no evidence that they are generally effective (Dodes & Dodes, 2014). Thus, if AA does not systematically succeed in reducing or eliminating problem-drinking, which it was developed to treat, one wonders whether there is any reason to believe that SAA, SLAA, and SCA 12-step programs would be effective for treating sexual variations that cause substantial pain and distress.

Critical *THINK*ing Skill

USING DIAGNOSTIC LABELS ACCURATELY

In this chapter, we discuss sexual behaviours that depart from the norm in Canadian society. In order to bring some clarity and structure to the discussion, we rely on the *Diagnostic and Statistcal Manual-5* classification system. It identifies a number of *paraphilias,* which are intense and persistent atypical sexual interests. Paraphilias are distinct from *paraphilic disorders,* which are paraphilias that are recurrent, last at least six months, and create distress or impairment to the individual.

A highly publicized paraphilia in North America is pedophilic disorder, in which the objects of the recurrent, intense, sexually arousing fantasies, urges, or sexual behaviours are prepubescent children (generally under 13 years of age). Media frequently report authorities are looking for or have arrested someone for (attempted) sexual contact with a 9- or 11- or 13-year-old youth. Many people immediately jump to the conclusion that the person is a pedophile (a "dirty old man"), is mentally ill, and should be imprisoned or hospitalized for life. The application of this diagnostic label is more likely if there are reports that the person has engaged in similar activity in the past—that is, "has a history" of such behaviours.

A search of the law enforcement and clinical literature will quickly reveal that many different kinds of people engage in sexual contact with children or adolescents, and many do not fit the *DSM* criteria. Some persons who are arrested for sexual contact with children ("child molesters") are relatives or even parents of the children. They may have no history of sexual contact with other children. Legally, these are cases of incest, and the perpetrators may not fit *DSM* criteria. There are numerous cases of school teachers engaging in sexual activity with 15- or 16-year-old students, but that does not fit the definition of pedophilia because the students are not prepubescent children. (Note that we are not saying that such behaviours between students and teachers are acceptable—just that it is not correct to call such a teacher a pedophile.)

Critical thinking means that we must think carefully before we apply such labels to people. Often, we don't think critically; we infer from publicity about one incident that the person is a pedophile, "child-molester," or a "monster." The media often contribute by uncritically applying the label, or repeating hearsay about the person's past. Applying the label can lead to tremendous hostility directed at the suspect, and even vigilante groups and death threats, often before a thorough investigation has been conducted. These incidents can ruin lives and devastate communities. Furthermore, even if there was sexual contact with a child and thus against the law, the perpetrator may not fit other *DSM* criteria, and may be wrongfully labelled.

Of course, perpetrators of violence or sexual violence toward children (or anyone else) need to be dealt with appropriately. What should be done needs to be determined by careful investigation of what happened, the perpetrator's circumstances, and the perpetrator's history. Some persons truly are characterized by pedophilic disorder, with long histories of sexual contact exclusively with children of a particular age and gender, and an inability to control their behaviour. They fit the diagnosis and should be treated accordingly. On the other hand, the 23-year-old teacher who has sex with a "consenting" 16-year-old has broken the law because they are in a position of trust (see Table 2.1 for the offence of sexual exploitation) and shown extremely poor judgment but should not be categorized as a pedophile.

SUMMARY

It seems reasonable to define *abnormal sexual behaviour* as behaviour that is uncomfortable for the person, inefficient, bizarre, or physically or psychologically harmful to the person or others. The American Psychiatric Association defines a *paraphilia* as an intense and persistent atypical sexual interest. Paraphilias are distinct from *paraphilic disorders* which are paraphilias that are recurrent, last at least six months, and create distress or impairment to the individual. Some of these behaviours are against the law, but most are not.

Four theoretical approaches have been used in understanding the paraphilias: learning theory, cognitive theory, the sexual addiction or compulsion model, and sociological theory. Several explanations have been proposed for the fact that there are many more men than women with paraphilias.

A fetishist is a person who becomes erotically attached to some object other than another human being. Most likely, fetishism arises from conditioning, and provides a good example of the continuum from normal to abnormal behaviour.

The cross-dresser derives sexual satisfaction from dressing as a member of the other gender. Like many other sexual variations, it is much more common among men than among women.

Three interrelated styles of sexual interaction, jointly termed BDSM, involve differences in control over sexual interactions. Dominance and submission (D-S) involve a consensual exchange of power and the enacting of scripted performances. Bondage and discipline (B-D) involve the use of physical restraints or verbal commands by one person to control the other. Both D-S and B-D may occur without genital contact or orgasm. Sexual sadism and masochism involve deriving sexual gratification from giving and receiving pain. Both are recognized as paraphilic disorders if they are recurrent, persistent, last more than six months, and cause impairment, distress, or harm to others.

The voyeur is sexually aroused by looking at an unsuspecting person who is nude, undressing, or engaging in sexual activity. The exhibitionist displays his or her sex organs to others. Both are generally harmless.

Nymphomania and satyriasis are terms used to describe women and men with an extraordinarily high sex drive. Both terms are ambiguous and subject to misuse. The term *hypersexuality* is potentially more precise, particularly if it is defined behaviourally. The definition may need to be different for women than men.

Use of the Internet to access sexually oriented material or engage in sexual activity may become compulsive. The Internet may facilitate sexual compulsion because of the three As—anonymity, accessibility, and affordability.

Other sexual variations include asphyxiophilia, use of oxygen deprivation in an attempt to enhance sexual sensations; zoophilia, sexual contact with animals; and frotteurism, touching or rubbing one's genitals against the body of a nonconsenting person. Others include coprophilia, urophilia, and necrophilia. If any these become recurrent, intense, and persist for more than six months, they may be diagnosed as paraphilic disorders.

It is important to prevent harmful sexual variations before they develop. Available treatment programs include medical and hormonal treatments, cognitive-behavioural therapy, skills training, and AA-type 12-step programs. While each form of treatment may help some people whose sexual behaviour is problematic, only CBT-based programs are consistently shown to reduce the frequency of behaviour or reoffending.

CHAPTER 16

Sexual Coercion

© Brand X Pictures/Punchstock

Are YOU Curious?

1. What percentage of middle school and high school students in Canada have experienced sexual coercion?
2. What factors predispose men to be sexually aggressive?
3. When child molesters are released from prison, how likely are they to reoffend?
4. What behaviours in the workplace count as sexual harassment?

Read this chapter to find out.

LEARNING OBJECTIVES

After studying this chapter, you will be able to

LO1 Describe the offences in the *Criminal Code of Canada* that relate to sexual assault, and contrast these with the statute on rape before 1983.

LO2 Discuss the Canadian data on the reported frequency of sexual assault and sexual coercion.

LO3 Describe theories used to explain and factors that contribute to sexual assault.

LO4 Describe the emotional reactions and common physical injuries of victims of a sexual assault.

LO5 Profile men as victims of sexual assault.

LO6 Identify strategies that can prevent sexual assault and child sexual abuse.

LO7 Describe the offences in the *Criminal Code of Canada* that relate to child sexual abuse.

LO8 Summarize the Canadian data on the prevalence of child sexual abuse.

LO9 Describe the impact of child sexual abuse on the victim.

LO10 Differentiate child molesters from pedophiles, and discuss the characteristics of pedophiles.

LO11 Give examples of the treatment options available for sex offenders, and explain the controversy surrounding the National Sex Offender Registry.

LO12 Define and discuss, with examples, the different forms of sexual harassment.

Eboni's basic education about sex came from what she saw and the direct experiences that she had. When she was 5, she and her brother were wrestling with their uncle. Suddenly her uncle locked her brother out of the room and began taking off Eboni's clothes. He held her down on the bed and began to penetrate her but stopped abruptly. Eboni was frightened of him from then on. She didn't really understand what he intended to do or why he wanted to do it, but she knew that his behavior was unexpected and strange. . . .

Eboni's grandmother and father insisted that she not talk to strangers or take money from them. Eboni understood why—she knew that being molested meant being raped. But strangers were not the predators.*

*Wyatt (1997, pp. 72–73).

This chapter is about sexual activity that involves coercion and is not between consenting adults; specifically, we will consider sexual assault, child sexual abuse, and sexual harassment at work, in education, and by professionals. All these topics have been highly publicized in the last 20 years, and much good scientific research on them has appeared.

LO1

Sexual Assault

In the last two decades, there has been a movement toward seeing crimes involving force in sexual relations as crimes of violence and victimization rather than as sex crimes. In 1983, the *Criminal Code of Canada* was amended to accommodate this different understanding and to protect victims. Before 1983, the *Criminal Code* had four sections that prohibited forced sexual activity: rape, attempted rape, indecent assault against a female, and indecent assault against a male. At that time, the legal definition of rape was forced heterosexual intercourse by a man with a woman who was not his wife (see Table 16.1). The rape law was criticized on a number of grounds. First, rape was limited to forced heterosexual intercourse. Second, it defined the assailant as male and the victim as female. Thus, women could not be charged with rape, and men could not be victims of rape. Third, husbands could not be charged with raping their wives, meaning that a woman could not legally refuse her husband's demands. Fourth, the victim's prior sexual activities could be considered as evidence of her consent and of the credibility of her testimony, effectively putting her past on trial. In addition, the law had a number of provisions that made the criminal justice system unresponsive to sexual assault complaints. It specifically required corroboration that the crime of rape actually took place. The judge was obliged to inform the jury that they should not convict only based on the complainant's testimony (Los, 1994). Finally, rape complaints that were not made immediately after the

Table 16.1 The Offence of Rape in the *Criminal Code of Canada* in 1968

In 1983, three sexual assault offences replaced this offence (see Table 2.1 for a description of the current offences).

A male person commits rape when he has sexual intercourse with a female person who is not his wife,

a. Without her consent, or
b. With her consent if the consent
   i. Is extorted by threats or fear of bodily harm
   ii. Is obtained by impersonating her husband, or
   iii. Is obtained by false and fraudulent representations as to the nature and quality of the act.

attack were invalidated. These provisions meant that it was extremely difficult to get a conviction if there was no physical evidence (such as physical injury) or when the complaint was not filed immediately. In fact, the majority of complaints of rape did not result in a conviction (Clark & Lewis, 1977; Siegel & McCormick, 1999).

In 1983, the *Criminal Code* was amended so that the offences of rape and indecent assault were replaced with three gender-neutral crimes of sexual assault. The differences in these crimes depend on the amount of force used to carry out the assault and the degree of injury sustained by the victim, not on the nature of the forced sexual activity. The purpose of these changes was to de-emphasize the sexual nature of the offence, stress their violent nature, encourage victims to report these crimes to the police, and improve the court procedure to reduce trauma to victims and increase the rate of convictions (Roberts & Gebotys, 1992). The three levels of sexual assault parallel the three levels of physical assault in the *Criminal Code:* (simple) sexual assault, sexual assault with a weapon causing serious injury or endangering the life of the victim or causing bodily harm, and aggravated sexual assault (refer to Table 2.1 for a description of these offences).

Sexual assault[1] includes a variety of nonconsensual sexual experiences ranging from unwanted touching to forced oral, anal, or vaginal intercourse and sexual violence causing serious physical injury or disfigurement to the victim. In keeping with the equality provisions of the *Charter of Rights and Freedoms,* the law is written in gender-neutral terms so that either men or women can be the victim of a sexual assault and can be charged with sexual assault, and the statute no longer discriminates against married people. The crucial point is that the activity is nonconsensual—that is, the victim did not consent to it. The *Criminal Code* also defines *consent* for the purposes of sexual assault offences. Consent must be actively established. Silence, inaction, or ambiguous conduct is not consent. There is no consent if the complainant is drunk or unconscious, if the complainant shows by his or her actions that he or she is not in agreement, or if the complainant consents to engage in sexual activity and then changes his or her mind. Children under age 16 cannot be considered to have consented to sexual activity with an adult as this is considered child sexual abuse (discussed later in this chapter).

There were also some provisions that related to court proceedings, such as limiting the questioning of victims about their sexual history in sexual assault trials (often referred to as the *rape shield laws*) and no longer requiring corroboration of the victim's testimony. However, because of court challenges, there are now some conditions under which the judge can admit the victim's sexual history as evidence. Advocacy groups, such as the Women's Legal Education and Action Fund (LEAF), argue that myths and stereotypes about sexual assault still influence many judges, such as the mistaken belief that many women make false allegations about sexual assault, and thus, contrary to the will of Parliament, judges frequently permit sexual history evidence (Busby, 1999).

L02 Statistics

The 2009 Canadian General Social Survey asked both women and men under age 65 about their experiences of criminal sexual assault: 3.4 percent of the women and 1.5 percent of the men reported that they had experienced sexual assault in the previous 12 months (Perreault & Brennan, 2010). Most of the perpetrators (87 percent) were male. Most of these sexual assaults (81 percent) were the least serious type of sexual assault; the remainder involved threats or actual violence. In about half of these incidents, the perpetrator was someone the victim knew.

What about university students specifically? A survey of university students at 82 public and private universities and colleges across Canada found that, in the previous year, 10.7 percent had experienced sexual

touching without their consent, 3.6 percent nonconsensual attempted sexual penetration, and 2.0 percent nonconsensual sexual penetration. Between three and five times as many women as men reported having had these nonconsensual sexual experiences (American College Health Association, 2016).

Few of these individuals had reported their experience to the police. Thus, statistics from police reports represent only a small proportion of sexual assaults in Canada. In 2015, there were 21 362 sexual assaults reported to the police. The rate of reported sexual assault has been decreasing since the 1990s. Some of the reasons that women choose not to report their sexual assault to the police were believing that the police could not do anything, wanting to keep the event private, feeling ashamed or embarrassed, being afraid of not being believed, fearing the perpetrator, and not wanting the perpetrator to be arrested (Kong et al., 2003; Lievore, 2003). Another reason why women may choose not to report is that there is an extremely low probability that doing so will result in a criminal conviction (SIECCAN, 2015).

> **What percentage of middle school and high school students in Canada have experienced sexual coercion?**

Individuals with disabilities are at greater risk of experiencing sexual assault than are individuals without disabilities—more than four times as likely in one study (Martin et al., 2006).

The following discussion starts with sexual assault by men against women because this is the most common type of sexual assault.

L03 Sexual Assault of Women by Acquaintances

Sexual assault by someone who is known to the victim, often called *date rape* (although it often doesn't occur on dates) or sexual assault by an acquaintance, is much more frequent than sexual assault by a stranger. How many women report these types of unwanted sexual experiences? Few, if we go by police reports; for example, in 2011 in Canada, 75 percent of the assaults that women reported to the police (10 680 women) were by someone they knew (Sinha, 2013). These figures likely underestimate the true rate of sexual assault because many women do not report their sexual assault to the police, particularly if it involves an acquaintance.

Indeed, research that examined sexual coercion in university or community samples found considerably higher numbers. These studies typically ask respondents about a range of unwanted sexual activity not only from threats or physical force but also from verbal coercion, such as continual

> **sexual assault:** Any nonconsensual sexual activity ranging from unwanted touching; to forced oral, anal, or vaginal intercourse; to sexual violence in which the victim is wounded or maimed or his or her life is endangered or when the victim is incapable of giving consent.

---

[1]Although many Canadians still use the term *rape* in everyday conversation—usually meaning forced sexual intercourse—in keeping with the *Criminal Code of Canada* we have chosen to use the term *sexual assault* in this chapter, except when studies specifically used the term *rape*.

arguments and pressure. Thus, some but not all of these unwanted experiences would meet a legal definition of sexual assault. A study in Ontario found that 48 percent of university women reported having experienced coerced sexual activity involving pressure or force (Hartwick et al., 2007). Another Ontario study found that 59 percent of women had experienced some form of sexual victimization, with 24 percent reporting forced oral, anal, or vaginal sex (Senn et al., 2014). Similarly, 44 percent of middle school and high school girls in New Brunswick reported having had a sexually coercive experience with a boyfriend; 17 percent of boys reported that they had been sexually abusive (Sears & Byers, 2010; Sears et al., 2007). More than half of these girls (57 percent) were upset by the experience. Many women do not recognize that what happened to them was sexual assault because it occurred in a dating situation, often after the couple had engaged in consensual sexual activity at a lower level (e.g., kissing). Nonetheless, research in Ontario has demonstrated that sexual coercion by a dating partner is associated with depression, lower self-esteem, and more negative sexual self-perceptions (Offman & Matheson, 2004).

Miscommunication may contribute to sexual assault in dating relationships. Research has shown that many men still hold to the traditional view that a woman who says "no" really means "yes" (Osman, 2003). Others believe that because a woman gave consent to, for example, kissing at the beginning of a sexual encounter, she has given consent to engaging in sexual intercourse. Films that portray women as enjoying sex resulting from sexual coercion by men reinforce this myth. Men need to learn that "No" means "No" whether it occurs before or during the sexual encounter. They also need to learn that only "Yes" means "Yes" (Muehlenhard et al., 2016). Consider this example of miscommunication and different perceptions in a case of sexual assault by an acquaintance:

Bob: Patty and I were in the same statistics class together. She usually sat near me and was always very friendly. I liked her and thought maybe she liked me, too. Last Thursday I decided to find out. After class I suggested that she come to my place to study for midterms together. She agreed immediately, which was a good sign. That night everything seemed to go perfectly. We studied for a while and then took a break. I could tell that she liked me, and I was attracted to her. I was getting excited. I started kissing her. I could tell that she really liked it. We started touching each other and it felt really good. All of a sudden she pulled away and said "Stop." I figured she didn't want me to think that she was "easy" or "loose." A lot of girls think they have to say "no" at first. I knew once I showed her what a good time she could have, and that I would respect her in the morning, it would be OK. I just ignored her protests and eventually she stopped struggling. I think she liked it but afterward she acted bummed out and cold. Who knows what her problem was?

Patty: I knew Bob from my statistics class. He's cute and we are both good at statistics, so when a tough midterm was scheduled, I was glad that he suggested we study together. It never occurred to me that it was anything except a study date. That night everything went fine at first, we got a lot of studying done in a short amount of time, so when he suggested we take a break I thought we deserved it. Well, all of a sudden he started acting really romantic and started kissing me. I liked the kissing but then he started touching me below the waist. I pulled away and tried to stop him but he didn't listen. After a while I stopped struggling; he was hurting me and I was scared. He was so much bigger and stronger than me. I couldn't believe it was happening to me. I didn't know what to do. He actually forced me to have sex with him. I guess looking back on it I should have screamed or done something besides trying to reason with him but it was so unexpected. I couldn't believe it was happening. I still can't believe it did. (Hughes & Sandler, 1987, p. 1)

Excerpted with permission from *Friends Raping Friends: Could It Happen to You?* Copyright 1987 by the Association of American Colleges and Universities.

Two factors seem to explain why sexually aggressive men misperceive women's communications. First, men in general tend to misperceive women's warmth and friendliness as indicating sexual interest, a pattern found in numerous studies (Farris et al., 2008; Perilloux et al., 2012). Second, sexually aggressive men are likely to have a "suspicious schema," meaning that they generally believe that women do not communicate honestly, particularly when the woman communicates clearly and assertively that she is rejecting an advance (Malamuth & Brown, 1994). These men choose to ignore verbal and nonverbal refusals, even when they are clear (Senn, 2013). However, recent research has questioned the miscommunication hypothesis and suggests that for the most part men do understand women's refusals as refusals (Beres et al., 2013; Muehlenhard et al., 2016).

This raises the question of what constitutes consent to sexual activity; that is, many sexual assault awareness programs emphasize the importance of obtaining consent before engaging in sexual activity, but often these programs do not clearly define what does and does not count as consent. It is quite complicated to define consent (Muehlenhard et al., 2016). Is it a person's internal state of willingness? If so, how can someone know what the other person's internal state is? Is it an act of explicitly agreeing to an activity, such as saying "I will have sex with you"? If so, does one only have to obtain explicit consent once or is obtaining consent a continuous process? Another complication is that explicit consent is not part of most people's sexual script and thus is rarely used. Rather most people communicate consent nonverbally. Or, can consent be inferred from various behaviours even if explicit consent is not given? If so, what are the behaviours from which we can and cannot infer consent? An affirmative consent standard (such as in Canadian law) makes it clear that consent cannot be assumed just because a person does not express nonconsent (there can be lots of reasons why someone does not express nonconsent, including being drunk and afraid).

A frightening problem today is the emergence of the so-called date-rape drugs. There are three major types: Rohypnol, GHB, and ketamine. Numerous cases have been reported of men who slipped the drug into a woman's drink and then sexually assaulted her. Rohypnol (row-HIP-nawl; *roofie, roachie, La Rocha, forget pills, pasta, peanuts, whiteys, ropes*) is the drug name for flunitrazepam. The drug causes drowsiness or sleep, and the man sexually assaults the woman while she is incapacitated. The drug also causes the woman not to remember the event the next day. GHB (*liquid G, G, Georgia home boy, easy lay, grievous bodily harm*), the drug name for gamma hydroxybutyrate, produces similar effects to alcohol but can cause hallucinations in larger doses and when mixed with alcohol can lead to loss of consciousness. Ketamine (*K, vitamin K, special K*) causes a combination of amnesia and hallucinations. Ecstasy (*Adam, XTC, bean, E, M, roll*) and Foxy Methoxy are also sometimes used as date-rape drugs. Several strategies for avoiding this situation have been suggested, including, especially, not accepting a drink from a stranger and never leaving your drink unattended. In addition to these drugs, there are a number of other substances that have been used to facilitate sexual assault, often termed *drug-facilitated sexual assault* because they result in disinhibition, drowsiness, or amnesia. These drugs include alcohol, marijuana, and tranquilizers (du Mont et al., 2009).

Partner Sexual Assault of Women

The definition of sexual assault in the *Criminal Code of Canada* includes nonconsensual sex with a spouse, common-law partner, or other intimate partner. How common is **partner sexual assault**? Community-based surveys indicate that of women who have experienced forced intercourse, more than half (51 percent) were assaulted by an intimate partner (Black et al., 2011). However, few of these women report the assault to the police; for example, between 2009 and 2014 in 2011, only 2 percent of sexual assaults reported to police were by a legal or common-law spouse. The trauma to the woman who is sexually assaulted by an intimate partner is, of course, no less severe than other forms of sexual assault (Bennice & Resick, 2003; Brousseau et al., 2011).

One phenomenon that emerges from the research is an association between nonsexual and sexual violence in long-term relationships—that is, the man who batters his female partner is also likely to force her to have sex. Quebec researchers have shown that 80 percent of the women in a shelter for battered women reported having experienced both physical and sexual violence in their relationship (Moreau et al., 2015).

A man might sexually assault his female partner from many motives, including anger, power and domination, sadism, or a desire for sex regardless of whether she is willing (Russell, 1990). In some cases the man is extremely angry, perhaps in the middle of a family argument, and he expresses his anger toward his partner by sexually assaulting her. In other cases, power and domination of the female partner seem to be the motive; for example, the woman may be threatening to leave him. Finally, some sexual assaults occur because the man believes his female partner "owes" him sex.

L04 The Impact of Sexual Assault on Women

Compared with nonvictimized women, women who have experienced sexual assault are more likely to show several types of psychological distress, including anxiety, depression, suicide ideation and attempts, and **post-traumatic stress disorder (PTSD)** (Martin et al., 2011). This is true of both women sexually assaulted by a stranger and those sexually assaulted by an acquaintance or a date (Koss, 1993; Neville & Heppner, 1999). PTSD is defined as the long-term psychological distress suffered by someone who has experienced a terrifying, uncontrollable event (Figure 16.1). Originally developed to describe the long-term psychological distress suffered by war veterans, most of whom are men, it later became clear that female

> **partner sexual assault:** The sexual assault of a person by his or her current or former marital or common-law spouse or other intimate partner.
> **post-traumatic stress disorder (PTSD):** Long-term psychological distress suffered by someone who has experienced a terrifying event.

Figure 16.1 Many women experience severe emotional distress after a sexual assault, and it is important that crisis counselling be available to them.

© Photofusion Picture Library/Alamy

First Person

A Sexual Assault Victim Tells Her Story

During my second year at university, I realized that I wanted to socialize more. I broke up with my hometown honey, began attending parties, started drinking, and dated other guys at my school. I was a virgin and didn't want to be anymore. I met my second boyfriend in physics. "G" was a football player and a big, handsome man, the best-looking man I'd ever met. We began to date and at first it was wonderful. He even carried me home once from a party, and I thought, "This is the one." Our first attempt at intercourse was difficult, and I began to beg him to stop, but he just kept trying until he was successful and there was blood everywhere. It was awful.

I continued to date G, but he began to act very differently. When he drank, he became extremely violent, and on different occasions I watched him break a vending machine and pull a toilet out of a wall at a university residence. He was unhappy with the way he was treated on the football team. He demanded to know where I was at all times and accused me of cheating on him. I wanted to break up with him, especially since sex was rough and not always consensual, but I was scared of him. I tried avoiding him but he always found me.

One night, G arrived very drunk at a party I was attending. I tried to sneak out of the party. He noticed I left and ran out after me. I didn't want trouble so I drove him to his dorm. He claimed he was too drunk to walk to his dorm, so I tried to help him into his room. When I turned around to leave, he sprang up and locked me in. He attacked me. I tried fighting him, but he wouldn't listen or stop. He hit my head into the wall several times and tried to force me to perform oral sex. I bit him, and that made him more angry. He then tried to force anal sex, and I fought as hard as I could. I finally started crying, and he stopped when he lost his erection. The rest of the night, I felt completely trapped in his dorm room. I lay awake all night and tried to leave, but he would wake up and stop me. I've never forgotten how scared I felt that entire night. He got up that morning and showered and acted as if nothing had happened. He was in all my classes for the rest of my university career.

I began to drink very heavily afterward. I told my roommate, J, and another woman on my floor, D. I never thought to report it, since he was my "boyfriend."

A year and a half later, I began to hear voices. It was a male voice calling me a fucking bitch, whore, and other names. I thought I was going crazy and became very depressed. I decided I must be schizophrenic and decided to kill myself.

Soon after, I was shopping in a bookstore. I saw this title staring right at me, *I Never Called It Rape*. I started reading it right there in the store, and I began crying and thinking, "This is what happened to me." I spoke with a faculty member, who arranged for immediate counselling.

The first time I went to see the counsellor, I couldn't even speak. I sat in her office and cried for the entire hour. She kept saying, "It's not your fault, it's not your fault." I couldn't believe it. Later we discussed how most of the times G and I had sex had actually been sexual assault, including the first and the last. I participated in a "Take Back the Night March." Members of one male residence threw bottles at us.

I went through medical school and residency. During my first year of residency, I was assaulted again, this time by a man in a stairwell during a New Year's Eve party at a hotel. I started screaming, "You're raping me, you're raping me!" He stopped and I got away! But I didn't go to the ER, I just went home and crawled in bed. My old shame came back. I began to drink heavily again. One night I drank all night and never showed up to work that next morning. I finally rolled into my director's office, depressed, hung over, and still smelling of alcohol, and my boss said I had to stop and straighten up right away or he wouldn't let me back for the next year. So I stopped drinking. I also made two very good friends around the same time. Through their support, I really turned my life around.

Three years later, I moved to a different city. I was living alone for the first time and had a great deal of anxiety. I joined a Sexual Assault Survivors Support Group. Then in the spring, I was invited to speak at my old university for Career Day for high school students, so I went back there ten years after the incidents. I was finally successful in my career, had strong, loving relationships with my friends and parents, and was happy. I look back at what happened now and think that I really survived a lot. I feel it helps me to be a better physician because I can empathize with how bad life can be for people.

Source: Based on an interview conducted by Janet Hyde.

survivors of sexual assault show these same symptoms characteristic of PTSD (Koss & Figueredo, 2004). Typical symptoms can include anxiety, depression, nightmares, and not feeling safe.

According to the cognitive-behavioural view of PTSD, people who have experienced a terrifying event form a memory schema that involves information about the situation and their responses to it (Foa et al., 1989). Because the schema is large, many cues can trigger it and thereby evoke the feelings of terror that occurred at the time; the schema is probably activated at some level all the time. The consequences can be far-reaching and long-lasting.

Most women who experience a sexual assault have negative psychological reactions immediately afterward. Many, but not all, show significant recovery within a year (Martin et al., 2011). A number of factors are associated with worse psychological outcomes: whether the woman has experienced sexual violence previously (i.e., this is a revictimization), the severity of the violence (more severe violence is associated with worse outcomes), and the reactions of others when the woman discloses the assault (negative reactions from others produce worse psychological outcomes). See First Person for one woman's account of these effects on her life. The good news is that psychotherapeutic treatments for PTSD are available and they are successful in treating sexual assault survivors (Resick et al., 2012).

Some women experience self-blame (Cairns, 1993). A woman may spend hours agonizing over what she did to bring on the sexual assault or what she might have done to prevent it: "If I hadn't worn that tight sweater . . ."; "If I hadn't been dumb enough to walk on that dark street . . ."; "If I hadn't been stupid enough to trust that guy. . . ." Or she may *know* that she is not to blame but nonetheless feel guilty—that is, experience emotional self-blame but not cognitive self-blame (Glenn & Byers, 2009). Self-blame is a result of a tendency on the part of society to *blame the victim* and excuse the perpetrator and is linked to worse long-term psychological outcomes for victims (Glenn & Byers, 2009; Koss & Figueredo, 2004). People are particularly likely to blame the victim if she voluntarily used alcohol or drugs, even when the perpetrator used physical force (Girard & Senn, 2008).

Researchers are finding increased evidence of the damage to women's *physical health* that may result from sexual assault (de Visser et al., 2007; Golding, 1999; Paras et al., 2009). Women may suffer physical injuries, such as cuts and bruises and vaginal pain and bleeding. Women who have been forced to have oral sex may suffer irritation or damage to the throat. Women forced to have anal intercourse report rectal bleeding and pain. A sexually assaulted woman may contract a sexually transmitted infection, such as HIV/AIDS or herpes. In about 5 percent of cases involving forced intercourse,

pregnancy results (Koss et al., 1991). Women who have been sexually or physically assaulted at some time in the past visit their physician twice as often per year as non-victimized women (Koss et al., 1991).

Sexual assault affects many people in addition to the victim—women in general, partners of victims, and the victim's friends. For example, most women routinely do a number of things that stem from fears of sexual assault even though they have never experienced sexual assault. That is, many women, when getting into their car at night, almost reflexively check the back seat to make sure no one is hiding there. In addition, most university women avoid walking alone through dark parts of the campus at night. In the Violence Against Women Survey (Statistics Canada, 1993), 60 percent of women reported feeling worried when walking alone in their neighbourhood after dark. Most women experience the fear of sexual assault, if not sexual assault itself, and this fear restricts their activities (Parrot & Cummings, 2006; Senn & Dzinas, 1996).

Spouses or partners of victims and the victim's friends may also be profoundly affected. At the same time, they can provide important support for the woman as she recovers (see First Person).

New research in psychology indicates that not everyone who experiences a serious traumatic event develops PTSD. Some, in fact, display **post-traumatic growth**—that is, positive life changes and psychological development following exposure to trauma (Tedeschi et al., 1998). Research with sexual assault survivors confirms that some do report positive life changes, such as an increased ability to take care of themselves, a greater sense of purpose in life, and greater concern for others in similar situations (Frazier et al., 2004).

Causes of Sexual Assault against Women

To provide a perspective for the discussion that follows, we can distinguish among three major theoretical views of the nature of sexual assault (Baron & Straus, 1989; Zurbriggen, 2010).

1. *Psychopathology of sex offenders:* This theoretical view holds that sexual assault is an act committed by a psychologically disturbed man. His deviance is responsible for the crime occurring.
2. *Feminist:* Feminist theorists and learning theorists view sexual assault as the product of gender-role socialization in our culture, which reinforces and legitimizes male aggression in general and sexual coercion specifically. Feminists also have theorized about the complex

post-traumatic growth: Positive life changes and psychological development following exposure to trauma.

links between sex and power: In some assaults, men use sex to demonstrate their power over women; in other assaults, men use their power over women to get sex. Feminists also point to the eroticization of violence in our society. Gender inequality is both the cause and the result of sexual assault in this view.

3. *Social disorganization:* Sociologists believe that crime rates, including sexual assault rates, increase after disruption to the social organization of a community. Under such conditions the community cannot enforce its norms against crime.

You personally may subscribe to one or more of these views. It is also true that researchers in this area have generally based their work on one of these theoretical models, which may influence their research. Keep these models in mind as you read the rest of this chapter.

> **What factors predispose men to be sexually aggressive?**

What do the data say? Research indicates that a number of factors contribute to sexual assault, ranging from forces at the cultural level to factors at the individual level. These factors include the following: cultural values, sexual scripts, early family influences, peer-group influences, characteristics of the situation, miscommunication, sex and power motives, and masculinity norms and men's attitudes. The data on each of these factors are considered here.

Cultural values can serve to support sexual assault. In the International Dating Violence Study, researchers collected data from university students at 38 sites around the world, including in the United States, Asia, Europe, Latin America, and the Middle East (Hines, 2007). The results indicated that the more hostility that men from a culture expressed toward women on questionnaires, the higher the rate of women reporting being sexually coerced.

Sexual scripts play a role in sexual aggression as well (Byers, 1996; Krahé et al., 2007). Adolescents quickly learn society's expectations about dating and sex through culturally transmitted sexual scripts. These scripts support sexual assault when they convey the message that the man is supposed to be oversexed and be the sexual "aggressor" (see Chapter 13 for a discussion of the traditional sexual script). By adolescence, both girls and boys endorse scripts that justify sexual aggression. A New Brunswick study of almost 1700 middle school and high school students found that about 11 percent of boys believe that it is acceptable for boys to be sexually coercive with a girlfriend (Price & Byers, 1999; Sears et al., 2007). Boys who were sexually abusive but not abusive in other ways (i.e., physically or psychologically) were more accepting of sexual dating violence and had friends who were sexually abusive. This suggests that these boys see sexual coercion as a normal part of the sexual script.

Early family influences may play a role in shaping a man into becoming a sexual aggressor. Specifically, young men who are sexual aggressors are more likely to have been sexually abused themselves in childhood (Seto et al., 2010).

The peer group can be a powerful factor in men's sexually aggressive behaviour. For example, a national study of 1300 Canadian male college and university students found that men who had abusive friends were more likely to have used sexual aggression (DeKeseredy & Kelly, 1993; DeKeseredy & Schwartz, 1998). It may be that aggressive friends encourage men to be sexually aggressive. It also may be that sexually aggressive men choose friends who have similar attitudes.

Characteristics of the situation play a role. Sexual assault is more likely to occur in secluded places or at parties at which excessive alcohol is used (Koss et al., 1994). Another situational factor is social disorganization, as noted earlier. An extreme example is war, in which sexual assault of women is common (Zurbriggen, 2010). We see graphic examples in Darfur, Sudan, where roving units called *Janjaweed* (armed men on horses) terrorize the local civilians, including through sexual assault of the women (Parrot & Cummings, 2006).

Miscommunication between women and men is a factor. In our discussion of sexual assault in dating relationships, we saw a case in which the man and the woman had totally different understandings of what had occurred. Because many people in Canada find it difficult to discuss sex, they most often do not ask their partner for sexual consent directly but rather try to infer sexual interest from subtle nonverbal cues, a process that is highly prone to errors (Humphreys & Brousseau, 2010). For example, some men may interpret a woman's friendly or affectionate behaviour or sexy clothing as carrying a sexual message that she did not intend (Farris et al., 2006; Lindgren et al., 2008).

Sex and power motives are involved in sexual assault. Feminists have stressed that sexual violence is an expression of power and dominance by men over women (Parrot & Cummings, 2006; Zurbriggen, 2010). Current theory emphasizes that sexual motives and power motives are both involved and interact with each other. For example, using phallometric assessment, researchers in Ontario examined differences in physiological arousal to consensual and nonconsensual sexual scenarios between a group of men convicted of sexual assault, a group of men convicted of nonsexual crimes, and a group of men from the community. The violent nonsexual criminals and men from the community were more aroused by hearing about consensual sex than by hearing about forced sex. However, the sex offenders showed little difference in their arousal to consenting and sexual assault scenarios (Lalumière et al., 2003).

What to Do after a Sexual Assault

If You Have Been Sexually Assaulted

Tell someone you trust. Sexual assault is a traumatic violation of the person. Especially in the beginning it is helpful to be with someone who will listen to your feelings and help you carry out your decisions. If you can't tell a friend or a family member, call a sexual assault crisis line.

Decide whether to report the assault to the police. This is your decision. If you decide to report, call the police as soon as possible and preserve evidence of the crime. Do not wash, change your clothes, bathe, shower, or douche until you have a medical exam. Save anything that was involved as it may be needed as evidence.

Seek medical attention. Whether or not you decide to report the assault to the police, it is important that you see a doctor to treat any physical injuries and check for STIs and pregnancy. If pregnancy seems likely, emergency contraception can be used (see Chapter 7). You have the right to have forensic evidence collected, whether or not you choose to report the sexual assault to the police at that time, so that the evidence is available if you later decide to report it. The hospital will use a sexual assault forensic kit to collect evidence such as scrapings, semen, blood, and hair. It is important that this be done within 72 hours of the assault.

Understand that it is normal to experience a wide range of emotions. Emotions such as anger, sadness, detachment, depression, fear, and being out of control are normal responses to sexual assault. It will take time to recover. Taking control over the little things in your life, and later the bigger things, can be one step on the road to recovery.

Understand that the assault was not your fault. You may feel guilty or that you were somehow to blame and the attack was somehow your fault. Sexual assault is a crime, and it was not your fault.

If Someone You Know Has Been Sexually Assaulted

Believe them. Sexual assault survivors may fear not being believed. Accept their version of the facts and be supportive. Sexual assault survivors react differently; not having an emotional reaction may indicate that they are in shock.

Listen to them. Find somewhere to be alone with them, and let them talk. Be patient. Let them tell their story at their own speed and in their own way. They may need to talk at odd hours or a great deal in the beginning.

Comfort them and provide security. Try to calm and ground them if they are anxious or upset. Do this in a soothing, not a disapproving, way. They may not want to be held or touched, but you can still nurture them by offering tea, a blanket, a comfortable chair, a favourite object, and so on. Help them feel safe by offering to find them a secure place to sleep and companionship when they return home.

Tell them it was not their fault. Do not judge. Avoid questions that seem to blame them for their actions. Avoid "why" questions such as "Why didn't you fight harder?" or "Why did you go to their room?" Let them know that it was the aggressor's fault, not theirs.

Encourage action. Suggest calling a sexual assault crisis centre. A sexual assault crisis worker is experienced in talking to survivors and can understand the survivors' needs and offer useful resources. Medical assistance also may be important, depending on the nature of the assault. If they agree to medical assistance, go with them to the hospital, clinic, or doctor's office. Stay during the examination if they want you to.

Let them make the decisions. Sexual assault survivors need to regain their feeling of control. You can help with this by giving referrals and resources but letting them make the decisions.

Help them decide whether to report the assault. If they decide to report the assault, encourage them to preserve any evidence. They should not take a shower or remove their clothes until they are examined at a hospital. However, even if the person did take a shower and then decided to be examined, evidence may still be collected.

Recognize your own limitations. Take time out when you need it. Recognize when you have reached the limits of your abilities. Help them create a network of support and referrals. Put aside your feelings and deal with them elsewhere. If you have strong feelings, talk to another friend or a local hotline.

Source: Condensed from Hughes and Sandler (1987) and from materials developed by the Fredericton Sexual Assault Crisis Centre.

Finally, *masculinity norms and men's attitudes* are another factor (Abram et al., 2003; Zurbriggen, 2010), as we will see in the next section. Supporting the feminist theoretical view, research shows that men who have more hypermasculine attitudes are more likely to have a history of sexual aggression (Murnen et al., 2002).

The Role of Alcohol in Sexual Assault of Women

Research has established a link between alcohol consumption and sexual assault (Abbey, 2011; Abbey et al., 2014). Men who are intoxicated are more likely to commit a sexual assault than men who are not intoxicated. That finding is a correlation, though. Does it mean that alcohol actually plays a causal role? Or might it be that a man who wants to commit a sexual assault drinks to get himself ready, or perhaps to give himself an excuse. Or could it be that some third factor, such as impulsivity, accounts for the correlation? A man who is highly impulsive drinks too much and commits sexual assault. Researchers have spent a great deal of effort sorting out these possibilities.

First, let's consider the *effects of alcohol on the perpetrator*. Scientists have documented two categories of effects: pharmacological effects and psychological effects. *Pharmacological effects*, the actual effects of the drug on the body and behaviour, have been detected in laboratory experiments. Alcohol impairs higher cognitive functions such as complex decision-making, planning, and response inhibition (Abbey et al., 2014). These effects can be found at blood-alcohol concentrations (BAC) as low as 0.04, which is the equivalent of two drinks consumed over two hours. At a BAC of 0.08, the effects are large. For a man who is predisposed to commit sexual assault, alcohol can turn the predisposition into actual behaviour.

As for the *psychological effects*, alcohol is glamorized in our culture and is widely believed to improve men's sexual outcomes (Abbey, 2011). People believe that drinking alcohol will make them more sociable and sexually uninhibited. These beliefs create expectancy effects and they can be powerful. Moreover, the expectancy effects can amplify the actual pharmacological effects.

Let's consider one particular study to illustrate how researchers go about studying the pharmacological and psychological effects (Abbey et al., 2009). Male undergraduates first completed measures including past sexual assault perpetration and the trait of general hostility. A month later—so that they wouldn't perceive a connection with the earlier measures—the men were brought to the lab. They were randomly assigned to one of three experimental conditions: intoxicated, sober, or placebo. Those in the intoxicated group drank four vodka and tonics to bring their BAC to 0.08. The sober group

was given an equivalent amount of tonic. Those in the placebo group were told they were getting the vodka and tonic, but in fact there was no vodka in their drinks. Each participant then watched an eight-minute video designed to simulate a potential sexual assault situation with a date. The characters were Lisa and Mark, and participants were asked to imagine themselves as Mark. In a series of scenes, Lisa and Mark talk after a class and then meet at a party and spend time together, after which Mark invites Lisa to his apartment. They proceed to kiss and touch and the film fades out. The men were then asked a series of questions about whether they (Mark) would be justified in forcing sex.

The results indicated that alcohol consumption did not have a simple main effect on ratings of how justified it would be to force sex. However, there was an interaction between alcohol consumption and a man's trait level of hostility; among those in the intoxicated group, the higher the level of hostility, the greater the belief that forcing sex was justified. These findings demonstrate that, among men who are at risk of being a perpetrator (in this case, have high levels of hostility), alcohol consumption makes them feel more justified in committing sexual assault.

Turning now to the *effects of alcohol on victims*, the basic pharmacological effects are the same as they are for perpetrators. Alcohol consumption leads to a decline in cognitive functioning such as decision-making. Alcohol also leads to a reduction in anxiety, so that a woman may miss signs of danger in her environment. And alcohol consumption may lead women to be less effective in resisting an assault if one occurs (Stoner et al., 2007). Individuals who are consuming alcohol are perceived as being more sexually interested than those who are not drinking (Muehlenhard et al., 2016). None of these research findings are meant to blame the victim, of course. Instead, they point to the complex interactions between the perpetrator's drinking and the victim's drinking that contribute to sexual assault.

Men Who Are Sexually Aggressive against Women

There is no typical sexually aggressive man. Men who commit sexual assault against women vary tremendously in occupation, education, relationship status, previous criminal record, and motivation for committing sexual assault.

One thing we do know about sexually aggressive men is that they tend to be repeat offenders. In one study of men who admitted to sexual assault on a survey but had never been prosecuted, the majority had committed the crime more than once (Lisak & Miller, 2002). Those who were repeat offenders averaged about six sexual assaults each.

Compared with other men, men who commit sexual assault tend to have the following characteristics (Gannon & Ward, 2008; Thakker et al., 2008):

1. They hold a number of social cognitions or *implicit theories* that support sexual assault. They believe that women are sexual objects, that women are dangerous and deceptive, that the world in general is dangerous, that certain behaviours are uncontrollable in the face of strong urges, and they have a sense of entitlement involving male superiority and control.

2. They are more likely to have had brain injuries as a child, which may be related to the next deficit. Nonetheless, only about 4 percent of men who have committed sexual assault have had traumatic head injuries.

3. They are characterized by poor inhibition and self-regulation. In particular, they are unable to inhibit aggressive impulses.

4. They lack empathy (Senn et al., 2000). Specifically, they fail to understand the suffering that a sexual assault victim experiences.

5. They may have experienced environmental triggers, such as being in a war.

6. They are more likely themselves to have been victims of child sexual abuse (Jesperson et al., 2009).

These research findings have important implications for programs of therapy aimed at reducing the chance of men convicted of sexual assault reoffending (Marshall, 1993; Pithers, 1993; Thakker et al., 2008). They need training in empathy. In addition, therapy must challenge their cognitive distortions and denial that they did anything wrong.

Ethnicity and Sexual Assault against Women

We have seen how cultural context can promote or inhibit sexual assault. The cultural heritages of various ethnocultural groups in Canada provide different cultural contexts for people of those groups, so it is important to consider the incidence of sexual assault in Canadian ethnocultural communities. Participants in three of the communities that participated in the Ethnocultural Communities Facing AIDS study were asked whether they had ever been coerced or forced to have sex with someone against their will. The incidence of sexual coercion differed markedly from one community to the other. In the English-speaking Caribbean communities, 37 percent of the women and 19 percent of the men reported that they had experienced sexual coercion, compared to 8 percent of the women and 1 percent of the men in the

Latin American communities, and 5 percent of the men from the South Asian communities (Maticka-Tyndale et al., 1996). Interestingly, in the English-speaking Caribbean communities, people who had been in Canada longer were more likely to indicate that they had experienced sexual coercion. This suggests that sexual coercion is a more common experience in Canada than it is in the Caribbean.

Sometimes ethnic heritage can help. In Asian cultures, saving face is very important. For men from Asian communities in Canada, the potential for loss of face by committing sexual assault is a deterrent to such activity (Hall et al., 2005).

Historical factors may also affect the meaning of sexual assault. For example, many Canadian immigrants are refugees from conflict zones (for example, Bosnia and more recently Syria) where invading military forces instituted systematic campaigns of sexual violence against women (Valentich, 1994; Wolfe, 2013). Similarly, sexual assault has a highly charged meaning in the history of African Americans (Sommerville, 2004). In the period following the American Civil War, a black man convicted of rape or attempted rape of a white woman was typically castrated or lynched. In sharp contrast, there was no penalty for a white man who raped a black woman.

In some cultures, it is considered a wife's duty to have sex with her husband when he wants to. Might these cultural expectations affect how sexual assault—particularly spousal assault—is defined in these countries?

L05 Sexual Assault against Men

The sexual assault provisions in the *Criminal Code of Canada* apply equally to men and to women as victims. However, men were the victims in only 8 percent of sexual assault reported to the police (Sinha, 2013). Some authors believe, based on self-report studies, that there are more female sex offenders than indicated by police reports (Denov, 2003). Further, gay men also experience sexual coercion from their sexual partners (Gavey et al., 2009). For example, in one study 20 percent of a sample of gay and bisexual men reported having experienced unwanted sexual intercourse resulting from threats or use of force as an adult (Kalichman et al., 2001). It is important for counsellors and others in helping professions to recognize the possibility of male victims of sexual assault.

As with the statistics for women, estimates of the number of men who have experienced sexual coercion are higher when the data are based on university and community samples than when they are based on police reports. For example, research with undergraduate students across Canada found that 4.3 percent of the men reported sexual touching without their consent,

1.0 percent reported nonconsensual attempted penetration, and 0.5 percent reported nonconsensual penetration (American College Health Association, 2016). Many men are upset by these experiences (Byers & O'Sullivan, 1998; O'Sullivan et al., 1998). In a study of New Brunswick middle school and high school students, 33 percent of the boys reported that they had experienced sexual coercion; 5 percent of the girls reported that they had been sexually abusive (Sears & Byers, 2010; Sears et al., 2007). Only 19 percent of these boys were upset by the experience, however. Although both these studies showed that girls and women are more likely to experience sexual coercion than are boys and men, they also indicate that sexual coercion of men by women is not that infrequent.

These experiences are very upsetting for some men. For example, some men (straight and gay) who have been sexually assaulted experience symptoms of PTSD (Dunmore et al., 2001; Gold et al., 2007). Men who have been sexually assaulted also experience self-blame, guilt, and shame (Byers & Glenn, 2012). Research in Quebec has shown that in 20 percent of couples, sexual coercion is reciprocal (Brousseau et al., 2011).

Some of the same factors that contribute to sexual aggression by men also contribute to sexual aggression by women. They occur in similar heterosexual dating situations, and men and women use similar strategies to influence their partner to engage in the unwanted sexual activities, most often verbal forms of pressure or ignoring requests to stop (Byers & Glenn, 2012; Hartwick et al., 2007; O'Sullivan et al., 1998). Sexual scripts play a role as well. Research in Ontario has shown that many women believe the stereotype that men are always interested in sex (Clements-Schreiber et al., 1998). Thus, they may not believe that when a man says "No" he really means "No." For example, in a study of sexual coercion in a sample of university students, 58 percent of the men (and 78 percent of the women) reported being the objects of sexual persistence after they had refused sexual advances (Struckman-Johnson et al., 2003). Sexual persistence included using any of a number of tactics to have sexual contact with the respondent despite their initial refusal of the sexual advances. The persistence tactics assessed included persistent kissing and touching, the perpetrator taking off his or her own clothes, telling lies, and using physical restraints. One man said,

> At a party, she came up and began talking to me. I was already drinking some at the time. While playing cards, she talked me into finishing several of her drinks and beers. She said there was another party and convinced me to go. I was too drunk to drive so she drove us. The "party" seemed to lack other people. After about a half-hour of kissing/making out, I was tired and wanted to go home. She said no and told me she wanted to have sex. I said no, but she continued to kiss me and try to talk me into it. When she produced a condom, I gave in. (Struckman-Johnson et al., 2003, p. 83)

Research in Ontario found that male victims tend to be blamed more harshly for their victimization than female victims and female perpetrators blamed more leniently for their behaviour than male perpetrators (Rye et al., 2006). Men may be particularly unlikely to report a sexual assault if they are aware that they may be blamed for their own victimization.

Having recognized that some men are sexually coerced by women, it is important to note that the great majority of male victims of forced intercourse are sexually assaulted by men, not women (Calderwood, 1987). In particular, sexual coercion can be a problem in the relationships of men who have sex with men (Kalichman et al., 2001). Men who have been sexually assaulted by other men can experience very negative behavioural and psychological consequences (Walker et al., 2005). Sexual coercion also exists in women's same-sex relationships. This suggests that we need programs, as we have for heterosexual individuals, aimed at reducing sexual coercion in same-sex relationships (Kalichman et al., 2001).

Sexual Assault in Prison

According to a study of 516 male and female prisoners in U.S. prisons, 22 percent of the men and 7 percent of the women had been the objects of sexual coercion while in prison (Struckman-Johnson et al., 1996). Prison staff were the perpetrators in 18 percent of the cases, fellow prisoners in the remainder. Among the male victims, 53 percent had been forced to have receptive anal sex, sometimes with multiple male perpetrators, and 8 percent were forced to have receptive oral sex. The men reported severe emotional consequences.

Sexual assault in prison is a particularly clear example of the way in which sexual assault is an expression of power and aggression; prisoners—most of whom would identify as heterosexual—use it as a means of establishing a dominance hierarchy.

 ## Preventing Sexual Assault

Strategies for preventing sexual assault need to be aimed at both men and women. Although most programs are aimed at teaching women ways to avoid victimization, it is perhaps more important to develop programs for men.

To eliminate sexual assault of women, our society would need to make a radical change in the way it socializes males (Hall & Barongan, 1997). If little boys were not so pressed to be aggressive and tough, and were encouraged to express their feelings and to be nurturant to others there would be far fewer sexually aggressive men. If adolescent boys did not have to demonstrate that they are hypersexual, perhaps there would be few sexually aggressive men.

We also need prevention programs aimed at changing attitudes that contribute to sexual assault. These programs need to stress the importance of obtaining verbal consent and to provide behavioural strategies for doing so. Research in Ontario has shown that women more than men stress a need for active verbal consent in both new and ongoing relationships (Humphreys, 2007; Humphreys & Herold, 2007). Programs need to foster a climate in which sexually coercive behaviour is seen as unacceptable in such a way that men do not perceive the presenters to be "male bashing" (Figure 16.2). These types of perceptions can result in a backlash that increases attitudes and statements justifying men's use of sexual coercion. An infamous example is the response of some men to a "No Means No" campaign at Queen's University in Kingston—they hung banners out of the windows of male residences that read "No means more beer" and "No means tie her up."

Unfortunately, until society makes large changes, we still need to teach women to be vigilant and to recognize that they are in a sexual assault situation and to respond more strongly in these situations, while at the same time avoiding victim-blaming (Humphreys & Kennett, 2010; Jozkowski & Humphreys, 2014).

Research shows that fighting back—fighting, yelling, and fleeing—increases a woman's likelihood of thwarting a sexual assault attempt (Ahrens et al., 2008; Brecklin & Ullman, 2005; Zoucha-Jensen & Coyne, 1993). However, we also need to change how we socialize girls so that women are more comfortable being assertive and using self-defence.

Finally, to prevent sexual assault of men, we need to combat the cultural stereotype that men are always interested in sex. This belief may make it difficult for men to clearly and repeatedly refuse a sexual invitation, and may make men's partners less likely to believe men when they do say no. However, for people to be honest and open about their sexual interests, they will first need to become more comfortable talking about sex and less reliant on nonverbal communication.

A variety of types of sexual assault prevention programs have been tested, often in academic settings, such as with incoming first-year postsecondary students. A crucial aspect of effective programs involves having the participants actively practise skills (Gidycz et al., 2011). Passive programs with an expert lecturing to a

Figure 16.2 Students protest a video of a frosh-week chant at St. Mary's University in Halifax in 2013 that condoned nonconsensual sex with underage girls, correctly naming it sexual assault.

© THE CANADIAN PRESS/Andrew Vaughan

class are less effective. Peer-led programs that focus on a single gender in a small group (e.g., an athletic team) and for multiple sessions seem to be most effective. The programs generally are based on one of several strategies (Gidycz et al., 2011):

1. *Awareness-based programs* aim to raise people's awareness of the prevalence of sexual assault and thereby create community change.

2. *Empathy-based programs* seek to increase the audience's understanding of the consequences for victims, thereby increasing empathy for them.

3. *Social norms-based programs* encourage individuals to question the gender-role norms that support violence against women.

4. *Skills-based programs* teach people, especially women, skills that will decrease their risk of being the objects of sexual violence (e.g., avoid excessive drinking).

5. *Bystander intervention programs* encourage people to intervene if they see violence occurring. A three-hour bystander intervention program has been shown to increase students' confidence that they could intervene and change a number of attitudes and beliefs that would make them more ready to intervene (Senn & Forrest, 2015).

A sexual assault resistance program recently developed by Charlene Senn at the University of Windsor is designed to enhance women's ability to physically, verbally, and psychologically resist sexual coercion and assault (Senn et al., 2011; Senn, 2011, 2013). It has four three-hour units. Unit 1 focuses on increasing women's awareness of personal risk, helping them become more aware of situations that pose risk, and helping them develop problem-solving strategies to reduce risk and avoid the assault. Unit 2 helps women more quickly admit to themselves when they are in a coercive situation and deal with their emotional barriers to taking strong action in those situations. Unit 3 teaches women about the most successful tactics for resisting sexual coercion in different situations, including self-defence training. Unit 4 provides sexuality education to broaden women's sexual assertiveness (Figure 16.3). Research with high school and undergraduate students found that the program resulted in significant attitude change, greater confidence that they could defend themselves if attacked, and use of more effective methods of self-defence in hypothetical situations. A more recent evaluation of the program at the Universities of Windsor, Guelph, and Calgary found that one year after participating in the program, women were 46 percent less likely to reporting having experienced sexual assault compared to a control group (Senn et al., 2015).

Figure 16.3 Self-defence classes for women. Many experts believe that all women should take such classes to gain the skills necessary to defend themselves in the case of an attempted sexual assault.

© kolvenbach/Alamy Stock Photo

LO7

Child Sexual Abuse

In this section we discuss the broad category of child sexual abuse and one specific subcategory, intrafamilial sexual abuse—sexual abuse that occurs within the family.

There are currently several statutes in the *Criminal Code of Canada* related to the sexual exploitation of children, including sexual assault, sexual interference, invitation to sexual touching, and sexual exploitation (refer to Table 2.1). These offences apply to any type of sexual contact with a child by a man or a woman, showing pornography to a child, having a child witness sexual intercourse, or using a computer to facilitate committing a sexual offence against a child. Making, possessing, and distributing child pornography is also illegal and is discussed in Chapter 17.

The laws that seek to prevent the sexual exploitation of children and young people were amended in

1985, and new laws have been added since then. Many of the criticisms of the repealed rape law discussed earlier in this chapter also applied to the laws pertaining to sexual exploitation of children. For example, in most cases they applied only to girls (Busby, 1999). In contrast, the current provisions are gender-neutral and based on a combination of age, whether the accused is in a position of trust, and the specific activities that occurred. The age of consent is normally 16. This means that an adult accused of engaging in sexual activity with someone under 16 cannot defend himself or herself on the basis that the child agreed to the sexual activity. However, as shown in Figure 16.4, there are what are called "close in age" exceptions: a child who is 14 or 15 years old can legally have sex with someone who is less than five years older; a child of who is 12 or 13 years old can consent to nonexploitative sexual activity with adolescents less than two years older. A study conducted in British Columbia found that very few adolescents who had engaged in first intercourse at 14 or 15 years old had had a partner who was not "close in age"; however, 25 percent of the boys and 49 percent of the girls who had engaged in first intercourse at 12 or 13 had a first partner who would not fit the "close in age" exemption (Miller et al., 2010). The age of consent for anal intercourse is 18 and thus is higher than for vaginal intercourse. However, although the Supreme Court has ruled that this constitutes discrimination against gay youth and so the government has introduced legislation to change it to 16. The age of consent is also higher if the adult is in a position of trust or authority with a child, such as a teacher or sports coach. Under the sexual exploitation provision, it is an offence for a person in a position of trust to have sex with a child who is under 18 years old, whether or not the child consents to it.

The *Criminal Code* includes a law against incest. This statute prohibits sexual intercourse with a person who is a blood relative—that is, a parent, child, brother, sister, grandparent, or grandchild. Most prosecutions are cases involving children and adult relatives, although the incest statute is not specific to child sexual abuse. The nearly universal taboo against incest seems to have as its purposes the promise to children that the home will be a place where they can be free from sexual pressure and the prevention of the genetic problems of inbreeding.

The latest form of child sexual abuse involves **Internet sexual solicitation of youth** (Wolak et al., 2008). In such cases, a sexual predator meets a child or adolescent online, gains the youth's confidence, and arranges a face-to-face meeting. A well-sampled survey of youth between the ages of 10 and 17 found that 18 percent of girls and 8 percent of boys had received a sexual solicitation on the Internet (Mitchell et al., 2007). Only a few of those incidents resulted in an actual meeting, but the sexual solicitation itself can be distressing.

The court process can be stressful for the child who discloses the abuse. A number of Child Advocacy Centres have been established across Canada to help children through the aftermath of reporting the abuse.

 L08 ## Patterns of Child Sexual Abuse

How common is child sexual abuse? According to a meta-analysis of data across 22 countries, including Canada,

> **Internet sexual solicitation of youth:** Cases in which a sexual predator meets a child or adolescent online, gains the youth's confidence, and arranges a face-to-face meeting.

Figure 16.4 Ages of consent. Consent laws can often be confusing to understand, and are subject to change. The chart below may be useful when deciding if a particular relationship is consensual in the eyes of the law. Can consent be given if . . .

The youth is . . . → And the other person is . . . ↓	Under 12	12	13	14	15	16	17	18	19	20
Under 12	*	No	No	No	No	No	No	No	No	No
Same Age	No	Yes**	Yes**	Yes**	Yes**	Yes**	Yes**	Yes	Yes	Yes
Less Than 1 Year Older	No	Yes**	Yes**	Yes**	Yes**	Yes**	Yes**	Yes	Yes	Yes
Less Than 2 Years Older	No	Yes**	Yes**	Yes**	Yes**	Yes**	Yes**	Yes	Yes	Yes
Less Than 3 Years Older	No	No	No	Yes**	Yes**	Yes**	Yes**	Yes	Yes	Yes
Less Than 4 Years Older	No	No	No	Yes**	Yes**	Yes**	Yes**	Yes	Yes	Yes
Less Than 5 Years Older	No	No	No	Yes**	Yes**	Yes**	Yes**	Yes	Yes	Yes
More Than 5 Years Older	No	No	No	No	No	Yes**	Yes**	Yes	Yes	Yes

Other considerations: The law also provides for the protection of persons with mental or physical disabilities without any age restrictions.

*Children under the age of 12 cannot consent to any sexual activity with any other age. However, it is not an offence if two children under 12 engage in sexual activities.

**This does not apply if one of the individuals is in a position of trust or authority over the other, one is in a relationship of dependency with the other, or if the relationship between them is found to be exploitative.

22 percent of women and 8 percent of men had suffered some form of sexual abuse prior to age 18 (Pereda et al., 2009). Age 18 represents a broad definition of "child," but the statistics do not go down much if the age is set at 15 or even 12 (Freyd et al., 2005; Pereda et al., 2009). How about in Canada, specifically? According to the General Social Survey, 12 percent of women and 4 percent of men had experienced sexual abuse as a child. Similarly, research in Quebec using a telephone survey of 1002 adults found that 22 percent of the women and 10 percent of the men reported unwanted sexual activities by an adult or a child three or more years older than them before the age of 18 (Hébert et al., 2009). It seems clear that child sexual abuse is not rare and that girls are more often its victims than boys are.

Most cases of child sexual abuse are never reported. For example, in the National Population Survey, only about 20 percent of the victims had told anyone. Similarly, in the Quebec survey described above, 21 percent of adult who had experienced child sexual abuse (and more men than women) had never told anyone about the abuse. only 21 percent had disclosed the abuse within a month of its occurrence, and 51 percent did not disclose it until more than five years after the event (Hébert et al., 2009).

How many of these incidents are reported to the authorities? In 2012, there were 3.4 reported sexual offences against children per 1000 children in Canada. Reported sexual assaults for girls were more than three times as high as for boys; reports for youth between the ages of 12 to 17 were more than twice as high as for younger children. Of those complaints substantiated by police, most involve touching and fondling of the genitals (68 percent), attempted or completed sexual activity (35 percent), or adults exposing their genitals (12 percent) (Trocmé et al., 2001). Thus, in the great majority of cases, both for boys and girls, the sexual activity involves touching of the genitals without penetration (see also Hébert et al., 2009).

The great majority of perpetrators of child sexual abuse are men. According to the National Health and Social Life Survey (NHSLS), for girls, almost all the reported cases involved sexual contact with men; for boys, most cases involved men although some cases involved women. A number of factors probably account for this great imbalance. Men in our culture are socialized more toward seeing sexuality as focused on sexual acts rather than as part of an emotional relationship. The sexual script for men involves partners who are smaller and younger than them, whereas women's sexual script involves partners who are larger and older than they are.

Reports from 155 police departments in 2012 provide information regarding reported cases of sexual assault of children and youth in Canada (Cotter & Beaupré,

Table 16.2 Categories of People Who Were Accused of Sexual Offences against Children and Youth (ages 0 to 17 years) in 2012

Perpetrators	Percentage of Victims	
	Girls	Boys
Acquaintance*	44%	43%
Family	38	40
Stranger	12	6
Intimate partner	6	10

*Acquaintance includes any relationship in which the perpetrator and victim were familiar with each other but were not related or in a legal guardianship arrangement.

Source: Statistics Canada, 2011.

2014). Most (81 percent) of the child and youth victims of sexual offences were girls. Some of the sexual abuse was of children at very young ages (some under three years old); about 10 percent of cases of child sexual abuse occur before the child is 6 (Hébert et al., 2009). However, the rates are highest for 14- and 15-year-olds. Table 16.2 shows the relationship between these adults and their victims. Notice that sexual assault by a stranger is quite uncommon, accounting for only 12 percent of offences. In contrast, 38 percent of children and youth were sexually assaulted by a family member, including parents, siblings, and extended family members such as stepparents or grandparents.

Of particular concern is sexual abuse of children by a person in a position of trust or authority (Figure 16.5). One of the most publicized cases of this type of abuse was that of eight Roman Catholic priests and ten lay members of the Christian Brothers of Ireland in Canada, who were convicted of sexually abusing 77 boys at Mount Cashel Orphanage in St. John's, Newfoundland, in the 1970s. A number of priests in other parts of Canada and in the United States, as well as coaches, Scout leaders, teachers, and so on, have also been convicted of child sexual abuse. Many First Nations children attending residential schools and Aboriginal and non-Aboriginal boys in youth detention centres were sexually abused by persons charged with their care. In all these situations, individuals who had responsibility to protect the welfare of children used their power and authority to coerce children into engaging in sexual activity with them.

Intrafamilial Sexual Abuse

Incest is defined in the *Criminal Code of Canada* as sexual contact between blood relatives. Of particular concern is sexual abuse of children by an adult family

Figure 16.5 Sexual abuse outside the family is most often perpetrated by a person in a position of trust, such as (a) in the sexual abuse of Theo Fleury by his junior hockey coach, and (b) the sexual and physical abuse of Aboriginal children attending residential schools run by several different Christian churches—the subject of an Edmonton-to-Ottawa walk for justice by Robert Desjarlais in June 2000.

(a) © THE CANADIAN PRESS/Chris Young

(b) © CP Picture Archive/Jonathan Hayward

member, often called **intrafamilial sexual abuse**. Intrafamilial abuse includes child sexual abuse both by a blood relative and by a nonrelative who is the child's caregiver (e.g., by a stepfather) and is typically prosecuted under the sexual assault provisions of the *Criminal Code* (see Table 2.1).

The overwhelming majority of cases of intrafamilial child sexual abuse go unreported to authorities and so are not prosecuted. Nonetheless, court statistics (see Table 16.2) show that in 2009 family members were accused of 34 percent of the sexual assaults against children (Brzozowski, 2007). Data from the NHSLS based on adult recollections of incidents of sexual abuse in childhood, most of which were never reported, also show that a large percentage of cases are perpetrated by family members. Researchers found that 54 percent of the women and 20 percent of the men reported that the perpetrator was a family member.

LO9 Impact on the Victim

Child sexual abuse can have serious and long-lasting effects on the victim (Kendall-Tackett et al., 1993; Figure 16.5). Children who have experienced child sexual abuse are more likely to experience a variety of symptoms, including anxiety, depression, behaviour problems, health complaints, and thoughts of suicide

(Blanchard-Daillaire & Hébert, 2014; Brabant et al., 2013; Cyr & Hébert, 2011; Kendall-Tackett et al., 1993). For example, research in Quebec has shown that sexually abused children experience more symptoms associated with PTSD than do children who have experienced other life stressors, such as an orthopedic problem (Collin-Vézina & Hébert, 2005; Tremblay et al., 2000). They also have more social difficulties (Blanchard-Daillaire & Hébert, 2014). Boys who have experienced child sexual abuse are also more likely to engage in risky sexual behaviour in adolescence (Homma et al., 2012). Note that although children who have experienced sexual abuse are more likely to experience each of these symptoms, some sexually abused children do not experience any severe negative consequences. These resilient children appear to benefit from having both personal qualities and parents with qualities that protect them against the adverse consequences of child sexual abuse (Hébert et al., 2014). (See Milestones in Sex Research for a discussion of whether children who were victims of sexual abuse or other severe trauma can forget or suppress the memory.)

If a case is reported and prosecuted, the child may be as traumatized by testifying in court as by the abuse itself. Repeatedly testifying about severe abuse is

intrafamilial sexual abuse: Sexual contact between a child and an adult who is the child's relative or caregiver, such as a stepfather.

Milestones in Sex Research

False Memory Syndrome? Recovered Memory?

A topic that is extremely controversial concerns the issue of what some call *recovered memory* and what others call *false memory syndrome.* The issue is whether the child victim of sexual abuse or other severe trauma can forget (suppress) the memory of the event and later recover that memory.

On one side of the argument, the *recovered memory* side, psychotherapists see adult clients who display serious symptoms of prior trauma, such as severe depression and anxiety. Sometimes these clients have clear memories of being sexually abused in childhood and have always remembered the events but have never told anyone until they told the therapist. In other cases, the client does not remember that any abuse occurred but, during the process of therapy, or sometimes spontaneously before therapy, something triggers the memory and the client then recalls the sexual abuse.

On the other side, some psychologists believe that these memories for events that had been forgotten and then are remembered are actually *false memories;* that is, the events never occurred. They argue that unscrupulous or overzealous therapists may induce these memories by hypnotizing clients or strongly suggesting to clients that they had been abused in childhood. Even subtle suggestions by a well-intentioned therapist can produce false memories in susceptible individuals.

What do the data say? Research on the issue of child sexual abuse provides support for the idea that forgetting does occur in some cases. In one study, 129 women who were known to have been sexually abused as children—they had been brought to a hospital for treatment at the time and the abuse had been medically verified—were interviewed 17 years later; 38 percent did not remember the abuse (Williams, 1994). The possible flaw in this study is that some of the respondents may have remembered but not have reported it to the interviewer. However, they were reporting many other intimate sexual experiences, so it seems likely that they would report accurately about this one, too. In a study of adult women who reported to a researcher that they had been a victim of child sexual abuse, 30 percent said that they had completely blocked out any memory of the abuse for a full year or more (Gold et al., 1994). In an especially elegant study, children who were sexually abused and the cases prosecuted were studied at the time. A follow-up study more than ten years later, when the individuals were in their 20s, tested their memory for the earlier events (Alexander et al., 2005). Frequency of abuse was associated with worse memory for the events. Poor support from the mother at the time was also associated with worse memory.

Therefore, the evidence seems to indicate that in 30 to 40 percent of cases, memories of childhood sexual abuse

associated with worse mental health outcomes (Quas et al., 2005). Interestingly, the perpetrator receiving a light sentence is also associated with worse mental health outcomes for the child.

Research has demonstrated that many of the negative effects of child sexual abuse persist into adulthood. Canadian research has shown that, compared with controls, adults who were sexually abused as children display more depression, anxiety, eating disorders, psychological distress, and alcohol and drug dependence (Dion et al., 2016; LeClerc et al., 2010; Runtz & Roche, 1999). They also have more negative feelings about sexuality; have more sexual difficulties; have difficulty forming stable, safe romantic relationships; and are more likely to engage in extradyadic sexual activity (Frias et al., 2014; Lacelle et al., 2012a, 2012b;

Leclerc et al., 2010; Lemieux & Byers, 2008). The risk of these difficulties is greater if attempted or completed intercourse occurred, if the abuse was by a relative, and if the victim told someone and received a negative response from that person (Bulik et al., 2001; Feiring et al., 2009; Lemieux & Byers, 2008; Rellini & Meston, 2011). Adult survivors of child sexual abuse are also more likely to experience sexual assault as an adult, as well as sexual disorders such as fears of sex, lack of sexual desire, and lack of arousal (Meston et al., 2006; Najman et al., 2005). Women who were sexually abused as children are also more likely to be preoccupied with sex, younger at the time of their first voluntary intercourse, and more likely to be teen mothers (Noll et al., 2003). Their sexuality is ambivalent—they experience both sexual aversion and a preoccupation with sex.

are forgotten for a period and then remembered again. In fact, it has been theorized that amnesia for traumatic events of this kind, particularly when the child has been betrayed by someone in a position of trust like a parent, is an adaptive response that helps the child survive in a terribly distressed family situation (Freyd, 1996).

The other question is, Can memories of events that did not occur be implanted in someone? In one study, the researcher was able to create false memories of childhood events in 25 percent of the adults given the treatment (Loftus, 1993). Certain conditions seem to increase the chances that people will think they remember things that did not actually occur, including suggestion by an authority figure and suggestion under hypnosis.

Two studies shed additional light on this debate. One was a study of women admitted to a hospital unit specializing in the treatment of trauma-related psychological disorders (Chu et al., 1999). Among those reporting childhood sexual abuse, 26 percent had partial amnesia for it and 27 percent had complete amnesia for a period of time before recalling it. These patients also displayed dissociative symptoms. *Dissociative amnesia* is an inability to recall important personal information, usually of a traumatic nature (American Psychiatric Association, 2000a). The great majority of those who suffered child sexual abuse had been able to corroborate the occurrences by some method, such as medical records. Importantly, most of them first remembered the abuse while at home, and about half were not involved in any kind of treatment or counselling at the time they remembered, ruling out the possibility of suggestion by a therapist.

In another study, normal participants' brains were scanned by using fMRI (functional magnetic resonance imaging) while they were suppressing unwanted memories (Anderson et al., 2004). Neural systems underlying suppression were clearly identified and included a region in the prefrontal cortex and the hippocampus. From this study we can see that suppression of memories is not just hocus-pocus but has a real basis in the brain.

What is the bottom line? There is evidence that some people do forget childhood sexual abuse and remember it later. There is also evidence that some people can form false memories based on suggestions made by another person. It seems likely that most of the cases of recovered memory of child sexual abuse are true but that some are false and the product of suggestion. It is also probably true that false accusations of past child abuse are made, often by a well-intentioned "victim" who is highly suggestible to press reports of other cases or who has been influenced by a therapist. This may result in an arrest of an innocent person. There are errors of justice on both sides. Nonetheless, there are many more cases of unreported and unpunished perpetrators than of falsely convicted persons.

Sources: Alexander et al., 2005; Anderson et al., 2004; Chu et al., 1999; Dalenberg et al., 2012; Freyd, 1996; Gold et al., 1994; Loftus, 1993; Williams, 1994.

Again, though, not all adults who report sexual contact with an adult as a child show these long-term negative consequences.

Child sexual abuse has effects not only on mental health but also on physical health. Adults who were sexually abused as children are one-and-a-half times as likely as those who were not abused to have had health problems in the past year (Sachs-Ericsson et al., 2005).

In most cases, child sexual abuse is psychologically damaging and may lead to symptoms such as depression and PTSD. Patterns of sexual abuse can range from five minutes of fondling by a neighbour to repeated forced intercourse by a father or stepfather over a period of several years. The effects of sexual abuse are most severe when it involved intercourse, occurred repeatedly over years, and was committed by a father or stepfather (Fleming et al., 1999; Kendler & Bulik et al., 2000). In addition, Canadian studies have shown that adjustment is affected by both the abused child's coping style and the quality of family relationships (Hébert et al., 2006; Runtz & Schallow, 1997; Tremblay et al., 1999).

Treatments such as cognitive-behavioural therapy are available and effective in treating adults with PTSD following child sexual abuse (McDonagh et al., 2005).

 The Offenders

Many child molesters abuse more than one child. In particular, child sexual abusers who abuse boys outside the family are likely to have multiple victims (Abel et al., 1987). For example, in 2000, Carl Toft came up for parole

Milestones in Sex Research

What Causes Pedophilia?

It is very difficult to think of a group more hated than pedophiles—people who are sexually aroused by children (Cantor et al., 2009). This anger is fuelled by the media, which tend to focus on alarming cases of sexual offences against children. It is also fuelled by the commonly held view that anyone sexually attracted to children is invariably a sexual predator who will act on that attraction and harm children. Not all pedophiles are also child molesters, however; not all act on their sexual attraction. The proportion of people who experience a sexual attraction to children and never act on it at all is not known. Activist and sex/relationship columnist Dan Savage (2010) referred to pedophiles remaining celibate for their whole lives rather than risk harm to a child as "gold star pedophiles" and suggested that society should be helping rather than automatically demonizing such people.

In contrast, and counterintuitively, most people who sexually abuse children are *not* pedophiles. That is, most cases of child sexual abuse are committed by people who actually prefer adults as sexual partners. This phenomenon is common in cases of intrafamilial sexual abuse (e.g., parent–child) and in sexual activity (both consensual and coercive) between siblings. Typically,

nonpedophiles who sexually abuse children also exhibit generally antisocial behaviour, use drugs and alcohol, or have histories of childhood adversity themselves, such as violence and neglect (but only sometimes sexual abuse).

What causes pedophilia? For most of the twentieth century, pedophilia was believed to be the result of having been sexually abused as a child. This has often been called the *abused-abuser hypothesis*. But does experiencing sexual abuse as a child cause a person to become a pedophile? There is evidence that children who experience adversity in childhood—whether sexual abuse, nonsexual physical abuse, or neglect—are more likely to engage in criminal behaviour in adulthood. However, there is little solid evidence for any specific association between having been sexually abused and becoming a sexual abuser (U.S. General Accounting Office, 1996). Also, almost all child molesters are male, whereas the majority of their victims are female. If the abused-abuser hypothesis of pedophilia were true, one would expect the sex ratio to be the same among victims and perpetrators—that is, that most abusers would be female not male.

More recently, researchers have used neuroimaging and other procedures to show that there are differences

---

after serving 8 years of a 13-year sentence for molesting more than 200 boys at the New Brunswick Training Centre. In 2005, he was released into the community after completing 10 years of that 13-year sentence. Critics argued that he should be denied parole because, by his own admission, he was not cured.

What do the data say about child sexual abusers? Are they likely to repeat the offence? Are there effective treatments for them?

Pedophilia involves an adult who has a sexual preference for prepubescent children, generally ages 13 or younger. A *pedophilic disorder* (one of the paraphilic disorders identified in the *DSM-5;* see Chapter 15 for more information on paraphilic disorders) can be diagnosed when an individual experiences

pedophilia: Paraphilia in which an adult has a sexual preference for prepubescent children.

recurrent intense fantasies or urges involving children and the person has either acted on these urges or the urges cause marked distress or interpersonal difficulties (American Psychiatric Association, 2013). (See Milestones in Sex Research for a discussion of the causes of pedophilia.) Although the vast majority of pedophiles are male, some women also sexually abuse young children (Seto, 2004). An Alberta study of convicted adolescent sex offenders showed a high frequency of deviant sexual fantasies (Aylwin et al., 2005). Not all pedophiles are child molesters—that is, some people who experience pedophilic urges never act on them (Seto, 2009). In addition, not all child molesters are pedophiles—that is, not all have a sexual preference for prepubescent children. Research in Ontario has shown that most men convicted of child pornography offences are

in the brains of pedophiles compared with men who commit nonsexual crimes and with healthy noncriminals. The evidence suggests that at least some of these biological differences existed before birth.

First, relative to sex offenders against adults and to people with atypical sexualities other than pedophilia, pedophiles score lower on IQ and memory tests (Blanchard et al., 2007; Cantor et al., 2004; Cantor et al., 2005). Because pedophilic sexual offenders against children score lower than nonpedophilic sexual offenders (i.e., sex offenders who offend against adults), we cannot attribute the difference merely to less intelligent people getting caught.

Second, more than one-third of pedophiles are not right-handed (they are left-handed or ambidextrous), compared with approximately 10 percent in the mainstream population (Cantor et al., 2005). Pedophiles also are more likely to show minor physical anomalies (Dyshniku et al., 2015; Fazio et al., 2015). Because handedness and these physical anomalies result from prenatal brain organization, these differences suggest that whatever chain of events leads to pedophilia, the first links of that chain were present before birth. Finally, there are differences in the white matter in the brain that are not a result of child adversity (Cantor et al., 2015).

Third, MRI and fMRI studies have compared the brain structure and brain function of pedophiles with both healthy controls and people who have committed nonsexual offences. Pedophiles demonstrate significant differences from nonsexual offenders in white matter tissue (Cantor et al., 2008; Cantor & Blanchard, 2012), the bundles of axons that connect neurons with each other. The affected tissues appear to be those that connect the brain areas that respond to sexual stimuli. Interestingly, fMRI studies have shown that in both pedophiles and nonpedophiles, the same areas of the brain respond to people they find sexually attractive. They only differ in whom they find sexually attractive (Polisois-Keating & Joyal, 2013).

This growing body of research suggests that people do not choose to be sexually attracted to children. However, they do remain entirely in control of their behaviour. When it comes to pedophilia, almost all of society's attention is on punishment to help prevent a second offence. The more we learn about what causes pedophilia, however, the better we might prevent the first offence.

Sources: Blanchard et al. (2007), Cantor et al. (2004, 2008, 2009), Cantor & Blanchard (2012), Cantor, Blanchard, et al. (2005); Cantor, Klassen, et al. (2005), Savage (2010), U.S. General Accounting Office (1996).

Written by James M. Cantor, Ph.D., Centre for Addiction and Mental Health, Toronto.

---

pedophiles; they show a preference for prepubescent children (Seto et al., 2006). Child pornography is discussed in Chapter 17.

Pedophiles fall into a number of categories, depending on the gender of the children they are attracted to and other factors. In one study of 678 pedophiles, all of them men, 27 percent were attracted to boys, 47 percent to girls, and 25 percent to both (Blanchard et al., 1999). Child molesters also differ in whether their victims are their biological children, stepchildren, children they know, or children they do not know (Guay et al., 2001). Pedophiles who molest children tend to be repeat offenders, and their patterns of preference tend to be stable over time.

Pedophiles score low on measures of heterosocial competence (Dreznick, 2003). That is, they lack the interpersonal skills to function well in adult heterosexual relationships. They are more likely to have experienced sexual and nonsexual abuse as children (Brotto & Klein, 2007). Canadian research shows that pedophiles have poorer cognitive functioning than controls and are more likely than controls (11 percent compared with 5 percent) to have had accidents involving head injury and unconsciousness before the age of 6 (Blanchard et al., 2002; Cantor et al., 2004; Cantor, Blanchard, et al., 2005). This suggests that problems with early brain development or some injury to the developing brain may create this disorder in some cases.

Researchers are very interested in developing measures that might identify pedophiles who have not been arrested and perhaps have not even offended yet (Seto, 2004). Implicit association tests (see Chapter 3 for a description of these types of measures) using reaction times indicate that pedophiles have a strong mental association between children and sex, whereas nonpedophiles have an association between adults and sex (Babchishin et al., 2013; Gray et al., 2005). Research in Ontario using phallometric measures, such as those discussed in Chapters 3 and 11, indicate that men who are attracted to child pornography but have not sexually offended against children show greater arousal to child photos than to adult photos, and their arousal to child photos is even greater than the arousal of men who have actually sexually offended against children (Seto et al., 2006). Possession of child pornography itself might be an indicator of pedophilia (Seto, 2004). Measures such as these may provide ways to identify men who are likely to offend even before they commit their crime.

> When child molesters are released from prison, how likely are they to reoffend?

One study that attempted to answer the question of recidivism (repeat offending) followed a sample of 206 child molesters and found a recidivism rate of 23 percent (Moulden et al., 2009). This is no doubt an underestimate of the actual rates of reoffending, because so much child sexual abuse goes unreported (Hanson, 2000). Ontario researchers have shown that recidivism is much higher for sex offenders who had not received treatment (participation in treatment is voluntary) (Hanson & Bussière, 1998). It was also higher for certain subgroups of child molesters, such as those men who had committed previous sexual offences, had begun sexual offending at an early age, and had targeted male victims. Ontario researchers have also demonstrated that the recidivism rate is higher for extrafamilial offenders than for intrafamilial offenders, as well as for offenders with general feelings of hostility (Firestone et al., 2000, 2005; Greenberg et al., 2000). Several Canadian studies have found that men who show greater sexual arousal to children as measured through phallometric assessment are more likely to commit another sexual offence (Firestone et al., 2000; Proulx et al., 1997; Seto et al., 2000).

Most experts believe that pedophilia itself—the sexual attraction to children—cannot be changed; the best that we can hope for with treatment is to increase the individual's voluntary control over acting on those urges (Seto, 2009).

LO11 Treatment of Sex Offenders

Canadian researchers have been leaders in the development of assessment and treatment strategies for child sexual abusers (Bradford & Greenberg, 1996; Hall, 1995; Marshall & Barbaree, 1988; Marshall & Pithers, 1994). Among the treatments in use in Canada are anti-androgen drugs, hormones, antidepressant drugs (SSRIs, such as Prozac), and cognitive-behavioural therapy. Cyproterone acetate (CPA) is an anti-androgen drug—it reduces the action of testosterone

in the body with the hope of a corresponding reduction of the sexually aggressive behaviour—that has been used in the treatment of child sexual abusers and other sex offenders. It does seem to be effective in reducing sexual urges (Seto, 2009). Other anti-androgen drugs seem to be less effective. One problem is that sex offenders have to agree voluntarily to this treatment. Few sex offenders are willing to continue to take anti-androgens because they also suppress normal sexual arousal. Between 30 and 100 percent of men who start hormonal treatment later drop out (Barbaree & Seto, 1997). One class of antidepressants (the SSRIs, which include Prozac and Zoloft) has also been tried in the treatment of sex offenders (Bradford & Greenberg, 1996). Its use is based on the assumption that sex offending can be a particular kind of obsessive-compulsive disorder, and such disorders generally respond well to these antidepressants. Although there have not yet been any blind clinical trials, there is some research evidence that use of SSRIs can be a helpful addition to other interventions, such as therapy (Hall & Hall, 2007).

Behavioural treatment generally aims to teach pedophiles to control their sexual arousal to children (Seto, 2009). One method involves aversive classical conditioning, in which an unpleasant stimulus (e.g., the smell of ammonia) is repeatedly paired with sexual pictures of children. This method does seem to increase the individual's voluntary control of his sexual arousal to children. Behavioural treatments to increase pedophiles' positive, appropriate sexual arousal to adults—which would be another important component to the solution—have been less successful. Correctional Service Canada uses *cognitive-behavioural treatment* that targets not only behaviours but also attitudes and beliefs.

Canadian researchers conducted a follow-up of high-risk sex offenders (high risk because they had a history of multiple offences or violent offences) (Abracen & Looman, 2004). They found that the recidivism rate was 52 percent for untreated sex offenders and 24 percent for treated sex offenders, a significant improvement with treatment. The treatment was cognitive-behavioural therapy (CBT). A more recent well-controlled study by these authors found that the rate of sexually reoffending over more than a nine-year period were low (about 10 percent) for both offenders who received sex offender treatment and those who received other treatment programs (Abracen et al., 2010).

However, some experts question whether, at present, there are any successful treatments for pedophiles (Camilleri & Quinsey, 2008; Seto, 2009). A major review of both drug and psychotherapy interventions with sex offenders concluded that there is no strong evidence of the success of either kind of treatment (Långström et al.,

2013). This conclusion is due, in part, to a shortage of studies, and especially a shortage of high-quality studies. More attention to interventions and evaluating them well is needed.

Mandatory Notification of the Release of Sex Offenders

Many Canadians are concerned that sex offenders released into the community after serving their sentence will reoffend—that is, commit another sexual assault or molest another child. Media coverage of high-profile cases in which offenders have reoffended after their release adds to public fears and has resulted in calls for mandatory public notification of the release of sex offenders. The rationale is that if people are aware that there is a released sex offender in their community, they can protect themselves and their children from sexual violence.

Since 1994, organizations (but not individuals) have been able to have potential employees and volunteers screened by police to ensure that they do not have a prior conviction for child sexual abuse. In addition, in December 2004, the federal government, with unanimous support of the provinces and territories, implemented the National Sex Offender Registry, which is available only to law enforcement officials and is intended to help them investigate unsolved crimes of a sexual nature. In 2011, the National Sex Offender Registry was strengthened in several ways, including automatic inclusion of all convicted sex offenders, mandatory DNA sampling, and proactive use of the registry by police to help prevent sexual crimes.

Some people argue that there should be a comparable national registry of child molesters available to the public (Canadian Centre for Justice Statistics, 1999). Most authorities raise a number of concerns with doing this, including misidentification of innocent people and sex offenders' rights to privacy if they do not pose a risk to the public. They also fear that some citizens might take the law into their own hands. Finally, public notification may drive sex offenders underground so that it becomes more difficult for police to keep track of them. The issue of public warnings about the release of sex offenders pits the rights of the community to be informed about the risk of significant harm against the privacy rights of the offender (Canadian Centre for Justice Statistics, 1999). Therefore, at present, community notification is restricted to offenders believed to pose an immediate risk to the public. The police use a great deal of discretion in determining which offenders pose such a risk, leaving the issue open to continued public debate.

Is the National Sex Offender Registry working? That is, does it help to reduce the likelihood that convicted sex offenders will reoffend? We do not know because there has been no published research evaluating its effectiveness at reducing recidivism (Murphy et al., 2009).

Preventing Child Sexual Abuse

With increasing awareness of the prevalence and potential negative consequences of child sexual abuse, most elementary schools in Canada have implemented sexual abuse prevention programs (these often go by names such as *personal safety*). The goal of these programs is to empower children and to provide them with the necessary skills to resist people who attempt to abuse them sexually. it is important to have these programs in schools because few children receive this type of information from their parents (Tutty, 2014). Most programs share certain concepts (Hébert et al., 2001; Hébert & Tourigny, 2004). For example, they help children to distinguish between good touches and bad touches, as well as to recognize potentially abusive situations. They teach them strategies to deal assertively with potential abuse, such as yelling "No." They emphasize the importance of the child telling a trusted adult about the abuse or attempted abuse. Finally, they reassure children that they are not to blame in the event that sexual abuse does occur. However, the programs differ in their length, the way the program is delivered (e.g., video, puppets, books), and who delivers it (teachers, parents, police officers) (Hébert & Tremblay, 2000; Hébert et al., 2001). A few programs offer concurrent programs for parents to assist them in talking to their children about sexual abuse. Researchers in Quebec evaluated the impact of such a parent workshop (Hébert et al., 2002). They found that the workshop had a positive impact on parents' knowledge and on their reactions to a hypothetical situation involving child sexual abuse, compared with parents who did not attend the workshop. However, only 20 percent of the invited parents chose to attend the workshop.

How effective are these programs? Do children learn the concepts? Do they remember them? A review of studies on the effectiveness of child sexual abuse prevention programs found that these programs do increase elementary school children's knowledge (Hébert & Tourigny, 2004). Further, in role-play scenarios, the children are better able to identify potentially abusive situations and implement the skills that they learned. Older children tend to show greater gains than younger children do. However, the gains are sometimes small and tend to decrease over time. Further, more recent research in Quebec suggests they may not be effective with children who are from lower socio-economic status immigrant families who have little knowledge of sexual abuse (Daigneault et al., 2012). This suggests that children will need to have booster sessions—that is, have sexual abuse prevention skills reviewed regularly—if they are to retain their skills. Longer programs and programs that allow children to practise and role-play their self-protection skills, rather than relying only on instruction, tend to be more effective.

There are some concerns that are often raised about child abuse prevention programs. First, are children able to put the skills they learn into practice (Finkelhor & Daro, 1997)? That is, how many children actually use the skills they learned in a sexual abuse prevention program when faced with a sexual abuser, particularly when the abuser is a family member? Second, will the program have negative effects on the children, such as increasing their anxieties or their fear of appropriate physical affection (Reppucci et al., 1999)? Although some children do show these types of responses, according to parental reports, most children do not (Hébert et al., 2001; Tutty, 1997).

Sexual Harassment

Under Canadian federal and provincial law, sexual harassment is a form of sex discrimination. However, unless it involves sexual assault, it is not a *Criminal Code* offence and is not dealt with in a court of law. Rather, victims can lodge a complaint with the Human Rights Commission. The issue is a powerful one—it can interfere with a person's ability to do a job or obtain a service. It may force a victim out of a job, but it can also force a perpetrator from a job.

Canadian courts and human rights tribunals have used the following definition of sexual harassment developed by the U.S. Equal Employment Opportunity Commission (Aggarwal, 1992):

> Unwelcome sexual advances, requests for sexual favors, and other verbal or physical conduct of a sexual nature constitute sexual harassment when
> A. Submission to such conduct is made either explicitly or implicitly a term or condition of an individual's employment or academic advancement,
> B. Submission to or rejection of such conduct by an individual is used as the basis for academic or employment decisions affecting that individual, or
> C. Such conduct has the purpose or effect of unreasonably interfering with an individual's work or academic performance or creating an intimidating, hostile, or offensive working or educational environment.

> What behaviours in the workplace constitute sexual harassment?

According to the New Brunswick Human Rights Commission, sexual harassment is any "vexatious comment or conduct of a sexual nature, that is known or ought reasonably to be known to be unwanted"—that is, that a reasonable person should have known was unwelcome. Sexual harassment can be divided into two categories: sexual coercion and sexual annoyance (Aggarwal, 1992). The key ingredient for sexual coercion is that compliance with the sexual advances has some direct link to employment or educational status or opportunity, or to receipt of a public service. This is termed "quid pro quo harassment" (*quid pro quo* meaning "I'll do something for you if you do something for me"). Sexual annoyance or environmental harassment is sexually related behaviour that creates a hostile, intimidating work environment so that the person cannot work effectively, such as constant lewd innuendoes, verbal intimidation, or practical jokes that cause embarrassment. Individuals who are gay, lesbian, or transgender are particularly likely to experience harassment based on their sexual or gender identity. A survey of homophobia, biphobia, and transphobia in Canadian schools found that 55 percent of the sexual minority students had been verbally harassed about their gender expression or perceived sexual orientation (Taylor et al., 2011).

Sexual harassment can occur at work and in education, as well as in other contexts, such as psychotherapy or on the street.

Sexual Harassment at Work

Sexual harassment at work may take a number of different forms (Figure 16.6). A prospective employer may make it clear that sexual activity is a prerequisite to being hired. Stories of such incidents are rampant among actors. Once on the job, sexual activity may become a condition for continued employment, for a promotion, or for other benefits, such as a raise. Or it can involve creating a hostile work environment. Here is one case:

> I work at a family-owned restaurant. Because I am a bartender, it is often just me behind the bar. On numerous occasions, I have caught one of the owners staring at my backside as I am getting things out of the refrigerator behind the bar. He has also blatantly stared at my legs, if I am wearing a skirt, while I am trying to speak with him. He has also shown me how to clean the nozzle used to foam milk for coffee drinks, but does so in a fashion that looks much like someone manually stimulating a certain piece of the male anatomy, and then looks at me with a grin on his face. There have been times when the dishwasher wasn't working and he made comments to the male bartender, as I was standing right there, such as, "Be gentle with her . . . you have to go slowly so you don't hurt it . . . it needs lubrication." He has walked up behind me and blown on my neck. All of the comments and actions are very unnerving. (from a student essay)

It is clear how psychologically damaging such environments are to the victim. Surveys indicate that sexual

Figure 16.6 Sexual harassment at work: This man is engaging in inappropriate touching, but if he is her supervisor, she may be hesitant to protest.

© Ryan McVay/Getty Images

harassment at work is far more common than many people realize, particularly for women, although the estimates vary depending on the definition of sexual harassment. A 2014 Angus Reid poll asked about unwelcome sexual advances, requests for sexual favours, non-consensual contact, and verbal harassment of a sexual nature at work. The poll found that 43 percent of women and 20 percent of men reported that they had experienced some form of sexual harassment at work; for 12 percent of the women and 9 percent of the men this involved unwanted sexual contact. About a quarter of these experienced had occurred within the previous two years. However, 20 percent reported the incidents to their employer.

Sexual harassment and sexual assault in the RCMP and military have become a serious problem. For example, results from the 2016 Survey on Sexual Misconduct in the Canadian Armed Forces found that 1.7 percent of members, and four times as many women as men, reported being sexually victimized in the previous year either in the military workplace or in situations involving military members. More than one-quarter of the women (27 percent) reported experiencing sexual assault at least once while serving in

the Armed Forces. Furthermore, the report showed that inappropriate sexualized and discriminatory behaviours based on sex were very common—31 percent of the women and 15 percent of them reported being the target of these types of behaviours in the previous year. In 2016, the RCMP agreed to a compensation package for female employee who were victims of sexual harassment and abuse after hundreds of women came forward to describe the sexual harassment that they had experience, often over many years. Despite efforts to address sexual harassment in both the RCMP and military, many women still have concerns about possible repercussions from reporting their harassment experiences (Gill & Febbraro, 2013).

Both female and male victims report that harassment has negative effects on their emotional and physical health, their ability to work with others on the job, and their feelings about work (Chan et al., 2008; Willness et al., 2007). However, men are more likely to feel that the overtures from women ended up being reciprocal and mutually enjoyable. Women, on the other hand, are more likely to report damaging consequences, including being fired or quitting their job (Gutek, 1985). There is evidence linking the experience of sexual harassment to depression, anxiety, and PTSD (Rederstorff et al., 2007). Even subtle sexual harassment, such as asking, "Do you have a boyfriend?" in a job interview, can damage women's performance in the interview (Woodzicka & LaFrance, 2005).

Why does sexual harassment at work occur? According to one theory proposed, it results from a combination of gender stereotyping and men's ambivalent motives (Fiske & Glick, 1995; Krings & Facchin, 2009). Stereotypes of women in our culture are complex and include three distinct clusters: *sexy, nontraditional* (e.g., feminist), and *traditional* (e.g., mother). Many men have ambivalent motives in their interactions with women because they desire both dominance and intimacy. Fiske and Glick (1995) argue that there are four types of harassment of women by men. With the first, *earnest harassment,* the man is truly motivated by a desire for sexual intimacy, but he will not take no for an answer and persists with unwelcome sexual advances. He stereotypes women as sexy. With the second type, *hostile harassment,* the man's motivation is domination of the woman, often because he perceives her as being in competition with him in the workplace. He holds the stereotype of women as nontraditional and therefore competitive with him. His response to rejection by a woman is increased harassment. The third and fourth types of harassment involve ambivalent combinations of the two basic motives: dominance and a desire for intimacy. In the third type, *paternalistic-ambivalent harassment,* the man is motivated by a desire for sexual intimacy but also by a paternalistic desire to be like a father to the woman. This type of harassment may be particularly insidious because the man thinks of himself as acting benevolently toward the woman. Finally, the fourth type, *competitive-ambivalent harassment,* mixes real sexual attraction and a stereotype of women as sexy with the man's hostile desire to dominate the woman, which is based on his belief that she is nontraditional and competitive with him. This theory gives us an excellent view of the complex motives that underlie men's sexual harassment of women.

Social psychologists have developed a clever method for studying sexual harassment experimentally in the laboratory, called the Computer Harassment Paradigm (Maass et al., 2003). In one study, university men were first exposed to a female confederate of the experimenters, who expressed either strong feminist beliefs (intentions to get a high-level career in an area usually reserved for men and involvement in an organization for women's rights) or traditional beliefs. The men then had the opportunity to harass the woman by sending her pornographic material on a computer (she did not actually receive it). The men exposed to the feminist sent significantly more pornography than did men in the control group. However, not all men in the feminist-threat condition responded with harassment; those who did so were mainly men who identified strongly with the male role. The findings of this experiment are consistent with the type of harassment known as hostile environment harassment.

Sexual harassment at work is more than just an annoyance. Particularly for women, because they are more likely to be harassed by supervisors, it can make a critical difference in career advancement. For the woman who supports her family, being fired for sexual noncompliance is a catastrophe. The power of coercion is enormous.

Sexual Harassment in Education

Sexual harassment on campus is not rare (Pyke, 1996). For example, a 1989 survey at the University of Prince Edward Island found that 29 percent of the female students reported that a faculty member had sexually harassed them personally (Mazer & Percival, 1989). Harassment ranged from sexual teasing and jokes to unwanted touching and offers of favours for sex. More than 85 percent of male and female students had experienced sexual harassment in class, most commonly sexual jokes and other remarks by faculty that put down women, men, gay men, or lesbians. Women report dropping courses, changing majors, or dropping out of university because of sexual harassment (Fitzgerald, 1993). Many Canadian universities have

sexual harassment policies and have set up reporting and grievance procedures for dealing with sexual harassment cases.

Sexual harassment in an educational context is not confined either to universities or to teachers harassing students. One survey of 14- and 15-year-olds in the Netherlands found that 24 percent of the girls and 11 percent of the boys had been the objects of sexual harassment (Timmerman, 2003). Of those cases, 73 percent represented harassment by peers and 27 percent harassment by teachers (or other school-related adults, such as a tutor or principal). Of the teachers who were harassers, 90 percent were men. The psychological consequences were more severe when the harassment was done by a teacher than by a peer. An Ontario study of 1213 youth in Grades 6 to 8 found that 36 percent of boys and 21 percent of girls reported having perpetrated sexual harassment; 42 percent of boys and 38 percent of girls reported having experienced sexual harassment (McMaster et al., 2002). The two most common sexually harassing behaviours were homophobic name-calling and sexual comments, jokes, gestures, and looks. Indeed, Canadian research has shown that 49 percent of trans students, 41 percent of male sexual minority students, and 36 percent of female sexual minority students reported that they had experienced sexual harassment (Taylor & Peter, 2011).

Sex between Health Care Professionals and Clients or Patients

There is another category of coercive and potentially damaging sexual encounters—those between a client or patient and a health care professional, such as a psychotherapist, physician, physiotherapist, or chiropractor (Plaut, 2008). Professional associations, such as the Canadian Psychological Association (1995), state clearly in their codes of ethics that such behaviours are unethical. Nonetheless, professional sexual misconduct does occur and can be extremely damaging.

Experts regard this kind of situation as having the potential for serious emotional damage to the client (Pope, 2001). Like the cases of sexual harassment discussed earlier, it is a situation of unequal power, in which the more powerful person, the health care professional, imposes sexual activity on the less powerful person, the patient or client. The situation is regarded as particularly serious in psychotherapy because clients have opened themselves up emotionally to the therapist and therefore are extremely vulnerable. Some provinces, such as Ontario and New Brunswick, have passed legislation that defines sexual contact between a patient or client and any health professional in a position of trust as sexual abuse or misconduct.

How do professionals accused of sexual misconduct respond? According to two Quebec researchers, they generally fall into three groups: *deniers, rationalizers,* and *repentants.* Deniers refuse to acknowledge that the sexual activities occurred. Rationalizers tend to avoid responsibility for their behaviour by minimizing its impact. Those in the repentant group take full responsibility for their action, are sincerely sorry that it occurred, and take steps to ensure that it will not occur again (Assalian & Ravart, 2003).

ANALYZING AN ARGUMENT

Critical thinking needs to be informed by accurate information (Halpern, 2002). Consider the following case, which occurred in 2014.

Justice Robin Camp presided over the trial of *R v Wager,* in which a homeless male youth was accused of sexually assaulting a homeless 19-year-old woman in a bathroom. During the trial, Justice Camp asked the following questions of the alleged victim:

> Q. *But when—when he was using—when he was trying to insert his penis, your bottom was down in the basin. Or am I wrong?*
> A. *My—my vagina was not in the bowl of the basin when he was having intercourse with me.*
> Q. *All right. Which then leads me to the question: Why not—why didn't you just sink your bottom down into the basin so he couldn't penetrate you?*
> A. *I was drunk.*
> Q. *And when your ankles were held together by your jeans, your skinny jeans, why couldn't you just keep your knees together?*
> A. *[no verbal response]*
> Q. *You're shaking your head.*
> A. *I don't know.*

Justice Camp also questioned the complainant's morals and suggested her attempts to fight off the accused were feeble. The trial resulted in an acquittal. Answer the following questions before reading the discussion in the paragraph that follows:

1. What beliefs and attitudes may have led Justice Camp to ask those particular questions?

2. How accurate are those beliefs?

The Crown appealed the acquittal. The Alberta Court of Appeal ruled that Justice Camp had relied on discredited stereotypes about women and violence, treated the victim as less worthy of belief than the accused in questioning the victim and arriving at his decision, and appeared to be blaming the victim. As a result, the Court of Appeal overturned the acquittal. Subsequently, the Canadian Judicial Council organized a disciplinary hearing to review Justice Camp's behaviour and determine whether his continued presence on the bench would undermine public confidence in the judiciary. They recommended that he be removed from the bench. After this ruling, Justice Camp resigned from the bench.

Inaccurate stereotypes can influence our perceptions of situations, even situations as serious as criminal proceedings. They can also have some serious negative impacts. For example, the complainant who was 19 at the time of the first trial reported that the experience made her hate herself and contemplate suicide. People in positions of authority, such as judges, are expected to demonstrate knowledge of social issues and changes in social values. However, critical thinking requires that we all become aware of and question our underlying assumptions that are inaccurate and harmful to others.

SUMMARY

In the *Criminal Code of Canada,* sexual assault is any sexual activity to which the victim did not consent, ranging from unwanted touching to forced oral, anal, or vaginal intercourse. There are three levels of sexual assault, depending on the amount of force used not on the nature of the sexual activity. The law is gender-neutral in that it applies equally to men and women as victims and perpetrators.

The Violence Against Women Survey found that 39 percent of Canadian women reported having been sexually assaulted. Other surveys have found that some men report having experienced sexual coercion, although a smaller percentage of men than women report these experiences. Victims may experience post-traumatic stress disorder (PTSD) as a result of the assault.

Sexual assault by a dating or romantic partner or spouse is quite common. There are three major theoretical views of sexual assault: psychopathology of sex offenders, feminist, and social disorganization. Compared with other men, men who commit sexual assault tend to hold beliefs that support forced sex and to lack empathy. The incidence of sexual assault differs markedly between the various ethnocultural communities in Canada.

Approximately 18 percent of women and 8 percent of men report that they had experienced unwanted sexual contact with an adult or an older adolescent by age 16. There are currently several offences related to the sexual abuse of children in the *Criminal Code of Canada,* including sexual assault, sexual interference, invitation to sexual touching, and sexual exploitation. Most sexual abuse of children is committed by a relative or by a family friend. People who were sexually abused as children are more likely than other people to have symptoms such as anxiety, PTSD, depression, and health complaints. More severe psychological consequences are likely to occur when the perpetrator is a close family member who is an adult (sibling incest seems less likely to be harmful) and when the sexual contact is extensive and involves penetration. Pedophiles are more likely to be attracted to girls than to boys. Some types of child molesters have a low rate of recidivism, but certain types are highly likely to repeat their offence. Experts debate whether treatments for pedophiles are effective. There is a controversy among professionals over whether adults can recover memories of child sexual abuse that they had forgotten (recovered memory) or whether these are cases of false memory syndrome, in which the supposedly remembered incidents never actually occurred. Most schools offer child abuse prevention programs. Their goals are to provide children with the knowledge and skills to resist people who attempt to abuse them.

Sexual harassment, whether on the job or in education, involves unwelcome sexual advances when there is some coercion involved, such as making the sexual contact a condition of being hired or receiving an A grade in a course. In another form of sexual harassment, the work or educational environment is made so hostile on a sexual and gender basis that the employee cannot work effectively. Surveys show that sexual harassment at work is fairly common. In severe cases it can lead to damaging psychological consequences, such as PTSD for the victim. In education, the data indicate that about one-third of female students have been individually harassed by professors, although many more have experienced sexual harassment in class. This abuse can lead to negative consequences for the student, such as being forced to change majors or drop out of school. Sex between health care professionals and patients or clients is a violation of professional ethics and is also illegal in many provinces.

CHAPTER 17

Sex for Sale

© Jonkmanns/laif/Aurora

Are YOU Curious?

1. Why do some men and women pay for sex?
2. What types of pornography are illegal in Canada?
3. What are the effects of viewing erotica and pornography on sexual behaviour?

Read this chapter to find out.

LEARNING OBJECTIVES

After studying this chapter, you will be able to

LO1 Describe Canadian laws regarding prostitution and pornography and why they are controversial.

LO2 Describe and compare various kinds of sex workers and sex work.

LO3 Outline the role of third parties in the lives of sex workers.

LO4 Describe the "career development" (or history) and well-being of a typical sex worker.

LO5 Describe the customers of sex workers and their motivations.

LO6 Discuss the primary issues surrounding sex tourism.

LO7 Distinguish between pornography, obscenity, and erotica, and explain the community standards of tolerance test.

LO8 Outline the various types of pornography and the typical consumer.

LO9 Identify the reasons some people object to pornography and evaluate research on the effects of pornography on its users.

Parliament has the power to regulate against nuisances, but not at the cost of the health, safety, and lives of prostitutes. . . . The prohibitions all heighten the risks [to prostitutes]. . . . They do not merely impose conditions on how prostitutes operate. They go a critical step further, by imposing *dangerous* conditions on prostitution; they prevent people engaged in a risky—but legal—activity from taking steps to protect themselves from the risks.*

---

*Chief Justice Beverley McLachlin, Supreme Court of Canada, December 20, 2013.

The exchange of sexual gratification for money is a prominent feature of many contemporary societies and one that involves large amounts of money. In this chapter, we consider two ways in which sex can be bought and sold: commercial sex work and pornography. Both involve complex legal issues and public controversy, but both also attract a steady stream of eager customers. Other commercial ventures related to sexuality—such as the selling of sex toys and fetish objects—are discussed elsewhere in this book (e.g., Chapters 9 and 15).

LO1

Commercial Sex Work

Sex workers are individuals who work as prostitutes, escorts, erotic dancers, phone sex workers, and pornographic models and actors, as well as in nontherapeutic massage parlours. According to Ontario sociologist Eleanor Maticka-Tyndale and her colleagues (2000b), what is common to all these types of activities is that they involve the sale of a service to "satisfy a sexual fantasy, produce sexual excitement or arousal, and/or provide sexual satisfaction to the customer" (p. 88). We use the term *sex worker* as much as possible throughout this chapter because the term focuses on the activity and does not imply that a person's identity is determined by the activities he or she engages in. **Commercial sex workers** who engage in prostitution (*hookers*) receive money, material gifts, or some other form of payment (such as drugs) for engaging in partnered sexual activities or interactions. As social critics have pointed out, some dating and living arrangements, and some long-term relationships, including certain marriages, also fall in this category. For example, a Quebec study found that 3 percent of adolescents reported that they had received "money, drugs, alcohol, or gifts" for sex, and 4 percent reported that they

commercial sex workers: Persons who engage in sexual acts in return for money or drugs and do so in a fairly nondiscriminating fashion; prostitutes.

common bawdy house: A place kept, occupied, or used by one or more persons to engage in prostitution or indecency.

had provided something for sex at least once (Lavoie et al., 2010). Most of the time (95 percent of buyers and 88 percent of sellers), the other person was a friend or an acquaintance. Similarly, a B.C. study found that among youth who had ever used alcohol or drugs, 2 percent of the boys and 3 percent of the girls had exchanged sex for substances (Homma et al., 2012).

Until recently, prostitution per se—that is, the buying and selling of sex—was not illegal in Canada. However, various activities related to prostitution were criminal offences, such as stopping cars, impeding the flow of traffic, or communicating in public for the purposes of engaging in prostitution or obtaining the sexual services of a prostitute. These offences were often called "communication offences." In addition, cities attempt to control sex work through by-laws pertaining to zoning, traffic, and licensing of businesses. Prostitution was considered a minor offence, punishable usually by a fine or by a short jail term for repeat offenders. In addition, keeping or being found in a **common bawdy house** (the legal term for a place in which prostitution occurs), procuring (pimping), and living on money made from prostitution were also illegal, and the maximum sentences for these offences were significantly higher than for the communication offences.

There were many criticisms of these laws. One criticism was that although prostitution was legal, there were no clear guidelines on where it could take place. Another was that these laws were difficult to enforce, and the probability of arrest was low. A third was that the laws were enforced inconsistently (Gemme, 1998; Shaver, 1993, 1994, 1996b). Almost all charges were for communication offences involving street prostitution—people working within massage parlours, escort services, brothels, and call operations rarely got charged. More sex workers than customers are charged, and their sentences are more severe. In addition, more men who pay for sex with women were charged than men who pay for sex with men, in part because male police officers do not like to pose as prostitutes to entrap clients. Charges were disproportionately laid against female sex workers.

Figure 17.1 In 2013, the Supreme Court of Canada struck down Canada's prostitution laws as violating the *Charter of Rights and Freedoms*. As a result, in 2014, the government brought in new legislation making the buying of sex but not the selling of sex illegal.

THE CANADIAN PRESS/Adrian Wyld

However, the major criticism was that they imposed dangerous conditions on prostitution (a legal activity) by putting vulnerable women at increased risk of violence. In 2013, the Supreme Court unanimously struck down the sections of the *Criminal Code* dealing with prostitution as violating the *Charter of Rights and Freedoms* (Figure 17.1). The Court ruled that although Parliament has the power to impose conditions on how prostitutes operate, the current conditions prevent sex workers from protecting themselves from the risks associated with their work and therefore violate Canadians' basic values. The Court cited specific harms caused by each of the prostitution laws: the ban on brothels, the law against living off the avails of prostitution, and the ban on street soliciting.

In 2014, the government passed new legislation related to sex work, the *Protection of Communities and Exploited Persons Act*. The current offences are listed in Table 2.1. These laws make the buying but not the selling of sex illegal; that is, they prohibit purchasing sexual services or communicating for this purpose and receiving material benefit from purchasing sexual services. They are based on the view that buying sex inherently exploits and objectifies women, and the stated intent is, thus, to protect women from exploitation (Davies, 2015). They also prohibit advertising sexual services for sale. Many people argue that the new laws do not in fact protect sex workers from risk of violence, because it forces sex work underground. Thus, they do not address the harms that were found unconstitutional in the previous law. For example, they force sex workers to continue to live and work in unsafe conditions. The Canadian Alliance for Sex Work Law Reform, a group of 28 sex workers rights and allied groups based in 17 Canadian cities, continues to call for repeal of the current laws.

Some people argue that sex work is a victimless crime and that because both parties in prostitution are consenting, buying (or selling) sex should not be illegal. The argument against the criminalization of sex work assumes that if these activities were legal, or at least decriminalized, they could be regulated and the problems of crime, public offence, and the spread of sexually transmitted infections associated with sex work would be reduced. Enhancing the safety of sex workers is a particularly important issue (Young, 2008). Researchers interviewed women engaged in sex work in Vancouver (Farley et al., 2005). Almost all had been physically assaulted (90 percent) or sexually assaulted (78 percent) in the course of their work. Further, an average of seven prostitutes are killed each year while practising their trade in Canada (Beattie & Cotter, 2010). Under decriminalization, sex work is viewed as a personal choice and therefore a private matter between adults rather than a crime. The law could still be involved to ensure that people, particularly children, are not forced into prostitution and to penalize pimps and other people who profit from sex work.

Quebec sexologist Robert Gemme argued that while we need to eliminate the legal consequences of prostitution, we also need to remove the negative effects that result from the social stigma attached to prostitution—thus the term *sex worker*. From this perspective, prostitution is sex *work* (emphasis on the word "work") and is a trade to be regulated like any other trade. Thus, sex workers should be entitled to all the benefits and protection given to other workers, such as freedom from harassment, proper pay, humane living and working conditions, the right to be treated with respect, and access to workers' compensation benefits (MacDonald & Jeffrey, 2000; Lewis et al., 2005). In several Canadian cities, there are movements to unionize sex workers.

Based on these arguments, the current federal government has met with a number of groups about the current laws and is considering making changes to the law. In addition, some police forces, for example in Saskatoon, Calgary, Montreal, Victoria, and Vancouver, are not enforcing the law and/or have not changed the way they are dealing with sex work (Eschner, 2015).

How do Canadians view sex work and the current legislation? According to a 2016 Angus Reid poll, more than half of Canadians believe that buying (65 percent) and selling (63 percent) sex is morally wrong; however, more Canadians believe that having an affair (89 percent) or not declaring income to avoid paying taxes (79 percent) is morally wrong. Older women are particularly likely to see the buying and selling of sex as morally wrong. Another Angus Reid poll (2014) asked Canadians about support for the current laws related to prostitution before they came into effect; 35 percent supported the proposed law and 47 percent opposed it. In particular, 56 percent of men and 34 percent of women feel that buying sex should be legal (it is currently illegal). Men tend to be more accepting of sex work than are women.

Female Sex Workers

Research has focused primarily on female sex workers providing services to male workers, so we start our discussion there. However, keep in mind that there are heterosexual male and female, gay, lesbian, bisexual, and transgender sex workers and clients.

Venues

Commercial sexual activity occurs in a number of settings or venues. The nature of the venue or of the social or sexual context influences the type of sex worker and client found there (e.g., race, social class), the activity that occurs, and its associated risks. In New Brunswick, 80 percent of sex workers work the streets; the remainder work for an escort agency or strip club (Lee & Coates, 2007). In Vancouver, on the other hand, most sex workers work in a variety of venues, sometimes more than one at a time (Benoit & Millar, 2001). The discussion that follows focuses on female workers and their male clients, but keep in mind that there are male, female, gay, lesbian, bisexual, and transgender sex workers and clients.

The **call girl** (notice the diminutive "girl") works out of her own residence, making appointments with clients by a landline, cellphone, or the Internet. She is often from a middle-class background and may be a university graduate. She dresses expensively and lives in an upscale neighbourhood. A call girl in a medium-sized city may charge a minimum of $150 per hour, and more if she engages in atypical activities; call girls in major metropolitan areas charge $200 or more per hour. A call girl can earn a great deal of money. But she also has heavy business expenses: an expensive residence, an extensive wardrobe, bills for makeup and hairdressers, online marketing, and tips for porters and landlords.

A call girl may have a number of regular customers and may accept new clients only on referral. Because she makes dates by telephone or over the Internet, she can exercise close control over whom she sees and over her schedule. She usually sees clients in her residence, which also allows her to control the setting in which she works. In addition to sexual

gratification, she often provides an illusion of intimacy (Leaver & Dolnick, 2010). She may provide other services, such as accompanying clients to business and social gatherings. Call girls have considerable autonomy, and their physical and health risks are reduced by the setting in which they work. Many call girls advertise on specialized websites (Bernstein, 2007).

Another venue for commercial sex work is the **brothel**. In the nineteenth century and early twentieth century, there were many successful brothels in North America. They varied from storefront clip joints, where the customer's money was stolen while he was sexually occupied, to elegant mansions where the customer was treated like a distinguished dinner guest. Brothels declined in number after World War II.

The contemporary equivalent is the **in-call service**, which employs women working regular shifts in an apartment or condominium, servicing clients who come to the apartment. In major cities, the charge is $150 or $200 per hour; in exchange, the client can participate in standard sexual activity, including fellatio, cunnilingus, and vaginal intercourse. Many in-call services require initial contact by telephone, although others advertise their location in specialized media or even telephone books. A sex worker in this setting generally has less autonomy than a call girl has; there is usually a manager or madam (discussed shortly) who determines the conditions of work and the fees to be charged, and collects a substantial percentage of each fee. In-call workers have less choice of clients and may be expected to service several per shift.

Another contemporary setting for commercial sex is the **massage parlour**. Some massage parlours provide legitimate massage therapy. In others, the employees sell sexual services; these often advertise "sensual massage" or "erotic massage," making it pretty clear which type of parlour they are. Some parlours offer a standard list of services and prices; others allow the masseuse or masseur to decide what she or he will do with a particular client and possibly how much of a "tip" is required for that activity. Massage parlours vary greatly in decor and price. Some are located in professional buildings, are expensively decorated, and provide food and drinks in addition to sexual gratification. Charges may range from $100 to $300 or more. Such parlours may accept charge cards, with the business listed on the monthly statement as a restaurant. At the other end of the scale, storefront parlours, often located in commercial sex districts, offer no amenities and charge rates of $40 to $100.

The fact that massage parlours vary from high-end settings with expensive services to storefronts that provide no amenities and cheap services is not unusual. The sex industry in Vietnam consists of three distinct

call girl: The most expensive and exclusive category of sex workers.
brothel (BRAH-thul): A house of prostitution where sex workers and customers meet for sexual activity.
in-call service: A residence in which sex workers work regular shifts, selling sexual services on an hourly basis.
massage parlour: A place where massages and sexual services can generally be purchased.

Figure 17.2 Escort services are another venue for sex work and provide a range of services. They are frequently advertised online. (NOTE: The models whose photos are shown here are being used for illustrative purposes only.)

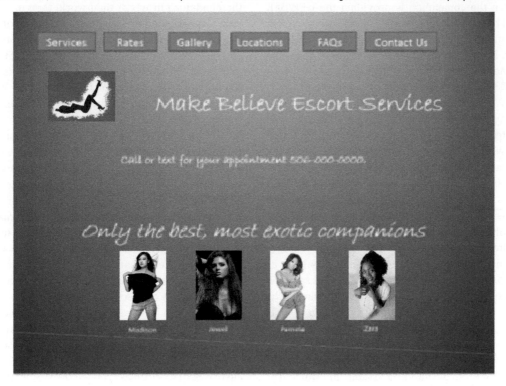

venues, organized by the social class status of both clients and workers (Hoang, 2011). The "low-end sector" consists of barber shops where local poor, often migrant women serve local working-class men. The middle sector consists of bars in which young, attractive women work as bartenders and provide services to clients; the clients are often tourists. The high end is upscale bars where women of high status "hang out" and meet high-status Vietnamese men, and they may develop continuing relationships with them. The fact that sex workers and their clients are of similar social status is characteristic of sex work in many parts of the world.

Another venue for a sex business is the *escort service*. These services have revealing names, such as Alternative Lifestyle Services, First Affair, All Yours, Versatile Entertainment, and Hubbies for Hire (Figure 17.2). Most escort services employ both men and women who will engage in sexual activity; like massage parlours, the service may have a standard menu, or the escort may have the autonomy to decide what activities he or she will do with a client. Sex work in this setting is referred to as an **out-call service** since the escorts go to the clients. This is obviously a more risky business in that the escort cannot control the setting in which the services are provided. Escorts are usually required to telephone the service when they arrive and when they leave the client's location. This not only contributes to their safety but also allows the service to monitor how long the escort spent with the client and therefore the amount owed the service. Several Canadian cities license escorting, including Calgary, Edmonton, Saskatoon, Winnipeg, and Windsor. The by-law in Windsor differs from that in some other Canadian cities because it allows escorts to work out of their own homes instead of requiring them to set up offices in specially zoned areas of the city. This was an attempt to treat escorts the same as other independent business people (Maticka-Tyndale et al., 2005).

In major Canadian cities, there are upscale (and very expensive) escort services, such as Executive's Choice in Windsor, Diamonds Escorts in the Niagara Region, A Touch of Class Escorts in Alberta, and VIP Escorts for Eastern Canada. These services provide male and female companions, and their websites include disclaimers that sexual services are not being offered. (Compare that with the poses and dress of the companions shown in the online

out-call service: A service that sends a sex worker to a location specified by the client to provide sexual services.

photo galleries!) As a result, charges are a single rate and do not depend on what services the companion provides. Often the companion is providing the GFE/BFE (girlfriend/boyfriend experience), including personalized attention, conversation, and ego-stroking. Rates are by the hour, with many agencies offering discounts for multi-hour appointments. Hourly rates are between $150 and $350; daily rates are between $1000 and $2500. They also offer rates for weddings, weekends, and dinner dates. The reach of the Internet allows these agencies to develop ties to companions and clients all over the world. Some agencies provide or encourage communication via Skype. Have you ever wondered what a $5000 escort looks like? See Figure 17.3.

In most communities, the most visible sex worker is the **streetwalker**. She sells her wares on the streets of cities. She is generally less attractive and less fashionably dressed than the call girl, and she charges correspondingly less for services, perhaps as little as $20 for a "quickie," usually a hand-job or oral sex. She is more likely to impose strict time constraints on the customer. In one study, female street sex workers in Montreal earned between $1800 and $2000 per week. On the other hand, a study in Vancouver found that the median annual income of the sex workers they

> **streetwalker:** A lower-status sex worker who works on the streets selling sexual services.
> **strip club:** A place that provides sexualized interactions, not necessarily physically intimate contact.

interviewed was only $18 000 (Benoit & Millar, 2001). Because streetwalkers have relatively little control over the conditions in which they work, they are at greater risk of disease and of violence at the hands of their customers, pimps, and even police officers. In one study of 30 female sex workers in Montreal, 14 had been sexually assaulted and 22 had been physically assaulted in the previous 12 months (Shaver, 1996b). In Vancouver, more than 50 women, most of them street sex workers, were murdered between 1983 and 2001.

Child or juvenile sex workers also work as street prostitutes. A recent Vancouver study of 508 sex workers found that 38 percent entered the trade when they were under 18 years old (Goldenberg et al., 2014). These individuals were more likely to be born in Canada, inject drugs, and have worked for a manager or been coerced into sex work. They were also more likely to be infected with HIV. There has been an increasing demand in recent years for child prostitutes. In 1988, Parliament passed specific legislation prohibiting the purchase of sexual services from someone under 18 years old. The Federal/Provincial/Territorial Working Group on Prostitution has recommended that youths involved in prostitution be treated as persons in need of assistance and not as offenders (Canadian Centre for Justice Statistics, 1999).

The **strip club** provides sexualized interactions, not necessarily physically intimate contact. Like massage parlors, strip clubs exist along a continuum, from very elegant "gentlemen's clubs" employing attractive, articulate young women who provide companionship and female attention in exchange for tips, to "dive" bars where women engage in (almost) nude dance routines and lap dances (Frank & Carnes, 2010). Each club attracts a particular race, class, and gender of workers and clients. Clubs catering to straight men are common; they provide a space for traditionally male behaviour, including rowdiness and vulgarity, and consumption (cigars, alcohol). Men seek escape from their daily lives and personal and sexual acceptance from the workers. Thus, the interaction is often traditionally gendered and sexualized. Less common are clubs where men dance for heterosexual women (Scull, 2013). Whereas male clients often come to the club alone, females usually come in groups, often to celebrate a special occasion. Male dancers engage in hypermasculine displays of gender, and generally dominate the female clients, occasionally mistreating them. There are clubs or events that cater to same-sex desiring women (SSDW). Carnes studied events designed for black SSDWs. Like heterosexual male clients, these women desired sexualized interactions with women in a public space; their experiences were connected to a sense of belonging to a political and erotic community, and feelings of acceptance.

Figure 17.3 "Kristen," a high-end escort, offers companionship for as much as $5000.

The Internet and cellphones have had a major impact on the delivery of commercial sexual services since 2001 (Delap, 2014). They have made entry into work as an in-call or out-call provider much easier. They also have made access by clients to workers much easier. Potential customers can browse the web or specialized apps in complete privacy and arrange a meeting by e-mail, text, or cellphone. In some cities, these technologies have markedly reduced demand for and provision of services by street workers (Venkatesh, 2011). Researchers for *The Economist* analyzed 190 000 female workers' profiles posted on an international website. The data are for the period 1999 to 2014; the majority of the women work(ed) in the U.S. From 2006 to 2014, the average price for an hour with one of the women fell from about $340 to $260. The price varied greatly across cities, and also by the characteristics of the woman and services offered. The authors suggest the decline reflects rapidly increasing numbers of providers due to several factors: increasing ease of entry, migration of young women (especially immigrants) to large cities, and the entry of local women into the market due to the ability to engage in sex work discreetly and anonymously (Delap, 2014).

Research on commercial sex workers in a large Canadian city has found that the same person may work in several different venues over time (Lewis et al., 2004). For example, in areas with cold winters, people who work on the streets in the summer and fall may work in in-call services or bars during the winter. Women also may move back and forth between an escort service and working as a call girl.

L03 The Role of Third Parties

Research in Ontario, Quebec, and the Maritimes has shown that most sex workers work with third parties, whether working for themselves or working for an agency (Clamen et al., 2013). A third party is anyone involved who is neither the client nor the worker. These third parties take a variety of different roles. They may be supervisors, owners, managers, receptionists, security, drivers, personal assistants, advertisers, or webmasters. They may hire, work with, or work for third parties. Sex workers themselves can be third parties if they facilitate another sex worker's activities. The researchers found that these relationships are complex and that they challenge the stereotypes about third parties involved with commercial sex workers. That is, they found that many of these relationships are not abusive or exploitative and provide important services that increase safety, security, and well-being. Of course, some relationships are abusive and exploitative.

Many people associate sex workers with a **pimp** ("The Man"), portrayed as the companion-master. If a sex worker has a pimp, she supports him with her earnings, and in return he may provide her with companionship and sex, bail her out of jail, and provide her with food, shelter, clothing, and drugs. If he keeps an eye on her when she is working, he may provide some protection against theft and violence. But the same pimp also may exercise considerable control over her and engage in verbal, physical, and sexual abuse if she fails to do what he tells her. The stereotype of all sex workers having pimps is not accurate. In Canada, a majority of adult sex workers work *without* a pimp. For example, in New Brunswick, 74 percent of sex workers work for themselves (Lee & Coats, 2007) (see Milestones in Sex Research for some of their stories). However, many child prostitutes do have pimps.

Just as many call girls and exotic dancers have day jobs, so do pimps. Many are in the food trades or services (Venkatesh, 2011). Some are students. One pimp worked his way through university connecting male students with women to go on dates, dance at parties, and provide sexual services in a variety of places, or deliver the GFE (Adshade, 2010). He knew many of the men and women from school; a man would request a service, and he kept asking women until one agreed. His take depended on the woman's attractiveness and skill, the service, the venue, and the client's willingness to pay—from $20 (for a hand-job in a car) to $700 (all night in a luxury hotel). He described his role as helping "women, friends of mine, to find paying customers."

Another third party in commercial sex work is the **madam**, a woman who manages or owns an in-call service, out-call service, brothel, or escort service. A madam is usually experienced and skilled at managing sex workers and businesses. Sometimes she also is socially skilled with a network of contacts in the community.

In other venues, there may be other third parties. Massage parlours employ managers who are on the premises at all times and may exercise close control of their employees. The importance of these third parties is that they reduce the autonomy of the sex workers they supervise and may coerce them to perform activities or work with clients that they do not want to. There is sharp disagreement among observers over the extent to which a sex worker can exercise choice with regard to his or her activities. Some argue that workers choose whom they serve and what acts they perform; others argue that they have little choice if they need the money. The reality depends, in part, on the involvement of the third parties in the worker's daily life.

pimp: A sex worker's companion, protector, and master.
madam: A woman who manages a brothel, an in-call service, an out-call service, or an escort service.

Sex Trafficking

Sex trafficking refers to the recruitment and control of persons, by threat or use of force or deception, for purposes of sexual exploitation (Hynes & Raymond, 2002). In one scenario, girls and young women are recruited in developing countries by ads or by people who promise them education, a good job (as a dancer, nanny, secretary), or a husband in a developed country. Recruiters may even supply forged travel documents, often for a price. When the women arrive in the destination country, they find themselves captives; often their travel documents are taken away, the money they earn goes to those who control them, and their controllers threaten physical harm to the women or their families if they disobey or run away. The women often work in bars, brothels, and massage parlours, and they may be moved every few weeks. It is estimated that trafficking produces $7 billion profit per year (Parrot & Cummings, 2006). The United Nations estimates that tens of thousands of young women and girls are trafficked each year; half are children, with most of these victims ending up in Germany, the United States, and Italy. Many of these women are brought to Canada every year to work in the sex trade; some are kept as virtual prisoners (McClelland, 2001).

A different image is of the child sex slave, an image vigorously railed against by some celebrities (e.g., Ashton Kutcher) and numerous media including the *New York Times, Fox News,* and *CNN.* Here the scenario is a girl aged 10 or 11 to 17 seduced or kidnapped by an older man and forced into prostitution in various venues—strip clubs, brothels, massage parlors, private homes. Their exploiters use threats of and actual physical violence, and threats to their families to control them. The usual quoted figure is "100,000 to 300,000 child sex slaves in the United States today" (Cizmar et al., 2011). The problem is that the number is false. It began as a "guesstimate" by researchers at the University of Pennsylvania in 2001 of the number of children *at risk in all of North America.*

Three American studies using three different methods do not support the assertion that there are even 100 000 "child sex slaves" in the United States or that the number of foreign nationals trafficked for sexual exploitation is equally large (Banks & Kyckelhahn, 2011; Hinman, 2011). It shouldn't really matter whether the number is large or small, or whether the victims are children or adults, male or female. Sexual exploitation is wrong, a crime, and very damaging to the victim. We need to increase efforts to eradicate it based on a realistic picture of the problem. Vastly exaggerated estimates do not help.

Some girls are definitely forced into prostitution in Canada, although it is impossible to know how many. The Canadian Women's Foundation is funding grassroots organizations across the country to help prevent trafficking and help girls and women escape sex trafficking. Two researchers worked for more than two years to recruit underage sex workers in New York City in order to find out who they are (Hinman, 2011). They interviewed 249 underage prostitutes. Forty-five percent were boys; 90 percent were born in the United States. Half said they were recruited by a friend, and only 10 percent had a pimp. Nearly all said they exchanged sex for money in order to support themselves.

LO4 **The Career of a Sex Worker**

Given the stigmatized and often risky nature of sex work, many scholars and social service professionals have studied entry into it (see First Person). There are two general explanations. One emphasizes negative experiences in childhood and adolescence, such as physical and sexual abuse, family instability, poverty, homelessness, and contact with exploitative men such as pimps or drug dealers. The other explanation emphasizes factors in the environment at the point of entry, especially economic need, the lack of job skills (often reflecting poor education), and limited employment opportunity (McCarthy et al., 2014). Past research generally studied small samples of workers in a particular venue or part of the industry, giving a narrow picture of the influences on their entry. New research compared predictors of entry into sex work with predictors of entry into two other service occupations in Sacramento, California, and Victoria, British Columbia: food and beverage service, and barbering and hair-styling. Workers in the three occupations (about 200 from each) were located in two metropolitan areas, using telephone directories, lists of businesses, and municipal licensing lists. Workers in each occupation were recruited and trained to conduct face-to-face interviews. The interviews collected data on numerous early and more recent life experiences. The results indicated that family background measures related to becoming a sex worker were an additional parent or guardian (instability) and parents receiving public assistance; childhood experience variables included experiencing physical and sexual abuse and living in a foster home; and influences in emerging adulthood included fewer years of education and indicators of economic need—being single or living with an unemployed partner. So, in fact, the data support both of the explanations. Of course, individual sex workers experienced some of these but not all. For example, an Ontario study found that sex workers do not identify their childhood experiences as a cause of their decision to enter the sex trade (Orchard et al., 2014).

Force or coercion is another factor. Some women report being coerced physically or psychologically by a husband or lover into selling sex for money. As noted earlier, coercion is a major factor in sex trafficking. Some women become involved in prostitution through

sex trafficking: The recruitment and control of persons for sexual exploitation.

a family member or friend who is already a sex worker and can teach them the ropes (Miller, 1986).

On entering, most sex workers go through an apprenticeship in which they learn the skills of the trade. The apprentice learns sexual techniques, especially fellatio, since many customers want oral sex. She learns how to hustle, how to successfully negotiate her services and price with potential customers. She learns how to maintain control over the interaction so that she can protect herself as much as possible from being hurt or robbed by clients (and many sex workers are hurt or robbed). She learns values, like "the customer is always right," and fairness to other "working girls." Women who are recruited into the life by a pimp may be trained by one of his more experienced "wives." Some women are trained by an experienced madam, in exchange for a large percentage of their fees.

There has been relatively little research on the "mid-career" sex worker. We have noted that a sex worker may work in several different venues over time. After learning the ropes, women may work in the in-call or out-call services and try to establish a list of regular clients. If successful, they usually begin to work independently (Bernstein, 2007). A woman might move from in-call to out-call as she becomes more experienced at managing clients. She might move from the street into work in bars or at truck stops in response to changes in the weather or her health. Sex workers who are addicted to drugs may be forced to work long hours and service many customers in more than one venue to support their habit. Again, some of these changes may result from coercion or exploitation by a pimp or a sex trafficker.

Research in New Brunswick and Nova Scotia found that when asked "What is the best part of sex work?" almost all sex workers replied "the money" (Jeffrey & MacDonald, 2006a, 2006b). This did not mean that they were forced into sex work by economic factors but rather that they chose sex work over their other alternatives, such as a minimum-wage job or social assistance. They also identified independence and flexibility of work as a positive part of their work. Thus, these sex workers chose sex work as a way of earning a better income (between $30 and $300 per night for outdoor work and between $50 and $150 per hour for indoor work) in a relatively short period while being able to set their own schedule.

The major hazards associated with being a sex worker are being a victim of a "bad trick" (i.e., physical or sexual assault or even murder), drug addiction, and sexually transmitted infections (Church et al., 2001; Jeffrey & MacDonald, 2006a, 2006b). The worst risk is of being murdered.

Sex Workers' Well-Being

There are a variety of images of the contemporary sex worker: young, attractive, autonomous, healthy, "the happy hooker"; young, brazen, aggressive, "the tough chick"; not-so-young, bruised emotionally and physically, a victim. Which one is valid?

According to a landmark study (Vanwesenbeeck, 1994), all these images are accurate. Researchers in the Netherlands recruited 100 women who had been working for at least one year for a study of "sex and health"; these women were interviewed and completed several measures of coping style and well-being. The samples included women who worked on the street, in windows, in clubs and brothels (Figure 17.4), for escort services, and in their own homes. The results indicated that one-quarter of the women were doing well. They had few physical or psychosocial complaints, used problem-focused coping strategies, and were satisfied with their lives. Another quarter were at the opposite end. They complained of headaches, backaches, anxiety, and depression; their coping strategies involved dissociation (seeing problems as unrelated to the self) and denial, and they were dissatisfied with sex work. The remaining women were in the middle.

Figure 17.4 Brothels in a few cities around the world display available workers in windows on the sidewalk. These workers have cleaner and safer working conditions.

© NB Photos/Alamy

Milestones in Sex Research

Talking Back: Stories of Sex Work in the Maritimes

One really does not expect a sex worker to be articulate, to resist, or to "talk back" to dominant stereotypes of her or his work, but that is what we found when we started asking for and recording the words of sex workers in the Maritimes.

Many of us have stereotypes of people in sex work. Sex workers are often depicted by the media, some police, and certain conservative religious groups as victims or as deserving of a certain fate. Rarely are sex workers depicted as the people they are—mothers, friends, sisters, brothers, fathers, grandparents, lovers, or workers. Equally problematic is the view that sex workers are passive and lacking agency, the ability to act in the social world, to make choices, or to resist dominant, negative beliefs about their lives. In our study, we asked 62 sex workers (men, women, and transgender) in three Maritime cities about their perceptions and attitudes about the work they do, as well as about others' views of them. In answering our questions, they were articulate, witty, and courageous. They did not hesitate to "talk back" to dominant, erroneous images of them. Their words were the most important part of our study because we saw ourselves as engaged in a politics of solidarity rather than a politics of saving. Here we share some of their insights.

We asked about the best and worst aspects of sex work that they encountered. The best parts of the work they claimed were "the money, honey." Colleen from Moncton could not understand why anyone would not do her work, given the amount of money she makes compared with other service work:

> There's one woman at my work (call centre), she's a psychology major, and she has her master's. And she's working at a call centre for $8.00 an hour. I think she's making a little bit more now 'cause she's been there for a long time. I think she's making $8.40 an hour. Like, still, you spent $50,000 on university, to make $8.40 an hour?

On the other hand, Eric from Moncton claimed he'd never go back to sex work, and that he'd "rather work for twelve hours a day than go out and stand for an hour in the cold. It's degrading." Money was talked about in terms of refusal to "budget" according to what the state (read social assistance) was demanding. As Jacqueline of Saint John said: "It's cash in my pocket. Welfare doesn't know. It gives my son better clothes, better food. . . . I spend all my money on him." Sex workers' refusal to "be poor" and to accept "handouts," and their desire to be their own boss was a common theme as well.

Violence was the worst part of sex work; all participants reported an increase in violence. Dana, of Halifax, blamed the increase in violence as being squarely connected to people's stereotypes:

> The reason I feel that [clients have become more violent] is because the media portrays us as non-people. And yeah, they do, they make us more . . . like the word *prostitute*, this is where I have the big problem,

The risks to a woman and thus her well-being varied according to the venue in which she worked. In the Netherlands, where sex work is legal, women who worked in windows and on the streets were at greater risk. Similarly, research in Canada has found that working the streets is associated with greater risk of violence by clients (Lewis et al., 2005; Shaver, 2005). This obviously influences physical and mental health. Women who worked in windows or on the streets worked faster, had more clients, and earned less per customer than those working in in-call and out-call services. In a more recent study of indoor sex workers in the Netherlands, workers reported having an average nine-hour workday; more than one-third worked more than 40 hours per week, and half had taken no holidays in the preceding year (Venicz & Vanwesenbeeck, 2000). The scores of indoor sex workers on measures of burnout—depersonalization and emotional exhaustion—were compared with the scores of female health-care workers and persons in treatment for work-related problems. Sex workers scored significantly higher on depersonalization, which was mainly explained by contextual factors: working because of coercion, experiences of violence, and lack of control

it dehumanizes people . . . they use the word "prostitute" or "hooker" as opposed to "a woman who was working as a prostitute." It's a job—it's not a person.

They've made it a person and they've made it a stereotypical low-life person and a disposable person and the more that the media continues to do that, the more the tricks feel that they are allowed to be violent.

Stigma was also cited by Jason in Moncton:

Okay, how can I put this? We're not scum because you're the ones paying. . . . You guys are looking down on us . . . yeah, but who's paying us? It's you guys. How do we make our money? You guys.

Stigma extends beyond behaviour on the street. Many reported the kind of experience that Jill, from Saint John, had when she went to emergency services at the local hospital:

I've gone in for a coffee burn, and you know what I mean, all of a sudden it's turned into my drug use, and the way I was dressed and stuff: "Well, you're just a prostitute, you know and you probably deserved it." And it was a coffee burn, so you know what I mean, so . . . . They make you feel like you're diseased or something.

Others, such as Denise, an ex-worker in Halifax, spoke of how much they grew in the experience of sex work, how much they learned:

I learned a lot. I learned a lot about myself: how strong I really could be. I met a lot of other people, like girls like myself. We were all normal, and then things happened. And I learned a lot about people in general. . . . I can survive, and I have survived. I have

become strong. You look into the face of death every day and you're either gonna make it or break it. You're gonna be found dead, or you're gonna survive. . . . But I never forget the times and I'm not embarrassed. I learned a lot about society, and the law.

Felicity from Halifax reported that her clients were one of the best parts of her job and that she deplored any kind of discrimination they might face:

They [her clients] are missing something, whether they don't have a wife at home that's giving them enough attention, or they have no one in their lives. You know, some of them just need to be close to someone, or they just need somebody to love them even if it's a half-hour or an hour at a time. . . .

In sum, the world of sex workers is far from the usual stereotypes that people create. It isn't always safe, it isn't always pretty, but as they point out, many other jobs have similar types of stories—of exploitation, of addiction, and of liberation and independence.

The last words belong to Alexis, a 17-year-old former sex worker from Moncton:

If I had a chance to tell the media so that they—so the world would hear what I had to say, something I'd tell them is, "Don't speak. You want to know about a whore, you get to know a whore and you'll see that she's just like you." That's what I'd tell them.

Written by Gayle MacDonald based on Leslie Ann Jeffrey and Gayle MacDonald. (2006). *Sex Workers in the Maritimes Talk Back.* Vancouver: UBC Press.

in interaction with clients (Vanwesenbeeck, 2005). An important caveat in interpreting these studies is that they were conducted in the context of legalized prostitution in the Netherlands. Doubtless, the health outcomes would be worse in countries in which prostitution was illegal and therefore sex workers have little recourse if, for example, they are assaulted.

A unique study of the geography of sex worker victimization used reports filed by sex workers in New South Wales in Australia (Prior et al., 2012). An outreach project there encourages workers to voluntarily report instances of victimization they experience. An analysis

of 333 reports filed over eight years identified 528 criminal acts. One-fifth involved theft including stealing, defrauding, and nonpayment. One-sixth involved harassment including stalking, nuisance behaviour, and threats. Other actions included disorderly conduct, assault, and abduction. Most incidents occurred indoors, regardless of the venue; victimization occurred in the assailant's car (street work), the premises (brothels), the assailant's home (out-call), or the worker's residence (in-call). The authors concluded that privacy and the worker's lack of control are major situational contributors to victimization.

In an attempt to reduce street prostitution and to reduce risks for sex workers, Zurich, Switzerland, has created "sex drive-ins." Nine garage-style structures have been built; they are equipped with alarm buttons and guarded by security personnel to ensure the safety of the sex workers. Men enter the area and select from the women who are present. They drive into one of the structures. Customers are not allowed to leave the area with the sex workers. Social and health-care services are offered on-site for the workers. Similar sites exist in Utrecht, Netherlands, and Cologne, Germany.

Risks are especially high for women who are being trafficked because they are at risk of suffering abuse and injury by both clients and masters, experiencing illness and infection, and facing medical neglect (Hynes & Raymond, 2002).

There is also the risk of exposure to sexually transmitted infections, especially HIV/AIDS. Sex workers infected with HIV are often workers who are also injecting drugs; research indicates that the injection is the greater risk. In the Western world, studies show that the sex worker's risk of HIV infection is greater in his or her private sex life than in the sex work. The risk varies greatly in other parts of the world, with high rates of HIV/AIDS in some cities and countries but low rates in others (Vanwesenbeeck, 2001).

Some suggest that the high levels of violence and of psychological distress found among sex workers are not due to the nature of the sex work per se, but instead reflect the stigma associated with sex work (Bernstein, 2007). Sex workers are at risk of sexual assault because of attitudes such as the view that sex workers cannot be sexually assaulted so no harm is done if you do force them to have sex (Miller & Schwartz, 1995). The risk of arrest and mistreatment by law enforcement personnel, and the resulting anxiety and distress, reflect the fact that some aspects of sex work are illegal.

Sex workers use a variety of strategies to cope with the risks of their work. Some use drugs and alcohol to increase their confidence and decrease their guilt. Others use a strategy of shutting down their feelings and focusing narrowly on the task. The consequences of this distancing are often referred to as *depersonalization* (not, of course, an experience unique to sex work). Independent women may view themselves as professionals, providing therapy, "sexual healing," or sex education. They may take courses to enhance their skills, such as massage certification, or use prior training as a therapist or social worker. These women perceive their work as offering opportunities for personal growth (Bernstein, 2007). Some emphasize the rewarding aspects of the work, perhaps that it supports their children. Many sex workers use as a coping technique the careful management of time and place, locating their sex work in a specific physical and temporal place

separated from their private sexual and familial relationships (also not unique to sex work). Sex workers also may use the network of contacts with other sex workers as a source of support; workers on one "stroll" worked together to protect a pregnant colleague by giving her all the customers who wanted a blow-job and protecting her from clients known to be rough (Anderson, 2004).

"Squaring up" or "leaving the life" refers to giving up sex work. Financially and psychologically, it is a difficult thing to do, particularly for the person with no job skills. Recognizing this, some analysts call for comprehensive programs that provide education and job training, shelters, and counselling for women (and men) who want to leave commercial sex work (Hynes & Raymond, 2002). There are promising approaches available that can reduce harm, including education (especially job training), empowerment, preventive health care, and improved occupational and safety conditions. For example, PEERS, which stands for Prostitutes, Empowerment, Education, and Resource Society, has branches in several Canadian cities and provides support, training, and resources to help male and female sex workers leave the trade. Stella is an organization in Quebec that provides support and information to sex workers and is working to educate the public, fight discrimination against sex workers, and promote decriminalization of their work (chezstella.org).

The Role of Early Abuse

The study of women working in the Netherlands found that in addition to their work venue, having a history of victimization and trauma as children or adolescents before they entered prostitution was associated with poorer well-being (Vanwesenbeeck, 1994). Researchers in Ontario conducted semi-structured, life history interviews with women engaged in sex work (Orchard et al. 2014). One section focused on childhood and family life. Analyses of interviews with 14 women ages 24 to 60 identified several themes. Most of the women grew up with their mothers and fathers; many reported difficult relationships with their mothers, and complicated and painful relationships with their fathers. One-third reported sexual abuse by their fathers or other men in childhood and adolescence. They described "childhood as being largely devoid of the freedom and protection normally associated with this phase" and early "adoption of roles normally reserved for adults (i.e., work at home and caregiving)" (p. 16). The women grew up in economically deprived neighbourhoods, and sex work was a readily available option. Clearly, any adult who has experienced childhood victimization may have poor well-being. Coercive sexual activity in adolescence or young adulthood is associated with a variety of adverse health and social outcomes (Ganju et al., 2004).

Working Their Way through University

Economic need has been recognized for decades as one reason women enter the commercial sex industry. It has frequently been cited as one reason young women, often with limited employment prospects, become strippers, streetwalkers, or escorts. In the past decade, there have been reports of women students engaging in sex work. The first widely publicized case was that of Brooke Magnanti. Beginning in 2003, writing under the pen name *Belle du Jour*, she blogged about her life as a £300 per hour escort. She worked in London for 14 months. Subsequently, her diary and two books were published detailing her career; the books were best-sellers. In 2007, a television series based on her books began broadcasting in England, *Secret Diary of a Call Girl*. The books and the TV series created widespread name recognition. In 2009, fearing her identity was going to be revealed, she announced her identity publicly as Dr. Brooke Magnanti, a child health-care specialist. She stated that she worked as an escort between the time she submitted her PhD thesis and took her oral exams.

Sophie (a pseudonym) is a 22-year-old university student working as an escort to pay for her education. Her student loans don't cover her living costs, and she is enrolled in an intensive program. She was 19 when she started; she says she had no idea what she was doing, and "suddenly it [sex work] was the better option." She advertises on an adult site, and picks her clients based on feedback. She performs both in-call and out-call work. She acknowledges the risk; there is no safety net. She schedules clients around her classes, and sometimes does not see clients for weeks (Buchanan, 2014). Another student working a few hours per week as an escort said, "I made the choice . . . in hopes of having a smaller debt when I am done" (Anonymous, 2012). Both women acknowledge the psychological toll of the work, one stating that she experienced PTSD.

Vaughn Jackson, Amanda Pena, and Maran Gorham all work as strippers at the Show Palace in Queens, New York. Mike Diaz, manager of the all-nude club, is happy to employ students. He sees the jobs he provides as preventing them from accumulating huge debts while they are in school. Plus, he says, they can schedule the work around school. Vaughn, Amanda, and Maran each work, on the average, three nights per week and earn $1500 to $2000 per week. All three seem proud of what they do; one finds it "empowering" (Schuster, 2014). Stripping, of course, is less risky, since the worker is surrounded by co-workers, customers, and management.

How common are the experiences described by these women? Research in the U.K. involved recruiting students on 29 university campuses by approaching students in various areas on campus, and online. Most participants were full-time undergraduates. About six percent of the sample (all but one female) reported currently working in the sex industry, as erotic dancers, strippers, or escorts (Roberts et al., 2013).

Research in Berlin obtained data from 4386 students in "major" universities in that city; questionnaires were distributed via student mailing lists (Betzer, Kohler, & Schleman, 2015). Participants' average age was 24, average semester in school was fifth, and 44 percent were women. Seven percent indicated they were or had been involved in sex work, most reporting they had engaged in sexual intercourse in direct exchange for money or escort services. Students reporting sex work reported receiving significantly less financial support from their families and fewer scholarships. The researchers conclude that sex work results from financial hardship, and its appeal is the higher income for fewer hours of work. Sex workers were more likely to report being homosexual or bisexual, and to have an STI.

According to Statistics Canada, about 2.1 million persons are enrolled full-time in post-secondary education programs. Six percent is 125 000, so if the estimates from the two surveys reported above apply to Canadian students, over 100 000 are engaging in sex work. Many of these students are engaging in sex work because of (a) the steady increase in college and university costs over the past decade; (b) the low and unpredictable wages paid by jobs typically available to students, such as wait staff, student hourly work on campus, and door-to-door soliciting; (c) high cost of living in some cities; and (d) higher rates of youth unemployment. Given the risks of commercial sex work, student involvement in it is becoming a serious concern. In England, the Student Sex Work Project (SSWP; www.thestudentsexworkproject.co.uk) is developing programs to provide information and resources to student sex workers, with a focus on their safety and sexual health. In the United States, the Sex Workers Outreach Project (SWOP) is a national project focusing on sex worker rights and advocacy, staffed by a number of former student sex workers (www.swopusa.org). Improved access to and financial support for higher education for all qualified persons should be a national priority.

Early coercion is associated with subsequent nonconsensual sex (e.g., trafficking), unintended pregnancy, and abortion. Adverse mental health outcomes include low self-esteem as well as substance abuse.

Customers

At the time of the Kinsey research, about 69 percent of all white males had had some experience with sex workers (Kinsey et al., 1948). In 1992, the National Health and Social Life Survey (NHSLS) in the U.S. asked all respondents whether they had had sex with someone they paid or who paid them (Laumann et al., 1994). Only 17 percent of men and 2 percent of women reported that they had had sex with such a partner since age 18. According to the National Survey of Sexual Health and Behavior (NSSHB), in the United States in 2009, 4.3 percent of men ages 18 to 59 and 0.8 percent of women ages 18 to 59 reported paying or being paid for sex in the last year (Herbenick et al., 2010c). Thus, the use of prostitutes has declined dramatically in the past 50 years. This likely reflects the increased frequency of nonmarital and casual sexual activity during this same period (see Chapters 10 and 11).

Sex workers refer to their customers as "johns." A Canadian study of johns developed a detailed questionnaire; it could be filled out on the Internet, printed and returned by mail, or completed in-person, by telephone, or through an Internet interview (Atchison, 2010). Participants were recruited by ads placed in newspapers, magazines, newsletters, adult clubs and businesses, and online discussion boards. Participants had to be at least 19, have paid for sex at least once in their lifetime, and reside in Canada. The author analyzed completed questionnaires from 861 people. The mean age was 42, and 99.4 percent were male. At the time of the survey, one-half were married or in a common-law relationship, and 39 percent were single. Of those who were not married, 25 percent had regular sex partners. Two-thirds earned at least $50 000 per year. On average, participants had purchased sex 100 times in their lives and had visited indoor sex establishments 4.8 times in the previous 12 months. Eighty-six percent preferred female workers, and 10.5 percent preferred male workers. The most recent time they paid for sex, they paid for multiple activities (25 percent), half-oral and half-vaginal sex (17 percent), the GFE (16 percent), and vaginal intercourse (16 percent). Thus, most of these johns were heterosexual, in a relationship, and middle class by income (and occupation), and had visited commercial sex workers several times per year. Some johns are occasional johns; they may be businessmen who seek only occasional contacts with sex workers, perhaps while on business trips; some are compulsive johns, who use sex workers for their major sexual outlet. They are driven

> **Why do some people pay for sex?**

to them and cannot stay away (see Chapter 15).[1] Nearly 50 percent of johns are repeat clients who seek a regular relationship with one particular sex worker or a small group of them (Freund et al., 1991).

A study of 46 female sex workers, one-half working in Tijuana and one-half in Ciudad Juarez, Mexico, asked them a series of questions about their current, regular, and non-regular clients (Robertson et al., 2014). These interviews were part of a much larger study of sex workers and their noncommercial partners, so the researchers had much background data. Analyses identified four types of clients. *One-time clients* were men the worker did not expect to see again; the transaction was strictly commercial. Some women preferred to avoid such clients, but accepted them when other types of clients were scarce. *Regular clients/"friends"* were repeat clients the worker had known for some time. The workers developed friendships with these men and trusted them; the men treated the woman with kindness and respect. Several women had clients who had *fallen in love* with them. These men were very difficult to manage because they sought noncommercial relationships and commitments (e.g., living together). Occasionally, a worker would report that her current intimate partner was a former client who had fallen in love with her. The fourth type was *long-term financial providers*. These men provided consistent, substantial financial support, often paying for major expenses on a regular basis. In exchange, the client expected special services such as spending the night or travelling together. These were often wealthy older men living in the U.S.

For many clients, a major appeal is the clear and bounded nature of the sexual interaction. Money is paid and services are received. The exchange is limited in time and space, and requires no effort to develop or maintain a relationship. The client wants "bounded authenticity"—real sex, a sense that she or he matters and is desirable, without the effort, expense, and hassles of commitment (Bernstein, 2007).

Commercial sex work is common in locations where there are large numbers of men separated from their usual social contacts, such as military bases. In the twenty-first century, the provision of sex workers near bases often involves women who have been trafficked, especially in places like South Korea. Interviews with a random sample of Hispanic men in North Carolina, where men outnumber Hispanic women 2.3 to 1, found that 28 percent had visited a commercial sex worker in the preceding year. Forty-six percent of single men and 40 percent of married men not living with their wives

---

[1] Some Canadian cities have implemented programs designed to increase johns' awareness of the risks of street prostitution. Instead of receiving criminal charges, the johns attend a full-day seminar that provides information on community concerns, health risks, and sexual addictions and compulsions (Symbalauk & Jones, 1999).

reported using a sex worker. The men reported an average of five or more visits in the preceding year (Parrado et al., 2004).

Male Sex Workers

Most male sex workers serve a male clientele. However, some sell their services to women or to both women and men.

Male sex workers serving a female clientele work in three settings. Some male sex workers work for escort services and provide companionship and sexual gratification on an out-call basis. Working in such a setting is much less risky for men than for women. Some men work in massage parlours, under the same conditions as female employees. These male sex workers virtually never work in the street, in contrast to female streetwalkers and male *hustlers* (discussed shortly). This reflects gender-role socialization; female clients are unlikely to cruise the streets and pick up a sex worker, because they have been taught to let the man take the initiative.

A third type is the **gigolo**, a man who provides companionship and sexual gratification on a continuing basis to a woman in exchange for money. A gigolo often, though not always, has only one client at a time. The demand for gigolos reflects the fact that women, like

men, desire sexual gratification on a continuing basis and will pay for it when circumstances require or allow them to do so. On the other hand, most women prefer their sexual activity to be part of an ongoing relationship.

Many male sex workers sell their services primarily or exclusively to men; some of their clients identify as gay, others identify as heterosexual. Women who engage in sex work are acting in ways that are consistent with their feminine identity, providing emotional and sexual labour for others. Men who engage in sex work with male clients find that their masculine identity is challenged, triggering a stigma not faced by other types of sex workers. Contemporary male sex workers catering to men work in four settings (Minichiello, Scott, & Callander, 2013). *Outdoor workers* are often young, and identify as heterosexual; they typically solicit pedestrians and motorists and engage in sex in cars, homes, or other locations. Some work in the vicinity of public toilets. Advantages are minimal overhead and the ability to retain their earnings; like women who work the streets, they face the risks of assault and stigma. Male street workers are sometimes referred to as **hustlers** (Figure 17.5). To emphasize their masculinity,

> **gigolo (JIG-uh-loh):** A male who provides companionship and sexual gratification on a continuing basis to a woman in exchange for money.
> **hustlers:** Male sex workers who sell their services to men.

Figure 17.5 Sex for sale on Jarvis Street in Toronto.

© Mats Bakken

they may wear tight jeans and leather jackets. In some cities there are specific areas known as places where hustlers operate. *Bar workers* are found in gay-identified spaces—gyms, bars, clubs, and hotels. Since these are spaces where casual and same-sex activities are common, these men face less stigma than outdoor workers. These men typically work part-time. A minority of men work in *brothels,* providing sexual services on an in-call basis. Their working conditions and risks are similar to those experienced by women in this setting. Usually a brothel will have only a few male employees. Prices for specific activities are typically fixed, and management retains a significant amount of the fee. The clients may be primarily women. The largest group is *escorts or "call boys,"* the male counterpart of the "call girl." They often identify as gay or bisexual. They work in both in-call and out-call services, and their clientele locates them through gay media. Their clients are usually middle- and upper-class men, and these workers can earn large incomes for relatively few hours of work. One study interviewed 40 men working for a single escort agency (Smith et al., 2015). The escorts reported that a variety of social and emotional activities were required both to provide good service to clients and to cope with their fear of being stigmatized if they disclosed their sex work to persons outside the agency. Sex work in this setting is not just about sex.

In one study of male sex workers in Montreal between the ages of 16 and 29, the main reason for engaging in sex work, stated by 88 percent, was money, although some said they engaged in sex work as a way to meet people (Earls & David, 1989). Many of these young men came from troubled home environments, often leaving home at an early age. The majority (78 percent) reported using drugs on a regular basis.

Researchers wanted to study the male clients of male escorts. In 2012, they posted an invitation to complete an online survey on DaddyReviews.com, an escort website (Grov et al., 2014). The survey asked about the client's most recent hire, and was completed by 495 men. Most were white (88 percent), employed full-time (71 percent), and single (59 percent). Three-fourths identified as gay, 18 percent bisexual, and 4 percent heterosexual. Clients paid an average of $250 per hour, and oral and anal sex were the most common sexual activities engaged in. Given the use of the Internet to recruit the sample and the fee paid per hour, these are clearly well-to-do clients and may not be a representative sample.

Transgender Sex Workers

Some trans women work as sex workers. They are typically taking estrogen, which feminizes their body, including giving them breasts. Transgender sex workers serve a male clientele. A study of 46 cisgender women, 46 cisgender men, and 48 trans women working as street sex workers found that the transgender sex workers were more similar to the female sex workers than to the male sex workers in keeping regular hours and spending less time with each client (Weinberg et al., 1999). Most reported that they enjoyed sexual activities with clients at least sometimes; in this way, they were more similar to the male than to the female sex workers in the study. The transgender sex workers typically provided oral sex, manual stimulation, and receptive anal intercourse. More than half never or rarely told their customers that they were male; they would deceive their customers by restricting services (e.g., to oral sex), taping or tucking their penis back between their legs, and providing an excuse not to remove their skirt or panties (e.g., having their period).

L06 Sex Tourism

An increasingly important type of commercial sex is **sex tourism**, which refers to varieties of leisure travel that have as their purpose the purchase of sexual services (Wonders & Michalowski, 2001). Both men and women engage in sex tourism, although women may be more likely to identify their behaviour as *romance tourism* resulting in sexual activity (Jacobs, 2009; Perrott, 2012). Sex tourism is made possible by three large-scale social forces: the migration of men and women from less-developed nations, or from rural to urban areas, in search of jobs; the commodification of sexual intimacy, making all types of sex a commodity or service for sale; and increased travel for recreational purposes. All three of these forces are tied to increasing globalization, the movement of information and people freely across national boundaries.

The migration of people in search of economic opportunities provides a large group of young men and women in search of work. In some locales, they are aggressively recruited into sex work by pimps or persons with ties to sex trafficking. In other places, they enter into the life more or less voluntarily, often because there are few other opportunities for persons of their racial or ethnic background. In Amsterdam, where the attitude toward sex work can be described as regulated tolerance, a few individuals control much of the commercial sex work, recruiting foreign migrants to work in windows and brothels. In contrast, in Havana, Cuba, commercial sex work is decentralized, with many men and women working independently. They contact potential clients in hotels, bars, and on the street, hoping to connect with someone who will employ them, perhaps for several days.

sex tourism: Leisure travel with the purpose of purchasing sexual services.

In some countries, sex tourism is the most rapidly growing economic sector and a major source of hard currency; in such places, governments have little incentive to reduce or eliminate it. One estimate places the value of the global sex industry at $20 billion per year.

The tourists who can purchase sexual services are obviously wealthy enough to travel, which in turn often means they are citizens of developed countries and members of the middle and upper classes in their home societies. The sex workers are often from a different national and ethnic background. One of the attractions for the tourist is sex with this "dark-skinned other," perhaps someone from a group stereotyped as sexually free and uninhibited. The encounter is appealing because it is a sharp contrast to the tourist's usual sexual experience (Brennan, 2010; Padilla, 2007). Unfortunately, one such appeal for men is sex with a young girl, and in some Asian cities girls as young as 12 and 13 are available in brothels, where they are tightly controlled by their managers. Of importance, Canadian citizens and permanent residents who engage in sexual activities with children in a foreign country that are illegal in Canada (see Table 2.1) can be charged and prosecuted in Canada.

The search for the type of sex workers—gender, age, sexual orientation—and experience that the tourist seeks is facilitated by the Internet (Padilla, 2007). Websites publish information about sex work, cruising areas and meeting places, and prices; past visitors review their experiences. Sex workers advertise on some of these sites, and some have their own web pages.

L07

Pornography

Pornography refers to sexually arousing material (focusing on the consumer) or material intended to produce sexual arousal (focusing on the producer). In either case, we are talking about a very broad range of material/experiences, many of which we will discuss in this section. The debate over pornography has been raging for decades. Some conservatives, religious fundamentalists, and some feminists (strange bedfellows, indeed!) agree that some kinds of pornography should be made illegal. Each group has overlapping but also different reasons for taking this position (Cowan et al., 1989; Luff, 2001). In contrast, some civil liberties groups, liberals, and some other feminists argue that freedom of expression, guaranteed in the *Charter of Rights and Freedoms*, must be preserved and therefore pornography should not be restricted by law. Meanwhile, Joe Brown downloads *All New Beaver Hunt, v. 13* for a pleasurable evening's entertainment.

Terms

We can distinguish among pornography, obscenity, and erotica. Pornography comes from the Greek words *porneia*, which means, quite simply, "prostitution," and *graphos*, which means "writing." In general usage today, **pornography** refers to magazines, films, and so on that are intended to be sexually arousing (Malamuth, 1998). The term is often used by people to refer to any image they don't like.

The *Criminal Code of Canada* uses the term *obscenity*, not pornography, in defining what sexual explicit material involving adults is illegal. It is a crime to sell or possess for the purposes of distribution any material that is obscene. It is also illegal to present an "immoral, indecent, or obscene" play, film, or other live performance. **Obscenity** refers to "any publication a dominant characteristic of which is the undue exploitation of sex." Because "undue exploitation" is rather vague, the courts have used the **community standards of tolerance test** to determine whether material is obscene. Community standards of tolerance do not refer to what Canadians would look at themselves; they refer to what Canadians would accept other Canadians being exposed to. Using the community standards of tolerance test means that standards can and do change over time as societal attitudes change. In 2005, the Supreme Court of Canada ruled that the test for indecency should not just be whether an activity violates community standards but whether it actually causes harm.

In the debate over pornography, some people make the distinction between pornography (which is unacceptable to them) and erotica (which is acceptable to them). According to this distinction, *pornography* depicts sexually explicit activities that are coupled with violence, are degrading or dehumanizing (usually to women), or include children (Russell, 1980). In contrast, **erotica** depicts explicit sex that is not violent and is neither degrading nor dehumanizing. According to this definition, a movie of a woman being sexually assaulted would be pornography, whereas a movie of two mutually consenting adults who are both enjoying having intercourse together would be considered erotica.

In keeping with this distinction, the Supreme Court of Canada in *R. v. Butler* ruled in 1992 that sexually explicit material depicting adults engaging in

What types of pornography are illegal in Canada?

pornography: Sexually arousing art, literature, or films.

obscenity: Something that is offensive according to accepted standards of decency; the legal term for pornography.

community standards of tolerance test: The test used by courts to determine whether something is obscene based on what Canadians would accept other Canadians being exposed to and whether it causes harm.

erotica: Sexually arousing material that is not violent, degrading, or demeaning and does not include children.

consensual sexual activity that does not depict violence and is not degrading or dehumanizing is not obscene. This decision divided pornography into three categories: (1) explicit sex with violence, (2) explicit sex without violence but in which people are treated in a way that is degrading or dehumanizing, and (3) explicit sex that is neither degrading nor dehumanizing. The Court ruled that the first category, sex with violence, constitutes "undue exploitation of sex" and thus fits the definition of obscenity in the *Criminal Code*. The Court indicated that the third category (erotica) is generally accepted in Canadian society (unless it involves children) and thus is not obscene. However, explicit sex that is degrading or dehumanizing may or may not be obscene depending on the risk of harm involved and whether the material has artistic merit. Although the Supreme Court decision gave a good deal of guidance to the courts, there is still ambiguity in the law. For example, what exactly constitutes degrading or dehumanizing sex? What criteria should be used to determine whether material has artistic merit? Should material depicting sadomasochistic activity in which partners consensually participate in some types of pain rituals or degrading activities (see Chapter 15) be considered obscene?

Another complication is that Canada Border Services Agency officials have the power to refuse to allow books, magazines, DVDs, and other materials deemed to be obscene to enter Canada without having to lay criminal charges or have the materials reviewed by the courts. In 1994, the Little Sisters Bookstore and Art Emporium in Vancouver challenged the right of customs officials to do so. They argued that customs officials specifically target gay and lesbian bookstores and that they deem material that does not include violence or degradation to be obscene just because it depicts gay or lesbian sex. Ultimately, the Supreme Court of Canada upheld the *Customs Act* but criticized customs inspectors for unfairly targeting the store.

Overview

Our discussion of pornography will consider several aspects of it. We begin with a brief discussion of the size and scope of the industry. Then we will consider in detail the various ways in which sexually arousing material is packaged and delivered in the contemporary world. This leads naturally to a consideration of the people who produce these materials. Next we will consider the consumers, who, after all, keep the industry booming (or not). Then we will discuss one of the major areas of research for the past four decades: the effects of pornography on users. Finally, we will discuss the larger perspective. Throughout, we pay particular attention to social scientists' research.

L08 The Pornography Industry

Pornography is a multibillion-dollar business in North America. Included in this industry are many different products and services: Internet porn, including "adult" websites, chat rooms, news groups, and bulletin boards; DVDs, videos, and films; magazines; live entertainment; and kiddie porn. Some of this activity is legal (e.g., publishing *Playboy* online); some of it is illegal (e.g., producing videos of children engaging in sex); and some is legal depending upon the county you live in (e.g., strip clubs featuring complete nudity and bodily contact). It is impossible to obtain precise data on the economics of pornography. One analysis estimated that in 2006, retail sales of all types in Canada totalled $1 billion (Mandese, 2007). According to Wikipedia (2012), the global market for Internet pornography alone is worth almost $5 billion.

Internet Pornography

In the past 15 years, the Internet has made available a wide variety of sex-related services for every computer in Canada with a connection to a DSL, satellite, or modem, whether at work, school, or home. According to Trekkie Monster in the musical *Avenue Q*, "The Internet is for porn!" Is that really true? Well, in 2010, 4 percent of the most-trafficked websites in the world were sex-related (Ruvalo, 2011). From July 2009 to July 2010, 13 percent of web searches were for erotic content. The day on which the most people look at pornography on the Internet? Monday. The busiest month? January. About 40 million Americans (13 percent of the population) regularly visit porn sites.

Pornhub is one of the world's largest porn sites; it has 38 million daily users (Anthony, 2014). In 2016, Canadians were the third-most frequent viewers (after the U.S. and the U.K.). Most (75 percent) of users were men. The most common sex-related search terms used by Canadians? "Lesbian." The next two most popular were related to youth (e.g., "teen") and "older women" (e.g., MILF). The average Canadian user spends between nine and ten minutes on-site, and views seven to ten pages; 58 percent of the users accessed the site with smartphones. A technical analysis of the infrastructure needed to service such sites suggests that porn certainly drives Internet technology. The most visited site has 4.4 billion page views per month, three times the size of CNN. And each viewer spends an average of 15 to 20 minutes (Anthony, 2012). The storage needed for the thousands of videos, and the bandwidth needed to meet the download demand is huge. Downloads of porn videos at peak may absorb the equivalent of one-fifteenth of the bandwidth available between New York and London.

The services provided online include access to sexually arousing videos, photos, and stories; an array of goods (sex toys, lingerie, even panties worn by porn stars) and services for sale; online chats with like-minded others; and access to bulletin boards with a variety of specialized materials.

Adult Websites

Adult websites display and sell a variety of sexual materials and services. According to Alexa.com, in May 2015, the most visited sites were Xnxx, Youporn, and Livejasmin. They are in the top 250 most-visited sites on the Internet. Xnxx and Youporn are "tube sites," featuring sexually explicit videos that can be viewed online or purchased, explicit photos, profiles of the women, and message forums for communicating about each woman. Livejasmin provides live sex online and the opportunity to chat with the actors. There are hundreds of other sites with names like Amateurs Gone Wild, Asian Pleasures, Lovely Cheerleaders, and Lydia Lashes. Each site typically includes thousands of photos organized by content, pornographic videos that can be viewed on your computer screen, stories, links to live sex shows, and links to live video cameras in such places as men's and women's locker rooms. Some also sell videos, CD-ROMs, sex toys, and costumes. Some also include interactive sex shows where the viewer can request that the actor perform specific acts. Many

of these sites specialize, featuring "teenagers" (if the actors are under 18, the material violates the law); Black, Asian, or Hispanic women; gay men; lesbians; pregnant women; and on and on (Figure 17.6). Each site charges a daily, weekly, or monthly membership fee for access; the fee can usually be paid by supplying a valid credit card number.

Researchers have analyzed the content of television programs for decades. Recently, similar techniques have been applied to the content posted on websites. Most sites organize videos into categories for ease of user access. Research indicates that two of the most popular search terms are teen and MILF. A team of researchers in New Brunswick analyzed five teen and five MILF videos from each of ten free sites. Across all of the videos, vaginal intercourse and fellatio were most frequently depicted; use of toys, condoms, and coercion were rare. There were no gender differences in who initiated the activity or use of persuasion. MILF videos portrayed the female as more agentic and more in control than teen videos, consistent with the presumed greater experience of a mature woman (Vannier et al., 2014). Another group analyzed the content of 302 videos featuring male performers posted on five sites. Masturbation and anal intercourse were the most common behaviours portrayed, with condoms used in about one-half of the portrayals

Figure 17.6 The newest innovation in the porn business is computer porn.

of intercourse. Longer videos portrayed a larger number of behaviours, including a larger number of high-risk behaviours (Downing et al., 2014).

Viewing pornography on the Internet can be a positive alternative sexual outlet. Further, it allows people access to sexually explicit images in privacy, letting them explore their individual interests without experiencing shyness or shame (Nosko et al., 2007). However, Internet pornography may also be a cause for concern, for several reasons. One is that the large and ever-increasing number of chat rooms, news groups, and websites lead to some people becoming dependent on or addicted to (see Chapter 15) this type of sexual content (Yellowlees & Marks, 2007). None of these involves face-to-face social interaction, which is central to most sexual relationships; the risk is that these encounters become a substitute. However, only a small percentage of people who use the Internet for sexual activities (1 percent in one study) develop a sexual addiction or compulsion (Griffiths, 2001).

Finally, the Internet facilitates the distribution of child pornography, which is illegal in Canada. Existing Canadian laws governing child pornography apply to the Internet, and some law enforcement agencies seek out and arrest offenders. However, this material can be easily transferred across borders and may be legal in the country where it originated, making enforcement of the child pornography laws difficult (Canadian Centre for Justice Statistics, 1999).

Chat Rooms

Chat rooms, or Internet relay chat groups, provide a location where individuals can meet and carry on conversations electronically. These rooms are often oriented toward persons with particular sexual interests, often captured by their names. The conversations often involve graphic descriptions of sexual activities or fantasies. The telephone sex conversation reproduced later in the chapter could have taken place electronically, with the words displayed on a computer screen or through audio connections instead of spoken over a phone line. In this context, an interesting feature of these chats can be that the other person cannot see you. This allows you to present yourself in any way you desire, to rehearse or try out a broad range of identities (Turkle, 1995).

News Groups

People can also log on to sex-oriented news or discussion groups, read messages posted by others, and post messages themselves. The messages may include personal information, or they may be a story or a file containing pornographic pictures in digital format. Stories can be printed by the user; picture files can be downloaded and viewed through a plug-in. Often, the messages are simply advertisements for or links to sex-oriented websites that sell pornographic material.

Commercial Bulletin Boards

There are numerous commercial bulletin boards (BBS) that contain sexually explicit photographs in digital form. Users may log on to these bulletin boards and download images for a fee. Each image is listed in an electronic catalogue with a short description. Sites specialize, and many of the images are hard-core, paraphilic, or pedophilic (see Chapter 15). "The 'adult' BBS market is driven largely by the demand for paraphilic and pedophilic imagery. The availability of, and the demand for, vaginal sex imagery is relatively small" (Rimm, 1995, p. 1890). Possessing such images is illegal in Canada (see Table 2.1).

DVDs, Videos, and Films

Sexually explicit movies were made as early as 1915. The technology remained primitive and distribution very limited until the 1960s. The *hard-core film* industry began to emerge in a big way around 1970. Two films were especially important in this breakthrough. *I Am Curious (Yellow),* appearing in the late 1960s, showed sexual intercourse explicitly. In part because it was a foreign film with an intellectual tone, it became fashionable for people, including married couples, to see it. The other important early film was *Deep Throat,* appearing in 1972. With its humour and creative plot, it was respectable and popular among the middle class. After the success of *Deep Throat,* many more full-length, technically well-made hard-core films appeared. *Deep Throat* had made it clear that there were big profits to be made. It cost US$24 000 to make, yet by 1982 it had yielded US$25 million in profits.

Loops are short (ten-minute) hard-core videos. They are set up in coin-operated computers in private booths, usually in adult bookstores. The patron can enter and view the film in private and perhaps masturbate while doing so. They cater to both the straight and gay communities.

In the early 1980s, X-rated videocassettes for home viewing began to replace porn theatres. For example, *Deep Throat* became available on cassette in 1977, and by 1982, 300 000 copies had been sold (Cohn, 1983). Cable and satellite television also entered the arena, with porn channels thriving in some areas (Figure 17.7). Next came the DVD. This *privatization* of pornography was furthered by the development of the Internet, which vastly expanded the potential market.

Figure 17.7 Anne-Marie Losique recently launched Canada's first adult channels in English and French, Vanessa TV, which shows the softer and more erotic side of sex. It recently merged with an American giant and become Vivid TV Canada, a bilingual on-demand channel.

François Roy/La Presse

There are also increasing numbers of adult videos made for gay men and lesbians. Canadian gay men criticize pornography aimed at gay men for depicting hypermasculine men, being nonegalitarian, and simulating a heterosexual model (Morrison, 2004). Research with lesbians in Canada identified two types of lesbian pornography: "pseudo-lesbian" pornography, which is actually created to cater to meet the erotic interests and fantasies of male viewers, and lesbian pornography, which is created by and designed for lesbians. In lesbian-created pornography, performers do not necessarily have "ideal" bodies, there is a greater attempt to convey intimacy and emotion, and there is a focus on the body rather than on genitals and penetration (Morrison & Tallack, 2005). However, even in lesbian-created pornography women's bodies are still unrealistic in terms of weight and breast size. Further, too much focus on intimacy and emotion sometimes results in depictions that are not sexually arousing.

Many hard-core films and X-rated DVDs are made for a heterosexual audience. In the United States, adult videos earn US$4 billion per year and account for more than 700 million rentals annually (Rich, 2001). Based on an informal survey, an adult video distributor estimated that in 1998 more than 38 000 adult videos were rented each day in Ontario, resulting in annual revenue of more than $52 million. There are no national data available.

These videos portray couples engaging in both fellatio and cunnilingus, and in vaginal and anal intercourse in various settings and positions. Less often, films and videos show sexual activity involving three or more people, or two women (Davis & Bauserman, 1993). First Person offers a look at the making of X-rated videos from the perspective of the actors.

A rapidly expanding part of the porn industry is the amateur video. The development of the home video camera has enabled anybody with a willing partner, friends, or neighbours to produce homemade porn. Such videos cost virtually nothing to make, and distributors are eager to purchase them. These films account for at least 20 percent of all adult videos made in the United States ("Sex Industry," 1998). Amateur videos are available free on numerous Internet sites. Perhaps as a result, sales and rentals of adult videos fell 30 percent from 2004 to 2006 (Baram, 2007). Sales fell an additional 50 percent from 2006 to 2010 (Johansmeyer, 2010).

In the 1990s, a number of companies began marketing videos designed to educate people about various aspects of human sexuality. With names like the "Better Sex" video series, these include explicit portrayals of a wide variety of consenting heterosexual activities. As such, these are erotica, not pornography. They often include commentary by a psychologist or sex therapist, reassuring viewers that the activities portrayed are normal and

Behind the Scene: Making X-Rated Videos

Dave Cummings bounces out of bed. He's working today, so he goes through his routine: he showers, shaves extremely close to get a smooth face, trims his fingernails and his pubic hair, applies lotion to his groin, and finishes with hand lotion. He dresses casually and drives to a large, expensive home in Beverly Hills rented for the shoot. When he arrives, he greets the other performers, mostly young women and men in their 20s and 30s. In this group, Dave is the odd man out. He is 59 years old, balding, and looks like your doctor, not the typical male performer in an X-rated video. It is that appearance that gets him work. Dave provides the realism in the video; he is believable as a doctor, lawyer, judge, or schoolteacher in roles where a hard-bodied, bronzed guy in his 20s is not credible (Kikuras, 2004).

Dave points to one of the most important qualifications for a male actor in the world of X-rated videos: the ability to perform sexually. Many videos budget for a three-day shoot. The script calls for six to nine episodes of sex, each requiring one or more erect penises; the majority are to end with visible ejaculation. In other words, these videos place a premium on male sexual performance, perhaps not surprising in a performance-oriented culture. It costs money and frustrates everyone involved if a male actor has a long refractory period (see Chapter 9). To make it in the industry, a man has to demonstrate that he is up to the demands. Dave is lucky; he has good genes and stamina. In his own words, he can "get it up, keep it up, not come before [I am] told to, and can climax on cue." In years past, a man without Dave's talents would not last in this line of work. But a pharmaceutical breakthrough—Viagra—changed all that. Many male porn actors routinely use Viagra or similar medications, which enable them to get and keep an erection. As a result, there are hundreds of men competing for the available jobs.

One consequence of this competition is pressure to perform acts and take risks that the actor might prefer to avoid. Even in this era of widespread knowledge of HIV/AIDS, condom use is rare in the porn industry; some viewers don't like to see them, some directors and producers don't allow them, some actors and actresses don't like the resulting hassle or change in sensation. The risk became very real in May 2004, when it was announced that five performers had positive HIV tests. One of these performers was Lara Roxx, who was from Quebec. There was a Canadian documentary about her, *Inside Lara Roxx*.

Another consequence of the competition is low pay. Men may be paid as little as $500 for a video. The industry is built primarily around women (even older women; Figure 17.8). It is the women who achieve a kind of stardom, whose names appear in the publicity and on the video boxes, and whose bodies are featured in the videos. Relatively new performers may be paid $350 to $1000 for a film featuring conventional sex. Engaging in unconventional or rough sex brings a higher fee. Needless to say, there are no royalties paid to the performers. The typical film is budgeted at $5000 to $35 000 (Huffstutter & Frammolino,

providing factual information. These series are advertised in national magazines and some daily newspapers.

There is a continuum from the subtle to the explicit in portrayals of sex. The subtle end is found in *music videos*. The sexual content of many videos is unmistakable (Figure 17.9). A content analysis of lead performers in 34 music videos found significant gender differences in how men and women are portrayed (Wallis, 2011). The authors divided the videos that appeared on MTV and MTV2 over a three-week period into 30-second segments. They coded behaviours such as suggestive dancing, sultry looks, showing force, and sexual self-touch. The authors found that portrayals reinforced male and female stereotypes; that is, women tended to be portrayed as subordinate whereas the men tended to be portrayed as aggressive. In addition, the women engaged in more sexually suggestive

2001). A typical release sells 1000 to 2000 copies; only the rare hit brings in $1 million (e.g. "How Big," 2001). Thus, there is constant pressure to keep costs to a minimum.

Just as there are a variety of pathways into commercial sex work, individuals enter the porn industry in different ways. Dave Cummings voluntarily entered the industry at age 54. Once he had demonstrated his prowess, he found himself in continuing demand. In fact, he is now producing his own line of videos. Cummings says he does it because he enjoys sex and for the opportunity to have sex with lots of attractive young women. A 21-year-old starlet, Sienna, drifted into performing in adult videos. She had worked in a fast-food outlet and bagel shop; she saw an ad in the newspaper for "nude modelling" and tried it. For the first year, she did still photo shoots, $350 to $400 for a few hours. Then she moved to working for an Internet company, engaging in masturbation while clients watched her via the Net. After a few months she thought, "If I'm gonna do this, I might as well do porn and make more money." Sienna says she may leave the industry soon; "I've just been pounded so much in these movies that I'm starting to get tired" (Petkovich, 2004). Some performers report being coerced into performing for stills or movies through the use of alcohol, drugs, or physical force by others on-camera.

The emphasis on sexual performance reflects the larger North American culture, and it is often chemically enhanced, as are many other performances in the contemporary world. The distribution and sale of the DVDs reflects the commercialization of sex, turning access to sexual images and sexual gratification into a commodity to be sold for cash or credit.

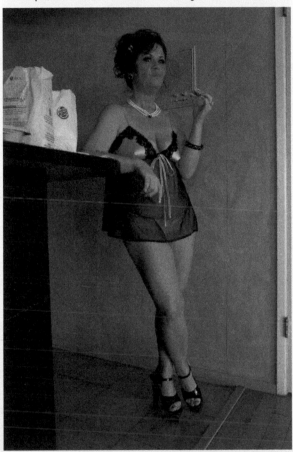

Figure 17.8 The greying pornography: As baby boomers get older, the demand for older performers is increasing. Here De'Bella, 50, waits for the director's call for her closeups; her male costars are usually in their 20s.

© Axel Koester/The New York Times/Redux

behaviour, such as sexual self-touch and suggestive dancing. Other research on music videos, including rap music videos, has found that men are portrayed as dominant over women, as wanted by women, and as having sex with attractive women (Conrad et al., 2009; Ward et al., 2005). Women are portrayed wearing revealing clothing and are valued almost exclusively for their physical appearance and sex appeal—that is, as sex objects.

Magazines

A declining share of the pornography market consists of magazines, ranging from *soft-core* (genital display, such as in *Playboy*) to *hard-core* (penetrative sex, threesomes, such as in *Hustler*). The number and sales of slick, colour magazines mushroomed in the 1970s and 1980s following the success of *Playboy*. Launched in 1953, *Playboy*'s circulation peaked in 1972 at 7.2 million. In the 1980s,

Figure 17.9 The sexual content of many music videos and live performances is unmistakable. Clothing, body language, and physical contact between performers evoke sexual images.

© Kevin Mazur/AMA2012/WireImages

Penthouse and *Hustler* provided stiff competition with more graphic and daring photo and editorial content, and there were dozens of less well-known competitors. Fierce legal and public-relations battles were fought in the 1980s and 1990s over the display and sale of these magazines, forerunners of today's battles over sexual content on the Internet. The development of the high-quality mass-produced videos available on VHS and later DVD caused the magazine market to go into a long decline. *Penthouse* declared bankruptcy in 2003; by 2010, *Playboy*'s circulation had declined to 1.6 million, and it no longer publishes every month.

Magazines catering to specialized tastes remain on the market. They include material designed for gay men, leather fetishists, swingers, people interested in interracial sex, and people interested in girl-on-girl sex.

Hard-core magazines have a no-holds-barred approach to content. Photographs may include vaginal fisting, anal intercourse and fisting, dual penetration, sadomasochism, bondage, and sex with animals. A study of the titles of magazines and books found in adult bookstores in the United States revealed that 17 percent were about a paraphilia or sexual variation (see Chapter 15) (Lebeque, 1991). Of those, 50 percent featured sadomasochism. An additional 21 percent dealt with incest.

The profit on magazines is high. Photos are often outtakes from commercial or amateur videos. Sets and lighting are minimal. The markups may be as high as 600 percent. The number of outlets selling these magazines appears to have declined in the past decade. Repeat, frequent customers account for a substantial percentage of the sales in such stores.

Live Entertainment

Shows providing live, sexualized entertainment are yet another part of the sex industry. Burlesque, which featured women seductively undressing on a stage in a theatre, has been transformed into strip clubs. These provide seminude (i.e., with pasties and a G-string) or nude dancing in a lounge setting; often, dancers circulate among the patrons when not on stage. These clubs range in style from converted neighbourhood bars to upscale gentlemen's clubs. Participant observation research, supplemented by interviews, indicates that many of the customers are regulars; they come not for sexual release but for the opportunity to interact with attractive young women and the pleasure of a sexualized interaction without the need to perform sexually (Frank, 2005).

The Lion's Den, a club in a New England town, is typical of how strip clubs are run. There is a gendered division of labour. Men, in the roles of manager, bartenders, deejays, and bouncers, run the club and manage the women—the waitresses and strippers. The club employs as many as 51 strippers, mostly white, mostly with a high school education. The strippers work seven-hour shifts, dividing their time between stage performances lasting 15 to 30 minutes and circulating to solicit private or table dances. A number of the dancers are single mothers; working at night allows them to spend the days with their children (Price-Glynn, 2010).

In 1997, there were 2478 licensed exotic dancers in Toronto alone (Maticka-Tyndale et al., 1999). Dancers perform stage shows, table dances, and lap dances. Dancers earn only a small wage for dancing on stage and are typically expected to offer table dances or lap dances if requested. Lap dances can be performed either in public or in private areas of the club. In the private areas, the stripper allows the patron to touch her body, excluding her genitals, as she dances. Most often she will gyrate in his lap and rub herself against him. An Ontario study found that lap dancers made between $10 and $20 per dance, although customers pay more for dances in private rooms (Lewis & Maticka-Tyndale, 1998). Some strip clubs also offer VIP rooms in which a greater level of sexual activity takes place, although not all strippers provide these services. Typically, this involves fellatio and manual stimulation to ejaculation, as well as a lap dance. The price is typically between $100 and $150.

The question of whether lap dancing is legal or constitutes an "indecent performance," particularly when done in a private room, has not been fully settled by the courts (Figure 17.10). However, in general, the courts have ruled that the community's level of tolerance can be quite high when activities occur in private. This is complicated by the fact that lap dancing is safest for dancers if it is done in a public area of the club where they are less likely to be assaulted or forced to go beyond dancing (Lewis & Maticka-Tyndale, 1998; Maticka-Tyndale et al., 2000b). There is also more protection for the customer in these public areas from pressure to engage in activities beyond watching the dancer. Some cities, such as Toronto, have enacted bylaws that prohibit physical contact, including touching,

Figure 17.10 Canadians are divided in their opinions about lap dancing. The Supreme Court of Canada banned lap dancing in public areas because it inflicts "attitudinal harm" to those watching but ruled that lap dancing in private cubicles, where people passing by can't see it, is not indecent.

© evan Hurd/Alamy Stock Photo

between patrons and persons providing services in adult entertainment parlours as a way of restricting table dancing and lap dancing.

The blog lettersfromstripclubs contains posts by men who visit the clubs. One poster, engaged to a "knockout," goes to the club to indulge his fetish for large, fake breasts; he frequents clubs where the women allow him to fondle them. A gay man goes with male friends to celebrate events in their lives and to people-watch. A third man considers it therapy: Where else can you talk completely openly to someone who won't judge you?

Male strippers catering to a female audience are less common but perform periodically in many communities. In the commercial sex districts of large cities, there are also live sex shows featuring couples or groups engaging in sexual acts onstage. These shows are second cousins to the elaborately staged reviews in major casinos and hotels, which often feature nudity and simulated sexual activity in a lavish setting.

Telephone Sex

Telephone sex provides another example of enlisting technology to provide sexual excitement. It refers to sexually explicit conversations between one or more persons; often the participant(s) engage in masturbation. Note "one or more"; one type of commercial phone sex involves listening to prerecorded narratives. Another type involves live conversations with a paid phone sex operator. Of course, phone sex may be noncommercial, involving separated lovers; in this case, both may masturbate. And, of course, lovers can now add video, in what might be called Skype sex.

A study of a sample of prerecorded messages identified several patterns (Glascock & LaRose, 1993). The typical recording was of a female voice describing a series of sexual activities in which the caller was a participant. Callers were likely to hear fantasies involving masturbation, vaginal intercourse, and oral sex. Few descriptions included violence or forced sex.

There are a number of companies that provide phone sex services. They employ dispatchers who direct calls and may process payment information, and erotic performers who provide conversation. Performers may work in company office suites or from their home. The Sexy Smart Girls Agency (a pseudonym) employs 40 workers, some part-time and some full-time (Guidroz & Rich, 2010). It is mostly night work, since most calls come between 11 p.m. and 5 a.m. Callers may want to discuss straight sex, anal sex, adult baby/diaper lover, incest (with the operator playing mom or sis), BDSM, bestiality, and fetishism. Some companies/workers limit topics they will discuss; others advertise "no taboos." Sexy Smart Girls advertises in men's sex magazines. Operators who were interviewed were 21 to 45, but all presented in calls as 20 to 23. All were white, with at least a high school education. Most had worked in phone sex less than 18 months, suggesting a high turnover. They typically concealed their phone sex work from family, friends, and other employers. Most had unconventional sexual/intimate relationship arrangements; this is also true of some strippers. Live sex work in clubs and on the telephone undoubtedly creates stress in many intimate relationships.

In some cases, phone sex workers work for themselves rather than for a company. For example, a student who needed money for tuition and books set up a 1-900 line in her home after reading an advertisement for phone sex operators in a Winnipeg newspaper (Schroeder, 2000). Callers were charged by the minute.

Here is a phone sex call recounted to an interviewer:

I say, "When you give a guy a blow job, what's your favorite way to do it?" She says, "Well, I love being on my knees, cause being on my knees with him standing is so submissive." I said, "Do you like looking at his cock in his pants, does that really turn you on?" She says, "I love that." I say, "I would love to be standing in front of you." She says, "Oh, that would really turn me on." "Do you like having your breasts played with when you're giving a blow job?" "Yes, I like it very much. I also like to be fingered." "How many fingers do you like inside you?" "I love two fingers." "And why do you like blowing a guy so much?" "Because I'm getting him excited and I know I can't wait for him to fuck me." "Do you like to fuck for a long time?" "Yes, I get lost in it." So then I said, "Well, I've really been thinking about you on top of me, and while you're riding me, I'll be spanking you." She said, "Oh God, I love that." I was masturbating and I came. It was great. (Maurer, 1994, pp. 349–350)

Harry Maurer, *Sex: An Oral History*. Copyright © 1994 by Harry Maurer. Used by permission of Viking Penguin, a division of Penguin Group USA Inc., and by permission of International Creative Management.

Child Pornography

Child pornography refers to any visual depiction—photo, film, video, audio—of sexually explicit conduct involving a person under 18 years of age; it may include images of nude genitalia, or even clothed genitals if the images are sexual. It is viewed by many as the most reprehensible part of the porn industry because it produces such an obvious victim: the child model. Children, by virtue of their developmental level, cannot give truly informed consent to participation in such activities, and the potential for doing psychological and physical damage to them is great.

The *Criminal Code of Canada* prohibits people from possessing, making, or distributing child pornography. Child pornography is defined as any representation of a person who is or is depicted to be under the age of 18 engaging in explicit sexual activity or that depicts their genitals for sexual purposes; any written or audio material that advocates sexual activity with someone under 18; and any written material or audio recordings that describes, for sexual purposes, sex with someone under 18 (see Table 2.1). The sections of the statute use the term "pornography" rather than "obscenity" as with the adult provisions, and they specifically prohibit the making, sale, or possession of child pornography. The purpose of these laws is to protect children from harm by ensuring that they are not involved in the making of pornography and by preventing child sexual abuse by users of child pornography. Indeed, research in Ontario has shown that most men convicted of child pornography offences are pedophile; that is, they show a preference for prepubescent children and thus are at risk to offend against children (Seto et al., 2006). A child is defined as anyone under the age of 18. These statutes also outlaw "pseudo-child pornography"—that is, pornography that uses adults but makes them look like children.

Child pornography offences differ from offences governing adult pornography in three primary ways. Displaying or offering to sell pornography to persons under 16 is an offence, whether or not these materials would be viewed as obscene under the *Criminal Code*. In addition, the sentences for child pornography offences are greater than for obscenity offences. Finally, it is an offence to be in the possession of child pornography, whereas it is only illegal to sell or distribute obscene material involving adults.

In 2001, the Supreme Court upheld the law criminalizing the possession of child pornography with two narrow exceptions. It ruled that possessing private works of imagination that have artistic merit and photographic depictions of oneself are legal. Thus, it is legal to write or draw sexually explicit depictions of children for one's own personal pleasure. In response to this ruling, Parliament passed amendments to the child pornography legislation in 2002 that broadened the definition of child pornography, prohibited advertising child pornography, increased penalties, and ensured that people using the artistic merit defence will have to show that they have a legitimate purpose for possessing the child pornography.

There are commercial websites that distribute sexual images of what appear to be persons under 18. These sites include words like "nymphet" and variations of "lolita" in their names, and display terms like "little girls/boys." In May 2015, there was a "Lovely Nymphet Network" on Tumblr with a variety of photos of young women of ambiguous age. Viewing sexual explicit material of individuals depicting to be under 18 is illegal in Canada.

child pornography: Visual depictions of explicit sexual activities or genitalia involving children.

The most explicit child pornography is thought to be distributed on the Internet via "peer-to-peer" (p2p) networks. These networks involve individuals who produce and/or distribute all sorts of materials surreptitiously; they often develop elaborate online distribution systems that are difficult to identify or trace. Most publicized cases of law enforcement arrests involve participants in such networks. In August 2012, as a result of an investigation code-named Holitna, authorities arrested 43 men across seven countries and charged them with sexually abusing children and producing and distributing the resulting images.

The Canadian Centre for Child Protection operates a tip line for reporting online child pornography. Over an eight-year period, most (78 percent) reports were of images and videos of children under 12 years of age, although some depicted infants and toddlers. About half depicted explicit sexual activity/assaults. Almost two-thirds (69 percent) appeared to be in a home setting. The number of police-reported child pornography increased from 2003 to 2012. This could reflect increase incidents; it could also reflect increased reporting and/or more effective police surveillance.

There is a continuing debate about the link between child pornography (CP) offenses and child molesting/pedophilic behaviour (see Chapter 16 for a discussion of the distinction between pedophilia and child molestation). Clearly, some instances of production involve sexual activity with a child. A study of offenders found that about 17 percent of those arrested had molested the child (Wolak et al., 2011a). Of course, many persons involved in CP never get arrested. Seto (2004) assessed 685 men referred to a mental health clinic for various reasons including child pornography. About 43 percent of those involved in CP had a history of offences against children. On the other hand, studies of sex offenders find that they are no more likely than male nonoffenders to have been exposed to hard-core pornography (Malamuth & Huppin, 2007). Some producers are pedophiles and are motivated by their own sexual interest in children, but others are motivated by profit (Quayle, 2008).

Some major, well-known films could easily be classified as CP. *Taxi Driver* featured Jodie Foster as a 12-year-old prostitute. And *Pretty Baby* launched the career of Brooke Shields, playing the role of a 12-year old brothel prostitute in New Orleans. Shields herself was 12 years old when the film was made. *The Girl Next Door* features abuse and molestation of a 13-year-old by family and friends.

Advertising

Let's close our discussion of the types of pornography by considering a mating of sex and money that all of us encounter every day—*sex in advertising*. Both subtle and obvious sexual promises are used to sell a wide variety of products. A muscular young man wearing low-slung jeans and no shirt sells Calvin Klein. Abercrombie & Fitch catalogues feature photos of nude young people in bed or in pools. Perfumes promise that they will make women instantly sexually attractive. One brand of coffee seems to guarantee a warm, romantic, sensuous evening for the couple who drink it.

How much sexual content is there in advertising? One study analyzed the sexual content of magazine advertising in 1983 and 2003 (Reichert & Carpenter, 2004). Sexual clothing and portrayals of intimate contact became more frequent. In 2003, for example, 78 percent of women in ads in men's magazines were attired in sexually suggestive clothing. Sexually provocative behaviour is another aspect of sex found in magazine advertising; in ads portraying heterosexual couples, 53 percent engage in sexual contact (passionate kissing, simulated intercourse) (Reichert, 2002).

Television advertising uses not only bodily display or nudity and sexually suggestive interaction but also context (a Caribbean beach, a bed or bedroom), language including double entendre (a message with two meanings, one being sexual), and talk about sexual activity. Some advertisers, such as Victoria's Secret and Calvin Klein, cultivate a sexually suggestive image (Figure 17.11). A study of prime-time commercials broadcast on NBC found that 12 percent of the female models and 2 percent of the male models were dressed to be sexually suggestive. Network promotional ads were more likely to include sexual content. Sexual contact in ads increased from 12 percent in 1990 to 21 percent in 1998. A review of the research on the effects of advertising concludes that sexual information attracts attention, and viewers are more likely to remember the sexual image; paradoxically, however, they are less likely to remember the brand name (Reichert, 2002). Beyond the effects of ads on brand images and purchasing, there is concern that continuing exposure to ads that contain gender-stereotyped ideas and images, such as thin, attractive females and taut, buff males, may affect attitudes toward one's body. In one study, male and female university students were shown either 15 sexist and 5 neutral ads, 20 neutral ads, or no ads. The results indicated that exposure to the sexist ads was associated with dissatisfaction with one's own body among *both* men and women (Lavine et al., 1999).

The Producers

In the 1980s and 1990s, the largest component of the porn industry was the production and distribution of X-rated videos on DVD. Some of the major production companies were (are) Adam and Eve, Hustler, Playboy, Vivid, and Wicked. These companies often use a traditional business structure (CEOs, vice-presidents, producers, etc.),

Figure 17.11 Sex in advertising. Many advertisers, including Calvin Klein, use sexual images to sell products. Do you consider this image lascivious? Some people do.

and each produced dozens of videos per year. The heads of these firms were generally entrepreneurs interested in making money who saw the X-rated film industry as a business opportunity. Most of these companies had permanent studios resembling those of major film makers, which require a substantial investment, high maintenance costs, and numerous employees to manage.

The development of hand-held cameras and portable equipment allowed movement away from studio-based production. As noted in First Person, Dave Cummings drives to a large home in Beverly Hills, rented for just three or four days for the filming. Thus, today videos can be made by a small crew that can travel anywhere, allowing much easier access to the production side. In 2015, Wikipedia lists 75 production companies that make heterosexual and lesbian videos, and 99 companies that make gay and bisexual videos. Note that heterosexual, lesbian, gay, and bisexual refer to the target audience for the video. The sexual orientation of the performers may not be consistent with that of the target population. Thus, some straight men perform in gay pornography and some lesbians perform in heterosexual pornography.

As noted earlier, the Internet has displaced the production and marketing of DVDs with online access to X-rated films, and especially short clips taken from

them. Like YouTube, these sites accept uploads from almost anyone. Many of the clips on tube sites have the logo of the production company prominently displayed, and may include links so the viewer can purchase the full version.

Many of the performers, or artists if you prefer, in hard- and soft-core materials are probably like some of your friends and co-workers. In the discussion of commercial sex work, we noted that more than 100 000 students may be employed in the industry in Canada, including appearing in videos and stills, performing on sex-cam sites, and stripping and working other jobs (servers) in strip clubs. We noted that a large component of Internet videos are made by amateurs, ordinary singles and couples who perhaps have some exhibitionist tendencies, like extra money, or just like to imagine other people finding them sexually attractive. The many niche markets for web porn—for videos featuring Black, Asian, or Hispanic women, gays, lesbians, trans persons, pregnant women—create a demand for all kinds of people to perform. The videos can be easily uploaded to a tube site.

There are a variety of pathways into commercial sex work. *Playboy* visits major campuses every year and advertisers for "models," often turning away aspiring

"Playmates" because there are too many applicants! Some video producers recruit young women at large parties or popular Spring Break locations. Dave Cummings (First Person) voluntarily entered the industry at age 54.

There are a wide variety of beliefs (stereotypes, myths) about actresses in X-rated films. Researchers recruited 177 female performers in adult films through the Adult Industry Medical Healthcare Foundation. Each completed a survey. Researchers then recruited a comparison sample of women, matched on age, marital status, and ethnicity, in university and community (e.g., airports) settings. Actresses were more likely to identify as bisexual, report an earlier age of first intercourse (15.1 versus 17.3), have more sexual partners in the previous year, and report greater enjoyment of sex. Actresses were not more likely to report sexual abuse in childhood (Griffith et al., 2013a). In a related study, undergraduates were asked to estimate various characteristics of male and female pornography actors. Their estimates were compared with data from surveys of male and female performers. Students underestimated the sexual experience and enjoyment of sex reported by actors, and overestimated their earnings by 300 percent! (Griffith et al., 2013b) (see Table 17.1).

Stories, available on many websites, the largest being Literotica.com, can be written by anyone with a fertile imagination. The stories are usually posted by their authors who receive no payment. Still photos can be taken and uploaded to the web by anyone with a smartphone; there are a number of sites that feature "selfies" showing women and men in very explicit poses, or engaging in partnered activity, posted by the taker.

The wide variety of people engaging in the production of X-rated materials suggests that the stigma associated with it has declined substantially in the past 40 years. In many ways, porn has become part of mainstream culture, with celebrities, annual awards shows, and industry conventions showcasing the latest products and young talent. This makes it easier for a person with the requisite talents and appearance to enter the field, so a wider variety of men and women do.

The Customers

Who is consuming/buying/using all of these sexually explicit materials? It has long been taken as fact that pornography is used primarily by men. The General Social Survey has asked a question about viewing an X-rated movie of representative samples of U.S. adults almost every year since 1973. From 1987 to 2010, the percentage of men reporting that they have has fluctuated between 30 percent and 40 percent (Wright, 2013). Men who are younger and non-white are more likely to report viewing. Note that the question does not specify a venue; the viewing could have occurred in a commercial theatre, at a private party, or on the Internet or a smartphone. The most common venue has probably changed over the years, but viewership is quite stable. Across the same time period, fewer women report viewing an X-rated movie. In recent years, men make up more than two-thirds of those who report viewing (Smith & Son, 2013). The GSS data show that from 1987 to 2010, the percentage of women has fluctuated between 10 and 15 percent; among women 18 to 30, the percentage reporting

Table 17.1 Comparison of College Student Perceptions and Pornography Actors' Reports of Work

	Porn Actors		College Students			
	M	**SD**	**M**	**SD**	***t***	***r***
Female targets						
Number of different sexual partners in the adult entertainment industry	72.21	94.96	78.67	127.84	<1	.03
Earning in the adult entertainment industry	74,010	124,699.36	250,711.00	666,734.02	2.75*	−.17
Enjoy work	8.50	1.52	7.62	1.95	4.80**	−.24
Male targets						
Number of different sexual partners in the adult entertainment industry	312.27	647.08	97.14	296.17	3.93***	−.22
Earning in the adult entertainment industry	79,997	138,151.87	224,431	529,995.26	−2.19*	.15
Enjoy work	8.38	1.83	8.13	1.87	1.12	−.05

*p < .05

**p < .01

***p < .001

Source: James D. Griffith, Michelle Hayworth, Lea T. Adams, Sharon Mitchell, and Christian Hart (2013), "Characteristics of Pornography Film Actors: Self-Report versus Perceptions of College Students," *Archives of Sexual Behavior, 42,* 637–647.

viewing is about one-third. Non-white women are more likely to report having viewed an X-rated film (Wright, Bae, & Funk, 2013).

On university campuses, viewing pornography is gendered. A study in New Brunswick found that 89 percent of male students and 39 percent of female students had looked at sexually explicit pictures or videos online in the previous month (Shaughnessy, Byers, & Walsh, 2011). Men also report viewing pornography significantly more frequently than women do (Shaughnessy et al., 2014). In a study that compared undergraduate students in Canada, the U.S., Germany, and Sweden, the men reported viewing pornography three times more often than did the women (Döring et al., 2015). Other research suggests that the main reasons for viewing it are curiosity and to experience sexual arousal. Salmon (2012) suggested that women are not attracted to pornography because it emphasizes impersonal sex and sexual variety. Women, she argues, are aroused by an emphasis on relationships, and women are aroused by finding Mr. or Ms. Right. Heterosexual women find both of these in romance novels. Romance novels account for 7 percent of paperback book sales in Canada.

Women purchase and watch pornographic videos. Research conducted in Australia in 1999 reported that 65 percent of X-rated videos were purchased by a woman or a heterosexual couple. In data from 280 women, 20 percent said they selected the video, 50 percent said both selected it, 18 percent said the partner selected it with both their preferences in mind, and 9 percent said the partner selected it (Contessini, 2003). Female interest in erotica was recognized 30 years ago by Candida Royale, then a film star, who became a producer and director; her company, *Femme Productions*, has made more than 20 films directed toward women. A growing number of men and women are attempting to market to women, producing what is called *female-empowered* adult entertainment, including films, cable TV programs, sex toy stores, and Web sites (see Figure 17.12). Recently, a Montrealer created Bellesa, a feminist porn site specifically for women, as a platform where women can celebrate their sexuality.

A study of 617 married or cohabiting heterosexual couples collected data from each partner (Paulsen et al., 2013). Questions included, "During the last 12 months, on how many days did you view or read pornography (i.e., movies, magazines, Internet sites, adult romantic novels)?" Notice that this is a very broad question, and includes romantic novels. Data were collected in 2009 and 2010; the sample was primarily white (83 percent) and well-educated (56 percent of both men and women had bachelor's degrees or higher). Ninety-four percent of the women reported using these materials once a month or less, compared to only 31 percent of the men; the difference was highly significant. Ten percent of the men reported using three or more days per week, and 16 percent reported using once or twice per week. Obviously, most couples were not using

Figure 17.12   Not all producers of pornography are men. Women are increasingly involved in the production of sexually explicit video and Internet materials.

© Dan Callister/Online USA/Getty Images

the materials together. Users of both genders reported lower religiosity.

We noted earlier that most strip clubs cater to a heterosexual male audience. Most women who enter are with male customers, but increasingly a single woman or groups of two or more women are in the audience (Figure 17.13). Participant observation research found that even if women actively demonstrated interest, such as by tipping dancers on the stage, dancers often *passed over* (avoided) them as they circulated on the floor (Wosick et al., 2008). Some dancers acknowledged them as women, by complaining to them about costumes or male customers. Some more experienced dancers treated them as customers and gave them dances; these dances were *tailored* to a woman's body (e.g., involved breast play) and were individualized.

Computer porn attracts a more varied clientele. Chat rooms and news groups attract both men and women of diverse ages (assuming that those who describe themselves online are doing so accurately). Some of these people are married. There have been news reports of a man or woman leaving a spouse or partner in order to

live with someone he or she met via the Internet. Depending on the focus of the room or group, participants may be from diverse racial or ethnic backgrounds and have varied sexual interests. The data on gender of consumers suggests that bulletin boards and adult websites probably attract middle-class white men—although some emphasize materials oriented toward other clienteles. Table 17.2 presents results from an online survey that

Figure 17.13 While there are differences between men and women in their response to pornography, some women enjoy watching a stripper as much as some men do.

© Oliver Knight / Alamy Stock Photo

Table 17.2 Do You Use Porn? A Survey by the Kinsey Institute (N = 10 453)	
Sex	
Male	80%
Female	17%
Age	
18 to 20	11%
21 to 30	31%
31 to 40	29%
40 to 50	15%
51 to 60	7%
61 to 70	2%
71 or order	1%
Viewed sexual images in the past month?	
Never have viewed them	3%
Not once, but I have in the past	20%
One or two times	16%
Once a week	10%
A few times a week	27%
Once a day	9%
Several times a day	10%
How much time per week in the past month?	
I did not use porn in the past	11%
Month	18%
Less than one hour	37%
1 to 5 hours	16%
6 to 15 hours	6%
26 to 50 hours	3%
More than 50 hours	3%
Why do you use porn? (top 5 answers)	
To masturbate / for physical release	72%
To sexually arouse myself and/or others	69%
Out of curiosity	54%
To fantasize about things I would not necessarily want in real life	43%
To distract myself	38%

Based on an online survey conducted in association with Public Broadcasting System. Results at http://www.pbs.org/wgbh/pages/frontline/shows/porn/etc/surveyres.html.

assessed the number of times and number of hours per month that users view sexual materials.

A wide variety of people patronize adult retail stores (and their online cousins). As the manager of one store said,

> We get everyone in here from millionaires to scum of the earth. The blue-collar and white-collar men come for the tapes. Married couples come in for things to help their sex life. The gay crowd cruises the booths in back. Groups of women come in for gag items. (Moore, 1994)

LO9 The Effects of Pornography

People have debated the effects of sexually themed media since they were created. For decades, the debates relied on common sense and religious dogma. In the mid-1960s, social scientists began to conduct research to provide a more rigorous foundation for these debates. Today, we have a wide array of data to draw on.

The fundamental question, perhaps, is how do media portrayals affect the user's sexuality? What is the mechanism involved? One answer is provided by *sexual script theory* (see our discussion of sexual scripts in Chapters 2 and 8). Scripts define appropriate sexual interactions by identifying actors, behaviours, and contexts for sexual activity. As media portrayals have become more common, they have become a major socializing influence on persons exposed to them. Wright (2013) specifies three ways in which media portrayals influence the person: acquisition, or learning via exposure; activation, or cueing a script already learned; and application, using the script to guide behaviour or interaction.

> **What are the effects of viewing erotica and pornography on sexual behaviour?**

Four questions can be asked about the effects of using pornography:

1. Does it produce sexual arousal?
2. Does it affect users' attitudes about sexual activities or relationships?
3. Does it affect the sexual behaviour of users?
4. Does it affect the aggressive or criminal behaviour of users, particularly aggressive behaviour toward women?

Many studies have examined the effect of sexually explicit material on sexual arousal. This research consistently finds that exposure to *material that the viewer finds acceptable* does produce arousal (Davis & Bauserman, 1993). Exposure to portrayals that the viewer finds objectionable produces a negative reaction.

Most people disapprove of paraphilic behaviours (see Chapter 15), sexual assault, and sexual activity involving children, so they react negatively to hard-core and child pornography.

There are gender differences in self-reports of response to sexually explicit materials. Men report higher levels of arousal to such portrayals than do women (Kingston et al., 2009; Malamuth, 1998). The differences are larger in response to pornography than to erotica, and the difference is much larger among university students than among older persons (Murnen & Stockton, 1997). This difference between men and women is often attributed to the fact that most erotica and pornography is male oriented. The focus is almost exclusively on sexual behaviour, with little character development or concern for relationships. There is limited foreplay and afterplay; the male typically ejaculates on some part of the woman's body (the *cum shot*) rather than inside her. Former porn film star Candida Royale produces videos made for women. An experiment found that male university students responded positively to and were aroused by videos made for men and for women; females reported negative responses to the videos intended for men and positive responses and sexual arousal to the videos designed for women (Mosher & MacIan, 1994).

How does pornography affect attitudes? The research indicates that a single exposure to stories, photographs, or videos has little or no effect. Massive exposure (such as viewing videos for five hours) does lead to more permissive attitudes. In this situation, viewers become more tolerant of the behaviour observed and less in favour of restrictions on it (Davis & Bauserman, 1993). What about attitudes toward aggression against women? Some studies show that exposure to portrayals of forced intercourse lead men to be more tolerant of sexual assault, but other studies do not find a relationship between exposure and attitudes (Fisher & Grenier, 1994). Men exposed to portrayals of sexual aggression against women do not report a greater willingness to sexually assault a woman (Davis & Bauserman, 1993). On the other hand, individuals classified as high risk to commit sexual aggression are particularly influenced by exposure, showing negative attitudes toward women (Kingston et al., 2009).

There is particular concern about the effects of exposure to child pornography. It would be illegal (and therefore unethical) to show research participants sexual images of persons under 18. So researchers exposed college students to "barely legal" images, of persons who are over 18 but look (much) younger (Paul & Linz, 2008). Images were either in web page format, or in the same format on the page but with web banners, ads, and so on removed. The researchers wondered whether exposure would create an association or schema relating sex and eroticism to youth. To test for such an association they used the *priming paradigm,* where target words are tested for speed of recognition, images are viewed, and then speed of recognition is measured again. Men and women exposed to "barely legal" images exhibited faster recognition of the words "erotic" and "beautiful" than men and women exposed to similar images of models over 21 years of age, suggesting that exposure to the images did create an association.

With regard to sexual behaviour, the research shows that in response to erotic portrayals of consenting heterosexual activity, both men and women may report an increase in sexual thoughts and fantasies and in behaviours such as masturbation and intercourse. A survey of early adolescents in the United States questioned them about exposure to sexually explicit content in adult magazines, X-rated movies, and the Internet (Brown & L'Engle, 2009). Two-thirds of the boys and 39 percent of the girls had seen at least one sexually explicit medium in the past year. Being Black, being older, having a lower socio-economic status, and having less-educated parents were related to greater exposure for both boys and girls. Follow-up data were collected two years later. For both boys and girls, early exposure predicted less progressive gender-role attitudes, having oral sex, and having intercourse; among boys, it also predicted more permissive attitudes about sex. Exposure to portrayals of behaviour the person has not personally engaged in did *not* lead to an increase in these behaviours (Davis & Bauserman, 1993).

Finally, there has been great interest in whether exposure to portrayals of sexual aggression (which almost always involve men behaving aggressively toward women) increases aggressive behaviour. A number of laboratory studies have shown that men who are insulted or provoked by a woman and have been exposed to violent pornography are significantly more aggressive toward the woman in the experimental situation compared with men exposed to sexually explicit but nonviolent material. If the comparison group is men exposed to nonsexual violent films, many studies find no difference between the two, but some find that exposure to sexual violence increases aggression toward a woman more than exposure just to violence (Davis & Bauserman, 1993). Laboratory exposure has greater negative impact on men who report high levels of use compared with men with low levels of use (Kingston et al., 2009). Research in Ontario suggests that men with lower IQs may be more influenced by violent pornography than men with higher IQs (Bogaert et al., 1999). However, few men (5 to 6 percent in one Ontario study) choose to watch violent pornography when given the opportunity (Bogaert, 1993, 2001).

Ontario psychologists William Fisher and Guy Grenier have questioned the extent to which these laboratory studies capture the relationship between pornography and aggression in the real world (Fisher & Grenier, 1994). They point out that, in these laboratory studies, the men are told by the experimenter to send some level of shock to the female confederate. Although in these studies they can choose the level of shock to administer, they are not given the opportunity to engage in a nonaggressive response. However, in a real-life situation, a man could choose to speak to a woman who angered him or to walk away from the situation, instead of engaging in an aggressive response. The researchers found that when given the choice, 86 percent of the men chose not to make an aggressive response. Thus, it is not clear that exposure to pornography causes sexual aggressive behaviour in men who are not already predisposed to sexual violence (Seto et al., 2001).

The research reviewed above examined effects of exposure on individuals. An alternative approach is to assess the effects of making sexually explicit materials more widely available, for example by legalizing their sale and distribution in a city, province or territory, or country. Diamond (2009) has been studying this issue for some time, examining the effects of increased availability on sex-crime rates. If exposure to such materials causes sexual aggression, we would expect an increase in rates of sexual assault and other sexual offences, and perhaps in prostitution, in the jurisdiction after such materials become available. In fact, every methodologically sound investigation finds that "as pornography has increased in availability, sex crimes have either decreased or not increased" (p. 304).

In sum, then, we can conclude that exposure to sexually explicit material that the viewer finds acceptable is arousing to both men and women. Exposure to aggressive pornography does increase men's aggression toward women under certain laboratory conditions. The extent to which these results are generalizable to a real-life situation is not known, however. Exposure to aggressive pornography may also affect men's attitudes, making them more accepting of violence against women, particularly men at high risk. Researchers in Ontario have concluded that men who are already predisposed to sexual aggression are the most likely to be affected by pornography; men who are not predisposed toward violence are unlikely to be affected (Seto et al., 2001).

What about the effects of pornography on women? Researchers in Ontario found that exposure to violent and dehumanizing pornography, but not to erotica, has a negative emotional impact on women (Senn & Radtke, 1990). Of particular interest is that women who reported having had more forceful sexual experiences in the past were particularly negative in their evaluations of pornography but not of erotica. It may be that, for these women, violent sexual images bring back painful memories.

A final question is what do people perceive the outcomes for themselves of using pornography to be? Researchers in New Brunswick studied the views of male and female undergraduate students and heterosexual and sexual minority individuals from the community (Shaughnessy et al., 2014). They found that, in general, participants believed that viewing pornography had little effect on them, although they believed that it had significantly greater positive than negative outcomes on themselves, their life, and their relationship. Similarly, research in Nova Scotia found that young adults saw their use of pornography as resulting in a number of health benefits, although they also identified some resulting health challenges (Hare et al., 2014).

Issues Related to Pornography

In general, Canadians have neutral to slightly positive attitudes toward use of pornography (Byers & Shaughnessy, 2014). However, as we stated in the introduction to this section, some groups want to ban most or all "pornography" (though they may disagree about exactly what it is). Political conservatives, religious fundamentalists, and some feminists are very critical of it. Why would feminists (e.g., Griffin, 1981; Lederer, 1980; Morgan, 1978), who prize sexual liberation, be opposed to pornography? There are three basic reasons some feminists and many others object to pornography. First, they argue that pornography debases women. In the milder, soft-core versions, it portrays women as sex objects whose breasts, legs, and genitalia can be purchased and then ogled. In the hard-core versions, women may be shown being held down, penetrated by several men simultaneously, or urinated upon. Does mainstream pornography demean and objectify women? The answer depends in part on how one defines the term, and there is controversy over that. Defining objectification as including treating another person as an object, one partner dominating another, and penis worship, one researcher performed a content analysis of the 50 best-selling pornographic videos in Australia (McKee, 2005). Many of the videos were imports from the United States and Europe. Seven measures allowed direct comparison of portrayal of men and portrayals of women. On one measure, not having an orgasm, women were significantly higher than men. On

three measures—less time spent looking at the camera, less time spent talking to the camera, and less likely to initiate sex—men were significantly higher than women. On three final measures— having a name, being a central character, and time spent talking—there were no significant differences. One can also argue that pornography objectifies men. Most men depicted in pornography videos have large penises, are continuously aroused, have buff bodies, and will engage in any type of intercourse with any female. That is probably as unrealistic as the portrayals of women.

Second, they argue that pornography associates sex with violence toward women and, as such, contributes to sexual assault and other forms of violence against women and girls. One feminist writer has put it bluntly: "Pornography is the theory and rape is the practice" (Morgan, 1980, p. 139). We have just reviewed the empirical evidence on this point. There is some evidence that exposure of men to aggressive pornography can increase aggression toward women under certain conditions, but so does exposure to aggressive films without sex. The evidence suggests that it is exposure to aggression, not sex, that produces the effect. Research suggests that there are some men who are at high risk due to predisposing factors for whom exposure to aggressive pornography does elicit aggressive sexual scripts. However, this association may be due to higher sex drive in these men (Baer et al., 2015).

Third, they argue that pornography shows—indeed, glamorizes— unequal power relationships between women and men. A common theme in pornography is boss-secretary, doctor-nurse, or professor-student sex, or men forcing women to have sex, so that the power of men and subordination of women are emphasized. Consistent with this point, feminists and others do not object to sexual materials that portray women and men in equal, humanized relationships—what we have termed *erotica*. Feminists also note the intimate relationship between pornography and traditional gender roles Pornography is enmeshed as both cause and effect; that is, pornography in part results from traditional gender roles and sexual script that make it socially acceptable for men to use and require hypersexuality and aggressiveness as part of the male role. In turn, pornography may serve to perpetuate traditional gender roles. By seeing or reading about dominant males and submissive, dehumanized females, each new generation of adolescent boys is socialized to accept these roles.

A growing concern over the past decade, particularly in the media, is *pornography addiction* (Montgomery-Graham et al., 2015). The data in Table 17.2 indicate that about 10 percent of respondents to the survey "viewed sexual images" more than once a day in the preceding month, and that 12 percent spent 16 or more hours per week. Some commentators and some health professionals believe that exposure to these images at these levels is problematic, that very high levels of viewing reflect an addiction, behaviour that is compulsive and out of control. There is no question that excessive viewing can negatively affect one's life—grades, productivity at work, interpersonal relationships. Also, we reviewed data showing that exposure to pornographic material affects one's sexual scripts and behaviour, and can lead to poorer-quality sexual relationships; these effects are more likely the more time one spends consuming these materials. On the other hand, these data are correlational, so it is not known whether pornography use negatively affects relationships or poor relationships lead to greater pornography use (Montgomery-Graham et al., 2015). Further, it is debatable whether this is an addiction in the scientific meaning of that term (see Chapter 15). Critics of the addiction perspective on excessive consumption of X-rated materials argue that it is another effort to medicalize sexual behavior (see Chapter 2), that it is an issue of deficient self-regulation (Sirianni & Vishwanath, 2015), and that it provides a convenient label/excuse for someone whose pornography use is bothering himself or others.

These are disturbing issues. What is the solution? Should pornography be censored or made illegal? Or would this only make it forbidden and therefore more attractive, and still available on the black market? Or should all forms of pornography be legal and readily available, and should we rely on other methods—such as education of parents and students through the school system—to abolish its use? Or should we adopt some in-between strategy, making some forms of pornography—say child pornography and violent pornography— illegal, while allowing free access to erotica? Note that the 1992 Supreme Court decision in the *Butler* case and child pornography legislation adopted this last approach.

Our own opinion is that legal restrictions—known less politely as censorship—are probably not the solution. We agree with the view put forth by a group of researchers that a better solution is education (Donnerstein et al., 1987; Linz et al., 1987). In their experiments, they have debriefed male participants at the conclusion of the procedures. They convey to the participants that media depictions are unreal and that the portrayal of women enjoying forced sex is fictitious. They dispel common myths about sexual assault ("rape myths"), especially any that were shown in the film used in the experiment. Participants who have been debriefed in this way show less acceptance of rape myths and more sensitivity to victims of sexual assault than participants shown a neutral film do (Donnerstein et al., 1987). More recently, researchers in Ontario examined the effects of a similar intervention on men's responses to Internet pornography (Isaacs & Fisher, 2008). This intervention reduced the men's attraction to and enjoyment of violent pornography compared with men who did not get the intervention. The experimental group was also more able to recognize and reject violent pornography.

Subsequently, some researchers introduced *prebriefing* of participants in research involving exposure to sexually explicit materials. The typical briefing— pre or post—consists of a short audiotape or a printed handout pointing out that the material is fictional. It reminds participants that women do not enjoy forced sex and that sexual assault is a serious crime. Researchers identified ten studies that included prebriefing or debriefing, and measures of the effects of exposure to the material. All ten found that there were no negative effects of exposure accompanied by an educational briefing. In six of the studies, participants were less accepting of rape myths at the conclusion of the study than at the beginning (Allen et al., 1996). This research provides solid evidence that education can eliminate at least negative effects of pornography on attitudes.

More generally, the research points to the need for pornography education. Programs that involve exposing adolescents in a controlled environment to pornographic material, and then working with them to analyze it, to consider its realism, objectification, gender role portrayals, and so on could go a long way to reducing the negative effects of sexually explicit media. These programs could be implemented by individual families, religious groups, boys and girls clubs, schools. As in so many other areas of sexuality and sexual health, for both individuals and society, the best answer is evidence-based education.

IDENTIFYING THE DIFFERENCE BETWEEN EVERYDAY BELIEFS AND SCIENTIFIC EVIDENCE

Each of us has a set of beliefs about ourselves, our behaviour, and the influences on us. These everyday beliefs are sometimes referred to as common sense. Often, there is a good deal of research that is relevant to these beliefs. One of the functions of this book is to summarize in an accessible way the research relevant to our sexual beliefs and behaviour.

In this chapter, we summarized the research that has been conducted over the past 30 years on the effects of exposure to pornography or sexually explicit material. Some of this research is correlational, and some of it is experimental; the experimental results are the basis for making causal claims about the effects of viewing these materials. Let's review the evidence:

- Exposure to portrayals the viewer finds acceptable produces sexual arousal for both men and women.
- Exposure to portrayals of consensual heterosexual activity leads to increased sexual thoughts and behaviour.
- Exposure to violent pornography may create more tolerance toward violence toward women.
- Exposure to portrayals of violence toward women increases men's aggression against women, at least in the laboratory.

Now, how much sexually explicit material have you been exposed to in the past month? In films, on TV, on DVDs, online? In video games? What was the content? How much was consensual, how much involved violence directed toward women? Toward men? If you are a typical undergraduate student, chances are you have been exposed to porn weekly or more often, perhaps of several types.

Now, apply the scientific evidence summarized above to your exposure. Does pornography arouse you? Do you think about sex more often and engage in more sex after you watch porn (not just in the hours after but for two or three days)? Are you more tolerant of violence against women than you used to be? Chances are you will admit to being aroused, and maybe to thinking more about sex. But you're not sure it affects your behaviour, and you are sure you don't tolerate violence against women, right?

We like to think we are different, that things that influence others, including friends and family members, don't influence us. When we professors discuss the research on the effects of exposure to advertising, or mass media, or pornography, or consumption of alcohol, on sexual attitudes or behaviour, our students assure us that these things affect their friends, but NOT them! Time for some critical thinking. If these studies have been done on large samples of students, and they have, and you are a student, why would you not be affected, especially if your friends are? Pornography users, especially those who watch 11 hours per week or more (whom the experts consider compulsive viewers or addicts), tell us that it doesn't affect them.

The everyday belief that you are not affected by mass media is in direct contradiction to research evidence. Obviously, the effect varies depending upon what content you watch and how much of it. But regular viewers are affected. Critical thinking involves following the scientific evidence, not just everyday beliefs.

SUMMARY

Commercial sex is a major industry in Canada and increasingly around the world. Two prominent aspects of it are sex work and pornography.

Although selling sex is not illegal in Canada, purchasing sex is illegal. It is also a crime to see or distribute any material that is obscene. Obscenity is determined by using the community standards of tolerance test. Possession of child pornography is also illegal.

Commercial sex workers engage in partnered sexual activity in return for payment, such as money, gifts, or drugs. There are several venues in which they work in Canada including their own homes, in-call services, out-call services, and massage parlours. The working conditions, risks, and income of a sex worker depend on the setting. Third parties who may be involved include a pimp, madam, or manager; the involvement of these people generally limits a worker's autonomy. Sex trafficking involves exploitation and is a major problem. Research suggests that a female sex worker's well-being depends on the risk level of the setting in which she works, the reasons she entered sex work, and whether she experienced victimization as a child or an adolescent.

Data indicate that the use of sex workers has declined substantially in North America in the past 50 years. About one-half of the clients of female sex workers are occasional johns; the other 50 percent are repeat clients. Some men rely on sex workers for their sexual outlet.

Some male sex workers serve a female clientele. They may work as escorts, employees of massage parlours, or gigolos. More common are hustlers who cater to a male clientele.

Distinctions are made among pornography (sexually arousing art, literature, or film), obscenity (material offensive to Canadians), and erotica (sexual material that shows men and women in equal, humane relationships). Pornography on the Internet has mushroomed in the past 20 years; people can discuss explicit sexual activity online, read sexually arousing stories, download sexually explicit images, or purchase a variety of goods and services at adult websites. Pornographic magazines, films, and DVDs, both soft-core (erotica) and hard-core, are a multibillion-dollar business. Children are the victims in child pornography.

Social psychological research indicates that exposure to portrayals that the viewer finds acceptable is arousing to both men and women. Men are more likely to report arousal than are women. Massive exposure leads to more favourable attitudes toward the behaviour observed. Some studies find that exposure to violent pornography creates more tolerant attitudes toward violence against women, but others find no such effect. Exposure of heterosexuals to portrayals of consenting heterosexual activity leads to an increase in sexual thoughts and behaviour. Exposure to portrayals of sexual or nonsexual violence toward women increases men's aggression against women in the laboratory, although the extent to which these results generalize to real-life situations is not known. Some of the issues raised about pornography are that it debases women and portrays unequal relationships between men and women. Research suggests that it does not generally contribute to violence against women, although it may in individual cases. Education about the effects of pornography is probably the best solution to the problems created by violent and dehumanizing pornography.

CHAPTER 18

Sexual Disorders and Sex Therapy

©Ryan McVay/Getty Images

LEARNING OBJECTIVES

After studying this chapter, you will be able to

LO1 Describe each of the sexual disorders listed in the *DSM-5*.

LO2 Discuss the physical (organic), drug, and psychological factors that may cause or maintain sexual disorders.

LO3 Contrast the traditional diagnoses of female sexual disorders with the New View of women's sexual problems.

LO4 Compare and contrast the different approaches to sex therapy.

LO5 Describe the specific therapeutic and biomedical treatments for specific sexual disorders.

LO6 Discuss the primary criticisms of sex therapy techniques.

LO7 Describe ways to prevent sexual dysfunctions, and list strategies for choosing a sex therapist.

Are YOU Curious?

1. What counts as premature (early) ejaculation?
2. What can a woman do if she has trouble having orgasms?
3. How does Viagra work?

Read this chapter to find out.

Telling it in plain words makes me see how I feared the wrong thing.*

* Margaret Avison. (1982). The Agnes Cleves Papers, *In Winter Sun/The Dumbfounding: Poems 1940–66*, Toronto: McClelland & Stewart.

Many people experience occasional sexual problems and concerns that go away without treatment. When a problem with sexual response causes significant psychological distress or interpersonal difficulty, it is called a *sexual disorder*. The term *sexual dysfunction* is also used. Examples are a man's difficulty getting an erection and a woman's difficulty having an orgasm.

This definition seems fairly simple. As we will see, however, in practice it can be difficult to determine exactly when something is a sexual disorder. Indeed, whether we define something as a sexual disorder is affected by the social and cultural context in which we live. In addition, there is a tendency to think in terms of only two categories, people with a sexual disorder and "normal" people. In fact, there is a continuum. Most of us have had, at one time or another, a sexual problem that went away in a day or a few months without treatment. In one New Brunswick study, 59 percent of the men and 68 percent of the women reported experiencing a sexual problem in the previous 18 months, but none had sought treatment (MacNeil & Byers, 1997). Another New Brunswick study showed that sexual problems can start at a young age—on average almost all university students reported one or more sexual problems (six different problems on average), although most problems were not chronic (O'Sullivan & Majerovich, 2008). Most young people who experience a sexual problem find this distressing (O'Sullivan et al., 2014, 2016). In another study, in which 16- to 21-year-old adolescents were followed for two years, these researchers showed that 79 percent of male and 84 percent of female adolescents reported experiencing a persistent sexual problem (O'Sullivan et al., 2016). Students from the Chinese and other Asian ethnocultural community groups are more likely than Euro-Canadian students to experience sexual problems (Woo & Brotto, 2008). These cases represent the shades of grey that lie between absolutely great sexual functioning and long-term difficulties that require sex therapy.

Long-term sexual difficulties can cause a great deal of psychological distress to individuals and their partners, and many of these people seek out treatment. Until the 1960s, the only available treatment was long-term psychoanalysis, which was costly and not particularly effective. A new era in understanding and treatment was ushered in with the publication, in 1970, of *Human Sexual Inadequacy* by Masters and Johnson. This book reported on the team's research on sexual disorders, as well as on their rapid-treatment program of behaviour therapy. Since then, many additional developments have taken place in the field, including cognitive behaviour therapy and medical (drug) treatments.

Sexual disorders and treatments for them are the topics of this chapter. First we will consider the kinds of sexual disorders. Following that, we will review the causes of these disorders and then the treatments for them.

LO1

 Sexual Disorders

In Chapter 15, we introduced the American Psychiatric Association's manual of disorders, called the *Diagnostic and Statistical Manual,* now in its fifth edition, the *DSM-5* (APA, 2013b). It is controversial and not all experts agree with some of the decisions made about diagnoses. Nonetheless, in this section we will consider seven categories of **sexual disorders** listed in the *DSM-5:* male hypoactive sexual desire disorder, erectile disorder, premature (early) ejaculation, delayed ejaculation, female orgasmic disorder, female sexual interest/arousal disorder, and genito-pelvic pain/penetration disorder. Notice that the first four refer to men and the last three refer to women.

Of course, sexual disorders do not always fall so neatly into these distinct categories. For example, a person who has difficulty with orgasm or who experiences sexual pain is likely to develop low desire as a result. In this case, a person can have more than one disorder. Although each disorder corresponds to different aspects of the sexual response cycle (see Chapter 9), in all disorders the person is not able to respond sexually or to feel sexual pleasure because of the disorder and experiences distress because of it. The *DSM-5* also includes substance/medication-induced sexual dysfunction and a category for other sexual disorders. Of note, a number of Canadian researchers were instrumental in spearheading needed changes to the *DSM* diagnostic categories for sexual disorders in the recent update to the *DSM-5*—indeed, Dr. Ken Zucker from Toronto was the chair of the committee reviewing needed changes.

Each disorder can be seen to vary along two dimensions. It can be a **lifelong sexual disorder** or it can be an **acquired sexual disorder**. A lifelong sexual disorder occurs when the individual

sexual disorders: Problems with sexual response that cause a person mental distress.

lifelong sexual disorder: A sexual disorder that has been present since the person began sexual functioning.

acquired sexual disorder: A sexual disorder that develops after a period of normal functioning.

has always had that disorder (e.g., the person has never had an orgasm). An acquired sexual disorder occurs when the individual currently has the problem but did not have the problem in the past (e.g., has had orgasms in the past but is currently unable to orgasm). Sexual disorders can also be either *generalized,* that is, occurring in all situations, or *situational.* A **situational sexual disorder** is a disorder that occurs in some situations but not in others. Many sexual disorders are not absolute. They may occur with one partner (e.g., the spouse) but not another (e.g., the lover), or in one situation (e.g., at home) but not another (e.g., on vacation). Sexual disorders can occur with a partner of the same or other sex. The clinician needs to assess a number of factors that may be affecting the problem before deciding whether the individual has a sexual disorder—such as whether the person is receiving effective stimulation and what the relationship between the partners is like. These are discussed in more detail below.

✳Disorders in Men

The disorders that can be diagnosed for men include male hypoactive sexual desire disorder, erectile disorder, premature (early) ejaculation, and delayed ejaculation.

Male Hypoactive Sexual Desire Disorder

Sexual desire, or *libido,* refers to an interest in sexual activity, leading the individual to seek out sexual activity or to be pleasurably receptive to it. The term **hypoactive sexual desire disorder (HSDD)** (the prefix *hypo* means "low") is used when an individual does not have spontaneous thoughts or fantasies about sexual activity and is not interested in sexual activity (Basson, 2004; Brotto et al., 2010). It is also sometimes termed *inhibited sexual desire* or *low sexual desire.* The defining characteristics are persistent or recurrent low or lack of sexual thoughts or fantasies and low or absent interest in sex that is distressing to the individual. For many people, desire occurs before sexual activity begins and leads them to initiate sex; other people begin to feel desire after their partner initiates or after sexual activity starts. This latter pattern is called *responsive desire.* It is not uncommon for men to report problems with sexual desire: About 6 percent of young men and 41 percent of men over the age of 65 report this problem (APA, 2013b). However, less than 2 percent of men meet the criteria for a diagnosis of male hypoactive sexual desire disorder.

Like other sexual disorders, HSDD poses complex problems of definition. There are many circumstances when it is

situational sexual disorder: A sexual disorder that a person has in some situations but not in others.
hypoactive sexual desire (HSDD): A sexual disorder in which there is a lack of interest in sexual activity; also termed inhibited sexual desire or low sexual desire.
discrepancy of sexual desire: A sexual problem in which the partners have considerably different levels of sexual desire.
erectile (eh-REK-tile) disorder: The inability to have or maintain an erection.

perfectly normal for a person not to experience sexual desire. For example, one cannot be expected to be turned on by every potential partner. Men who experience anxiety about erection or ejaculation may lose interest in sex. (See Chapter 14 for a discussion of the difference between asexuality and hypoactive sexual desire disorder.)

This disorder is only diagnosed in men because in women sexual desire and arousal are often linked. Thus, they were combined into a single disorder for women (see *female sexual interest/arousal disorder* below). This decision is still controversial.

It is also often true that the problem is not the individual's absolute level of sexual desire but a discrepancy between the partners' levels (Willoughby & Vitas, 2012). That is, if one partner wants sex considerably less frequently than the other partner does, there is a conflict, even if neither partner is experiencing a sexual disorder. This problem is termed a **discrepancy of sexual desire** and is a couple problem, not a sexual disorder. Researchers in Ontario have shown that partners' perceptions of a greater desire discrepancy between them but not the extent of the actual desire discrepancy is associated with lower sexual satisfaction (Sutherland et al., 2015).

Erectile Disorder

Erectile disorder (ED) is the inability to have an erection or maintain one on almost all or all occasions. Other terms for it are *erectile dysfunction* and *inhibited sexual excitement.* Although erectile disorder used to be called *impotence* (a term many laypeople still use), many professionals prefer not to use this term because of the negative connotations associated with it. One result of erectile disorder is that the man cannot engage in sexual intercourse. Using terminology discussed earlier, cases of erectile disorder can be classified as either *lifelong erectile disorder* (which is quite rare) or *acquired erectile disorder,* depending on whether the man has ever been able to have and maintain an erection that is satisfactory for penetration in the past. It can also be *generalized* or *situational* (i.e., it happens only with certain types of stimulation or types of partners).

According to surveys in North America and Europe, erectile disorder occurs in fewer than 10 percent of men under 40 but then increases to about 30 percent for men in their 60s (Lewis et al., 2010). Erectile disorder is the most common of the disorders among men who seek sex therapy, particularly since the introduction of Viagra.

Psychological reactions to erectile disorder may be severe. For many men, it is one of the most embarrassing things they can imagine. Depression may follow from repeated episodes. The man may avoid sexual encounters. It may also cause embarrassment or worry to the man's partner.

Premature (Early) Ejaculation

Premature (early) ejaculation occurs when a man persistently has an orgasm and ejaculates sooner than desired during sexual activity with a partner and is significantly distressed about the problem (APA, 2013b). For individuals who engage in penile–vaginal intercourse, ejaculation must occur within one minute following penetration; although premature (early) ejaculation also applies to men with a same-sex partner, specific time criteria have not been specified for other sexual activities. This definition is similar to the definition adopted by the International Society for Sexual Medicine to create consistency in both research and diagnosis (Althof et al., 2010). Both definitions involve three parts: (1) ejaculation that always or almost always occurs before or within one minute of vaginal penetration (note the heteronormativity of both of the definitions); (2) the inability to delay ejaculation; and (3) distress about the problem. This definition therefore includes a time component, a lack of control component, and a distress component. Premature (early) ejaculation can be lifelong or acquired and situational or generalized.

In extreme cases, ejaculation may take place so soon after erection that it happens before penetration can occur. In other cases, the man is able to delay the orgasm to some extent, but not as long as he would like or not long enough to meet his partner's preferences. This definition is an improvement over previous definitions because it specifies what is meant by "premature" or "early"—at least for penile–vaginal intercourse. In the past, the definitions used by clinicians and researchers in the field varied widely (Bettocchi et al., 2008; Grenier & Byers, 1995, 2001).

Psychiatrist and sex therapist Helen Singer Kaplan (1974; Grenier & Byers, 2001; McCarthy, 1989) believed that the key to defining rapid ejaculation is the absence of voluntary control of orgasm; that is, the real problem is that the man with premature (early) ejaculation has little or no control over when he orgasms. Another good definition is self-definition, even if the man does not meet the criteria for a formal diagnosis: if a man finds that he has become greatly concerned about his lack of ejaculatory control or that it is interfering with his ability to form intimate relationships, or if a couple agree that it is a problem in their relationship, it is entirely legitimate to seek professional assistance for these concerns.

Estimates are that between 1 and 3 percent of men would be diagnosed with premature (early) ejaculation (APA, 2013b). However, many more men report poor ejaculatory control. Our research has shown that 24 percent of Canadian men report having a current problem with climaxing "too early" (Grenier & Byers, 2001). Although the average time to ejaculation after penetration reported by the men in this study was about eight minutes, 7 percent reported ejaculating within one minute (which would fit within the *DSM-5* guidelines), and 17 percent reported ejaculating within two minutes. Not all of the men who reported that they had a problem with early

ejaculation actually ejaculated quickly; some had unrealistic expectations about how long intercourse should last. It might be some relief for them to know that their female partners were less likely to see the timing of their ejaculation as a problem—only 10 percent of the partners felt the man had a problem related to early ejaculation compared with 24 percent of the men (Byers & Grenier, 2003). Further, early ejaculation was associated with lower sexual satisfaction for the men but not for their partners, and it was not associated with relationship satisfaction for either partner. In another study, 53 percent of university men in New Brunswick reported limited ejaculatory control; 59 percent were very concerned about ejaculating sooner than they wanted to (Grenier & Byers, 1997). Very few of these men had ever sought therapy for the problem.

> **What counts as premature (early) ejaculation?**

Like erectile disorder, premature ejaculation may create a web of related psychological problems. Because the ability to postpone ejaculation and "satisfy" a partner is so important in our concept of a man who is a competent lover, early ejaculation can cause a man to become anxious about his sexual competence. Furthermore, the partner may become frustrated because she or he is not having a satisfying sexual experience either. So the condition may create friction in the relationship.

The negative psychological effects of early ejaculation are illustrated by a young man in one of our sexuality classes who handed in an anonymous question. He described himself as a premature ejaculator and said that after several humiliating experiences during intercourse with dates, he was now convinced that no woman would want him in that condition. He no longer had the courage to ask for dates, so he had stopped dating entirely. He wanted to know how the women in the class would react to a man with such a problem. The question was discussed in class, and most of the women agreed that their reaction to his problem would depend a great deal on the quality of the relationship they had with him. If they cared deeply for him, they would be sympathetic and patient and help him overcome the difficulty. The point is, though, that the early ejaculation had created problems so severe that the young man not only had stopped having sex but had also stopped dating.

Men have developed (mostly ineffective) home remedies for dealing with early ejaculation, such as doubling up on condoms and using desensitizing creams. Perhaps the most common is to think of something else. We had university men in New Brunswick report the thoughts they used to delay ejaculation (Grenier & Byers, 1997). These thoughts fell into five categories: sex negative (thinking of an unattractive TV personality); sex positive (thinking "we're in no hurry" or visualizing a past episode of prolonged intercourse); nonsexual and negative (thinking of a

> **premature (early) ejaculation:** A sexual disorder in which the man ejaculates too soon and feels he cannot control when he ejaculates.

sad event, unpaid debts); sex neutral (counting backward from 100); and sexually incongruous (thinking of your grandmother, reciting the Lord's Prayer). Of these options, we recommend the sex-positive alternative because it not only delays ejaculation but also allows both partners to remain in the moment. However, to some extent, any distraction technique may detract from attention to the sensations, and the proximity to the "point of no return." Thus, many clinicians encourage men to remain focused on sensations and the stop-start technique (described later in the chapter) to maintain arousal at manageable levels.

Delayed Ejaculation

Delayed ejaculation (also sometimes called *male orgasmic disorder*) is the opposite of rapid (early) ejaculation. The man is consistently (for a period of at least six months) unable to orgasm, or orgasm is greatly delayed when engaging in sexual activity with a partner, even though he has a solid erection and has had more than adequate stimulation, and he is distressed about this (APA, 2013b; Perelman, 2014). In the most common version, the man is incapable of orgasm during intercourse but may be able to orgasm as a result of hand or mouth stimulation. Fortunately, these problems are rare.

Male orgasmic disorder is far less common than premature ejaculation. About 10 percent of men experience this problem (Mitchell et al., 2013). However, likely less than 1 percent of men would meet the criteria for a diagnosis of delayed ejaculation, although it is more common among men over 50 than among younger men (APA, 2013b). As discussed later, some medications can result in delayed ejaculation (APA, 2013b).

Male orgasmic disorder is, to say the least, a frustrating experience for a man. In addition, some people react negatively to this condition, seeing their partner's inability to have an orgasm as a personal rejection. Some men, anticipating these negative reactions, have adopted the practice of faking orgasm. In other cases, the couple engages in prolonged thrusting so that the man can orgasm, which results in exhaustion or painful intercourse for the partner.

✱Disorders in Women

The disorders that can be diagnosed for women include female sexual interest/arousal disorder, female orgasmic disorder, and genito-pelvic pain/penetration disorder.

Female Sexual Interest/Arousal Disorder

Female sexual interest/arousal disorder refers to a lack of or significantly reduced sexual interest or arousal (APA, 2013b). To meet the criteria for this disorder, the woman would experience at least three of the following persistent symptoms that cause clinically significant distress: lack of interest in sexual activity; lack of sexual thoughts; lack of desire as demonstrated by not initiating sex with a partner and not being responsive to the partner's initiations (i.e., responsive desire); absent or reduced sexual excitement or pleasure in all or almost all sexual encounters; absent or reduced response to sexual stimuli; and absent or reduced physiological response during all or almost all sexual encounters. The disorder cannot be due to psychological or relationship distress. This definition takes into account that different women may experience female sexual interest/arousal disorder differently and may exhibit different symptoms. For some women, the disorder may primarily affect her sexual interest and thoughts—that is, her sexual desire. In fact, about 39 percent of Canadian women report diminished sexual desire (Fisher et al., 1999b).

In other women, female sexual interest/arousal disorder may primarily affect their ability to become aroused and respond sexually—that is, their arousal. In still other women, it may affect both.

Note that, as noted above, a *discrepancy of sexual desire* between members of the couple (in which the woman has lower desire than her partner) is not sufficient to diagnose female sexual interest/arousal disorder.

Difficulties with arousal and lubrication are common. However, most are not persistent and, particularly in older women, they may not cause distress (APA, 2013b). These problems become particularly frequent among women during and after menopause (Rosen, Connor, et al., 2012). As estrogen levels decline, vaginal lubrication decreases. The use of sterile lubricants is an easy way to deal with this problem. The absence of subjective feelings of arousal is more complex to treat.

Female Orgasmic Disorder

Female orgasmic disorder refers to a woman's recurrent difficulty having an orgasm or reduced orgasm intensity during almost all sexual activity (APA, 2013b). As with the other disorders, the woman must be distressed about the situation (see First Person for one woman's story). This condition goes by a variety of other terms, including *orgasmic dysfunction, anorgasmia,* and *inhibited female orgasm.* Laypersons may call it *frigidity,* but sex therapists reject this term because it has derogatory connotations and is imprecise because it may refer to a variety of conditions ranging from total lack of sexual arousal to arousal without orgasm. Therefore, the term *female orgasmic disorder* is preferred.

Like other sexual disorders, cases of female orgasmic disorder may be classified into *lifelong* and *acquired* depending on whether the woman has ever had orgasms in the past (APA, 2013b). A common pattern is *situational*

delayed ejaculation: A sexual disorder in which the man cannot have an orgasm or the orgasm is greatly delayed, even though he has an erection and has had a great deal of sexual stimulation.

female sexual interest/arousal disorder: A sexual disorder in which the woman's sexual interest or arousal is significantly reduced.

female orgasmic disorder: A sexual disorder in which the woman is unable to have an orgasm.

orgasmic disorder, in which the woman has orgasms in some situations but not others. For example, she may be able to have orgasms while masturbating but not while being stimulated by a partner. Orgasmic disorders are common among women (Heiman, 2007). Younger women are more likely to report infrequent orgasms than are older women (Fisher et al., 1999b).

Worldwide, approximately 10 percent of women have never experienced an orgasm in their lifetime (APA, 2013b). However, 21 percent of Canadian women report that they do not usually have an orgasm during intercourse (Fisher et al., 1999b). These women don't necessarily have a disorder (APA, 2013b). Consider the case of the heterosexual woman who orgasms as a result of masturbation or hand or mouth stimulation by a partner but who does not orgasm during penile–vaginal intercourse. Is this really a sexual disorder? The notion that it is a disorder can be traced to sexual scripts and beliefs that there is a "right" way to have sex—with the penis inside the vagina—and a corresponding "right" way to have orgasms. Because this pattern of situational orgasmic disorder is so common, the *DSM-5* explicitly states that women who need clitoral stimulation to reach orgasm should not be diagnosed with this disorder. Often the woman who orgasms as a result of hand or mouth stimulation, but not penile thrusting, is simply having orgasms when she is adequately stimulated and is not having them when she is inadequately stimulated.

Nonetheless, there should be room for self-definition of sexual concerns and problems as deserving of attention, even if not a diagnosis. If a woman is truly distressed that she is not able to orgasm during vaginal intercourse and wants therapy, then it may be appropriate to provide it even if she does not meet the criteria for having a disorder. The therapist, however, should be careful to explain to her the problems of cultural definition just raised to be sure that her request for therapy stems from her own dissatisfaction with her sexual responding rather than from an overly idealistic sexual script. Therapy in such cases probably is best viewed as an effort to enrich the client's experience rather than to fix a problem.

Genito-Pelvic Pain/Penetration Disorder

In the *DSM-5*, two separate disorders (dyspareunia and vaginismus) were combined into one disorder genito-pelvic pain/penetration disorder. Part of the reason for the merger is that the two tend to occur together. **Genito-pelvic pain/penetration disorder** refers to any one of four symptoms that typically occur together: difficulty having intercourse/penetration; marked genital and/or pelvic pain during penetration attempts (sometimes termed **dyspareunia**); fear of pain associated with vaginal penetration; and marked tension or tightening of the pelvic floor muscles during attempts at vaginal penetration (APA, 2013b). The symptoms must occur for more than six months and must cause the woman significant

distress. Difficulty having intercourse may be situational or generalized, although it is more typical for women who experience pain with a partner to also experience pain in other situations, such as during a gynaecological exam (Boyer & Pukall, 2014). Approximately, 15 percent of women report recurrent pain during sexual intercourse. Of particular concern, research in Quebec found that dyspareunia is common in girls between the ages of 12 and 19 who are engaging in intercourse; 20 percent of these girls reported experiencing regular pain during intercourse for at least six months (Landry & Bergeron, 2009).

Although complaints of occasional pain during intercourse are fairly common among women, persistent genito-pelvic pain is not as common. The location of the pain, its nature, and its intensity may vary. It may be felt in the vagina, around the vaginal entrance and clitoris, or deep in the pelvis. It may be generalized or localized to a particular area (Damsted-Petersen et al., 2009). The pain may also differ in quality and in intensity (Pukall et al., 2003). Some women describe a burning sensation, others a sharp pain or an aching feeling. It can be lifelong or develop after a period of experiencing pain-free penetration (acquired) (Sutton et al., 2015). To put it mildly, dyspareunia decreases a woman's enjoyment of the sexual experience, frequently causes problems with arousal and orgasm, and may lead to avoiding sexual situations; it also adversely affects the partner's sexual functioning and satisfaction (Chernler & Reissing, 2013; Smith & Pukall, 2013; 2014). Some women experience reflexive muscle spasm of the outer third of the vagina making penetration impossible; this is often referred to as **vaginismus**. For other women, whose pelvic floor muscles tighten involuntarily, penetration may be possible if they learn to relax their muscles. Although there is no equivalent male disorder in the *DSM-5*, about 2 percent of men experience pain during sex (Mitchell et al., 2013b).

Quebec psychologist Yitzchak Binik and his colleagues have criticized the notion of a sexual pain disorder (Binik et al., 2007; Meana et al., 1997; Pukall et al., 2000). They point out that just because pain interferes with sexual activity such as intercourse, this does not make it a sexual disorder. They use the analogy of lower back pain that interferes with work. Although lower back pain may prevent a person from working, this pain is classified by its location (i.e., lower back pain) rather than by the activity it interferes with (i.e., work pain). Further, the pain associated with intercourse often also occurs in nonsexual situations, such as inserting a tampon or physical exercise. Thus they argue that painful intercourse should be reclassified and treated as a pain disorder that interferes with

> **genito-pelvic pain/penetration disorder:** Any one of four symptoms that typically occur together related to genital pain during actual or attempted sexual intercourse.
> **dyspareunia (dis-pah-ROO-nee-uh):** Painful intercourse.
> **vaginismus:** A reflexive spasm of the muscles surrounding the entrance to the vagina, in some cases so severe that intercourse is impossible.

First Person

A Case of Female Orgasmic Disorder

J ane was a self-employed, attractive, divorced woman who came to the clinic at the University of Minnesota at the age of 43, with an acquired inability to reach orgasm, which had then led to a decline in her sexual desire. She had been divorced from her husband, Tom, for 5½ years after a 17-year marriage. Even though she was not in love with him, Jane had married Tom because he was the first man with whom she had sexual intercourse. Jane and Tom had two sons from this marriage, ages 13 (Bruce) and 18 (Dean). Bruce was attending a costly private school paid for by Jane. Dean had a history of emotional and behavioural problems.

At the time she sought help at our clinic, Jane was in a three-year-long relationship with Frank, a 45-year-old divorced man. Frank directed their sexual relationship. Jane was compliant with Frank's sexual requests, never asking that her needs be met. She reported having an orgasm only once with Frank, although she still reported becoming aroused during their sexual interactions. This lack of orgasm was in contrast to the pattern during her marriage, when she was able to have an orgasm at least half of the time by rubbing her clitoris against her husband's pelvic area when she was on top (her husband did not always have an erection). This difficulty having an orgasm, along with the lack of a supportive response from her partner, affected Jane's sexual desire, which declined precipitously.

Jane came to therapy believing that there was something wrong with her physically—that she was broken sexually. This belief originated from her boyfriend's assertion that she had a small clitoris, which interfered with her ability to orgasm. She lacked an adequate sexual vocabulary and experienced difficulty talking about sex, often becoming red-faced or tearful. These problems with sexual communication were partially the result of her upbringing in a small rural town in a fundamentalist religious family, where sex was rarely discussed. Jane grew up with her biological parents, two brothers, and two sisters. She described her family as "fundamentally religious," her father as the dominant decision-maker, and her mother as "puritanical." In therapy, it emerged that she had been sexually abused by both older brothers, beginning when she was 12 years old.

Jane's treatment proceeded over several years because of the need to help her recover from the child sexual abuse and the PTSD and depression that resulted from it. Treatment used the Sexual Health Model developed at the University of Minnesota and involved multiple treatment methods described in this chapter, including individual, couple, and group therapy and psychiatric care. Jane found a new partner who was more supportive, and treatment ended with Jane feeling sexually confident.

Source: Robinson et al. (2011). Names have been changed to preserve anonymity. Read this article if you want the full details of the therapy.

---

sexual activity rather than as a sexual disorder (Binik, 2005; Payne, Reissing, et al., 2005). As with other pain disorders, psychological and cognitive factors, such as the fear of pain, increase the intensity of the pain experienced (Desrochers et al., 2008, 2009).

What Causes Sexual Disorders?

biopsychosocial model: A general model that argues that physical, psychological, and social factors all contribute to sexual disorders.

There are many causes of sexual disorders, varying from person to person and from one disorder to another. Several categories of factors may be related to sexual disorders: physical factors, drugs, individual psychological factors, and interpersonal factors. These factors interact with each other so that the causes of most disorders can best be understood from a biopsychosocial perspective (Brotto et al., 2015). According to the **biopsychosocial model**, biological, psychological, and social factors all play a role in the development and maintenance of sexual disorders. For example, disorders that are largely due to physical factors affect people's thoughts, feelings, and relationships; in turn, their thoughts and feelings may make the problem worse (or better). Conversely, disorders that are primarily due to psychological or social factors nonetheless affect nerves and blood vessels in a physical way. Each of these categories is discussed separately.

Physical Causes

Physical factors that cause sexual disorders include **organic factors of sexual disorders** (physical factors, such as diseases) and drugs.

Erectile Disorder

Diseases associated with the heart and the circulatory system are particularly likely to be associated with erectile disorder, since erection itself depends on the circulatory system (Rosen, 2007). Any kind of vascular pathology (problems in the blood vessels supplying the penis) can produce erection problems. Erection depends on having a great deal of blood flowing into the penis via the arteries, with simultaneous constricting of the veins so that the blood cannot flow out as rapidly as it is coming in. Thus, damage to either these arteries or the veins may produce erectile disorder.

Erectile disorder is associated with diabetes mellitus. Several aspects of diabetes are involved including circulation problems and peripheral nerve damage (Sáenz de Tejada et al., 2004). In fact, in some cases erectile disorder may be the earliest symptom of diabetes. Of course, not all diabetic men have erectile disorders; indeed, the majority do not. One estimate is that 28 percent of men with diabetes have an erectile disorder (Sáenz de Tejada et al., 2004). Diabetes is also associated with sexual disorders in women (Giraldi & Kristensen, 2010).

Hypogonadism—an underfunctioning of the testes so that testosterone levels are very low—is associated with ED (Morales & Heaton, 2001). ED is also associated with a condition called hyperprolactinemia in which there is excessive production of prolactin (Johri et al., 2001).

Any disease or injury that damages the lower part of the spinal cord may cause erectile disorder, since that is the location of the erection reflex centre (see Chapter 9). Finally, some—though not all—kinds of prostate surgery may cause the condition (Libman & Fichten, 1987; Libman et al., 1989).

With erectile disorders, as with most sexual disorders, it is important to recognize that the distinction between organic causes and psychological causes is too simple (Rosen, 2007). In keeping with the biopsychosocial model, most sexual disorders result from a complex interplay of the two causes. For example, a man who has circulatory problems that initially cause him to have erection problems is likely to develop anxieties about erection, which in turn may create further difficulties. This notion of dual causes has important implications for therapy. A comprehensive approach to treatment should include attention to physical, psychological, and interpersonal factors.

Premature (Early) Ejaculation

Premature (early) ejaculation is more often caused by psychological than physical factors. However, for some men rapid ejaculation may be due to a malfunctioning of the ejaculatory reflexes (Grenier & Byers, 1995). These men have a physiological hypersensitivity that results in faster ejaculation. (See Chapter 9 for a discussion of ejaculation.) Physical factors may also be involved in cases of acquired premature ejaculation, in which the man at one time had ejaculatory control but later lost it. A local infection, such as prostatitis, may be the cause, as may degeneration in the related parts of the nervous system, which may occur in neural disorders, such as multiple sclerosis.

An intriguing explanation for early ejaculation comes from the sociobiologists (Hong, 1984). Their idea is that rapid ejaculation has been selected for in the process of evolution—what we might call "survival of the fastest." Monkeys and apes (and humans) who copulated and ejaculated rapidly, the argument goes, would be more likely to survive and reproduce in that the female would be less likely to get away, and the male would be less likely to be attacked by other sexually aroused males while he was copulating. In fact, the average time from intromission (insertion of the penis into the vagina) to ejaculation among chimpanzees is rapid—about seven seconds (Tutin & McGinnis, 1981). However, primates engage in lengthy courtship and foreplay behaviours that would not be predicted by sociobiologists (Bixler, 1986). Nonetheless, according to sociobiologists, the genes for rapid ejaculation are still around.

Delayed Ejaculation

Delayed ejaculation may be associated with a variety of medical or surgical conditions, such as multiple sclerosis, spinal cord injury, and prostate surgery (Rosen & Leiblum, 1995b). Most commonly, though, it is associated with psychological factors.

Female Orgasmic Disorder

Orgasmic disorder in women may be caused by severe illness, general ill health, or extreme fatigue. Injury to the spinal cord can cause orgasm problems (Sipski et al., 2001). However, most cases are primarily caused by psychological factors.

Genito-pelvic Pain/Penetration Disorder

Although genito-pelvic pain in women is often caused by organic factors, research suggests that psychosocial and interpersonal factors also contribute (Bergeron et al., 2010; Rosen & Leiblum, 1995a). Further, the experience of pain

> **organic factors of sexual disorders:** Physical factors, such as disease or injury, that cause sexual disorders.

during sexual activity is influenced by psychological factors (Bergeron et al., 2010; Desrochers et al., 2008; Desrochers et al., 2009).

Organic factors for genito-pelvic pain/penetration disorder include the following:

1. *Disorders of the vaginal entrance:* Irritated remnants of the hymen; painful scars, perhaps from an episiotomy or sexual assault; or infection of the Bartholin glands

2. *Disorders of the vagina:* Vaginal infections; allergic reactions to spermicidal creams or the latex in condoms or diaphragms; a thinning of the vaginal walls, which occurs naturally with age or chemically induced menopause; or scarring of the roof of the vagina, which can occur after hysterectomy

3. *Pelvic disorders:* Pelvic infection, such as pelvic inflammatory disease; endometriosis; tumours; cysts; or tearing of the ligaments supporting the uterus

4. *Dysfunction of the pelvic floor muscles:* Higher pelvic floor muscle tone; lower vaginal flexibility; higher mucosal sensitivity; lower muscle strength (Bergeron et al., 2010)

Sexual pain in men is typically caused by a variety of organic factors. It may be caused by infection. For an uncircumcised man, poor hygiene may be a cause; if the penis is not washed thoroughly with the foreskin retracted, material may collect under the foreskin, causing infection. An allergic reaction to spermicidal creams or to the latex in condoms may also be involved. Finally, various prostate problems may cause pain during intercourse, after intercourse, or on ejaculation (Smith et al., 2007).

Drugs

Some drugs may have side effects that cause sexual disorders (APA, 2013b; Ashton, 2007; Segraves & Balon, 2003, 2010). For example, hormonal contraceptives interfere with sexual desire and arousal in some women. Some drugs used to treat high blood pressure increase problems with erection in men and decrease sexual desire in both men and women. Similarly, many antidepressants can have a range of sexual side effects. Indeed, there are so many substances and drugs that can cause problems with sexual functioning that the *DSM-5* includes a diagnostic category for *substance/medication-induced sexual dysfunction.* Although it would be impossible to list every drug effect on every aspect of sexual functioning, a list of some of the major drugs that may cause sexual disorders is provided in Table 18.1. Here we will consider the effects of alcohol, illicit drugs, and prescription drugs.

Alcohol

The effects of alcohol on sexual responding vary considerably. We can think of these effects as falling into three categories: (1) short-term pharmacological effects, (2) expectancy effects, and (3) long-term effects of chronic alcohol abuse. In the last category, people who abuse alcohol, particularly in the later stages of alcoholism, frequently have sexual disorders, typically including erectile disorder, orgasmic disorder, and loss of desire (Segraves & Balon, 2003). These sex problems may be the result of any of a number of organic effects of long-term alcoholism. For example, chronic alcoholism in men may cause disturbances in sex hormone production because of atrophy of the testes or liver damage. Chronic alcohol abuse, too, generally has negative effects on the person's interpersonal relationships, which may contribute to sexual disorders.

What about the person who is not an alcoholic but has had one or many drinks on a particular evening and then proceeds to a sexual interaction (Figure 18.1a)? As noted earlier, there is an interplay of two effects: expectancy effects and actual pharmacological effects (George & Stoner, 2000; George et al., 2006). Many people have the expectation that alcohol will loosen them up, making them more sociable and sexually uninhibited. These expectancy effects in themselves produce increased physiological arousal and subjective feelings of arousal. Expectancy effects, though, interact with the pharmacological effects and work mainly at low doses, that is, when only a little alcohol has been consumed. At high dosage levels, alcohol acts as a depressant and sexual arousal is markedly suppressed, in both men[1] and women.

Illicit or Recreational Drugs

There is a widespread belief that marijuana (*cannabis, pot, weed*) has aphrodisiac properties. Scientific research is limited. Therefore, we can provide only tentative ideas about the effects of marijuana on sexual functioning. In surveys of users, many respondents report that it increases sexual desire and makes sexual interactions more pleasurable (McKay, 2005a). In regard to potential negative effects, there is concern that marijuana use contributes to risky sexual behaviour, such as unprotected sex (Collins et al., 2005). Chronic users report decreased sexual desire (Segraves & Balon, 2003). In community studies, marijuana use has been associated with orgasmic disorder (Johnson et al., 2004).

To make matters more complicated, B.C. researchers have found that the effects of cannabinoids (the active drugs in marijuana) depend on gender (Gorzalka et al., 2010). In women, low doses of cannabis are associated

---

[1] Some refer to the resulting erection problems as "whisky dick."

Table 18.1 Drugs That May Impair or Improve Sexual Response

Drug	How It Affects Sexual Functioning	Common Medical Uses
1. Psychoactive Drugs		
Antianxiety drugs/tranquilizers		Anxiety, panic disorders
Buspirone	Enhanced desire, orgasm	
Benzodiazepines (Librium, Valium, Ativan)	Decreased hypoactive desire, improvement of premature ejaculation	
Antidepressants I: Tricyclics and MAO inhibitors	Desire disorders, erection problems, orgasm problems, ejaculation problems	Depression
	May treat hypersexuality, premature ejaculation	
Antidepressants II: Serotonin reuptake inhibitors (Paxil, Prozac, Zoloft)	Desire disorders, erection problems, orgasm problems	Depression, obsessive-compulsive disorder, panic disorders
Lithium	Desire disorders, erection problems	Bipolar disorder
Antipsychotics (Thorazine, Haldol)	Desire disorders, erection problems, orgasm problems, ejaculation problems	Schizophrenia
2. Antihypertensives		
Reserpine, methyldopa	Desire disorders, erection difficulties, orgasm delayed or blocked	High blood pressure
ACE inhibitors (Vasotec)	Erection difficulties	
3. Substance Use and Abuse		
Alcohol	At low doses, increases desire	
	At high doses, decreases erection, arousal, orgasm	
	Alcoholism creates many disorders and atrophied testicles, infertility	
Nicotine	Decreases blood flow to penis, creates erectile disorder	
Opioids		
Endogenous: Endorphins (neurotransmitter, not a drug)	Sense of well-being and relaxation	
Heroin	Decreased desire, orgasm, ejaculation, replacement for sex	
Marijuana	Enhanced sexual pleasure but not actual "performance"; chronic use decreases desire	

Sources: Ashton (2007); Meston et al. (2004); Segraves & Balon (2003).

with increased sexual desire and sexual pleasure. It is possible that cannabis boosts the production of androgens in women, leading to the positive sexual effects. At higher doses, though, cannabis creates sexual problems. In men, moderate doses of cannabis appear to increase sexual desire while at the same time creating erection problems.

Among drug users, cocaine is reported to be one of the drugs of choice for enhancing sexual experiences (Figure 18.1b). It is said to increase sexual desire, enhance sensuality, and delay orgasm. Chronic use of cocaine, however, is associated with loss of sexual desire, orgasmic disorders, and erectile disorders (Segraves & Balon, 2003). The effects also depend on the means of

administration—whether the cocaine is inhaled, smoked, or injected. The most negative effects on sexual functioning occur among those who regularly inject the drug. Crack cocaine is highly addictive and the crack epidemic, especially in city downtown areas, often involves the exchange of sex for drugs (Green et al., 2005).

Stimulant drugs, notably amphetamines, are associated with increased sexual desire and better control of orgasm in some studies (Segraves & Balon, 2003). Injection of amphetamines itself causes a physical sensation that is described by some as a total-body orgasm. In some cases, though, orgasm becomes difficult or impossible when using amphetamines.

(a) © Jeff Greenberg/PhotoEdit

(b) The McGraw-Hill Companies, Inc./Gary He, photographer

Figure 18.1   Alcohol and cocaine are popular recreational drugs that many people believe enhance sexual experience. Research shows, though, that high levels of alcohol suppress sexual arousal, and repeated use of cocaine is associated with loss of sexual desire, orgasm disorders, and erection problems.

Crystal methamphetamine (also known as *ice* or *crystal meth*) is a popular recreational drug. This drug is of particular concern because, while high on it, people have a tendency to engage in risky sexual behaviours (Semple et al., 2004; Semple et al., 2009; Urbina & Jones, 2004; Wohl et al., 2002). One study of heterosexual, HIV-negative adults using crystal meth indicated that, over a two-month period, they averaged 22 acts of unprotected vaginal sex and nine different sex partners (Semple et al., 2004). Crystal meth can also lead to paranoia, hallucinations, and violent behaviour (Brecht et al., 2004).

The opiates, such as morphine, heroin, and methadone, have strong suppression effects on sexual desire and response (Segraves & Balon, 2003). Long-term use of heroin, in particular, leads to decreased testosterone levels in males.

Prescription Drugs

Some *psychiatric drugs*—that is, drugs used in the treatment of psychological disorders—may affect sexual functioning (Segraves & Balon, 2003). In general, these drugs have their beneficial psychological effects because they alter the functioning of the central nervous system (CNS). But these CNS alterations in turn affect sexual functioning. For example, the drugs used to treat schizophrenia may cause delayed orgasm or "dry orgasm" in men—that is, orgasm with no ejaculation. Tranquilizers and antidepressants often improve sexual responding by improving the person's mental state. However, there may also be negative effects.

Many of the antidepressants, especially selective serotonin reuptake inhibitors (SSRIs) are associated with desire, arousal, and delayed orgasm problems in men and women. This is a problem because, according to Health Canada, there were over 16 million prescriptions for SSRI antidepressants filled in Canada in 2011, and these are very common side effects—between 30 and 60 percent of people taking SSRIs experience a sexual disorder (Gregorian et al., 2002; Hemels et al., 2002). On the other hand, they are sometimes used to treat premature ejaculation precisely because they delay orgasm. A few antidepressants—most notably bupropion (Wellbutrin)—have fewer sexual side effects and are becoming popular for that very reason.

The list of other prescription drugs that can affect sexual functioning is long, so we will mention just two examples. Some of the antihypertensive drugs (used to treat high blood pressure) can cause erection problems (Segraves & Balon, 2003). Most of the research on antihypertensive drug effects has been done with men, so we know less about their effects on women, although sexual problems have been reported among women using antihypertensive medication. Some of the medications used to treat epilepsy appear to cause erection problems and decreased sexual desire, although epilepsy by itself also seems to be associated with sexual disorders. Women who are treated with drugs called aromatase inhibitors following breast cancer and surgery, are highly likely to experience problems with sexual desire (Panjari et al., 2011).

Psychological Causes

The psychological sources of sexual disorders can be separated into predisposing factors and maintaining or ongoing causes (Wincze & Carey, 2001). **Predisposing factors** are people's prior life experiences—for example, things that happened in childhood—that now inhibit the sexual response. **Maintaining factors** are ongoing life circumstances, personal characteristics, and characteristics of lovemaking that help explain why the problem continues.

There are eight factors that are often maintaining psychological causes of sexual disorder. Six of these factors are within the individual: myths or misinformation; negative attitudes; anxieties or inhibition; cognitive interference; individual psychological distress, such as depression; and behavioural or lifestyle factors. Two of the factors are interpersonal: failure to engage in effective, sexually stimulating behaviour, often caused by failure of the partners to communicate; and relationship distress. To be effective, treatment needs to address these maintaining factors.

Maintaining Individual Causes

Myths or misinformation can be a source of sexual dysfunction. Many people have beliefs about lovemaking that are incorrect, or they are unaware of sexual information (such as the effects of aging on the sexual response) that is important to sexual functioning. For example, some couples seek sex therapy because of a woman's failure to orgasm; the therapist soon discovers that neither partner is aware of the location of the clitoris, much less its fantastic erotic potential. Misinformation can lead to a sexual script that does not fully enhance sexual arousal and pleasure or to anxiety and worry. These cases can often be cleared up by simple educational techniques.

A second possible source of sexual dysfunction is *negative attitudes* about sexual activity, one's own body, or one's partner's body. For example, the beliefs that "good" people do not enjoy sex or that one is ugly or fat may result in anxiety or other negative feelings during sexual activity that may affect sexual functioning. Researchers in B.C. found that sex guilt—feeling that one

is violating "proper" sexual conduct—is associated with lower sexual desire in women, and sex guilt accounts for why South Asian women tend to report lower sexual desire than Euro-Canadian women (Woo et al., 2011, 2012). Sometimes negative attitudes are so strong that they result in a feeling of disgust—a strong emotion that is the enemy of arousal (de Jong et al., 2013). Disgust—whether it is associated with a particular person, a body part, or an object—makes a person want to avoid sex. High internalized homonegativity (see Chapter 14) may result in sexual dysfunction for individuals with same-sex partners (Armstrong & Reissing, 2013).

Anxiety during sexual activity can be a source of sexual disorders. Anxiety may be caused by negative or traumatic experiences in the past, such as child sexual abuse. Indeed, experiences of child sexual abuse have been linked to a range of sexual problems and disorders (Desrochers et al., 2008; Lemieux & Byers, 2008). Women who experience genito-pelvic pain typically experience anxiety about the possibility of experiencing pain during sexual activity, which, in turn, tends to make the pain worse when they do engage in sex (Anderson et al., 2016).

Anxiety also may be caused by fear of failure—that is, fear of being unable to perform. Anxiety itself can block sexual response in some people. Often anxiety can create a vicious circle of self-fulfilling prophecy in which fear of failure produces a failure, which produces more fear, which produces another failure, and so on. For example, a man may have one episode of erectile dysfunction, perhaps after drinking too much at a party. The next time he has sex, he anxiously wonders whether he will "fail" again. His anxiety is so great that he cannot get an erection. At this point he is convinced that the condition is permanent, and all future sexual activity is marked by such intense fear of failure that erectile disorder results. The prophecy is fulfilled. The effects of anxiety, though, are complicated and depend on the individual, as we will see in the research of David Barlow described later in this section.

In Chapter 9, we discussed the sexual excitation–inhibition model, or the dual control model of sexual response (Bancroft et al., 2009). In brief, the model proposes that two basic processes underlie human sexual response: excitation (responding with arousal to sexual stimuli) and inhibition (inhibiting sexual arousal, not responding to sexual stimuli). This model can be applied directly to understanding the origins of sexual disorders. In general, the idea is that people who are low on sexual excitation, high on sexual inhibition, or both, are likely to develop sexual disorders. For example, in research with a community

> **predisposing factors:** Experiences that people have had in the past—for example, in childhood—that now affect their sexual response.
> **maintaining factors:** Various ongoing life circumstances, personal characteristics, and lovemaking patterns that inhibit sexual response.

sample of men, scores on the sexual inhibition scale correlated strongly with the men's reports of difficulties in obtaining or maintaining an erection (Bancroft et al., 2009). Similarly, research with a community sample of women showed that sexual inhibition scores were correlated with their reports of sexual problems (Sanders et al., 2008).

Cognitive interference is a fourth maintaining cause of sexual disorders. Cognitive interference refers to thoughts that distract the person from focusing on the erotic experience. The problem is basically one of attention (de Jong, 2009). Is the person focusing his or her attention on erotic thoughts and feelings or on distracting thoughts? (Will my technique be good enough to please her? Will my body be beautiful enough to arouse him?) Research in Ontario asked undergraduate students about the nonerotic thoughts they had during their most recent sexual encounter that took away from their sexual experience (Purdon & Holdaway, 2006; Purdon & Watson, 2011). More than 90 percent of participants reported having at least one such nonerotic thought. These thoughts most often related to performance concerns; concerns related to external consequences (e.g., STIs) and emotional consequences (e.g., for relationship); and body image. Men are more likely to have thoughts related to performance, and women are more likely to have thoughts related to body image (Nelson & Purdon, 2011; Purdon & Watson, 2011). Students who reported more nonerotic thoughts, particularly nonerotic thoughts that caused anxiety, had poorer sexual functioning. Similarly, research in New Brunswick has shown that poor body image is associated with poorer sexual functioning in women, beyond the effects of actual body size (Weaver & Byers, 2006, 2013). This is likely because poor body image leads to increased nonerotic thoughts and anxiety about the body and ones own attractiveness in sexual situations. Researchers in Quebec have shown that, among women with genito-pelvic pain, negative thoughts about the meaning of pain is associated with experiencing more intense pain (Desrochers et al., 2010; Rosen, Bergeron, Lambert, et al., 2012).

Spectatoring, a term coined by Masters and Johnson, is one kind of cognitive interference. The person behaves like a spectator or judge of his or her own sexual "performance." People who do this are constantly (mentally) stepping outside the sexual activities in which they are engaged to evaluate how they are doing, mentally commenting, "Good job," or "Lousy," or "Could stand improvement." These ideas on the importance of cognition in sexual disorder derive from the cognitive theories of sexual responding discussed in Chapter 2.

cognitive interference: Negative thoughts that distract a person from focusing on the erotic experience.
spectatoring: Masters and Johnson's term for acting as an observer or judge of one's own sexual performance; hypothesized to contribute to sexual disorders.

Sex researcher David Barlow (1986; Wiegel et al., 2007) ran an elegant series of experiments to test the ways in which anxiety and cognitive interference affect sexual functioning. He studied men with and without sexual disorders, particularly erectile disorder, whom he calls the "dysfunctionals" and the "functionals." He found that functionals and dysfunctionals respond very differently to stimuli in sexual situations. For example, anxiety (induced by the threat of being shocked) *increases* the arousal of functional men but *decreases* the arousal of dysfunctional men while watching erotic films. Similarly, demands for performance (e.g., the experimenter says the research participant must have an erection or he will be shocked) increase the arousal of functionals but are distracting to (create cognitive interference in) and decrease the arousal of dysfunctionals. When both self-reports of arousal and physiological measures of arousal (the penile strain gauge) are used, dysfunctional men consistently underestimate their physical arousal, whereas functional men are accurate in their reporting.

From these laboratory findings, Barlow (1986) constructed a model that describes how anxiety, positive and negative emotions (affect), and cognitive interference act together to produce sexual disorders, such as erectile disorder. When dysfunctionals are in a sexual situation, there is a performance demand. This causes them to feel anxiety and other negative emotions. They then experience cognitive interference and focus their attention on nonerotic thoughts, such as thinking about how awful it will be when they don't have an erection. This increases arousal of their autonomic nervous system. To them, that feels like anxiety and generates more negative affect, whereas a functional person would experience it as sexual arousal. For the dysfunctionals, the anxiety creates further cognitive interference, and eventually the sexual performance is dysfunctional—they don't manage to get an erection. The situation is amplified because the dysfunctionals have various negative cognitive biases. For example, they expect to perform poorly. All this leads them to avoid future sexual encounters or, when they are in one, to experience negative feelings, and the cycle repeats itself. This model recognizes the importance of cognitive processes, such as cognitive interference and the effect of emotion.

Research in Quebec suggests there may be a similar process in women who experience sexual pain. That is, anxiety and fear about sexual pain lead women who experience pain to focus their attention on possible pain cues rather than on erotic stimuli (Payne et al., 2005). In turn, this cognitive interference may interfere with the sexual response over and above any pain experienced.

It is important to note that anxiety produces sex problems only in some men. For the majority of men, who function well sexually, anxiety does not impair sexual responding, at least in the lab. The same is true for women (Elliott & O'Donohue, 1997).

A fifth possible cause of sexual disorders is individual *psychological distress;* that is, sexual disorder may be one symptom of a more general psychological disorder. For example, individuals who are depressed often experience low sexual desire or have difficulty becoming aroused (Brotto & Klein, 2010; Frohlich & Meston, 2002; McCabe et al., 2010). Emotions such as anger and sadness (as well as anxiety, as we saw earlier) can interfere with sexual responding in some people (Araujo et al., 2000; Brotto & Klein, 2010). These are examples of the mind–body connection.

Behavioural and lifestyle factors can also affect sexual functioning. Smoking, alcohol consumption, and obesity are all behaviours that are associated with higher rates of sexual disorders (Derby et al., 2000; Segraves & Balon, 2003). However, these behaviours are quite modifiable. A study of obese men between the ages of 35 and 55 showed that regular physical exercise reduced their body mass index (BMI) and the incidence of erectile disorder (Esposito et al., 2004). A stressful lifestyle, such as a difficult work environment, long work hours, or a lack of privacy in the home, may also affect sexual functioning. Surprisingly, couples often fail to recognize how their lifestyle impairs their sexual functioning.

Maintaining Interpersonal Factors

The last two maintaining factors relate to the couple's interactions and relationship. Sexual disorders may be caused by *failure to engage in effective sexually stimulating behaviour.* Sometimes this is a result of simple ignorance—that is, myths and misinformation. More often, poor technique is due to the failure of the partners to communicate with each other about their sexual preferences. We often expect our partners to read our minds (which most of us are not particularly good at) to determine what we like and don't like. In fact, a survey of more than 3000 Canadian men and women found that only 28 percent had had even one serious discussion about sex in their relationship in the previous year (Auld et al., 2002). New Brunswick researchers examined whether sexual self-disclosure does, in fact, enhance sexual functioning in dating and long-term relationships (MacNeil & Byers, 2005, 2009). They had 74 heterosexual couples independently complete measures of their sexual likes and dislikes, their partner's sexual likes and dislikes, and their own sexual satisfaction. They found that, for both the men and the women, individuals who self-disclosed more about their sexual preferences had partners who had a better understanding of what pleased them sexually. In turn, the more the partner understood their sexual likes, the more the couple engaged in mutually pleasing and the less they engaged in displeasing sexual activities during lovemaking; the more pleasing and less displeasing the sexual script, the more sexually satisfied they were.

In short, you are the leading expert in the field of what feels good to you, and your partner will never know what turns you on or what you desire at a particular moment unless you make this known, either verbally or nonverbally. But many people do not communicate their sexual desires. For example, a woman who needs a great deal of clitoral stimulation to have an orgasm may never tell her partner this; as a result, her partner provides some clitoral stimulation but not the amount of stimulation she needs. Consequently, she does not orgasm.

Relationship distress, that is, disturbances in a couple's relationship, is another leading cause of sexual disorders (Althof et al., 2004; McCabe et al., 2010). That is, the relational context in which sex occurs is key to understanding an individual's sexual functioning and interest in and ability to respond sexually. Frequent arguments or anger and resentment toward one's partner do not create an optimal environment for sexual enjoyment (Figure 18.2). Intimacy problems in the relationship can be a factor in sexual disorders. Poor communication, not feeling understood, a lack of common interests, and a lack of trust may interfere with the feelings of closeness and intimacy that are important to

Figure 18.2 Relationship distress is a leading cause of sexual disorders.

© Royalty-free/Corbis

quality lovemaking and to being able to respond sexually (Basson, 2001b; Bois et al., 2015). Researchers in Ontario have shown that individuals who have a partner who respond negatively when they experience a sexual difficulty, experience poorer sexual functioning and lower sexual satisfaction (Fallis et al., 2013). Researchers in Nova Scotia have shown that, for women with genito-pelvic pain, having a male partner whose responses are more negative or solicitous and less facilitative is associated with experiencing more intense pain (Rosen et al., 2013, 2014, 2015). In contrast, high-quality couple communication is associated with lower pain intensity (Rancourt et al., 2016). A lack of quality time together because of an overly hectic lifestyle can also contribute to reduced feelings of intimacy and closeness and thus to relationship distress. In turn, relationship distress may result in a sexual disorder.

Predisposing Factors

The immediate or maintaining causes of sexual dysfunction are often a result of things that were learned or experienced in childhood, adolescence, or even adulthood. These early events result in negative attitudes, misinformation, cognitive interference, difficulty communicating, and so on.

Growing up in a family that communicates negative messages about sex is often a predisposing factor to sexual disorders because it creates negative attitudes. The person who grew up in a very strict, religious family and was taught that sex is dirty and sinful may believe that sex is not pleasurable, that it should be gotten over with as quickly as possible, and that it is for purposes of procreation only. It is the rigid belief in sexual rights and wrongs (particularly wrongs), not religiosity per se, that likely impacts sexual functioning (Kleinplatz & Krippner, 2000). The child who is punished severely for masturbating and told never to "touch herself" again may develop negative attitudes about her genitals and about genital touching. Parents who teach their children the double standard may contribute to sexual disorders, particularly in daughters who were told that no nice woman is interested in sex or enjoys it. Growing up in a homonegative family or culture may contribute to internalized homonegativity among gays and lesbians, which in turn may affect their sexual functioning. Such learning inhibits the enjoyment of a full sexual response.

In some cases, the person's first sexual act was traumatic. An example would be a young man who could not get an erection the first time he attempted penetration and was laughed at by his partner. Such an experience sets the stage for future erectile disorder.

Child sexual abuse by parents or other adults is probably the most serious of the traumatic early experiences that lead to later sexual disorders (Najman et al., 2005). A history of sexual abuse is frequently reported by people seeking therapy for sexual problems (Berthelot et al., 2014; Leonard & Follette, 2002; Loeb et al., 2002). For example, researchers in Quebec have shown that young women with chronic genito-pelvic pain are more likely than young women without pain to have experienced sexual abuse (Landry & Bergeron, 2011).

Combined Cognitive and Physiological Factors

According to the cognitive–physiological model of sexual functioning and dysfunction, we function well sexually when we are physiologically aroused and we interpret it as sexual arousal rather than something else, like nervousness (Palace, 1995a, 1995b). As Barlow's research shows, people with sexual disorders tend to interpret their arousal as anxiety. In addition, the physiological processes and cognitive interpretations form a feedback loop. That is, interpreting arousal as sexual arousal increases arousal further.

In a clever experiment, British Columbia women with sexual disorders were exposed, in a laboratory setting, to a frightening movie that increased their general autonomic arousal (Palace, 1995b). The women were then shown a brief erotic video and given feedback (actually false) that their genitals had shown a strong arousal response to it. This feedback created a cognitive interpretation for the way they were feeling. The combination of general autonomic arousal and the belief that they were responding with strong sexual arousal led these women, compared with the controls, to greater vaginal arousal responses and subjective reports of arousal in subsequent sessions. This demonstration of the effectiveness of combined physiological and cognitive factors is particularly striking because the women began with problems in sexual responding.

 L03 **A New View of Women's Sexual Problems and Their Causes**

Over the past decade, a group of sex therapists specializing in treating women's sex problems worked together to formulate what they call a New View of the nature of women's sexual problems and their causes (Tiefer, 2001). The New View was critical of the categories of disorders formulated by the American Psychiatric Association in the *DSM-IV-TR*, the diagnostic manual that has recently been updated to the *DSM-5*. It argues that these diagnostic categories had three flaws: (1) They treat male sexuality and female sexuality as totally equivalent, when they differ in some important ways; (2) they ignore the relational context of sexuality and desires for emotional intimacy; and (3) they ignore differences among women and naturally occurring variations in women's sexuality.

In keeping with the New View critique of the *DSM* and emphasis on contextual factors that influence sexual functioning, the *DSM-5* stipulates that clinicians need to consider a number of factors in arriving at a diagnosis, including partner factors, relationship factors, individual vulnerability factors, cultural or religious factors, and medical factors. In some cases, the *DSM-5* specifically prohibits diagnosing a disorder when one of these factors is present—for example, severe relationship distress. They also have changed some of the diagnostic categories to better fit women's experience so that, as you saw earlier in the chapter, the diagnostic categories for men and women are not parallel. Still, many of the New View criticisms of the *DSM* approach are still relevant.

What did these experts propose instead of the approach taken in the *DSM*? As described below, they defined a sexual problem as dissatisfaction with any emotional, physical, or relational aspect of sexual experience. Their definition takes social, cultural and relationship factors into account.

Sexual Problems Due to Socio-cultural, Political, or Economic Factors

The category of socio-cultural, political, or economic factors includes problems that are due to (1) ignorance and anxiety because of inadequate sexuality education, lack of access to health services, or other social constraints; (2) sexual avoidance or distress because of perceived inability to meet cultural norms regarding ideal sexuality (e.g., anxiety about one's body or about sexual orientation); (3) inhibitions caused by conflict between the norms of one's culture of origin and those of the dominant culture; and (4) lack of interest or fatigue caused by family and work obligations.

Sexual Problems Relating to Partner and Relationship

Problems in the category relating to the partner and relationship involve (1) sexual inhibition or distress arising from betrayal or fear of the partner because of abuse; (2) discrepancies in desire or preferences for sexual activities; (3) ignorance or inhibition about sexual communications; (4) loss of sexual interest as a result of conflicts over issues, such as money, or resulting from traumatic experiences, such as infertility; and (5) loss of arousal because of a partner's health or sexual problems.

Sexual Problems Due to Psychological Factors

The category of psychological factors includes the following problems: (1) sexual aversion or inhibition of sexual pleasure because of past experiences of physical, sexual, or emotional abuse; (2) personality problems with attachment or rejection, or depression or anxiety; and (3) sexual inhibition caused by fear of sexual acts or

their possible consequences, such as pain during intercourse or fear of pregnancy or STIs.

Sexual Problems Due to Medical Factors

When sexual problems arise despite a supportive interpersonal situation, adequate sexual knowledge, and positive attitudes, they may be a result of (1) any number of medical conditions that affect neurological, circulatory, endocrine, or other systems of the body; (2) pregnancy or STIs; (3) side effects of medications.

As you can see, this way of thinking about sexual disorders and their causes in women is considerably different from the dominant ways of thinking and the categories listed in the *DSM-IV-TR* or *DSM-5*. New research is beginning to support this alternative view (King et al., 2007). For example, official diagnoses of disorders do not correlate well with women's perception that they have a problem or with their psychological distress. This suggests that the traditional diagnostic categories are missing the mark for some women.

LO4

Therapies for Sexual Disorders

A variety of therapies for sexual disorders are available, each relying on a different theoretical understanding of what causes sexual disorders. Here we examine four major categories of therapies: behaviour therapy, cognitive behaviour therapy, couple therapy, and biomedical therapies. Effective treatments for sexual disorders focus on factors that are currently maintaining the sexual disorder rather than on predisposing factors.

Behaviour Therapy

Behaviour therapy has its roots in learning theory. The basic assumption is that sex problems are the result of prior learning and that they are maintained by ongoing reinforcements and punishments (immediate causes). It follows that these problem behaviours can be unlearned by new conditioning. One of the key techniques is *in vivo desensitization*, in which the client is gradually led through exercises that reduce anxiety.

In 1970, Masters and Johnson reported on their development of a set of techniques for sex therapy with heterosexual couples and ushered in a new era of sex therapy. They operated from a behaviour therapy model because they saw sexual disorders as learned behaviours rather than as symptoms of mental illness. Masters and Johnson used a rapid two-week program of intensive daily therapy that consisted mainly of education and specific behavioural exercises, or "homework assignments."

Often a first step in behavioural sex therapy is to help clients learn more about their own bodies and what they like and do not like sexually. Because each person is unique, this is often done by assigning an exercise, sometimes called *body mapping*, which the client does alone (that is, without a partner present). Clients map out their own sensations by touching their body all over (usually first excluding breasts and genitals) to find out what parts of the body and what ways of touching produce pleasure. They later communicate what they have learned to their partner.

One of the basic goals of Masters and Johnson's therapy was to eliminate goal-oriented sexual performance. Many clients believe that in sex they must perform and achieve certain things. If sex is an achievement situation, it also can become the scene of failure, and perceived failures lead people to believe that they have a sexual problem. In one technique used in behaviour therapy to eliminate a goal-oriented attitude toward sex, the couple is forbidden to engage in sexual activity (although they are encouraged to engage in lots of affectionate activity) until they are specifically permitted to by the therapists. They are assigned sensate focus exercises that reduce the demands on them. As the couple successfully completes each of these exercises, the sexual component of subsequent exercises is gradually increased. The couple chalk up a series of successes until eventually they are having intercourse and the disorder has disappeared. This exercise also works to condition a new response to sexual stimuli that were previously experienced as anxiety-producing by pairing relaxation and intimacy with these stimuli.

Sensate focus exercises are based on the notion that touching and being touched are important forms of sexual expression and that touching is also an important form of communication; for example, a touch can express affection, desire, understanding, or a lack of caring. In the exercises, one member of the couple plays the giving role (touches and strokes the other), while the other person plays the receiving role (is touched by the other). The giving partner is instructed to take an exploratory, experimental approach and try out differing ways of touching or caressing the partner, while the receiving partner is instructed to communicate to the giver what is most pleasurable. Thus the exercise fosters communication. The partners switch roles after a certain period. In the first exercises, the giver is not to stroke the genitals or breasts (nor should the receiver ask for this) but may touch any other area. As the couple progress through the exercises, they are instructed to begin touching the genitals and breasts. These exercises also encourage the partners to focus their attention on the sensuous pleasures they are receiving. Many people's sexual response is dulled because they are distracted; they are thinking about how to solve a family financial problem or are spectatoring their own performance. They are victims of cognitive interference. The sensate focus exercises train people to concentrate only on their sexual experience, thereby increasing the pleasure of it. In addition to these exercises, behaviour therapists provide simple education. The couple is given thorough instruction in the anatomy and physiology of the male or female sexual organs (depending on whether the couple are of the same sex or not). Some couples, for example, have no idea what or where the clitoris is. These instructions may also clear up myths and misinformation that either member of the couple may have had since childhood. For example, a man with an erectile disorder may have been told as a child that men can have only a fixed number of orgasms in their lifetime. As he approaches middle age, he starts to worry because his erections may come and go during lovemaking (see Chapter 11) or about whether he may have used up almost all of his orgasms, and this creates the erectile disorder. It is important for such men to learn that nature has imposed no quota on them.

Masters and Johnson collected data on the success and failure rates of their therapy. In their book *Human Sexual Inadequacy*, they reported on the treatment of 790 persons. Of these, 142 still had a disorder at the end of the two-week therapy program. This translates to a failure rate of 18 percent or a *success rate of 82 percent*. Although the failure rate ran around 18 percent for most disorders, there were two exceptions: Therapy for rapid ejaculation had a very low failure rate (2.2 percent), and therapy for lifelong erectile disorder had a high failure rate (40.6 percent). That is, rapid ejaculation was quite easy to treat, and lifelong erectile disorder very difficult. Masters and Johnson's success rate is impressive, although their results have been called into question, as we shall see later in this chapter.

In Masters and Johnson's initial development of their therapy techniques, all the couples were mixed-sex. They later used the same techniques in treating sexual disorders in same-sex couples, with a comparable success rate (Masters & Johnson, 1979).

Cognitive Behaviour Therapy

Paralleling the increased importance of cognitive theories in psychology (see Chapter 2) is the increased importance of cognitive approaches to psychotherapy. Today, many sex therapists use a combination of the behavioural exercises pioneered by Masters and Johnson and cognitive therapy (Heiman, 2007). This is termed **cognitive behaviour therapy** or CBT.

sensate focus exercises: A part of the sex therapy developed by Masters and Johnson in which one partner caresses the other, the other communicates what is pleasurable, and there are no performance demands.

cognitive behaviour therapy: A form of therapy that combines behaviour therapy and restructuring of negative thought patterns.

First Person

A Case of Low Sexual Desire

Sarah, age 27, was referred to a sex therapist by an endocrinologist, to be considered for testosterone treatment for her complaints of low sexual desire. Sarah had no ovarian tissue. One ovary that had a large cyst had been removed when she was 13, and her other ovary had undergone torsion (twisting that cut off the blood supply) and had to be removed when she was 16. She had been given estrogen and progesterone replacement immediately so that her menstrual periods never stopped.

When Sara met with the therapist, she explained that sex with her partner Carl was enjoyable. They had been together four years and were sexual approximately once a week. Carl would have preferred to be sexual every day, but Sarah resisted. She said that even though sex was enjoyable and satisfying, if she never had sex again, it would be fine with her. She reported that both Carl and her endocrinologist thought that she was very abnormal.

Sarah had very few sexual thoughts about arousal or anticipating sexual activity. Her sexual thoughts were instead troubling and focused on her guilt that their sexual interactions were infrequent and that she was abnormal. During sexual interactions with Carl, she was aroused, enjoyed the experience, and had orgasms. She found arousing Carl to be pleasurable and arousing for her.

Using the New View of women's sexual problems, the therapist explained to Sarah that her experience was within normal limits. In a meeting with Carl, the therapist described the range of women's sexual experiences. The next question was whether some factors were causing Sarah's behaviour to be toward the end of the spectrum. Both biological and psychological factors seemed to be involved. Because of the removal of her ovaries, she was manufacturing no testosterone, although androgens manufactured by the adrenal gland were present. Sarah's life history also gave clues regarding possible psychological factors. Sarah grew up with an alcoholic father who was prone to shouting, arguing, and engaging in emotional abuse; Sarah coped by retreating to her bedroom. She suppressed her feelings of anger and did not rebel even when she was a teenager. This coping style worked well at the time. However, as an adult, she was probably still in the habit of suppressing emotions generally. Sarah agreed about this and understood that her sexual emotions were probably also suppressed.

The therapist decided against testosterone treatment and instead focused on encouraging Sarah to deliberately attempt to feel more nonsexual emotion throughout the day. In addition, she was to deliberately allow more sexual stimuli in her life, such as music, movies, dancing, and erotic conversations.

The therapist met with Carl to explain the situation and assess his own family history. His parents had a bitter divorce when he was just 10. He felt that neither parent had really loved him. For Carl, having sex with his partner was a sign that he was loved. Carl was able to realize that pressuring Sarah did not help the situation, and he ceased doing so, which Sarah appreciated. In addition, when Sarah realized the origins and extent of Carl's need to feel loved, she became strongly motivated to find the triggers that were able to make her feel more sexual. Salsa dancing proved to be one of those triggers, combined with encouraging Carl to flirt with her more often. Sarah's sexual self-image increased markedly, as did her sexual desire.

Rosemary Basson, "Sexual Desire/Arousal Disorders in Women," in S. Leiblum (Ed.), *Principles and Practice of Sex Therapy*, 4e, 2007, pp. 42–43. Reprinted by permission of the Guilford Press.

Cognitive restructuring is an important technique in the CBT approach to sex therapy (Wincze & Carey, 2001). In cognitive restructuring, the therapist essentially helps the client restructure his or her thought patterns, helping him or her to become more positive (for an example, see First Person). Cognitive restructuring is particularly useful in addressing two of the maintaining causes of sexual disorders described earlier in this chapter—negative attitudes and cognitive interference. In one form of cognitive restructuring, the therapist challenges the client's negative attitudes. These attitudes may be as general as a woman's distrusting attitudes toward all men or as specific as a man's negative attitudes toward masturbation. The client is helped to reshape these attitudes into more positive ones.

In CBT, therapists also like to address cognitive interference. The general idea is to reduce the presence of interfering thoughts during sex. First the therapist must help the client identify the presence of such thoughts. The therapist then suggests techniques for reducing these thoughts, generally by replacing them with erotic thoughts—perhaps focusing attention on a particular part of one's body and how it is responding with arousal, or having an erotic fantasy. Out go the bad thoughts, and in come the good thoughts.

Recently some therapists have added mindfulness training as part of sex therapy. Mindfulness training helps individuals focus their attention on the present moment and create nonjudgmental present-moment sexual awareness (Brotto & Basson, 2014; Brotto et al., 2008, 2014; Dunkley & Brotto, 2016). For example, Canadian psychologist Lori Brotto explains to clients,

> Many of us go through life not living in the present moment. We fluctuate between thinking in the future (worrying, planning, thinking) and living in the past (reviewing events, conversations, plans). We miss out on valuable and meaningful experiences in the present. . . . In instances when we want to be present, such as the sexual scenario, it is difficult if not impossible for us to turn off the cerebral chatter. The net effect is a reduction in arousal, thereby making the sexual experience less rewarding and pleasurable.

She then assigns clients a series of exercises, first in nonsexual situations and then in sexual situations, that help them learn to be fully present (Brotto et al., 2008).

Couple Therapy

As we noted earlier, poor communication and relationship distress are important maintaining causes of sexual disorders. Accordingly, many sex therapists use couple therapy as part of the treatment. This approach rests on the assumption that there is a reciprocal relationship between interpersonal conflict and sex problems. Sex problems can cause conflicts, and conflicts can cause sex problems. Even if a couple is not experiencing relationship distress, it is also usually helpful to have both partners participate in resolving the problem. In couple therapy, the relationship itself is treated, with the goal of reducing antagonisms and tensions between the partners and improving intimacy, empathy, and communication. As the relationship improves, the couple is better able to make the changes that will help resolve the sex problem. Canadian researchers have shown that for women with genito-pelvic pain, their partner's response

to their pain can either help alleviate it or can make it worse (Rosen et al., 2010, 2012). This suggests that it is helpful to involve the partner in the therapy (Corsini-Munt et al., 2014).

For certain disorders and certain couples, therapists may use a combination of cognitive behaviour and couple therapy. For example, sex therapists Raymond Rosen, Sandra Leiblum, and Ilana Spector (1994) used a five-part model in treating men with erectile disorder:

1. *Sexual- and performance-anxiety reduction:* Individuals with sexual disorders, particularly men with erectile disorder, often have a great deal of performance anxiety. This can be treated using such techniques as sensate focus exercises.

2. *Education and cognitive intervention:* As noted earlier, people with sexual disorders often lack sexual information. Many also have unrealistic expectations about sexual functioning and satisfaction. Cognitive interventions may help men with erection problems to overcome "all or nothing" thinking—that is, the belief that if any aspect of his sexual performance is not perfect, the whole interaction is a disaster. An example is the belief that "I failed sexually because my erection was not 100 percent rigid."

3. *Script assessment and modification:* All couples have a sexual script that they enact together. People with sexual disorders typically have a restricted, repetitive, and inflexible script, using a small number of techniques that they never change. Novelty is one of the greatest turn-ons, so therapy is designed to help the couple break out of their restricted script and develop a new, mutually pleasurable sexual script.

4. *Conflict resolution and relationship enhancement:* As we have discussed, conflicts in a couple's relationship can lead to sexual disorders. In therapy, these conflicts are identified and the couple works to resolve them. Couples also work to increase their positive interactions.

5. *Relapse prevention training:* Sometimes a relapse—a return of the disorder—occurs following therapy. Therapists have developed techniques to help couples avoid or deal with such relapses. For example, they are told to engage in sensate focus sessions at least once a month.

Notice that part 1 represents the behaviour therapy techniques pioneered by Masters and Johnson; parts 2 and 3 are cognitive therapy techniques; and part 4 is couple therapy. Most skilled sex therapists today use combined or integrated techniques such as these, tailored to the specific disorder and situation of the couple.

L05 Specific Treatments for Specific Problems

Some very specific techniques have been developed for the treatment of certain sexual disorders. Of course, each of these techniques is typically only one part of a comprehensive treatment approach.

The Stop-Start Technique

The stop-start technique is used in the treatment of premature (early) ejaculation (see Figure 18.3). The man first learns to identify sensations before the point of ejaculatory inevitability (see Chapter 9). The partner manually stimulates the man to erection and then stops the stimulation before that point. Gradually the man loses his erection. The partner resumes stimulation, the man gets another erection, the partner stops, and so on. After doing this three or four times, the man can allow himself to orgasm. The man learns that he can have an erection and be highly aroused without having an orgasm. Using this technique, the couple may extend their sex play to 15 or 20 minutes, and the man gains control over his orgasm. Another version of this method that is occasionally used is the squeeze technique, in which the partner adds a squeeze around the coronal ridge, which also stops orgasm.

Masturbation

The most effective form of therapy for women with orgasmic disorder is a program of directed masturbation (LoPiccolo & Stock, 1986; Meston et al., 2004). The data indicate that masturbation is the technique most likely to produce orgasm in women; it is therefore a logical treatment for women who have problems with having orgasms, many of whom have never masturbated. Women can use a vibrator to learn to bring themselves to orgasm. Masturbation is sometimes recommended as therapy for men as well—for example, in learning to have greater control over the timing of ejaculation.

Kegel Exercises

One technique that is used with women is **Kegel exercises**, named for the physician who devised them (Kegel, 1952). They are designed to exercise and strengthen the *pubococcygeal muscle,* or PC muscle, which runs along the sides of the entrance of the vagina. The exercises are particularly helpful for women who have had this muscle stretched in childbirth, who have poor muscle tone, or who have vaginismus. The woman is instructed first to find her PC muscle by sitting on a toilet with her legs spread apart, beginning to urinate, and stopping the flow of urine voluntarily. The muscle that stops the flow is the PC muscle. After that, the woman is told to contract the muscle ten times during each of six sessions per day. Gradually, she can work

> **Kegel (KAY-gul) exercises:** A part of sex therapy for women with orgasmic disorder, in which the woman exercises the muscles surrounding the vagina; also called pubococcygeal or PC muscle exercises.

Figure 18.3 The stop-start technique for treating rapid ejaculation and the position of the couple while using the stop-start technique.

up to more.[2] These exercises seem to enhance arousal and facilitate orgasm by increasing women's awareness of and comfort with their genitals (Heiman, 2007). They also permit the heterosexual woman to stimulate her partner more because her vagina can grip his penis more tightly, and they are a cure for women who have problems with involuntarily urinating as they orgasm.

Pelvic floor muscle exercises and therapy can be used on their own and should be used as part of the comprehensive, multidisciplinary treatment of genito-pelvic pain/penetration disorder that includes both pelvic floor rehabilitation and cognitive behaviour therapy (Bergeron et al., 2010; Brotto et al., 2015; van Lankveld et al., 2010). Physiotherapists provide physical assistance to make sure that the woman is doing the exercises correctly—about half of women do not do them correctly with just verbal instructions (Rosenbaum, 2005, 2007a). Often physiotherapists use biofeedback to help women learn to isolate and contract the correct muscles of the pelvic floor. Research in Ontario has shown that pelvic floor physiotherapy is effective at treating genito-pelvic pain and vaginismus in women (Gentilcore-Saulnier et al., 2010; Goldfinger et al., 2009, 2015; Reissing et al., 2013). A variation on the Kegel exercises is reverse Kegels, in which the focus is on learning to relax the muscles in the pelvic area. Women who have genito-pelvic pain accompanied by tensing or tightening of the pelvic floor muscles during attempted penetration can use vaginal dilators to help them overcome their involuntary muscle contraction (see Figure 18.4). The set of dilators are graduated in size so that women can start with inserting a very small dilator and then build up to larger dilators. Some women prefer to use their own or their partner's fingers (starting with the tip of the little finger) instead of dilators.

Pelvic floor muscle exercises are sometimes also used in treating men with premature ejaculation.

Bibliotherapy

Bibliotherapy refers simply to the use of a self-help book to treat a disorder. Research shows that bibliotherapy is effective for orgasmic disorders in women (van Lankveld, 1998). Julia Heiman and Joseph LoPiccolo's *Becoming Orgasmic: A Sexual Growth Program for Women* (1988) has been used extensively for this purpose. Bibliotherapy has also been shown to be effective for couples with a mixture of male and female sexual disorders (van Lankveld et al., 2001; van Lankveld, 2009). In addition, many people

> **bibliotherapy:** The use of a self-help book to treat a disorder.

Figure 18.4 This is a set of vaginal dilators that vary in size. Women who have genito-pelvic pain accompanied by tensing or tightening of the pelvic floor muscles during attempted penetration can use them to help overcome their involuntary muscle contraction.

Come As You Are Co-Operative

describe Bernie Zilbergeld's self-help book *The New Male Sexuality* (1999) and Michale Metz and Barry McCarthy's book *Coping with Premature Ejaculation: How to Overcome PE, Please Your Partner and Have Great Sex* (2003) (among others) as helpful. Other couples find sex therapy videotapes to be helpful. Interestingly, as early as 1973, Steven Neiger, a Canadian pioneer in sex therapy and sex education, developed a series of 12 audiotapes to help couples overcome sexual problems (Alexander, 1990). It may be that in the future the Internet will replace bibliotherapy as self-help methods for treating sexual disorders. The advice columns at self-help websites can provide accurate, explicit, and nonjudgmental information. Specialized message boards and chat rooms for people who share a common interest (e.g., bisexuals, persons with disabilities) can help to create a sense of community and provide useful information, especially for those who are geographically isolated or in countries where sex therapy is unknown.

Biomedical Therapies

Beginning in the 1990s, there was increased recognition of the biological bases of some sexual disorders. Consistent with this emphasis, many developments in medical and drug treatments and even surgical treatment have occurred. From the biopsychosocial perspective, biomedical therapies need to be used in conjunction with other interventions that address the psychosocial factors associated with the sexual disorder. The medicalization of sexuality, with its emphasis on performance and medical treatment, is discussed later in this chapter.

---

[2] Students should recognize the exciting possibilities for doing these exercises. For example, they are a good way to amuse yourself in the middle of a lecture, and no one will ever know you are doing them.

Drug Treatments

Many promising advances have been made in the identification of drugs that cure sexual disorders or work well when used together with CBT or other psychological forms of sex therapy (Ashton, 2007; Rosen, 2007; Rowland & Burnett, 2000). Some are drugs that have direct sexual effects, whereas others are psychotherapeutic drugs (such as antidepressants) that work by improving the person's mood but, as discussed earlier in this chapter, may also affect sexual functioning.

Certainly the most widely publicized breakthrough among these treatments was the approval of **Viagra** (sildenafil) for the treatment of erectile disorder (Figure 18.5). Earlier biomedical treatments, such as intracavernosal injections, were unsatisfactory for various reasons (these are discussed in the next section). Viagra is taken by mouth approximately one hour before anticipated sexual activity. It does not, by itself, produce an erection. Rather, when the man is stimulated sexually after taking Viagra, the drug facilitates the physiological processes that produce erection. Specifically, it relaxes the smooth muscles in the corpora cavernosa, allowing blood to flow in and create an erection. Averaged over 27 clinical trials, about 57 percent of men respond successfully to Viagra, compared with 21 percent responding to the placebo (Fink et al., 2002). Men have generally been quite satisfied with Viagra. Side effects are not common;

Figure 18.5 Viagra, one of the prescription drugs available for treating erectile disorder.

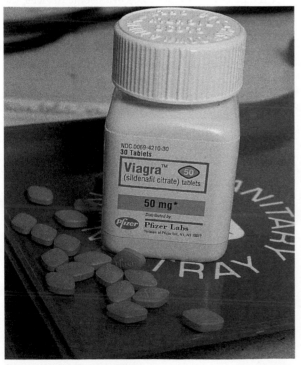

© Larry Mulvehill/The Image Works

if present, they include headache, flushing, and vision disturbances (Ashton, 2007).

On balance, Viagra seems to be quite safe (Morales et al., 1998; Rosen & McKenna, 2002). It does not seem to cause priapism (an erection that just won't go away). Yet the very ease of its use may lead physicians to overprescribe it and men to demand it in inappropriate circumstances. Today it is easily available on the Internet. If the erection difficulties are due to relationship problems or individual issues, Viagra will provide at most a temporary solution. It is not helpful for sexual disorders other than erectile disorder. And there is no evidence that it enhances sexual performance in men who function sexually within the normal range. In addition, its recreational or high-performance uses are causes for concern (Harte & Meston, 2011).

> **How does Viagra work?**

Viagra was such a success, financially and otherwise, that drug companies immediately sought successors—drugs that would be more convenient or would work in cases that were not effectively treated with Viagra. One of these, Cialis (tadalafil), is very much like Viagra in that it relaxes the smooth muscle surrounding the arteries to the penis, facilitating engorgement (Brock et al., 2002; Montorsi et al., 2004; Padma-Nathan et al., 2001). Whereas Viagra lasts only a maximum of 8 to 10 hours, Cialis can be effective for as long as 24 to 36 hours. Drugs such as Cialis have been shown to have no negative effects on sperm production or sex hormone production (Hellstrom et al., 2003a).

Levitra (vardenafil) and Zydena (udenafil) are other drugs that work like Viagra, have slightly different formulations, and are as effective as Viagra (Chen et al., 2015). All of these drugs are in the category of *PDE5 inhibitors;* that is, they inhibit or block an enzyme (PDE5), and by doing so, they relax smooth muscles in the arteries to the penis, thereby allowing more blood to flow into it.

And what about a Viagra for women? The drug company Pfizer, as well as many scientists, hoped that Viagra also would work for women; that is, it would cure their desire and orgasm problems. The problem is that Viagra works by increasing vasocongestion, and insufficient vasocongestion is probably not what causes most women's sexual difficulties. After many failed clinical trials, Pfizer announced in 2004 that it would give up on testing Viagra for women (Harris, 2004). For example, British Columbia researcher Rosemary Basson and her colleagues found that Viagra does not increase either arousal or orgasm in either premenopausal or postmenopausal women with sexual dysfunction (Basson & Brotto, 2003; Basson et al., 2002).

In another attempt at a female Viagra, German pharmaceutical company Boehringer developed the drug flibanserin (trade name Addyi). It had originally been developed to be an antidepressant, but it

> **Viagra:** A drug used in the treatment of erectile disorder; sildenafil.

didn't work very well for that purpose. It acts to reduce levels of the neurotransmitter serotonin and increase levels of dopamine and norepinephrine. To use terms from the dual control model discussed in Chapter 9, serotonin is thought to have an inhibitory effect on sexual desire and dopamine and norepinephrine are thought to have excitatory effects. All that sounds good on paper, but the U.S. Food and Drug Administration (FDA) investigated it and issued a negative report in 2010 and again in 2013, based on clinical trials that showed no actual increase in sexual desire in women taking it, compared with controls. Boehringer decided not to pursue further work on the drug.

In 2014 and 2015, the plot thickened for flibanserin (Moynihan, 2014). The drug was acquired by a new company, Sprout Pharmaceutical. A feminist campaign materialized, pressuring the FDA to approve flibanserin because of the need for a "pink Viagra," and arguing that the FDA was discriminating against women by not approving it. As it turned out, the "feminist" campaign was actually funded by Sprout. And flibanserin still doesn't work. But the FDA approved it in 2015 because of the pink Viagra campaign. It is marketed under the name Addyi. Addyi is not approved for sale in Canada but is under review.

Women's sexual problems most commonly involve orgasm difficulties and low sexual desire/arousal, the latter being a problem particularly as women age and their ovaries decline in production of testosterone. One possibility is administration of testosterone or some other androgen (Basaria & Dobs, 2006; Baulieu et al., 2000), although use of testosterone in women is still quite controversial. For example, researchers in B.C. found no difference in testosterone levels between women with and without hypoactive sexual desire disorder (Basson et al., 2010). Intrinsa is a testosterone patch designed for postmenopausal women experiencing low sexual desire. However, initial results have not been sufficiently positive to receive approval to market the patch in Canada or the United States.

The other issue concerning women and Viagra involves the partners of men with Viagra-aided erections. Not all partners, some of whom had adjusted to a relationship without intercourse, welcome the man's new capacity, an issue that has been ignored in the medical fix approach (Potts et al., 2003; Rosen & McKenna, 2002). For example, for a couple with relationship problems, it may create additional problems if taking Viagra results in pressure to engage in unwanted sexual activity. Often it is important to combine couple therapy with drug therapy. Some women, of course, are absolutely delighted with the results (Montorsi & Althof, 2004).

Intracavernosal Injection

Intracavernosal injection (ICI) is a treatment for erectile disorders (Hsiao et al., 2011; Shabsigh et al., 2000). It involves injecting a drug (such as alprostadil, or Edex)

into the corpora cavernosa of the penis. The drugs used are vasodilators—that is, they dilate the blood vessels in the penis so that much more blood can accumulate there, producing an erection.

Since the introduction of Viagra, ICI is now used mainly in cases in which the erection problem is organic and the man does not respond to Viagra or its successors (Shabsigh et al., 2000). It can also be used in conjunction with CBT in cases that have combined organic and psychological causes. Like Viagra, ICI can have positive psychological effects because it restores the man's confidence in his ability to get erections. It also reduces his performance anxiety because he is able to engage in intercourse successfully. However, according to research in British Columbia, about 50 percent of men who begin using ICI discontinue its use (Basson and VHHSC Centre, 1998). ICI can also result in a prolonged erection that does not go away, even in the absence of stimulation, called *priapism*. This condition is painful and requires medical treatment. There are also potential abuses. Men who have normal erections should not use ICI in an attempt to produce a "super erection."

Alprostadil is now also available as a suppository to place inside the urethra or as a cream to rub on, eliminating the need for the needle. This system is often called MUSE, which stands for "medicated urethral system for erections." However, MUSE is not as effective as ICI.

Suction Devices

Suction devices are another treatment for sexual arousal disorders. Essentially, they pump you up! A tube is placed over the penis (see Figure 18.6). With some devices, the mouth can produce enough suction; with others, a small hand pump is used. Once a reasonably firm erection is present, the tube is removed and a rubber ring is placed around the base of the penis to maintain the penis's

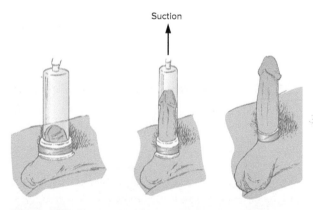

Suction

Figure 18.6 A treatment for erectile disorder. An external tube, with a rubber ring around it, is placed over the lubricated penis. Suction applied to the tube produces erection, which is maintained by the constricting action of the rubber ring once the plastic tube has been removed.

engorgement with blood. These devices have been used successfully with, for example, diabetic men. They can also be helpful in combination with cognitive-behavioural couple therapy for cases of erectile dysfunction that are mainly psychological in origin (Wylie et al., 2003).

There is also now a suction device to assist women with clitoral engorgement called EROS. However, there is little research supporting the effectiveness of this device; for most women the subjective aspects of arousal are at least equally important as is clitoral engorgement per se.

Surgical Therapy

There is promising evidence that surgery (e.g., vestibulectomy) can help women with some types of genito-pelvic pain (Bergeron et al., 2001; Lambert et al., 2012; Landry et al., 2008). Nonetheless, most surgical treatments are currently focused on male sexual problems.

For severe cases of erectile disorder, surgical therapy is possible. The surgery involves implanting a **penile prosthesis** (Hellstrom, 2003). A sac or bladder of sterile fluid is implanted in the lower abdomen, connected to two inflatable tubes running the length of the corpus spongiosum, with a pump in the scrotum. Thus the man can literally pump up or inflate his penis so that he has a full erection.

It should be emphasized that this is a radical treatment that should be reserved only for those cases that have not been successfully treated by sex therapy or drug therapy. The patient must understand that the surgery itself destroys some portions of the penis, so that a natural erection will never again be possible. Although the treatment is radical and should be used conservatively, it is right for some men who have been incapable of erection because of organic difficulties.

In another version of a surgical approach, a semi-rigid, silicone-like rod is implanted into the penis (Fathy et al., 2007; Ferguson & Cespedes, 2003). This noninflatable device is less costly than the inflatable version and has a lower rate of complications (Rosen & Leiblum, 1995b).

✳ Evaluating Sex Therapy

One of the most basic questions we must ask about sex therapy is, Is it effective? As described earlier in this chapter, since Masters and Johnson created their therapy approach, many additional therapies have been developed. Many studies have evaluated the effectiveness of these therapies. At this point, there is sufficient evidence evaluating certain treatments for certain disorders to reach the following conclusions (Althof, 2007; Fruhauf et al., 2013; Heiman, 2007; McCabe et al., 2010):

- Lifelong orgasmic dysfunction in women is successfully treated with directed masturbation, and the treatment can be enhanced with sensate focus exercises.
- Treatments for acquired orgasmic dysfunction in women are somewhat less successful. Therapy that combines some or all of the following components seems to be most effective: sex education, sexual skills training, communication skills training, and body image therapy. The problem here, most likely, is that there are many different patterns of secondary anorgasmia, with a need to match treatment to the pattern of the disorder, something that research has not been able to untangle.
- Vaginismus can be successfully treated with progressive vaginal dilators, relaxation, and physiotherapy. Kegel exercises may also be helpful, but the evidence is not as strong.
- For premature ejaculation, drugs, specifically some antidepressants (SSRIs), may be combined with CBT to improve effectiveness (Hellstrom, 2011).
- Erectile disorder can be treated successfully with a combination of CBT and couple therapy, as described in the section on couple therapy.
- Hypoactive sexual desire disorder in women can be treated successfully with the kind of therapy developed by Masters and Johnson and with CBT.

For some disorders, research is insufficient to conclude that there is an effective treatment. Of course, this does not mean that current treatments are not effective; just that the research has not been done to determine one way or the other.

One critique of sex therapy points out the *medicalization* of sexual disorders (Kleinplatz, 2003a; Tiefer, 1994, 2000). Research has increasingly identified organic sources of male erectile disorder, and with these advances have come attempts to identify drugs and surgeries, rather than psychotherapies, to treat problems. In part, political and financial issues are involved, as physicians try to seize the treatment of sexual disorders from psychologists and other therapists. But there is also a cost to the patient as the disorder may be given a quick fix with drugs while the patient's anxieties and relationship problems are ignored. That is, we treat the symptoms, not the problem (Kleinplatz, 2003b). For biomedical treatments to be successful over the long term, the cognitive, affective, and interpersonal issues must also be addressed (Basson and VHHSC Centre, 1998). The New View of women's sexual problems, discussed earlier in this chapter, was proposed in part as an alternative to medicalization; of importance, it takes socio-cultural and relationship factors into account.

> **penile prosthesis (prahs-THEE-sis):** A surgical treatment for erectile dysfunction, in which inflatable tubes are inserted into the penis.

In contrast to these scientific criticisms, sex therapy has also been criticized on philosophical grounds. Ottawa psychologist and sex therapist Peggy Kleinplatz (1992, 1998) has argued that the current approach to sex therapy is goal-oriented rather than pleasure-oriented. By defining problems in terms of sexual disorders, sex therapists and their clients may focus on physiological and mechanical outcomes (getting an erection, having an orgasm) rather than on clients' subjective experience of sexuality, sexual satisfaction, and eroticism (Kleinplatz, 2003b). Sexual satisfaction is not just the absence of a sexual disorder (Byers, 1999). Often individuals get aroused and have orgasms but experience disappointment with the quality of their sexual encounters with their partner. Evaluation of the success of sex therapy should include more attention to whether therapy has resulted in enhanced sexual satisfaction. Resolving a sexual disorder often results in a decrease in sexual *dissatisfaction*, but it does not necessarily result in increased sexual satisfaction.

Psychiatrist Thomas Szasz (1980) argued that sex therapists have essentially produced a lot of illness by creating the (somewhat arbitrary) diagnostic categories of sexual disorder. For example, the man who cannot have intercourse because he cannot get an erection is said to have "erectile dysfunction," yet the man who cannot bring himself to perform cunnilingus is not regarded as having any dysfunction. Why should the first problem be an illness and the second one not? A man who ejaculates rapidly is termed a "premature ejaculator" and considered in need of therapy, but what exactly is wrong with ejaculating rapidly?

This criticism may especially apply to individuals with disabilities. Ontario researcher Gina Di Giulio (2003) has argued that the diagnostic categories for sexual dysfunction do not fit for such persons. In particular, the focus on genital response may imply that persons with disabilities cannot experience a highly pleasurable and satisfying sex life. Yet a woman with a spinal cord injury who has little genital sensation might get great pleasure from having her breasts or other parts of her body stroked, and reach orgasm from this type of pleasuring. That is, she has adapted her lovemaking to meet her own needs and situation. It is important for sex therapists to communicate to their clients with disabilities that they are fully sexual and that there is no right way to make love.

LO7
Some Practical Information

✳Avoiding Sexual Disorders

People can use some of the principles that emerge from sex therapists' work to avoid having sexual disorders in the first place. As the saying goes, an ounce of prevention is worth a pound of cure. In Chapter 1, we introduced the concept of sexual health. The following are some principles of good sexual mental health:

1. *Communicate with your partner.* Don't expect him or her to be a mind reader concerning what is pleasurable to you. One way to do this is to make it a habit to talk to your partner while you are having sex; verbal communication then does not come as a shock. Some people, though, feel uncomfortable talking at such times; nonverbal communication, such as placing your hand on top of your partner's and moving it where you want it, works well too although not as well (see Chapter 12 for more detail about good sexual communication).

2. *Try to stay in the moment.* Don't be a spectator, feeling as if you are putting on a sexual performance that you constantly need to evaluate. Concentrate as much as possible on the giving and receiving of sensual pleasures, not on how well you are doing.

3. *Relax and enjoy yourself.* Don't set up goals for sexual performance. If you have a goal, you can fail, and failure can produce disorders. Don't set your heart on having simultaneous orgasms or, if you are a woman, on having five orgasms before your partner has one. Just relax and enjoy yourself.

4. *Be choosy about the situations in which you have sex.* Don't have sex when you are in a terrific hurry or are afraid you will be disturbed. Also, be choosy about who your partner is. Trusting your partner is essential to good sexual functioning; similarly, a partner who really cares for you will be understanding if things don't go well and will not laugh or be sarcastic.

5. *Accept that disappointments will occur.* They do in any sexual relationship. What is important is how you interpret them. It is important that you don't see yourself as a failure and don't let them ruin the relationship. Instead, try to think, "How can we make this turn out well anyhow?"

✳Choosing a Sex Therapist

No provinces or territories require specific licensing or certification to practise sex therapy. This means that anyone can hang out a shingle saying "sex therapist," and some people with no training in the field have done so.

How do you go about finding a good, qualified sex therapist? Since 2013, Quebec has required sexologists to be licensed, as they do other professions (see www.opsq.org). Although they are not required by law to do so, some Ontario sex therapists choose to become certified by the Board of Examiners in Sexual Therapy and Counselling (BESTCO). These organizations ensure that people who identify themselves as sex therapists have the knowledge and training to effectively treat sexual disorders (Kleinplatz, 2009). However, the other provinces and territories do not have such boards. A very few Canadian sex therapists choose to be certified by a U.S. organization. However, most sex therapists in Canada operate under their discipline licences—such as psychology, clinical social work, or psychiatry—and therefore do not seek additional certification as a sex therapist even if they have training in sex therapy. Your local medical or psychological association can provide a list of therapists in your area and may be able to tell you which ones have special training in sex therapy.

Unfortunately, most therapists have only limited training in assessing and treating sexual difficulties (Miller & Byers, 2009, 2010; Reissing & Di Giulio, 2010). As a result, many are not confident in their abilities to provide treatment for sexual concerns and, as a result, do not routinely address their clients' sexual issues and concerns (Miller & Byers, 2012). Thus, it is important to ask potential therapists about their specific training in sex therapy and about their approach to it to make sure that they are qualified to provide sex therapy. Choose a therapist or clinic that offers an individualized *integrated biopsychosocial approach* that recognizes the potential biological, psychological, and relationship influences on any sexual disorder and is prepared to address all these and work in conjunction with professionals from other disciplines if needed.

What about people who live in an area where there are no sex therapists? Some therapists provide sex therapy online. What are its advantages and disadvantages (McCabe et al., 2010)? Proponents of sex therapy online argue that it is more affordable than traditional in-person therapy and that its anonymity is a major advantage. Interactions with a therapist online can break the wall of isolation surrounding a person with a sexual disorder. There are disadvantages, too. Currently, there is no system for licensing online sex therapists, so unqualified and perhaps unethical persons could easily present themselves as therapists. In fact, it is difficult to find legitimate sex therapy websites because searching for terms such as "sex therapy" leads to a deluge of porn sites. Moreover, online sex therapists probably will not be able to give true intensive therapy of the kind one would get in multiple in-person sessions with a therapist. However, qualified online therapists can affirm that a behaviour is not problematic and provide positive encouragement as well as accurate information, and that's enough to solve many people's problems. Unfortunately, many people who would benefit from sex therapy are unlikely to seek help, even over the Internet, for religious or cultural reasons, because they are embarrassed about it, or because they are erotophobic.

USING DIAGNOSTIC LABELS ACCURATELY

In this chapter, we revisit a critical thinking skill introduced in Chapter 15, thinking clearly about diagnostic labels and applying them accurately. Consider the following case.

Josh is 22. He has engaged in sexual intercourse on ten different occasions, with three different women, over the last two years. On the first three occasions, he got so excited during foreplay that he had an orgasm and ejaculated before he was able to insert his penis into her vagina. On the next three occasions, when he got excited he distracted himself by thinking about his grandmother and managed to insert his penis into his partner's vagina, but he still had his orgasm about 30 seconds later. For the most recent four occasions, distracting himself by thinking about his grandmother hasn't worked and he is back to having his orgasm before he can even insert his penis into his partner's vagina. He is very upset about the problem but doesn't know what to do about it.

Does Josh's case qualify as premature ejaculation? What should he do about it? Answer these questions before you proceed to read the paragraphs that follow.

To decide whether Josh's case qualifies as premature ejaculation, we need to look at the experts' definition and we will use the one given by the International Society for Sexual Medicine. To meet the criteria for premature ejaculation, the following must occur:

- Ejaculation must always or almost always occur prior to or within one minute of vaginal penetration. Every one of Josh's attempts at intercourse meet this criterion.

- In addition, there must be an inability to control or delay when ejaculation occurs. Josh also meets this criterion. Try though he might, he has not been able to delay his orgasms.

- In addition, the man must feel distressed about the problem, and Josh does.

Therefore, Josh meets all three criteria and his case would qualify as premature ejaculation (although only a trained clinician could actually make this diagnosis, and then only after a thorough interview).

Knowing that he meets the criteria, what should Josh do then? First, if he hadn't met the criteria—for example, maybe this had happened to him only once and on all other occasions he functioned fine—we might advise him to ignore the situation because most men have occasional experiences like this and then go on to function well. But Josh does meet the criteria. It is therefore reasonable for him to seek help. A good strategy would be to go to a licensed therapist with specific training in sex therapy. Their licensing association might provide information about their areas of expertise; if not, it's fine for him to ask potential training about whether they have expertise and experience treating sexual problems. Going to his family physician is probably not the best strategy because family physicians receive little or no training in sex therapy. Another strategy would be to try self-help before seeking professional help, choosing a book written by one or more individuals who are trained and experienced sex therapists. He could ask a willing partner to help him with the start-stop technique described earlier in this chapter.

SUMMARY

There are seven main sexual disorders according to the *DSM-5:* male hypoactive sexual desire disorder, erectile disorder, premature (early) ejaculation, delayed ejaculation, female sexual interest/arousal disorder, female orgasmic disorder, and genito-pelvic pain/penetration disorder.

Sexual disorders may be caused by physical factors, individual psychological factors, and interpersonal factors. Organic causes include some illnesses, infections, and damage to the spinal cord. Certain drugs may also create problems with sexual functioning. Psychological causes are categorized into predisposing factors and maintaining causes including myths and misinformation, negative attitudes, anxiety and inhibition, cognitive interference, psychological distress, and behavioural or lifestyle factors. Interpersonal factors include failure to engage in effective stimulation, often cause by poor sexual communication, and relationship distress caused by, for example, conflict in the couple's relationship or lack of intimacy.

Therapies for sexual disorders include behaviour therapy (pioneered by Masters and Johnson), cognitive behaviour therapy (CBT), couple therapy, specific treatments for specific problems (e.g., stop-start for premature ejaculation), and a variety of biomedical treatments, which include drug treatments (e.g., Viagra).

Evaluations of the effectiveness of sex therapy provide evidence that certain disorders can be effectively treated by certain therapies. Criticisms of sex therapy focus on the medicalization of sexual disorders, and the entire enterprise of identifying and labeling particular patterns of behaviour as disorders. Steps to prevent the occurrence of sexual disorders include good couple communication and not setting up sexual performance goals. When choosing a sex therapist, it is important that the person is licensed or certified in their field and has specific sex therapy training.

CHAPTER 19

Sexuality Education

© Creatas/Punchstock

Are YOU Curious?

1. What do Canadians think about sex education in schools?
2. What kinds of sex education programs work?
3. Why don't parents provide sex education for their kids?

Read this chapter to find out.

LEARNING OBJECTIVES

After studying this chapter, you will be able to

LO1 Outline the purpose and desired positive outcomes of the *Canadian Guidelines for Sexual Health Education.*

LO2 Discuss the attitudes of Canadian parents, teachers, and students toward sex education in school and at home.

LO3 Describe what sexual information should be taught to children at different ages and how this relates to children's knowledge and sexual interest.

LO4 Discuss and evaluate the components of the various types of sex education curriculum available.

LO5 Outline the controversies surrounding condom distribution in schools and the inclusion of sexual orientation issues in sex education programs.

LO6 Describe the qualities necessary to be a good sexuality education teacher.

LO7 Explain why parents do not provide much explicit sex education to their children and how parents can prepare themselves to communicate with their children about sexuality topics.

LO8 Describe the role that the media, health professionals, and the Internet can play in providing sex education in the community.

LO9 Discuss the pertinent issues surrounding teaching sexual health education to persons from different cultures and to persons with developmental disabilities.

Formal sex education in Canadian schools goes back at least to the early 1900s when Arthur W. Beall gave his "Advanced Purity Lectures." . . . Those involved in Public and school sex education saw themselves at the forefront of "modern thinking." Nevertheless, their message strongly reinforced conventional morality. . . . [T]hey appear to have been 100% successful in eliminating masturbatory insanity as a social problem. You hardly hear about that these days.*

* Michael Barrett (1990), Chair, Sex Information and Education Council of Canada (SIECCAN).

As we look to the future, a top priority for society has to be comprehensive sexuality education. If you have studied this textbook, you should be prepared to be a good sex educator for your own children. You should also be a well-informed citizen who can make thoughtful decisions about sexuality education. However, it is not just children who require sex education. Most people need additional information about sexuality throughout their lives so that they can adapt to changes in their life circumstances (e.g., becoming single again, physical changes caused by aging and illness). This chapter concerns **sexuality education**. Sexuality education is the lifelong process of acquiring information about sexual behaviour and forming attitudes, beliefs, and values about identity, relationships, and intimacy (SIECUS, 1991). Sex education can occur in many settings: home, school, church or synagogue, youth programs, relationships, and via the Internet.

Purposes of Sexuality Education

The goal of sexuality education is to promote healthy sexuality. What is healthy sexuality? The Public Health Agency of Canada (PHAC, 2008a) has adopted the definition of sexual health put forward by the World Health Organization (see Chapter 1):

> Sexual health is a state of physical, emotional, mental, and social well-being in relation to sexuality; it is not merely the absence of disease, dysfunction, or infirmity. Sexual health requires a positive and respectful approach to sexuality and sexual relationships, as well as the possibility of having pleasurable and safe sexual experiences, free of coercion, discrimination, and violence. For sexual health to be attained and maintained, the sexual rights of all persons must be respected, protected, and fulfilled.

Notice that this definition emphasizes positive sexuality, not just freedom from disease or dysfunction. The Sex Information and Education Council of Canada

(**SIECCAN**) is active in promoting high-quality sex education in Canada and coordinated the development of the *Canadian Guidelines for Sexual Health Education* (PHAC, 2008a). The Guidelines provide a framework for sexual health education for persons of all ages and from diverse populations that balances the well-being and desires of the individual with the needs and rights of others and of society. According to the Guidelines, sexuality education should help people both to achieve positive outcomes and to avoid negative ones. Positive outcomes include sexual self-esteem, respect for self and others, nonexploitative sexual satisfaction and sexual pleasure, rewarding human relationships, and the joy of desired parenthood. Negative outcomes include unwanted pregnancy, sexually transmitted infections, sexual coercion, and sexual dysfunction. Effective sexual health education integrates four key components through a variety of activities. These allow individuals to develop:

1. A deeper understanding that is relevant to their specific health needs and concerns

2. The confidence, motivation, and personal insight needed to act on that knowledge

3. The skills necessary to enhance sexual health and to avoid negative sexual health outcomes

4. A safe, secure, and inclusive environment that is conducive to promoting optimal sexual health (PHAC, 2008a, p. 14)

To achieve these goals, youth need to have an opportunity to explore attitudes, feelings, and values that may influence their decisions and behaviour. Sex education should emphasize the self-worth and dignity of the individual, and encourage respect for diversity in values, background, and sexual orientation. The Guidelines recognize that students need to make their own informed and responsible choices rather than have choices imposed on them. For

sexuality education: The lifelong process of acquiring information about sexual behaviour and forming attitudes, beliefs, and values about identity, relationships, and intimacy. **SIECCAN:** The Sex Information and Education Council of Canada, a national resource for up-to-date information, research, and publications on human sexuality, including sexual health.

example, some adolescents will choose abstinence over sexual involvement; others will choose to have sexual relationships. Of note, research in New Brunswick has shown that abstinence means different things to different people (Byers et al., 2009). Almost all students agreed that a person can engage in deep kissing and still be abstinent. However, students are quite mixed on whether a person can engage in oral sex or genital fondling and still consider themselves to be abstinent.

The Sexuality Information and Education Council of the United States, in partnership with Advocates for Youth and Answers, has developed specific standards for comprehensive and responsible sexuality education in their document *National Sexuality Education Standards: Core Content and Skills* (Future of Sex Education Initiative, 2012). This document identifies seven topics as the minimum, essential content: anatomy and physiology, puberty and adolescent development, identity, pregnancy and reproduction, sexually transmitted infections and HIV, healthy relationships, and personal safety. It also identifies key indicators that students have mastered content and skills in each area for Kindergarten through Grade 12.

 LO2

In the Home, in the School, or Somewhere Else?

Invariably some people object to providing sexuality education in schools. They might say that sex education promotes sexual intercourse, teenage pregnancy, or HIV/AIDS, and they are sure that it should take place only in the home (or possibly the church), but certainly not in the schools. Other people accept sexuality education in schools but object to specific aspects of the curriculum or the grade level at which topics are covered (for example, you might recall the controversy in 2010 about the Ontario sexuality education curriculum).

As shown in Table 19.1, school is the main source of sexuality education for Grade 9 students in Canada; 41 percent of the girls and 51 percent of the boys gave this response (Boyce et al., 2003). In contrast, only 6 percent of the boys and 14 percent of the girls identified parents or other family members as their main source of sexuality information. The fact is that many children are given little or no sexuality education at home; of course, not talking about sex with one's children is also a form of communication and sends a variety of negative messages. Further, individuals for whom sex was not discussed at home may have difficulty talking about sex with their partner or children, may develop negative attitudes about their own sexuality or about sex in general, or may not be equipped to make good sexual choices for themselves. Notice that TV, movies,

Table 19.1 Main Sources of Grade 9 Students' Information about Sex

	Boys	Girls
Parents or other family members	6%	14%
Friends	9	17
Internet	12	3
School	51	41
Magazines, newspapers, books	5	12
Television/movies	9	5
Physician or nurse	5	5

Source: Boyce, W., M. Doherty-Poirier, C. Fortin, & D. MacKinnon. (2003). *Canadian Youth, Sexual Health and HIV/AIDS Study*. Toronto: Council of Ministers of Education.

printed materials such as magazines, and the Internet are important sources of information for many youth, as are friends. In many cases, the information provided on TV and in movies is sensationalized and unrealistic (see Milestones in Sex Research in Chapter 10). Relying on friends for information is unwise; they likely know no more than you do. Teens are increasingly turning to the Internet for information about sex. More than 50 percent of students in Grades 7 to 12 report that they have searched for health information online (Rideout et al., 2010). The problem with the Internet as the primary source of sexuality information for youth is that there is no quality control; there are some sites with excellent and accurate information but others that promote misinformation. For example, one study of 177 sites found that 46 percent of those discussing contraception and 35 percent of those discussing abortion contained inaccurate information (Buhi et al., 2010). One of the best sites is www.sexualityandu.ca. Possibly the worst source? Pornography; some teens say they got their information from watching pornography on the web. Thus, it is fortunate and appropriate that school has become the main and preferred source of information (McKay & Holowaty, 1997). Of concern, though, is that youth who have immigrated to Canada within the previous three years are more likely than other youth to report not having received sex education (Salehi et al., 2010).

Sex education in the school is not "instead of" education in the home. Most Canadian parents, teachers, and students feel that both parents and schools have a role to play in providing sex education (Byers et al., 2003a, 2003b; Cohen et al., 2004; McKay & Holowaty, 1997; McKay et al., 1998; Weaver et al., 2002). For example, in a survey of parents in New Brunswick, 95 percent felt that responsibility for sexual health education should be shared by parents and schools (Weaver et al., 2002); somewhat fewer high school students (77 percent) and middle school students (69 percent) shared this view

(Byers et al., 2003a, 2003b). Some sexuality education programs actively involve parents by including homework to be done jointly by parent and child. The evaluation of one program of this type found that students receiving classroom instruction plus homework felt more able to refuse high-risk behaviours and more often intended to delay initiation of intercourse compared with students receiving only classroom instruction (Blake et al., 2003). The homework assignments appeared to reinforce the school-based program, and resulted in greater parent–child communication about sex.

How well are parents and schools doing in providing sex education? According to parents and students who participated in four New Brunswick studies, only between 24 percent (according to middle school students) and 38 percent (according to the parents) of children are getting excellent or very good sex education at home. According to the teachers and students, the schools are not doing much better: Between 13 percent (according to high school students) and 37 percent (according to middle school students) rated the sexual health education they had received in school as very good or excellent. Of interest, research in Ontario has shown that university students who were less satisfied with the sex education they received in high school were more likely to take a university-level sexuality course (Rye et al., 2014). Is this one of the reasons you chose to take this course?

One study involved interviews with 40 rural and urban youth in Nova Scotia and British Columbia about their sexual experiences, including their experiences with sexual health education (Shoveller et al., 2004). The youth indicated that neither schools nor parents promoted meaningful discussions about sex. Rather they perceived that both sexual health education and discussion with parents (if they had any) focused on prevention of pregnancy and STIs; what was missing for these youth was discussion of issues related to sexual relationships, especially the emotional and potentially positive aspects of sexual relationships. For example, one male youth described the sexual health education he had received in school:

> It [sex] was only talked about in Sex Ed . . . it was very *technical* and, of course, you couldn't ask *real* questions about your own experience. I think I understand the physical stuff but it's so emotional. And, it's the emotional stuff that you are always fucked up about when you are young. So, that's the part that was difficult. There's no question-and-answer period for that. You would never do that [emotional stuff] in a science class. (Shoveller et al., 2004, p. 480)

Similarly, youth indicated that they picked up subtle and not-so-subtle messages from their parents that certain kinds of questions and discussions about sex were off limits.

The goal of this chapter is to describe effective sex education, with particular focus on sex education in school and at home. We will also look at the potential of the Internet for providing sexual education. However, we first examine what research can tell us about what children should be taught about sex at different ages.

What to Teach at Different Ages

Sexuality education, whether at home or at school, is not something that can be carried out all at once in one week during Grade 5 or by having "the talk." Like teaching math or life skills, it is a process that must begin when children are small. They should learn simple concepts first, progressing to more complex ones as they grow older. Although sex education should always come before experience, what is taught at any particular age depends, in part, on the child's sexual behaviour (see Chapter 10), sexual knowledge, and sexual interests at that age. This section will concentrate on theories and research that provide information on the last two points.

Children's Sexual Knowledge

A few researchers have investigated what children in Western countries know about sex and reproduction at various ages. Children begin to develop an understanding of pregnancy and birth at a very early age. Very young children may believe that a baby has always existed, that it existed somewhere else before it got inside the mother. The following dialogue demonstrates this:

> (How did the baby happen to be in your Mommy's tummy?) It just grows inside. (How did it get there?) It's there all the time. Mommy doesn't have to do anything. She waits until she feels it. (You said that the baby wasn't in there when you were there.) Yeah, then he was in the other place . . . in America. (In America?) Yeah, in somebody else's tummy. (Bernstein & Cowan, 1975, p. 86)

As children get older, they develop—we hope—a more accurate understanding!

By age 7 or 8, children have a more sophisticated understanding of reproduction. They may know that three things are involved in making a baby: a social relationship between two people, such as love or marriage; sexual activity; and the union of sperm and egg. However, they may not understand that the sexual activity involves intercourse. At age 12, some children can give a good physiological explanation of reproduction that includes the idea that the embryo begins its biological existence at the moment of conception and is the product of genetic material from both parents. As one preteen explained:

The sperm encounters one ovum, and one sperm breaks into the ovum which produces, the sperm makes like a cell, and the cell separates and divides. And so it's dividing, and the ovum goes through a tube and embeds itself in the wall of the, I think it's the fetus of the woman. (Bernstein & Cowan, 1975, p. 89)

Some 10- and 11-year-olds understand that one of the reasons parents want to be alone is to have sex; others are reluctant to recognize the sexual dimension of their parents' relationship (De La Vega Salas & Thériault, 2001).

As we discussed in Chapter 10, research suggests that many children engage in sexual play and exploration. How does sexual behaviour relate to sexual knowledge? One review of the literature concluded that young children often engage in sexual behaviour without having a clear understanding of what it means (Gordon & Schroeder, 1995). These findings have important implications for sex education. Educators need to be aware of the level of the child's understanding and should not inundate him or her with information inappropriate for his or her age. Instead, the educator should attempt to clarify misunderstandings in the child's beliefs. For example, if a child believes a baby has always existed, the educator might say, "To make a baby, you need two grownups: a man and a woman."

Children's Sexual Interests

Children's knowledge of and interest in sex are reflected in the questions they ask. At age 5, kids may be asking where babies come from. At age 9, a boy or girl may ask about sexual behaviours: "What's oral sex?" Such questions are often stimulated by hearing the term in conversation or in the media. A 10-year-old may be interested in bodily processes and ask, "What's a period?" By age 11, many kids are asking questions related to puberty, such as "When will I get breasts?" or "When will I grow taller?" Such questions typically reflect an awareness that other youth are experiencing such growth. At age 13 or 14, many youth have specific questions about sexual activity. One young man asked, "Do girls move a lot when they have sex?" A 14-year-old girl asked her mom, "Where do people have sex?" (Blake, 2004). It is important that sex education for a particular age group addresses the questions of that age group, rather than questions children of that age thought about but answered long ago (Figure 19.1).

High school students agree that sex education should begin in early elementary school and should progress from the simple to the complex (Byers et al., 2003a). They believe that it should cover a wide range of topics including reproduction, pregnancy, abortion, birth control options, disease prevention, sexual violence, relationships and gender roles, sexual pleasure, sexual orientation and attraction, and sexual decision-making. They would like

Figure 19.1 In a sexual health education class for middle school students, the questions range from "How do you know when you need a bra?" to "Can you have sex at 12?"

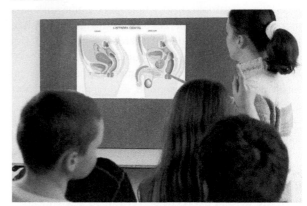

© LEMOINE/SCIENCE PHOTO LIBRARY

all these topics presented by Grade 8 but then revisited in high school. In particular, they want sexual health education that talks more about sex—feelings, arousal, foreplay, contraception, condoms, weighing alternatives, healthy relationships, sexual pleasure, sexual communication (that is, not just biological topics)—and is respectful of their choices (Caputo, 2000; Causarano et al., 2010; Langille, 2000; Maticka-Tyndale, 2001).

The sexual knowledge of preschool children in the United States was assessed by interviewing 147 children, ages 2 to 6 (Volbert, 2000). Drawings were used to initiate discussion. The results indicated that sexual knowledge evolves during the preschool years. At age 2, children can identify the sex of others and use slang to refer to the genitals. At age 3, children explain gender differences using cultural characteristics (clothing, earrings). At age 5, children explain gender identity based on genital differences; and at age 6, children have some knowledge of vaginal or Caesarian birth. There were no significant differences in knowledge between boys and girls.

An analysis of questions e-mailed to a reproductive health website found that 23 percent of the questions involved misconceptions about reproduction (Wynn et al., 2009). The authors suggest that two causes of this lack of information are poor sex education and confusing media messages.

Attitudes toward School-Based Sexuality Education

Surveys in Ontario, Nova Scotia, and New Brunswick have found very high levels of support for sex education in schools among parents, teachers, and students

Table 19.2 Responses of Parents, Teachers, and Students

	Percentage Agreeing with Each Statement			
	Parents	Teachers	Middle School Students	High School Students
Sexual health education should be provided in the schools.	94%	93%	93%	92%
The schools and parents should share responsibility for providing children with sexual health education.	95%	95%	69%	77%
Sexual health education should start in Grades K–5.	65%	78%	30%	23%

Sources: Byers et al., 2003a and b; Cohen et al., 2004; Weaver et al., 2002

(Langille et al., 1996; McKay, 1996; McKay et al., 2014; Weaver et al., 2002). For example, we surveyed 4206 parents, 336 teachers, 745 middle school students, and 1666 high school students in New Brunswick about their ideas about sex education. Some of the results are presented in Table 19.2. The four groups were consistent with each other in many of their views. For example, all four groups were strongly in support of sexual health education in the schools—more than 90 percent agreed that sexual health education should be provided in schools. Further, they were in favour of a broadly based curriculum that covers a wide range of topics, including HIV/AIDS and other STIs, sexual decision-making, sexual communication, sexual assault, birth control, abortion, and homosexuality. Similar results have been found in the other provinces. Further, there is strong support for sex education in schools by parents with children in both public and Catholic schools (McKay et al., 2014). The point is that in Canada, there is strong support for broad-based sex education in schools, beginning in the primary grades.

You may be surprised to learn that most adults favour sex education. The media regularly publicize controversies, cases in which parents are protesting sex education in the schools. There are three things to keep in mind about such episodes. First, they are rare. The vast majority of schools with sex education programs have not experienced such conflict. Second, the protesters are usually in a minority. Third, the controversy is often not over whether there should be a program but over the use of a particular curriculum, book, or video.

LO4

The Curriculum

The term *sexuality education* has been used to refer to a wide variety of programs. With the exception of Quebec, all Canadian provinces and territories have, as part of their health programs, province-wide, school-based

sexual health curricula (Health Canada, 2003; Joint Consortium for School Health [JCSH], 2007). In 2005, Quebec changed its health curriculum and removed sexual health education. Instead, all teachers are asked to incorporate teaching of sexual health into other subjects such as math, science, or history. Critics say this is not working; students are not getting the sex education they need and are campaigning to bring sex education back as part

What do Canadians think about sex education in schools?

of the health curriculum. In addition, there are major differences in how fully these curricula are implemented in different communities (Barrett, 1990). The comprehensiveness of the curriculum that is taught varies considerably across schools, school boards, and provinces and territories. For example, a study in British Columbia concluded that sexual health education in that province does not meet the criteria set out by the *Canadian Guidelines for Sexual Health Education* and that it is "hit or miss" as to whether students get quality sexual health education (Options for Sexual Health, 2004).

Other problems with the curricula are that they tend to only go up to Grade 8 or 9 even though students in Grades 10 to 12 are the most likely to be engaging in sexual activity, there is little discussion of the positive and pleasurable aspects of sexual relationships, and there are few resources tailored for specific groups, such as GLBT youth, youth with disabilities, or youth from specific ethnocultural or indigenous communities (JCSH, 2007). There is also considerable controversy over specific aspects of the curriculum. These controversies reflect cultural attitudes toward children and sexuality, with people who object often arguing that sexuality education should not provide specific types of information too early, in order to protect "the innocence of children." Of course, children are not really "innocent" and know a lot more about sex than some parents may suspect (see Chapter 10 for a discussion of childhood sexuality). Also, having sexual knowledge is helpful and not harmful to children.

One area that is particularly controversial is whether the curriculum should address homonegativity. Toronto's Human Sexuality Program was developed following the fatal beating of a gay student in Toronto in 1985 and provides classroom presentations on sexual-minority issues. However, there was a strong public outcry in 1997 in some parts of British Columbia when the B.C. Teachers Federation announced a decision to develop resources to help teachers address homonegativity in the classroom. For example, the conservative Citizens Research Institute developed a pamphlet to help parents demand that children not "be exposed to and/or involved in any activity or program which: discusses or portrays the lifestyle of gays, lesbians, bisexual and/or transgendered individuals as one which is normal, acceptable or must be tolerated" (Dwyer & Farran, 1997). They do not represent the majority; most Canadian parents, teachers, and students want sexual orientation included in sex education programs (Byers et al., 2003a, 2003b; Cohen et al., 2004; McKay et al., 1998; Weaver et al., 2002). Most classrooms will have one or two students who are LBGT or questioning their sexual orientation. Thus, discussion of sexual orientation helps to meet their needs as well as to increase acceptance of diversity among their classmates (McKay, 2000).

We will focus in the next section on the more substantial programs.

Early Sex Education Programs

The first programs, developed 30 years ago, were concerned with the transmission of knowledge. The goal of these programs was to reduce the number of teen pregnancies. Accordingly, the emphasis was on teaching students about sexual intercourse, pregnancy and birth control, and the consequences of having a baby. Later programs retained the informational content of the first ones, but the emphasis was placed on values clarification and decision-making skills. Proponents of these programs believed that young people engage in sexual risk-taking because they are unsure of their values and have difficulty making decisions. These programs also taught skills designed to improve communication with partners. Subsequent evaluations demonstrated that these programs were not particularly effective at reducing teenage pregnancy or sexual risk-taking behaviour (Kirby, 1992).

HIV/AIDS Risk Education

In the 1990s, the focus of sex education shifted from pregnancy prevention to HIV/AIDS and other STIs. All provinces and territories (with the exception of Quebec) have school-based programs that include information about HIV and AIDS (Barrett, 1994). Research has shown that more than 99 percent of Canadian parents approve of HIV/AIDS education in the schools (Weaver et al., 2002).

abstinence-only programs of sex education: Programs that promote sexual abstinence until marriage as the sole means of preventing pregnancy and exposure to sexually transmitted infections.

Programs of this type are often sharply focused on disease prevention. They have a variety of goals, including removing myths about HIV/AIDS and other STIs, encouraging delay of sexual intercourse, and supporting condom use or abstinence from unprotected intercourse. Each curriculum relies on lectures and class discussion facilitated by a teacher, a public health nurse or, more recently, a peer educator (Dunn et al., 1998). On occasion, someone with HIV/AIDS is brought in to talk with the class. These programs were usually short, often lasting only one or two class periods. A review of the effectiveness of these programs found that they improved knowledge significantly (Kim et al., 1997). In addition, many studies reported positive changes in respondents' intentions to use condoms.

One example of an HIV/AIDS education program in Canadian schools is the 20-hour Skills for Healthy Relationships program developed jointly by the federal and provincial governments. This program is designed for Grade 9 students and includes components aimed at delaying sexual activity, increasing condom use, creating compassion for persons living with HIV/AIDS, combating homonegativity, and improving communications and negotiating skills. It is based on a theoretical model that includes acquiring knowledge, developing responsible attitudes, increasing motivation, and developing skills (Fisher & Fisher, 1998). The program uses students as peer-group leaders and encourages parental involvement. An evaluation of the effectiveness of the program found that, compared with the regular program, students gained significantly in knowledge, became more positive in their attitudes toward people living with HIV/AIDS, increased their intentions to communicate assertively in sexual situations, and improved their skills in being able to use condoms correctly. However, the program did not affect the likelihood that students would engage in sexual intercourse or use a condom when they did engage in intercourse (Boyce et al., 2000).

The Canada Youth Sexual Health and HIV/AIDS Study (CYSHHAS) found that students in 2002 had *less* knowledge about HIV/AIDS than students who participated in the 1989 Canada Youth and AIDS Study (Boyce et al., 2003). This may be because of decreased focus on the disease in schools and in the media, and it is of concern because it might increase the risk of acquiring an infection (Brooke et al., 2010).

Abstinence-Only Programs

Abstinence-only programs of sex education developed out of opposition to sex education in the schools. Some people were opposed to any sex education in the

Figure 19.2 Reacting to controversy, in 2010 Dalton McGuinty, who was premier at the time, postponed the launch of a revamped school curriculum in Ontario that was developed after two years of work and extensive discussion. Some religious leaders and parents objected to children being taught about masturbation, homosexuality, and anal sex. The curriculum has now been updated.

© Fred Chartrand/CP Images

schools; others felt that the existing programs were too liberal or permissive. The concerns led to passage by the U.S. Congress of an act that limits the use of U.S. federal funds to abstinence-only programs that "promote sexual abstinence as the sole means of preventing pregnancy and exposure to sexually transmitted diseases" (Wilcox & Wyatt, 1997, p. 4). Millions of dollars have been spent by U.S. state and federal governments to support the development and widespread use of these programs. The two most widely known of these curricula are called Sex Respect and Teen Aid. Sex Respect is designed for middle school students and includes catchy slogans for children to chant in class, such as "Don't be a louse, wait for your spouse!"; "Do the right thing, wait for the ring!"; and "Pet your dog, not your date!" All students take a "chastity pledge," and there is a chart of physical intimacy in which a prolonged kiss is characterized as the "beginning of danger." The curriculum teaches that condoms can be the road to ruin because many fail, resulting in pregnancy (which as you know from Chapter 7 is not accurate).

Sex Respect throws in a lot of gender-role stereotypes as well, characterizing boys as "sexual aggressors" and girls as "virginity protectors." It presents the two-parent, heterosexual couple as "the sole model of a healthy, 'real' family." Another problematic characteristic of abstinence-only programs is that sexual diversity is not accepted or respected.

Neither the federal nor the provincial governments in Canada have supported the development or implementation of abstinence-only sexuality education in the schools. In general, school-based sexuality education in Canada has taken the approach of not promoting a particular set of values; that is, teaching about both abstinence and about birth control and safer sex (JCSH, 2007; PHAC, 2008a; SIECCAN, 2009). Nonetheless, these abstinence-only programs are being offered in some Canadian schools (Figure 19.2). For example, in 1992 Teen Aid was taught to more than 20 000 students in 203 Saskatchewan schools, even though the Department of Education in that province offers a broadly based sexuality education curriculum. School boards paid $150 to $250 a day to the Teen Aid organization for it to offer the program. More often the programs are offered in the community, by church groups, for example.

So, how effective are these curricula? Researchers who assessed the content of Sex Respect concluded that it omits a number of important topics, including sexual anatomy (!), sexual physiology, sexual response, contraception, and abortion (Goodson & Edmundson, 1994). We noted earlier that high school students say that all of these topics should be included in sex education. There have been many evaluations of these programs' effects on student attitudes and behaviour. A review of 52 evaluations concluded that, for the most part, the research shows these programs do not delay the onset of sexual activity or reduce the percentage of students having sex, getting pregnant, or acquiring an STI (Wilcox & Wyatt, 1997). That is, contrary to claims, these programs are not effective at delaying intercourse or reducing the rates of teenage pregnancy (Bennett & Assefi, 2005; Technical Working Group, 2002; Trenholm et al., 2007). In fact, data indicate that an emphasis on abstinence-only curricula is associated with higher teen pregnancy rates (Stanger-Hall & Hall, 2011). These programs also put youth at greater risk when they do start having sex, because they are less likely to use condoms.

Comprehensive, Theoretically Based Programs

The newest programs are comprehensive and are explicitly based on social science theories of health promotion, including social inoculation theory, social learning theory, the information–motivation–behavioural skills approach, and the health belief model (McKay, 1993). *Social inoculation theory* proposes that people are better able to resist social pressure when they recognize the pressure, are motivated to resist it, and have rehearsed resisting it. These programs include discussion of the social pressures to engage in sex, and ways to resist these influences (based on inoculation theory). *Social learning theory* emphasizes the importance of practising new skills that can be easily translated into behaviour, so these curricula include rehearsal and role-playing activities. The *information–motivation–behavioural skills model*, developed by Dr. William Fisher at Western University (see Milestones in Sex Research in Chapter 3) not only emphasizes the importance of health-related information but also enhances both skills and the motivation to use those skills. The *health belief model* includes attitudes, expectations, and self-efficacy—that is, the confidence that one can enact needed behaviours.

In light of the continuing high levels of teenage pregnancy—about 2.8 percent of Canadian teenagers became pregnant in 2010 (McKay, 2012)—the sharp increases in rates of STIs among persons 15 to 24 years of age, and the increasing rate of HIV infection in adolescents, it is imperative that we identify sex education programs that are effective in reducing sexual risk-taking behaviour. Although most programs increase students' knowledge, many programs are not effective at changing behaviour. Unfortunately, there are few published studies evaluating school-based sex education programs in Canada (Barrett, 1990; DiCenso et al., 2002). The effectiveness of school-based programs in the United States has been reviewed, however (Kirby et al., 1994). Researchers identified six characteristics that, according to the scientific evidence, are associated with delaying the initiation of intercourse, reducing the frequency of intercourse, reducing the number of sexual partners, and increasing the use of condoms and other contraceptives:

What kinds of sex education programs work?

- *Effective programs focus on reducing risk-taking behaviour.* Such programs have a small number of specific goals. They do not emphasize general issues such as gender equality and dating.

- *Effective programs are based on theories of social learning.* Programs that use theory in designing the curriculum are more effective than nontheoretical programs. The theories suggest that, to be effective, the program must increase knowledge, elicit or increase motivation to protect oneself, demonstrate that specific behaviours will protect the person, and teach the person how to use those behaviours effectively.

- *Effective programs teach through experiential activities that personalize the messages.* Such programs avoid lectures and videos; instead they use small-group discussions, simulation and games, role-playing, rehearsal, and similar educational techniques (Figure 19.3). Some of these programs rely on peer educators.

- *Effective programs address media and other social influences that encourage sexual risk-taking behaviours.* Some programs look at how the media use sex to sell products. All the effective programs analyze the lines that young people use to try to get someone else to engage in sex and teach ways of responding to these approaches.

- *Effective programs reinforce clear and appropriate values.* These programs are not value-free. They emphasize the values of postponing sex and avoiding unprotected sex and high-risk partners. The values and norms must be tailored to the target population. Different programs are needed for middle school students, for white middle-class high school students, and for ethnic-minority-group high school students.

- *Effective programs enhance communication skills.* Such programs provide models of good communication and opportunities for practice and skill rehearsal.

The length of the program and teacher training are also important. Effective programs are long enough to complete all these components and activities and are delivered by teachers or peers who believe in the program and have received training in how to deliver it (Kirby, 2002).

A review of the impact of 55 curriculum-based programs found that two-thirds of the programs that emphasized condoms and contraceptives as well as abstinence had positive effects. Youth who receive these programs are more likely to delay initiation of sexual activity, reduce sexual activity, and increase condom or contraceptive use (Kirby & Laris, 2009). Similar results were

Figure 19.3 Research indicates that sex education programs are most effective when they include experiential and skill-building activities that personalize the message. Here students learn how to use a condom.

© Act Up AIDS / Alamy Stock Photo

found in a review of the effectiveness of sexuality education programs by the United Nations Program on HIV/AIDS, with data from countries as diverse as Mexico, France, Thailand, and the United States (UNAIDS, 1997). The review focused on 53 studies that measured the impact of educational programs on behaviour. Three studies found an increase in sexual behaviour following a program. Twenty-two of the studies reported that the program delayed the initiation of sexual activity, led to a reduction in the number of partners, or reduced rates of unwanted pregnancy and STIs. The characteristics of the most effective programs were similar to those just identified.

We need to ensure that such programs are fully implemented and that teachers receive adequate training and support. Provincial and territorial governments and school boards also need to stand firm against vocal opponents of these programs. We also need to make sure that the curriculum is aimed not only at reducing negative outcomes, such as unwanted teenage pregnancies, STIs, and HIV/AIDS, but also at helping youth achieve positive outcomes, such as sexual self-esteem, sexual comfort, and fulfilling interpersonal relationships.

L05 Condom Distribution

One visible conflict has been over whether schools should distribute condoms to students. Different schools and school districts in Canada have widely differing policies on making condoms available in the schools. In some schools, condoms are available through the sex education program. In other schools, clinics providing health care services to adolescents dispense condoms. In still other schools, condoms are sold in vending machines—one high school in Ottawa and two on Vancouver Island were the first to install condom machines, in 1989. Again, data indicate widespread support in Canada for the distribution of condoms in schools (Ornstein, 1989).

The most visible opposition to condom distribution programs is by the Roman Catholic Church and other religious groups. These groups oppose such programs on the grounds that they will encourage sexual intercourse outside of marriage. However, research does not support their fears. For example, in a study comparing students in Massachusetts high schools that did and did not have such programs, students in schools with condoms available were *less* likely to report having ever had intercourse and *less* likely to report recent intercourse (Blake et al., 2003). In addition, sexually active students in schools that made condoms available were twice as likely to use condoms.

Research indicates that condom distribution programs are associated with reductions in teenage pregnancies and abortions. For example, making condoms available through specialized health units in high schools in one county in rural Ontario resulted in a 21 percent drop in the pregnancy rate and an 11 percent drop in the number of abortions among teenagers ages 18 years and younger.

Sexual Diversity

Whether or not they are out to teachers and classmates, it is likely that in every classroom there are at least one or two gay, lesbian, bisexual, or transgender students (PHAC, 2010c; SIECCAN, 2009). Other students have sexual-minority family members or friends. It is important that sex education programs address the needs of all students, including students who are members of sexual minorities, and include discussion of sexual diversity (SIECCAN, 2009). A study of LGB youth in Ontario found that they perceived that the sex education they received neglected them and their experiences (Brooke et al., 2010). Because bullying and harassment of LGBT youth in Canadian schools is so common (see Chapter 14), it is important that sex education address heterosexism, homonegativity, transphobia, and discrimination on the basis of sexual orientation and gender identity (Grace & Wells, 2001; McKay, 2005b; Taylor et al., 2011; Wells, 2009). In fact, in 2005 the B.C. Court of Appeal ruled that schools have a duty to take strong action to address homonegativity to ensure that no students experience discrimination and harassment at school.

This ruling was the result of a complaint by Azmi Jubran, a student in North Vancouver's Handsworth Secondary School, who was the victim of homophobic bullying, including being called names like "faggot" and "queer" and being pushed, punched, and spat on because the other students thought he was gay. The court ruled that it was not enough that the school punished the offending students. Instead, the school had a duty to provide "anti-homophobia" education to all students. This is important because although more and more high school students are coming out and there are more gay–straight alliance clubs in schools, LGBT students frequently experience psychological and physical harassment from other students, as well as a lack of support from homophobic school teachers and principals (Grace & Wells, 2001). A lesbian high school student in Alberta living in a safe house described her experience:

> The high school I went to in Grades 10 and 11 was awful. It was very, very homophobic. It's funny. When I got involved in going to gay bars, I even saw some of my teachers that are gay. But why aren't they out in school? I don't know, but I wish they were. Then at least I could have gone to them. But I can understand why they're not because it is a really homophobic high school. If I ever did hear a queer-related topic, it was always something negative. So I always had to shut up because I was too scared. (Grace & Wells, 2001, pp. 138–139)

In a tragic case, 15-year-old Jamie Hubley, a gay Ottawa teenager, committed suicide as a result of homophobic bullying. What changes are needed? First, sex education needs to include discussion of sexual orientation, including being gay, bisexual, and transgender. In this way, straight and questioning students would learn about being gay, lesbian, or bisexual. Second, LGBT students need to see themselves represented throughout the curriculum. For example, elementary school children could read books that feature same-sex parents. Math problems might feature a same-sex couple (e.g., "Jim wanted to give David an engagement ring that cost . . ."). Third, schools need to be supportive of LGBT teachers so that these teachers can serve as respected role models for LGBT and questioning students. Fourth, all schools need to be proactive in establishing a gay-positive environment. This would mean hanging gay-positive posters where all students can see them. Schools could hand out student bookmarks that list contact information for a number of support groups including LGBT youth groups. All schools should establish **gay–straight alliance clubs** (Figure 19.4). These are school-based clubs run by students and, importantly, supported by teachers, that work to create a safe, caring, and inclusive environment for LGBT students. They are open to all students, regardless of sexual orientation. There are currently 150 Canadian GSA clubs

gay–straight alliance clubs: School-based clubs run by students and, importantly, supported by teachers that work to create a safe, caring, and inclusive environment for LGBT students.

Figure 19.4 While a Grade 12 student in Coquitlam, British Columbia, Brent Power formed a gay–straight alliance club to combat homophobia; some B.C. parents strongly objected to discussion of homosexuality in the classroom.

© Chuck Stoody/CP Images

registered on the Egale Canada website (check them out at www.myGSA.ca). Research legislation in Ontario requires schools to allow students to form groups to raise awareness and understanding of sexual orientation and gender identity; in the past some schools did not allow such organizations. Finally, schools must have clear policies that protect students from discrimination on the basis of sexual orientation (Grace & Wells, 2001, 2006, 2007).

The Teacher

Suppose you have decided to start a program of sexuality education. You have found a curriculum that is consistent with your objectives. Wherever the program is to be carried out—in the home, the school, the place of worship, or someplace else—the next resource you need is the teacher. There are two essential qualifications: The person must be educated about sexuality, and he or she must be comfortable and skillful in interacting with learners about sexual topics (Health Canada, 2003). Interviews with female high school students in Amherst, Nova Scotia, identified teacher discomfort and lack of knowledge as important barriers in sex education (Langille et al., 1999). This is in large part because many of the teachers providing sexual health education have had no training to teach the subject (Cohen et al., 2012). Students also see as important the ability of teachers to personalize the information—that is, to relate the material to the students' lives (Eisenberg et al., 1997).

Sex education teachers need to be educated about sex. Reading a comprehensive text, such as this one, or taking a college or university course in sexuality are good ways to acquire the needed information. The teacher does not have to have a degree in sexology; the important qualifications are a good basic knowledge, a willingness to admit when he or she does not know the answer to a question, and the patience to look things up. A survey of Canadian BEd programs found that only 16 percent of them included sexuality as part of a required course (10 to 13 hours on average); about a quarter had an optional sexuality course (McKay & Barrett, 1999). In contrast, undergraduate students in the Department of Sexology at the University of Quebec in Montreal take 28 courses related to sexuality, and the department offers a master's degree in sexual health education (Dupras, 2001). A national survey found that only about half of school districts regularly offer in-service training in sexuality education, and teachers do not feel comfortable or competent in teaching sex (McCall et al., 1999). A survey of junior high school teachers in Newfoundland and Labrador who were responsible for sexual health education found that none had received specific training to teach sex education (Ninomiya, 2010). Perhaps as a result, most teachers do not cover the more sensitive

issues associated with sexuality and do not use active learning strategies, such as role-playing and small-group discussions (Cohen et al., 2004; Ninomiya, 2010). Clearly, there is a need for more training in sexuality to prepare teachers to teach sex education.

Equally important is the teacher's comfort with sexual topics. Even when parents or other adults willingly give factual information about sex to a child or an adolescent, they may convey negative attitudes because they become anxious, or they blush, or they use euphemisms rather than explicit sexual language. According to one 16-year-old girl, "The personal development classes are a joke. Even the teacher looks uncomfortable. There is no way anybody is going to ask a serious question" (Stodghill, 1998). Teachers who are comfortable with the subject matter are willing to ask students questions to determine what they know and to find out about any myths and misinformation they may have. They will encourage students to ask questions and be able to answer the questions asked. They will use a variety of active and interactive teaching techniques.

Some people are relaxed and comfortable in discussing sex. Others must work to learn this attitude. There are a number of ways to do this. For example, the teacher can role-play, with another adult, having sexual discussions with children. Some communities periodically offer programs designed to increase the comfort of the sexuality teacher or to enhance awareness of his or her own sexual values and attitudes. A good teacher is also a good listener who can assess what the learner knows from the questions asked and who can understand what a child really wants to know when she or he asks a question. As one joke had it, little Billy ran into the kitchen one day after Kindergarten and asked his mother where he had come from; she gritted her teeth, realized the time had come, and proceeded with a 15-minute discussion of intercourse, conception, and birth, blushing the whole time. Billy listened, but at the end he appeared somewhat confused and walked away shaking his head, saying, "That's funny. Jimmy says he came from Winnipeg."

Finally, it is important that teachers receive training and professional development to address their own homonegativity, to learn how to help make schools safe for and inclusive of LGBT students, and to learn to be supportive of students questioning their sexual orientation or going through the coming-out process (Grace & Wells, 2006; PHAC, 2010c).

How are Canadian teachers doing? A survey of university students in Ontario found that students gave the sexual health education teachers they had in middle school and high school a rating between average and good in terms of their confidence, knowledge, approachability, and comfort with sexual topics (Meaney et al., 2009). Middle school students in New Brunswick on average rated their teachers as doing a "good" rather than a "very good" or "excellent" job of providing them with sex education

(Byers, Sears, et al., 2013). Boys and girls in lower grades and with less sexual experience tended to rate their teachers more highly, suggesting that the content focused on pubertal development rather than issues related to sexuality within romantic relationships. Students who perceived their teacher as covering sexual health topics that matched their interests more adequately, as more comfortable talking about these topics, and as doing a better job of answering their questions rated the quality of the sex education they received more positively. That is, student perceptions of both the content and the delivery of sex education affected their views of its quality.

LO7
Home-Based Sexuality Education

Some Canadian youth identify their parents as an important source of sexuality information (Frappier et al., 2008). Others are given little or poor sex education at home. For example, a New Brunswick study asked parents of elementary and middle school students about the extent to which they had discussed a number of sexual topics with their child (Weaver et al., 2002). The topics they had discussed in the most detail were child sexual abuse and the correct names for genitals, but even these topics most parents had discussed only in some detail but not in a lot of detail. On average, the parents said that they had discussed the other topics, including puberty, STIs, birth control, and sexual decision-making, in general terms or not at all. Few parents of even the middle school students had discussed these topics in a lot of detail. Perhaps as a result, less than half of parents (38 percent), middle school students (42 percent), and high school students (36 percent) indicated that the quality of sex education provided by parents was very good or excellent (Byers, 2011). Similarly, in a more recent New Brunswick study, 29 percent of mothers had engaged in sexual discussions with their middle school adolescent in some detail and an additional 22 percent intended to do so in the next six months (Byers & Sears, 2012). Of concern is that 49 percent did not intend to discuss sexuality with their adolescent in the next six months even though these adolescents likely will be going through puberty and starting to date.

> **Why don't some parents provide sex education for their kids?**

The results of these studies also point to four major reasons why parents do not provide much explicit education to their children. First, many people are embarrassed about discussing sexuality. We see few models of how to have an explicit, matter-of-fact discussion; we are much more likely to see people discussing sex indirectly, with euphemisms and innuendo, or telling dirty jokes. (As a partial corrective, we have tried to write this book in an explicit, straightforward way.) Parents who are more comfortable talking about sex do a better job providing their children with sex education, including encouraging their children to ask questions more frequently (Byers et al., 2008; Foster et al., 2011).

Second, many parents lack *self-efficacy*—that is confidence that they can talk to their child about these topics. This may be because they perceive themselves as not knowing enough about various sexual topics. Many parents did not have good sexuality education themselves, and they may be painfully aware of their ignorance. In one Canadian survey, 76 percent of mothers indicated that they were not able to find some of the information they needed to have these discussions with their adolescent (Frappier et al., 2008). Interestingly, parents who had good sex education themselves in high school or university tend to talk more to their children about sexuality than do parents who did not take a human sexuality course. Parents who are more satisfied with the sex education they received from their own parents also provide better sex education to their own children (Byers et al., 2008). It appears that parents tend to replicate the sex education they received themselves (Byers, 2011).

Third, parents do not know how to provide sex education to their children (Figure 19.5). They also do not know at what ages they should discuss various topics. Of course, whether or not sexuality is openly discussed in the home (and many of our students say that it was never talked about in their home), parents communicate to their children about sex. Thus, just as parents convey

Figure 19.5 Parents who want to communicate with their children about sex can use books like this one to open the discussion. *What Makes a Baby* is notable because it is written and illustrated to include all kinds of kids, adults, and families.

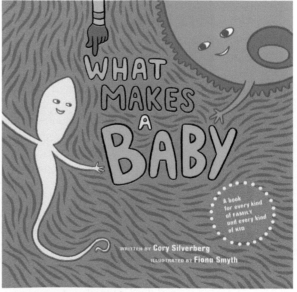

What Makes a Baby by Cory Silverberg. Used with permission.

First Person

Talking to Your Children about Sex

M any parents want to be able to communicate with their children about sexuality but feel nervous about doing so. Here are a few guidelines for parents taken in part from the materials prepared by SIECCAN for the Canadian Health Network:

Be prepared. This means that you should educate yourself about sexuality. If you are fortunate and had a good sex education course in high school or university, you may already feel knowledgeable enough to answer your children's questions. However, many parents do not feel that they know as much as they should and are afraid that their children will ask them questions that they can't answer. It's okay not to know everything about sex; after all, most children can get the facts from the sex education they receive at school. Besides, sharing your feelings and values, not teaching facts, is the most important contribution that you can make to your children's sexuality education. Nonetheless, you may want to take steps to fill in some of the gaps you have in your knowledge about sexuality. To do this you can read books, such as this textbook, on human sexuality or books on talking to children about sexuality, or you can attend a workshop for parents on that subject. You can also find out what is in your child's sex education curriculum at school. Remember, you need to talk to your children about both the positive aspects of sex (e.g., pleasure, sexual self-esteem) and the negative aspects of sex (e.g., sexual abuse, sexual coercion, and STIs).

Work to increase your comfort level. One of the most important contributions you can make to your children's sex education is increasing their comfort in talking about and asking questions about sex. Children's comfort will largely reflect the parents' comfort (Figure 19.6). You need to acknowledge to yourself the areas and topics that make you uncomfortable and take steps to increase your comfort level. Books and workshops about talking to your children about sexuality are good ways to increase your comfort level. Planning what to say and practising saying it (preferably in front of the mirror or with a partner) may also help to increase your comfort.

Plan ahead. Most of us did not have parents who talked to us about sex, so we can't base our own approach to educating our children about sexuality on our own experiences. As a result, it is important for you to decide how you want to approach sex education

Figure 19.6 It is important to be prepared, proactive, and honest when talking with your child about sex.

© SW Productions/Getty Images

with your children. For example, you need to decide what you want to tell your children at various ages, how you plan to share your values with them, how you want to respond to questions about things your child hears at school, and so on. Remember that positive messages are more likely to have an influence than are lectures and threats. Also, you need to plan for what you might say if your teenager tells you something that you find upsetting. It is important for you to discuss these matters with your teen calmly, without yelling, or you will close the doors to further discussions.

(continued)

(*continued*)

(For examples of key topics that you should cover at different stages of development, you can check out www .sexandu.ca/resources/resource-library.)

Be proactive. Too many parents wait for their children to ask them questions. Children are naturally curious about sex, but they are unlikely to ask questions if they have been getting nonverbal messages that you are uncomfortable talking about sex, or you never mention it at all. If you take the first steps, it will be easier for your children to raise questions and concerns at a later date. Opening the lines of communication is as important as the information you provide.

A good way to start talking to your children about sex is to use what we often call "teachable moments." For example, bath time is a good opportunity to provide your children with the correct term for their genitals just as you provide them with the correct name for their other body parts—nose, knee, and toes. Other teachable moments occur when someone your child knows becomes pregnant or gives birth, when something sexual is mentioned on television, or when a sexually related story is on the news. You can use these teachable moments to raise the topic of where babies come from, under what circumstances it is okay for teenagers to have sex, whether a couple in a movie are engaging in safer sex, and so on.

Another way to be proactive is to provide children and youth with books and DVDs about sexuality. For example, children's author Robie Harris has written excellent illustrated books for parents to read with children ages 4 and up (*It's Not the Stork!*, 2006), 7 and up (*It's So Amazing!*, 2004), and 10 and up (*It's Perfectly Normal*, 1994). You will need to read the books or watch the DVDs with your young and preadolescent children. Each page or DVD segment can lead to interesting discussions on the topics raised in the book or video. Your teen likely will prefer to read books on his or her own, but you should nonetheless initiate a discussion about the material to answer questions or concerns that the teenager has. You also need to initiate discussions with your teen on sexual decision-making and to try to ensure that he or she has the skills to apply decisions in real-life situations. For example, you can help your teen become more comfortable talking to a partner about their sexual decisions or, if they do decide to have sex, about safer sex and birth control.

Listen first and then answer all questions truthfully, honestly, and accurately. Before answering their question, listen carefully to what your child is saying so that you are clear about what he or she is asking. For young children, answering questions truthfully, honestly, and accurately will involve providing short answers containing direct explanations. As your children grow older, they will want and need more detail and will be more likely to ask questions if you've created an open environment. You do not need to worry about providing your children with too much information too early. Children take the information they need and tend to ignore the rest. Unless you are a sex educator yourself, it is likely that your children will eventually ask you a question and you will not know the answer. It's okay not to know everything about sex. By admitting that you don't know the answer, you give your children permission not to have to know everything about sex, and communicate that having to seek out answers is normal and healthy at any time in life. Of course, it's important for you to then try to find the answer with your child.

---

a positive attitude toward sexuality by, for example, providing children with the correct names for their genitals and comfortably answering their sexual questions, parents convey their negative attitudes toward sex by not doing these things and by not talking about sex. As such, sexual education starts at birth through the nonverbal messages we give that lead to children feeling either good about their bodies or uncomfortable with their bodies and genitals.

Fourth, some parents have attitudes that are not supportive of sex education. Some are not convinced that parent–child sexual communication (particularly with younger children) will have positive outcomes and not negative outcomes for them and for their child. Some believe that the people who are significant in their lives would not approve of these discussions. As a result, they do not initiate these conversations. Changing parents' attitudes would likely change their intentions to talk to their children and their behaviour (Byers & Sears, 2012).

Many Canadian parents want to talk to their children about sex. However, they feel that they need to be more knowledgeable about sexuality and more comfortable talking about sex before they can do so. They also feel that they need guidance on when and how to communicate with their children about sexuality (Byers, 2011). First Person provides some suggestions to parents who want to communicate with their children about sexuality.

What are the results of better parent–child sexual communication? Research suggests that more extensive sexual communication between parents and their adolescent is associated with a number of positive outcomes for the adolescent, including increased sexual knowledge, greater confidence about using condoms, and later initiation of sexual intercourse (DiIorio et al., 1999; Hutchison & Cooney, 1998). Researchers in Ontario also have shown that young women who had more conversations with their parents about dealing with unwanted sexual advances were more *sexually resourceful;* that is, they had more skills to resist, say no, or leave situations involving noncoercive unwanted sexual activity rather than give in to them (Kennett et al., 2012). Women who are more sexually resourceful give in to unwanted sexual behaviour less frequently.

Sexuality Education in the Community

The need for accurate sexual information does not end when people graduate from high school. For example, about 15 000 students in Canadian colleges and universities take a human sexuality course, perhaps like the one you are taking, each year—this number likely could be higher, but some schools do not offer courses in human sexuality. In addition, people need additional information about sexuality throughout their lives as they reach different life stages. The pregnant woman may need to learn about pregnancy and childbirth. New parents may want to increase their understanding of sexuality in childhood or of child sexual abuse. LGBT individuals may want information about other people's coming-out process. The middle-age woman may want to learn more about menopause. Older adults may need to learn about the effects of aging on the sexual response. Even for children and youth, sex education can and does occur outside the home and the classroom. For example, HIV/STI prevention interventions occur in public health clinics, in community settings, or through the media. These efforts can be directed at the population at large, or at specific subgroups with specific needs—for example, men who have sex with men, street youth, or members of specific ethnocultural minority groups. Community groups, health care professionals, and the Internet can all provide sex education outside the school or home setting.

Sex Education by Health Care Professionals

Physicians and other health professionals have an important role to play in educating youth about sexual health (McCall & McKay, 2004). For example, by routinely asking about sexual involvement in a nonjudgmental way, physicians make it more likely that teenagers will approach them for advice on contraception when they do begin having sexual intercourse. However, many physicians are not comfortable talking about sex with their patients, particularly their adolescent patients, and thus do not routinely ask these questions. Others do not feel knowledgeable about sexuality. A survey of Canadian medical schools indicated that 14 of 18 sexual topics listed were covered in the curriculum, mostly through lecture and clinical experience (Barrett et al., 2012). However, two-thirds of programs in Canada and the United States provide medical students with less than ten hours of instruction related to sexual issues (Solursh et al., 2003). Perhaps as a result, a Nova Scotia study found that few high school students had ever discussed with their family doctor whether they were sexually active. Even among students who were engaging in intercourse, only 56 percent of the girls and 16 percent of the boys had discussed this with their family physician (Langille et al., 2001). A notable exception to the dearth of sexuality instruction in medical schools is l'Université de Québec à Sherbrooke, where medical students attend a four-day retreat related to sexuality. At the retreat they examine their attitudes and biases related to sexuality, with the goal of making it more comfortable to discuss sexual concerns with their clients (Solursh et al., 2003).

Even some specialists who are routinely consulted about sexual issues do not feel confident in their sexuality training. For example, researchers in Ontario found that obstetrics and gynaecology residents had significant knowledge gaps in some, but not all, areas (Garcia & Fisher, 2007). To fill this gap in physician training related to sexuality, the Society for Gynaecologists and Obstetricians released two sets of guidelines for physicians who treat women's sexual health concerns (Burnett et al., 2011; Lamont et al., 2012). However, studies of patients diagnosed with an illness that affected their sexual functioning (e.g., cancer) indicate that they were not fully educated by their health care providers about the sexual changes they might experience (Archibald et al., 2006; Letts et al., 2010). For example, one woman with breast cancer commented about changes to her sexual functioning resulting from treatment:

> I would have liked to have known ahead of time to know what to expect. Like is this normal? Is it just something I am feeling? . . . I would have been prepared for it. Like I wouldn't have been as worried about it, or as concerned about it. (Archibald et al., 2006)

It is important that health care workers ensure that their patients' information and support needs are met with respect to the sexual changes they experience as a result of their disease or treatment.

Therapists also have a role in providing sexual health information to their clients (Miller & Byers, 2009, 2010). To do so, therapists need to be knowledgeable about topics about which their clients might have sexual concerns (Fisher & Holzapfel, 2014). As one example, they need to be knowledgeable about STI transmission and prevention so that they can help their clients make decisions that do not put them at risk for infection. They also need knowledge about issues related to the sexual response, sexual orientation, gender identity, and aging, to name just a few. Yet Canadian researchers have shown that many lack confidence that they can relay accurate sexual health information (Miller & Byers, 2012).

Sex Education on the Internet

The media can be used to increase awareness of specific sexual issues, such as prenatal nutrition, sexual minorities, or sexual violence. In particular, the Internet may be useful in providing information about sexuality. This can be an addition to formal school-based sex education, or a way of providing sexual information to people throughout their lives. Certainly, many Canadians already seek out sexuality information on the Internet. For example, in an online survey of 760 university students in British Columbia, about half (52.5 percent) had looked for sexuality information on the Internet within the past year (Boies, 2002). Further, 21 percent of the students reported that their first sexuality education material had come from the Internet. A New Brunswick study found that 18 percent of male university students and 31 percent of female students had looked for sexuality information online in the previous month (Shaughnessy, Byers, & Walsh, 2011). The Internet is particularly attractive because it is an affordable, available, anonymous, and acceptable way to access sexuality information, and people can do so without being observed (Barak & Fisher, 2001; Cooper, 1998). There are several other advantages to sex education on the Internet (Barak & Fisher, 2001):

- Materials are easily revised, so all users can have access to the most up-to-date information.
- Websites can use multimedia communications, including text, sound, pictures, animation, and videos.
- The material can be accessed from any computer, at any time.
- Users can exchange information with other users.
- A website can provide access to information and services outside its own site by providing links to other sites.

- Potentially, information and programs provided can be individualized to the needs of each user based on responses to prescreening questions administered on the site.

There are also potential problems with sex education on the Internet. Anybody can establish an Internet site, and nobody monitors these sites for the accuracy of their content, so the unsuspecting user may be getting incorrect information (Fisher & Barak, 2000). Indeed, as noted earlier, there is also a great deal of misinformation provided on the web, which is a huge problem. Finally, not everybody has access to the Internet; people who are socio-economically disadvantaged and who belong to ethnocultural minority groups tend to have less access. Nonetheless, the Internet certainly has the potential to enhance traditional approaches to sex education.

Effective Multicultural Sexuality Education

Much of the discussion in this chapter has assumed that the participants in a sexuality education program are homogeneous, that they are all from the same ethnocultural community. In some situations that assumption is valid, but in other settings the learners may be from diverse ethnocultural backgrounds.

Cultures vary in a number of ways that may affect the success or failure of a sexuality education program (Irvine, 1995). There are cultural differences in sexual practices; some of these were discussed in Chapter 1. The acceptability of explicit sexual language or of particular types of language, such as street slang, varies from one cultural community to another. Cultures vary in the meaning they attach to sexuality. The majority cultures in Europe and North America have emphasized sex for the purpose of reproduction and thus tend to regard vaginal intercourse as the norm (see Chapter 20). Other cultures place greater emphasis on the pleasure that can be derived from sexual stimulation. Finally, cultures vary in the definition of and the roles expected within the family.

Of necessity, sexuality education programs use language. Street slang might enhance rapport with street youth but deeply offend recent immigrants. Curriculum developers and teachers base their programs on assumptions about the prevalence of specific sexual practices, such as vaginal and anal intercourse. They implicitly or explicitly identify some practices as desirable—for example, condom use. They also reflect assumptions about the purposes of sexual intimacy; for example, abstinence-based programs assume that sexual intercourse is most or only meaningful within marriage.

If sexuality education is to be successful, it must reflect, or at least accept, the cultures of the participants. The educator must assess the audience, the intended messages, and the context, and target the program accordingly (Irvine, 1995). Educators must recognize their own sexual culture, learn about the sexual cultures of the participants, and be aware of the power differences between groups in our society. In the classroom, they should use this knowledge to enhance the effectiveness of the presentation. The use of communication styles and media common to the cultures of the participants—for example, music—can be a valuable tool. Finally, it is important that the program not advocate beliefs and practices that are incompatible with participants' cultures. Such programs are doomed to failure. This is true for school-based sexuality education and for workshops and outreach programs. For example, researchers in Toronto documented a need for educational outreach and services specifically for East Asian and Southeast Asian men who have sex with men. They used the results of a needs assessment to make specific recommendations about how to best provide culturally appropriate services (Poon et al., 2001). It also means that sex education programs developed in one country will not necessarily be accepted or be effective in another country (Figure 19.7).

Rather, they typically will have to be modified to fit the culture of that country.

The First Nations HIV/TB Training Kit is designed to train community health educators to deliver culturally based training sessions on HIV and TB (tuberculosis) (Association of Iroquois and Allied Indians, 1997). Training emphasizes cultural sensitivity to distinct rituals, cultural practices, and methods within each First Nations community, such as storytelling, the talking circle, traditional medicines, and the medicine wheel. Resources like this one, and the programs that result from this type of training, respond to the call for sexuality education that incorporates the family and community context in which our sexuality is grounded (PHAC, 2008a; Maddock, 1997; Young, 1996).

Another group that needs to have sexuality education tailored to its needs is those with disabilities. We cannot assume that curricula designed for students in Grade 6 can be presented to 12-year-olds with disabilities (Di Giulio, 2003). Instead, these youth need sex education programs that are tailored to their unique learning needs, concerns, and styles. This includes individuals with intellectual disabilities (see First Person). It also includes youth on the autism spectrum who may need sex education that integrates core social and relationship skills

Figure 19.7 Sex education around the world. At this family-planning clinic in India, an educator explains the female reproductive system to these mothers.

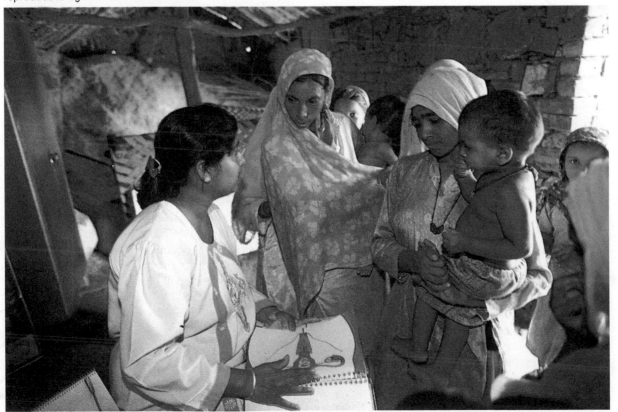

© Robert Nickelsberg/Getty Images

First Person

Sex Education for Persons with Developmental Disabilities

Persons with IQs below 70 are generally classified as having an intellectual or a developmental disability. There is a great range of capacities among individuals with developmental disabilities, from some who require constant care to those who function quite well in the community, who can read and write and hold simple jobs. It is important to recognize that the great majority of persons with intellectual disabilities in the moderate range (IQs between 50 and 70) are in the category of near-normal functioning. Programs need to assess the cognitive and emotional abilities of each child and adolescent and then present developmentally appropriate materials.

In the past, society has regarded persons with disabilities, including developmental disabilities, as asexual. Although many of these attitudes remain, society, parents, and caregivers are increasingly recognizing that persons with developmental disabilities have normal sexual desires. However, because these children are often slower to learn the norms of society, they may express themselves sexually in ways that are not acceptable to others, such as masturbating in public. Further, persons with developmental disabilities may be particularly vulnerable to sexual exploitation and abuse.

Unfortunately, not all youth with developmental disabilities have access to adequate sex education; in fact, many receive little or no such education. For students enrolled in regular classes, the sexual health education curriculum may not fit their learning style or level of understanding. For these reasons and others, careful sexuality education for persons with intellectual disabilities is essential. Fortunately, there are now a number of comprehensive guides and curricula that have been developed precisely to teach youth with developmental disabilities about their sexuality.

It is important that persons with developmental disabilities be educated about contraception and that contraceptives be made available to them (Figure 19.8). Because persons with developmental disabilities have normal sexual desires, they may engage in sexual activity, including intercourse. In one study, 24 percent of boys and 8 percent of girls with developmental delays had engaged in intercourse by age 16 (Cheng & Udry, 2003). If these youth lack sexuality education, they may not realize that pregnancy and STIs can result. An unwanted pregnancy for a woman or couple with developmental disabilities may be a difficult situation; they may be able to function well when taking care of themselves but not with the added burden of a baby. On the other hand, some persons with developmental disabilities do function sufficiently well to care for

Figure 19.8 There is a need to provide sex education to children and adults with disabilities.

© Mikael Vaisanen/Getty Images

a child. The important thing is that they make as educated a decision as possible and that they have access to contraceptives. Many experts recommend an IUD or other methods that do not require memory or forethought for effective use for women with developmental disabilities. Information about forms of romantic and sexual expression may have to emphasize social norms about what is appropriate, and discourage inappropriate behaviours in public. Also, programs for persons with disabilities must recognize their vulnerability to exploitation and make special efforts to teach them self-protection skills.

In the 1920s, both Alberta and British Columbia passed laws allowing sterilization without consent of people deemed to have "mental retardation." While we now view this as a violation of human rights, the law was not repealed in Alberta until 1972, after 2900 such operations had been performed. In 1996, an Alberta woman successfully sued the government for damages related to her involuntary sterilization. She had been sterilized at the age of 14 without her knowledge or consent.

In summary, persons with developmental disabilities have sexual needs and desires. Because of their special needs, it is especially important that they receive appropriate sexual health education.

Sources: Ames, 1991; Baladerian, 1991; Di Giulio, 2003; Kempton & Kahn, 1991; Nemeth, 1995.

development with more traditional sexuality content (Byers et al., 2012). Youth with physical disabilities may need additional information in addition to the mainstream sex education pertaining to self-esteem and body image (Krupa & Esmail, 2010; Parrott & Esmail, 2010).

As we increasingly recognize diversity both within Canada and around the world, creating developmentally and culturally effective sexuality educational programs should be an important priority. Happily, research has consistently shown that, internationally, a large majority of parents support the provision of school-based sexual health education—for example, 75 percent of parents in Tanzania and 92 percent of parents in Nigeria (Mkumbo & Ingham, 2010; Ogunjimi, 2006). Another important priority is helping parents from diverse cultures talk to their children about sexuality in ways that promote the children's sexual health. For example, research in Pakistan has found that youth do not consider their parents to be reliable sources of information about sex (Khan & Pine, 2003). Similarly, few parents in a study conducted in rural Nigeria had discussed sexual issues with their children; the ones that had done so typically had provided incorrect, frightening information in an attempt to prevent them from engaging in sexual activity (Izugbara, 2008).

Critical *THINK ing Skill*

USING SCIENCE IN FORMING PUBLIC POLICY

It is often said that sexual health education in schools is the most controversial topic in education. In particular, politicians, principals, and teachers are highly concerned about possible negative parental reactions to providing sex education in the schools. They fear that parents do not want their adolescents to receive sex education and that there will be a public backlash to a curriculum that goes beyond the biological aspects. This can prevent implementation and delivery of a comprehensive sexual health curriculum.

One example is the decision by the Ontario government in 2010 to withdraw the proposed revision to the sexual health curriculum (OPHEA, 2012). This was a result of complaints from some parents about the curriculum as well as media reports that a large percentage of Ontario parents were opposed to broadly based, comprehensive sexual health education. In short, the decision was based on anecdotal evidence not on science.

An alternative would have been for the government to review scientific studies that have been done in Canada (including in Ontario) or commission a survey about parents' actual attitudes toward sexual health education. They would have found out that, as reported earlier in this chapter, a number of Canadian surveys in different provinces (including Ontario) have shown that the vast majority of Canadian parents (85 to 95 percent) support providing broad-based sexual health education in school. This would have made it clear that the public outcry represented the views of a vocal minority of parents, not the views of the majority of parents as reported in the media and as the government feared.

SUMMARY

School is the primary source of sexuality information in Canada. However, many children receive their sex education from their peers or other sources, not from their parents. The vast majority of Canadians support sex education in the school. Cases of opposition to sex education involve a small number of people.

The purposes of sexuality education include providing children with adequate knowledge of the physical and emotional aspects of sex, with an opportunity to develop their own values and interpersonal skills, and with the maturity to take responsibility for their sexuality. Sex education should help people achieve positive outcomes and avoid negative outcomes.

What is taught at each age should depend on what children are thinking about at that age. Children pass through various stages in their understanding of sexuality. For example, at first they believe that a baby has always existed. Later, they realize that the parents caused the baby's creation, but they don't know exactly how. Older children acquire a more scientific understanding of reproduction. Children's sexual play seems to precede rather than follow the development of sexual knowledge.

Sexuality education curricula have evolved a great deal over the past three decades. The early programs focused on preventing adolescent pregnancy and HIV/AIDS through knowledge, values clarification, and decision-making skills. They resulted in increased knowledge and intentions to use condoms. Conservative programs, such as Sex Respect, emphasize abstinence and are limited in content. The evidence indicates they are not effective and may lead to increased risk. Contemporary, broadly based programs are based on social science theory and emphasize the importance of not only providing information but also allowing students to practise new behaviours such as communication skills. Research suggests that sexuality education programs that are effective at delaying the onset of intercourse, reducing the frequency of intercourse and the number of partners, and increasing condom use share several characteristics: they focus on specific risk-taking behaviours, are based on theory, use experiential activities, address social influences on sexual behaviour, reinforce values, and provide opportunities to practise new skills.

There is a good deal of conflict over the distribution of condoms in high schools. There is widespread support among both high school students and their parents for such programs, but the Catholic Church, among others, is a vocal opponent.

It is important that sex education programs address the needs of LGBT students as well as heterosexism, homonegativity, and discrimination on the basis of sexual orientation.

A good sexuality education instructor must have accurate knowledge about sexuality, be comfortable discussing it, and be good at listening to the questions learners ask. Students say that the instructor's ability to relate the material to their lives is also important.

It also is important that parents talk to their children about sexuality. Some guidelines for parents are (1) be prepared, (2) work to increase your comfort level, (3) plan ahead, (4) be proactive, and (5) answer all questions truthfully, honestly, and accurately.

People have a need for continuing sex education throughout their lives. Physicians, other health professionals, and the Internet are all important sources of ongoing sex education.

To be effective, multicultural sexuality education must reflect or be consistent with the culture(s) of participants. It should present messages that are compatible with their beliefs and practices. Such programs should use language and styles of communication that are appropriate.

Aasheim, V., Nilsen, A. B. V., Lukasse, M., & Reinar, L. M. (2011). Perineal techniques during the second stage of labour for reducing perineal trauma. *Cochrane Database of Systematic Reviews, 12,* CD006672.

Abbey, A. (2011). Alcohol's role in sexual violence perpetration: Theoretical explanations, existing evidence and future directions. *Drugs and Alcohol Review, 30,* 481–489.

Abbey, A., Parkhill, M. R., Jacques-Tiura, A. J., & Saenz, C. (2009). Alcohol's role in men's use of coercion to obtain unprotected sex. *Substance Use & Misuse, 44,* 1329–1348.

Abbey, A., Wegner, R., Woerner, J., Pegram, S. E., & Pierce, J. (2014). Review of survey and experimental research that examines the relationship between alcohol consumption and men's sexual aggression perpetration. *Trauma, Violence, and Abuse, 15,* 265–282.

Abbott, A. (2010). Baby boom bags Nobel prize. *Nature, 467,* 641–642.

Abdool Karim, Q., Abdool Karim, S. S., Frohlich, J. A., Grobler, A. C., Baxter, C., Mansoor, L. E., . . . CAPRISA 004 Trial Group. (2010). Effectiveness and safety of tenofovir gel, an antiretroviral microbicide, for the prevention of HIV infection in women. *Science, 329,* 1168–1174.

Abel, G. G., Becker, J. V., Mittelman, M., Cunningham-Rathner, J., Rouleau, J. L., & Murphy, W. D. (1987). Self-reported sex crimes of nonincarcerated paraphiliacs. *Journal of Interpersonal Violence, 2,* 3–25.

Abel, G. G., Osborn, C., Anthony, D., & Gardos, P. (1992). Current treatments of paraphiliacs. *Annual Review of Sex Research, 3,* 255–290.

Abel, G., & Rouleau, J.-L. (1990). The nature and extent of sexual assault. In W. L. Marshall, D. R. Laws, & H. E. Bartarce (Eds.), *Handbook of sexual assault* (pp. 9–21). New York: Plenum.

Abracen, J., & Looman, J. (2004). Issues in the treatment of sexual offenders: Recent development and directions for future research. *Aggression and Violent Behavior, 9,* 229–246.

Abracen, J., Looman, J., Ferguson, M., Harkins, L., & Mailloux, D. (2010). Recidivism among treated sexual offenders and comparison subjects: Recent outcome data from the Regional Treatment Centre (Ontario) high-intensity sex offender treatment programme. *Journal of Sexual Aggression.* doi:10.1080/13552600903511980

Abram, D., Viki, G., Masser, B., & Bohner, G. (2003). Perceptions of stranger and acquaintance rape: The role of benevolent and hostile sexism in victim blame and rape proclivity. *Journal of Personality and Social Psychology, 84,* 111–125.

Acevedo, B., Aron A., Fisher, H. E., & Brown, L. (2012). Neural correlates of long-term intense romantic love. *Social Cognitive and Affective Neuroscience, 7,* 145–159.

Acker, M., & Davis, M. (1992). Intimacy, passion and commitment in adult romantic relationships: A test of the triangular theory of love. *Journal of Social and Personal Relationships, 9,* 21–50.

Acton, W. (1857). *The functions and disorders of the reproductive organs in childhood, youth, adult age, and advanced life, considered in their physiological, social, and moral relations.* Philadelphia: Lindsay and Blakiston.

Adam, B. D. (2007). Why be queer? In G. Pavlich & M. Hird (Eds.), *Questioning sociology* (pp. 71–79). Don Mills, ON: Oxford University Press.

Adam, B. D., Betacourt, G., & Serrano-Sánchez, A. (2011). Development of an HIV prevention and life skills program for Spanish-speaking gay and bisexual newcomers to Canada. *Canadian Journal of Human Sexuality, 20,* 11–17.

Adam, B. D., Elliott, R., Husbands, W., Murray, J., & Maxwell, J. (2008). Effects of the criminalization of HIV transmission in Cuerrier on men reporting unprotected sex with men. *Canadian Journal of Law and Society, 23,* 143–159.

Adams, M. A., Banting, J. D., Maurice, D. H., Morales, A., & Heaton, J. P. W. (1997). Vascular control mechanisms in penile erection: Phylogeny and the inevitability of multiple and overlapping systems. *International Journal of Impotence Research, 9,* 85–91.

Addiego, F., Belzer, E. G., Comolli, J., Moger, W., Perry, J. D., & Whipple, B. (1981). Female ejaculation: A case study. *Journal of Sex Research, 17,* 13–21.

Adkins-Regan, E. (2002). Development of sexual partner preference in the zebra finch: A socially monogamous, pair-bonding animal. *Archives of Sexual Behavior, 31,* 27–34.

Adoya-Osiguwa, S. A., Markoulaki, S., Pocock, V., Milligan, S. R., & Fraser, L. R. (2003). 17B-estradiol and environmental estrogens significantly affect mammalian sperm function. *Human Reproduction, 18,* 101–107.

Adshade, M. (2010). Confessions of a college pimp. Retrieved from http://www.bigthink.com/ideas/24377

Afifi, M. (2009). Women's empowerment and the intention to continue the practice of female genital cutting in Egypt. *Archives of Iranian Medicine, 12,* 154–160.

Aggarwal, A. P. (1992). *Sexual harassment: A guide for understanding and prevention.* Toronto: Butterworths.

Agnew, T. (1997). *A multicultural perspective of breastfeeding in Canada.* Ottawa: Minister of Public Works and Government Services Canada.

Ahlborg, T., Rudeblad, K., Linnér, S., & Linton, S. J. (2008). Sensual and sexual marital contentment in parents of small children—A follow-up study when the first child is four years old. *Journal of Sex Research, 45,* 295–304.

Ahluwalia, I. B., Merritt, R., Beck, L. E., & Rogers, M. (2001). Multiple lifestyle and psychosocial risks and delivery of small for gestational age infants. *Obstetrics and Gynecology, 97,* 649–656.

Ahmadi, N. (2003). Rocking sexualities: Iranian migrants' views on sexuality. *Archives of Sexual Behavior, 32,* 317–326.

Ahrens, C. E., Dean, K., Rozee, P. D., & McKenzie, M. (2008). Understanding and preventing rape. In F. L. Denmark & M. Paludi (Eds.), *Psychology of women: A handbook of issues and theories* (pp. 509–554). Westport, CT: Praeger.

Ainsworth, C. (2005). The secret life of sperm. *Nature, 436,* 770–771.

Aksglaede, L., Sörensen, K., Petersen, J. H., Skakkebæk, N. E., & Juul, A. (2009). Recent decline in age at breast development: The Copenhagen Puberty Study. *Pediatrics, 123,* e932–e939.

Albanesi, H. P. (2010). *Gender and sexual agency: How young people make choices about sex.* Lanham, MD: Lexington Books.

Albright, J. M. (2008). Sex in America online: an exploration of sex, marital status, and sexual identity in Internet sexseeking and its impacts. *Journal of Sex Research, 45,* 175–186.

Alcid, S. & Miller, A. (2014). Environmental toxins threaten reproductive health and justice. Retrieved from https://www.nwhn.org/environmental-toxins-threaten-reproductive-health-and-justice/

Alderson, K. G. (2004). A phenomenological investigation of same-sex marriage. *Canadian Journal of Human Sexuality, 13,* 107–122.

Alexander, E. (1990). Sexual therapy in English-speaking Canada. *SIECCAN Journal, 5*(1), 37–43.

Alexander, K. W., Quas, J. A., Goodman, G. S., Ghetti, S., Edelstein, R. S., Redlich, A. D., . . . Jones, D. P. H. (2005). Traumatic impact predicts long-term memory for documented child sexual abuse. *Psychological Science, 16,* 33–40.

Alexander, M. G., & Fisher, T. D. (2003). Truth and consequences: Using the bogus pipeline to examine sex differences in self-reported sexuality. *Journal of Sex Research, 40,* 27–35.

Aliyu, M., Wilson, R., Zoorob, R., Chakrabarty, S., Alio, A. P., Kirby, R. S., & Salihu, H. M. (2008). Alcohol consumption during pregnancy and the risk of stillbirth among singletons. *Alcohol, 42,* 369–374.

Allen, D. M. (1980). Young male prostitutes: A psychological study. *Archives of Sexual Behavior, 9,* 399–426.

Allen, E. S., & Atkins, D. C. (2014). The association of divorce and extramarital sex in a representative U.S. sample. *Journal of Family Issues, 33,* 477–493.

Allen, K. R., & Goldberg, A. E. (2009). Sexual activity during menstruation: A qualitative study. *Journal of Sex Research, 46,* 535–545.

Allen, M., & Burrell, N. A. (2002). Sexual orientation of the parent: The impact on the child. In M. Allen, R. W. Preiss, B. M. Gayle, & N. A. Burrell (Eds.), *Interpersonal communication research: Advances through meta-analysis* (pp. 125–143). Mahwah, NJ: Erlbaum.

Allen, M., D'Alessio, D., Emmers, T., & Gebhardt, L. (1996). The role of educational briefings in mitigating effects of experimental exposure to violent sexually explicit material. *Journal of Sex Research, 33,* 135–141.

Allen, U. D., Robinson, J. L., & Canadian Paediatric Society, Infectious Diseases and Immunization Committee. (2014). Prevention and management of neonatal herpes simplex virus infections. *Paediatrics & Child Health, 19,* 201–206.

Allman, D. (1999). *M is for mutual A is for acts: Male sex work and AIDS in Canada.* Ottawa: Health Canada.

Almroth, L., Almroth-Berggren, V., & Hassanein, O. M. (2001). Male complications of female genital mutilation. *Social Science & Medicine, 53,* 1455–1460.

Al-Sahab, B., Ardern, C. I., Hamadeh, M. J., & Tamim, H. (2010). Age at menarche in Canada: Results from the National Longitudinal Survey of Children & Youth. *BMC Public Health, 10,* 736.

Al-Sahab, B., Saqib, M., Hauser, G., & Tamim, H. (2010). Prevalence of smoking during pregnancy and associated risk factors among Canadian women: A national survey. *BMC Pregnancy and Childbirth, 10,* 24.

Althof, S. E. (2007). Treatment of rapid ejaculation: Psychotherapy, pharmacotherapy, and combined therapy. In S. Leiblum (Ed.), *Principles and practice of sex therapy* (4th ed., pp. 212–240). New York: Guilford.

Althof, S. E., Abdo, C. H. N., Dean, J., Hackett, G., McCabe, M., McMahon, C. G., . . . Tan, H. M. (2010). International Society for Sexual Medicine's guidelines for the diagnosis and treatment of premature ejaculation. *Journal of Sexual Medicine, 7,* 2947–2969.

Althof, S. E., Leiblum, S. R., Chevret-Measson, M., Hartmann, U., Levine, S. B., McCabe, M., . . . Wylie, K. (2004). Psychological and interpersonal dimensions of sexual function and dysfunction. In T. F. Lue, R. Basson, R. Rosen, F. Giuliano, S. Khoury, & F. Montorsi (Eds.), *Sexual medicine: Sexual dysfunctions in men and women* (pp. 73–115). Paris: Editions 21.

Ambert, A. (2009). Divorce: Facts, causes, and consequences (3rd ed.). *Contemporary Family Trends.* Vanier Institute of the Family. Retrieved from http://www.vifamily.ca

American Academy of Pediatrics Committee on Genetics. (2000). Evaluation of the newborn with developmental anomalies of the external genitalia. *Pediatrics, 106,* 138–142.

American Academy of Pediatrics. (2010). Policy statement—sexuality, contraception, and the media. *Pediatrics, 126,* 576–582.

American Cancer Society. (2009). *Cancer facts and figures.* Atlanta: American Cancer Society.

American Cancer Society. (2012). Cancer facts and figures 2012. Retrieved from http://www.cancer.org

American Cancer Society. (2014). Breast cancer facts and figures 2013–2014. Retrieved from http://www.cancer.org/acs/groups/content/@research/documents/document/acspc-042725.pdf

American College Health Association. (2016). *National college health assessment II: Canadian reference group executive summary Spring 2016.* Hanover, MD: American College Health Association.

American Congress of Obstetricians and Gynecologists. (2007, September 1). ACOG advises against cosmetic vaginal procedures due to lack of safety and efficacy data. Retrieved from http://www.acog.org

American Psychiatric Association. (2000a). Position statement on therapies focused on attempts to change sexual orientation (reparative or conversion therapies). *American Journal of Psychiatry, 157,* 1719–1721.

American Psychiatric Association. (2000b). *Diagnostic and statistical manual of mental disorders* (4th ed.). Washington, DC: Author.

American Psychiatric Association. (2010). *The American Psychiatric Publishing Textbook of Psychiatry* (5th ed.). Arlington, VA: Author. Retrieved from http://www.psychiatryonline.com

American Psychiatric Association. (2013a). *Diagnostic and statistical manual of mental disorders* (5th ed.). Washington, DC: Author.

American Psychiatric Association. (2013b). Sexual dysfunctions. *Diagnostic and Statistical Manual of Mental Disorders* (5th ed., pp. 423–450.) Washington, DC: Author.

American Psychological Association, Task Force on the Sexualization of Girls. (2007). *Report of the APA Task Force on the Sexualization of Girls.* Washington, DC: Author. Retrieved from http://www.apa.org/pi/wpo/sexualization.html

American Psychological Association. (2008). *Answers to your questions: For a better understanding of sexual orientation and homosexuality.* Washington, DC: Author. Retrieved from http://www.apa.org/topics/sorientation.pdf

American Psychological Association. (2009). *Publication manual of the American Psychological Association* (6th ed.). Washington, DC: Author.

American Urological Association Practice Guidelines Committee. (2003). AUA guideline on management of benign prostatic hyperplasia (2003). Chapter 1: Diagnosis and treatment recommendations. *Journal of Urology, 170,* 530–547.

Ames, T.-R. (1991). Guidelines for providing sexuality-related services to severely and profoundly retarded individuals: The challenge for the 1990s. *Sexuality and Disability, 9,* 113–122.

Anderson, A. (2001). The perfect woman. *The Weekend Post.* Retrieved from http://www.nationaldream.ca/2001Feb10.pdf

Anderson, A. B., Rosen, N. O., Price, L., & Bergeron, S. (2016). Associations between penetration cognitions, genital pain, and sexual well-being in women with provoked vestibulodynia. *Journal of Sexual Medicine, 13,* 444–452.

Anderson, B., & Coletto, D. (2016a, July 9). Canadians' moral compass set differently from that of our neighbours to the south [News release]. Abacus Data. Retrieved from http://abacusdata.ca/canadians-moral-compass-set-differently-from-that-of-our-neighbours-to-the-south/

Anderson, B., & Coletto, D. (2016b, July 10). How big are Canadian differences on questions of morality? [News release]. Abacus Data. Retrieved from http://abacusdata.ca/how-big-are-canadian-regional-differences-on-questions-of-morality/

Anderson, K., Kaplan, H., & Lancaster, J. (2001). *Men's financial expenditures on genetic children and stepchildren from current and former relationships* (Report No. 01–484). Ann Arbor, MI: Population Studies Center.

Anderson, M. C., Ochsner, K. N., Kuhl, B., Cooper, J., Robertson, E., & Gabrieli, S. W. (2004). Neural systems underlying the suppression of unwanted memories. *Science, 303,* 232–235.

Anglican Bishops of Canada. (1997). Human sexuality: A statement by the Anglican bishops of Canada. Retrieved from http://www.anglican.ca/faith/identity/hob-statement.htm

Anglican Church of Canada. (1989). *Abortion in a new perspective: Report on the task force on abortion.* Toronto: Anglican Book Centre.

Angus Reid Global. (2014, June 10). *Gender split reveals deep divide between men, women on issues surrounding the sex trade.* Retrieved from http://angusreid.org/gender-split-reveals-deep-divide-between-men-women-on-issues-surrounding-the-sex-trade/

Angus Reid Institute. (2014, December 5). *Three-in-ten Canadians say they've been sexually harassed at work, but very few* have reported this to their employees. Retrieved from www.angus-reid.com/polls

Angus Reid Institute. (2015, March 26). *Religion and faith in Canada today: Strong belief, ambivalence and rejection define our views.* Retrieved from www.angusreid.org/faith-in-canada

Angus Reid Institute. (2016, January 13). *Canadians say our moral values are weakening four-to-one over those who say they're getting stronger.* Retrieved from http://angusreid.org/morality

Angus Reid Public Opinion. (2009a). Gender shapes views on debate over prostitution in Canada. Retrieved from http://www.visioncritical.com/category/global-opinions-and-trends

Angus Reid Public Opinion. (2009b). Household income levels define what is morally acceptable for Canadians. Retrieved from http://www.visioncritical.com/category/global-opinions-and-trends

Angus Reid Strategies. (2007, December 20). Canada open-minded on relationships and sexual behaviour, but not drugs. Retrieved from http://www.angusreidstrategies.com

Anonymous. (2012). Student to sex worker: My life as an escort. Retrieved from http://feminspire.com/student-to-sex-worker-my-life-as-an-escort

Anthony, S. (2012). Just how big are porn sites? Retrieved from http://www.extremetech.com/computing/123929

Anthony, S. (2014). Pornhub delivers: Apple users surf the most porn, while Chrome users are the quickest. ExtremeTech.com. Retrieved from http://www.extremetech.com/computing/183663-pornhub-delivers-apple-users-surf-the-most-porn-while-opera-users-are-the-quickest

Antoni, M. H., Lehman, J. M., Kilbourn, K. M., Boyers, A. E., Culver, J. L., Alferi, S. M., . . . Carver, C. S. (2001). Cognitive-behavioural stress management intervention decreases the prevalence of depression and enhances benefit finding among women under treatment for early-stage breast cancer. *Health Psychology, 20,* 20–32.

Aos, S., Miller, M., & Drake, E. (2006). *Evidence-based adult corrections programs: What works and what does not.* Olympia, WA: Washington State Institute for Public Policy.

Appleby, B. M. (1999). *Responsible parenthood: Decriminalizing contraception in Canada.* Toronto: University of Toronto Press.

Aquinas, St. Thomas. (1968). *Summa theologica* (Vol. 43). In T. Gilly (Trans.). New York: McGraw-Hill.

Araujo, A. B., Johannes, C. B., Feldman, H. A., Derby, C. A., & McKinlay, J. B. (2000). Relation between psychosocial risk factors and incident erectile dysfunction: Prospective results from the Massachusetts Male Aging Study. *American Journal of Epidemiology, 152,* 533–541.

Archer, J. (2004). Sex differences in aggression in real-world settings: A meta-analytic review. *Review of General Psychology, 8,* 291–322.

Archibald, S. A., Lemieux, S., Byers, E. S., Tamlyn, K., & Worth, J. (2006). Chemically-induced menopause and the sexual functioning of breast cancer survivors. *Women and Therapy, 29,* 83–106. doi:10.1300/J015v29n01_05

Armstrong, E. A., England, P., & Fogarty, A. C. K. (2012). Accounting for women's orgasm and sexual enjoyment in college hookups and relationships. *American Sociological Review, 77,* 435–462.

Armstrong, H. L., & Reissing, E. D. (2013). Women who have sex with women: a comprehensive review of the literature and conceptual model of sexual function. *Sexual and Relationship Therapy, 28,* 364–399.

Armstrong, H. L., & Reissing, E. D. (2014). Attitudes toward casual sex, dating, and committed relationships with bisexual partners. *Journal of Bisexuality, 14,* 236–264.

Armstrong, H. L., & Reissing, E. D. (2015). Women's motivations to have sex in casual and committed relationships with male and female partners. *The Archives of Sexual Behavior.* doi:10.1007/s10508-014-0462-4

Arnett, J. J., & Tanner, J. (2011). In defense of emerging adulthood as a life stage: Rejoinder to Kloep's and Hendry's Chapters 4 and 5. In J. J. Arnett (Ed.), *Debating emerging adulthood: Stage or process* (pp. 212–234). New York: Oxford University Press.

Arnold, A. P. (2003). The gender of the voice within: The neural origin of sex differences in the brain. *Current Opinion in Neurobiology, 13,* 759–764.

Arnow, B. A., Desmond, J. E., Banner, L. L., Glover, G. H., Solomon, A., Polan, M. L., . . . Atlas, S. W. (2002). Brain activation and sexual arousal in healthy, heterosexual males. *Brain, 125,* 1014–1023.

Ashby, S. L., Arcari, C. M., & Edmonson, M. B. (2006). Television viewing and risk of sexual initiation by young adolescents. *Archives of Pediatric & Adolescent Medicine, 160,* 375–380.

Ashton, A. K. (2007). The new sexual pharmacology: A guide for the clinician. In S. Leiblum (Ed.), *Principles and practice of sex therapy* (4th ed., pp. 509–542). New York: Guilford Press.

Assalian, P., & Ravart, M. (2003). Management of professional sexual misconduct: Evaluation and recommendations. *Journal of Sexual & Reproductive Medicine, 3,* 89–92.

Assisted Human Reproduction Canada. (2011). Risks associated with AHR. Retrieved from http://www.ahrc-pac.gc.ca

Association of Iroquois and Allied Indians. (1997). *First Nations HIV/TB training Kit.* Ottawa: Medical Services Branch-Health Canada.

Aubrey, J. S. (2004). Sex and punishment: An examination of sexual consequences and the sexual double standard in teen programming. *Sex Roles, 50,* 505–514.

Aucoin, M. W., & Wasserug, R. J. (2006). The sexuality and social performance of androgen-deprived (castrated) men throughout history: Implications for modern day cancer patients. *Social Science & Medicine, 63,* 3162–3173.

Auld, B. R., & Brock, G. (2002). Sexuality and erectile dysfunction: Results of a national survey. *Journal of Sexual & Reproductive Medicine, 2,* 50–54.

Autry, A. M., Hayes, E. C., Jacobson, G. F., & Kirby, R. S. (2002). A comparison of medical induction and dilation and evacuation for second trimester abortion. *American Journal of Obstetrics and Gynecology, 187,* 393–397.

Avis, N. E., & McKinlay, S. M. (1995, March–April). The Massachusetts Women's Health Study: An epidemiological investigation of the menopause. *Journal of the American Medical Women's Association, 50,* 45–63.

Aylor, B. A. (2003). Maintaining long-distance relationships. In D. J. Canary & M. Dainton (Eds.), *Maintaining relationships through communication: Relational, contextual, and cultural variations* (pp. 127–139). Mahwah, NJ: Lawrence Erlbaum Associates.

Aylwin, A. S., Reddon, J. R., & Burke, A. R. (2005). Sexual fantasies of adolescent male sex offenders in residential treatment: A descriptive study. *Archives of Sexual Behavior, 34,* 231–239.

Babchishin, K. M., Nunes, K. L., & Hermann, C. A. (2013). The validity of Implicit Association Test (IAT) measures of sexual attraction to children: A meta-analysis. *Archives of Sexual Behavior, 42,* 487–499.

Bach, G., & Wyden, P. (1969). *The intimate enemy: How to fight fair in love and marriage.* New York: Morrow.

Bachmann, G. A., & Leiblum, S. R. (1991). Sexuality in sexagenarian women. *Maturitas, 13,* 43–50.

Backstrom, L., Armstrong, E. A., & Puentes, J. (2012). Women's negotiation of cunnilingus in college hookups and relationships. *Journal of Sex Research, 49,* 1–12.

Badeau, D., & Bergeron, A. (1997). *Bien vieillir. En santé sexuelle. Pour une approche globale des adultes agés.* Montreal: Meridien.

Badgley, R. (1984). *Sexual offences against children: Report of the Committee on Sexual Offences Against Children and Youths.* Ottawa: Canadian Government Publishing.

Baer, J. L., Kohut, T., & Fisher, W. A. (2015). Is pornography use associated with anti-woman sexual aggression? Re-examining the confluence model with third variable considerations. *Canadian Journal of Human Sexuality, 24,* 160–173.

Bagemihl, B. (1999). *Biological exuberance: Animal homosexuality and natural diversity.* New York: St. Martin's Press.

Bailey, J. M., & Pillard, R. C. (1991). A genetic study of male sexual orientation. *Archives of General Psychiatry, 48,* 1089–1096.

Bailey, J. M., Pillard, R. C., Neale, M. C., & Agyei, Y. (1993). Heritable factors influence sexual orientation in women. *Archives of General Psychiatry, 50,* 217–223.

Bailey, J. M., Willerman, L., & Parks, C. (1991). A test of the maternal stress theory of human male homosexuality. *Archives of Sexual Behavior, 20,* 277–294.

Bailey, J., Kim, P. Y., Hills, A., & Linsenmeier, J. W. (1997). Butch, femme, or straight acting? Partner preferences of gay men and lesbians. *Journal of Personality and Social Psychology, 73,* 960–973.

Bailey, R. C., Moses, S., Parker, C. B., Agot, K., Maclean, I., Krieger, J. N., . . . Ndinya-Achola, J. O. (2007). Male circumcision for HIV prevention in young men in Kisumu, Kenya: A randomised controlled trial. *Lancet, 369,* 643–656.

Bain, J. (2007). The many faces of testosterone. *Clinical Interventions in Aging, 2*(4), 1–10.

Bain, J. (2010). Testosterone and the aging male: To treat or not to treat? *Maturitas, 66,* 16–22.

Baird, T. L., & Flinn, S. K. (2001). *Manual vacuum aspiration: Expanding women's access to safe abortion.* Chapel Hill, NC: Ipas.

Baker, F. C., Driver, H. S., Paiker, J., Rogers, G. G., & Mitchell, D. (2002). Acetaminophen does not affect 24-h body temperature or sleep in the luteal phase of the menstrual cycle. *Journal of Applied Physiology, 92,* 1684–1691.

Baker, M. (2008). Embryonic-like stem cells from a single human hair. *Nature Reports Stem Cells.* doi:10.1038/stemcells.2008.142

Baladerian, N. J. (1991). Sexual abuse of people with developmental disabilities. *Sexuality and Disability, 9,* 323–335.

Baldwin, J. D., & Baldwin, J. I. (1989). The socialization of homosexuality and heterosexuality in a non-Western society. *Archives of Sexual Behavior, 18,* 13–30.

Baldwin, J. D., & Baldwin, J. I. (1997). Gender differences in sexual interest. *Archives of Sexual Behavior, 26,* 181–210.

Baldwin, S. B., Wallace, D. R., Papenfuss, M. R., Abrahamsen, M., Vaught, L. C., & Giuliano A. R. (2004). Condom use and other factors affecting penile human papillomavirus detection in men attending a sexually transmitted disease clinic. *Sexually Transmitted Diseases, 31,* 601–607.

Balsam, K. F. (2004, August). *Identity, community, and outness: Comparing bisexual and lesbian/gay adults.* Paper presented at the 111th Annual Convention of the American Psychological Association, Toronto.

Balsam, K. F., Lehavot, K., & Beadnell, B. (2011). Sexual revictimization and mental health: a comparison of lesbians, gay men, and heterosexual women. *Journal of Interpersonal Violence, 26,* 1798–1814.

Balsam, K. F., Rothblum, E. D., & Beauchaine, T. P. (2005). Victimization over the life span: a comparison of lesbian, gay, bisexual, and heterosexual siblings. *Journal of Consulting and Clinical Psychology, 73,* 477–487.

Bancroft, J. (1978). The prevention of sexual offenses. In C. B. Qualls, J. P. Wincze, & D. H. Barlow (Eds.), *The prevention of sexual disorders* (pp. 95–116). New York: Plenum.

Bancroft, J. (2004). Alfred C. Kinsey and the politics of sex research. *Annual Review of Sex Research, 15,* 1–39.

Bancroft, J. (2010). Sexual desire and the brain revisited. *Sexual and Relationship Therapy, 25*(2), 166–171.

Bancroft, J., & Vikadinovic, Z. (2004). Sexual addiction, sexual compulsivity, sexual impulsivity, or what? Toward a theoretical model. *Journal of Sex Research, 41,* 225–234.

Bancroft, J., Graham, C., Janssen, E., & Sanders, S. A. (2009). The dual control model: Current status and future directions. *Journal of Sex Research, 46,* 121–142.

Bancroft, J., Herbenick, D., & Reynolds, M. (2003). Masturbation as a marker of sexual development. In J. Bancroft (Ed.), *Sexual development in childhood.* Bloomington, IN: Indiana University Press.

Bandura, A. (1982). Self-efficacy mechanism in human agency. *American Psychologist, 37,* 122–147.

Bandura, A. J. (1977). *Social learning theory.* Englewood Cliffs, NJ: Prentice-Hall.

Bandura, A., & Walters, R. H. (1963). *Social learning and personality development.* New York: Holt.

Bang, A. K., Carlsen, E., Holm, M., Petersen, J. H., Skakkebæk, N. E., & Jørgensen, N. (2005). A study of finger lengths, semen quality and sex hormones in 360 young men from the general Danish population. *Human Reproduction, 20,* 3109–3113.

Banks, D., & Kyckelhahn, T. (2011). *Characteristics of suspected human trafficking incidents, 2008–2010.* Washington, DC: U.S. Department of Justice, Bureau of Justice Statistics, NCJ 233732.

Barak, A., & Fisher, W. A. (2001). Toward an Internet-driven, theoretically based, innovative approach to sex education. *Journal of Sex Research, 38,* 324–332.

Baram, M. (2007). Free porn threatens adult film industry. *ABC News.* Retrieved from http://abcnews.com

Barash, D. P. (1982). *Sociobiology and behavior* (2nd ed.). New York: Elsevier.

Barbaree, H. E., & Seto, M. C. (1997). Pedophilia: Assessment and treatment. In D. R. Laws & W. O'Donohue (Eds.), *Sexual deviance: Theory, assessment, and treatment* (pp. 175–193). New York: Guilford Press.

Barlow, D. H. (1986). Causes of sexual dysfunction: The role of cognitive interference. *Journal of Consulting and Clinical Psychology, 54,* 140–148.

Barlow, D. H., Leitenberg, H., & Agras, W. S. (1969). Experimental control of sexual deviation through manipulation of noxious scenes in covert sensitization. *Journal of Abnormal Psychology, 74,* 596–601.

Baron, L., & Straus, M. A. (1989). *Four theories of rape in American society.* New Haven, CT: Yale University Press.

Barr, H. M., Streissguth, A. P., Darby, B. L., & Sampson, P. D. (1990). Prenatal exposure to alcohol, caffeine, tobacco and aspirin: Effects on fine and gross motor performance in 4-year-old children. *Developmental Psychology, 26,* 339–348.

Barrett, J. R. (2006). Fertile grounds of inquiry: Environmental effects on human reproduction. *Environmental Health Perspectives, 114,* A644–A649.

Barrett, M. (1990). Selected observations of sex education in Canada. *SIECCAN Journal, 5*(1), 21–30.

Barrett, M. (1994). Sexuality education in Canadian schools: An overview in 1994. *Canadian Journal of Human Sexuality, 3,* 199–225.

Barrett, M., King, A., Levy, J., Maticka-Tyndale, E., & McKay, A. (1997). *The international encyclopdia of sexuality* (Vol. 1, pp. 221–343). New York: Continuum Publishing.

Barrett, M., McKay, A., Dickson, C., Seto, J., Fisher, W., Read, R., . . . Wong, T. (2012). Sexual health curriculum and training in Canadian medical schools: A study of family medicine, obstetrics and gynaecology and undergraduate medicine programs in 2011 with comparisons to 1996. *Canadian Journal of Human Sexuality, 21,* 63–73.

Bartels, A., & Zeki, S. (2004). The neural correlates of maternal and romantic love. *Neuroimage, 21,* 1155–1166.

Bartholomew, K., & Horowitz, L. M. (1991). Attachment styles among young adults: A test of a 4-category model. *Journal of Personality and Social Psychology, 61,* 226–244.

Bartlett, N. B., & Vasey, P. L. (2006). A retrospective study of childhood gender-atypical behavior in Samoan *fa'afafine. Archives of Sexual Behavior, 35,* 559–566.

Bartlett, N. H., Vasey, P. L., & Bukowski, W. M. (2000). Is gender identity disorder in children a mental disorder? *Sex Roles, 43,* 753–785.

Bartos, S., Berger, I., & Hegarty, P. (2014). Interventions to reduce sexual prejudice: A study-space analysis and meta-analytic review. *Journal of Sex Research, 51,* 363–382.

Basaria, S., & Dobs, A. (2006). Controversies regarding transdermal androgen therapy in postmenopausal women. *Journal of Clinical Endocrinology and Metabolism, 91,* 4743–4752.

Basson, R. (2001a). Human sex-response cycles. *Journal of Sex & Marital Therapy, 27,* 33–43.

Basson, R. (2001b). Using a different model for female sexual response to address women's problematic low sexual desire. *Journal of Sex & Marital Therapy, 27,* 395–403.

Basson, R. (2004). Summary of the recommendations on women's sexual dysfunctions. In T. F. Lue, R. Basson, R. Rosen, F. Giuliano, S. Khoury, & F. Montorsi (Eds.), *Sexual medicine: Sexual dysfunctions in men and women* (pp. 975–990). Paris: Editions 21.

Basson, R. (2005). Women's sexual dysfunction: Revised and expanded definitions. *Canadian Medical Association Journal, 172,* 1327–1333.

Basson, R. (2006). Sexual desire and arousal disorders in women. *New England Journal of Medicine, 354*, 1497–1506.

Basson, R. (2007). Sexual desire/arousal disorders in women. In S. Leiblum (Ed.), *Principles and practice of sex therapy* (4th ed., pp. 25–53). New York: Guilford.

Basson, R., & Brotto, L. A. (2003). Sexual psychophysiology and effects of sildenafil citrate in oestrogenised women with acquired genital arousal disorder and impaired orgasm: A randomised controlled trial. *BJOG: International Journal of Obstetrics and Gynaecology, 110*, 1014–1024.

Basson, R., & VHHSC Centre for Sexuality, Gender Identity, & Reproductive Health. (1998). Integrating new biomedical treatments into the assessment and management of erectile dysfunction. *Canadian Journal of Human Sexuality, 7*, 213–229.

Basson, R., Berman, J., Burnett, A., Derogatis, L., Ferguson, D., Fourcroy, J., . . . Whipple, B. (2001). Report of the International Consensus Development Conference on female sexual dysfunction: Definitions and classifications. *Journal of Sex & Marital Therapy, 27*, 83–94.

Basson, R., Brotto, L. A., Petkau, A. J., & Labrie, F. (2010). Role of androgens in women's sexual dysfunction. *Menopause, 17*, 1–10.

Basson, R., McInnes, R., Smith, M., Hodgson, G., & Koppiker, N. (2002). Efficacy and safety of sildenafil citrate in women with sexual dysfunction associated with female sexual arousal disorder. *Journal of Women's Health & Gender-Based Medicine, 11*, 367–377.

Bauer, G. R., Scheim, A. I., for the Trans PULSE Project Team. (2015). *Transgender People in Ontario, Canada: Statistics to Inform Human Rights Policy*. London, ON.

Bauer, G. R., Scheim, A. I., Pyne, J., Travers, R., & Hammond, R. (2015). Intervenable factors associated with suicide risk in transgender persons: a respondent driven sampling study in Ontario, Canada. *BMC Public Health, 15*, 525–539.

Baulieu, E. E., Thomas, G., Legrain, S., Lahlou, N., Roger, M., Debuire, B., . . . Forette, F. (2000). Dehydroepiandrosterone (DHEA), DHEA sulfate, and aging: Contributions of the DHEAge study to a sociobiomedical issue. *Proceedings of the National Academy of Sciences, 97*, 4279–4284.

Baumeister, R. F. (1988a). Masochism as escape from the self. *Journal of Sex Research, 25*, 28–59.

Baumeister, R. F. (1988b). Gender differences in masochistic scripts. *Journal of Sex Research, 25*, 478–499.

Baumeister, R. F., Catanese, K., & Vohs, K. (2001). Is there a gender difference in strength of sex drive? Theoretical views, conceptual distinctions, and a review of relevant evidence. *Personality and Social Psychology Review, 5*, 242–273.

Baxter, J., Brabazon, C., Gunter, K., & Willms, D. (1993a). *Many voices: HIV/AIDS in the context of culture: Report for the communities from the Horn of Africa. Ethnocultural communities facing AIDS: A national study.* Ottawa: National Health Research and Development Program (Health Canada)/AIDS Education and Prevention Unit (National AIDS Strategy) Health Canada.

Baxter, J., Brabazon, C., Gunter, K., & Willms, D. (1993b). *Many voices: HIV/AIDS in the context of culture: Report for the English-speaking Caribbean communities. Ethnocultural communities facing AIDS: A national study.* Ottawa: National Health Research and Development Program (Health Canada)/AIDS Education and Prevention Unit National AIDS Strategy) Health Canada.

Bazelon, E. (2007, January 21). Is there a post-abortion syndrome? *New York Times Magazine.*

Beach, F. A. (Ed.). (1976). *Human sexuality in four perspectives.* Baltimore, MD: Johns Hopkins University Press.

Beall, A., & Sternberg, R. (1995). The social construction of love. *Journal of Social and Personal Relationships, 12*, 417–438.

Beattie S., & Cotter, A. (2010). Homicide in Canada, 2009. *Juristat, 30*(3). Retrieved from http://www.statcan.gc.ca/pub/85-002-x/2010003/article/11352-eng.pdf

Beauchamp, D. L. (2008). Canadian Centre for Justice Statistics profile series: Sexual orientation and victimization 2004. Retrieved from http://www.mtroyal.ca/cs/groups/public/documents/pdf/psc_orientation_victimisation.pdf

Beaulieu, M. (1994). Screening for D (Rh) sensitization in pregnancy. *The Canadian guide to clinical preventive health care.* Ottawa: Public Health Agency of Canada.

Beaupré, P. (2008). I do. Take two? Changes in intentions to remarry among divorced Canadians during the past 20 years. *Matter of Fact, 5*, 1–3.

Beier, E. G., & Sternberg, D. P. (1977). Marital communication. *Journal of Communication, 27*, 92–103.

Bell, S., Reissing, E. D., Henry, L. A., & Van-Zuylen, H. (2016). Sexual activity after 60: A systematic review of associated factors. *Sexual Medicine Reviews*, 1–29.

Belzer, E. G. (1981). Orgasmic expulsions of women: A review and heuristic inquiry. *Journal of Sex Research, 17*, 1–12.

Bem, D. J. (1996). Exotic becomes erotic: A developmental theory of sexual orientation. *Psychological Review, 103*, 320–335.

Bem, D. J. (1998). Is EBE theory supported by the evidence? Is it androcentric? A reply to Peplau et al. (1998). *Psychological Review, 105*, 395–398.

Bem, S. L. (1981). Gender schema theory: A cognitive account of sex typing. *Psychological Review, 88*, 354–364.

Bem, S. L. (1989). Genital knowledge and gender consistency in preschool children. *Child Development, 60*, 649–662.

Bem, S. L. (1993). *The lenses of gender: Transforming the debate on sexual inequality.* New Haven, CT: Yale University Press.

Bennett, S., & Assefi, N. (2005). School-based teenage pregnancy prevention programs: A systematic review of randomized controlled trials. *Journal of Adolescent Health, 36*, 72–81.

Bennice, J. A., & Resick, P. (2003). Marital rape: History, research, and practice. *Trauma, Violence, & Abuse, 4*, 228–246.

Benoit, C., & Millar, A. (2001). *Dispelling myths/understanding realities: Working conditions, health status and exiting experiences of sex workers.* Report prepared for the Prostitutes Empowerment and Resource Society. Vancouver, BC: British Columbia Health Research Foundation.

Benoit, C., Jannson, M., Millar, A., & Phillips, R. (2005). Community-academic research on hard-to-reach populations: Benefits and challenges. *Qualitative Health Research, 15*, 263–282.

Bentz, E., Hefler, L., Kaufmann, U., Huber, J., Kolbus, A., & Tempfer, C. (2008). A polymorphism of the CYP17 gene related to sex steroid metabolism is associated female-to-male but not male-to-female transsexualism. *Fertility and Sterility, 90*, 56–59.

Ben-Ze'ev, A. (2004). *Love online: Emotions on the Internet.* Cambridge, UK: Cambridge University Press.

Berenbaum, S. A. (2006). Psychological outcome in children with disorders of sex development: Implications for understanding typical development. *Annual Review of Sex Research, 17*, 1–38.

Beres, M. A., Herold, E., & Maitland, S. B. (2004). Sexual consent behaviours in same-sex relationships. *Archives of Sexual Behavior, 33*, 475–486.

Beres, M. A., Senn, C. Y., & McCaw, J. (2013). Navigating ambivalence: How heterosexual young adults make sense of desire differences. *Journal of Sex Research, 0*, 1–12.

Berg, B. L. (2007). *Qualitative research methods for the social sciences.* Boston: Allyn and Bacon.

Berg, J. H., & Derlega, V. J. (1987). Themes in the study of self-disclosure. In V. J. Derlega & J. H. Berg (Eds.), *Self-disclosure: Theory, research and therapy* (pp. 1–8). New York: Plenum.

Bergdall, A. R., Kraft, J. M., Andes, K., Carter, M., Hatfield-Timajchy, K., & Hock-Long, L. (2012). Love and hooking up in the new millennium: Communication technology and relationships among urban African American and Puerto Rican young adults. *Journal of Sex Research, 49*, 570–582.

Bergen, D. J., & Williams, J. E. (1991). Sex stereotypes in the United States revisited: 1972–1988. *Sex Roles, 24*, 413–423.

Bergeron, S., Binik, Y. M., Khalifé, S., Pagidas, K., Glazer, H. I., Meana, M., & Amsel, R. (2001). A randomized comparison of group cognitive-behavioral therapy, surface electromyographic biofeedback, and vestibulectomy in the treatment of dyspareunia resulting from vulvar vestibulitis. *Pain, 91*, 297–306.

Bergeron, S., Morin, M., & Lord, M. (2010). Integrating pelvic floor rehabilitation and cognitive-behavioural therapy for sexual pain: What have we learned and where do we go from here? *Sexual and Relationship Therapy, 25,* 289–298.

Berglund, H., Lindström, P., & Savic, I. (2006). Brain response to putative pheromones in lesbian women. *Proceedings of the National Academy of Sciences, 103,* 8269–8274.

Bergman, K. M., Sarkar, P., O'Connor, T. G., Modi, N., & Glover, V. (2007). Prenatal stressful life events predict child cognitive outcomes. *Early Human Development, 83,* 136.

Bergstrand, C., & Williams, J. B. (2000, October 10). Today's alternative marriage styles: The case of swingers. *Electronic Journal of Human Sexuality, 3.* Retrieved from http://www.ejhs.org

Berkman, C., & Zinberg, G. (1997). Homophobia and heterosexism in social workers. *Journal of the National Association of Social Workers, 42,* 319–332.

Berman, J. R., Adhikari, S. P., & Goldstein, I. (2000). Anatomy and physiology of female sexual function and dysfunction. *European Urology, 38,* 20–29.

Berman, L., Berman, J., Miles, M., Pollets, D., & Powell, J. A. (2003). Genital self-image as a component of sexual health: Relationship between genital self-image, female sexual function, and quality of life measures. *Journal of Sex & Marital Therapy, 29,* 11–21.

Bermant, G., & Davidson, J. M. (1974). *Biological bases of sexual behavior.* New York: Harper & Row.

Bernstein, A. C., & Cowan, P. A. (1975). Children's concepts of how people get babies. *Child Development, 46,* 77–92.

Bernstein, E. (2007). *Temporarily yours: Intimacy, authenticity, and the commerce of sex.* Chicago: University of Chicago Press.

Bersamin, M. M., Paschall, M. J., Saltz, R. F., & Zamboanga, B. L. (2012). Young adults and casual sex: The relevance of college drinking settings. *Journal of Sex Research, 49,* 274–281.

Berscheid, E., & Hatfield, E. (1978). *Interpersonal attraction* (2nd ed.). Reading, MA: Addison-Wesley.

Berscheid, E., & Walster, E. (1974). A little bit about love. In T. L. Huston (Ed.), *Foundations of interpersonal attraction.* New York: Academic.

Berthelot, N., Godbout, N., Hébert, M., Goulet, M., & Bergeron, S. (2014). Prevalence and correlates of childhood sexual abuse in adults consulting for sexual problems. *Journal of Sex & Marital Therapy, 40,* 434–443.

Best, D. L. (2001). Gender concepts: Convergence in cross-cultural research and methodologies. *Cross-Cultural Research, 35,* 23–43.

Bettocchi, C., Verze, P., Palumbo, F., Arcaniolo, D., & Mirone, V. (2008). Ejaculatory disorders: Pathophysiology and management. *Nature Clinical Practice Urology, 5,* 93–103.

Betzer, F., Kohler, S., & Schlemm, L. (2015). Sex work among students of higher education: A survey-based, cross-sectional study. *Archives of Sexual Behavior, 44,* 525–528.

Bhattacharya, S., Townend, J., Shetty, A., Campbell, D., & Bhattacharya, S. (2008). Does miscarriage in initial pregnancy lead to adverse obstetric and perinatal outcomes in the next continuing pregnancy? *BJOG, 115,* 1623–1629.

Bibby, R. (1987). *Fragmented gods: The poverty and potential of religion in Canada.* Toronto: Irwin.

Bibby, R. (1993). *Unknown gods: The ongoing story of religion in Canada.* Toronto: Stoddart.

Bibby, R. W. (1995). *The Bibby report: Social trends Canadian style.* Toronto: Stoddart.

Bibby, R. W. (2001). *Canada's teens: Today, yesterday, and tomorrow.* Toronto: Stoddart.

Bibby, R. W. (2002). Homosexuality in Canada: A national reading. Retrieved from http://www.reginaldbibby.com/images/PCReleaseHomosexualityMay02.pdf

Bibby, R. W. (2004). *The future families project.* Vanier Institute of the Family. Retrieved from http://www.vifamily.ca

Bibby, R. W. (2006). *The boomer factor: What Canada's most famous generation is leaving behind.* Toronto: Bastian Books.

Bibby, R. W., Russell, S., & Rolheiser, R. (2009). *The emerging millennials: How Canada's newest generation is responding to change & choice.* Lethbridge, AB: Project Canada Books.

Biggs, M. L., & Schwartz, S. M. (2007). Cancer of the testis. In L. A. G. Ries, J. L. Young, G. E. Keel, M. P. Eisner, Y. D. Lin, & M.-J. D. Horner (Eds.), *SEER survival monograph: cancer survival among adults: U.S. SEER program, 1988–2001, patient and tumor characteristics* (Chapter 21, NIH publication no. 07-6215). Bethesda, MD: National Cancer Institute, SEER Program.

Billings, A. (1979). Conflict resolution in distressed and non-distressed married couples. *Journal of Consulting and Clinical Psychology, 47,* 368–376.

Binik, Y. M. (2005). Should dyspareunia be retained as a sexual dysfunction in *DSM-V*? A painful classification decision. *Archives of Sexual Behavior, 34,* 11–21.

Binik, Y. M., Bergeron, S., & Khalifé, S. (2007). Dyspareunia and vaginismus: So-called sexual pain. In S. Leiblum (Ed.), *Principles and practice of sex therapy* (4th ed., pp. 124–156). New York: Guilford.

Bird, S. E. (1999). Gendered construction of the American Indian in popular media. *Journal of Communication, 49,* 61–83. doi:10.1111/j.1460-2466.1999.tb02805.x

Birnie, C., McClure, M. J., Lydon, J. E., & Holmberg, D. (2009). Attachment avoidance and commitment aversion: A script for relationship failure. *Personal Relationships, 16,* 79–97.

Bissell, M. (2000). Socio-economic outcomes of teen pregnancy and parenthood: A review of the literature. *Canadian Journal of Human Sexuality, 9,* 191–204.

Bivona, J., & Critelli, J. (2009). The nature of women's rape fantasies: An analysis of prevalence, frequency and contents. *Journal of Sex Research, 46,* 33–45.

Bixler, R. H. (1986). Of apes and men (including females). *Journal of Sex Research, 22,* 255–267.

Black, A., Bucio, A., Butt, C., Crangle, M., & Lalonde, A. (2009). *Improving sexual and reproductive health: Integrating women's empowerment and reproductive rights* (2nd ed.). Retrieved from http://iwhp.sogc.org/uploads/File/ISRH_booklet_web.pdf

Black, A., Yang, Q., Wu Wen, S., Lalonde, A. B., Guilbert, E., & Fisher, W. (2009). Contraceptive use among Canadian women of reproductive age: Results of a national survey. *Journal of Obstetrics and Gynaecology Canada, 31,* 627–640.

Black, M. C., et al. (2011). The National Intimate Partner and Sexual Violence Survey (NISVS): 2010 Summary Report. Atlanta: Centers for Disease Control and Prevention. Retrieved from http://www.cdc.gov/violenceprevention

Blackless, M., et al. (2000). How sexually dimorphic are we? Review and synthesis. *American Journal of Human Biology, 12,* 151–166.

Blair, C. D., & Lanyon, R. I. (1981). Exhibitionism: Etiology and treatment. *Psychological Bulletin, 89,* 439–463.

Blair, K. L. (2016). Ethical research with sexual and gender minorities. In A. E. Goldberg (Ed.), *The SAGE encyclopedia of LGBTQ studies* (pp. 375–380). Thousand Oaks, CA: Sage.

Blair, K. L., & Pukall, C. F. (2014). Can less be more? Comparing duration vs. frequency of sexual encounters in same-sex and mixed-sex relationships. *Canadian Journal of Human Sexuality, 23,* 123–136.

Blais, M., Gervais, J., & Hébert, M. (2014). Internalized homophobia as a partial mediator between homophobic bullying and self-esteem among youths of sexual minorities in Quebec (Canada). *Ciência & Saúde Coletiva, 19,* 727–735.

Blais, M., Gervais, J., Boucher, K., Hébert, M., Lavoie, F., & l'équipe de recherché PAJ. (2013). Prevalence of prejudice based on sexual minority status among 14- to 22-year-old youths in the province of Quebec (Canada). *International Journal of Victimology, 11*(2), December.

Blake, J. (2004). *Words can work: When talking with kids about sexual health.* Gloucester, MA: Blake Works, Inc.

Blake, S., Ledsky, R., Goodenow, C., Sawyer, R., Lohrmann, D., & Windsor, R. (2003). Condom availability programs in Massachusetts high schools: Relationships with condom use and sexual behavior. *American Journal of Public Health, 93,* 955–962.

Blakemore, J., Berenbaum, S., & Liben, L. S. (2009). *Gender development.* New York: Psychology Press.

Blanchard, R. (1997). Birth order and sibling sex ratio in homosexual versus heterosexual males and females. *Annual Review of Sex Research, 8,* 27–67.

Blanchard, R. (2004). Quantitative and theoretical analyses of the relation between older brothers and homosexuality in men. *Journal of Theoretical Biology, 230,* 173–187.

Blanchard, R., & Bogaert, A. F. (2004). Proportion of homosexual men who owe their sexual orientation to fraternal birth order: An estimate based on two national probability samples. *American Journal of Human Biology, 16,* 151–157.

Blanchard, R., Christensen, B. K., Strong, S. M., Cantor, J. M., Kuban, M. E., Klassen, P., . . . Blak, T. (2002). Retrospective self-reports of childhood accidents causing unconsciousness in phallometrically diagnosed pedophiles. *Archives of Sexual Behavior, 31,* 511–526.

Blanchard, R., Dickey, R., & Jones, C. (1995). Comparison of height and weight in homosexual versus nonhomosexual gender dysphorics. *Archives of Sexual Behavior, 24,* 543–554.

Blanchard, R., Kolla, N. J., Cantor, J. M., Klassen, P. E., Dickey, R., Kuban, M. E., & Blak, T. (2007). IQ, handedness, and pedophilia in adult male patients stratified by referral source. *Sexual Abuse: A Journal of Research and Treatment, 19,* 285–309.

Blanchard, R., Steiner, B. W., & Clemmenson, L. H. (1985). Gender dysphoria, gender reorientation and the clinical management of transsexualism. *Journal of Consulting & Clinical Psychology, 53,* 295–304.

Blanchard, R., Watson, M. S., Choy, A., Dickey, R., Klassen, P., Kuban, M., & Ferran, D. J. (1999). Pedophiles: Mental retardation, maternal age, and sexual orientation. *Archives of Sexual Behavior, 28,* 111–127.

Blanchard, V., et al. (2009). Investigating the effects of marriage and relationship education on couples' communication skills: A meta-analytic study. *Journal of Family Psychology, 23,* 203–214.

Blanchard-Dallaire, D., & Hébert, M. (2014a). Le rôle des attributions et des enjeux sociaux des enfants victimes d'agression sexuelle dans la prediction des troubles intériorisés et extériorises. *Revue de psychoéducation, 43,* 251–271.

Blanchard-Dallaire, D., & Hébert, M. (2014b). Social relationships in sexually abused children: Self-reports and teachers' evaluation. *Journal of Child Sexual Abuse, 23,* 326–344.

Bleakley, A., Hennessy, M., & Fishbein, M. (2011). A model of adolescents' seeking of sexual content in their media choices. *Journal of Sex Research, 48,* 309–315.

Bleakley, A., Hennessy, M., Fishbein, M., & Jordan, A. (2008). It works both ways: The relationship between exposure to sexual content in the media and adolescent sexual behavior. *Media Psychology, 11,* 443–461.

Blumberg, E. (2003). The lives and voices of highly sexual women. *Journal of Sex Research, 40,* 146–157.

Blumstein, P. W., & Schwartz, P. (1983). *American couples.* New York: Morrow.

Boag, S. (2007). "Real processes" and the explanatory status of repression and inhibition. *Philosophical Psychology, 20,* 375–392.

Bockting, W. O. (1999, October/November). From construction to context: Gender through the eyes of the transgendered. *SIECUS Report,* 3–7.

Bockting, W. O. (2004). Plastic and reconstructive surgery for transgender and transsexual patients. In D. B. Sarwer et al. (Eds.), *Psychological aspects of plastic surgery.* Philadelphia: Lippincott Williams & Wilkins.

Bodner, L. M., Markovic, N., Harger, G., & Roberts, J. M. (2004). Prepregnancy body mass index and the risk of preeclampsia. *Federation of American Societies for Experimental Biology Journal, 18*(5), A928.

Bogaert, A. F. (1993). *The sexual media: The role of individual differences.* Unpublished doctoral dissertation. University of Western Ontario, London, Ontario.

Bogaert, A. F. (1996). Volunteer bias in human sexuality research: Evidence for both sexuality and personality differences in males. *Archives of Sexual Behavior, 25,* 125–140.

Bogaert, A. F. (2001). Personality, individual differences, and preferences for the sexual media. *Archives of Sexual Behavior, 30,* 29–53.

Bogaert, A. F. (2003). Number of older brothers and sexual orientation: New tests and the attraction/behaviour distinction in two national probability samples. *Journal of Personality and Social Psychology, 84,* 644–652.

Bogaert, A. F. (2004). Asexuality: Prevalence and associated factors in a national probability sample. *Journal of Sex Research, 41,* 279–287.

Bogaert, A. F. (2005). Age at puberty and father absence in a national probability sample. *Journal of Adolescence, 28,* 541–546.

Bogaert, A. F. (2015). Asexuality: What it is and why it matters. *Journal of Sex Research, 52,* 362–379.

Bogaert, A. F., & Sadava, S. (2002). Adult attachment and sexual behavior. *Personal Relationships, 9,* 191–204.

Bogaert, A. F., & Skorska, M. (2011). Sexual orientation, fraternal birth order, and the maternal immune hypothesis: A review. *Frontiers in Neuroendocrinology, 32,* 247–254.

Bogaert, A. F., Visser, B. A., & Pozzebon, J. A. (2015). Gender differences in object of desire self-consciousness sexual fantasies. *Archives of Sexual Behavior, 44,* 2299–2310.

Bogaert, A. F., Woodard, U., & Hafer, C. L. (1999). Intellectual ability and reactions to pornography. *Journal of Sex Research, 26*(3), 283–291.

Bogle, K. (2008). *Hooking up.* New York: New York University Press.

Boies, S. C. (2002). University students uses of and reactions to online sexual information and entertainment: Links to online and offline sexual behaviour. *Canadian Journal of Human Sexuality, 11,* 77–89.

Bois, K., Bergeron, S., Rosen, N., Mayrand, M.-H., Brassard, A., & Sadikaj, G. (2016). Intimacy, sexual satisfaction, and sexual distress in vulvodynia couples: An observational study. *Health Psychology, 35,* 531–540.

Boislard, P. M.-A., & Poulin, F. (2011). Individual, familial, friends-related and contextual predictors of early sexual intercourse. *Journal of Adolescence, 34,* 289–300.

Bolton, M., McKay, A., & Schneider, M. (2010). Relational influences on condom use discontinuation: A qualitative study of young adult women in dating relationships. *Canadian Journal of Human Sexuality, 19,* 91–104.

Boon, S. L., & Alderson, K. G. (2009). A phenomenological study of women in same-sex relationships who were previously married to men. *Canadian Journal of Human Sexuality, 18,* 149–168.

Boonstra, H. (2001). Islam, women and family planning: A primer. *Guttmacher Report on Public Policy, 4,* 4–7.

Booth, C. L., & Meltzoff, A. N. (1984). Expected and actual experience in labour and delivery and their relationship to maternal attachment. *Journal of Reproductive and Infant Psychology, 2,* 79–91.

Bornstein, K. (1994). *Gender outlaw: On men, women, and the rest of us.* New York: Routledge.

Bornstein, R. F. (1989). Exposure and affect: Overview and meta-analysis of research, 1968–1987. *Psychological Bulletin, 106,* 265–289.

Boroditsky, R., Fisher, W., & Sand, M. (1996, December). The 1996 Canadian contraceptive study. *Journal of the Society of Obstetricians and Gynaecologists of Canada.*

Bossio, J. A., Pukall, C. F., & Steele, S. (2016). Examining penile sensitivity in neonatally circumcised and intact men using quantitative sensory testing. *Journal of Urology, 195,* 1848–1853. doi:10.1016/j.juro.2015.12.080

Boston Women's Health Book Collective. (2005). *Our bodies, ourselves for the new century.* New York: Simon and Schuster.

Boswell, J. (1980). *Christianity, social tolerance, and homosexuality.* Chicago: University of Chicago Press.

Boswell, J. (1994). *Same-sex unions in premodern Europe.* New York: Villard Books.

Bouyer, J., Coste, J., Shojaei, T., Pouly, J. L., Fernandez, H., Gerbaud, L., & Job-Spira, N. (2003). Risk factors for ectopic pregnancy: a comprehensive analysis based on a large case-control, population-based study in France. *American Journal of Epidemiology, 157,* 185–194.

Bowe, J. (2006, November 19). Gay donor or gay dad? *New York Times Magazine,* 66–73.

Bowen, A. (2005). Internet sexuality research with rural men who have sex with men: Can we recruit and retain them? *Journal of Sex Research, 42,* 317–323.

Bower, J., Gurevich, M., & Mathieson, C. (2002). (Con)tested identities: Bisexual women reorient sexuality. *Journal of Bisexuality, 2*, 23–52.

Boyarin, D. (1995). Are there any Jews in 'The History of Sexuality'? *Journal of the History of Sexuality, 5*, 333–355.

Boyce, W. F., Doherty-Poirier, M., Fortin, C., & MacKinnon, D. (2003). *Canadian youth, sexual health and HIV/AIDS study.* Counsel of Ministers of Education, Canada.

Boyce, W. F., Doherty-Poirier, M., MacKinnon, D., Fortin, C., Saab, H., King, M., & Gallupe, O. (2006). Sexual health of Canadian youth: Findings from the Canadian youth, sexual health and HIV/AIDS Study. *Canadian Journal of Human Sexuality, 15*, 59–68.

Boyce, W. F., Gallupe, O., & Fergus, S. (2008). Characteristics of Canadian youth reporting a very early age of first sexual intercourse. *Canadian Journal of Human Sexuality, 17*, 97–108.

Boyce, W. F., King, A. J. C., & Warren, W. K. (2000). The effectiveness of a school-based HIV education program: A longitudinal comparative evaluation. *Canadian Journal of Program Evaluation, 15*, 93–116.

Boyer, S. C., & Pukall, C. F. (2014). Pelvic examination experiences in women with and without chronic pain during intercourse. *Journal of Sexual Medicine, 11*, 3035–3050.

Boynton, P. M. (2003). "I'm just a girl who can't say no"? Women, consent, and sex research. *Journal of Sex & Marital Therapy, 29*(Suppl.), 23–32.

Brabant, M., Hébert, M., & Chagnon, F. (2013). Identification of sexually abused female adolescents at risk for suicidal ideations: A classification and regression tree analysis. *Journal of Child Sexual Abuse, 22*, 153–172.

Brabazon, C., Bercovitz, E., Dospital, L., Gunter, K., Mangat, S. S., Manson Singer, S., . . . West, J. (1993a). *Many voices: HIV/AIDS in the context of culture: Report for the Chinese communities. Ethnocultural communities facing AIDS: A national study.* Ottawa: National Health Research and Development Program (Health Canada)/AIDS Education and Prevention Unit (National AIDS Strategy), Health Canada.

Brabazon, C., Bercovitz, E., Dospital, L., Gunter, K., Mangat, S. S., Manson Singer, S., . . . West, J. (1993b). *Many voices: HIV/AIDS in the context of culture: Report for the South Asian communities. Report for the Chinese communities. Ethnocultural communities facing AIDS: A national study.* Ottawa: National Health Research and Development Program (Health Canada)/AIDS Education and Prevention Unit (National AIDS Strategy), Health Canada.

Bradford, J. M. W. (2000). The treatment of sexual deviation using a pharmacological approach. *Journal of Sex Research, 37*, 248–257.

Bradford, J. M. W., & Greenberg, D. M. (1996). Pharmacological treatment of deviant sexual behaviour. *Annual Review of Sex Research, 7*, 283–306.

Brankley, A. E., Goodwill, A. M., & Abracen, J. (2016). A cognitive-behavioural case conceptualization approach to the assessment and treatment of necrophilia. In L. Mellor, A. Aggrawal, & E. W. Hickey (Eds.), *Understanding necrophilia: A global multidisciplinary approach.* San Diego, CA: Cognella.

Brassard, A., Dupuy, E., Bergeron, S., & Shaver, P. R. (2015). Attachment insecurities and women's sexual function and satisfaction: The mediating roles of sexual self-esteem, sexual anxiety, and sexual assertiveness. *Journal of Sex Research, 52*, 110–119.

Brassard, A., Shaver, P. R., & Lussier, Y. (2007). Attachment, sexual experience, and sexual pressure in romantic relationships: A dyadic approach. *Personal Relationships, 14*, 475–493.

Braun, V., & Kitzinger, C. (2001). "Snatch," "hole," or "honey-pot"? Semantic categories and the problem of nonspecificity in female genital slang. *Journal of Sex Research, 38*, 146–158.

Brecher, E. M. (1984). *Love, sex, and aging.* Mount Vernon, NY: Consumers Union.

Brecht, M. L., O'Brien, A., von Mayrhauser, C., & Anglin, M. D. (2004). Methamphetamine use behaviors and gender differences. *Addictive Behaviors, 29*, 89–106.

Brecklin, L. R., & Ullman, S. E. (2005). Self-defense or assertiveness training and women's responses to sexual attacks. *Journal of Interpersonal Violence, 20*, 738–762.

Brennan, D. (2010). Sex tourism, and sex workers' aspirations. In R. Weitzer (Ed.), *Sex for sale: Prostitution, pornography, and the sex industry* (2nd ed., pp. 307–323). New York: Routledge.

Brennan, P. A., & Zufall, F. (2006). Pheromonal communication in vertebrates. *Nature, 444*, 308–315.

Brenton, M. (1972). *Sex talk.* New York: Stein and Day.

Breslow, N., Evans, L., & Langley, J. (1985). On the prevalence and roles of females in the sadomasochistic subculture: Report of an empirical study. *Archives of Sexual Behavior, 14*, 303–318.

Breton, S., Smith, P. J. S., Lut, B., & Brown, D. (1996). Acidification of the male reproductive tract by a proton pumping (H1)-ATPase. *Nature Medicine, 2*, 470–472.

Broad, K. D., & Keverne, E. B. (2011). Placental protection of the fetal brain during short-term food deprivation. *Proceedings of the National Academy of Science, 108*, 15237–15241.

Brock, G., McMahon, C. G., Chen, K K., Costigan, T., Shen, W., Watkins, V., et al. (2002). Efficacy and safety of tadalafil in men with erectile dysfunction: An integrated analysis of registration trials. *Journal of Urology, 167*, 178.

Brock, G., Nehra, A., Lipshultz, L. I., Karlin, G. S., Gleave, M. P., Seger, M., et al. (2003). Safety and efficacy of vardenafil for the treatment of men with erectile dysfunction after radical retropubic prostatectomy. *Journal of Urology, 170*, 1278–1283.

Brooke, C. L., Adam, B. D., McCauley, J., & Bortolin, S. (2010). Perceptions of HIV risk among lesbian, gay, and bisexual youth. *Our Schools/Our Selves, 19*(2), 39–54.

Brotman, H. (1984, Jan. 8). Human embryo transplants. *New York Times Magazine,* 42ff.

Brotto, L. A., & Gorzalka, B. B. (2002). Genital and subjective sexual arousal in postmenopausal women: Influence of laboratory-induced hyperventilation. *Journal of Sex & Marital Therapy, 28*, 39–53.

Brotto, L. A., & Heiman, J. R. (2007). Mindfulness in sex therapy: Applications for women with sexual difficulties following gynecologic cancer. *Sexual and Relationship Therapy, 22*, 3–11.

Brotto, L. A., & Klein, C. (2007). Sexual and gender identity disorders. In M. Hersen, S. M. Turner, & D. Beidel (Eds.) *Adult psychopathology and diagnosis* (5th ed., pp. 504–570). Hoboken, NJ: John Wiley & Sons.

Brotto, L. A., & Klein, C. (2010). Psychological factors involved in women's sexual dysfunctions. *Expert Reviews in Obstetrics and Gynecology, 5*, 93–104.

Brotto, L. A., & Luria, M. (2008). Menopause, aging, and sexual response in women. In D. L. Rowland, & L. Incrocci (Eds.), *Handbook of sexual and gender identity disorders* (pp. 251–283). Hoboken, NJ: John Wiley & Sons.

Brotto, L. A., & Yule, M. A. (2011). Physiological and subjective sexual arousal in self-identified asexual women. *Archives of Sexual Behavior, 40*, 699–712.

Brotto, L. A., Chik, H. M., Ryder, A. G., Gorzalka, B. B., & Seal, B. N. (2005). Acculturation and sexual function in Asian women. *Archives of Sexual Behaviour, 34*, 613–626.

Brotto, L. A., Chou, A. Y., Singh, T., & Woo, J. S. T. (2008). Reproductive health practices among Indian, Indo-Canadian, Canadian East Asian, and Euro-Canadian Women: The role of acculturation. *Journal of Obstetrics and Gynaecology Canada, 30*, 229–238.

Brotto, L. A., Heiman, J. R., Goff, B., Greer, B., Lentz, G., Swisher, E., . . . Van Blaricom, A. (2008). A psychoeducational intervention for sexual dysfunction in women with gynecologic cancer. *Archives of Sexual Behavior, 37*, 317–329.

Brotto, L. A., Knudson, G., Inskip, J., Rhodes, K., & Erskine, Y. (2010). Asexuality: A mixed-methods approach. *Archives of Sexual Behavior, 39*, 599–618.

Brotto, L. A., Mehak, L., & Kit., C. (2009). Yoga and sexual functioning: A review. *Journal of Sex & Marital Therapy, 35*, 378–390.

Brotto, L. A., Woo, J. S. T., & Ryder, A. G. (2007). Acculturation and sexual function in Canadian East Asian men. *Journal of Sexual Medicine, 4*, 72–82.

Brotto, L., & Basson, R. (2014). Group mindfulness-based therapy significantly improves sexual desire in women. *Behaviour Research and Therapy, 57*, 43–54.

Brotto, L., Atallah, S., Johnson-Agbakwu, C., Rosenbaum, T., Abdo, C., Byers, E. S., . . . Wylie, K. (2016). Psychological and interpersonal dimensions of sexual function and dysfunction. *Journal of Sexual Medicine, 13,* 538–571.

Brotto, L., Basson, R., Smith, K. B., Driscoll, M., & Sadownik, L. (2014). Mindfulness-based group therapy for women with provoked vestibulodynia. *Mindfulness, 6,* 417–432.

Brotto, L., et al. (2009). Asexuality: A mixed-methods approach. *Archives of Sexual Behavior.* doi:10.1007/s10508-008-9434-x

Brousseau, M. M., Bergeron, S., Hébert, M., & McDuff, P. (2011). Sexual coercion victimization and perpetration in heterosexual couples: A dyadic investigation. *Archives of Sexual Behavior, 40,* 363–372. doi:10.1007/s10508-010-9617-0

Brousseau, M. M., et al. (2011). Sexual coercion victimization and perpetration in heterosexual couples: A dyadic investigation. *Archives of Sexual Behavior, 40,* 363–372.

Brown, G., Maycock, B., & Burns, S. (2005). Your picture is your bait: Use and meaning of cyberspace among gay men. *Journal of Sex Research, 42,* 63–73.

Brown, J. D. (2002). Mass media influences on sexuality. *Journal of Sex Research, 39,* 42–45.

Brown, J. D., L'Engle, K. L., Pardun, C. J., Guo, G., Kenneavy, K., & Jackson, C. (2006). Sexy media matter: exposure to sexual content in music, movies, television, and magazines predicts black and white adolescents' sexual behavior. *Pediatrics, 117*(4), 1018–1027.

Brown, J., & L'Engle, K. (2009). X-rated: Sexual attitudes and behaviors associated with U.S. early adolescents' exposure to sexually explicit media. *Communication Research, 36,* 129–151.

Brown, Z. A., et al. (2005). Genital herpes complicating pregnancy. *Obstetrics & Gynecology, 106,* 845–856.

Bruggemann, O., et al. (2007). Support to a woman by a companion of her choice during childbirth: A randomized controlled trial. *Reproductive Health, 4,* 5.

Brym, R. J., & Lenton, R. L. (2001). Love online: A report on digital dating in Canada. Retrieved from http://www.nelson.com

Brym, R. J., & Lenton, R. L. (2003). Love at first byte: Internet dating in Canada. Retrieved from http://www.societyinquestion4e.nelson.com/article2.html

Brzozowski, J. A. (2007). Family violence against children and youth. In L. Ogrodnik (Ed.), *Family violence in Canada: A statistical profile, 2007.* (Catalogue no. 85-224-XIE). Ottawa: Canadian Centre for Justice Statistics.

Buchanan, K. M. (1986). *Apache women warriors.* El Paso, TX: Texas Western Press.

Buchanan, R. T. (2014). The truth about student sex workers: It's far from Belle Du Jour. Retrieved from http://www.independent.co.uk/life-style/health-and-families/features/the-truth-about-student-sex-workers-its-far-from-belle-du-jour-9757719.html

Buck, L. G. M., Sundaram, R., Sweeney, A. M., Schisterman, E. F., Maisog, J., & Kannan, K. (2014). Urinary bisphenol A, phthalates, and couple fecundity: the Longitudinal Investigation of Fertility and the Environment (LIFE) Study. *Fertility and Sterility, 101,* 1359–1366.

Buhi, E. R., et al. (2010). Quality and accuracy of sexual health information web sites visited by young people. *Journal of Adolescent Health, 47,* 206–208.

Bulik, C., Prescott, C., & Kendler, K. (2001). Features of childhood sexual abuse and the development of psychiatric and substance use disorders. *British Journal of Psychiatry, 179,* 444–449.

Bullivant, S. B., Sellergren, S. A., & Stern, K. (2004). Women's sexual experience during the menstrual cycle: Identification of the sexual phase by noninvasive measurement of luteinizing hormone. *Journal of Sex Research, 41,* 82–93.

Bullough, B., & Bullough, V. (1997). Are transvestites necessarily heterosexual? *Archives of Sexual Behavior, 26,* 1–12.

Bullough, V. L. (1976). *Sexual variance in society and history.* New York: Wiley.

Bullough, V. L. (1994). *Science in the bedroom: A history of sex research.* New York: Basic Books.

Bumpass, L. L., Sweet, J. A., & Cherlin, A. (1991). The role of cohabitation in declining rates of marriage. *Journal of Marriage and the Family, 53,* 913–927.

Burack, J. H., et al. (1993). Depressive symptoms and CD4 lymphocyte decline among HIV-infected men. *Journal of the American Medical Association, 270,* 2568–2573.

Bureau of Labor Statistics. (2016). *American Time Use Survey.* Washington, DC: Author.

Burgess, A. W. (1984). *Child pornography and sex rings.* Lexington, MA: Lexington Books.

Burke, S. M., Cohen-Kettenis, P. T., Veltman, D. J., Klink, D. T., & Bakker, J. (2014). Hypothalamic response to the chemo-signal androstadienone in gender dysphoric children and adolescents. *Frontiers in Endocrinology, 5,* 60.

Burleson, B. R. (2003). The experience and effects of emotional support: What the study of cultural and gender differences can tell us about close relationships, emotion, and interpersonal communication. *Personal Relationships, 10,* 1–23.

Burleson, B., & Denton, W. (1997). The relationship between communication skill and marital satisfaction: Some moderating effects. *Journal of Marriage and the Family, 59,* 884–902.

Burleson, M. H., et al. (2007). In the mood for love or vice versa? Exploring the relations among sexual activity, physical affection, affect and stress in the daily lives of mid-aged women. *Archives of Sexual Behavior, 36,* 357–368.

Burnett, M., Aggarwal, A., Davis, V., Dempster, J., Fisher, W., ...Wagner, M- (2011). SOGC policy statement: Sexual and reproductive health counselling by health care professionals. *Journal of Obstetrics and Gynaecology of Canada, 33,* 870–871.

Burrows, M., & Bird, S. R. (2005). Velocity at VO2 (max) and peak treadmill velocity are not influenced within or across the phases of the menstrual cycle. *European Journal of Applied Physiology, 93,* 575–580.

Burt, S. (2014). Mansplaining cross-dressing. *The New Yorker.*

Burton, D. L. (2000). Were adolescent sexual offenders children with sexual behavior problems? *Sex Abuse, 12,* 37–48.

Burton, F. D. (1970). Sexual climax in *Macaca mulatta. Proceedings of the Third International Congress on Primatology, 3,* 180–191.

Busby, K. (1999). Not a victim until the conviction is entered: Sexual violence, prosecutions and legal "truth." In *Locating law: Race/class/gender connections.* Halifax, NS: Fernwood Publishing.

Bushnik, T., Cook, J. L., Yuzpe, A. A., Tough, S., & Collins, J. (2012). Estimating the prevalence of infertility in Canada. *Human Reproduction, 27,* 738–746.

Buss, A. (1966). *Psychopathology.* New York: Wiley.

Buss, D. M. (1988). The evolution of human intra-sexual competition: Tactics of mate attraction. *Journal of Personality and Social Psychology, 54,* 616–628.

Buss, D. M. (1989). Sex differences in human mate preferences: Evolutionary hypotheses tested in 37 cultures. *Behavioral and Brain Sciences, 12,* 1–49.

Buss, D. M. (1991). Evolutionary personality psychology. *Annual Review of Psychology, 45,* 459–491.

Buss, D. M. (1994). *The evolution of desire: Strategies of human mating.* New York: Basic Books.

Buss, D. M. (2000). *The dangerous passion: Why jealousy is as necessary as love and sex.* New York: The Free Press.

Buss, D. M. (2009). The great struggles of life: Darwin and the emergence of evolutionary psychology. *American Psychologist, 64,* 140–148.

Buss, D. M., & Schmitt, D. P. (1993). Sexual strategies theory: An evolutionary perspective on human mating. *Psychological Review, 100,* 204–232.

Buss, D., & Shackelford, T. (1997a). From vigilance to violence: Mate retention tactics in married couples. *Journal of Personality and Social Psychology, 72,* 346–361.

Buss, D., & Shackelford, T. (1997b). Susceptibility to infidelity in the first year of marriage. *Journal of Research in Personality, 31,* 193–221.

Butzer, B., & Campbell, L. (2008). Adult attachment, sexual satisfaction, and relationship satisfaction: A study of married couples. *Personal Relationships, 15,* 141–154.

Byard, R., Hucker, S., & Hazelwood, R. (1993). Fatal and near-fatal autoerotic asphyxial episodes in women. *The American Journal of Forensic Medicine and Pathology, 14,* 70–73.

Byers, E. S. (1996). How well does the traditional sexual script explain sexual coercion?

Review of a program of research. *Journal of Psychology and Human Sexuality, 8,* 7–25.

Byers, E. S. (1999). The interpersonal exchange model of sexual satisfaction: Implications for sex therapy with couples. *Canadian Journal of Counselling, 33*(2), 95–111.

Byers, E. S. (2011). Beyond the birds and the bees and was it good for you?: Thirty years of research on sexual communication. *Canadian Psychology, 52,* 20–28.

Byers, E. S., & Demmons, S. (1999). Sexual satisfaction and sexual self disclosure within dating relationships. *Journal of Sex Research, 36,* 180–189.

Byers, E. S., & Glenn, S. A. (2012). Gender differences in cognitive and affective responses to sexual coercion. *Journal of Interpersonal Violence, 27,* 827–845.

Byers, E. S., & Grenier, G. (2003). Premature or rapid ejaculation: Heterosexual couples' perceptions of men's ejaculatory behavior. *Archives of Sexual Behavior, 32,* 261–270.

Byers, E. S., & Heinlein, L. (1989). Predicting initiation and refusals of sexual activities in married and cohabiting heterosexual couples. *Journal of Sex Research, 26,* 210–231.

Byers, E. S., & MacNeil, S. (2006). Further validation of the interpersonal exchange model of sexual satisfaction. *Journal of Sex & Marital Therapy, 32,* 53–69.

Byers, E. S., & O'Sullivan, L. F. (1998). Similar but different: Men's and women's experiences of sexual coercion. In P. B. Anderson & C. Strickman-Johnson (Eds.), *Sexually aggressive women.* New York: Guilford Press.

Byers, E. S., & Rehman, U. (2013). Sexual well-being. In D. Tolman & L. Diamond (Eds.), *APA handbook of sexuality and psychology.* Washington, DC: APA Books.

Byers, E. S., & Sears, H. A. (2012). Mothers who do and do not intend to discuss sexual health with their young adolescents. *Family Relations, 61,* 851–863.

Byers, E. S., & Shaughnessy, K. (2014). Attitudes toward online sexual activities. *Cyberpsychology: Journal of Psychosocial Research on Cyberspace, 8,* article 10.

Byers, E. S., & Slattery, G. (1997). Sexology in Russia and Estonia: Reflections on an exchange. *Canadian Journal of Human Sexuality, 6,* 53–64.

Byers, E. S., & Wang, A. (2004). Understanding sexuality in close relationships from the social exchange perspective. In J. H. Harvey, A. Wenzel, & S. Sprecher (Eds.), *The handbook of sexuality in close relationships* (pp. 203–234). Mahwah, NJ: Lawrence Erlbaum.

Byers, E. S., Crooks, R., Griffiths, B., Mackin, B., MacDonald, G., Mac-Donald, G., . . . Yates, P. (1997). *The extent of sex offences and the nature of sex offenders in New Brunswick: A research project.* Submitted to the New Brunswick Department of the Solicitor General and Correctional Services Canada.

Byers, E. S., Demmons, S., & Lawrance, K.-A. (1998). Sexual satisfaction within dating relationships: A test of the interpersonal

exchange model of sexual satisfaction. *Journal of Social and Personal Relationships, 15*(2), 257–267.

Byers, E. S., Goldsmith, K., & Miller, A. (2016). If given the choice, would you choose to be a man or a woman? *Canadian Journal of Human Sexuality.* Advance online publication. doi:10.3138/cjhs.252-A7

Byers, E. S., Henderson, J., & Hobson, K. (2009). University students' definitions of sexual abstinence and having sex. *Archives of Sexual Behavior, 38,* 665–674. doi:10.1007/s10508-007-9289-6

Byers, E. S., Nichols, S., & Voyer, S. D. (2013). Challenging stereotypes: Sexual functioning of single adults with high functioning autism spectrum disorder. *Journal of Autism and Developmental Disorders.* doi:10.1007/s10803-013-1813-z

Byers, E. S., Nichols, S., Voyer, S. D., & Reilly, G. (2012). Sexual well-being of a community sample of high-functioning adults on the autism spectrum who have been in a romantic relationship. *Autism.* doi:10.1177/1362631311431950

Byers, E. S., O'Sullivan, L. F., & Brotto, L. A. (2016). Time out from sex or romance: Sexually experienced adolescents' decisions to purposefully avoid sexual activity or romantic relationships. *Journal of Youth and Adolescence, 45,* 831–845.

Byers, E. S., Purdon, C., & Clark, D. (1998). Sexual intrusive thoughts of college students. *Journal of Sex Research, 35,* 359–369.

Byers, E. S., Sears, H. A., & Foster, L. R. (2013). Factors associated with middle school students' perceptions of the quality of school-based sexual health education. *Sex Education, 13,* 214–227.

Byers, E. S., Sears, H. A., & Weaver, A. D. (2008). Parents' reports of sexual communication with children in kindergarten to grade 8. *Journal of Marriage and Family, 70*(1), 86–96.

Byers, E. S., Sears, H. A., Voyer, S. D., Thurlow, J. L., Cohen, J. N., & Weaver, A. D. (2003a). An adolescent perspective on sexual health education at school and at home: I. High school students. *Canadian Journal of Human Sexuality, 12,* 1–17.

Byers, E. S., Sears, H. A., Voyer, S. D., Thurlow, J. L., Cohen, J. N., & Weaver, A. D. (2003b). An adolescent perspective on sexual health education at school and at home: II. Middle school students. *Canadian Journal of Human Sexuality, 12,* 19–32.

Byers, L. J., Menzies, K. S., & W. L. O'Grady (2004). The impact of computer variables on the viewing and sending of sexually explicit material on the Internet: Testing Cooper's "triple-A engine." *Canadian Journal of Human Sexuality, 13,* 157–169.

Byers, M. E. (2005). *Growing up Degrassi.* Toronto: Sumach Press.

Byne, W., Lasco, M. S., Kemether, E., Shinwari, A., Edgar, M. A., & Morgello, S. (2000). The interstitial nuclei of the human anterior hypothalamus: Assessment for sexual

variation in volume and neuronal size, density, and number. *Brain Research, 856,* 254–258.

Byrne, D. (1971). *The attraction paradigm.* New York: Academic.

Byrne, D. (1983). Sex without contraception. In D. Byrne & W. A. Fisher (Eds.), *Adolescents, sex, and contraception.* Hillsdale, NJ: Lawrence Erlbaum.

Byrne, D. (1997). An overview (and underview) and research and theory within the attraction paradigm. *Journal of Social and Personal Relationships, 14,* 417–431.

Byun, S., et al. (2009). Internet addiction: Metasynthesis of 1996–2006 quantitative research. *CyberPsychology & Behavior, 12,* 203–207.

Cacioppo, S., Bianchi-Demicheli, F., Frum, C., Pfaus, J. G., & Lewis, J. W. (2012a). The common neural bases between sexual desire and love: A multilevel kernel density fMRI analysis. *Journal of Sexual Medicine, 9,* 1048–1054.

Cacioppo, S., Bianchi-Demicheli, F., Hatfield, E., & Rapson, R. L. (2012b). Social neuroscience of love. *Clinical Neuropsychiatry, 9,* 3–13.

Cado, S., & Leitenberg, H. (1990). Guilt reactions to sexual fantasies during intercourse. *Archives of Sexual Behavior, 19,* 49–64.

Cahill, L. (2005). His brain, her brain. *Scientific American, 292,* 40–47.

Cahill, L. S. (1985). The "seamless garment": Life in its beginnings. *Theological Studies, 46,* 64–80.

Cairns, K. V. (1993). Sexual entitlement and sexual accommodations: implications for female and male experience of sexual coercion. *Canadian Journal of Human Sexuality, 2,* 203–213.

Calderwood, D. (1987, May). The male rape victim. *Medical Aspects of Human Sexuality,* 53–55.

Call, V., Sprecher, S., & Schwartz, P. (1995). The incidence and frequency of marital sex in a national sample. *Journal of Marriage and the Family, 57,* 639–652.

Callahan, D. (1986, February). How technology is reframing the abortion debate. *Hastings Center Report,* 33–42.

Calzavara, L. M., Burchell, A. N., Myers, T., Bullock, S. L., Escobar, M., & Cockerill, R. (1998). Condom use among Aboriginal people in Ontario, Canada. *International Journal of STD & AIDS, 9,* 272–279.

Calzo, J. P., & Ward, L. M. (2009). Media exposure and viewers' attitudes toward homosexuality: Evidence for mainstreaming or resonance? *Journal of Broadcasting and Electronic Media, 53,* 280–299.

Cameron, J. J., & Ross, M. (2007). In times of uncertainty: Predicting the survival of long-distance relationships. *Journal of Social Psychology, 147,* 581–606.

Camilleri, J. A., & Quinsey, V. L. (2008). Pedophilia: Assessment and treatment. In D. R. Laws & W. T. O'Donohue (Eds.), *Sexual deviance* (pp. 183–212). New York: Guilford.

Campbell, A., Shirley, L., & Caygill, L. (2002). Sex-typed preferences in three domains: Do two-year-olds need cognitive variables? *British Journal of Psychology, 93,* 201–217.

Campbell, D. A., Lake, M. F., Falk, M., & Backstrand, J. (2006). A randomized control trial of continuous support in labor by a lay doula. *Journal of Obstetric, Gynecologic, & Neonatal Nursing, 35,* 456–464.

Canadian AIDS Society. (2011). Rapid HIV testing in Canada. Retrieved from http://www.cdnaids.ca/rapidhivtestingincanada

Canadian Association for Adolescent Health. (2006). Teens face significant barriers seeking information about STIs and other sexual health matters. *Proteen, 15,* 12–16.

Canadian Association of Midwives. (2004). *Position statement on elective cesarean section.* Retrieved from http://www.canadianmidwives.org

Canadian Cancer Society. (2012). *Canadian cancer statistics 2012.* Toronto: Author.

Canadian Cancer Society. (2013a). *Risk factors for prostate cancer.* Toronto: Author.

Canadian Cancer Society. (2013b). What is breast cancer? Retrieved from http://www.cancer.ca/en/cancer-information/cancer-type/breast/breast-cancer/

Canadian Cancer Society. (2013c). *Risk factors for testicular cancer.* Retrieved from http://www.cancer.ca

Canadian Cancer Society. (2016a). *Breast cancer statistics.* Toronto: Author.

Canadian Cancer Society. (2016b). *Testicular cancer statistics.* Toronto: Author.

Canadian Centre for Justice Statistics. (1999). Integration and analysis program: Sex offenders. *Juristat, 19*(3). Retrieved from http://publications.gc.ca/Collection-R/Statcan/85-002-XIE/0039985-002-XIE.pdf

Canadian Federation for Sexual Health (2007). *Sexual Health in Canada: Baseline 2007.* Ottawa: Author.

Canadian Fertility & Andrology Society. (2013). Guidelines. Retrieved from https://cfas.ca/clinical-practice-guidelines/

Canadian HIV/AIDS Legal Network. (2002). *HIV vaccines in Canada: Legal and ethical issues: An Overview.* Retrieved from http://www.aidslaw.ca/publications/publicationsdocEN.php?ref=368

Canadian HIV/AIDS Legal Network. (2009). *Canada's immigration policy as it affects people living with HIV/AIDS.* Retrieved from http://www.aidslaw.ca/publications/publicationsdocEN.php?ref=97

Canadian HIV/AIDS Legal Network. (2014). *Criminal law & HIV non-disclosure in Canada.* Toronto: Author.

Canadian Institute for Health Information. (2010). Number of induced abortions reported in Canada. Retrieved from http://www.cihi.ca/CIHI-ext-portal/pdf/internet/TA_08_ALLDATATABLES20101124_EN

Canadian Institute for Health Information. (2011). Number of induced abortions reported in Canada in 2011. Retrieved from http://www.cihi.ca/cihi-ext-portal/pdf/internet/ta_11_alldatatables20130221_en

Canadian Midwifery Regulators Consortium. (2007). What is a Canadian registered midwife? Retrieved from http://cmrcccosf.ca/node/18

Canadian Paediatric Society. (2013, January 30). Reaffirmed position statement: Testing for HIV infection in pregnancy. *Paediatric Child Health 2008, 13,* 221–224.

Canadian Psychological Association. (1995). *Companion manual to the Canadian Code of Ethics for Psychologists, 1991.* Ottawa: Author.

Canadian Psychological Association. (2003, August 6). Gays and lesbians make bad parents: There is no basis in the scientific literature for this perception [Press release]. Ottawa: Author.

Cantor, J. M., & Blanchard, R. (2012). White matter volumes in pedophiles, hebephiles, and teleiophiles [Letter to the editor]. *Archives of Sexual Behavior, 41,* 749–752. doi:10.1007/s10508-012-9954-2

Cantor, J. M., & Sutton, K. S. (2014). Paraphilia, gender dysphoria, and hypersexuality. In P. H. Blaney & T. Millon (Eds.), *Oxford textbook of psychopathology* (3rd ed.) (pp. 589–614). New York: Oxford University Press.

Cantor, J. M., Blanchard, R., & Barbaree, H. E. (2009). Sexual disorders. In P. H. Blaney & T. Millon (Eds.), *Oxford textbook of psychopathology* (2nd ed., pp. 527–548). New York: Oxford University Press.

Cantor, J. M., Blanchard, R., Christensen, B. K., Dickey, R., Klassen, P. E., Beckstead, A. L., . . . & Kuban, M. E. (2004). Intelligence, memory, and handedness in pedophilia. *Neuropsychology, 18,* 3–14.

Cantor, J. M., Blanchard, R., Paterson, A. D., & Bogaert, A. F. (2002). How many gay men owe their sexual orientation to fraternal birth order? *Archives of Sexual Behavior, 31,* 63–71.

Cantor, J. M., Blanchard, R., Robichaud, L., & Christensen, B. (2005). Quantitative reanalysis of aggregate data on IQ in sexual offenders. *Psychological Bulletin, 131,* 555–568.

Cantor, J. M., Kabani, N., Christensen, B. K., Zipursky, R. B., Barbaree, H. E., Dickey, R., . . . Blanchard, R. (2008). Cerebral white matter deficiencies in pedophilic men. *Journal of Psychiatric Research, 42,* 167–183.

Cantor, J. M., Klassen, P. E., Dickey, R., Christensen, B. K., Kuban, M. E., Blak, T., . . . Blanchard, R. (2005). Handedness in pedophilia and hebephilia. *Archives of Sexual Behavior, 34,* 447–459.

Cantor, J. M., Klein, C., Lykins, A., Rullo, J. E., Thaler, L., & Walling, B. R. (2013). A treatment-oriented typology of self-identified hypersexuality referrals. *Archives of Sexual Behavior, 42,* 883–893.

Cantor, J. M., Lafaille, S., Soh, D. W., Moayedi, M., Mikulis, D. J., & Girard, T. A. (2015). Diffusion tensor imaging of pedophilia. *Archives of Sexual Behavior, 44,* 2161–2172.

Caplan, P. (1995). *How do they decide who is normal?* Reading, MA: Addison-Wesley.

Cappon, P., Adrien, A., Godin, G., Manson Singer, S., Maticka-Tyndale, E., Willms, D., & Daus, T. (1996). HIV/AIDS in the context of culture: Selection of ethnocultural communities for study in Canada. *Canadian Journal of Public Health, 87*(1), S11–S25.

Caputo, T. (2000). *Hearing the voices of youth: Youth participation in selected Canadian municipalities.* Ottawa: Health Canada.

CARAL. (n.d.). *Historical biography of Henry Morgentaler.* Ottawa: CARAL.

Carani, C., Zini, D., Baldini, A., Della Casa, L., Ghizzani, A., & Marrama, P. (1990). Effects of androgen treatment in impotent men with normal and low levels of free testosterone. *Archives of Sexual Behavior, 19,* 223–234.

Carnes, P. (1983). *The sexual addiction.* Minneapolis: Compcare Publications.

Caron, A., Lafontaine, M-F., Bureau, J-F., Levesque, C., & Johnson, S. M. (2012). Comparisons of close relationships: An evaluation of relationship quality and patterns of attachment to parents, friends, and romantic partners in young adults. *Canadian Journal of Behavioural Science, 44,* 245–256.

Carpenter, L. M. (2001). The ambiguity of "having sex": The subjective experience of virginity loss in the United States. *Journal of Sex Research, 38,* 127–139.

Carter, C. S. (1992). Hormonal influences on human sexual behavior. In J. B. Becker et al. (Eds.), *Behavioral endocrinology* (pp. 131–142). Cambridge, MA: MIT Press.

Cashdan, E. (2008). Waist-to-hip ratio across cultures: Trade-offs between androgen- and estrogen-dependent traits. *Current Anthropology, 49,* 1099–1107.

Catania, J. A., Binson, D., Van Der Straten, A., & Stone, V. (1995). Methodological research on sexual behavior in the AIDS era. *Annual Review of Sex Research, 6,* 77–125.

Catania, J. A., Gibson, D., Marin, B., Coates, T., & Greenblatt, R. (1990). Response bias in assessing sexual behaviors relevant to HIV transmission. *Evaluation and Program Planning, 13,* 19–29.

Catellsagué, X., Bosch, F. X., Muñoz, N., Meijer, C. J. L. M., Shah, K. V., de Sanjosé, S., . . . International Agency for Research on Cancer Multicenter Cervical Cancer Study Group. (2002). Male circumcision, penile human papillomavirus infection, and cervical cancer in female partners. *New England Journal of Medicine, 346,* 1105–1112.

Causarano, N., Pole, Flicker, S., & the Toronto Teen Survey Team (2010). Exposure to and desire for sexual health eduation among urban youth: Associations with religion and other factors. *Canadian Journal of Human Sexuality, 19,* 169–184.

CBC News. (2004, May 10). Man raised as girl dies. Retrieved from http://www.cbc.ca/news/canada/manitoba/man-raised-as-girl-dies-1.511287

Cénat, J. M., Blais, M., Hébert, M., Lavoie, F., & Guerrier, M. (2015). Correlates of bullying in Quebec high school students: The vulnerability of sexual-minority youth. *Journal of Affective Disorders, 183,* 315–321.

Centers for Disease Control. (2004). *Intimate partner violence: Fact sheet*. Retrieved from http://www.cdc.gov/ncipc/factsheets/ipv-facts.htm

Cerny, J. A., & Janssen, E. (2011). Patterns of sexual arousal in homosexual, bisexual, and heterosexual men. *Archives of Sexual Behavior, 40,* 687–697.

Chalker, R. (1995, November/December). Sexual pleasure unscripted. *Ms.,* 49–52.

Chalmers, B., & Hashi, K. O. (2000). 432 Somali women's birth experiences in Canada after earlier female genital mutilation. *Birth, 27,* 227–234.

Chan, C. S. (1995). Issues of sexual identity in an ethnic minority: The case of Chinese American lesbians, gay men, and bisexual people. In A. R. D'Augelli & C. J. Patterson (Eds.), *Lesbian, gay, and bisexual identities over the lifespan* (pp. 87–101). New York: Oxford University Press.

Chan, D. K-S., Lam, C. B., Chow, S. Y., & Cheung, S. F. (2008). Examining the job related, psychological, and physical outcomes of workplace sexual harassment: A meta-analytic review. *Psychology of Women Quarterly, 32,* 362–376.

Chandra, A., Mosher, W., & Coopen, C. (2011). Sexual behavior, sexual attraction, and sexual identity in the United States: Data from the 2006–2008 National Survey of Family Growth. *National Health Statistics Reports, 36.*

Chang, S. C. H., Woo, J. S. T., Gorzalka, B. B., & Brotto, L. A. (2010). A questionnaire study of cervical cancer screening beliefs and practices of Chinese and Caucasian mother-daughter pairs living in Canada. *Journal of Obstetrics and Gynaecology Canada, 32,* 254–262.

Chapman, H., Hobfoll, S., & Ritter, C. (1997). Partners' stress underestimations lead to women's distress: A study of pregnant inner-city women. *Journal of Personality and Social Psychology, 73,* 418–425.

Charon, J. (1995). *Symbolic interactionism: An introduction, interpretation, and integration* (5th ed). Englewood Cliffs, NJ: Prentice Hall.

Chatterjee, A., Rathore, A., Vidyant, S., Kakkar, K., & Dhole, T. N. (2012), Chemokines and chemokine receptors in susceptibility to HIV-1 infection and progression to AIDS. *Disease Markers, 32,* 143–151.

Chavarro, J., Rich-Edwards, J. W., Rosner, B. A., & Willett, W. C. (2007). Diet and lifestyle in the prevention of ovulatory disorder infertility. *Obstetrics & Gynecology, 110,* 1050–1058.

Chen, L., Staubli, S. E. L., Schneider, M. P., Kessels, A. G., Ivic, S., Bachmann, L. M., & Kessler, T. M. (2015). Phosphodiesterase 5 inhibitors for the treatment of erectile dysfunction: A trade-off network meta-analysis. *European Urology, 68,* 674–680.

Cheng, D., Schwarz, E. B., Douglas, E., & Horon, I. (2009). Unintended pregnancy and associated maternal preconception, prenatal, and postpartum behaviors. *Contraception, 79,* 194–198.

Cheng, J., Elam-Evans, L. D., Berg, C. J., Herndon, J., Flowers, L., Seed, K. A., & Syverson, C. J. (2003, February 21). Pregnancy-related mortality surveillance: United States, 1991–1999. *Morbidity & Mortality Weekly Report, 52,* 1–8.

Cheng, M. M., & Udry, J. R. (2003). How much do mentally disabled adolescents know about sex and birth control? *Adolescent & Family Health, 3,* 28–38.

Cherner, R. A., & Reissing, E. D. (2013). A comparative study of sexual function, behavior, and cognitions of women with lifelong vaginismus. *Archives of Sexual Behavior, 42,* 1605–1614.

Chesler, E. (1992). *Woman of valor: Margaret Sanger and the birth control movement.* New York: Simon & Schuster.

Childbirth by Choice Trust. (2003). Contraceptive use in Canada. Retrieved from http://www.cbctrust.com

Chiu, Y. H., Afeiche, M. C., Gaskins, A. J., Williams, P. L., Petrozza, J. C., Tanrikut, C., ... & Chavarro, J. E. (2015). Fruit and vegetable intake and their pesticide residues in relation to semen quality among men from a fertility clinic. *Human Reproduction, 30,* 1342–1351.

Chivers, M. L. (2005). A brief review and discussion of sex differences in the specificity of sexual arousal. *Sexual and Relationship Therapy, 20,* 377–390.

Chivers, M. L., & Bailey, J. M. (2000). Sexual orientation of female-to-male transsexuals: A comparison of homosexual and nonhomosexual types. *Archives of Sexual Behavior, 29,* 259–278.

Chivers, M. L., Rieger, G., Latty, E., & Bailey, J. M. (2004). A sex difference in the specificity of sexual arousal. *Psychological Science, 15,* 736–744.

Chivers, M. L., Seto, M. C., & Blanchard, R. (2007). Gender and sexual orientation differences in sexual response to sexual activities versus gender of actors in sexual films. *Journal of Personality and Social Psychology, 93,* 1108–1121. doi:10.1037/0022-351493.6.1108

Chivers, M. L., Seto, M. C., Lalumière, M. L., Laan, E., & Grimbos, T. (2010). Agreement of self-reported and genital measures of sexual arousal in men and women: A meta-analysis. *Archives of Sexual Behavior, 39,* 5–56.

Chivers, M., & Blanchard, R. (1996). Prostitution advertisements suggest association of transvestism and masochism. *Journal of Sex & Marital Therapy, 22*(2), 97–102.

Chivers, M., & Timmers, A. (2012). Effects of gender and relationship context in audio narratives on genital and subjective sexual response in heterosexual women and men. *Archives of Sexual Behavior, 41*(1), 185–197. doi:10.1007/s10508-012-9937-3

Choi, E. J., Ha, C. M, Choi, J., Kang, S. S., Choi, W. S., Park, S. K., ... Lee, B. J. (2001). Low-density DNA array-coupled to PCR differential display identifies new estrogen-responsive genes during the postnatal differentiation of the rat hypothalamus. *Molecular Brain Research, 97,* 115–128.

Choi, Y., Bishai, D., & Minkovitz, C. (2009). Multiple births are a risk factor for postpartum maternal depression. *Pediatrics, 123,* 1147–1154.

Chong, Y. M. G., Teng, K. Z. S., Siew, S. C. A., & Skorik, M. M. (2012). Cultivation effects of video games: A longer-term experimental test of first- and second-order effects. *Journal of Social & Clinical Psychology, 31,* 952–971.

Chrisler, J. C., Rose, J. G., Dutch, S. E., Sklarsky, K. G., & Grant, M. C. (2006). The PMS illusion: Social cognition maintains social construction. *Sex Roles, 54,* 371–376.

Christensen, C. V. (1971). *Kinsey: A biography.* Bloomington, IN: Indiana University Press.

Christopher, F. S., & Sprecher, S. (2000). Sexuality in marriage, dating, and other relationships: A decade review. *Journal of Marriage and the Family, 62,* 999–1017.

Chu, J. A., Frey, L. M., Ganzel, B., & Mattews, J. (1999). Memories of childhood abuse: Dissociation amnesia, and corroboration. *American Journal of Psychiatry, 156,* 749–755.

Chu, M., & Lobo, R. (2004). Formulations and use of androgens in women. *Journal of Family Practice, 53,* S3.

Church, S., Henderson, M., Barnard, M., & Hart, G. (2001). Violence by clients towards female prostitutes in different work settings: Questionnaire survey. *British Medical Journal, 322,* 524–525.

CIHI (Canadian Institute for Health Information, 2016). *Health indicators interactive tool.* Retrieved from www.cihi.ca

CIHI (Canadian Institute for Health Information, 2016a). *Childbirth indicators by place of residence.* Retrieved from www.cihi.ca

Cimbalo, R. S., Faling, B., & Mousaw, P. (1976). The course of love: A cross-sectional design. *Psychological Reports, 38,* 1292–1294.

Cizmar, M., Conklin, E., & Hinman, K. (2011). Real men get their facts straight. Retrieved from http://www.villagevoice.com/content/printVersion/2651144/

Clamen, J., Bruckert, C., & Mensah, M. N. (2013). Managing sex work: Information for third parties and sex workers in the incall and outcall sectors of the sex industry. Retrieved from http://www.sciencessociales.uottawa.ca/gis-msi/eng/publications.asp

Clark, L., & Lewis, D. (1977). *Rape: The price of coercive sexuality.* Toronto: Women's Educational Press.

Clark, R. D., & Hatfield, E. (1989). Gender differences in receptivity to sexual offers. *Journal of Psychology & Human Sexuality, 2,* 39–45.

Clark, W., & Crompton, S. (2006). Till death do us part? The risk of first and second marriage dissolution. *Canadian Social Trends* (Catalogue no. 11-008E). Ottawa: Statistics Canada.

Clarke, J. N. (2006). Homophobia out of the closet in the media portrayal of HIV/AIDS 1991, 1996 and 2001: Celebrity, heterosexism and the silent victims. *Critical Public Health, 16*, 317–330.

Clark-Flory, T. (2011). I cross-dress and my wife doesn't know it. Retrieved from http://www.salon.com/2011/11/25/

Clausell, E., & Roisman, G. I. (2009). Outness, big five personality traits, and same-sex relationship quality. *Journal of Social and Personal Relationships, 26*, 211–226.

Cleland, K., Zhu, H., Goldstuck, N., Cheng, L., & Trussell, J. (2012). The efficacy of intrauterine devices for emergency contraception. *Human Reproduction, 27*, 1994–2000.

Clemente, C. D. (1987). *Anatomy: A regional atlas of the human body* (3rd ed.). Baltimore, MD: Urban & Schwarzenberg.

Clements-Schreiber, M. E., Rempel, J. K., & Desmarais, S. (1998). Women's sexual pressure tactics and adherence to related attitudes: A step towards prediction. *Journal of Sex Research, 35*(2), 197–205.

Clutton-Brock, T. (2007). Sexual selection in males and females. *Science, 318*, 1882–1885.

Cochran, S. D., Mays, V. M., Alegria, M., Ortega, A. N., & Takeuchi, D. (2007). Mental health and substance use disorders among Latino and Asian American lesbian, gay, and bisexual adults. *Journal of Consulting and Clinical Psychology, 75*, 785–794.

Cochran, S., Sullivan, J. G., & Mays, V. (2003). Prevalence of mental disorders, psychological distress, and mental health services use among lesbian, gay, and bisexual adults in the United States. *Journal of Consulting and Clinical Psychology, 71*, 53–61.

Cochran, W. G., Mosteller, F., & Tukey, J. W. (1953). Statistical problems of the Kinsey report. *Journal of the American Statistical Association, 48*, 673–716.

Cohen, B. B., Zhang, Z., Nannini, A., Farr, S. L., Anderson, J. E., Jamieson, D. J., & Tepper, N. K. (2009). Assisted reproductive technology and trends in low birthweight – Massachusetts, 1997–2004. *MMWR, 58*, 49–52.

Cohen, J. (1988). *Statistical power analysis for the behavioral sciences*. Hillsdale, NJ: Erlbaum.

Cohen, J. (1997). Exploiting the HIV-chemokine nexus. *Science, 275*, 1261–1264.

Cohen, J. (1998). Exploring how to get at- and eradicate-hidden HIV. *Science, 279*, 1854–1855.

Cohen, J. (2009). Beyond Thailand: Making sense of a qualified AIDS vaccine "success." *Science, 326*, 652–653.

Cohen, J. (2011a). The emerging race to cure HIV infections. *Science, 332*, 784–789.

Cohen, J. N., & Byers, E. S. (2014). Beyond lesbian bed death: Enhancing our understanding of the sexuality of sexual-minority women in relationships. *Journal of Sex Research, 51*, 893–903.

Cohen, J. N., & Byers, E. S. (2015). Minority stress, protective factors, and sexual functioning of women in a same-sex relationship. *Psychology of Sexual Orientation and Gender Diversity, 2*, 391–403.

Cohen, J. N., Byers, E. S., & Sears, H. A. (2012). Factors affecting Canadian teachers' willingness to teach sexual health education. *Sex Education, 12*, 299–316.

Cohen, J. N., Byers, E. S., & Walsh, L. P. (2008). Factors influencing the sexual relationships of lesbians and gay men. *International Journal of Sexual Health, 20*, 162–176.

Cohen, J. N., Byers, E. S., Sears, H. A., & Weaver, A. D. (2004). Sexual health education: Attitudes, knowledge, and comfort of teachers in New Brunswick schools. *Canadian Journal of Human Sexuality, 13*, 1–15.

Cohen, K. M. (2002). Relationships among childhood sex-atypical behavior, spatial ability, handedness, and sexual orientation in men. *Archives of Sexual Behavior, 31*, 129–144.

Cohen, M. S., Chen, Y. Q., McCauley, M., Gamble, T., Hosseinipour, M. C., Kumarasamy, N., . . . Fleming, T. R. (2011). Prevention of HIV-1 infection with early antiretroviral therapy. *New England Journal of Medicine, 365*, 493–505.

Cohn, L. (1983, November 16). Pix less able but porn is stable. *Variety, 313*(3), 1–2.

Colagross-Schouten, A., Lemoy, M.-J., Keesler, R. I., Lissner, E., & VandeVoort, C. A. (2017). The contraceptive efficacy of intravas injection of Vasalgel for adult male rhesus monkeys. *Basic and Clinical Andrology, 27*, doi:10.1186/s12610-017-0048-9.

Colapinto, J. (2004, June 3). Gender gap: What were the real reasons behind David Reimer's Suicide? *Slate*. Retrieved from http://www.slate.com/id/2101678/

Cole, E. R. (2009). Intersectionality and research in psychology. *American Psychologist, 64*, 170–180.

Cole, L. (2011). The utility of six over-the counter(home) pregnancy tests. *Clinical Chemistry and Laboratory Medicine, 49*, 1317–1322.

Cole, L., Khantian, S., Sutton, J., Davies, S., & Rayburn, W. (2004). Accuracy of home pregnancy tests at the time of missed menses. *American Journal of Obstetrics and Gynecology, 190*, 100–105.

Coleman, E. (1991). Compulsive sexual behavior: New concepts and treatments. *Journal of Psychology and Human Sexuality, 4*(2), 37–51.

Coleman, E., Bockting, W., Botzer, M., Cohen-Kettenis, P., DeCuypere, G., Feldman, J., . . . & Zucker, K. (2012). Standards of care for the health of transsexual, transgender, and gender-nonconforming people, version 7. *International Journal of Transgenderism, 13*, 165–232.

Coleman, E., Miner, M., Ohlerking, F., & Raymond, N. (2001). Compulsive Sexual Behavior inventory: A preliminary study of reliability and validity. *Journal of Sex and Marital Therapy, 27*, 325–332.

Coleman, E., Raymond, N., & McBean, A. (2003, July 2003). Assessment and treatment of compulsive sexual behaviour. *Minnesota Medicine, 86*, 42–47.

Collaborative Group on Hormonal Factors in Breast Cancer. (2002). Breast cancer and breast-feeding. *Lancet, 360*, 187–195.

Collins, N. L., & Miller, L. C. (1994). Self-disclosure and liking: A metaanalytic review. *Psychological Bulletin, 116*, 457–475.

Collins, R. L., Ellickson, P. L., Orlando, M., & Klein, D. J. (2005). Isolating the nexus of substance use, violence and sexual risk for HIV infection among young adults in the United States. *AIDS and Behavior, 9*, 73–87.

Collins, R. L., Elliott, M. N., Berry, S. H., Kanouse, D. E., Kunkel, D., Hunter, S. B., & Miu, A. (2004). Watching sex on television predicts adolescent initiation of sexual behavior. *Pediatrics, 114*(3), e280–e209.

Collins, W. A., Welsh, D. P., & Furman, W. (2009). Adolescent romantic relationships. *Annual Review of Psychology, 60*, 631–652.

Collin-Vézina, D., & Hébert, M. (2005). Comparing dissociation and PTSD in sexually abused school-aged girls. *Journal of Mental & Nervous Disease, 193*, 47–52.

Comet (Comparative Obstetric Mobile Epidural Trial) Study Group. (2001). Effect of low-dose mobile versus traditional epidural techniques on mode of delivery: A randomised controlled trial. *Lancet, 358*, 19–23.

Comfort, A. (1991). *The new joy of sex: A gourmet guide to lovemaking for the nineties*. New York: Crown.

Compas Inc. (2005, February 14). Valentine's Day poll for the *National Post*. Toronto: Author.

Compas, B. E., & Luecken, L. (2002). Psychological adjustment to breast cancer. *Current Directions in Psychological Science, 11*, 111–114.

Congregation for the Doctrine of the Faith. (1986). The pastoral care of homosexual persons. *Origins, 26*, 378–382.

Congregation for the Doctrine of the Faith. (1987). Instruction on respect for human life in its origin and on the dignity of procreation. *Origins, 16*, 198–211.

Congregation for the Doctrine of the Faith. (2008, September 8). Regarding the instruction dignitas personae. Retrieved from http://www.religiousinstitute.org/statement/regarding-the-instruction-dignitas-personaesummary

Conley, T. D. (2011). Perceived proposer personality characteristics and gender differences in acceptance of casual sex offers. *Journal of Personality and Social Psychology, 100*, 309–329.

Conley, T. D., Moors, A. C., Matsick, J. L., Ziegler, A., & Valentine, B. A. (2011). Women, men, and the bedroom: Methodological and conceptual insights that narrow, reframe, and eliminate gender differences in sexuality. *Current Directions in Psychological Science, 20*, 296–300.

Connell, E., & Hunt, A. (2006). Sexual ideology and sexual physiology in the discourses of sex advice literature. *Canadian Journal of Human Sexuality, 15*, 23–45.

Conrad, K., Dixon, T., & Zhang, Y. (2009). Controversial rap themes, gender portrayals and skin tone distortion: A content analysis of rap music videos. *Journal of Broadcasting & Electronic Media, 53*, 134–156.

Conron, K. J., Scott, G., Stowell, G. S., & Landers, S. J. (2012). Transgender health in Massachusetts: Results from a household probability sample of adults. *American Journal of Public Health, 102*, 118–122.

Contessini, C. (2003). Personal Communication.

Cook, K., & Rice, E. (2003). Social exchange theory. In J. DeLamater (Ed.), *The handbook of social psychology* (pp. 53–76). New York: Kluwer-Plenum.

Cooper, A. (1998). Sexuality and the Internet: Surfing into the new millennium. *CyberPsychology & Behavior, 1*, 187–193.

Cooper, A., & Griffin-Shelley, E. (2002). Introduction. The Internet: The next sexual revolution. In A. Cooper (Ed.), *Sex and the internet: A guidebook for clinicians* (pp. 1–15). New York: Brunner-Routledge.

Cooper, A., Delmonico, D. L., Griffin-Shelley, E., & Mathy, R. M. (2004). Online sexual activity: An examination of potentially problematic behaviors. *Sexual Addiction & Compulsivity, 11*, 129–143.

Cooper, A., Delmonico, D., & Burg, R. (2000). Cybersex users, abusers, and compulsives: New findings and implications. In A. Cooper (Ed.), *Cybersex: The dark side of the force* (pp. 5–29). Philadelphia: Brunner Routledge.

Cooper, A., Putnam, D. E., Planchon, L. A., & Boies, S. C. (1999a). Online sexual compulsivity: Getting tangled in the Net. *Sexual Addiction & Compulsivity: Journal of Treatment and Prevention, 6*, 79–104.

Cooper, A., Scherer, C. R., Gordon, B. L., & Boies, S. C. (1999b). Sexuality on the Internet: From sexual exploration to pathological expression. *Professional Psychology: Research & Practice, 30*(2), 154–164.

Cordova, M. J., Cunningham, L., Carlson, C., & Andrykowski, M. (2001). Posttraumatic growth following breast cancer: A controlled comparison study. *Health Psychology, 20*, 176–185.

Corey, L., & Wald, A. (2008). Genital herpes. In K. Holmes et al. (Eds.), *Sexually transmitted diseases* (4th ed., pp. 399–438). New York: McGraw-Hill.

Corsini-Munt, S., Bergeron, S., Rosen, N. O., Mayrand, M.-H., & Delisle, I. (2014). Feasibility and preliminary effectiveness of a novel cognitive-behavioral couple therapy for provoked vestibulodynia: A pilot study. *Journal of Sexual Medicine, 11*, 2515–2527.

Cortini, F., Hanson, R. K., & Coache, M. (2010). The recidivism rates of female sexual offenders are low: A meta-analysis. *Sex Abuse, 22*, 387–401.

Cotter, A., & Beaupré, P. (2014). Police-reported sexual offences against children and youth in Canada, 2012. *Juristat*. Statistics Canada catalogue no. 85-002-X.

Coughlan, C. (2008). Surgical management of tubal disease and infertility. *Obstetrics, Gynaecology, and Reproductive Medicine, 11*, 013.

Countryman, L. W. (1987). The AIDS crisis: Theological and ethical reflections. *Anglican Theological Review, 69*, 125–134.

Countryman, L. W. (1994). New Testament sexual ethics and today's world. In J. B. Nelson & S. P. Longfellow (Eds.), *Sexuality and the sacred* (pp. 28–53). Louisville, KY: Westminster/John Knox Press.

Coustan, D. (1995). Obstetric analgesia and anesthesia. In D. R. Coustan, R. V. Hunning, Jr., & D. Singer (Eds.), *Human reproduction: Growth and development* (pp. 327–340). Boston: Little, Brown & Co.

Coustan, D., & Angelini, D. (1995). The puerperium. In D. R. Coustan, R. V. Hunning, Jr., & D. Singer (Eds.), *Human reproduction: Growth and development* (pp. 341–358). Boston: Little, Brown & Co.

Couzinet, B., Le Strat, N., Ulmann, A., Baulieu, E. E., & Schaison, G. (1986). Termination of early pregnancy by the progesterone antagonist RU486 (mifepristone). *New England Journal of Medicine, 315*, 1565–1569.

Cowan, G., Chase, C. J., & Stahly, G. B. (1989). Feminist and fundamentalist attitudes toward pornography control. *Psychology of Women Quarterly, 13*, 97–112.

Cowley, J. J., & Brooksbank, B. W. L. (1991). Human exposure to putative pheromones and changes in aspects of social behavior. *Journal of Steroid Biochemistry and Molecular Biology, 39*, 647–659.

Cox, D. J. (1988). Incidence and nature of male genital exposure behavior as reported by college women. *Journal of Sex Research, 24*, 227–234.

Cox, W. T. L., Devine, P. G., Bischmann, A., & Hyde, J. S. (2016). Inferences about sexual orientation: The role of stereotypes, faces, and the gaydar myth. *Journal of Sex Research, 53*, 157–171.

Coyle, C. T., & Enright, R. D. (1997). Forgiveness intervention with post-abortion men. *Journal of Consulting and Clinical Psychology, 65*, 1042–1046.

Cramer, E. H., Jones, P., Keenan, N. L., & Thompson, B. L. (2003). Is naturopathy as effective as conventional therapy for treatment of menopausal symptoms? *Journal of Alternative and Complementary Medicine, 8*, 529–538.

Crawford, J., Kippax, S., & Waldby, C. (1994). Women's sex talk and men's sex talk: Different worlds. *Feminism and Psychology*, 571–587.

Crawford, M., & Popp, D. (2003). Sexual double standards: A review and methodological critique of two decades of research. *Journal of Sex Research, 40*, 13–26.

Craze, R. (2003). *Teach yourself tantric sex*. Whitby, ON: McGraw-Hill.

Creighton, J. (1992). *Don't go away mad*. New York: Doubleday.

Creighton, S. M., & Minto, C. (2001). Managing intersex: Most vaginal surgery in childhood should be deferred. *British Medical Journal, 323*, 1264–1265.

Creighton, S. M., Minto, C., & Steele, S. (2001). Objective cosmetic and anatomical outcomes at adolescence of feminising surgery for ambiguous genitalia done in childhood. *Lancet, 358*, 124–125.

Crocker, D., & Kalemba, V. (1999). The incidence and impact of women's experiences of sexual harassment in Canadian workplaces. *Canadian Review of Sociology and Anthropology, 36*, 541–558.

Crompton, L. (2003). *Homosexuality and civilization*. Cambridge, MA: Harvard University Press.

Crompton, S. (2005). Always the bridesmaid: People who don't expect to marry. *Canadian Social Trends* (Catalogue no. 11-008E). Ottawa: Statistics Canada.

Cruess, S., Antoni, M. H., Hayes, A., Penedo, F. J., Ironson, G. H., Fletcher, M. A., . . . Schneiderman, N. (2002). Changes in mood and depressive symptoms and related change processes during cognitive-behavioral stress management in HIV-infected men. *Cognitive Therapy & Research, 26*, 373–392.

Cunningham, F. G., MacDonald, P. C., Gant, N. F., Leveno, K. J., & Gilstrap, L. C., III. (1993). *Williams obstetrics* (19th ed.). Norwalk, CT: Appleton and Lange.

Cunningham, M., Roberts, A., Wu, C.-H., Burbee, A., & Druen, P. (1995). "Their ideas of beauty are, on the whole, the same as ours": Consistency and variability in the cross-cultural perception of female physical attractiveness. *Journal of Personality and Social Psychology, 68*, 261–279.

Curran, C. E. (1988). Roman Catholic sexual ethics: A dissenting view. *Christian Century, 105*, 1139–1142.

Curtis, J. T., & Wang, Z. X. (2003). The neurochemistry of pair bonding. *Current Directions in Psychological Science, 12*, 49–53.

Cutler, W. B. (1999). Human sex-attractant hormones. *Psychiatric Annals, 29*, 54–59.

Cyr, M. V., & Hébert, M. (2011). Analyse comparative des caractéristiques de l'agression sexuelle et des conséquences associées en fonction du sexe. *Service Social, 57*, 15–30.

D'Augelli, A. (2002). Mental health problems among lesbian, gay, and bisexual youths ages 14 to 21. *Clinical Child Psychology and Psychiatry, 7*, 433–456.

D'Augelli, A. R. (2006). Developmental and contextual factors and mental health among lesbian, gay, and bisexual youths. In A. E. Omoto & H. M. Kurtzman (Eds.), *Recent research on sexual orientation*. Washington, DC: APA Books.

D'Souza, G., Kreimer, A. R., Viscidi, R., Pawlita, M., Fakhry, C., Koch, W. M., . . . Gillison, M. L. (2007). Case-control study of human papillomavirus and oropharyngeal cancer. *New England Journal of Medicine, 356*, 1944–1956.

Da Costa, D., Brender, W., & Larouche, J. (1998) A prospective study of the impact of psychosocial and lifestyle variables on pregnancy complications. *Journal of Psychosomatic Obstetrics and Gynaecology, 19*, 28–37.

Dahl, B., Fylkesnes, A. M., Sòrlie, V., & Malterud, K. (2013). Lesbian women's experiences with healthcare providers in the birthing context: A meta-ethnography. *Midwifery, 29*, 674–681.

Daigneault, I., Hébert, M., McDuff, P., & Frappier, J. (2012). Evaluation of a sexual abuse prevention workshop in a multicultural, impoverished urban area. *Journal of Child Sexual Abuse, 21,* 521–542.

Dailard, C. (2006). The public health promise and potential pitfalls of the world's first cervical cancer vaccine. *Guttmacher Policy Review, 9,* 6–9.

Dalenberg, C. J., Brand, B. L., Gleaves, D. H., Dorahy, M. J., Loewenstein, R. J., Cardeña, E., . . . Spiegel, D. (2012). Evaluation of the evidence for the trauma and fantasy models of dissociation. *Psychological Bulletin, 138,* 550–558.

Damgaard, I., Jensen, T., Petersen, J. H., Skakkebæk, N. E., Toppari, J., Main, K. M., & the Nordic Cryptorchidism Study Group. (2006). Cryptorchidism and maternal alcohol consumption during pregnancy. *Environmental Health Perspectives, 115,* 272–277. doi:10.1289/ehp.9608

Damsted-Petersen, C., Boyer, S. C., & Pukall, C. F. (2009). Current perspectives in vulvodynia. *Women's Health, 5,* 423–436.

Daneback, K., Cooper, A., & Månsson, S. (2005). An internet study of cybersex participants. *Archives of Sexual Behavior, 34,* 321–329.

Daneback, K., Cooper, A., & Mansson, S.-A. (2004). An investigation of cybersex: Who participates, reasons that they do, and resulting consequences. Unpublished manuscript.

Daniluk, J. C. (1999). When biology isn't destiny: Implications for the sexuality of women without children. *Canadian Journal of Counselling, 33,* 79–94.

Daniluk, J. C. (2001a). "If we had it to do over again . . .": Couples' reflections on their experiences of infertility treatments. *The Family Journal: Counseling and Therapy for Couples and Families, 9,* 122–133.

Daniluk, J. C. (2001b). Reconstructing their lives: A longitudinal, qualitative analysis of the transition to biological childlessness for infertile couples. *Journal of Counseling & Development, 79,* 439–449.

Daniluk, J. C., & Koert, E. (2013). The other side of the fertility coin: a comparison of childless men's and women's knowledge of fertility and assisted reproductive technology. *Fertility and Sterility, 99,* 839–846.

Daniluk, J. C., & Koert, E. (2015). Fertility awareness online: the efficacy of a fertility education website in increasing knowledge and changing fertility beliefs. *Human Reproduction, 30,* 353–363.

Daniluk, J. C., Koert, E., & Cheung, A. (2012). Childless women's knowledge of fertility and assisted human reproduction: identifying the gaps. *Fertility and Sterility, 97,* 420–426.

Dargie, E., Blair, K. L., Goldfinger, C., & Pukall, C. F. (2015). Go long! Predictors of positive relationship outcomes in long-distance dating relationships. *Journal of Sex & Marital Therapy, 41,* 181–202.

Darling, C. A., Davidson, J. K., & Conway-Welch, C. (1990). Female ejaculation: Perceived origins, the Gräfenberg spot/ area, and sexual responsiveness. *Archives of Sexual Behavior, 19,* 29–48.

Darroch, J. E., Frost, J. J., Singh, S., and the Study Team. (2001). *Teenage sexual and reproductive behavior in developed countries: Can more progress be made?* New York: Alan Guttmacher Institute.

Darroch, J. E., Singh, S., Frost, J. J., & the Study Team. (2001). Differences in teenage pregnancy rates among five developed countries: The roles of sexual activity and contraceptive use. *Family Planning Perspectives, 33,* 244–250.

Darwich, L., Hymel, S., & Waterhouse, T. (2012). School avoidance and substance use among lesbian, gay, bisexual, and questioning youths: The impact of peer victimization and adult support. *Journal of Educational Psychology, 104,* 381–392.

Das, A., Waite, L., & Laumann, Ed. (2012). Sexual expression over the life course. In L. Carpenter & J. DeLamater (Eds.), *Sex for life: From virginity to Viagra, how sexuality changes throughout our lives* (pp. 236–259). New York: New York University Press.

Davé, S., Petersen, I., Sherr, L, & Nazareth, I. (2010). Incidence of maternal and paternal depression in primary care. *Archives of Pediatric and Adolescent Medicine, 164,* 1038–1044. doi:10.1001/archpediatrics.2010.184

David, A. (2011). The joy of spanking. *Salon.com.* Accessed at http://www.salon.com/2011/02/11/inside_world_of_spanking

David, H. P., Dytrych, Z., & Matejcek, Z. (2003). Born unwanted: Observations from the Prague study. *American Psychologist, 58,* 224–229.

Davies, J. M. (2015). The criminalization of sexual commerce in Canada: Context and concepts for critical analysis. *Canadian Journal of Human Sexuality, 24,* 78–91.

Davies, M. J., Moore, V. M., Willson, K. J., Van Essen, P., Priest, K., Scott, H., . . . Chan, A. (2012). Reproductive technologies and the risk of birth defects. *The New England Journal of Medicine, 366,* 1803–1813.

Davis, C. M., & Bauserman, R. (1993). Exposure to sexually explicit materials: An attitude change perspective. *Annual Review of Sex Research, 4,* 121–210.

Davis, D., Shaver, P. R., & Vernon, M. L. (2003). Physical, emotional, and behavioral reactions to breaking up: The roles of gender, age, emotional involvement, and attachment style. *Personality and Social Psychology Bulletin, 29*(7), 871–884.

Davis, D., Shaver, P. R., Widaman, K. F., Vernon, M. L., Follette, W. C., & Beitz, K. (2006). "I can't get no satisfaction": Insecure attachment, inhibited sexual communication, and sexual dissatisfaction. *Personal Relationships, 13*(4), 465–483.

Dawson, S. J., & Chivers, M. L. (2014). Gender differences and similarities in sexual desire. *Current Sexual Health Report, 6,* 211–219.

Dawson, S. J., Bannerman, B. A., & Lalumière, M. (2016). Paraphilic interests: An examination of sex differences in a nonclinical sample. *Sex Abuse: A Journal of Research and Treatment, 28,* 20–45.

Dawson, S. J., Sawatsky, M. L., & Lalumiere, M. L. (2015). Assessment of introital lubrication. *Archives of Sexual Behavior, 44,* 1527–1535.

Dawson, S. J., Suschinsky, K. D., & Lalumière, M. L. (2012). Sexual fantasies and viewing times across the menstrual cycle: A diary study. *Archives of Sexual Behavior, 41,* 173–183.

Day, L. C., Muise, A. , Joel, S., & Impett, E. A. (2015). To do it or not to do it? How communally motivated people navigate sexual interdependence dilemmas. *Personality and Social Psychology Bulletin, 41,* 791–804.

Day, M. V., Kay, A. C., Holmes, J. G., & Napier, J. L. (2011). System justification and the defense of committed relationship ideology. *Journal of Personality and Social Psychology, 101,* 291–306.

De Cuypere, G., T'Sjoen, G., Beerten, R., Selvaggi, G., De Sutter, P., Hoebeke, P., . . . Rubens, R. (2005). Sexual and physical health after sex reassignment surgery. *Archives of Sexual Behavior, 34,* 679–690.

De Graaf, H., & Rademakers, J. (2006). Sexual behavior of prepubertal children. *Journal of Psychology & Human Sexuality, 18,* 1–21.

De Graaf, H., & Rademakers, J. (2011). The psychological measurement of childhood sexual development in western societies: Methodological challenges. *Journal of Sex Research, 48,* 118–129.

De Graaf, H., Vanwesenbeeck, I., Meijer, S., Woertman, L., & Meeus, W. (2009). Sexual trajectories during adolescence: Relation to demographic characteristics and sexual risk. *Archives of Sexual Behavior, 38*(2), 276–282.

De Jong, D. C. (2009). The role of attention in sexual arousal: Implications for treatment of sexual dysfunction. *Journal of Sex Research, 46,* 237–248.

De Jong, P. J., van Overveld, M., & Borg, C. (2013). Giving in to arousal or staying stuck in disgust? Disgust-based mechanisms in sex and sexual dysfunction. *Journal of Sex Research, 50,* 247–262.

De La Vega Salas, M. L., & Thériault, J. (2001). Sexualité parental et relation intime du couple parental: Conceptualisations des enfants âgés de dix et 11 ans. *Gynécologie, obstétrique, & fertilité, 29,* 226–233.

De Visser, R. O., et al. (2007). The impact of sexual coercion on psychological, physical, and sexual well-being in a representative sample of Australian women. *Archives of Sexual Behavior, 36,* 676–686.

de Vries, A. L. C., McGuire, J. K., Steensma, T. D., Wagenaar, E. C. F., Doreleijers, T. A. H., & Cohen-Kettenis, P. T. (2014). Young adult psychological outcome after puberty suppression and gender reassignment. *Pediatrics, 134,* 1–9.

De Waal, F. (2002). Evolutionary psychology: The wheat and the chaff. *Current Directions in Psychological Science, 11,* 187–191.

De Waal, F. B. M. (1995). The behavior of a close relative challenges assumptions about male supremacy in human evolution. *Scientific American*, 82–88.

DeBruine, L. M., Jones, B. C., Crawford, J. R., Welling, L. L. M., & Little, A. C. (2010). The health of a nation predicts their mate preferences: Crosscultural variation in women's preferences for masculinized male faces. *Proceedings of the Royal Society: Biological Sciences, 277*, 1692–2405.

DeKeseredy, W. S., & Kelly, K. (1993). Woman abuse in university and college dating relationships: The contribution of the ideology of familial patriarchy. *Journal of Human Justice, 4*(2), 25–52.

DeKeseredy, W. S., & Schwartz, M. D. (1998). *Women abuse on campus: Results from the Canadian national survey*. Thousand Oaks, CA: Sage Publications.

Dekker, A., & Schmidt, G. (2002). Patterns of masturbatory behaviour: Changes between the sixties and the nineties. *Journal of Psychology & Human Sexuality, 14*, 35–48.

Del Giudice, M., Angeleri, R., & Manera, V. (2009). The juvenile transition: A developmental switch point in human life history. *Developmental Review, 29*, 1–3

DeLamater, J. (1987). A sociological perspective. In J. H. Geer & W. T. O'Donohue (Eds.), *Theories of human sexuality* (pp. 237–256). New York: Plenum.

DeLamater, J., & Moorman, S. (2007). Sexuality and aging. In K. Markides (Ed.), *Encyclopedia of health and aging*. Thousand Oaks, CA: Sage Publications.

DeLamater, J., Wagstaff, D. A., & Havens, K. K. (2000). The impact of a culturally appropriate STD/AIDS education intervention on Black male adolescents' sexual and condom use behavior. *Health Education and Behavior, 27*, 454–470.

Delap, J. (2014, August 9). The changing business of sex: How the Internet affects prostitution. *The Economist.*

Delemarre-van de Waal, H., & Cohen-Kettenis, P. (2006). Clinical management of gender identity disorder in adolescents: A protocol on psychological and paediatric endocrinology aspects. *European Journal of Endocrinology, 155*, S131–S137.

Deligeor-Oglov, E. (2000). Dysmenorrhea. *Annals of the New York Academy of Sciences, 900*, 237–244.

DeMaris, A. (2009). Distal and proximal influences on the risk of extramarital sex: A prospective study of longer duration marriages. *Journal of Sex Research, 46*, 597–607.

Demers, A. A., Kliewer, E. V., Remes, O., Onysko, J., Dinner, K., Wong, T., & Jayaraman, G. C. (2012). Cervical cancer among Aboriginal women in Canada. *Canadian Medical Association Journal, 184*, 743–744.

Dennerstein, L., Alexander, J. L., & Kotz, K. (2003). The menopause and sexual functioning: A review of the population-based studies. *Annual Review of Sex Research, 14*, 64–82.

Dennis, C. (2005). Psychosocial and psychological interventions for prevention of post-natal depression: Systematic review. *British Medical Journal, 331*, 15.

Denov, M. S. (2003). The myth of innocence: Sexual scripts and the recognition of child sexual abuse by female perpetrators. *Journal of Sex Research, 40*, 303–314.

Denzin, N. K., & Lincoln, Y. S. (1994). Introduction: Entering the field of qualitative research. In N. K. Denzin, & Y. S. Lincoln (Eds.), *Handbook of qualitative research* (pp. 1–17). Thousand Oaks, CA: Sage.

Denzin, N. K., & Lincoln, Y. S. (Eds.). (2005). *The Sage handbook of qualitative research* (3rd ed.). Thousand Oaks, CA: Sage.

DePaulo, B. (2006). *Singled out: How singles are stereotyped, stigmatized, and ignored, and still live happily ever after*. New York: St. Martin's Press.

Derby, C. A., Mohr, B. A., Goldstein, I., Feldman, H. A., Johannes, C. B., & McKinlay, J. B. (2000). Modifiable risk factors and erectile dysfunction: Can lifestyle changes modify risk? *Urology, 56*, 302–306.

Descamps, M. J., Rothblum, E., Bradford, J., & Ryan, C. (2000). Mental health impact of child sexual abuse, rape, intimate partner violence, and hate crimes in the National Lesbian Health Care Survey. *Journal of Gay & Lesbian Social Services, 11*, 27–55.

Desrochers, G., Bergeron, S., Khalifé, S., Dupuis, M., & Jodoin, M. (2009). Fear avoidance and self-efficacy in relation to pain and sexual impairment in women with provoked vestibulodynia. *Clinical Journal of Pain, 25*, 520–527.

Desrochers, G., Bergeron, S., Khalifé, S., Dupuis, M., & Jodoin, M. (2010). Provoked vestibulodynia: Psychological predictors of topical and cognitive-behavioral treatment outcome. *Behaviour Research and Therapy, 48*, 106–115.

Desrochers, G., Bergeron, S., Landry, T., & Jodoin, M. (2008). Do psychosexual factors play a role in the etiology of provoked vestibulodynia? A critical review. *Journal of Sex & Marital Therapy, 34*, 198–226.

DeSteno, D., Valdesolo, P., & Bartlett, M. (2006). Jealousy and the threatened self: Getting to the heart of the green-eyed monster. *Journal of Personality and Social Psychology, 91*, 626–641.

Devor, A. (2014). The transgender archives: Foundations for the future. Victoria, BC: University of Victoria Libraries.

Devor, A. H. (1989). *Gender blending: Confronting the limits of duality*. Bloomington, IN: Indiana University Press.

Devor, A., & Dominic, K. (2015). "Trans*Sexualities." In John DeLamater and Rebecca F. Plante (Eds.), *Handbook of the sociology of sexualities* (pp. 181–199). Switzerland: Springer International Publishing.

Devor, H. (1996). Female gender dysphoria in context: Social problem or personal problem? *Annual Review of Sex Research: An Integrative & Interdisciplinary Review, 7*, 44–89.

Devor, H. (1997a). *FTM: Female-to-male transsexuals in society*. Bloomington, IN: Indiana University Press.

Devor, H. (1997b). More than manly women: How female to male transsexuals reject lesbian identities. In B. Bullough, V. Bullough, & J. Elias (Eds.), *Gender blending*. Amherst, NJ: Prometheus.

Di Giulio, G. (2003). Sexuality and people living with physical or developmental disabilities: A review of key issues. *Canadian Journal of Human Sexuality, 12*, 53–68.

Di Giulio, G., & Reissing, E. D. (2006). Premenstrual dysphoric disorder: Prevalence, diagnostic considerations, and controversies. *Journal of Psychosomatic Obstetrics & Gynecology, 27*, 201–210.

Diamanti-Kandarakis, E., & Gore, A. C. (2009). Endocrine-disrupting chemicals: An Endocrine Society scientific statement. *Endocrine Review, 30*, 293–342.

Diamond, L. M. (2003). Was it a phase? Young women's relinquishment of lesbian/bisexual identities over a 5-year period. *Journal of Personality and Social Psychology, 84*, 352–364.

Diamond, L. M. (2004). Emerging perspectives on distinctions between romantic love and sexual desire. *Current Directions in Psychological Science, 13*, 116–119.

Diamond, L. M. (2005). A new view of lesbian subtypes: Stable versus fluid identity trajectories over an 8-year period. *Psychology of Women Quarterly, 29*, 119–128.

Diamond, L. M. (2008a). *Sexual fluidity: Understanding women's love and desire*. Cambridge, MA: Harvard University Press.

Diamond, L. M. (2008b). Female bisexuality from adolescence to adulthood: Results from a 10-year longitudinal study. *Developmental Psychology, 44*, 5–14.

Diamond, M. (1996). Prenatal predisposition and the clinical management of some pediatric conditions. *Journal of Sex and Marital Therapy, 22*, 139–147.

Diamond, M. (1999). Pediatric management of ambiguous and traumatized genitalia. *Journal of Urology, 162*, 1021–1028.

Diamond, M. (2009). Pornography, public acceptance, and sex-related crime: A review. *International Journal of Law and Psychiatry, 32*, 304–314.

Diamond, M., & Sigmundson, H. K. (1997). Sex reassignment at birth: Long-term review and clinical implications. *Archives of Pediatric and Adolescent Medicine, 151*, 298–304.

DiCenso, A., Gyatt, G., Willan, A., & Griffith, L. (2002). Interventions to reduce unintended pregnancies among adolescents: Systematic review of randomized controlled trials. *British Medical Journal, 324*, 1426.

Dickey, R. P. (2000). *Managing contraceptive pill patients* (10th ed.). Dallas, TX: EMIS.

Dickson, N., Paul, C., & Herbison, P. (2003). Same-sex attraction in a birth cohort: Prevalence and persistence in early adulthood. *Social Science & Medicine, 56*, 1607–1615.

Dill, K. E., & Thill, K. (2007). Video game characters and the socialization of gender roles: Young people's perceptions mirror sexist media depictions. *Sex Roles, 57,* 851–864.

Dion, J., Matte-Gagné, C., Daigneault, I., Blackburn, M.-E., Hébert, M., McDuff, P., . . . Perron, M. (2016). A prospective study of the impact of child maltreatment and friend support on psychological distress trajectory: From adolescence to emerging adulthood. *Journal of Affective Disorders, 189,* 336–343.

Dion, K. K. (1973). Young children's stereotyping of facial attractiveness. *Developmental Psychology, 9,* 183–188.

Dion, K. K., & Dion, K. L. (1993b). Individualistic and collectivistic perspectives on gender and the cultural content of love and intimacy. *Journal of Social Issues, 49,* 53–69.

Dion, K. L. (1977). The incentive value of physical attractiveness for young children. *Personality and Social Psychology Bulletin, 3,* 67–70.

Dion, K. L., & Dion, K. K. (1993a). Gender and ethnocultural comparisons in styles of love. *Psychology of Women Quarterly, 17,* 463–474.

Dixson, B. J., Grimshaw, G. M., Linklater, W. L., & Dixson, A. F. (2011). Eye-tracking of men's preferences for waist-to-hip ratio and breast size of women. *Archives of Sexual Behavior, 40,* 43–50.

Docter, R. F., & Prince, V. (1997). Transvestism: A survey of 1032 crossdressers. *Archives of Sexual Behavior, 26,* 589–606.

Dodes, L., & Dodes, Z. (2014). *The Sober Truth.* Boston: Beacon Press.

Dodge, B., Reece, M., Cole, S., & Sandfort, T. (2004). Sexual compulsivity among heterosexual college students. *Journal of Sex Research, 41,* 343–350.

Doing it and enjoying it. (1999, December 20). *Maclean's, 112*(51).

Donadio, R. (2010, December 21). Vatican adds nuance to Pope's condom remarks. *The New York Times.*

Donahue, J. E., Stopa, E. G, & Chorsky, R. L. (2000). Cells containing immunoreactive estrogen receptor-a in the human basal forebrain. *Brain Research, 856,* 142–151.

Donnelly, D. A. (1993). Sexually inactive marriages. *Journal of Sex Research, 30,* 171–179.

Donnelly, D., Burgess, E., Anderson, S., Davis, R., & Dillard, J. (2001). Involuntary celibacy: A life course analysis. *Journal of Sex Research, 38,* 159–169.

Donnerstein, E., Linz, D., & Penrod, S. (1987). *The question of pornography: Research findings and policy implications.* New York: Free Press.

Doran, T. A. (1990). Chorionic villus sampling as the primary diagnostic tool in prenatal diagnosis. *Journal of Reproductive Medicine, 35,* 935–940.

Döring, N., Daneback, K., Shaughnessy, K., Grov, C., & Byers, E. S. (2015). Online sexual activity experiences among college students: A four-country comparison. *Archives of Sexual Behavior.* doi:10.1007/s10508-015-0656-4

Dorrie, N., Focker, M., Freunscht, I., & Hebebrand, J. (2014). Fetal alcohol spectrum disorders. *European Child and Adolescent Psychiatry, 23,* 863–875.

Douglas, M. (1970). *Purity and danger: An analysis of concepts of pollution and taboo.* Baltimore, MD: Penguin.

Downing, M., Jr., Schrimshaw, E., Antebi, N., & Siegel, K. (2014). Sexually explicit media on the Internet: A content analysis of sexual behaviors, risk, and media characteristics in gay male adult videos. *Archives of Sexual Behavior, 43,* 811–821.

Drea, C. M. (2009). Endocrine mediators of masculinization in female mammals. *Current Directions in Psychological Science, 18,* 221–226.

Dreznick, M. T. (2003). Heterosocial competence of rapists and child molesters: A meta-analysis. *Journal of Sex Research, 40,* 170–178.

Driedger, S. D. (2002, September 30). What parents don't know (or won't admit). *Maclean's.*

Driscoll, R., Davis, K. E., & Lipetz, M. E. (1972). Parental interference and romantic love: The Romeo and Juliet effect. *Journal of Personality and Social Psychology, 24,* 1–10.

Drolet, M., Brisson, M., Maunsell, E., Franco, E. L., Coutlée, F., Ferenczy, A., . . . Mansi, J. A. (2011). The impact of anogenital warts on health-related quality of life: A 6-month prospective study. *Sexually Transmitted Diseases, 38,* 949–956.

Dryer, P. C., & Horowitz, L. (1997). When do opposites attract? Interpersonal complementarity vs. similarity. *Journal of Personality and Social Psychology, 72,* 592–603.

du Mont, J., Macdonald, S., Rotbard, N., Asllani, E., Bainbridge, D., & Cohen M. M. (2009). Factors associated with suspected drug-facilitated sexual assault. *CMAJ, 180,* 513–519.

Duchesne, D. (1999). Street prostitution in Canada. In *The Juristat reader: A statistical overview of the Canadian justice system.* Toronto: Thomson Educational Publishing.

Duerr, A., Corey, L., & Wasserheit, J. N. (2008). HIV vaccines. In K. Holmes et al. (Eds.), *Sexually transmitted diseases* (4th ed., pp. 1937–1954). New York: McGraw-Hill.

Duff, S. J., & Hampson, E. (2000). A beneficial effect of estrogen on working memory in postmenopausal women taking hormone replacement therapy. *Hormones and Behavior, 38,* 262–276.

Dunbar, E. (2006). Race, gender, and sexual orientation in hate crime victimization: Identity politics or identity risk? *Violence and Victims, 21,* 323–337.

Duncan, S., Phillips, M., Roseneil, S., Carter, J., & Stoilova, M. (2013). *Living apart together: Uncoupling intimacy and co-residency.* Birkbeck, University of London.

Dunkley, C. R., & Brotto, L. A. (2016). Psychological treatments for provoked vestibulodynia: Integration of mindfulness-based and cognitive behavioral therapies. *Journal of Clinical Psychology, 0,* 1–14.

Dunmore, E., Clark, D. M., & Ehlers, A. (2001). A prospective investigation of the role of cognitive factors in persistent posttraumatic stress disorder (PTSD) after physical or sexual assault. *Behaviour Research and Therapy, 39,* 1063–1084.

Dunn, L., Ross, B., Caines, T., & Howorth, P. (1998). A school-based HIV/AIDS prevention education program: Outcomes of peer-led versus community health nurse-led interventions. *Canadian Journal of Human Sexuality, 7,* 339–345.

Dunn, M. E., & Trost, J. E. (1989). Male multiple orgasms: A descriptive study. *Archives of Sexual Behavior, 18,* 377–388.

Dunn, S., & Guilbert, E. (2003). Emergency contraception. *SOGC Clinical Practice Guidelines, 131,* 1–7.

Dunne, M. P., Martin, N. G., Bailey, J. M., Heath, A. C., Bucholz, K. K., Madden, P. A. F., & Statham, D. J. (1997). Participation bias in a sexuality survey: Psychological and behavioural characteristics of responders and non-responders. *International Journal of Epidemiology, 26,* 844–854.

Dupras, A. (2001). Sexology as innovation. *Scandinavian Journal of Sexology, 4,* 139–148.

Durante, K. M., Griskevicius, V., Hill, S. E., Perilloux, C., & Li, N. P. (2011). Ovulation, female competition, and product choice. Hormonal influences on consumer behavior. *Journal of Consumer Research, 37,* 921–934.

Dutton, D. G., & Aron, A. P. (1974). Some evidence for heightened sexual attraction under conditions of high anxiety. *Journal of Personality and Social Psychology, 30,* 470–517.

Dwyer, V., & Farran, S. (1997, May 19). Class action: Fighting homophobia at school. *Maclean's.*

Dyshniku, F., Murray, M. E., Fazio, R. L., Lykins, A. M., & Cantor, J. M. (2015). Minor physical anomalies as a window into the prenatal origins of pedophilia. *Archives of Sexual Behavior, 44,* 2151–2159.

Earls, C. M., & David, H. (1989). A psychosocial study of male prostitution. *Archives of Sexual Behavior, 18,* 401–420.

Earls, C. M., & Lalumière, M. L. (2002). A case study of preferential bestiality (zoophilia). *Sexual Abuse: A Journal of Research and Treatment, 14,* 83–88.

Earls, C. M., & Lalumière, M. L. (2009). A case study of preferential bestiality. *Archives of Sexual Behavior, 38,* 605–609.

Eason, E., Labrecque, M., Wells, G., & Feldman P. (2000). Preventing perineal trauma during childbirth: A systematic review. *Obstetrics & Gynecology, 95,* 464–471.

Ebsworth, M., & Lalumière, M. L. (2012). Viewing time as a measure of bisexual sexual interest. *Archives of Sexual Behavior, 41,* 161–172.

Edgar, T., & Fitzpatrick, M. A. (1993). Expectations for sexual interaction: A cognitive test of the sequencing of sexual communication behaviors. *Health Communication, 5,* 239–261. doi:10.1207/s15327027hc0504_1

Edwards, W. M., & Coleman, E. (2004). Defining sexual health: A descriptive overview. *Archives of Sexual Behavior, 33,* 189–196.

Eisenberg, M. E., Wagenaar, A., Neumark-Sztainer, D. (1997). Viewpoints of Minnesota students on school-based sexuality education. *Journal of School Health, 67,* 322–326.

Elder, G. (1969). Appearance and education in marriage mobility. *American Sociological Review, 34,* 519–533.

Elias, J., & Gebhard, P. (1969). Sexuality and sexual learning in childhood. *Phi Delta Kappan, 50,* 401–405.

Eliot, L. (2009). *Pink brain, blue brain: How small differences grow into troublesome gaps–and what we can do about it.* Boston: Houghton Mifflin.

Elliott, A. N., & O'Donohue, W. T. (1997). The effects of anxiety and distraction on sexual arousal in a nonclinical sample of heterosexual women. *Archives of Sexual Behavior, 26,* 607–624.

Elliott, S., Latini, D. M., Walker, L. M., Wasserug, R., Robinson, J. W., & the ADT Survivorship Working Group. (2010). Androgen deprivation therapy for prostate cancer: Recommendations to improve patient and partner quality of life. *Journal of Sexual Medicine, 7*(9), 2996–3010.

Ellis, H. H. (1939). *My life.* Boston: Houghton Mifflin.

Ellis, L. (1996). The role of perinatal factors in determining sexual orientation. In R. C. Savin-Williams & K. M. Cohen (Eds.), *The lives of lesbians, gays, and bisexuals* (pp. 35–70). Fort Worth, TX: Harcourt Brace.

Ellis, L., & Cole-Harding, S. (2001). The effects of prenatal stress, and of prenatal alcohol and nicotine exposure, on human sexual orientation. *Physiology & Behavior, 74,* 213–226.

Emmers-Sommer, T., Allen, M., Bourhis, J., Sahlstein, E., Laskowski, K., Falato, W., . . . Cashman, L. (2004). A meta-analysis of the relationship between social skills and sexual offenders. *Communication Reports, 17,* 1–10.

Endocrine Society. (2009). Endocrine treatment of transsexual persons: An Endocrine Society clinical practice guideline. *Journal of Clinical Endocrinology and Metabolism, 94,* 3132–3154.

England, P., Allison, P. D., & Sayer, L. C. (2014). When one spouse has an affair, who is more likely to leave? *Demographic Research, 30,* 535–546.

Enns, Carolyn Z. (2004). *Feminist theories and feminist psycho-therapies* (2nd ed.). New York: Haworth.

Epting, L. K., & Overman, W. H. (1998). Sex-sensitive tasks in men and women: A search for performance fluctuations across the menstrual cycle. *Behavioral Neuroscience, 112,* 1304–1317.

Erens, B., Phelps, A., Clifton, S., Mercer, C. H., Tanton, C., Hussey, D, . . . Johnson, A. M. (2014). Methodology of the third British National Survey of Sexual Attitudes and Lifestyles (Natsal-3). *Sexually Transmitted Infections, 90,* 84–89.

Erikson, E. H. (1950). *Childhood and society.* New York: Norton.

Erikson, E. H. (1968). *Identity, youth and crisis.* New York: Norton.

Eriksson, J., & Humphreys, T. P. (2013). Development of the Virginity Beliefs Scale. *Journal of Sex Research.* doi:10.1080/00224499.2 012.724475

Ernulf, K. E., & Innala, S. M. (1995). Sexual bondage: A review and unobtrusive investigation. *Archives of Sexual Behavior, 24,* 631–654.

Eschner, K. (2015, March 18). Cops tread cautiously on feds' new sex worker law. *NOW Magazine.* Retrieved from https://now-toronto.com/news/cops-tread-cautiously-on-feds-new-sex-worker-law/

Espin, O. (1987). Issues of identity in the psychology of Latina lesbians. In Boston Lesbian Psychologies Collective, *Lesbian psychologies.* Urbana, IL: University of Illinois Press.

Esposito, K., et al. (2004). Effect of lifestyle changes on erectile dysfunction in obese men: A randomized controlled trial. *Journal of the American Medical Association, 291,* 2978–2984.

Euling, S. Y., Herman-Giddens, M. E., Lee, P. A., Selevan, S. G., Juul, A., Sorensen, T. I., . . . Swan, S. H. (2008). Examination of US puberty-timing data from 1940 to 1994 for secular trends: Panel findings. *Pediatrics 121* (Suppl. 3), S172–S191.

Everett, G. M. (1975). Amyl nitrate ("poppers") as an aphrodisiac. In M. Sandler and G. L. Gessa (Eds.), *Sexual behavior: Pharmacology and biochemistry.* New York: Raven.

Everitt, B. J., & Bancroft, J. (1991). Of rats and men: The comparative approach to male sexuality. *Annual Review of Sex Research, 2,* 77–118.

Exton, M. S., Bindert, A., Kruger, T., Scheller, F., Hartmann, U., & Schedlowski, M. (1999). Cardiovascular and endocrine alterations after masturbation-induced orgasm in women. *Psychosomatic Medicine, 61,* 280–289.

Eyler, A. E., & Wright, K. (1997, July–September). Gender identification and sexual orientation among genetic females with gender-blended self-perception in childhood and adolescence [Electronic version]. *The International Journal of Transgenderism, 1.* Retrieved from http://www.symposium.com

Ezzell, C. (1994). Breast cancer genes: Cloning BRCA1, mapping BRCA2. *Journal of NIH Research, 6*(10), 33–35.

Fallis, E. E., Purdon, C., & Rehman, U. S. (2013). Development and validation of the response to sexual difficulties scale. *Archives of Sexual Behavior, 42,* 67–79.

Farley, M. A. (1994). Sexual ethics. In J. B. Nelson & S. P. Longfellow (Eds.), *Sexuality and the sacred* (pp. 54–67). Louisville, KY: Westminster/John Knox Press.

Farley, M., Lynne, J., & Cotton, A. J. (2005). Prostitution in Vancouver, Canada: Violence and the colonization of First Nations women. *Transcultural Psychiatry, 42,* 242–271.

Farr, R. H., Forssell, S., & Patterson, C. J. (2010). Parenting and child development in adoptive families: Does parental sexual orientation matter? *Applied Developmental Science, 14,* 164–176.

Farris, C., Treat, T. A., Viken, R. J., & McFall, R. M. (2008). Perceptual mechanisms that characterize gender differences in decoding women's sexual intent. *Psychological Science, 19,* 348–354.

Farris, C., Viken, R. J., Treat, T. A., & McFall, R. M. (2006). Heterosocial perceptual organization: Application of the choice model to sexual coercion. *Psychological Science, 17,* 869–875.

Fathy, A., Shamloul, R., AbdelRahim, A., Zeidan, A., El-Dakhly, R., & Ghanem, H. (2007). Experience with Tube® (Promedon) malleable penile implant. *Urologia Internationalis, 79,* 244–247.

Faulkner, E. (1997). *Anti-Gay/Lesbian Violence in Toronto, Canada: The Impact on Individuals and Communities.* Ottawa: Department of Justice Canada: Research and Statistics Division/Policy Sector. TR1997–5e. A Project of the 519 Church Street Community Centre Victim Assistance Programme, Toronto.

Fazekas, A., Senn, C. Y., & Ledgerwood, D. M. (2001). Predictors of intention to use condoms among university women: An application and extension of the theory of planned behaviour. *Canadian Journal of Behavioural Science, 33,* 103–117.

Fazio, R. L., Dyshniku, F., Lykins, A. M., & Cantor, J. M. (2015). Leg length versus torso length in pedophilia: Further evidence of atypical physical development early in life. *Sexual Abuse: A Journal of Research and Treatment, 1,* 1–15.

Federman, D. D. (2006). The biology of human sex differences. *New England Journal of Medicine, 354,* 1507–1514.

Federoff, J. P. (1995). Antiandrogens vs. serotonergic medications in the treatment of sex offenders: A preliminary compliance study. *Canadian Journal of Human Sexuality, 4,* 111–122.

Federoff, J. P., & Moran, B. (1997). Myths and misconceptions about sex offenders. *Canadian Journal of Human Sexuality, 6,* 263–276.

Federoff, J. P., Fishell, A., & Federoff, B. (1999). A case series of women evaluated for paraphilic sexual disorders. *Canadian Journal of Human Sexuality, 8,* 127–140.

Federoff, P. (2007, October). *The long and winding road: How the concept of "love-map" has changed.* Paper presented at the meeting of the Canadian Sex Research Forum, Banff, AB.

Feinberg, L. (1996). *Transgender warriors: Making history from Joan of Arc to Dennis Rodman.* Boston: Beacon Press Books.

Feingold, A. (1990). Gender differences in effects of physical attractiveness on romantic attraction. *Journal of Personality and Social Psychology, 59,* 981–993.

Feiring, C., Simon, V. A., & Cleland, C. M. (2009). Childhood sexual abuse, stigmatization, internalizing symptoms, and the development of sexual difficulties and dating aggression. *Journal of Consulting and Clinical Psychology, 77,* 127–137.

Feldman, R., Weller, A., Zagoory-Sharon, O., & Levine, A. (2007). Evidence for a neuroendocrinological foundation of human affiliation. *Psychological Science, 18,* 965–970.

Felmlee, D., Orzechowicz, D., & Fortes, C. (2010). Fairy tales: Attraction and stereotypes in same-gender relationships. *Sex Roles, 62,* 226–240.

Felton, G., & Segelman, F. (1978). Lamaze childbirth training and changes in belief about person control. *Birth and the Family Journal, 5,* 141–150.

Fenaughty, J., & Harré, N. (2003). Life on the seesaw: A qualitative study of suicide resiliency factors for young gay men. *Journal of Homosexuality, 45,* 1–22.

Ferguson, K. H., & Cespedes, R. D. (2003). Prospective long-term results and quality-of-life assessment after Dura-II penile prosthesis placement. *Urology, 61,* 437–441.

Fergusson, D. M., Horwood, L. J., & Boden, J. M. (2009). Reactions to abortion and subsequent mental health. *The British Journal of Psychiatry, 195,* 420–426.

Ferri, M., Amato, L., & Davoli, M. (2009). Alcoholics anonymous (AA) is a self-help group. *Cochrane Database Systems Review.* Retrieved from http://www.cochrane.org/CD005032/ADDICTN_alcoholics-anonymous

Feuer, A. (2015, February 13). On tinder, taking a swipe at love, or sex, or something, in New York. *New York Times,* MB1.

Ficara, L. C., & Mongeau, P. A. (2000, November). *Relational uncertainty in long distance college student dating relationships.* Paper presented at the annual meeting of the National Communication Association, Seattle, WA.

Field, D., & Rabinovitch, J. (Eds.) (2003). *Stories from the margins: Writing by sex trade workers past and present.* Retrieved from http://peers.bc.ca/images/Stories-BookletWeb.pdf

Fielder, R. L., & Carey, M. P. (2010). Predictors and consequences of sexual "hookups" among college students: A short-term prospective study. *Archives of Sexual Behavior, 39,* 1105–1119.

Fields, R. D. (2007). Sex and the secret nerve. *Scientific American Mind, 18,* 20–27.

Filipp, D., Alizadeh-Khiavi, K., Richardson, C., Palma, A., Paredes, N., Takeuchi, O., . . . Julius, M. (2001). Soluble CD14 enriched in colostrums and milk induces B cell growth and differentiation. *Proceedings of the National Academy of Sciences, 98,* 603–608.

Findlay, M. W., Doldere, J., Trost, N., Craft, R., Cao, Y., Cooper-White, J., . . . Morrison, W. (2011). Tissue-engineered breast reconstruction: Bridging the gap toward large-volume tissue engineering in humans. *Plastic and Reconstructive Surgery, 128,* 1206–1215.

Fink, H., Mac Donald, R., Rutks, I. R., Nelson, D. B., & Wilt, T. J. (2002). Sildenafil for male erectile dysfunction: A systematic review and meta-analysis. *Archives of Internal Medicine, 162,* 1349–1360.

Finkel, E. J., Eastwick, P. W., Karney, B. R., Reis, H. T., & Sprecher, S. (2012). Online dating: A critical analysis from the perspective of psychological science. *Psychological Science in the Public Interest, 13,* 3–66.

Finkelhor, D., & Daro, D. (1997). Prevention of child sexual abuse. In M. E. Helfer & R. S. Kempe (Eds.), *The battered child* (5th ed., pp. 615–626). Chicago: University of Chicago Press.

Finkelhor, D., & Russell, D. (1984). Women as perpetrators: Review of the evidence. In D. Finkelhor (Ed.), *Child sexual abuse: New theory and research.* New York: The Free Press.

Finkelhor, D., Mitchell, K., & Wolak, J. (2000). *Online victimization: A report on the nation's youth.* Washington, DC: National Center for Missing & Exploited Children.

Firestone, P., Bradford, J. M., McCoy, M., Greenberg, D. M., Curry, S., & Larose, M. R. (2000). Prediction of recidivism in extrafamilial child molesters based on court-related assessments. *Sexual Abuse: A Journal of Research and Treatment, 12,* 203–221.

Firestone, P., Nunes, K. L., Moulden, H., Broom, I., & Bradford, J. M. (2005). Hostility and recidivism in sexual offenders. *Archives of Sexual Behavior, 34,* 277–283.

Fischtein, D. S., Herold, E. S., & Desmarais, S. (2005). Canadian attitudes toward female topless behaviour: A national survey. *Canadian Journal of Human Sexuality, 14,* 63–75.

Fisher, D. A., Hill, D. L., Grube, J. W., & Gruber, E. L. (2007). Gay, lesbian, and bisexual content on television: A quantitative analysis across two seasons. *Journal of Homosexuality, 52,* 167–188.

Fisher, H. (1992). *Anatomy of love: The mysteries of mating, marriage and why we stray.* New York: Ballantine Books.

Fisher, H., Aron, A., & Brown, L. (2006). Romantic love: A mammalian brain system for mate choice. *Philosophical Transactions of the Royal Society, B, 361,* 2173–2186.

Fisher, J. A., Bowman, M., & Thomas, T. (2003). Issues for South Asian Indian patients surrounding sexuality, fertility, and childbirth in the U.S. health care system. *Journal of the American Board of Family Medicine, 16*(2), 151–155.

Fisher, M., & Cox, A. (2009). The influence of male facial attractiveness on women's receptivity. *Journal of Social, Evolutionary, and Cultural Psychology, 3,* 49–61.

Fisher, T. D., Moore, Z. T., & Pittenger, M. J. (2012). Sex on the brain? An examination of frequency of sexual cognitions as a function of gender, erotophilia, and social desirability. *Journal of Sex Research, 49,* 69–77.

Fisher, W. A., & Barak, A. (2000). Online sex shops: Phenomenological, psychological, and ideological perspectives on Internet sexuality. *Cyberpsychology & Behavior, 3,* 575–589.

Fisher, W. A., & Boroditsky, R. (2000). Sexual activity, contraceptive choice, and sexual and reproductive health indicators among single Canadian women aged 15–29: Additional findings from the Canadian contraception study. *Canadian Journal of Human Sexuality, 9,* 79–93.

Fisher, W. A., & Fisher, J. D. (1992). Understanding and promoting AIDS preventive behaviour: A conceptual model of educational tools. *Canadian Journal of Human Sexuality, 1,* 99–106.

Fisher, W. A., & Fisher, J. D. (1998). Understanding and promoting sexual and reproductive health behaviour: Theory and method. *Annual Review of Sex Research, 9,* 39–76.

Fisher, W. A., & Grenier, G. (1994). Violent pornography, antiwoman thoughts, and antiwoman acts: In search of reliable effects. *Journal of Sex Research, 31,* 23–38.

Fisher, W. A., & Holzapfel, S. (2014). Suppose they gave an epidemic and sex therapy didn't attend? Sexually transmitted infection concerns in the sex therapy context. In Y. M. Binik & K. S. K. Hall (Eds.), *Principles and practice of sex therapy* (5th ed., ch. 22). New York: Guilford.

Fisher, W. A., Boroditsky, R., & Bridges, M. L. (1999a). Familiarity with opinions about and use of contraceptive methods among Canadian women. *Canadian Journal of Human Sexuality, 18,* 167–174.

Fisher, W. A., Boroditsky, R., & Bridges, M. L. (1999b). The 1998 contraception study. *Canadian Journal of Human Sexuality, 8,* 161–216.

Fisher, W. A., Boroditsky, R., & Morris, B. (2004). The 2002 Canadian contraception study: Part 2. *Journal of Obstetrics and Gynaecology Canada, 26,* 646–656.

Fisher, W. A., Byrne, D., & White, L. A. (1983). Emotional barriers to contraception. In D. Byrne and W. A. Fisher (Eds.), *Adolescents, sex, and contraception.* Hillsdale, NJ: Lawrence Erlbaum.

Fisher, W. A., Byrne, D., White, L. A., & Kelley, K. (1988). Eroto-phobiaerotophilia as a dimension of personality. *Journal of Sex Research, 25,* 123–151.

Fisher, W. A., Kohut, T., & Fisher, J. D. (2009). AIDS exceptionalism: On the social psychology of HIV prevention research. *Social Issues and Policy Review, 3,* 45–77.

Fisher, W. A., Sukhbir, S. S., Shuper, P. A., Carey, M., Otchet, F., MacLean-Brine, D., . . . Gunter, J. (2005). Characteristics of women undergoing repeat induced abortion. *Canadian Medical Association Journal, 172,* 637–641.

Fiske, S. T., & Glick, P. (1995). Ambivalence and stereotypes cause sexual harassment: A theory with implications for organizational change. *Journal of Social Issues, 51*(1), 97–115.

Fitch, R. H., & Bimonte, H. A. (2002). Hormones, brain, and behavior: Putative biological contributions to cognitive sex differences. In A. McGillicuddy-DeLisi & R. DeLisi (Eds.), *Biology, society, and behavior: The development of sex differences in cognition* (pp. 55–92). Westport, CT: Ablex.

Fitzgerald, L. F. (1993). Sexual harassment. *American Psychologist, 48*, 1070–1076.

Flack, W. F., Jr., Daubman, K. A., Caron, M. L., Asadorian, J. A., D'Aureli, N. R., Gigliotti, S. N., . . . Stine, E. R. (2007). Risk factors and consequences of unwanted sex among university students: Hooking up, alcohol, and stress response. *Journal of Interpersonal Violence, 22*(2), 139–157.

Flak, A. L., Su, S., Bertrand, J., Denny, C. H., Kesmodel, U. S., & Cogswell, M. E. (2014). The association of mild, moderate, and binge prenatal alcohol exposure and child neuropsychological outcomes: A meta-analysis. *Alcoholism: Clinical and Experimental Research, 38*, 214–226.

Flak, V., Beech, A., & Fisher, D. (2007). Forensic assessment of deviant sexual interests: The current position. *Issues in Forensic Psychology, 6*, 70–83.

Flaxman, S. M., & Sherman, P. W. (2000). Morning sickness: A mechanism for protecting mother and embryo. *Quarterly Review of Biology, 75*, 113–148.

Fleming, A., Ruble, D., Krieger, H., & Wong, P. Y. (1997). Hormonal and experiential correlates of internal responsiveness during pregnancy and the puerperium in human mothers. *Hormones and Behavior, 31*, 145–158.

Fleming, J., Mullen, P., Sibthorpe, B., & Bammer, G. (1999). The long-term impact of childhood sexual abuse in Australian women. *Child Abuse & Neglect, 23*, 145–159.

Fletcher, J. (1966). *Situation ethics: The new morality.* Philadelphia: Westminster Press.

Foa, E. B., Steketee, G., & Olasov, B. (1989). Behavioral/cognitive conceptualization of post-traumatic stress disorder. *Behavior Therapy, 20*, 155–176.

Foldès, P., Cuzin, B., & Andro, A. (2012). Reconstructive surgery after female genital mutilation: A prospective cohort study. *The Lancet, 380*, 134–141.

Forbes, E. E., & Dahl, R. E. (2010). Pubertal development and behavior: Hormonal activation of social and motivational tendencies. *Brain and Cognition, 72*, 66–72.

Ford, C. S., & Beach, F. A. (1951). *Patterns of sexual behavior.* New York: Harper & Row.

Ford, J. G. (2001). Healing homosexuals: A psychologist's journey through the ex-gay movement and the pseudo-science of reparative therapy. In A. Shidlo, M. Schroeder, & J. Drescher (Eds.), *Sexual conversion therapy: Ethical, clinical, and research perspectives* (pp. 69–86). New York: Haworth.

Ford, K., & Norris, A. (1991). Methodological considerations for survey research on sexual behavior: Urban African American and Hispanic youth. *Journal of Sex Research, 28*, 539–555.

Fortenberry, J. D. (2002). Clinic-based service programs for increasing responsible sexual behavior. *Journal of Sex Research, 39*, 63–66.

Fortenberry, J. D., Temkit, M., Tu, W., Graham, C. A., Katz, B. P., & Orr, D. P. (2005). Daily mood, partner support, sexual interest, and sexual activity among adolescent women. *Health Psychology, 24*, 252–257.

Forum Research Inc. (2012). Canada-wide abortion issues: Six in ten believe abortion should be legal in all circumstances. Retrieved from http://www.forumresearch.com

Foster, C. A., Witcher, B. S., Campbell, W. K., & Green, J. D. (1998). Arousal and attraction: Evidence for automatic and controlled processes. *Journal of Personality and Social Psychology, 74*, 86–101.

Foster, L. R., & Byers, E. S. (2008). Predictors of stigma and shame related to sexually transmitted infections: Attitudes, education, and knowledge. *Canadian Journal of Human Sexuality, 17*, 193–202.

Foster, L. R., & Byers, E. S. (2016). Predictors of the sexual well-being of individuals diagnosed with herpes and human papillomavirus. *Archives of Sexual Behavior, 45*, 403–414.

Foster, L. R., Byers, E. S., & Sears, H. A. (2011). Middle school students' perceptions of the quality of the sexual health education received from their parents. *Canadian Journal of Human Sexuality, 20*, 55–65.

Fox, D. (2002). Gentle persuasion. *New Scientist, 173*, 32.

Fox, N., Gelber, S., & Chasen, S. (2008). Physical and sexual activity during pregnancy and near delivery. *Journal of Women's Health, 17*, 1431–1435.

Fox, R. C. (1995). Bisexual identities. In A. R. D'Augelli & C. J. Patterson (Eds.), *Lesbian, gay, and bisexual identities over the lifespan.* New York: Oxford University Press.

Fraley, R. C., Roisman, G. I., Booth-LaForce, C., Owen, M. T., & Holland, A. (2013). Interpersonal and genetic origins of adult attachment styles: A longitudinal study from infancy to early adulthood. *Journal of Personality and Social Psychology, 104*, 817–838.

Frank, K. (2005). Exploring the motivations and fantasies of strip club customers in relation to legal regulations. *Archives of Sexual Behavior, 34*, 487–504.

Frank, K., & DeLamater, J. (2010). Deconstructing monogamy: Boundaries, identities, and fluidities across relationships. In M. Barker & D. Langdridge (Eds.), *Understanding non-monogamies* (pp. 9–22). New York: Routledge.

Frappier, J.-Y., Kaufman, M., Baltzer, F., Elliott, A., Lane, M., Pinzon, J., & McDuff, P. (2008). Sex and sexual health: A survey of Canadian youth and mothers. *Pediatric and Child Health, 13*, 25–30.

Frayser, S. G. (1985). *Varieties of sexual experience: An anthropological perspective on human sexuality.* New Haven, CT: Human Relations Area Files Press.

Frayser, S. G. (1994). Defining normal childhood sexuality: An anthropological approach. *Annual Review of Sex Research, 5*, 173–217.

Frazier, P., Tashiro, T., Berman, M., Steger, M., & Long, J. (2004). Correlates of levels and patterns of positive life changes following sexual assault. *Journal of Consulting and Clinical Psychology, 72*, 19–30.

Frederick, D., Peplau, A., & Lever, J. (2008). The Barbie mystique: Satisfaction with breast size and shape across the lifespan. *International Journal of Sexual Health, 20*, 200–211.

Freese, J., & Meland, S. (2002). Seven-tenths incorrect: Heterogeneity and change in the waist-to-hip ratios of Playboy centerfold models and Miss America pageant winners. *Journal of Sex Research, 39*, 133–138.

Freud, S. (1924). *A general introduction to psychoanalysis.* New York: Permabooks, 1953 (Boni & Liveright edition, 1924).

Freund, M., Lee, N., & Leonard, T. (1991). Sexual behavior of clients with street prostitutes in Camden, NJ. *Journal of Sex Research, 28*, 579–591.

Freyd, J. J. (1996). *Betrayal trauma theory.* Cambridge, MA: Harvard University Press.

Freyd, J. J., Putnam, F. W., Lyon, T. D., Becker-Blease, K. A., Cheit, R. E., Siegel, N. B., & Pezdek, K. (2005). The science of child sexual abuse. *Science, 308*, 501.

Frias, M. T., Brassard, A., & Shaver, P. (2014). Childhood sexual abuse and attachment insecurities as predictors of women's own and perceived-partner extradyadic involvement. *Child Abuse & Neglect, 38*, 1450–1458.

Frisch, R. E., & McArthur, J. W. (1974). Menstrual cycles: Fatness as a determinant of minimum weight for height necessary for their maintenance or onset. *Science, 185*, 949–951.

Frishman, G. (1995). Abortions, miscarriages, and ectopic pregnancies. In D. R. Carstrin, R. V. Hunning Jr., & E. D. B. Singer (Eds.), *Human reproduction: Growth and development.* Boston: Little, Brown.

Frohlich, P., & Meston, C. (2002). Sexual functioning and self-reported depressive symptoms among college women. *Journal of Sex Research, 39*, 321–325.

Frühauf, S., Gerger, H., Schmidt, H. M., Munder, T., & Barth, J. (2013). Efficacy of psychological interventions for sexual dysfunction: A systematic review and meta-analysis. *Archives of Sexual Behavior, 42*, 6, 915–933.

Fryar, C., Hirsch, R., Porter, K. S., Kottiri, B., Brody, D. J., & Louis, T. (2007). Drug use and sexual behaviors reported by adults: United States, 1999–2002. *Advance Data from Vital and Health Statistics; 384.* Hyattsville, MD: National Center for Health Statistics.

Fryhofer, S. (2012). Preconception checklist for women planning pregnancy. *Medscape Internal Medicine.* Retrieved from http://www.medscape.com/viewarticle/762801

Fudge, M. C., & Byers, E. S. (2016). "I have a nice gross vagina": Understanding young women's genital self-perceptions. *Journal of Sex Research, 00*, 1–11. doi:10.1080/0022449 9.2016.1155200.

Fujimoto, V., Luke, B., Brown, M. B., Jain, T., Armstrong, A., Grainger, D. A., . . . Society for Assisted Reproductive Technology Writing Group. (2008). Racial and ethnic disparities in assisted reproductive technology outcomes in the United States. *Fertility and Sterility, 10*, 61.

Fullerton, T., Rye, B. J., Meaney, G. J., & Loomis, C. (2013). Condom and hormonal contraceptive use by young women: An information-motivation-behavioral skills assessment. *Canadian Journal of Behavioural Science, 45*, 196–209.

Furman, W. (2002). The emerging field of adolescent romantic relationships. *Current Directions in Psychological Science, 11*, 177–180.

Furnish, V. P. (1994). The Bible and homosexuality: Reading the texts in context. In J. S. Siker (Ed.), *Homosexuality in the church* (pp. 18–35). Louisville, KY: Westminster/John Knox Press.

Furstenberg, F. F., Brooks-Gunn, J., & Morgan, S. P. (1987). *Adolescent mothers in later life.* New York: Cambridge University Press.

Future of Sex Education Initiative. (2012). National sexuality education standards: Core content and skills, K-12 [a special publication of Journal of School Health]. Retrieved from http://www.futureofsexeducation.org

Gager, C., & Yabiku, S. (2010). Who has the time? The relationship between household labor time and sexual frequency. *Journal of Family Issues, 31*, 135–163.

Gagnon, J. H. (1977). *Human sexualities.* Glenview, IL: Scott, Foresman.

Gagnon, J. H. (1990). The explicit and implicit use of the scripting perspective in sex research. *Annual Review of Sex Research, 1*, 1–44.

Gagnon, J. H., & Simon, W. (1973). *Sexual conduct: The social origins of human sexuality.* Chicago: Aldine.

Gaither, G. A., Sellbom, M., & Meier, B. P. (2003). The effect of stimulus content on volunteering for sexual interest research among college students. *Journal of Sex Research, 40*, 240–248.

Galbreath, N., Berlin, F., & Sawyer, D. (2002). Paraphilias and the Internet. In A. Cooper (Ed.), *Sex and the Internet: A guidebook for clinicians* (pp. 187–205). New York: Brunner-Routledge.

Gallant, P. (2003). Count'em up. *DailyXtra.* Retrieved from http://dailyxtra.com/toronto/count-em

Gallant, S. J., Popiel, D. A., Hoffman, D. M., Chakraborty, P. K., & Hamilton, J. A. (1992). Using daily ratings to confirm premenstrual syndrome/late luteal phase dysphoric disorder: What makes a real difference? *Psychosomatic Medicine, 54*, 167–181.

Gallup Canada Inc. (1988). Canadian Gallup Poll, July 1988.

Gallup. (2014, May 22). Birth control, divorce top list of morally acceptable issues. Retrieved from http://www.gallup.com/poll/170249/split-abortion-pro-choice-pro-life.aspx

Gallup. (2016, June 8). U.S. still split on abortion: 47% pro-choice, 46% pro-life. Retrieved from http://www.gallup.com/poll/192404/birth-control-divorce-top-list-morally-acceptable-issues.aspx

Galvani, A., & Slatkin, M. (2003). Evaluating plague and smallpox as historical selective pressures for the CCR5-Delta 32 HIV-resistance allele. *Proceedings of the National Academy of Sciences, 100*, 15276–15279.

Gangestad, S. W., & Buss, D. M. (1993). Pathogen prevalence and human mate preferences. *Ethology and Sociobiology, 14*, 89–96.

Gangestad, S. W., & Thornhill, R. (1997). Human sexual selection and developmental stability. In J. A. Simpson & D. T. Kenrick (Eds.), *Evolutionary social psychology* (pp. 169–195). Mahwah, NJ: Lawrence Erlbaum Associates.

Gannon, T. A., & Ward, T. (2008). Rape: Psychopathology and theory. In D. R. Laws & W. T. O'Donohue (Eds.), *Sexual deviance* (pp. 336–355). New York: Guilford.

Ganz, T. (2002). Versatile defensins. *Science, 298*, 977–979.

Garcia, J. R., MacKillop, J., Aller, E. L., Merriweather, A. M., Wilson, D. S., & Lum, J. K. (2010). Associations between dopamine D4 receptor gene variation with both infidelity and sexual promiscuity. *PLoS ONE, 5*, e14162.

Garcia, M., & Fisher, W. A. (2007). Obstetrics and gynaecology residents' self-rated knowledge, motivation, skill, and practice patterns in counselling for contraception, STI prevention, sexual dysfunction, and intimate partner violence and sexual coercion. *Journal of Obstetrics and Gynaecology of Canada, 30*, 59–65.

Garcia-Velasco, J., & Mondragon, M. (1991). The incidence of the vomeronasal organ in 1000 human subjects and its possible clinical significance. *Journal of Steroid Biochemistry and Molecular Biology, 39*, 561–563.

Garnets, L., & Peplau, L. A. (2006). Sexuality in the lives of adult lesbian and bisexual women. In D. C. Kimmel, T. Rose, & S. David (Eds.) *Research and clinical perspectives on lesbian, gay, bisexual, and transgender aging* (pp. 70–90). New York: Columbia University Press.

Gartrell, N. K., Bos, H. M., & Goldberg, N. G. (2011). Adolescents of the U.S. National Longitudinal Lesbian Family Study: Sexual orientation, sexual behavior, and sexual risk exposure. *Archives of Sexual Behavior, 40*, 1199–1209.

Gartrell, N., Rodas, C., Deck, A., Peyser, H, & Banks, A. (2005). The National Lesbian Family Study: 4. Interviews with the 10-year-old children. *American Journal of Orthopsychiatry, 75*, 5181–5524.

Gathorne-Hardy, J. (2000). *Sex, the measure of all things: A life of Alfred C. Kinsey.* Bloomington, IN: Indiana University Press.

Gavey, N., Schmidt, J., Braun, V., Fenaughty, J., & Eremin, M. (2009). Unsafe, unwanted sexual coercion as a barrier to safer sex among men who have sex with men. *Journal of Health Psychology, 14*, 1021–1026.

Gay, P. (1984). *The bourgeois experience: Victoria to Freud.* New York: Oxford University Press.

Gebhard, P. H. (1976). The Institute. In M. S. Weinberg (Ed.), *Sex research: Studies from the Kinsey Institute.* New York: Oxford University Press.

Gemme, R. (1998). Legal and sexological aspects of adult street prostitution: A case for sexual pluralism. In J. Elias, V. J. Bullough, V. Elias, & G. Brewer (Eds.), *Prostitution: On whores, hustlers & johns.* Amherst, NY: Prometheus Books.

Gemme, R., Murphy, A., Bourque, A., Nemeh, M. A., & Payment, N. (1984). *A report on prostitution in Quebec* (Working Paper sec11). Ottawa: Department of Justice Canada.

Gender Identity Research and Education Society. (2006). Atypical gender development: A review. *International Journal of Transgenderism, 9*, 29–43.

Genel, M. (2000). Gender verification no more? *Medscape Women's Health, 5*(3).

Genovesi, V. J. (1987). *In pursuit of love: Catholic morality and human sexuality.* Wilmington, DE: Michael Glazier.

Gentilcore-Saulnier, E., McLean, L., Goldfinger, C., Pukall, C. F., & Chamberlain, S. (2010). Pelvic floor muscle assessment outcomes in women with and without provoked vestibulodynia and the impact of a physical therapy program. *Journal of Sexual Medicine, 7*, 1003–1022.

Gentile, D. A., Lynch, P. J., Linder, J. R., & Walsh, D. A. (2004). The effects of violent video game habits on adolescent attitudes and behaviors. *Journal of Adolescence, 27*, 5–22.

George, W. H., & Stoner, S. A. (2000). Understanding acute alcohol effects on sexual behavior. *Annual Review of Sex Research, 11*, 92–124.

George, W. H., Stoner, S. A., Davis, K. C., Lindgren, K. P., Norris, J., & Lopez, P. A. (2006). Postdrinking sexual perceptions and behaviors toward another person: Alcohol expectancy set and gender differences. *Journal of Sex Research, 43*, 282–291.

Georges, E. (1996). Abortion policy and practice in Greece. *Social Science & Medicine, 42*, 509–519.

Georgiadis, J. R., & Kringelbach, M. L. (2012). The human sexual response cycle: Brain imaging evidence linking sex to other pleasures. *Progress in Neurobiology, 98*, 49–81.

Gerbner, G., Gross, L., & Morgan, M. (2002). Growing up with television: Cultivation processes. In J. Bryant & D. Zillman (Eds.), *Media effects: Advances in theory and research* (2nd ed., pp. 43–67). Mahwah, NJ: Erlbaum.

Gerlach, N., McGlothlin, J. W., Parker, P. G., & Ketterson, E. D. (2012). Promiscuous mating produces offspring with higher lifetime fitness. *Proceedings of the Royal Society B, 279*(1730), 860–866.

Gervais, S. J., Vescio, T., & Allen, J. (2011). When what you see is what you get: The consequences of the objectifying gaze for women and men. *Psychology of Women Quarterly, 35*, 5–17.

Gidycz, C. A., Orchowski, L. M., & Edwards, K. (2011). Primary prevention of sexual violence. In J. White et al. (Eds.), *Violence against women and children* (vol. 2, pp. 159–180). Washington, DC: American Psychological Association.

Gijs, L., & Gooren, L. (1996). Hormonal and psychopharmacological interventions in the treatment of paraphilias. *Journal of Sex Research, 33*, 273–290.

Gilbert, L., Basso, O., Sampalis, J., Karp, I., Martins, C., Feng, J., . . . DOvE Study Group. (2012). Assessment of symptomatic women for early diagnosis of ovarian cancer: Results from the prospective DOvE pilot project. *Lancet Oncology, 13*(3), 285–291.

Gill, R., & Febbraro, A. R. (2013). Experiences and perceptions of sexual harassment in the Canadian Forces Combat Arms. *Violence Against Women, 19*, 269–287.

Gillath, O., Mikulincer, M., Birnbaum, G. E., & Shaver, P. R. (2008). When sex primes love: Subliminal sexual priming motivates relationship goal pursuit. *Personality and Social Psychology Bulletin, 34*, 1057–1069.

Gilligan, C. (1982). *In a different voice: Psychological theory and women's development.* Cambridge, MA: Harvard University Press.

Gilmore, M. R., Leigh, B. C., Hoppe, M. J., & Morrison, D. M. (2010). Comparison of daily and retrospective reports of vaginal sex in heterosexual men and women. *Journal of Sex Research, 47*, 279–284.

Ginsberg, T. B., Pomerantz, S. C., & Kramer-Feeley, V. (2005). Sexuality in older adults: Behaviours and preferences. *Age and Ageing, 34*, 475–480.

Ginsburg, F. (1989). *Contested lives: The abortion debate in an American community.* Berkeley, CA: University of California Press.

Giordano, P. C., Manning, W. D., & Longmore, M. A. (2010). Affairs of the heart: Qualities of adolescent romantic relationships and sexual behavior. *Journal of Research on Adolescence, 20*, 983–1013.

Giraldi, A., & Kristensen, E. (2010). Sexual dysfunction in women with diabetes mellitus. *Journal of Sex Research, 47*, 199–211.

Girard, A. L., & Senn, C. Y. (2008). The role of the new "date rape drugs" in attributions about date rape. *Journal of Interpersonal Violence, 23*, 3–20.

Giuliano, F., & Clement, P. (2005). Neuroanatomy and physiology of ejaculation. *Annual Review of Sex Research, 15*, 190–216.

Gjerdingen, D. (2003). The effectiveness of various postpartum depression treatments and the impact of antidepressant drugs on nursing infants. *Journal of the American Board of Family Practice, 16*, 372–382.

Glascock, J., & LaRose, R. (1993). Dial-a-porn recordings: The role of the female participant in male sexual fantasies. *Journal of Broadcasting & Electronic Media*, 313–324.

Glass, S. J., & Johnson, R. W. (1944). Limitations and complications of organotherapy in male homosexuality. *Journal of Clinical Endocrinology, 4*, 540–544.

Glenn, S. A., & Byers, E. S. (2009). The roles of situational factors, attributions, and guilt in the well-being of women who have experienced sexual coercion. *Canadian Journal of Human Sexuality, 18*, 201–219.

Glowacka, M., Rosen, N. O., Vannier, S., & MacLellan, M. C. (2016). Development and validation of the sexual contingent self-worth scale. *Journal of Sex Research.* doi:10.1080/00224499.2016.1186587

Glowacka, M., Rosen, N., Chorney, J., Snelgrove-Clarke, E., & George, R. B. (2014). Prevalence and predictors of genito-pelvic pain in pregnancy and postpartum: The prospective impact of fear avoidance. *Journal of Sexual Medicine, 11*, 3021–3034.

Gold, E. R. (1986). Long-term effects of sexual victimization in childhood: An attributional approach. *Journal of Consulting and Clinical Psychology, 54*(4), 471–475.

Gold, S. D., Marx, B. P., & Lexington, J. M. (2007). Gay male sexual assault survivors: The relations among internalized homophobia, experiential avoidance, and psychological symptom severity. *Behaviour Research and Therapy, 45*, 549–562.

Gold, S. N., Hughes, D., & Hohnecker, L. (1994). Degrees of repression of sexual abuse memories. *American Psychologist, 49*, 441–442.

Goldberg, M. (1987). Understanding hypersexuality in men and women. In G. R. Weeks & L. Hof (Eds.), *Integrating sex and marital therapy.* New York: Brunner-Mazel.

Goldberg, S. (1983). Parent-infant bonding: Another look. *Child Development, 54*, 1355–1382.

Goldenberg, S. M., Chettiar, J., Simo, A., Silverman, J. G., Strathdee, S. A., Montaner, J., & Shannon, K. (2014). Early sex work initiation independently elevates odds of HIV infection and police arrest among adult sex workers in a Canadian setting. *Journal of Acquired Immune Deficiency Syndrome, 65*, 122–128.

Goldfarb, M. R., Trudel, G., Boyer, R., & Préville, M. (2007). Marital relationship and psychological distress: Its correlates and treatments. *Sexual and Relationship Therapy, 22*, 109–126.

Goldfinger, C., Pukall, C. F., Gentilcore-Saulnier, E., McLean, L., & Chamberlain, S. (2009). A prospective study of pelvic floor physical therapy: Pain and psychosexual outcomes in provoked vestibulodynia. *Journal of Sexual Medicine, 6*, 1955–1968.

Goldfinger, C., Pukall, C. F., Thibault-Gagnon, S., McLean, L., & Chamberlain, S. (2016). Effectiveness of cognitive-behavioral therapy and physical therapy for provoked vestibulodynia: A randomized pilot study. *Journal of Sexual Medicine, 13*, 88–94.

Goldfoot, D. A., Westerberg-van Loon, W., Groeneveld, W., & Koos Slob, A. (1980). Behavioral and physiological evidence of sexual climax in the female stump-tailed macaque (*Macaca arctoides*). *Science, 208*, 1477–1478.

Golding, J. M. (1999). Sexual assault history and medical care seeking. *Psychology & Health, 14*, 949–957.

Goldsmith, K. M., & Byers, E. S. (2016). Perceived impact of body feedback from romantic partners on young adults' body image and sexual well-being. *Body Image, 17*, 161–170.

Goldstein, J. M., Seidman, L. J., Horton, N. J., Makris, N., Kennedy, D. N., Caviness, V., . . . Tsuang, M. T. (2001). Normal sexual dimorphism of the adult human brain assessed by in vivo magnetic resonance imaging. *Cerebral Cortex, 11*, 490–497.

Golub, S. (1992). *Periods: From menarche to menopause.* Newbury Park, CA: Sage.

Gonsiorek, J. C. (1996). Mental health and sexual orientation. In R. C. Savin-Williams & K. M. Cohen (Eds.), *The lives of lesbians, gays, and bisexuals* (pp. 462–478). Fort Worth, TX: Harcourt Brace.

Gonzaga, G., Turner, R., Keltner, D., Campos, B., & Altemus, M. (2006). Romantic love and sexual desire in close relationships. *Emotion, 6*, 163–179.

Gonzalez, F., & Espin, O. (1996). Latino men, Latina women, and homosexuality. In R. Cabaj & T. Stein (Eds.), *Textbook of homosexuality and mental health* (pp. 583–601). Washington, DC: American Psychiatric Association.

Goodson, P., & Edmundson, E. (1994). The problematic promotion of abstinence: An overview of Sex Respect. *Journal of School Health, 64*, 205–210.

Goodson, P., McCormic, D., & Evans, A. (2001). Searching for sexually explicit materials on the internet: An exploratory study of college students' behavior and attitudes. *Archives of Sexual Behavior, 30*, 101–118.

Gooren, L. (2006). The biology of human psychosexual differentiation. *Hormones and Behavior, 50*, 589–601.

Gordon, B., & Schroeder, C. (1995). *Sexuality: A developmental approach to problems.* New York: Plenum Press.

Gordon, R. A., Crosnoe, R., & Wang, X. (2013). Physical attractiveness and the accumulation of social and human capital in adolescence and young adulthood. *Monographs of the Society for Research in Child Development, 78*, No. 6. Hoboken, NJ: Wiley.

Gordts, S., Campo, R., Puttemans, P., & Gordts, S. (2009). Clinical factors determining pregnancy outcome after microsurgical tubal reanastomosis. *Fertility and Sterility, 92*, 1198–1202.

Gorzalka, B. B., & Hill, M. N. (2006). Cannabinoids, reproduction, and sexual behavior. *Annual Review of Sex Research, 17*, 132–161.

Gorzalka, B. B., Hill, M. N., & Chang, S. C. (2010). Male-female differences in the effects of cannabinoids on sexual behavior and gonadal hormone function. *Hormones and Behavior, 58,* 91–99.

Gosling, S. D., Vazire, S., Srivastava, S., & John, O. P. (2004). Should we trust web-based studies? A comparative analysis of six preconceptions about internet questionnaires. *American Psychologist, 59,* 93–104.

Gosselin, C., & Wilson, G. (1980). *Sexual variations: Fetishism, sadomasochism, transvestism.* New York: Simon & Schuster.

Gottlieb, L. (2006, March). How do I love thee? *Atlantic Monthly,* 58–70.

Gottman, J. M. (1994). *Why marriages succeed or fail.* New York: Simon & Schuster.

Gottman, J. M., & Notarius, C. I. (2002). Marital research in the 20th century and a research agenda for the 21st century. *Family Process, 41,* 159–197.

Gottman, J., & Silver, N. (1999). *The seven principles for making marriage work.* New York: Three Rivers/Random House.

Gottman, J., Conn, J., Carrere, S., & Swanson, C. (1998). Predicting marital happiness and stability from newlywed interactions. *Journal of Marriage and the Family, 60,* 5–22.

Gottman, J., Markman, H., & Notarius, C. (1977). The topography of marital conflict: A sequential analysis of verbal and nonverbal behavior. *Journal of Marriage and the Family, 39,* 461–478.

Gottman, J., Notarius, C., Gonso, J., & Markman, H. (1976). *A couple's guide to communication.* Champaign, IL: Research Press.

Gould, S. J. (1987). *An urchin in the storm.* New York: Norton.

Gouliquer, L. (2000). Negotiation sexuality: Lesbians in the Canadian military. In B. Miedema, J. Stoppard, & V. Anderson (Eds.), *Women's bodies/women's lives: health, well-being and body image.* Toronto: Second Story Press.

Gower, D. B., & Ruparelia, B. A. (1993). Olfaction in humans with special reference to odorous 16-androstenes: Their occurrence, perception and possible social, psychological and sexual impact. *Journal of Endocrinology, 137,* 167–187.

Grabe, S., Ward, L. M., & Hyde, J. S. (2008). The role of the media in body image concerns among women: A meta-analysis of experimental and correlational studies. *Psychological Bulletin, 134,* 460–476.

Grace, A. P., & Wells, K. (2001). Getting an education in Edmonton, Alberta: The case of queer youth. *Journal of the Canadian Lesbian and Gay Studies Association, 3,* 137–151.

Grace, A. P., & Wells, K. (2006). The quest for a queer inclusive cultural ethics: Setting directions for teachers' preservice and continuing professional development. *New Directions for Adult and Continuing Education, 112,* 51–61.

Grace, A. P., & Wells, K. (2007). Gay and bisexual male youth as educator activists and cultural workers: The queer critical praxis of three Canadian high-school students. *International Journal of Inclusive Education,* 1–22.

Graham, B. S. (2009). What does the report of the USMHRP Phase III study in Thailand mean for HIV and for vaccine developers? *Clinical and Experimental Immunology, 158,* 257–259.

Graham, C. A., Sanders, S. A., Milhausen, R. R., & McBride, K. R. (2004). Turning on and turning off: A focus group study of the factors that affect women's sexual arousal. *Archives of Sexual Behavior, 33,* 527–538.

Grant, J. M., Mottet, L., Tanis, J. E., Harrison, J., Herman, J., & Keisling, M. (2011). *Injustice at every turn: A report of the National Transgender Discrimination Survey.* National Center for Transgender Equality.

Grant, R. M., Anderson, P. L., McMahan, V., Liu, A., Amico, K. R., Mehrotra, M., . . . & Glidden, D. V. (2014). Uptake of pre-exposure prophylaxis, sexual practices, and HIV incidence in men and transgender women who have sex with men: A cohort study. *The Lancet, 14,* 820–829.

Grau, I., & Kimpf, M. (1993). Love, sexuality, and satisfaction: Interventions of men and women. *Zeitschrift fur Sozial Psychologie, 24,* 83–93.

Gravel, E. E., Pelletier, L. G., & Reissing, E. D. (2016). "Doing it" for the right reasons: Validation of a measurement of intrinsic motivation, extrinsic motivation, and amotivation for sexual relationships. *Personality and Individual Differences, 92,* 164–173.

Gravel, E. E., Young, M., Olavarria-Turner, M., & Lee, A. M. S. (2011). Ethnic differences in sexual guilt between Anglo-Canadians and Franco-Québécois emerging adults: The mediating roles of family and religion. *Canadian Journal of Human Sexuality, 20,* 129–142.

Gray, N. S., et al. (2005). An implicit test of the associations between children and sex in pedophiles. *Journal of Abnormal Psychology, 114,* 304–308.

Gray, P. B., Garcia, J. R., Crosier, B. S., & Fisher, H. E. (2015). Dating and sexual behavior among single parents of young children in the United States. *Journal of Sex Research, 52,* 121–128.

Grazian, D. (2008). *On the make: The hustle of urban nightlife.* Chicago: University of Chicago Press.

Greeley, A. (1994). Review of the *Janus report on sexual behavior. Contemporary Sociology, 23,* 221–223.

Greely, H. (2011). Get ready for the flood of fetal gene screening. *Nature, 469,* 289–291.

Green, A. I. (2014). Toward a sociology of collective sexual life. In A. Green (Ed.), *Sexual fields: Toward a sociology of collective sexual life* (pp. 1–24). Chicago: University of Chicago Press.

Green, L. L., Fullilove, M. T., & Fullilove, R. E. (2005). Remembering the lizard: Reconstructing sexuality in the rooms of Narcotics Anonymous. *Journal of Sex Research, 42,* 28–34.

Green, R. (1975). Adults who want to change sex; adolescents who crossdress; and children called "sissy" and "tomboy." In R. Green (Ed.), *Human sexuality: A health practitioner's text.* Baltimore, MD: Williams & Wilkins.

Green, R. M. (1984). Genetic medicine in Jewish legal perspective. *The Annual of the Society of Christian Ethics,* 249–272.

Green, R. M. (2007). *Babies by design: The ethics of genetic choice.* New Haven, CT: Yale University Press.

Greenberg, D. M., Bradford, J., Firestone, P., & Curry, S. (2000). Relationships of child molesters: A study of victim relationship with the perpetrator. *Child Abuse and Neglect, 24,* 1485–1494.

Greenberg, S., Rabinowitz, R., Firestone, P., Bradford, J. M., & Greenberg, D. M. (2002). Prediction of recidivism in exhibitionists: Psychological, phallometric, and offence factors. *Sexual Abuse: A Journal of Research and Treatment* (329–347).

Gregersen, E. (1996). *The world of human sexuality: Behaviors, customs, and beliefs.* New York: Irvington.

Gregor, T. (1985). *Anxious pleasures: The sexual lives of an Amazonian people.* Chicago: University of Chicago Press.

Gregorian, R. S., Golden, K. A., Bahce, A., Goodman, C., Kwong, W. J., & Khan, Z. M. (2002). Antidepressant-induced sexual dysfunction. *The Annals of Pharmacotherapy, 36,* 1577–1589.

Grello, C. M., Welsh, D., & Harper, M. (2006). No strings attached: The nature of casual sex in college students. *Journal of Sex Research, 43,* 255–267.

Grenier, G., & Byers, E. S. (1995). Rapid ejaculation: A review of conceptual, etiological, and treatment issues. *Archives of Sexual Behavior, 24,* 447–474.

Grenier, G., & Byers, E. S. (1997). The relationships among ejaculatory control, ejaculatory latency, and attempts to prolong heterosexual intercourse. *Archives of Sexual Behavior, 26,* 27–48.

Grenier, G., & Byers, E. S. (2001). Operationalizing premature or rapid ejaculation. *Journal of Sex Research, 38,* 369–378.

Griffin, S. (1981). *Pornography and silence.* New York: Harper & Row.

Griffith, J., Hayworth, M., Adams, L., Mitchell, S., & Hart, C. (2013). Characteristics of pornography film actors: Self-report versus perceptions of college students. *Archives of Sexual Behavior, 42,* 637–647.

Griffith, J., Mitchell, S., Hart, C., Adams, L., & Gu, L. (2013). Pornography actresses: An assessment of then damaged good hypothesis. *Journal of Sex Research, 50,* 621–632.

Grimbos, T., et al. (2010). Sexual orientation and the second to fourth finger length ratio: A meta-analysis in men and women. *Behavioral Neuroscience, 124,* 278–287.

Grimes, D. A., Lopez, L. M., Schulz, K. F., Van Vliet, H. A., & Helmerhorst, F. M. (2006). Triphasic versus monophasic oral contraceptives for contraception. *Cochrane*

Database of Systematic Reviews 2006, Issue 3. Art. No.: CD003553. doi:10.1002/14651858. CD003553.pub2

Grov, C., Wolff, M., Smith, M. D., Koken, J., & Parsons, J. T. (2014). Male clients of male escorts: Satisfaction, sexual behavior, and demographic characteristics. *Journal of Sex Research, 51,* 827–837.

Gruenbaum, E. (2000). *The female circumcision controversy: An anthropological perspective.* Philadelphia: University of Pennsylvania Press.

Grumbach, M. M., & Styne, D. M. (1998). Puberty: Ontogeny, neuroendocrinology, physiology, and disorders. In J. D. Wilson et al. (Eds.), *Williams textbook of endocrinology* (9th ed., pp. 1509–1625). Philadelphia: Saunders.

Guay, J.-P., Proulx, J., Cusson, M., & Ouimet, M. (2001). Victim-choice polymorphia among serious sex offenders. *Archives of Sexual Behavior, 30,* 521–534.

Guay, S., Boisvert, J., & Freeston, M. H. (2003). Validity of three measures of communication for predicting relationship adjustment and stability among a sample of young couples. *Psychological Assessment, 15,* 392–398.

Guéguen, N. (2011). Effects of solicitor sex and attractiveness on receptivity to sexual offers: A field study. *Archives of Sexual Behavior, 40,* 915–919.

Guerrero, L., Spitzberg, B., & Yoshimura, S. (2004). Sexual and emotional jealousy. In J. H. Harvey, A. Wenzel, & S. Sprecher (Eds.), *The handbook of sexuality in close relationships* (pp. 311–345). Mahwah, NJ: Lawrence Erlbaum.

Guidroz, K., & Rich, G. J. (2010). Commercial telephone sex: Fantasy and reality. In R. Weitzer (Ed.), *Sex for sale: Prostitution, pornography, and the sex industry* (2nd ed., pp. 139–159). New York: Routledge.

Guise, J.-M., Palda, V., Westhoff, C., Chan, B. K. S., Helfand, K., & Lieu, T. A. (2003). The effectiveness of primary care-based interventions to promote breastfeeding: Systematic evidence review and meta-analysis for the US Preventive Services Task Force. *Annals of Family Medicine, 1,* 70–78.

Gunby, J., Bissonnette, F., Librach, C., & Cowan, L. (2011). Assisted reproductive technologies (ART) in Canada: 2007 results from the Canadian ART register. *Fertility and Sterility, 95,* 542–547.

Gunter, K., Maticka-Tyndale, E., Godin, G., Manson-Singer, S., & Bradet, R. (1993a). *Beliefs and behaviors related to HIV/AIDS: Report for the Caribbean communities. Ethnocultural communities facing AIDS: A national study.* Ottawa: National Health Research and Development Program Cross-Cultural Views of Disability and Sexuality (Health Canada)/AIDS Education and Prevention Unit (National AIDS Strategy) Health Canada.

Gunter, K., Maticka-Tyndale, E., Godin, G., Manson-Singer, S., & Bradet, R. (1993b). *Beliefs and behaviors related to HIV/AIDS:*

Report for the South Asian communities. Ethnocultural communities facing AIDS: A national study. Ottawa: National Health Research and Development Program (Health Canada)/AIDS Education and Prevention Unit (National AIDS Strategy) Health Canada.

Gurevich, M., Mathieson, C. M., Bower, J., & Dhayanandhan, B. (2007). Disciplining bodies, desires and subjectivities: Sexuality and HIV-positive women. *Feminism & Psychology, 17,* 9–38.

Gursoy, A. (1996). Abortion in Turkey: A matter of state, family, or individual decision. *Social Science & Medicine, 42,* 531–542.

Gutek, B. A. (1985). *Sex and the workplace.* San Francisco: Jossey-Bass.

Guterman, M. A. (2008). Observance of the laws of family purity in modern Orthodox Judaism. *Archives of Sexual Behavior, 37,* 340–345.

Hackney, A. C. (2008). Effects of endurance exercise on the reproductive system of men: The "exercise-hypogonadal male condition." *Journal of Endocrinological Investigation, 31,* 932–938.

Haig, D. (1996). Altercation of generations: Genetic conflicts of pregnancy. *American Journal of Reproductive Immunology, 35,* 226–232.

Halbreich, U., & Kahn, L. (2001). Role of estrogen in the aetiology and treatment of mood disorders. *CNS Drugs, 15,* 797–817.

Haldeman, D. C. (1994). The practice and ethics of sexual orientation conversion therapy. *Journal of Consulting and Clinical Psychology, 62,* 221–227.

Haldeman, D. C. (2001). Therapeutic antidotes: Helping gay and bisexual men recover from conversion therapies. In A. Shidlo, M. Schroeder, & J. Drescher (Eds.), *Sexual conversion therapy: Ethical, clinical, and research perspectives* (pp. 117–130). New York: Haworth.

Hall, G. C. N. (1995). Sexual offender recidivism revisited: A meta-analysis of recent treatment studies. *Journal of Consulting and Clinical Psychology, 63,* 802–809.

Hall, G. C. N., & Barongan, C. (1997). Prevention of sexual aggression. *American Psychologist, 52,* 5–14.

Hall, G. C. N., Teten, A. L., DeGarmo, D. S., Sue, S., & Stephens, K. A. (2005). Ethnicity, culture, and sexual aggression: Risk and protective factors. *Journal of Consulting and Clinical Psychology, 73,* 830–840.

Hall, J. A. (1998). How big are nonverbal sex differences? The case of smiling and sensitivity to nonverbal cues. In D. Canary & K. Dindia (Eds.), *Sex differences and similarities in communication* (pp. 155–178). Mahwah, NJ: Erlbaum.

Hall, R. C. W., & Hall, R. C. W. (2007). A profile of pedophilia: Definition, characteristics of offenders, recidivism, treatment outcomes, and forensic issues. *Mayo Clinic Proceedings, 82,* 457–471.

Halldorsson, T., Ström, M., Petersen, S. B., & Olsen, S. F. (2010). Intake of artificially

sweetened soft drinks and risk of preterm delivery: A prospective cohort study in 59,334 Danish pregnant women. *American Journal of Clinical Nutrition, 92,* 626–633.

Halpern, C. T. (2010). Reframing research on adolescent sexuality: Health sexual development as part of the life course. *Perspectives on Sexual and Reproductive Health, 42,* 6–7.

Halpern, D. F. (1998). Teaching critical thinking for transfer across domains. *American Psychologist, 53,* 449–455.

Halpern, D. F. (2002). Teaching for critical thinking: A four-part model to enhance thinking skills. In S. F. Davis & W. Buskist (Eds.), *The teaching of psychology: Essays in honor of Wilbert J. McKeachie and Charles L. Brewer* (pp. 91–105). Mahwah, NJ: Erlbaum.

Hamilton, L. D., Van Dam, D., & Wassersug, R. J. (2015). The perspective of prostate cancer patients and patients' partners on the psychological burden of androgen deprivation and the dyadic adjustment of prostate cancer couples. *Psycho-Oncology, 25,* 823–831.

Hamilton, M. C., Anderson, D., Broaddus, M., & Young, K. (2006). Gender stereotypes and under-representation of female characters in 200 popular children's picture books: A twenty-first century update. *Sex Roles, 55,* 757–766.

Hampson, E., & Moffat, S. D. (2004). The psychobiology of gender: Cognitive effects of reproductive hormones in the adult nervous system. In A. H. Eagly, A. E. Beall, & R. J. Sternberg (Eds.), *The psychology of gender* (2nd ed.). New York: Guilford Press.

Hampton, M. R., Jeffery, B., McWatters, B., & Smith, P. (2005). Influence of teens' perceptions of parental disapproval and peer behaviour on their initiation of sexual intercourse. *Canadian Journal of Human Sexuality, 14,* 105–121.

Hampton, M. R., McKay-McNabb, K., Racette, S. F., & Byrd, N. J. (2007). Aboriginal elders as healers: Saskatchewan elders speak about sexual health. In J. D. Pappas, W. E. Smythe, & A. Baydala (Eds.), *Cultural healing and belief systems* (pp. 236–259). Calgary, AB: Detselig Enterprises Ltd.

Hampton, M. R., McWatters, B., & Jeffery, B. (2000). Method-related experiences of Canadian women using Depo-Provera for contraception. *Canadian Journal of Human Sexuality, 9,* 247–257.

Handy, L. C., Valentich, M., Cammaert, L. P., & Gripton, J. (1985). Feminist issues in sex therapy. In M. Valentich & J. Gripton (Eds.), *Feminist perspectives on social work and human sexuality.* New York: Haworth Press.

Hanson, R. K. (2000). Will they do it again? Predicting sex-offense recidivism. *Current Directions in Psychological Science, 9,* 106–109.

Hanson, R. K., & Bussière, M. T. (1998). Predicting relapse: A meta-analysis of sexual offender recidivism studies. *Journal of Consulting and Clinical Psychology, 66,* 348–362.

Hanson, R. K., Gordon, A., Harris, A. J. R., Marques, J. K., Murphy, W., Quinsey, V. L., & Seto, M. C. (2002). First report of the collaborative outcome data project on the effectiveness of psychological treatment for sex offenders. *Sexual Abuse: A Journal of Research and Treatment, 14*, 169–194.

Hardwick, D., & Patychuk, D. (1999). Geographic mapping demonstrates the association between social inequality, teen births and STDs among youth. *Canadian Journal of Human Sexuality, 8*(22), 77–90.

Hardwick, D., McKay, A., & Ashem, M. (2007). Chlamydia screening of adolescent and young women by general practice physicians in Toronto, Canada: Baseline survey data from a physician education campaign. *Canadian Journal of Human Sexuality, 16*, 63–75.

Hare, K., Gahagan, J., Jackson, L., & Steenbeek, A. (2014). Perspectives on "Pornography": Exploring sexually explicit Internet movies' influences on Canadian young adults' holistic sexual health. *Canadian Journal of Human Sexuality, 23*, 148–158.

Hare, L., Bernard, P., Sánchez, F. J., Baird, P. N., Vilain, E., Kennedy, T., & Harley, V. R. (2008). Androgen receptor repeat length polymorphism associated with male-to-female transsexualism. *Biological Psychiatry, 65*, 93–96.

Harlow, H. F., Harlow, M. K., & Hause, F. W. (1963). The maternal affectional system of rhesus monkeys. In II. L. Rheingold (Ed.), *Maternal behavior in mammals*. New York: Wiley.

Harper, C. C., Cheong, M., Rocca, C. H., Darney, P. D., & Raine, T. R. (2005). The effect of increased access to emergency contraception among young adolescents. *Obstetrics & Gynecology, 106*, 483–491.

Harrington, P. R., & Swanstrom, R. (2008). The biology of HIV, SIV, and other lentiviruses. In K. Holmes et al. (Eds.), *Sexually transmitted diseases* (4th ed., pp. 323–339). New York: McGraw-Hill.

Harris, C. R. (2002). Sexual and romantic jealousy in heterosexual and homosexual adults. *Psychological Science, 13*, 7–12.

Harris, G. (2004, February 28). Pfizer gives up testing Viagra on women. *New York Times*, pp. C1.

Harris, G. E., & Alderson, K. G. (2006). Gay men living with HIV/AIDS: The potential for empowerment. *Journal of HIV/AIDS & Social Services, 5*, 9–24.

Harris, G. W., & Levine, S. (1965). Sexual differentiation of the brain and its experimental control. *Journal of Physiology, 181*, 379–400.

Harris/Decima. (2007, December 15). The average Canadian is a 6.7 out of 10 [Press release].

Harte, C. B., & Meston, C. M. (2011). Recreational use of erectile dysfunction medications in undergraduate men in the United States: Characteristics and associated risk factors. *Archives of Sexual Behavior, 40*, 597–606.

Hartley, T., & Mazzuca, J. (2001, December 12). Fewer Canadians favour legalized abortion under any circumstance. *The Gallup Poll, 61*(85). Toronto: Gallup Canada Inc.

Hartman, W., & Fithian, M. (1984). *Any man can: The multiple orgasmic technique for every loving man*. New York: St. Martin's Press.

Hartmann, K., Viswanathan, M., Palmieri, R., Gartlehner, G., Thorp, J., & Lohr, K. (2005). Outcomes of routine episiotomy: A systematic review. *Journal of the American Medical Association, 293*, 2141–2148.

Hartwick, C., Desmarais, S., & Hennig, K. (2007). Characteristics of male and female victims of sexual coercion. *Canadian Journal of Human Sexuality, 16*, 31–44.

Hatcher, R. A., Trussell, J., Nelson, A. L., Cates, W., Jr., Stewart, F. H., & Kowal, D. (2007). *Contraceptive technology* (19th ed). New York: Ardent Media.

Hatcher, R. A., Trussell, J., Nelson, A. L., Cates, W., Jr., Stewart, F. H., & Kowal, D. (2011). *Contraceptive technology* (20th ed.). New York: Ardent Media.

Hatfield, E. (1978). Equity and extramarital sexuality. *Archives of Sexual Behavior, 7*, 127–141.

Hatfield, E., & Rapson, R. (1993a). Historical and cross-cultural perspectives on passionate love and sexual desire. *Annual Review of Sex Research, 4*, 67–97.

Hatfield, E., & Rapson, R. (1993b). *Love, sex, and intimacy*. New York: HarperCollins.

Hatfield, E., & Sprecher, S. (1986). Measuring passionate love in intimate relations. *Journal of Adolescence, 9*, 383–410.

Hatfield, E., & Walster, G. W. (1978). *A new look at love*. Reading, MA: Addison-Wesley.

Hatfield, E., Walster, G. W., & Berscheid, E. (1978). *Equity theory and research*. Boston: Allyn & Bacon.

Hatzichristou, D., Montorsi, F., Buvat, J., Laferriere, N., Bandel, T. J., & Porst, H. (2004). The efficacy and safety of flexible-dose vardenafil (Levitra) in a broad population of European men. *European Urology, 45*, 634–641.

Hawkins, A. J., & Fackrell, T. A. (2010). Does relationship and marriage education for lower-income couples work? A meta-analytic study of emerging research. *Journal of Couple and Relationship Therapy, 9*, 181–191.

Hawkins, A., Blanchard, V. L., Baldwin, S. A., & Fawcett, E. B. (2008). Does marriage and relationship education work? A meta-analytic study. *Journal of Consulting and Clinical Psychology, 76*, 723–734.

Hayashi, K., Ogushi, S., Kurimoto, K., Shimamoto, S., Ohta, H., & Saitou, M. (2012, November 16). Offspring from oocytes derived from in vitro primordial germ cell-like cells in mice. *Science, 338*(6109), 971–975.

Hayes, T. B., Collins, A., Lee, M., Mendoza, M., Noriega, N., Stuart, A. A., & Vonk, A. (2002). Hermaphroditic, demasculinized frogs after exposure to the herbicide atrazine at low ecologically relevant doses. *Proceedings of the National Academy of Sciences, 99*, 5476–5480.

Haynes, B. F., Gilbert, P. B., McElrath, M. J., Zolla-Pazner, S., Tomaras, G. D., Alam, S. M., . . . & Kim, J. H. (2012). Immune-correlates analysis of an HIV-1 vaccine efficacy trial. *New England Journal of Medicine, 366*, 1275–1286.

Health Canada. (1994a). *Many voices: HIV/AIDS in the context of culture. Report for the communities from and the English-speaking Caribbean communities*. Ottawa: Author.

Health Canada. (1994b). *Many voices: HIV/AIDS in the context of culture. Report for the communities from the Horn of Africa*. Ottawa: Author.

Health Canada. (1994c). *Many voices: HIV/AIDS in the context of culture. Report for the South Asian communities*. Ottawa: Author.

Health Canada. (1994d). *Many voices: HIV/AIDS in the context of culture. Report for the Latin American community*. Ottawa: Author.

Health Canada. (1994e). *Many voices: HIV/AIDS in the context of culture. Report for the Chinese communities*. Ottawa: Author.

Health Canada. (1996a). *Breastfeeding*. Canadian Perinatal Surveillance System—Fact Sheets, 1–6.

Health Canada. (1996b). *HIV/AIDS and Aboriginal people in Canada*. Ottawa: Author.

Health Canada. (1996c). *HIV/AIDS Epidemiology among Aboriginal peoples in Canada. Epi Update*. Laboratory Centre for Disease Control. Ottawa: Health Canada.

Health Canada. (1998a). *Cervical cancer in Canada—cancer updates*. Laboratory Centre for Disease Control, 1–8.

Health Canada. (2000). What everyone should know about human papillomavirus (HPV): Questions and Answers. *Bureau of HIV/AIDS, STD and TB Update Series: Population and Public Health Branch, STD Epi Update*. Ottawa: Author.

Health Canada. (2001). HIV and AIDS in Canada, Surveillance Report to December 31, 2000. *Division of HIV/AIDS Epidemiology and Surveillance, Bureau of HIV/AIDS, STD and TB, Centre for Infectious Disease Prevention and Control*. Ottawa: Health Canada.

Health Canada. (2003). *Canadian guidelines for sexual health education*. Ottawa: Health Canada.

Health Canada. (2004). *Health Canada advises of potential adverse effects of SSRIs and other anti-depressants on newborns*. [Advisory 2004-44]. Retrieved October 12, 2004 from http://www.hcsc.gc.ca

Hearn, K. D., O'Sullivan, L. F., & Dudley, C. D. (2003). Assessing reliability of early adolescent girls' reports of romantic and sexual behavior. *Archives of Sexual Behavior, 32*, 513–522.

Heatherington, L., & Lavner, J. A. (2008). Coming to terms with coming out: Review and recommendations for family systems-focused research. *Journal of Family Psychology, 22,* 329–343

Heaton, J. P. W. (2000). Central neuropharmacological agents and mechanisms in erectile dysfunction: The role of dopamine. *Neuroscience and Biobehavioral Reviews, 24,* 561–569.

Heaton, J. P. W. (2001). Key issues from the clinical trials of apomorphine SL. *World Journal of Urology, 19,* 25–31.

Hébert, A., & Weaver, A. (2014). An examination of personality characteristics associated with BDSM orientations. *Canadian Journal of Human Sexuality, 23,* 106–115.

Hébert, A., & Weaver, A. (2015). Perks, problems, and the people who play: A qualitative exploration of dominant and submissive BDSM roles. *Canadian Journal of Human Sexuality, 24,* 49–62.

Hébert, M., & Tourigny, M. (2004). Child sexual abuse prevention: A review of evaluative studies and recommendations for program development. *Advances in Psychology Research, 32,* 109–142.

Hébert, M., & Tremblay, C. (2000). La prévention de l'agression sexuelle à l'égard des enfants. In F. Vitaro & C. Gagnon (Eds.), *Prévention des problèmes d'adaptation chez les enfants et les adolescents*-Tome 1 *Les problèmes internalisès* (pp. 429–503). Ste-Foy: Presses de l'Université du Québec.

Hébert, M., Langevin, R., & Charest, F. (2014). Factors associated with resilience in preschoolers reporting sexual abuse: A typological analysis. *International Journal of Child and Adolescent Resilience, 2,* 46–58.

Hébert, M., Lavoie, F., & Parent, N. (2002). An assessment of outcomes following parents' participation in a child abuse prevention program. *Victims and Violence, 17,* 355–372.

Hébert, M., Lavoie, F., Piché, C., & Poitras, M. (2001). Proximate effects of a child sexual abuse prevention program in elementary school children. *Child Abuse & Neglect, 25,* 505–522.

Hébert, M., Tourigny, M., Cyr, M., McDuff, P., & Joly, J. (2009). Prevalence of childhood sexual abuse and timing of disclosure in a representative sample of adults from Québec. *Canadian Journal of Psychiatry, 54,* 631–636.

Hébert, M., Tremblay, C., Parent, N., Daignault, I. V., & Piché, C. (2006). Correlates of behavioral outcomes in sexually abused children. *Journal of Family Violence, 21,* 287–299.

Heffron, R., Donnell, D., Rees, H, Celum, C., Mugo, N., Were, E., . . . Baeten, J. M. (2012). Use of hormonal contraceptives and risk of HIV-1 transmission: A prospective cohort study. *Lancet Infectious Diseases, 12,* 19–26.

Heiman, J. R. (1975). The physiology of erotica: Women's sexual arousal. *Psychology Today, 8*(11), 90–94.

Heiman, J. R. (2007). Orgasmic disorders in women. In S. Leiblum (Ed.), *Principles and practice of sex therapy* (4th ed., pp. 84–123). New York: Guilford.

Heiman, J. R., & LoPiccolo, J. (1988). *Becoming orgasmic: A sexual and personal growth program for women.* New York: Simon & Schuster.

Heine, S. J., & Norenzayan, A. (2006). Toward a psychological science for a cultural species. *Perspectives in Psychological Science, 1,* 251–269.

Heino, A., & Gissler, M. (2013, March 20). "Pohjoismaiset raskaudenkeskeytykset 2011 (Induced fs in the Nordic countries 2011)". Helsinki: Terveyden ja hyvinvoinnin laitos (National Institute for Health and Welfare), Finland.

Heldman, C., & Wade, L. (2010). Hook-up culture: Setting a new research agenda. *Sexuality Research and Social Policy, 7,* 323–333.

Helgeson, V. S., Cohen, S., & Schulz, R. (2001). Long-term effects of educational and peer discussion group interventions on adjustment to breast cancer. *Health Psychology, 20,* 387–392.

Hellerstedt, W. L., Peterson-Hickey, M., Rhodes, K. L., & Garwick, A. (2006). Environmental, social, and personal correlates of having ever had sexual intercourse among American Indian youths. *American Journal of Public Health, 96,* 2228–2234.

Hellstrom, W. (2003). Three-piece inflatable penile prosthesis components (surgical pearls on reservoirs, pumps, and rear-tip extenders). *International Journal of Impotence Research, 15,* S136–S138.

Hellstrom, W. J. (2011). Update on treatments for premature ejaculation. *International Journal of Clinical Practice, 65,* 16–26.

Hellstrom, W. J., Gittelman, M., Karlin, G., Segerson, T., Thibonnier, M., & Taylor, T. (2003b). Sustained efficacy and tolerability of vardenafil, a highly potent selective phosphodiesterase type 5 inhibitor, in men with erectile dysfunction: results of a randomized, double-blind, 26-week placebo-controlled pivotal trial. *Urology, 61,* 8–14.

Hellstrom, W., Overstreet, J. W., Yu, A. S., Saikali, K., Shen, W., Beasley, C. M., & Watkins, V. S. (2003a). Tadalafil has no detrimental effect on human spermatogenesis or reproductive hormones. *Journal of Urology, 170,* 887–891.

Helminiak, D. A. (2001a). Sexual ethics in college textbooks: A survey. *Journal of Sex Education and Therapy, 26,* 106–114.

Helminiak, D. A. (2001b). Sexual ethics in college textbooks: A suggestion. *Journal of Sex Education and Therapy, 26,* 320–327.

Helminiak, D. A. (2004). The ethics of sex: A call to the gay community. *Pastoral Psychology, 52,* 259–267.

Hemels, M. E., Koren, G., & Einarson, T. R. (2002). Increased use of antidepressants in Canada: 1981–2000. *The Annals of Pharmacotherapy, 36,* 1375–1379.

Henderson, A. J. Z., Bartholomew, K., Trinke, S. J., & Kwong, M. J. (2005). When loving means hurting: An exploration of attachment and intimate abuse in a community sample. *Journal of Family Violence, 20,* 219–230

Hendrick, C., & Hendrick, S. (2004). Sex and romantic love: Connects and disconnects. In J. H. Harvey, A. Wenzel, & S. Sprecher (Eds.), *The handbook of sexuality in close relationships* (pp. 159–182). Mahwah, NJ: Lawrence Erlbaum.

Hendrick, S. S., Hendrick, C., & Adler, N. L. (1988). Romantic relationships: Love, satisfaction, and staying together. *Journal of Personality and Social Psychology, 54,* 980–988.

Hendrick, S., & Hendrick, C. (1992). *Liking, loving, and relating* (2nd ed.). Pacific Grove, CA: Brooks/Cole.

Henningsson, S., Westberg, L., Nilsson, S., Lundström, B., Ekselius, L., Bodlund, O., . . . Landén, M. (2005). Sex steroid-related genes and male-to-female transsexualism. *Psychoneuroendocrinology, 30,* 657–664.

Henrich, J., Boyd, R., & Richerson, P. J. (2012). The puzzle of monogamous marriage. *Philosophical Transactions of the Royal Society, 367,* 657–669.

Henrich, J., Heine, S. J., & Norenzayan, A. (2010). The weirdest people in the world? *Behavioral and Brain Sciences, 33,* 61–135.

Herbenick, D., & Reece, M. (2010). Development and validation of the female genital self-image scale. *Journal of Sexual Medicine, 7*(5), 1822–1830. doi:10.1111/j.1743–6109.2010.01728.x

Herbenick, D., Reece, M., Sanders, S., Dodge, B., Ghassemi, A., & Fortenberry, J. D. (2009). Prevalence and characteristics of vibrator use by women in the United States: Results from a nationally representative study. *Journal of Sexual Medicine, 6,* 1857–1866.

Herbenick, D., Reece, M., Schick, V., Sanders, S. A., Dodge, B., & Fortenberry, J. D. (2010a). Sexual behavior in the United States: Results from a national probability sample of men and women ages 14–94. *Journal of Sexual Medicine, 7*(SS05), 255–265.

Herbenick, D., Reece, M., Schick, V., Sanders, S. A., Dodge, B., & Fortenberry, J. D. (2010b). Sexual behaviors, relationships and perceived health status among adult women in the United States: Results from a national probability sample. *Journal of Sexual Medicine, 7*(SS05), 277–290.

Herbenick, D., Reece, M., Schick, V., Sanders, S. A., Dodge, B., & Fortenberry, J. D. (2010c). An event-level analysis of the sexual characteristics and composition among adults ages 18 to 59: Results from a national probability sample in the United States. *Journal of Sexual Medicine, 7* (SS05), 346–361.

Herdt, G. (1990). Mistaken gender: 5-alpha reductase herma phroditism and biological reductionism in sexual identity reconsidered. *American Anthropologist, 92,* 433–446.

Herdt, G. H. (1984). *Ritualized homosexuality in Melanesia.* Berkeley, CA: University of California Press.

Herek, G. M. (2000). The psychology of sexual prejudice. *Current Directions In Psychological Science, 9,* 19–22.

Herek, G. M. (2002). Heterosexuals' attitudes toward bisexual men and women in the United States. *Journal of Sex Research, 39,* 264–274.

Hergenhahn, B. R. (2001). *An introduction to the history of psychology* (4th ed.). Toronto: Wadsworth/Thomas Learning.

Herold, E. (1981). Contraceptive embarrassment and contraceptive behaviour among young single women. *Journal of Youth & Adolescence, 10*(3), 233–242.

Herold, E. S., & Way, L. (1988). Sexual self disclosure among university women. *Journal of Sex Research, 24,* 1–14.

Heron, A. (1963). *Towards a Quaker view of sex.* London, UK: Friends Home Service Committee.

Herrero, R., Castellsague, X., Pawlita, M., Lissowska, J., Kee, F., Balaram, P., Rajkumar, T., . . . IARC Multicenter Oral Cancer Study Group. (2003). Human papilloma virus and oral cancer: The International Agency for Research on Cancer multicenter study. *Journal of the National Cancer Institute, 95*(23), 1772–1783.

Hess, J. S., & Coffelt, T. A. (2012). Verbal communication about sex in marriage: Patterns of language use and its connection with relational outcomes. *Journal of Sex Research, 49,* 603–612.

Hessell, A. J., & Haigwood, N. L. (2015). Animal models in HIV-1 protection and therapy. *Current Opinion in HIV and AIDS, 10,* 170–176.

Hetherington, M. E., & Parke, R. D. (2003). *Child Psychology: A contemporary viewpoint updated* (5th ed.). McGraw-Hill.

Hewlett, B. S., & Hewlett, B. L. (2010). Sex and searching for children among Aka foragers and Ngandu farmers of Central Africa. *African Study Monographs, 31*(3), 107–125.

Hightower, M. (1997). Effects of exercise participation on menstrual pain and symptoms. *Women & Health, 26,* 15–27.

Hill, D. B. (2000). Categories of sex and gender: Either/or, both/and, and neither/nor. *History and Philosophy of Psychology Bulletin, 12,* 25–33.

Hill, D. B., Rozanski, C., Carfagnini, J., & Willoughby, B. (2007). Gender identity disorders in childhood and adolescence: A critical inquiry. *International Journal of Sexual Health, 1,* 95–122.

Hill, M. (2002). Skin color and the perception of attractiveness among African Americans: Does gender make a difference? *Social Psychology Quarterly, 65,* 77–91.

Hines, A. L., & Jiang, H. J. (2102). Rates of obstetric trauma, 2009 (Statistical Brief #129). Agency for Healthcare Research and Quality. Retrieved from http://www.hcup-us.ahrq.gov/reports/statbriefs/sb129.pdf

Hines, D. A. (2007). Predictors of sexual coercion against women and men: A multilevel, multinational study of university students. *Archives of Sexual Behavior, 36,* 403–422.

Hinman, K. (2011, November 3). Lost boys. *LA Weekly.* Retrieved from http://www.laweekly.com/content/printVersion/1535565/

Hipp, L. E., Low, L. K., & van Anders, S. M. (2012). Exploring women's postpartum sexuality: Social, psychological, relational and birth-related contextual factors. *Journal of Sexual Medicine, 9,* 2330–2341.

Hirschenhauser, K., Frigerio, D., Grammer, K., & Magnusson, M. S. (2002). Monthly patterns of testosterone and behavior in prospective fathers. *Hormones and Behavior, 42,* 172–181.

Hite, S. (1976). *The Hite report.* New York: Macmillan.

Hite, S. (1981). *The Hite report on male sexuality.* New York: Alfred Knopf.

Hobbs, M. M., Seña, A. C., Swygard, H., & Schwebbe, J. R. (2008). *Trichomonas vaginalis* and trichomoniasis. In K. Holmes et al. (Eds.), *Sexually transmitted diseases* (4th ed., pp. 771–794). New York: McGraw-Hill.

Hobfoll, S., Ritter, C., Lavin, J., Hulsizer, M., & Cameron, R. P. (1995). Depression prevalence and incidence among inner-city pregnant and postpartum women. *Journal of Consulting and Clinical Psychology, 63,* 445–453.

Hoffmann, H., Janssen, E., & Turner, S. L. (2004). Classical conditioning of sexual arousal in women and men: Effects of varying awareness and biological relevance of the conditioned stimulus. *Archives of Sexual Behavior, 33,* 43–54.

Hollander, D. (1996). Programs to bring down cesarean section rate prove to be successful. *Family Planning Perspectives, 28,* 182–185.

Holman, A., & Sillars, A. (2012). Talk about "hooking up": The influence of college student social networks on nonrelationship sex. *Health Communication, 27,* 205–216.

Holmberg, D., & Blair, K. L. (2009). Sexual desire, communication, satisfaction, and preferences of men and women in same-sex versus mixed-sex relationships. *Journal of Sex Research, 46,* 57–66.

Holmberg, D., Blair, K. L., & Phillips, M. (2010). Women's sexual satisfaction as a predictor of well-being in same-sex versus mixed-sex relationships. *Journal of Sex Research, 47*(1), 1–11.

Holmes, M. (2002). Rethinking the meaning and management of intersexuality. *Sexualities, 5,* 159–180.

Holstege, G., Georgiadis, J. R., Paans, A. M., Meiners, L. C., van der Graaf, F. H., & Reinders, A. A. (2003). Brain activation during human male ejaculation. *Journal of Neuroscience, 23,* 9185–9193.

Holter, H., Anderheim, L., Bergh, C., & Möller, A. (2006). First IVF treatment—shortterm impact on psychological well-being and the marital relationship. *Human Reproduction, 21,* 3295–3302.

Homma, Y., Nicholson, D., & Saewyc, E. (2012). Profile of high school students exchanging sex for substances in rural Canada. *Canadian Journal of Human Sexuality, 21*(1), 29–40.

Homma, Y., Saewyc, E. M., Wong, S. T., & Zumbo, B. D. (2013). Sexual health and risk behaviour among East Asian adolescents in British Columbia. *Canadian Journal of Human Sexuality, 22,* 13–24.

Homma, Y., Wang, N., Saewyc, E., & Kishor, N. (2012). The relationship between sexual abuse and risky sexual behavior among adolescent boys: A meta-analysis. *Journal of Adolescent Health, 51,* 18–24.

Homma, Y., Wong, S. T., Zumbo, B. D., & Saewyc, E. M. (2014). Ethnic identity and sexual initiation among East Asian youth in Canada. *Journal of Immigrant Minority Health.* doi:10.1007/s10903-014-0101-0

Hong, L. K. (1984). Survival of the fastest: On the origin of premature ejaculation. *Journal of Sex Research, 20,* 109–122.

Hook, E. W., & Handsfield, H. H. (2008). Gonococcal infections in the adult. In K. Holmes et al. (Eds.), *Sexually transmitted diseases* (4th ed., pp. 627–646). New York: McGraw-Hill.

Hopwood, N. J., Kelch, R. P., Hale, P. M., Mendes, T. M., Foster, C. M., & Beitins, I. Z. (1990). The onset of human puberty: Biological and environmental factors. In J. Bancroft & J. M. Reinisch (Eds.), *Adolescence and puberty.* New York: Oxford University Press.

Horney, K. (1973). The flight from womanhood (1926). In K. Horney, *Feminine psychology.* New York: Norton.

Horrocks, R. (1997). *An introduction to the study of sexuality.* New York: St. Martin's Press.

Hou, F., & Myles, J. (2007). The changing role of education in the marriage market: Asortative marriage in Canada and the United States since the 1970s. *Analytical Studies Branch Research Paper Series* (Catalogue no. 11F0019MIE). Ottawa: Statistics Canada.

House, C. (1997). Navajo warrior women: An ancient tradition in a modern world. In S. Jacobs, et al. (Eds.), *Two-spirit people* (pp. 223–227). Urbana, IL: University of Illinois Press.

How big is porn? (2001, May 25). *Forbes.*

Hsiao, W., Bennett, N., Guhring, P., Narus, J., & Mulhall, J. P. (2011). Satisfaction profiles in men using intracavernosal injection therapy. *Journal of Sexual Medicine, 8,* 512–517.

Hubacher, D. (2002). The checkered history and bright future of intrauterine contraception in the United States. *Perspectives on Sexual and Reproductive Health, 34,* 98–103.

Huber, J. D., & Herold, E. S. (2006). Sexually overt approaches in singles bars. *Canadian Journal of Human Sexuality, 15,* 133–146.

Hucker, S. (2008). Sexual masochism: Psychopathology and theory. In D. Richard Laws & W. O'Donohue (Eds.), *Sexual deviance: Theory, assessment, and treatment* (2nd ed., pp. 250–263). New York: Guilford.

Hucker, S., & Blanchard, R. (1992). Death scene characteristics in 118 fatal cases of autoerotic asphyxia compared with suicidal asphyxia. *Behavioural Sciences and the Law, 10,* 509–523.

Huffstutter, P. J., & Frammolino, R. (2001, July 6). Lights, camera, Viagra: When the show must go on, sometimes a little chemistry helps. *Los Angeles Times*, A1.

Hughes, J. O., & Sandler, B. R. (1987). *"Friends" raping friends: Could it happen to you?* Washington, DC: Association of American Colleges.

Hughes, T. L., Johnson, T., & Wilsnack, S. C. (2001). Sexual assault and alcohol abuse: A comparison of lesbians and heterosexual women. *Journal of Substance Abuse, 13,* 515–532.

Hugh-Jones, S., Gough, B., & Littlewood, A. (2005). Sexual exhibitionism as "sexuality and individuality": A critique of the psycho-medical discourse from the perspectives of women who exhibit. *Sexualities, 8,* 259–281.

Huh, J., Park, K., Hwang, I. S., Jung, S. I., Kim, H. J., Chung, T. W., & Jeong, G. W. (2008). Brain activation areas of sexual arousal with olfactory stimulation in men. A preliminary study using functional MRI. *Journal of Sexual Medicine, 5,* 619–625.

Hulshoff, H. E., Cohen-Kettenis, P. T., Van Haren, N. E. M., Peper, J. S., Brans, R. G. H., Cahn, W., . . . Kahn, R. S. (2006). Changing your sex changes your brain: Influences of testosterone and estrogen on adult human brain structure. *European Journal of Endocrinology, 155,* S107–S114.

Humphreys, T. P. (2007). Perceptions of sexual consent: The impact of relationship history and gender. *Journal of Sex Research, 44,* 307–315.

Humphreys, T. P. (2012). Cognitive frameworks of virginity and first intercourse. *Journal of Sex Research.* doi:10.1080/00224499.2012.677868

Humphreys, T. P., & Brousseau, M. M. (2010). The Sexual Consent Scale-Revised: Development, reliability, and preliminary validity. *Journal of Sex Research, 47*(5), 420–428.

Humphreys, T. P., & Herold, E. (2007). Sexual consent in heterosexual relationships: Development of a new measure. *Sex Roles, 57,* 305–315.

Humphreys, T. P., & Kennett, D. J. (2010). The reliability and validity of instruments supporting the sexual self-control model. *Canadian Journal of Human Sexuality, 19*(1–2), 1–13.

Hunt, M. (1974). *Sexual behavior in the 1970s.* Chicago: Playboy Press.

Hust, S. J., Brown, J., & L'Engle, K. (2008). Boys will be boys and girls better be prepared: An analysis of the rare sexual health messages in young adolescents' media. *Mass Communication and Society, 11,* 3–23.

Hutchinson, K. A. (1995). Androgens and sexuality. *American Journal of Medicine, 98* (Suppl. 1A), 1A111S–1A115S.

Hutchinson, M. K., & Cooney, T. M. (1998). Patterns of parent-teen sexual risk communication: Implications for intervention. *Family Relations, 47,* 185–94.

Hutton, E. K., Reitsma, A. H., & Kaufman, K. (2009). Outcomes associated with planned home and planned hospital births in low-risk women attended by midwives in Ontario, Canada, 2003-2006: a retrospective cohort study. *Birth, 36,* 180–189.

Hyde, J. S., & Else-Quest, N. (2012). *Half the human experience: The psychology of women* (8th ed.). Boston: Houghton Mifflin.

Hyde, J. S., & Jaffee, S. R. (2000). Becoming a heterosexual adult: The experiences of young women. *Journal of Social Issues, 56,* 283–296.

Hyde, J. S., DeLamater, J., & Hewitt, E. (1998). Sexuality and the dualearner couple: Multiple rules and sexual functioning. *Journal of Family Psychology, 12,* 354–368.

Hyde, J. S., DeLamater, J., Plant, E. A., & Byrd, J. M. (1996). Sexuality during pregnancy and the year postpartum. *Journal of Sex Research, 33,* 143–151.

Hynes, H. P., & Raymond, J. G. (2002). Put in harm's way: The neglected health consequences of sex trafficking in the United States. In J. Silliman, & A. Bhattacharjee (Eds.), *Policing the national body: Sex, race, and criminalization* (pp. 197–229). Cambridge, MA: South End Press.

Hynie, M., & Lydon, J. E. (1995). Women's perceptions of female contraceptive behaviour: Experimental evidence of the social double standard. *Psychology of Women Quarterly, 19,* 563–581.

Hynie, M., Lydon, J. E., & Taradash, A. (1997). Commitment, intimacy, and women's perceptions of premarital sex and contraceptive readiness. *Psychology of Women Quarterly, 21,* 447–464.

Hynie, M., Lydon, J. E., Cote, S., & Weiner, S. (1998). Relational sexual scripts and women's condom use: The importance of internalized norms. *Journal of Sex Research, 35*(4), 370–380.

Ibañez, G. E., Van Oss Marin, B., Flores, S. A., Millett, G., & Diaz, R. M. (2009). General and gay-related racism experienced by Latino gay men. *Cultural Diversity and Ethnic Minority Psychology, 15,* 215–222.

Idso, C. (2009). Sexually transmitted infection prevention in newly single older women: A forgotten health promotion need. *Journal for Nurse Practitioners, 5,* 440–446.

Ilies, R., Hauserman, N., Schwochau, S., & Stibal, J. (2003). Reported incidence rates of work-related sexual harassment in the United States: Using meta-analysis to explain reported rate disparities. *Personnel Psychology, 56,* 607–631.

Ilkkaracan, P. (2001). Islam and women's sexuality. In P. B. Jung, M. E. Hunt, & R. Balakrishnan (Eds.), *Good sex: Feminist perspectives from the world's religions* (pp. 61–76). New Brunswick, NJ: Rutgers University Press.

Imperato-McGinley, J., Guerrero, L., Gautier, T., & Peterson, R. E. (1974). Steroid 5 reductase deficiency in man: An inherited form of male pseudohermaphroditism. *Science, 186,* 1213–1215.

Impett, E. A., Muise, A., & Rosen, N. O. (2015). Is it good to be giving in the bedroom? A prosocial perspective on sexual health and well-being in romantic relationships. *Current Sexual Health Reports, 7,* 180–190.

Institute of Medicine. (2004). *New frontiers in contraceptive research.* Washington, DC: National Academies Press.

Ipsos. (2013, June). *A global advisory: Same-sex marriage.* Retrieved from http://ipsos-na.com/download/pr.aspx?id=12795

Irvine, J. M. (1995). *Sexuality education across cultures: Working with differences.* San Francisco: Jossey-Bass.

Isaacs, C. R., & Fisher, W. A. (2008). A computer-based educational intervention to address potential negative effects of Internet pornography. *Communication Studies, 59,* 1–18.

Israel, D. D., Sheffer-Babila, S., de Luca, C., Jo, Y-H., Liu, S. M., Xia, Q., . . . Chua, S. C., Jr. (2012). Effects of leptin and melanocortin signaling interactions on pubertal development and reproduction. *Endocrinology, 153,* 2408–2419.

Iwaniuk, A. N., Koperski, D. T., Cheng, K. M., Elliott, J. E., Smith, L. K., Wilson, L. K., & Wylie, D. R. (2006). The effects of environmental exposure to DDT on the brain of a songbird: Changes in structures associated with mating and song. *Behavioural Brain Research, 173,* 1–10.

Izugbara, C. O. (2008). Home-based sexuality education: Nigerian parents discussing sex with their children. *Youth & Society, 39,* 575–600.

Jaakkola, J., & Gissler, M. (2004). Maternal smoking in pregnancy, fetal development and childhood asthma. *American Journal of Public Health, 94,* 136–141.

Jackson, G. (2009). Sexual response in cardiovascular disease. *Journal of Sex Research, 46,* 233–236.

Jackson, T., Chen, H., Guo, C., & Gao, X. (2006). Stories we love by: Conceptions of love among couples from the People's Republic of China, and the United States. *Journal of Cross-Cultural Psychology, 37,* 446–464.

Jacobs, J. (2009). Have sex will travel: Romantic "sex tourism" and women negotiating modernity in the Sinai. *Gender, Place, and Culture, 16,* 43–61.

Jacobs, S., Thomas, W., & Lang, S. (Eds.). (1997). *Two-spirit people.* Urbana, IL: University of Illinois Press.

Jacobson, S. W., Jacobson, J. L., & Sokol, R. J. (1994). Effects of fetal alcohol exposure on infant reaction time. *Alcoholism: Clinical and Experimental Research, 18,* 1125–1132.

Jacobson, S. W., Jacobson, J. L., Sokol, R. J., Marticr, S. S., & Ager, J. W. (1993). Prenatal alcohol exposure and infant information processing ability. *Child Development, 64,* 1706–1721.

Jamieson, D. J., Kaufman, S. C., Costello, C., Hillis, S. D., Marchbanks, P. A., & Peterson, H. B. (2002). A comparison of women's regret after vasectomy versus tubal sterilization. *Obstetrics and Gynecology, 99,* 1073–1079.

Janicek, M. F., & Averette, H. E. (2001). Cervical cancer: Prevention, diagnosis, and therapeutics. *CA: Cancer Journal for Clinicians, 51*, 92–114.

Janowsky, J. S., Chavez, B. Zamboni, B., & Orwoll, E. (1998). The cognitive neuropsychology of sex hormones in men and women. *Developmental Neuropsychology, 14*, 421–440.

Janssen, E., Vorst, H., Finn, P., & Bancroft, J. (2002a). The Sexual Inhibition (SIS) and Sexual Excitation (SES) Scales: I. Measuring sexual excitation proneness in men. *Journal of Sex Research, 39*(2), 114–126.

Janssen, E., Vorst, H., Finn, P., & Bancroft, J. (2002b). The Sexual Inhibition (SIS) and Sexual Excitation (SES) Scales: II. Predicting psychophysiological response patterns. *Journal of Sex Research, 39*(2), 127–132.

Janssen, P. A., Thiessen, P., Klein, M. C., Whitfield, M. F., MacNab, Y. C., & Cullis-Kuhl, S. C. (2007). Standards for the measurement of birth weight, length and head circumference at term in neonates of European, Chinese and South Asian ancestry. *Open Medicine, 1*, e74–e88.

Janus, S. S., & Janus, C. L. (1993). *The Janus report on sexual behavior.* New York: Wiley.

Jefferson, E. A. (2005, November 15). Grown up parties are turning up the heat. *Denver Post.*

Jeffrey, L. A., & MacDonald, G. (2006a). "It's the money, Honey": The economy of sex work in the Maritimes. *The Canadian Review of Sociology and Anthropology, 43*, 313–327.

Jeffrey, L. A., & MacDonald, G. (2006b). *Sex workers in the Maritimes talk back.* Vancouver: UBC Press.

Jemail, J. A., & Geer, J. (1977). Sexual scripts. In R. Gemme & C. C. Wheeler (Eds.), *Progress in sexology.* New York: Plenum.

Jenkins, J. S., & Nussey, S. S. (1991). The role of oxytocin: Present concepts. *Clinical Endocrinology, 34*, 515–525.

Jenks, R. (1998). Swinging: A review of the literature. *Archives of Sexual Behavior, 27*, 507–521.

Jenks, R. J. (1985). Swinging: A replication and test of a theory. *Journal of Sex Research, 21*, 199–210.

Jenny, C., Roesler, T. A., & Poyer, K. A. (1994). Are children at risk for sexual abuse by homosexuals? *Pediatrics, 94*, 41–44.

Jensen, R. (2007). *Getting off: Pornography and the end of masculinity.* Cambridge, MA: South End Press.

Jensen, T., Gottschau, M., Madsen, J. O. B., Andersson, A., Lassen, T., Skakkebaek, N., . . . Jörgensen, N. (2014). Habitual alcohol consumption associated with reduced semen quality, and changes in reproductive hormones: a cross-sectional study among 1221 young Danish men. *BMJ Open, 4*, e005462. doi:10.1136/bmjopen-2014-005462

Jesperson, A., Lalumiere, M., & Seto, M. (2009). Sexual abuse history among adult sex offenders and non-sex offenders: A meta-analysis. *Child Abuse and Neglect, 33*, 179–192.

Jha, P., Kumar, R., Vasa, P., Dhingra, N., Thiruchelvam, D., & Maineddin, R. (2006). Low male-to-female sex ratio of children born in India: National survey of 1.1 million households. *The Lancet, 367*, 211–218.

Joel, D. (2011). Male or female? Brains are intersex. *Frontiers in Integrative Neuroscience, 5*, 57.

Johansmeyer, T. (2010). Even porn stars get the recession blues. Retrieved from http://www.dailyfinance.com/2010/01/08/even-porn-stars-get-the-recession-blues/

Johansson, A., Sundbom, E., Höjerback, T., & Bodlund, O. (2010). A five-year follow up study of Swedish adults with gender identity disorder. *Archives of Sexual Behavior, 39*, 1429–1437.

John, E. M., Savitz, D. A., & Sandler, D. P. (1991). Prenatal exposure to parents' smoking and childhood cancer. *American Journal of Epidemiology, 133*, 123–132.

Johnsdotter, S., & Essén, B. (2010). Genitals and ethnicity: The politics of genital modifications. *Reproductive Health Matters, 18*, 29–37.

Johnson, A. M., Mercer, C. H., Erens, B., Copas, A. J., McManus, S., Wellings, K., . . . Field, J. (2001). Sexual behaviour in Britain: Partnerships, practices, and HIV risk behaviours. *Lancet, 358*, 1835–1842.

Johnson, A. M., Wadsworth, J., Wellings, K., Bradshaw, S., & Field, J. (1992). Sexual lifestyles and HIV risk. *Nature, 360*, 410–412.

Johnson, B. R., Horga, M., & Andronache, L. (1996). Women's perspectives on abortion in Romania. *Social Science & Medicine, 42*, 521–530.

Johnson, S. D., Phelps, D., & Cottier, L. (2004). The association of sexual dysfunction and substance use among a community epidemiological sample. *Archives of Sexual Behavior, 33*, 55–64.

Johri, A., Heaton, J., & Morales, A. (2001). Severe erectile dysfunction is a marker for hyperprolactinemia. *International Journal of Impotence Research, 13*, 176–182.

Joint Consortium for School Health. (2007). *Sexual health: Quick scan of activities and resources in Canadian schools.* Retrieved from http://www.jcshcces.ca/upload/Sexual/20Health.pdf

Joint SOGC-CFAS Guidelines. (2008). Guidelines for the number of embryos to transfer following in vitro fertilization. *International Journal of Gynecology and Obstetrics, 102*, 203–216.

Jonah, Metropolitan of All America and Canada. (2010, January 24). Sanctity of Life Sunday 2010. Retrieved from http://www.oca.org

Jonason, P. K., & Fisher, T. D. (2009). The power of prestige: Why young men report having more sex partners than young women. *Sex Roles, 60*, 151–159.

Jonason, P. K., Li, N. P., & Cason, M. J. (2009). The "booty call": A compromise between men's and women's ideal mating strategies. *Journal of Sex Research, 46*, 460–470.

Jonason, P. K., Li, N. P., & Richardson, J. (2011). Positioning the booty-call relationship on the spectrum of relationships: Sexual but more emotional than one-night stands. *Journal of Sex Research, 48*, 486–495.

Jones, C., Chan, C., & Farine, D. (2011). Sex in pregnancy. *Canadian Medical Association Journal.* doi:10.1503/cmaj.091580

Jones, H. (2006). Drug addiction during pregnancy: Advances in maternal treatment and understanding child outcomes. *Current Directions in Psychological Science, 15*, 126–130.

Jones, J. H. (1997). *Alfred C. Kinsey: A public/private life.* New York: Norton.

Jones, J., Pelham, B., Carvallo, M., & Mirenberg, M. (2004). How do I love thee? Let me count the Js: Implicit egotism and interpersonal attraction. *Journal of Personality and Social Psychology, 87*, 665–683.

Jones, L. M., Mitchell, K. J., & Finkelhor, D. (2012). Trends in youth internet victimization: Findings from three youth internet safety surveys 2000–2010. *Journal of Adolescent Health, 50*, 179–186.

Jones, R. K., & Henshaw, S. K. (2002). Mifepristone for early medical abortion: Experiences in France, Great Britain and Sweden. *Perspectives on Sexual and Reproductive Health, 34*, 154–161.

Jones, R. K., & Kooistra, K. (2011). Abortion incidence and access to services in the United States, 2008. *Perspectives on Sexual and Reproductive Health, 43*(1), 41–50.

Joshi, S. P., Peter, J., & Valkenburg, P. M. (2011). Scripts of sexual desire and danger in U.S. and Dutch teen girl magazines: A cross-national content analysis. *Sex Roles, 64*, 463–474.

Jozkowski, K. N., & Humphreys, T. P. (2014). Sexual consent on college campuses: Implications for sexual assault prevention education. *The Health Education Monograph Series, 31*, 30–35.

Julien, D., Chartrand, E., Simard, M. C., Bouthillier, D., & Begin, J. (2003). Conflict, social support, and relationship quality: An observational study of heterosexual, gay male, and lesbian couples' communication. *Journal of Family Psychology, 17*, 419–428.

Julien, D., Jouvin, E., Jodoin, E., l'Archevêque, A., & Chartrand, E. (2008). Adjustment among mothers reporting same-gender sexual partners: A study of a representative population sample from Quebec province (Canada). *Archives of Sexual Behavior, 37*, 864–876.

Kabir, A., Pridjian, G., Steinmann, W., Herrera, E., & Khan, M. (2005). Racial differences in cesareans: An analysis of U.S. 2001 national inpatient sample data. *Obstetrics and Gynecology, 195*, 710–718.

Kaestle, C. E., & Allen, K. R. (2011). The role of masturbation in healthy sexual development: Perceptions of young adults. *Archives of Sexual Behavior, 40*, 983–994.

Kafka, M., & Hennen, J. (2002). A DSM-IV Axis I comorbidity study of males (n = 120) with paraphilias and paraphilia-related disorders. *Sex Abuse, 14*, 349–366.

Kahr, B. (2008). *Who's been sleeping in your head? The secret world of sexual fantasies.* New York: Basic Books.

Kai, L., & Pourier, D. J. (2001). Using the National Longitudinal Study of Youth in the U.S. to study the birth process: A Bayesian approach. *Research in Official Statistics, 4,* 127–150.

Kaiser Family Foundation. (1998). *Sex in the 90s: 1998 national survey of Americans on sex and sexual health* (Publication No. 1430). Menlo Park, CA: Author.

Kaiser Family Foundation. (2001). *Biennial report on sex in the media: Executive summary.* Menlo Park, CA: Author.

Kaiser Family Foundation. (2003). *A biennial report of the Kaiser Family Foundation on Sex on TV3: Executive summary.* Menlo Park, CA: Author.

Kalichman, S. C., & Cain, D. (2004). The relationship between indicators of sexual compulsivity and high risk sexual practices among men and women receiving services from a sexually transmitted infection clinic. *Journal of Sex Research, 41,* 235–241.

Kalichman, S. C., & Rompa, D. (1995). Sexual sensation seeking and compulsivity scales: Reliability, validity, and predicting HIV risk behavior. *Journal of Personality Assessment, 62,* 586–601.

Kalichman, S. C., Benotsch, E., & Simpson, D. (2001). Unwanted sexual experiences and sexual risks in gay and bisexual men: Associations among revictimization, substance use, and psychiatric symptoms. *Journal of Sex Research, 38,* 1–9.

Kalick, S. M., Zebowitz, L., Langlois, J., & Johnson, R. (1998). Does human facial attractiveness honestly advertise health? Longitudinal data on an evolutionary question. *Psychological Science, 9,* 8–13.

Kalil, K., Gruber, J., Conley, J., & Sytniac, M. (1993). Social and family pressures on anxiety and stress during pregnancy. *Pre- and Perinatal Psychology Journal, 8,* 113–118.

Kallstrom-Fuqua, A. C., Weston, R., & Marshall, L. (2004). Childhood and adolescent sexual abuse of community women: Mediated effects on psychological distress and social relationships. *Journal of Consulting and Clinical Psychology, 72,* 980–992.

Kaplan, H. S. (1974). *The new sex therapy.* New York: Brunner/Mazel.

Kaplan, H. S. (1979). *Disorders of sexual desire.* New York: Simon & Schuster.

Kaplan, H. S., & Sager, C. J. (1971, June). Sexual patterns at different ages. *Medical Aspects of Human Sexuality,* 10–23.

Kaplan, M., & Krueger, R. (2010). Diagnosis, assessment, and treatment of hypersexuality. *Journal of Sex Research, 47,* 181–198.

Karama, S., Lecours, A. R., Leroux, J. M., Bourgouin, P., Beaudoin, G., Joubert, S., & Beauregard, M. (2002). Areas of brain activation in males and females during viewing of erotic film excerpts. *Human Brain Mapping, 16,* 1–13.

Karraker, A., & DeLamater, J. (2013). Past year sexual inactivity among older married persons and their partners. *Journal of Marriage and Family, 75,* 142–163.

Karraker, A., DeLamater, J., & Schwartz, C. (2011). Sexual frequency decline from midlife to later life. *Journals of Gerontology Series B: Psychological Sciences & Social Sciences, 66B*(4), 502–512.

Katz-Wise, S. (2012). *Beyond labels: Sexual fluidity and sexual identity development in sexual minority young adults.* Doctoral dissertation, University of Wisconsin–Madison.

Kaufmann, J.-C. (2012). *Love online.* Cambridge, UK: Polity Press.

Keefe, D. L. (2002). Sex hormones and neural mechanisms. *Archives of Sexual Behavior, 31,* 401–404.

Keelan, P. R., Dion, K. L., & Dion, K. K. (1994). Attachment style and heterosexual relationships among young adults: A short-term panel study. *Journal of Social and Personal Relationships, 11,* 201–214.

Keenan, T., & Ward, T. (2000). A theory of mind perspective on cognitive, affective, and intimacy deficits in child sex offenders. *Sex Abuse, 12,* 49–60.

Kegel, A. H. (1952). Sexual functions of the pubococcygeus muscle. *Western Journal of Surgery, 60,* 521–524.

Kelly, M. P., Strassberg, D. S., & Turner, C. M. (2006). Behavioral assessment of couples' communication in female orgasmic disorder. *Journal of Sex & Marital Therapy, 32*(2), 81–95.

Kelmer, G., Rhoades, G. K., Stanley, S., & Markman, H. J. (2013). Relationship quality, commitment, and stability in long-distance relationships. *Family Process, 52,* 257–270.

Kempf, D. J., Marsh, K. C., Denissen, J. F., McDonald, E., Vasavanonda, S., Flentge, C. A., . . . Kong, X. P. (1995). ABT-538 is a potent inhibitor of human immunodeficiency virus protease. *Proceedings of the National Academy of Sciences, 92,* 2484.

Kempton, W., & Kahn, E. (1991). Sexuality and people with intellectual disabilities: A historical perspective. *Sexuality and Disability, 9,* 93–111.

Kendall-Tackett, K., Williams, L., & Finkelhor, D. (1993). Impact of sexual abuse on children: A review and synthesis of recent empirical studies. *Psychological Bulletin, 113,* 164–180.

Kendler, K. S., Bulik, C. M., Silberg, J., Hettema, J. M., Myers, J., & Prescott, C. A. (2000). Childhood sexual abuse and adult psychiatric and substance use disorders in women: An epidemiological and cotwin control analysis. *Archives of General Psychiatry, 57,* 953–959.

Kendler, K. S., Thornton, L., Gilman, S., & Kessler, R. (2000). Sexual orientation in a US national sample of twin and nontwin sibling pairs. *American Journal of Psychiatry, 157,* 1843–1846.

Kennedy, R., & Suttenfield, K. (2001). Postpartum depression. *Medscape Mental Health 6*(4), 1.

Kennett, D., Humphreys, T. P., & Schultz, K. E. (2012). Sexual resourcefulness and the impact of family, sex education, media and peers. *Sex Education, 12,* 351–368.

Kenny, M. C., & Wurtele, S. K. (2012). Child sexual behavior inventory: A comparison between Latino and normative samples of preschoolers. *Journal of Sex Research.* doi: 10.1080/00224499.2011.652265

Kero, A., Lalos, A., Högberg, U., & Jacobssen, L. (1999). The male partner involved in legal abortion. *Human Reproduction, 14,* 2669–2675.

Keverne, E. B. (1999). The vomeronasal organ. *Science, 286,* 716–720.

Khan, A., & Pine, P. (2003). *Adolescent reproductive health in Pakistan: Status, policies, programs, and issues.* Washington, DC, Futures Group International, POLICY Project (USAID Contract No. HRN-C-00–00–00006–00).

Kiefer, A. K., & Sanchez, D. T. (2007). Scripting sexual passivity: A gender role perspective. *Personal Relationships, 14,* 269–290.

Kikuras, A. (2004). An interview with Dave Cummings, Unchain the underground. Retrieved from http://www.unchain.com

Kim, J. L., Sorsoli, C. L., Collins, K., Zylbergold, B. A., Schooler, D., & Tolman, D. L. (2007). From sex to sexuality: Exposing the heterosexual script on primetime network television. *Journal of Sex Research, 44,* 145–157.

Kim, N., Stanton, B., Li, X., Dickersin, K., & Galbraith, J. (1997). Effectiveness of the 40 adolescent AIDS-risk reduction interventions: A quantitative review. *Journal of Adolescent Health, 20,* 204–215.

King, A. J. C., Beazley, R. P., Warren, W. K., Hankins, C. A., Robertson, A. S., & Radford, J. L. (1988). *Canada youth and AIDS study.* Kingston, ON: Social Program Evaluation Group, Queen's University.

King, D. B., DeCicco, T. L., & Humphreys, T. P. (2009). Investigating sexual dream imagery in relation to daytime sexual behaviours and fantasies among Canadian university students. *Canadian Journal of Human Sexuality, 18*(3), 135–146.

King, M., Holt, V., & Nazareth, I. (2007). Women's views of their sexual difficulties: Agreement and disagreement with clinical diagnoses. *Archives of Sexual Behavior, 36,* 281–288.

King, M., Marks, J., & Mandell, J. (2003). Breast and ovarian cancer risks due to inherited mutations in BRCA1 and BRCA2. *Science, 302,* 643–646.

King, M., Semlyen, J., Tai, S. S., Killaspy, H., Osborn, D., Popelyk, D., & Nazareth, I. (2008). A systematic review of mental disorder, suicide, and deliberate self harm in lesbian, gay and bisexual people. *BMC Psychiatry, 8,* 70.

Kingston, D. A., Malamuth, N. M., Federoff, P., & Marshall, W. L. (2009). The importance of individual differences in pornography use: Theoretical perspectives and implications for treating sexual offenders. *Journal of Sex Research, 46,* 216–232.

Kinnish, K. K., Strassberg, D., & Turner, C. (2005). Sex differences in the flexibility of sexual orientation: A multidimensional retrospective assessment. *Archives of Sexual Behavior, 34,* 173–184.

Kinsey, A. C., Pomeroy, W. B., & Martin, C. E. (1948). *Sexual behavior in the human male.* Philadelphia: Saunders.

Kinsey, A. C., Pomeroy, W. B., Martin, C. E., & Gebhard, P. H. (1953). *Sexual behavior in the human female.* Philadelphia: Saunders.

Kinsman, G. (1996). *The regulation of desire: Sexuality in Canada.* Montreal: Black Rose Books.

Kiragu, K. (2001). Youth and HIV/AIDS: Can we avoid catastrophe? *Population Reports (Series L), No. 12.* Johns Hopkins University School of Public Health.

Kirby, D. (1992). School-based programs to reduce sexual risktaking behavior. *Journal of School Health, 62,* 281–287.

Kirby, D. (2002). Effective approaches to reducing adolescent unprotected sex, pregnancy, and childbearing. *Journal of Sex Research, 39,* 51–57.

Kirby, D., & Laris, B. A. (2009). Effective curriculum-based sex and STD/HIV education programs for adolescents. *Child Development Perspectives, 3,* 21–29.

Kirby, D., Short, L., Collins, J., Rugg, D., Kolbe, L., Howard, M., . . . Zabin, L. S. (1994). School-based programs to reduce sexual risk behaviors: A review of effectiveness. *Public Health Reports, 109,* 339–360.

Kirk, K., Bailey, J., Dunne, M., & Martin, N. (2000). Measurement models for sexual orientation in a community twin sample. *Behavior Genetics, 30,* 345–356.

Kiselica, M., & Scheckel, S. (1995). The couvade syndrome (sympathetic pregnancy) and teenage fathers: A brief primer for counselors. *School Counselor, 43,* 42–51.

Klaus, M., & Kennell, J. (1976). Human maternal and paternal behavior. In M. Klaus & J. Kennell (Eds.), *Maternal infant bonding.* St. Louis, MO: Mosby.

Klebanov, P. K., & Jemmott, J. B. (1992). Effects of expectations and bodily sensations on self-reports of premenstrual symptoms. *Psychology of Women Quarterly, 16,* 289–310.

Klein, C., & Gorzalka, B. B. (2009). Sexual functioning in transsexuals following hormone therapy and genital surgery: A review. *Journal of Sexual Medicine, 6,* 2922–2939.

Klein, V., Rettenberger, M., & Briken, P. (2014). Self-report indicators of hypersexuality and its correlates in a female online sample. *Journal of Sexual Medicine, 11,* 1974–1981.

Kleinhaus, K., Perrin, M., Friedlander, Y., Paltiel, O., Malaspina, D., & Harlap, S. (2006). Paternal age and spontaneous abortion. *Obstetrics and Gynecology, 108,* 369–377.

Kleinplatz, P. J. (1992). The erotic experience and the intent to arouse. *Canadian Journal of Human Sexuality, 1*(3), 133–139.

Kleinplatz, P. J. (1998). Sex therapy for vaginismus: A review, critique, and humanistic alternative. *Journal of Humanistic Psychology, 38*(2), 51–81.

Kleinplatz, P. J. (2003a). Beyond sexual mechanics and hydraulics: Humanizing the discourse surrounding erectile dysfunction. *Journal of Humanistic Psychology, 43,* 1–29.

Kleinplatz, P. J. (2003b). What's new in sex therapy? From stagnation to fragmentation. *Sexual & Relationship Therapy, 18,* 95–106.

Kleinplatz, P. J. (2009). Consumer protection is the major purpose of sex therapy certification. *Archives of Sexual Behavior, 38,* 1031.

Kleinplatz, P. J. (2010). Lessons from great lovers. In S. Levine, S. Althof, & C. Risen (Eds.), *Handbook of clinical sexuality for mental health professionals* (2nd ed., pp. 57–72). New York: Brunner-Routledge.

Kleinplatz, P. J., & Krippner, S. (2005). Spirituality and sexuality: Celebrating erotic transcendence and spiritual embodiment. In S. G. Mijares, & G. S. Khalsa (Eds.), *The psychospiritual clinician's handbook: Alternative methods for understanding and treating mental disorders.* Binghamton, NY: Haworth Press, Inc.

Kleinplatz, P. J., & Ménard, A. D. (2007). Building blocks toward optimal sexuality: Constructing a conceptual model. *The Family Journal: Counseling and Therapy for Couples and Families, 15,* 72–78.

Kleinplatz, P. J., Ménard, A. D., & Campbell, M. (2013). Relational contributions to optimal sexual experiences. In A. C. Michalos (Ed.), *Encyclopedia of quality of life research.* New York: Springer.

Kleinplatz, P. J., Ménard, A. D., Paquet, M.-P., Paradis, N., Campbell, M., Zuccarini, D., & Mehak, L. (2009). The components of optimal sexuality: A portrait of "great sex." *Canadian Journal of Human Sexuality, 18*(1–2), 1–13.

Kleinplatz, P. J., Ménard, A. D., Paradis, N., Campbell, M., Dalgleish, T., Segovia, A., & Davis, K. (2009). From closet to reality: Optimal sexuality among the elderly. *Irish Psychiatrist, 10*(1), 15–18.

Klemetti, R., Sevón, T., Gissler, M., & Hemminki, E. (2006, November). Health of children born as a result of in vitro fertilization. *Pediatrics, 118,* 1819–1827.

Kline, G., Stanley, S., Markman, H., Olmos-Gallo, P. A., St. Peters, M., Whitton, S., & Prado, L. (2004). Timing is everything: Pre-engagement cohabitation and increased risk for poor marital outcomes. *Journal of Family Psychology, 18,* 311–318.

Kloas, W., Urbatzka, R., Opitz, R., Würtz, S., Behrends, T., Hermelink, B., . . . Lutz, I. (2009). Endocrine disruption in aquatic vertebrates. *Trends in Comparative Endocrinology and Neurobiology: Annals of the New York Academy of Sciences, 1163,* 187–200.

Knäuper, B., & Kornik, R. (2004). Perceived transmissibility of STIs: Lack of differentiation between HIV and chlamydia. *Sexually Transmitted Infections, 80,* 74–78.

Knäuper, B., Kornik, R., Atkinson, K., Guberman, C., & Aydin, C. (2005). Motivation influences the underestimation of cumulative risk. *Personality and Social Psychology Bulletin, 31,* 1511–1523.

Kniffin, K. M., & Wilson, D. S. (2004). The effect of nonphysical traits on perception of physical attractiveness: Three naturalistic studies. *Evolution and Human Behavior, 25,* 88–101.

Knobloch-Westerwick, S., & Hoplamazian, G. J. (2012). Gendering the self: Selective magazine reading and reinforcement of gender conformity. *Communication Research, 39,* 358–384.

Koch, P. B., Mansfield, P., Thurau, D., & Carey, M. (2005). "Feeling frumpy": The relationships between body image and sexual response changes in midlife women. *Journal of Sex Research, 42,* 215–223.

Koelman, C. A., Coumans, A. B., Nijman, H. W., Doxiadis, I. I., Dekker, G. A., & Claas, F. H. (2000). Correlation between oral sex and a low incidence of preeclampsia: A role for soluble HLA in seminal fluid? *Journal of Reproductive Immunology, 46,* 155–166.

Kolata, G. (2001, March 25). Researchers find grave defect risk in cloning animals. *New York Times,* p. 1ff.

Kolbenschlag, M. (1985). Abortion and moral consensus: Beyond Solomon's choice. *Christian Century, 102,* 179–183.

Kolker, A. (1989). Advances in prenatal diagnosis. *International Journal of Technology Assessment in Health Care, 5,* 601–617.

Komisaruk, B. R., & Whipple, B. (2005). Function MRI of the brain during orgasm in women. *Annual Review of Sex Research, 15,* 62–86.

Kong, R., Johnson, H., Beattie, S., & Cardillo, A. (2003). Sexual offences in Canada. *Juristat, 23,* 6.

Korber, B., & Gnanakaran, S. (2011). Converging on an HIV vaccine. *Science, 333,* 1589–1590.

Korff, J., & Geer, J. H. (1983). The relationship between sexual arousal experience and genital response. *Psychophysiology, 20,* 121–127.

Kosfeld, M., Heinrichs, M., Zak, P., Fischbacher, U., & Fehr, E. (2005). Oxytocin increases trust in humans. *Nature, 435* (June 2), 673–676.

Kosnick, A. (1977). *Human sexuality: New directions in American Catholic thought.* New York: Paulist Press.

Koss, M. P. (1993). Rape: Scope, impact, interventions, and public policy response. *American Psychologist, 48,* 1062–1063.

Koss, M. P., Koss, P. G., & Woodruff, W. J. (1991). Deleterious effects of criminal victimization on women's health and medical utilization. *Archives of Internal Medicine, 151,* 342–347.

Koss, M., & Figueredo, A. (2004). Change in cognitive mediators of rape's impact on psychosocial health across 2 years of recovery. *Journal of Consulting and Clinical Psychology, 72,* 1063–1072.

Kothari, P. (1984). For discussion: Ejaculatory disorders—a new dimension. *British Journal of Sexual Medicine, 11,* 205–209.

Kovacs, P. (2002a). Congenital anomalies and low birth weight associated with assisted reproductive technologies (Article 435963). *Medscape Women's Health 7*(3), 3.

Kovacs, P. (2002b). Preconception sex selection. *Medscape Ob/Gyn & Women's Health, 7*(2). Retrieved from http://www.medscape.com/viewarticle/441313

Krahé, B., Bieneck, S., & Scheinberger-Olwig, R. (2007). The role of sexual scripts in sexual aggression and victimization. *Archives of Sexual Behavior, 36,* 687–701.

Kramer, M. S., Platt, R. W., Wen, S. W., Joseph, K. S., Allen, A., Abrahamowicz, M., . . . Breart, G. (2001). A new and improved population-based Canadian reference for birth weight for gestational age. *Pediatrics, 108,* e35.

Kraut, R., Olson, J., Banaji, M., Bruckman, A., Cohen, J., & Couper, M. (2004). Psychological research online: Report of the Board of Scientific Affairs' Advisory Group on the Conduct of Research on the Internet. *American Psychologist, 59,* 105–117.

Krings, F., & Facchin, S. (2009). Organizational justice and men's likelihood to sexually harass: The moderating role of sexism and personality. *Journal of Applied Psychology, 94,* 501–510.

Krippendorff, K. (2004). *Content analysis: An introduction to its methodology.* Thousand Oaks, CA: Sage.

Kroeber, A. L., & Kluckhohn, C. (1963). *Culture: A critical review of concepts and definitions.* New York: Vintage Books.

Krueger, R. B., & Kaplan, M. S. (2001). Depo-leuprolide acetate for treatment of paraphilias: A report of twelve cases. *Archives of Sexual Behavior, 30,* 409–422.

Kruger, B. S. (2006). The post-orgasmic prolactin increase following intercourse is greater than following masturbation and suggests greater satiety. *Biological Psychology, 71,* 312–315.

Krüger, T. H., Haake, P., Hartmann, U., Schedlowski, M., & Exton, M. S. (2002). Orgasm-induced prolactin secretion: Feedback control of sexual drive? *Neuroscience and Biobehavioral Reviews, 26,* 31–44.

Kruijver, F. P., Zhou, J. N., Pool, C. W., Hofman, M. A., Gooren, L. J., & Swaab, D. F. (2000). Male-to-female transsexuals have female neuron numbers in a limbic nucleus. *Journal of Clinical Endocrinology and Metabolism, 85,* 2034–2041.

Krupa, C., & Esmail, S. (2010, June). Sexual health education for children with visual impairments: Talking about sex is not enough. *Journal of Visual Impairment & Blindness,* 327–337.

Kukkonen, T. M., Binik, Y. M., Amsel, R., & Carrier, S. (2007). Thermography as a physiological measure of sexual arousal in both men and women. *Journal of Sexual Medicine, 4,* 93–105.

Kukkonen, T. M., Binik, Y. M., Amsel, R., & Carrier, S. (2010). An evaluation of the validity of thermography as a physiological measure of sexual arousal in a non-university adult sample. *Archives of Sexual Behavior, 39,* 861–873.

Kunkel, D., Eyal, K., Finnerty, K., Biely, E., & Donnerstein, E. (2005). *Sex on TV 4.* Menlo Park, CA: Kaiser Family Foundation.

Kunkel, D., Farrar, K. M., Eyal, K., Biely, E., Donnerstein, E., & Rideout, V. (2007). Sexual socialization messages on entertainment television: Comparing content trends 1997–2002. *Media Psychology, 9,* 595–622.

Kuper, L. E., Coleman, B. R., & Mustanski, B. S. (2014). Coping with LGBT and racial-ethnic-related stressors: A mixed-methods study of LGBT youth of color. *Journal of Research on Adolescence, 24,* 703–719.

Kurdek, L. A. (2005). What do we know about gay and lesbian couples? *Current Directions in Psychological Science, 14,* 251–254.

Kuyper, L., de Wit, J., Adam, P., & Woertman, L. (2012). Doing more good than harm? The effects of participation in sex research on young people in the Netherlands. *Archives of Sexual Behavior, 41,* 497–506.

Kwak-kim, J., Agcaoili, M. S., Aleta, L., Liao, A., Ota, K., Dambaeva, S., . . . Gilman-Sachs, A. (2013). Management of women with recurrent pregnancy losses and antiphospholipid syndrome. *American Journal of Reproductive Immunology, 69,* 596–607.

Kwon, P. (2013). Resilience in lesbian, gay, and bisexual individuals. *Personality and Social Psychology Review, 17,* 371–383.

La Rocque, C. L., & Cioe, J. (2011). An evaluation of the relationship between body image and sexual avoidance. *Journal of Sex Research, 48,* 397–408.

Laan, E., Everaerd, W., van Bellen, G., & Hanewald, G. (1994). Women's sexual and emotional responses to male- and female-produced erotica. *Archives of Sexual Behavior, 23,* 153–170.

Labrecque, M., Eason, E., Marcoux, S., Lemieux, F., Pinault, J., Feldman, P., & Laperrière, L. (1999). Randomized controlled trial of prevention of perineal trauma by perineal massage during pregnancy. *American Journal of Obstetrics and Gynecology, 180,* 593–600.

Lacelle, C., Hébert, M., Lavoie F., Vitaro, F., & Tremblay, R. E. (2012a). Child sexual abuse and women's sexual health: The contribution of CSA severity and exposure to multiple forms of childhood victimization. *Journal of Child Sexual Abuse, 21,* 571–592.

Lacelle, C., Hébert, M., Lavoie F., Vitaro, F., & Tremblay, R. E. (2012b). Sexual health in women reporting a history of child sexual abuse. *Child Abuse & Neglect, 36,* 247–259.

Lacroix, N. (2003). *Kama Sutra: A modern guide to the ancient art of sex.* New York: Hylas Publishing.

LaFromboise, T. D., Heyle, A. M., & Ozer, E. J. (1990). Changing and diverse roles of women in American Indian cultures. *Sex Roles, 22,* 455–476.

Lahey, K. A. (1999). *Are we "persons" yet? Law and sexuality in Canada.* Toronto: University of Toronto Press.

Laliberté, L. (2006). New vaginas for old. *National Review of Medicine, 3*(2).

Lalumière, M. L., & Quinsey, V. L. (1998). Pavlovian conditioning of sexual interests in human males. *Archives of Sexual Behavior, 27,* 241–252.

Lalumière, M. L., Blanchard, R., & Zucker, K. J. (2000). Sexual orientation and handedness in men and women: A meta-analysis. *Psychological Bulletin, 126,* 575–592.

Lalumière, M. L., Quinsey, V. L., Harris, G. T., Rice, M. E., & Trautrimas, C. (2003). Are rapists differentially aroused by coercive sex in phallometric assessments? *Annals of the New York Academy of Sciences, 989,* 211–224.

LaMarre, A. K., Paterson, L. Q., & Gorzalka, B. B. (2003). Breastfeeding and postpartum maternal sexual functioning: A review. *Canadian Journal of Human Sexuality, 12,* 151–168.

Lamb, M. E., & Hwang, C. (1982). Maternal attachment and mother-neonate bonding: A critical review. In M. E. Lamb & A. L. Brown (Eds.), *Advances in developmental psychology* (Vol. 2). Hillsdale, NJ: Lawrence Erlbaum.

Lambert, B., Bergeron, S., Desrosiers, M., & Lepage, Y. (2012). Introital primary and secondary dyspareunia: Multimodal clinical and surgical control. *Sexologies, 21,* 9–12.

Lambert, T. A., Kahn, A., & Apple, K. (2003). Pluralistic ignorance and hooking up. *Journal of Sex Research, 40,* 129–133.

Lamberts, S. W., van den Beld, A. W., & van der Lely, A. J. (1997). The endocrinology of aging. *Science, 278,* 419–424.

Lammers, J., Stoker, J. I., Jordan, J., Pollmann, M., & Stapel, D. A. (2011). Power increases infidelity among men and women. *Psychological Science, 22,* 1191–1197.

Lamont, J., Bajzak, K., Bouchard, C., Burnett, M., Byers, E. S., Cohen, T., . . . Senikas, V. (2012). Female sexual health consensus clinical guidelines. *Journal of Obstetrics & Gynaecology Canada, 34,* 769–775.

Landott, M. A., Bartholomew, K., Saffrey, C., Oram, D., & Perlman, D. (2004). Gender nonconformity, childhood rejection, and adult attachment: A study of gay men. *Archives of Sexual Behavior, 33,* 117–128.

Landry, T., & Bergeron, S. (2009). How young does vulvo-vaginal pain begin? Prevalence and characteristics of dyspareunia in adolescents. *Journal of Sexual Medicine, 6*(4), 927–935.

Landry, T., & Bergeron, S. (2011). Biopsychosocial factors associated with dyspareunia in a community sample of adolescent girls. *Archives of Sexual Behavior, 40,* 877–889.

Landry, T., Bergeron, S., Dupuis, M-J., & Desrochers, G. (2008). The treatment of provoked vestibulodynia: A critical review. *Clinical Journal of Pain, 24,* 155–171.

Laner, M. R., & Ventrone, N. A. (2000). Dating scripts revisited. *Journal of Family Issues, 21,* 488–500.

Langfeldt, T. (1981). Childhood masturbation. In L. L. Constantine & F. M. Martinson (Eds.), *Children and sex* (pp. 63–74). Boston: Little, Brown.

Langille, D. (2000). *Adolescent sexual health services and education: Options for Nova Scotia.* Maritime Centre of Excellence for Women's Health. Policy discussion series paper #8. Halifax, NS: Maritime Centre of Excellence for Women's Health.

Langille, D. B., Beazley, R., Shoveller, J., & Johnston, G. (1994). Prevalence of high risk sexual behaviour in adolescents attending school in a county in Nova Scotia. *Canadian Journal of Public Health, 85*(4), 227–230.

Langille, D. B., Murphy, G. T., Hughes, J., & Rigby, J. A. (2001). Nova Scotia high school students' interactions with physicians for sexual health information and services. *Canadian Journal of Public Health, 92,* 219–222.

Langille, D. B., Proudfoot, K., Rigby, J., Aquino-Russell, C., & Forward, K. (2008). A pilot project for chlamydia screening in adolescent females using self-testing: Characteristics of participants and non-participants. *Canadian Journal of Public Health, 99,* 117–120.

Langille, D., Beazley, R., & Doncaster, H. (1996). *Amherst parents' attitudes towards school-based sexual health education.* Amherst, NS: Amherst Initiative for Healthy Adolescent Sexuality.

Langille, D., Graham, J., Marshall, E., Blake, M., Chittey, C., & Doncaster-Scott, H. (1999). *Developing understanding from young women's experiences in obtaining sexual health services and education in a Nova Scotia community.* Maritime Centre of Excellence for Women's Health.

Långström, N., & Seto, M. (2006). Exhibitionistic and voyeuristic behavior in a Swedish national population survey. *Archives of Sexual Behavior, 35,* 427–435.

Långström, N., & Zucker, K. J. (2005). Tranvestic fetishism in the general population: Prevalence and correlates. *Journal of Sex & Marital Therapy, 31,* 87–95.

Langstrom, N., Enebrink, P., Lauren, E.-M., Lindblom, J., Werko, S., & Hanson, R. K. (2013). Preventing sexual abusers of children from reoffending: Systematic review of medical and psychological interventions. *British Medical Journal, 347,* f4630.

Lansford, J. E., Yu, T., Erath, S., Pettit, G. S., Bates, J. E., & Dodge, K. A. (2010). Developmental precursors of number of sexual partners from age 16 to 22. *Journal of Research on Adolescence, 20*(3), 651–677.

Larroque, B., Ancel, P-Y., Marret, S., Marchand, L., André, M., Arnaud, C., . . . Kaminski, M. (2008). Neurodevelopmental disabilities and special care of 5-year-old children born before 33 weeks of gestation (the EPIPAGE study): A longitudinal cohort study. *The Lancet, 371,* 813–820.

Larsen, J., Urry, J., & Axhausen, K. (2006). *Mobilities, networks, geographics.* Hampshire, UK: Ashgate.

Larsson, A., & Dykes, A. (2009). Care during pregnancy and childbirth in Sweden: Perspectives of lesbian women. *Midwifery, 25,* 682–690.

Larsson, I., & Svedin, C. G. (2002a). Teachers' and parents' reports on 3- to 6-year-old children's sexual behaviour: A comparison. *Child Abuse & Neglect, 26,* 247–266.

Larsson, I., & Svedin, C. G. (2002b). Sexual experiences in childhood: Young adults' recollections. *Archives of Sexual Behavior, 31,* 263–274.

Lassek, W. D., & Gaulin, S. (2007). Menarche is related to fat distribution. *American Journal of Physical Anthropology, 133,* 1147–1151.

Latty-Mann, H., & Davis, K. (1996). Attachment theory and partner choice: Preference and actuality. *Journal of Social and Personal Relationships, 13,* 5–23.

Lau, J. T. F., Tsui, H. Y., & Wang, Q. S. (2003). Effects of two telephone survey methods on the level of reported risk behaviours. *Sexually Transmitted Infections, 79,* 325–331.

Laughon, S. K., Branch, D. W., Beaver, J., & Zhang, J. (2012). Changes in labor patterns over 50 years. *American Journal of Obstetrics and Gynecology, 206,* 419 (e1–e9).

Laumann, E. O., Gagnon, J. H., Michael, R. T., & Michaels, S. (1994). *The social organization of sexuality: Sexual practices in the United States.* Chicago: University of Chicago Press.

Laumann, E. O., Paik, A., & Rosen, R. (1999). Sexual dysfunction in the United States: Prevalence and predictors. *Journal of the American Medical Association, 281,* 537–544.

Laurenceau, J.-P., Feldman, B., & Pietromonaco, P. R. (1998). Intimacy as an interpersonal process: The importance of self-disclosure, partner disclosure, and perceived partner responsiveness in interpersonal exchanges. *Journal of Personality and Social Psychology, 74,* 1238–1251.

Lavin, M. (2008). Voyeurism: Psychopathology and theory. In D. R. Laws, & W. O'Donohue (Eds.), *Sexual deviance: Theory, assessment, and treatment* (2nd ed., pp. 305–319). New York: Guilford.

Lavine, H., Sweeney, D., & Wagner, S. (1999). Depicting women as sex objects in television advertising: Effects on body dissatisfaction. *Personality and Social Psychology Bulletin, 25,* 1049–1058.

Lavoie, F., Thibodeau, C., Gagné, M., & Hébert, M. (2010). Buying and selling sex in Québec adolescents: A study of risk and protective factors. *Archives of Sexual Behavior, 39,* 1147–1160.

Law Reform Commission of Canada. (1992). *Medically assisted procreation working paper 65.* Ottawa: Canada Communication Group-Publishing, cat. #J32–1/65–1992.

Lawrance, K.-A., & Byers, E. S. (1995). Sexual satisfaction in long-term heterosexual relationships: The interpersonal exchange model of sexual satisfaction. *Personal Relationships, 2,* 267–285.

Lawrance, K.-A., Taylor, D., & Byers, E. S. (1996). Differences in men's and women's global, sexual and ideal-sexual expressiveness and instrumentality. *Sex Roles, 34*(5 & 6), 337–357.

Le Bourdais, C., & Lapierre-Adamcyk, E. (2004). Changes in conjugal life in Canada: Is cohabitation progressively replacing marriage? *Journal of Marriage and Family, 66,* 929–942.

Leader, A. (1999). New reproductive technologies: Why are we limiting choices for infertile couples? *Canadian Medical Association Journal, 161,* 1411–1412.

Leaper, C., & Ayres, M. M. (2007). A meta-analytic review of gender variations in adults' language use: Talkativeness, affiliative speech, and assertive speech. *Personality and Social Psychology Review, 11,* 328–363.

Leaper, C., & Friedman, C. (2007). The socialization of gender. In J. E. Grusec & P. D. Hastings (Eds.), *Handbook of socialization: Theory and research* (pp. 561–587). New York: Guilford Press.

Leaver, J., & Dolnick, D. (2010). Call girls and street prostitutes: Selling sex and intimacy. In R. Weitzer (Ed.), *Sex for sale: Prostitution, pornography, and the sex industry* (2nd ed., pp. 187–203). New York: Routledge.

Lebacqz, K. (1987). Appropriate vulnerability: A sexual ethic for singles. *Christian Century, 104,* 435–438.

Lebeque, B. (1991). Paraphilias in U.S. pornography titles: "Pornography made me do it" (Ted Bundy). *Bulletin of the American Academy of Psychiatry and Law, 19,* 43–48.

Leca, J-B., Gunst, N., & Vasey, P. L. (2014). Male homosexual behavior in a free-ranging all-male group of Japanese macaques at Minoo, Japan. *Archives of Sexual Behavior, 43,* 853–861. doi:10.1007/s10508-014-0310-6

Lechner, S. C., Antoni, M. H., Lydston, D., LaPerriere, A., Ishii, M., Devieux, J., . . . Weiss, S. (2003). Cognitive-behavioral interventions improve quality of life in women with AIDS. *Journal of Psychosomatic Research, 54,* 253–261.

Leclerc, B., Bergeron, S., Binik, Y. M., & Khalifé, S. (2010). History of sexual and physical abuse in women with dyspareunia: Association with pain, psychosocial adjustment, and sexual functioning. *Journal of Sexual Medicine, 7,* 971–980.

Lederer, L. (Ed.). (1980). *Take back the night: Women on pornography.* New York: Morrow.

Lee, B. H., & O'Sullivan, L. F. (2014). The ex-factor: Characteristics of online and offline post-relationship contact and tracking among Canadian emerging adults. *Canadian Journal of Human Sexuality, 23,* 96–105.

Lee, J. A. (1979). The social organization of sexual risk. *Alternative Lifestyles, 2,* 69–100.

Lee, P. A., Houk, C. P., Ahmed, S. F., & Hughes, I. A. (2006). Consensus statement on management of intersex disorders. *Pediatrics, 118,* e488–e500.

Lee, S., & Coates, J. (2007). *Sex trade research initiative, New Brunswick.* Report prepared for Provincial Government's Executive Council Office, Women's Issues Branch.

Lee, T. K., Handy, A. B., Kwan, W., Oliffe, J. L., Brotto, L. A., Wassersug, R. J., & Dowsett, G. W. (2015). Impact of prostate cancer treatment on the sexual quality of life for men-who-have-sex-with-men. *Journal of Sexual Medicine, 12,* 2378–2386.

Leger Marketing. (2012). Religiosity and atheism 2005–2012. Retrieved from http://www.leger360.com/admin/upload/publi_pdf/Religion_in_Canada_0812.pdf

Leifer, M. (1980). *Psychological effects of motherhood: A study of first pregnancy.* New York: Praeger.

Leitenberg, H., & Henning, K. (1995). Sexual fantasy. *Psychological Bulletin, 117,* 469–496.

Lemelin, C., Lussier, Y., Sabourin, S., Brassard, A., & Naud, C. (2014). Risky sexual behaviours: The role of substance use, psychopathic traits, and attachment insecurity among adolescents and young adults in Quebec. *Canadian Journal of Human Sexuality, 23,* 189–199.

Lemieux, R., & Hale, J. (2002). Cross-sectional analysis of intimacy, passion, and commitment: Testing the assumptions of the triangular theory of love. *Psychological Reports, 90,* 1009–1014.

Lemieux, S. R., & Byers, E. S. (2008). The sexual well-being of women who have experienced child sexual abuse. *Psychology of Women Quarterly, 32,* 126–144.

Leonard, L. (2000). Interpreting female genital cutting: Moving beyond the impasse. *Annual Review of Sex Research, 11,* 158–190.

Leonard, L. M., & Follette, V. M. (2002). Sex functioning in women reporting a history of child sexual abuse: Clinical and empirical considerations. *Annual Review of Sex Research, 13,* 346–388.

Lerman, H. (1986). From Freud to feminist personality theory. *Psychology of Women Quarterly, 10,* 1–18.

LeTourneau, E., Henggeler, S. W., Borduin, C. M., Schewe, P. A., McCart, M. R., Chapman, J. E., & Saldana, L. (2009). Multisytemic therapy for juvenile sexual offenders: 1-year results from a randomized effectiveness trial. *Journal of Family Psychology, 23,* 89–102.

Letts, C., Tamilyn, K., & Byers, E. S. (2010). Exploring the impact of prostate cancer on men's sexual well-being. *Journal of Psychosocial Oncology, 28,* 490–510.

Levaque, E., Sawatsky, M. L., & Lalumière, M. L. (2016). Hypersexualité chez les étudiants universitaires hétérosexuels. *Canadian Journal of Behavioural Science/Revue canadienne des sciences du comportement, 48,* 182–192.

LeVay, S. (1991). A difference in hypothalamic structure between heterosexual and homosexual men. *Science, 253,* 1034–1037.

LeVay, S. (1996). *Queer science: The use and abuse of research into homosexuality.* Cambridge, MA: MIT Press.

Lever, J. (1994, August). Sexual revelations. The 1994 Advocate Survey of Sexuality and Relationships: The Men. *The Advocate,* 17–24.

Lever, J. (1995, August). Lesbian sex survey. The 1995 Advocate Survey of Sexuality and Relationships: The Women. *The Advocate,* 22–30.

Lever, J., Frederick, D. A., & Peplau, L. (2006). Does size matter? Men's and women's views on penis size across the lifespan. *Psychology of Men & Masculinity, 7*(3), 129–143. doi:10.1037/1524-9220.7.3.129

Lever, J., Grov, C., Royce, T., & Gillespie, B. J. (2008). Searching for love in all the "write" places: Exploring Internet personal use by sexual orientation, gender, and age. *International Journal of Sexual Health, 20,* 233–246.

Levin, D. (2009). So sexy, so soon: The sexualization of childhood. In S. Olfman (Ed.), *The sexualization of childhood* (pp. 75–88). Westport, CT: Praeger.

Levin, I., & Trost, J. (1999). Living apart together. *Community, Work & Family 2*(3): 279–294.

Levin, R. J. (2003). Is prolactin the biological "off switch" for human sexual arousal? *Sexual and Relationship Therapy, 18,* 237–243.

Levin, R. J. (2005). Sexual arousal—its physiological roles in human reproduction. *Annual Review of Sex Research, 15,* 154–189.

Levine, R., Sato, S., Hashimoto, T., & Verma, J. (1995). Love and marriage in eleven cultures. *Journal of Cross-Cultural Psychology, 26,* 554–571.

Levitas, E., Weiss, N., Lunenfeld, E., & Potashnik, G. (2003). Are semen parameters related to abstinence? Analysis of 7,233 semen samples. Paper presented at European Society for Human Reproduction and Embryology, Madrid.

Levitt, E., Moser, C., & Jamison, K. (1994). The prevalence and some attributes of females in the sadomasochistic subculture: A second report. *Archives of Sexual Behavior, 23,* 465–473.

Levy, J. J., Maticka-Tyndale, E., & Lew, V. A. (1992). Pratique contraceptives et preventive face au sida parmi un groupe de cegepiens de Montreal: Variations interethniques. *Novelles Pratique Sociale, 5*(2), 25–36.

Lewis, J., & Maticka-Tyndale, E. (1998). *Final report: Erotic/exotic dancing: HIV-related risk factors.* Ottawa: Health Canada.

Lewis, J., Maticka-Tyndale, E., Shaver, F., & Schramm, H. (2005). Managing risk and safety on the job: The experiences of Canadian sex workers. *Journal of Psychology and Human Sexuality, 17,* 147–167.

Lewis, R. W., et al. (2004). Definitions, classification, and epidemiology of sexual dysfunction. In T. F. Lue, R. Basson, R. Rosen, F. Giuliano, S. Khoury, & F. Montorsi (Eds.). *Sexual medicine: Sexual dysfunctions in men and women* (pp. 39–72). Paris, France: Editions 21.

Lewis, R. W., Fugl-Meyer, K. S., Corona, G., Hayes, R. D., Laumann, E. O., Moreira, E. D., Jr., . . . Segraves, T. (2010). Definitions/epidemiology/risk factors for sexual dysfunction. *Journal of Sexual Medicine, 7,* 1598–1607.

Lewis, W. J. (1997). Factors associated with post-abortion adjustment problems: Implications for triage. *Canadian Journal of Human Sexuality, 6,* 9–16.

Ley, D., Prause, N., & Finn, P. (2014). The emperor has no clothes: A review of the "Pornography Addiction" model. *Current Sexual Health Reports, 6,* 94–105.

Liao, M., L., & Creighton, S. (2010). Labial surgery for well women: A review of the literature. *British Journal of Obstetrics and Gynecology, 117,* 20–25.

Libman, E. (1989). Sociocultural and cognitive factors in aging and sexual expression: Conceptual and research issues. *Canadian Psychology, 3*(3), 560–567.

Libman, E., & Fichten, C. S. (1987). Prostatectomy and sexual function. *Urology, 24*(5), 467–478.

Libman, E., Fichten, C. S., Creti, L., Weinstein, N., Amsel, R., & Brender, W. (1989). Transurethral prostatectomy: Differential effects of age category and presurgery sexual functioning on postprostatectomy sexual adjustment. *Journal of Behavioural Medicine, 12*(5), 469–485.

Lichtenstein, B. (2012). Starting over: Dating risks and sexual health among midlife women after relationship dissolution. In L. Carpenter & J. DeLamater (Eds.) *Sex for life: From virginity to Viagra, how sexuality changes throughout our lives* (pp. 180–197). New York: New York University Press.

Liebmann-Smith, J. (1987). *In pursuit of pregnancy: How couples discover, cope with, and resolve their fertility problems.* New York: Newmarket Press.

Lievore, D. (2003). *Non-reporting and hidden recording of sexual assault: An International literature review.* Canberra: Commonwealth Government of Australia.

Liljeros, F., Edling, C. R., Amaral, L. A., Stanley, H. E., & Aberg, Y. (2001). The web of human sexual contacts. *Nature, 411,* 907–908.

Lindgren, K. P., Parkhill, M. R., George, W. H., & Hendershot, C. S. (2008). Gender differences in perceptions of sexual intent: A qualitative review and integration. *Psychology of Women Quarterly, 32,* 423–439.

Linz, D., Donnerstein, E., & Penrod, S. (1987). The findings and recommendations of the Attorney General's Commission on Pornography: Do the psychological "facts" fit the political fury? *American Psychologist, 42,* 946–953.

Lippa, R. A. (2013). Men and women with bisexual identities show bisexual patterns of sexual attraction to male and female "swimsuit models." *Archives of Sexual Behavior, 42,* 187–196.

Lipsey, M. W., & Wilson, D. B. (2001). *Practical meta-analysis.* Thousand Oaks, CA: Sage.

Lisak, D., & Miller, P. M. (2002). Repeat rape and multiple offending among undetected rapists. *Violence & Victims, 17,* 73–84.

Liskin, L., Kak, N., Rutledge, A. H., Smit, L. C., & Stewart, L. (1985, November–December). Youth in the 1980s: Social and health concerns. *Population Reports, XIII*, No. 5, M350–M388.

Liu, C. (2003). Does quality of marital sex decline with duration? *Archives of Sexual Behavior, 32*, 55–60.

Ljunger, E., Cnattingius, S., Lundin, C., & Anneren, G. (2005). Chromosomal anomalies in first-trimester miscarriages. *Acta Obstetrica et Gynecologica Scandinavica, 84*, 1103–1107.

Loeb, T. B., Rivkin, I., Williams, J. K., Wyatt, G. E., Vargas Carmona, J., & Chin, D. (2002). Child sexual abuse: Associations with the sexual functioning of adolescents and adults. *Annual Review of Sex Research, 13*, 307–345.

Loffreda, B. (2000). *Losing Matt Shepard: Life and politics in the aftermath of anti-gay murder*. New York: Columbia University Press.

Löfgren-Mårtenson, L., & Månsson, S. (2010). Lust, love, and life: A qualitative study of Swedish adolescents' perceptions and experiences with pornography. *Journal of Sex Research, 47*(6), 568–579.

Loftus, E. F. (1993). The reality of repressed memories. *American Psychologist, 48*, 518–537.

Logan, T. D. (2010). Personal characteristics, sexual behaviors, and male sex work: A quantitative approach. *American Sociological Review, 75*, 679–704.

Lombardi, E. L., Wilchins, R., Priesing, D., & Malouf, D. (2001). Gender violence: Transgender experiences with violence and discrimination. *Journal of Homosexuality, 42*, 89–101.

London Department of Health. (2013, July 11). *Abortion statistics, England and Wales: 2012*. London: Department of Health, United Kingdom.

Longo, D. J., Clum, G. A., & Yaeger, N. J. (1988). Psychosocial treatment for recurrent genital herpes. *Journal of Consulting and Clinical Psychology, 56*, 61–66.

LoPiccolo, J., & Stock, W. E. (1986). Treatment of sexual dysfunction. *Journal of Consulting and Clinical Psychology, 54*, 158–167.

Lorius, C. (1999). *Tantric sex: Making love last*. London, UK: Thorsons/Harper-Collins.

Los, M. (1994). The struggle to redefine rape in the early 1980s. In J. V. Roberts & R. M. Mohr (Eds.), *Confronting sexual assault: A decade of legal change*. Toronto: University of Toronto Press.

Lottes, I. L., & Alkula, T. (2011). An investigation of sexuality-related attitudinal patterns and characteristics related to those patterns for 32 European countries. *Sexuality Research and Social Policy, 8*, 77–92.

Lue, Y., Wang, C., Cui, Y., Wang, X., Sha, J., Zhou, Z., . . . Swerdloff, R. S. (2009). Levonorgestrel enhances spermatogenesis suppression by testosterone with greater alteration in testicular gene expression in men. *Biology of Reproduction, 80*, 484–492.

Luff, D. (2001). "The downright torture of women": Moral lobby women, feminists, and pornography. *The Sociological Review, 49*, 78–99.

Luke, B. (1994). Nutritional influences on fetal growth. *Clinical Obstetrics and Gynecology, 37*, 538–549.

Lunny, C. A., & Fraser, S. N. (2010). The use of complementary and alternative medicines among a sample of Canadian menopausal-aged women. *Journal of Midwifery & Women's Health, 55*, 335–343.

Luo, M., Fee, M., & Katz, L. (2003). Encoding pheromonal signals in the accessory olfactory bulb in behaving mice. *Science, 299*, 1196–1201.

Luo, S., & Klohnen, E. (2005). Assortative mating and marital quality in newly weds: A couple-centered approach. *Journal of Personality and Social Psychology, 88*, 304–326.

Luong, M. (2008). Life after teenage motherhood. *Perspectives* (Catalogue no. 75-001-X, p. 5–13). Ottawa: Statistics Canada.

Lussier, P., & Piché, L. (2008). Frotteurism: Psychopathology and theory. In D. R. Laws & W. O'Donohue (Eds.), *Sexual deviance: Theory, assessment, and treatment* (2nd ed., pp. 131–149). New York: Guilford.

Luzuriaga, K., Newell, M. L., Dabis, F., Excler, J. L., & Sullivan, J. L. (2006). Vaccines to prevent transmission of HIV-1 via breastmilk: Scientific and logistical priorities. *The Lancet, 368*, 511–521.

Lydon-Rochelle, M., Holt, V., Easterling, T., & Martin, D. (2001). Risk of uterine rupture during labor among women with a prior cesarean delivery. *New England Journal of Medicine, 345*, 3–8.

Maass, A., Cadinu, M., Guarnieri, G., & Grasselli, A. (2003). Sexual harassment under social identity threat: The computer harassment paradigm. *Journal of Personality and Social Psychology, 85*, 853–870.

Maccoby, E. E. (2002). Gender and group process: A developmental perspective. *Current Directions in Psychological Science, 11*, 54–58.

MacCulloch, M., Gray, N., & Watt, A. (2000). Brittain's sadistic murderer syndrome reconsidered: An associative account of the aetiology of sadistic sexual fantasies. *Journal of Forensic Psychiatry, 11*, 401–418.

MacDonald, G., & Jeffrey, L. (2000). The ethics of social control in researching the sex trade: Prostitutes and professors. Prepared for Gendering Ethics/Ethics of Gender Conference at the Centre for Interdisciplinary Gender Studies on June 21, 2000, at the University of Leeds, UK.

MacDonald, N., & Wong, T. (2007). Canadian guidelines on sexually transmitted infections, 2006. *Canadian Medical Association Journal, 176*, 175–176.

MacDonald, T. K., & Ross, M. (1999). Assessing the accuracy of predictions about dating relationships: How and why do lovers' predictions differ from those made by

observers? *Personality and Social Psychology Bulletin, 25*, 1417–1429.

MacFarlane, G. R., Blomberg, S. P., & Vasey, P. L. (2010). Homosexual behaviour in birds: Frequency of expression is related to parental care disparity between the sexes. *Animal Behaviour, 80*, 375–390.

MacInnis, C. C., & Hodson, G. (2012). Intergroup bias toward "Group X": Evidence of prejudice, dehumanization, avoidance, and discrimination against asexuals. *Group Processes and Intergroup Relations, 15*, 725–743.

MacIntosh, H., Reissing, E. D., & Andruff, H. (2010). Same-sex marriage in Canada: The impact of legal marriage on the first cohort of gay and lesbian Canadians to wed. *Canadian Journal of Human Sexuality, 19*(3), 79–90.

Mackie, M. (1991). *Gender relations in Canada: Further explorations*. Toronto: Harcourt Brace Canada.

MacKinnon, C. A. (1982). Feminism, Marxism, method, and the state: An agenda for theory. *Feminist Theory, 7*, 515–544.

Maclean's/CTV Poll. (1994, Jan. 3). Canada under the covers. *Maclean's, 107*(1).

Maclean's/CTV Poll. (1995, Jan. 2). Looking inward. *Maclean's*.

Maclean's/Global Poll. (2000, December 25). Politics, social attitudes, and sex. *Maclean's, 113*(52), 52–54.

MacMillan, H. L., Fleming, J. E., Trocmé, N., Boyle, M. H., Wong, M., Racine, Y. A., . . . Offord, D. R. (1997). Prevalence of child physical and sexual abuse in the community: Results from the Ontario Health Supplement. *Journal of the American Medical Association, 278*, 131–135.

MacNeil, S., & Byers, E. S. (1997). The relationship between sexual problems, communication and sexual satisfaction. *Canadian Journal of Human Sexuality, 6*, 277–283.

MacNeil, S., & Byers, E. S. (2005). Dyadic assessment of sexual self-disclosure and sexual satisfaction in heterosexual dating couples. *Journal of Social and Personal Relationships, 22*, 169–181.

MacNeil, S., & Byers, E. S. (2009). Role of sexual self-disclosure in the sexual satisfaction of long-term heterosexual couples. *Journal of Sex Research, 46*, 1–12. doi:10.1080/00224490802398399

Madden, M., & Lenhart, A. (2006). *Online dating*. Retrieved from http://www.pew-internet.org/pdfs/PIP_Online_Dating.pdf

Maddock, J. W. (1997). Sexuality education: A history lesson. In J. W. Maddock (Ed.), *Sexuality education in post-secondary and professional training settings* (pp. 1–22). Binghamton, NY: The Haworth Press.

Magaña, J. R., & Carrier, J. M. (1991). Mexican and Mexican American male sexual behavior and spread of AIDS in California. *Journal of Sex Research, 28*, 425–441.

Maguire, D. C. (2001). *Sacred choices: The right to contraception and abortion in ten world religions*. Minneapolis: Augsburg Fortress.

Mah, K., & Binik, Y. M. (2001). The nature of human orgasm: A critical review of major trends. *Clinical Psychology Review, 21*, 823–856.

Mah, K., & Binik, Y. M. (2002). Do all orgasms feel alike? Evaluating a two-dimensional model of the orgasm experience across gender and sexual context. *Journal of Sex Research, 39*, 104–113.

Mah, K., & Binik, Y. M. (2005). Are orgasms in the mind or the body? Psychosocial versus physiological correlates of orgasmic pleasure and satisfaction. *Journal of Sex and Marital Therapy, 31*, 187–200.

Mahoney, E. R. (1983). *Human sexuality.* New York: McGraw-Hill.

Maines, R. P. (1999). *The technology of orgasm: "Hysteria," the vibrator, and women's sexual satisfaction.* Baltimore, MD: Johns Hopkins University Press.

Major, B., Appelbaum, M., Beckman, L., Dutton M. A., Russo, N. F., & West, C. (2009). Abortion and mental health. *American Psychologist, 64*(9), 863–890.

Malamuth, N. M. (1998). The confluence model as an organizing framework for research on sexually aggressive men: Risk moderators, imagined aggression and pornography consumption. In R. Geen & E. Donnerstein (Eds.), *Aggression: Theoretical and empirical reviews.* New York: Academic Press.

Malamuth, N. M., & Brown, L. M. (1994). Sexually aggressive men's perceptions of women's communications. *Journal of Personality and Social Psychology, 67*, 699–712.

Malta, S., & Farquharson, K. (2014). The initiation and progression of late-life romantic relationships. *Journal of Sociology, 50*, 237–251.

Maltz, W., & Boss, S. (1997). *In the garden of desire. The intimate world of women's sexual fantasies.* New York: Broadway Books.

Mandese, J. (2007). Feeling blue: Americans consume more adult content. *Media Post.* Retrieved from http://www.mediapost.com

Manson Singer, S., Willms, D. G., Adrien, A., Baxter, J., Brabazon, C., Leaune, V., . . . Cappon, P. (1996). Many voices—Sociocultural results of the ethnocultural communities facing AIDS study in Canada. *Canadian Journal of Public Health, 8*(Supp. 1), S26–S32.

Manson, J. E. (2012). Menopausal HT: 15 top medical organizations endorse new consensus statement. Retrieved from http://www.medscape.com/viewarticle/767206

Mark, K., Janssen, E., & Milhausen, R. (2011). Infidelity in heterosexual couples: Demographic, interpersonal, and personality related predictors of extradyadic sex. *Archives of Sexual Behavior, 40*, 971–982.

Markman, H., & Kadushin, F. (1986). Preventive effects of human training for first-time parents: A short-term longitudinal study. *Journal of Consulting and Clinical Psychology, 54*, 872–874.

Markman, H., Rhoades, G. K., Stanley, S. M., Ragan, E. P., & Whitton, S. W. (2010). The premarital communication roots of marital distress and divorce: The first five years of marriage. *Journal of Family Psychology, 24*, 289–298.

Marsan, C. D. (2008, February 7). The hottest trends in online dating. Retrieved from http://www.networkworld.com/news/2008/020708-valentines-online-dating.html

Marshall, B. L. (2012). Medicalization and the refashioning of age-related limits on sexuality. *Journal of Sex Research, 49*, 337–343.

Marshall, D. C. (1971). Sexual behavior on Mangaia. In D. S. Marshall & R. C. Suggs (Eds.), *Human sexual behavior* (pp. 103–162). New York: Basic Books.

Marshall, T. C. (2008). Cultural differences in intimacy: The influence of gender-role ideology and individualism-collectivism. *Journal of Social and Personal Relationships, 25*, 143–168.

Marshall, W. L. (1993). A revised approach to the treatment of men who sexually assault adult females. In G. N. Hall, et al. (Eds.), *Sexual aggression* (pp. 143–165). Washington, DC: Taylor & Francis.

Marshall, W. L., & Barbaree, H. E. (1988). The long-term evaluation of a behavioural treatment program for child molesters. *Behaviour Research and Therapy, 6*, 499–511.

Marshall, W. L., & Pithers, W. D. (1994). A reconsideration of treatment outcome with sex offenders. *Criminal Justice and Behavior, 21*, 10–27.

Marshall, W. L., Marshall, L. E., & Serran, G. A. (2006). Strategies in the treatment of paraphilias: A critical review. *Annual Review of Sex Research, 17*, 162–182.

Marshall, W. L., Payne, K., Barbaree, H. E., & Eccles, A. (1991). Exhibitionists: Sexual preferences for exposing. *Behavioural Research Therapy, 20*(1), 37–40.

Martin, C. L., & Halverson, C. F. (1983). The effects of sex-typing schemas on young children's memory. *Child Development, 54*, 563–574.

Martin, C. L., & Ruble, D. (2004). Children's search for gender cues: Cognitive perspectives on gender development. *Current Directions in Psychological Science, 13*, 67–70.

Martin, C. L., Ruble, D., & Szkrybalo, J. (2002). Cognitive theories of early gender development. *Psychological Bulletin, 128*, 903–933.

Martin, S. L., Macy, R. J., & Young, S. K. (2011). Health and economic consequences of sexual violence. In J. W. White, M. P. Koss, & A. E. Kazdin (Eds.), *Violence against women and children: Navigating solutions* (vol. 1, pp. 173–196). Washington, DC: American Psychological Association.

Martin, S. L., Ray, N., Sotres-Alvarez, D., Kupper, L. L., Moracco, K. E., Dickens, P. A., . . . Gizlice, Z. (2006). Physical and sexual assault of women with disabilities. *Violence Against Women, 12*, 823–837.

Martins, Y., Preti, G., Crabtree, C. R., Runyan, T., Vainius, A. A., & Wysocki, C. (2005). Preference for human body odors is influenced by gender and sexual orientation. *Psychological Science, 16*, 694–701.

Martins, Y., Tiggemann, M., & Churchett, L. (2008). Hair today, gone tomorrow: A comparison of body hair removal practices in gay and heterosexual men. *Body Image, 5*, 312–316.

Martinson, F. M. (1994). *The sexual life of children.* Westport, CT: Bergin & Garvey.

Masters, W. H., & Johnson, V. (1966). *Human sexual response.* Boston: Little, Brown.

Masters, W. H., & Johnson, V. (1970). *Human sexual inadequacy.* Boston: Little, Brown.

Masters, W. H., & Johnson, V. (1979). *Homosexuality in perspective.* Boston: Little, Brown.

Masters, W. H., Johnson, V. E., & Kolodny, R. C. (1982). *Human sexuality.* Boston: Little, Brown.

Mathieson, C., & Endicott, L. (1998). Lesbian and Bisexual Identity: Discourse of difference. *Atlantis, 23*, 38.

Mathy, R., & Cooper, A. (2003). The duration and frequency of Internet use in a nonclinical sample: Suicidality, behavioral problems, and treatment history. *Psychotherapy: Theory, Research, Practice, Training, 40*, 125–135.

Maticka-Tyndale, E. (1992). Social construction of HIV transmission and prevention among heterosexual young adults. *Social Problems, 39*(93), 238–252.

Maticka-Tyndale, E. (1997). Reducing the incidence of sexually transmitted disease through behavioural and social change. *Canadian Journal of Human Sexuality, 6*, 89–104.

Maticka-Tyndale, E. (2001). Sexual health and Canadian youth: How do we measure up? *Canadian Journal of Human Sexuality, 10*, 1–17.

Maticka-Tyndale, E. (2008). Sexuality and sexual health of Canadian adolescents: Yesterday, today and tomorrow. *Canadian Journal of Human Sexuality, 17*, 85–95.

Maticka-Tyndale, E., & Bicher, M. (1996). The impact of medicalization on women. In B. Schissel & L. Mahood (Eds.), *Social control in Canada: A reader on the social construction of deviance.* Toronto: Oxford University Press.

Maticka-Tyndale, E., & Smylie, L. (2008). Sexual rights: Striking a balance. *International Journal of Sexual Health, 20*, 7–24.

Maticka-Tyndale, E., Adams, B. D., & Cohen, J. (2002) Sexual desire and practice among people living with HIV and using combination anti-retroviral therapies. *Canadian Journal of Human Sexuality, 11*, 33–40.

Maticka-Tyndale, E., Barrett, M., & McKay, A. (2000). Adolescent sexual and reproductive health in Canada: A review of national data sources and their limitations. *Canadian Journal of Human Sexuality, 9*, 41–65.

Maticka-Tyndale, E., Godin, G., LeMay, G., Adrien, A., Manson-Singer, S., Willms, D., . . . Bradet, R. (1996). Canadian ethnocultural communities facing AIDS: Overview and summary of survey results from phase III. *Canadian Journal of Public Health, 87*(Supp. 1), S38–S43.

Maticka-Tyndale, E., Herold, E., & Oppermann, M. (2003). Casual sex among Australian schoolies. *Journal of Sex Research, 40,* 158–169.

Maticka-Tyndale, E., Lewis, J., & Street, M. (2005). Making a place for escort work: A case study. *Journal of Sex Research, 42,* 46–53.

Maticka-Tyndale, E., Lewis, J., Clark, J. P., Zubick, J., & Young, S. (1999). Social and cultural vulnerability to sexually transmitted infection: The work of exotic dancers. *Canadian Journal of Public Health, 90,* 19–22.

Maticka-Tyndale, E., Lewis, J., Clark, J. P., Zubrick, J., & Young, S. (2000). Exotic dancing and health. *Women & Health, 31,* 87–108.

Matthews, J. E., Stephenson, R., & Sullivan, P. S. (2012). Factors associated with self-reported HBV vaccination among HIV-negative MSM participating in an online sexual health survey: A cross-sectional study. *PLoS ONE, 7*(2), e30609. doi:10.1371/journal.pone.0030609

Mattson, S., & Riley, E. (1998). A review of the neurobehavioral deficits in children with fetal alcohol syndrome or prenatal exposure to alcohol. *Alcoholism: Clinical and Experimental Research, 22,* 279–294.

Maurer, H. (1994). *Sex: Real people talk about what they really do.* New York: Penguin Books.

Mayo Clinic. (2012a). Maximizing fertility. Retrieved from http://www.mayoclinic.com/health/how-to-get-pregnant/PR00103

Mayo Clinic. (2012b). Male infertility: Lifestyle and home remedies. Retrieved from http://www.mayoclinic.com/health/male-infertility/DSO1038/lifestyle-and-home-remedies

Mazer, D. B., & Percival, E. F. (1989). Students' experiences of sexual harassment at a small university. *Sex Roles, 20*(1 & 2), 1–22.

Mazzuca, J. (2004, November 2). Origin of homosexuality? Britons, Canadians say "nature." *Gallup News Service.* Washington DC: The Gallup Organization.

McCabe, M., Althof, S. E., Assalian, P., Chevret-Measson, M., Leiblum, S. R., Simonelli, C., & Wylie, K. (2010). Psychological and interpersonal dimensions of sexual function and dysfunction. *Journal of Sexual Medicine, 7,* 327–336.

McCall, D., & McKay, A. (2004). SOGC policy statement: School-based and school-linked sexual health education and promotion in Canada. *Journal of Obstetrics and Gynaecology Canada, 146,* 596–600.

McCall, D., Beazley, R., Doherty-Poirier, M., Lovato, C., MacKinnon, D., Otis, J., & Shannon, M. (1999). *Schools, public health, sexuality and HIV: A status report.* Toronto: Council of Ministers of Education.

McCallum, E. B., & Peterson, Z. D. (2012). Investigating the impact of inquiry mode on self-reported sexual behavior: Theoretical considerations and review of the literature. *Journal of Sex Research, 49,* 212–226.

McCarthy, B. W. (1989). Cognitive-behavioral strategies and techniques in the treatment of early ejaculation. In S. R. Leiblum & R. C. Rosen (Eds.), *Principles and practice of sex therapy* (2nd ed.). New York: Guilford.

McCarthy, B., Benoit, C., & Jansson, M. (2014). Sex work: A comparative study. *Archives of Sexual Behavior, 43,* 1379–1390.

McClelland, S. (2001, December 3). Inside the sex trade. *Maclean's.*

McClintock, M. K. (1971). Menstrual synchrony and suppression. *Nature, 229,* 244–245.

McClintock, M. K. (1998). Whither menstrual synchrony? *Annual Review of Sex Research, 9,* 77–95.

McClintock, M. K. (2000). Human pheromones: Primers, releasers, signalers, or modulators? In K. Wallen & J. Schneider (Eds.), *Reproduction in context* (pp. 355–420). Cambridge, MA: MIT Press.

McClintock, M., & Herdt, G. (1996). Rethinking puberty: The development of sexual attraction. *Current Directions in Psychological Science, 5,* 178–183.

McClure, R., & Brewer, R. T. (1980). Attitudes of new parents towards child and spouse with Lamaze or non-Lamaze methods of childbirth. *Journal of Human Behavior, 17,* 45–48.

McCoy, N. L. (1996). Menopause and sexuality. In M. K. Beard (Ed.), *Optimizing hormone replacement therapy: Estrogen-androgen therapy in postmenopausal women* (pp. 32–36). Minneapolis: McGraw-Hill Healthcare.

McCoy, N. L. (1997). Sexual issues for postmenopausal women. *Topics in Geriatric Rehabilitation, 12,* 28–39.

McCoy, N. L., & Pitino, L. (2002). Pheromonal influences on sociosexual behavior in young women. *Physiology & Behavior, 75,* 367–375.

McCreary Centre Society. (2007). *Not yet equal: The health of lesbian, gay, and bisexual youth in BC.* Vancouver, BC: Author.

McCutcheon, J., & Morrison, M. A. (2014). The effect of parental gender roles on students' attitudes toward lesbian, gay, and heterosexual adoptive couples. *Adoption Quarterly, 18,* 138–167.

McDermid, S. A., Zucker, K. J., Bradley, S. J., & Maing, D. M. (1998). Effects of physical appearance on masculine trait ratings of boys and girls with gender identity disorder. *Archives of Sexual Behavior, 27*(3), 253–267.

McDonagh, A., Friedman, M., McHugo, G., Ford, J., Sengupta, A., Mueser, K., . . . Descamps, M. (2005). Randomized trial of cognitive-behavioral therapy for chronic posttraumatic stress disorder in adult female survivors of childhood sexual abuse. *Journal of Consulting and Clinical Psychology, 73,* 515–524.

McEwen, B. S. (1997). Meeting report–Is there a neurobiology of love? *Molecular Psychiatry, 2,* 15–16.

McEwen, B. S. (2001). Estrogen effects on the brain: Multiple sites and molecular mechanisms. *Journal of Applied Physiology, 91,* 2785–2801.

McFarland, W. P. (2001). The legal duty to protect gay and lesbian students from violence in school. *Professional School Counseling, 4,* 171–180.

McFarlane, J. M., & Williams, T. M. (1994). Placing premenstrual syndrome in perspective. *Psychology of Women Quarterly, 18,* 339–374.

McFarlane, J., Martin, C. L., & Williams, T. M. (1988). Mood fluctuations: Women versus men and menstrual versus other cycles. *Psychology of Women Quarterly, 12,* 201–224.

McGuire, J. K., & Barber, B. L. (2010). A person-centered approach to the multifaceted nature of young adult sexual behavior. *Journal of Sex Research, 47,* 301–313.

McKay, A. (1993). Research supports broadly-based sex education. *Canadian Journal of Human Sexuality, 2,* 89–98.

McKay, A. (1996). Rural parents' attitudes toward school-based sexual health education. *Canadian Journal of Human Sexuality, 5,* 15–29.

McKay, A. (2000). Common questions about sexual health education. *SIECCAN Newsletter, 35,* 129–137.

McKay, A. (2004). Oral sex among teenagers: Research, discourse and education. *Canadian Journal of Human Sexuality, 13,* 201–203.

McKay, A. (2005a). Sexuality and substance use: The impact of tobacco, alcohol, and selected recreational drugs on sexual function. *Canadian Journal of Human Sexuality, 14,* 47–56.

McKay, A. (2005b). *Sexual health education in the schools: Questions and answers.* Toronto: SIECCAN.

McKay, A. (2006a). Chlamydia screening programs: A review of the literature. Part 1. Issues in the promotion of chlamydia testing of youth by primary care physicians. *Canadian Journal of Human Sexuality, 15,* 1–11.

McKay, A. (2006b). Trends in teen pregnancy in Canada with comparisons to U.S.A. and England/Wales. *Canadian Journal of Human Sexuality, 15,* 157–161.

McKay, A. (2007). The effectiveness of latex condoms for prevention of STI/HIV. *Canadian Journal of Human Sexuality, 16,* 57–61.

McKay, A. (2012). Trends in Canadian national and provincial/territorial teen pregnancy rates: 2001-2010. *Canadian Journal of Human Sexuality, 21,* 161–175.

McKay, A., & Barrett, M. (1999). Pre-service sexual health education training of elementary, secondary, and physical health education teachers in Canadian faculties of education. *Canadian Journal of Human Sexuality, 8,* 91–101.

McKay, A., & Barrett, M. (2010). Trends in teen pregnancy rates from 1996–2006: A comparison of Canada, Sweden, U.S.A., and England/Wales. *Canadian Journal of Human Sexuality, 19,* 43–52.

McKay, A., & Holowaty, P. (1997). Sexual health education: A study of adolescents' opinions, self-perceived needs, and current and preferred sources of information. *Canadian Journal of Human Sexuality, 6*, 29–38.

McKay, A., Byers, E. S., Voyer, S. D., Humphreys, T. P., & Marham, C. (2014). Ontario parents' opinions and attitudes towards sexual health education in the schools. *Canadian Journal of Human Sexuality, 23*, 159–166.

McKay, A., Pietrusiak, M.-A., & Holowaty, P. (1998). Parents' opinions and attitudes towards sexuality education in schools. *Canadian Journal of Human Sexuality, 7*, 139–145.

McKee, A. (2005). The objectification of women in mainstream pornographic videos in Australia. *Journal of Sex Research, 42*, 277–290.

McKenna, B., Hampton, M. R., Bourassa, C., McKay-McNabb, K., & Baydala, A. (2010). Voices from the moon lodge. In S. Geissler, L. Loutzenhiser, J. Praud, & L. Streifler (Eds.). *Mothering Canada: Interdisciplinary voices* (pp. 231–240). Toronto: Demeter Press.

McKenna, K. E. (2000). Some proposals regarding the organization of the central nervous system control of penile erection. *Neuroscience and Biobehavioral Reviews, 24*, 535–540.

McKenzie-Mohr, D., & Zanna, M. P. (1990). Treating women as sexual objects: Look to the (gender schematic) male who has viewed pornography. *Personality and Social Psychology Bulletin, 16*(2), 296–308.

McKinlay, S. M., Brambilla, D. J., & Posner, J. G. (1992). The normal menopause transition. *American Journal of Human Biology, 4*, 37–46.

McMahon, S., Hansen, L., Mann, J., Sevigny, C., Wong, T., & Roache, M. (2004). Contraception. *BMC Women's Health, 4*(Suppl 1), S25.

McManus, A. J., Hunter, L. P., & Renn, H. (2006). Lesbian experiences and needs during childbirth: Guidance for health care providers. *JOGNN, 35*, 13–23.

McMaster, L. E., Connolly, J., Pepler, D., & Craig, W. M. (2002). Peer to peer sexual harassment in early adolescence: A developmental perspective. *Development and Psychopathology, 14*, 91–105.

McNair, R., Dempsey, D., Wise, S., & Perlesz, A. (2002). Lesbian parenting: Issues, strengths and challenges. *Family Matters, 63*, 40–49.

McNeill, J. J. (1987). Homosexuality: Challenging the Church to grow. *Christian Century, 104*, 242–246.

Meana, M., Binik, Y. M., Khalife, S., & Cohen, D. R. (1997). Bio psychosocial profile of women with dyspareunia. *Obstetrics & Gynecology, 90*, 583–589.

Meaney, G. J., & Rye, B. J. (2010). Gendered egos: Attitude functions and gender as predictors of homonegativity. *Journal of Homosexuality, 57*, 1274–1302.

Meaney, G. J., Rye, B. J., Wood, E., & Solovieva, E. (2009). Satisfaction with school-based sexual health education in a sample of university students recently graduated from Ontario high schools. *Canadian Journal of Human Sexuality, 18*, 107–125.

Mehta, A., & Sheth, S. (2006). Postpartum depression: How to recognize and treat this common condition. *Medscape Psychiatry and Mental Health, 11*, article 529930.

Meischke, H. (1995). Implicit sexual portrayals in the movies: Interpretations of young women. *Journal of Sex Research, 32*, 29–36.

Ménard, A. D., & Kleinplatz, P. J. (2008). Twenty-one moves guaranteed to make his thighs go up in flames: Depictions of "great sex" in popular magazines. *Sexuality and Culture, 12*(1), 1–20.

Mercer, B. M., Gilbert, S., Landon, M. B., Spong, C. Y., Leveno, K. J., Rouse, D. J., . . . Ramin, S. M. (2008). Labor outcomes with increasing number of prior vaginal births after Caesarean delivery. *Obstetrics & Gynecology, 111*, 285–291.

Mercer, C. H., Tanton, C., Prah, P., Erens, B., Sonnenberg, P., Clifton, S, . . . Johnson, A. M. (2013). Changes in sexual attitudes and lifestyles in Britain through the life course and over time: findings from the National Surveys of Sexual Attitudes and Lifestyles (Natsal). *Lancet, 382*, 1781–1794.

Merolla, A. J. (2012). Connecting here and there: A model of long-distance relationship maintenance. *Personal Relationships, 19*, 775–795.

Messenger, J. C. (1993). Sex and repression in an Irish folk community. In D. N. Suggs & A. W. Miracle (Eds.), *Culture and human sexuality* (pp. 240–261). Pacific Grove, CA: Brooks/Cole.

Messineo, M. J. (2008). Does advertising on Black Entertainment Television portray more positive gender representations compared to broadcast networks? *Sex Roles, 59*, 752–764.

Meston, C. M., Levin, R. J., Sipski, M. L., Hull, E. M., & Heiman, J. R. (2004). Women's orgasm. *Annual Review of Sex Research, 15*, 173–257.

Meston, C. M., Rellini, A. H., & Heiman, J. R. (2006). Women's history of sexual abuse, their sexuality, and sexual self schemas. *Journal of Consulting and Clinical Psychology, 74*, 229–236.

Meston, C. M., Trapnell, P. D., & Gorzalka, B. B. (1996). Ethnic and gender differences in sexuality: Variations in sexual behavior between Asian and non-Asian university students. *Archives of Sexual Behavior, 25*, 33–72.

Meston, C. M., Trapnell, P., & Gorzalka, B. (1998). Ethnic, gender, and length-of-residency influences on sexual knowledge and attitudes. *Journal of Sex Research, 35*, 176–188.

Meston, C., & Buss, D. (2007). Why humans have sex. *Archives of Sexual Behavior, 36*, 477–507.

Metcalf, M. G., Skidmore, D. S. Lowry, G. F., & Mackenzie, J. A. (1983). Incidence of ovulation in the years after the menarche. *Journal of Endocrinology, 97*, 213–219.

Metz, M., & McCarthy, B. (2003). *Coping with premature ejaculation: How to overcome PE, please your partner and have great sex.* Oakland, CA: New Harbinger Publications, Inc.

Meyer, I. H. (2003). Prejudice, social stress, and mental health in lesbian, gay, and bisexual populations: Conceptual issues and research evidence. *Psychological Bulletin, 129*, 674–697.

Meyer-Bahlburg, H. F. L., Dolezal, C., Baker, S. W., Carlson, A. D., Obeid, J. S., & New, M. I. (2004). Prenatal androgenization affects gender-related behavior but not gender identity in 5–12-year-old girls with congenital adrenal hyperplasia. *Archives of Sexual Behavior, 33*, 97–104.

Meyer-Bahlburg, H. F. L., Dolezal, C., Baker, S. W., Ehrhardt, A. A., & New, M. I. (2006). Gender development in women with congenital adrenal hyperplasia as a function of disorder severity. *Archives of Sexual Behavior, 35*, 667–684.

Mezzacappa, E., & Katkin, E. (2002). Breastfeeding is associated with reduced perceived stress and negative mood in mothers. *Health Psychology, 21*, 187–193.

Michael, R. T., Gagnon, J. H., Laumann, E. O., & Kolata, G. (1994) *Sex in America: A definitive survey.* Boston: Little, Brown.

Mihan, R., Kerr, J. Maticka-Tyndale, E., & The ACBY Team. (2016). HIV-related stigma among African, Caribbean, and Black youth in Windsor, Ontario. *AIDS Care, 28*, 758–763.

Miki, Y., Swensen, J., Shattuck-Eidens, D., Futreal, P. A., Harshman, K., Tavtigian, S., . . . Skolnick, M. H. (1994). A strong candidate for the breast and ovarian cancer susceptibility gene BRCA1. *Science, 266*, 66–71.

Miklos, J. R., & Moore, R. D. (2008). Labiaplasty of the labia minora: Patients' indications for pursuing surgery. *Journal of Sexual Medicine, 5*, 1492–1495.

Milam, J. (2006). Posttraumatic growth and HIV disease progression. *Journal of Consulting and Clinical Psychology, 74*, 817–827.

Milan, A., Maheux, H., & Chui, T. (2010). A portrait of couples in mixed unions. *Canadian Social Trends* (Catalogue no. 11-008). Ottawa: Statistics Canada.

Milan, R. J., & Kilmann, P. R. (1987). Interpersonal factors in premarital contraception. *Journal of Sex Research, 23*, 289–321.

Milhausen, R. R., Buchholz, A. C., Opperman, E. A., & Benson, L. E. (2014). Relationships between body image, body composition, sexual functioning, and sexual satisfaction among heterosexual young adults. *Archives of Sexual Behavior, 6*, 1621–1633.

Miller, B. B., Cox, D. N., & Saewyc, E. M. (2010). Age of sexual consent law in Canada: Population-based evidence for law and policy. *Canadian Journal of Human Sexuality, 19*, 105–119.

Miller, E. M. (1986). *Street woman.* Philadelphia: Temple University Press.

Miller, J., & Schwartz, M. (1995). Rape myths and violence against street prostitutes. *Deviant Behavior, 76,* 1–23.

Miller, L. C., & Fishkin, S. A. (1997). On the dynamics of human bonding and reproductive success: Seeking windows on the adapted-for-human-environmental interface. In J. A. Simpson & D. T. Kenrick (Eds.), *Evolutionary social psychology* (pp. 197–235). Mahwah, NJ: Lawrence Erlbaum.

Miller, N. (1992). *Out in the world: Gay and lesbian life from Buenos Aires to Bangkok.* New York: Random House.

Miller, R. S., & Lefcourt, H. M. (1982). The assessment of social intimacy. *Journal of Personality Assessment, 46,* 514–518.

Miller, S. A., & Byers, E. S. (2004). Actual and desired duration of foreplay and intercourse: Discordance and misperceptions within heterosexual couples. *Journal of Sex Research, 41,* 301–309.

Miller, S. A., & Byers, E. S. (2009). Psychologists' continuing education and training in sexuality. *Journal of Sex & Marital Therapy, 35,* 206–219.

Miller, S. A., & Byers, E. S. (2010). Psychologists' sexual education and training in graduate school. *Canadian Journal of Behavioural Science, 42,* 93–100.

Miller, S. A., & Byers, E. S. (2012). Practicing psychologists' sexual intervention self-efficacy and willingness to treat sexual issues. *Archives of Sexual Behavior, 41*(4), 1041–1050.

Miller, S. L., & Maner, J. (2010). Scent of a woman: Men's testosterone responses to olfactory ovulation cues. *Psychological Science, 21,* 276–283.

Miller, S., Corrales, R., & Wachman, D. B. (1975). Recent progress in understanding and facilitating marital communication. *The Family Coordinator, 24,* 143–152.

Miller, W. J., Nair, R., & Wadhera, S. (1996). Declining cesarean section rates: A continuing trend? *Health Reports, 8,* 17–24.

Milner, J., Dopke, C., & Crouch, J. (2008). Paraphilia not otherwise specified: Psychopathology and theory. In D. R. Laws & W. T. O'Donohue (Eds.), *Sexual deviance: Theory, assessment, and treatment* (2nd ed., pp. 384–418). New York: Guilford.

Miner, M., & Coleman, E. (2001). Advances in sex offender treatment and challenges for the future. *Journal of Psychology and Human Sexuality, 13,* 5–24.

Minichiello, V., Scott, J., & Callander, D. (2013). New pleasures and old dangers: Reinventing male sex work. *Journal of Sex Research, 50,* 263–275.

Minkoff, H., & Chervenak, F. A. (2003). Elective primary cesarean delivery. *The New England Journal of Medicine, 348,* 946–950.

Minto, C. L., Liao, L. M., Woodhouse, C. R. J., Ransley, P. G., & Creighton, S. M. (2003). The effect of clitoral surgery on sexual outcome in individuals who have intersex conditions with ambiguous genitalia: A cross-sectional study. *Lancet, 361,* 1252–1257.

Misovich, S. J., Fisher, J. D., & Fisher, W. A. (1997). Close relationships and elevated HIV risk behavior: Evidence and possible underlying psychological processes. *Review of General Psychology, 1,* 72–107.

Mitchell, K. J., Jones, L. M., Finkelhor, D., & Wolak, J. (2013). Understanding the decline in unwanted online sexual solicitations for U.S. youth 2000-2-1-: Findings from three Youth Internet Safety Surveys. *Child Abuse & Neglect, 37,* 1225–1236.

Mitchell, K. J., Wolak, J., & Finkelhor, D. (2007). Trends in youth reports of sexual solicitations, harassment and unwanted exposure to pornography on the Internet. *Journal of Adolescent Health, 40,* 116–126.

Mitchell, K., Roberts, A., Gilber, M., Homma, Y., Warf, C., Daly, L. K., & Saewyc, E. M. (2015). Improving the accuracy of chlamydia trachomatis incidence rate estimates among adolescents in Canada. *Canadian Journal of Human Sexuality, 24,* 12–18.

Mitchell, M. E., Bartholomew, K., & Cobb, R. J. (2014). Need fulfillment in polyamorous relationships. *Journal of Sex Research, 51,* 329–339.

Mkumbo, K. A. K., & Ingham, R. (2010). What Tanzanian parents want (and do not want) covered in school-based sex and relationships education. *Sex Education, 10,* 67–78.

Moir, S., Chun, T. W., & Fauci, A. S. (2008). Immunology and pathogenesis of human immunodeficiency virus infection. In K. Holmes et al. (Eds.), *Sexually transmitted diseases* (4th ed., pp. 341–358). New York: McGraw-Hill.

Molitch, M. E. (1995). Neuroendocrinology. In P. Felig et al. (Eds.), *Endocrinology and metabolism.* New York: McGraw-Hill.

Money, J. (1986). *Lovemaps: Clinical concepts of sexual/erotic health and pathology, paraphilia, and gender transposition in childhood, adolescence, and maturity.* New York: Irvington Publishers.

Money, J. (1987). Sin, sickness, or status: Homosexual gender identity and psychoneuroendocrinology. *American Psychologist, 42,* 384–399.

Money, J., & Ehrhardt, A. (1972). *Man and woman, boy and girl.* Baltimore, MD: Johns Hopkins. Reissued in a facsimile edition by Jason Aronson, Northvale, NJ, 1996.

Monro, S. (2000). Theorizing transgender diversity: Towards a social model of health. *Sexual and Relationship Therapy, 15,* 33–45.

Montazeri, A. (2008). Health-related quality of life in breast cancer patients: A bibliographic review of the literature from 1974 to 2007. *Journal of Experimental & Clinical Cancer Research, 27.*

Montesi, J. L., Conner, B. T., Gordon, E. A., Fauber, R. L., Kim, K. H., & Heimberg, R. G. (2013). On the relationship among social anxiety, intimacy, sexual communication, and sexual satisfaction in young couples. *Archives of Sexual Behavior, 42,* 81–91.

Montesi, J. L., Fauber, R. L., Gordon, E. A., & Heimberg, R. G. (2010). The specific importance of communicating about sex to couples' sexual and overall relationship satisfaction. *Journal of Social and Personal Relationships, 28,* 591–609

Montgomery-Graham, S., Kohut, T., Fisher, W., & Campbell, L. (2015). How the popular media rushes to judgment about pornography and relationships while research lags behind. *Canadian Journal of Human Sexuality.* doi:10.3138/cjhs.243-A4.

Montorsi, F., & Althof, S. (2004). Partner responses to sildenafil citrate (Viagra) treatment of erectile dysfunction. *Urology, 63,* 762–767.

Montorsi, F., Perani, D., Anchisi, D., Salonia, A., Scifo, P., Rigiroli, P., ... Fazio, F. (2003a). Apomorphine-induced brain modulation during sexual stimulation: A new look at central phenomena related to erectile dysfunction. *International Journal of Impotence Research, 15,* 203–209.

Montorsi, F., Perani, D., Anchisi, D., Salonia, A., Scifo, P., Rigiroli, P., ... Fazio, F. (2003b). Brain activation patterns during video sexual stimulation following the administration of apomorphine. *European Urology, 43,* 405–411.

Montorsi, F., Verheyden, B., Meuleman, E., Junemann, K. P., Moncada, I., Valiquette, L., ... Watkins, V. S. (2004). Long-term safety and tolerability of tadalafil in the treatment of erectile dysfunction. *European Urology, 45,* 339–345.

Montoya, R. M. (2008). I'm hot, so I'd say you're not: The influence of objective physical attractiveness on mate selection. *Personality and Social Psychology Bulletin, 34,* 1315–1331.

Montoya, R. M., Horton, R., & Kirchner, J. (2008). Is actual similarity necessary for attraction? A meta-analysis of actual and perceived similarity. *Journal of Social and Personal Relationships, 25,* 889–922.

Moody, C., & Simth, N. G. (2013). Suicide protective factors among trans adults. *Archives of Sexual Behavior, 42,* 739–752.

Moore, A. J. (1987). Teenage sexuality and public morality. *Christian Century, 104,* 747–750.

Moore, F. R., Cassidy, C., Smith, M. J. L., & Perrett, D. I. (2006). The effects of female control of resources on sex-differentiated mate preferences. *Evolution and Human Behavior, 27,* 193–205.

Moore, T. (1994, January 3). Porn shop enjoys brisk business yearround. *The Capital Times,* pp. 5A–6A.

Moores, A., Phillips, J. C., O'Byrne, P., & MacPherson, P. (2015). Anal cancer screening knowledge, attitudes, and experiences among men who have sex with men in Ottawa, Ontario. *Canadian Journal of Human Sexuality, 24,* 228–236.

Moracco, K. E., Runyan, C. W., Bowling, J. M., & Earp, J. A. L. (2007). Women's experiences with violence: A national study. *Women's Health Issues, 17,* 3–12.

Morales, A., & Heaton, J. (2001). Hormonal erectile dysfunction: Evaluation and management. *Urologic Clinics of North America, 28,* 279.

Morales, A., Gingell, C., Collins, M., Wicker, P. A., & Osterloh, I. H. (1998). Clinical safety of oral sildenafil (Viagra) in the treatment of erectile dysfunction. *International Journal of Impotence Research, 10,* 69–74.

Morales, A., Heaton, J., & Carson, C. (2000). Andropause: A misnomer for a true clinical entity. *Journal of Urology, 163,* 705–712.

More women going from jobless to topless. (2009). Associated Press. Retrieved from http://www.today.com/id/29824663/

Moreau, C., Boucher, S., Hébert, M., & Lemelin, J. (2015). Capturing sexual violence experiences among battered women using the Revised Sexual Experiences Survey and the Revised Conflict Tactics Scales. *Archives of Sexual Behavior, 44,* 223–231.

Morell, V. (1998). A new look at monogamy. *Science, 281,* 1982–1983.

Moreno, M. A., Parks, M. R., Zimmerman, F. J., Brito, T. E., & Christakis, D. A. (2009). Display of health risk behaviors on MySpace by adolescents: Prevalence and associations. *Archives of Pediatric and Adolescent Medicine, 163,* 27–34.

Morgan, E. M. (2011). Associations between young adults' use of sexually explicit materials and their sexual preferences, behaviors, and satisfaction. *Journal of Sex Research, 48,* 520–530.

Morgan, R. (1980). Theory and practice: Pornography and rape. In L. Lederer (Ed.), *Take back the night: Women on pornography.* New York: Morrow.

Morison, L., Scherf, C., Ekpo, G., Paine, K., West, B., Coleman, R., & Walraven, G. (2001). The long-term reproductive health consequences of female genital cutting in rural Gambia: A community-based survey. *Tropical Medicine & International Health, 6,* 643–653.

Morrison, M. A., & Morrison, T. G. (2002). Development and validation of a scale measuring modern prejudice toward gay men and lesbians. *Journal of Homosexuality, 43,* 15–37.

Morrison, M. A., Jewell, L., McCutcheon, J., & Cochrane, D. B. (2014). In the face of anti-LGBQ behaviour: Saskatchewan high school students' perceptions of school climate and consequential impact. *Canadian Journal of Education, 37,* 1–29.

Morrison, M. A., Morrison, T. G., & Franklin, R. (2009). Modern and old-fashioned homonegativity among samples of Canadian and American university students. *Journal of Cross-Cultural Psychology, 40,* 523–542.

Morrison, T. G. (2004). "He was treating me like trash, and I was loving it." Perspectives on gay male pornography. *Journal of Homosexuality, 47,* 167–183.

Morrison, T. G., & Tallack, D. (2005). Lesbian and bisexual women's interpretations of lesbian and ersatz lesbian pornography. *Sexuality & Culture, 9,* 3–30.

Morrison, T. G., Ellis, S. R., Morrison, M. A., Bearden, A., & Harriman, R. L. (2006).

Exposure to sexually explicit material and variations in body esteem, genital attitudes, and sexual esteem among a sample of Canadian men. *Journal of Men's Studies, 14,* 209–222.

Morrison, T. G., Ryan, T. A., Fox, L., McDermott, D. T., & Morrison, M. A. (2008). Canadian university students' perception of the practices that constitute "normal" sexuality for men and women. *Canadian Journal of Human Sexuality, 17,* 161–171.

Morris-Rush, J., & Bernstein, P. (2002). Postpartum depression. *Medscape Women's Health, 7.*

Morry, M. M. (2007). The attraction-similarity hypothesis among crosssex friends: Relationship satisfaction, perceived similarities, and selfserving perceptions. *Journal of Social and Personal Relationships, 24,* 117–138.

Moser, C. (1998). S/M (Sadomasochistic) interactions in semi-public settings. *Journal of Homosexuality, 36,* 19–29.

Moser, C. (2001). Paraphilia: Another confused sexological concept. In P. J. Kleinpatz (Ed.), *New directions in sex therapy: Innovations and alternatives* (pp. 91–108), Philadelphia: W. B. Saunders Company.

Moser, C., & Kleinpatz, P. J. (2002). Transvestic fetishism: Psychopathology or iatrogenic artifact? *New Jersey Psychologist, 52,* 16–17.

Moser, C., & Kleinpatz, P. J. (2005). DSM-IV-TR and the paraphilias: An argument for removal. *Journal of Psychology and Human Sexuality, 17,* 91–109.

Moser, C., Kleinplatz, P. J., & Zuccarini, D. (2004). Situating unusual child and adolescent sexual behavior in context. *Child & Adolescent Psychiatric Clinics of North America, 13,* 569–589.

Moses, S., Bradley, J., Nagelkerke, N., Roland, A., Ndinya-Achola, J., & Plummer, F. (1990). Geographical patterns of male circumcision practices in Africa: Association with HIV seroprevalence. *International Journal of Epidemiology, 19,* 693–697.

Mosher, D., & MacIan, P. (1994). College men and women respond to X-rated videos intended for male or female audiences: Gender and sexual scripts. *Journal of Sex Research, 31,* 99–113.

Mosher, W. D., Chandra, A., & Jones, J. (2005). Sexual behavior and selected health measures: Men and women 15–44 years of age in the U.S., 2002. *Advance Data, 362,* 1–55.

Moskovtsev, S. I., Dacanay, D., Baratz, A., Sharma, P., Glass, K., Librach, C. L., & CReATe Fertility Center (2013). *Significant increase in utilization of donor sperm by Lesbian couples after the legalization of same sex marriages in Ontario, Canada.* Presented at the International Federation of Fertility Societies and the American Society for Reproduction Medicine annual conference.

Moss, B. F., & Schwebel, A. I. (1993). Marriage and romantic relationships: Defining

intimacy in romantic relationships. *Family Relations, 42,* 31–37.

Moulden, H. M., Firestone, P., Kingston, D., & Bradford, J. (2009). Recidivism in pedophiles: An investigation using different diagnostic methods. *Journal of Forensic Psychiatry & Psychology, 20,* 680–701.

Mouritsen, A., Aksglaede, L., Sörensen, K., Sloth Mogensen, S., Leffers, H., & Juul, A. (2010). Hypothesis: Exposure to endocrine-disrupting chemicals may interfere with timing of puberty. *International Journal of Andrology, 33,* 346–359.

Muehlenhard, C. L., Humphreys, T. P., Jozkowski, K. N., & Peterson, Z. D. (2016). The complexities of sexual consent among college students: A conceptual and empirical review. *Journal of Sex Research, 53,* 457–487.

Muehlenhard, C., & Skippee, S. (2010). Men's and women's reports of pretending orgasm. *Journal of Sex Research, 47,* 552–567.

Mueller, K., Rehman, U. S., Fallis, E. E., & Goodnight, J. A. (2016). An interpersonal investigation of sexual self-schemas. *Archives of Sexual Behavior, 45,* 281–290.

Muise, A., & Impett, E. A. (2015). Good, giving, and game: The relationship benefits of communal sexual motivation. *Social Psychology and Personality Science, 6,* 164–172.

Muise, A., Impett, E. A., Kogan, A., & Desmarais, S. (2012). Keeping the spark alive: Being motivated to meet a partner's sexual needs sustains sexual desire in long-term romantic relationships. *Social Psychology and Personality Science, 4,* 267–273.

Muller, J., Mittleman, M., Maclure, M., Sherwood, J., & Tofler, G. (1996). Triggering myocardial infarction by sexual activity. *Journal of the American Medical Association, 275,* 1405–1409.

Munk-Olsen, T., Laursen, T. M., Pedersen, C. B., Lidegaard, Ø., & Mortensen, P. B. (2011). Induced first trimester abortion and risk of mental disorder. *New England Journal of Medicine, 364,* 332–339.

Murnen, S. K., & Stockton, M. (1997). Gender and self-reported sexual arousal in response to sexual stimuli: A meta-analytic review. *Sex Roles, 37,* 135–154.

Murnen, S. K., Wright, C., & Kaluzny, G. (2002). If "boys will be boys," then girls will be victims? A meta-analytic review of the research that relates masculine ideology to sexual aggression. *Sex Roles, 46,* 359–376.

Murphy, L., Federoff, J. P., & Martineau, M. (2009). Canada's sex offender registries: Background, implementation, and social policy considerations. *Canadian Journal of Human Sexuality, 18,* 61–72.

Murray, S. L., & Holmes, J. G. (1997). A leap of faith? Positive illusions in romantic relationships. *Personality and Social Psychology Bulletin, 23,* 586–604.

Murray, S. L., Holmes, J. G., & Griffin, D. W. (1996). The benefits of positive illusions: Idealization and the construction of satisfaction in close relationships. *Journal of*

Personality and Social Psychology, 70(1), 79–98.

Murray, S. O. (2000). *Homosexualities*. Chicago: University of Chicago Press.

Mustanski, B. S., Dupree, M. G., Nievergelt, C. M., Bocklandt, S., Schork, N. J., & Hamer, D. H. (2005). A genomewide scan of male sexual orientation. *Human Genetics, 116*, 272–278.

Mustanski, B. S., Garofalo, R., & Emerson, E. M. (2010). Mental health disorders, psychological distress, and suicidality in a diverse sample of lesbian, gay, bisexual, and transgender youths. *American Journal of Public Health, 100*, 2426–2432.

Myers, B. J. (1984). Mother-infant bonding: The status of this critical period hypothesis. *Developmental Review, 4*, 240–274.

Myers, K., & Raymond, L. (2010). Elementary school girls and heteronormativity: The girl project. *Gender & Society, 24*, 167–188.

Myers, P. N., & Biocca, F. A. (1992). The elastic body image: The effect of television advertising and programming on body image distortions in young women. *Journal of Communication, 42*, 108–133.

Myers, T., Bullock, S. L., Calzavara, L. M., Cockerill, R., Marshall, V. W., & George-Mandoka, C. (1999). Culture and sexual practices in response to HIV among Aboriginal people living on reserve in Ontario. *Culture, Health & Sexuality, 1*(1), 19–37.

Myers, T., Calzavara, L. M., Bullock, S., Cockerill, R., & Marshall, V. (1994). The Ontario First Nations AIDS and Healthy Lifestyle Survey: A model for community-based research in diverse reserve communities. *Arctic Medical Research, 53*(Suppl. 2), 726–731.

Myers, T., Godin, G., Calzavara, L., Lambert, J., & Locker, D. (1993). *The Canadian survey of gay and bisexual men and HIV infection: Men's survey*. Ottawa: Canadian Aids Society.

Nack, A. (2008). *Damaged goods: Women living with incurable STDs*. Philadelphia: Temple University Press.

Najman, J. M., Dunne, M. P., Purdie, D. M., Boyle, F. M., & Coxeter, P. D. (2005). Sexual abuse in childhood and sexual dysfunction in adulthood: An Australian population-based study. *Archives of Sexual Behavior, 34*, 517–526.

Narod, S. A., Douglas, G. R., Nestmann, E. R., & Blakey, D. H. (1988). Human mutagens: Evidence from paternal exposure? *Environmental and Molecular Mutagenesis, 11*, 401–415.

National Campaign to Prevent Teen and Unplanned Pregnancy. (2009). *Sex and tech: Results from a survey of teens and young adults*. http://www.thenationalcampaign.org/sextech/PDF/SexTech_Summary.pdf

Naz, R. K. (2011). Antisperm contraceptive vaccines: Where we are and where we are going. *American Journal of Reproductive Immunology, 66*, 5–12.

Ndovi, T. T., Parsons, T., Choi, L., Caffo, B., Rohde, C., & Hendrix, C. W. (2007). A new method to estimate quantitatively seminal vesicle and prostate gland contributions to ejaculate. *British Journal of Clinical Pharmacology, 63*, 404–420.

Negash, S., Cui, M., Fincham, F. D., & Pasley, K. (2014). Extradyadic involvement and relationship dissolution in heterosexual women university students. *Archives of Sexual Behavior, 43*, 531–539.

Nelson, A. L., & Purdon, C. (2011). Non-erotic thoughts, attentional focus, and sexual problems in a community sample. *Archives of Sexual Behavior, 40*, 395–406.

Nelson, J. B. (1978). *Embodiment: An approach to sexuality and Christian theology*. Minneapolis: Augsburg.

Nelson, J. B. (1992). *Body theology*. Louisville, KY: Westminster/John Knox Press.

Nemeth, M. (1995, June 26). Nobody has the right to play God. *Maclean's*.

Neville, V. A., & Heppner, M. S. (1999). Contextualizing rape: Reviewing sequelae and proposing a culturally inclusive ecological model of sexual assault recovery. *Applied and Preventive Psychology, 8*, 41–62.

Newhouse, D. (1998). Magic & joy: Traditional aboriginal views of human sexuality. *Canadian Journal of Sexuality, 7*, 183–187.

Ngun, T. C., Ghahramani, N., Sanchez, F., Bocklandt, S., & Vilain, E. (2011). The genetics of sex differences in brain and behavior. *Frontiers in Neuroendocrinology, 32*, 227–246.

Nichols, S., & Byers, E. S. (2016). Sexual well-being and relationships in adults with Autism Spectrum Disorder. In S. D. Wright (Ed.), *Autism spectrum disorder in mid and later life* (pp. 257–271). London and Philadelphia: Jessica Kingsley Publishers.

Nicol, M. R., Emerson, C. W., Prince, H. M. A., Nelson, J. A. E., Fedoriw, Y., Sykes, C., . . . & Kashuba, A. D. M. (2015). Models for predicting effective HIV chemoprevention in women. *Journal of Acquired Immune Deficiency Syndromes, 68*, 369–376.

Ninomiya, M. M. (2010). Sexual health education in Newfoundland and Labrador schools: Junior high school teachers' experiences, coverage of topics, comfort levels and views about professional practice. *Canadian Journal of Human Sexuality, 19*, 15–26.

Noll, J., Trickett, P., & Putnam, F. (2003). A prospective investigation of the impact of childhood sexual abuse on the development of sexuality. *Journal of Consulting and Clinical Psychology, 71*, 575–586.

Norris, S. (2006). Reproductive technologies: Surrogacy, and egg and sperm donation (Report PRB 00–35E). Library of Parliament. Retrieved from http://www.parl.gc.ca/Content/LOP/ResearchPublications/prb0035-e.htm

Nosek, B. A., Banaji, M. R., & Greenwald, A. G. (2002). Math = male, me = female, therefore math me. *Journal of Personality and Social Psychology, 83*, 44–59.

Nosko, A., Wood, E., & Desmarais, S. (2007). Unsolicited online sexual material: What affects our attitudes and likelihood to search for more? *Canadian Journal of Human Sexuality, 16*, 1–10.

Noss, J. B. (1963). *Man's religions* (3rd ed.). New York: Macmillan.

Nova Scotia Department of Community Services. (1991). *Mothers and children: One decade later*. Halifax, NS: Author.

Novembre, J., Galvani, A. P., & Slatkin, M. (2005). The geographic spread of the CCR5 Delta 32 HIV-resistance allele. *PLoS Biology, 3*, e339.

O'Byrne, P., & Dias, R. (2008). Urine drop-off testing: A self-directed method for STI screening and prevention. *Canadian Journal of Human Sexuality, 17*, 53–59.

O'Connell, H. E., & DeLancey, J. (2005). Clitoral anatomy in nulliparous, healthy, premenopausal volunteers using unenhanced magnetic resonance imaging. *Journal of Urology, 173*, 2060–2063.

O'Connor, A. (1987). Female sex offenders. *British Journal of Psychiatry, 150*, 615–620.

O'Connor, M. J., Sigman, M., & Kasari, C. (1993). Interactional model for the association among maternal alcohol use, mother-infant interaction, and infant cognitive development. *Infant Behavior and Development, 16*, 177–192.

O'Hara, M. W., & Swain, A. M. (1996). Rates and risk of postpartum depression: A meta-analysis. *International Review of Psychiatry, 8*, 37–54.

O'Neill, S., & Blackmer, J. (2015). *Assisted reproduction in Canada: An overview of ethical and legal issues and recommendations for the development of national standards*. Ottawa: Canadian Medical Association.

O'Shea, P. A. (1995). Congenital defects and their causes. In D. R. Constan, R. V. Haning, Jr., & D. B. Singer (Eds.), *Human reproduction: Growth and development*. Boston: Little, Brown.

O'Sullivan, L. F. (2011, April). *Tweeting, texting, teens & chat: The Internet and sex in the lives of youth*. Ideas that matter, UNB Fredericton, New Brunswick.

O'Sullivan, L. F., & Byers, E. S. (1992). College students' incorporation of initiator and restrictor role in sexual dating interactions. *Journal of Sex Research, 29*, 435–446.

O'Sullivan, L. F., & Byers, E. S. (1996). Gender differences in responses to discrepancies in desired level of sexual intimacy. *Journal of Psychology & Human Sexuality, 8*(1 & 2), 49–67.

O'Sullivan, L. F., & Majerovich, J. (2008). Difficulties with sexual functioning in a sample of male and female late adolescent and young adult university students. *Canadian Journal of Human Sexuality, 17*, 109–121.

O'Sullivan, L. F., & Meyer-Bahlburg, H. (2003). African-American and Latina inner-city girls' reports of romantic and sexual development. *Journal of Social and Personal Relationships, 20*, 221–238.

O'Sullivan, L. F., & Ronis, S. T. (2013). Virtual cheating hearts: Extradyadic and poaching interactions among adolescents with links to online sexual activities. *Canadian Journal of Behavioural Science, 45*, 175–184.

O'Sullivan, L. F., Brotto, L. A., Byers, E. S., Majerovich, J. A., & Wuest, J. A. (2014). Prevalence and characteristics of sexual functioning among sexually experienced middle to late adolescents. *Journal of Sexual Medicine, 11*, 630–641.

O'Sullivan, L. F., Byers, E. S., & Finkelman, L. (1998). A comparison of male and female college students' experiences of sexual coercion. *Psychology of Women Quarterly, 22*, 177–195.

O'Sullivan, L. F., Byers, E. S., Brotto, L. A., Majerovich, J. A., & Fletcher, J. (2016). A longitudinal study of problems in sexual functioning and related sexual distress among middle to late adolescents. *Journal of Adolescent Health, 59*, 318–324.

Ochs, E. P., Mah, K., & Binik, Y. (2002). Obtaining data about human sexual functioning from the Internet. In A. Cooper (Ed.), *Sex and the Internet: A guidebook for clinicians* (pp. 245–262). New York: Routledge.

Ochs, E., & Binik, Y. M. (1999). The use of couple data to determine the reliability of self-reported sexual behaviour. *Journal of Sex Research, 36*, 374–384.

Offman, A., & Kleinplatz, P. J. (2004). Does PMDD belong in the DSM? Challenging the medicalization of women's bodies. *Canadian Journal of Human Sexuality, 13*, 17–27.

Offman, A., & Matheson, K. (2004). The sexual self-perceptions of young women experiencing abuse in dating relationships. *Sex Roles, 51*, 551–560.

Offman, A., & Matheson, K. (2005). Sexual compatibility and sexual functioning in intimate relationships. *Canadian Journal of Human Sexuality, 14*, 21–29.

Ogletree, S. M., & Ginsburg, H. J. (2000). Kept under the hood: Neglect of the clitoris in common vernacular. *Sex Roles, 43*, 917–926.

Ogolsky, B. G., & Bowers, J. R. (2012). A meta-analytic review of relationship maintenance and its correlates. *Journal of Social and Personal Relationships, 30*, 343–367.

Ogunjimi, L. O. (2006). Attitudes of students and parents towards the teaching of sex education in secondary schools in Cross Rivers States. *Education Research and Review, 1*, 347–349.

Ojeda, S. R. & Lomniczi, A. (2014). Puberty in 2013: Unravelling the mystery of puberty. *Nature Reviews Endocrinology, 10*, 67–69.

Okami, P., Olmstead, R., & Abramson, P. (1997). Sexual experiments in early childhood: 18-year longitudinal data from the UCLA Family Lifestyles Project. *Journal of Sex Research, 34*, 339–347.

Okoronkwo, C., Sieswerda, L. E., Cooper, R., Binette, D., & Todd, M. (2012). Parental consent to HPV vaccination for their daughters: The effects of knowledge and attitudes. *Canadian Journal of Human Sexuality, 21*, 117–126.

Olson, J., Schrager, S. M., Belzer, M., Simons, L. K., & Clark, L. F. (2015). Baseline physiologic and psychosocial characteristics of transgender youth seeking care for gender dysphoria. *Journal of Adolescent Health, 57*, 374–380.

Olsson, S., & Möller, A. R. (2003). On the incidence and sex ratio of transsexualism in Sweden, 1972–2002. *Archives of Sexual Behavior, 32*(4), 381–386.

Olyan, S. M. (1994). And with a male you shall not lie the lying down of a woman: On the meaning and significance of Leviticus 18:22 and 20:13. *Journal of the History of Sexuality, 5*, 179–206.

Omarzu, J., Miller, A. N., Schultz, C., & Timmerman, A. (2012). Motivations and emotional consequences related to engaging in extramarital relationships. *International Journal of Sexual Health, 24*, 154–162.

Ontario Physical and Health Education Association (OPHEA). (2012). Time to take action for Ontario's kids. Toronto: OPHEA. Retrieved from https://www.ophea.net/sites/default/files/file_attach/HPEA_AdvocacyPieceFINAL_02OC12.pdf

Oosterhuis, H. (2000). *Step children of nature: Krafft-Ebing, psychiatry, and the making of sexual identity.* Chicago: University of Chicago Press.

Options for Sexual Health. (2004). *An assessment of the effectiveness of sexual health education in BC schools.* Retrieved from http://www.optionsforsexualhealth.org

Orchard, T., Farr, S., Macphail, S., Wender, C., & Wilson, C. (2014). Expanding the scope of inquiry: Exploring accounts of childhood and family life among sex workers in London, Ontario. *Canadian Journal of Human Sexuality, 23*, 9–18.

Ormond, G., Nieuwenhuijsen, M. J., Nelson, P., Toledano, M. B., Iszatt, N., Geneletti, S., & Elliott, P. (2008). Endocrine disruptors in the workplace, hair spray, folate supplementation, and risk of hypospadias: Case-control study. *Environmental Health Perspectives, 117*, 303–307.

Ornstein, M. (1989). *AIDS in Canada: Knowledge, behaviour, and attitudes of adults.* Toronto: Institute for Social Research, York University.

Osman, S. L. (2003). Predicting men's rape perceptions based on the belief that "no" really means "yes." *Journal of Applied Social Psychology, 33*, 683–692.

Ott, M. A., Millstein, S. G., Ofner, S., & Halpern-Felsher, B. L. (2006). Greater expectations: Adolescents' positive motivations for sex. *Perspectives on Sexual and Reproductive Health, 38*(2), 84–89.

Owen, J., & Fincham, F. D. (2011a). Effects of gender and psychosocial factors on "friends with benefits" relationships among young adults. *Archives of Sexual Behavior, 40*, 311–320.

Owen, J., & Fincham, F. D. (2011b). Young adults' emotional reactions after hooking up encounters. *Archives of Sexual Behavior, 40*, 321–330.

Pachankis, J. E. (2007). The psychological implications of concealing a stigma: A cognitive-affective-behavioral model. *Psychological Bulletin, 133*, 328–345.

Padilla, M. (2007). *Caribbean pleasure industry: Tourism, sexuality, and AIDS in the Dominican Republic.* Chicago: University of Chicago Press.

Padma-Nathan, H., McMurray, J. G., Pullman, W. E., Whitaker, J. S., Saoud, J. B., Ferguson, K. M., & Rosen, R. C. (2001). On-demand IC351 (Cialis trademark) enhances erectile function in patients with erectile dysfunction. *International Journal of Impotence Research, 13*, 2–9.

Page, S. T., Amory, J. K., Anawalt, B. D., Irwig, M. S., Brockenbrough, A. T., Matsumoto, A. M., & Bremner, W. J. (2006). Testosterone gel combined with depomedroxyprogesterone acetate is an effective male hormonal contraceptive regimen and is not enhanced by the addition of a GnRH antagonist. *Journal of Clinical Endocrinology and Metabolism, 91*, 4374–4380.

Paik, A. (2010). The contexts of sexual involvement and concurrent sexual partnerships. *Perspectives on Sexual and Reproductive Health, 42*, 33–42.

Pakenham, K. I., Dadds, M. R., & Terry, D. J. (1994). Relationships between adjustment to HIV and both social support and coping. *Journal of Consulting and Clinical Psychology, 62*, 1194–1203.

Pakzad, K., Boucher, B. A., Kreiger, N., & Cotterchio, M. (2007). The use of herbal and other non-vitamin, non-mineral supplements among pre- and post-menopausal women in Ontario. *Canadian Journal of Public Health, 98*, 383–388.

Palace, E. M. (1995a). A cognitive-physiological process model of sexual arousal and response. *Clinical Psychology: Science and Practice, 2*, 370–384.

Palace, E. M. (1995b). Modification of dysfunctional patterns of sexual response through autonomic arousal and false physiological feedback. *Journal of Consulting and Clinical Psychology, 63*, 604–615.

Paliwal, P., Gelfand, A. E., Abraham, L., Barlow, W., & Elmore, J. G. (2006). Examining accuracy of screening mammography using an event order model. *Stat Med, 25*, 267–283.

Panay, N., Hamoda, H., Arya, R., & Savvas, M. (2013). The 2013 British Menopause Society and Women's Health Concern recommendations on hormone replacement therapy. *Menopause International, 19*, 59–68.

Panjari, M., Bell, R. J., Davis, S. R. (2011). Sexual function after breast cancer. *Journal of Sexual Medicine, 8*, 294–302.

Paras, M. L., Murad, M. H., Chen, L. P., Goranson, E. N., Sattler, A. L., Colbenson, K. M., . . . Zirakzadeh, A. (2009). Sexual abuse and lifetime diagnosis of somatic disorders: A systematic review and meta-analysis. *Journal of the American Medical Association, 302*, 550–561.

Parker, G. (1983). The legal regulation of sexual activity and the protection of females. *Osgoode Hall Law Journal, 21*, 187–244.

Parker, R., di Mauro, D., Filiano, B., Garcia, J., Munoz-Laboy, M., & Sember, R. (2004). Global transformations and intimate relations in the 21st century: Social science research on sexuality and the emergence of Sexual Health and Sexual Rights frameworks. *Annual Review of Sex Research, 15,* 362–398.

Parrinder, G. (1980). *Sex in the world's religions.* New York: Oxford University Press.

Parrot, A., & Cummings, N. (2006). *Forsaken females: The global brutalization of women.* New York: Rowman & Littlefield.

Parrott, Y., & Esmail, S. (2010). Burn survivors' perceptions regarding relevant sexual education strategies. *Health Education, 110,* 84–97.

Parsons, J. T., Kelly, B. C., Bimbi, D. S., DiMaria, L., Wainberg, M. L., & Morgenstern, J. (2008). Explanations for the origins of sexual compulsivity among gay and bisexual men. *Archives of Sexual Behavior, 37,* 817–826.

Pasqualotto, F. F., Umezu, F. M., Salvador, M., Borges, E., Jr., Sobreiro, B. P., & Pasqualotto, E. B. (2008). Effect of cigarette smoking on antioxidant levels and presence of leukocytospermia in infertile men: A prospective study. *Fertility and Sterility, 90,* 278–283.

Patrick, M. E., & Lee, C. M. (2010). Sexual motivations and engagement in sexual behaviour during the transition to college. *Archives of Sexual Behavior, 39,* 674–681.

Patterson, C. J. (2000). Family relationships of lesbians and gay men. *Journal of Marriage and the Family, 62,* 1052–1069.

Patterson, C. J. (2006). Children of lesbian and gay parents. *Current Directions in Psychological Science, 15,* 241–244.

Patterson, C. J. (2009). Children of lesbian and gay parents: Psychology, law, and policy. *American Psychologist, 64,* 727–736.

Paul, B., & Linz, D. (2008). The effects of exposure to virtual child pornography on viewer cognitions and attitudes toward deviant sexual behavior. *Communication Research, 35,* 3–38.

Paul, C., Teng, S., & Saunders, P. T. K. (2008). A single, mild, transient scrotal heat stress causes DNA damage, subfertility and impairs formation of blastocysts in mice. *Reproduction, 136,* 73–84.

Payne, K. A., & Binik, Y. M. (2006). Reviving the labial thermistor clip. *Archives of Sexual Behavior, 35,* 111–113.

Payne, K. A., Binik, Y. M., Amsel, R., & Khalifé, S. (2005). When sex hurts, anxiety and fear orient attention towards pain. *European Journal of Pain, 9,* 427–436.

Payne, K. A., Reissing, E. D., Lahaie, M., Binik, Y. M., Amsel, R., & Khalifé, S. (2005). What is sexual pain? A critique of DSM's classification of dyspareunia and vaginismus. *Journal of Psychology & Human Sexuality, 17,* 141–154.

Payne, K. A., Thaler, L., Kukkonen, T., Carrier S., & Binik, Y. (2007). Sensation and sexual arousal in circumcised and uncircumcised men. *Journal of Sexual Medicine, 4,* 667–674.

Pedersen, W., Miller, L. C., Putcha-Bhagavatula, A., & Yang, Y. (2002). Evolved sex differences in the number of partners desired? The long and short of it. *Psychological Science, 13,* 157–159.

Péloquin, K., Bigras, N., Brassard, A., & Godbout, N. (2014). Perceiving that one's partner is supportive moderates the associations among attachment insecurity and psychosexual variables. *Canadian Journal of Human Sexuality, 23,* 178–188.

Péloquin, K., Brassard, A., Lafontaine, M-F., & Shaver, P. R. (2013). Sexuality examined through the lens of attachment theory: Attachment, caregiving, and sexual satisfaction. *Journal of Sex Research.* doi:10.1080/00224499.2012.757281

Pennisi, E. (1996). Homing in on a prostate cancer gene. *Science, 274,* 1301.

Peplau, L. A. (2003). Human sexuality: How do men and women differ? *Current Directions in Psychological Science, 12,* 37–40.

Peplau, L. A., Fingerhut, A., & Beals, K. P. (2004). Sexuality in the relationships of lesbians and gay men. In J. Harvey, A. Wenzel, & S. Sprecher (Eds.), *Handbook of sexuality in close relationships* (pp. 349–369). Mahwah, NJ: Lawrence Erlbaum Associates, Inc.

Peplau, L. A., Garnets, L. D., Spalding, L. R., Conley, T. D., & Veniegas, R. C. (1998). A critique of Bem's "Exotic becomes erotic" theory of sexual orientation. *Psychological Review, 105,* 387–394.

Perel, E. (2006). *Mating in captivity: Unlocking erotic intelligence.* New York: Harper.

Perelman, M. A., & Rowland, D. L. (2006). Retarded ejaculation. *World Journal of Urology.* doi:10.1007/s00345-006-0127-6

Perez, M. A., Skinner, E. C., & Meyerowitz, B. E. (2002). Sexuality and intimacy following radical prostatectomy: Patient and partner perspectives. *Health Psychology, 21,* 288–293.

Perilloux, C., Easton, J. A., & Buss, D. M. (2012). The misperception of sexual interest. *Psychological Science, 23,* 146–151.

Perlman, D., & Fehr, B. (1987). The development of intimate relationships. In D. Perlman & S. Duck (Eds.), *Intimate relationships: Development, dynamics, and deterioration.* Newbury Park, CA: Sage.

Perreault, S., & Brennan, S. (2010). Criminal victimization in Canada, 2009. *Juristat, 30*(2).

Perrott, S. (2012). Reforming policing of sex tourism in the Philippines and the Gambia: Can we avoid confusing messages? In S. C. Taylor, D. J. Torpy, & D. K. Das (Eds.), *Policing global movement: Tourism, migration, human trafficking, and terrorism.* Boca Raton, FL: CRC Press.

Perry, J. D., & Whipple, B. (1981). Pelvic muscle strength of female ejaculators: Evidence in support of a new theory of orgasm. *Journal of Sex Research, 17,* 22–39.

Persson, G. (1980). Sexuality in a 70-year-old urban population. *Journal of Psychosomatic Research, 24,* 335–342.

Petersen, J. L., & Hyde, J. S. (2010). A meta-analytic review of research on gender differences in sexuality, 1993 to 2007. *Psychological Bulletin, 136,* 21–38.

Petkovich, A. (2004). From gonzo porn to mainstream? Porn starlet Sienna. *Spectator.* Retrieved from http://www.spectator.net

Pew Research. (2013, June 4). *The global divide on homosexuality: Greater acceptance in more secular and affluent countries.* Retrieved from http://www.pewglobal.org/2013/06/04/the-global-divide-on-homosexuality/

Pew Research Center. (2010). The decline of marriage and the rise of new families. Pew Research Center Report.

Pfaus, J. (2009). Pathways of sexual desire. *Journal of Sexual Medicine, 6,* 1506–1533.

Pfaus, J. G., Kippin, T. E., & Coria-Avila, G. (2003). What can animal models tell us about human sexual response? *Annual Review of Sex Research, 14,* 1–63.

Pfaus, J. G., Kippin, T. E., Coria-Avila, G. A., Gelez, H., Afonso, V. M., Ismail, N., & Parada, M. (2012). Who, what, where, when (and maybe even why)? How the experience of sexual reward connects sexual desire, preference, and performance. *Archives of Sexual Behavior, 41,* 31–62.

Pfeiffer, E. (1975). Sex and aging. In L. Gross (Ed.), *Sexual issues in marriage.* New York: Spectrum.

Pfeiffer, E., Verwoerdt, A., & Wang, H. S. (1968). Sexual behavior in aged men and women. *Archives of General Psychiatry, 19,* 753–758.

Phillips, P. (2012). Pregnancy test review. Retrieved from http://www.early-pregnancy-tests.com/compare.html

Phoenix, C. H., Goy, R. W., Gerall, A. A., & Young, W. C. (1959). Organizing action of prenatally administered testosterone propionate on the tissues mediating mating behavior in the female guinea pig. *Endocrinology, 65,* 369–382.

Pike, J. J., & Jennings, N. A. (2005). The effects of commercials on children's perceptions of gender appropriate toy use. *Sex Roles, 52,* 83–92.

Pilkington, N. W., & Lydon, J. E. (1997). The relative effect of attitude similarity and attitude dissimilarity and interpersonal attraction: Investigating the moderating roles of prejudice and group membership. *Journal of Personality and Social Psychology Bulletin, 23*(2), 107–122.

Pinheiro, R. C., Lambert, J., Benard, F., Mauffette, F., & Miron, P. (1999). Effectiveness of in vitro fertilization with intracytoplasmic sperm injection for severe male infertility. *Canadian Medical Association Journal, 161,* 1397–1442.

Pinkerton, J., Stovall, D., & Kightlinger, R. (2009). Advances in the treatment of menopausal symptoms. Medscape CME. Retrieved from http://cme.medscape.com/viewarticle/705445

Pithers, W. D. (1993). Treatment of rapists. In G. N. Hall et al. (Eds.), *Sexual aggression* (pp. 167–196). Washington, DC: Taylor & Francis.

Pittenger, W. N. (1970). *Making sexuality human.* Philadelphia: Pilgrim Press.

Pittman, F., III. (1993, May–June). Beyond betrayal: Life after infidelity. *Psychology Today*, 32–38ff.

Pitts, M. K., Smith, A., Grierson, J., O'Brien, M., & Mission, S. (2004). Who pays for sex and why? An analysis of social and motivational factors associated with male clients of sex workers. *Archives of Sexual Behavior, 33*, 353–368.

Planned Parenthood Federation of Canada. (n.d.). *A history of birth control in Canada.*

Plaud, J. J., Gaither, G. A., Hegstadc, H. J., Rowan, L., & Devitt, M. K. (1999). Volunteer bias in human psychophysiological sexual arousal research: To whom do our research results apply? *Journal of Sex Research, 36*, 171–179.

Plaut, S. M. (2008). Sexual and nonsexual boundaries in professional relationships: Principles and teaching guidelines. *Sexual and Relationship Therapy, 23*, 85–94.

Ploem, C., & Byers, E. S. (1997). The effects of two AIDS risk-reduction interventions on heterosexual college women's AIDS-related knowledge and condom use. *Journal of Psychology & Human Sexuality, 9*(1), 1–24.

Plummer, K. (1975). *Sexual stigma: An interactionist account.* London, UK: Routledge & Kegan Paul.

Poasa, K. H., Blanchard, R., & Zucker, K. J. (2004). Birth order in transgendered males from Polynesia: A quantitative study of Samoan *Fa'afa–fine. Journal of Sex & Marital Therapy, 30*, 13–23.

Poh, H. L., Koh, S. S., & He, H.-G. (2014). An integrative review of fathers' experiences during pregnancy and childbirth. *International Nursing Review, 61*, 543–554.

Polisois-Keating, A., & Joyal, C. C. (2013). Functional neuroimaging of sexual arousal: A preliminary meta-analysis comparing pedophilic to non-pedophilic men. *Archives of Sexual Behavior, 42*, 1111–1113.

Pollack, A., Dean, C., & Dreifus, C. (2004, February 13). Medical and ethical issues cloud plans to clone for therapy. *New York Times.*

Pollet, T., & Nettle, D. (2008). Driving a hard bargain: sex ratio and male marriage success in a historical U.S. population. *Biology Letters, 4*, 31–33.

Polzer, J. C., & Knabe, S. M. (2012). From desire to disease: Human papillomavirus (HPV) and the medicalization of nascent female sexuality. *Journal of Sex Research, 49*, 344–352.

Pomeroy, W. B. (1972). *Dr. Kinsey and the Institute for Sex Research.* New York: Harper & Row.

Ponseti, J., & Bosinski, H. (2010). Subliminal sexual stimuli facilitate genital response in women. *Archives of Sexual Behavior, 39*, 1073–1079.

Poole, N. A. (2008). Fetal alcohol spectrum disorder (FASD) Prevention: Canadian

Perspectives (2008). Retrieved from http://www.phac-aspc.gc.ca/fasd-etcaf/cp-pc-eng.php

Poon, M. K-L., Ho, Peter T-T, & Wong, J. P-H. (2001). Developing a comprehensive AIDS prevention outreach program: A needs assessment survey of MSM of East and Southeast Asian descent who visit bars and/or bath houses in Toronto. *Canadian Journal of Human Sexuality, 10*, 25–37.

Poon, M. K-L., Wong, J. P-H., Sutdhibhasilp, N., Ho, P. T-T., & Wong, B. (2011). HIV and STI testing among East and Southeast Asian men who have sex with men in Toronto. *Canadian Journal of Human Sexuality, 20*, 157–166.

Pope John Paul II. (1995, March 25). *Evangelium Vitae:* Encyclical Letter on the Value and Inviolability of Human Life.

Pope Paul VI. (1968, July 30). *Humanae vitae.* (English text in the *New York Times*, p. 20.)

Pope, K. (2001). Sex between therapists and clients. In J. Worell (Ed.), *Encyclopedia of women and gender* (pp. 955–962). New York: Academic Press.

Popenoe, D. (2009). Cohabitation, marriage, and child wellbeing: A cross-national perspective. *Society, 46*(5), 429–436. doi:10.1007/s12115-009-9242-5

Posner, R. (1992). *Sex and reason.* Cambridge, MA: Harvard University Press.

Posner, R. B. (2006). Early menarche: A review of research on trends in timing, racial differences, etiology, and psychosocial consequences. *Sex Roles, 54*, 315–322.

Poteat, V. P., Kimmel, M. S., & Wilchins, R. (2011). The moderating effects of support for violence beliefs on masculine norms, aggression, and homophobic behavior during adolescence. *Journal of Research on Adolescence, 21*, 434–447.

Poteat, V. P., O'Dwyer, L. M., & Mereish, E. H. (2012). Changes in how students use and are called homophobic epithets over time: Patterns predicted by gender, bullying, and victimization status. *Journal of Educational Psychology, 104*, 393–406.

Potts, A., Gavey, N., Grace, V. M., & Vares, T. (2003). The downside of Viagra: Women's experiences and concerns. *Sociology of Health & Illness, 25*, 697–719.

Poulin, C., & Gouliquer, L. (2003). Part-time disabled lesbian passing on roller blades, or PMS, Prozac, and essentializing women's ailments. *Women & Therapy: A Feminist Quarterly, 26*, 95–108.

Powdermaker, H. (1933). *Life in Lesu.* New York: Norton.

Practice Committee of the American Society for Reproductive Medicine. (2008). Obesity and reproduction: An educational bulletin. *Fertility and Sterility, 90* (Suppl. 3), S21–S29.

Prager, K. J. (1997). *The psychology of intimacy.* New York: Guilford Press.

Prather, R. S. (2000). Pigs is pigs. *Science, 289*, 1886–1887.

Pratto, F., & Walker, A. (2004). The bases of gendered power. In A. H. Eagly, A. E. Beall,

& R. J. Sternberg (Eds.), *The psychology of gender* (2nd ed.) (pp. 242–268). New York: Guilford Press.

Prause, N., & Graham, C. A. (2007). Asexuality: Classification and characterization. *Archives of Sexual Behavior, 36.*

Price, E. L., Byers, E. S., & the Dating Violence Research Team. (1999). The Attitudes Towards Dating Violence Scales: Development and initial validation. *Journal of Family Violence, 14*, 351–375.

Price, E. L., Byers, E. S., Sears, H., Whelan, J., & Saint-Pierre, M. (2000, January). Dating violence amongst New Brunswick adolescents: A summary of two studies. *Research Paper Series, #2.* Muriel McQueen Fergusson Centre for Family Violence Research.

Price, J., Allensworth, D., & Hillman, K. (1985). Comparison of sexual fantasies of homosexuals and heterosexuals. *Psychological Reports, 57*, 871–877.

Price, M., & Hyde, J. S. (2009). When two isn't better than one: Predictors of early sexual activity in adolescence using a cumulative risk model. *Journal of Youth and Adolescence, 38*, 1059–1071.

Price-Glynn, K. (2010). *Strip club: Gender, power and sex work.* New York: New York University Press.

Prior, J., Hubbard, P., & Birch, P. (2012). Sex worker victimization, modes of working, and location in New South Wales, Australia: A geography of victimization. *Journal of Sex Research.* doi:10.1080/00224499.2012.668975

Propper, C. R. (2005). The study of endocrine-disrupting compounds: Past approaches and new directions. *Integrative and Comparative Biology, 45*, 194–200.

Proulx, J., Pellerin, B., Paradis, Y., McKibben, A., Aubut, J., & Ouimet, M. (1997). Static and dynamic predictors of recidivism in sexual aggressors. *Sexual Abuse: A Journal of Research and Treatment, 9*, 7–27.

Puar, J. K. (2001). Global circuits: Transnational sexualities and Trinidad. *Signs: Journal of Women in Culture and Society, 26*, 1039–1065.

Public Health Agency of Canada. (2005). *Fetal alcohol spectrum disorder (FASD).* Cat. No H124–4/2004. Retrieved from http://www.phac-aspc.gc.ca/fasd-etcaf/pdf/faq_fasd_e.pdf

Public Health Agency of Canada. (2007a). *Frequently asked questions on emergency contraception.* Retrieved from http://www.phac-aspc.gc.ca/stdmts/ec_cu_e.html

Public Health Agency of Canada. (2007b). *Sexually transmitted infections.* Retrieved from http://www.publichealth.gc.ca/sti

Public Health Agency of Canada. (2008a). *Canadian guidelines for sexual health education.* Ottawa: Author.

Public Health Agency of Canada. (2008b). *Canadian perinatal health report.* Ottawa: Author.

Public Health Agency of Canada. (2009a). *What mothers say: The Canadian maternity experiences survey.* Ottawa: Author.

Public Health Agency of Canada. (2009b). *HIV and AIDS in Canada. Surveillance report to December 31, 2008.* Surveillance and Risk Assessment Division, Centre for Infectious Disease Prevention and Control, Public Health Agency of Canada.

Public Health Agency of Canada. (2010a). Perinatal HIV transmission in Canada. *HIV/AIDS Epi Update.* Catalog HP40–56/8–2010E-PDF.

Public Health Agency of Canada. (2010b). *Hepatitis B-Get the Facts.* Retrieved from http://www.phac-aspc.gc.ca

Public Health Agency of Canada. (2010c). *Questions & answers: Sexual orientation in schools.* Ottawa: Author.

Public Health Agency of Canada. (2011b). *What everyone should know about human papillomavirus (HPV): Questions and answers.* Ottawa:Author.

Public Health Agency of Canada. (2012a). *Canadian hospitals maternity policies and practices survey.* Ottawa: Author.

Public Health Agency of Canada. (2012b). *The healthy pregnancy guide.* Ottawa: Author.

Public Health Agency of Canada. (2012c). Update on human papillomavirus (HPV) vaccines. *Canada Communicable Disease Report, 38,* ACS-1.

Public Health Agency of Canada. (2013). *Canadian guidelines on sexually transmitted infections.* Ottawa: Author. Retrieved from http://www.phac-aspc.gc.ca/std-mts/sti-its/cgsti-ldcits/index-eng.php

Public Health Agency of Canada. (2016). Report of sexually transmitted infections in Canada: 2012. Ottawa: Author. Retrieved from http://www.phac-aspc.gc.ca/sti-its-surv-epi/rep-rap-2012/rep-rap-3-eng.php

Pukall, C. F., Payne, K. A., Binik, Y. M., & Khalifé, S. (2003). Pain measurement in vulvodynia. *Journal of Sex & Marital Therapy, 29*(Suppl.), 111–120.

Pukall, C. F., Reissing, E. D., Binik, Y. M., Khalifé, S., & Abbott, F. V. (2000). New clinical and research perspectives on the sexual pain disorders. *Journal of Sex Education and Therapy, 25,* 36–44.

Purdon, C., & Holdaway, L. (2006). Non-erotic thoughts: Content and relation to sexual functioning and sexual satisfaction. *Journal of Sex Research, 43,* 154–162.

Purdon, C., & Watson, C. (2011). Non-erotic thoughts and sexual functioning. *Archives of Sexual Behavior, 40,* 891–902.

Purnine, D., & Carey, M. (1997). Interpersonal communication and sexual adjustment: The roles of understanding and agreement. *Journal of Consulting & Clinical Psychology, 65,* 1017–1025.

Pyke, S. (1996). Sexual harassment and sexual intimacy in learning environments. *Canadian Psychology, 37*(1), 13–22.

Quadagno, D., et al. (1991). The menstrual cycle: Does it affect athletic performance? *Physician & Sports Medicine, 19,* 121–124.

Quas, J. A., Goodman, G. S., Ghetti, S., Alexander, K. W., Edelstein, R., Redlich, A. D., . . . Jones, D. P. (2005). Childhood sexual assault victims: Long-term outcomes after testifying in criminal court. *Monographs of the Society for Research in Child Development, 70,* 1–127.

Quayle, E. (2008). Online sex offending: Psychopathology and theory. In D. R. Laws, & W. O'Donohue (Eds.), *Sexual deviance: Theory, assessment, and treatment* (2nd ed., pp. 439–458). New York: Guilford.

Quinn, T. C., Wawer, M. J., Sewankambo, N., Serwadda, D., Li, C., Wabwire-Mangen, F., . . . Gray, R. H. (2000). Viral load and heterosexual transmission of human immunodeficiency virus type 1. *New England Journal of Medicine, 342,* 921–929.

Rabe, Thomas. (2007). Contraception—update and trends. *Journal Reproduktionsmed Endokrinol, 4,* 337–357.

Rachman, S. (1966). Sexual fetishism: An experimental analogue. *Psychological Record, 16,* 293–296.

Rako, S., & Friebely, J. (2004). Pheromonal influences on sociosexual behavior in postmenopausal women. *Journal of Sex Research, 41,* 372–380.

Ramchandani, P., Stein, A., Evans, J., O'Connor, T., & the ALSPAC Study Team. (2005). Paternal depression in the postnatal period and child development: A prospective population study. *Lancet, 365,* 2201–2205.

Rametti, G., Carrillo, B., Gómez-Gil, E., Junque, C., Segovia, S., Gomez, A., & Guillamon, A. (2011). White matter microstructure in female to male transsexuals before cross-sex hormonal treatment: A diffusion tensor imaging study. *Journal of Psychiatric Research, 45,* 199–204.

Ramsey, S., Sweeney, C., Fraser, M., & Oades, G. (2009). Pubic hair and sexuality: A review. *Journal of Sexual Medicine, 6,* 2102–2110.

Rancourt, K. M., Rosen, N. O., Bergeron, S., & Nealis, L. J. (2016). Talking about sex when sex is painful: Dyadic sexual communication is associated with women's pain, and couples' sexual and psychological outcomes in provoked vestibulodynia. *Archives of Sexual Behavior, 45,* 1933–1944.

Randall, H. E., & Byers, E. S. (2003). What is sex?: Students' definitions of having sex, sexual partner, and unfaithful sexual behaviour. *Canadian Journal of Human Sexuality, 12,* 87–96.

Ratnam, S., Franco, E., & Ferenczy, A. (2000). Human papillomavirus testing for primary screening of cervical cancer precursors. *Cancer Epidemiology Biomarkers & Prevention, 9,* 945–951.

Rawlins, D. (2003). *Anything Goes.* New York: Harlequin Blaze.

Ray, J. G., Henry, D. A., & Urquia, M. L. (2012). Sex ratios among Canadian liveborn infants of mothers from different countries. *CMAJ, 184,* E492–E496.

Raymond, N. C., Grant, J. E., Kim, S. W., & Coleman, E. (2002). Treatment of compulsive sexual behaviour with naltrexone and serotonin reuptake inhibitors: Two case studies. *International Clinical Psychopharmacology 127,* 201–205.

Reamy, K. J., & White, S. E. (1987). Sexuality in the puerperium: A review. *Archives of Sexual Behavior, 16,* 165–186.

Rederstorff, J. C., Buchanan, N. T., & Settles, I. H. (2007). The moderating roles of race and genderrole attitudes in the relationship between sexual harassment and psychological well-being. *Psychology of Women Quarterly, 31,* 50–61.

Reece, M., Herbenick, D., & Sherwood-Puzzello, C. (2004). Sexual health promotion and adult retail stores. *Journal of Sex Research, 41,* 173–180.

Reece, M., Herbenick, D., Sanders, S. A., Dodge, B., Ghassemi, A., & Fortenberry, J. D. (2009). Prevalence and characteristics of vibrator use by men in the United States. *Journal of Sexual Medicine, 6,* 1867–1874.

Reece, M., Herbenick, D., Schick, B., Sanders, S. A., Dodge, B., & Fortenberry, J. D. (2010a). Background and considerations on the National Survey of Sexual Health and Behavior (NSSHB) from the investigators. *Journal of Sexual Medicine, 7*(SS05), 243–246.

Reece, M., Herbenick, D., Schick, V., Sanders, S. A., Dodge, B., & Fortenberry, J. D. (2010b). Sexual behaviors, relationships, and perceived health among adult men in the United States. *Journal of Sexual Medicine, 7*(SS05), 291–304.

Reefhuis, J., Honein, M. A., Schieve, L. A., Correa, A., Hobbs, C. A., & Rasmussen, S. A. (2009). Assisted reproductive technology and major structural birth defects in the United States. *Human Reproduction, 24,* 360–366.

Reeves, A., & Reading, C. (2013). Constructions of sexuality for First Nation women in Atlantic Canada: Results from a qualitative study. In D. Castaneda (Ed.), *The essential handbook of women's sexuality* (pp. 93–114). Santa Barbara, CA: ABC-CLIO.

Regan, P. (2004). Sex and the attraction process: Lessons from science (and Shakespeare) on lust, love, chastity, and fidelity. In J. H. Harvey, A. Wenzel, & S. Sprecher (Eds.), *The handbook of sexuality in close relationships* (pp. 159–182). Mahwah, NJ: Lawrence Erlbaum.

Regnerus, M. (2007). *Forbidden fruit: Sex and religion in the lives of American teenagers.* New York: Oxford University Press.

Rehman, U., Fallis, E., & Byers, E. S. (2013). Sexual satisfaction in heterosexual women. In D. Cataneda (Ed.), *The essential handbook of women's sexuality* (Vol. 1, pp. 25–45). Santa Barbara, CA: Praeger.

Rehor, J. E. (2015). Sensual, erotic, and sexual behaviors of women from the "Kink" community. *Archives of Sexual Behavior, 44,* 825–836.

Reichert, T. (2002). Sex in advertising research: A review of content, effects, and functions of sexual information in consumer advertising. *Annual Review of Sex Research, 13,* 241–273.

Reichert, T., & Carpenter, C. (2004). An update on sex in magazine advertising: 1983 to

2003. *Journalism and Mass Communication Quarterly, 81,* 823–837.

Reid, R., Garos, S., & Carpenter, B. (2011). Reliability, validity, and psychometric development of the Hypersexual Behavior Inventory in an outpatient sample of men. *Sexual Addiction and Compulsivity, 18,* 30–51.

Reis, E. (2007). Divergence or disorder? The politics of naming intersex. *Perspectives in Biology and Medicine, 50,* 535–543.

Reisenzein, R. (1983). The Schachter theory of emotion: Two decades later. *Psychological Bulletin, 94,* 239–264.

Reisner, S. L., Greytak, A., Parsons, J. P., & Ybarra, M. (2015). Gender minority social stress in adolescence: Disparities in adolescent bullying and substance use by gender identity. *Journal of Sex Research, 52,* 243–256.

Reiss, I. L. (1986). *Journey into sexuality: An exploratory voyage.* Englewood Cliffs, NJ: Prentice-Hall.

Reissing, E. D., & Di Giulio, G. (2010). Practicing clinical psychologists' provision of sexual health care services. *Professional Psychology: Research, and Practice, 41,* 57–63.

Reissing, E. D., Armstrong, H. L., & Allen, C. (2013). Pelvic floor physical therapy for lifelong vaginismus: A retrospective chart review and interview study. *Journal of Sex & Marital Therapy, 39,* 306–320.

Rellini, A. H., & Meston, C. M. (2011). Sexual self-schemas, sexual dysfunction, and the sexual responses of women with a history of childhood sexual abuse. *Archives of Sexual Behavior, 40,* 351–362.

Rempel, J. K., & Baumgartner, B. (2003). The relationship between attitudes towards menstruation and sexual attitudes, desires, and behavior in women. *Archives of Sexual Behavior, 32,* 155–163.

Rempel, L. A., & Rempel, J. K. (2004). Partner influence on health behavior decision-making: Increasing breastfeeding duration. *Journal of Social and Personal Relationships, 21,* 92–111.

Renaud, C. A., & Byers, E. S. (1999). Exploring the frequency, diversity, and content of university students' positive and negative sexual cognitions. *Canadian Journal of Human Sexuality, 8,* 17–30.

Renaud, C. A., & Byers, E. S. (2001). Positive and negative sexual cognitions: Subjective experience and relationships to sexual adjustment. *Journal of Sex Research, 38,* 252–262.

Renaud, C., Byers, E. S., & Pan, S. (1997). Sexual and relationship satisfaction in mainland China. *Journal of Sex Research, 34,* 399–410.

Renne, E. P. (1996). The pregnancy that doesn't stay: The practice and perception of abortion by Ekiti Yoruba women. *Social Science & Medicine, 42,* 483–494.

Repke, J. T. (1994). Calcium and vitamin D. *Clinical Obstetrics and Gynecology, 37,* 550–557.

Reppucci, N. D., Land, D., & Haugaard, J. J. (1999). Child sexual abuse prevention programs that target young children. In P. K. Trickett, & C. J. Schellenbach (Eds.), *Violence against children in the family and the community.* Washington, DC: American Psychological Association.

Resick, P. A., Williams, L. F., Suvak, M. K., Monson, C. M., & Gradus, J. L. (2012). Long-term outcomes of cognitive-behavioral treatments for posttraumatic stress disorder among female rape survivors. *Journal of Consulting and Clinical Psychology, 80,* 201–210.

Reuther, R. R. (1985). Catholics and abortion: Authority vs. dissent. *Christian Century, 102,* 859–862.

Rhoades, G. K., Stanley, S. M., & Markman, H. J. (2006). Pre-engagement cohabitation and gender asymmetry in marital commitment. *Journal of Family Psychology, 20,* 553–560.

Rhoades, G. K., Stanley, S. M., & Markman, H. J. (2009). The pre-engagement cohabitation effect: A replication and extension of previous findings. *Journal of Family Psychology, 23,* 107–111.

Ribner, D. S., & Kleinplatz, P. J. (2007). The hole in the sheet and other myths about sexuality and Judaism. *Sex and Relationship Therapy, 22,* 445–456.

Rice, W. R., Friberg, U., & Gavrilets, S. (2012). Homosexuality as a consequence of epigenetically canalized sexual development. *The Quarterly Review of Biology, 87,* 343–368.

Rich, F. (2001, May 20). Naked capitalists. *New York Times Magazine.*

Richard-Davis, G., & Wellons, M. (2013). Racial and ethnic differences in the physiology and clinical symptoms of menopause. *Seminar in Reproductive Medicine, 31,* 380–386.

Richters, J., de Visser, R. O., Rissel, C. E., Grulich, A. E., & Smith, A. M. A. (2008). Demographic and psychosocial features of participants in bondage and discipline, "sadomasochism" or dominance and submission (BDSM): Data from a national survey. *Journal of Sexual Medicine, 5,* 1660–1668.

Richters, J., de Visser, R., Rissel, C., & Smith, A. (2006). Sexual practices at last heterosexual encounter and occurrence of orgasm in a national survey. *Journal of Sex Research, 43,* 217–226.

Rideout, V. J., Foehr, U. G., & Roberts, D. F. (2010). Generation M^2: Media in the lives of 8- to 18-year-olds. Retrieved from http://www.kff.org

Ridgeway, C., & Bourg, C. (2004). Gender as status: An expectation states theory approach. In A. H. Eagly, A. E. Beall, & R. J. Sternberg (Eds.), *The psychology of gender* (2nd ed.) (pp. 217–241). New York: Guilford Press.

Ridley, C. A., Cate, R. M., Collins, D. M., Reesing, A. L., Lucero, A. A., Gilson, M. S., & Almeida, D. M. (2006). The ebb and flow of marital lust: A relational approach. *Journal of Sex Research, 43,* 144–153.

Ridley, C., Ogolsky, B., Payne, P., Totenhagen, C., & Cate, R. (2008). Sexual expression: Its emotional context in heterosexual, gay, and lesbian couples. *Journal of Sex Research, 45,* 305–314.

Rieger, G., Linsenmeier, J. A., Gygax, L., & Bailey, J. M. (2008). Sexual orientation and childhood gender nonconformity: Evidence from home videos. *Developmental Psychology, 44,* 46–58.

Riessing, E. D., Andruff, H. L., & Wentland, J. J. (2011). Looking back: the experience of first sexual intercourse and current sexual adjustment in young heterosexual adults. *Journal of Sex Research, 49*(1), 27–35.

Rigdon, S. M. (1996). Abortion law and practice in China: An overview with comparisons to the United States. *Social Science & Medicine, 42,* 543–560.

Rimm, M. (1995). Marketing pornography on the information superhighway: A survey of 917,410 images. *Georgetown Law Journal, 83,* 1849–1925.

Ringheim, K., & Gribble, J. (2009). *Expanding contraceptive choice: Five promising innovations.* New York: Population Reference Bureau.

Rini, C., Dunkel Schetter, C., Hobel, C., Glynn, L., & Sandman, C. (2006). Effective social support: Antecedents and consequences of partner support during pregnancy. *Personal Relationships, 13,* 207–229.

Riportella-Muller, R. (1989). Sexuality in the elderly: A review. In K. McKinney & S. Sprecher (Eds.), *Human sexuality: The societal and interpersonal context* (pp. 210–236). New York: Ablex.

Rissel, C. E., Richters, J., Grulich, A. E., de Visser, R. O., & Smith, A. M. A. (2003a). Sex in Australia: Attitudes towards sex in a representative sample of adults. *Australian and New Zealand Journal of Public Health, 27,* 118–123.

Rissel, C. E., Richters, J., Grulich, A. E., de Visser, R. O., & Smith, A. M. A. (2003b). Sex in Australia: First experiences of vaginal intercourse and oral sex among a representative sample of adults. *Australian and New Zealand Journal of Public Health, 27,* 131–137.

Rissel, C. E., Richters, J., Grulich, A. E., de Visser, R. O., & Smith, A. M. A. (2003c). Sex in Australia: Selected characteristics of regular sexual relationships. *Australian and New Zealand Journal of Public Health, 27,* 124–130

Ritchie, A., & Barker, M. (2006). There aren't words for what we do or how we feel so we have to make them up: Constructing polyamorous languages in a culture of compulsory monogamy. *Sexualities, 9,* 584–601.

Roach, K. (2000). *Criminal law* (2nd ed.). Toronto: Irwin.

Roberts, A. L., Austin, S. B., Corliss, H. L., Vandermorris, A. K., & Koenen, K. C. (2010). Pervasive trauma exposure among U.S. sexual orientation minority adults and risk of posttraumatic stress disorder. *American Journal of Public Health, 100,* 2433–2441.

Roberts, A., & Pistole, M. C. (2009). Long distance romantic relationships: Attachment, closeness, and satisfaction. *Journal of College Counseling, 12,* 5–17.

Roberts, J., & Gebotys, R. (1992). Reforming rape laws. *Law and Human Behaviour, 16,* 555–573.

Roberts, R., Jones, A., & Sanders, T. (2013). Students and sex work in the UK: Providers and purchasers. *Sex Education, 13,* 349–363.

Robertson, A., Syvertson, J., Amaro, H., Martinez, G., Rangel, M. G., Patterson, T., & Strathdee, S. (2014). Can't buy me love: A typology of female sex workers' commercial relationships on the Mexico-US border. *Journal of Sex Research, 51,* 711–720.

Robertson, S., & Sharkey, D. (2001). The role of semen in induction of maternal immune tolerance to pregnancy. *Seminars in Immunology, 13,* 243.

Robinson, B. E., Munns, R. A., Weber-Main, A. M., Lowe, M. A., & Raymond, N. C. (2011). Application of the Sexual Health Model in the long-term treatment of hypoactive sexual desire and female orgasmic disorder. *Archives of Sexual Behavior, 40,* 469–478.

Robinson, J. P., & Espelage, D. L. (2011). Inequities in educational and psychological outcomes between LGBTQ and straight students in middle and high school. *Educational Researcher, 40,* 315–330.

Rodrigue, C., Blais, M., Lavoie, F., Adam, B. D., Magontier, C., & Goyer, M.-F. (2015). The structure of casual sexual relationships and experiences among single adults aged 18-30 years old: A latent profile analysis. *Canadian Journal of Human Sexuality, 24,* 215–227.

Roehr, B. (2007). Dramatic drop in HIV infections halts circumcision trials. *British Medical Journal, 334,* 11.

Rogen, S. (2008, July 20). Quoted in the *New York Times Sunday Magazine,* p. 49.

Romans, S. E., Kreindler, D., Asllani, E., Einstein, G., Laredo, S., Levitt, A., . . . & Stewart, D. E. (2013). Mood and the menstrual cycle. *Psychotherapy and Psychosomatics, 82,* 53–60.

Romer, D., Hornik, R., Stanton, B., Black, M., Li, X., Ricardo, I., & Feigelman, S. (1997). "Talking computers": A reliable and private method to conduct interviews on sensitive topics with children. *Journal of Sex Research, 34,* 3–9.

Ronald, A., Pennell, C., & Whitehouse, A. (2011). Prenatal maternal stress associated with ADHD and autistic traits in early childhood. *Frontiers in Psychology, 1* (article 223), 1–7.

Ronis, S. T., & LeBouthillier, D. M. (2013). University students' attitudes toward purchasing condoms. *Canadian Journal of Human Sexuality, 22,* 86–94. doi:10.3138/CJHS.2013.2201

Rosaldo, M. A. (1974). Woman, culture and society: A theoretical overview. In M. S. Rosaldo & L. Lamphere (Eds.), *Woman, culture, and society.* Stanford, CA: Stanford University Press.

Rosario, M., Meyer-Bahlburg, H., Hunter, J., Exner, T., Swadz, M., & Keller, A. (1996). The psychosexual development of urban lesbian, gay and bisexual youths. *Journal of Sex Research, 33,* 113–126.

Roscoe, B., Cavanaugh, L., & Kennedy, D. (1988). Dating infidelity: Behaviors, reasons, and consequences. *Adolescence, 89,* 36–43.

Roscoe, B., Kennedy, D., & Pope, T. (1987). Adolescents' views of intimacy: Distinguishing intimate from nonintimate relationships. *Adolescence, 22,* 511–516.

Rose, A. J., & Rudolph, K. D. (2006). A review of sex differences in peer relationship processes: Potential trade-offs for the emotional and behavioral development of girls and boys. *Psychological Bulletin, 132,* 89–131.

Roselli, C. E., Resko, J. A., & Stormshak, F. (2002). Hormonal influences on sexual partner preference in rams. *Archives of Sexual Behavior, 31,* 43–49.

Rosen, D. H. (1974). *Lesbianism: A study of female homosexuality.* Springfield, IL: Charles C. Thomas.

Rosen, N. O., & Pukall, C. (2016). Comparing the prevalence, risk factors, and repercussions of postpartum genito-pelvic pain and dyspareunia. *Sexual Medicine Reviews, 4,* 126–135.

Rosen, N. O., Bergeron, S., Glowacka, M., Delisle, I., & Baxter, M. L. (2012). Harmful or helpful: Perceived solicitous and facilitative partner responses are differentially associated with pain and sexual satisfaction in women with provoked vestibulodynia. *Journal of Sexual Medicine, 9,* 2351–2360.

Rosen, N. O., Bergeron, S., Lambert, B., & Steben, M. (2012). Provoked vestibulodynia: Mediators of the associations between partner responses, pain, and sexual satisfaction. *Archives of Sexual Behavior.* doi:10.1007/s10508-012-9905-y

Rosen, N. O., Bergeron, S., Leclerc, B., Lambert, B., & Steben, M. (2010). Woman and partner-perceived partner responses predict pain and sexual satisfaction in provoked vestibulodynia (PVD) couples. *Journal of Sexual Medicine, 7,* 3715–3724.

Rosen, N. O., Bergeron, S., Sadikaj, G., & Delisle, I. (2015). Daily associations among male partner responses, pain during intercourse, and anxiety in women with vulvodynia and their partners. *Journal of Pain, 16,* 1312–1320.

Rosen, N. O., Bergeron, S., Sadikaj, G., Glowacka, M., Delisle, I., & Baxter, M.-L. (2014). Impact of male partner responses on sexual function in women with vulvodynia and their partners: A dyadic daily experience study. *Health Psychology, 33,* 823–831.

Rosen, N. O., Knauper, B., Mozessohn, L., & Ho, M. R. (2005). Factors affecting knowledge of sexually transmitted infection transmissibility in healthcare providers: Results from a national survey. *Sexually Transmitted Diseases, 32,* 619–624.

Rosen, R. C. (2007). Erectile dysfunction: Integration of medical and psychological approaches. In S. Leiblum (Ed.), *Principles and practice of sex therapy* (4th ed., pp. 277–312). New York: Guilford.

Rosen, R. C., & Leiblum, S. R. (1995a). Hypoactive sexual desire. *Psychiatric Clinics of North America, 18,* 107–121.

Rosen, R. C., & Leiblum, S. R. (1995b). Treatment of sexual disorders in the 1990s: An integrated approach. *Journal of Consulting and Clinical Psychology, 63,* 877–890.

Rosen, R. C., & McKenna, K. E. (2002). PDE-5 inhibition and sexual response: Pharmacological mechanisms and clinical outcomes. *Annual Review of Sex Research, 13,* 36–88.

Rosen, R. C., Connor, M. K., Miyasato, G., Link, C., Shifren, J. L., Fisher, W. A., . . . Schobelock, M. J. (2012). Sexual desire problems in women seeking healthcare: A novel study design for ascertaining prevalence of hypoactive sexual desire disorder in clinic-based samples of U.S. women. *Journal of Women's Health, 21,* 505–515.

Rosen, R. C., Leiblum, S. R., & Spector, I. P. (1994). Psychologically based treatment for male erectile disorder: A cognitive-interpersonal model. *Journal of Sex & Marital Therapy, 20,* 67–85.

Rosenbaum, T. Y. (2005). Physiotherapy treatment of sexual pain disorders. *Journal of Sex & Marital Therapy, 31,* 329–340.

Rosenbaum, T. Y. (2007a). Pelvic floor involvement in male and female sexual dysfunction and the role of pelvic floor rehabilitation in treatment: A literature review. *Journal of Sexual Medicine, 4,* 4–13.

Rosenbaum, T. Y. (2007b). Physical therapy management and treatment of sexual pain disorders. In S. R. Leiblum (Ed.), *Principles and practice of sex therapy* (4th ed., pp. 157–180). New York: Guilford.

Rosenberg, Z. F., Gross, M., Hiller, S., & Cates, W. (2008). Topical microbicides and other chemical barriers for the prevention of STD/HIV infection. In K. Holmes et al. (Eds.), *Sexually transmitted diseases* (4th ed., pp. 1831–1848). New York: McGraw-Hill.

Rosenblatt, K. A., Wicklund, K., & Stanford, J. (2001). Sexual factors and the risk of prostate cancer. *American Journal of Epidemiology, 153,* 1152–1158.

Rosenfeld, M. J., & Thomas, R. J. (2012). Searching for a mate: The rise of the Internet as a social intermediary. *American Sociological Review, 77,* 523–547.

Rosner, F. (1983). In vitro fertilization and surrogate motherhood: The Jewish view. *Journal of Religion and Health, 22,* 139–160.

Ross, L. E., & Steiner, M. (2003). A biopsychosocial approach to premenstrual dysphoric disorder. *Psychiatric Clinics of North America, 26,* 529–546.

Ross, L. R., & Spinner, B. (2001). General and specific attachment representations in adulthood: Is there a relationship? *Journal of Social and Personal Relationships, 18,* 747–766.

Ross, M. N., Paulsen, J. A., & Stalstrom, O. W. (1988). Homosexuality and mental health: A cross-cultural review. *Journal of Homosexuality, 15,* 131–152.

Ross, M. W. (2005). Typing, being, and doing: Sexuality and the internet. *Journal of Sex Research, 42*, 342–354.

Ross, M. W. (2008). Psychological perspectives on sexuality and sexually transmissible diseases and HIV infection. In K. Holmes et al. (Eds.), *Sexually transmitted diseases* (4th ed., pp. 137–148). New York: McGraw-Hill.

Ross, M. W., Rosser, B. R., McCurdy, S., & Feldman, J. (2007). The advantages and limitations of seeking sex online: A comparison of reasons given for online and offline sexual liaisons by men who have sex with men. *Journal of Sex Research, 44*, 59–71.

Rotello, G. (1997). *Sexual ecology: AIDS and the destiny of gay men.* New York: Dutton.

Rotermann, M. (2005). Sex, condoms, and STDs among young people. *Health Reports, 16*, 39–45.

Rotermann, M. (2007a). Marital breakdown and subsequent depression. *Health Reports, 18*(2), 33–44.

Rotermann, M. (2007b). Second or subsequent births to teenagers. *Health Reports, 18*, 39–42.

Rotermann, M. (2008). Trends in teen sexual behaviour and condom use. *Health Reports, 19*, 1–5.

Rotermann, M. (2012). Sexual behaviour and condom use of 15- to 24-year-olds in 2003 and 2009/10. *Health Reports, 23*, 1–5.

Rotermann, M., Langlois, K. A., Severini, A., & Totten, S. (2013). Prevalence of chlamydia trachomatis and herpes simplex virus type 2: Results from the 2009 to 2011 Canadian Health Measures survey. *Health Reports, 24*, 10–15.

Rothblum, E. D. (1994). "I only read about myself on bathroom walls": The need for research on the mental health of lesbians and gay men. *Journal of Consulting and Clinical Psychology, 62*, 213–220.

Rousseau, S., Lord, J., Lepage, Y., & Van Campenhout, J. (1983). The expectancy of pregnancy for "normal" infertile couples. *Fertility & Sterility, 40*, 768–772.

Rowland, D. A., & Slob, A. K. (1997). Premature ejaculation: Psychophysiological considerations in theory, research, and treatment. *Annual Review of Sex Research, 8*, 224–253.

Rowland, D. L., & Burnett, A. L. (2000). Pharmacotherapy in treatment of male sexual dysfunction. *Journal of Sex Research, 37*, 226–243.

Royal Commission on New Reproductive Technologies. (1993). *Proceed with care: Final report of the Royal Commission on New Reproductive Technologies.* Ottawa: Minister of Government Services Canada.

Rubel, A. N., & Bogaert, A. F. (2015). Consensual nonmonogamy: Psychological well-being and relationship quality correlates. *Journal of Sex Research, 52*, 961–982.

Rubin, Z., Hill, C. T., Peplau, L. A., & Schetter, C. D. (1980). Self-disclosure in dating couples: Sex roles and the ethic of openness. *Journal of Marriage and the Family, 42*, 305–317.

Ruble, D. N. (1977). Premenstrual symptoms: A reinterpretation. *Science, 197*, 291–292.

Ruble, D. N., & Stangor, C. (1986). Stalking the elusive schema: Insights from developmental and social-psychological analyses of gender schemas. *Social Cognition, 4*, 227–261.

Rule, N. O., & Ambady, N. (2008). Brief exposures: Male sexual orientation is accurately perceived at 50-ms. *Journal of Experimental Social Psychology, 44*, 1100–1105.

Rule, N. O., Ambady, N., & Hallett, K. C. (2009). Female sexual orientation is perceived accurately, rapidly, and automatically from the face and its features. *Journal of Experimental Social Psychology, 45*, 1245–1251.

Rule, N. O., Ambady, N., Adams, R. B., Jr., & Macrae, C. N. (2008). Accuracy and awareness in the perception and categorization of male sexual orientation. *Journal of Personality and Social Psychology, 95*, 1019–1028.

Rule, N. O., Ishii, K., Ambady, N., Rosen, K. S. & Hallett, K. C. (2011). Found in translation: Cross-cultural consensus in the accurate categorization of male sexual orientation. *Personality and Social Psychology Bulletin, 37*, 1449–1507.

Runtz, M. G., & Roche, D. N. (1999). Validation of the trauma symptom inventory in a Canadian sample of university women. *Child Maltreatment, 4*(1), 69–80.

Runtz, M. G., & Schallow, J. R. (1997). Social support and coping strategies as mediators of adult adjustment following childhood maltreatment. *Child Abuse & Neglect, 21*, 211–226.

Rupp, H. A., & Wallen, K. (2008). Sex differences in response to visual sexual stimuli: A review. *Archives of Sexual Behavior, 37*, 206–218.

Rusbult, C. (1983). A longitudinal test of the investment model: The development (and deterioration) of satisfaction and commitment in heterosexual involvements. *Journal of Personality and Social Psychology, 45*, 101–117.

Rusbult, C., Johnson, D. J., & Morrow, G. D. (1986). Predicting satisfaction and commitment in adult romantic involvements: An assessment of the generalizability of the investment model. *Social Psychology Quarterly, 49*, 81–89.

Russell, D. E. H. (1980). Pornography and violence: What does the new research say? In L. Lederer (Ed.), *Take back the night: Women on pornography.* New York: Morrow.

Russell, D. E. H. (1990). *Rape in marriage* (Rev. ed.). Bloomington, IN: Indiana University Press.

Russell, G. M., & Richards, J. A. (2003). Stressor and resilence factors for lesbians, gay men, and bisexuals confronting antigay politics. *American Journal of Community Psychology, 31*, 313–328.

Rust, P. C. (2000a). Bisexuality: A contemporary paradox for women. *Journal of Social Issues, 56*, 205–221.

Rust, P. C. (2000b). *Bisexuality in the United States: A social science reader.* New York: Columbia University Press.

Rust, P. C. (2001). Two many and not enough: The meaning of bisexual identities. *Journal of Bisexuality, 1*, 31–68.

Rust, P. C. (2002). Bisexuality: The state of the union. *Annual Review of Sex Research, 13*, 180–240.

Ruvalo, J. (2011). How much of the internet actually is for porn? Retrieved from http://www.forbes.com/sites/julieruvalo/2011/09/07/how-much-of-the-internet-isactuallyfor-porn

Ryan, C., Huebner, D., Diaz, R. M., & Sanchez, J. (2009). Family rejection as a predictor of negative health outcomes in White and Latino lesbian, gay, and bisexual young adults. *Pediatrics, 123*, 346–352.

Rye, B. J., & Meaney, G. J. (2007a). The pursuit of sexual pleasure. *Sexuality & Culture, 11*, 28–51.

Rye, B. J., & Meaney, G. J. (2007b). Voyeurism: It is good as long as we do not get caught. *International Journal of Sexual Health, 19*, 47–56.

Rye, B. J., & Meaney, G. J. (2009). Impact of a homonegativity awareness workshop on attitudes toward homosexuality. *Journal of Homosexuality, 56*, 31–55.

Rye, B. J., & Meaney, G. J. (2010). Measuring homonegativity: A psychometric analysis. *Canadian Journal of Behavioral Science, 42*, 158–167.

Rye, B. J., Greatrix, S. A., & Enright, C. S. (2006). The case of the guilty victim: The effects of gender of victim and gender of perpetrator on attributions of blame and responsibility. *Sex Roles, 54*, 639–649.

Rye, B. J., Mashinter, C., Meaney, G. J., Wood, E., & Gentile, S. (2014). Satisfaction with previous sexual health education as a predictor of intentions to pursue further sexual health education. *Sex Education: Sexuality, Society and Learning, 15*, 93–107.

Rylko-Bauer, B. (1996). Abortion from a cross-cultural perspective. *Social Science & Medicine, 42*, 479–482.

Sachs-Ericsson, N., Blazer, D., Plant, E. A., & Arnow, B. (2005). Childhood sexual and physical abuse and the 1-year prevalence of medical problems in the National Comorbidity Survey. *Health Psychology, 24*, 32–40.

Sacred Congregation for the Doctrine of the Faith. (1976, January 16). Declaration on certain questions concerning sexual ethics. (English text in the *New York Times*, p. 2).

Saegert, S., Swap, W., & Zajonc, R. B. (1973). Exposure, context, and interpersonal attraction. *Journal of Personality and Social Psychology, 25*, 234–242.

Sáenz de Tejada, I., Angulo, J., Cellek, S., González-Cadivid, N., Heaton, J., Pickard, R., & Simonsen, U. (2004). Physiology of erectile dysfunction and pathophysiology of erectile dysfunction. In T. F. Lue, R. Basson, R. Rosen, F. Giuliano, S. Khoury, & F. Montorsi (Eds.), *Sexual medicine: Sexual dysfunctions in men and women* (pp. 287–343). Paris, France: Editions 21.

Saewyc, E. M. (2007). Contested conclusions: Claims that can (and cannot) be made from the current research on gay, lesbian, and bisexual teen suicide attempts. *Journal of LGBT Health Research, 3*(1), 79–87.

Saewyc, E. M. (2011). Research on adolescent sexual orientation: Development, health disparities, stigma, and resilience. *Journal of Research on Adolescence, 21,* 256–272.

Saewyc, E. M., Taylor, D., Homma, Y., & Ogilvie, G. (2008). Trends in sexual health and risk behaviours among adolescent students in British Columbia. *Canadian Journal of Human Sexuality, 17,* 1–13.

Saewyc, E., Clark, T. C., Barney, L., Brunanski, D., & Homma, Y. (2014). Enacted stigma and HIV risk behaviours among sexual minority Indigenous youth in Canada, New Zealand, and the United States. *Pimatisiwin: A Journal of Aboriginal and Indigenous Community Health, 11*(3), 411–420.

Sagarin, E. (1973). Power to the peephole. *Sexual Behavior, 3,* 2–7.

Sakaluk, J. K., Todd, L. M., Milhausen, R., Lachowsky, N. J., & Undergraduate Research Group in Sexuality (URGiS). (2014). Dominant heterosexual scripts in emerging adulthood: Conceptualization and measurement. *Journal of Sex Research, 51,* 516–531.

Saleh, F. M., & Berlin, F. S. (2003). Sex hormones, neurotransmitters, and psychopharmacological treatments in men with paraphilic disorders. *Journal of Child Sexual Abuse, 12,* 233–253.

Saleh, F. M., Niel, T., & Fishman, M. J. (2004). Treatment of paraphilia in young adults with leuprolide acetate: A preliminary case report series. *Journal of Forensic Science, 49,* 1343–1348.

Salehi, R., Flicker, S., & the Toronto Teen Survey Team. (2010). Predictors of exposure to sexual health education among teens who are newcomers to Canada. *Canadian Journal of Human Sexuality, 19,* 157–168.

Salem, R. N. (2005). World Health Organization updates guidance on how to use contraceptives. *INFO Reports, 4.* Baltimore, MD: Johns Hopkins University.

Salganik, M., & Heckathorn, D. (2004). Sampling and estimation in hidden populations using respondent-driven sampling. *Sociological Methodology, 34,* 193–239.

Salisbury, C. M., & Fisher, W. A. (2014). "Did you come?" A qualitative exploration of gender differences in beliefs, experiences, and concerns regarding female orgasm occurrence during heterosexual sexual interactions. *Journal of Sex Research, 51,* 616–631.

Salmon, C. (2012). The pop culture of sex: An evolutionary window on the worlds of pornography and romance. *Review of General Psychology, 16,* 152–160.

Samson, J.-M., Levy, J. J., Dupras, A., & Tessier, D. (1991). Coitus frequency among married or cohabiting heterosexual adults: A survey in French Canada. *Australian Journal of Marriage & Family, 12,* 103–109.

Samson, J.-M., Levy, J. J., Dupras, A., & Tessier, D. (1993). Active oralgenital sex among married and cohabiting heterosexual adults. *Sexological Review, 1,* 143–156.

Sanchez, D. T., Fetterolf, J. C., & Rudman, L. A. (2012). Eroticizing inequality in the United States: The consequences and determinants of traditional gender role adherence in intimate relationships. *Journal of Sex Research, 49,* 168–183.

Sanchez, D. T., Kiefer, A. K., & Ybarra, O. (2006). Sexual submissiveness in women: Costs for sexual autonomy and arousal. *Personality and Social Psychology Bulletin, 32,* 512–524.

Sánchez-Fuentes, M. M., Santos-Iglesias, P., Byers, E. S., & Sierra, J. C. (2015). Validation of the Interpersonal Exchange Model of Sexual Satisfaction Questionnaire in a Spanish sample. *Journal of Sex Research, 52,* 1028–1041.

Sand, M., & Fisher, W. A. (2007). Women's endorsement of models of female sexual response: The nurses' sexuality study. *Journal of Sexual Medicine, 4,* 708–719.

Sandberg, J. (2006). Infant mortality, social networks, and subsequent fertility. *American Sociological Review, 71,* 288–309.

Sanders, S., Graham, C. A., & Milhausen, R. (2008). Predicting sexual problems in women: The relevance of sexual excitation and sexual inhibition. *Archives of Sexual Behavior, 37,* 241–251.

Sandfort, T., & Ehrhardt, A. (2004). Sexual health: A useful public health paradigm or a moral imperative? *Archives of Sexual Behavior, 33,* 181–187.

Sanghavi, D. M. (2006, October 17). Preschool puberty, and a search for the causes. *New York Times.*

Sansone, R. A., & Sansone, L. A. (2007). Cosmetic surgery and psychological issues. *Psychiatry, 4*(12), 65–68.

Santilla, P., Sandnabba, N. K., Laurence, A., & Nordling, N. (2002). Investigating the underlying structure in sadomasochistically oriented behavior. *Archives of Sexual Behavior, 31,* 185–196.

Sardell, R. J., Arcese, P., Keller, L. F., & Reid, J. M. (2012). Are there indirect fitness benefits to female extra-pair reproduction? Lifetime reproductive success of within-pair and extra-pair offspring. *The American Naturalist, 179.* Retrieved from www.jstor.org/stable/10.1086/665665.

Sauvageau, A., & Racette, S. (2006). Autoerotic deaths in the literature from 1954 to 2004: A review. *Journal of Forensic Science, 51,* 140–146.

Savage, D. (2010, February 4). Gold star pedophiles. *The Stranger.* Retrieved from http://www.thestranger.com/seattle/SavageLove?oid=3347526

Savic, I., Berglund, H., & Lindström, P. (2005). Brain response to putative pheromones in homosexual men. *Proceedings of the National Academy of Sciences, 102,* 7456–7361.

Savin-Williams, R. C. (1995). An exploratory study of pubertal maturation timing and self-esteem among gay and bisexual male youths. *Developmental Psychology, 31,* 56–64.

Savin-Williams, R. C. (2001). Suicide attempts among sexual-minority youths: Population and measurement issues. *Journal of Consulting and Clinical Psychology, 69,* 983–991.

Savin-Williams, R. C. (2006). Who's gay? Does it matter? *Current Directions in Psychological Science, 15,* 40–44.

Savin-Williams, R. C., & Cohen, K. M. (2007). Development of same-sex attracted youth. In I. H. Meyer & M. E. Northridge (Eds.), *The health of sexual minorities* (pp. 27–47). New York: Springer. doi:10.1007/978-0-387-31334-4_2

Savin-Williams, R. C., & Ream, G. L. (2003). Suicide attempts among sexual-minority male youth. *Journal of Clinical Child and Adolescent Psychology, 32,* 509–522.

Savin-Williams, R. F., & Vrangalova, Z. (2013). Mostly heterosexual as a distinct sexual orientation group: A systematic review of the empirical evidence. *Developmental Review, 33,* 58–88.

Sayle, A. E., Savitz, D. A., Thorpe, J. M., Jr., Hertz-Picciotto, L., & Wilcox, A. J. (2001). Sexual activity during late pregnancy and risk of preterm delivery. *Obstetrics and Gynecology, 97,* 283–289.

Schachter, S. (1964). The interaction of cognitive and physiological determinants of emotional state. In L. Berkowitz (Ed.), *Advances in experimental social psychology* (Vol. I). New York: Academic.

Schaefer, M. T., & Olson, D. H. (1981). Assessing intimacy: The PAIR Inventory. *Journal of Marital and Family Therapy,* 47–60.

Schafer, G. (2008). Romantic love in heterosexual relationships: Women's experiences. *Journal of Social Science, 16,* 187–197.

Schaffir, J. (2006). Sexual intercourse at term and onset of labor. *Obstetrics and Gynecology, 107,* 1310–1314.

Scharfe, E., & Bartholomew, K. (1995). Accommodation and attachment representations in young couples. *Journal of Social and Personal Relationships, 12,* 389–401.

Scheim, A. I., & Bauer, G. R. (2016). Sex and gender diversity among transgender persons in Ontario, Canada: Results from a respondent-driven sampling survey. *Journal of Sex Research, 52,* 1–14.

Schenck, C., Arnulf, I., & Mahowald, M. (2007). Sleep and sex: What can go wrong? *Sleep, 30,* 683–702.

Schiavi, R. C., Mandeli, J., & Schreiner-Engel. (1994). Sexual satisfaction in healthy aging men. *Journal of Sex and Marital Therapy, 20,* 3–13.

Schick, V. R., Calabrese, S. K., Rima, B. N., & Zucker, A. N. (2010). Genital appearance dissatisfaction: Implications for women's genital image self-consciousness, sexual esteem, sexual satisfaction, and sexual risk. *Psychology of Women Quarterly, 34,* 394–404.

Schieffelin, E. L. (1976). *The sorrow of the lonely and the burning of the dancers.* New York: St. Martin's Press.

Schmidt, L. (2006). Psychosocial burden of infertility and assisted reproduction. *The Lancet, 367,* 379–380.

Schmiege, S., & Russo, N. F. (2005). Depression and unwanted first pregnancy: Longitudinal cohort study. *British Medical Journal, 331,* 1303.

Schmitt, D. P. (2003). Universal sex differences in the desire for sexual variety: Tests from 52 nations, 6 continents, and 13 islands. *Journal of Personality and Social Psychology, 85,* 85–104.

Schmucker, M., & Losel, F. (2008). Does sexual offender treatment work? A systematic review of outcome evaluations. *Psicothema, 2,* 10–19.

Schneider, M. (1991). Developing service for lesbian and gay adolescents. *Canadian Journal of Community Mental Health, 10,* 133–151.

Schoeb, G., Belzile, M., Brassard, A., Desruisseaus, L.-M., Potvin, C., Blais, M., & Bruyninx, S. (2013). The perceived equity and equality of sexual practices scale: Validation of a measure of equity and equality within couples. *Canadian Journal of Human Sexuality, 22,* 25–39.

Schofield, A. T., & Vaughan-Jackson, P. (1913). *What a boy should know.* New York: Cassell.

Schooler, D., Sorsoli, C. L., Kim, J. L., & Tolman, D. L. (2009). Beyond exposure: A person-oriented approach to adolescent media diets. *Journal of Research on Adolescence, 19,* 484–508.

Schroeder, A. (2000, January 28). The money was great, risks were real. Student reflects on her year as a phone sex operator. *The Brunswickan.*

Schubach, G. (2002). The G-spot is the female prostate. *American Journal of Obstetrics and Gynecology, 186,* 850.

Schultz, W. C. M., Wiel, H. B. M., Klatter, J. A., Sturm, B. E., & Nauta, J. (1989). Vaginal sensitivity to electric stimuli: Theoretical and practical implications. *Archives of Sexual Behavior, 18*(2), 87–96.

Schultz, W. W., van Andel, P., Sabelis, I., & Mooyaart, E. (1999). Magnetic resonance imaging of male and female genitals during coitus and female sexual arousal. *British Medical Journal, 319,* 1596–1600.

Schuster, D. (2014). These NYC coeds are students by day, strippers by night. *New York Post.* Retrieved from http://nypost.com/2014/04/28/these-nyc-coeds-are-students-by-day-strippers-by-night

Schwartz, L. B. (1997, December 20/27). Understanding human parturition. *The Lancet, 350,* 1792–1793.

Scott, J. P. (1964). The effects of early experience on social behavior and organization. In W. Etkin (Ed.), *Social behavior and organization among vertebrates.* Chicago: University of Chicago Press.

Scott, V. M., Mottarella, K. E., & Lavooy, M. J. (2006). Does virtual intimacy exist? A brief exploration into reported levels of intimacy in online relationships. *Cyberpsychology & Behavior, 9,* 759–761.

Scull, M. T. (2011). Reinforcing gender roles at the male strip show: A qualitative analysis of men who dance for women (MDW). *Deviant Behavior, 34,* 557–578.

Sears, H. A., & Byers, E. S. (2010). Adolescent girls' and boys' experiences of psychologically, physically and sexually aggressive behaviors in their dating relationships: Co-occurrence and emotional reaction. *Journal of Aggression, Maltreatment, & Trauma, 19,* 517–539.

Sears, H. A., Byers, E. S., & Price, E. L. (2007). The co-occurrence of adolescent boys' and girls' use of psychologically, physically, and sexually abusive behaviours in their dating relationships. *Journal of Adolescence, 30,* 487–504.

Sedgh, G., Henshaw, S. K., Singh, S., Bankole, A., & Drescher, J. (2007). Legal abortion worldwide: Incidence and recent trends. *Perspectives on Sexual and Reproductive Health, 39*(4), 216–225.

Segraves, R. T., & Balon, R. (2003). *Sexual pharmacology: Fast facts.* New York: Norton.

Segraves, R. T., & Balon, R. (2010). Recognizing and reversing sexual side effects of medications. In S. Levine (Ed.), *Handbook of clinical sexuality for mental health professionals* (2nd ed., pp. 311–327). London, UK: Routledge.

Séguin, L. J., Milhausen, R. R., & Kukkonen, T. (2015). The development and validation of the motives for feigning orgasms scale. *Canadian Journal of Human Sexuality, 24,* 31–48.

Sell, R. L. (1997). Defining and measuring sexual orientation: A review. *Archives of Sexual Behavior, 26,* 643–658.

Sell, R. L., Wells, J. A., & Wypij, D. (1995). The prevalence of homosexual behavior and attraction in the United States, the United Kingdom and France. *Archives of Sexual Behavior, 24,* 235–248.

Sellors, J. W., Mahoney, J. B., Kczorowski, J., Lytwyn, A., Bangura, H., Chong, S., . . . the Survey of HPV in Ontario Women (SHOW) group. (2000). Prevalence and predictors of human papillomavirus infection in women in Ontario, Canada. *Canadian Medical Association Journal, 163,* 503–509.

Selvaggi, G., & Elander, A. (2008). Penile reconstruction/formation. *Current Opinion in Urology, 18,* 589–597.

Semple, S. J., Patterson, T. L., & Grant, I. (2004). The context of sexual risk behavior among heterosexual methamphetamine users. *Addictive Behaviors, 29,* 807–810.

Semple, S. J., Zians, J., Strathdee, S. A., & Patterson, T. L. (2009). Sexual marathons and methamphetamine use among HIV positive men who have sex with men. *Archives of Sexual Behavior, 38,* 583–590.

Senn, C. Y. (2011). An imperfect feminist journey: Reflections on the process to develop an effective sexual assault resistance program for university women. *Feminism & Psychology, 21*(1), 121–137.

Senn, C. Y. (2013). Education on resistance to acquaintance sexual assault: Preliminary promise of a new program for young women in high school and university. *Canadian Journal of Behavioural Science, 45,* 24–33.

Senn, C. Y., & Desmarais, S. (2001). Are our recruitment practices for sex studies working across gender? The effect of topic and gender of recruiter on participation rates of university men and women. *Journal of Sex Research, 38,* 111–117.

Senn, C. Y., & Dzinas, K. (1996). Measuring fear of rape: A new scale. *Canadian Journal of Behavioural Science, 28,* 141–144.

Senn, C. Y., & Forrest, A. (2016). "And then one night when I went to class. . .": The impact of sexual assault bystander intervention workshops incorporated in academic courses. *Psychology of Violence, 6,* 607–618.

Senn, C. Y., & Radtke, H. L. (1990). Women's evaluations of and affective reactions to mainstream violent pornography, nonviolent pornography and erotica. *Violence and Victims, 5,* 143–155.

Senn, C. Y., Desmarais, S., Verberg, N., & Wood, E. (2000). Predicting coercive sexual behaviour across the lifespan in a random sample of Canadian men. *Journal of Social and Personal Relationships, 17,* 95–113.

Senn, C. Y., Eliasziw, M., Barata, P. C., Thurston, W. E., Newby-Clark, I. R., Radtke, H. L., & Hobden, K. L. (2015). Efficacy of a sexual assault resistance program for university women. *The New England Journal of Medicine, 372,* 2326–2335.

Senn, C. Y., Eliasziw, M., Barata, P. C., Thurston, W. E., Newby-Clark, I. R., Radtke, H. L., . . . & SARE Study Team. (2014). Sexual violence in the lives of first-year university women in Canada: no improvements in the 21st century. *BMC Women's Health, 14,* 135–142.

Senn, C. Y., Gee, S. S., & Thake, J. (2011). Emancipatory sexuality education and sexual assault resistance: Does the former enhance the latter? *Psychology of Women Quarterly, 35,* 72–91.

Seto, M. C. (2004). Pedophilia and sexual offenses against children. *Annual Review of Sex Research, 15,* 321–361.

Seto, M. C. (2009). Pedophilia. *Annual Review of Clinical Psychology, 5,* 391–407.

Seto, M. C., Cantor, J. M., & Blanchard, R. (2006). Child pornography offenses are a valid diagnostic indicator of pedophilia. *Journal of Abnormal Psychology, 115,* 610–615.

Seto, M. C., Kjellgren, C., Priebe, G., Mossige, S., Svedin, C. G., & Långström, N. (2010b). Sexual coercion experience and sexually coercive behavior: A population study of Swedish and Norwegian male youth. *Child Maltreatment, 15,* 219–228.

Seto, M. C., Lalumière, M. L., & Blanchard, R. (2000). The discriminative validity of a phallometric test for pedophilic interests among adolescent sex offenders against children. *Psychological Assessment, 12,* 319–327.

Seto, M. C., Lalumière, M. L., Harris, G. T., & Chivers, M. L. (2012). The sexual responses of sexual sadists. *Journal of Abnormal Psychology.* doi:10.1037/a0028714

Seto, M. C., Maric, A., & Barbaree, H. E. (2001). The role of pornography in the etiology of sexual aggression. *Aggression and Violent Behavior, 6*, 35–53.

Seto, M. C., Murphy, W. D., Page, J., & Ennis, L. (2003). Detecting anomalous sexual interests in juvenile sex offenders. *Annals of the New York Academy of Sciences, 898*, 118–130.

Setty-Venugopal, V., & Upadhyay, U. D. (2002). Three to five saves lives. Population Reports, Series L, Number 13. Baltimore, MD: Johns Hopkins University School of Public Health.

Sex survey results. (n.d.). *NOW* Toronto. Retrieved from http://www.nowtoronto.com/love/survey.cfm

Shabsigh, R., Padma-Nathan, H., Gittleman, M., McMurray, J., Kaufman, J., & Goldstein, I. (2000). Intracavernous alprostadil alfadex (Edex/viridal) is effective and safe in patients with erectile dysfunction after failing sildenafil (Viagra). *Urology, 55*, 477–480.

Shamloul, R. (2005). Treatment of men complaining of short penis. *Urology, 65*, 1183–1185.

Shapiro, C., Trajanovic, N., & Federoff, J. P. (2003). Sexsomnia—A new parasomnia? *Canadian Journal of Psychiatry, 48*, 311–317.

Shapiro, H. T. (1997). Ethical and policy issues in human cloning. *Science, 277*, 195–196.

Sharpstein, D. J., & Kirkpatrick, L. (1997). Romantic jealousy and adult romantic attachment. *Journal of Personality and Social Psychology, 72*, 627–640.

Shattock, R. J., Warren, M., McCormack, S., & Hankins, C. A. (2011). Turning the tide against HIV. *Science, 333*, 42–43.

Shattuck-Eidens, D., McClure, M., Simard, J., Labrie, F., Narod, S., Couch, F., ... Erdos, M. (1995). A collaborative survey of 80 mutations in the BRCA1 breast and ovarian cancer susceptibility gene. *JAMA, 273*, 535–541.

Shaughnessy, K., & Byers, E. S. (2013). Seeing the forest with the trees: Cybersex as a case study of single-item versus multi-item measures of sexual behaviour. *Canadian Journal of Behavioural Science, 45*, 220–229.

Shaughnessy, K., Byers, E. S., & Thornton, S. J. (2011a). What is cybersex?: Heterosexual students' definitions. *International Journal of Sexual Health, 23*, 79–89.

Shaughnessy, K., Byers, E. S., & Walsh, L. (2011b). Online sexual activity experience of heterosexual students: Gender similarities and differences. *Archives of Sexual Behavior, 40*, 419–427.

Shaughnessy, K., Byers, E. S., Clowater, S. L., & Kalinowski, A. (2014). Self-appraisals of arousal-oriented online sexual activities in university and community samples. *Archives of Sexual Behavior, 43*, 1187–1197.

Shaver, F. M. (1993). Prostitution: A female crime? In E. Adelberg & C. Currie (Eds.), *In conflict with the law: Women and the Canadian justice system* (pp. 153–173). Vancouver: Press Gang Publishers.

Shaver, F. M. (1994). The regulation of prostitution: Avoiding morality traps. *CHS/RCDS, 9*(1), 123–145.

Shaver, F. M. (1996a). Prostitution: On the dark side of the service industry. In Tom Fleming (Ed.), *Post critical criminology*. Scarborough, ON: Prentice Hall.

Shaver, F. M. (1996b). Regulation of prostitution: Setting the morality trap. In B. Schissel & L. Mahood (Eds.), *Social control in Canada*. Toronto: Oxford University Press.

Shaver, F. M. (2005). Sex work research: Methodological and ethical challenges. *Journal of Interpersonal Violence, 20*, 296–319.

Shaw, A. M. M., Rhoades, G. K., Allen, E. S., Stanley, S. M., & Markham, H. J. (2013). Predictors of extradyadic sexual involvement in unmarried opposite-sex relationships. *Journal of Sex Research, 50*, 598–610.

Shaw, J. (2006). *Reality check: A close look at accessing abortion services in Canadian hospitals*. Ottawa: Canadians for Choice.

Sheff, E. (2005). Polyamorous women, sexual subjectivity, and power. *Journal of Contemporary Ethnographics, 34*, 251–283.

Shell-Duncan, B. (2008). From health to human right: Female genital cutting and the politics of intervention. *American Anthropologist, 110*, 225–236.

Sherwin, B. B. (1991). The psychoendocrinology of aging and female sexuality. *Annual Review of Sex Research, 2*, 181–198.

Shidlo, A., Schroeder, M., & Drescher, J. (2001). What needs fixing? An introduction. *Journal of Gay & Lesbian Psychotherapy, 5*, 1–4.

Shifren, J. L., Braunstein, G. D., Simon, J. A., Casson, P. R., Buster, J. E., & Redmond, G. P. (2000). Transdermal testosterone treatment in women with impaired sexual function after oophorectomy. *New England Journal of Medicine, 343*, 682–688.

Shifren, J. L., Nahum, R., & Mazer, N. A. (1998). Incidence of sexual dysfunction in surgically menopausal women. *Menopause, 5*, 189–190.

Shirpak, K. R., Maticka-Tyndale, E., & Chinichian, M. (2007). Iranian immigrants' perceptions of sexuality in Canada: A symbolic interactionist approach. *Canadian Journal of Human Sexuality, 16*, 113–128.

Shoveller, J. A., Johnson, J. L., Langille, D. B., & Mitchell, T. (2004). Sociocultural influences on young people's sexual development. *Social Sciences & Medicine, 59*, 473–487.

SIECCAN. (2004). Adolescent sexual and reproductive health in Canada: A report card in 2004. *Canadian Journal of Human Sexuality, 13*, 67–81.

SIECCAN. (2009). Sexual health education in the schools: Questions & answers (3rd ed.). *Canadian Journal of Human Sexuality, 18*, 47–60.

SIECCAN. (2015). *Sexual assault in Canada: Legal definitions, statistics, and frontline responses*. Toronto: Author.

Siegel, L. J., & McCormick, C. (1999). *Criminology in Canada: Theories, patterns and typologies*. Scarborough, ON: ITP Nelson.

Signorile, M. (1997). *Life on the outside: The Signorile report on gay men*. New York: HarperCollins.

Sik Ying Ho, P. (2006). The (charmed) circle game: Reflections on sexual hierarchy through multiple sexual relationships. *Sexualities, 9*, 547–564.

Siker, J. S. (Ed.). (1994). *Homosexuality in the church: Both sides of the debate*. Louisville, KY: Westminster/John Knox Press.

Silvera, M. (1990). Man royal and sodomites: Some thought on the invisibility of Afro-Caribbean lesbians. In S. D. Stone (Ed.), *Lesbians in Canada*. Toronto: Between the Lines.

Silverberg, C., & Odette, F. (2011). *Sexuality and access project: Survey summary*. Retrieved from http://sexuality-and-access.com

Simms, D. C., & Byers, E. S. (2013). Heterosexual daters' sexual initiation behaviors: Use of the theory of planned behavior. *Archives of Sexual Behavior, 42*, 105–116.

Simon, V., Ho, D., & Karim, Q. (2006). HIV/AIDS epidemiology, pathogenesis, prevention, and treatment. *The Lancet, 368*, 489–504.

Simpson, J. A. (1990). Influence of attachment styles on romantic relationships. *Journal of Personality and Social Psychology, 59*, 971–980.

Simpson, J., Collins, W. A., Tran, S., & Haydon, K. (2007). Attachment and the experience and expression of emotions in romantic relationships: A developmental perspective. *Journal of Personality and Social Psychology, 92*, 355–367.

Singh, D. (1993). Adaptive significance of female physical attractiveness: Role of waist-to-hip ratio. *Journal of Personality and Social Psychology, 65*, 293–307.

Singh, S., & Darroch, J. E. (2000). Adolescent pregnancy and childbearing: Levels and trends in developed countries. *Family Planning Perspectives, 32*, 14–23.

Singh, S., Darroch, J. E., Frost, J. J., & the Study Team. (2001). Socioeconomic disadvantage and adolescent women's sexual and reproductive behavior: The case of five developed countries. *Family Planning Perspectives, 33*, 251–258, 289.

Sinha, M. (2012). Family violence in Canada: A statistical profile, 2010. *Juristat* (Catalogue no. 85-002-X). Ottawa: Statistics Canada.

Sinha, M. (2013). Measuring violence against women: Statistical trends. *Juristat* (Catalogue no. 85-002-X). Ottawa: Statistics Canada.

Sipski, M. L., Alexander, C., & Rosen, R. (2001). Sexual arousal and orgasm in women: Effects of spinal cord injury. *Annals of Neurology, 49*, 35–44.

Sirianni, J., & Vishwanath, A. (2016). Problematic online pornography use: A media attendance perspective. *Journal of Sex Research, 53*, 21–34.

Skaletsky, H., Kuroda-Kawaguchi, T., Minx, P. J., Cordum, H. S., Hillier, L., Brown, L. G., ... Page, D. C. (2003). The male-specific region of the human Y chromosome is a mosaic of discrete sequence classes. *Nature, 423,* 825–837.

Small, M. F. (1993). *Female choices: Sexual behavior of female primates.* Ithaca, NY: Cornell University Press.

Smith, A. M. A., Rissel, C. E., Richters, J., Grulich, A. E., & de Visser, R. O. (2003). Sex in Australia: Sexual identity, sexual attraction and sexual experience among a representative sample of adults. *Australian and New Zealand Journal of Public Health, 27,* 138–145.

Smith, G., Frankel, S., & Yarnell, J. (1997). Sex and death: Are they related? Findings from the Caerphilly cohort study. *British Medical Journal, 315,* 1641–1645.

Smith, J. R., Smith, J. R., Freije, D., Carpten, J. D., Grönberg, H., Xu, J., . . . Isaacs, W. B. (1996). Major susceptibility locus for prostate cancer on chromosome 1 suggested by a genome-wide search. *Science, 274,* 1371–1373.

Smith, K. B., & Pukall, C. F. (2014). Sexual function, relationship adjustment, and the relational impact of pain in male partners of women with provoked vulvar pain. *Journal of Sexual Medicine, 11,* 1283–1293.

Smith, K. B., Pukall, C. F., Tripp, D. A., & Nickel, J. C. (2007). Sexual and relationship functioning in men with chronic prostatitis/chronic pelvic pain syndrome and their partners. *Archives of Sexual Behavior, 36,* 301–311.

Smith, M. (1999). *Lesbian and gay rights in Canada: Social movements and equality seeking, 1971–1995.* Toronto: University of Toronto Press.

Smith, M., Grov, C., Seal, D., Bernhardt, N., & McCall, P. (2015). Social-emotional aspects of male escorting: Experiences of men working for an agency. *Archives of Sexual Behavior, 44,* 1047–1058.

Smith, R. J., Okano, J. T., Kahn, J. S., Bodine, E. N., & Blower, S. (2010). Evolutionary dynamics of complex networks of HIV drug-resistant strains: The case of San Francisco. *Science, 327,* 697–701.

Smith, T. (2003). *American sexual behavior: Trends, sociodemographic differences, and risk behavior.* University of Chicago, National Opinion Research Center, GSS Topical Report No. 25.

Smith, T., & Son, J. (2013). *Trends in public attitudes about sexual morality.* Chicago: National Opinion Research Center.

Smith, Y. L. S., van Goozen, S., Kuiper, A., & Cohen-Ketteris, P. (2005). Transsexual subtypes: Clinical and theoretical significance. *Psychiatry Research, 137,* 151–160.

Snowdon, C. T., Pieper, B. A., Boe, C. Y., Cronin, K. A., Kurian, A. V., & Ziegler, T. E. (2010). Variation in oxytocin is related to variation in affiliative behaviour in monogamous, pair bonded tamarins. *Hormones and Behavior, 58,* 614–618.

Snowdon, C. T., Ziegler, T. E., Schultz-Darken, N. J., & Ferris, C. F. (2006). Social odours, sexual arousal and pairbonding in primates.

Philosophical Transactions of the Royal Society B, 361, 2079–2089.

Soble, A. (2009). A history of erotic philosophy. *Journal of Sex Research, 46,* 104–120.

Society of Obstetricians and Gynaecologists of Canada. (2006). Canadian consensus conference on menopause, 2006 update. *Journal of Obstetrics and Gynaecology of Canada, 171,* S7–S10.

Society of Obstetricians and Gynaecologists of Canada. (2007a). Committee Opinion: Mid-trimester amniocentesis fetal loss rate. *Journal of Obstetrics and Gynaecology Canada, 194,* 586–590.

Society of Obstetricians and Gynaecologists of Canada. (2007b). Canadian consensus guideline on continuous and extended hormonal contraception, 2007. *Journal of Obstetrics and Gynaecology of Canada, 29*(7), Supplemental 2.

Society of Obstetricians and Gynaecologists of Canada. (2012). SOGC Committee Opinion: Delayed child-bearing. *Journal of Obstetrics and Gynaecology Canada, 34,* 80–93.

Society of Obstetricians and Gynaecologists of Canada. (2013, February 19). *Position Statement: Hormonal Contraception and risk of venous thromboembolism (VTE).* Ottawa: Author.

Sokol, R. J., Delaney-Black, V., & Nordstrom, B. (2003). Fetal alcohol spectrum disorder. *Journal of the American Medical Association, 290,* 2996–2999.

Solms, M. (1997). *The neuropsychology of dreams: A clinico-anatomical study.* Mahwah, NJ: Erlbaum.

Solomon, S. E., Rothblum, E., & Balsam, K. (2005). Money, housework, sex, and conflict: Same-sex couples in civil unions, those not in civil unions, and heterosexual married siblings. *Sex Roles, 52,* 561–576.

Solursh, D. S., Ernst, I. L., Lewis, R. W., Prisant, L. M., Mills, T. M., Solursh, L. P., . . . The Human Sexuality Multispecialty Group. (2003). The human sexuality education of physicians in North American medical schools. *International Journal of Impotence Research, 15,* S41–S45.

Sommerville, D. M. (2004). *Rape and race in the nineteenth-century South.* Chapel Hill, NC: University of North Carolina Press.

Soon, J. A., Levine, M., Osmond, B. L., Ensom, M. H. H., & Fielding, D. W. (2005). Effects of making emergency contraception available without a physician's prescription: A population-based study. *Canadian Medical Association Journal, 172,* 878–883.

Sorokan, S. T., Finlay, J. C., & Jefferies, A. L. (2015). Newborn male circumcision. *Paediactric Child Health, 20,* 311–315.

Sparling, S., & Cramer, K. (2015). Choosing the danger we think we know: Men and women's faulty perceptions of sexually transmitted infection risk with familiar and unfamiliar new partners. *Canadian Journal of Human Sexuality, 24,* 237–242.

Special, W. P., & Li-Barber, K. T. (2012). Self-disclosure and student satisfaction with

Facebook. *Computers in Human Behavior, 28,* 624–630.

Spehr, M., Gisselmann, G., Poplawski, A., Riffell, J. A., Wetzel, C. H., Zimmer, R. K., & Hatt, H. (2003). Identification of a testicular odorant receptor mediating human sperm chemotaxis. *Science, 299,* 2054–2058.

Spiers, H., Hannon, E., Schalkwyk, L. C., Smith, R., Wong, C. C. Y., O'Donovan, M. C., . . . Mill, J. (2015). Methylomic trajectories across human fetal brain development. *Genome Research, 25,* 338–352.

Spourk, R. F. (2002). Dehydroepiandrosterone: A springboard hormone for female sexuality. *Fertility and Sterility, 77,* S19–S25.

Sprecher, S. (1987). The effects of self-disclosure given and received on affection for an intimate partner and stability of the relationship. *Journal of Social and Personal Relationships, 4,* 115–127.

Sprecher, S., Sullivan, Q., & Hatfield, E. (1994). Mate selection preferences: Gender differences examined in a national sample. *Journal of Personality and Social Psychology, 66,* 1074–1080.

Springen, K., & Noonan, D. (2002). Sperm banks go online. MSNBC News 899016.

Sritharan, R., Heilpern, K., Wilbur, C. J., & Gawronski, B. (2010). I think I like you: Spontaneous and deliberate evaluations of potential romantic partners in an online dating context. *European Journal of Social Psychology, 40*(6), 1062–1077.

St. Augustine. (1950). *The city of God.* (Marcus Dods, Trans.). New York: Modern Library.

Stack, S., & Gundlach, J. H. (1992). Divorce and sex. *Archives of Sexual Behavior, 21,* 359–368.

Stafford, L., & Merolla, A. J. (2007). Idealization, reunions, and stability in long distance dating relationships. *Journal of Social and Personal Relationships, 24,* 37–54.

Stamm, W. E. (2008). *Chlamydia trachomatis* infections. In K. Holmes et al. (Eds.), *Sexually transmitted diseases* (4th ed., pp. 575–594). New York: McGraw-Hill.

Stanger-Hall, K., & Hall, D. (2011). Abstinence-only education and teen pregnancy rates: Why we need comprehensive sex education in the U.S. *PLoS ONE, 6*(10), e24658. doi:10:1371/journal.pone.0024658

Stanley, S. M., Rhoades, G. K., & Markham, H. J. (2006). Sliding versus deciding: Inertia and the premarital cohabitation effect. *Family Relations, 55,* 499–509.

Stanton, A. L., Lobel, M., Sears, S., & DeLuca, R. (2002). Psychosocial aspects of selected issues in women's reproductive health: Current status and future directions. *Journal of Consulting and Clinical Psychology, 70,* 751–770.

Starks, K. J., & Morrison, E. S. (1996). *Growing up sexual* (2nd ed.). New York: HarperCollins.

Statistics Canada. (1993). The violence against women survey. *The Daily.* Ottawa: Author.

Statistics Canada. (1995). Therapeutic abortions. *Statistical report on the health of*

Canadians: Conditions and diseases (Catalogue no. 82-219-XPB). Ottawa: Author.

Statistics Canada. (2007, June 13). General Social Survey: Navigating family transitions. *The Daily*.

Statistics Canada. (2008a). Pregnancy Outcomes 2005. Catalogue no. 82–224-X. Ottawa: Author.

Statistics Canada. (2008b). Report on the demographic situatuation in Canada 2005 and 2006. Statistics Canada Catalogue no. 91–209-X. Ottawa: Industry Canada.

Statistics Canada. (2010, May 10). Canadian Internet use survey. *The Daily*. Retrieved from http://www.statcan.gc.ca/daily-quotidien/100510/dq100510a-eng.htm

Statistics Canada. (2011a). *Health fact sheets: Breastfeeding, 2009* (Catalogue no. 982-625-X). Ottawa: Author.

Statistics Canada. (2011b). *Conjugal status, Opposite/same-sex status and presence of children for the couple census families in private households of Canada, provinces, territories and census metropolitan areas, 2011 census* (Catalogue no. 98-312-XCB2011046). Ottawa: Author.

Statistics Canada. (2011c). *Family violence in Canada: A statistical profile* (Catalogue no. 85-224-X). Ottawa: Author.

Statistics Canada. (2012). Census: Families, households and marital status—Portrait of families and living arrangements in Canada, census year 2011, no. 1: Families, households and marital status, 2011 (Catalogue No. 98–312-X2011001). Ottawa: Author.

Statistics Canada. (2013a). *Breastfeeding trends in Canada*. Catalogue no. 82-624-X. Ottawa: Author.

Statistics Canada. (2013b). *National household survey, 2011: Immigration and ethnocultural diversity in Canada*. Ottawa: Author.

Statistics Canada. (2014). *Canadian Internet Use & E-commerce in Canada - Data from the 2012 Canadian Internet User Survey*. Catalogue no. 11-627-M. Ottawa: Author.

Statistics Canada. (2015). *Canadian community health survey: Combined data, 2013/2014*. Catalogue no. 11-001-X. Ottawa: Author.

Statistics Canada. (2016). Health fact sheets: *Trends in Canadian births, 1992-2012*. Catalogue no. 82-625-X. Ottawa: Author.

Statistics Canada. (2016, November 28). Sexual misconduct in the Canadian Armed Forces, 2016. *The Daily*. Ottawa: Author.

Steensma, T. D., Biemond, R., de Boer, F., & Cohen-Kettenis, P. T. (2011). Desisting and persisting gender dysphoria after childhood: A qualitative follow-up study. *Clinical Child Psychology and Psychiatry, 16*, 499–516.

Steensma, T. D., van der Ende, J., Verhulst, F. C., & Cohen-Kettenis, P. T. (2012). Gender variance in childhood and sexual orientation in adulthood: A prospective study. *Journal of Sexual Medicine, 10*, 2723–2733.

Steinberg, L. (2011). *Adolescence* (9th ed). New York: McGraw-Hill.

Steiner, M. J., & Cates, W. (2006). Condoms and sexually-transmitted infections. *New England Journal of Medicine, 354*, 2642–2643.

Steiner, M. J., Warner, L., Stone, K. M., & Cates, W., Jr. (2008). Condoms and other barrier methods for prevention of STD/HIV infection and pregnancy. In K. Holmes et al. (Eds.), *Sexually transmitted diseases* (4th ed., pp. 1821–1829). New York: McGraw-Hill.

Steiner, M., Dunn, E., & Born, L. (2003). Hormones and mood: From menarche to menopause and beyond. *Journal of Affective Disorders, 74*, 67–83.

Stephure, R. J., Boon, S. D., MacKinnon, S. L., & Deveau, V. L. (2009). Internet initiated relationships: Associations between age and involvement in online dating. *Journal of Computer-Mediated Communication, 14*(3), 658–681. doi:10.1111/j.1083-6101.2009.01457.x

Stern, K., & McClintock, M. K. (1998). Regulation of ovulation by human pheromones. *Nature, 392*, 177–179.

Sternberg, R. J. (1986). A triangular theory of love. *Psychological Review, 93*, 119–135.

Sternberg, R. J. (1987). Liking versus loving: A comparative evaluation of theories. *Psychological Bulletin, 102*, 331–345.

Sternberg, R. J. (1996). Love stories. *Personal Relationships, 3*, 59–79.

Sternberg, R. J. (1997). Construct validation of a triangular love scale. *European Journal of Social Psychology, 27*, 313–335.

Sternberg, R. J. (1998). *Love is a story: A new theory of relationships*. New York: Oxford University Press.

Sternberg, R. J., Hojjat, M., & Barnes, M. L. (2001). Empirical tests of aspects of a theory of love as a story. *European Journal of Personality, 15*, 199–218.

Stevenson, M. R. (1995). Searching for a gay identity in Indonesia. *Journal of Men's Studies, 4*, 93–108.

Stevinson, C., & Ernst, E. (2001). Complementary/alternative therapies for premenstrual syndrome: A systematic review of randomized controlled trials. *American Journal of Obstetrics and Gynecology, 185*, 227–235.

Stobert, S., & Kemeny, A. (2003, Summer). *Childfree by choice* (Catalogue No. 11–008). Ottawa: Statistics Canada.

Stoddard, J. P., Dibble, S. L., & Fineman, N. (2009). Sexual and physical abuse: A comparison between lesbians and their heterosexual sisters. *Journal of Homosexuality, 56*, 407–420.

Stodghill, R., II. (1998, June 15). Where'd you learn that? *Time, 151*, 52–59.

Stone, K. M. (1994). HIV, other STDs, and barriers. In C. Mauck et al. (Eds.), *Barrier contraceptives: Current status and future prospects* (pp. 203–212). New York: Wiley.

Stoneburner, R. L., & Low-Beer, D. (2004). Population-level HIV declines and behavioral risk avoidance in Uganda. *Science, 304*, 714–718.

Stoner, S. A., George, W. H., Peters, L. M., & Norris, J. (2007). Liquid courage: Alcohol fosters risky sexual decision-making in individuals with sexual fears. *AIDS and Behavior, 11*, 227–237.

Storey, A. E., Walsh, C. J., Quinton, R. L., & Wynne-Edwards, K. E. (2000). Hormonal correlates of paternal responsiveness in new and expectant fathers. *Evolution and Human Behavior, 21*, 79–95.

Storms, M. D. (1980). Theories of sexual orientation. *Journal of Personality and Social Psychology, 38*, 783–792.

Stothard, K. J., Tennant, P. W., Bell, R., & Rankin, J. (2009). Maternal overweight and obesity and the risk of congenital abnormalities: A systematic review and meta-analysis. *Journal of the American Medical Association, 301*, 636–650.

Strachan, T., & Read, A. P. (2004). *Human molecular genetics* (3rd ed.). New York: Garland Science.

Strandberg-Larsen, K. (2008). Binge drinking in pregnancy and risk of fetal death. *Obstet Gynecol, 111*, 602–609.

Stranges, E., Wier, L., & Elixhauser, A. (2011). *Complicating conditions of vaginal deliveries and Cesarean sections, 2009* (HCUP Statistical Brief #113). Rockville, MD: Agency for Healthcare Research and Quality. Retrieved from http://www.hcup-us.ahrq.gov/reports/statbriefs/sb113.pdf

Streissguth, A. P., Barr, H. M., Bookstein, F. L., Sampson, P. D., & Olson, H. C. (1999). The long-term neurocognitive consequences of prenatal alcohol exposure: A 14-year study. *Psychological Science, 10*, 186–190.

Striepe, M. I., & Tolman, D. I. (2003). Mom, Dad, I'm straight: The coming out of gender ideologies in adolescent sexual-identity development. *Journal of Clinical Child and Adolescent Psychology, 32*, 523–530.

Strohm, C. Q., Seltzer, J. A., Cochran, S. D., & Mays, V. M. (2009). "Living apart together" relationships in the United States. *Demographic Research, 21*, 177–214.

Strong, C. (1997). *Ethics in reproductive and perinatal medicine*. New Haven, CT: Yale University Press.

Struckman-Johnson, C., Struckman-Johnson, D., & Anderson, P. B. (2003). Tactics of sexual coercion: When men and women won't take no for an answer. *Journal of Sex Research, 40*, 76–86.

Struckman-Johnson, C., Struckman-Johnson, D., Rucker, L., Bumby, K., & Donaldson, S. (1996). Sexual coercion reported by men and women in prison. *Journal of Sex Research, 33*, 67–76.

Stryker, S. (1987). The vitalization of symbolic interactionism. *Social Psychology Quarterly, 50*, 83–94.

Stubbs, M. L. (2008). Cultural perceptions and practices around menarche and adolescent menstruation in the United States. *Annals of the New York Academy of Sciences, 1135*, 58–66.

Štulhofer, A., Buško, V., & Landripet, I. (2010). Pornography, sexual socialization, and satisfaction among young men. *Archives of Sexual Behavior, 39*(1), 168–178. doi:10.1007/s10508-008-9387-0

Sue, D. W. (2010). *Microaggressions in everyday life: Race, gender, and sexual orientation.* Hoboken, NJ: John Wiley & Sons.

Sue, D. W., Capodilupo, C. M., Torino, G. C., Bucceri, J. M., Holder, A. M., Nadal, K. L., & Esquilin, M. (2007). Racial microaggressions in everyday life: implications for clinical practice. *The American Psychologist, 62,* 271–286. doi:10.1037/0003-066X.62.4.271

Sullivan, N. (2003). *A critical introduction to queer theory.* New York: NYU Press.

Sun, S. S., Schubert, C. M., Chumlea, W. C., Roche, A. F., Kulin, H. E., Lee, P. A., . . . Ryan, A. S. (2002). National estimates of the timing of sexual maturation and racial differences among US children. *Pediatrics, 110,* 911–919.

Suschinsky, K. D., & Lalumière, M. L. (2011). Category-specific and sexual concordance: The stability of sex differences in sexual arousal patterns. *Canadian Journal of Human Sexuality, 20,* 93–108.

Suschinsky, K. D., Lalumière, M. L., & Chivers, M. L. (2009). Sex differences in patterns of genital sexual arousal: Measurement artifacts or true phenomena?. *Archives of Sexual Behavior, 38*(4), 559–573. doi:10.1007/s10508-008-9339-8

Suschinsky, K. D., Shelley, A. J., Gerritsen, J., Tuiten, A., & Chivers, M. L. (2015). The clitoral photoplethysmograph: A pilot study examining discriminant and convergent validity. *Journal of Sexual Medicine, 12,* 2324–2338.

Sutcliffe, P. A., Dixon, S., Akehurst, R. L., Wilkinson, A., Shippam, A., White, S., . . . Caddy, C. M. (2009). Evaluation of surgical procedures for sex reassignment: a systematic review. *Journal of Plastic, Reconstructive & Aesthetic Surgery, 62,* 294–308.

Sutherland, S. E., Rehman, U. S., Fallis, E. E., & Goodnight, J. (2015). Understanding the phenomenon of sexual desire discrepancy in couples. *Canadian Journal of Human Sexuality, 24,* 141–150.

Sutton, K. S., Boyer, S. C., Goldfinger, C., Ezer, P., & Pukall, C. F. (2012). To lube or not to lube: Experiences and perceptions of lubricant use in women with and without dyspareunia. *Journal of Sexual Medicine, 9,* 240–250.

Sutton, K. S., Stratton, N., Pytyck, J., Kolla, N. J., & Cantor, J. M. (2014). Patient characteristics by type of hypersexuality referral: A quantitative chart review of 115 consecutive male cases. *Journal of Sex & Marital Therapy, 41,* 563–580.

Sutton, K., Pukall, C., Wild, C., Johnsrude, I., & Chamberlain, S. (2015). Cognitive, psychophysical, and neural correlates of vulvar pain in primary and secondary provoked vestibulodynia: A pilot study. *Journal of Sexual Medicine, 12,* 1283–1297.

Swaab, D. F. (2005). The role of the hypothalamus and endocrine system in sexuality. In J. Hyde (Ed.), *Biological substrates of human*

sexuality. Washington, DC: American Psychological Association.

Swaab, D. F., Gooren, L. J., & Hofman, M. A. (1995). Brain research, gender and sexual orientation. *Journal of Homosexuality, 28,* 283–301.

Swami, V. (2009). An examination of the love-is-blind bias among gay men and lesbians. *Body Image, 6,* 149–151.

Swamy, G., Ostbye, T., & Skjaerven, R. (2008). Association of preterm birth with long-term survival, reproduction, and next generation preterm birth. *Journal of the American Medical Association, 299,* 1429–1436.

Swygard, H., Sena, A. C., Hobbs, M. M., & Cohen, M. S. (2004). Trichomoniasis: Clinical manifestations, diagnosis, and management. *Sexually Transmitted Infections, 80,* 91–95.

Symbalauk, D. G., & Jones, K. M. (1999). Prostitution offender programs: An educational alternative to sentencing. *Law Now, 23,* 38.

Szabo, R. (2000). How does male circumcision protect against HIV infection? *British Medical Journal, 320,* 1592.

Szasz, T. S. (1973). Sex. In *The second sin.* London, UK: Routledge & Kegan Paul.

Szasz, T. S. (1980). *Sex by prescription.* Garden City, NY: Anchor Press/Doubleday.

Szielasko, A. L., Symons, D. K., & Price, E. L. (2013). Development of an attachment-informed measure of sexual behavior in late adolescence. *Journal of Adolescence.* doi:10.1016/j.adolescence.2012.12.008

Taberner, P. V. (1985). *Aphrodisiacs: The science and the myth.* Philadelphia: University of Pennsylvania Press.

Tafoya, T., & Wirth, D. A. (1996). Native American two-spirit men. In J. F. Longres (Ed.), *Men of color* (pp. 51–67). New York: Haworth.

Tag-Eldin, M. A., Gadallah, M. A., Al-Tayeb, M. N., Abdel-Aty, M., Mansour, E., & Sallema, M. (2008). Prevalence of female genital cutting among Egyptian girls. *Bulletin of the World Health Organization, 86,* 269–274.

Talamini, J. T. (1982). *Boys will be girls: The hidden world of the heterosexual male transvestite.* Washington, DC: University Press of America.

Talge, N. M., Neal, C., Glover, V., & Early Stress Translational Research and Prevention Science Network. (2007). Antenatal maternal stress and long-term effects on child neurodevelopment: How and why? *Journal of Child Psychology and Psychiatry, 48,* 245–261.

Tannahill, R. (1980). *Sex in history.* New York: Stein & Day.

Tannen, D. (1991). *You just don't understand: Women and men in conversation.* New York: William Morrow.

Tanner, J. M. (1967). Puberty. In A. McLaren (Ed.), *Advances in reproductive physiology* (Vol. II). New York: Academic.

Taylor, C., & Peter, T., with McMinn, T. L., Schachter, K., Beldom, S., Ferry, A., Gross, Z., & Paquin, S. (2011). Every class in every school: The final report on the first national

climate survey on homophobia, biphobia, and transphobia in Canadian schools. Toronto: EGALE Canada Human Rights Trust. Retrieved from http://www.egale.ca

Taylor, C., Peter, T., Schachter, K., Paquin, S., Beldom, S., Gross, Z., & McMinn, T. L. (2008). *Youth speak up about homophobia and transphobia: The first National Climate survey on homophobia in Canadian Schools. Phase one report.* Toronto: Egale Canada Human Rights Trust.

Taylor, D. (2006). From "It's all in your head" to "Taking back the month": Premenstrual syndrome (PMS) research and the contributions of the society for Menstrual Cycle Research. *Sex Roles, 54,* 377–392.

Taylor, L. S., Fiore, A. T., Mendelsohn, G. A., & Cheshire, C. (2011). "Out of my league": A real-world test of the matching hypothesis. *Personality and Social Psychology Bulletin, 37,* 942–954.

Tebbe, E. A., Moradi, B., & Ege, E. (2014). Revised and abbreviated forms of the Genderism and Transphobia Scale: Tools for assessing anti-trans prejudice. *Journal of Counseling Psychology, 61,* 581–592.

Technical Working Group. (2002). *Evaluation of abstinence education programs funded under Title V, Section 510: Interim Report.* U.S. Department of Health and Human Services: Office of the Assistant Secretary for Planning and Evaluation.

Tedeschi, R. G., Park, C. L., & Calhoun, L. G. (Eds.). (1998). *Posttraumatic growth: Positive changes in the aftermath of crisis.* Mahwah, NJ: Erlbaum.

Templeman, T. L., & Stinnett, R. D. (1991). Patterns of sexual arousal and history in a "normal" sample of young men. *Archives of Sexual Behavior, 20,* 137–150.

Tennant, P. W. G., Rankin, J., & Bell, R. (2011). Maternal body mass index and the risk of fetal and infant death: A cohort study from the North of England. *Human Reproduction, 26,* 1501–1511.

Terasawa, E., Kurian, J. R., Keen, K. L., Shiel, N. A., Colman, R. J., & Capuano, S. V. (2012). Body weight impact on puberty: Effects of high-calorie diet on puberty onset in female rhesus monkeys. *Endocrinology, 153,* 1696–1705.

Terman, L. M. (1948). Kinsey's *Sexual Behavior in the Human Male:* Some comments and criticisms. *Psychological Bulletin, 45,* 443–459.

Terman, L., et al. (1938). *Psychological factors in marital happiness.* New York: McGraw-Hill.

Terry, L. L., & Vasey, P. L. (2010). Feederism in a woman. *Archives of Sexual Behavior.* doi:10.1007/s10508-009-9580-9

Tessler Lindau, S., Schumm, L. P., Laumann, E. O., Levinson, W., O'Muircheartaigh, C. A., & Waite, L. J. (2007). A study of sexuality and health among older adults in the United States. *The New England Journal of Medicine, 357,* 762–774.

Testa, M., VanZile-Tamsen, C., & Livingston, J. A. (2005). Childhood sexual abuse, relationship satisfaction, and sexual risk taking in a community sample of women. *Journal of Consulting and Clinical Psychology, 73,* 1116–1124.

Testa, R. J., Habarth, J., Peta, J., Balsam, K., & Bockting, W. (2015). Development of the Gender Minority Stress and Resilience Measure. *Psychology of Sexual Orientation and Gender Diversity, 2,* 65–77.

Testa, R. J., Sciacca, L. M., Wang, F., Hendricks, M. L., Goldblum, P., Bradford, J., & Bongar, B. (2012). Effects of violence on transgender people. *Professional Psychology: Research and Practice, 42,* 452–459.

Thakker, J., Collie, R. M., Gannon, T. A., & Ward, T. (2008). Rape: Assessment and treatment. In D. R. Laws & W. T. O'Donohue (Eds.), *Sexual deviance* (pp. 356–383). New York: Guilford.

The sex industry. (1998, February 14). *The Economist,* 21–23.

Thibaut, F., De La Barra, F., Gordon, H., Cosyns, P., Bradford, J. M., & WFSBP Task Force on Sexual Disorders. (2010). The World Federation of Societies for Biological Psychiatry (WFSBP) guidelines for the biological treatment of paraphilias. *The World Journal of Biological Psychiatry, 11,* 604–655.

Thompson, A. E., & Byers, E. S. (2016). Heterosexual young adults' interest, attitudes, and experiences related to mixed-gender, multiperson sex. *Archives of Sexual Behavior.* doi:10.1007/s10508-016-0699-1

Thompson, A. E., & O'Sullivan, L. F. (2012). Gender differences in associations of sexual and romantic stimuli: Do young men really prefer sex over romance? *Archives of Sexual Behavior, 41,* 949–957.

Thompson, A. E., O'Sullivan, L. F., Byers, E. S., & Shaughnessy, K. (2014). Young adults' implicit and explicit attitudes towards the sexuality of older adults. *Canadian Journal on Aging, 33,* 259–270.

Thompson, A. P. (1983). Extramarital sex: A review of the research literature. *Journal of Sex Research, 19,* 1–22.

Thompson, S. K. (1975). Gender labels and early sex role development. *Child Development, 46,* 339–347.

Thorne, N., & Amrein, H. (2003). Vomeronasal organ: Pheromone recognition with a twist. *Current Biology, 13,* R220–R222.

Thorpe, L. P., Katz, B., & Lewis, R. T. (1961). *The psychology of abnormal behavior.* New York: Ronald Press.

Tiefer, L. (1991). Historical, scientific, clinical, and feminist criticisms of "The Human Sexual Response Cycle" model. *Annual Review of Sex Research, 2,* 1–24.

Tiefer, L. (1994). Three crises facing sexology. *Archives of Sexual Behavior, 23,* 361–374.

Tiefer, L. (2000). Sexology and the pharmaceutical industry: The threat of co-optation. *Journal of Sex Research, 37,* 273–283.

Tiefer, L. (2001). Arriving at a "new view" of women's sexual problems: Background, theory, and activism. In E. Kachak & L. Tiefer (Eds.), *A new view of women's sexual problems* (pp. 63–98). New York: Haworth Press.

Tiefer, L. (2004). *Sex is not a natural act and other essays* (2nd ed.). Boulder, CO: Westview Press.

Tiefer, L. (2008). Female genital cosmetic surgery: Freakish or inevitable? Analysis from medical marketing, bioethics, and feminist theory. *Feminism Psychology, 18,* 466–479.

Tiggemann, M., & Hodgson, S. (2008). The hairlessness norm extended: Reasons for and predictors of women's body hair removal at different body sites. *Sex Roles, 59,* 889–897.

Timmerman, G. (2003). Sexual harassment of adolescents perpetrated by teachers and by peers: An exploration of the dynamics of power, culture, and gender in secondary schools. *Sex Roles, 48,* 231–244.

Tjepkema, M. (2008). Health care use among gay, lesbian and bisexual Canadians. *Health Reports, 19,* 53–64.

Tobin, D. D., Menon, M., Menon, M., Spatta, B. C., Hodges, E. E., & Perry, D. G. (2010). The intrapsychics of gender: A model of self-socialization. *Psychological Review, 117*(2), 601–622.

Tolman, D. L., & Diamond, L. M. (Eds.) (2014). *APA handbook of sexuality and psychology.* Washington, DC: American Psychological Association.

Tolman, D. L., & McClelland, S. I. (2011). Normative sexuality development in adolescence: A decade in review, 2000–2009. *Journal of Research on Adolescence, 21,* 242–255.

Toppari, J., & Juul, A. (2010). Trends in puberty timing in humans and environmental modifiers. *Molecular and Cellular Endocrinology, 324,* 39–44.

Townsend, J. W. (2003). Reproductive behavior in the context of global population. *American Psychologist, 58,* 197–2004.

Tracy, S. K., Hartz, D. L., Tracy, M. B., Allen, J., Forti, A., Hall, B., . . . Kildea, S. (2013). Caseload midwifery care versus standard maternity care for women of any risk: M@NGO, a randomised, controlled trial. *The Lancet, 382,* 1723–1732.

Traish, A. M., Kim, N. N., Munarriz, R., Moreland, R., & Goldstein, I. (2002). Biochemical and physiological mechanisms of female genital sexual arousal. *Archives of Sexual Behavior, 31,* 393–400.

Traven, S., Cuyllen, K., & Protter, B. (1990). Female sexual offenders: Severe victims and victimizers. *Journal of Forensic Sciences, 35,* 140–150.

Tremblay, C., Hébert, M., & Piché, C. (1999). Coping strategies and social support as mediators of consequences in child sexual abuse victims. *Child Abuse & Neglect, 23,* 929–945.

Tremblay, C., Hébert, M., & Piché, C. (2000). Type I and type II posttraumatic stress disorder in sexually abused children. *Journal of Child Sexual Abuse, 9,* 65–90.

Tremblay, L., & Frignon J. (2004). Biobehavioural and cognitive determinants of adolescent girls' involvement in sexual risk behaviours: A test of three theoretical models. *Canadian Journal of Human Sexuality, 13,* 29–43.

Trenholm, C., Devaney, B., Fortson, K., Quay, L., Wheeler, J., & Clark, M. (2007). *Impacts of four Title V section 510 abstinence education programs: Final report* (MPR Ref. No. 8549–110). Princeton, NJ: Mathematica Policy Research Inc.

Triandis, H. C., McCusker, C., & Hui, C. H. (1990). Multimethod probes of individualism and collectivism. *Journal of Personality and Social Psychology, 59,* 1006–1020.

Trocmé, N., MacLaurin, B., Fallon, B., Daciuk, J., Billingsley, D., Tourigny, M., . . . McKenzie, B. (2001). *Canadian Incidence Study of Reported Child Abuse and Neglect: Final Report.* Ottawa: Minister of Public Works and Government Services Canada.

Trotter, E. C., & Alderson, K. G. (2007). University students' definitions of having sex, sexual partner, and virginity loss: The influence of participant gender, sexual experience, and contextual factors. *Canadian Journal of Human Sexuality, 16,* 11–29.

Trudel, G. (2002). Sexuality and marital life: Results of a survey. *Journal of Sex & Marital Therapy, 28,* 241–261.

Truitt, W. A., & Coolen, L. (2002). Identification of a potential ejaculation generator in the spinal cord. *Science, 297,* 1566–1569.

Trynka, S., & Tucker, N. (1995). Overview. In N. Tucker (Ed.), *Bisexual politics: Theories, queries, and visions.* New York: Harrington Park Press.

Tsui, L., & Nicoladis, E. (2004). Losing it: Similarities and differences in first intercourse experiences of men and women. *Canadian Journal of Human Sexuality, 13,* 95–106.

Turkle, S. (1995). *Life on the screen: Identity in the age of the Internet.* New York: Simon & Schuster.

Turner, P. K., Runtz, M. G., & Galambos, N. L. (1999). Sexual abuse, pubertal timing, and subjective age i adolescent girls: A research note. *Journal of Reproductive and Infant Psychology, 17*(2), 111–118.

Tutin, C. E. G., & McGinnis, P. R. (1981). Chimpanzee reproduction in the wild. In C. E. Graham (Ed.), *Reproductive biology of the great apes* (pp. 239–264). New York: Academic Press.

Tutty, L. M. (1997). Child sexual abuse prevention programs: Evaluating who do you tell. *Child Abuse & Neglect, 21,* 869–881.

Tutty, L. M. (2014). Listen to the children: Kids' impressions of who do you tell. *Journal of Child Sexual Abuse, 23,* 17–37.

U.S. Bureau of the Census. (2004). Current population survey, Annual social and economic supplement. Table 2: Marital status of the population 15 years and older by age and gender. Retrieved from http://www.census.gov/population/socdemo/gender/2004gender_table2.xls

U.S. General Accounting Office. (1996). *Cycle of sexual abuse: Research inconclusive about whether child victims become adult abusers* (Report number GAO/GGD-96-178). Retrieved from http://www.gpo.gov/fdsys/pkg/GAOREPORTS-GGD-96-178/html/GAOREPORTS-GGD-96-178.htm

Udry, J. R. (1988). Biological predispositions and social control in adolescent sexual behavior. *American Sociological Review, 53*, 709–722.

Udry, J. R., & Eckland, B. K. (1984). Benefits of being attractive: Differential payoffs for men and women. *Psychological Reports, 54*, 47–56.

Udry, J. R., Billy, J. O., Morris, N. M., Groff, T. R., & Raj, M. H. (1985). Serum androgenic hormones motivate sexual behavior in adolescent boys. *Fertility and Sterility, 43*, 90–94.

Ueno, K. (2005). Sexual orientation and psychological distress in adolescence: Examining interpersonal stressors and social support processes. *Social Psychology Quarterly, 68*, 258–277.

Ulmann, A., Teutsch, G., & Philibert, D. (1990, June). RU-486. *Scientific American, 262*, 42–48.

UNAIDS. (1997). *Impact of HIV and sexual health education on the sexual behavior of young people*. Geneva, Switzerland: Author.

UNAIDS. (2016). *Global AIDS Update 2016*. Retrieved from http://www.unaids.org

Underwood, M. K., Rosen, L. H., More, D., Ehrenreich, S. E., & Gentsch, J. K. (2011). The BlackBerry project: Capturing the content of adolescents' text messaging. *Developmental Psychology, 48*, 295–302.

UNESCO. (2005). *Human cloning: Ethical issues* (2nd ed.). Retrieved from http://unesdoc.unesco.org/images/0013/001359/135928e.pdf

UNICEF. (2016). *Female genital mutilation/cutting: A global concern*. Retrieved from http://www.unicef.org/media/files/FGMC_2016_brochure_final_UNICEF_SPREAD.pdf

Union for Reform Judaism. (2004). What is the Reform perspective on abortion? Retrieved from http://uahc.org

United Church of Canada, General Council 1980.

United Church of Canada, General Council 1989.

United Synagogue of Conservative Judaism. (1989). Retrieved from http://www.uscj.org

Upadhyay, U. D., Adhikary, I., Robey, B., Blackburn, R. D., & Richey, C. (2005). Microbicides: new potential for protection. *Inforeports, 3*. Baltimore: Johns Hopkins School of Public Health. Retrieved from http://www.infoforhealth.org

UPI. (1981, November 5). Toxicologist warns against butyl nitrite. *Delaware Gazette*, p. 3.

Urbina, A., & Jones, K. (2004). Crystal methamphetamine, its analogues, and HIV infection; Medical and psychiatric aspects of a new epidemic. *Clinical Infectious Diseases, 38*, 890–894.

Uy, J. M., Parsons, J. T., Bimbi, D. S., Koken, J. A., & Halkitis, P. N. (2004). Gay and bisexual male escorts who advertise on the Internet: Understanding reasons for and effects of involvement in commercial sex. *International Journal of Men's Health, 3*, 11–26.

Vaillancourt, T., & Aanchai, S. (2011). Intolerance of sexy peers: Intrasexual competition among women. *Aggressive Behavior, 37*, 569–577.

Valentich, M. (1994). Rape revisited: Sexual violence against women in the former Yugoslavia. *Canadian Journal of Human Sexuality, 3*, 53–64.

Valkenburg, P. M., Sumter, S. R., & Peter, J. (2011). Gender differences in online and offline self-disclosure in pre-adolescence and adolescence. *British Journal of Developmental Psychology, 29*, 253–269.

Valkenburg, P., & Peter, J. (2009). Social consequences of the Internet for adolescents: A decade of research. *Current Directions in Psychological Science, 18*, 1–5.

Van Anders, S. M., & Watson, N. V. (2006). Menstrual cycle irregularities are associated with testosterone levels in healthy premenopausal women. *American Journal of Human Biology, 18*, 841–844.

Van Anders, S. M., Brotto, L., Farrell, J., & Yule, M. (2009). Associations among physiological and subjective sexual response, sexual desire, and salivary steroid hormones in healthy premenopausal women. *Journal of Sexual Medicine, 6*, 739–751.

Van Anders, S. M., Hamilton, L. D., & Watson, N. V. (2007). Multiple partners are associated with higher testosterone in North American men and women. *Hormones and Behavior, 51*, 454–459.

Van Dongen, S., & Gangestad, S. (2011). Human fluctuating asymmetry in relation to health and quality: A meta-analysis. *Evolution and Human Behavior, 32*, 380–396.

Van Goozen, S. H. M., Wiegant, V. M., Endert, E., Helmond, F. A., & Van de Poll, N. E. (1997). Psychoendocrinological assessment of the menstrual cycle: The relationship between hormones, sexuality, and mood. *Archives of Sexual Behavior, 26*, 359–382.

Van Horn, K. R., Arnone, A., Nesbitt, K., Desilets, L., Sears, T., Giffin, M., & Brudi, R. (1997). Physical distance and interpersonal characteristics in college students' romantic relationships. *Personal Relationships, 4*, 25–34.

Van Lankveld, J. (1998). Bibliotherapy in the treatment of sexual dysfunctions: A meta-analysis. *Journal of Consulting and Clinical Psychology, 66*, 702–708.

Van Lankveld, J. (2009). Self-help therapies for sexual dysfunction. *Journal of Sex Research, 46*, 143–155.

Van Lankveld, J., Everaerd, W., & Grotjohann, Y. (2001). Cognitive-behavorial bibliotherapy for sexual dysfunctions in heterosexual couples: A randomized waiting-list controlled clinical trial in the Netherlands. *Journal of Sex Research, 38*, 51–67.

Van Lankveld, J., ter Kuile, M. M., de Groot, H. E., Melles, R., Nefs, J., & Zandbergen, M. (2006). Cognitive-behavioral therapy for women with lifelong vaginismus: A randomized waiting-list controlled trial of efficacy. *Journal of Consulting and Clinical Psychology, 74*, 168–178.

van Lankweld, J., Granot, M., Weijmar Schultz, W., Binik, Y., Wesselmann, U., . . . Achtrari, C. (2010). Women's sexual pain disorders. *Journal of Sexual Medicine, 7*, 615–631.

Van Lent, P. (1996). Her beautiful savage: The current sexual image of the Native American male. In S. E. Bird (Ed.), *Dressing in feathers: The construction of the Indian in American popular culture* (pp. 211–228). Boulder, CO: Westview.

Vance, E. B., & Wagner, N. N. (1976). Written descriptions of orgasm: A study of sex differences. *Archives of Sexual Behavior, 5*, 87–98.

Vancouver Coastal Health Authority. (2009). Supporting sexual health and intimacy in care facilities: Guidelines for supporting adults living in long-term care facilities and group homes in British Columbia, Canada. Retrieved from http://www.sfu.ca

VanderLaan, D. P., & Vasey, P. L. (2008). Mate retention behavior of men and women in heterosexual and homosexual relationships. *Archives of Sexual Behavior, 37*, 572–585.

VanderLaan, D. P., Gothreau, L., Bartlett, N. H., & Vasey, P. L. (2011). Separation anxiety in feminine boys: Pathological or prosocial? *Journal of Gay and Lesbian Mental Health, 15*, 1–16.

Vannier, S. A., & O'Sullivan, L. F. (2008). The feasibility and acceptability of handheld computers in a prospective diary study of adolescent sexual behaviour. *Canadian Journal of Human Sexuality, 17*, 183–192.

Vannier, S. A., & O'Sullivan, L. F. (2011). Communicating interest in sex: Verbal and nonverbal initiation of sexual activity in young adults' romantic dating relationships. *Archives of Sexual Behavior, 40*, 961–969.

Vannier, S. A., & O'Sullivan, L. F. (2012). Who gives and who gets: Why, when, and with whom young people engage in oral sex. *Journal of Youth and Adolescence, 41*, 572–582.

Vannier, S., Currie, A., & O'Sullivan, L. (2014). Schoolgirls and soccer moms: A content analysis of free "Teen" and "MILF" online pornography. *Journal of Sex Research, 51*, 253–264.

Vanwesenbeeck, I. (1994). *Prostitutes' well-being and risk*. Amsterdam: VU University Press.

Vanwesenbeeck, I. (2001). Another decade of social scientific work on sex work: A review of research 1990–2000. *Annual Review of Sex Research, 12*, 242–289.

Vanwesenbeeck, I. (2005). Burnout among female indoor sex workers. *Archives of Sexual Behavior, 34*, 627–640.

Vanwesenbeeck, I. (2008). Sexual violence and the MDGs. *International Journal of Sexual Health, 20*, 25–49.

Varghese, B., Maher, J. E., Peterman, T. A., Branson, B. M., & Steketee, R. W. (2002). Reducing the risk of sexual HIV transmission: quantifying the per-act risk for HIV on the basis of choice of partner, sex act, and condom use. *Sexually Transmitted Diseases, 29*, 38–43.

Vasey, P. L. (2002). Sexual partner preference in female Japanese macaques. *Archives of Sexual Behavior, 31*, 51–62.

Vasey, P. L., & Bartlett, N. H. (2007). What can the Samoan "fa'afafine" teach us about the Western concept of gender identity disorder in childhood? *Perspectives in Biology and Medicine, 50*, 481–490.

Vasey, P. L., & Bartlett, N. H. (2007). What can the Samoan *fa'afafine* teach us about the Western concept of "Gender Identity Disorder in Childhood"? *Perspectives in Biology and Medicine, 50*, 481–490.

Vasey, P. L., & Duckworth, N. (2008). Female-male mounting in Japanese macaques: The proximate role of sexual reward. *Behavioural Processes, 77*, 405–407. doi:10.1016/j.beproc.2007.07.004

Vasey, P. L., Foroud, A., Duckworth, N., & Kovacovsky, S. D. (2006). Male-female and female-female mounting in Japanese Macaques: A comparative study of posture and movement. *Archives of Sexual Behavior, 35*, 117–129.

Vasey, P. L., Leca, J-B., Gunst, N., & VanderLaan, D. P. (2014). Female homosexual behavior and inter-sexual mate competition in Japanese macaques: Possible implications for sexual selection theory. *Neuroscience and Biobehavioral Reviews, 46*, 573–578.

Vasey, P. L., VanderLaan, D. P., Gothreau, L. M., & Bartlett, N. H. (2009). Traits of separation anxiety in childhood: A retrospective study of Samoan men, women and *Fa'afafine*. *Archives of Sexual Behavior*. doi:10.1007/s10508-9009-9589-0

Vasey, P. L., VanderLaan, D. P., Gothreau, L., &, Bartlett, N. H. (2011). Traits of separation anxiety in childhood: A comparison of Samoan men, women and *fa'afafine*. *Archives of Sexual Behavior, 40*, 511–517.

Ve Ard, C., & Veaux, F. (2003). Polyamory 101. Retrieved from http://www.xeromag.com/poly101.pdf

Veale, J. F., Watson, R. J., Peter, T., & Saewyc, E. M. (2017). Mental health disparities among Canadian transgender youth. *Journal of Adolescent Health, 60*, 44–49.

Venicz, L., & Vanwesenbeeck, I. (2000). *Something is going to change in prostitution: Social position and the psychological well being of indoor prostitutes before the law reform*. Utrecht/The Hague, The Netherlands: NISSO/Ministry of Justice.

Venkatesh, S. (2011). How tech tools transformed New York's sex trade. *Wired*. Retrieved from http://www.wired.com/magazine/2011/01/ff_sextrade/all

Vilain, E. (2000). The genetics of sexual development. *Annual Review of Sex Research, 11*, 1–25.

Vincent, J. P., Friedman, L. C., Nugent, J., & Messerly, L. (1979). Demand characteristics in observations of marital interaction. *Journal of Consulting and Clinical Psychology, 47*, 557–566.

Volbert, R. (2000). Sexual knowledge of preschool children. *Journal of Psychology and Human Sexuality, 12*, 5–26.

Volgsten, H., Skoog Svanberg, A., Ekselius, L., Lundkvist, Ö, & Sundström Poromaa, I. (2008). Prevalence of psychiatric disorders in infertile women and men undergoing *in vitro* fertilization treatment. *Human Reproduction, 23*, 2056–2063.

Von Hertzen, H., Piaggio, G., Ding, J., Chen, J., Song, S., & Bartfai, G. (2002). Low dose mifepristone and two regimens of levonorgestrel for emergency contraception: A WHO multicentre randomised trial. *Lancet, 360*, 1803–1810.

Von Krafft-Ebing, R. (1886). *Psychopathia sexualis*. (Reprinted by Putnam, New York, 1965.)

Von Kries, R., Koletzko, B., Sauerwald, T., von Mutius, E., Barnert, D., Grunert, V., & von Voss, H. (1999). Breast feeding and obesity: Cross sectional study. *British Medical Journal, 319*, 147–150.

Wade, L., & DeLamater, J. (2002). Relationship dissolution as a life stage transition: Effects on sexual attitudes and behaviors. *Journal of Marriage and the Family, 64*, 898–914.

Wagner, A. C., McShane, K. E., Hart, T. A., & Margolese, S. (2016). A focus group qualitative study of HIV stigma in the Canadian healthcare system. *Canadian Journal of Human Sexuality, 25*, 61–71.

Waite, L., & Joyner, K. (2000). Emotional and physical satisfaction with sex in married, cohabitating, and dating sexual unions: Do men and women differ? In Edward Laumann & Robert Michael (Eds.), *Sex, love, and health in America: Private choices and public policy* (pp. 239–269). Chicago: University of Chicago Press.

Wald, A., Langenberg, A. G., Krantz, E., Douglas, J. M., Jr., Handsfield, H. H., DiCarlo, R. P., . . . Corey, L. (2005). The relationship between condom use and herpes simplex virus acquisition. *Annals of Internal Medicine, 143*, 707–713.

Walen, S. R., & Roth, D. (1987). A cognitive approach. In J. H. Geer & W. T. O'Donohue (Eds.), *Theories of human sexuality*. New York: Plenum.

Walker, C. (2009). Lest we forget: The Tuskegee experiment. *Journal of Theory Construction & Testing, 13*, 5–6.

Walker, J., Archer, J., & Davies, M. (2005). Effects of rape on men: A descriptive analysis. *Archives of Sexual Behavior, 34*, 69–80.

Walker, L. M., Wassersug, R. J., & Robinson, J. W. (2015). Psychosocial perspectives on sexual recovery after prostate cancer treatment. *Nature Reviews Urology, 12*, 167–176.

Wallen, K. (2001). Sex and context: Hormones and primate sexual motivation. *Hormones and Behavior, 40*, 339–357.

Wallen, K., & Lloyd, E. (2011). Female sexual arousal: Genital anatomy and orgasm in intercourse. *Hormones and Behavior*. doi:10:1016/j.yhbeh.2010.12.004

Wallen, K., & Parsons, W. A. (1997). Sexual behavior in same-sexed nonhuman primates: Is it relevant to understanding human homosexuality? *Annual Review of Sex Research, 8*, 195–223.

Wallen, K., & Zehr, J. L. (2004). Hormones and history: The evolution and development of primate female sexuality. *Journal of Sex Research, 41*, 101–112.

Wallerstein, E. (1980). *Circumcision: An American health fallacy*. New York: Springer.

Wallin, P. (1949). An appraisal of some methodological aspects of the Kinsey report. *American Sociological Review, 14*, 197–210.

Wallis, C. (2011). Performing gender: A content analysis of gender display in music videos. *Sex Roles, 64*, 160–172.

Walster, E., Walster, W., & Berscheid, E. (1978). *Equity: Theory and research*. Boston: Allyn and Bacon.

Wang, P. J., McCarrey, J., Yang, F., & Page, D. (2001). An abundance of X-linked genes expressed in spermatogonia. *Nature Genetics, 27*, 422–426.

Ward, L. M., & Harrison, K. (2005). The impact of media use on girls' beliefs about gender roles, their bodies, and sexual relationships: A research synthesis. In E. Cole & J. H. Daniel (Eds.), *Featuring females: Feminist analyses of media* (pp. 3–24). Washington, DC: American Psychological Association

Ward, L. M., Hansbrough, E., & Walker, E. (2005). Contributions of music video exposure to Black adolescents' gender and sexual schemas. *Journal of Adolescent Research, 20*, 143–166.

Ward, O. B., Ward, I. L., Denning, J. H., Hendricks, S. E., & French, J. A. (2002). Hormonal mechanisms underlying aberrant sexual differentiation in male rats prenatally exposed to alcohol, stress, or both. *Archives of Sexual Behavior, 31*, 9–16.

Ward, T., Gannon, T., & Yates, P. (2008). The treatment of offenders: Current practice and new developments with an emphasis on sex offenders. *International Review of Victimology, 15*, 179–204.

Wassersug, R. J. (2010). On the invisibility of the emasculated. *Anthropology Today, 26*, 1–3.

Wassersug, R. J., McKenna, E., & Lieberman, T. (2012). Eunuch as a gender identity after castration. *Journal of Gender Studies, 21*, 253–270.

Wassersug, R. J., Zelenietz, S. A., & Squire, G. F. (2004). New age eunuchs: Motivation and rationale for voluntary castration. *Archives of Sexual Behavior, 33*, 433–442.

Waxman, S. E., & Pukall, C. F. (2009). Laser doppler imaging of genital blood flow: A direct measure of female sexual arousal. *Journal of Sexual Medicine, 6*, 2278–2285.

Waynforth, D., Hurtadoa, A. M., & Hillary, K. (1998). Environmentally contingent reproductive strategies in Mayan and Ache Males. *Evolution and Human Behavior, 19*, 369–385.

Weaver, A. D., & Byers, E. S. (2006). The relationships among body image, body mass index, exercise, and sexual functioning in heterosexual women. *Psychology of Women Quarterly, 30*, 333–339.

Weaver, A. D., & Byers, E. S. (2013). Eye of the beholder? Sociocultural factors in the body image and sexual well-being of heterosexual women. *International Journal of Sexual Health, 25,* 128–147.

Weaver, A. D., Byers, E. S., Sears, H. A, Cohen, J. N., & Randall, H. E. S. (2002). New Brunswick parents' attitudes towards sexual health education at school and at home. *Canadian Journal of Human Sexuality, 11,* 19–31.

Weaver, A. D., Claybourn, M., & MacKeigan, K. L. (2013). Evaluations of friends-with-benefits relationship scenarios: Is there evidence of a sexual double standard? *Canadian Journal of Human Sexuality, 22,* 152–159.

Weaver, A. D., MacKeigan, K. L., & MacDonald, H. A. (2011). Experiences and perceptions of young adults in friends with benefits relationships: A qualitative study. *Canadian Journal of Human Sexuality, 20,* 41–53.

Weideger, P. (1976). *Menstruation and menopause.* New York: Knopf.

Weinberg, M. S., Shaver, F. S., & Williams, C. J. (1999). Gendered sex work in the San Francisco tenderloin. *Archives of Sexual Behavior, 28,* 503–521.

Weinberg, M. S., Williams, C. J., & Pryor, D. W. (1994). *Dual attraction: Understanding bisexuality.* New York: Oxford University Press.

Weinberg, M., Williams, C., & Calhan, C. (1995). "If the shoe fits . . .": Exploring male homosexual foot fetishism. *Journal of Sex Research, 32,* 17–27.

Weinberg, T. S. (1987). Sadomasochism in the United States: A review of recent sociological literature. *Journal of Sex Research, 23,* 50–69.

Weinberg, T. S. (1994). Research in sadomasochism: A review of sociological and social psychological literature. *Annual Review of Sex Research, 5,* 257–279.

Weller, L., Weller, A., & Avinir, O. (1995). Menstrual synchrony: Only in roommates who are close friends? *Physiology and Behavior, 58,* 883–889.

Wellings, K., Collumbien, M., Slaymaker, E., Singh, S., Hodges, Z., Patel, D., & Bajos, N. (2006). Sexual and reproductive health 2: Sexual behaviour in context: A global perspective. *The Lancet, 368,* 1706–1728.

Wells, B. E., & Twenge, J. M. (2005). Changes in young people's sexual behavior and attitudes, 1943–1999: A cross-temporal meta-analysis. *Review of General Psychology, 9,* 249–261.

Wells, K. (2009). Research exploring the health, wellness, and safety concerns of sexual minority youth. *Canadian Journal of Human Sexuality, 18,* 221–229.

Wenk, M., & Nieschlag, E. (2006). Male contraception; A realistic option? *The European Journal of Contraception and Reproductive Health Care, 11,* 69–80.

Wentland, J. J., & Reissing, E. D. (2011). Taking casual sex not too casually: Exploring definitions of casual sexual relationships. *Canadian Journal of Human Sexuality, 20,* 75–91.

Wentland, J. J., & Reissing, E. D. (2011). Taking casual sex not too casually: Exploring definitions of casual sexual relationships. *Canadian Journal of Human Sexuality, 20,* 75–91.

Wentland, J. J., Herold, E. S., Desmarais, S., & Milhausen, R. R. (2009). Differentiating highly sexual women from less sexual women. *Canadian Journal of Human Sexuality, 18,* 169–182.

Wheeler, G. D., Wall, S. R., Belcastro, A. N., & Cumming, D. C. (1984). Reduced serum testosterone and prolactin levels in male distance runners. *Journal of the American Medical Association, 252,* 514–516.

Wheeler, J., Newring, K., & Draper, C. (2008). Transvestic fetishism: Psychopathology and theory. In D. R. Laws & W. O'Donohue (Eds.), *Sexual deviance: Theory, assessment, and treatment* (2nd ed., pp. 272–284). New York: Guilford.

Whipple, B., Ogden, G., & Komisanak, B. (1992). Physiological correlates of imagery-induced orgasm in women. *Archives of Sexual Behavior, 21,* 121–133.

Whitam, F. L. (1983). Culturally invariable properties of male homosexuality: Tentative conclusions from cross-cultural research. *Archives of Sexual Behavior, 12,* 207–226.

White, G. L., & Mullen, P. E. (1989). *Jealousy: Theory, research, and clinical strategies.* New York: Guilford.

White, G. L., Fishbein, S., & Rutstein, J. (1981). Passionate love and the misattribution of arousal. *Journal of Personality and Social Psychology, 41,* 56–62.

White, L. J. (2001). Romans 1:26–27: The claim that homosexuality is unnatural. In P. Jung & J. Coray (Eds.), *Sexual diversity and Catholicism* (pp. 133–149). Collegeville, MN: The Liturgical Press.

Whitley, B., Jr. (1993). Reliability and aspects of the construct validity of Sternberg's Triangular Love Scale. *Journal of Social and Personal Relationships, 10,* 475–480.

Wibowo, E., & Wassersug, R. J. (2013). The effect of estrogen on the sexual interest of castrated males: implications to prostate cancer patients on androgen-deprivation therapy. *Critical Reviews in Oncology/Hematology, 87*(3), 224–238.

Wichström, L., & Hegna, K. (2003). Sexual orientation and suicide attempt: A longitudinal study of the general Norwegian adolescent population. *Journal of Abnormal Psychology, 112,* 144–151.

Wickler, W. (1973). *The sexual code.* New York: Anchor Books.

Widmer, M., Villar, J., Benigni, A., Conde-Agudelo, A., Karumanchi, S. A., & Lindheimer, M. (2007). Mapping the theories of preeclampsia and the role of angiogenic factors: A systematic review. *Obstetrics & Gynecology, 109,* 168–180.

Wiederman, M. W., & Hurd, C. (1999). Extradyadic involvement during dating. *Journal of Social and Personal Relationships, 16,* 265–274.

Wiegel, M., Scepkowski, L., & Barlow, D. (2007). Cognitive-affective processes in sexual arousal and sexual dysfunction. In

E. Janssen (Ed.), *The psychophysiology of sex* (pp. 143–165). Bloomington, IN: Indiana University Press.

Wierckx, K., Van Caenegem, E., Elaut, E., Dedecker, D., Van de Peer, F., Toye, K., . . . T'Sjoen, G. (2011). Quality of life and sexual health after sex reassignment surgery in Transsexual men. *Journal of Sexual Medicine, 8,* 3379–3388.

Wikipedia. (2012). Internet pornography statistics.

Wilcox, A. J., Weinberg, C. R., & Baird, D. D. (1995). Timing of sexual intercourse in relation to ovulation. *New England Journal of Medicine, 333,* 1517–1521.

Wilcox, B. L., & Wyatt, J. (1997). *Adolescent abstinence education programs: A meta-analysis.* Presented at the annual meeting, Society for the Scientific Study of Sexuality, Arlington, VA.

Wilkinson, R. (1995). Changes in psychological health and the marital relationship through child bearing: Transition or process as stressor. *Australian Journal of Psychology, 47,* 86–92.

Willetts, M., Sprecher, S., & Beck, F. (2004). Overview of sexual practices and attitudes within relational contexts. In J. H. Harvey, A. Wenzel, & S. Sprecher (Eds.), *The handbook of sexuality in close relationships* (pp. 57–85). Mahwah, NJ: Lawrence Erlbaum.

Williams, C., & Weinberg, M. (2003). Zoophilia in men: A study of sexual interest in animals. *Archives of Sexual Behavior, 32,* 523–535.

Williams, L. M. (1994). Recall of childhood trauma: A prospective study of women's memories of child sexual abuse. *Journal of Consulting and Clinical Psychology, 62,* 1167–1176.

Williams, S., & Lettieri, C. (2012). Sexsomnia: Clinical analysis of an underdiagnosed parasomnia. *Medscape.* Retrieved from http://www.medscape.com

Willness, C. R., Steel, P., & Lee, K. (2007). A meta-analysis of the antecedents and consequences of workplace sexual harassment. *Personnel Psychology, 60,* 127–162.

Willoughby, B. J., & Vitas, J. (2012). Sexual desire discrepancy: The effect of individual differences in desired and actual sexual frequency on dating couples. *Archives of Sexual Behavior, 41,* 477–486.

Wilson, G. (1997). Gender differences in sexual fantasy: An evolutionary analysis. *Personality and Individual Differences, 22,* 27–31.

Wilson, G. D. (1987). An ethological approach to sexual deviation. In G. D. Wilson (Ed.), *Variant sexuality: Research and theory.* Baltimore, MD: Johns Hopkins University Press.

Wilson, R. J., Looman, J., Abracen, J., & Pake, D. R., Jr. (2013). Comparing sexual offenders at the Regional Treatment Centre (Ontario) and the Florida Civil Commitment Center. *International Journal of Offender Therapy and Comparative Criminology, 57,* 377–395.

Wimpissinger, F., Tscherney, R., & Stackl, W. (2009). Magnetic resonance imaging of female prostate pathology. *Journal of Sexual Medicine, 6,* 1704–1711.

Wincze, J. P., & Carey, M. P. (2001). *Sexual dysfunction: A guide for assessment and treatment* (2nd ed.). New York: Guilford Press.

Winer, R. L., & Koutsky, L. A. (2008). Genital human papillomavirus infection. In K. Holmes et al. (Eds.), *Sexually transmitted diseases* (4th ed., pp. 489–508). New York: McGraw-Hill.

Winer, R. L., Hughes, J. P., Feng, Q., O'Reilly, S., Kiviat, N. B., Holmes, K. K., & Koutsky, L. A. (2006). Condom use and the risk of genital human papillomavirus infection in young women. *New England Journal of Medicine, 354,* 2645–2654.

Winn, R. L., & Newton, N. (1982). Sexuality in aging: A study of 106 cultures. *Archives of Sexual Behavior, 11,* 283–298.

Winter, J. S. D., & Couch, R. M. (1995). Sexual differentiation. In P. Felig, J. D. Baxter, & L. A. Frohman (Eds.), *Endocrinology and metabolism* (3rd ed., pp. 1053–1104). New York: McGraw-Hill.

Winters, J., Christoff, K., & Gorzalka, B. B. (2009). Conscious regulation of sexual arousal in men. *Journal of Sex Research, 46,* 330–343.

Wisborg, K., Barklin, A., Hedegaard, M., & Henriksen, T. B. (2008). Psychological stress during pregnancy and stillbirth: Prospective study. *BJOG, 115,* 882–885.

Wisniewski, A. B., Migeon, C. J., Gearhart, J. P., Rock, J. A., Berkovitz, G. D., Plotnick, L. P., . . . Money, J. (2001). Congenital micropenis: Long-term medical, surgical, and psychosexual follow-up of individuals raised male or female. *Hormone Research, 56,* 3–11.

Wisniewski, A. B., Migeon, C. J., Meyer-Bahlburg, H. F., Gearhart, J. P., Berkovitz, G. D., Brown, T. R., & Money, J. (2000). Complete androgen insensitivity syndrome: Long-term medical, surgical, and psychosexual outcome. *Journal of Clinical Endocrinology & Metabolism, 85,* 2664–2669.

Wiswell, T. E., Enzenauer, R. W., Cornish, J. D., & Hawkins, C. T. (1987). Declining frequency of circumcision: Implications for changes in the absolute incidence and male to female sex ratio of urinary tract infections in early infancy. *Pediatrics, 79,* 338–342.

Woertman, L., & van den Brink, F. (2012). Body image and female sexual functioning and behavior: A review. *Journal of Sex Research, 49,* 184–211.

Wohl, A. R., Johnson, D. F., Lu, S., Jordan, W., Beall, G., Currier, J., et al. (2002). HIV risk behaviors among African American men in Los Angeles County who self-identify as heterosexual. *Journal of Acquired Immune Deficiency Syndromes, 31,* 354–360.

Wolak, J., Finkelhor, D., Mitchell, K. J., & Ybarra, M. L. (2008). Online "predators" and their victims. *American Psychologist, 63,* 111–128.

Wolak, J., Mitchell, K., & Finkelhor, D. (2007). Unwanted and wanted exposure to online pornography in a national sample of youth Internet users. *Pediatrics, 119,* 247–257.

Wolfe, L. (2013, April 3). Syria has a massive rape crisis. *The Atlantic.* Retrieved from https://www.theatlantic.com/international/archive/2013/04/syria-has-a-massive-rape-crisis/274583

Wolff, L., & Geissel, D. (1994). Street prostitution in Canada. *Canadian Social Trends* (Catalogue no. 11-008E). Ottawa: Statistics Canada.

Wonders, N. A., & Michalowski, R. (2001). Bodies, borders, and sex tourism in a globalized world: A tale of two cities—Amsterdam and Havana. *Social Problems, 48,* 645–571.

Wong, J. K., Hezareh, M., Günthard, H. F., Havlir, D. V., Ignacio, C. C., Spina, C. A., & Richman, D. D. (1997). Recovery of replication-competent HIV despite prolonged suppression of plasma viremia. *Science, 278,* 1291–1295.

Wong, J. P-H., Chan, K. B. K., Boi-Doku, R., & McWatt, S. (2012). Risk discourse and sexual stigma: Barriers to STI testing, treatment and care among young heterosexual women in disadvantaged neighbourhoods in Toronto. *Canadian Journal of Human Sexuality, 21,* 75–89.

Woo, J. S. T., & Brotto, L. A. (2008). Age of first sexual intercourse and acculturation: Effects on adult sexual responding. *Journal of Sexual Medicine, 5,* 571–582.

Woo, J. S. T., Brotto, L. A., & Gorzalka, B. B. (2009). The role of sexuality in cervical cancer screening among Chinese women. *Health Psychology, 28,* 598–604. doi:10.1037/a0015986

Woo, J. S. T., Brotto, L. A., & Gorzalka, B. B. (2010). Sex guilt and culture-linked barriers to testicular examinations. *International Journal of Sexual Health, 22,* 144–154.

Woo, J. S. T., Brotto, L. A., & Gorzalka, B. B. (2011). The role of sex guilt in the relationship between culture and women's sexual desire. *Archives of Sexual Behavior, 40,* 385–394.

Woo, J. S. T., Brotto, L. A., & Gorzalka, B. B. (2012). The relationship between sex guilt and sexual desire in a community sample of Chinese and Euro-Canadian women. *Journal of Sex Research, 49,* 290–298.

Wood, J. R., McKay, A., Komarnicky, T., & Milhausen, R. R. (2016). Was it good for you too?: An analysis of gender differences in oral sex practices and pleasure ratings among heterosexual Canadian university students. *Canadian Journal of Human Sexuality, 25,* 21–29.

Wood, J. R., Milhausen, R. R., & Jeffrey, N. K. (2014). Why have sex? Reasons for having sex among lesbian, bisexual, queer, and questioning women in romantic relationships. *Canadian Journal of Human Sexuality, 23,* 75–88.

Wood, N. S., Marlow, N., Costeloe, K., Gibson, A. T., & Wilkinson, A. R. (2000). Neurologic and developmental disability after extreme preterm birth. *New England Journal of Medicine, 343,* 378–384.

Wood, W., Kressel, L., Joshi, P. D., & Louie, B. (2014). Meta-analysis of menstrual cycle effects on women's mate preferences. *Emotion Review, 6,* 229–249.

Woods, L. N., & Emery, R. E. (2002). The cohabitation effect on divorce: Causation or selection? *Journal of Divorce & Remarriage, 37,* 101–122.

Woods, N. F., Mitchell, E. S., Percival, D. B., & Smith-DiJulio, K. (2009). Is the menopausal transition stressful? Observations of perceived stress from the Seattle Midlife Women's Health Study. *Menopause, 16,* 90–97.

Woods, S., & Raju, U. (2001). Maternal smoking and the risk of congenital birth defects: A cohort study. *Journal of the American Board of Family Practice, 14,* 330–334.

Woodzicka, J. A., & LaFrance, M. (2005). The effects of subtle sexual harassment on women's performance in a job interview. *Sex Roles, 53,* 67–78.

Working Group for a New View of Women's Sexual Problems. (2001). Part I: A new view of women's sexual problems. In E. Kachak & L. Tiefer (Eds.), *A new view of women's sexual problems* (pp. 1–8). New York: Haworth Press.

Workowski, K. A., & Berman, S. (2010). Sexually transmitted disease treatment guidelines, 2010. *Morbidity and Mortality Weekly Report, 59,* RR-12.

World Association for Transgender Health. (2001). *Standards of care* (6th ed.). Retrieved from http://www.wpath.org/publications_standards.cfm

World Health Organization. (1980). *International classification of Impairments, disabilities, and handicaps.* Geneva, Switzerland: Author.

World Health Organization. (2004). *Unsafe abortion: Global and regional estimates of incidence of unsafe abortion and associated mortality in 2000* (4th ed.). Retrieved from http://www.who.int

World Health Organization. (2006). Defining sexual health: Report of a technical consultation on sexual health, 28–31 January 2002, Geneva. Retrieved from http://www.who.int/reproductivehealth/topics/gender_rights/defining_sexual_health.pdf

World Health Organization. (2007). *Male circumcision: Global trends and determinants of prevalence, safety and acceptability.* Geneva, World Health Organization. Retrieved from http://www.who.int

World Health Organization. (2009). *Epidemiological fact sheet on HIV and AIDS: 2008 Update.* Geneva SU. Retrieved from http://www.who.int

World Health Organization. (2016). *Female genital mutilation.* Fact sheet No. 241. Retrieved from http://www.who.int/mediacentre/factsheets/fs241/en/

World Professional Association for Transgender Health. (2012). Standards of care. Retrieved from http://www.wpath.org

Worthington, E., Martin, G., Shumate, M., & Carpenter, J. (1983). The effect of brief Lamaze training and social encouragement on pain endurance in a cold pressor task. *Journal of Applied Social Psychology, 13,* 223–233.

Wosick-Correa, K., & Joseph, L. (2008). Sexy ladies sexing ladies: Women as consumers in strip clubs. *Journal of Sex Research, 45,* 201–216.

Wright, J. L., Lin, D. W., & Stanford, J. L. (2012). Circumcision and the risk of prostate cancer. *Cancer, 118,* 4437–4443.

Wright, P. (2013). U.S. males and pornography, 1973-2010: Consumption, predictors, correlates. *Journal of Sex Research, 50,* 60–71.

Wright, P. J. (2009). Sexual socialization messages in mainstream entertainment mass media: A review and synthesis. *Sexuality & Culture, 13,* 181–200.

Wright, P. J. (2011). Mass media effects on youth sexual behavior: Assessing the claim for causality. *Communication Yearbook, 35,* 343–385.

Wright, P., Bae, S., & Funk, M. (2013). United States women and pornography through four decades: Exposure, attitudes, behavior, individual differences. *Archives of Sexual Behavior, 42,* 1131–1144.

Wright, V., Schieve, L., Reynolds, M., & Jeng, G. (2005). Assisted reproductive technology surveillance—United States, 2002. *Morbidity and Mortality Weekly Report, 54*(SS02), 1–24.

Wyatt, G. E. (1997). *Stolen women: Reclaiming our sexuality, taking back our lives.* New York: Wiley.

Wyatt, G. E., Peters, S. D., & Guthrie, D. (1988). Kinsey revisited, Part I: Comparisons of the sexual socialization and sexual behavior of white women over 33 years. *Archives of Sexual Behavior, 17,* 201–240.

Wyatt, T. D. (2003). *Pheromones and animal behaviour.* New York: Cambridge University Press.

Wylie, K. R., Jones, R., & Walters, S. (2003). The potential benefit of vacuum devices augmenting psychosexual therapy for erectile dysfunction: A randomized controlled trial. *Journal of Sex & Marital Therapy, 29,* 227–236.

Wynn, L. L., Foster, A., & Trussell, J. (2009). Can I get pregnant from oral sex? Sexual health misconceptions in emails to a reproductive health website. *Contraception, 71,* 91–97.

Yee, J., Apale, A. N., & Deleary, M. (2011). Sexual and reproductive health, rights and realities and access to services for First Nations, Inuit, and Métis in Canada. *Journal of Obstetrics & Gynaecology Canada, 33,* 633–637.

Yeh, H-C., Lorenz, F., Wickrama, K. A. S., Conger, R., and Elder, G. H., Jr. (2006). Relationships among sexual satisfaction, marital quality and marital instability at midlife. *Journal of Family Psychology, 20,* 336–343.

Yellowlees, P., & Marks, S. (2007). Problematic Internet use or Internet addiction? *Computers in Human Behavior, 23,* 1447–1453.

Yoder, P. S., Abderrahim, N., & Zhuzhuni, A. (2004). *Female genital cutting in the demographic and health surveys: A critical and comparative analysis.* DHS Comparative Reports No. 7. Calverton, MD: ORC Macro.

Yost, M. R., & Thomas, G. (2012). Gender and binegativity: Men's and women's attitudes toward male and female bisexuals. *Archives of Sexual Behavior, 41,* 691–702.

Yost, M. R., & Zurbriggen, E. L. (2006). Gender differences in the enactment of sociosexuality: An examination of implicit social motives, sexual fantasies, coercive sexual attitudes, and aggressive sexual behavior. *Journal of Sex Research, 43,* 163–173.

Young, A. (2008). The state is still in the bedrooms of the nation: The control and regulation of sexuality in Canadian criminal law. *Canadian Journal of Human Sexuality, 17,* 203–220.

Young, I. (1996). Education for sexuality—the role of the school. *Journal of Biological Education, 30,* 250–255.

Young, K., Griffin-Shelley, E., Cooper, A., O'Mara, J., & Buchanan, J. (2000). Online infidelity: A new dimension in couple relationships with implications for evaluation and treatment. *Sexual Addiction and Compulsivity, 7,* 59–74.

Yule, M. A. (2011). *Furthering our understanding of asexuality: An investigation into biological markers of asexuality, and the development of the Asexuality Identification Scale.* Masters dissertation, University of British Columbia.

Yule, M. A., Brotto, L. A., & Gorzalka, B. B. (2014). Sexual fantasy and masturbation among asexual individuals. *Canadian Journal of Human Sexuality, 23,* 89–95.

Yule, M. A., Brotto, L. A., & Gorzalka, B. B. (2014a). Biological markers of asexuality: Handedness, birth order, and finger length ratios in self-identified asexual men and women. *Archives of Sexual Behavior, 43,* 299–310.

Zaidi, A. U., Couture-Carron, A., Maticka-Tyndale, E., & Arif, M. (2014). Ethnic identity, religion, and gender: An exploration of intersecting identities creating diverse perceptions and experiences with intimate cross-gender relationships amongst South Asian youth in Canada. *Canadian Ethnic Studies, 46,* 27–54.

Zak, P. J., Kursban, R. O., & Matzner, W. L. (2004). The neurobiology of trust. *Annals of the New York Academy of Science, 1032,* 224–227.

Zala, S. M., & Penn, D. J. (2004). Abnormal behaviours induced by chemical pollution: A review of the evidence and new challenges. *Animal Behaviour, 68,* 649–664.

Zaviačič, M. (1994). Sexual asphyxiophilia (Koczwarism) in women and the biological phenomenon of female ejaculation. *Medical Hypotheses, 42,* 318–322.

Zaviačič, M., Ablin, R., Ružič, M., Štvrtina, S., Galbavý, S., Danihel, L., . . . Holomáč, K. (2000a). Immunohistochemical study of prostatespecific antigen in normal and pathological human tissues: Special reference to the male and female prostate and breast. *Journal of Histotechnology, 23,* 105–111.

Zaviačič, M., Zajíčková, M., Blažeková, J., Donárová, L., Stvrtina, S., Mikulecký, M., . . . Breza, J. (2000b). Weight, size, macroanatomy, and histology of the normal prostate in the adult human female: A mini-review. *Journal of Histotechnology, 23,* 61–69.

Zax, M., Sameroff, A., & Farnum, J. (1975). Childbirth education, maternal attitude and delivery. *American Journal of Obstetrics and Gynecology, 123,* 185–190.

Zentner, M., & Miture, K. (2012). Stepping out of the caveman's shadow: Nations' gender gap predicts degree of sex differentiation in mate preferences. *Psychological Science, 23,* 1176–1185.

Zhou, J., Hogman, M., Gooren, L., & Swaab, D. (1995). A sex difference in the human brain and its relation to transsexuality. *Nature, 378,* 68–70.

Zilbergeld, B. (1992). *The new male sexuality.* New York: Bantam Books.

Zilbergeld, B. (1999). *The new male sexuality* (Rev. ed.). New York: Bantam Books.

Zilbergeld, B., & Evans, M. (1980, August). The inadequacy of Masters and Johnson. *Psychology Today, 14,* 28–43.

Zillmann, D., Schweitzer, K. J., & Mundorf, N. (1994). Menstrual cycle variations of women's interest in erotica. *Archives of Sexual Behavior, 23,* 579–598.

Zivony, A., & Lobel, T. (2014). The invisible stereotypes of bisexual men. *Archives of Sexual Behavior, 43,* 1165–1176.

Zlidar, V. M., Gardner, R., Rutstein, S. O., Morris, L., & Goldberg, H. (2003). New survey findings: The reproductive revolution continues. *Population Reports,* Series M, No. 17, 1–42. Baltimore, MD: Johns Hopkins University School of Public Health.

Zoucha-Jensen, J. M., & Coyne, A. (1993). The effects of resistance strategies on rape. *American Journal of Public Health, 83,* 1633–1634.

Zucker, K. J. (2000). Gender identity disorder. In A. J. Sameroff et al. (Eds.), *Handbook of developmental psychopathology* (2nd ed., pp. 671–686).

Zucker, K. J., Bradley, S. J., Kuksis, M., Pecore, K., Birkenfeld-Adams, A., Doering, R. W., & Wild, J. (1999). Gender constancy judgments in children with gender identity disorder: Evidence for a developmental lag. *Archives of Sexual Behavior, 28*(6), 475–502.

Zucker, K. J., Owen, A., Bradley, S. J., & Ameeriar, L. (2002). Gender-dysphoric children and adolescents: A comparative analysis of demographic characteristics and behavioral problems. *Clinical Child Psychology and Psychiatry, 7*(3), 398–411.

Zucker, K. J., Wilson-Smith, D. N., Kurita, J. A., & Stern, A. (1995). Children's appraisals of sex-typed behaviour in their peers. *Sex Roles, 33,* 703–725.

Zuger, A. (1987, June). AIDS on the wards: A residency in medical ethics. *Hastings Center Report,* 16–20.

Zumpe, D., & Michael, R. P. (1968). The clutching reaction and orgasm in the female rhesus monkey (*Macaca mulatta*). *Journal of Endocrinology, 40,* 117–123.

Zurbriggen, E. L. (2010). Rape, war, and the socialization of masculinity: Why our refusal to give up war ensures that rape cannot be eradicated. *Psychology of Women Quarterly, 34,* 538–549.

Zurbriggen, E. L., & Morgan, E. M. (2006). Who wants to marry a millionaire? Reality dating television programs, attitudes toward sex, and sexual behaviors. *Sex Roles, 54,* 1–17.

Zussman, L., Zussman, S., Sunley, R., & Bjornson, E. (1981). Sexual response after hysterectomy-oophorectomy. *American Journal of Obstetrics and Gynecology, 140,* 725–729.

Index